Standard & Poor's 500 Guide to STAR Performing Stocks

ABOUT THE AUTHOR

Standard & Poor's, a division of The McGraw-Hill Companies, Inc., is the nation's leading securities information company. It provides a broad range of financial services, including the respected Standard & Poor's ratings and stock rankings, advisory services, data guides, and the most closely watched and widely reported gauges of stock market activity—the S&P 500, S&P MidCap 400, S&P SmallCap 600, and the S&P Super Composite 1500 stock price indexes. Standard & Poor's products are marketed around the world and used extensively by financial professionals and individual investors.

Contents

How to Read a Stock Report

This easy-to-follow overview tear sheet combines Standard & Poor's analysts' evaluation with key statistics to give you a definitive picture of the stock's overall value.

1 **DATE OF REPORT**
Stock Reports are updated weekly (selected Reports more often, as needed) so you know the information is always current.

2 **SUMMARY**
Gives you a concise, informative description of the company's business.

3 **STANDARD & POOR'S ANALYST OPINION***
Provides an overall buy, hold or sell recommendation based on STARS (Stock Appreciation Ranking System), which measures short-term appreciation potential for over 1,100 select stocks. Over the past 14 years, our "buy" stocks have appreciated more than 10-fold—a performance few professional money managers have been able to achieve!

4 **OUTLOOK***
Brings you a proven, easy-to-follow stock evaluation system that uses our own exclusive proprietary quantitative model. Stocks with an Outlook of 5 are expected to generally outperform all other stocks, and those rated 1 are expected to underperform all other stocks on average.

5 **FAIR VALUE***
Helps you quickly determine if the stock is a good buy based on Standard & Poor's proprietary quantitative model and our analysis of what the stock is currently worth.

6 **RISK**
Rates the volatility of the stock's price over the past year.

7 **EARNINGS/DIVIDENDS RANKING**
Offers a quick appraisal of the company's long-term standings with our Earnings/Dividends Rankings—from A+ to D—which assess relative growth and stability of earnings and dividends over the past 10 years.

8 **TECHNICAL EVALUATION***
Indicates whether the technical analysis signals a bullish, neutral or bearish outlook on the stock.

RELATIVE STRENGTH RANK
Shows you—on a scale of 1 to 99—how the stock has performed compared to all other companies in our universe on a rolling 13-week basis.

INSIDER ACTIVITY
Gives you an insight as to insider sentiment by showing whether directors, officers and key employees are buying or selling the company's stock during the most recent six months.

PRICE CHART
Concisely conveys almost four years of price movement—presented in a logarithmic format that illustrates true percent changes in price. It shows you at a glance weekly price ranges, weekly volume, a measure of how the stock is performing compared to the S&P 500, and 10 and 30 week moving averages. The triangles indicate if reported quarterly earnings were up ▲, down ▼ or the same ▶ as last year's earnings for the same quarter.

12 **OVERVIEW AND VALUATION**
Gives you our analyst's in-depth evaluation of the company's current situation and expected future stock performance.

13 **KEY STOCK STATISTICS**
Highlights important statistics and estimates, including the value today of a $10,000 investment in the stock made five years ago, which assumes year-end reinvestment of dividends.

14 **EARNINGS HISTORY**
Provides, in easy-to-read tables, a quick look at the actual quarterly revenues, income and earnings per share data for the five previous years and for the quarters that have already been reported in the current year.

15 **DIVIDEND DATA**
Brings you a recent history of dividends paid, as well as dates for declaration, ex-dividend, stock of record and payment.

Please note: For stocks not currently followed by a Standard & Poor's analyst, you get a Business Profile, Operational Review and Stock Performance Report in place of the Analyst Opinion, Overview and Valuation.

*Please see page 14 for more detailed information on our Analyst Opinion, Outlook, Fair Value, and Technical Evaluation.

STANDARD &POOR'S STOCK REPORTS

Coca-Cola

NYSE Symbol **KO**

In S&P 500

1 **27-MAY-00** **Industry:** Beverages (Non-Alcoholic)

2 **Summary:** Coca-Cola is the world's largest soft-drink company and has a sizable fruit juice business. Its bottling interests include a 40% stake in NYSE-listed Coca-Cola Enterprises.

3 S&P Opinion Hold (★★★)

Recent Price • 54⅝ | Yield • 1.2%
52 Wk Range • 69⅞-42⅞ | 12-Mo. P/E • 82.7

Quantitative Evaluations

4 Outlook (1 Lowest—5 Highest) • **1**

5 Fair Value • **38⅝**

6 Risk • **Low**

7 Earn./Div. Rank • **A**

8 Technical Eval. • **Neutral** since 5/00

9 Rel. Strength Rank (1 Lowest—99 Highest) • **91**

10 Insider Activity • **NA**

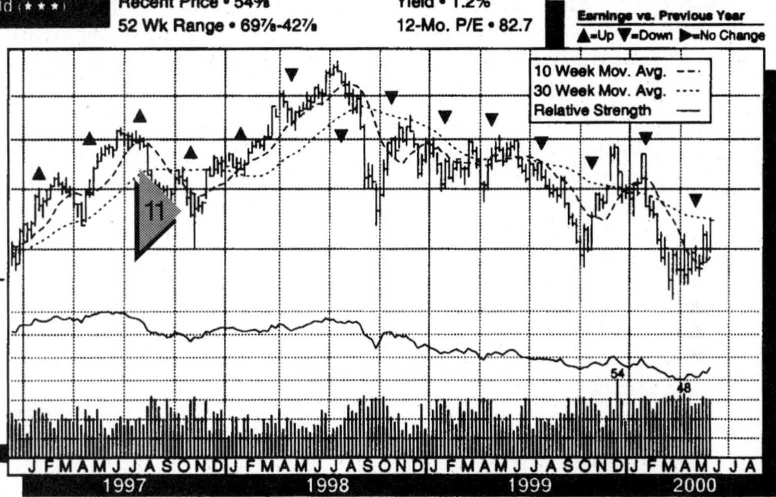

OPTIONS: ASE, CBOE, P, Ph

12 **Overview - 24-MAY-00**

Revenues should rise at a high single digit rate in 2 13 as 5% to 6% higher volumes and 5% to 7% higher concentrate prices outweigh unfavorable currency e change translations. We expect negative currency translations to have less of an impact on earnings than in recent years. Operating margins should widen, aided by operating efficiencies and initial benefits of the company's organizational realignment and headcount reductions. A modest rise in equity income is seen, reflec g an improved earnings outlook for bottlers. Rising fre 14 cash flow should allow for debt reduction and a resumption of share repurchases. We anticipate that E S before special items will rise 10% in 2000, to $1.44, from 1999's $1.31. Our estimate includes the net effect of reductions in bottler concentrate inventories and realignment savings for 2000. For the longer term, a return to EPS growth in excess of 15% is possible.

Valuation - 24-MAY-00

We continue our hold opinion on the shares, reflecting concerns about KO's ability to achieve its long-term volume growth objectives as the company implements a massive organizational realignment. While its new decentralized operating structure should improve KO's ability to operate in local markets, we believe the ris of near-term business disruptions warrants a more cau 15 tious stance. As far as KO's international troubles a concerned, we believe the worst may be over, as k international markets continue to improve and stabil e. In addition, the 1999 acquisition of Cadbury Schweppes beverage brands in 161 countries worldwide has enhanced international growth prospects. Despite trading recently at 37X our 2000 EPS estimate, a significant premium to the S&P 500, we believe KO's superior margin structure and dominant market position make the shares a worthwhile holding.

Key Stock Statistics

S&P EPS Est. 2000	1.44	Tang. Bk. Value/Share	3.06
P/E on S&P Est. 2000	37.9	Beta	1.02
S&P EPS Est. 2001	1.75	Shareholders	388,641
Dividend Rate/Share	0.68	Market cap. (B)	$135.0
Shs. outstg. (M)	2475.1	Inst. holdings	50%
Avg. daily vol. (M)	5.396		

Value of $10,000 invested 5 years ago: $ 22,402

Fiscal Year Ending Dec. 31

	2000	1999	1998	1997	1996	1995
Revenues (Million $)						
1Q	4,391	4,428	4,457	4,138	4,194	3,854
2Q	—	5,379	5,151	5,075	5,253	4,936
3Q	—	5,195	4,747	4,954	4,656	4,895
4Q	—	4,931	4,458	4,701	4,443	4,333
Yr.	—	19,805	18,813	18,868	18,546	18,018
Earnings Per Share ($)						
1Q	-0.02	0.30	0.34	0.39	0.28	0.25
2Q	—	0.38	0.48	0.52	0.42	0.35
3Q	—	0.32	0.36	0.40	0.38	0.32
4Q	—	-0.02	0.24	0.33	0.30	0.26
Yr.	—	0.98	1.42	1.64	1.38	1.18

Next earnings report expected: mid July

Dividend Data (Dividends have been paid since 1893.)

Amount ($)	Date Decl.	Ex-Div. Date	Stock of Record	Payment Date
0.160	Jul. 15	Sep. 13	Sep. 15	Oct. 01 '99
0.160	Oct. 21	Nov. 29	Dec. 01	Dec. 15 '99
0.170	Feb. 17	Mar. 13	Mar. 15	Apr. 01 '00
0.170	Apr. 19	Jun. 13	Jun. 15	Jul. 01 '00

16 **BUSINESS SUMMARY**

Gives you a comprehensive background of the company's business position—with practical information about such topics as its industry, key products and services, subsidiaries, sources of revenue, joint ventures with other companies, and more.

17 **PER SHARE DATA**

Brings you a complete historical perspective on the most important per share data. Includes the Payout Ratio which can aid your evaluation of dividend policy on a historical basis.

18 **INCOME STATEMENT ANALYSIS**

Facilitates year-to-year comparisons—with the percent changes—of revenues, operating income, depreciation, interest expense, pretax profits, net income, and more.

19 **BALANCE SHEET AND OTHER FINANCIAL DATA**

Gives you an easy-to-follow look at major company finances, including cash position, assets and liabilities, long-term debt, total capitalization, and cash flow.

20 **RATIO ANALYSIS**

Provides a close-up look at the company's financial picture through comprehensive analysis of past performance, including long-term debt as a percentage of invested capital and percent return on assets and equity.

STANDARD
&POOR'S
STOCK REPORTS

The Coca-Cola Company

27-MAY-00

16 **Business Summary - 24-MAY-00**

The Coca-Cola Company is the world's largest producer of soft drink concentrates and syrups, as well as the world's largest producer of juice and juice-related products. Finished soft drink products bearing the company's trademarks have been sold in the U.S. since 1886, and are now sold in nearly 200 countries. Sales and operating profit in 1999 by geographic region were distributed as follows: North America (38% of revenues, 32% of profits), Greater Europe (23%, 23%), Middle & Far East (26%, 23%), Latin America (10%, 18%), and Africa (3%, 4%).

The company's business may be the most focused and efficient of any in the world, and is, quite simply, the production and sale of soft drink and non-carbonated beverage concentrates and syrups. These products are sold to the company's authorized independent and company-owned bottling/canning operations, and fountain wholesalers. These customers then either combine the syrup with carbonated water, or combine the concentrate with sweetener, water and carbonated water to produce finished soft drinks. The finished soft drinks are packaged in authorized containers bearing the company's well-known trademarks, which include Coca-Cola (best-selling soft drink in the world, including Coca-Cola classic), caffeine free Coca-Cola (classic), diet Coke (sold as Coke light in many markets outside the U.S.), Cherry Coke, diet Cherry Coke, Fanta, Sprite, diet Sprite, Barq's, Surge, Mr. PiBB, Mello Yello, TAB, Fresca, PowerAde, Minute Maid, Hi-C, Fruitopia, and other products developed for specific markets, including Georgia ready to drink coffees. KO has equity positions in approximately 42 unconsolidated bottling, canning and distribution operations for its products worldwide, including bottlers that accounted for about 58% of the company's U.S. unit case volume in 1999.

In the third quarter of 1999, the company completed the $970 million acquisition of Cadbury Schweppes plc beverage brands in 161 countries worldwide (excluding the U.S.), representing 85% of the world's population. Brands acquired include Schweppes and Canada Dry mixers (such as tonic water, club soda and ginger ale), Crush, Dr. Pepper, and certain regional brands. The proposed acquisition of these brands in several remaining countries is still undergoing regulatory review.

KO enters into forward exchange contracts, and purchases currency options (principally European currencies and Japanese yen) to reduce the risk that its eventual dollar net cash inflows resulting from sales outside the U.S. will be adversely affected by changes in exchange rates.

17

Per Share Data ($) **(Year Ended Dec. 31)**	**1999**	**1998**	**1997**	**1996**	**1995**	**1994**	**1993**	**1992**	**1991**	**1990**
Tangible Bk. Val.	3.06	3.19	2.67	2.18	1.77	1.79	1.55	1.34	1.55	1.31
Cash Flow	1.30	1.67	1.89	1.59	1.36	1.14	0.97	0.83	0.70	0.60
Earnings	0.98	1.42	1.64	1.40	1.19	0.99	0.84	0.71	0.60	0.51
Dividends	0.64	0.60	0.56	0.50	0.44	0.39	0.34	0.28	0.24	0.20
Payout Ratio	65%	42%	34%	36%	37%	39%	40%	39%	39%	39%
Prices - High	$70\frac{7}{8}$	$88\frac{7}{8}$	$72\frac{5}{8}$	$54\frac{1}{4}$	$40\frac{1}{4}$	$26\frac{3}{4}$	$22\frac{5}{8}$	$22\frac{3}{4}$	$20\frac{1}{2}$	$12\frac{1}{4}$
- Low	$47\frac{1}{4}$	$53\frac{5}{8}$	$51\frac{1}{8}$	$36\frac{1}{8}$	$24\frac{3}{8}$	$19\frac{1}{2}$	$18\frac{3}{4}$	$17\frac{3}{4}$	$10\frac{3}{4}$	$8\frac{1}{8}$
P/E Ratio - High	72	63	44	39	34	27	27	32	34	24
- Low	48	38	31	26	21	20	22	25	18	16

18

Income Statement Analysis (Million $)										
Revs.	19,805	18,813	18,868	18,546	18,018	16,172	13,957	13,074	11,572	10,236
Oper. Inc.	4,774	5,612	5,627	4,394	4,546	4,090	3,485	3,080	2,586	2,237
Depr.	792	645	626	479	454	382	333	310	254	236
Int. Exp.	337	277	258	286	272	199	178	171	185	231
Pretax Inc.	3,819	5,198	6,055	4,596	4,328	3,728	3,185	2,746	2,383	2,014
Eff. Tax Rate	36%	32%	32%	24%	31%	32%	31%	31%	32%	31%
Net Inc.	2,431	3,533	4,129	3,492	2,986	2,554	2,188	1,884	1,618	1,382

19

Balance Sheet & Other Fin. Data (Million $)										
Cash	1,812	1,807	1,737	1,658	1,315	1,531	1,078	1,063	1,117	1,492
Curr. Assets	6,480	6,380	5,969	5,910	5,450	5,205	4,434	4,248	4,144	4,143
Total Assets	21,623	19,145	16,940	16,161	15,041	13,873	12,021	11,052	10,222	9,278
Curr. Liab.	9,856	8,640	7,379	7,416	7,348	6,177	5,171	5,303	4,118	4,296
LT Debt	854	687	801	1,116	1,141	1,426	1,428	1,120	985	536
Common Eqty.	9,513	8,403	7,311	6,156	5,392	5,235	4,584	3,888	4,426	3,774
Total Cap.	10,865	9,514	8,560	7,573	6,727	6,841	6,125	5,090	5,611	4,650
Cap. Exp.	1,069	863	1,093	990	937	878	808	1,083	792	642
Cash Flow	3,223	4,178	4,755	3,971	3,440	2,936	2,521	2,194	1,872	1,600

20

Curr. Ratio	0.7	0.7	0.8	0.8	0.7	0.8	0.9	0.8	1.0	1.0
% LT Debt of Cap.	7.9	7.2	9.4	14.7	17.0	20.8	23.3	22.0	17.6	11.5
% Net Inc.of Revs.	12.3	18.8	21.9	18.8	16.6	15.8	15.7	14.4	14.0	13.5
% Ret. on Assets	11.9	19.6	24.9	22.4	20.7	19.9	19.0	17.9	16.6	15.8
% Ret. on Equity	27.1	45.0	61.3	60.5	56.2	52.4	51.8	45.7	39.6	39.3

Data as orig. reptd.; bef. results of disc. opers. and/or spec. items. Per share data adj. for stk. divs. as of ex-div. date. Bold denotes diluted EPS (FASB 128). E-Estimated. NA-Not Available. NM-Not Meaningful. NR-Not Ranked.

Office—1 Coca-Cola Plaza, N.W., Atlanta, GA 30313. **Tel**—(404) 676-2121. **Website**—http://www.thecoca-colacompany.com **Chrmn & CEO**—D. N. Daft. **Pres & COO**—J. L. Stahl. **EVP's**—J. E. Chestnut, C. S. Frenette, J. R. Gladden, C. Ware. **SVP & CFO**—G. P. Fayard. **Secy**—S. E. Shaw. **Investor Contact**—Larry M. Mark. **Dirs**—H. A. Allen, R. W. Allen, C. P. Black, W. E. Buffet, D. N. Daft, S. B. King, D. F. McHenry, S. Nunn, P. F. Oreffice, J. D. Robinson III, P. V. Ueberroth, J. B. Williams. **Transfer Agent & Registrar**—First Chicago Trust Co. of New York, Jersey City, NJ. **Incorporated**—in Delaware in 1919. **Empl**— 37,400. **S&P Analyst:** Richard Joy

Glossary

Following is a glossary of terms and definitions used throughout this book. Please refer to this section as you encounter terms which need further clarification.

Stock Report Terms

Quantitative Evaluations

Standard & Poor's Opinion—Buy, hold or sell recommendations are provided using Standard & Poor's unique STARS (Stock Appreciation Ranking System), which measures short-term (six- to 12-month) appreciation potential of stocks. STARS performance is measured against the performance of the S&P 500 Index.

STARS Rankings are as follows:

- ***** Buy—Expected to be among the best performers over the next 12 months.
- **** Accumulate—Expected to be an above-average performer.
- *** Hold—Expected to be an average performer.
- ** Avoid—Likely to be a below-average performer.
- * Sell—Expected to be a well-below-average performer and fall in price.

Outlook—Using Standard & Poor's exclusive proprietary quantitative model, stocks are ranked in one of five Outlook Groups—ranging from Group 5, listing the most undervalued stocks, to Group 1, the most overvalued issues. Group 5 stocks are expected to generally outperform all others. To identify a stock that is in a strengthening or weakening position, a positive (+) or negative (–) Timing Index is placed next to the Outlook ranking. Using these rankings, here's what action should be taken:

5+ = Buy	2+ = Hold if in portfolio
5 = Hold if in portfolio	2– = Sell
4+ = Hold if in portfolio	1+ = Hold if in portfolio
4– = Sell	1– = Sell
3+ = Hold if in portfolio	
3– = Sell	

The Timing Index helps identify the right time to buy stocks, but its most important function is to indicate when it is time to sell. Because Group 5 stocks have historically produced the best results, Standard & Poor's recommends buying only Group 5 stocks with a positive Timing Index. Then, hold onto each one for as long as it remains in a positive trend (positive Timing Index), even if the ranking falls as the stock appreciates toward overvalued status. This will reduce transaction costs and substantially raise your chances of outperforming the market in the long run. It will also raise the number of transactions which qualify as long-term capital gains for tax purposes.

Fair Value—The price at which a stock should sell today as calculated by Standard & Poor's computers using our quantitative model based on the company's earnings, growth potential, return on equity relative to the S&P 500 and its industry group, price to book ratio history, current yield relative to the S&P 500, and other factors. The current fair price is shown given today's S&P 500 level.

Risk—Rates the volatility of the stock's price over the past year.

Technical Evaluation—In researching the past market history of prices and trading volume for each company, Standard & Poor's computer models apply special technical methods and formulas to identify and project price trends for the stock. They analyze how the price of the stock is moving and evaluate the interrelationships between the moving averages to ultimately determine buy or sell signals—and to decide whether they're bullish, neutral or bearish for the stock. The date the signals were initiated is also provided so you can take advantage of a recent or ongoing uptrend in price, or see how a stock has performed over time since our last technical signal was generated.

Relative Strength Rank—Shows, on a scale of 1 to 99, how the stock has performed compared with all other companies in Standard & Poor's universe of companies on a rolling 13-week basis.

Insider Activity—Gives an insight as to insider sentiment by showing whether directors, officers and key employees—who may have proprietary information not available to the general public—are buying or selling the company's stock during the most recent six months.

Key Stock Statistics

Avg. Daily Vol.—The average daily trading volume of the stock for the past 20 days on a rolling basis, shown in millions.

Market Cap.—The price of the stock multiplied by the number of shares outstanding, shown in billions.

Insider Holdings—The percentage of outstanding shares held by directors, officers and key employees of the company, and others who hold a minimum of 10% of the outstanding shares.

Value of $10,000 Invested 5 years ago—The value today of a $10,000 investment in the stock made five years ago, assuming year-end reinvestment of dividends.

Standard & Poor's Ranking

The investment process involves assessment of various factors—such as products and industry position, company resources and financial policy—with results that make some common stocks more highly esteemed than others. In this assessment, Standard & Poor's believes that earnings and dividend performance is the end result of the interplay of these factors and that, over the long run, the record of this performance has a considerable bearing on relative quality. The rankings, however, do not reflect all of the factors that may bear on stock quality.

Growth and stability of earnings and dividends are the key elements in Standard & Poor's earnings and dividend rankings for common stocks, which are designed to capsulize the nature of this record in a single symbol. It should be noted, however, that the process also takes into consideration certain adjustments and modifications deemed desirable in establishing such rankings.

These rankings are derived by means of a computerized scoring system based on per share earnings and dividend records of the most recent ten years. Basic scores are computed for earnings and dividends and then adjusted by a set of predetermined modifiers for growth, stability, and cyclicality. Adjusted scores for earnings and dividends are then combined to yield a final score.

The ranking system also makes allowance for the fact that, in general, corporate size imparts certain recognized advantages from an investment standpoint. Minimum size limits (in terms of corporate sales) are set for the various rankings, but exceptions may be made where a score reflects an outstanding earnings-dividend record.

Final scores are then translated into one of the following rankings:

A+ Highest
A High
A− Above Average
B+ Average
B Below Average
B− Lower
C Lowest
D In Reorganization
NR No Ranking

In some instances, rankings may be modified by special considerations, such as natural disasters, massive strikes, or nonrecurring accounting adjustments.

It is important to note that a ranking is not a forecast of future market price performance, but is basically an appraisal of past performance of earnings and dividends and relative current standing. Consequently, rankings should not be used as market recommendations: a high-score stock may at times be so overpriced as to justify its sale while a low-score stock may be attractively priced for purchase. Rankings based upon earnings and dividend records are no substitute for complete analysis. They cannot take into account the potential effects of management changes, internal company policies not yet fully reflected in the earnings and dividend record, public relations standings, recent competitive shifts, and a host of other factors that may be relevant in investment decision making.

Beta

The beta coefficient is a measure of the volatility of a stock's price relative to the S&P 500 Index (a proxy for the overall market). An issue with a beta of 1.5 for example, tends to move 50% more than the overall market, in the same direction. An issue with a beta of 0.5 tends to move 50% less. If a stock moved exactly as the market moved, it would have a beta of 1.0. A stock with a negative beta tends to move in a direction opposite to that of the overall market.

Per Share Data ($) Tables

Tangible Book Value; Book Value (See also: "Common Equity" under Industrial)—Indicates the theoretical dollar amount per common share one might expect to receive from a company's tangible "book" assets should liquidation take place. Generally, book value is determined by adding the stated value of the common stock, paid-in capital and retained earnings and then subtracting intangible assets (excess cost over equity of acquired companies, goodwill, and patents), preferred stock at liquidating value and unamortized debt discount. Divide that amount by the outstanding shares to get book value per common share.

Cash Flow—Net income plus depreciation, depletion, and amortization, divided by shares used to calculate earnings per common share. (Also see: "Cash Flow" for Industrial Companies.)

Earnings—The amount a company reports as having been earned for the year on its common stock based on generally accepted accounting standards. Earnings per share are presented on a *"Diluted"* basis pursuant to FASB 128, which became effective December 15, 1997, and are generally reported from continuing operations, before extraordinary items. This reflects a change from previously reported *Primary* earnings per share. INSURANCE companies report *operating earnings* before gains/losses on security transactions and *earnings* after such transactions.

Dividends—Generally total cash payments per share based on the ex-dividend dates over a twelve-month period. May also be reported on a declared basis where this has been established to be a company's payout policy.

Payout Ratio—Indicates the percentage of earnings paid out in dividends. It is calculated by dividing the annual dividend by the earnings. For INSURANCE companies *earnings* after gains/losses on security transactions are used.

Prices High/Low—Shows the calendar year high and low of a stock's market price.

P/E Ratio High/Low—The ratio of market price to earnings—essentially indicates the valuation investors place on a company's earnings. Obtained by dividing the annual earnings into the high and low market price for the year. For INSURANCE companies *operating earnings* before gains/losses on security transactions are used.

Net Asset Value—Appears on investment company reports and reflects the market value of stocks, bonds, and net cash divided by outstanding shares. The % DIFFERENCE indicates the percentage premium or discount of the market price over the net asset value.

Portfolio Turnover—Appears on investment company reports and indicates percentage of total security purchases and sales for the year to overall investment assets. Primarily mirrors trading aggressiveness.

Income/Balance Sheet Data Tables

Banks

Net Interest Income—Interest and dividend income, minus interest expense.

Loan Loss Provision—Amount charged to operating expenses to provide an adequate reserve to cover anticipated losses in the loan portfolio.

Taxable Equivalent Adjustment—Increase to render income from tax-exempt loans and securities comparable to fully taxed income.

Noninterest Income—Service fees, trading and other income, excluding gains/losses on securities transactions.

% Expenses/Op. Revenues—Noninterest expense as a percentage of taxable equivalent net interest income plus noninterest income (before securities gains/losses). A measure of cost control.

Commercial Loans—Commercial, industrial, financial, agricultural loans and leases, gross.

Other Loans—Gross consumer, real estate and foreign loans.

% Loan Loss Reserve—Contra-account to loan assets, built through provisions for loan losses, which serves as a cushion for possible future loan charge-offs.

% Loans/Deposits—Proportion of loans funded by deposits. A measure of liquidity and an indication of bank's ability to write more loans.

Earning Assets—Assets on which interest is earned.

Money Market Assets—Interest-bearing interbank deposits, federal funds sold, trading account securities.

Investment Securities—Federal, state, and local government bonds and other securities.

Gains/Losses on Securities Transactions—Realized losses on sales of securities, usually bonds.

Net Before Taxes—Amount remaining after operating expenses are deducted from income, including gains or losses on security transactions.

Effective Tax Rate—Actual income tax expense divided by net before taxes.

Net Income—The final profit before dividends (common/preferred) from all sources after deduction of expenses, taxes, and fixed charges, but before any discontinued operations or extraordinary items.

Net Interest Margin—A percentage computed by dividing net interest income, on a taxable equivalent basis, by average earning assets. Used as an analytical tool to measure profit margins from providing credit services.

% Return on Revenues—Net income divided by gross revenues.

% Return on Assets—Net income divided by average total assets. An analytical measure of asset-use efficiency and industry comparison.

% Return on Equity—Net income (minus preferred dividend requirements) divided by average common equity. Generally used to measure performance.

Total Assets—Includes interest-earning financial instruments—principally commercial, real estate, consumer loans and leases; investment securities/trading accounts; cash/money market investments; other owned assets.

Cash—Mainly vault cash, interest-bearing deposits placed with banks, reserves required by the Federal Reserve and items in the process of collection—generally referred to as float.

Government Securities—Includes United States Treasury securities and securities of other U.S. government agencies at book or carrying value. A bank's major "liquid asset."

State and Municipal Securities—State and municipal securities owned at book value.

Loans—All domestic and foreign loans (excluding leases), less unearned discount and reserve for possible losses. Generally considered a bank's principal asset.

Deposits—Primarily classified as either *demand* (payable at any time upon demand of depositor) or *time* (not payable within thirty days).

Deposits/Capital Funds—Average deposits divided by average capital funds. Capital funds include capital notes/debentures, other long-term debt, capital stock, surplus, and undivided profits. May be used as a "leverage" measure.

Long-Term Debt—Total borrowings for terms beyond one year including notes payable, mortgages, debentures, term loans, and capitalized lease obligations.

Common Equity—Includes common/capital surplus, undivided profits, reserve for contingencies and other capital reserves.

% Equity to Assets—Average common equity divided by average total assets. Used as a measure of capital adequacy.

% Equity to Loans—Average common equity divided by average loans. Reflects the degree of equity coverage to loans outstanding.

Industrial Companies

Following data is based on Form 10K Annual Report data as filed with SEC.

Revenues—Net sales and other operating revenues. Includes franchise/leased department income for retailers, and royalties for publishers and oil and mining companies. Excludes excise taxes for tobacco, liquor, and oil companies.

Operating Income—Net sales and operating revenues less cost of goods sold and operating expenses (including research and development, profit sharing, exploration and bad debt, but excluding depreciation and amortization).

% Operating Income of Revenues—Net sales and operating revenues divided into operating income. Used as a measure of operating profitability.

Capital Expenditures—The sum of additions at cost to property, plant and equipment and leaseholds, generally excluding amounts arising from acquisitions.

Depreciation—Includes noncash charges for obsolescence, wear on property, current portion of capitalized expenses (intangibles), and depletion charges.

Interest Expense—Includes all interest expense on short/long-term debt, amortization of debt discount/premium and deferred expenses (e.g., financing costs).

Net Before Taxes—Includes operating and nonoperating revenues (including extraordinary items not net of taxes), less all operating and nonoperating expenses, except income taxes and minority interest, but including equity in nonconsolidated subsidiaries.

Effective Tax Rate—Actual income tax charges divided by net before taxes.

Net Income—Profits derived from all sources after deduction of expenses, taxes, and fixed charges, but before any discontinued operations, extraordinary items, and dividends (preferred/common).

% Net Income of Revenues—Net income divided by sales/operating revenues.

Cash Flow—Net income (before extraordinary items and discontinued operations, and after preferred dividends) plus depreciation, depletion, and amortization.

Cash—Includes all cash and government and other marketable securities.

Current Assets—Those assets expected to be realized in cash or used up in the production of revenue within one year.

Current Liabilities—Generally includes all debts/obligations falling due within one year.

Current Ratio—Current assets divided by current liabilities. A measure of liquidity.

Total Assets—Current assets plus net plant and other noncurrent assets (intangibles and deferred items).

% Return on Assets—Net income divided by average total assets on a per common share basis. Used in industry analysis and as a measure of asset-use efficiency.

Long-Term Debt—Debts/obligations due after one year. Includes bonds, notes payable, mortgages, lease obligations, and industrial revenue bonds. Other Long-Term Debt, when reported as a separate account, is excluded. This account generally includes pension and retirement benefits.

Common Equity (See also: "Book Value" under Per Share Data Table)—Common stock plus capital surplus and retained earnings, less any difference between the carrying value and liquidating value of preferred stock.

Total Invested Capital—The sum of stockholders' equity plus long-term debt, capital lease obligations, deferred income taxes, investment credits, and minority interest.

% Long-Term Debt of Invested Capital—Long-term debt divided by total invested capital. Indicates how highly "lever aged" a business might be.

% Return on Equity—Net income less preferred dividend requirements divided by average common shareholders' equity on a per common share basis. Generally used to measure performance and industry comparisons.

Utilities

Operating Revenues—Represents the amount billed to customers by the utility.

Depreciation—Amounts charged to income to compensate for the decline in useful value of plant and equipment.

Maintenance—Amounts spent to keep plants in good operating condition.

Operating Ratio—Ratio of operating costs to operating revenues or the proportion of revenues absorbed by expenses. Obtained by dividing operating expenses including depreciation, maintenance, and taxes by revenues.

Fixed Charges Coverage—The number of times income before interest charges (operating income plus other income) after taxes covers total interest charges and preferred dividend requirements.

Construction Credits—Credits for interest charged to the cost of constructing new plant. A combination of allowance for equity funds used during construction and allowance for borrowed funds used during construction—credit.

Effective Tax Rate—Actual income tax expense divided by the total of net income and actual income tax expense.

Net Income—Amount of earnings for the year which is available for preferred and common dividend payments.

% Return on Revenues—Obtained by dividing net income for the year by revenues.

% Return on Invested Capital—Percentage obtained by dividing income available for fixed charges by average total invested capital.

% Return on Common Equity—Percentage obtained by dividing income available for common stock (net income less preferred dividend requirements) by average common equity.

Gross Property—Includes utility plant at cost, plant work in progress, and nuclear fuel.

Capital Expenditures—Represents the amounts spent on capital improvements to plant and funds for construction programs.

Net Property—Includes items in gross property less provision for depreciation.

% Earned on Net Property—Percentage obtained by dividing operating income by average net property for the year. A measure of plant efficiency.

Total Invested Capital—Sum of total capitalization (common-preferred-debt), accumulated deferred income taxes, accumulated investment tax credits, minority interest, contingency reserves, and contributions in aid of construction.

Total Capitalization—Combined sum of total common equity, preferred stock and long-term debt.

Long-Term Debt—Debt obligations due beyond one year from balance sheet date.

Capitalization Ratios—Reflect the percentage of each type of debt/equity issues outstanding to total capitalization. % DEBT is obtained by dividing total debt by the sum of debt, preferred, common, paid-in capital and retained earnings. % PREFERRED is obtained by dividing the preferred stocks outstanding by total capitalization. % COMMON, divide the sum of common stocks, paid-in capital and retained earnings by total capitalization.

Finally, at the very bottom of the right-hand page, you'll find general information about the company: its address and telephone number, the names of its senior executive officers and directors (usually including the name of the investor contact), the transfer agent and registrar for the stock, and the state in which the company is incorporated.

A Note on the Stock Selection and Organization of this Book

Stock Reports

The Standard & Poor's Stock Reports selected for this book include all Five STARS and selected Four STARS as of a date in late August 2001. The Stock Reports are organized by sector groupings, with the Five STARS alphabetically, followed by the Four STARS alphabetically.

In using the Stock Reports in this handbook, please pay particular attention to the dates attached to the Stock Report and each evaluation, recommendation, or analysis section. Opinions rendered are as of that date and may change often. It is strongly suggested that before investing in any security you should obtain the current analysis on that issue.

To order the latest Standard & Poor's Stock Report on a company, for as little as $3.00 per report, please call:

S&P Reports On-Demand at 1-800-292-0808.

Please also consult the Standard & Poor's website for information about Stock Reports and other S&P products, at www.standardandpoors.com. Standard & Poor's Stock Reports are also distributed by many brokerage and investment firms to individual investors. Further, you can learn more about Standard & Poor's equity analysis through the online version of Business Week, at www.businessweek.com, by selecting the Investing button.

Part One

Consumer Discretionary Stocks

STANDARD
&POOR'S
STOCK REPORTS

Liberty Media Corp. 'A'

NYSE Symbol **LMC.A**

20-AUG-01

Industry: Broadcasting (Television, Radio & Cable)

Summary: Liberty Media, with assets including equity interests in various media or communications companies, became an independent publicly traded company in August 2001.

S&P Opinion: Buy (★★★★★)

Recent Price • 15

52 Wk Range • 23.62-10.75

Yield • Nil

12-Mo. P/E • NM

Quantitative Evaluations

Outlook (1 Lowest—5 Highest) **• NA**

Fair Value **• NA**

Risk **• NA**

Earn./Div. Rank **• NR**

Technical Eval. **• NA**

Rel. Strength Rank (1 Lowest—99 Highest) **• 35**

Insider Activity **• NA**

Earnings vs. Previous Year
▲=Up ▼=Down ▶=No Change

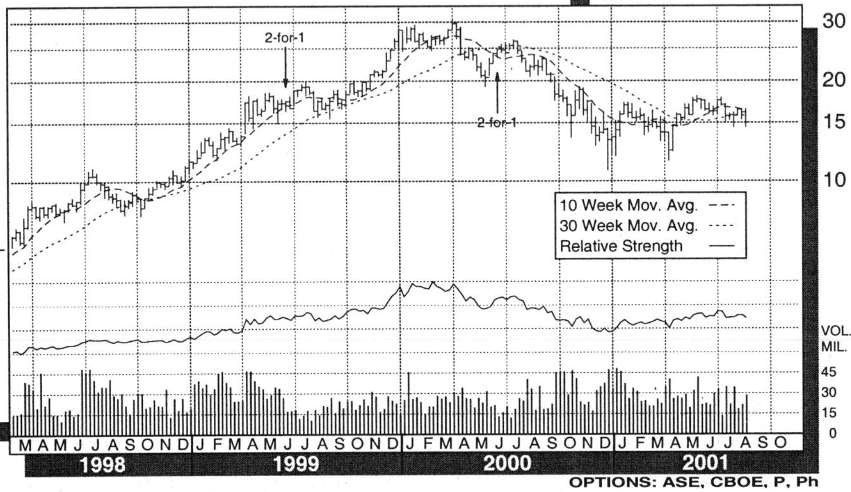

OPTIONS: ASE, CBOE, P, Ph

Overview - 20-AUG-01

On August 10, 2001, Liberty was split off as an independent publicly traded company. The stock now trades under a new symbol (LMC.A) In the past, Liberty-related shares were tracking stocks of AT&T. In 2001, we look for much of Liberty's revenue to come from ownership of Starz Encore Group LLC, a provider of premium movie services, and from a group of businesses outside of the U.S. that are part of Liberty Media International. However, we do not expect Liberty's income statement to fully reflect the value of its asset base, which includes minority equity interests in various publicly-owned companies, and between 40% and 50% ownership of privately-owned TV programming companies Discovery Communications, Inc., and QVC, Inc. The level of profit or loss reported on Liberty's income statement in 2001 is likely to be influenced by the extent to which there are gains on asset sales.

Valuation - 20-AUG-01

Through mid-August, this stock had outperformed the S&P 500 year to date, after sharply underperforming in full-year 2000. Overall, we were pleased with the second quarter cash flow growth from three privately-owned companies (Starz, Discovery Communications. and QVC) in which Liberty has a major equity interest. We have been disappointed by the recent performance of some publicly-owned stocks held by Liberty, but, we generally like the portfolio, and we look for both it and Liberty's privately-owned assets to rise in value. Also, we expect the recent separation of Liberty from AT&T to help the LMC.A stock's visibility and appeal to investors. We see LMC.A shares as an attractive way to benefit from the savvy of Liberty Chairman John Malone, and we recommend buying the stock.

Key Stock Statistics

S&P EPS Est. 0	NA	Tang. Bk. Value/Share	9.34
P/E on S&P Est. 0	NA	Beta	1.35
Dividend Rate/Share	Nil	Shareholders	6,842
Shs. outstg. (M)	2587.8	Market cap. (B)	$ 35.6
Avg. daily vol. (M)	5.057	Inst. holdings	63%

Value of $10,000 invested 5 years ago: $ 51,428

Fiscal Year Ending Dec. 31

	2000	1999	1998	1997	1996	1995
Revenues (Million $)						
1Q	235.0	71.00	—	—	—	—
2Q	382.0	221.0	—	—	—	—
3Q	436.0	214.0	—	—	—	—
4Q	473.0	223.0	—	—	—	—
Yr.	1,526	729.0	—	—	—	—
Earnings Per Share ($)						
1Q	—	—	—	—	—	—
2Q	—	—	—	—	—	—
3Q	—	—	—	—	—	—
4Q	—	—	—	—	—	—
Yr.	**0.57**	**-0.78**	—	—	—	—

Next earnings report expected: NA

Dividend Data

No cash dividends have been paid.

A Division of The McGraw-Hill Companies

Liberty Media Corp.

Business Summary - 20-AUG-01

Liberty Media Corp. owns interests in a broad range of videoprogramming, communications and Internet businesses in the U.S., Europe, South America and Asia. In early August 2001, Liberty was split off as independent publicly traded company, after having previously been a subsidiary of AT&T Corp. The stock now trades under a new symbol (LMC.A). In the past, Liberty-related shares were tracking stocks of AT&T.

At August 13, 2001, Liberty-owned equity stakes in various publicly owned companies had a market value of $28.3 billion. In addition, there were underlying collars and exchangeable features that the company said added another $2.5 billion of value. Liberty's holdings in publicly-owned companies with the largest value included AOL Time Warner ($7.4 billion), News Corp. ($6.3 billion), Sprint Corp. (PCS Group) ($4.7 billion), and USA Networks ($3.9 billion).

Liberty's ownership stakes in privately-owned companies include 100% of Starz Encore Group LLC, a supplier of premium movie services; 49% of Discovery Communications, Inc., which operates various cable TV programming services; and 42% of QVC, Inc., which operates home shopping television programming services.

Liberty's most significant consolidated subsidiaries at December 31, 2000, were Starz Encore Group LLC, Liberty Livewire Corp., and On Command Corp. These businesses were either wholly or majority owned, and, accordingly, the results of operations of such businesses are included in Liberty's consolidated results for the periods in which they were wholly or majority owned.

In June 2001, Liberty said that it had approved key elements of an agreement through which it would acquire 100% ownership of six regional cable television companies owned by German company Deutche Telecom. Also, Liberty has reached an agreement in principle to grant a third party an option to acquire a related interest of up to 24.9%.

Liberty also has ownership interests of 20% to 50% in various companies. As of year-end 2000, these businesses included USA Networks, Inc., Discovery Communications, Inc., QVC, Inc., Gemstar-TV Guide International, Inc., UnitedGlobalCom, Inc., and Telewest Communications plc. In addition, it holds interests in companies that are neither consolidated subsidiaries nor affiliates accounted for using the equity method. The most significant of these include AOL Time Warner Inc., Sprint Corp., News Corp. and Motorola, Inc.

Aggregate gains from dispositions during 2000 amounted to $7.3 billion, most of which came from the acquisition of TV Guide by Gemstar, and the acquisition of General Instrument by Motorola.

Per Share Data ($) **(Year Ended Dec. 31)**	**2000**	**1999**	**1998**	**1997**	**1996**	**1995**	**1994**	**1993**	**1992**	**1991**
Tangible Bk. Val.	9.27	11.06	NA	NA	NA	NA	NA	NA	NA	NA
Cash Flow	0.90	-0.56	NA	NA	NA	NA	NA	NA	NA	NA
Earnings	0.57	-0.78	NA	NA	NA	NA	NA	NA	NA	NA
Dividends	Nil	Nil	NA	NA	NA	NA	NA	NA	NA	NA
Payout Ratio	Nil	Nil	NA	NA	NA	NA	NA	NA	NA	NA
Prices - High	30.71	28.40	NA	NA	NA	NA	NA	NA	NA	NA
- Low	10.75	10.95	NA	NA	NA	NA	NA	NA	NA	NA
P/E Ratio - High	54	NM	NA	NA	NA	NA	NA	NA	NA	NA
- Low	19	NM	NA	NA	NA	NA	NA	NA	NA	NA
Income Statement Analysis (Million $)										
Revs.	1,526	729	NA	NA	NA	NA	NA	NA	NA	NA
Oper. Inc.	1,290	-1,651	NA	NA	NA	NA	NA	NA	NA	NA
Depr.	854	562	NA	NA	NA	NA	NA	NA	NA	NA
Int. Exp.	246	288	NA	NA	NA	NA	NA	NA	NA	NA
Pretax Inc.	3,082	-3,071	NA	NA	NA	NA	NA	NA	NA	NA
Eff. Tax Rate	48%	NM	NA	NA	NA	NA	NA	NA	NA	NA
Net Inc.	1,485	-2,020	NA	NA	NA	NA	NA	NA	NA	NA
Balance Sheet & Other Fin. Data (Million $)										
Cash	1,795	2,092	NA	NA	NA	NA	NA	NA	NA	NA
Curr. Assets	2,954	3,369	NA	NA	NA	NA	NA	NA	NA	NA
Total Assets	54,268	58,658	NA	NA	NA	NA	NA	NA	NA	NA
Curr. Liab.	29.6	3,370	NA	NA	NA	NA	NA	NA	NA	NA
LT Debt	5,269	2,723	NA	NA	NA	NA	NA	NA	NA	NA
Common Eqty.	34,290	38,435	NA	NA	NA	NA	NA	NA	NA	NA
Total Cap.	51,244	55,264	NA	NA	NA	NA	NA	NA	NA	NA
Cap. Exp.	221	40.0	NA	NA	NA	NA	NA	NA	NA	NA
Cash Flow	2,339	-1,458	NA	NA	NA	NA	NA	NA	NA	NA
Curr. Ratio	1.0	1.0	NA	NA	NA	NA	NA	NA	NA	NA
% LT Debt of Cap.	10.3	4.9	NA	NA	NA	NA	NA	NA	NA	NA
% Net Inc.of Revs.	97.3	NM	NA	NA	NA	NA	NA	NA	NA	NA
% Ret. on Assets	2.6	NM	NA	NA	NA	NA	NA	NA	NA	NA
% Ret. on Equity	4.1	NM	NA	NA	NA	NA	NA	NA	NA	NA

Data as orig reptd.; or from recent SEC filing; bef. results of disc opers/spec. items. Data related to 1999 income statement is for 10-month period. Per share data adj. for stk. divs. Bold denotes diluted EPS (FASB 128)-prior periods restated. E-Estimated. NA-Not Available. NM-Not Meaningful. NR-Not Ranked.

Office—9197 South Peoria St., Englewood, CO 80112. **Tel**—(720) 875-5400. **Website**—http://www.libertymedia.com **Chrmn**—J. C. Malone. **Pres & CEO**—R. R. Bennett. **EVP & COO**—G. S. Howard. **SVP & Treas**—D. J. A. Flowers. **Dirs**—R. R. Bennett, P. A. Gould, H. R. Handler, G. S. Howard, J. H. Kern, F. J. Macchiarola, J. C. Malone, M. T. Ricks, L. E. Romrell. **Transfer Agent**—Boston EquiServe. **Incorporated**—in Delaware in 1994. **Empl**— 6,940. **S&P Analyst:** Tom Graves, CFA

STANDARD &POOR'S STOCK REPORTS

Barnes & Noble

NYSE Symbol **BKS**

In S&P MidCap 400

18-AUG-01 **Industry:** Retail (Specialty)

Summary: BKS is the largest U.S. operator of book stores, and the world's largest operator of video game and PC entertainment stores.

S&P Opinion: Buy (★★★★★)

Recent Price • 40.66 | Yield • Nil
52 Wk Range • 41.70-16.43 | 12-Mo. P/E • NM

Quantitative Evaluations

Outlook (1 Lowest—5 Highest)
• **1**

Fair Value
• **32**

Risk
• **Average**

Earn./Div. Rank
• **NR**

Technical Eval.
• **Neutral** since 7/01

Rel. Strength Rank (1 Lowest—99 Highest)
• **89**

Insider Activity
• **Unfavorable**

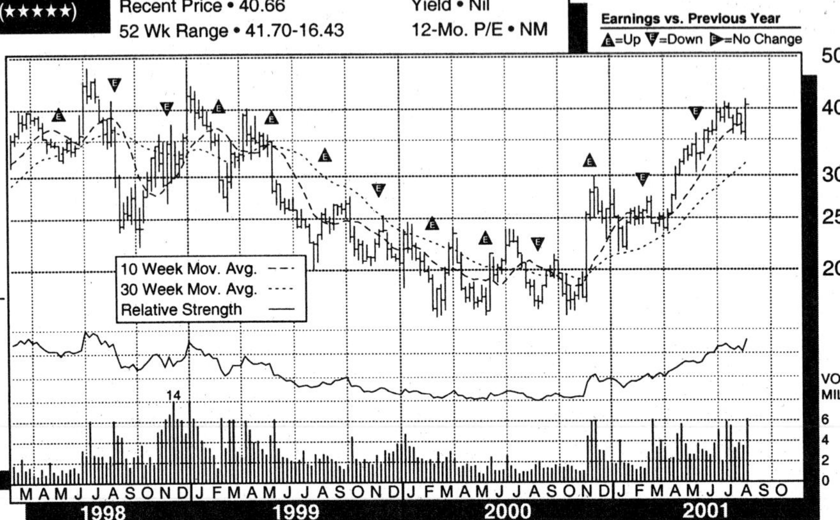

OPTIONS: ASE, CBOE

Overview - 15-AUG-01

We see a 3.5% to 4.5% gain in same-store superstore sales in FY 02 (Jan.) despite the impact of a softer economy and the absence of the Harry Potter (HP) phenomenon. The fifth book in the HP cycle could be released in late 2002 or early 2003. The launch of three new game platforms in 2001, plus the launch of Sony's PlayStation 2 in October 2000, should boost same-store gamestore sales by well over 40% in FY 02, and at least 25% in FY 03. For FY 02, we project consolidated EPS of $1.77. Bookstore earnings should rise 7%, to $1.98 from $1.85. Babbages should report profits of at least $0.09, versus a loss of $0.16. BKS's share of BNBN's losses should decline to about $0.28, from $0.55. Other equity losses should decline to $0.02, from $0.06. For FY 03, we see consolidated EPS of $2.30. By segment, we project $2.20 of bookstore earnings; $0.33 from Babbages; online losses of $0.21; and other losses of $0.02.

Valuation - 15-AUG-01

We reiterate our strong buy recommendation on the shares. Although year to date the shares were recently up 48% in 2001, following a 29% advance in calendar 2000, BKS continues to offer solid value. At 22X our FY 02 EPS estimate, and 17X our FY 03 estimate, the shares continue to trade toward the lower end of their average P/E range over the past four years. BKS is trading at a P/E considerably less than one times its anticipated earnings growth in FY 02 (67%) and FY 03 (30%). In addition, we believe BKS provides protection against further economic softness in the retailing sector, because most of its anticipated growth will come from an unusually strong product cycle at Babbages, relatively stable growth of same-store sales at the Barnes & Noble superstores, and declining Internet losses, mostly through cutting costs.

Key Stock Statistics

S&P EPS Est. 2002	1.77	Tang. Bk. Value/Share	5.90
P/E on S&P Est. 2002	23.0	Beta	1.03
S&P EPS Est. 2003	2.30	Shareholders	2,064
Dividend Rate/Share	Nil	Market cap. (B)	$ 2.7
Shs. outstg. (M)	65.6	Inst. holdings	64%
Avg. daily vol. (M)	0.870		

Value of $10,000 invested 5 years ago: $ 25,215

Fiscal Year Ending Jan. 31

	2002	2001	2000	1999	1998	1997
Revenues (Million $)						
1Q	1,010	894.3	718.3	666.3	595.7	508.8
2Q	—	924.3	727.2	675.0	617.8	524.3
3Q	—	951.8	49.05	674.1	614.8	532.6
4Q	—	1,605	1,325	1,029	968.5	882.5
Yr.	—	4,376	3,486	3,006	2,797	2,448
Earnings Per Share ($)						
1Q	**-0.18**	**0.06**	**-0.02**	**-0.05**	**-0.06**	**-0.08**
2Q	—	**-0.13**	**0.33**	**-0.08**	**-0.02**	**-0.04**
3Q	—	**-0.08**	**-0.15**	**-0.07**	Nil	**-0.04**
4Q	—	**-0.52**	**1.48**	**1.47**	**0.98**	**0.91**
Yr.	—	**-0.81**	**1.81**	**1.29**	**0.93**	**0.75**

Next earnings report expected: mid August

Dividend Data

No cash dividends have been paid.

A Division of The McGraw·Hill Companies

Barnes & Noble, Inc.

Business Summary - 15-AUG-01

Barnes & Noble is the world's largest bookseller. It is the leading U.S. operator of book superstores, and the second largest operator of mall bookstores (primarily through B. Dalton). In 2000, its share of the U.S. consumer book market rose to 16%, from 15%. Barnes & Noble.com, Inc., is the second largest online book seller, through its website http://www.bn.com. The service offers every book in print (approximately 1.5 million titles), including immediate delivery of more than 400,000 in-stock books. It also offers more than 12 million listings from its nationwide network of out-of-print, rare and used book dealers. In October 1998, the company sold a 50% interest in BN.com to the German media conglomerate Bertelsmann AG. The partners sold an 18% stake in the venture to the public in a May 1999 IPO. In November 2000, the website acquired Fatbrain.com, Inc., the third largest online bookseller; the stock transaction cut BKS's stake in the online business to 36%, from 40%.

BKS's rapidly expanding superstore operations consist of 569 stores (at February 3, 2001) in 49 states across the U.S., under the Barnes & Noble Booksellers, Bookstop, and Bookstar trade names. Mall operations consist of 339 stores in 46 states, under the B. Dalton Bookseller, Doubleday Book Shops, and Scribner's Bookstores tradenames.

The company also publishes books under the Barnes & Noble Books imprint, for exclusive sale through its retail stores and mail-order catalogs, sent to more than 1 million customers worldwide. BKS is the world's largest catalog bookseller. The company is the largest U.S. retailer in every segment of its sales: bargain books, magazines, newspapers, children's books, art books, calendars, etc.

The superstores, which account for 88% of total bookstore sales, have their heaviest concentrations in California, Texas, Florida and New York. Each superstore stocks more than 175,000 titles. BKS opened 32 superstores in FY 01 (Jan.), down from 38 in FY 00.

In less than a year, BKS became the world's largest specialty retailer of video games and PC entertainment. In October 1999, it acquired Babbage's Etc., a chain operated under the Babbage's, Software Etc. and GameStop trade names, and a website, gamestop.com. In June 2000, the company acquired Funco, Inc., a retail marketer of new and used video games, related hardware and accessories. At the end of January 2001, combined retail stores totaled 978. BKS plans to open 80 new gamestores and 40 book superstores in FY 02.

BKS also owns equity stakes in Chapters Inc., Canada's leading bookstore chain; NuvoMedia; iUniverse.com, the Internet's largest publishing portal; and Calendar Club LLC, an operator of seasonal calendar kiosks both in the U.S. and internationally.

Per Share Data ($) (Year Ended Jan. 31)	2001	2000	1999	1998	1997	1996	1995	1994	1993	1992
Tangible Bk. Val.	6.43	8.37	8.61	6.50	5.46	4.61	3.72	3.19	2.39	NA
Cash Flow	1.47	3.39	2.53	2.05	1.63	-0.05	0.99	0.58	0.53	NA
Earnings	-0.81	1.81	1.29	0.93	0.74	-0.85	0.41	0.03	0.03	NA
Dividends	Nil	Nil	Nil	Nil	Nil	Nil	Nil	Nil	NA	NA
Payout Ratio	Nil	Nil	Nil	Nil	Nil	Nil	Nil	Nil	NA	NA
Cal. Yrs.	2000	1999	1998	1997	1996	1995	1994	1993	1992	1991
Prices - High	29.93	44.37	48.00	33.93	18.87	21.12	15.68	17.00	NA	NA
- Low	16.31	20.06	22.18	12.87	11.62	13.06	10.00	11.25	NA	NA
P/E Ratio - High	NM	25	37	36	26	NM	39	NM	NA	NA
- Low	NM	11	17	14	16	NM	25	NM	NA	NA
Income Statement Analysis (Million $)										
Revs.	4,376	3,486	3,006	2,797	2,448	1,977	1,623	1,337	1,087	NA
Oper. Inc.	387	345	277	226	181	139	105	71.2	55.8	NA
Depr.	146	113	88.7	78.6	61.7	50.2	36.6	29.1	25.1	NA
Int. Exp.	54.5	25.2	25.4	38.1	40.6	30.3	26.0	27.6	27.1	NA
Pretax Inc.	-33.0	219	157	110	81.4	-63.3	45.6	16.3	5.8	NA
Eff. Tax Rate	NM	41%	41%	41%	37%	NM	44%	53%	77%	NA
Net Inc.	-52.0	129	92.4	64.7	51.2	-53.0	25.5	7.8	1.3	NA
Balance Sheet & Other Fin. Data (Million $)										
Cash	26.0	24.2	31.1	12.7	12.4	9.3	55.0	138	NA	NA
Curr. Assets	1,455	1,242	1,088	978	867	848	614	546	NA	NA
Total Assets	2,557	2,414	1,808	1,591	1,447	1,315	1,026	896	737	NA
Curr. Liab.	935	923	772	713	654	622	458	364	NA	NA
LT Debt	667	432	249	285	290	262	190	190	190	NA
Common Eqty.	778	846	679	532	456	400	358	329	292	NA
Total Cap.	1,519	1,403	960	817	746	662	548	519	482	NA
Cap. Exp.	134	146	141	122	172	155	88.8	81.1	NA	NA
Cash Flow	94.4	242	181	143	113	-2.8	62.1	30.7	26.4	NA
Curr. Ratio	1.6	1.3	1.4	1.4	1.3	1.4	1.3	1.5	NA	NA
% LT Debt of Cap.	43.9	30.8	25.9	34.8	38.9	39.6	34.7	36.6	39.4	NA
% Net Inc.of Revs.	NM	3.7	3.1	2.3	2.1	NM	1.6	0.6	0.1	NA
% Ret. on Assets	NM	6.1	5.4	4.3	3.7	NM	2.6	0.6	NA	NA
% Ret. on Equity	NM	16.9	15.3	13.1	12.0	NM	7.4	0.6	NA	NA

Data as orig reptd.; bef. results of disc opers/spec. items. Per share data adj. for stk. divs. Bold denotes diluted EPS (FASB 128)-prior periods restated. E-Estimated. NA-Not Available. NM-Not Meaningful. NR-Not Ranked.

Office—122 Fifth Ave., New York, NY 10011. **Tel**—(212) 633-3300. **Website**—http://www.shareholder.com/bks **Chrmn & CEO**—L. Riggio. **Vice Chrmn**—S. Riggio. **CFO**—Maureen O'Connell. **COO**—J. A. Kahn. **EVP-Fin & Investor Contact**—Marie Toulantis.**Secy**—M. N. Rosen. **Dirs**—M. A. Berdon, M. J. Del Guidice, W. Dillard II, R. Miller, M. T. Monaco, L. Riggio, S. Riggio, W. Sheluck Jr., M. N. Rosen. **Transfer Agent & Registrar**—Bank of New York, NYC. **Incorporated**—in Delaware. **Empl**— 27,200. **S&P Analyst:** William H. Donald

STANDARD
&POOR'S
STOCK REPORTS

Charter Communications

Nasdaq Symbol **CHTR**

18-AUG-01

Industry:
Broadcasting (Television, Radio & Cable)

Summary: This holding company is the fourth largest U.S. operator of cable TV systems.

S&P Opinion: Buy (★★★★★)

Recent Price • 20.01
52 Wk Range • 24.45-14

Yield • Nil
12-Mo. P/E • NM

Quantitative Evaluations

Outlook
(1 Lowest—5 Highest)
• **NA**

Fair Value
• **NA**

Risk
• **NA**

Earn./Div. Rank
• **NR**

Technical Eval.
• **NA**

Rel. Strength Rank
(1 Lowest—99 Highest)
• **29**

Insider Activity
• **Neutral**

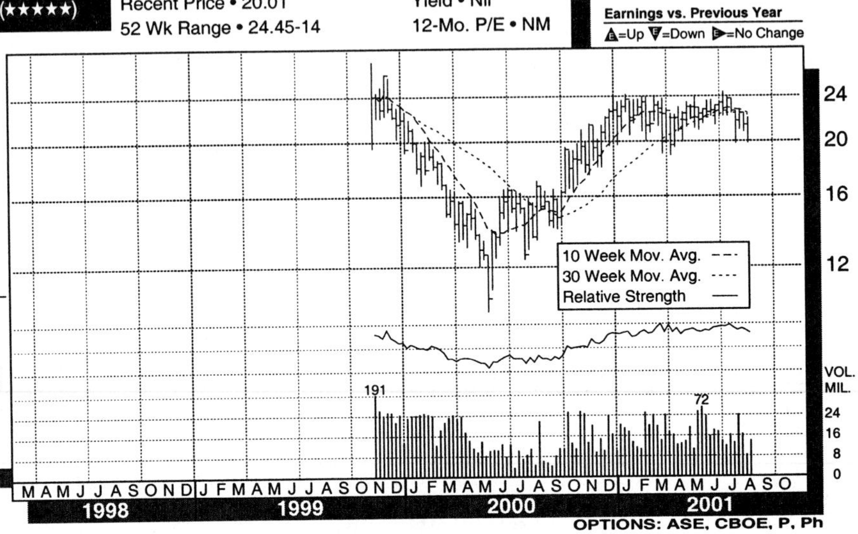

OPTIONS: ASE, CBOE, P, Ph

Overview - 23-JUL-01

We expect proforma revenues to increase about 15% in 2001, primarily reflecting increased demand for digital cable and high speed Internet access. With a high rate of subscriber additions for these services, we believe CHTR should have nearly 2 million digital cable, and more than 500,000 high-speed data subscribers, by the end of 2001. Revenue growth will also be supported by increased advertising and new video-on-demand (VOD) services. The company is one of the first U.S. operators to launch VOD in a major market. Core cable revenues should benefit from rate increases, and from a higher penetration rate. However, operating profit margins are expected to narrow slightly, as a result of higher marketing costs related to satellite competition, and programming costs associated with VOD services. We expect proforma EBITDA to grow 14% in 2001, to $2.74, from 2000's $2.40.

Valuation - 23-JUL-01

We maintain a buy opinion on the shares, based on our belief that CHTR will continue to experience high growth rates and improving industry fundamentals. Growth rates for the company in core basic, digital cable, and high speed Internet access subscribers are among the highest in the industry. In light of the fact that CHTR operates in regions with healthy DBS competition, we attribute its success to its marketing prowess. Concerns about the company's ability to raise capital have been mostly alleviated by a recent sale of $1.2 billion in senior notes, providing capital that will fund most of the company's plant upgrades. At recent levels, the stock is attractively valued, at about 8X projected 2001 EBITDA, representing a significant discount to the valuation accorded CHTR's slower growing peers.

Key Stock Statistics

S&P EPS Est. 2001	-4.29	Tang. Bk. Value/Share	NM
P/E on S&P Est. 2001	NM	Beta	NA
S&P EPS Est. 2002	-4.03	Shareholders	176,045
Dividend Rate/Share	Nil	Market cap. (B)	$ 4.7
Shs. outstg. (M)	233.8	Inst. holdings	70%
Avg. daily vol. (M)	3.117		

Value of $10,000 invested 5 years ago: NA

Fiscal Year Ending Dec. 31

	2001	2000	1999	1998	1997	1996
Revenues (Million $)						
1Q	873.8	721.6	—	—	—	—
2Q	928.5	794.8	—	—	—	—
3Q	—	839.0	—	—	—	—
4Q	—	893.9	—	—	—	—
Yr.	—	3,249	1,428	2,692	—	—
Earnings Per Share ($)						
1Q	**-1.20**	**-0.81**	—	—	—	—
2Q	**-1.07**	**-0.89**	—	—	—	—
3Q	**E-1.02**	**-0.93**	—	—	—	—
4Q	**E-1.05**	**-1.04**	—	—	—	—
Yr.	**E-4.29**	**-3.67**	**-2.22**	**-3.16**	—	—

Next earnings report expected: NA

Dividend Data

No cash dividends have been paid.

Charter Communications, Inc.

Business Summary - 23-JUL-01

Charter Communications has forged an aggressive acquisition strategy under chairman Paul Allen, becoming the fourth largest U.S. operator of cable TV systems, with approximately 6.2 million customers. Upon completion in 2002 of a system upgrade and rebuild program, the company expects to have one of the most robust broadband networks in the U.S., capable of providing a variety of new services.

The company's program centers on upgrading from analog to digital technology, thereby enabling it to provide expanded cable programming services, high speed Internet access and email, and interactive television. Future services will likely include Internet telephony. Capital spending is expected to total about $7.0 billion from 2000 through 2003, excluding acquisitions. About $2.9 billion will be used to upgrade system bandwidth to allow two way communications and the infrastructure to offer advanced data and video services, and the remainder will be used for extensions of systems, development of new products and services, purchase of digital converters, and system maintenance.

CHTR has achieved subscriber growth well above the level of rest of the cable industry in recent years. In 1999, organic subscriber growth of 3.6% was about twice the national average. At December 31, 1999, the basic service penetration rate (pro forma for a subsequent acquisition) was 62.3% of 9.85 million homes passed. At that time, 155,400 customers subscribed to digital video services, and the company provided 91,500 homes and commercial customers with Internet access. About 4.7 million homes were passed by cable systems capable of providing digital video, and 4.9 million were passed by Internet access-capable systems. By December 31, 2000, CHTR expects digital video and Internet access capable systems to pass approximately 70% of homes.

In the November 1999 IPO, 195.5 million shares were sold at $19 each. On a pro forma basis for the January 2000 acquisition of cable systems owned by Bresnan Communications, CHTR owns a 40% interest in its cable systems operations. The remaining 60% interest, as represented by membership units in the company's operating subsidiary, are convertible into common shares, and are reflected as minority interests on financial statements. As the minority interest units are exchanged for common stock, CHTR's ownership in its systems will rise.

On July 6, 2000, the company ceased negotiations to exchange certain cable systems with AT&T Broadband. Under a letter of intent signed in December 1999, CHTR would have traded systems with 632,000 customers, scattered in five states, plus an undisclosed amount of cash, for systems with 704,000 customers in the vicinity of St. Louis and Birmingham, as well as in Illinois and Georgia.

Per Share Data ($) (Year Ended Dec. 31)	2000	1999	1998	1997	1996	1995	1994	1993	1992	1991
Tangible Bk. Val.	NM	NM	NM	NA	NA	NA	NA	NA	NA	NA
Cash Flow	7.29	22.78	6.89	NA	NA	NA	NA	NA	NA	NA
Earnings	-3.67	-2.22	-3.16	NA	NA	NA	NA	NA	NA	NA
Dividends	Nil	Nil	NA	NA	NA	NA	NA	NA	NA	NA
Payout Ratio	Nil	Nil	NA	NA	NA	NA	NA	NA	NA	NA
Prices - High	24.18	27.75	NA	NA	NA	NA	NA	NA	NA	NA
- Low	10.00	19.00	NA	NA	NA	NA	NA	NA	NA	NA
P/E Ratio - High	NM	NM	NA	NA	NA	NA	NA	NA	NA	NA
- Low	NM	NM	NA	NA	NA	NA	NA	NA	NA	NA
Income Statement Analysis (Million $)										
Revs.	3,249	1,428	2,692	NA	NA	NA	NA	NA	NA	NA
Oper. Inc.	3,445	559	1,228	NA	NA	NA	NA	NA	NA	NA
Depr.	2,473	745	1,708	NA	NA	NA	NA	NA	NA	NA
Int. Exp.	1,059	478	1,065	NA	NA	NA	NA	NA	NA	NA
Pretax Inc.	-2,055	-638	-1,556	NA	NA	NA	NA	NA	NA	NA
Eff. Tax Rate	NM	NM	Nil	NA	NA	NA	NA	NA	NA	NA
Net Inc.	-829	-66.2	-537	NA	NA	NA	NA	NA	NA	NA
Balance Sheet & Other Fin. Data (Million $)										
Cash	131	134	NA	NA	NA	NA	NA	NA	NA	NA
Curr. Assets	433	263	NA	NA	NA	NA	NA	NA	NA	NA
Total Assets	23,044	18,967	NA	NA	NA	NA	NA	NA	NA	NA
Curr. Liab.	1,367	720	NA	NA	NA	NA	NA	NA	NA	NA
LT Debt	14,165	8,936	7,774	NA	NA	NA	NA	NA	NA	NA
Common Eqty.	3,123	3,011	2,879	NA	NA	NA	NA	NA	NA	NA
Total Cap.	21,377	17,329	10,653	NA	NA	NA	NA	NA	NA	NA
Cap. Exp.	2,825	742	753	NA	NA	NA	NA	NA	NA	NA
Cash Flow	1,644	679	1,171	NA	NA	NA	NA	NA	NA	NA
Curr. Ratio	0.3	0.4	NA	NA	NA	NA	NA	NA	NA	NA
% LT Debt of Cap.	66.3	51.6	73.0	NA	NA	NA	NA	NA	NA	NA
% Net Inc.of Revs.	NM	NM	NM	NA	NA	NA	NA	NA	NA	NA
% Ret. on Assets	NM	NM	NA	NA	NA	NA	NA	NA	NA	NA
% Ret. on Equity	NM	NM	NA	NA	NA	NA	NA	NA	NA	NA

Data as orig reptd.; pro forma in 1998, bal. sh. & bk.val. as of Jun. 30, 1999; bef. results of disc opers/spec. items. Per share data adj. for stk. divs. Bold denotes diluted EPS (FASB 128)-prior periods restated. E-Estimated. NA-Not Available. NM-Not Meaningful. NR-Not Ranked.

Office—12444 Powerscourt Dr., St. Louis, MO 63131. **Tel**—(314) 543-2218. **Website**—www.chartercom.com **CEO & Pres**—J. L. Kent. **EVP & COO**—D. Barford. **EVP & CFO**—K. D. Kalkwarf. **Investor Contact**—K. Picha. **Dirs**—P. G. Allen, J. L. Kent, M. B. Nathanson, N. B. Peretsman, W. D. Savoy. **Transfer Agent & Registrar**—ChaseMellon Shareholder Services. **Incorporated**—in Delaware in 1999. **Empl**— 4,980. **S&P Analyst:** Howard Choe

STANDARD &POOR'S
STOCK REPORTS

The Children's Place

Nasdaq Symbol **PLCE**

18-AUG-01

Industry: Retail (Specialty-Apparel)

Summary: This specialty retailer sells value-priced apparel and accessories for newborns and girls and boys up to age twelve.

S&P Opinion: Buy (★★★★★)

Recent Price • 25.25
52 Wk Range • 33.75-14.93

Yield • Nil
12-Mo. P/E • 14.7

Quantitative Evaluations

Outlook
(1 Lowest—5 Highest)
• **5**

Fair Value
• **47**

Risk
• **NA**

Earn./Div. Rank
• **NR**

Technical Eval.
• **Bearish** since 7/01

Rel. Strength Rank
(1 Lowest—99 Highest)
• **56**

Insider Activity
• **Unfavorable**

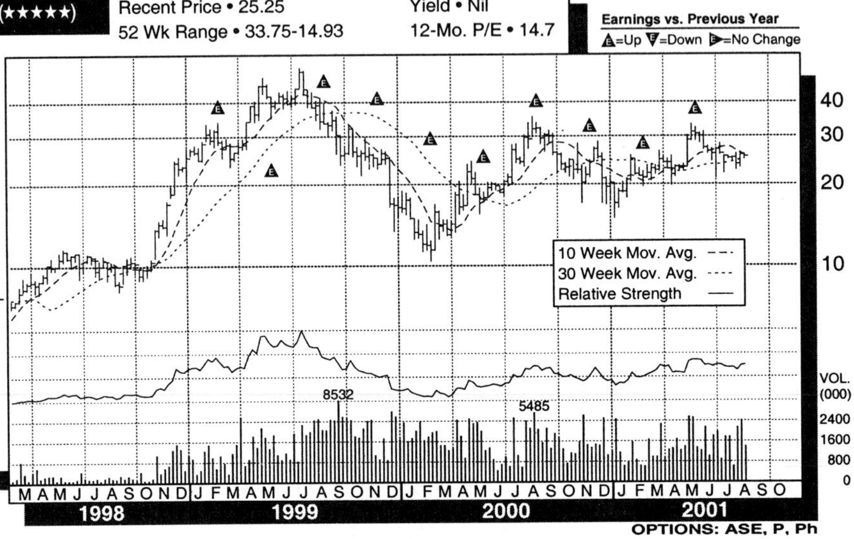

OPTIONS: ASE, P, Ph

Overview - 09-JUL-01

PLCE continues to open new stores and expand as part of a multi-year plan to grow to more than 1,000 stores nationwide. In the first quarter of FY 02 (Jan.), it opened 37 new stores of the 120 scheduled for the year. After a weak 2000 holiday period and lackluster sales in the first two months of FY 02, combined March/April same-store sales (these two months are often lumped together because of the importance and varied timing of Easter) were flat. Comparatively, sales have been better than those across the industry, which suggests that PLCE is gaining market share. For all of FY 02, we expect same-store sales to be up about 1%, with total sales up 19%. Narrower gross margins will be countered by leveraging of corporate overhead, resulting in flat margins. We expect EPS to rise 13% to $1.80.

Valuation - 09-JUL-01

S&P is initiating coverage of PLCE with a strong buy recommendation. We believe The Children's Place concept of offering fashionable, well made children's clothing at attractive prices in a well designed store is on target. The brand is becoming increasingly well known so that parents think of The Children's Place first for their children's apparel. The company continues to locate new stores in malls and other shopping destinations around the country; we expect the number of stores to grow from 400 as of January 31, 2001, to more than 1,000 within five years. S&P thinks PLCE offers excellent appreciation potential at a very attractive valuation of 13 times estimated FY 02 EPS.

Key Stock Statistics

S&P EPS Est. 2002	1.80	Tang. Bk. Value/Share	6.88
P/E on S&P Est. 2002	14.0	Beta	NA
S&P EPS Est. 2003	2.28	Shareholders	4,500
Dividend Rate/Share	Nil	Market cap. (B)	$0.663
Shs. outstg. (M)	26.2	Inst. holdings	46%
Avg. daily vol. (M)	0.329		

Value of $10,000 invested 5 years ago: NA

Fiscal Year Ending Jan. 31

	2002	2001	2000	1999	1998	1997
Revenues (Million $)						
1Q	160.5	130.1	92.62	56.00	—	—
2Q	—	107.7	73.92	48.01	—	—
3Q	—	165.8	119.4	82.50	—	—
4Q	—	183.6	135.5	97.34	65.33	—
Yr.	—	587.4	421.5	283.9	192.6	143.8
Earnings Per Share ($)						
1Q	**0.48**	**0.36**	**0.28**	**0.11**	—	—
2Q	—	**0.06**	**0.05**	**-0.02**	—	—
3Q	—	**0.63**	**0.48**	**0.33**	—	—
4Q	—	**0.56**	**0.51**	**0.38**	**0.17**	—
Yr.	—	**1.60**	**1.32**	**0.80**	**0.29**	**1.28**

Next earnings report expected: late August

Dividend Data

The company does not anticipate paying cash dividends on its common stock in the foreseeable future, but rather intends to retain earnings to finance operations and the expansion of its business.

The Children's Place Retail Stores, Inc.

Business Summary - 09-JUL-01

One could ask which is growing faster -- this specialty retail chain, or the kids for whom it sells clothing and accessories. This is not an overstatement, as The Children's Place Retail Stores nearly quadrupled the number of stores it operates from 108 in early 1997 to 431 as of April 1, 2001.

The company sells apparel and accessories under The Children's Place brand for children from newborn to 12 years of age. The company targets a broad demographic mix by offering high-quality, fashionable clothing at prices generally 20% to 30% below that of mall-based competitors.

The apparel and related merchandise is intended to create a coordinated look distinctive to The Children's Place brand. The company offers a new collection each season -- spring, summer, back-to-school and holiday -- and typically offers a new merchandise line each month that is built around a central color pallette. Each line includes a stylish assortment of coordinated apparel with complementary accessories designed to spark multiple item purchases.

The company utilizes a team approach toward merchandising, including groups from management, trend and design, and sourcing and procurement. Trend and design teams analyze and interpret current and emerging fashion trends to develop a broad selection of clothing and accessories for each upcoming season, while still maintaining the look of The Children's Place brand. The merchandise management team, in conjunction with senior management, reviews prior season results to aid in creating a detailed purchasing plan for the season covering each department, category and key item, as well as allocating merchandise to each store.

The sourcing and procurement teams have developed long term relationships with over 150 independent manufacturers located primarily in Asia. The personnel of these parties assist the company's own staff in sourcing, pre-production approval, quality inspection and delivery assurance. In addition to its manufacturers' own quality testing abilities, the company augments quality assurance with an in-house laboratory to test and evaluate fabric, trimming materials and pre-production samples. The company purchases about 65% of its merchandise from independent agents in Taiwan and Turkey and a trading company based in Hong Kong.

The company's 431 stores are located in 43 states, with the heaviest concentration in the eastern half of the country. The prototype store is 4,200 square feet and is designed to be open and bright. The company distributes merchandise to its stores from a 204,000 sq. ft. center in Secaucus, NJ, and, beginning in the summer of 2001, a new 250,000 sq. ft. facility in Ontario, California.

Per Share Data ($) **(Year Ended Jan. 31)**	**2001**	**2000**	**1999**	**1998**	**1997**	**1996**	**1995**	**1994**	**1993**	**1992**
Tangible Bk. Val.	6.39	4.67	3.23	2.38	2.13	-85.73	NA	NA	NA	NA
Cash Flow	2.38	1.83	1.17	0.53	2.69	37.59	NA	NA	NA	NA
Earnings	1.60	1.32	0.80	0.29	1.28	NA	NA	NA	NA	NA
Dividends	Nil	Nil	Nil	Nil	Nil	NA	NA	NA	NA	NA
Payout Ratio	Nil	Nil	Nil	Nil	Nil	NA	NA	NA	NA	NA
Cal. Yrs.	2000	1999	1998	1997	1996	1995	1994	1993	1992	1991
Prices - High	35.50	53.87	27.25	16.12	NA	NA	NA	NA	NA	NA
- Low	10.37	13.37	4.93	4.37	NA	NA	NA	NA	NA	NA
P/E Ratio - High	22	41	34	56	NA	NA	NA	NA	NA	NA
- Low	6	10	6	15	NA	NA	NA	NA	NA	NA
Income Statement Analysis (Million $)										
Revs.	587	421	284	193	144	122	NA	NA	NA	NA
Oper. Inc.	92.2	71.7	44.1	20.4	16.8	7.6	NA	NA	NA	NA
Depr.	20.9	13.8	8.6	6.0	4.0	3.5	NA	NA	NA	NA
Int. Exp.	1.0	0.3	0.3	2.6	2.9	1.9	NA	NA	NA	NA
Pretax Inc.	70.2	57.4	35.0	11.7	9.5	1.7	NA	NA	NA	NA
Eff. Tax Rate	39%	39%	41%	40%	NM	2.13%	NA	NA	NA	NA
Net Inc.	42.7	35.0	20.7	7.0	30.4	1.7	NA	NA	NA	NA
Balance Sheet & Other Fin. Data (Million $)										
Cash	8.1	2.2	16.4	0.9	3.4	0.6	NA	NA	NA	NA
Curr. Assets	99	73.6	62.5	38.4	27.7	16.2	NA	NA	NA	NA
Total Assets	232	171	111	79.4	64.5	32.1	NA	NA	NA	NA
Curr. Liab.	58.0	46.2	27.0	18.2	15.7	33.8	NA	NA	NA	NA
LT Debt	Nil	Nil	Nil	Nil	19.1	8.2	NA	NA	NA	NA
Common Eqty.	167	120	80.6	58.5	27.3	-11.7	NA	NA	NA	NA
Total Cap.	167	120	80.6	58.5	46.4	-3.5	NA	NA	NA	NA
Cap. Exp.	53.1	58.2	19.8	17.2	8.5	6.9	NA	NA	NA	NA
Cash Flow	63.6	48.9	29.3	12.9	34.5	5.2	NA	NA	NA	NA
Curr. Ratio	1.7	1.6	2.3	2.1	1.8	0.5	NA	NA	NA	NA
% LT Debt of Cap.	Nil	Nil	Nil	Nil	41.2	NM	NA	NA	NA	NA
% Net Inc.of Revs.	7.3	8.3	7.3	2.7	21.2	1.4	NA	NA	NA	NA
% Ret. on Assets	21.1	24.9	18.7	8.8	47.2	5.2	NA	NA	NA	NA
% Ret. on Equity	29.7	34.9	25.6	11.9	111.5	NM	NA	NA	NA	NA

Data as orig reptd.; bef. results of disc opers/spec. items. Per share data adj. for stk. divs. Bold denotes diluted EPS (FASB 128)-prior periods restated. E-Estimated. NA-Not Available. NM-Not Meaningful. NR-Not Ranked.

Office—915 Secaucus Rd., Secaucus, NJ 07094.**Tel**—(201) 558-2400. **Website**—http://www.childrensplace.com **Chrmn & CEO**—E. Dabah. **VP-Fin, & CFO**—S. L. Udasin. **VP & Secy**—S. Balasiano. **Investor Contact Info**—(201) 558-2400, ext. 4500; investor relations@childrensplace.com **Dirs**—E. Dabah, S. F. Kasaks, J. F. Megrue, D. J. Oddi, S. Silverstein.**Transfer Agent & Registrar**—American Stock Transfer & Trust Co. **Incorporated**—in Delaware in 1988. **Empl**— 7,818. **S&P Analyst:** Mark S. Basham

STANDARD &POOR'S
STOCK REPORTS

Clayton Homes

NYSE Symbol **CMH**

In S&P MidCap 400

18-AUG-01 **Industry:** Homebuilding

Summary: This producer and retailer of low- to medium-priced manufactured homes also provides related financing and insurance services, and manages manufactured housing communities.

S&P Opinion: Buy (★★★★★)

Recent Price • 15.22 | 52 Wk Range • 16.55-8.31 | Yield • 0.4% | 12-Mo. P/E • 19.8

Quantitative Evaluations

Outlook (1 Lowest—5 Highest) • **4+**

Fair Value • **20.50**

Risk • **Average**

Earn./Div. Rank • **A-**

Technical Eval. • **Bullish** since 6/01

Rel. Strength Rank (1 Lowest—99 Highest) • **53**

Insider Activity • **NA**

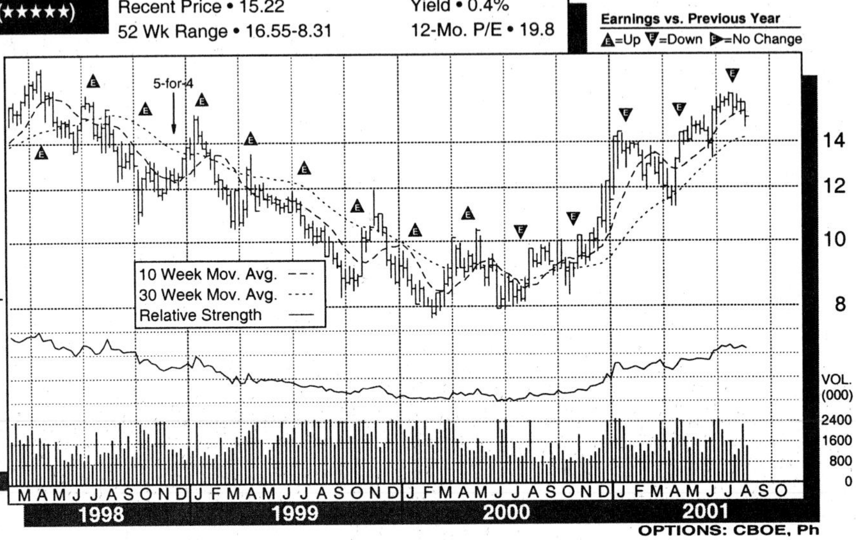

OPTIONS: CBOE, Ph

Overview - 10-AUG-01

We expect revenues to rebound by about 5% in FY 02 (Jun.), with modest gains likely in both the housing and finance divisions. A continuing excess of industry retail sites and restrictive financing will likely keep the manufactured home industry sluggish for a while longer. However, the sector's ongoing idling of plants and closing of retail units should firm trends by mid-FY 02, giving CMH's sales a lift. Our forecasted improvement in financial services revenues should be driven by a larger loan servicing portfolio and improving manufactured housing trends. Margins should be limited for a while by difficult revenue trends, but our projected stabilization of the manufactured housing sector will likely boost margins as FY 02 moves along. CMH should also be aided by a greater focus on multi-section homes, a larger proportion of higher-margined company dealer sales, and cost controls.

Valuation - 10-AUG-01

The shares have recovered since late 2000, as investors began to foresee a conclusion to the current downturn in manufactured housing. Clayton has been battling a sharp reduction in industry shipments, with retail center overcapacity causing a supply glut and restrictive financing slowing demand. Substantial industry sales of repossessed homes have also taken dollars away from new home sales. Those severe conditions have provided a major challenge, but CMH's business has been steadied by its strong management team, conservative operating strategy and solid financial services business. In addition, we think aggressive industry actions to overcome its woes will finally have their intended impact by mid-FY 02. Based on our outlook, and with the shares trading in the the lower to middle end of their traditional forward P/E multiple, the stock should greatly outperform the broad market in the coming year.

Key Stock Statistics

S&P EPS Est. 2002	0.90	Tang. Bk. Value/Share	7.54
P/E on S&P Est. 2002	16.9	Beta	0.90
Dividend Rate/Share	0.06	Shareholders	11,380
Shs. outstg. (M)	137.8	Market cap. (B)	$ 2.1
Avg. daily vol. (M)	0.297	Inst. holdings	51%

Value of $10,000 invested 5 years ago: $ 12,632

Fiscal Year Ending Jun. 30

	2001	2000	1999	1998	1997	1996
Revenues (Million $)						
1Q	300.8	337.3	314.7	262.7	236.2	215.3
2Q	284.9	309.2	319.1	251.1	234.7	211.2
3Q	272.1	307.0	308.3	268.4	226.6	211.4
4Q	293.2	399.9	402.2	345.6	324.2	290.9
Yr.	1,151	1,293	1,344	1,128	1,022	928.7
Earnings Per Share ($)						
1Q	**0.21**	**0.25**	**0.22**	0.20	0.17	0.15
2Q	**0.20**	**0.25**	**0.24**	**0.21**	0.18	0.15
3Q	**0.17**	**0.26**	**0.24**	**0.21**	0.18	0.16
4Q	**0.19**	**0.27**	**0.36**	**0.30**	0.27	0.25
Yr.	**0.77**	**1.03**	**1.06**	**0.92**	**0.80**	**0.71**

Next earnings report expected: mid October

Dividend Data (Dividends have been paid since 1995.)

Amount ($)	Date Decl.	Ex-Div. Date	Stock of Record	Payment Date
0.016	Jul. 26	Sep. 25	Sep. 27	Oct. 18 '00
0.016	Nov. 01	Dec. 22	Dec. 27	Jan. 17 '01
0.016	Jan. 25	Mar. 26	Mar. 28	Apr. 18 '01
0.016	Apr. 25	Jun. 25	Jun. 27	Jul. 18 '01

A Division of The McGraw-Hill Companies

Clayton Homes, Inc.

Business Summary - 10-AUG-01

Reflecting dismal industry conditions, the fourth quarter of FY 00 (Jun.) marked the first year to year quarterly earnings decline in 14 years for Clayton Homes; profits also faltered in the four following quarters. The company has generally posted impressive earnings consistency in light of the highly cyclical nature of the manufactured housing industry. Clayton strives for steady long-term growth through a disciplined operating strategy. It refuses to overpay for factories and sales centers during industry upturns, and prides itself on snaring additional capacity at bargain prices during tougher industry times. The company also achieves earnings stability through activities in financial services and manufactured home communities, where mortgage payments, insurance premiums and rental incomes persist during most market and economic conditions.

The company makes a wide variety of single- and multi-section manufactured homes, which are factory-built, completely finished, constructed to be transported by trucks, and designed as permanent, primary residences when sited. CMH's homes had retail prices in FY 00 (latest available) ranging from $10,000 to $75,000, and were sized from 500 sq. ft. to 2,400 sq. ft.

CMH sells homes through company-owned dealers (51% of revenues in FY 01) and independent dealers (19%). In addition to selling homes built by Clayton, company-owned centers also offer new and used homes produced by others. The number of dealers selling CMH homes has grown strongly, with company-owned dealers increasing 55% (at June 30, 2001) since FY 95 year end, and independents rising 51%. However, since the industry started to suffer in recent periods from an oversaturation of retail dealers, CMH has undertaken a moderate consolidation. At FY 00 year end, it operated 318 company-owned retail centers, and supplied homes to 707 independent dealers, but those totals had fallen to 297 and 634, respectively, at FY 01 year end. CMH sold 26,215 homes in FY 01, down 17% from 31,520 in FY 00.

CMH believes its provision of financing options plays a big part in its sale of homes. It offers lending through its Vanderbilt Mortgage and Finance unit and also maintains relationships with conventional lenders. In FY 00 (latest available), 76% of CMH's retail home sales were financed through Vanderbilt. CMH also offers insurance policies issued by non-related insurance concerns.

Clayton also operates manufactured housing communities. At FY 01 year end, it owned a total of 21,121 sites at 81 communities, which sported an occupancy rate of 75%. The company attributes the typically low occupancy rates of its communities to its strategy of acquiring weaker, underperforming developments.

The company repurchased 5.4 million of its shares in FY 00, for a total of $50 million. Further substantial buybacks seem unlikely in the near term, as a severe industry downturn has started to give CMH opportunities to expand through bargain asset purc hases.

Per Share Data ($) (Year Ended Jun. 30)	2001	2000	1999	1998	1997	1996	1995	1994	1993	1992
Tangible Bk. Val.	NA	7.54	6.66	5.94	5.10	4.38	3.69	3.14	2.55	2.15
Cash Flow	NA	1.18	1.18	1.27	0.89	0.79	0.64	0.53	0.42	0.32
Earnings	0.77	1.03	1.06	0.92	0.80	0.72	0.59	0.48	0.39	0.29
Dividends	0.06	0.06	0.06	0.06	0.06	0.04	0.03	Nil	Nil	Nil
Payout Ratio	8%	6%	6%	7%	8%	6%	5%	Nil	Nil	Nil
Prices - High	16.55	13.06	15.43	18.10	15.60	14.50	14.96	10.95	10.07	8.51
- Low	11.25	7.68	8.25	10.64	10.10	9.90	7.16	6.30	6.75	3.60
P/E Ratio - High	21	13	15	20	20	20	25	23	26	27
- Low	15	7	8	12	13	14	12	13	17	12
Income Statement Analysis (Million $)										
Revs.	NA	1,293	1,344	1,128	1,022	929	758	628	476	371
Oper. Inc.	NA	247	277	231	201	179	140	115	88.4	80.5
Depr.	NA	20.4	17.8	14.7	13.1	11.1	8.3	6.7	4.9	3.4
Int. Exp.	NA	6.8	13.3	2.0	Nil	NM	NM	0.4	1.4	20.2
Pretax Inc.	NA	59.4	246	222	193	172	136	108	83.4	60.1
Eff. Tax Rate	NA	NM	37%	38%	38%	NM	36%	36%	36%	35%
Net Inc.	NA	144	155	138	120	107	87.0	69.3	53.8	39.3
Balance Sheet & Other Fin. Data (Million $)										
Cash	NA	141	103	1.7	89.7	47.4	49.4	38.9	28.7	63.4
Curr. Assets	NA	NA	NA	NA	NA	NA	NA	NA	NA	NA
Total Assets	NA	1,506	1,417	1,458	1,046	886	761	701	587	555
Curr. Liab.	NA	NA	NA	NA	NA	NA	NA	NA	NA	NA
LT Debt	NA	96.1	96.5	248	22.8	30.2	49.0	71.0	112	163
Common Eqty.	NA	1,036	948	881	755	650	544	462	349	293
Total Cap.	NA	1,132	1,044	1,129	791	686	602	540	468	462
Cap. Exp.	NA	34.4	47.7	62.2	42.9	40.8	44.5	35.6	22.7	19.1
Cash Flow	NA	164	173	152	133	118	95.3	75.9	58.7	42.8
Curr. Ratio	NA	NA	NA	NA	NA	NA	NA	NA	NA	NA
% LT Debt of Cap.	NA	8.5	9.2	21.9	2.9	4.4	8.1	13.1	23.9	35.4
% Net Inc.of Revs.	NA	11.1	11.5	12.2	11.7	11.5	11.5	11.0	11.3	10.6
% Ret. on Assets	NA	9.9	10.8	11.0	12.4	12.9	11.9	10.7	9.4	7.3
% Ret. on Equity	NA	14.5	16.9	16.9	17.0	17.9	17.3	17.0	16.7	15.4

Data as orig. reptd.; bef. results of disc. opers. and/or spec. items. Per share data adj. for stk. divs. as of ex-div. date. Bold denotes diluted EPS (FASB 128). E-Estimated. NA-Not Available. NM-Not Meaningful. NR-Not Ranked.

Office—5000 Clayton Rd., Maryville, TN 37804. **Tel**—(865) 380-3000. **Website**—http://www.clayton.net **Chrmn**—J. L. Clayton. **Pres & CEO**—K. T. Clayton. **Secy & Investor Contact**—Carl Koella III. **Dirs**—B. J. Clayton, J. L. Clayton, K. T. Clayton, D. W. Evins, W. H. Jordan, J. J. Kalec, T. N. McAdams, C. W. Neel. **Transfer Agent & Registrar**—American Stock Transfer & Trust, NYC. **Incorporated**—in Tennessee in 1968. **Empl**— 7,429. **S&P Analyst:** Michael W. Jaffe

STANDARD
&POOR'S
STOCK REPORTS

Comcast Corp.

Nasdaq Symbol **CMCSK**

In S&P 500

18-AUG-01

Industry:
Broadcasting (Television, Radio & Cable)

Summary: Comcast is the third largest U.S. cable TV system operator, and is rapidly expanding its broadband and digital cable businesses. It also owns QVC.

S&P Opinion: Buy (★★★★★)

Recent Price • 36.87
52 Wk Range • 46.31-33.37
Yield • Nil
12-Mo. P/E • 13.0

Quantitative Evaluations

Outlook
(1 Lowest—5 Highest)
• **NA**

Fair Value
• **NA**

Risk
• **Average**

Earn./Div. Rank
• **B-**

Technical Eval.
• **Bearish** since 7/01

Rel. Strength Rank
(1 Lowest—99 Highest)
• **35**

Insider Activity
• **NA**

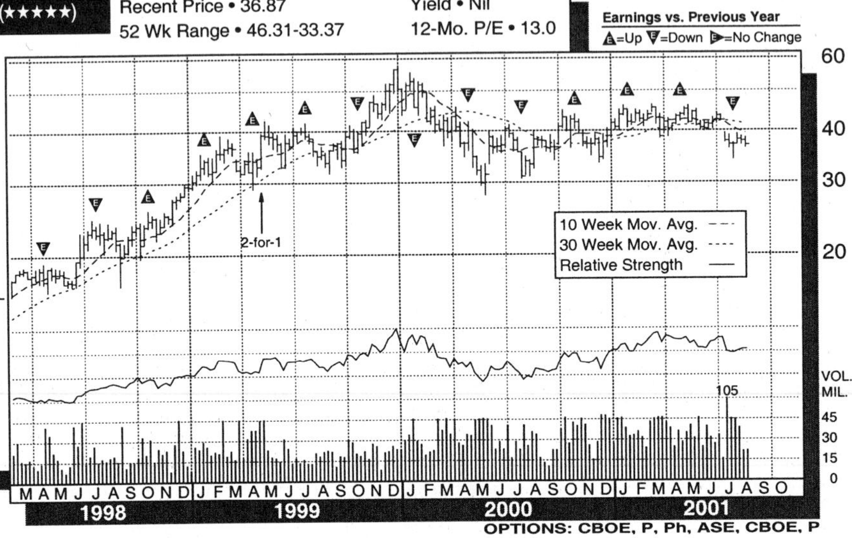

OPTIONS: CBOE, P, Ph, ASE, CBOE, P

Overview - 10-AUG-01

We expect pro forma revenues to grow around 11% in 2001, reflecting increased demand for digital services and high speed Internet access lines, and continued strength at QVC. Cable revenues should climb nearly 9%, mainly due to subscriber upgrades to digital cable, increased high-speed data subscribers and advertising revenue. QVC revenues should grow 12%, reflecting strong domestic and German sales growth. Content sales should be driven by E! Network and the Golf channel. Operating cash flow should increase a solid 10%, but margins are expected to narrow slightly due to higher costs associated with the new business communications division. We expect operating cash flow per share to increase to $2.98 in 2001, from $2.61 in 2000.

Valuation - 10-AUG-01

We recommend buying CMCSK, reflecting strong company qualities and favorable industry fundamentals. CMCSK was recently trading at 13X our estimate of 2001 operating cash flow per share, representing a slight discount to its peers. The shares have been pressured by the prospect of CMCSK acquiring the cable assets of AT&T. While we believe such an acquisition may weaken CMCSK's financial condition in the short term, we believe management would create superior value for shareholders in the long run. The company has a long history of turning around underperforming cable operations and extracting synergies from the combined cable systems. CMCSK is the only cable operator that has recently enjoyed accelerating growth in both digital cable and high-speed data services. The company's ability to bundle television and broadband services should contribute to solid revenue growth over the next few years.

Key Stock Statistics

S&P EPS Est. 2001	0.67	Tang. Bk. Value/Share	NM
P/E on S&P Est. 2001	55.0	Beta	0.77
S&P EPS Est. 2002	-0.56	Shareholders	3,662
Dividend Rate/Share	Nil	Market cap. (B)	$ 33.7
Shs. outstg. (M)	945.0	Inst. holdings	72%
Avg. daily vol. (M)	6.304		

Value of $10,000 invested 5 years ago: $ 48,023

Fiscal Year Ending Dec. 31

	2001	2000	1999	1998	1997	1996
Revenues (Million $)						
1Q	2,196	1,939	1,374	1,360	1,131	950.7
2Q	2,299	1,912	1,479	1,322	1,185	945.6
3Q	—	1,960	1,525	1,355	1,204	974.6
4Q	—	2,408	1,832	1,447	1,393	1,168
Yr.	—	8,219	6,209	5,145	4,913	4,038
Earnings Per Share ($)						
1Q	**1.06**	**-0.23**	**0.12**	**-0.12**	**-0.10**	**-0.07**
2Q	**0.04**	**0.20**	**1.10**	**-0.13**	**-0.03**	**0.04**
3Q	**E-0.18**	**1.29**	**0.07**	**0.88**	**-0.09**	**-0.02**
4Q	**E-0.25**	**0.81**	**-0.23**	**0.52**	**-0.12**	**-0.05**
Yr.	**E0.67**	**2.16**	**0.95**	**1.25**	**-0.33**	-0.10

Next earnings report expected: early November

Dividend Data

The shares were split two for one in May 1999. The most recent cash payment was $0.01 a share (as adjusted) in March 1999.

Comcast Corporation

Business Summary - 10-AUG-01

Comcast is principally engaged in three businesses: the development, management and operation of broadband communications networks; electronic commerce via its QVC retailing subsidiary; and the content business, through certain consolidated subsidiaries and programming assets.

At the end of 2000, CMCSK served 7.7 million cable subscribers, making it the third largest U.S. cable system operator. The company is rapidly deploying digital video cable and high-speed Internet access service to develop the array of products it offers on its cable communications networks. CMCSK is currently deploying fiber optic cable and upgrading the technical quality of its cable communications networks, in order to increase the reliability and capacity of its systems. The upgraded systems let the company provide additional video programming and other services, such as digital video, high speed Internet access, and ultimately telephony. As of January 31, 2001, 84% of CMCSK's cable customers were served by a cable system of at least 550 MHz, and 70% were served by a system of at least 750 MHz. Digital cable was available to more than 95% of customers. More than 1,354,000 customers subscribed to digital cable.

Cable revenues are derived primarily from subscription services, which are typically paid on a monthly basis. Subscription rates are dependent on the level of programming packages chosen by the customer. Other sources of revenue include premium cable channels, advertising sales, pay-per-view services, installation services, commissions from electronic retailing, and other services.

Through a joint venture with Excite@Home, the company offers high-speed cable modem services as Comcast@Home in areas served by its cable communications systems. This service allows subscribers to connect their personal computers, via cable modems, to the Internet at speeds much greater than those offered by a conventional analog modem. At the end of 2000, Comcast@Home service was available to more than 6.3 million homes, and had 400,000 subscribers.

Comcast owns a 57% interest in QVC, an electronic retailing business. QVC is engaged in domestic and international electronic media of general merchandise over television programs which are transmitted to subscribers. At QVC, a program host describes and demonstrates the products, which viewers order directly from QVC. Products sold include jewelry, housewares, electronics, apparel and accessories, collectibles, toys and cosmetics.

Comcast's investments in the content business include 100% ownership of CN8-The Comcast Network and Comcast Sports Southeast, and stakes in Comcast SportsNet (53%), E! Entertainment (40%), Style (40%), The Golf Channel (60%), In Demand (11%), Outdoor Life (17%), Speedvision (15%), and the Sunshine Network (16%).

Per Share Data ($) (Year Ended Dec. 31)	2000	1999	1998	1997	1996	1995	1994	1993	1992	1991
Tangible Bk. Val.	NM	NM	NM	NM	NM	NM	-1.52	-1.97	-0.45	0.05
Cash Flow	4.90	2.40	2.38	1.05	1.30	1.36	0.56	0.56	0.04	0.03
Earnings	2.16	0.95	1.25	-0.33	-0.10	-0.08	-0.16	-0.23	-0.54	-0.43
Dividends	Nil	0.01	0.01	0.01	0.01	0.01	0.01	0.01	0.01	0.01
Payout Ratio	Nil	1%	4%	NM	NM	NM	NM	NM	NM	NM
Prices - High	55.68	57.68	30.12	16.53	10.68	11.18	12.00	14.06	6.56	6.06
- Low	27.87	28.90	14.75	7.31	6.87	6.87	7.00	5.81	4.50	3.62
P/E Ratio - High	26	61	24	NM	NM	NM	NM	NM	NM	NM
- Low	13	30	12	NM	NM	NM	NM	NM	NM	NM
Income Statement Analysis (Million $)										
Revs.	8,219	6,209	5,145	4,913	4,038	3,363	1,375	1,338	900	721
Oper. Inc.	2,470	1,880	1,497	1,469	1,207	1,019	576	606	397	309
Depr.	2,631	1,216	940	936	698	689	336	342	232	164
Int. Exp.	691	538	467	565	541	525	313	347	268	205
Pretax Inc.	3,602	1,500	1,558	-229	-16.1	-45.4	-85.0	-84.0	-158	-98.0
Eff. Tax Rate	40%	48%	38%	NM	NM	NM	NM	NM	NM	NM
Net Inc.	2,045	781	1,008	-209	-52.5	-37.8	-75.0	-99	-218	-156
Balance Sheet & Other Fin. Data (Million $)										
Cash	652	922	4,524	578	540	910	465	680	348	596
Curr. Assets	5,144	9,759	5,624	1,560	1,406	1,654	609	777	429	645
Total Assets	35,745	28,686	14,817	12,804	12,089	9,580	6,763	4,948	4,272	2,794
Curr. Liab.	4,042	5,527	3,093	1,418	1,365	1,122	661	595	392	264
LT Debt	10,517	8,707	5,464	6,559	7,103	6,944	4,811	4,163	3,974	2,165
Common Eqty.	28,113	9,772	3,242	1,101	520	-828	-727	-870	-182	19.0
Total Cap.	45,734	23,159	10,779	10,317	9,796	6,116	5,475	3,292	3,792	2,472
Cap. Exp.	1,637	894	899	926	670	623	270	NA	NA	NA
Cash Flow	4,653	1,967	1,919	712	646	651	261	243	14.0	9.0
Curr. Ratio	1.3	1.8	1.8	1.1	1.0	1.5	0.9	1.3	1.1	2.4
% LT Debt of Cap.	23.0	37.6	50.7	63.4	72.5	113.5	87.9	126.4	104.8	87.6
% Net Inc.of Revs.	24.9	12.6	19.6	NM	NM	NM	NM	NM	NM	NM
% Ret. on Assets	6.3	3.6	6.5	NM	NM	NM	NM	NM	NM	NM
% Ret. on Equity	8.4	11.5	46.4	NM	NM	NM	NM	NM	NM	NM

Data as orig reptd.; bef. results of disc opers/spec. items. Per share data adj. for stk. divs. Bold denotes diluted EPS (FASB 128)-prior periods restated. E-Estimated. NA-Not Available. NM-Not Meaningful. NR-Not Ranked.

Office—1500 Market St., Philadelphia, PA 19102-2148. **Tel**—(215) 665-1700. **Website**—http://www.comcast.com **Chrmn**—R. J. Roberts. **Vice Chrmn**—J. A. Brodsky. **Pres**—B. L. Roberts. **EVP & Treas**—John R. Alchin. **EVP & Secy**—D. L. Wang. **Investor Contact**—Marlene Dooner (215-981-7392). **Dirs**—D. Anstrom, S. M. Bonovitz, J. A. Brodsky, J. L. Castle, F. G. Rohatyn, B. L. Roberts, R. J. Roberts, B. C. Watson, I. A. Wechsler, A. Wexler. **Transfer Agent**—Bank of New York, NYC. **Incorporated**—in Pennsylvania in 1969. **Empl**— 35,000. **S&P Analyst:** Howard Choe

STANDARD
&POOR'S
STOCK REPORTS

Electronics Boutique Hldgs.

Nasdaq Symbol **ELBO**

18-AUG-01

Industry:
Retail (Specialty)

Summary: This specialty retailer focuses on the sale of video games and PC entertainment software through over 770 locations in the U.S. and abroad.

S&P Opinion: Buy (★★★★★)

Recent Price • 35.60
52 Wk Range • 36.45-14.37
Yield • Nil
12-Mo. P/E • 72.7

Quantitative Evaluations

Outlook
(1 Lowest—5 Highest)
• **3**

Fair Value
• **30.70**

Risk
• **NA**

Earn./Div. Rank
• **NR**

Technical Eval.
• **Bearish** since 8/01

Rel. Strength Rank
(1 Lowest—99 Highest)
• **93**

Insider Activity
• **NA**

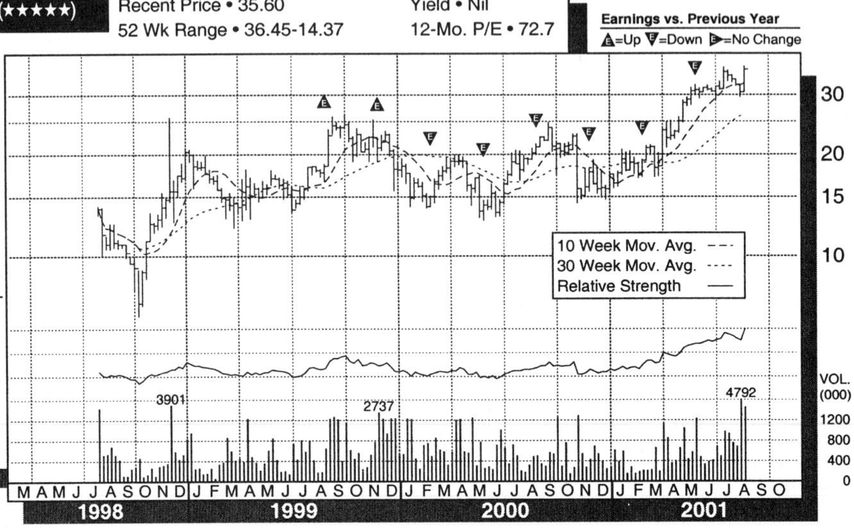

Overview - 25-MAY-01

Revenue growth of 6% in FY 01 (Jan.) strayed from the historical four-year compound average annual growth rate of 23%, due to the transition to new-technology video game hardware platforms. We forecast revenue growth of over 30% in FY 02, to approximately $1.0 billion, driven by sales of new-technology platforms from Sony, Nintendo and Microsoft, and from related video game software and accessories. The gross margin should narrow by approximately 80 basis points in 2001, as a greater degree of lower margin hardware sales dominates. In 2002, increasing levels of software sales will lead the margin wider. Leverage over SG&A expenses and depreciation & amortization charges, despite the opening of 175 gross new stores, should widen the EBIT margin by 50 basis points. We expect EPS to increase 36% in FY 02, to $0.90, and 41% in FY 03, to $1.27.

Valuation - 25-MAY-01

ELBO shares have risen 78% thus far in 2001, compared to a 2.9% decline in the S&P 500 Index, due to the introduction of new game consoles. ELBO's focus on the sale of entertainment software has enabled it to build significant brand awareness among "gamers" as the premier destination to find titles; unsuspecting moms aren't lost either, with stores mostly located in heavily trafficked malls. With 175 stores planned for opening, we expect ELBO to slingshot its way into the new product cycle, which typically runs four to five years. ELBO's inventory intelligence, gathered through its pre-sell program, helps it manage inventory effectively, and is valuable to manufacturers as well. Trading at 24.5X our FY 03 EPS estimate of $1.27, the shares are 35% discounted to our forecast for growth through the two-year period. Our valuation of future free cash flows also supports our case for purchase.

Key Stock Statistics

S&P EPS Est. 2002	0.90	Tang. Bk. Value/Share	5.78
P/E on S&P Est. 2002	39.6	Beta	NA
S&P EPS Est. 2003	1.27	Shareholders	39
Dividend Rate/Share	Nil	Market cap. (B)	$0.893
Shs. outstg. (M)	25.1	Inst. holdings	34%
Avg. daily vol. (M)	0.489		

Value of $10,000 invested 5 years ago: NA

Fiscal Year Ending Jan. 31

	2002	2001	2000	1999	1998	1997
Revenues (Million $)						
1Q	179.9	151.1	123.6	—	—	—
2Q	—	125.0	113.1	102.5	—	—
3Q	—	157.8	176.5	111.3	—	—
4Q	—	334.0	314.6	252.9	—	—
Yr.	—	770.8	728.7	573.9	—	339.6
Earnings Per Share ($)						
1Q	**-0.06**	**0.11**	**0.14**	—	—	—
2Q	**E-0.21**	**-0.09**	**0.03**	**-0.02**	—	—
3Q	**E0.11**	**0.06**	**0.19**	**0.08**	—	—
4Q	**E1.06**	**0.58**	**0.71**	**0.81**	—	—
Yr.	**E0.90**	**0.66**	**1.10**	**1.11**	**0.74**	**0.50**

Next earnings report expected: mid August

Dividend Data

No cash dividends have been paid.

Electronics Boutique Holdings Corp.

Business Summary - 25-MAY-01

Electronics Boutique specializes in the retail sale of electronic games. ELBO sells video games and PC entertainment software, supported by the sale of video game hardware, PC productivity software, PC accessories and related products. ELBO's store base is comprised of over 770 locations in 46 states and Puerto Rico, Canada, Australia, New Zealand, Denmark, Norway and South Korea. At January 2000, 61.5% of the outstanding common shares were beneficially owned by EB Nevada Inc., a company indirectly controlled by James Kim, his wife and certain trusts for his children.

ELBO's store portfolio at year-end FY 01 (Jan.) was primarily comprised of Electronics Boutique locations, and also included stores under the names EBX, BC Sports Collectibles, EBKids and Stop 'N Save Software. Averaging 1,200 square feet in size, most of the stores are located in high traffic areas in regional shopping malls. The company anticipates the opening of 175 new stores in FY 02. Online shoppers are served by EBWORLD.com, its e-commerce subsidiary that generated revenues of $14.1 million in FY 00.

Domestic retail sales of video game titles, hardware and accessories were approximately $7.2 billion in 1999. At year-end 1999, the installed base of video game hardware systems in the U.S. totaled 21.8 million Sony Playstation units, 13.2 million Nintendo 64 units, and 1.3 million Sega Dreamcast units. In October 2000, Sony introduced the Sony Playstation 2, a 128 bit system employing DVD technology. In the fall of 2001, the introduction of new systems from Nintendo and Microsoft is expected to further ignite industry sales.

ELBO's operating strategy is geared toward winning over the core gamer, who demands immediate access to new releases and generally purchases more video and PC game titles than the average consumer. ELBO's extensive breadth of title selection helps draws gamers, with approximately 1,350 titles offered.

Strong demand often precedes game introductions, and the company gears its strategy toward satisfying that demand through its "EB Pre-Sell Program," which guarantees customers a copy of a new release immediately upon launch. In addition, the company's "EB Reserve List" entitles participants to be notified when a game has arrived in stores. ELBO also maintains a price matching policy to support customer loyalty.

With nearly 2,000 SKUs and about 10 new SKUs introduced each day, the company must maintain strict inventory policies. ELBO's inventory management system enables it to maximize sales of new releases and avoid markdowns as titles mature. Risk is minimized through: extensive research on new-releases for forecasting; utilization of point-of-sale polling technology; local preference consideration; and replenishment of store-level inventories daily from fully automated distribution centers. Inventory turnover was 5.4X in FY 00.

Per Share Data ($) (Year Ended Jan. 31)	**2001**	**2000**	**1999**	**1998**	**1997**	**1996**	**1995**	**1994**	**1993**	**1992**
Tangible Bk. Val.	5.83	5.17	2.33	NA	NA	NA	NA	NA	NA	NA
Cash Flow	1.37	1.69	1.49	NA	NA	NA	NA	NA	NA	NA
Earnings	0.66	1.10	0.99	1.40	0.50	NA	NA	NA	NA	NA
Dividends	NA	Nil	Nil	Nil	Nil	NA	NA	NA	NA	NA
Payout Ratio	NA	Nil	Nil	Nil	Nil	NA	NA	NA	NA	NA
Cal. Yrs.	2000	1999	1998	1997	1996	1995	1994	1993	1992	1991
Prices - High	NA	26.31	25.75	NA	NA	NA	NA	NA	NA	NA
- Low	NA	12.12	6.62	NA	NA	NA	NA	NA	NA	NA
P/E Ratio - High	NA	24	23	NA	NA	NA	NA	NA	NA	NA
- Low	NA	11	6	NA	NA	NA	NA	NA	NA	NA
Income Statement Analysis (Million $)										
Revs.	771	729	574	454	340	NA	NA	NA	NA	NA
Oper. Inc.	35.9	48.7	42.2	28.5	16.9	NA	NA	NA	NA	NA
Depr.	15.9	12.3	9.8	8.0	6.6	NA	NA	NA	NA	NA
Int. Exp.	0.1	1.4	1.1	2.6	2.4	NA	NA	NA	NA	NA
Pretax Inc.	24.7	37.8	32.0	22.9	8.5	NA	NA	NA	NA	NA
Eff. Tax Rate	40%	40%	37%	3.69%	6.50%	NA	NA	NA	NA	NA
Net Inc.	14.9	22.8	20.3	22.1	7.9	NA	NA	NA	NA	NA
Balance Sheet & Other Fin. Data (Million $)										
Cash	45.1	88.4	42.0	20.6	44.7	NA	NA	NA	NA	NA
Curr. Assets	163	199	118	83.7	102	NA	NA	NA	NA	NA
Total Assets	267	276	172	143	139	NA	NA	NA	NA	NA
Curr. Liab.	133	156	121	101	92.1	NA	NA	NA	NA	NA
LT Debt	Nil	Nil	Nil	10.5	24.2	NA	NA	NA	NA	NA
Common Eqty.	131	116	48.8	28.4	20.4	NA	NA	NA	NA	NA
Total Cap.	131	116	48.9	38.9	44.6	NA	NA	NA	NA	NA
Cap. Exp.	44.8	31.8	19.6	18.5	8.6	NA	NA	NA	NA	NA
Cash Flow	30.7	35.1	30.1	30.1	14.5	NA	NA	NA	NA	NA
Curr. Ratio	1.2	1.3	1.0	0.8	1.1	NA	NA	NA	NA	NA
% LT Debt of Cap.	Nil	Nil	0.0	27.1	54.3	NA	NA	NA	NA	NA
% Net Inc.of Revs.	1.9	3.1	3.5	4.9	2.3	NA	NA	NA	NA	NA
% Ret. on Assets	5.5	10.2	12.9	15.5	5.7	NA	NA	NA	NA	NA
% Ret. on Equity	12.0	27.6	52.5	77.7	38.8	NA	NA	NA	NA	NA

Data as orig reptd.; bef. results of disc opers/spec. items. Per share data adj. for stk. divs. Bold denotes diluted EPS (FASB 128)-prior periods restated. E-Estimated. NA-Not Available. NM-Not Meaningful. NR-Not Ranked.

Office—931 South Matlack St., West Chester, PA 19382. **Tel**—(610) 430-8100. **Website**—http://www.ebholdings.com **Chrmn**—J. J. Kim. **Pres & CEO**—J. J. Firestone. **SVP & CFO**—J. R. Panichello. **SVP-Fin & Investor Contact**—J. Smith. **Dirs**—D. S. Adler, J. J. Firestone, J. J. Kim, S. Y. Kim, L. J. Siana, S. Steinberg. **Transfer Agent**—First Chicago Trust Co. of New York, Jersey City, NJ. **Empl**— 5,000. **S&P Analyst:** Markos N. Kaminis

STANDARD
&POOR'S
STOCK REPORTS

Gemstar-TV Guide Intl.

Nasdaq Symbol **GMST**

18-AUG-01

Industry: Electrical Equipment

Summary: This company is a leading global technology and media company focused on consumer entertainment.

S&P Opinion: Buy (★★★★★)

Recent Price • 33.53
52 Wk Range • 91.62-20.25
Yield • Nil
12-Mo. P/E • NM

Quantitative Evaluations

Outlook
(1 Lowest—5 Highest)
• **NA**

Fair Value
• **NA**

Risk
• **High**

Earn./Div. Rank
• **B-**

Technical Eval.
• **Neutral** since 8/01

Rel. Strength Rank
(1 Lowest—99 Highest)
• **18**

Insider Activity
• **NA**

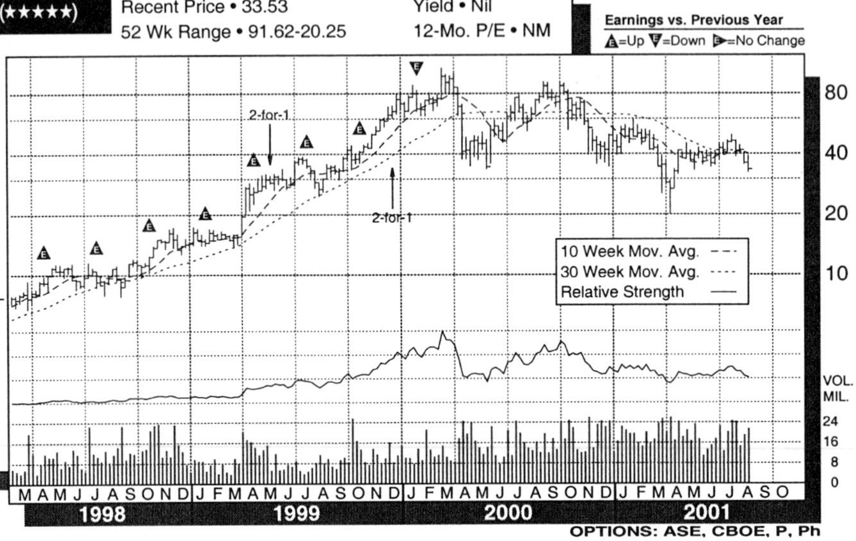

OPTIONS: ASE, CBOE, P, Ph

Overview - 23-JUL-01

While we expect GMST's technology & licensing and interactive platform division revenues to accelerate 34% and 400%, respectively, in 2001, pro forma consolidated revenues should be flat due to declining TV Guide print circulation and a planned reduction in the C-Band satellite business. Technology & licensing revenue growth should be driven by increased deployment of interactive programming guides in set-top boxes and growth in the number of digital cable subscribers. Revenue growth in the interactive platform division should be driven by a significant ramp-up in advertising revenues. We expect operating expenses to fall, reflecting cost-cutting in anticipation of the slowdown in the print and C-Band divisions. As a result, pro forma EBITDA should rise 6% to $1.02 per share. Due mainly to depreciation and amortization charges, GMST should incur a loss of $1.18 per share.

Valuation - 23-JUL-01

Our buy recommendation reflects the company's high growth prospects in light of increasing demand for digital and interactive TV. We believe GMST's growth will be primarily driven by strong industry and consumer demand for its interactive program guides. The company's interactive guide will likely be deployed in most digital set-top boxes in the future and should generate substantial licensing and advertising revenues. The company is currently providing this service to over 100 multi-channel service operators, recently signing long-term agreements with major operators Charter Communications and Comcast Corp. GMST maintains a potent library of 125 domestic issued patents, which has thwarted competition and has increasingly persuaded major cable operators to adopt the company's guides. In light of the tremendous growth potential for GMST, we view the shares as attractively valued currently trading at 45X our 2001 EBITDA estimate.

Key Stock Statistics

S&P EPS Est. 2001	-1.18	Tang. Bk. Value/Share	NM
P/E on S&P Est. 2001	NM	Beta	1.63
S&P EPS Est. 2002	-0.86	Shareholders	600
Dividend Rate/Share	Nil	Market cap. (B)	$ 13.8
Shs. outstg. (M)	411.9	Inst. holdings	30%
Avg. daily vol. (M)	3.952		

Value of $10,000 invested 5 years ago: $ 56,950

Fiscal Year Ending Dec. 31

	2001	2000	1999	1998	1997	1996
Revenues (Million $)						
1Q	352.5	—	43.10	33.90	25.63	13.08
2Q	334.2	63.23	47.21	37.03	27.68	13.12
3Q	—	309.8	61.82	41.50	30.53	19.12
4Q	—	358.1	83.99	54.03	42.72	25.05
Yr.	—	731.1	241.4	166.5	126.5	71.12
Earnings Per Share ($)						
1Q	**-0.30**	—	**0.09**	**0.07**	-0.02	0.03
2Q	**-0.32**	**0.12**	**0.10**	**0.07**	0.05	0.03
3Q	**E-0.30**	**-0.30**	**0.13**	**0.08**	**0.06**	0.04
4Q	**E-0.26**	**-0.31**	**0.11**	**0.12**	**0.09**	0.07
Yr.	**E-1.18**	**-0.64**	**0.33**	**0.33**	**0.19**	**-0.04**

Next earnings report expected: NA

Dividend Data

No cash dividends have been paid.

Gemstar-TV Guide International, Inc.

Business Summary - 23-JUL-01

Gemstar-TV Guide International, Inc., is a leading global technology and media company focused on consumer entertainment. Gemstar-TV Guide International Inc. develops, markets and licenses proprietary technologies and systems that simplify and enhance consumers' interaction with electronics products and other platforms that deliver video, programming information and other data.

The technology and licensing division is responsible for the development, licensing and protection of intellectual property and proprietary technology. Gemstar's technology includes the VCR Plus+ system, the interactive program guide marketed under the Guide Plus+ and TV Guide Interactive brands and the electronic book. Revenue is derived from technology and licensing fees earned through the provision of technology to service providers and users.

The interactive platform division owns, operates and derives recurring income from advertising, interactive services, content sales and e-commerce on the company's various proprietary technologies and platforms.

The media and services division operates the TV Guide magazines, TV Guide Channel, and other television media properties, as well as a media sales group that services all of the company's media platforms. Revenues are derived primarily in the form of subscription fees and advertising revenues from the TV Guide magazines and TV Guide Channel.

The investments and holdings division operates the company's other satellite-delivered video services, including Superstar/Netlink Group, LLC, a provider of programming packages to consumers in the C-band industry, UVTV, a distributor of superstations and other distant signal networks to programming service providers and TVG Network, a channel devoted to the horse racing industry.

In January 2000, Gemstar entered the electronic book publishing business through the acquisition of the two leading eBook companies NuvoMedia(R), Inc., the maker of the Rocket eBook, and SoftBook Press, Inc. maker of the SoftBook Reader. This business opportunity will permit Gemstar to create a platform for the distribution and sale, in a secure and protected distribution environment, of electronically based reading material, using consumer-friendly state-of-the-art reading devices, offering a broad range of books, magazines, newspapers and other materials.

On July 12, 2000, the company acquired all of the outstanding common stock of TV Guide, Inc., in a deal valued at $7.9 billion, issuing 0.6573 of a share of Gemstar common stock for each share of TV Guide Class A and B common stock outstanding.

Per Share Data ($) (Year Ended Dec. 31)	2000	1999	1998	1997	1996	1995	1994	1993	1992	1991
Tangible Bk. Val.	1.77	1.77	0.84	0.45	0.39	0.47	0.05	NA	NA	NA
Cash Flow	0.35	0.35	0.40	0.22	0.16	0.15	0.11	NA	NA	NA
Earnings	-0.64	0.33	0.33	0.19	0.14	0.13	0.08	NA	NA	NA
Dividends	Nil	Nil	Nil	Nil	Nil	Nil	Nil	NA	NA	NA
Payout Ratio	Nil	Nil	Nil	Nil	Nil	Nil	Nil	NA	NA	NA
Prices - High	107.43	79.50	17.29	6.53	10.06	10.43	NA	NA	NA	NA
- Low	33.50	13.87	5.18	2.40	3.06	3.00	NA	NA	NA	NA
P/E Ratio - High	NM	NM	53	34	74	80	NA	NA	NA	NA
- Low	NM	NM	16	13	22	23	NA	NA	NA	NA
Income Statement Analysis (Million $)										
Revs.	241	241	166	127	71.1	53.4	41.7	NA	NA	NA
Oper. Inc.	133	133	102	67.9	24.4	21.2	14.8	NA	NA	NA
Depr.	5.9	5.9	4.5	4.4	2.0	1.7	1.4	NA	NA	NA
Int. Exp.	24.8	Nil	Nil	Nil	Nil	Nil	Nil	NA	NA	NA
Pretax Inc.	125	125	104	59.1	26.5	21.6	12.5	NA	NA	NA
Eff. Tax Rate	35%	35%	29%	35%	32%	25%	29%	NA	NA	NA
Net Inc.	81.3	81.3	73.9	38.7	18.1	16.1	8.8	NA	NA	NA
Balance Sheet & Other Fin. Data (Million $)										
Cash	286	286	218	154	50.1	63.1	12.7	NA	NA	NA
Curr. Assets	358	358	227	163	84.7	66.8	16.2	NA	NA	NA
Total Assets	467	467	253	186	96.8	78.4	23.2	NA	NA	NA
Curr. Liab.	44.4	44.4	37.0	53.0	37.9	12.3	11.0	NA	NA	NA
LT Debt	586	Nil	Nil	Nil	Nil	Nil	Nil	NA	NA	NA
Common Eqty.	386	386	184	103	52.3	61.2	8.9	NA	NA	NA
Total Cap.	1,007	420	214	103	52.3	61.2	8.9	NA	NA	NA
Cap. Exp.	4.2	4.2	0.5	0.8	0.9	2.1	0.9	NA	NA	NA
Cash Flow	87.2	87.2	78.4	43.1	20.1	17.8	10.2	NA	NA	NA
Curr. Ratio	8.1	8.1	6.1	3.1	2.2	5.4	1.5	NA	NA	NA
% LT Debt of Cap.	58.2	Nil	Nil	Nil	Nil	Nil	Nil	NA	NA	NA
% Net Inc.of Revs.	33.7	33.7	44.4	30.6	25.4	30.1	33.6	NA	NA	NA
% Ret. on Assets	NA	22.5	33.7	27.4	20.6	31.7	38.0	NA	NA	NA
% Ret. on Equity	NA	28.5	51.4	49.7	31.9	45.9	99.0	NA	NA	NA

Data as orig reptd.; prior to 2000 (9 mos.), yrs. ended Mar. 31 of the fol. cal. year; bef. results of disc opers/spec. items. Per share data adj. for stk. divs. Bold denotes diluted EPS (FASB 128)-prior periods restated. E-Estimated. NA-Not Available. NM-Not Meaningful. NR-Not Ranked.

Office—135 North Los Robles Avenue, Suite 800, Pasadena, CA 91101. **Tel**—(626) 792 5700. **Website**—http://www.tvguideinc.com **CEO & Pres**—H. C. Yuen. **CFO, Co-Pres & Co-COO**—E. M. Leung. **Co-Pres & Co-COO**—P. C. Boylan III. **Investor Contact**—L. Lloyd da Silva. **Dirs**—P. C. Boylan III, C. Carey, G. F. Carrier, D. F. DeVoe, N. Donatiello Jr., E. M. Leung, D. B. Macrae, J. E. Meyer, L. K. Murdoch, K. R. Murdoch, J. B. Orlick, H. C. Yuen. **Transfer Agent & Registrar**—American Stock Transfer Co. **Incorporated**—in Delaware in 2000. **Empl**— 3,000. **S&P Analyst:** Howard Choe

STANDARD
&POOR'S
STOCK REPORTS

Home Depot

NYSE Symbol **HD**

In S&P 500

18-AUG-01

Industry:
Retail (Building Supplies)

Summary: HD operates a chain of more than 1,200 retail warehouse-type stores, selling a wide variety of home improvement products for the do-it-yourself and home remodeling markets.

S&P Opinion: Buy (★★★★★)

Recent Price • 49.23
52 Wk Range • 56.81-34.68
Yield • 0.3%
12-Mo. P/E • 43.2

Quantitative Evaluations

Outlook
(1 Lowest—5 Highest)
• **3**

Fair Value
• **48.50**

Risk
• **Low**

Earn./Div. Rank
• **A+**

Technical Eval.
• **Bullish** since 7/01

Rel. Strength Rank
(1 Lowest—99 Highest)
• **62**

Insider Activity
• **Unfavorable**

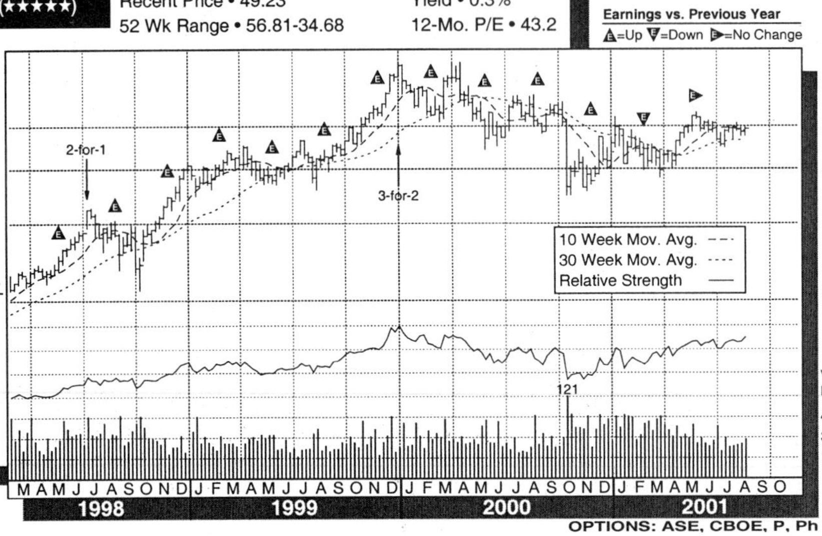

OPTIONS: ASE, CBOE, P, Ph

Overview - 15-AUG-01

We expect sales to grow 15% to 20% in the second half of FY 02 (Jan.), fueled by the addition of another 89 new stores, and by same-store sales gains of approximately 2% to 3%. Gross margins are expected to benefit from firming lumber prices, a more effective merchandise mix, and a greater percentage of imported merchandise. However, margin gains could be limited by greater sales penetration of lower margin appliances, which were added to stores in mid-2000. Higher payroll costs to support new service departments are likely to be offset by greater leverage in advertising expenses and vendor contributions, and new productivity initiatives. Over the longer term, the company should continue to gain market share via its accelerated rollout of newer format stores, such as EXPO Design Centers and Villager's Hardware, and by increased international exposure. We project that FY 02 EPS will rise 15%, to $1.27, and see a further gain, to $1.50, in FY 03.

Valuation - 15-AUG-01

We continue to recommend that investors buy HD. We believe the stock will outperform the market over the next six to 12 months, as investors continue to move toward interest rate sensitive shares. In addition, improving consumer confidence should translate into greater demand for home improvement merchandise. Although the company will continue to face near-term margin pressures resulting from depressed lumber and building materials prices, comparisons will become easier during the second half of FY 02. For the longer term, we believe HD will continue to build on its already dominant position in the highly fragmented, $600 billion do-it-yourself home improvement and building materials markets. We believe the shares are an attractive portfolio addition.

Key Stock Statistics

S&P EPS Est. 2002	1.27	Tang. Bk. Value/Share	6.57
P/E on S&P Est. 2002	38.8	Beta	0.94
S&P EPS Est. 2003	1.50	Shareholders	196,126
Dividend Rate/Share	0.16	Market cap. (B)	$114.9
Shs. outstg. (M)	2333.6	Inst. holdings	56%
Avg. daily vol. (M)	5.043		

Value of $10,000 invested 5 years ago: $ 40,575

Fiscal Year Ending Jan. 31

	2002	2001	2000	1999	1998	1997
Revenues (Million $)						
1Q	12,200	11,112	8,952	7,123	5,657	4,362
2Q	14,576	12,618	10,431	8,139	6,550	5,293
3Q	—	11,545	9,877	7,699	6,217	4,922
4Q	—	10,463	9,174	7,258	5,731	4,959
Yr.	—	45,738	38,434	30,219	24,156	19,536
Earnings Per Share ($)						
1Q	**0.27**	**0.27**	**0.21**	**0.15**	**0.12**	**0.09**
2Q	**0.39**	**0.36**	**0.29**	**0.21**	**0.16**	**0.12**
3Q	**E0.33**	**0.28**	**0.25**	**0.17**	**0.11**	**0.10**
4Q	**E0.28**	**0.20**	**0.25**	**0.18**	**0.14**	**0.11**
Yr.	**E1.27**	**1.10**	**1.00**	**0.71**	**0.51**	**0.43**

Next earnings report expected: NA

Dividend Data (Dividends have been paid since 1987.)

Amount ($)	Date Decl.	Ex-Div. Date	Stock of Record	Payment Date
0.040	Nov. 16	Nov. 28	Nov. 30	Dec. 14 '00
0.040	Feb. 22	Mar. 06	Mar. 08	Mar. 22 '01
0.040	May. 30	Jun. 12	Jun. 14	Jun. 28 '01
0.040	Aug. 16	Aug. 29	Aug. 30	Sep. 13 '01

A Division of The McGraw-Hill Companies

The Home Depot, Inc.

Business Summary - 15-AUG-01

The Home Depot is a do-it-yourselfer's paradise. The company, founded in 1978, is the world's largest home improvement retailer and the second largest U.S. retailer. HD operates retail warehouse-type stores that sell a wide assortment of building materials and home improvement products, primarily to the do-it-yourself and home remodeling markets. At July 29, 2001, it was operating 1,249 stores, including 1,125 Home Depots, 33 EXPO Design Centers, four Villager's Hardware stores in the U.S., and one Floor Store in Texas. There were 73 Home Depots in Canada, five in Chile, two in Argentina, two in Puerto Rico and four in Mexico. The company's stores in Chile are operated through a joint venture with S.A.C.I. Falabella, the largest department store chain in Chile.

Stores average 108,000 sq. ft., plus 24,000 sq. ft. of garden center and storage space. They stock 40,000 to 50,000 product items. HD aims to provide a broad range of merchandise, consisting of many different kinds of building and home improvement materials, at competitive prices. The company trains employees to be knowledgeable about the products in the stores; employees may also have trade skills or direct experience in using the products.

EXPO Design Centers, with about 100,000 sq. ft. of selling space, market upscale interior design products. The company currently operates 26 such units, and plans to open 200 stores in the next five to six years. HD also operates four Villager's Hardware test stores in New Jersey, and one Floor Store test store in Texas.

The company also offers its products through direct marketing channels. Its Maintenance Warehouse subsidiary is a leading direct mail marketer of maintenance, repair and operations products serving primarily the multi-family housing and lodging facilities management market. National Blinds & Wallpaper is a telephone mail order service for wallpaper and custom window treatments. During FY 01, HD began selling its products over the Internet at its e-commerce site, www.homedepot.com, in three markets. Orders are filled at the stores, and customers can either pick up their purchases or have them delivered. During FY 02, the company plans to expand its e-commerce site to additional areas of the U.S. for UPS delivery.

The company also operates several subsidiaries. Atlanta-based Georgia Lighting offers an extensive collection of decorative lighting fixtures and accessories to commercial and retail customers. Apex Supply company is a wholesale distributor of plumbing, HVAC, appliances and other related products.

During FY 02, HD planned to open approximately 200 new stores, including 17 new locations in Canada, and 17 EXPO units.

Per Share Data ($)										
(Year Ended Jan. 31)	**2001**	**2000**	**1999**	**1998**	**1997**	**1996**	**1995**	**1994**	**1993**	**1992**
Tangible Bk. Val.	6.32	5.22	3.83	3.17	2.71	2.28	1.64	1.38	1.14	0.88
Cash Flow	1.35	1.19	0.86	0.63	0.53	0.42	0.34	0.27	0.21	0.16
Earnings	1.10	1.00	0.71	0.52	0.43	0.34	0.29	0.22	0.18	0.13
Dividends	0.16	0.13	0.07	0.06	0.05	0.04	0.03	0.03	0.02	0.01
Payout Ratio	15%	13%	10%	12%	12%	12%	11%	12%	10%	9%
Cal. Yrs.	2000	1999	1998	1997	1996	1995	1994	1993	1992	1991
Prices - High	70.00	69.75	41.33	20.16	13.22	11.11	10.72	11.30	11.43	7.79
- Low	34.68	34.58	18.43	10.61	9.22	8.13	8.11	7.77	6.60	2.57
P/E Ratio - High	64	70	58	39	31	32	48	50	63	58
- Low	32	35	26	21	21	24	36	35	36	19
Income Statement Analysis (Million $)										
Revs.	45,738	38,434	30,219	24,156	19,536	15,470	12,477	9,239	7,148	5,137
Oper. Inc.	4,792	4,258	3,034	2,299	1,766	1,361	1,117	793	615	434
Depr.	601	463	373	283	232	181	130	85.9	65.6	52.3
Int. Exp.	21.0	28.0	37.0	42.0	39.0	25.0	53.5	44.6	48.6	24.0
Pretax Inc.	4,217	3,804	2,654	1,914	1,543	1,195	980	737	576	396
Eff. Tax Rate	39%	39%	39%	39%	39%	39%	38%	38%	37%	37%
Net Inc.	2,581	2,320	1,614	1,160	938	732	605	457	363	249
Balance Sheet & Other Fin. Data (Million $)										
Cash	167	168	62.0	172	558	108	58.0	431	414	395
Curr. Assets	7,777	6,390	4,933	4,460	3,709	2,672	2,133	1,967	1,562	1,158
Total Assets	21,385	17,081	13,465	11,229	9,342	7,354	5,778	4,701	3,932	2,510
Curr. Liab.	4,385	3,656	2,857	2,456	1,842	1,416	1,214	973	755	534
LT Debt	1,545	750	1,566	1,303	1,247	720	983	882	844	271
Common Eqty.	15,004	12,341	8,740	7,098	5,955	4,988	3,442	2,814	2,304	1,691
Total Cap.	16,755	13,188	10,400	8,595	7,366	5,822	4,496	3,724	3,164	1,969
Cap. Exp.	3,558	2,581	2,059	1,525	1,194	1,278	1,101	900	437	432
Cash Flow	3,182	2,783	1,987	1,443	1,170	913	734	543	428	301
Curr. Ratio	1.8	1.7	1.7	1.8	2.0	1.9	1.8	2.0	2.1	2.2
% LT Debt of Cap.	9.2	5.7	15.1	15.2	16.9	16.9	21.9	23.7	26.7	13.7
% Net Inc.of Revs.	5.6	6.0	5.3	4.8	4.8	4.7	4.8	5.0	5.1	4.9
% Ret. on Assets	13.4	15.2	13.1	11.3	11.2	11.1	11.5	10.5	11.0	11.2
% Ret. on Equity	18.9	22.0	20.4	17.8	17.1	17.4	19.2	17.8	17.8	19.9

Data as orig reptd.; bef. results of disc opers/spec. items. Per share data adj. for stk. divs. Bold denotes diluted EPS (FASB 128)-prior periods restated. E-Estimated. NA-Not Available. NM-Not Meaningful. NR-Not Ranked.

Office—2455 Paces Ferry Rd., Atlanta, GA 30339. **Tel**—(770) 433-8211. **Website**—www.HomeDepot.com **Chrmn**—B. Marcus. **Pres & CEO**—R. L. Nardelli. **CFO**—D. Carey. **Secy**—L. Smith. **Investor Contact**—James Grant (770-384-3039). **Dirs**—G. D. Brenneman, R. H. Brown, J. L. Clendenin, B. R. Cox, W. S. Davila, C. X. Gonzalez, M. A. Hart III, B.G. Hill, K. G. Langone, B. Marcus, R. L. Nardelli, R. S. Penske. **Transfer Agent & Registrar**—Fleet National Bank (c/o EquiServe L.P.), Boston. **Incorporated**—in Delaware in 1978. **Empl**— 227,000. **S&P Analyst:** Maureen C. Carini

STANDARD & POOR'S STOCK REPORTS

Lennar Corp.

NYSE Symbol **LEN**

In S&P MidCap 400

18-AUG-01 **Industry:** Homebuilding

Summary: This builder of moderate priced homes greatly expanded its operations through the acquisition of U.S. Home in May 2000.

S&P Opinion: Buy (★★★★★)

Recent Price • 39.59
52 Wk Range • 49.88-24.87
Yield • 0.1%
12-Mo. P/E • 8.3

Quantitative Evaluations

Outlook
(1 Lowest—5 Highest)
• **4-**

Fair Value
• **49**

Risk
• **Average**

Earn./Div. Rank
• **A-**

Technical Eval.
• **Bearish** since 8/01

Rel. Strength Rank
(1 Lowest—99 Highest)
• **35**

Insider Activity
• **NA**

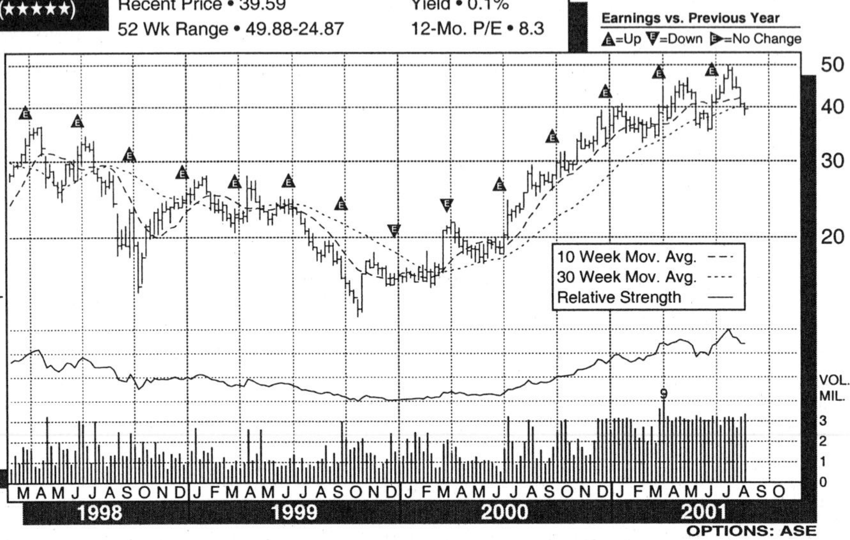

OPTIONS: ASE

Overview - 01-AUG-01

Home sales should grow almost 30% in FY 01 (Nov.), with a gain of about 10% likely in FY 02. The FY 01 gains will be led by the full-year inclusion of U.S. Home (UH; acquired in May 2000) and a downturn in mortgage rates since the spring of 2000. New community openings and modestly higher average prices should assist sales in both years. Weak labor markets and softer consumer confidence pose threats, and mortgage rates have likely approached their cycle bottom, but rates should stay accommodating enough to keep orders at a decent pace into FY 02. Financial services revenues should also pick up somewhat in both years, with FY 01 aided by the addition of UH's business and both years helped by a better mortgage capture rate. Margins should widen sharply in FY 01, largely on merger benefits, especially the formation of a national purchasing program. The absence of purchase accounting adjustments taken in FY 00 should also help, as will LEN's low cost land positions. Supplementary merger benefits should bring slightly better FY 02 margins.

Valuation - 01-AUG-01

The shares have moved sharply higher since late 1999, on better interest rate trends and enthusiasm for the U.S. Home deal. We think the Fed's rate easing program will lift the faltering economy, restore consumer confidence, and ease current threats of a slowdown in housing markets. We also like the demographics of LEN's geographic markets and its conservative operating strategy. Shares in the cyclical homebuilding industry typically trade at a large discount to the broad market. However, at a recent level of about 7X our FY 02 EPS forecast, the shares are near the lower end of their traditional P/E multiple range. Based on our positive expectations for LEN's business, and our belief that its earnings gains will continue through at least FY 02, we view the shares as well undervalued.

Key Stock Statistics

S&P EPS Est. 2001	5.35	Tang. Bk. Value/Share	17.83
P/E on S&P Est. 2001	7.4	Beta	1.17
S&P EPS Est. 2002	6.10	Shareholders	2,200
Dividend Rate/Share	0.05	Market cap. (B)	$ 2.1
Shs. outstg. (M)	63.8	Inst. holdings	77%
Avg. daily vol. (M)	0.929		

Value of $10,000 invested 5 years ago: NA

Fiscal Year Ending Nov. 30

	2001	2000	1999	1998	1997	1996
Revenues (Million $)						
1Q	1,104	640.4	590.6	440.7	232.5	226.5
2Q	1,392	968.2	738.4	532.1	271.9	258.3
3Q	—	1,376	819.5	620.8	332.6	320.1
4Q	—	1,722	970.1	823.1	466.1	376.3
Yr.	—	4,707	3,119	2,417	1,303	1,181
Earnings Per Share ($)						
1Q	**0.75**	**0.40**	**0.45**	**0.30**	0.27	0.48
2Q	**1.40**	**0.64**	**0.63**	**0.47**	0.35	0.51
3Q	**E1.40**	**0.90**	**0.72**	**0.59**	0.55	0.66
4Q	**E1.80**	**1.59**	**0.95**	**1.06**	0.19	0.79
Yr.	**E5.35**	**3.64**	**2.74**	**2.49**	**1.34**	2.43

Next earnings report expected: NA

Dividend Data (Dividends have been paid since 1978.)

Amount ($)	Date Decl.	Ex-Div. Date	Stock of Record	Payment Date
0.013	Sep. 21	Nov. 02	Nov. 06	Nov. 16 '00
0.013	Jan. 23	Feb. 01	Feb. 05	Feb. 15 '01
0.013	Apr. 03	May. 03	May. 07	May. 17 '01
0.013	Jun. 21	Aug. 02	Aug. 06	Aug. 16 '01

Lennar Corporation

Business Summary - 01-AUG-01

This leading homebuilder greatly expanded its operations through the May 2000 acquisition of U.S. Home Corp. (UH; $1.8 billion of revenues in 1999), for a total of $510 million in cash and common stock, plus the assumption of $650 million of debt. Lennar offers homes for first-time, move-up and active adult buyers, and also provides a number of financial services.

Prior to the merger, LEN ranked as the leading homebuilder in Florida, and had sizable operations in California, Texas, Arizona and Nevada. UH also had a significant presence in Florida, Texas and Arizona, added big positions in Denver, Minneapolis, and the Eastern Seaboard, and a major presence in the retirement/active adult segment. More than 50% of the nation's new home starts occur in those combined geographic regions; prior to the merger, Lennar built homes in areas that collectively accounted for about one-third of the nation's residential construction.

The merger with UH linked two different marketing strategies. LEN has sold homes on an Everything's Included basis, with most popular options and upgrades included as standard, and only limited customer ability to select additional options. UH, on the other hand, ran a design studio program in each of its major markets, where buyers put together more customized homes. LEN now operates communities offering both of these complementary programs (in both new and existing communities).

In FY 00 (Nov.), LEN delivered 18,236 homes (plus 342 through joint ventures), at an average price of $226,000, up 45% from 12,589 units (plus 17 through joint ventures) in FY 99 ($212,000); much of the gain reflected the inclusion of UH since its acquisition. LEN mostly sells single-family detached units, and the homes tend to be moderately priced for their locations. LEN takes part in all phases of planning and building, and subcontracts nearly all development and construction work.

Lennar recorded a 69% year to year surge in unit orders (7,230units, including orders through joint ventures) in the second quarter of FY 01 (9% on a pro forma basis). This brought order backlog to $2.8 billion (11,545 homes, including joint ventures) at May 31, 2001, or 20% (18%) above the year earlier level.

The Financial Services division provides mortgage financing, title insurance and closing services for LEN homebuyers and others; and acquires, packages and resells mortgage loans and mortgage-backed securities. UH's mortgage banking operations have been added to the division.

Effective October 31, 1997, LEN spun off its commercial real estate business as a new public company, LNR Property. It believed the value of its commercial real estate business was restricted by its mix with homebuilding operations. Immediately thereafter, LEN acquired Pacific Greystone Corp. in exchange for 17 million shares, making LEN a major California builder.

Per Share Data ($) (Year Ended Nov. 30)	2000	1999	1998	1997	1996	1995	1994	1993	1992	1991
Tangible Bk. Val.	17.83	14.16	12.31	8.26	19.36	16.95	14.93	13.09	10.49	9.61
Cash Flow	4.46	3.39	2.87	1.57	2.76	2.24	2.12	1.80	1.29	0.95
Earnings	3.64	2.74	2.49	1.34	2.43	1.95	1.89	1.51	0.95	0.70
Dividends	0.05	0.05	0.05	0.09	0.10	0.10	0.10	0.08	0.08	0.08
Payout Ratio	1%	2%	2%	7%	4%	5%	5%	5%	8%	11%
Prices - High	39.37	27.87	36.18	44.68	27.25	25.50	25.16	24.00	20.75	12.50
- Low	15.25	13.06	14.87	15.00	21.62	15.25	14.25	18.00	11.66	5.08
P/E Ratio - High	11	10	15	33	11	13	13	16	22	18
- Low	4	5	6	11	9	8	8	12	12	7
Income Statement Analysis (Million $)										
Revs.	4,707	3,119	2,417	1,303	1,181	870	789	641	426	323
Oper. Inc.	533	382	NA	149	187	145	94.1	68.5	61.5	38.1
Depr.	58.5	47.7	24.4	9.0	12.0	10.3	8.4	10.0	10.6	7.3
Int. Exp.	99	48.9	47.6	25.0	31.3	42.7	25.0	19.7	16.8	14.2
Pretax Inc.	376	285	240	85.7	144	115	112	82.1	45.4	33.0
Eff. Tax Rate	39%	39%	40%	41%	39%	39%	39%	36%	36%	36%
Net Inc.	229	173	144	50.6	88.0	70.4	68.2	52.5	29.1	21.1
Balance Sheet & Other Fin. Data (Million $)										
Cash	288	83.3	34.7	52.9	NA	NA	NA	NA	NA	NA
Curr. Assets	NA	NA	NA	NA	NA	NA	NA	NA	NA	NA
Total Assets	3,778	2,058	1,918	1,343	1,766	1,442	1,293	1,195	980	862
Curr. Liab.	NA	NA	NA	NA	NA	NA	NA	NA	NA	NA
LT Debt	1,240	524	799	614	858	636	566	230	307	350
Common Eqty.	1,229	881	716	439	695	608	534	467	319	291
Total Cap.	2,468	1,405	1,515	1,053	1,553	1,301	1,151	757	688	708
Cap. Exp.	16.0	15.3	13.2	70.8	26.3	10.1	55.1	21.4	11.7	4.5
Cash Flow	288	220	168	59.6	100	80.7	76.6	62.5	39.7	28.5
Curr. Ratio	NA	NA	NA	NA	NA	NA	NA	NA	NA	NA
% LT Debt of Cap.	50.2	37.3	52.7	41.7	55.2	48.9	49.2	30.4	44.6	49.4
% Net Inc.of Revs.	4.9	5.5	6.0	3.9	7.5	8.1	8.6	8.2	6.8	6.5
% Ret. on Assets	7.9	8.7	8.8	3.3	5.5	5.1	5.5	4.5	3.2	2.5
% Ret. on Equity	21.7	21.6	25.0	8.9	6.2	12.3	13.6	12.5	9.5	7.5

Data as orig. reptd.; bef. results of disc. opers. and/or spec. items. Per share data adj. for stk. divs. as of ex-div. date. Bold denotes diluted EPS (FASB 128). E-Estimated. NA-Not Available. NM-Not Meaningful. NR-Not Ranked.

Office—700 Northwest 107th Ave., Miami, FL 33172. **Tel**—(305) 559-4000. **Website**—http://www.lennar-homes.com **Chrmn**—L. Miller. **Vice Chrmn & COO**—R. J. Strudler. **Pres & CEO**—S. A. Miller. **VP & Investor Contact**—Marshall Ames (305-485-2092). **Dirs**—I. Bolotin, S. L. Gerard, J. M. Jaffe, R. K. Landon, S. Lapidus, L. Miller, S. A. Miller, H. Ripault, A. P. Rosen, S. J. Saiontz, R. J. Strudler. **Transfer Agent & Registrar**—BankBoston, N.A., Canton, MA. **Incorporated**—in Delaware in 1969. **Empl**— 7,140. **S&P Analyst:** Michael W. Jaffe

STANDARD &POOR'S STOCK REPORTS

Linens 'n Things

NYSE Symbol **LIN**

In S&P SmallCap 600

18-AUG-01

Industry: Retail (Specialty)

Summary: This retailer operates a nationwide chain of superstores selling home textiles, housewares and home accessories at everyday low prices.

S&P Opinion: Buy (★★★★★)

Recent Price • 25.56 | 52 Wk Range • 37.88-20 | Yield • Nil | 12-Mo. P/E • 16.8

Quantitative Evaluations

Outlook (1 Lowest—5 Highest) • **4-**

Fair Value • **32.80**

Risk • **NA**

Earn./Div. Rank • **B**

Technical Eval. • **Bearish** since 6/01

Rel. Strength Rank (1 Lowest—99 Highest) • **41**

Insider Activity • **NA**

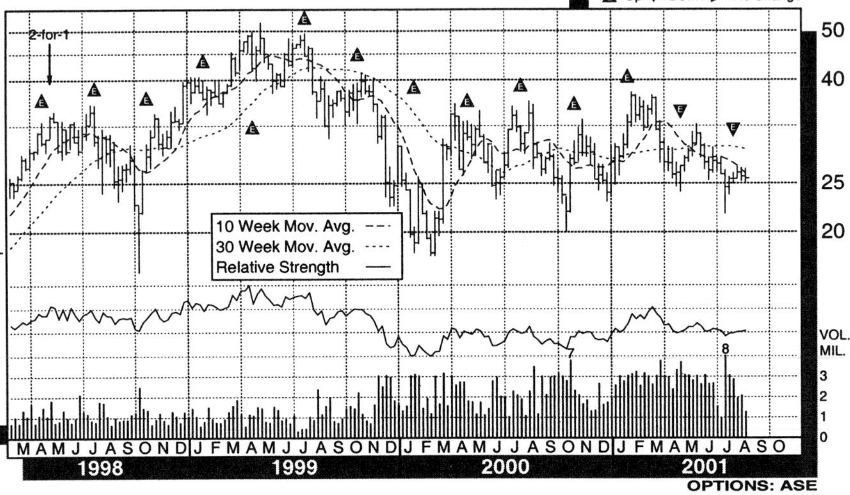

OPTIONS: ASE

Overview - 23-JUL-01

We expect total sales to increase 17% in 2001, aided by the addition of about 60 new stores and a same-store sales gain of about 1%. Gross margins will continue to benefit from a shift toward a more profitable sales mix of higher margin "things", consisting of housewares and home accessories, an improved centralized logistics system, and fewer markdowns. LIN will also focus on increasing sales of its more profitable private label merchandise, with a goal of reaching 15% of total sales by the end of 2001, up from 10% currently. As sales trends improve, operating margins should widen slightly, as the benefits of improved operating leverage and a more favorable product mix are mostly offset by higher occupancy and payroll costs. For 2001, we project EPS will decline 3% to $1.55, from the $1.60 reported for 2000. However, we expect EPS to reach $1.85 in 2002.

Valuation - 23-JUL-01

We recently raised our opinion on LIN shares to buy from accumulate. In 2001, the shares have come under selling pressure as same-store sales comparisons succumbed to unfavorable weather conditions early in the year, a weaker economy and pressure from liquidation sales at a going-out-of-business competitor. However, we expect recent interest rate cuts and anticipated tax refund checks to spur consumer spending and consequently boost same-store sales over the next six to 12 months. For the longer term, we remain positive about LIN's prospects and believe that EPS will grow 18% to 20% annually, as LIN continues to gain market share from department stores and weaker specialty store competitors. With the shares recently trading at only 13X our FY 02 EPS estimate, a significant discount to both its peers and our growth rate projections, we believe the shares are undervalued.

Key Stock Statistics

S&P EPS Est. 2001	1.55	Tang. Bk. Value/Share	10.98
P/E on S&P Est. 2001	16.5	Beta	NA
S&P EPS Est. 2002	1.85	Shareholders	7,300
Dividend Rate/Share	Nil	Market cap. (B)	$ 1.0
Shs. outstg. (M)	40.5	Inst. holdings	0%
Avg. daily vol. (M)	0.406		

Value of $10,000 invested 5 years ago: NA

Fiscal Year Ending Dec. 31

	2001	2000	1999	1998	1997	1996
Revenues (Million $)						
1Q	379.3	327.0	273.5	218.0	179.9	138.1
2Q	387.7	339.7	271.6	222.1	185.2	147.7
3Q	—	410.4	341.1	278.6	225.2	180.4
4Q	—	495.6	414.3	347.4	283.4	229.8
Yr.	—	1,573	1,301	1,066	874.2	696.1
Earnings Per Share ($)						
1Q	0.11	0.13	0.09	0.04	0.01	-0.05
2Q	0.11	0.17	0.12	0.07	0.03	-0.01
3Q	E0.45	0.45	0.36	0.28	0.19	0.13
4Q	E0.88	0.84	0.70	0.56	0.42	0.32
Yr.	E1.55	1.60	1.27	0.94	0.65	0.39

Next earnings report expected: mid October

Dividend Data

The company intends to retain all its earnings for the foreseeable future for use in the operation and expansion of its business and accordingly has no plans to pay dividends on its common stock.

Linens 'n Things, Inc.

Business Summary - 23-JUL-01

Linen's 'n Things (LIN) is one of the leading, national large-format retailers of home textiles, housewares and home accessories. It holds an approximately 2% share of the $75 billion industry. Founded in 1975, LIN was acquired by CVS Corp. (formerly Melville Corp.) in 1983, and spun off in November 1996. By the end of 1997, CVS had sold its 32.5% interest in the company. LIN's strategy is to offer a broad assortment of high-quality, brand name merchandise at everyday low prices, while providing efficient customer service and maintaining low operating costs. Prices are substantially below regular department store prices and comparable to or lower than department store sale prices. The company offers more than 28,000 items across six departments: bath, home accessories, housewares, storage, bedding, and window treatments.

LIN's growth strategy includes new superstore expansion and increased productivity of the existing store base. During 2000, the company opened 57 new stores and closed four smaller locations, and opened another 11 stores while closing one during the first quarter of 2001. As of March 31, 2001, the company operated 293 stores in 40 states and three provinces in Canada. Since 1990, the company has replaced essentially all of its traditional stores (7,500 sq. ft. to 10,000 sq. ft.) with a superstore format that has evolved to about 30,000 sq. ft. to 60,000 sq. ft. Total square footage at March 31, 2001, was 10.2 million sq. ft., up from 9.8 million at the end of 1999 and just 1.2 million sq. ft. in January 1991. The company expects to add an additional 60 to 65 net new stores in 2001.

To increase existing-store productivity, the company has been moving to boost the sale of "things" merchandise (housewares and home accessories) to 50% of total sales, from 40% currently. "Things" carry higher margins than linens products (bedding, towels and pillows), and buying is more impulse driven. LIN also sells private-label merchandise, which accounts for about 10% of sales.

Over the past several years the company has invested significant capital in building a centralized infrastructure, including two distribution centers, located in Greensboro, NC, and southern NJ, and a management information system.

In 2000, the company launched its e-commerce capability on its website, linensnthings.com. The site allows access to the company's bridal and gift registry and allows customers to purchase items through the site.

Per Share Data ($)										
(Year Ended Dec. 31)	**2000**	**1999**	**1998**	**1997**	**1996**	**1995**	**1994**	**1993**	**1992**	**1991**
Tangible Bk. Val.	10.98	9.22	7.76	6.69	5.90	5.58	1.60	NA	NA	NA
Cash Flow	2.39	1.92	1.47	1.11	0.77	0.34	0.69	0.49	NA	NA
Earnings	1.60	1.27	0.94	0.65	0.39	Nil	0.45	0.30	NA	NA
Dividends	Nil	Nil	Nil	Nil	Nil	Nil	Nil	Nil	NA	NA
Payout Ratio	Nil	Nil	Nil	Nil	Nil	Nil	Nil	Nil	NA	NA
Prices - High	36.37	52.06	40.62	22.25	9.87	NA	NA	NA	NA	NA
- Low	17.93	22.43	16.62	8.75	7.75	NA	NA	NA	NA	NA
P/E Ratio - High	23	41	43	34	25	NA	NA	NA	NA	NA
- Low	11	18	18	13	20	NA	NA	NA	NA	NA
Income Statement Analysis (Million $)										
Revs.	1,573	1,301	1,066	874	696	555	440	333	NA	NA
Oper. Inc.	142	111	83.3	63.5	45.2	32.0	41.8	29.1	NA	NA
Depr.	32.4	26.5	21.3	18.0	14.5	12.9	9.6	7.4	NA	NA
Int. Exp.	1.9	0.0	0.1	1.0	4.7	7.1	3.2	1.4	NA	NA
Pretax Inc.	105	84.5	61.9	44.5	25.9	1.1	29.1	20.3	NA	NA
Eff. Tax Rate	38%	38%	39%	42%	42%	103%	41%	42%	NA	NA
Net Inc.	64.9	52.1	38.1	25.8	15.0	0.0	17.2	11.7	NA	NA
Balance Sheet & Other Fin. Data (Million $)										
Cash	38.5	45.8	42.6	39.9	26.9	2.9	NA	NA	NA	NA
Curr. Assets	533	431	355	290	257	234	NA	NA	NA	NA
Total Assets	822	680	561	472	424	400	NA	NA	NA	NA
Curr. Liab.	306	249	201	167	146	177	NA	NA	NA	NA
LT Debt	Nil	Nil	Nil	Nil	13.5	13.5	NA	NA	NA	NA
Common Eqty.	459	384	324	280	250	237	NA	NA	NA	NA
Total Cap.	459	431	360	306	281	251	NA	NA	NA	NA
Cap. Exp.	70.1	70.1	46.3	35.3	46.4	41.3	39.1	30.6	NA	NA
Cash Flow	97.4	78.6	59.4	43.8	29.6	12.8	26.8	19.1	NA	NA
Curr. Ratio	1.7	1.7	1.8	1.7	1.8	3.0	NA	NA	NA	NA
% LT Debt of Cap.	Nil	Nil	Nil	Nil	4.8	5.4	NA	NA	NA	NA
% Net Inc.of Revs.	4.1	4.0	3.6	3.0	2.2	NM	3.9	3.5	NA	NA
% Ret. on Assets	8.6	8.4	7.4	5.8	3.9	NA	NA	NA	NA	NA
% Ret. on Equity	15.4	14.7	12.6	9.7	9.2	NA	NA	NA	NA	NA

Data as orig reptd.; bef. results of disc opers/spec. items. Per share data adj. for stk. divs. Bold denotes diluted EPS (FASB 128)-prior periods restated. E-Estimated. NA-Not Available. NM-Not Meaningful. NR-Not Ranked.

Office—6 Brighton Rd., Clifton, NJ 07015. **Tel**—(973) 778-1300. **Website**—http://www.linensnthings.com **Pres, Chrmn & CEO**—N. Axelrod. **CFO & Investor Contact**—William T. Giles (973-815-2929). **Dirs**—N. Axelrod, P. E. Beekman, H. F. Compton, C. C. Conaway, S. P. Goldstein, M. Handel. **Transfer Agent**—BankBoston, NA. **Incorporated**—in Delaware in 1996. **Empl**— 12,200. **S&P Analyst:** Maureen C. Carini

STANDARD &POOR'S
STOCK REPORTS

P.F. Chang's China Bistro

Nasdaq Symbol **PFCB**

In S&P SmallCap 600

18-AUG-01

Industry: Restaurants

Summary: This company owns and operates two Asian restaurant concepts: P.F. Chang's China Bistro and Pei Wei Asian Diner.

S&P Opinion: Buy (★★★★★)

Recent Price • 42.25
52 Wk Range • 46.87-27.37
Yield • Nil
12-Mo. P/E • 40.6

Quantitative Evaluations

Outlook
(1 Lowest—5 Highest)
• **5**

Fair Value
• **55.80**

Risk
• **NA**

Earn./Div. Rank
• **NR**

Technical Eval.
• **Bullish** since 7/01

Rel. Strength Rank
(1 Lowest—99 Highest)
• **82**

Insider Activity
• **NA**

Overview - 31-JUL-01

Revenues should climb 36% in 2001, driven by the opening of 14 P.F. Chang's China Bistro restaurants and four Pei Wei Asian Diner locations, as well as by consumers' receipt of tax refunds. We anticipate same-store growth of 3%-4%, compared to 11.7% in 2000, as the entire industry is hurt by a weaker U.S. economy. We expect an improved economy and growing awareness of the company's brand to boost same-store revenue growth in 2002. The restaurant operating margin should narrow in 2001, due to higher labor costs following an early 2001 increase in California's minimum wage rate. Over time, we expect the margin to widen, as PFCB gains power over food purchases. With leverage over restaurant preopening costs and G&A expenses, the EBITDA margin should widen about 50 basis points. Following depreciation charges, minority interest, and a lower effective tax rate, EPS should climb over 37% in 2001, to $1.18.

Valuation - 31-JUL-01

The shares have progressed upward since their late 1998 IPO, and were recently up 31% in 2001, compared to an 8.9% decline in the S&P 500. Even so, we believe PFCB shares have room for further upside. The Asian segment is a large and fragmented market, as evidenced by PFCB's leadership with just over 50 locations. The company's P/E multiple of 35X our 2001 EPS estimate is above the 19X multiple of the industry, but our five-year projection for 30% EPS growth also surpasses the consensus expectation for 15% industry growth. In addition, the shares' P/E of 27X our 2002 EPS estimate is 21% discounted to the 34% EPS growth rate we forecast through the two-year period. This comparison and our valuation of projected free cash flow from operations have strengthened our view that the shares' intrinsic value lies at approximately $55, 34% above the current market price.

Key Stock Statistics

S&P EPS Est. 2001	1.18	Tang. Bk. Value/Share	9.94
P/E on S&P Est. 2001	35.8	Beta	NA
S&P EPS Est. 2002	1.55	Shareholders	65
Dividend Rate/Share	Nil	Market cap. (B)	$0.503
Shs. outstg. (M)	11.9	Inst. holdings	0%
Avg. daily vol. (M)	0.270		

Value of $10,000 invested 5 years ago: NA

Fiscal Year Ending Dec. 31

	2001	2000	1999	1998	1997	1996
Revenues (Million $)						
1Q	72.42	51.41	30.47	—	—	—
2Q	76.46	53.50	32.96	—	—	—
3Q	—	61.18	40.96	—	—	—
4Q	—	68.82	48.91	24.86	—	—
Yr.	—	234.9	153.3	78.03	39.77	—
Earnings Per Share ($)						
1Q	0.31	0.21	0.11	—	—	—
2Q	0.27	0.19	0.09	—	—	—
3Q	E0.28	0.19	0.12	—	—	—
4Q	E0.32	0.27	0.22	-0.10	—	—
Yr.	E1.18	0.86	0.54	-0.25	-1.03	—

Next earnings report expected: late October

Dividend Data

No cash dividends have been paid. The company currently intends to retain earnings for use in the operation and expansion of its business and therefore does not anticipate paying any cash dividends for the foreseeable future.

P.F. Chang's China Bistro, Inc.

Business Summary - 31-JUL-01

An operator of restaurant concepts in the Asian niche, P.F. Chang's China Bistro (PFCB) believes its recipe for success is a blend of traditional Chinese cuisine and American hospitality, served up in a sophisticated, contemporary bistro setting. As of December 31, 2000, the company owned and operated 52 full-service, bistro-style restaurants across the U.S. PFCB has also developed a second concept, Pei Wei Asian Diner, that offers a quicker, more casual dining experience; the first Pei Wei diner opened in July 2000, in the Phoenix, AZ, area.

The menu selection at P.F. Chang's China Bistro restaurants focuses on dishes designed to replicate the flavors and styles of China's five major culinary regions: Canton, Hunan, Mongolia, Shanghai and Szechwan. The P.F. Chang's menu adheres to the Chinese culinary concepts of fan and t'sai, a balance of rice, noodles and grains with meat, seafood and vegetables, to offer dishes with an array of taste, texture and color. In addition to its core menu, the company also offers special lunch and dinner selections. PFCB's research effort includes annual trips to China by the company's corporate executive chef.

Each P.F. Chang's restaurant features a display kitchen and exhibition wok cooking areas, and is decorated with terra cotta replicas of Xi'an warriors and narrative murals depicting 12th century China. Entrees at the restaurants range in price from $8 to $13, and appetizers range in price from $3 to $8. The average check per guest, including alcoholic beverages, is approximately $17 to $18. About 20% of PFCB's revenues are attributable to the sale of alcoholic beverages. Lunch and dinner contribute about 30% and 70% of revenues, respectively.

Under PFCB's incentive system, certain managers and executive chefs (culinary partners) are allowed to participate in the cash flows of the restaurants for which they have responsibility. The company believes this approach allows it to expand without sacrificing restaurant-level operating performance.

The company was formed in 1996 with the acquisition of the four original P.F. Chang's restaurants. In the years that followed, it has embarked on a strategic expansion of the concept targeted at major metropolitan areas throughout the U.S. PFCB added 17 restaurants in 2000, and plans to open 14 Bistros and four Pei Wei restaurants in 2001.

Based on the company's development schedule of 14 Bistros and four Pei Wei Asian Diners, and assuming modest customer traffic growth, PFCB expects 2001 revenues to increase over 30%, with earnings rising more due to the anticipated revenue gain and related leverage of the company's corporate infrastructure and pre-opening expenses. PFCB projects 2001 EPS at $1.14 to $1.18.

Per Share Data ($) (Year Ended Dec. 31)	2000	1999	1998	1997	1996	1995	1994	1993	1992	1991
Tangible Bk. Val.	6.69	5.59	4.94	-4.90	NA	NA	NA	NA	NA	NA
Cash Flow	1.55	1.07	0.25	-0.24	NA	NA	NA	NA	NA	NA
Earnings	0.86	0.54	-0.25	-1.03	NA	NA	NA	NA	NA	NA
Dividends	Nil	Nil	Nil	NA	NA	NA	NA	NA	NA	NA
Payout Ratio	Nil	Nil	Nil	NA	NA	NA	NA	NA	NA	NA
Prices - High	46.87	31.12	23.37	NA	NA	NA	NA	NA	NA	NA
- Low	23.12	18.12	12.00	NA	NA	NA	NA	NA	NA	NA
P/E Ratio - High	55	58	NM	NA	NA	NA	NA	NA	NA	NA
- Low	27	34	NM	NA	NA	NA	NA	NA	NA	NA
Income Statement Analysis (Million $)										
Revs.	235	153	78.0	39.8	NA	NA	NA	NA	NA	NA
Oper. Inc.	27.9	15.8	4.4	1.1	NA	NA	NA	NA	NA	NA
Depr.	7.9	5.0	2.4	1.1	NA	NA	NA	NA	NA	NA
Int. Exp.	0.4	0.2	1.4	0.4	NA	NA	NA	NA	NA	NA
Pretax Inc.	20.0	11.3	0.9	-0.3	NA	NA	NA	NA	NA	NA
Eff. Tax Rate	30%	25%	5.54%	NM	NA	NA	NA	NA	NA	NA
Net Inc.	9.7	6.0	0.1	-1.7	NA	NA	NA	NA	NA	NA
Balance Sheet & Other Fin. Data (Million $)										
Cash	6.4	5.3	18.9	2.7	NA	NA	NA	NA	NA	NA
Curr. Assets	12.0	9.3	23.2	5.7	NA	NA	NA	NA	NA	NA
Total Assets	116	81.7	69.2	28.5	NA	NA	NA	NA	NA	NA
Curr. Liab.	18.7	14.3	8.9	12.6	NA	NA	NA	NA	NA	NA
LT Debt	1.5	1.5	1.8	2.4	NA	NA	NA	NA	NA	NA
Common Eqty.	77.3	64.8	58.2	-4.4	NA	NA	NA	NA	NA	NA
Total Cap.	82.2	66.8	60.2	15.9	NA	NA	NA	NA	NA	NA
Cap. Exp.	37.4	31.1	24.8	8.7	NA	NA	NA	NA	NA	NA
Cash Flow	17.6	11.0	2.5	-0.6	NA	NA	NA	NA	NA	NA
Curr. Ratio	0.6	0.7	2.6	0.5	NA	NA	NA	NA	NA	NA
% LT Debt of Cap.	1.8	2.3	3.0	15.0	NA	NA	NA	NA	NA	NA
% Net Inc.of Revs.	4.1	3.9	0.2	-4.3	NA	NA	NA	NA	NA	NA
% Ret. on Assets	9.8	7.4	-1.1	-9.0	NA	NA	NA	NA	NA	NA
% Ret. on Equity	13.7	9.3	-1.3	57.9	NA	NA	NA	NA	NA	NA

Data as orig reptd.; bef. results of disc opers/spec. items. Per share data adj. for stk. divs. Bold denotes diluted EPS (FASB 128)-prior periods restated. E-Estimated. NA-Not Available. NM-Not Meaningful. NR-Not Ranked.

Office—15210 N. Scottsdale Rd., Suite 300, Scottsdale, AZ 85254. **Tel**—(602) 957-8986. **Website**—http://www.pfchangs.com **Chrmn & CEO**—R. L. Federico. **Pres & CFO**—R. T. Vivian. **Secy**—K. K. Cashman. **Dirs**—F. L. Cardwell Jr., R. L. Federico, P. M. Fleming, J. G. Shennan Jr., R. M. Welborn, K. J. Wessels. **Transfer Agent & Registrar**—First Chicago Trust Co. of New York. **Incorporated**—in Delaware in 1996.**Empl**— 7,000. **S&P Analyst:** Markos N. Kaminis

STANDARD &POOR'S
STOCK REPORTS

SCP Pool

Nasdaq Symbol **POOL**

In S&P SmallCap 600

18-AUG-01 **Industry:** Leisure Time (Products)

Summary: This company is the largest independent distributor of swimming pool supplies and related products in the U.S.

S&P Opinion: Buy (★★★★★) Recent Price • 40.54 52 Wk Range • 40.63-22.75 Yield • Nil 12-Mo. P/E • 21.7

Quantitative Evaluations
Outlook (1 Lowest—5 Highest) **• 3**
Fair Value **• 41**
Risk **• Low**
Earn./Div. Rank **• NR**

Technical Eval. **• Bullish** since 7/01
Rel. Strength Rank (1 Lowest—99 Highest) **• 90**
Insider Activity **• NA**

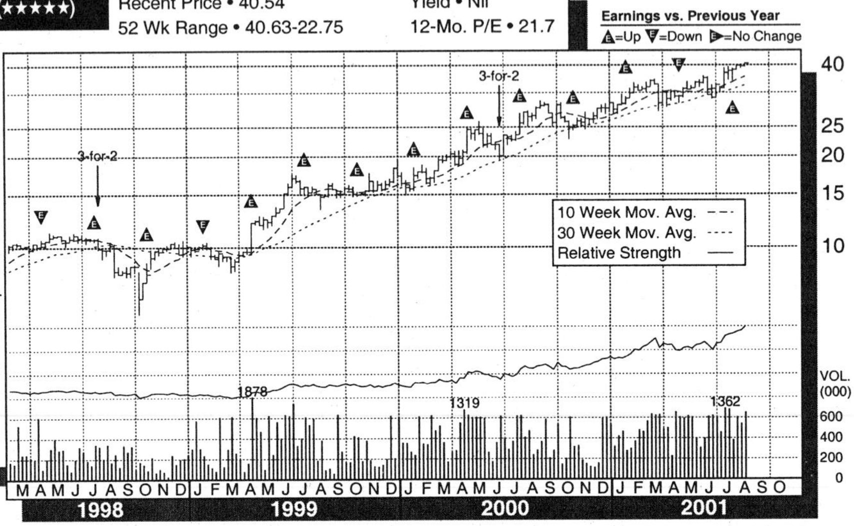

Overview - 24-JUL-01

Revenues should climb 28% in 2001, driven by the acquisitions of Superior Pool Products and the pool division of Hughes Supply, Inc. Same-store sales growth is seen in mid-single digits through the second half, after a first half burdened by heavy rainfall in the Southeast. Gross margins will widen, exceeding 25%, on leverage over pricing, supply costs, and payment terms. Selling and administrative expenses will increase as a percentage of sales, due to the absorption of less profitable acquired operations. However, operating margins have widened steadily historically, and should benefit in 2002 as POOL gains leverage on existing service center operations. We expect further improvement to result from market share gains and tighter operational controls. We forecast EPS of $1.94 for 2001, representing 23% growth from 2000 levels.

Valuation - 24-JUL-01

After appreciating 74% in 2000, the shares were recently up 28% in 2001, versus a 1.7% rise for the S&P Small Cap 600 Index, reflecting strong revenue growth coupled with a trend of improving operating margins. The company has benefited from the aging of the baby boomer population, as the average age of pool owners is 45 to 50. In addition, we believe the recent housing boom has helped drive growth. POOL has gained economies of scale through consolidation in a fragmented industry, as shown by gross margin of 24% in 2000, versus 17.7% in 1997. Return on equity increased to 25.4% in 2000, from 13.6% in 1997, even as debt leverage decreased. We view the shares as undervalued, trading at a P/E multiple of about 20X our 2001 EPS estimate, an 11% discount to our projection for EPS growth. Based on this, and on our valuation of discounted future free cash flows, we value the shares at approximately $53, 37% above recent levels.

Key Stock Statistics

S&P EPS Est. 2001	1.94	Tang. Bk. Value/Share	3.92
P/E on S&P Est. 2001	20.9	Beta	0.60
S&P EPS Est. 2002	2.33	Shareholders	51
Dividend Rate/Share	Nil	Market cap. (B)	$0.693
Shs. outstg. (M)	17.1	Inst. holdings	84%
Avg. daily vol. (M)	0.133		

Value of $10,000 invested 5 years ago: $ 74,175

Fiscal Year Ending Dec. 31

	2001	2000	1999	1998	1997	1996
Revenues (Million $)						
1Q	155.5	120.6	98.91	73.99	63.57	41.14
2Q	232.1	254.0	225.1	178.4	124.8	85.87
3Q	—	190.5	163.3	133.9	98.49	62.34
4Q	—	104.7	82.79	71.28	48.18	46.49
Yr.	—	669.8	569.8	457.6	335.0	235.8
Earnings Per Share ($)						
1Q	**0.06**	**0.07**	**0.04**	**-0.07**	**-0.04**	**0.00**
2Q	**1.42**	**1.12**	**0.89**	**0.69**	**0.44**	**0.39**
3Q	—	**0.55**	**0.45**	**0.33**	**0.24**	**0.15**
4Q	—	**-0.16**	**-0.17**	**-0.18**	**-0.15**	**-0.24**
Yr.	—	**1.58**	**1.21**	**0.77**	**0.47**	**0.31**

Next earnings report expected: mid October

Dividend Data

Amount ($)	Date Decl.	Ex-Div. Date	Stock of Record	Payment Date
3-for-2	Jul. 30	Sep. 10	Aug. 15	Sep. 07 '01

SCP Pool Corporation

Business Summary - 24-JUL-01

Founded in 1981, SCP Pool Corp. (POOL) distributes swimming pool supplies and related products to pool remodelers and builders, independent retail stores and pool repair and service companies. The company distributes about 60,000 national brand and private label products to about 38,000 customers. As of February of 2001, the company operated 160 service centers in 35 states, the U.K. and France. Domestic sales accounted for 97% of the total in 2000.

Products include both non-discretionary pool maintenance products, such as chemicals and replacement parts, packaged pools (kits to build swimming pools which include walls, liners, bracing and other materials); and pool equipment, including cleaners, filters, heaters, pumps and lights. In 2000, the company enhanced its breadth of complementary products offered to include toys and games, hand tools, building materials, electrical supplies, and water features such as fountains.

POOL's principal marketing activities are conducted by its sales force of 149 salespersons and by its 148 service center managers. No customer accounted for over 1% of the company's sales in 2000. The company initiated a preferred vendor program in 1999, whereby service centers are encouraged to purchase products from a smaller number of vendors in order to effect more efficient purchasing and inventory management.

The company has focused on distributing products to the residential in-ground and above-ground swimming pools and small commercial markets. POOL believes about 60% of total pool industry revenues are based on a number of ongoing maintenance and repair requirements associated with pool ownership. The maintenance of proper chemical balance and the related maintenance and repair of swimming pool equipment, such as pumps, heaters, filters and cleaners create a non-discretionary demand for pool chemicals and other swimming pool supplies and services.

POOL completed two acquisitions in 2000. The company purchased substantially all of the net assets of Superior Pool Products, Inc., and Pool-Rite, Inc. in July and October, respectively, for an aggregate price of $25 million. The Superior distribution network encompassed 19 service centers in California, Arizona and Nevada; it had 1999 sales exceeding $80 million.

In January 2001, the company acquired the pool division of Hughes Supply, Inc., for about $48 million. The purchase added 31 service centers to POOL's distribution network in the eastern half of the U.S. Because both Superior and Hughes had historically been prominent forces in the industry, and had a significant degree of customer loyalty, POOL adopted a strategy of offering two distinct distribution choices for customers, including the Superior Pool Products and SCP brands.

Per Share Data ($) **(Year Ended Dec. 31)**	**2000**	**1999**	**1998**	**1997**	**1996**	**1995**	**1994**	**1993**	**1992**	**1991**
Tangible Bk. Val.	3.92	2.89	2.10	1.96	0.27	0.18	NA	NA	NA	NA
Cash Flow	1.87	1.47	1.01	0.71	0.49	0.66	0.28	NA	NA	NA
Earnings	1.58	1.21	0.77	0.48	0.32	0.35	0.17	NA	NA	NA
Dividends	Nil	Nil	Nil	Nil	Nil	Nil	Nil	NA	NA	NA
Payout Ratio	Nil	Nil	Nil	Nil	Nil	Nil	Nil	NA	NA	NA
Prices - High	31.62	19.41	11.27	10.66	6.37	3.33	NA	NA	NA	NA
- Low	14.91	8.25	6.00	5.77	2.96	2.88	NA	NA	NA	NA
P/E Ratio - High	20	16	15	22	20	10	NA	NA	NA	NA
- Low	9	7	8	12	9	8	NA	NA	NA	NA
Income Statement Analysis (Million $)										
Revs.	670	570	458	335	236	161	102	NA	NA	NA
Oper. Inc.	53.4	42.4	28.9	18.5	13.1	12.3	8.9	NA	NA	NA
Depr.	5.1	4.6	4.4	3.4	2.5	2.1	1.6	NA	NA	NA
Int. Exp.	3.6	3.1	3.5	4.5	3.2	5.1	4.2	NA	NA	NA
Pretax Inc.	45.2	34.5	21.8	11.4	7.4	3.8	NA	NA	NA	NA
Eff. Tax Rate	38%	37%	37%	38%	39%	39%	NA	NA	NA	NA
Net Inc.	28.1	21.6	13.7	7.1	4.5	2.3	2.4	NA	NA	NA
Balance Sheet & Other Fin. Data (Million $)										
Cash	3.4	4.0	4.9	22.3	4.6	2.0	0.8	NA	NA	NA
Curr. Assets	178	132	112	96.5	73.1	39.9	19.7	NA	NA	NA
Total Assets	252	194	164	136	113	75.4	50.7	NA	NA	NA
Curr. Liab.	89.3	68.7	50.5	33.1	38.4	18.7	11.2	NA	NA	NA
LT Debt	34.7	22.8	28.7	33.1	35.9	23.6	36.0	NA	NA	NA
Common Eqty.	123	97.6	80.6	66.6	36.8	32.3	3.0	NA	NA	NA
Total Cap.	163	125	113	103	74.8	56.7	39.4	NA	NA	NA
Cap. Exp.	4.3	3.2	2.0	1.1	0.8	0.9	0.4	NA	NA	NA
Cash Flow	33.2	26.2	18.1	10.5	7.0	4.4	4.0	NA	NA	NA
Curr. Ratio	2.0	1.9	2.2	2.9	1.9	2.1	1.8	NA	NA	NA
% LT Debt of Cap.	21.4	18.1	25.3	32.0	48.0	41.6	91.4	NA	NA	NA
% Net Inc.of Revs.	4.2	3.8	3.0	2.1	1.9	14.0	2.4	NA	NA	NA
% Ret. on Assets	12.6	12.1	9.2	5.7	4.8	3.7	NA	NA	NA	NA
% Ret. on Equity	25.4	24.3	18.7	13.6	13.1	13.2	NA	NA	NA	NA

Data as orig reptd.; bef. results of disc opers/spec. items. Per share data adj. for stk. divs. Bold denotes diluted EPS (FASB 128)-prior periods restated. E-Estimated. NA-Not Available. NM-Not Meaningful. NR-Not Ranked.

Office—109 Northpark Blvd., 4th Flr., Covington, LA 70433-5001. **Tel**—(985) 892-5521. **Website**—http://www.scppool.com **Chrmn**—W. B. Sexton. **Pres & CEO**— M. J. Perez de la Mesa. **CFO, Treas, Secy & Investor Contact**—Craig K. Hubbard. **Dirs**—A. W. Code, J. J. Gaffney, M. P. de la Mesa, F. J. St. Romain, W. B. Sexton, R. C. Sledd, J. E. Stokely. **Transfer Agent & Registrar**—EquiServe, Jersey City, NJ. **Incorporated**—in Delaware in 1993. **Empl**— 1,800. **S&P Analyst:** Markos N. Kaminis

STANDARD &POOR'S
STOCK REPORTS

United Rentals

NYSE Symbol **URI**

In S&P MidCap 400

18-AUG-01

Industry: Services (Commercial & Consumer)

Summary: URI offers for rent a wide range of equipment to contractors, industrial and commercial customers and homeowners, through a number of locations in the U.S. and Canada.

S&P Opinion: Buy (★★★★★)

Recent Price • 23.72
52 Wk Range • 26.40-11.68
Yield • Nil
12-Mo. P/E • 15.8

Quantitative Evaluations

Outlook (1 Lowest—5 Highest)
• **1+**

Fair Value
• **21.40**

Risk
• **NA**

Earn./Div. Rank
• **NR**

Technical Eval.
• **Bearish** since 8/01

Rel. Strength Rank (1 Lowest—99 Highest)
• **68**

Insider Activity
• **Unfavorable**

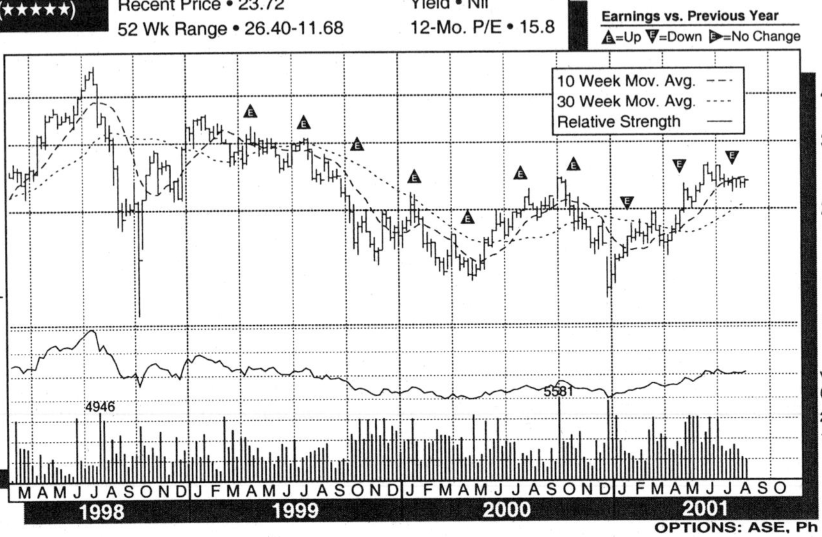

OPTIONS: ASE, Ph

Overview - 30-JUL-01

As the economy slows in 2001, URI's revenue growth rate should decelerate to about 2%. Equipment rental revenues are expected to increase 13%, driven by solid utilization rates and newly won national client accounts. The company is expected to postpone sales of old equipment and purchases of new equipment to help generate free cash flow of $390 million in 2001. We expect URI to strengthen its balance sheet with the funds. Sales of new equipment and other merchandise should rise about 8%. In 2002, we expect economic recovery to restore revenue growth of over 10%. Over time, as URI benefits from economies of scale, gross margin should widen. URI is already winning better terms on equipment purchases through the reduction of its supplier base. By 2002, SG&A expense leverage will widen the EBITDA margin; the net margin should narrow in 2001, then widen to 6.4% in 2002. After a 3.7% decrease in 2001, EPS should rise 25% in 2002.

Valuation - 30-JUL-01

Following a 22% decline in 2000, the shares were recently up 78% in 2001, versus an 8.7% decline for the S&P 500 Index. We believe the relative outperformance of the shares is due to the cyclical nature of URI's business, which should benefit from lower interest rates and a potentially restored economy. URI spent the past few years consolidating its fragmented industry. As a result, we expect the company to begin benefiting from economies of scale. With the building of brand value and the ability to win national accounts, URI has recently been able to raise prices without significant consequences. With a P/E multiple of 13X our 2001 EPS estimate, the shares were at a discount to the 24X multiple of the S&P 500. Based on our expectations of an improved economy in 2002, we recommended URI for aggressive investors.

Key Stock Statistics

S&P EPS Est. 2001	1.82	Tang. Bk. Value/Share	NM
P/E on S&P Est. 2001	13.0	Beta	NA
S&P EPS Est. 2002	2.27	Shareholders	246
Dividend Rate/Share	Nil	Market cap. (B)	$ 1.7
Shs. outstg. (M)	70.1	Inst. holdings	57%
Avg. daily vol. (M)	0.206		

Value of $10,000 invested 5 years ago: NA

Fiscal Year Ending Dec. 31

	2001	2000	1999	1998	1997	1996
Revenues (Million $)						
1Q	619.1	579.0	392.3	171.1	—	—
2Q	768.0	730.0	503.7	254.1	—	—
3Q	—	859.0	668.6	379.1	—	—
4Q	—	750.9	669.0	416.0	—	—
Yr.	—	2,919	2,234	1,220	10.63	51.89
Earnings Per Share ($)						
1Q	**0.04**	**0.19**	**0.18**	**0.11**	—	—
2Q	**0.26**	**0.51**	**0.28**	**0.27**	—	—
3Q	—	**0.79**	**0.60**	**-0.13**	—	—
4Q	—	**0.40**	**0.48**	**0.24**	—	—
Yr.	—	**1.89**	**1.53**	**0.48**	Nil	0.20

Next earnings report expected: late October

Dividend Data

No cash dividends have been paid. The company intends to retain all earnings for the foreseeable future for use in the operation and expansion of its business.

United Rentals, Inc.

Business Summary - 30-JUL-01

United Rentals was formed in September 1997 for the purpose of creating a large, geographically diversified equipment rental company in North America. URI began equipment rental operations in October 1997, acquiring six established companies. As of June 1999, the company served more than 900,000 customers through a network of 506 locations in 41 states, Canada and Mexico. Equipment is rented, as well as sold, to a diverse customer base, primarily consisting of construction industry participants, industrial companies, and homeowners.

The company offers for rent a broad array of equipment, including light to heavy construction and industrial equipment and general tools and equipment.

Construction and industrial equipment consists primarily of aerial lifts, air compressors, backhoes, boom lifts, bulldozers, cranes, ditching equipment, forklifts, generators, high reach equipment, pumps, scissor lifts, and tractors.

General tools and equipment consists mainly of garden and landscaping equipment, hand tools, high-pressure washers, paint sprayers, power tools, and roto tillers.

URI routinely sells used rental equipment, and is generally able to achieve favorable prices, due to its preventive maintenance program and its national salesforce that can access many resale markets across North America. The company typically sells used equipment through its salesforce. It also sells used equipment to dealers and through public auctions.

New equipment is distributed at several locations, for tool and equipment manufacturers that include Genie Industries, Grove Worldwide, JLG Industries and Snorkel (aerial lifts); Ingersoll-Rand (air compressors, tools, pumps): Kubota (earthmoving equipment): Trak International (loaders and forklifts): and Edco Manufacturing (surfacing equipment).

Sales of related merchandise and parts involve the sale, at most locations, of a variety of merchandise (such as saw blades, fasteners, drill bits, hard hats, gloves, and other safety equipment) that may be used in conjunction with rental equipment.

In 1998, the company completed 84 acquisitions. Among the more significant was the September 1998 purchase U.S. Rentals, in exchange for about 29.6 million common shares. URI also acquired, Wynne Systems, Inc., for 1,456,997 common shares. In August 1999, the company purchased Rental Tools, for 2,744,368 shares.

In October 1999, URI placed privately a total of $150 million of Series B perpetual convertible preferred stock. Each preferred share is convertible into URI common stock at $30 a share. Earlier, in August 1999, URI placed privately $300 million of seven-year senior secured term loan C notes.

Per Share Data ($) (Year Ended Dec. 31)	2000	1999	1998	1997	1996	1995	1994	1993	1992	1991
Tangible Bk. Val.	NM	NM	NM	4.49	4.56	NA	NA	NA	NA	NA
Cash Flow	5.95	5.23	3.37	0.02	0.62	NA	NA	NA	NA	NA
Earnings	1.89	1.53	0.48	Nil	0.20	NA	NA	NA	NA	NA
Dividends	Nil	Nil	Nil	Nil	NA	NA	NA	NA	NA	NA
Payout Ratio	Nil	Nil	Nil	Nil	NA	NA	NA	NA	NA	NA
Prices - High	24.31	35.68	48.06	19.31	NA	NA	NA	NA	NA	NA
- Low	11.68	14.31	10.56	13.50	NA	NA	NA	NA	NA	NA
P/E Ratio - High	13	23	NM	NM	NA	NA	NA	NA	NA	NA
- Low	6	9	NM	NM	NA	NA	NA	NA	NA	NA
Income Statement Analysis (Million $)										
Revs.	2,919	2,234	1,220	10.6	51.9	NA	NA	NA	NA	NA
Oper. Inc.	962	753	404	1.9	14.4	NA	NA	NA	NA	NA
Depr.	414	344	211	1.3	7.2	NA	NA	NA	NA	NA
Int. Exp.	248	159	72.0	0.5	1.8	NA	NA	NA	NA	NA
Pretax Inc.	301	242	78.3	0.1	5.8	NA	NA	NA	NA	NA
Eff. Tax Rate	42%	41%	56%	38%	40%	NA	NA	NA	NA	NA
Net Inc.	176	143	34.8	NM	3.5	NA	NA	NA	NA	NA
Balance Sheet & Other Fin. Data (Million $)										
Cash	34.4	23.8	20.4	68.6	58.2	NA	NA	NA	NA	NA
Curr. Assets	NA	NA	NA	NA	NA	NA	NA	NA	NA	NA
Total Assets	5,124	4,498	2,635	169	1,513	NA	NA	NA	NA	NA
Curr. Liab.	NA	NA	NA	NA	NA	NA	NA	NA	NA	NA
LT Debt	Nil	374	359	0.8	0.3	NA	NA	NA	NA	NA
Common Eqty.	1,546	1,397	726	158	145	NA	NA	NA	NA	NA
Total Cap.	1,546	1,852	1,129	159	145	NA	NA	NA	NA	NA
Cap. Exp.	962	842	564	0.8	NA	NA	NA	NA	NA	NA
Cash Flow	591	486	246	1.3	10.7	NA	NA	NA	NA	NA
Curr. Ratio	NA	NA	NA	NA	NA	NA	NA	NA	NA	NA
% LT Debt of Cap.	Nil	20.2	31.8	0.5	NA	NA	NA	NA	NA	NA
% Net Inc.of Revs.	6.0	6.4	2.9	0.3	6.7	NA	NA	NA	NA	NA
% Ret. on Assets	3.7	4.0	2.6	NA	NA	NA	NA	NA	NA	NA
% Ret. on Equity	12.0	13.4	8.9	NA	NA	NA	NA	NA	NA	NA

Data as orig reptd.; bef. results of disc opers/spec. items. Per share data adj. for stk. divs. Bold denotes diluted EPS (FASB 128)-prior periods restated. E-Estimated. NA-Not Available. NM-Not Meaningful. NR-Not Ranked.

Office—Four Greenwich Office Park, Greenwich, CT 06083. **Tel**—(203) 622-3131. **Website**—www.unitedrentals.com **Chrmn & CEO**—B. S. Jacobs. **Pres & COO**—W. R. Hicks. **Vice Chrmn & Secy**—J. N. Milne. **CFO**—M. J. Nolan. **Dirs**—L. D. Black, W. F. Berry, R. D. Colburn, R. M. DeFeo, M. S. Gross, R. J. Heckmann, W. R. Hicks, B. S. Jacobs, J. S. McKinney, J. N. Milne, G. Tsai Jr., C. M. Weyer. **Transfer Agent & Registrar**—American Stock Transfer & Trust Co. **Incorporated**—in Delaware in 1997. **Empl**— 8,501. **S&P Analyst:** Markos N. Kaminis

STANDARD
&POOR'S
STOCK REPORTS

USA Networks

Nasdaq Symbol **USAI**

21-AUG-01

Industry: Broadcasting (Television, Radio & Cable)

Summary: This company owns and operates a diverse stable of leading media, cable and electronic commerce businesses, including the flagship USA Network cable channel.

S&P Opinion: Buy (★★★★★)

Recent Price • 23.75
52 Wk Range • 28.44-16.18
Yield • Nil
12-Mo. P/E • NM

Quantitative Evaluations

Outlook (1 Lowest—5 Highest)
• **NA**

Fair Value
• **NA**

Risk
• **NA**

Earn./Div. Rank
• **NR**

Technical Eval.
• **Bullish** since 4/01

Rel. Strength Rank (1 Lowest—99 Highest)
• **29**

Insider Activity
• **Neutral**

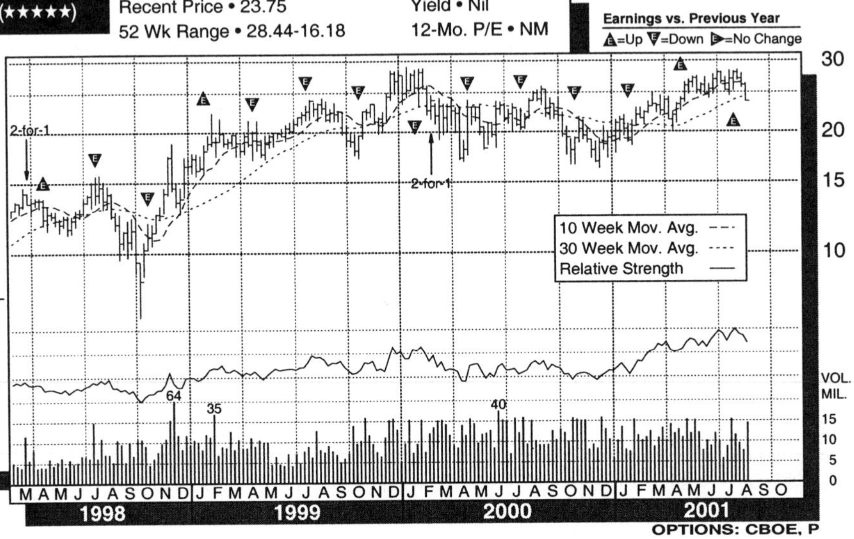

OPTIONS: CBOE, P

Overview - 21-AUG-01

In 2001, despite a difficult advertising market, revenues are expected to increase 17% to $5.4 billion. Growth in cash flow, as measured by EBITDA (non-GAAP), will approximate 37% in 2001, after a 29% gain in 2000. After substantial depreciation and amortization charges, income taxes and minority interest, we estimate reported earnings per share of $0.15 in 2001, compared to a reported loss of $0.15 in 2000. In 2002, we forecast a revenue increase of 20%-21%, including the consolidated results of Expedia. The planned acquisition of a majority interest in Expedia is expected to be accretive to cash flow and neutral to reported EPS in 2002. We also expect a rebound in advertising rates and minutes sold during 2002. Projected cash flow, at $1.4 billion, represents a 27% increase over estimated 2001 cash flow. Reported EPS are estimated at $0.25.

Valuation - 21-AUG-01

S&P is maintaining its buy opinion on USAI. Under CEO Barry Diller's strong leadership, USA Networks will content to redefine what a "media" company is. USAI's drive to create synergy between presumably distinct businesses will be furthered by the planned acquisition of a majority interest in Expedia, Inc. Together with USAI's majority owned Hotel Reservation Network, and vacation package and cruise services provider National Leisure Group, USAI will be the market leader in interactive travel services with about $4 billion in annual gross bookings. These operations will also provide the foundation for a new USA Travel cable channel. Based on projected annual 30% growth over the next three years in cash flow, we value USAI at 20 times estimated 2002 EBITDA, or approximately $36 per share.

Key Stock Statistics

S&P EPS Est. 2001	0.15	Tang. Bk. Value/Share	NM
P/E on S&P Est. 2001	NM	Beta	1.12
S&P EPS Est. 2002	0.25	Shareholders	30,000
Dividend Rate/Share	Nil	Market cap. (B)	$ 18.0
Shs. outstg. (M)	733.6	Inst. holdings	27%
Avg. daily vol. (M)	2.195		

Value of $10,000 invested 5 years ago: $ 32,758

Fiscal Year Ending Dec. 31

	2001	2000	1999	1998	1997	1996
Revenues (Million $)						
1Q	1,316	1,003	729.0	523.1	279.6	11.11
2Q	—	1,098	777.4	703.4	265.7	10.92
3Q	—	1,150	793.3	640.5	326.3	11.21
4Q	—	1,316	936.1	767.1	390.3	—
Yr.	—	4,601	3,236	2,634	1,262	1,068
Earnings Per Share ($)						
1Q	**-0.05**	**-0.06**	**0.02**	**0.09**	0.02	-0.02
2Q	—	**-0.08**	**-0.03**	**-0.01**	0.01	-0.01
3Q	—	**-0.05**	**-0.02**	**-0.02**	0.02	-0.01
4Q	—	**-0.08**	**-0.03**	**0.11**	**0.02**	—
Yr.	—	**-0.15**	**-0.04**	**0.21**	**0.06**	-0.02

Next earnings report expected: NA

Dividend Data

The company does not anticipate paying cash dividends in the immediate future.

USA Networks, Inc.

Business Summary - 21-AUG-01

Founded in 1986, USA Networks (USAI) operates diversified media, broadcasting and cable, and electronic commerce businesses, and controls a cluster of related businesses. The company operates through three principal units: USA Entertainment (35.2% of 2000 net revenues), USA Electronic Retailing (40.4%), and USA Information and Services (24.4%). Various emerging business units (not included in the percentage breakdown) generated revenues of $254 million in 2000.

USA Entertainment conducts the company networks and television production, filmed entertainment, broadcasting and developing networks segments. Networks and television production consists of the USA Network and Sci-Fi Channel cable networks, as well as the Studios USA unit, which produces original programming for USA Network, other broadcast and cable networks, pay television, and for syndication. Series include Law & Order, Xena: Warrior Princess, and several talk shows: The Sally Jesse Raphael Show, The Jerry Springer Show, and Maury. The unit is also the exclusive domestic distributor of the television library of Universal Studios, Inc. Feature film production and distribution consists of the October Films and Gramercy Pictures production units, and home video distribution through USA Home Entertainment.

Electronic Retailing consists primarily of the Home Shopping Network and America's Store, which sell consumer goods and services by means of live, customer-interactive electronic retail sales programs which are transmitted via satellite to cable television systems, affiliated broadcast television stations and satellite dish receivers. As of December 31, 1999, HSN was available in about 73.7 million unduplicated households, including 60.6 million cable households.

Information and Services operates the company's ticketing, hotel reservations, teleservices, interactive and electronic commerce and services segments. Ticketing operations consist of Ticketmaster, the leading provider of automated ticketing services in the U.S., and majority-owned Ticketmaster.com, Ticketmaster's exclusive agent for online ticket sales. The Hotel Reservations Network (71% owned) is a leading consolidator of hotel rooms for resale in the consumer market in the U.S. Internet Services are conducted through Styleclick, Inc., a leading enabler of e-commerce for manufacturers and retailers. Teleservices was formed via the April 2000 acquisition of Precision Response Corp., a leading provider of third-party customer care services. The interactive and electronic commerce and services segment consists of various operations associated with the company's other businesses, including the CitySearch city guide operations of Ticketmaster Online/CitySearch.

On July 16, 2001, USAI agreed to acquire a controlling interest in Expedia, Inc., for a combination of common, warrants, and preferred stock. Microsoft currently holds approximately 69% of Expedia. At the closing of the transaction, which is expected in 2001, USAI will own 67% to 75% of Expedia's outstanding equity, with the remainder held by the public and potentially Microsoft.

Per Share Data ($) (Year Ended Dec. 31)	2000	1999	1998	1997	1996	1995	1994	1993	1992	1991
Tangible Bk. Val.	NM	NM	NM	NM	NM	NM	NA	NA	NA	NA
Cash Flow	1.68	0.99	0.54	0.49	0.21	0.39	NA	NA	NA	NA
Earnings	-0.15	-0.04	0.21	0.06	-0.02	0.00	NA	NA	NA	NA
Dividends	Nil	Nil	Nil	Nil	Nil	Nil	NA	NA	NA	NA
Payout Ratio	Nil	Nil	Nil	Nil	Nil	Nil	NA	NA	NA	NA
Prices - High	29.06	28.43	18.81	12.93	8.68	10.06	NA	NA	NA	NA
- Low	16.18	15.56	6.90	5.00	5.25	2.18	NA	NA	NA	NA
P/E Ratio - High	NM	NM	87	NM	NM	NM	NA	NA	NA	NA
- Low	NM	NM	32	NM	NM	NM	NA	NA	NA	NA
Income Statement Analysis (Million $)										
Revs.	4,601	3,236	2,634	1,262	75.2	47.9	NA	NA	NA	NA
Oper. Inc.	750	573	464	192	19.1	22.9	NA	NA	NA	NA
Depr.	694	360	246	97.0	15.5	14.7	NA	NA	NA	NA
Int. Exp.	75.2	79.7	121	31.6	11.8	11.0	NA	NA	NA	NA
Pretax Inc.	71.4	261	284	56.5	-4.9	1.3	NA	NA	NA	NA
Eff. Tax Rate	NM	NM	45%	73%	NM	91%	NA	NA	NA	NA
Net Inc.	-88.6	-27.6	76.9	13.1	-6.5	0.1	NA	NA	NA	NA
Balance Sheet & Other Fin. Data (Million $)										
Cash	373	424	445	116	42.6	22.1	NA	NA	NA	NA
Curr. Assets	1,776	1,388	1,268	421	249	27.2	NA	NA	NA	NA
Total Assets	10,474	9,253	8,327	2,671	2,116	143	NA	NA	NA	NA
Curr. Liab.	1,173	1,032	863	360	273	21.2	NA	NA	NA	NA
LT Debt	848	575	776	448	271	97.9	NA	NA	NA	NA
Common Eqty.	3,440	2,770	2,571	1,447	1,159	13.2	NA	NA	NA	NA
Total Cap.	9,203	7,842	6,981	2,267	1,786	126	NA	NA	NA	NA
Cap. Exp.	177	139	87.0	NA	NA	NA	NA	NA	NA	NA
Cash Flow	605	332	323	110	8.9	14.3	NA	NA	NA	NA
Curr. Ratio	1.5	1.3	1.5	1.2	0.9	1.3	NA	NA	NA	NA
% LT Debt of Cap.	9.2	7.3	11.1	19.8	15.2	77.9	NA	NA	NA	NA
% Net Inc.of Revs.	NM	NM	2.9	1.0	NM	0.3	NA	NA	NA	NA
% Ret. on Assets	NM	NM	1.4	0.5	NM	0.1	NA	NA	NA	NA
% Ret. on Equity	NM	NM	3.8	1.0	NM	8.0	NA	NA	NA	NA

Data as orig reptd.; bef. results of disc opers/spec. items. Per share data adj. for stk. divs. Bold denotes diluted EPS (FASB 128)-prior periods restated. E-Estimated. NA-Not Available. NM-Not Meaningful. NR-Not Ranked.

Office—152 West 57th St. **Tel**—(212) 314-7300. **Website**—www.usanetworks.com **Chrmn & CEO**—B. Diller. **Exec VP**—D. Khosrowshahi. **SVP & CFO**—M. Sileck.**Dirs**—P. G. Allen, E. Bronfman Jr., A. M. Busquet, B. Diller, P. Germond, V. A. Kaufman, D. R. Keough, G. Kofler, M. Kravis, P. Lescure, J. Messier, W. D. Savoy, H. N. Schwarzkopf, D. von Furstenberg.**Transfer Agent & Registrar**—Mellon Investor Services, SF. **Incorporated**—in Delaware in 1986.**Empl**— 20,780. **S&P Analyst:** Mark S. Basham

STANDARD
&POOR'S
STOCK REPORTS

Abercrombie & Fitch

NYSE Symbol **ANF**

In S&P MidCap 400

18-AUG-01 **Industry:** Retail (Specialty-Apparel)

Summary: An apparel retailer specializing in lifestyle branding, Abercrombie & Fitch operates more than 400 retail apparel stores.

S&P Opinion: Accumulate (★★★★) Recent Price • 31.29 52 Wk Range • 47.50-14.75 Yield • Nil 12-Mo. P/E • 19.2

Quantitative Evaluations

Outlook
(1 Lowest—5 Highest)
• 5+

Fair Value
• 50.70

Risk
• High

Earn./Div. Rank
• B

Technical Eval.
• **Bearish** since 7/01

Rel. Strength Rank
(1 Lowest—99 Highest)
• 18

Insider Activity
• Neutral

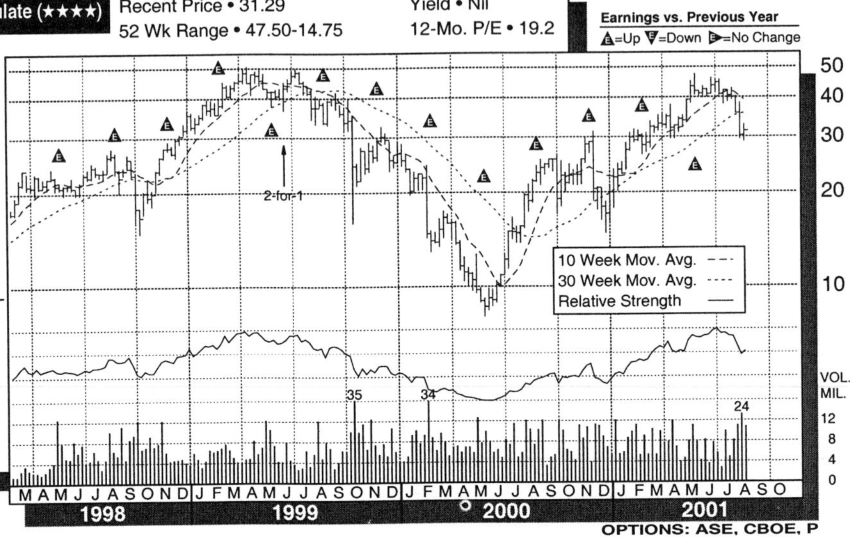

OPTIONS: ASE, CBOE, P

Overview - 16-AUG-01

We expect sales to rise approximately 23% in the second half of FY 02 (Jan.), driven by the addition of about 29 adult stores, 37 abercrombie kids stores and 22 Hollister stores, a new concept targeted to high school guys and girls. Strength in the women's business should continue to offset weakness in men's clothing sales. Same-store sales should advance modestly. Gross margins should benefit from reduced markdowns and improved sourcing, partially offset by higher occupancy costs. However, general, administrative and store operating expenses should decline as a percentage of sales, reflecting stringent cost controls. Capital expenditures are projected to rise substantially, to about $115 million to $120 million, mostly for new store growth. New channels of distribution, such as catalogs and Internet sales, bode well for future growth. We project that EPS will increase 15% in FY 02, to $1.78, and see a 21% gain to $2.15 in FY 03.

Valuation - 16-AUG-01

Although the shares have more than doubled since late 2000, we continue to recommend investors accumulate ANF stock. The company's dynamic management team, strong brand awareness for the Abercrombie & Fitch name, and the potential for more stores, bode well for continued earnings growth. Strong sales and productivity levels reported at the new Hollister stores during the first half of the year are also encouraging. The company expects to add a total of 29 of these stores during FY 02, with a total potential of 600-800 locations. ANF generates strong cash flow, and has no long term debt, allowing it to fund its growth from internally generated funds. We anticipate that EPS can advance 18% to 20% annually, and believe the shares merit accumulation for long-term capital gains.

Key Stock Statistics

S&P EPS Est. 2002	1.78	Tang. Bk. Value/Share	4.50
P/E on S&P Est. 2002	17.6	Beta	NA
S&P EPS Est. 2003	2.15	Shareholders	7,000
Dividend Rate/Share	Nil	Market cap. (B)	$ 3.1
Shs. outstg. (M)	99.3	Inst. holdings	86%
Avg. daily vol. (M)	2.709		

Value of $10,000 invested 5 years ago: NA

Fiscal Year Ending Jan. 31

	2002	2001	2000	1999	1998	1997
Revenues (Million $)						
1Q	263.7	206.7	188.3	134.2	74.32	51.02
2Q	280.1	231.5	198.9	147.1	86.64	57.43
3Q	—	366.9	287.0	229.9	148.5	87.69
4Q	—	439.4	367.9	304.6	212.2	139.2
Yr.	—	1,238	1,042	815.8	521.6	335.4
Earnings Per Share ($)						
1Q	**0.20**	**0.16**	**0.12**	**0.06**	Nil	—
2Q	**0.24**	**0.21**	**0.17**	**0.10**	**0.02**	**0.01**
3Q	**E0.48**	**0.43**	**0.36**	**0.23**	**0.10**	**0.05**
4Q	**E0.86**	**0.76**	**0.73**	**0.56**	**0.34**	**0.20**
Yr.	**E1.78**	**1.55**	**1.39**	**0.96**	**0.47**	**0.27**

Next earnings report expected: early November

Dividend Data

ANF currently intends to retain future earnings for the development of its business and does not anticipate paying regular quarterly dividends on the common stock for the foreseeable future.

Abercrombie & Fitch Co.

Business Summary - 16-AUG-01

Abercrombie & Fitch (ANF) gained fame for outfitting expeditions for the likes of Teddy Roosevelt, Ernest Hemingway and Admiral Byrd, but it is best known today as a rapidly growing specialty retailer of casual apparel for men and women. The company was established in 1892, and became well known as a supplier of rugged, high-quality outdoor gear. ANF emphasized durable and dependable merchandise, and placed a premium on complete customer satisfaction for each item sold.

In 1988, Abercrombie & Fitch was acquired for $25 million by The Limited, Inc. (LTD). In October 1996, LTD completed an IPO of 8.05 million ANF Class A common shares; LTD retained an 84% stake in ANF in the form of Class B stock. In May 1998, LTD completed a tax free exchange offer with its shareholders; as a result, LTD no longer has a stake in ANF.

In 1992, a new management team repositioned the company as a more fashion-oriented casual apparel business. In reestablishing the Abercrombie & Fitch brand, the company combined its historical image of quality with a new emphasis on casual American style and youthfulness. The stores are located primarily in regional shopping malls across the U.S. As of August 4, 2001, ANF operated 405 stores, including 281 adult Abercrombie & Fitch stores, 112 abercrombie for kids (geared to boys and girls 7 to 14 years of age) and 12 Hollister locations (geared toward teens).

ANF's current merchandise assortment covers a broad range of classifications in men's and women's casual apparel. In recent years, the company has allocated more selling square footage to women's apparel, resulting in a significant increase in sales in that category. In addition, ANF offers a broad range of accessories, including belts, socks, caps, boxers, underwear and personal products. Although the company currently markets dress shirts and ties, it has de-emphasized these categories, as it decided they did not fit in with its focus on casual apparel. The company's stores produced net sales per selling sq. ft. in FY 01 (Jan.) of $474, down from $505 in FY 00. The company's catalog A&F Quarterly and its e-commerce site contributed 3.8% of net sales in FY 01, compared to 2.9% in FY 00.

The company plans to spend $115 million to $120 million in FY 02 for capital expenditures for new stores, remodeling and/or expansion of existing stores, and related improvements. A 30% increase in square footage in FY 02 is to comprise 45 Abercrombie & Fitch stores, 64 abercrombie stores and 29 Hollister Co. units. All future capital expenditures are expected to be covered by cash generated through operations.

Per Share Data ($) (Year Ended Jan. 31)	2001	2000	1999	1998	1997	1996	1995	1994	1993	1992
Tangible Bk. Val.	4.28	3.05	1.82	0.57	0.11	-0.34	NA	NA	NA	NA
Cash Flow	1.85	1.65	1.16	0.63	0.40	0.18	NA	NA	NA	NA
Earnings	1.55	1.39	0.96	0.47	0.27	0.10	NA	NA	NA	NA
Dividends	Nil	Nil	Nil	Nil	Nil	Nil	NA	NA	NA	NA
Payout Ratio	Nil	Nil	Nil	Nil	Nil	Nil	NA	NA	NA	NA
Cal. Yrs.	2000	1999	1998	1997	1996	1995	1994	1993	1992	1991
Prices - High	31.31	50.75	36.12	18.06	13.50	NA	NA	NA	NA	NA
- Low	8.00	21.00	14.43	6.25	7.87	NA	NA	NA	NA	NA
P/E Ratio - High	20	37	38	38	50	NA	NA	NA	NA	NA
- Low	5	15	15	13	29	NA	NA	NA	NA	NA
Income Statement Analysis (Million $)										
Revs.	1,238	1,042	816	522	335	236	NA	NA	NA	NA
Oper. Inc.	284	270	188	100	57.8	32.9	NA	NA	NA	NA
Depr.	30.7	27.7	20.9	16.3	11.8	9.1	NA	NA	NA	NA
Int. Exp.	Nil	Nil	Nil	3.6	4.9	8.1	NA	NA	NA	NA
Pretax Inc.	261	249	170	80.5	41.1	15.7	NA	NA	NA	NA
Eff. Tax Rate	40%	40%	40%	40%	40%	40%	NA	NA	NA	NA
Net Inc.	158	150	102	48.3	24.7	9.4	NA	NA	NA	NA
Balance Sheet & Other Fin. Data (Million $)										
Cash	138	194	164	42.7	1.9	1.4	NA	NA	NA	NA
Curr. Assets	304	300	218	109	44.9	63.2	NA	NA	NA	NA
Total Assets	588	458	319	183	106	109	NA	NA	NA	NA
Curr. Liab.	155	138	122	67.0	43.6	84.6	NA	NA	NA	NA
LT Debt	Nil	Nil	Nil	50.0	50.0	58.6	NA	NA	NA	NA
Common Eqty.	423	311	186	58.8	11.2	-34.4	NA	NA	NA	NA
Total Cap.	423	311	186	109	61.2	24.1	NA	NA	NA	NA
Cap. Exp.	153	83.8	41.9	29.5	24.3	24.5	NA	NA	NA	NA
Cash Flow	189	177	123	64.7	36.4	18.5	NA	NA	NA	NA
Curr. Ratio	2.0	2.2	1.8	1.6	1.0	0.7	NA	NA	NA	NA
% LT Debt of Cap.	Nil	Nil	Nil	46.0	81.6	243.0	NA	NA	NA	NA
% Net Inc.of Revs.	12.8	14.4	12.5	9.3	7.4	4.0	NA	NA	NA	NA
% Ret. on Assets	30.2	38.5	40.6	33.4	25.5	NA	NA	NA	NA	NA
% Ret. on Equity	43.1	60.2	83.4	138.0	NA	NA	NA	NA	NA	NA

Data as orig. reptd.; bef. results of disc. opers. and/or spec. items. Per share data adj. for stk. divs. as of ex-div. date. Bold denotes diluted EPS (FASB 128). E-Estimated. NA-Not Available. NM-Not Meaningful. NR-Not Ranked.

Office—6301 Fitch Path, New Albany, OH 43054. **Tel**—(614) 283-6500. **Website**—http://www.abercrombie.com **Chrmn & CEO**—M. S. Jeffries. **EVP & COO**—S. R. Johnson. **VP & CFO**—W. S. McDonald. **Dirs**—R. M. Gertmenian, J. A. Golden, A M. Griffin, M. S. Jeffries, S. R. Johnson, J. W. Kessler, S. N. Shahid Jr., K. D. Sullivan. **Transfer Agent & Registrar**—First Chicago Trust Co. of New York. **Incorporated**—in Delaware in 1996. **Empl**— 13,900. **S&P Analyst:** Maureen C. Carini

STANDARD &POOR'S STOCK REPORTS

American Eagle Outfitters

Nasdaq Symbol **AEOS**

In S&P MidCap 400

22-AUG-01

Industry: Retail (Specialty-Apparel)

Summary: This company is a specialty retailer of all-American, casual apparel, accessories, and footwear for men and women between the ages of 16 and 34.

S&P Opinion: Accumulate (★★★★)

Recent Price • 30.84 | 52 Wk Range • 43-14.33 | Yield • Nil | 12-Mo. P/E • 23.0

Quantitative Evaluations

Outlook (1 Lowest—5 Highest) • **3**

Fair Value • **31.30**

Risk • **High**

Earn./Div. Rank • **NR**

Technical Eval. • **Bearish** since 8/01

Rel. Strength Rank (1 Lowest—99 Highest) • **22**

Insider Activity • **Unfavorable**

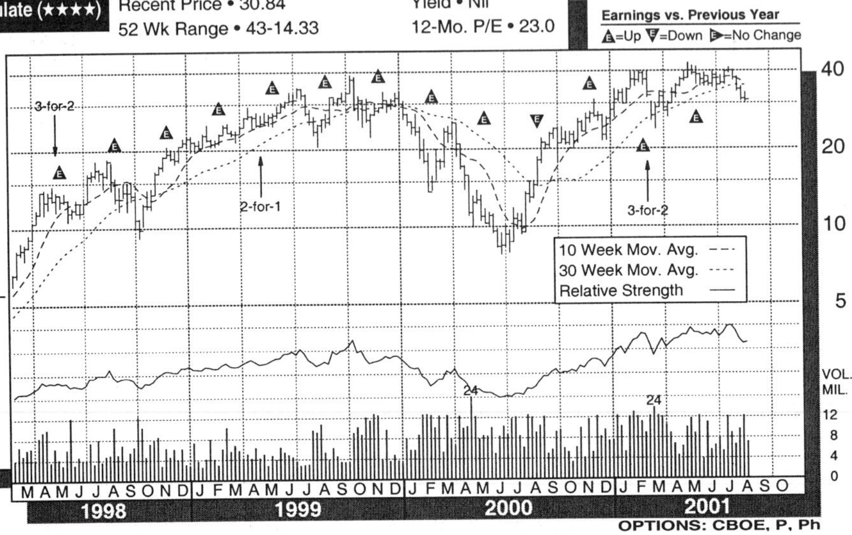

OPTIONS: CBOE, P, Ph

Overview - 22-AUG-01

We expect total sales for FY 02 (Jan.) to increase approximately 30% to 35%, reflecting the addition of about 45 new stores, contributions from the acquisition of the Thrifty's/Bluenotes chain in Canada, and same-store sales gains of approximately 1% to 3%. Although the Thrifty's/Bluenotes chain had a negative impact on earnings during the first half of FY 02, we expect the chain to contribute about $0.05 for for the full year. Gross margins should benefit from higher starting price points for core merchandise, partially offset by the inclusion of the lower margin Canadian businesses. The company believes that it can bring the newer chain up to the corporate average over time, however. SG&A expenses as a percent of sales should be flat. We expect earnings per share for FY 02 to reach $1.65, a 27% gain over the $1.30 reported in FY 01, and see a further rise to $2.06 in FY 03.

Valuation - 22-AUG-01

We continue to recommend investors accumulate AEOS shares. Since 1996, sales have grown at an average compounded annual growth rate of 25%, while earnings have climbed 61%. The shares have been volatile in recent weeks, reflecting uncertainty surrounding the important back-to-school selling season. Despite a slower economy, AEOS managed to post a 4.6% gain in same-store sales during the second quarter of FY 02, reflecting consumers' approval of the company's new merchandise presentation. Increases in other profit measures such as the average unit retail price, the number of transactions per average store, and the average transaction size also bode well for future results. We believe the shares, recently trading at only 15X our $1.65 estimate and with a projected EPS growth rate of 21% over the next three to five years, are undervalued and should be accumulated.

Key Stock Statistics

S&P EPS Est. 2002	1.65	Tang. Bk. Value/Share	5.16
P/E on S&P Est. 2002	18.7	Beta	2.08
S&P EPS Est. 2003	2.06	Shareholders	197
Dividend Rate/Share	Nil	Market cap. (B)	$ 1.7
Shs. outstg. (M)	71.5	Inst. holdings	70%
Avg. daily vol. (M)	2.876		

Value of $10,000 invested 5 years ago: $ 118,110

Fiscal Year Ending Jan. 31

	2002	2001	2000	1999	1998	1997
Revenues (Million $)						
1Q	251.6	178.0	145.4	99.7	60.95	54.40
2Q	292.4	209.0	178.6	125.7	86.16	70.30
3Q	—	282.8	222.7	149.1	104.9	78.85
4Q	—	423.7	285.4	213.1	153.7	122.9
Yr.	—	1,093	832.1	587.6	405.7	326.4
Earnings Per Share ($)						
1Q	0.21	0.17	0.17	0.08	-0.05	-0.05
2Q	0.21	0.04	0.23	0.13	0.01	0.00
3Q	E0.47	0.41	0.33	0.19	0.09	0.03
4Q	E0.76	0.68	0.51	0.34	0.22	0.10
Yr.	E1.65	1.30	1.24	0.75	0.28	0.09

Next earnings report expected: late November

Dividend Data

Amount ($)	Date Decl.	Ex-Div. Date	Stock of Record	Payment Date
3-for-2	Jan. 22	Feb. 26	Feb. 02	Feb. 23 '01

A Division of The McGraw·Hill Companies

American Eagle Outfitters, Inc.

Business Summary - 22-AUG-01

One of the largest specialty retailers targeting the teen-age demographic, American Eagle Outfitters has grown rapidly since it opened its first store in 1977. The company offers all-American casual apparel, accessories, and footwear for men and women between the ages of 16 and 34. AEOS sources, designs and markets a versatile line of timeless and relaxed clothing classics such as jeans, khakis, and T-shirts under its American Eagle Outfitters and AE brand names, for exclusive sale in its American Eagle Outfitters stores. As of August 20, 2001, the company offered merchandise through a network of 593 American Eagle Outfitters stores in 47 states and the District of Columbia and its e-commerce site, ae.com.

AEOS designs and sells virtually all of its merchandise under its own brands. Its merchandising strategy focuses on providing an in-season merchandise assortment within its primary merchandise groups: men's and women's apparel, footwear, and accessories. Merchandise is regularly updated with more styles, colors and fabrics. AEOS offers quality fashionable interpretations of fundamental wardrobe items such as jeans, sweaters, khakis, T-shirts, flannel shirts, and fleece.

Sales in FY 01 (Jan.) were obtained as follows: men's apparel 40%, women's apparel 52%, and footwear and accessories 8%.

In November 2000, the company entered Canada with the acquisition of the Thrifty's/Bluenotes retail chain, the Braemar chain and NLS, a distribution facility near Toronto. The Thrifty's/Bluenotes stores offer a more urban/suburban denim-driven collection for 12 to 22 year-olds. During 2001, the company plans to convert most of the Braemar stores to American Eagle Outfitters stores. As of March 15, 2001, AEOS operated 109 Thrifty's/Bluenotes stores in Canada.

In recent years, the company has concentrated on several core operating strategies, in an effort to differentiate itself from its competition and improve sales and profitability. These strategies include building on the American Eagle Outfitters brand; expanding distribution channels; and continuing to invest in infrastructure.

The company's primary store expansion strategy is to continue its geographic growth throughout the U.S. and to fill in existing markets. As of March 15, 2001, AEOS operated in 47 states, with the highest concentration of locations in Ohio, Pennsylvania, New York, Michigan, Illinois, and Virginia. The company opened 90 stores in FY 01, increasing its store base by 19%, and its selling square footage by over 29%. Of the 90 new stores opened in FY 01, 38 stores were in new markets in the Northwest and Southwest.

Per Share Data ($) (Year Ended Jan. 31)	2001	2000	1999	1998	1997	1996	1995	1994	1993	1992
Tangible Bk. Val.	4.97	3.77	2.20	2.02	1.59	1.44	1.11	1.22	NA	NA
Cash Flow	1.62	1.41	0.87	0.59	0.18	0.40	0.17	0.23	NA	NA
Earnings	1.30	1.24	0.75	0.28	0.13	0.25	0.15	0.18	NA	NA
Dividends	Nil	Nil	Nil	Nil	Nil	Nil	Nil	Nil	NA	NA
Payout Ratio	Nil	Nil	Nil	Nil	Nil	Nil	Nil	Nil	NA	NA
Cal. Yrs.	2000	1999	1998	1997	1996	1995	1994	1993	1992	1991
Prices - High	31.16	39.00	22.64	5.77	4.36	3.51	4.40	NA	NA	NA
- Low	7.75	19.62	4.77	1.05	0.86	0.81	1.85	NA	NA	NA
P/E Ratio - High	24	31	30	20	33	14	29	NA	NA	NA
- Low	6	16	6	4	7	3	12	NA	NA	NA
Income Statement Analysis (Million $)										
Revs.	1,093	832	588	406	326	227	297	198	NA	NA
Oper. Inc.	170	162	95.7	38.4	14.9	19.8	17.0	15.7	NA	NA
Depr.	23.2	12.2	8.6	7.3	6.1	4.1	5.0	3.6	NA	NA
Int. Exp.	Nil	Nil	Nil	Nil	Nil	0.8	0.8	0.8	NA	NA
Pretax Inc.	153	149	89.5	32.3	9.8	11.8	11.2	11.2	NA	NA
Eff. Tax Rate	39%	39%	40%	39%	40%	39%	40%	NM	NA	NA
Net Inc.	93.8	90.7	54.1	19.5	5.9	7.1	6.8	12.2	NA	NA
Balance Sheet & Other Fin. Data (Million $)										
Cash	133	76.6	71.9	48.4	34.3	20.0	0.5	0.2	NA	NA
Curr. Assets	319	263	155	102	73.8	56.3	95.8	59.9	NA	NA
Total Assets	543	355	211	145	110	95.4	134	82.9	NA	NA
Curr. Liab.	149	88.4	59.8	54.0	39.4	31.6	76.6	32.7	NA	NA
LT Debt	Nil	Nil	Nil	Nil	Nil	Nil	Nil	Nil	NA	NA
Common Eqty.	368	265	151	90.8	71.1	63.8	57.9	50.1	NA	NA
Total Cap.	368	265	151	90.8	71.1	63.8	57.9	50.1	NA	NA
Cap. Exp.	87.8	45.6	24.9	12.6	NA	NA	NA	NA	NA	NA
Cash Flow	117	103	62.7	26.9	12.0	11.2	11.7	15.8	NA	NA
Curr. Ratio	2.1	3.0	2.6	1.9	1.9	1.8	1.3	1.8	NA	NA
% LT Debt of Cap.	Nil	Nil	Nil	Nil	Nil	Nil	Nil	Nil	NA	NA
% Net Inc.of Revs.	8.6	10.9	9.2	4.8	1.8	3.1	2.3	6.2	NA	NA
% Ret. on Assets	20.9	32.1	30.4	15.3	5.8	NM	6.2	19.8	NA	NA
% Ret. on Equity	29.7	43.6	44.7	24.1	8.7	NM	12.5	44.8	NA	NA

Data as orig reptd.; bef. results of disc opers/spec. items. Data for 1996 is for six mos. ended Jan. 31. Prior to 1996 yrs. ended Jul. 31. Per share data adj. for stk. divs. Bold denotes diluted EPS (FASB 128)-prior periods restated. E-Estimated. NA-Not Available. NM-Not Meaningful. NR-Not Ranked.

Office—150 Thorn Hill Drive, Warrendale, PA 15086-7528. **Tel**—(724) 776-4857. **Website**—http://www.ae.com **Chrmn & CEO**—J. L. Schottenstein. **Vice Chrmn**—G. Kolber. **Pres**—R. S. Markfield. **COO**—J. O'Donnell. **EVP & CFO**—L. A. Weil. **VP, Treas & Secy**—W. P. Tait. **Dirs**—A. Deshe, J. P. Diamond, M. P. Doolan, G. W. Harrison, M. G. Jesselson, T. R. Ketteler, G. Kolber, J. L. Marakas, R. S. Markfield, J. O'Donnell, J. L. Schottenstein, S. Schottenstein, D. W. Thompson, G. E. Wedren. **Transfer Agent & Registrar**—National City Bank, Cleveland. **Incorporated**—in Delaware in 1998. **Empl**— 9,799. **S&P Analyst:** Maureen C. Carini

STANDARD
&POOR'S
STOCK REPORTS

AnnTaylor Stores

NYSE Symbol **ANN**
In S&P SmallCap 600

18-AUG-01

Industry: Retail (Specialty-Apparel)

Summary: This leading specialty retailer of women's better-quality apparel, shoes and accessories operates more than 475 stores in 42 states, the District of Columbia and Puerto Rico.

S&P Opinion: Accumulate (★★★★)

Recent Price • 33.68
52 Wk Range • 44.87-18.25
Yield • Nil
12-Mo. P/E • 22.0

Quantitative Evaluations

Outlook (1 Lowest—5 Highest)
• **5**

Fair Value
• **44.30**

Risk
• **Average**

Earn./Div. Rank
• **B**

Technical Eval.
• **Bearish** since 7/01

Rel. Strength Rank (1 Lowest—99 Highest)
• **74**

Insider Activity
• **Neutral**

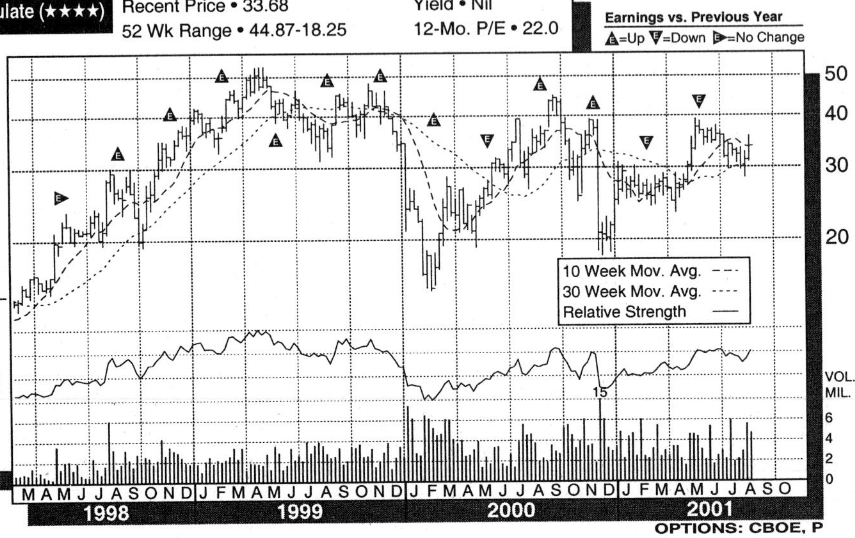

OPTIONS: CBOE, P

Overview - 17-AUG-01

We expect total sales to rise about 10% to 12% in FY 02 (Jan.), aided by the addition of about 60 new Loft stores and 18 new traditional AnnTaylor locations. After dropping 8.4% in the first half of FY 02, same-store sales should grow about 2% to 4% during the second half of the year. Recent weakness reflected both a general slowdown in consumer spending, and an unfavorable response by ANN's core consumers to a merchandise assortment too heavily weighted with contemporary fashion-forward looks at the expense of tradition classic career wear. We believe ANN has taken the correct steps to reposition itself for growth during the fall season, with a renewed focus on its core customers. Gross margins should continue to benefit from higher full-priced sales at both divisions, and from effective inventory management. SG&A margins should begin to stabilize as sales volume grows. We expect EPS to grow 28% in FY 02, to $2.25, and see a further rise, to $2.45, in FY 03.

Valuation - 17-AUG-01

We continue to recommend that investors accumulate the shares. We continue to believe that the second half FY 02 will show a turnaround in sales and earnings for the company. In reporting results for the second quarter, ANN indicated that inventories were clean and that its new merchandise offerings were being well received by its traditional customers. In addition, we expect consumer spending in the second half of the year to get a boost from lower interest rates and pent-up demand for the classic style apparel that ANN had been lacking. In light of the company's strong brand franchise, we view the shares, recently trading at 14X our EPS estimate for FY 03, as an attractive portfolio addition for long-term investors.

Key Stock Statistics

S&P EPS Est. 2002	2.25	Tang. Bk. Value/Share	9.89
P/E on S&P Est. 2002	15.0	Beta	1.04
S&P EPS Est. 2003	2.45	Shareholders	562
Dividend Rate/Share	Nil	Market cap. (B)	$0.980
Shs. outstg. (M)	29.1	Inst. holdings	0%
Avg. daily vol. (M)	0.759		

Value of $10,000 invested 5 years ago: $ 25,228

Fiscal Year Ending Jan. 31

	2002	2001	2000	1999	1998	1997
Revenues (Million $)						
1Q	307.1	277.1	249.4	198.2	197.1	184.5
2Q	310.3	306.3	265.8	223.4	185.0	187.9
3Q	—	305.9	272.3	227.5	187.2	212.7
4Q	—	343.6	297.1	262.8	211.8	213.1
Yr.	—	1,233	1,085	911.9	781.0	798.1
Earnings Per Share ($)						
1Q	**0.37**	**0.38**	**0.51**	**0.25**	0.25	0.08
2Q	**0.22**	**0.45**	**0.42**	**0.27**	0.04	0.03
3Q	**E1.00**	**0.78**	**0.65**	**0.50**	0.08	0.13
4Q	**E0.66**	**0.13**	**0.50**	**0.42**	**0.09**	0.12
Yr.	**E2.25**	**1.76**	**2.08**	**1.44**	**0.47**	**0.36**

Next earnings report expected: NA

Dividend Data

No dividends have been paid.

A Division of The McGraw·Hill Companies

AnnTaylor Stores Corporation

Business Summary - 17-AUG-01

Long known as a leading specialty retailer of women's better-quality apparel, shoes and accessories, AnnTaylor Stores offers its customers a distinct fashion point of view. The company believes its customer base is made up primarily of relatively affluent, fashion-conscious women who prefer classic styles, updated to reflect current fashion trends. ANN stores offer a collection of career and casual separates, weekend wear, dresses, tops, accessories, and shoes. As of February 3, 2001, the company operated 478 stores in 42 states, the District of Columbia and Puerto Rico. Of these stores, 332 were Ann Taylor stores, 133 were Ann Taylor Loft stores, and 13 were Ann Taylor Factory Stores.

The company emphasizes a total wardrobing strategy, whereby it trains its sales associates to assist customers in coordinating their wardrobe, helping them to achieve the Ann Taylor look, while reflecting each customer's personal style. The company believes its customer base consists of women between 25 and 55 years old, with limited time to shop. Stores offer a variety of coordinated apparel and an assortment of shoes and accessories to enable customers to assemble complete outfits. Newer moderate-priced stores are also being operated under the name Ann Taylor Loft. Merchandise is designed uniquely for these stores and is sold under the Ann Taylor Loft label.

The company's stores are located primarily in malls and upscale specialty retail centers, with the balance located in downtown and village locations.

Substantially all of the merchandise offered at the stores is developed by ANN's in-house product design and development teams, which design merchandise only for the company. Merchandising groups determine inventory needs for the upcoming season, edit the assortments developed by the design teams, plan monthly merchandise flows, and arrange for the production of merchandise either through ANN's sourcing division, or with manufacturers who are private label specialists. The company sources merchandise from about 232 manufacturers and vendors, none of which accounted for more than 5% of ANN's merchandise purchases in FY 01 (Jan.). Merchandise is manufactured in over 22 countries, with approximately 33% made in China, 17% in Korea, 11% in the Philippines, and 10% in Hong Kong.

Product extensions introduced over the last several years include petite sizes in the company's apparel offerings, and fragrance and personal care products in both the Ann Taylor and Ann Taylor Loft stores. In the Fall of 2000, ANN began a test of its own line of color cosmetics in a select group of Ann Taylor stores.

In November 2000, the company launched anntaylor.com, to offer merchandise to consumers over the Internet.

Per Share Data ($)										
(Year Ended Jan. 31)	**2001**	**2000**	**1999**	**1998**	**1997**	**1996**	**1995**	**1994**	**1993**	**1992**
Tangible Bk. Val.	9.44	7.06	4.24	2.03	1.02	0.36	0.13	-3.42	-4.69	-6.24
Cash Flow	3.15	3.25	2.55	1.98	1.82	1.18	2.32	1.47	1.08	0.87
Earnings	1.76	2.08	1.44	0.47	0.36	-0.04	1.40	0.66	0.28	0.05
Dividends	NA	Nil	Nil	Nil	Nil	Nil	Nil	Nil	Nil	Nil
Payout Ratio	NA	Nil	Nil	Nil	Nil	Nil	Nil	Nil	Nil	Nil
Cal. Yrs.	2000	1999	1998	1997	1996	1995	1994	1993	1992	1991
Prices - High	NA	53.06	40.25	25.25	24.25	38.00	44.87	30.00	25.00	36.50
- Low	NA	31.18	11.25	13.00	9.25	9.87	20.50	17.50	14.50	12.00
P/E Ratio - High	NA	26	28	54	67	NM	32	45	89	NM
- Low	NA	15	8	28	26	NM	15	27	52	NA
Income Statement Analysis (Million $)										
Revs.	1,233	1,085	912	781	798	731	666	508	474	444
Oper. Inc.	144	166	135	88.8	89.9	53.6	99	69.0	59.5	58.9
Depr.	46.1	41.4	39.8	38.8	36.3	28.3	21.3	18.0	17.0	15.7
Int. Exp.	7.3	11.8	18.1	20.0	24.4	21.0	14.2	17.7	21.3	34.0
Pretax Inc.	93.4	116	72.9	29.5	21.6	4.3	62.9	31.5	17.1	8.7
Eff. Tax Rate	44%	43%	46%	59%	60%	1.21%	48%	55%	65%	88%
Net Inc.	52.4	65.5	39.3	12.0	8.7	-0.9	32.6	14.3	5.9	1.0
Balance Sheet & Other Fin. Data (Million $)										
Cash	32.0	35.1	67.0	31.4	7.0	1.3	1.6	0.3	0.2	0.2
Curr. Assets	314	272	298	210	197	199	168	121	108	99
Total Assets	848	765	775	684	688	679	598	513	488	492
Curr. Liab.	141	120	130	87.9	78.0	112	65.9	68.1	78.5	72.4
LT Debt	116	114	201	105	131	232	200	180	158	186
Common Eqty.	574	606	433	384	371	326	326	259	245	229
Total Cap.	690	720	633	489	598	559	526	440	404	415
Cap. Exp.	83.3	53.4	45.1	22.9	16.1	78.4	61.3	25.1	4.3	10.0
Cash Flow	98.4	107	79.1	50.8	45.0	27.4	53.9	32.3	22.9	16.7
Curr. Ratio	2.2	2.3	2.3	2.4	2.5	1.8	2.6	1.8	1.4	1.4
% LT Debt of Cap.	16.8	15.9	31.7	21.5	21.9	41.5	38.0	41.0	39.2	44.8
% Net Inc.of Revs.	4.2	6.0	4.3	1.5	1.1	NM	4.9	2.8	1.2	0.2
% Ret. on Assets	6.5	8.5	5.4	1.7	1.3	NM	5.7	2.8	1.2	0.1
% Ret. on Equity	9.6	12.6	9.6	3.2	2.5	NM	10.8	5.6	2.4	0.6

Data as orig. reptd.; bef. results of disc. opers. and/or spec. items. Per share data adj. for stk. divs. as of ex-div. date. Bold denotes diluted EPS (FASB 128). E-Estimated. NA-Not Available. NM-Not Meaningful. NR-Not Ranked.

Office—142 W. 57th St., New York, NY 10019. **Tel**—(212) 541-3300. **Website**—www.anntaylor.com **Chrmn & CEO**—J. P. Spainhour. **SEVP & COO**—B. Erdos. **SVP & Secy**—J. F. L. Barandiaran. **SVP, CFO & Treas**—J. M. Smith. **Dirs**—G. S. Armstrong, J. J. Burke Jr., W. E. Cantrell, R. C. Grayson, R. W. Hovsepian, R. B. Lazarus, H. M. Merriman, J. P. Spainhour. **Transfer Agent & Registrar**—Mellon Investor Services, LLC, Ridgefield Park, NJ. **Incorporated**—in Delaware in 1988. **Empl**— 9,000. **S&P Analyst:** Maureen C. Carini

STANDARD
&POOR'S
STOCK REPORTS

AOL Time Warner

NYSE Symbol **AOL**

In S&P 500

18-AUG-01

Industry: Entertainment

Summary: This leading media company has significant operations in areas that include online access and content, cable systems and networks, publishing, filmed entertainment, and music.

S&P Opinion: Accumulate (★★★★)

Recent Price • 39.70
52 Wk Range • 62.27-31.50
Yield • Nil
12-Mo. P/E • NM

Quantitative Evaluations

Outlook
(1 Lowest—5 Highest)
• **5**

Fair Value
• **67.90**

Risk
• **High**

Earn./Div. Rank
• **B**

Technical Eval.
• **Bearish** since 7/01

Rel. Strength Rank
(1 Lowest—99 Highest)
• **20**

Insider Activity
• **Unfavorable**

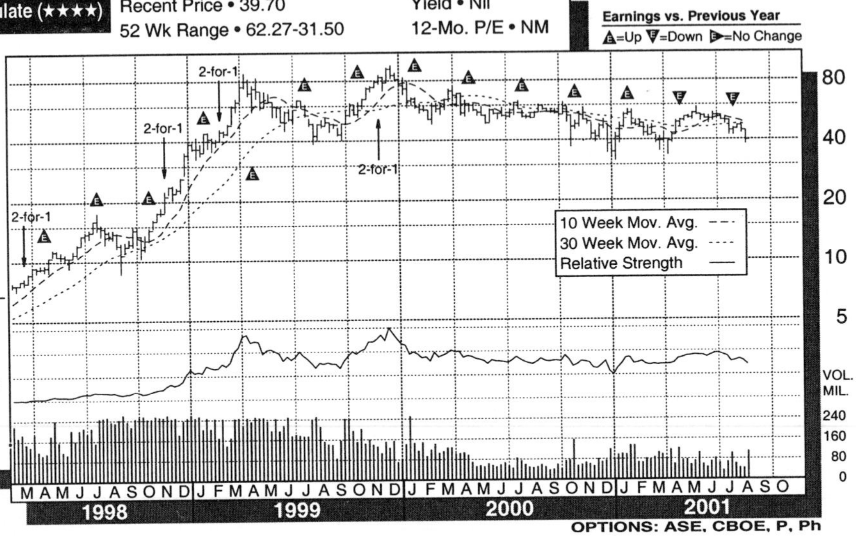

OPTIONS: ASE, CBOE, P, Ph

Overview - 14-AUG-01

Pro forma revenues should rise over 10% in 2001, driven by gains in both the subscriptions and advertising and commerce areas. For the longer term, we believe sales can grow about 20% annually. Our current expectations are for subscribers to AOL's flagship online service to approach 33 million by the end of 2001, up 18% from the level at December 2000. Even with a sluggish economy, we expect unique opportunities available to AOL to pay significant dividends. We anticipate AOL will continue to successfully cross-promote its offerings. In addition, advertisers have gravitated to AOL, not only because it is arguably the world's leading media company, but also due to the compelling audience, brand and value proposition it offers clients. Cost savings of note have also accrued. For 2001, we project EBITDA growth of 29%. Note that our forecasts use cash EPS, which excludes the impact of amortization and non-recurring items.

Valuation - 14-AUG-01

In August 2001, we downgraded the shares to accumulate from buy, in light of a high risk-reward profile resulting from a very challenging third quarter selling climate for advertising and content, and an above-market valuation. AOL is perhaps the world's best-positioned media company, due to its valuable subscriber and asset bases, which management has begun to effectively leverage to deliver growth. We believe the best is yet to come for 2001, as the release schedules for AOL's new feature films and music albums (accounting for 21% of 2000 revenues) are skewed notably toward the fourth quarter. Although our discounted cash flow analysis suggests that AOL's intrinsic value was recently significantly above its share price, the possibility of light third quarter revenues and rich P/E and EBITDA multiples make the shares attractive, but not compelling.

Key Stock Statistics

S&P EPS Est. 2001	1.27	Tang. Bk. Value/Share	2.51
P/E on S&P Est. 2001	31.3	Beta	2.52
S&P EPS Est. 2002	1.61	Shareholders	42,800
Dividend Rate/Share	Nil	Market cap. (B)	$169.1
Shs. outstg. (M)	4430.6	Inst. holdings	54%
Avg. daily vol. (M)	12.502		

Value of $10,000 invested 5 years ago: $ 200,855

Fiscal Year Ending Dec. 31

	2001	2000	1999	1998	1997	1996
Revenues (Million $)						
1Q	9,080	8,316	1,467	858.1	521.6	350.0
2Q	9,202	8,908	1,621	960.0	592.0	409.4
3Q	—	8,758	1,836	1,253	693.6	450.1
4Q	—	10,231	1,929	1,377	792.0	475.7
Yr.	—	36,213	6,886	4,777	2,000	1,685
Earnings Per Share ($)						
1Q	**-0.31**	**0.20**	**0.07**	**0.05**	0.02	-0.24
2Q	**-0.17**	**0.23**	**0.10**	**0.06**	**0.02**	-0.09
3Q	**E0.30**	**0.22**	**0.17**	**0.17**	**0.01**	Nil
4Q	**E0.41**	**0.14**	**0.13**	**0.07**	**0.01**	-0.01
Yr.	**E1.27**	**0.79**	**0.48**	**0.30**	**0.05**	**-0.33**

Next earnings report expected: mid October

Dividend Data

No cash dividends have been paid. The company intends to retain its earnings to finance growth and does not expect to pay cash dividends in the foreseeable future.

A Division of The ***McGraw·Hill*** *Companies*

AOL Time Warner Inc.

Business Summary - 14-AUG-01

In January 2001, online access and content company America Online, Inc. merged with cable systems and media concern Time Warner Inc., in a transaction valued at over $106 billion.

The global leader in online services, America Online has successfully melded its own proprietary offering with the Internet. As of June 2001, the number of subscribers to both the company's AOL and CompuServe online services was more than 32 million, with hundreds of millions more using its Internet services such as Digital City (local guide), MapQuest (mapping and navigation), AOL Moviefone (movie information and tickets), AOL Messaging ICQ, AOL Instant Messenger, Spinner (streaming music), and Winamp (music player).

The Networks group is home to CNN, the world's best known news brand; HBO and Cinemax, the two leading U.S. premium pay services; leading television entertainment brands such as TBS Superstation, TNT, Cartoon Network and Turner Classic Movies; and WB, a television network popular with teens and young adults.

Time Warner Cable provides cable service to more than 12.8 million customers throughout the U.S. The segment has upgraded over 92% of its cable plant, allowing provision of digital services such as high-resolution video, CD-quality sound, and video-on-demand. Major clusters include New York City, Tampa, Houston and Milwaukee.

Time Inc., which accounts for most of AOL's publishing revenues, owns more than 60 magazines, reaching 268 million readers. Titles include four of the five most popular consumer magazines: People, Time, Sports Illustrated, and Fortune, as well as Entertainment Weekly, Money, and In Style. In late 2000, the company acquired Times Mirror Magazines, Inc., the publisher of 26 magazines including Golf, Popular Science and Field & Stream, from Tribune Co., in a transaction valued at about $475 million.

The largest part of the filmed entertainment segment is Warner Bros., a global entertainment company with leading positions in feature films, television, home video, animation, and product/brand licensing. Properties include The Matrix, Batman, ER, Friends, The West Wing, DC Comics, and MAD Magazine, as well as production rights for the first four Harry Potter books. New Line Cinema is a leading independent producer and distributor of feature films.

Warner Music Group includes record companies Atlantic, Elektra, London-Sire Records Inc. and Rhino, and artists Madonna, Faith Hill, matchbox twenty, Kid Rock, and Red Hot Chili Peppers.

Revenues are categorized by the company into three segments: subscriptions (62% of 2000 revenues, and 68% of 1999 revenues), advertising and commerce (31%, 22%), and content and other (7%, 11%).

Per Share Data ($) (Year Ended Dec. 31)	2000	1999	1998	1997	1996	1995	1994	1993	1992	1991
Tangible Bk. Val.	2.51	2.44	1.17	0.12	0.03	0.08	0.07	0.11	0.03	0.03
Cash Flow	0.61	0.61	0.42	0.11	-0.25	0.11	0.04	0.01	0.00	0.00
Earnings	0.79	0.48	0.30	0.05	-0.33	0.02	-0.03	0.01	0.00	0.00
Dividends	Nil	Nil	Nil	Nil	Nil	Nil	Nil	Nil	Nil	Nil
Payout Ratio	Nil	Nil	Nil	Nil	Nil	Nil	Nil	Nil	Nil	Nil
Prices - High	83.37	83.37	95.81	40.00	5.69	4.43	2.89	0.91	0.54	0.22
- Low	32.75	32.75	32.50	5.15	1.98	1.39	0.76	0.37	0.13	0.08
P/E Ratio - High	NM	NM	NM	NM	NM	NM	NM	NM	NM	73
- Low	NM	NM	NM	NM	NM	NM	NM	NM	NM	27
Income Statement Analysis (Million $)										
Revs.	7,703	6,886	4,777	2,600	1,685	1,094	394	104	40.0	27.0
Oper. Inc.	2,271	1,776	851	341	101	249	103	9.3	5.1	3.8
Depr.	444	363	298	132	124	159	72.1	1.3	0.6	0.5
Int. Exp.	55.0	40.0	20.0	13.0	1.6	1.4	1.0	NA	NA	NA
Pretax Inc.	1,884	2,014	1,096	92.0	-499	62.3	-18.5	10.0	5.0	3.6
Eff. Tax Rate	39%	39%	30%	NM	NM	52%	NM	38%	38%	38%
Net Inc.	1,152	1,232	762	92.0	-499	29.8	-33.6	6.2	3.1	2.2
Balance Sheet & Other Fin. Data (Million $)										
Cash	2,610	2,490	887	631	125	129	64.1	67.7	14.3	14.0
Curr. Assets	4,671	4,428	1,979	930	323	271	133	105	25.0	19.0
Total Assets	10,827	10,673	5,348	2,214	847	959	406	148	32.0	24.0
Curr. Liab.	2,328	2,395	1,725	894	554	290	133	40.4	8.6	4.4
LT Debt	1,411	1,630	348	372	50.0	19.3	19.5	5.8	Nil	Nil
Common Eqty.	6,778	6,161	3,033	598	100	513	218	99	23.8	18.9
Total Cap.	8,189	7,791	3,381	970	205	668	273	108	24.0	19.0
Cap. Exp.	485	642	301	297	150	50.3	57.8	17.5	1.8	0.7
Cash Flow	1,596	1,595	1,060	224	-375	189	38.4	7.5	3.7	2.7
Curr. Ratio	2.0	1.8	1.1	1.0	0.6	0.9	1.0	2.6	3.0	4.4
% LT Debt of Cap.	17.2	20.9	10.3	38.4	24.4	2.9	7.1	5.4	Nil	Nil
% Net Inc.of Revs.	15.0	17.9	16.0	3.5	NM	2.7	NM	5.9	7.7	8.3
% Ret. on Assets	10.9	15.3	18.5	6.0	NM	4.4	NM	6.6	10.7	7.4
% Ret. on Equity	17.6	26.6	37.8	25.3	NM	8.2	NM	9.7	13.9	NM

Pro forma data for 2000. Prior to 2000, years ended Jun. of the fol. cal. yr. Data as orig reptd.; bef. results of disc opers/spec. items. Per share data adj. for stk. divs. Bold denotes diluted EPS (FASB 128)-prior periods restated. E-Estimated. NA-Not Available. NM-Not Meaningful. NR-Not Ranked.

Office—75 Rockefeller Plaza, New York, NY 10019. **Tel**—(212) 484-8000. **Website**—http://www.aoltimewarner.com **Chrmn**—S. M. Case. **Vice Chrmn & Sr Advsr**—R. E. Turner. **Vice Chrmn**—K. J. Novack. **CEO**—G. M. Levin. **Co-COO**—R. W. Pittman. **EVP & CFO**—J. M. Kelly. **EVP & Secy**—P. T. Cappuccio. **Dirs**—D. F. Akerson, J. L. Barksdale, S. F. Bollenbach, S. M. Case, F. J. Caufield, M. R. Gilburne, C. A. Hills, G. M. Levin, R. Mark, M. A. Miles, K. J. Novack, R. D. Parsons, R. W. Pittman, F. D. Raines, R. E. Turner, F. T. Vincent Jr. **Transfer Agent & Registrar**—EquiServe. **Incorporated**—in Delaware in 1985. **Empl**— 88,500. **S&P Analyst:** Scott H. Kessler

STANDARD &POOR'S STOCK REPORTS

Clear Channel Communications

NYSE Symbol **CCU**

In S&P 500

22-AUG-01

Industry: Broadcasting (Television, Radio & Cable)

Summary: This radio broadcasting, outdoor advertising and live entertainment company merged with radio station operator AMFM Inc. and also acquired SFX Entertainment in August 2000.

S&P Opinion: Accumulate (★★★★)

Recent Price • 53
52 Wk Range • 84.75-43.87
Yield • Nil
12-Mo. P/E • NM

Quantitative Evaluations

Outlook
(1 Lowest—5 Highest)
• **NA**

Fair Value
• **NA**

Risk
• **Average**

Earn./Div. Rank
• **B**

Technical Eval.
• **Bearish** since 8/01

Rel. Strength Rank
(1 Lowest—99 Highest)
• **35**

Insider Activity
• **Neutral**

Earnings vs. Previous Year
▲=Up ▼=Down ▶=No Change

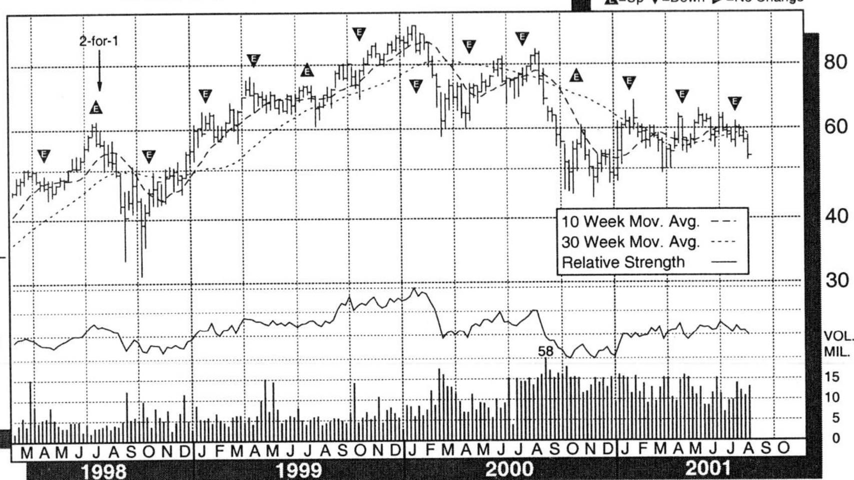

OPTIONS: ASE, CBOE, P, ASE, CBOE, P

Overview - 22-AUG-01

We expect pro forma revenues to decline 3% to 4% in 2001, mainly reflecting a weak advertising environment. Broadcast advertising has declined due to decreased advertising by dot-com companies and curbed spending by traditional advertisers amid a softer economy. We anticipate a modest rebound in the second half of the year. Although we expect operating margins to narrow, due to the lower margin SFX division, the company should continue to achieve cost efficiencies from its acquisitions. With higher interest expense and depreciation charges resulting from acquisitions, CCU should incur a net loss of $1.42 a share in 2001, versus a net loss of $0.57 a share in 2000. Pro forma 2001 EBITDA should decline 10% to $3.55, from $3.96 in 2000.

Valuation - 22-AUG-01

We recently downgraded the shares to accumulate from buy due to continued weakness in the advertising market. The soft economy has made advertisers cautious, holding back advertising spending until signs of an economic recovery emerge. However, with its strong market presence and distribution capabilities, CCU will be in a solid position to benefit from a recovery. The company is an industry leader and has continued to gain market share despite the weakened advertising market. CCU's channels of distribution are radio and outdoor billboards, segments that are more defensive in a weaker economy. Aside from external factors, CCU continues to execute well. The integration of SFX Entertainment and AMFM has proceeded smoothly, which should generate meaningful synergies and boost the profitability of acquired stations. With the shares trading at a 13% discount to its less competitive peers, we would accumulate on weakness.

Key Stock Statistics

S&P EPS Est. 2001	-1.42	Tang. Bk. Value/Share	NM
P/E on S&P Est. 2001	NM	Beta	1.01
S&P EPS Est. 2002	-0.93	Shareholders	3,120
Dividend Rate/Share	Nil	Market cap. (B)	$ 31.8
Shs. outstg. (M)	587.5	Inst. holdings	73%
Avg. daily vol. (M)	2.512		

Value of $10,000 invested 5 years ago: $ 25,932

Fiscal Year Ending Dec. 31

	2001	2000	1999	1998	1997	1996
Revenues (Million $)						
1Q	1,761	782.5	376.8	203.6	98.29	62.21
2Q	2,179	965.9	617.7	320.0	186.8	81.37
3Q	—	1,685	887.9	385.9	184.1	94.84
4Q	—	2,020	888.0	441.4	227.9	113.3
Yr.	—	5,345	2,678	1,351	697.1	351.7
Earnings Per Share ($)						
1Q	-0.53	-0.12	-0.02	0.02	0.05	0.05
2Q	-0.40	0.09	0.33	0.11	0.08	0.09
3Q	E-0.34	0.96	Nil	0.05	0.10	0.02
4Q	E-0.15	-0.33	-0.03	0.04	0.11	0.10
Yr.	E-1.42	-0.57	0.26	0.22	0.33	0.26

Next earnings report expected: late October

Dividend Data

The stock was split two for one in 1995, 1996 and 1998, and five-for-four stock splits were effected in 1992, 1993 and 1994.

Clear Channel Communications, Inc.

Business Summary - 22-AUG-01

Clear Channel Communications is a major diversified media company with three business segments: radio broadcasting, outdoor advertising, and live entertainment. As of December 31, 2000, CCU owned, programmed or sold airtime for 1,105 domestic radio stations, two international radio stations and 19 domestic television stations. The company is also one of the world's largest outdoor advertising companies, with an inventory of 149,171 domestic and 549,094 international display faces. In addition, CCU owned and operated 120 live entertainment venues.

On the broadcasting side of the business, as of December 31, 2000, the company owned, programmed or sold air time for 346 AM and 759 FM domestic radio stations, of which, 498 stations were in the top 100 markets, according to the Arbitron winter 2000 ranking of U.S. markets. CCU also owned one of the leading national radio networks, based on a total audience of over 180 million weekly listeners. Additionally, the company has equity interests in international radio stations located in Australia, New Zealand, Czech Republic, Great Britain, Mexico and Norway. CCU also owns a 26% non-voting equity interest in Hispanic Broadcasting Corporation.

In August 2000, CCU acquired AMFM Inc. in a stock and debt transaction valued at $23.8 billion, combining the two largest U.S. radio station owners.

As of December 31, 2000, the company owned, programmed or sold airtime for 19 televisions stations, which are affiliated with various television networks, including FOX, UPN, ABC, NBC, and CBS.

The outdoor advertising division operates in 52 domestic markets and over 43 countries. CCU's display faces include billboards of various sizes, wallscapes, transit displays, and street furniture displays. Revenues from this segment are mostly derived from local sales.

The company has quickly developed into one of the premier U.S. broadcasting and entertainment consolidators. In August 2000, CCU acquired SFX Entertainment for $2.9 billion in stock, plus the assumption of $1.5 billion of debt. With SFX, the company is one of the world's largest producers, promoters and marketers of live entertainment. In 2000, more than 60 million people attended approximately 26,000 of CCU's events including live music events, Broadway shows, family entertainment, sports and motor sports events. Venues include 65 theatres, 40 amphitheatres, 10 clubs, 3 arenas, a concert hall and an arena/motor racing circuit. In addition, SFX is a leading fully integrated sports marketing and management company, representing more than several hundred professional athletes. Revenues from this segment are derived primarily from ticket sales, rental income, corporate sponsorships and advertising, concessions, and merchandise.

Per Share Data ($) **(Year Ended Dec. 31)**	**2000**	**1999**	**1998**	**1997**	**1996**	**1995**	**1994**	**1993**	**1992**	**1991**
Tangible Bk. Val.	NM	NM	0.35	NM	NM	-1.00	-0.56	-0.04	-0.29	-0.11
Cash Flow	2.82	2.49	1.44	0.97	0.56	0.47	0.34	0.21	0.14	0.09
Earnings	0.57	0.26	0.22	0.34	0.25	0.23	0.16	0.07	0.04	0.01
Dividends	Nil	Nil	Nil	Nil	Nil	Nil	Nil	Nil	Nil	Nil
Payout Ratio	Nil	Nil	Nil	Nil	Nil	Nil	Nil	Nil	Nil	Nil
Prices - High	95.50	91.50	62.31	39.93	22.62	11.06	6.50	4.61	1.81	0.98
- Low	43.87	52.00	31.00	16.81	10.18	6.26	3.92	1.62	0.86	0.67
P/E Ratio - High	NM	NM	NM	NM	90	49	41	64	50	86
- Low	NM	NM	NM	NM	41	28	25	22	24	60
Income Statement Analysis (Million $)										
Revs.	5,345	2,678	1,351	697	352	244	173	118	82.2	74.1
Oper. Inc.	1,722	976	546	282	145	105	67.6	38.7	25.8	17.0
Depr.	1,401	722	305	114	45.8	33.8	24.7	17.4	12.3	7.6
Int. Exp.	383	192	136	75.1	30.1	20.8	7.7	5.4	4.7	5.4
Pretax Inc.	714	236	126	111	76.4	52.7	36.4	15.7	7.6	2.5
Eff. Tax Rate	65%	64%	57%	43%	37%	39%	40%	42%	43%	55%
Net Inc.	249	85.7	54.0	63.6	37.7	32.0	22.0	9.1	4.3	1.1
Balance Sheet & Other Fin. Data (Million $)										
Cash	825	81.1	36.5	24.7	16.7	5.4	6.8	5.5	2.8	3.8
Curr. Assets	2,343	925	410	199	113	70.5	53.9	38.2	24.8	20.5
Total Assets	50,056	16,822	7,540	3,456	1,325	563	412	228	147	92.0
Curr. Liab.	2,129	686	258	86.9	43.5	36.0	27.7	26.1	10.1	10.0
LT Debt	1,597	4,584	2,324	1,540	725	334	238	87.8	97.0	48.1
Common Eqty.	30,347	10,084	4,483	1,747	513	164	131	98.3	31.1	24.8
Total Cap.	38,777	15,987	7,206	3,318	1,256	510	371	190	132	75.8
Cap. Exp.	496	239	142	31.0	19.7	15.1	5.7	2.7	27.7	1.9
Cash Flow	1,650	808	359	178	83.5	65.8	46.7	26.6	16.5	8.8
Curr. Ratio	1.1	1.3	1.6	2.3	2.6	2.0	1.9	1.5	2.5	2.1
% LT Debt of Cap.	4.1	28.7	32.2	46.4	57.7	65.5	64.1	46.3	73.7	63.5
% Net Inc.of Revs.	4.7	3.2	4.0	9.1	10.7	13.2	12.7	7.7	5.2	1.5
% Ret. on Assets	0.7	0.7	1.0	2.7	4.0	6.6	6.9	4.6	3.5	1.0
% Ret. on Equity	1.2	1.2	1.7	5.6	11.1	21.8	19.1	13.6	15.1	8.0

Data as orig. reptd.; bef. results of disc. opers. and/or spec. items. Quarterly revs. incl. agency comm. pr to 1996. Per share data adj. for stk. divs. as of ex-div. date. Bold denotes diluted EPS (FASB 128). E-Estimated. NA-Not Available. NM-Not Meaningful. NR-Not Ranked.

Office—200 East Basse Road, San Antonio, TX 78209. **Tel**—(210) 822-2828. **Website**—http://www.clearchannel.com **Chrmn & CEO**—L. L. Mays. **Pres & COO**—M. P. Mays. **EVP & CFO**—R. T. Mays. **SVP & Secy**—K. E. Wyker. **VP & Investor Contact**—Randy Palmer. **Dirs**—R. L. Crandall, K. Eller, A. D. Feld, T. O. Hicks, V. E. Jordan Jr., M. J. Levitt, P. J. Lewis, L. L. Mays, M. P. Mays, R. T. Mays, B. J. McCombs, T. H. Strauss, J. H. Williams. **Transfer Agent & Registrar**—Bank of New York, NYC. **Incorporated**—in Texas in 1974. **Empl**— 36,350. **S&P Analyst:** Howard Choe

STANDARD
&POOR'S
STOCK REPORTS

Darden Restaurants

NYSE Symbol **DRI**

In S&P 500

18-AUG-01 **Industry:** Restaurants

Summary: This restaurant company operates the Red Lobster and Olive Garden chains.

S&P Opinion: Accumulate (★★★★)

Recent Price • 27.70
52 Wk Range • 32.50-16.62

Yield • 0.3%
12-Mo. P/E • 17.4

Quantitative Evaluations

Outlook (1 Lowest—5 Highest)
• **4+**

Fair Value
• **30.90**

Risk
• **Average**

Earn./Div. Rank
• **NR**

Technical Eval.
• **Neutral** since 8/01

Rel. Strength Rank (1 Lowest—99 Highest)
• **48**

Insider Activity
• **Neutral**

Earnings vs. Previous Year
E=Up E=Down E=No Change

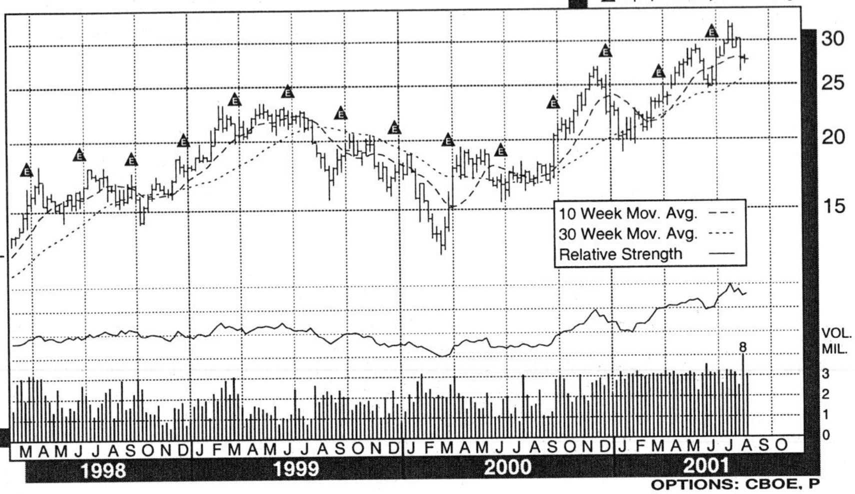

OPTIONS: CBOE, P

Overview - 27-JUN-01

Sales growth is expected to moderate to 3% to 4% in FY 02 (May), following strong same-store sales gains at Olive Garden and Red Lobster in FY 01. Food and beverage price inflation should increase moderately, and labor costs will continue to rise, putting some pressure on margins. Restaurant operating costs and general and administrative expenses are expected to continue to be well controlled. Operating income will advance about 8.0%, to 12.4% of sales, from an estimated 11.9% in FY 01. Depreciation charges and interest expense will increase modestly. EPS comparisons will benefit from a share buyback program. DRI repurchased a total of 8.4 million shares in FY 01. The company is rolling out its Bahama Breeze Caribbean-themed concept, and ended FY 01 with 21 units. Bahama Breeze is posting strong sales gains, boding well for profitability in FY 02. In addition, DRI's newest concept, Smokey Bones BBQ restaurants, is being aggressively rolled out, with nine units open at the end of FY 01. In FY 02, DRI plans to open eight to 10 Bahama Breeze restaurants, and a similar number of Smokey Bones units.

Valuation - 27-JUN-01

We have upgraded the shares to accumulate. In the fourth quarter, Olive Garden posted a 7.1% rise in same-store sales, and Red Lobster's same-store sales rose 3.8%. Operating income increased 11.9%, aided by lower restaurant labor expenses as a percentage of sales. We expect the casual dining sector's growing popularity to result in continued market share gains at the expense of the fast-food sector. Annual EPS growth should range from 16% to 18% over the next few years, aided by profitability at Bahama Breeze. We see room for moderate P/E multiple expansion.

Key Stock Statistics

S&P EPS Est. 2002	1.85	Tang. Bk. Value/Share	8.59
P/E on S&P Est. 2002	15.0	Beta	0.33
S&P EPS Est. 2003	2.15	Shareholders	31,896
Dividend Rate/Share	0.08	Market cap. (B)	$ 3.3
Shs. outstg. (M)	118.1	Inst. holdings	73%
Avg. daily vol. (M)	0.918		

Value of $10,000 invested 5 years ago: $ 34,521

Fiscal Year Ending May 31

	2001	2000	1999	1998	1997	1996
Revenues (Million $)						
1Q	1,018	929.4	866.1	809.3	805.6	886.1
2Q	932.0	848.2	791.2	745.3	748.8	731.2
3Q	988.6	917.5	866.9	811.3	800.9	795.1
4Q	1,082	1,006	914.0	921.2	816.6	829.5
Yr.	4,021	3,701	3,458	3,287	3,172	3,192
Earnings Per Share ($)						
1Q	**0.46**	**0.35**	**0.24**	0.16	0.13	-0.08
2Q	**0.24**	**0.18**	**0.11**	0.05	-0.07	0.10
3Q	**0.40**	**0.36**	**0.27**	**0.20**	0.10	0.22
4Q	**0.50**	**0.46**	**0.37**	**0.27**	0.19	-0.76
Yr.	**1.59**	**1.34**	**0.99**	**0.67**	**-0.59**	**0.46**

Next earnings report expected: mid September

Dividend Data (Dividends have been paid since 1995.)

Amount ($)	Date Decl.	Ex-Div. Date	Stock of Record	Payment Date
0.040	Sep. 20	Oct. 05	Oct. 10	Nov. 01 '00
0.040	Mar. 23	Apr. 06	Apr. 10	May. 01 '01

Darden Restaurants, Inc.

Business Summary - 27-JUN-01

Darden Restaurants (DRI) is a leader in the casual dining segment of the restaurant industry, with about 8% market share. This highly fragmented industry is characterized by thousands of independent operators and small chains. Chains account for only 22% of the full-service segment of eating out, while they dominate the fast-food segment, with 61% market share. The company, which was spun off from General Mills in May 1995, is named after William B. Darden, who founded the Red Lobster chain in 1968.

Red Lobster is the largest U.S. chain of full-service, seafood specialty restaurants, with 622 restaurants at the end of May 2000, and 32 in Canada. Total system sales were $2.07 billion in FY 00 (May), up 5.0% from the FY 99 level. Average restaurant sales were $3.2 million, a 10% gain. Same-store sales rose 7.6%. The restaurants feature fresh fish, shrimp, crab, lobster, scallops, and other seafood, served in a casual atmosphere. The company maintains about 100 different menus to reflect geographic differences in consumer preferences, prices and selections in its trade areas. The average check per person in FY 00 was between $14.00 and $15.00, with alcoholic beverages accounting for slightly more than 8% of sales.

Olive Garden is the largest U.S. chain of casual, full-service Italian-food restaurants with 464 restaurants at the end of May 2000 and five in Canada. System-wide sales grew nearly 7%, to $1.56 billion, in FY 00; same-restaurant sales were up 7.2%. The Olive Garden menu offers recipes from northern and southern Italy. Dinner entree prices at Olive Garden restaurants range from about $6.95 to $16.95, and lunch entree prices range from about $4.95 to $8.95. In February 1996, DRI opened the first unit of a Caribbean-themed restaurant concept, called Bahama Breeze. The company operated 14 Bahama Breeze units at the end of FY 00, and planned to add 10 units in FY 01. DRI also operates two Smokey Bones restaurants, which combine barbeque with a sports bar atmosphere.

In FY 00, the company closed 15 Red Lobsters and two Olive Gardens. In addition, three Red Lobsters were relocated to better sites. The company systematically reviews the performance of its restaurant sites to ensure that each unit meets its standards. When a unit falls below minimum standards, a thorough analysis is completed to determine the causes, and marketing and operational plans are implemented to improve the unit's performance. If performance does not improve to acceptable levels, the site is evaluated for relocation, closing, or conversion to one of the company's other concepts.

Per Share Data ($)										
(Year Ended May 31)	**2001**	**2000**	**1999**	**1998**	**1997**	**1996**	**1995**	**1994**	**1993**	**1992**
Tangible Bk. Val.	NA	7.63	7.22	7.03	7.22	7.58	7.37	6.61	NA	NA
Cash Flow	NA	2.33	2.01	1.51	0.30	1.32	1.17	1.54	NA	NA
Earnings	1.59	1.34	0.99	0.67	0.35	0.47	0.31	0.75	NA	NA
Dividends	0.08	0.08	0.08	0.08	0.08	0.08	Nil	NA	NA	NA
Payout Ratio	5%	6%	8%	12%	23%	17%	Nil	NA	NA	NA
Cal. Yrs.	2000	1999	1998	1997	1996	1995	1994	1993	1992	1991
Prices - High	27.00	23.37	18.93	12.50	14.00	12.12	NA	NA	NA	NA
- Low	12.43	15.62	11.75	6.75	7.50	9.12	NA	NA	NA	NA
P/E Ratio - High	17	17	19	19	40	26	NA	NA	NA	NA
- Low	8	12	12	10	21	19	NA	NA	NA	NA
Income Statement Analysis (Million $)										
Revs.	NA	3,701	3,458	3,287	3,172	3,192	3,163	2,963	NA	NA
Oper. Inc.	NA	421	352	300	235	345	316	331	NA	NA
Depr.	NA	130	125	126	137	135	135	125	NA	NA
Int. Exp.	NA	23.1	40.6	20.5	23.3	24.9	26.1	22.6	NA	NA
Pretax Inc.	NA	274	216	154	27.6	114	59.8	188	NA	NA
Eff. Tax Rate	NA	35%	35%	34%	NM	35%	18%	36%	NA	NA
Net Inc.	NA	177	141	102	-91.0	74.4	49.2	120	NA	NA
Balance Sheet & Other Fin. Data (Million $)										
Cash	NA	26.1	41.0	33.5	25.5	30.3	20.1	17.7	NA	NA
Curr. Assets	NA	290	328	398	337	288	308	250	NA	NA
Total Assets	NA	1,971	1,906	1,985	1,964	2,089	2,113	1,859	NA	NA
Curr. Liab.	NA	607	534	559	481	445	517	403	NA	NA
LT Debt	NA	304	314	311	313	301	304	304	NA	NA
Common Eqty.	NA	960	964	1,020	1,081	1,223	1,174	1,052	NA	NA
Total Cap.	NA	1,344	1,350	1,408	1,464	1,625	1,580	1,447	NA	NA
Cap. Exp.	NA	269	124	112	160	214	358	335	NA	NA
Cash Flow	NA	307	266	228	45.8	209	185	245	NA	NA
Curr. Ratio	NA	0.5	0.6	0.7	0.7	0.6	0.6	0.6	NA	NA
% LT Debt of Cap.	NA	22.6	23.3	22.0	21.4	18.5	19.2	21.0	NA	NA
% Net Inc.of Revs.	NA	4.8	4.1	3.1	NM	2.3	1.6	4.0	NA	NA
% Ret. on Assets	NA	9.2	7.2	5.2	NM	3.5	NA	NA	NA	NA
% Ret. on Equity	NA	18.4	14.2	9.7	NM	6.2	NA	NA	NA	NA

Data as orig reptd.; bef. results of disc opers/spec. items. Per share data adj. for stk. divs. Bold denotes diluted EPS (FASB 128)-prior periods restated. E-Estimated. NA-Not Available. NM-Not Meaningful. NR-Not Ranked.

Office—5900 Lake Ellenor Dr., Orlando, FL 32809. **Tel**—(407) 245-4000. **Website**—http://www.darden.com **Chrmn & CEO**—J. R. Lee. **SVP & Secy**—P. J. Shives. **SVP-Fin, Treas & Investor Contact**—Clarence Otis Jr. **Dirs**—B. D. Blum, D. B. Burke, O. C. Donald, J. Erving II, J. R. Lee, R. E. Rivera, M. D. Rose, H. de J. Ruiz, M. A. Sastre, J. A. Smith, B. Sweatt III, R. P. Wilson. **Transfer Agent & Registrar**—First Union National Bank, Charlotte, NC. **Incorporated**—in Florida in 1995. **Empl**— 122,300. **S&P Analyst:** Karen J. Sack, CFA

Disney (Walt)

NYSE Symbol **DIS**

In S&P 500

18-AUG-01 **Industry:** Entertainment

Summary: The operations of this major filmed entertainment and theme park company include the ABC television network.

S&P Opinion: Accumulate (★★★★)

Recent Price • 25.65
52 Wk Range • 41.93-25.10
Yield • 0.8%
12-Mo. P/E • NM

Quantitative Evaluations

Outlook
(1 Lowest—5 Highest)
• **1**

Fair Value
• **24.40**

Risk
• **Low**

Earn./Div. Rank
• **B+**

Technical Eval.
• **Neutral** since 8/01

Rel. Strength Rank
(1 Lowest—99 Highest)
• **29**

Insider Activity
• **Neutral**

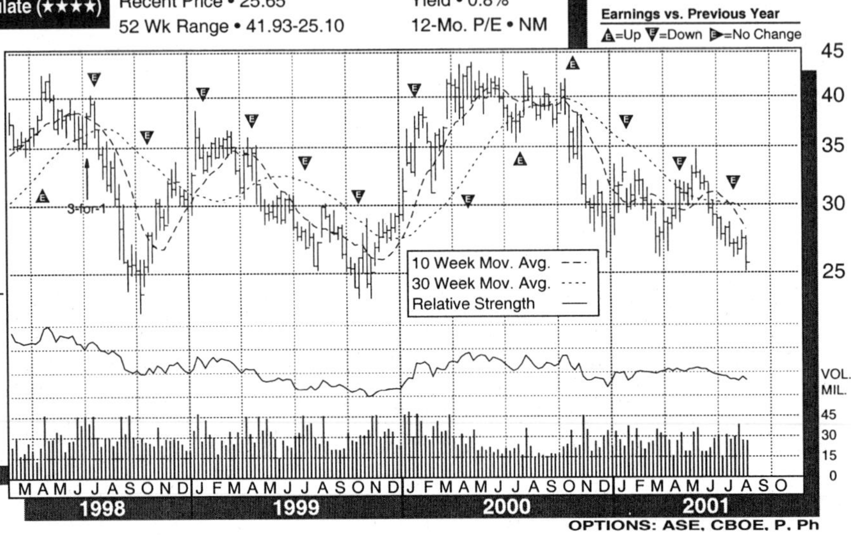

OPTIONS: ASE, CBOE, P, Ph

Overview - 08-AUG-01

We expect FY 02 (Sep.) revenues to rise moderately from the $25.4 billion estimated for FY 01, including at least a partial-year inclusion of the Fox Family Worldwide business, which DIS has agreed to acquire for about $3.0 billion in cash, plus the assumption of $2.3 billion in debt. We look for profit from DIS's media networks segment to be hurt by a relatively weak advertising environment, especially in advance (up-front) sales for the 2001-02 television season. We project that profit from the theme park segment will be up at least modestly, and that there will be improved profitability from the consumer products area and Disney's Internet-related segment. Net income for FY 02 is projected at $1.9 billion ($0.90 a share), compared to a pro forma $1.7 billion ($0.81), before special items, anticipated in FY 01. The projected EPS rise in FY 02 comes entirely from a change in the accounting for non-cash goodwill expense. Without this change, we would expect an EPS decline.

Valuation - 08-AUG-01

Through early August 2001, the stock was down moderately year to date, slightly outperforming the S&P 500. The shares were above $40 in late 2000, but we believe that the stock has been hurt, in part, by concerns about the strength of the U.S. television advertising environment and the overall U.S. economy. Looking ahead, we expect that prospects from continued growth of DVD sales and from new Disney-related international theme parks will help to bolster the stock. We look for this, plus the prospect of growing free cash flow and interest among small investors, to help offset various concerns about weakness in some of DIS's operations. With the company at an estimated enterprise value of 14 times projected FY 02 EBITDA, we view the stock as attractive.

Key Stock Statistics

S&P EPS Est. 2001	0.81	Tang. Bk. Value/Share	2.24
P/E on S&P Est. 2001	31.7	Beta	0.86
S&P EPS Est. 2002	0.90	Shareholders	882,000
Dividend Rate/Share	0.21	Market cap. (B)	$ 53.6
Shs. outstg. (M)	2090.0	Inst. holdings	51%
Avg. daily vol. (M)	6.010		

Value of $10,000 invested 5 years ago: $ 13,627

Fiscal Year Ending Sep. 30

	2001	2000	1999	1998	1997	1996
Revenues (Million $)						
1Q	7,433	6,932	6,589	6,339	6,278	3,837
2Q	6,049	6,303	5,510	5,242	5,481	4,543
3Q	5,975	6,051	5,522	5,248	5,194	5,087
4Q	—	6,116	5,781	6,147	5,520	5,272
Yr.	—	25,402	23,402	22,976	22,473	18,739
Earnings Per Share ($)						
1Q	**0.16**	**0.17**	**0.30**	**0.37**	**0.36**	0.31
2Q	**-0.26**	**0.08**	**0.11**	**0.18**	0.16	-0.01
3Q	**0.19**	**0.21**	**0.18**	**0.20**	0.23	0.20
4Q	—	**0.11**	**0.04**	**0.14**	0.20	0.16
Yr.	—	**0.57**	**0.62**	**0.89**	**0.95**	0.65

Next earnings report expected: early November

Dividend Data (Dividends have been paid since 1957.)

Amount ($)	Date Decl.	Ex-Div. Date	Stock of Record	Payment Date
0.210	Nov. 28	Dec. 06	Dec. 08	Dec. 22 '00

The Walt Disney Company

Business Summary - 08-AUG-01

The Walt Disney Co., with operations ranging from theme parks and retail stores to movies and broadcasting, aims to combine imaginative material with masterful marketing, as it delivers popular culture worldwide. In July 2001, DIS said that it had agreed to acquire Fox Family Worldwide, whose assets include the Fox Family Channel in the U.S. and interests in some international channels, for $3 billion in cash, plus the assumption of $2.3 billion in debt.

DIS's filmed entertainment operations include production and distribution of theatrical motion pictures, television shows and home videos. DIS also owns and operates about 10 television stations, the ABC TV network, and various radio stations. In cable television, DIS owns and operates The Disney Channel, has 80% ownership of various ESPN cable channels, and has an equity interest of 50% or less in various cable networks, including the Lifetime cable channel (50%), the E! Entertainment cable channel (39.6%), and the Arts & Entertainment cable network (37.5%).

Theme park and resort assets include the Walt Disney World Complex in Florida, which contains the Magic Kingdom, Epcot Center, the Disney-MGM Studio Theme Park, the Animal Kingdom, and at least 12 hotels owned by DIS. Also, DIS's operations in Anaheim, CA, include the Disneyland theme park, some hotels, and a new theme park called Disney's California Adventure, which opened in February 2001. In Japan, Tokyo Disneyland is owned and operated by Oriental Land Co., Ltd., pursuant to a licensing agreement. Oriental Land Co. is expected to open a second theme park, Tokyo DisneySea, in 2001. DIS also owns about 39% of Euro Disney S.C.A., a French company that operates the Disneyland Paris theme park business; a second DIS-related park is to open near Paris in 2002. In November 1999, planned development of a Disney-related theme park project in Hong Kong was announced. The project, in which DIS would initially have a 43% equity interest (excluding convertible subordinated shares to be owned by the Hong Kong government), would open in 2005. Much of the financing (equity and debt) would be provided by the Hong Kong government.

Other operations or assets include merchandise licensing, a chain of more than 600 Disney retail stores, ownership interests in two California professional sports teams, and the Disney Cruise Line.

In November 1999, DIS created a new common stock, Go.com, related to various Internet businesses and direct marketing operations. However, in January 2001, DIS said it would discontinue its Go.com Internet portal and would continue to focus on other Internet sites, including ones related to entertainment, sports and news. Effective March 2001, each outstanding share of Disney Internet Group stock was converted into 0.19353 of a share of DIS common stock.

Per Share Data ($) (Year Ended Sep. 30)	2000	1999	1998	1997	1996	1995	1994	1993	1992	1991
Tangible Bk. Val.	2.24	2.59	1.75	0.63	NM	4.23	3.31	2.89	2.75	2.27
Cash Flow	1.48	2.22	2.70	3.36	2.78	2.03	1.66	1.04	0.98	0.90
Earnings	0.57	0.62	0.89	0.95	0.65	0.87	0.68	0.41	0.51	0.40
Dividends	0.21	0.21	0.19	0.16	0.13	0.11	0.09	0.08	0.06	0.05
Payout Ratio	37%	34%	21%	17%	20%	13%	13%	19%	13%	13%
Prices - High	43.87	38.68	42.79	33.41	25.75	21.41	16.20	16.25	15.08	10.83
- Low	26.00	23.37	22.50	22.12	17.75	15.00	12.58	12.00	9.50	7.79
P/E Ratio - High	77	62	48	35	39	25	24	40	39	27
- Low	46	38	25	23	27	17	19	29	19	20
Income Statement Analysis (Million $)										
Revs.	25,402	23,402	22,976	22,473	18,739	12,112	10,055	8,529	7,504	6,182
Oper. Inc.	5,043	7,010	7,533	8,903	6,968	4,115	3,412	2,589	2,047	1,799
Depr.	2,195	3,323	3,754	4,958	3,944	1,853	1,608	1,028	760	795
Int. Exp.	558	717	685	741	545	236	172	184	152	142
Pretax Inc.	2,633	2,314	3,157	3,387	2,061	2,117	1,703	1,074	1,302	1,019
Eff. Tax Rate	61%	44%	41%	42%	41%	35%	35%	38%	37%	38%
Net Inc.	920	1,300	1,850	1,966	1,214	1,380	1,110	671	817	637
Balance Sheet & Other Fin. Data (Million $)										
Cash	842	414	127	317	732	1,943	187	363	765	886
Curr. Assets	10,007	10,200	9,375	NA	NA	NA	NA	NA	NA	NA
Total Assets	45,027	43,679	41,378	37,776	37,777	14,606	12,826	11,751	10,862	9,429
Curr. Liab.	8,402	7,707	7,525	NA	NA	NA	NA	NA	NA	NA
LT Debt	6,959	9,278	9,562	11,068	12,342	2,984	2,107	1,131	1,608	1,818
Common Eqty.	24,100	20,975	19,388	17,285	16,086	6,651	5,508	5,030	4,705	3,871
Total Cap.	34,248	32,913	31,438	30,032	29,172	10,702	8,554	6,834	7,201	6,443
Cap. Exp.	2,013	2,134	2,314	1,922	1,745	897	1,026	814	599	954
Cash Flow	3,115	4,623	5,604	6,924	5,158	3,233	2,719	1,700	1,576	1,431
Curr. Ratio	1.2	1.3	1.2	NA	NA	NA	NA	NA	NA	NA
% LT Debt of Cap.	20.3	28.2	30.4	36.9	42.3	27.9	24.6	16.5	22.3	28.2
% Net Inc.of Revs.	3.6	5.6	8.1	8.7	6.5	11.4	11.0	7.9	10.9	10.3
% Ret. on Assets	2.1	3.1	4.7	5.2	4.7	10.1	9.1	5.9	8.0	7.3
% Ret. on Equity	4.1	6.4	10.1	11.8	10.7	22.7	21.3	13.7	19.0	17.4

Data as orig. reptd.; bef. results of disc. opers. and/or spec. items. Per share data adj. for stk. divs. as of ex-div. date. Bold denotes diluted EPS (FASB 128). E-Estimated. NA-Not Available. NM-Not Meaningful. NR-Not Ranked.

Office—500 S. Buena Vista St., Burbank, CA 91521. **Tel**—(818) 560-1000. **Website**—www.disney.com/investors **Chrmn & CEO**—M. D. Eisner. **Pres & COO**—R. A. Iger. **SEVP & CFO**—T. O. Staggs. **Secy**—M. L. Reed. **SVP & Investor Contact**—W. M. Webb. **Dirs**—R. F. Bowers, J. E. Bryson, R. E. Disney, M. D. Eisner, J. Estrin, S. P. Gold, R. A. Iger, M. C. Lozano, G. J. Mitchell, T. S. Murphy, L. J. O'Donovan, S. Poitier, R. A. M. Stern, A. L. Van de Kamp, R. L. Watson, G. L. Wilson. **Transfer Agent & Registrar**—Co.'s office. **Incorporated**—in California in 1938; reincorporated in Delaware in 1987. **Empl**— 120,000. **S&P Analyst:** Tom Graves, CFA

STANDARD
&POOR'S
STOCK REPORTS

Dow Jones & Co.

NYSE Symbol **DJ**

In S&P 500

20-AUG-01

Industry:
Publishing (Newspapers)

Summary: Dow Jones publishes The Wall Street Journal and Barron's, provides newswire, news retrieval and financial information services, and publishes general circulation newspapers.

S&P Opinion: Accumulate (★★★★)

Recent Price • 55.95
52 Wk Range • 67.50-48.10
Yield • 1.8%
12-Mo. P/E • NM

Quantitative Evaluations

Outlook
(1 Lowest—5 Highest)
• 1+

Fair Value
• **35.80**

Risk
• **Average**

Earn./Div. Rank
• **B**

Technical Eval.
• **Bearish** since 8/01

Rel. Strength Rank
(1 Lowest—99 Highest)
• **47**

Insider Activity
• **NA**

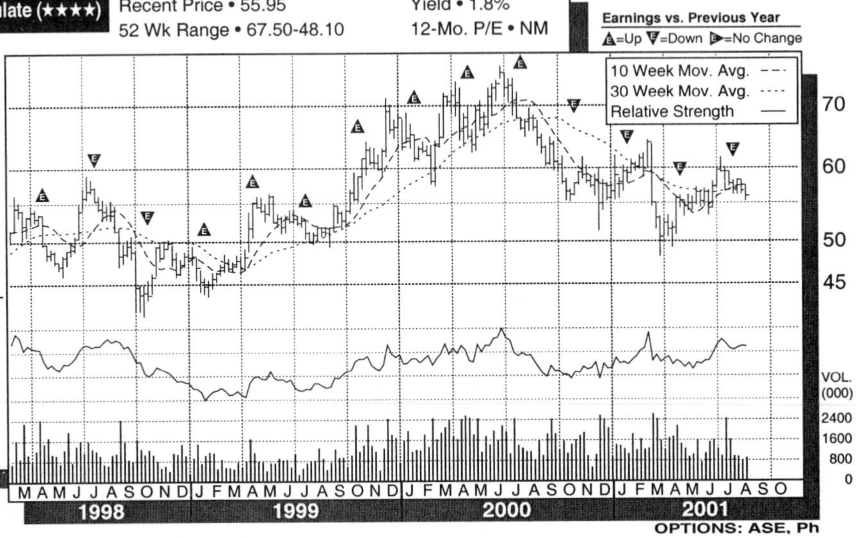

OPTIONS: ASE, Ph

Overview - 20-AUG-01

We are forecasting a 16.5% drop in advertising revenues for 2001, reflecting the continuing slump in demand for advertising combined with difficult comparisons against a very strong 2000. Electronic publishing revenues will continue to benefit from gains in newswire subscribers worldwide. Newsprint prices, although starting to decline, will be higher on average for the year 2001. Despite lower paper consumption, higher profits from electronic publishing and across-the-board cost controls, operating margins could narrow to about 14.0% from 22.6%. Net operating earnings, excluding nonrecurring items, are likely to drop 48%. We are projecting EPS in 2001 at $1.80, down 46% from $3.32. We anticipate an improving advertising environment in 2002, which, combined with wider operating margins, should contribute to a 39% EPS advance, to $2.50.

Valuation - 20-AUG-01

We continue to recommend accumulating DJ. The shares, which fell 2% year-to-date through mid-August 2001, outperformed the publishing index and the S&P 500. The publishing and broadcasting properties have been hurt by continuing economic softness and a lingering downturn in advertising. Although the timing of an advertising upturn is uncertain, we believe DJ will be an early beneficiary of improving market psychology. We also believe the shares will be among the first and strongest publishing stocks to react when the advertising outlook brightens. The company's attraction lies in generally favorable long-term prospects for both its print and electronic publishing operations, and for newer ventures. We believe DJ will average EPS gains in the five years 2002 through 2006 in the mid-to-high teens. As a result, the shares remain an attractive purchase for long-term value investors.

Key Stock Statistics

S&P EPS Est. 2001	1.80	Tang. Bk. Value/Share	NM
P/E on S&P Est. 2001	31.1	Beta	0.64
S&P EPS Est. 2002	2.50	Shareholders	10,992
Dividend Rate/Share	1.00	Market cap. (B)	$ 3.7
Shs. outstg. (M)	85.6	Inst. holdings	58%
Avg. daily vol. (M)	0.177		

Value of $10,000 invested 5 years ago: $ 15,325

Fiscal Year Ending Dec. 31

	2001	2000	1999	1998	1997	1996
Revenues (Million $)						
1Q	459.9	550.8	462.1	621.5	606.0	584.8
2Q	484.1	621.6	510.6	601.1	640.7	630.6
3Q	—	500.3	469.8	443.6	636.3	594.9
4Q	—	558.4	559.4	491.9	689.5	671.3
Yr.	—	2,203	2,002	2,158	2,573	2,482
Earnings Per Share ($)						
1Q	**0.07**	**0.98**	**0.56**	**0.35**	**0.26**	**0.38**
2Q	**0.50**	**1.13**	**0.62**	**-0.54**	**0.36**	**0.53**
3Q	—	**-0.39**	**1.13**	**0.27**	**0.28**	**0.42**
4Q	—	**-0.22**	**0.67**	**-0.01**	**-9.22**	**0.62**
Yr.	—	**-1.35**	**2.99**	**0.09**	**-8.36**	**1.95**

Next earnings report expected: mid October

Dividend Data (Dividends have been paid since 1906.)

Amount ($)	Date Decl.	Ex-Div. Date	Stock of Record	Payment Date
0.250	Oct. 18	Oct. 30	Nov. 01	Dec. 01 '00
0.250	Jan. 17	Jan. 30	Feb. 01	Mar. 01 '01
0.250	Apr. 18	Apr. 27	May. 01	Jun. 01 '01
0.250	Jun. 20	Jul. 30	Aug. 01	Aug. 31 '01

A Division of The McGraw-Hill Companies

Dow Jones & Company, Inc.

Business Summary - 20-AUG-01

Dow Jones & Co. is the parent of The Wall Street Journal and Barron's National Business and Financial Weekly. In addition to other publications, the company runs Dow Jones Newswires, Dow Jones Indexes, and the Ottaway group of community newspapers. DJ is co-owner with Reuters Group of Factiva, and with NBC of the CNBC television operations in Asia and Europe. DJ also provides news content to CNBC in the U.S. International operations accounted for 10% of consolidated revenues in 2000.

The Wall Street Journal, a financial and business daily, is the largest circulation daily newspaper in the U.S., with average daily circulation in 2000 of 1,789,000. DJ publishes two international editions. The Asian Wall Street Journal, with daily circulation of over 78,000, is the leader in its market. It is headquartered and published in Hong Kong and is transmitted by satellite to additional printing sites throughout Asia. The Wall Street Journal/Europe, with daily circulation of over 92,000, is the second largest business daily in Europe. The European paper is headquartered and published in Brussels, and printed in Belgium, Switzerland, England and Germany. DJ has expanded readership by introducing Wall Street Journal news content to Central and South America, as well as to other parts of the world.

The company publishes Barron's, a weekly magazine covering business and finance, and several other periodicals, including the Dow Jones Business and Financial Weekly, and SmartMoney magazine in partnership with Hearst Corp. Ottaway Newspapers publishes 19 daily and 15 weekly community newspapers. DJ also holds equity or other interests in international business and financial wire services, newspapers, and other publications. Dow Jones has a proprietary network of more than 1,650 business reporters and editors across 159 bureaus world-wide.

Electronic publishing includes the operations of WSJ.com, Dow Jones Newswires, Factiva, and Dow Jones Indexes. The Wall Street Journal Interactive Edition (WSJ.com) is the largest paid-subscription site on the World Wide Web, with more than 535,000 subscribers as of December 31, 2000. Other interactive sites include careerjournal.com, dowjones.com/Work.com, wine.wsj.com, collegejournal.com and others. Dow Jones Newswires delivers a spectrum of real-time global business and financial news across five asset classes to financial professionals around the world. Factiva was formed in 1999 from the combination of Dow Jones Interactive and Reuters Business Briefing. Factiva is an online, customizable research product that provides business and professional users with online access to the contents of more than 7,000 business, trade and local publications, including information sources in 22 languages.

Per Share Data ($)										
(Year Ended Dec. 31)	**2000**	**1999**	**1998**	**1997**	**1996**	**1995**	**1994**	**1993**	**1992**	**1991**
Tangible Bk. Val.	0.98	5.24	4.60	4.07	3.89	3.01	1.83	1.45	0.58	0.14
Cash Flow	-0.13	4.13	1.56	-5.74	4.22	4.08	3.90	3.37	2.94	2.53
Earnings	1.54	2.99	0.09	-8.36	1.96	1.96	1.83	1.48	1.17	0.71
Dividends	1.00	0.96	0.96	0.96	0.96	0.92	0.84	0.80	0.76	0.76
Payout Ratio	65%	32%	NM	NM	49%	47%	46%	54%	65%	106%
Prices - High	77.31	71.37	59.00	55.87	41.87	40.12	41.87	39.00	35.37	30.62
- Low	51.37	43.62	41.56	33.37	31.87	30.62	28.12	26.75	24.50	21.62
P/E Ratio - High	50	24	NM	NM	21	20	23	26	30	43
- Low	33	15	NM	NM	16	16	15	18	21	30
Income Statement Analysis (Million $)										
Revs.	2,203	2,002	2,158	2,573	2,482	2,284	2,091	1,932	1,818	1,725
Oper. Inc.	606	496	437	510	555	510	564	505	460	424
Depr.	108	104	142	251	218	206	205	189	179	183
Int. Exp.	2.0	5.3	7.2	19.4	18.8	18.3	16.9	22.6	30.4	41.2
Pretax Inc.	76.4	418	71.7	-763	331	323	339	286	234	159
Eff. Tax Rate	NM	35%	88%	NM	45%	43%	47%	49%	50%	55%
Net Inc.	-118	272	8.4	-801	190	190	181	148	118	72.0
Balance Sheet & Other Fin. Data (Million $)										
Cash	49.3	86.4	143	23.8	6.8	14.0	11.0	6.0	16.0	36.0
Curr. Assets	368	456	442	507	404	371	310	268	249	272
Total Assets	1,362	1,531	1,491	1,920	2,760	2,599	2,446	2,350	2,372	2,471
Curr. Liab.	587	579	600	672	601	582	531	471	462	457
LT Debt	151	150	150	229	332	254	296	261	335	448
Common Eqty.	159	3,071	509	781	1,644	1,602	1,482	1,493	1,449	1,436
Total Cap.	318	3,221	659	1,010	1,976	1,856	1,777	1,759	1,798	1,963
Cap. Exp.	187	191	226	348	232	219	222	161	126	106
Cash Flow	-11.1	376	151	-550	408	396	386	336	298	255
Curr. Ratio	0.6	0.8	0.7	0.8	0.7	0.6	0.6	0.6	0.5	0.6
% LT Debt of Cap.	47.4	4.7	22.7	22.7	16.8	13.7	16.6	14.8	18.6	22.8
% Net Inc.of Revs.	NM	13.6	0.4	NM	7.7	8.3	8.7	7.6	6.5	4.2
% Ret. on Assets	NM	18.1	0.5	NM	7.1	7.5	7.7	6.3	4.9	2.8
% Ret. on Equity	NM	9.3	1.3	NM	11.7	12.3	12.4	10.1	8.2	5.0

Data as orig reptd.; bef. results of disc opers/spec. items. Per share data adj. for stk. divs. Bold denotes diluted EPS (FASB 128)-prior periods restated. E-Estimated. NA-Not Available. NM-Not Meaningful. NR-Not Ranked.

Office—200 Liberty St., New York, NY 10281. **Tel**—(212) 416-2000. **Website**—http://www.dj.com **Chrmn & CEO**—P. R. Kann. **EVP & Secy**—P. G. Skinner. **EVP & CFO**—R.F. Zannino. **VP & Investor Contact**—Jerome Leshne. **Dirs**—R. V. Araskog, C. Bancroft, H. Golub, R. Hammer, L. Hill, I. O. Hockaday Jr., V. E. Jordan Jr., D. K. Li, M. P. P. McPherson, F. N. Newman, J. H. Ottaway Jr., W. C. Steere Jr. **Transfer Agent & Registrar**—Mellon Investor Services, L.L.C., Ridgefield Park, NJ. **Incorporated**—in Delaware in 1949. **Empl**— 8,574. **S&P Analyst:** William H. Donald

STANDARD
&POOR'S
STOCK REPORTS

eBay

Nasdaq Symbol **EBAY**

18-AUG-01 **Industry:** Computer (Software & Services)

Summary: EBAY operates the world's largest person-to-person on-line trading community. It also owns traditional auction businesses and the Half.com fixed-price marketplace.

S&P Opinion: Accumulate (★★★★) Recent Price • 59 | 52 Wk Range • 77.56-26.75 | Yield • Nil | 12-Mo. P/E • NM

Quantitative Evaluations

Outlook
(1 Lowest—5 Highest)
• **1−**

Fair Value
• **52.70**

Risk
• **NA**

Earn./Div. Rank
• **NR**

Technical Eval.
• **Bearish** since 8/01

Rel. Strength Rank
(1 Lowest—99 Highest)
• **41**

Insider Activity
• **Neutral**

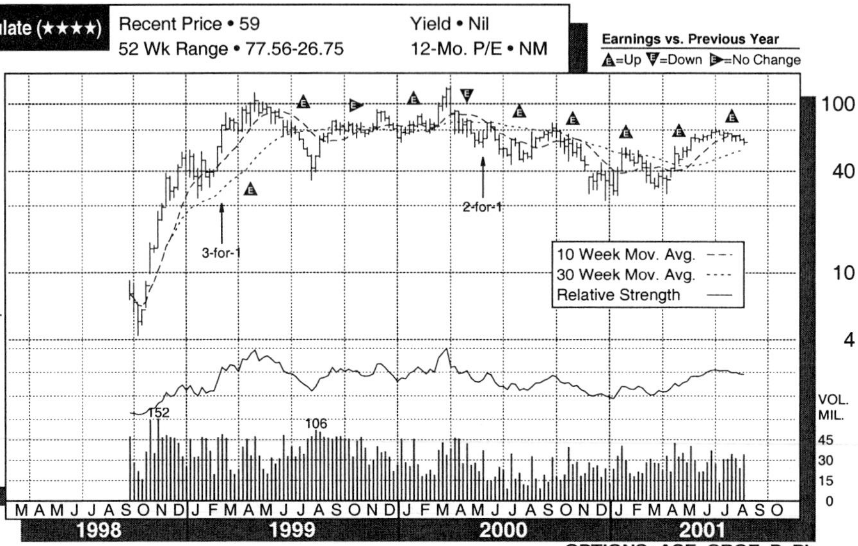

OPTIONS: ASE, CBOE, P, Ph

Overview - 23-JUL-01

We expect sales to climb over 69% in 2001 and 50% through 2005, driven by growth in the company's online business. International operations should continue to contribute significant additional listing and transaction fees and account for an increasing percentage of revenues. The ongoing expansion into the fixed-price market with the "Buy It Now" feature and Half.com platform should also bolster revenue growth. Gross margins should climb to the low 80% area in 2001, from the mid-70% level posted in 2000. Margins had been hurt by accelerated efforts to enhance network infrastructure capacity, as outages plagued the company previously. Site operation improvements have also been contributing to wider margins. We see operating expenses trending down as a percentage of sales, helped by the fast pace of revenue growth. We expect operating margins to exceed 24% in 2001.

Valuation - 23-JUL-01

We upgraded EBAY to accumulate, from hold, in early 2001. We admire the highly scalable business models of EBAY and its Half.com unit, letting buyers and sellers conduct online transactions. EBAY receives fees, but does not have to carry inventory or ship products. This allows for very wide gross margins relative to those of companies that sell goods directly to consumers. With a slowing economy, we believe individuals and businesses are more likely to use EBAY's platforms to obtain goods at more reasonable prices, and to sell items in a more cost efficient way. In addition, infrastructure investments have cut upload times and reduced the frequency and severity of outages. With huge market opportunities, dominant market share, sustainable competitive advantages, top-notch management, and a reasonable recent forward P/E to growth multiple of 1.8, we recommend accumulating the shares.

Key Stock Statistics

S&P EPS Est. 2001	0.49	Tang. Bk. Value/Share	3.72
P/E on S&P Est. 2001	NM	Beta	NA
S&P EPS Est. 2002	0.72	Shareholders	1,150
Dividend Rate/Share	Nil	Market cap. (B)	$ 15.9
Shs. outstg. (M)	270.2	Inst. holdings	33%
Avg. daily vol. (M)	6.130		

Value of $10,000 invested 5 years ago: NA

Fiscal Year Ending Dec. 31

	2001	2000	1999	1998	1997	1996
Revenues (Million $)						
1Q	154.1	85.89	34.01	—	—	—
2Q	180.9	98.15	49.48	—	—	—
3Q	—	113.4	58.53	12.94	—	—
4Q	—	134.0	73.92	19.50	—	—
Yr.	—	431.4	224.7	47.35	5.74	—
Earnings Per Share ($)						
1Q	**0.08**	**0.02**	**0.03**	Nil	—	—
2Q	**0.09**	**0.03**	**0.01**	Nil	—	—
3Q	**E0.12**	**0.05**	**0.01**	**0.01**	—	—
4Q	**E0.13**	**0.09**	**0.02**	**0.01**	—	—
Yr.	**E0.49**	**0.17**	**0.05**	**0.01**	**-0.01**	—

Next earnings report expected: mid October

Dividend Data

No cash dividends have been paid.

Business Summary - 23-JUL-01

eBay Inc. operates the world's largest and most popular online person-to-person trading community at ebay.com. As of June 2001, EBAY had 34.1 million registered users. At any one time, ebay.com has more than 5 million items for sale. Items are listed in more than 11,000 specific categories, with primary categories including Antiques & Art; Books; Business, Office & Industrial; Clothing & Accessories; Coins; Collectibles; Computers; Consumer Electronics; Dolls & Bears; Home & Garden; Jewelry, Gemstones & Watches; Movies; Music; Photo; Pottery & Glass; Real Estate; Sports; Stamps; Tickets & Travel; Toys & Hobbies; and Everything Else. Specialty sites include eBay Motors, eBay Premier (fine arts), Professional Services (through privately held eLance), and Half.com (fixed pricing).

The eBay service was introduced in September 1995, to establish an efficient marketplace for individuals to trade goods with one another. The online service lets users list items for sale, browse through listed items using a 24-hour-a-day service organized by topics, and bid on items of interest. Users can search online auction listings for specific items by category, key word, seller name and auction status (whether, i.e., the auction recently commenced or is about end).

EBAY's strategy is to build on its leading position in online person-to person trading by expanding its user base and strengthening its brand; broadening its trading platform across new product categories and geographies; fostering customer loyalty; and adding and enhancing features, functionality and value-added services (such as payment and insurance offerings).

The company operates some 60 local auction sites in the U.S. and country-specific websites for Australia, Canada, France, Germany, Ireland, Italy, Japan, New Zealand, South Korea, Switzerland and the U.K.

In May 1999, EBAY purchased Billpoint, Inc., which enables individuals to accept credit cards as payment for online sales, in exchange for 524,132 shares. In February 2000, Wells Fargo & Co. purchased a 35% stake in Billpoint, and entered into a long-term payment processing and customer care contract with EBAY.

In July 2000, the company acquired Half.com, a fixed-price marketplace to buy and sell used items for discounted prices, in exchange for 5.1 million EBAY shares, valued at $225 million. That website has become one of the Internet's most popular e-commerce destinations.

EBAY made several moves in early 2001 to bolster its international strategy. In the first quarter of 2001, the company acquired a majority stake in Internet Auction Co. Ltd., Korea's largest auction-style website, for about $120 million in cash. In May 2001, EBAY acquired iBazar S.A., an online auction company with marketplaces in Belgium, Brazil, France, Italy, the Netherlands, Portugal, Spain and Sweden, for approximately 2.25 million shares (recently valued at $150.8 million).

Per Share Data ($) (Year Ended Dec. 31)	2000	1999	1998	1997	1996	1995	1994	1993	1992	1991
Tangible Bk. Val.	3.72	3.25	0.34	0.01	NA	NA	NA	NA	NA	NA
Cash Flow	0.31	0.12	0.02	0.01	NA	NA	NA	NA	NA	NA
Earnings	0.17	0.05	0.01	0.01	NA	NA	NA	NA	NA	NA
Dividends	Nil	Nil	Nil	Nil	NA	NA	NA	NA	NA	NA
Payout Ratio	NM	Nil	Nil	Nil	NA	NA	NA	NA	NA	NA
Prices - High	127.50	117.00	51.87	NA	NA	NA	NA	NA	NA	NA
- Low	26.75	27.66	3.00	NA	NA	NA	NA	NA	NA	NA
P/E Ratio - High	NM	NM	NM	NA	NA	NA	NA	NA	NA	NA
- Low	NM	NM	NM	NA	NA	NA	NA	NA	NA	NA
Income Statement Analysis (Million $)										
Revs.	431	225	47.4	5.7	NA	NA	NA	NA	NA	NA
Oper. Inc.	74.6	23.8	8.7	1.6	NA	NA	NA	NA	NA	NA
Depr.	38.0	20.6	2.5	0.1	NA	NA	NA	NA	NA	NA
Int. Exp.	3.4	1.9	0.0	Nil	NA	NA	NA	NA	NA	NA
Pretax Inc.	78.0	20.5	7.0	1.5	NA	NA	NA	NA	NA	NA
Eff. Tax Rate	42%	46%	66%	43%	NA	NA	NA	NA	NA	NA
Net Inc.	48.3	10.8	2.4	0.9	NA	NA	NA	NA	NA	NA
Balance Sheet & Other Fin. Data (Million $)										
Cash	328	220	31.8	3.7	NA	NA	NA	NA	NA	NA
Curr. Assets	675	460	83.4	5.0	NA	NA	NA	NA	NA	NA
Total Assets	1,182	964	92.5	5.6	NA	NA	NA	NA	NA	NA
Curr. Liab.	137	88.8	8.0	1.1	NA	NA	NA	NA	NA	NA
LT Debt	11.4	15.0	Nil	0.3	NA	NA	NA	NA	NA	NA
Common Eqty.	1,014	852	84.4	1.0	NA	NA	NA	NA	NA	NA
Total Cap.	1,038	867	84.4	4.5	NA	NA	NA	NA	NA	NA
Cap. Exp.	49.8	141	8.9	NA	NA	NA	NA	NA	NA	NA
Cash Flow	86.3	31.5	4.9	0.7	NA	NA	NA	NA	NA	NA
Curr. Ratio	4.9	5.2	10.4	4.4	NA	NA	NA	NA	NA	NA
% LT Debt of Cap.	1.1	1.7	Nil	6.9	NA	NA	NA	NA	NA	NA
% Net Inc.of Revs.	11.2	4.8	5.1	15.2	NA	NA	NA	NA	NA	NA
% Ret. on Assets	4.5	1.9	4.9	NA	NA	NA	NA	NA	NA	NA
% Ret. on Equity	5.2	2.3	5.6	NA	NA	NA	NA	NA	NA	NA

Data as orig reptd.; bef. results of disc opers/spec. items. Per share data adj. for stk. divs. Bold denotes diluted EPS (FASB 128)-prior periods restated. E-Estimated. NA-Not Available. NM-Not Meaningful. NR-Not Ranked.

Office—2145 Hamilton Ave., San Jose, CA 95125. **Tel**—(408) 558-7400. **Website**—http://www.ebay.com **Chrmn**—P. M. Omidyar. **Pres & CEO**—M. C. Whitman. **EVP & COO**—B. T. Swette. **VP & CFO**—R. Dutta. **VP & Secy**—M. R. Jacobson. **Dirs**—P. Bourguignon, S. D. Cook, R. C. Kagle, D. G. Lepore, P. M. Omidyar, H. D. Schultz, M. C. Whitman. **Transfer Agent & Registrar**—ChaseMellon Shareholder Services, Ridgefield Park, NJ. **Incorporated**—in Delaware in 1998; formed in 1995. **Empl**— 1,927. **S&P Analyst:** Scott H. Kessler

STANDARD &POOR'S STOCK REPORTS

Family Dollar Stores

NYSE Symbol **FDO**

In S&P 500

18-AUG-01

Industry: Retail (Discounters)

Summary: This company operates a chain of more than 3,900 retail discount stores in 39 states throughout the U.S.

S&P Opinion: Accumulate (★★★★)

Recent Price • 30.03 | 52 Wk Range • 30.70-15.93 | Yield • 0.8% | 12-Mo. P/E • 27.8

Quantitative Evaluations

Outlook (1 Lowest—5 Highest) **• 3**

Fair Value **• 30**

Risk **• Low**

Earn./Div. Rank **• A**

Technical Eval. **• Bullish** since 7/01

Rel. Strength Rank (1 Lowest—99 Highest) **• 85**

Insider Activity **• Unfavorable**

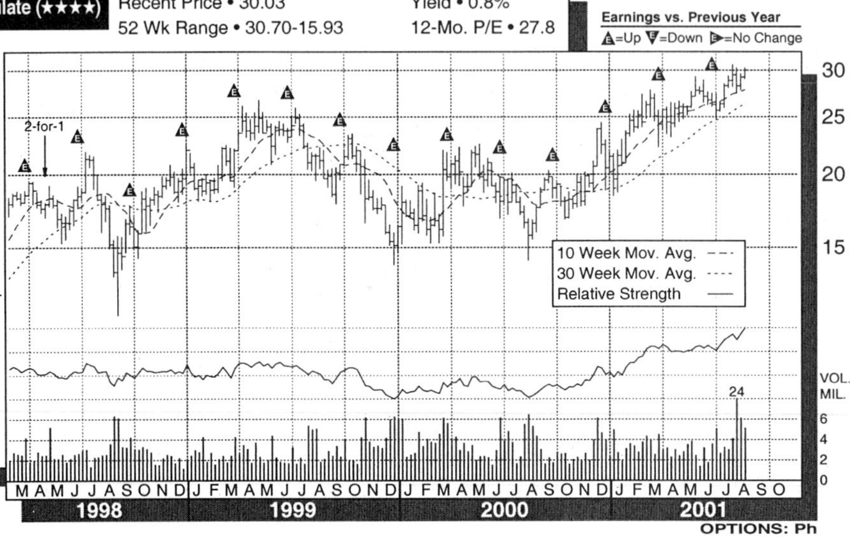

OPTIONS: Ph

Overview - 10-APR-01

We expect double-digit total sales growth in FY 01 (Aug.), spurred by the addition of about 450 (net) new stores. Same-store sales should increase 3.5% to 4.0%, reflecting strength in the sale of hardlines and weakness in apparel sales. Gross margins should narrow due to the extremely promotional retail environment but will begin to stabilize as year- to- year comparisons get easier due to a more complete annualization of the EDLP (everyday low price program). SG&A expense ratios should widen, in part reflecting higher labor costs and increased utility rates. Cost-cutting measures are in place, such as reducing the number of advertising circulars distributed. Pretax income will increase about 12%. The company continues to be financially strong, with no long-term debt and strong cash flow to fund its $165 to $175 million capital expenditure program. Three million shares of the November 1999 five million share repurchase authorization are remaining.

Valuation - 10-APR-01

The shares have risen almost 40% so far this year but are down slightly from their 52-week high. We recommend accumulating the stock. Moderate increases in same-store sales, customer count and the size of the average transaction have boosted investor confidence in the stock. Same-store sales rose 2.2% in the second quarter and the average transaction size rose 2.0% to $9.20, while customer count was unchanged from the preceding year. EPS increased only 10% hurt by a shift in the product mix and higher expenses. We anticipate the improvement in sales over the next few months to increase expense leverage. In addition, the implementation of new technology will improve store productivity. In light of our projected 17% growth in EPS for FY 02 to $1.35, we see room for P/E multiple expansion.

Key Stock Statistics

S&P EPS Est. 2001	1.15	Tang. Bk. Value/Share	5.42
P/E on S&P Est. 2001	26.1	Beta	0.99
S&P EPS Est. 2002	1.35	Shareholders	2,150
Dividend Rate/Share	0.24	Market cap. (B)	$ 5.2
Shs. outstg. (M)	171.8	Inst. holdings	82%
Avg. daily vol. (M)	1.998		

Value of $10,000 invested 5 years ago: $ 57,592

Fiscal Year Ending Aug. 31

	2001	2000	1999	1998	1997	1996
Revenues (Million $)						
1Q	820.1	713.5	628.0	542.8	454.9	396.2
2Q	1,037	858.5	752.2	635.9	530.3	448.3
3Q	887.0	770.8	678.9	585.8	498.4	427.9
4Q	—	789.8	692.1	597.5	511.4	442.3
Yr.	—	3,133	2,751	2,362	1,995	1,715
Earnings Per Share ($)						
1Q	**0.24**	**0.21**	**0.17**	**0.14**	0.10	0.09
2Q	**0.35**	**0.32**	**0.24**	**0.16**	0.12	0.09
3Q	**0.31**	**0.29**	**0.24**	**0.18**	0.14	0.11
4Q	**E0.23**	**0.18**	**0.16**	**0.12**	0.09	0.07
Yr.	**E1.15**	**1.00**	**0.81**	**0.60**	0.43	0.35

Next earnings report expected: late September

Dividend Data (Dividends have been paid since 1976.)

Amount ($)	Date Decl.	Ex-Div. Date	Stock of Record	Payment Date
0.055	Aug. 25	Sep. 13	Sep. 15	Oct. 16 '00
0.055	Nov. 06	Dec. 13	Dec. 15	Jan. 15 '01
0.060	Jan. 18	Mar. 13	Mar. 15	Apr. 16 '01
0.060	May. 15	Jun. 13	Jun. 15	Jul. 16 '01

Business Summary - 10-APR-01

The original predecessor of Family Dollar Stores was organized in 1959 to operate a self-service retail store in Charlotte, NC. In subsequent years, the company opened additional stores, and separate corporations were organized to operate these stores. Today, four indirect subsidiaries organized as North Carolina corporations provide distribution, trucking, operations, marketing and other services to FDO.

At November 1, 2000, there were 3,777 self-service retail discount stores in 39 states and the District of Columbia, operating under the Family Dollar name. The company's stores are highly concentrated, with 15 states having 100 or more stores as of November 1, 2000. States with large numbers of stores included Texas (404 stores), North Carolina (244), Ohio (238), Georgia (215), Florida (211), Tennessee (170), Virginia (169), Pennsylvania (168), New York (154), Michigan (145), Kentucky (143), Alabama (135), South Carolina (135), Indiana (125), and Louisiana (122).

In addition to expanding the number of stores, FDO has also focused on remodeling existing stores, with a new prototype interior layout designed to create a more customer-friendly environment. In FY 00 (Aug.), 41 stores were closed, 72 were relocated, 81 were expanded, and 122 were renovated. FDO planned to open about 500 stores and close about 50 stores in FY 01.

The stores offer a variety of merchandise, including men's, women's, boys', girls', and infants' clothing, shoes, domestics, household products, health and beauty aids, toys, school supplies, candy and snack food, housewares, paint and automotive supplies. Most items of merchandise are priced under $10.

The relatively small size of the company's stores permits FDO to open new units in rural areas and small towns, as well as in large urban areas, in locations convenient to the company's low and low-middle income customer base. As sales focus on low priced, basic merchandise, the stores offer customers a reasonable selection of competitively priced merchandise within a relatively narrow range of price points.

The company maintains a substantial variety and depth of basic and seasonal merchandise inventory in stock at its stores to attract customers and meet their shopping needs. During FY 00, hardlines accounted for 71.4% of company sales. This includes household chemicals and products, health and beauty aids, candy, snack and other food as well as electronics and hardware and automotive supplies. The balance of sales was softlines, consisting of hanging apparel and shoes (15.6%), basic apparel (5.3%) and domestics (7.7%).

FDO purchases its merchandise from approximately 1,800 suppliers. About 55% of merchandise is manufactured in the U.S., with substantially all such goods purchased directly from the manufacturer. Imported merchandise is purchased directly from the manufacturer or from importers.

Per Share Data ($) (Year Ended Aug. 31)	**2000**	**1999**	**1998**	**1997**	**1996**	**1995**	**1994**	**1993**	**1992**	**1991**
Tangible Bk. Val.	4.66	4.00	3.36	2.92	2.61	2.40	2.18	1.91	1.62	1.36
Cash Flow	1.31	1.06	0.80	0.60	0.50	0.47	0.48	0.48	0.42	0.32
Earnings	1.00	0.81	0.60	0.43	0.36	0.34	0.37	0.38	0.33	0.24
Dividends	0.21	0.20	0.17	0.15	0.14	0.12	0.11	0.09	0.08	0.07
Payout Ratio	21%	24%	28%	35%	39%	36%	29%	24%	24%	29%
Prices - High	24.50	26.75	22.43	15.06	7.00	6.58	6.12	7.87	8.20	5.70
- Low	14.25	14.00	11.50	6.25	3.66	3.62	3.37	5.04	4.37	1.91
P/E Ratio - High	25	33	37	35	20	19	17	21	25	23
- Low	14	17	19	14	10	11	9	13	13	8
Income Statement Analysis (Million $)										
Revs.	3,133	2,751	2,362	1,995	1,715	1,547	1,428	1,297	1,159	989
Oper. Inc.	325	266	201	151	123	117	120	120	103	76.0
Depr.	54.5	43.8	34.8	29.1	24.6	22.2	19.5	17.2	14.7	13.1
Int. Exp.	Nil	Nil	0.0	0.3	Nil	Nil	0.5	0.2	Nil	0.4
Pretax Inc.	271	223	166	121	99	94.0	100	103	88.9	63.7
Eff. Tax Rate	37%	37%	38%	39%	39%	39%	38%	37%	37%	37%
Net Inc.	172	140	103	74.7	60.6	58.0	62.0	64.4	55.7	40.2
Balance Sheet & Other Fin. Data (Million $)										
Cash	43.6	95.3	134	42.5	18.8	8.9	9.9	5.7	1.7	25.0
Curr. Assets	751	720	647	545	508	475	436	402	359	294
Total Assets	1,244	1,095	942	780	697	636	593	537	478	399
Curr. Liab.	412	379	343	261	234	210	206	197	188	158
LT Debt	Nil	Nil	Nil	Nil	Nil	Nil	Nil	Nil	Nil	Nil
Common Eqty.	798	691	578	500	445	408	370	323	272	227
Total Cap.	832	717	599	519	463	426	387	339	287	242
Cap. Exp.	172	125	96.4	77.1	54.3	27.7	42.6	32.5	30.1	14.8
Cash Flow	227	184	138	104	85.2	80.3	81.4	81.6	70.4	53.3
Curr. Ratio	1.8	1.9	1.9	2.1	2.2	2.3	2.1	2.0	1.9	1.9
% LT Debt of Cap.	Nil	Nil	Nil	Nil	Nil	Nil	Nil	Nil	Nil	Nil
% Net Inc.of Revs.	5.5	5.1	4.4	3.7	3.6	3.8	4.5	5.0	4.8	4.1
% Ret. on Assets	14.7	13.7	12.0	10.1	9.1	9.5	10.9	12.7	12.7	10.6
% Ret. on Equity	23.1	22.1	19.2	15.8	14.3	15.0	17.8	21.6	22.3	18.9

Data as orig reptd.; bef. results of disc opers/spec. items. Per share data adj. for stk. divs. Bold denotes diluted EPS (FASB 128)-prior periods restated. E-Estimated. NA-Not Available. NM-Not Meaningful. NR-Not Ranked.

Office—P.O. Box 1017, 10401 Old Monroe Rd., Charlotte, NC 28201-1017. **Tel**—(704) 847-6961. **Website**—http://www.familydollar.com **Chrmn**—L. Levine. **Vice Chrmn**—R. J. Kelly. **Pres & CEO**—H. R. Levine. **EVP & COO**—R. David Alexander Jr. **EVP, Secy & Investor Contact**—George R. Mahoney Jr. **SVP-Fin**—C. M. Sowers. **Dirs**—R. David Alexander Jr., M. R. Bernstein, S. A. Decker, J. H. Hance Jr., R. J. Kelly, L. Levine, H. R. Levine G. R. Mahoney Jr., J. G. Martin. **Transfer Agent & Registrar**—Mellon Investor Services, Ridgefield Park, NJ. **Incorporated**—in Delaware in 1969. **Empl**— 31,200. **S&P Analyst:** Karen J. Sack, CFA

STANDARD &POOR'S STOCK REPORTS

Harley-Davidson

NYSE Symbol **HDI**

In S&P 500

18-AUG-01

Industry: Leisure Time (Products)

Summary: This leading producer of heavyweight motorcycles also produces a line of motorcycle parts and accessories.

S&P Opinion: Accumulate (★★★★) Recent Price • 49.01 52 Wk Range • 54.35-34.25 Yield • 0.2% 12-Mo. P/E • 38.9

Quantitative Evaluations

Outlook (1 Lowest—5 Highest) • **1**

Fair Value • **40.50**

Risk • **Low**

Earn./Div. Rank • **A-**

Technical Eval. • **Bullish** since 7/01

Rel. Strength Rank (1 Lowest—99 Highest) • **56**

Insider Activity • **NA**

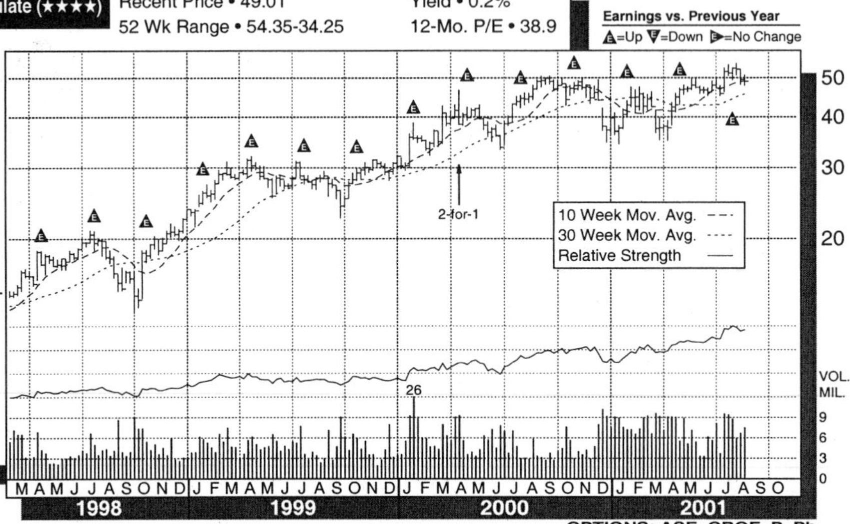

OPTIONS: ASE, CBOE, P, Ph

Overview - 17-JUL-01

We look for the company's net sales to increase about 14% in 2002, following a 15% rise projected for 2001. Growth is again expected to be fueled largely by higher unit sales of Harley-Davidson brand motorcycles. We look for HDI to ship at least 256,000 bikes in 2002, including initial shipments of the new high-performance dragster, up about 11% from the 231,000 expected to be shipped this year. The company shipped 204,592 bikes in 2000. HDI's operating margin should widen in 2001, leading to a 22% rise in operating profit. Narrower margins are anticipated for 2002, limiting the rise in profits to about 13%. We are forecasting EPS of $1.36 in 2001, up 23%, and $1.61 in 2002, up 18%. HDI is planning additional capacity that might come on stream around 2003.

Valuation - 17-JUL-01

We recently upgraded the shares to accumulate, from hold. Through mid-July, the stock had advanced 62% in 2001, strongly outperforming the S&P 500 year-to-date. Although the shares were trading at a premium P/E multiple of about 33X estimated 2002 EPS, we believe this high valuation is warranted, based on the prospects for average EPS gains in the high teens over the next five years. HDI should continue to outperform the general market. We like the company's market leadership position and its strong flagship brand. For the foreseeable future, we expect consumer demand for HDI bikes to exceed supply, as management continues to follow a strategy of carefully controlled production. The planned launch of a new high-performance dragster bike in the fourth quarter of 2001 should widen HDI's customer base, offering particular appeal to European and Japanese riders.

Key Stock Statistics

S&P EPS Est. 2001	1.36	Tang. Bk. Value/Share	5.20
P/E on S&P Est. 2001	36.0	Beta	1.23
S&P EPS Est. 2002	1.61	Shareholders	64,963
Dividend Rate/Share	0.12	Market cap. (B)	$ 14.9
Shs. outstg. (M)	304.0	Inst. holdings	71%
Avg. daily vol. (M)	1.436		

Value of $10,000 invested 5 years ago: $ 47,603

Fiscal Year Ending Dec. 31

	2001	2000	1999	1998	1997	1996
Revenues (Million $)						
1Q	767.3	681.1	558.6	466.5	427.1	371.1
2Q	850.9	755.0	608.7	517.2	444.1	392.8
3Q	—	714.1	623.2	517.2	444.2	385.8
4Q	—	756.2	662.5	563.1	447.2	381.5
Yr.	—	2,906	2,453	2,064	1,763	1,531
Earnings Per Share ($)						
1Q	**0.30**	**0.26**	**0.19**	**0.14**	0.13	0.11
2Q	**0.38**	**0.29**	**0.22**	**0.18**	0.16	0.13
3Q	**E0.33**	**0.27**	**0.21**	**0.17**	0.14	0.11
4Q	**E0.35**	**0.31**	**0.24**	**0.20**	**0.14**	0.12
Yr.	**E1.36**	**1.13**	**0.86**	**0.69**	**0.56**	**0.47**

Next earnings report expected: mid October

Dividend Data (Dividends have been paid since 1993.)

Amount ($)	Date Decl.	Ex-Div. Date	Stock of Record	Payment Date
0.025	Aug. 10	Sep. 06	Sep. 08	Sep. 19 '00
0.025	Dec. 06	Dec. 14	Dec. 18	Dec. 29 '00
0.025	Feb. 09	Mar. 08	Mar. 12	Mar. 23 '01
0.030	May. 05	Jun. 07	Jun. 11	Jun. 22 '01

A Division of The McGraw-Hill Companies

Harley-Davidson, Inc.

Business Summary - 17-JUL-01

Harley-Davidson is a leading supplier of heavyweight motorcycles. The company benefits from having one of the world's most recognized and respected brand names.

The company primarily manufactures and sells heavyweight (engine displacement of 651cc or more) touring, custom and performance motorcycles, and a broad range of related products, which include motorcycle parts, accessories, riding apparel, and collectibles. The touring segment of the heavyweight market includes motorcycles equipped for long-distance riding, including fairings, windshields, and saddlebags. Custom motorcycles are differentiated through the use of trim and accessories. The performance segment of the market emphasizes handling and acceleration. In 2000, based on new registrations, HDI's share of the U.S. heavyweight market was 47.4%, down from 50.2% in 1999, as a result of HDI's capacity restraints. The company's share of the worldwide heavyweight market was 28.2%, up from 26.7%. Competitors include Honda, Suzuki, Kawasaki and Yamaha.

HDI sells about 24 models of Harley-Davidson touring and custom heavyweight motorcycles, with suggested domestic retail prices ranging from approximately $5,595 to $18,980. It also makes and sells several models of Buell motorcycles, including a 492cc Buell Blast motorcycle, for which shipments began in early 2000. The Blast is targeted toward new riders; its retail price of $4,395 is about half the price of the next lowest-priced Buell motorcycle.

A transition to a new engine plant in Milwaukee was completed in 1997, and a new assembly plant in Kansas City is now being used for all of HDI's Sportster motorcycle production, thereby freeing up additional capacity at HDI's York, PA, assembly plant for larger, higher-margin motorcycles.

Despite continuous production increases, U.S. consumers often have to wait to purchase a new Harley-Davidson brand bike at list price. Studies by HDI indicate that a typical U.S. Harley-Davidson owner is a married male in his mid-40s, with household income of about $77,700, who purchases a motorcycle for recreational purposes, and who is an experienced motorcycle rider. HDI has a strong brand name, and offers about 95 years of heritage, something that other companies cannot match.

In 2000, shipments of Harley-Davidson brand motorcycles totaled 204,592 units, including 158,817 for the U.S. and 45,775 for export. This compared with 177,187 in 1999 (135,614 U.S.; 41,573 export).

In February 1998, the company acquired substantially all of the common stock of Buell Motorcycle Co., a business in which it had held a 49% equity interest since 1993. In 2000, there were shipments of 10,189 Buell motorcycles, including 5,146 of the relatively new Buell Blast. In 1999, HDI's Buell shipments totaled 7,767 bikes.

HDI's majority-owned Eaglemark Financial Services business provides services both to HDI dealers and to customers. HDI's licensing activity has included T-shirts, jewelry, small leat her goods, toys, and two cafes. Royalty revenues from licensing totaled about $31 million in 2000.

Per Share Data ($)										
(Year Ended Dec. 31)	**2000**	**1999**	**1998**	**1997**	**1996**	**1995**	**1994**	**1993**	**1992**	**1991**
Tangible Bk. Val.	4.47	3.65	3.20	2.58	2.06	1.51	1.40	1.06	0.92	0.63
Cash Flow	1.56	1.23	0.97	0.79	0.66	0.51	0.46	0.17	0.29	0.21
Earnings	1.13	0.86	0.69	0.56	0.47	0.37	0.34	0.06	0.19	0.13
Dividends	0.10	0.09	0.08	0.07	0.06	0.05	0.06	0.02	Nil	Nil
Payout Ratio	9%	10%	11%	12%	12%	12%	18%	24%	Nil	Nil
Prices - High	50.62	32.03	23.75	15.62	12.37	7.53	7.46	5.93	4.84	3.79
- Low	29.53	21.37	12.46	8.34	6.59	5.50	5.40	3.93	2.71	1.10
P/E Ratio - High	45	37	34	28	26	20	22	97	26	29
- Low	26	25	18	15	14	15	16	64	14	9
Income Statement Analysis (Million $)										
Revs.	2,906	2,453	2,064	1,763	1,531	1,351	1,542	1,217	1,105	940
Oper. Inc.	611	502	401	328	258	220	197	160	127	91.0
Depr.	133	114	87.4	70.2	55.2	42.3	36.9	33.0	29.4	22.6
Int. Exp.	Nil	Nil	Nil	Nil	Nil	1.4	2.4	2.0	5.9	9.4
Pretax Inc.	549	421	336	276	228	176	162	66.5	88.8	58.1
Eff. Tax Rate	37%	37%	37%	37%	37%	37%	36%	72%	39%	36%
Net Inc.	348	267	214	174	143	111	104	18.4	54.2	37.0
Balance Sheet & Other Fin. Data (Million $)										
Cash	420	183	165	147	142	31.5	59.3	77.7	44.1	30.9
Total Assets	2,436	2,112	1,920	1,599	1,320	1,001	739	583	522	474
LT Debt	355	280	280	280	258	164	9.4	3.4	2.0	47.0
Total Debt	355	280	427	371	258	167	27.7	24.8	19.3	88.0
Common Eqty.	1,406	1,161	1,080	827	663	495	433	325	335	238
Cap. Exp.	204	166	183	186	179	113	94.7	55.2	47.2	48.2
Cash Flow	481	381	301	244	199	153	141	51.4	83.6	59.6
% Ret. on Assets	15.3	13.3	12.2	11.9	12.3	13.4	15.5	3.3	10.6	8.4
% Ret. on Equity	27.1	24.4	23.0	23.4	24.6	23.9	27.5	5.6	18.4	16.9
% LT Debt of Cap.	20.2	19.4	21.4	25.3	NM	24.9	2.1	Nil	0.7	16.1

Data as orig reptd.; bef. results of disc opers/spec. items. Per share data adj. for stk. divs. Bold denotes diluted EPS (FASB 128)-prior periods restated. E-Estimated. NA-Not Available. NM-Not Meaningful. NR-Not Ranked.

Office—3700 West Juneau Ave., Milwaukee, WI 53208. **Tel**—(414) 342-4680. **Website**—www.harley-davidson.com **Chrmn & CEO**—J. L. Bleustein. **VP & CFO**—J. L. Ziemer. **VP & Treas**—J. M. Brostowitz. **VP & Secy**—G. A. Lione. **Investor Contact**—Patrick Davidson (414-343-8002). **Dirs**—B. K. Allen, R. I. Beattie, J. L. Bleustein, R. J. Hermon-Taylor, D. A. James, R. G. LeFauve, S. L. Levinson, J. A. Norling, R. F. Teerlink. **Transfer Agent & Registrar**—Computershare, Chicago. **Incorporated**—in Delaware in 1981; reincorporated in Wisconsin in 1991. **Empl**— 7,220. **S&P Analyst:** Tom Graves, CFA

STANDARD &POOR'S
STOCK REPORTS

Hilton Hotels

NYSE Symbol **HLT**
In S&P 500

18-AUG-01

Industry: Lodging - Hotels

Summary: This leading hospitality company owns, manages or franchises more than 1,800 hotels, resorts and vacation ownership properties.

S&P Opinion: Accumulate (★★★★)

Recent Price • 12.51 | Yield • 0.6%
52 Wk Range • 13.57-8.37 | 12-Mo. P/E • 17.4

Quantitative Evaluations

Outlook (1 Lowest—5 Highest)
• **4**

Fair Value
• **15.30**

Risk
• **Average**

Earn./Div. Rank
• **B+**

Technical Eval.
• **Bullish** since 7/01

Rel. Strength Rank (1 Lowest—99 Highest)
• **74**

Insider Activity
• **Neutral**

OPTIONS: ASE, CBOE, P, Ph

Overview - 08-AUG-01

In 2001, we look for HLT's revenue to be down at least modestly from the $3.5 billion reported for 2000, largely due to declines in revenue per available room (REVPAR) at owned hotels and the absence of some divested assets. In particular, we expect HLT's results to be hurt by weakness in U.S. business travel. We project that HLT's 2001 EBITDA, including corporate expense, will drop about 5%, to $1.2 billion. Net income is expected to decline 3%, to $265 million ($0.71 a share), from $249 million ($0.67), which excludes some year-ago non-recurring items. For 2002, including a benefit from a change in accounting for non-cash goodwill expense, we project net income of $318 million ($0.81). Long term, we expect that franchising and managing hotels will be of growing importance for HLT.

Valuation - 08-AUG-01

As of early August 2001, this stock had sharply outperformed the S&P 500, year to date, after topping the index by 20 percentage points in 2000. We believe that the stock has received support from prospects for a slowdown in the pace of new U.S. hotel construction coming on stream, and expectations of improved operating results in 2002. Based on estimated cash flow, the strength of HLT's brand, and the company's ownership of some difficult-to-replicate, highly regarded hotels, the stock has some appeal. Including estimated net debt of about $5 billion, the market is giving HLT an enterprise value that is approximately 8.2X estimated 2001 EBITDA (7.8X if corporate expense is excluded), and the stock is at a P/E of about 18X estimated 2001 EPS. We look for HLT's capital spending on property, plant and equipment to decline in 2002, and for the stock to increasingly become an attractive free cash flow story. The shares are at about 15X estimated 2002 free cash flow.

Key Stock Statistics

S&P EPS Est. 2001	0.71	Tang. Bk. Value/Share	NM
P/E on S&P Est. 2001	17.6	Beta	0.72
S&P EPS Est. 2002	0.81	Shareholders	23,300
Dividend Rate/Share	0.08	Market cap. (B)	$ 4.6
Shs. outstg. (M)	369.0	Inst. holdings	63%
Avg. daily vol. (M)	0.834		

Value of $10,000 invested 5 years ago: NA

Fiscal Year Ending Dec. 31

	2001	2000	1999	1998	1997	1996
Revenues (Million $)						
1Q	833.0	793.0	494.0	366.0	1,303	957.0
2Q	844.0	916.0	539.0	457.0	1,360	1,004
3Q	—	867.0	498.0	450.0	1,314	943.0
4Q	—	875.0	816.0	496.0	1,339	1,036
Yr.	—	3,451	3,161	1,769	5,316	3,940
Earnings Per Share ($)						
1Q	**0.15**	**0.16**	**0.16**	**0.14**	**0.26**	**0.19**
2Q	**0.23**	**0.23**	**0.25**	**0.25**	**0.34**	**0.30**
3Q	**E0.16**	**0.17**	**0.16**	**0.15**	**0.35**	**0.28**
4Q	**E0.17**	**0.17**	**0.07**	**0.17**	**-0.03**	**0.03**
Yr.	**E0.71**	**0.73**	**0.58**	**0.71**	**0.94**	**0.79**

Next earnings report expected: late October

Dividend Data (Dividends have been paid since 1946.)

Amount ($)	Date Decl.	Ex-Div. Date	Stock of Record	Payment Date
0.020	Nov. 09	Nov. 29	Dec. 01	Dec. 15 '00
0.020	Jan. 23	Feb. 28	Mar. 02	Mar. 16 '01
0.020	May. 09	May. 30	Jun. 01	Jun. 15 '01
0.020	Jul. 17	Aug. 29	Aug. 31	Sep. 14 '01

Hilton Hotels Corporation

Business Summary - 08-AUG-01

This hotel company includes more than 1,800 properties, operating under various brands. Although most of the hotels are franchises operated by others, HLT also owns or manages various lodging properties. Owned hotels include the Waldorf-Astoria in New York City and the Palmer House Hilton in Chicago. HLT's size was significantly increased through the November 1999 acquisition of Promus Hotel Corp., whose brands included Hampton Inn, Embassy Suites and Doubletree.

As of year-end 2000, HLT owned, managed or franchised 1,895 hotels with 317,823 rooms. This included 78 hotels (35,234 rooms) in which HLT had a majority or controlling ownership interest, including some of its largest and most profitable hotels; 73 leased and managed properties (12,602), including a number of hotels whose operating leases were sold by HLT in January 2001; 61 hotels (18,148) in which HLT had a minority or non-controlling ownership interest and operated; 191 hotels (51,122) that HLT managed but were owned wholly by others; and 1,492 franchised properties (200,717) owned and operated by third parties. In 2000, HLT had a net increase of 143 hotels (17,544 rooms), with the rise primarily coming from an increase in the number of franchise properties.

Based on number of properties (1,073) and rooms (111,231), HLT's largest brand at year-end 2000 was the Hampton business; however, the vast majority of these hotels were franchises. Another 228 hotels (85,243 rooms) were Hilton Hotels, and 89 hotels (12,575) were Hilton Garden Inn properties. HLT's Doubletree brand included 159 hotels (42,548 rooms), the Embassy Suites chain had 158 properties (38,510), and the Homewood Suites business included 94 properties (10,474). Other HLT hotels included 94 hotels with 17,242 rooms.

HLT has entered into agreements with British company Hilton Group Plc (formerly known as Ladbroke Group PLC), which owns rights to the Hilton name outside of the U.S. The agreements provided for a reunification of the Hilton brand worldwide through a strategic alliance between the two companies, including cooperation on sales and marketing, loyalty programs, and other operational matters.

As of early 2001, HLT was also managing 19 vacation ownership resorts in Florida, two in Nevada, and one in Hawaiii. Also, HLT was operating HGVClub, a point-based reservation and exchange system.

In November 1999, HLT acquired Promus Hotel Corp. (PRH) in a cash-and-stock transaction valued at about $2.9 billion (excluding assumption of debt). HLT paid about $1.7 billion for 55% of PRH's shares, and the remaining 45% of PRH's shares were exchanged for about 114 million HLT common shares. In December 1998, ownership of most of HLT's gaming assets was spun off to shareholders through a tax free distribution of equity in Park Place Entertainment (PPE).

Per Share Data ($) (Year Ended Dec. 31)	2000	1999	1998	1997	1996	1995	1994	1993	1992	1991
Tangible Bk. Val.	NM	NM	0.72	8.25	7.63	6.49	5.86	5.53	5.25	5.01
Cash Flow	1.67	1.25	1.09	2.21	1.34	1.62	1.28	1.12	1.06	0.99
Earnings	0.73	0.58	0.71	0.94	0.79	0.89	0.63	0.54	0.54	0.44
Dividends	0.08	0.08	0.32	0.32	0.30	0.30	0.30	0.30	0.30	0.30
Payout Ratio	11%	14%	45%	34%	39%	34%	48%	56%	55%	68%
Prices - High	12.12	17.12	35.50	35.81	31.75	19.93	18.50	15.25	13.31	12.46
- Low	6.37	8.37	12.00	24.00	15.28	15.09	12.43	10.37	9.93	8.56
P/E Ratio - High	17	30	50	38	40	22	29	29	25	28
- Low	9	14	17	26	19	17	20	19	18	19
Income Statement Analysis (Million $)										
Revs.	3,451	2,150	1,769	5,316	3,940	1,649	1,456	1,358	1,203	1,082
Oper. Inc.	1,212	682	589	896	507	496	354	316	294	249
Depr.	382	187	125	300	178	142	127	112	100	94.0
Int. Exp.	462	239	141	190	106	113	92.7	82.4	71.8	63.3
Pretax Inc.	479	313	336	448	267	280	201	161	159	123
Eff. Tax Rate	42%	42%	40%	42%	40%	37%	39%	36%	35%	31%
Net Inc.	272	176	188	250	156	173	122	103	104	84.0
Balance Sheet & Other Fin. Data (Million $)										
Cash	47.0	104	47.0	330	438	409	393	479	511	350
Curr. Assets	840	763	469	1,011	1,151	717	674	727	676	502
Total Assets	9,140	9,253	3,944	7,826	7,577	3,060	2,926	2,675	2,659	2,187
Curr. Liab.	646	629	506	941	998	535	328	278	365	195
LT Debt	5,693	6,085	3,037	2,709	2,606	1,070	1,252	1,113	1,087	789
Common Eqty.	3,284	3,252	187	3,368	3,196	1,254	1,128	1,057	1,003	953
Total Cap.	9,879	10,216	3,289	6,695	6,415	2,447	2,504	2,310	2,237	1,912
Cap. Exp.	458	254	171	531	242	187	254	157	221	78.0
Cash Flow	654	363	303	550	334	315	249	215	204	178
Curr. Ratio	1.3	1.2	0.9	1.1	1.1	1.3	2.1	2.6	1.9	2.6
% LT Debt of Cap.	57.6	59.6	92.3	40.5	40.6	43.8	50.0	48.2	48.6	41.3
% Net Inc.of Revs.	7.8	8.2	10.6	4.7	3.9	10.5	8.4	7.6	8.6	7.8
% Ret. on Assets	2.9	2.7	3.2	3.2	2.8	5.8	4.3	3.8	4.3	4.1
% Ret. on Equity	17.8	9.1	10.0	7.6	7.0	14.6	11.1	10.0	10.6	9.0

Data as orig. reptd.; bef. results of disc. opers. and/or spec. items. Per share data adj. for stk. divs. as of ex-div. date. E-Estimated. NA-Not Available. NM-Not Meaningful. NR-Not Ranked.

Office—9336 Civic Center Dr., Beverly Hills, CA 90210. **Tel**—(310) 278-4321. **Website**—http://www.hilton.com **Chrmn**—B. Hilton. **Pres & CEO**—S. F. Bollenbach. **EVP & CFO**—M. J. Hart. **EVP & Secy**—M. A. Kleiner. **SVP & Investor Contact**—Marc A. Grossman. **Dirs**—S. F. Bollenbach, A. S. Crown, P. M. George, B. Hilton, D. H. Huckestein, R. L. Johnson, B. V. Lambert, D. Michels, J. H. Myers, J. L. Notter, J. L. Shelton, D. F. Tuttle, P. V. Ueberroth, S. D. Young Jr. **Transfer Agent & Registrar**—The Bank of New York, NYC. **Incorporated**—in Delaware in 1946. **Empl**— 77,000. **S&P Analyst:** Tom Graves, CFA

STANDARD
&POOR'S
STOCK REPORTS

International Game Technology

NYSE Symbol **IGT**

In S&P MidCap 400

18-AUG-01

Industry: Gaming, Lottery & Pari-mutuel Cos.

Summary: This company is a leading maker of gaming machines and proprietary software systems for gaming machine networks.

S&P Opinion: Accumulate (★★★★)

Recent Price • 52.64 | Yield • Nil
52 Wk Range • 66.04-28.25 | 12-Mo. P/E • 19.2

Quantitative Evaluations

Outlook
(1 Lowest—5 Highest)
• 5+

Fair Value
• 70.20

Risk
• Average

Earn./Div. Rank
• B+

Technical Eval.
• Bearish since 7/01

Rel. Strength Rank
(1 Lowest—99 Highest)
• 40

Insider Activity
• Unfavorable

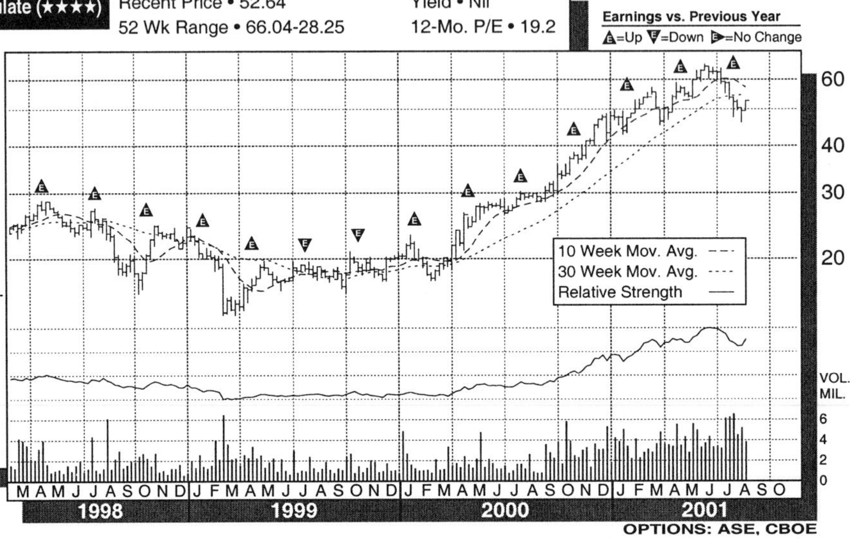

OPTIONS: ASE, CBOE

Overview - 09-AUG-01

We look for the company's revenues to rise sharply in FY 02 (Sep.), from the $1.2 billion projected for FY 01; the FY 01 estimate reflects a recent change in how results from unconsolidated joint ventures are presented. Revenue growth in FY 02 is expected to come largely from the pending acquisition of Anchor Gaming. Subject to various approvals, IGT would acquire Anchor in a stock-swap transaction currently valued at $1.2 billion, including the assumption of $430 million of Anchor debt. In FY 02, we expect IGT's already strong market position in the U.S. to be bolstered by new game introductions and by increased availability and sales of "EZ Pay" machines that enable gamblers to use tickets. Net income for FY 02 is projected at $281 million ($3.20 a share, with more shares outstanding), up from the $212 million ($2.78) projected for FY 01. These estimates exclude unusual or one-time items.

Valuation - 09-AUG-01

As of early August 2001, the stock had outperformed the S&P 500 Index, and by a smaller margin, the S&P 400 Index, year to date. However, the shares were down sharply from their 2001 high. During the past 18 months, we believe the stock has been helped by expectations of machine sales to Native American casinos in California, and by prospects for sales and utilization of IGT gaming devices with new themes and/or features. We look for the availability of newer IGT products to increase the pace at which casinos buy replacement machines. Although we have some concern about a lackluster outlook for new U.S. casino openings, we have become more optimistic about prospects for IGT's progressive jackpot systems business. We view the stock as attractive at 15X estimated FY 02 EPS. The shares could get some support from repurchase activity.

Key Stock Statistics

S&P EPS Est. 2001	2.78	Tang. Bk. Value/Share	NM
P/E on S&P Est. 2001	18.9	Beta	0.16
S&P EPS Est. 2002	3.20	Shareholders	4,631
Dividend Rate/Share	Nil	Market cap. (B)	$ 3.9
Shs. outstg. (M)	74.9	Inst. holdings	75%
Avg. daily vol. (M)	1.259		

Value of $10,000 invested 5 years ago: $ 28,337

Fiscal Year Ending Sep. 30

	2001	2000	1999	1998	1997	1996
Revenues (Million $)						
1Q	301.7	206.5	221.7	165.0	189.4	156.2
2Q	346.9	218.1	220.9	182.1	164.4	160.6
3Q	320.1	263.7	258.9	223.0	163.8	196.6
4Q	—	316.2	228.2	254.0	226.4	220.1
Yr.	—	1,004	929.7	824.1	744.0	733.5
Earnings Per Share ($)						
1Q	**0.64**	**0.49**	**0.32**	**0.26**	0.27	0.21
2Q	**0.70**	**0.33**	**0.32**	**0.31**	0.22	0.15
3Q	**0.73**	**0.51**	**0.39**	**0.40**	0.29	0.27
4Q	**E0.71**	**0.72**	**-0.45**	**0.37**	0.36	0.30
Yr.	**E2.78**	**2.00**	**0.65**	**1.33**	**1.13**	0.93

Next earnings report expected: early November

Dividend Data

Dividends, paid since 1993, were omitted in April 1999.

International Game Technology

Business Summary - 09-AUG-01

If you visit a U.S. casino, the odds are good that you'll see a gaming machine made by International Game Technology. More than 400,000 company machines, with features ranging from spinning fruit to video poker hands, can be found in U.S. gaming markets. This gives IGT, which also sells to international markets, a leading share of machine placements in the U.S. During the past decade, legalized gaming expanded rapidly in the U.S., but momentum for approval of new geographic locations appears to have slowed.

In July 2001, an agreement was reached through which IGT would acquire Anchor Gaming. Subject to various approvals, IGT would acquire Anchor in a stock-swap transaction which was valued in early August at $1.2 billion, including the assumption of $430 million of Anchor debt. Anchor is a joint venture partner with IGT in a portion of its gaming operations business, and also has other operations that include online lottery systems, two casinos in Colorado and another in California.

IGT's gaming operations segment includes proprietary systems that link gaming machines to a central computer, and build progressive jackpots. These systems are located in various markets, and are operated under such names as Megabucks and Quartermania. As of September 30, 2000, there were about 19,200 machines, including joint venture units, on 149 IGT MegaJackpot systems, versus about 15,100 machines on 137 systems a year earlier.

In FY 00 (Sep.), 60% of revenues came from product sales, down from 62% in FY 99. The remainder of revenues were from gaming operations, of which progressive systems are the biggest part.

Product sales in FY 00 included the sale of 107,000 machines, down from 116,000 in FY 99. FY 00 sales included 44,700 machines for the domestic market (likely including Canada), versus about 41,100 in FY 99. Shipments to international markets declined to 62,300 machines in FY 00, from 74,900 the year before. In March 1998, IGT acquired assets of two overseas machine manufacturers. International sales include some lower-priced machines with relatively low value prizes. In addition to machines for casinos, IGT has made video gaming terminals (VGTs) for government-sponsored programs, including lotteries.

In FY 00, IGT spent $55 million (5.5% of revenues) on research and development. IGT's ability to develop successful machines, with features that appeal to gamblers and casinos, should be a significant factor in the level of "replacement" machines it sells. A relatively new IGT product, the EZ Pay Ticket System, enables gaming machines to print and receive tickets, rather than coins.

In FY 00, IGT's earnings included about $0.23 a share from one-time items (primarily from a legal settlement), while FY 99's results included about $0.70 a share of impairment and restructuring charges related to operations in Australia and Brazil.

Per Share Data ($) (Year Ended Sep. 30)	2000	1999	1998	1997	1996	1995	1994	1993	1992	1991
Tangible Bk. Val.	NM	1.03	3.76	4.57	4.96	4.30	3.94	3.03	1.83	1.10
Cash Flow	2.70	1.17	1.69	1.41	1.17	0.92	1.22	1.02	0.69	0.36
Earnings	2.00	0.65	1.33	1.13	0.93	0.71	1.07	0.85	0.54	0.26
Dividends	Nil	0.12	0.12	0.12	0.12	0.12	0.12	0.06	Nil	Nil
Payout Ratio	Nil	18%	9%	11%	13%	17%	11%	7%	Nil	Nil
Prices - High	49.37	24.12	28.68	26.87	23.50	17.00	34.00	41.37	26.37	11.93
- Low	17.43	14.12	16.12	15.25	10.75	10.75	14.87	23.75	10.87	1.84
P/E Ratio - High	25	37	22	24	25	24	32	49	49	46
- Low	9	22	12	13	12	15	14	28	20	7
Income Statement Analysis (Million $)										
Revs.	1,004	930	824	744	733	621	674	478	399	237
Oper. Inc.	343	267	260	226	200	167	218	170	124	57.0
Depr.	54.4	52.3	41.5	35.0	30.5	27.9	20.1	20.2	19.0	12.0
Int. Exp.	102	72.8	41.0	30.4	23.5	20.4	11.8	12.7	13.8	9.2
Pretax Inc.	245	101	235	213	184	145	215	174	108	48.0
Eff. Tax Rate	36%	36%	35%	35%	36%	36%	35%	39%	39%	39%
Net Inc.	157	65.3	152	137	118	92.6	140	106	64.8	30.2
Balance Sheet & Other Fin. Data (Million $)										
Cash	245	426	175	152	231	289	203	217	149	126
Curr. Assets	814	975	671	572	616	607	559	460	323	227
Total Assets	1,624	1,765	1,544	1,215	1,154	972	868	647	490	346
Curr. Liab.	259	213	201	165	127	97.7	78.4	83.7	66.1	42.6
LT Debt	992	990	323	141	107	108	111	61.0	114	113
Common Eqty.	96.6	242	541	520	623	554	521	379	214	124
Total Cap.	1,088	1,233	865	661	730	662	643	456	351	254
Cap. Exp.	18.5	17.8	16.8	33.1	71.6	43.5	73.2	46.1	33.7	22.8
Cash Flow	211	118	194	172	149	121	161	126	83.7	42.2
Curr. Ratio	3.1	4.6	3.3	3.5	4.9	6.2	7.1	5.5	4.9	5.3
% LT Debt of Cap.	91.1	80.3	37.3	21.3	14.7	16.3	17.3	13.3	32.5	44.6
% Net Inc.of Revs.	15.6	7.0	18.5	18.4	16.1	14.9	20.8	22.1	16.2	12.7
% Ret. on Assets	9.3	3.9	11.1	11.6	11.1	10.1	18.1	18.0	15.3	10.9
% Ret. on Equity	92.6	16.7	28.7	24.0	42.1	17.2	30.5	34.8	37.8	28.0

Data as orig reptd.; bef. results of disc opers/spec. items. Per share data adj. for stk. divs. Bold denotes diluted EPS (FASB 128)-prior periods restated. E-Estimated. NA-Not Available. NM-Not Meaningful. NR-Not Ranked.

Office—9295 Prototype Drive, Reno, NV 89511. **Tel**—(775) 448-7777. **Website**—http://www.igt.com **Chrmn**—C. N. Mathewson. **Pres, CEO & COO**—G. T. Baker. **SVP, CFO & Treas**—M. T. Mullarkey. **SVP & Secy**—S. B. Brown. **Investor Contact**—Robert McIver (775-448-0110). **Dirs**—G. T. Baker, R. A. Bittman, A. J. Crosson, W. K. Keating, C. N. Mathewson, R. Miller, F. B. Rentschler, R. A. Schnabel. **Transfer Agent & Registrar**—Bank of New York, NYC. **Incorporated**—in Nevada in 1980. **Empl**— 3,600. **S&P Analyst:** Tom Graves, CFA

STANDARD &POOR'S
STOCK REPORTS

Jones Apparel Group

NYSE Symbol **JNY**

In S&P MidCap 400

18-AUG-01 **Industry:** Textiles (Apparel)

Summary: This company is the world's largest manufacturer of women's apparel, footwear and accessories, with brands such as Jones New York, Nine West, Rena Rowan, and Evan-Picone.

S&P Opinion: Accumulate (★★★★) Recent Price • 32.72 | 52 Wk Range • 47.43-23.31 | Yield • Nil | 12-Mo. P/E • 12.5

Quantitative Evaluations

Outlook (1 Lowest—5 Highest) • **5+**

Fair Value • **42.40**

Risk • **Average**

Earn./Div. Rank • **B+**

Technical Eval. • **Bearish** since 7/01

Rel. Strength Rank (1 Lowest—99 Highest) • **21**

Insider Activity • **Neutral**

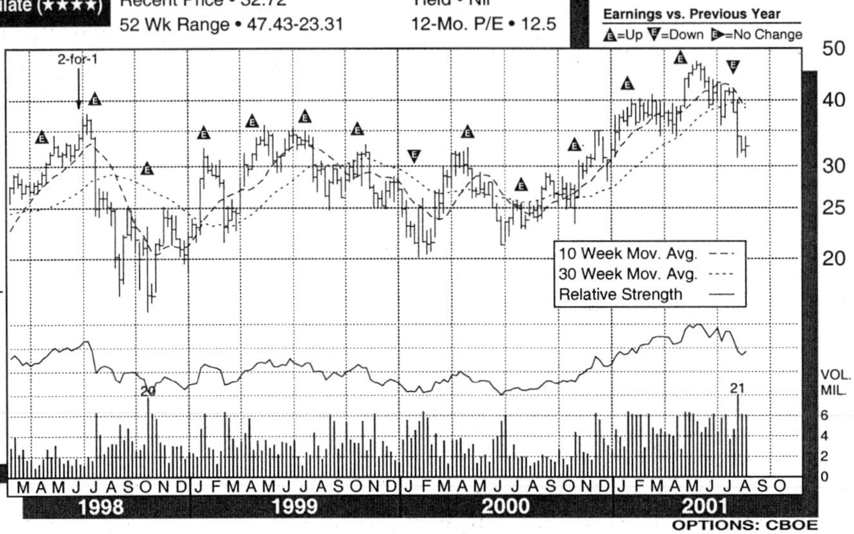

OPTIONS: CBOE

Overview - 01-AUG-01

We expect revenues to be flat in 2001, as contributions from new sales channels and recent acquisitions are offset by divestitures and lower retail same-store sales. Despite a weak economy, the company is continuing to see good sell-throughs of its core wholesale apparel merchandise. Capitalizing on demand for moderately priced apparel, JNY repositioned Bandolino as a moderate priced line, and plans to offer the Evan-Picone line, currently sold through J.C. Penney and May Co., to other chains as well. Nine and Co., a new brand, is also being sold through Kohl's and Mervyn's. Footwear sales have continued to be weak, however, with margins being pressured by heavy discounting. For 2001, savings from the Nine West restructuring, an exit from Asian stores, the elimination of weak products, and ongoing cost control will help boost operating margins. We expect EPS for 2001 to rise 11% to $2.75.

Valuation - 01-AUG-01

We continue to rate JNY shares as accumulate. Following the announcement that earnings per share were weaker than expected for the second quarter of 2001, the stock fell over 14% in one day. However, we believe the fundamentals for JNY remain intact and long-term prospects are favorable. Although results for the second half of 2001 may continue to be pressured by a weak macroeconomic environment, the company is well-positioned to take advantage of an expected economic recovery in early 2002. Indeed, JNY's multi-brand, multi-channel diversification, flexibility to change to keep up with fashion trends, and ability to make successful acquisitions should let earnings grow an average of about 12% annually for at least another three years. As a result, we believe the shares, recently trading at only 10X our EPS estimate of $3.39 for 2002, are attractive for long-term investors.

Key Stock Statistics

S&P EPS Est. 2001	2.75	Tang. Bk. Value/Share	0.16
P/E on S&P Est. 2001	11.9	Beta	1.18
S&P EPS Est. 2002	3.34	Shareholders	365
Dividend Rate/Share	Nil	Market cap. (B)	$ 4.1
Shs. outstg. (M)	123.9	Inst. holdings	85%
Avg. daily vol. (M)	1.984		

Value of $10,000 invested 5 years ago: $ 23,905

Fiscal Year Ending Dec. 31

	2001	2000	1999	1998	1997	1996
Revenues (Million $)						
1Q	1,070	1,082	579.1	383.8	321.5	260.4
2Q	889.0	906.6	510.4	308.6	266.3	193.3
3Q	—	1,192	1,147	500.3	450.5	309.0
4Q	—	962.2	914.5	492.6	349.2	258.4
Yr.	—	4,143	3,151	1,685	1,387	1,021
Earnings Per Share ($)						
1Q	**0.75**	**0.58**	**0.51**	**0.37**	0.28	0.19
2Q	**0.43**	**0.46**	**0.28**	**0.24**	0.18	0.13
3Q	—	**0.93**	**0.59**	**0.57**	0.45	0.29
4Q	—	**0.52**	**0.22**	**0.30**	**0.23**	0.15
Yr.	—	**2.48**	**1.60**	**1.47**	**1.13**	**0.76**

Next earnings report expected: late October

Dividend Data

No cash dividends have been paid.

A Division of The McGraw-Hill Companies

Jones Apparel Group, Inc.

Business Summary - 01-AUG-01

Jones Apparel Group aims to make itself a powerhouse of lifestyle megabrands in various distribution channels. The company designs, contracts for the manufacture of, and markets a broad range of women's career apparel, dresses, shoes, accessories and men's and women's sportswear.

The company's wholesale apparel (53% of 2000 sales) includes career and casual sportswear, jeanswear, dresses, suits, and a combination of all components termed lifestyle collection. Career and casual sportswear is marketed as groups of skirts, pants, jackets, blouses, sweaters and related accessories which, while sold as separates, are coordinated as to styles, color schemes and fabrics, and are designed to be worn together. Products are sold under brand names such as Jones New York, Evan-Picone, Rena Rowan, Todd Oldham, Ralph, Lauren, and Polo Jeans.

Wholesale footwear and accessories operations (23%) include the sale of both brand name and private label footwear and/or accessories through eight branded divisions, the Jervin private label division, and the Accessories division. The Accessories division makes and sells handbags and small leather goods primarily under the Nine West brand. Products are sold under brand names such as Nine West, Bandolino, Easy Spirit, Enzo Angiolini, and Calico.

JNY markets apparel, footwear and accessories directly to consumers through its specialty retail stores (24%) operating in malls, department stores, and urban retail centers worldwide, and in company outlet stores. Following the company's sale of 208 stores on January 1, 2001, as part of its divestiture of Nine West's operations in the United Kingdom, JNY operated 471 specialty retail stores. During 2001 it plans to open 10 to 15 new stores and close 35 to 50 underperforming domestic locations. At December 31, 2000 the company also operated 528 outlet stores in the U.S. and Canada.

Company stores generally sell either footwear, accessories or apparel (or a combination) primarily under their respective brand names. Nine West, Easy Spirit and Enzo Angiolini retail stores offer products not marketed to wholesale customers. Certain of the company's specialty retail stores also sell products licensed by the company, including belts, jewelry, legwear, outerwear, watches and sunglasses.

The company's newest product offering is costume jewelry, an addition emanating from the July 2000 acquisition of Victoria + Co Ltd. and its April 2001 purchase of Judith Jack. Products are sold under such notable brands as Napier, Judith Jack and under licenses from Tommy Hilfiger and Givenchy.

In April 2001, JNY agreed to acquire McNaughton Apparel Group Inc., a leading manufacturer and marketer of moderately-priced apparel, for approximately $572 million in cash and stock.

Per Share Data ($)										
(Year Ended Dec. 31)	**2000**	**1999**	**1998**	**1997**	**1996**	**1995**	**1994**	**1993**	**1992**	**1991**
Tangible Bk. Val.	0.16	NM	2.33	3.98	3.40	2.81	2.13	1.55	1.33	0.87
Cash Flow	3.37	2.05	1.68	1.26	0.83	0.66	0.56	0.49	0.42	0.37
Earnings	2.48	1.60	1.47	1.13	0.75	0.60	0.52	0.46	0.40	0.31
Dividends	Nil	Nil	Nil	Nil	Nil	Nil	Nil	Nil	Nil	Nil
Payout Ratio	Nil	Nil	Nil	Nil	Nil	Nil	Nil	Nil	Nil	Nil
Prices - High	35.00	35.87	37.75	28.71	18.68	9.90	8.93	10.25	10.50	7.46
- Low	20.12	21.50	15.87	16.06	8.90	5.65	5.50	4.65	5.75	3.40
P/E Ratio - High	14	22	26	25	25	17	17	22	26	24
- Low	8	13	11	14	12	9	11	10	14	11
Income Statement Analysis (Million $)										
Revs.	4,143	3,151	1,685	1,387	1,034	787	642	541	437	334
Oper. Inc.	714	431	283	211	139	107	92.1	82.5	70.2	54.9
Depr.	109	53.1	21.2	14.6	8.9	6.7	4.2	3.6	2.7	2.1
Int. Exp.	104	66.9	11.8	3.6	3.0	1.9	1.2	0.7	1.2	2.9
Pretax Inc.	503	315	252	195	128	100	87.3	79.0	66.6	50.1
Eff. Tax Rate	40%	40%	38%	37%	37%	36%	37%	39%	38%	32%
Net Inc.	302	188	155	122	80.8	63.5	54.9	48.4	41.3	34.1
Balance Sheet & Other Fin. Data (Million $)										
Cash	60.5	47.0	129	51.3	30.1	16.9	21.1	27.0	33.0	17.0
Curr. Assets	1,182	1,131	632	441	390	331	261	212	167	117
Total Assets	2,979	2,792	1,189	581	488	401	318	267	185	129
Curr. Liab.	887	661	174	110	96.0	71.0	54.4	52.8	45.1	37.7
LT Debt	576	834	415	27.3	12.1	10.1	8.0	9.6	4.8	5.2
Common Eqty.	1,477	1,241	594	436	377	315	249	189	135	85.8
Total Cap.	2,053	2,075	1,009	463	389	325	257	199	140	91.0
Cap. Exp.	46.8	29.7	48.5	32.1	34.1	16.0	9.5	11.6	7.1	2.5
Cash Flow	411	242	176	136	89.8	70.2	59.1	51.9	44.0	36.2
Curr. Ratio	1.3	1.7	3.6	4.0	4.1	4.7	4.8	4.0	3.7	3.1
% LT Debt of Cap.	28.1	40.2	41.1	5.9	3.1	3.1	3.1	4.8	3.4	5.8
% Net Inc.of Revs.	7.3	6.0	9.2	8.8	7.8	8.1	8.6	8.9	9.5	10.2
% Ret. on Assets	10.5	9.5	17.5	22.8	18.2	17.7	18.7	21.3	26.1	28.6
% Ret. on Equity	22.2	20.5	30.1	30.0	23.4	22.5	24.9	29.7	37.1	52.4

Data as orig. reptd.; bef. results of disc. opers. and/or spec. items. Per share data adj. for stk. divs. as of ex-div. date. Bold denotes diluted EPS (FASB 128). E-Estimated. NA-Not Available. NM-Not Meaningful. NR-Not Ranked.

Office—250 Rittenhouse Circle, Keystone Park, Bristol, PA 19007. **Tel**—(215) 785-4000. **Website**—http://www.jny.com **Chrmn**—S. Kimmel. **Pres**—J. Nemerov. **CFO & Investor Contact**—Wesley R. Card. **Dirs**—H. Gittis, S. Kimmel, J. Nemerov, E. A. Rothfeld, I. Samelman, A. F. Scarpa, G. Stutz. **Transfer Agent & Registrar**—Bank of New York, NYC. **Incorporated**—in Pennsylvania in 1975. **Empl**— 13,860. **S&P Analyst:** M. Carini

STANDARD
&POOR'S
STOCK REPORTS

Lowe's Companies

NYSE Symbol **LOW**

In S&P 500

23-AUG-01

Industry: Retail (Building Supplies)

Summary: This company retails building materials and supplies, lumber, hardware and appliances through more than 60 stores in 40 states.

S&P Opinion: Accumulate (★★★★)

Recent Price • 35.04
52 Wk Range • 39.86-17.12

Yield • 0.2%
12-Mo. P/E • 31.9

Quantitative Evaluations

Outlook
(1 Lowest—5 Highest)
• **3**

Fair Value
• **36.30**

Risk
• **Low**

Earn./Div. Rank
• **A+**

Technical Eval.
• **Neutral** since 8/01

Rel. Strength Rank
(1 Lowest—99 Highest)
• **46**

Insider Activity
• **Unfavorable**

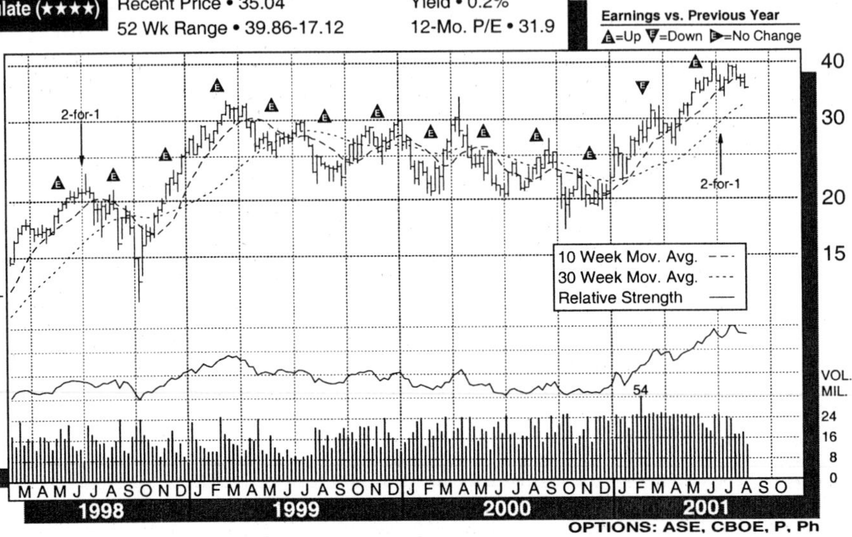

OPTIONS: ASE, CBOE, P, Ph

Overview - 23-AUG-01

We expect sales to rise about 20% in the second half of FY 02 (Jan.), reflecting the addition of about 60 new stores and same-store sales gains of approximately 2% to 4%. Gross margins should benefit from a firming of lumber and building materials prices, better inventory management, and a greater percentage of higher margin installed sales. The conversion of the former Eagle stores into the traditional Lowe's format was completed in the fourth quarter of FY 01. As a result, the company should begin to see improving sales and earnings trends at these locations as FY 02 progresses. Over the longer term, margins should benefit from increased leverage and economies of scale resulting from the addition of new and larger stores that offer a broad selection of merchandise with wider overall margins. We expect EPS to reach $1.25 in FY 02, and see a further gain to $1.50 in FY 03.

Valuation - 23-AUG-01

We continue to recommend investors accumulate LOW shares. The company reported better than expected EPS for the second quarter of FY 02. Same-store sales grew 1.7%, an improvement over the first quarter, when they declined 3%. Furthermore, the company continued to see trends improve as the quarter progressed and now expects same-store sales for the second half of FY 02 to rise about 2% to 4%. The company will experience easier sales and earnings comparisons, as the negative margin impact of lower building material and lumber prices and remerchandising disruptions at the former Eagle stores are alleviated. LOW's aggressive expansion plans, coupled with the maturation of the company's newer, larger stores, should continue to spur earnings growth of approximately 20% to 22% annually for the next several years.

Key Stock Statistics

S&P EPS Est. 2002	1.25	Tang. Bk. Value/Share	7.48
P/E on S&P Est. 2002	28.0	Beta	0.96
S&P EPS Est. 2003	1.48	Shareholders	15,446
Dividend Rate/Share	0.08	Market cap. (B)	$ 29.9
Shs. outstg. (M)	770.7	Inst. holdings	90%
Avg. daily vol. (M)	3.699		

Value of $10,000 invested 5 years ago: $ 37,793

Fiscal Year Ending Jan. 31

	2002	2001	2000	1999	1998	1997
Revenues (Million $)						
1Q	5,276	4,467	3,772	2,900	2,401	1,907
2Q	6,127	5,264	4,435	3,426	3,004	2,459
3Q	—	4,504	3,909	3,004	2,530	2,193
4Q	—	4,544	3,789	2,916	2,398	2,042
Yr.	—	18,779	15,906	12,245	10,137	8,600
Earnings Per Share ($)						
1Q	0.29	0.24	0.17	0.14	0.10	0.07
2Q	0.42	0.36	0.30	0.23	0.18	0.17
3Q	E0.31	0.27	0.22	0.17	0.13	0.11
4Q	E0.23	0.18	0.20	0.15	0.10	0.08
Yr.	E1.25	1.05	0.88	0.68	0.51	0.43

Next earnings report expected: mid November

Dividend Data (Dividends have been paid since 1961.)

Amount ($)	Date Decl.	Ex-Div. Date	Stock of Record	Payment Date
0.035	Sep. 19	Oct. 11	Oct. 13	Oct. 27 '00
0.035	Dec. 05	Jan. 17	Jan. 19	Feb. 02 '01
0.035	Apr. 03	Apr. 18	Apr. 20	May. 04 '01
2-for-1	May. 25	Jul. 02	Jun. 08	Jun. 29 '01

A Division of The McGraw-Hill Companies

Lowe's Companies, Inc.

Business Summary - 23-AUG-01

Lowe's Companies is the second largest U.S. do-it-yourself and home improvement retailer; it competes in the $300 billion, highly fragmented, home improvement industry. Capitalizing on a growing number of U.S. households (now 100 million), and on historically high rates of home ownership, LOW has grown from a chain of 15 stores in FY 62 (Jan.) to 700 stores in 40 states as of August 3, 2001. The company's stores serve both retail and commercial business customers. Retail customers are primarily do-it-yourself homeowners and other buying for personal and family use. Commercial business customers include repair and remodeling contractors, electricians landscapers, painters, plumbers and commercial and residential building maintenance professionals. Approximately 75% of FY 01 sales were to retail customers, with the balance from commercial business customers.

Since 1989, LOW has been transforming its store base from a chain of small stores into a chain of destination home improvement warehouses. The company's current prototype store has a 121,000 sq. ft. sales floor, and another 30,000 sq. ft. dedicated to lawn and garden products. A typical store stocks more than 40,000 items, with hundreds more available through the company's special order system. The company is in the midst of an aggressive expansion plan, opening more than two new stores per week. During FY 02, it expects to open 115 new stores, increasing its square footage by 19%.

The company is also strengthening its presence in metropolitan markets. During FY 01, the company entered nine of these markets; at the end of the year, 18% of its stores were in the top 25 U.S. markets. Sixty-five percent of new stores expected to open in FY 02 will be in metropolitan markets with populations greater than 500,000.

In 1998, the company began a major expansion into the western U.S., with plans to build more than 100 new stores over the next three to four years. In early 1999, LOW acquired Eagle Hardware and Garden, a 41-store chain of home improvement and garden centers in the western U.S. The acquisition accelerated LOW's West Coast expansion, and provided a stepping stone for the company into 10 new states and a number of key metropolitan markets. During FY 01, the company opened 18 stores in the west, with an additional 29 planned in FY 02.

Contributions to sales by product line in recent fiscal years were approximately as follows: fashion plumbing and electrical (12%); appliances (10%); lumber/plywood (9%); outdoor fashion (7%); nursery (7%); floors, windows and walls (7%); millwork (6%); building materials (6%); cabinets/furniture shelving (6%); tools (6%); hardware (6%); rough plumbing and electrical (5%); paint (5%); outdoor power equipment (2%); and other (4%).

Per Share Data ($)										
(Year Ended Jan. 31)	**2001**	**2000**	**1999**	**1998**	**1997**	**1996**	**1995**	**1994**	**1993**	**1992**
Tangible Bk. Val.	7.17	6.14	4.45	3.71	3.20	2.58	2.23	1.48	1.25	1.15
Cash Flow	1.59	1.32	1.07	0.86	0.73	0.58	0.54	0.36	0.26	0.11
Earnings	1.05	0.88	0.68	0.51	0.43	0.35	0.36	0.22	0.14	0.01
Dividends	0.07	0.06	0.06	0.06	0.05	0.05	0.04	0.08	0.04	0.03
Payout Ratio	7%	7%	9%	11%	12%	13%	12%	36%	25%	305%
Cal. Yrs.	2000	1999	1998	1997	1996	1995	1994	1993	1992	1991
Prices - High	33.62	33.21	26.09	12.28	10.87	9.71	10.34	7.48	3.17	2.32
- Low	17.12	21.50	10.79	7.90	7.15	6.50	6.64	3.00	2.00	1.43
P/E Ratio - High	32	38	38	24	25	28	29	34	22	NM
- Low	16	25	16	15	16	18	18	13	14	NM
Income Statement Analysis (Million $)										
Revs.	18,779	15,906	12,245	10,137	8,600	7,075	6,111	4,538	3,846	3,056
Oper. Inc.	1,811	1,511	1,105	865	701	540	481	297	211	151
Depr.	409	337	272	241	198	150	110	80.5	69.8	58.3
Int. Exp.	146	123	95.0	73.3	65.1	54.7	44.8	26.6	19.4	19.9
Pretax Inc.	1,283	1,065	758	559	454	352	344	198	126	5.0
Eff. Tax Rate	37%	37%	36%	36%	36%	35%	35%	34%	33%	NM
Net Inc.	810	673	482	357	292	226	224	132	84.7	6.5
Balance Sheet & Other Fin. Data (Million $)										
Cash	456	491	223	195	70.0	171	268	108	54.8	30.8
Curr. Assets	4,175	3,710	2,586	2,110	1,851	1,604	1,557	1,084	746	770
Total Assets	11,376	9,012	6,345	5,219	4,435	3,556	3,106	2,202	1,609	1,441
Curr. Liab.	2,929	2,386	1,765	1,449	1,349	950	946	681	500	589
LT Debt	2,698	1,727	1,283	1,046	767	866	681	592	314	114
Common Eqty.	5,494	4,695	3,136	2,601	2,217	1,657	1,420	874	733	669
Total Cap.	8,443	6,622	4,579	3,771	3,086	2,607	2,150	1,492	1,063	788
Cap. Exp.	2,332	1,472	928	773	677	520	414	337	243	140
Cash Flow	1,219	1,010	754	598	490	376	333	212	155	65.0
Curr. Ratio	1.4	1.6	1.5	1.5	1.4	1.7	1.6	1.6	1.5	1.3
% LT Debt of Cap.	32.0	26.1	28.0	27.7	24.9	33.3	31.7	39.7	29.5	14.4
% Net Inc.of Revs.	4.3	4.2	3.9	3.5	3.4	3.2	3.7	2.9	2.2	0.2
% Ret. on Assets	7.9	8.4	8.3	7.4	7.3	6.8	8.2	6.9	5.6	0.5
% Ret. on Equity	15.9	16.2	16.8	14.8	15.1	14.7	18.9	16.3	12.1	1.0

Data as orig reptd.; bef. results of disc opers/spec. items. Per share data adj. for stk. divs. Bold denotes diluted EPS (FASB 128)-prior periods restated. E-Estimated. NA-Not Available. NM-Not Meaningful. NR Not Ranked.

Office—1605 Curtis Bridge Road (P.O. Box 1111), North Wilkesboro, NC 28656. **Tel**—(336) 658-4000. **Website**—http://www.lowes.com **Chrmn, Pres & CEO**—R. L. Tillman. **SVP & Secy**—S. A. Hellrung. **SVP, CFO & Investor Contact**—Robert A. Niblock. **Dirs**—L. L. Berry, P. C. Browning, P. Fulton, D. E. Hudson, R. A. Ingram, K. Lewis, R. K. Lochridge, C. B. Malone, T. O'Malley, R. G. Schwartz, R. L. Tillman. **Transfer Agent & Registrar**—EquiServe Trust Co., N.A., Boston. **Incorporated**—in North Carolina in 1952. **Empl**— 94,601. **S&P Analyst:** Maureen C. Carini

STANDARD
&POOR'S
STOCK REPORTS

Mohawk Industries

NYSE Symbol **MHK**

In S&P MidCap 400

18-AUG-01

Industry: Textiles (Home Furnishings)

Summary: This company is the second largest U.S. carpet and rug maker.

S&P Opinion: Accumulate (★★★★)

Recent Price • 43.10
52 Wk Range • 45.45-19.06

Yield • Nil
12-Mo. P/E • 14.8

Quantitative Evaluations

Outlook
(1 Lowest—5 Highest)
• **5+**

Fair Value
• **73.50**

Risk
• **NA**

Earn./Div. Rank
• **B**

Technical Eval.
• **Bullish** since 5/01

Rel. Strength Rank
(1 Lowest—99 Highest)
• **92**

Insider Activity
• **Unfavorable**

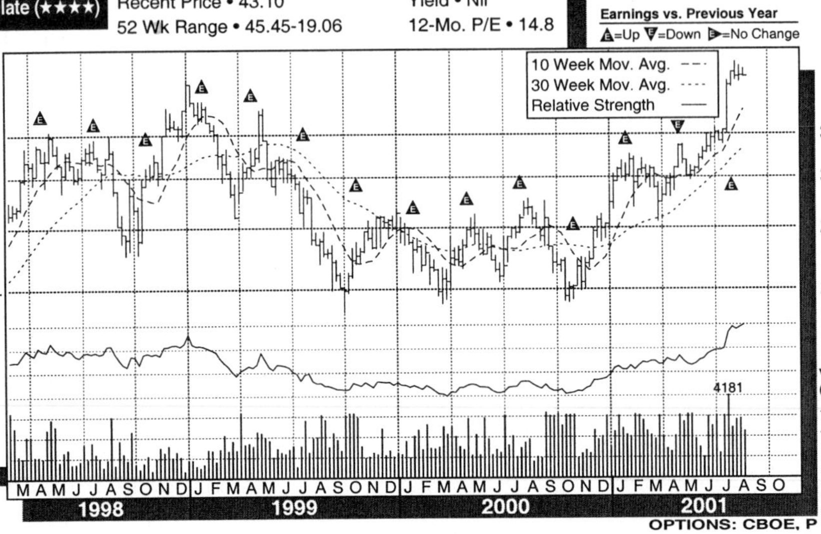

OPTIONS: CBOE, P

Overview - 17-JUL-01

We expect revenue in the second half of 2001 to remain lower than the year-ago level in both residential and commercial carpeting. Although housing sales have been strong, a lag effect will likely prevent a full benefit from occurring in 2001. We look for revenue growth to resume in 2002, helped by pent-up demand and higher consumer confidence, boosted by interest and tax rate cuts. Improved manufacturing efficiencies and cost containment efforts substantially expanded second quarter margins, allowing MHK to counter industry trends. With raw material prices and energy costs trending lower, we expect margins to remain near current improved levels. Up-front costs associated with launching hard surfaces distribution are expected to taper off by year end, and the segment should turn profitable in the first half of 2002. Net income for 2001 is projected at $164.5 million ($3.11 a share), up 1.2% from 2000's level. We expect 2002 earnings to increase to $3.40 per share.

Valuation - 17-JUL-01

We raised our opinion on the stock in July 2001 to accumulate, from avoid, as we expect investors to focus on expanding margins and the possibility of a cyclical rebound in 2002 sales. Also, MHK continues to repurchase shares and reduce debt, boosting EPS. Lower debt levels may encourage the company to resume pursuing acquisitions, as it has done regularly in recent years. With MHK having already built sales staff and distribution channels for hard surface flooring products, any acquisitions in this area would likely be accretive to earnings. We estimate that third quarter 2001 EPS will be about 4.7% above 2000's level, (excluding one time charges), with fourth quarter EPS 11% higher. At less than 12X projected 2002 EPS, we view MHK as attractively priced, particularly in light of the company's earnings growth prospects.

Key Stock Statistics

S&P EPS Est. 2001	3.11	Tang. Bk. Value/Share	12.28
P/E on S&P Est. 2001	13.9	Beta	0.95
S&P EPS Est. 2002	3.40	Shareholders	396
Dividend Rate/Share	Nil	Market cap. (B)	$ 2.3
Shs. outstg. (M)	52.4	Inst. holdings	81%
Avg. daily vol. (M)	0.259		

Value of $10,000 invested 5 years ago: $ 29,554

Fiscal Year Ending Dec. 31

	2001	2000	1999	1998	1997	1996
Revenues (Million $)						
1Q	743.7	765.1	709.2	561.7	412.8	383.7
2Q	828.4	852.8	790.8	662.6	479.2	474.6
3Q	—	838.5	809.9	692.0	500.8	471.2
4Q	—	799.4	775.5	723.0	516.1	465.6
Yr.	—	3,256	3,083	2,639	1,901	1,795
Earnings Per Share ($)						
1Q	**0.51**	**0.61**	**0.46**	**0.25**	0.17	0.11
2Q	**0.88**	**0.87**	**0.72**	**0.58**	0.37	0.32
3Q	**E0.90**	**0.79**	**0.74**	**0.60**	0.40	0.29
4Q	**E0.82**	**0.74**	**0.70**	**0.43**	**0.37**	0.24
Yr.	**E3.11**	**3.00**	**2.61**	**1.86**	**1.30**	**0.95**

Next earnings report expected: mid October

Dividend Data

No cash dividends have been paid.

Mohawk Industries, Inc.

Business Summary - 17-JUL-01

Mohawk Industries is a vertically integrated manufacturer of residential carpeting from extrusion of resin, to spinning of yarn, to weaving and shipping of finished carpet and rugs. The company is the second largest woven and tufted broadloom carpet and rug manufacturer in the U.S.

MHK was organized in 1988 to acquire Mohawk Carpet Corp. from its predecessor owner, Nohasco Corp., in a leveraged buyout. Subsequent to a 1992 initial public offering, MHK expanded the size and scope of its business through the acquisition of a number of companies including Horizon Industries, American Rug Craftsmen, Karastan Bigelow, Aladdin Mills, Galaxy Carpet Mills, Diamond Rug & Carpet Mills, Newmark & James, American Weavers, World Carpets, Image Industries, Durkan Patterned Carpets, and Crown Crafts.

MHK designs, makes and markets hundreds of carpet styles in a broad range of colors, textures and patterns. The company also offers a broad line of hard surface floorcovering products, which include tile, laminate, vinyl and wood, with products positioned in all price ranges. These products are marketed through carpet retailers, home centers, mass merchandisers, department stores, commercial dealers, and to commercial end users.

Broadloom carpet (over six by nine feet in size) accounted for 81% of the volume shipped by the industry in 1999. Tufted broadloom carpet (which refers to the manner of construction) accounted for 95% of broadloom industry volume shipped. The broadloom carpet industry has two primary markets, residential and commercial, with the residential market making up about 74% of industry volume and commercial comprising 26% in 1999. An estimated 55% of industry shipments are made in response to replacement demand, which usually involves exact yardage (or "cut order") shipments that provide wider profit margins than sale of carpet sold in full rolls.

Sales to residential customers provide a significant portion of total industry sales, and a majority of the company's total sales. MHK markets more than 750 residential products to more than 30,000 customers through its regional sales forces. Product distribution is conducted through regional hub-and-spoke networks. Carpet is delivered from mill sites to regional warehouses, and from there it is shipped to local distribution warehouses, then retailers.

The commercial market is segmented into several sub-markets: educational institutions, corporate office space, hospitality facilities, retail space and health care facilities. In addition, the company produces and sells carpet for the export market, the federal government and other niche businesses. The company believes that it is the largest producer of woven carpet in the U.S. and that it has several carpet weaving machines and processes that no other manufacturer has. This allows the company to differentiate itself from other manufacturers of commercial carpet.

Per Share Data ($) (Year Ended Dec. 31)	2000	1999	1998	1997	1996	1995	1994	1993	1992	1991
Tangible Bk. Val.	12.28	10.21	8.73	6.78	6.65	4.43	4.25	3.86	2.90	0.97
Cash Flow	4.51	4.35	3.03	2.43	2.01	1.17	1.65	1.55	0.89	0.66
Earnings	3.00	2.61	1.86	1.30	0.95	0.13	0.66	0.77	0.57	0.34
Dividends	Nil	Nil	Nil	Nil	Nil	Nil	Nil	Nil	Nil	Nil
Payout Ratio	Nil	Nil	Nil	Nil	Nil	Nil	Nil	Nil	Nil	Nil
Prices - High	29.12	42.00	42.43	22.00	18.58	12.83	24.33	23.16	9.58	NA
- Low	18.93	18.37	20.50	12.91	8.33	7.25	7.16	8.77	4.83	NA
P/E Ratio - High	10	16	23	17	20	NM	37	30	17	NA
- Low	6	7	11	10	9	NM	11	11	8	NA
Income Statement Analysis (Million $)										
Revs.	3,256	3,083	2,639	1,901	1,795	1,649	1,437	734	353	279
Oper. Inc.	399	400	299	209	179	137	148	74.4	33.5	25.9
Depr.	82.3	105	67.9	59.3	55.1	52.6	49.5	22.7	7.1	5.3
Int. Exp.	38.0	32.6	29.3	26.5	31.5	35.0	27.1	13.7	5.2	9.9
Pretax Inc.	268	260	182	112	82.7	10.5	58.2	39.3	21.6	10.5
Eff. Tax Rate	39%	40%	41%	39%	41%	39%	43%	42%	40%	39%
Net Inc.	163	157	108	68.0	49.0	6.4	33.0	22.7	13.1	6.4
Balance Sheet & Other Fin. Data (Million $)										
Cash	NA	Nil	Nil	Nil	Nil	Nil	Nil	Nil	Nil	2.9
Curr. Assets	1,024	934	807	573	556	508	454	287	166	78.0
Total Assets	1,793	1,683	1,331	961	961	903	855	561	278	116
Curr. Liab.	597	374	388	236	245	263	162	134	67.9	33.4
LT Debt	365	562	322	257	346	342	394	244	114	59.0
Common Eqty.	754	693	587	406	333	275	264	159	89.3	15.9
Total Cap.	1,196	1,308	938	692	706	638	691	426	208	81.0
Cap. Exp.	73.5	146	78.4	31.7	42.0	36.0	78.0	33.9	7.7	4.8
Cash Flow	245	263	176	127	104	59.0	82.5	45.4	20.0	11.0
Curr. Ratio	1.7	2.5	2.1	2.4	2.3	1.9	2.8	2.2	2.4	2.3
% LT Debt of Cap.	30.6	43.0	34.3	37.2	49.0	53.5	57.0	57.2	54.7	72.1
% Net Inc.of Revs.	5.0	5.1	4.1	3.6	2.7	0.4	2.3	3.1	3.7	2.3
% Ret. on Assets	9.4	10.2	9.4	7.1	5.3	0.7	3.6	5.1	5.8	5.3
% Ret. on Equity	22.5	24.1	21.7	18.4	16.1	2.4	12.3	17.1	23.0	43.7

Data as orig reptd.; bef. results of disc opers/spec. items. Per share data adj. for stk. divs. Bold denotes diluted EPS (FASB 128)-prior periods restated. E-Estimated. NA-Not Available. NM-Not Meaningful. NR-Not Ranked.

Office—160 S. Industrial Blvd., P.O. Box 12069, Calhoun, GA 30703. **Tel**—(706) 629-7721. **Website**—http://www.mohawkind.com **Chrmn & CEO**—D. L. Kolb. **Pres & COO**—J. S. Lorberbaum. **VP-Fin, CFO & Investor Contact**—John D. Swift. **Secy**—B. B. Lance. **Dirs**—L. Benatar, B. C. Bruckmann, D. L. Kolb, J. S. Lorberbaum, L. W. McCurdy, R. N. Pokelwaldt, S. H. Sharpe. **Transfer Agent & Registrar**—First Union National Bank of North Carolina, Charlotte. **Incorporated**—in Delaware in 1988. **Empl**— 24,005. **S&P Analyst:** Raymond Mathis

STANDARD & POOR'S STOCK REPORTS

Pacific Sunwear of California

Nasdaq Symbol **PSUN**

In S&P SmallCap 600

18-AUG-01

Industry: Retail (Specialty-Apparel)

Summary: This company is a leading mall-based specialty retailer of everyday casual apparel, accessories and footwear designed for active teens and young adults.

S&P Opinion: Accumulate (★★★★)

Recent Price • 17.20
52 Wk Range • 35.87-12.56
Yield • Nil
12-Mo. P/E • 18.1

Quantitative Evaluations

Outlook (1 Lowest—5 Highest) • **5**

Fair Value • **24.30**

Risk • **Average**

Earn./Div. Rank • **NR**

Technical Eval. • **Bearish** since 7/01

Rel. Strength Rank (1 Lowest—99 Highest) • **15**

Insider Activity • **Neutral**

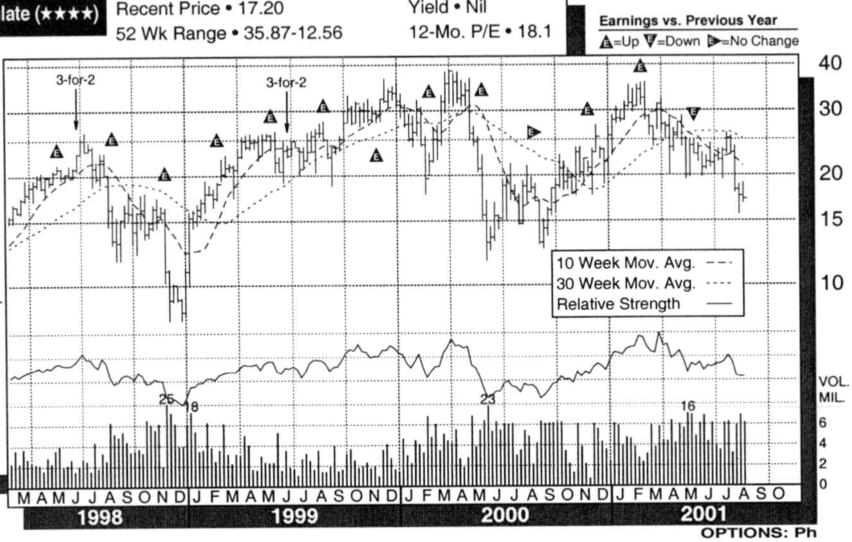

OPTIONS: Ph

Overview - 16-AUG-01

We expect total sales to grow 20% to 22% in FY 02 (Jan.), aided by 130 new locations, and by same-store sales gains of about 2%. Same-store sales slid 7.3% in the second quarter, reflecting the continued impact of a sluggish economy, and ongoing weakness in mens' bottoms. However, PSUN has been seeing a positive response to its back-to-school merchandise assortment which includes a higher mix of denim, more product sold at opening price points, and new brands. A new partnership with Hurley, a hot brand, is breathing some life into an otherwise lackluster men's sales environment. While the men's business is likely to remain difficult for the rest of the year, the girls' division should post modest gains. Margins, which narrowed during the first half, due to increased markdowns taken to clear out excess inventory, should improve as the year progresses. We expect EPS to grow 39%, to $1.60 in FY 03, from an estimated $1.15 in FY 02.

Valuation - 16-AUG-01

We continue to recommend investors accumulate PSUN shares. The shares have been volatile in 2001, reflecting conflicting investor sentiment between concerns over the effect of a weaker economy on consumer spending and optimism about the company's prospects for an earnings rebound in the second half. Despite a challenging first half, we believe PSUN has made strides in moving stagnant inventory out of its stores and positioning itself for future growth. We expect a more favorable merchandise mix and recent interest rate cuts to further boost sales. The shares were recently trading at about 17X our FY 01 EPS estimate of $1.15, a significant discount to PSUN's projected five-year growth rate of 21%. We believe P/E multiple expansion is likely, as investors focus on expected improvement in operations during the second half.

Key Stock Statistics

S&P EPS Est. 2002	1.15	Tang. Bk. Value/Share	6.52
P/E on S&P Est. 2002	15.0	Beta	1.24
S&P EPS Est. 2003	1.60	Shareholders	5,000
Dividend Rate/Share	Nil	Market cap. (B)	$0.563
Shs. outstg. (M)	32.7	Inst. holdings	0%
Avg. daily vol. (M)	1.574		

Value of $10,000 invested 5 years ago: $ 42,259

Fiscal Year Ending Jan. 31

	2002	2001	2000	1999	1998	1997
Revenues (Million $)						
1Q	137.7	112.6	81.44	61.16	38.93	27.64
2Q	156.5	132.0	100.5	73.20	48.33	34.57
3Q	—	163.7	124.0	91.78	65.31	43.25
4Q	—	181.2	130.9	94.98	74.56	49.81
Yr.	—	589.4	436.8	321.1	227.1	155.3
Earnings Per Share ($)						
1Q	**0.03**	**0.18**	**0.13**	**0.09**	**0.04**	**0.00**
2Q	**0.11**	**0.23**	**0.23**	**0.15**	**0.09**	**0.05**
3Q	—	**0.39**	**0.38**	**0.25**	**0.18**	**0.10**
4Q	—	**0.43**	**0.36**	**0.24**	**0.20**	**0.12**
Yr.	—	**1.22**	**1.10**	**0.73**	**0.53**	**0.26**

Next earnings report expected: early November

Dividend Data

No cash dividends have been paid. The shares were split three for two in October 1997, June 1998 and June 1999.

Pacific Sunwear of California, Inc.

Business Summary - 16-AUG-01

Pacific Sunwear of California has grown since 1980 from a Newport Beach, CA, surf shop selling surfboards and wax, to become a leading mall-based specialty retailer of everyday casual apparel, accessories and footwear designed to meet the needs of active teens and young adults.

As of August 5, 2001, the company was operating 677 stores, primarily in regional shopping malls, in 48 states and Puerto Rico. There were 523 PacSun stores, 63 PacSun outlet stores, and 91 d.e.m.o. stores. The stores were concentrated in the Northeast, Midwest, Southeast and California.

Customers are primarily young men aged 12 to 24, as well as young women of the same age, who generally prefer a casual look. PSUN believes its stores are differentiated by a carefully edited selection of popular and emerging brands, offered together with its own private brands.

Pacific Sunwear stores, the company's original and primary store format (also referred to as PacSun), average approximately 3,000 sq. ft. and offer a complete selection of shirts, shorts, pants, overshirts, sweatshirts, outerwear, footwear and accessories in order to satisfy the casual wardrobe needs of its customers. In each merchandise classification, Pacific Sunwear stores offer a broad selection, with the goal of being viewed by customers as the dominant retailer in their niche. Pacific Sunwear stores are located primarily in enclosed regional shopping malls.

The company's Pacific Sunwear outlet stores average approximately 4,000 sq. ft., and are located in value-oriented outlet malls, both open-air and enclosed. The stores offer a selection similar to that of the Pacific Sunwear mall stores, with emphasis on value pricing. Merchandise at Pacific Sunwear Outlets consists primarily of off-price brand merchandise, private-brand merchandise, and a smaller selection of full-priced branded merchandise.

The company's d.e.m.o. concept, introduced in FY 98 (Jan.), offers a broad assortment of hip hop music inspired casual apparel and accessories that primarily target young men aged 16 to 24, and, to a lesser extent, young women. There is no merchandise overlap with Pacific Sunwear stores or Pacific Sunwear Outlets.

PSUN's goal is to be the dominant nationwide specialty retailer of everyday casual apparel, footwear and accessories catering to the teen market. Its strategy includes offering a broad assortment, promoting the Pacific Sunwear and d.e.m.o. brand images, actively managing merchandise trends, maintaining strong vendor relationships, and providing attentive customer service. The company plans to open 125 new stores in FY 02: 85 PacSun stores, 20 outlet stores, and 20 d.e.m.o. locations.

Per Share Data ($)										
(Year Ended Jan. 31)	**2001**	**2000**	**1999**	**1998**	**1997**	**1996**	**1995**	**1994**	**1993**	**1992**
Tangible Bk. Val.	6.36	4.92	3.55	2.87	1.71	1.40	1.32	1.20	1.16	NA
Cash Flow	1.83	1.54	1.05	0.76	0.45	0.38	0.37	0.25	0.34	NA
Earnings	1.22	1.10	0.73	0.53	0.26	0.10	0.14	0.10	0.17	NA
Dividends	NA	Nil	Nil	Nil	Nil	Nil	Nil	Nil	Nil	NA
Payout Ratio	NA	Nil	Nil	Nil	Nil	Nil	Nil	Nil	Nil	NA
Cal. Yrs.	2000	1999	1998	1997	1996	1995	1994	1993	1992	1991
Prices - High	NA	36.75	26.25	15.33	8.74	3.06	3.50	3.55	NA	NA
- Low	NA	9.91	8.00	6.14	1.38	1.08	1.43	1.13	NA	NA
P/E Ratio - High	NA	33	36	29	33	31	24	34	NA	NA
- Low	NA	9	11	12	5	11	10	10	NA	NA
Income Statement Analysis (Million $)										
Revs.	589	437	321	227	155	113	85.3	54.9	45.8	NA
Oper. Inc.	83.5	70.8	48.3	32.7	17.3	8.4	8.7	5.7	5.9	NA
Depr.	19.9	14.3	10.4	6.9	5.3	4.3	2.9	1.7	1.3	NA
Int. Exp.	Nil	Nil	Nil	Nil	Nil	Nil	0.1	-0.4	0.1	NA
Pretax Inc.	65.0	57.4	38.9	27.1	12.2	4.2	6.1	4.3	3.9	NA
Eff. Tax Rate	39%	39%	40%	40%	39%	38%	37%	37%	22%	NA
Net Inc.	39.8	35.3	23.5	16.4	7.4	2.6	3.9	2.7	3.0	NA
Balance Sheet & Other Fin. Data (Million $)										
Cash	29.0	32.4	19.0	14.8	10.0	4.3	2.0	0.7	2.7	NA
Curr. Assets	128	104	70.1	66.9	34.9	23.7	23.3	23.1	8.2	NA
Total Assets	277	209	148	122	65.7	51.5	45.3	36.7	15.9	NA
Curr. Liab.	47.8	36.8	22.6	18.8	13.2	8.9	6.8	4.1	3.6	NA
LT Debt	1.1	Nil	Nil	Nil	Nil	0.4	0.8	Nil	NA	NA
Common Eqty.	213	162	117	97.7	47.9	38.5	35.6	31.2	1.0	NA
Total Cap.	215	162	118	99	49.4	38.8	36.4	31.2	NA	NA
Cap. Exp.	60.4	40.2	31.6	21.0	8.1	9.8	11.5	7.8	NA	NA
Cash Flow	59.6	49.6	34.0	23.3	12.7	6.9	6.7	4.3	4.2	NA
Curr. Ratio	2.7	2.8	3.1	3.6	2.6	2.7	3.4	5.6	2.3	NA
% LT Debt of Cap.	0.5	Nil	Nil	Nil	Nil	1.0	2.1	Nil	NA	NA
% Net Inc.of Revs.	6.7	8.1	7.3	7.2	4.8	2.3	4.5	4.9	6.6	NA
% Ret. on Assets	16.3	19.8	17.4	17.5	12.7	5.4	9.4	10.3	NA	NA
% Ret. on Equity	21.2	25.3	21.9	22.5	17.2	7.1	11.5	16.5	NA	NA

Data as orig reptd.; bef. results of disc opers/spec. items. Per share data adj. for stk. divs. Bold denotes diluted EPS (FASB 128)-prior periods restated. E-Estimated. NA-Not Available. NM-Not Meaningful. NR-Not Ranked.

Office—5200 East La Palma Ave., Anaheim, CA 92807. **Tel**—(714) 693-8066. **Website**—www.pacsun.com.com **Chrmn & CEO**—G. H. Weaver. **Pres**—T. M. Harmon. **SVP, CFO & Secy**—C. W. Womack. **Dirs**—P. C. Cummin III, S. F. Kasaks, P. L. Harris, J. Jensen III, G. H. Weaver. **Transfer Agent & Registrar**—U.S. Stock Transfer Corp., Glendale, CA. **Incorporated**—in California in 1982. **Empl**— 7,100. **S&P Analyst:** Maureen C. Carini

STANDARD & POOR'S STOCK REPORTS

Salton, Inc.

NYSE Symbol **SFP**

In S&P SmallCap 600

18-AUG-01 **Industry:** Housewares

Summary: This company is a leading designer, marketer and distributor of small appliances and tabletop products.

S&P Opinion: Accumulate (★★★★) Recent Price • 18.20 | 52 Wk Range • 41.50-12.85 | Yield • Nil | 12-Mo. P/E • 4.0

Quantitative Evaluations

Outlook (1 Lowest—5 Highest)
• **5**

Fair Value
• **34.60**

Risk
• **Average**

Earn./Div. Rank
• **B-**

Technical Eval.
• **Bearish** since 6/01

Rel. Strength Rank (1 Lowest—99 Highest)
• **51**

Insider Activity
• **NA**

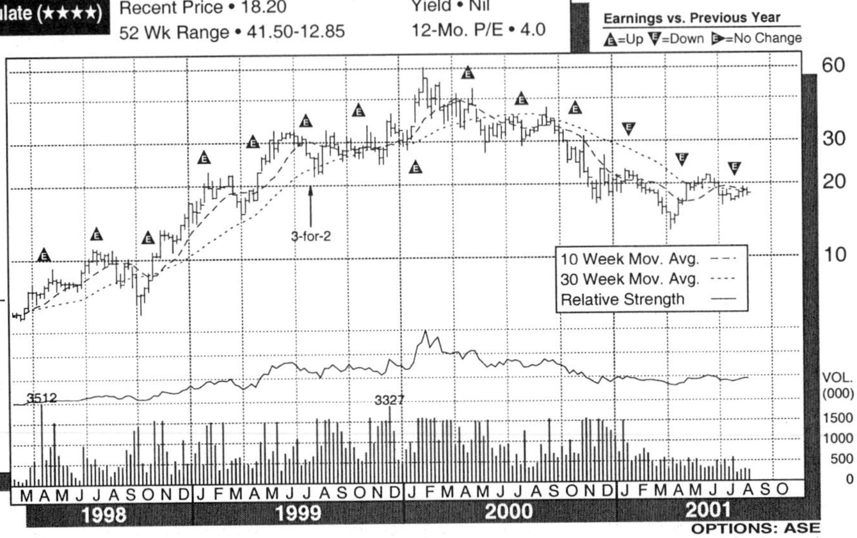

Overview - 17-MAY-01

We expect revenues to decrease 7% in FY 01 (Jun.), as the introduction of new products, including a new outdoor grill under the George Foreman brand, is offset by economic softening. In FY 02, we see top-line growth of about 3%, fueled by a steady stream of new product introductions. In addition, international sales (10% of total) should be boosted by the company's offer to acquire Pifco Holdings PLC. If consummated, the deal should allow for cross-sell opportunities in Europe and the U.S. We expect margins to narrow in FY 01 due to weakened product demand, higher freight costs and additional warehouse space. In the long term, margins will benefit from SG&A leverage related to the acquisition of the rights to the George Foreman name. We expect EPS of $4.17 in FY 01, followed by growth of 6% in FY 02, to $4.44, as operations and the economy likely recover.

Valuation - 17-MAY-01

SFP shares have retreated from their all-time high reached in early 2000, and were recently selling at 5.1X our calendar 2001 EPS estimate of $3.94. The shares are deeply discounted to the company's houseware industry peers in the S&P Super 1500 Index, which enjoy a P/E of 13.4. The shares are also discounted to our expectation for long-term growth of 10%. We attribute the stock's recent weakness to the deceleration of economic growth. Also, we believe the market is wary of Salton's ability to follow up on its successful George Foreman Grill products, but we see promise in the product pipeline. Market share may open up as well, as Sunbeam, SFP's competitor, recently filed for Chapter 11 bankruptcy. We believe the shares will benefit from a lower interest rate environment. Following 13 initial interest rate cuts since 1971, the S&P Household Products (Non-Durables) Index rose an average of 11.7%, in line with the S&P 500's average rise of 12.3%.

Key Stock Statistics

S&P EPS Est. 2001	4.17	Tang. Bk. Value/Share	4.12
P/E on S&P Est. 2001	4.4	Beta	1.42
S&P EPS Est. 2002	4.44	Shareholders	340
Dividend Rate/Share	Nil	Market cap. (B)	$0.208
Shs. outstg. (M)	11.4	Inst. holdings	58%
Avg. daily vol. (M)	0.050		

Value of $10,000 invested 5 years ago: $ 49,840

Fiscal Year Ending Jun. 30

	2001	2000	1999	1998	1997	1996
Revenues (Million $)						
1Q	207.3	196.3	104.4	65.77	34.86	23.28
2Q	262.2	292.8	142.7	102.2	58.84	36.37
3Q	153.6	172.1	124.3	68.10	41.69	20.19
4Q	—	176.1	134.7	69.57	47.42	19.36
Yr.	—	837.3	506.1	305.6	182.8	99.2
Earnings Per Share ($)						
1Q	**1.35**	**0.95**	**0.68**	**0.21**	**0.06**	0.11
2Q	**1.60**	**3.08**	**0.83**	**0.27**	**0.20**	0.24
3Q	**0.60**	**0.95**	**0.36**	**0.14**	**-0.03**	-0.07
4Q	**E0.67**	**0.98**	**0.48**	**0.37**	Nil	0.19
Yr.	**E4.17**	**5.91**	**2.37**	**0.99**	**0.23**	**0.46**

Next earnings report expected: mid September

Dividend Data

No cash dividends have been paid.

Salton, Inc.

Business Summary - 17-MAY-01

Most Americans have seen George Foreman selling grills on late-night infomercials, but do they know who actually manufacturers these widely popular products? The answer is Salton, a leading designer, marketer and distributor of a broad range of branded, high quality small appliances, tabletop products, and personal care and time products. The company believes it has the leading domestic market share in toasters, juice extractors, indoor grills, bread bakers, griddles, waffle makers and buffet ranges/hotplates.

In addition to the Salton name, some of the company's more recognizable brand names include Toastmaster, Maxim, Breadman, Juiceman, White-Westinghouse, Farberware, Melitta, Block, Atlantis, Sasaki, Rejuvenique, Ingraham, Timex, Indiglo, Calvin Klein, Sonex, Stiffel and Relaxor. The company is also a leading designer and distributor of small appliances in the U.S. under the names Kenmore and Magic Chef.

Typically, the company sells its products to mass merchandisers, department stores, specialty stores and mail order catalogs. Salton also sells certain of its products directly to consumers through infomercials and its website. The company's customers include such well known names as Kmart, Target Corp., Sears, Wal-Mart, Federated, May, QVC, Service Merchandise, Kohls and Bed, Bath and Beyond. In FY 00 (Jun.), Salton's five largest customers accounted for 46% of total revenues.

Among Salton's key strategies is the continuous introduction of new products. The company's product designers strive to develop new products and product line extensions that provide added value to consumers through enhanced functionality and improved aesthetics. During FY 00, Salton introduced 1,607 new stock keeping units (SKU), or products.

Another key strategy is growth through acquisitions, with a focus on companies that offer expansion into related or existing product categories, leverage Salton's existing distribution channels or provide growth into new distribution channels. Recent acquisitions include: Toastmaster, a manufacturer and marketer of kitchen and small appliances and time products; certain assets of Sasaki, Inc., a designer of high-quality tabletop products and accessories for the home; Sonex International Corp., a designer/distributor of electrically operated toothbrushes; certain assets and intellectual property of The Stiffel Co., a designer of lamps and related products; and the Relaxor brand business and certain inventory, including personal massagers and other personal care items.

One of Salton's hottest selling product lines over the past few years has been that associated with George Foreman, particularly the indoor grill. In late 1999, the company acquired the right to use the "George Foreman" name and image in connection with the marketing and sale of food preparation appliances. The aggregate purchase price payable to George Foreman and his partners was about $113,750,000, payable in five annual installments, an d 779,191 shares of common stock.

Per Share Data ($) (Year Ended Jun. 30)	2000	1999	1998	1997	1996	1995	1994	1993	1992	1991
Tangible Bk. Val.	4.12	0.80	2.67	1.73	1.67	1.20	1.00	NA	2.15	2.79
Cash Flow	7.14	2.87	1.20	0.38	0.68	0.30	-0.18	NA	-0.54	0.25
Earnings	5.91	2.37	0.99	0.23	0.46	0.07	-0.39	NA	NA	NA
Dividends	Nil	Nil	Nil	Nil	Nil	Nil	Nil	NA	NA	NA
Payout Ratio	Nil	Nil	Nil	Nil	Nil	Nil	Nil	NA	NA	NA
Prices - High	60.87	39.43	17.16	7.33	5.83	3.00	2.33	NA	4.50	8.50
- Low	16.56	14.00	5.33	3.75	1.50	1.08	0.83	NA	1.33	2.66
P/E Ratio - High	10	17	17	29	12	40	NM	NA	d	25
- Low	3	6	5	16	3	14	NM	NA	d	21
Income Statement Analysis (Million $)										
Revs.	837	506	306	183	99	77.0	48.8	NA	48.7	52.7
Oper. Inc.	195	76.7	32.8	13.6	7.3	5.7	0.7	NA	-1.1	6.8
Depr.	19.1	7.3	4.3	3.1	2.2	2.0	1.6	NA	1.5	1.2
Int. Exp.	28.8	15.5	5.3	4.1	3.9	3.1	2.0	NA	2.3	3.2
Pretax Inc.	147	53.9	32.2	6.4	1.1	0.7	-2.9	NA	-4.9	2.4
Eff. Tax Rate	37%	36%	38%	31%	NM	2.98%	NM	NA	NA	18%
Net Inc.	91.8	34.5	20.0	4.4	4.6	0.7	-2.9	NA	-4.9	0.7
Balance Sheet & Other Fin. Data (Million $)										
Cash	7.6	11.2	0.7	2.6	Nil	Nil	0.0	NA	0.0	0.0
Curr. Assets	371	261	128	76.8	48.0	34.0	32.8	NA	36.0	26.1
Total Assets	564	328	141	102	59.5	41.1	38.6	NA	40.7	30.3
Curr. Liab.	173	95.1	83.2	58.8	35.8	24.9	23.5	NA	20.9	23.5
LT Debt	215	182	Nil	Nil	Nil	NA	NA	NA	NA	NA
Common Eqty.	174	50.7	57.7	38.6	19.9	15.3	10.7	NA	16.8	0.1
Total Cap.	391	233	58.2	38.6	19.9	NA	NA	NA	NA	NA
Cap. Exp.	14.0	5.4	4.7	4.6	4.3	NA	NA	NA	NA	NA
Cash Flow	111	41.8	24.3	7.5	6.8	2.6	-1.4	NA	-3.3	1.8
Curr. Ratio	2.1	2.7	1.5	1.3	1.3	1.4	1.4	NA	1.7	1.1
% LT Debt of Cap.	54.9	78.2	NA	Nil	Nil	NA	NA	NA	NA	NA
% Net Inc.of Revs.	11.0	6.8	6.5	2.4	4.6	0.8	NM	NA	NA	1.3
% Ret. on Assets	20.6	14.7	16.4	5.4	9.1	1.6	NM	NA	NA	NA
% Ret. on Equity	81.8	63.7	41.5	15.0	26.1	5.0	NM	NA	NA	NA

Data as orig reptd.; bef. results of disc opers/spec. items. Per share data adj. for stk. divs. Bold denotes diluted EPS (FASB 128)-prior periods restated. E-Estimated. NA-Not Available. NM-Not Meaningful. NR-Not Ranked.

Office—550 Business Center Drive, Mount Prospect, IL 60056. **Tel**—(847) 803-4600. **Fax**—(847) 803-1186. **Website**—http://www.saltoninc.com **Chrmn**—D. C. Sabin. **CEO**—L. Dreimann. **SVP-Fin & CFO**—J. Thompson. **Pres, COO & Treas**—W. B. Rue. **Dirs**—R. A. Bergmann, F. Devine, B. Doornmalen, B. G. Pollack, D. C. Sabin. **Transfer Agent & Registrar**—LaSalle National Bank, Chicago. **Incorporated**—in Delaware. **Empl**—1,395. **S&P Analyst:** Markos N. Kaminis

STANDARD
&POOR'S
STOCK REPORTS

Scholastic Corp.

Nasdaq Symbol **SCHL**

In S&P MidCap 400

18-AUG-01

Industry: Publishing

Summary: This company is a leading publisher and distributor of children's books, classroom and professional magazines, and other educational materials.

S&P Opinion: Accumulate (★★★★)

Recent Price • 37
52 Wk Range • 49-31.18
Yield • Nil
12-Mo. P/E • 16.5

Quantitative Evaluations

Outlook
(1 Lowest—5 Highest)
• 3⁻

Fair Value
• 39.60

Risk
• High

Earn./Div. Rank
• B

Technical Eval.
• Bearish since 7/01

Rel. Strength Rank
(1 Lowest—99 Highest)
• 36

Insider Activity
• NA

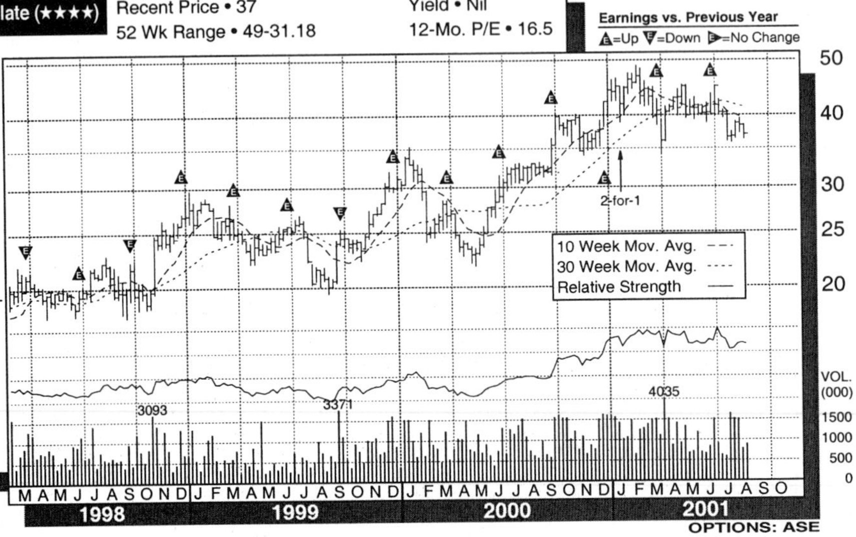

OPTIONS: ASE

Overview - 19-JUN-01

Despite the absence of new Harry Potter books until perhaps late in 2002, SCHL could sustain modest revenue gains in FY 02 (May), thanks to its increasingly popular supplemental reading programs for the educational market, an ever-growing slate of new products and services that include expansion in software offerings, and strength in its other trade book series. In April 2001, SCHL discontinued its basal textbook reading program, and incurred a mostly non-cash charge of between $1.05 and $1.15 a share. The reading program accounted for 2% of revenues, but its impact will be earnings neutral in FY 02. Its absence will favorably impact earnings and cash flow in FY 03. SCHL expects Grolier, which was acquired in June 2000, to be accretive by $0.15 to $0.20 a share in FY 02. We expect FY 02 EPS to rise 13% to $2.63 from the $2.32 estimated for FY 01.

Valuation - 19-JUN-01

The shares, which were recently off 5%, year to date, are attractively priced for long term capital gains. At 17.8X our FY 01 EPS estimate of $2.32 (before the reading program writeoff), and 15.7X the $2.63 projected for FY 02, SCHL is trading toward the low end of its historical P/E range. Since 1997, Scholastic's management has successfully refocused the company, emphasizing sustainable revenue and margin growth in its four core businesses. Management has instituted a strong focus on literacy and technology-based educational products, and on branded children's publishing properties that can be developed for television and multimedia. Healthy top line growth, combined with benefits from the Grolier acquisition, continuing cost control efforts, and emphasis on higher margin businesses, should contribute to average earnings growth in the high teens over the next five years.

Key Stock Statistics

S&P EPS Est. 2000	1.60	Tang. Bk. Value/Share	6.74
P/E on S&P Est. 2000	23.1	Beta	0.67
S&P EPS Est. 2001	2.24	Shareholders	5,000
Dividend Rate/Share	Nil	Market cap. (B)	$ 1.2
Shs. outstg. (M)	35.1	Inst. holdings	74%
Avg. daily vol. (M)	0.240		

Value of $10,000 invested 5 years ago: $ 11,202

Fiscal Year Ending May 31

	2001	2000	1999	1998	1997	1996
Revenues (Million $)						
1Q	362.1	180.0	150.2	166.6	158.6	135.2
2Q	668.3	507.8	403.2	354.8	342.2	294.6
3Q	433.0	312.8	267.3	239.0	210.7	216.1
4Q	—	394.0	334.0	297.9	254.8	282.7
Yr.	—	1,403	1,155	1,058	966.3	928.6
Earnings Per Share ($)						
1Q	**-0.31**	**-0.71**	**-0.54**	-0.41	-0.44	-0.31
2Q	**1.48**	**1.15**	**0.91**	0.80	1.18	0.96
3Q	—	**0.06**	**0.01**	**-0.10**	**0.39**	0.28
4Q	—	**0.86**	**0.64**	**0.41**	-0.36	0.05
Yr.	—	**1.48**	**1.10**	**0.72**	**0.01**	0.98

Next earnings report expected: NA

Dividend Data

Amount ($)	Date Decl.	Ex-Div. Date	Stock of Record	Payment Date
2-for-1	Dec. 14	Jan. 17	Dec. 29	Jan. 16 '01

A Division of The McGraw·Hill Companies

Scholastic Corporation

Business Summary - 19-JUN-01

Scholastic (SCHL) is a leading publisher and distributor of children's books, classroom and professional magazines, and other educational materials, with operations in the U.S., Canada, the U.K., Australia, New Zealand, Mexico, India, Ireland, Argentina and Southeast Asia. It also publishes educational computer software and produces family-oriented video and TV programming. For the most part, products are distributed directly to children and teachers in grade schools.

The company acquired Grolier Inc. in June 2000. Grolier is the leading operator of U.S. direct-to-home book clubs for children (mainly age five and under), and is the leading print and on-line publisher of children's non-fiction and reference products (including Children's Press and Franklin Watts imprints in the U.S., and major encyclopedias) sold primarily to U.S. school libraries. Grolier publishes children's books under the Orchard Books imprint for distribution through trade channels. It also has significant international operations in the U.K., Canada and Southeast Asia.

SCHL operates four core businesses: Children's Books (62% of FY 00 (May) revenues), Instructional Publishing (16%), Media & Technology (7%), and International (15%). SCHL's business strategy focuses strongly on literacy and technology-based educational products, branded children's publishing properties that can be developed for television and multimedia, and further expansion of its proprietary school-based distribution businesses. The company has accelerated investment spending on its Internet presence, to create the leading school-to-home learning site for students, teachers and parents. In April 2001, SCHL discontinued its basal textbook reading program.

The company's domestic book publishing business consists primarily of children's books in paperback editions distributed through school book clubs, school book fairs and classroom and library sales, as well as through sales in retail stores. Major titles include the Harry Potter and Star Wars series, Animorphs, Pokemon, Dear America, and I Spy.

SCHL publishes 34 magazines distributed to children in school classrooms, four magazines directed to teachers and other education professionals, and one consumer magazine directed at the growing home office market. Circulation of the classroom magazines in FY 00 was about 8 million.

Domestic operations also include publication and distribution of educational computer software, production of children's and family-oriented video and TV programming, and, through a joint venture, development and production of theatrical motion pictures.

Per Share Data ($) (Year Ended May 31)	2000	1999	1998	1997	1996	1995	1994	1993	1992	1991
Tangible Bk. Val.	11.24	8.74	7.72	7.09	7.79	7.97	6.64	4.99	4.70	3.96
Cash Flow	2.03	3.31	2.70	1.79	2.29	1.93	1.25	1.07	0.77	0.95
Earnings	1.48	1.10	0.72	0.01	0.98	1.19	1.02	0.89	0.54	0.65
Dividends	Nil	Nil	Nil	Nil	Nil	Nil	Nil	Nil	Nil	Nil
Payout Ratio	Nil	Nil	Nil	Nil	Nil	Nil	Nil	Nil	Nil	Nil
Cal. Yrs.	1999	1998	1997	1996	1995	1994	1993	1992	1991	1990
Prices - High	32.06	28.50	33.37	39.37	39.12	26.25	27.12	18.87	NA	NA
- Low	19.50	14.43	10.37	29.50	23.87	16.87	16.12	11.25	NA	NA
P/E Ratio - High	22	26	46	NM	40	22	27	21	NA	NA
- Low	13	13	14	NM	24	14	16	13	NA	NA
Income Statement Analysis (Million $)										
Revs.	1,403	1,155	1,058	966	929	750	632	552	489	423
Oper. Inc.	123	152	125	76.1	125	91.7	63.2	54.9	48.8	43.0
Depr.	24.1	73.6	64.9	58.4	42.5	24.0	7.6	5.8	5.5	6.8
Int. Exp.	18.6	19.0	20.1	16.7	11.2	6.1	3.0	2.8	12.0	14.4
Pretax Inc.	80.4	58.9	38.1	1.0	46.7	62.3	52.7	46.8	21.6	22.5
Eff. Tax Rate	36%	38%	38%	60%	32%	38%	38%	40%	40%	39%
Net Inc.	51.4	36.8	23.6	0.4	31.9	38.6	32.9	28.1	13.0	13.8
Balance Sheet & Other Fin. Data (Million $)										
Cash	9.0	5.9	5.1	4.9	4.3	3.7	4.1	4.1	17.1	12.7
Curr. Assets	540	434	383	396	350	279	220	166	154	124
Total Assets	983	842	765	784	673	506	390	263	226	188
Curr. Liab.	286	212	182	181	173	143	120	105	89.7	71.0
LT Debt	241	248	244	288	187	92.0	40.0	3.0	23.0	109
Common Eqty.	430	361	318	298	289	250	206	153	112	6.0
Total Cap.	671	609	562	585	475	342	245	157	135	115
Cap. Exp.	46.0	29.6	20.3	29.5	30.4	21.7	41.5	16.0	7.5	4.0
Cash Flow	75.5	110	88.5	58.8	74.4	62.6	40.5	33.9	18.5	20.6
Curr. Ratio	1.9	2.0	2.1	2.2	2.0	2.0	1.8	1.6	1.7	1.7
% LT Debt of Cap.	35.9	40.7	43.4	49.2	39.3	26.8	16.1	2.1	17.3	94.6
% Net Inc.of Revs.	3.7	3.2	2.2	Nil	3.4	5.1	5.2	5.1	2.6	3.3
% Ret. on Assets	5.6	4.6	3.0	0.1	5.4	8.6	10.1	9.9	4.8	7.8
% Ret. on Equity	13.0	10.8	7.7	0.1	11.8	16.9	18.3	16.4	21.2	NM

Data as orig reptd.; bef. results of disc opers/spec. items. Per share data adj. for stk. divs. Bold denotes diluted EPS (FASB 128)-prior periods restated. E-Estimated. NA-Not Available. NM-Not Meaningful. NR-Not Ranked.

Office—555 Broadway, New York, NY 10012. **Tel**—(212) 343-6741. **Website**—http://www.scholastic.com **Chrmn, Pres & CEO**—R. Robinson. **EVP & CFO**—K. McEnery. **VP-Fin & Investor Contact**—Ray Marchuk. **SVP & Secy**—C. B. Duell. **Treas**—V. M. Marzano. **Dirs**—H. V. Benham, R. M. Barrera, R. C. Cortines, C. T. Harris III, A. S. Hedden, M. C. Jemison, L. B. Keene, P. M. Mayer, J. G. McDonald, A. K. Oliver, R. Robinson, R. M. Spaulding. **Transfer Agent & Registrar**—Mellon Investor Services, NYC. **Incorporated**—in Delaware in 1986. **Empl**— 5,500. **S&P Analyst:** William H. Donald

STANDARD
&POOR'S
STOCK REPORTS

Superior Industries International

NYSE Symbol **SUP**

In S&P MidCap 400

23-AUG-01

Industry: Auto Parts & Equipment

Summary: This company is a leading maker of cast aluminum road wheels for automotive OEMs, as well as a manufacturer of automotive aftermarket products.

S&P Opinion: Accumulate (★★★★) | Recent Price • 39.33 | 52 Wk Range • 44.85-27.68 | Yield • 1.1% | 12-Mo. P/E • 15.0

Quantitative Evaluations

Outlook (1 Lowest—5 Highest) • **2**

Fair Value • **41**

Risk • **Low**

Earn./Div. Rank • **A**

Technical Eval. • **Bullish** since 7/01

Rel. Strength Rank (1 Lowest—99 Highest) • **43**

Insider Activity • **Neutral**

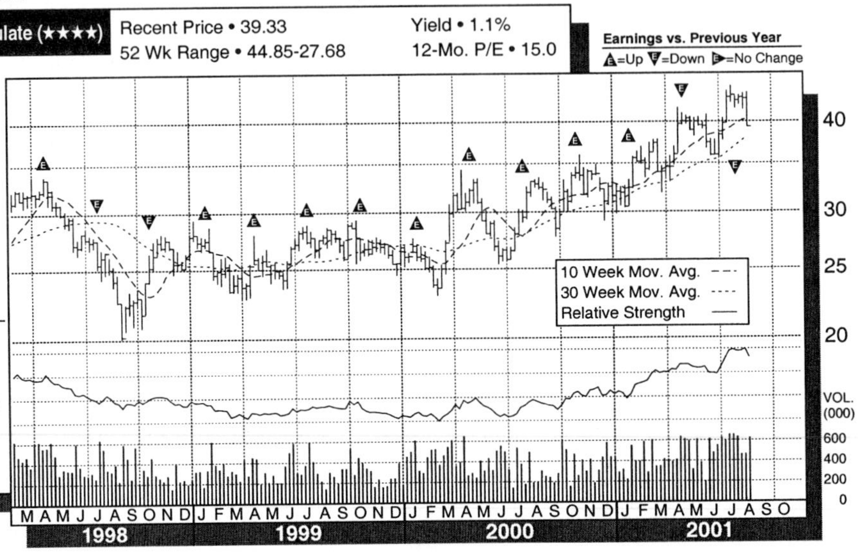

Overview - 23-AUG-01

Unit sales of cast aluminum automotive road wheels should grow in low single digits in 2002, reflecting increased worldwide demand for aluminum wheels, as well as new contracts. Total dollar sales could rise more rapidly, as increased production of cast aluminum wheels is aided by growing volume of chrome-plated aluminum wheels. Margins should widen, as income contributions from chrome sales rise, and SUP's Hungarian joint venture increases its profitability. With the exception of two relatively modest shortfalls in the first two quarters, the company has repeatedly exceeded analyst expectations. For 2001, we expect a decline in U.S. light vehicle sales to about 16.7 million units, from 2000's record of about million vehicles. We see a rebound to 16.9 million for 2002.

Valuation - 23-AUG-01

Investors have largely ignored recent shortfalls. SUP was unable to overcome sharply lower and erratic vehicle production schedules in the first quarter and reduced production and higher energy costs in the second quarter. The stock was aided in reaching a multi-year high by lower interest rates. However, the shares remain well below their record 1993 high of over $49. With little long term debt, the company has the financial flexibility to exploit diversification and expansion opportunities. Profit margins have consistently been among the widest in the auto industry, and this has been rewarded with a price to forecasted 2002 sales ratio of approximately 1.5X, above that of SUP's peers. With sufficient reserve cash on hand, the company could become more aggressive in repurchasing its common stock. The shares of this conservatively managed company, recently trading at a discount to the market P/E, offer an opportunity for above-average capital appreciation.

Key Stock Statistics

S&P EPS Est. 2001	2.45	Tang. Bk. Value/Share	15.45
P/E on S&P Est. 2001	16.1	Beta	0.91
S&P EPS Est. 2002	3.08	Shareholders	990
Dividend Rate/Share	0.44	Market cap. (B)	$ 1.0
Shs. outstg. (M)	25.9	Inst. holdings	65%
Avg. daily vol. (M)	0.173		

Value of $10,000 invested 5 years ago: $ 17,537

Fiscal Year Ending Dec. 31

	2001	2000	1999	1998	1997	1996
Revenues (Million $)						
1Q	166.1	155.4	136.9	136.4	125.9	121.5
2Q	161.9	175.8	155.0	138.1	142.1	137.6
3Q	—	144.8	131.4	112.3	130.2	120.5
4Q	—	168.9	148.4	152.7	150.9	124.8
Yr.	—	644.9	571.8	539.4	549.1	504.2
Earnings Per Share ($)						
1Q	**0.61**	**0.70**	**0.57**	**0.46**	**0.41**	**0.30**
2Q	**0.51**	**0.83**	**0.71**	**0.44**	**0.53**	**0.48**
3Q	**E0.56**	**0.66**	**0.54**	**0.28**	**0.47**	**0.40**
4Q	**E0.78**	**0.85**	**0.81**	**0.71**	**0.56**	**0.45**
Yr.	**E2.45**	**3.04**	**2.62**	**1.88**	**1.96**	**1.63**

Next earnings report expected: NA

Dividend Data (Dividends have been paid since 1985.)

Amount ($)	Date Decl.	Ex-Div. Date	Stock of Record	Payment Date
0.100	Oct. 23	Jan. 10	Jan. 12	Jan. 26 '01
0.100	Mar. 22	Apr. 04	Apr. 06	Apr. 20 '01
0.110	May. 11	Jun. 27	Jun. 29	Jul. 13 '01
0.110	Jul. 30	Oct. 03	Oct. 05	Oct. 19 '01

Superior Industries International, Inc.

Business Summary - 23-AUG-01

Superior Industries International produces cast aluminum road wheels for original equipment manufacturers (OEMs; 98% of sales in 2000) and various automotive aftermarket products (2%).

SUP is the leading supplier of aluminum wheels to Ford and GM, which together accounted for 90% of sales in 2000 (89% in 1999). Industrywide aluminum wheel installations on North American vehicles have increased greatly in recent years, reaching an estimated 54% share of the North American market in 1999.

SUP's long-term goal is to broaden its customer base. It has a joint venture with Topy Industries Ltd., Japan's largest wheel producer, through which it is developing sales in the U.S. and abroad to Japanese automakers. It has also won contracts from Jaguar and BMW. A joint venture with Otto Fuchs Metallwerke of Germany, operating a Hungarian plant with capacity to supply 1.5 million lightweight forged and low-pressure cast aluminum wheels to the European market, is nearing capacity as it supplies lightweight forged wheels to Audi and BMW. A joint project with Alcoa has developed a line of aluminum wheels for medium-duty trucks and buses.

The company operates six OEM casting plants, with combined annual capacity in excess of 12 million aluminum wheels. An aluminum wheel chrome-plating facility, added to the flagship Fayetteville plant in late 1994, could ultimately boost sales $100 million.

For the aftermarket, SUP makes one-piece cast aluminum, all-steel, composite steel and aluminum, and chrome-plated aluminum wheels, in styles to fit most vehicles. Related items include chrome-plated and locking lug nuts, hub covers and wire baskets. The company also makes steering wheel covers, suspension and other accessories.

In 1997, GM awarded SUP a contract to supply cast aluminum transmission brackets for a new Oldsmobile program, marking its entry into non-wheel aluminum components for the automotive market.

In 1998, as part of a strategy to expand its non-wheel aluminum components business, SUP entered into an exclusive licensing agreement for a unique proprietary hybrid aluminum casting/forging technology called Cobrapress. Cobrapress can be used to make non-wheel components that will be less expensive while maintaining the structural requirement of conventional forged aluminum and steel components.

The company has won eight contracts for the new aluminum components business with a significant follow on potential to manufacture aluminum suspensions and related underbody components.

In 1999 and 2000, SUP received new aluminum wheel supply contracts valued at over $350 million, with delivery expected over the next three years.

From 1995 through 2000, SUP repurchased 4.3 million common shares. In March 2000, directors authorized the buyback of up to an additional 4 million shares. As of mid-July 2001, 3.7 million shares remained authorized for purchase.

Per Share Data ($) (Year Ended Dec. 31)	2000	1999	1998	1997	1996	1995	1994	1993	1992	1991
Tangible Bk. Val.	15.45	13.35	11.42	10.30	8.87	7.89	6.75	5.88	4.56	3.58
Cash Flow	4.07	3.67	2.84	2.92	2.58	2.70	2.73	2.14	1.65	1.07
Earnings	3.04	2.62	1.88	1.96	1.63	1.78	1.85	1.47	0.95	0.63
Dividends	0.38	0.34	0.30	0.26	0.22	0.19	0.15	0.08	0.10	0.09
Payout Ratio	13%	13%	16%	13%	13%	11%	8%	6%	10%	14%
Prices - High	36.00	29.37	33.87	29.50	28.37	35.75	46.25	49.37	20.33	11.16
- Low	22.93	22.75	20.06	22.12	21.62	23.87	24.25	18.58	10.70	5.20
P/E Ratio - High	12	11	18	15	17	20	25	34	21	18
- Low	8	9	11	11	13	13	13	13	11	8
Income Statement Analysis (Million $)										
Revs.	645	572	539	549	504	522	457	393	325	273
Oper. Inc.	148	134	107	115	109	122	120	95.2	69.3	44.0
Depr.	26.9	28.5	26.7	26.9	27.3	27.7	26.6	20.6	21.5	12.4
Int. Exp.	0.1	0.1	0.2	0.5	1.5	3.3	4.8	4.7	5.6	6.8
Pretax Inc.	123	109	80.8	86.2	74.1	84.9	90.3	72.6	45.4	28.5
Eff. Tax Rate	35%	35%	35%	36%	37%	38%	38%	38%	37%	36%
Net Inc.	79.9	70.8	52.3	55.4	46.9	53.1	56.3	45.2	28.6	18.2
Balance Sheet & Other Fin. Data (Million $)										
Cash	93.5	108	86.6	73.7	42.1	11.0	27.0	36.6	39.8	63.6
Curr. Assets	246	264	236	200	164	143	161	141	134	147
Total Assets	492	460	427	383	358	342	358	310	267	271
Curr. Liab.	75.0	86.8	91.1	65.4	76.4	82.0	107	76.0	63.3	91.9
LT Debt	Nil	0.3	0.7	1.3	1.9	5.8	23.1	34.0	44.1	53.3
Common Eqty.	399	353	312	287	251	229	200	177	137	104
Total Cap.	404	360	321	301	263	235	234	223	195	173
Cap. Exp.	82.0	33.0	36.7	13.3	13.5	25.9	60.2	53.8	28.1	25.0
Cash Flow	107	99	79.0	82.3	74.2	80.8	82.9	65.8	50.1	30.6
Curr. Ratio	3.3	3.0	2.6	3.1	2.1	1.8	1.5	1.9	2.1	1.6
% LT Debt of Cap.	Nil	0.1	0.2	NM	1.0	2.5	9.9	15.2	22.6	30.8
% Net Inc.of Revs.	12.4	12.4	9.7	10.1	9.3	10.2	12.3	11.5	8.8	6.7
% Ret. on Assets	16.8	15.9	12.9	15.0	13.4	15.2	17.0	15.6	10.4	7.2
% Ret. on Equity	21.2	21.3	17.5	20.6	19.5	24.8	30.1	28.8	23.4	19.0

Data as orig reptd.; bef. results of disc opers/spec. items. Per share data adj. for stk. divs. Bold denotes diluted EPS (FASB 128)-prior periods restated. E-Estimated. NA-Not Available. NM-Not Meaningful. NR-Not Ranked.

Office—7800 Woodley Ave., Van Nuys, CA 91406. **Tel**—(818) 781-4973. **Fax**—(818) 780-3500. **Website**—www.supind.com **Chrmn & Pres**—L. L. Borick. **VP, CFO & Investor Contact**—R. Jeffrey Ornstein (818-902-2700). **Secy & Treas**—D. L. Levine. **Dirs**—S. I. Ausman, L. L. Borick, S. J. Borick, R. C. Brown, P. W. Colburn, V. B. Evans, R. J. Ornstein, J. H. Parkinson. **Transfer Agent & Registrar**—Mellon Investor Services, LA. **Incorporated**—in Delaware in 1969; reincorporated in California in 1994. **Empl**— 6,000. **S&P Analyst:** Efraim Levy

STANDARD & POOR'S
STOCK REPORTS

Venator Group

NYSE Symbol **Z**

18-AUG-01

Industry:
Retail (Specialty)

Summary: This company, which changed its name from Woolworth Corp. in June 1998, operates specialty stores under a number of formats worldwide.

S&P Opinion: Accumulate (★★★★)

Recent Price • 17.65
52 Wk Range • 18.30-9.75
Yield • Nil
12-Mo. P/E • NM

Quantitative Evaluations

Outlook
(1 Lowest—5 Highest)
• **1**

Fair Value
• **15.90**

Risk
• **Average**

Earn./Div. Rank
• **B-**

Technical Eval.
• **Bullish** since 6/01

Rel. Strength Rank
(1 Lowest—99 Highest)
• **92**

Insider Activity
• **Neutral**

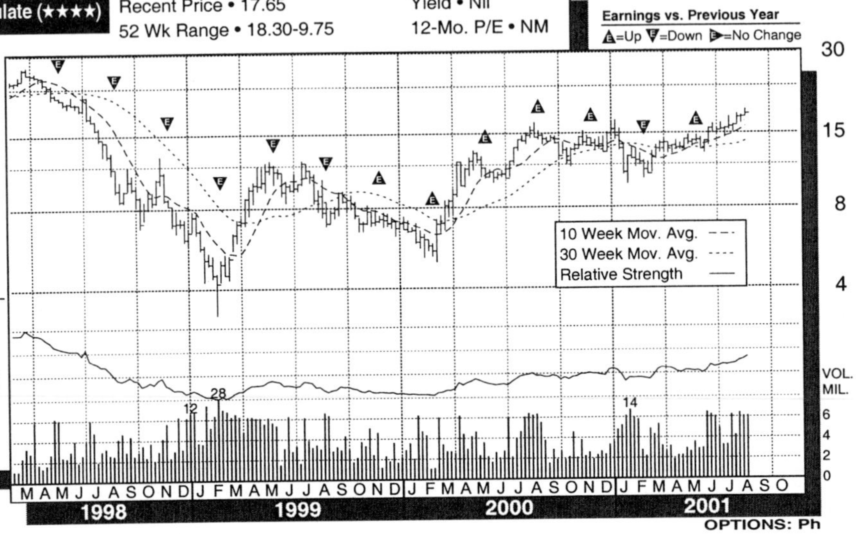

OPTIONS: Ph

Overview - 12-JUN-01

We expect total sales, on an as adjusted basis (reflecting the exclusion of non-core businesses disposed of or held for disposal, and the results of the stores in core operations that were targeted for closure) to grow 3% to 5% in FY 02 (Jan.), as the negative impact of fewer stores in operation is offset by a modest increase in same-store sales. Gross margins should continue to widen, aided by strong demand for athletic footwear, the closing of underperforming stores and businesses, and greater penetration of private label merchandise. Operating margins should benefit from the higher volume and increased operating efficiencies. Interest expense is expected to decline as Z continues to pay down debt. We expect FY 02 EPS to reach $0.94, a 22% gain over reported FY 01 results.

Valuation - 12-JUN-01

We continue to rate Z shares accumulate. Athletic footwear has come back into fashion, encouraged by a trend toward casual apparel both in the home and in the workplace. Retailers such as Venator have been benefiting from this trend. The industry remains quite promotional, but the company has been able to limit the increase in marketing costs. Although Z has a long way to go before attaining the profitability levels of its peers, it has been making substantial progress. Indeed, we look for operating margins to widen as much as four percentage points over the next three years, while free cash flow is used in part to eliminate debt net of cash over the next 24 months. This encourages us about the likelihood of meaningful price appreciation for the stock in the near to mid-term. We view Z, recently trading at 15X our FY 02 EPS estimate, as attractive for accumulation.

Key Stock Statistics

S&P EPS Est. 2002	0.94	Tang. Bk. Value/Share	6.27
P/E on S&P Est. 2002	18.8	Beta	0.86
S&P EPS Est. 2003	1.04	Shareholders	34,408
Dividend Rate/Share	Nil	Market cap. (B)	$ 2.5
Shs. outstg. (M)	139.5	Inst. holdings	85%
Avg. daily vol. (M)	1.378		

Value of $10,000 invested 5 years ago: $ 8,284

Fiscal Year Ending Jan. 31

	2002	2001	2000	1999	1998	1997
Revenues (Million $)						
1Q	1,072	1,108	1,079	1,466	1,766	1,820
2Q	—	1,041	1,063	1,465	1,500	1,856
3Q	—	1,160	1,178	1,122	1,583	2,048
4Q	—	1,256	1,327	1,332	2,002	2,368
Yr.	—	4,356	4,647	4,555	6,624	8,092
Earnings Per Share ($)						
1Q	**0.23**	**0.11**	**-0.08**	**-0.04**	0.01	-0.17
2Q	—	**0.07**	**-0.30**	**-0.09**	0.19	0.17
3Q	—	**0.19**	**0.05**	**-0.29**	0.41	0.52
4Q	—	**0.31**	**0.44**	**0.21**	**0.85**	0.74
Yr.	—	0.77	**0.13**	**0.02**	**1.57**	**1.44**

Next earnings report expected: mid August

Dividend Data

Prior to omission in April 1995, dividends had been paid since 1912. A dividend reinvestment plan is available.

Venator Group, Inc.

Business Summary - 12-JUN-01

Venator Group (formerly Woolworth Corp.) has come a long way from its five and dime store origins, and its name change reflects this. The company has eliminated or downsized mature formats (Woolworth general merchandise and Kinney shoe stores) to focus on high-return, specialty retailing formats. At the end of FY 01 (Jan.), Z operated 3,582 stores in its global athletic group, including Foot Locker, Lady Foot Locker, Kids Foot Locker and Champs Sports.

Foot Locker is the leading global athletic footwear and apparel retailer. Its stores offer the latest in athletic-inspired technical and performance products, manufactured primarily by the leading athletic brands. Its 1,936 stores are located mostly in the U.S., but also in Europe, Japan, Canada and Australia. Stores in the United States average 2,300 sq. ft. of selling space, while international stores comprise 1,800 sq. ft. There were also 662 Lady Foot Locker and 398 Kids Foot Locker stores in operation at the end of FY 01.

Champs Sports is, after Foot Locker, the second largest mall-based sporting goods retailer, selling both branded and private label sporting goods. Its 586 stores are located in the U.S. and Canada. The stores average 4,000 sq. ft. of selling space.

Eastbay is the largest direct mail marketer of athletic footwear, apparel and equipment in the U.S. Z changed the name of its e-commerce initiative from eVenator to Footlocker.com in FY 00. This subsidiary was formed in March 1999 to develop direct marketing over the Internet.

In the FY 00 second quarter, Z began a major restructuring program. It planned to sell or liquidate eight non-core businesses: The San Francisco Music Box Co., Randy River Canada, Foot Locker Outlets, Colorado, Team Edition, Going to the Game!, Weekend Edition, and Burger King franchises. It closed or planned to close all Foot Locker stores in Asia and, in North America, 150 Athletic Group stores and 208 Northern Group stores, including the Northern Getaway and Northern Elements formats in the U.S. It also planned a 30% reduction of sales and support staff in the continuing operations. The company incurred a related pretax charge of $155 million. Also in FY 00, it sold its Afterthoughts retail chain, and completed a public offering of its holding in Colorado Group, Ltd. in Australia in FY 00, for about $250 million and $55 million, respectively. During FY 01, the company discontinued its Northern casual apparel stores, including Northern Reflections and Northern Getaway stores.

Per Share Data ($)										
(Year Ended Jan. 31)	**2001**	**2000**	**1999**	**1998**	**1997**	**1996**	**1995**	**1994**	**1993**	**1992**
Tangible Bk. Val.	6.27	7.16	6.30	7.97	9.19	8.41	9.15	9.05	14.44	14.22
Cash Flow	1.86	1.44	1.14	2.80	2.66	0.56	2.12	-1.81	4.03	1.56
Earnings	0.77	0.13	0.02	1.57	1.26	-1.23	0.36	-3.76	2.14	-0.41
Dividends	Nil	Nil	Nil	Nil	Nil	Nil	0.74	1.16	1.12	1.08
Payout Ratio	Nil	Nil	Nil	Nil	Nil	Nil	NM	NM	52%	NM
Cal. Yrs.	2000	1999	1998	1997	1996	1995	1994	1993	1992	1991
Prices - High	16.50	12.00	27.25	28.75	25.25	19.37	26.25	32.75	35.00	36.37
- Low	5.00	3.18	5.81	18.25	9.37	12.25	12.87	20.50	26.00	23.50
P/E Ratio - High	21	92	NM	18	20	NM	73	NM	16	NM
- Low	6	25	NM	12	7	NM	36	NM	12	NM
Income Statement Analysis (Million $)										
Revs.	4,356	4,647	4,555	6,624	8,092	8,224	8,293	9,626	9,962	9,914
Oper. Inc.	334	188	56.0	521	505	323	466	264	773	650
Depr.	151	182	152	168	187	239	233	257	249	256
Int. Exp.	22.0	65.0	44.0	44.0	73.0	119	110	84.0	94.0	99
Pretax Inc.	176	28.0	-39.0	338	280	-233	96.0	-798	437	-83.0
Eff. Tax Rate	39%	39%	NM	37%	40%	NM	51%	NM	36%	NM
Net Inc.	107	17.0	3.0	213	169	-164	47.0	-495	280	-53.0
Balance Sheet & Other Fin. Data (Million $)										
Cash	109	162	193	116	321	13.0	72.0	57.0	49.0	69.0
Curr. Assets	1,000	1,089	1,275	1,459	1,823	1,618	2,069	2,494	2,654	2,590
Total Assets	2,232	2,515	2,876	3,182	3,476	3,506	4,173	4,593	4,692	4,618
Curr. Liab.	629	777	964	756	856	841	1,710	2,081	1,658	1,592
LT Debt	259	312	511	535	580	619	309	336	372	425
Common Eqty.	1,013	1,139	1,038	1,271	1,334	1,229	1,353	1,344	2,054	2,025
Total Cap.	1,272	1,451	1,549	1,854	1,972	1,936	1,767	1,767	2,536	2,545
Cap. Exp.	94.0	158	549	284	134	167	218	359	333	387
Cash Flow	258	199	155	381	356	75.0	280	-238	529	203
Curr. Ratio	1.6	1.4	1.3	1.9	2.1	1.9	1.2	1.2	1.6	1.6
% LT Debt of Cap.	20.4	21.5	33.0	28.9	29.4	32.0	17.5	19.0	14.7	16.7
% Net Inc.of Revs.	2.5	0.4	NM	3.2	2.1	NM	0.6	NM	2.8	NM
% Ret. on Assets	4.6	0.6	NM	6.4	4.8	NM	1.1	NM	6.0	NM
% Ret. on Equity	9.9	1.6	NM	16.4	13.2	NM	3.5	NM	13.7	NM

Data as orig reptd.; bef. results of disc opers/spec. items. Per share data adj. for stk. divs. Bold denotes diluted EPS (FASB 128)-prior periods restated. E-Estimated. NA-Not Available. NM-Not Meaningful. NR-Not Ranked.

Office—112 West 34th St., New York, NY 10120.**Tel**—(212) 720-3700.**Website**—http://www.venatorgroup.com **Chrmn**—J. C. Bacot. **CEO & Pres**—M. D. Serra. **VP & Treas**—J. H. Cannon. **VP & Secy**—G. M. Bahler. **Asst Treas & Investor Contact**—Peter D. Brown (212-720-4254). **Dirs**—J. C. Bacot, P. Crawford, P. H. Geier Jr., J. Gilbert Jr., J. E. Preston, D. Y. Schwartz, M. D. Serra, C. Sinclair, C. Turpin, D. D. Young. **Transfer Agents & Registrars**—First Chicago Trust Co. of New York, Jersey City, NJ; CIBC Mellon Trust Co., Toronto. **Incorporated**—in New York in 1911. **Empl**— 16,846. **S&P Analyst:** Maureen C. Carini

STANDARD
&POOR'S
STOCK REPORTS

Wal-Mart Stores

NYSE Symbol **WMT**

In S&P 500

18-AUG-01

Industry:
Retail (General Merchandise)

Summary: Wal-Mart is the largest retailer in North America, operating a chain of discount department stores, wholesale clubs and combination discount stores and supermarkets.

S&P Opinion: Accumulate (★★★★)

Recent Price • 50.80	Yield • 0.6%
52 Wk Range • 58.75-41.43	12-Mo. P/E • 35.8

Quantitative Evaluations

Outlook
(1 Lowest—5 Highest)
• 1

Fair Value
• 48.90

Risk
• Low

Earn./Div. Rank
• A+

Technical Eval.
• Bullish since 7/01

Rel. Strength Rank
(1 Lowest—99 Highest)
• 44

Insider Activity
• Neutral

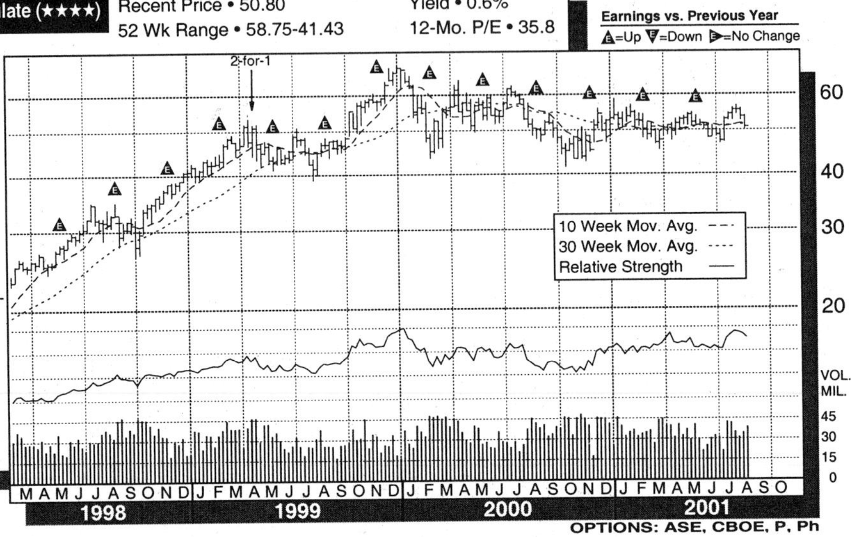

OPTIONS: ASE, CBOE, P, Ph

Overview - 17-AUG-01

Sales should increase about 12% in FY 02 (Jan.), with same-store sales up about 5% in each division. Discount stores and supercenters account for about 68% of total revenues. Supercenters and international expansion are driving growth. Gross margins should remain about level with those of FY 01. Expense ratios will decline, reflecting leverage over a growing store base, and operating income could increase about 13%. Interest expense could decline slightly. The company's supercenters are the key to WMT's domestic growth. Supercenters, which carry both groceries and general merchandise, are typically larger than WMT's traditional discount stores. The company operates more than 990 such units, generating over $60 million per unit annually, and is expected to add more than 160 units in FY 02, mostly replacing smaller discount units. International expansion also enhances long-term growth prospects. Directors have authorized the repurchase of up to $3 billion of common stock.

Valuation - 17-AUG-01

The shares of this premier discount chain have been in a narrow trading range over the past few months, and we are maintaining our accumulate recommendation. Second quarter earnings were in line with expectations, and total sales rose 13.2%. Operating profit increased 4.1% at Wal-Mart stores and 11.3% at Sam's Clubs, and soared 35.8% at the international division. We expect WMT to continue to benefit from a retail spending shift toward sellers of lower priced products, and from international growth. We see annual earnings gains of 14% to 16% resuming in FY 03 with a pickup in the economy. The shares of this well managed company will continue to receive a premium valuation, reflecting increased levels of free cash flow.

Key Stock Statistics

S&P EPS Est. 2002	1.50	Tang. Bk. Value/Share	5.22
P/E on S&P Est. 2002	33.9	Beta	0.87
S&P EPS Est. 2003	1.73	Shareholders	362,000
Dividend Rate/Share	0.28	Market cap. (B)	$227.1
Shs. outstg. (M)	4471.0	Inst. holdings	34%
Avg. daily vol. (M)	6.900		

Value of $10,000 invested 5 years ago: $ 43,662

Fiscal Year Ending Jan. 31

	2002	2001	2000	1999	1998	1997
Revenues (Million $)						
1Q	48,565	42,985	34,717	29,819	25,409	22,772
2Q	53,269	46,112	38,470	33,521	28,386	25,587
3Q	—	45,676	40,432	33,509	28,777	25,644
4Q	—	56,556	51,394	40,785	35,386	30,856
Yr.	—	191,329	165,013	137,634	117,958	104,859
Earnings Per Share ($)						
1Q	**0.31**	**0.30**	**0.25**	**0.18**	0.14	0.13
2Q	**0.36**	**0.36**	**0.28**	**0.23**	0.17	0.15
3Q	**E0.33**	**0.31**	**0.29**	**0.23**	0.17	0.15
4Q	**E0.50**	**0.45**	**0.43**	**0.35**	**0.28**	0.24
Yr.	**E1.50**	**1.40**	**1.25**	**0.99**	**0.78**	**0.67**

Next earnings report expected: mid November

Dividend Data (Dividends have been paid since 1973.)

Amount ($)	Date Decl.	Ex-Div. Date	Stock of Record	Payment Date
0.060	Nov. 16	Dec. 20	Dec. 22	Jan. 08 '01
0.070	Mar. 09	Mar. 21	Mar. 23	Apr. 09 '01
0.070	May. 31	Jun. 20	Jun. 22	Jul. 09 '01
0.070	Aug. 16	Sep. 19	Sep. 21	Oct. 09 '01

A Division of The McGraw-Hill Companies

Wal-Mart Stores, Inc.

Business Summary - 17-AUG-01

Wal-Mart, now the largest retailer in North America, has set its sights on other parts of the world. As of January 31, 2001, the company was operating 3,661 stores in the U.S. (1,736 Wal-Mart stores, 888 supercenters, and 475 Sam's Clubs); 499 in Mexico; 174 in Canada; 15 in Puerto Rico; 241 in the U.K.; and 142 in other countries, including Argentina (11), Brazil (20), Germany (94), and, under joint venture agreements, China (11) and South Korea (6).

The company's stores can be divided mainly into three categories: discount stores, supercenters, and Sam's Club stores. In FY 01 (Jan.), WMT's U.S. discount stores and supercenters had sales of $121.9 billion, up 12% from FY 00; Sam's Club sales in the U.S. totaled $26.8 billion, up 8.1%. In international markets, where WMT operates a variety of formats, some via joint ventures, sales were up 41.4%, to $32.1 billion.

The average Wal-Mart discount store in the U.S. has about 95,262 sq. ft.; the average supercenter is much larger, with 183,106 sq. ft. Most of the supercenters, which carry a broader assortment of groceries, developed from the relocation or expansion of WMT discount stores. Nationally advertised merchandise accounts for a majority of sales at WMT's U.S. discount stores and supercenters, but the company also markets limited lines of merchandise under store brands. WMT operated 18 Neighborhood Markets with an average size of 47,271 sq. ft.

Sam's Clubs are membership-only operations in about 48 states and Puerto Rico, averaging about 122,107 sq. ft. Merchandise includes bulk displays of name brand hard goods, some softgoods and institutional size grocery items. Each Sam's Club also carries products such as sporting goods, toys and books; most clubs have fresh food departments.

Capital spending in FY 01 totaled $8.0 billion. In FY 01, WMT added 167 Supercenters, 41 discount stores, 12 Neighborhood Markets, and 13 Sam's Clubs in the U.S., and 77 stores internationally. The company planned to finance these new units primarily from internally generated cash flows from operations. Cash flow from operations was $9.6 billion in FY 01, up 17% from FY 00.

The company, which has an annual technology and communications budget of about $500 million, has long been a leader in developing and implementing retail information technology. WMT is intent on increasing productivity, to pass on cost reductions to customers via an everyday low pricing strategy, and to provide a more complete assortment of merchandise in its stores. Walmart.com is a majority-owned subsidiary, formed in FY 00 to develop an Internet business.

Per Share Data ($) (Year Ended Jan. 31)	2001	2000	1999	1998	1997	1996	1995	1994	1993	1992
Tangible Bk. Val.	4.99	3.69	4.75	4.13	3.75	3.21	2.77	2.34	1.91	1.52
Cash Flow	2.04	1.78	1.41	1.15	0.98	0.88	0.81	0.69	0.57	0.46
Earnings	1.40	1.25	0.99	0.78	0.67	0.59	0.58	0.51	0.43	0.35
Dividends	0.20	0.18	0.15	0.14	0.10	0.10	0.09	0.07	0.05	0.04
Payout Ratio	14%	14%	16%	17%	16%	17%	15%	13%	11%	12%
Cal. Yrs.	2000	1999	1998	1997	1996	1995	1994	1993	1992	1991
Prices - High	69.00	70.25	41.37	20.96	14.12	13.81	14.62	17.06	16.46	14.96
- Low	41.43	38.68	18.78	11.00	9.54	10.25	10.50	11.50	12.53	7.12
P/E Ratio - High	49	56	42	27	21	23	25	33	38	43
- Low	30	31	19	14	14	17	18	23	29	20
Income Statement Analysis (Million $)										
Revs.	191,329	165,013	137,634	117,958	104,859	93,627	82,494	67,345	55,484	43,887
Oper. Inc.	12,392	10,684	8,418	6,796	5,871	5,416	5,120	4,389	3,615	2,892
Depr.	2,868	2,375	1,872	1,634	1,463	1,304	1,070	822	627	475
Int. Exp.	1,374	1,022	797	784	889	938	776	582	403	302
Pretax Inc.	10,116	9,083	7,323	5,719	4,850	4,346	4,262	3,692	3,166	2,553
Eff. Tax Rate	36%	37%	37%	37%	37%	37%	37%	37%	37%	37%
Net Inc.	6,295	5,575	4,430	3,526	3,056	2,740	2,681	2,333	1,995	1,608
Balance Sheet & Other Fin. Data (Million $)										
Cash	2,054	1,856	1,879	1,447	883	83.0	45.0	20.0	12.0	31.0
Curr. Assets	26,555	24,356	21,132	19,352	17,993	17,331	15,338	12,115	10,198	8,575
Total Assets	78,130	70,349	49,996	45,384	39,604	37,541	32,819	26,441	20,565	15,443
Curr. Liab.	28,949	25,803	16,762	14,460	10,957	11,454	9,973	7,406	6,754	5,004
LT Debt	15,655	16,674	9,607	9,674	10,016	10,600	9,709	7,960	4,845	3,278
Common Eqty.	31,343	25,834	21,112	18,503	17,143	14,756	12,726	10,752	8,759	6,990
Total Cap.	49,181	44,546	33,234	30,115	28,647	26,087	22,846	19,035	13,811	10,440
Cap. Exp.	NA	6,183	3,734	2,636	2,643	3,566	3,734	4,371	4,043	1,805
Cash Flow	9,163	7,950	6,302	5,160	4,519	4,044	3,751	3,155	2,622	2,084
Curr. Ratio	0.9	0.9	1.3	1.3	1.6	1.5	1.5	1.6	1.5	1.7
% LT Debt of Cap.	31.8	37.4	28.9	32.1	35.0	40.6	40.6	41.8	35.1	31.4
% Net Inc.of Revs.	3.3	3.4	3.2	3.0	2.9	2.9	3.3	3.5	3.6	3.7
% Ret. on Assets	8.5	9.3	9.3	8.3	7.9	7.8	9.1	9.9	11.1	12.0
% Ret. on Equity	22.0	23.8	22.4	19.8	19.2	19.9	19.9	23.9	25.3	26.0

Data as orig reptd.; bef. results of disc opers/spec. items. Per share data adj. for stk. divs. Bold denotes diluted EPS (FASB 128)-prior periods restated. E-Estimated. NA-Not Available. NM-Not Meaningful. NR-Not Ranked.

Office—702 Southwest 8th St. (P.O. Box 116), Bentonville, AR 72716-8611. **Tel**—(501) 273-4000. **Website**—http://www.wal-mart.com **Chrmn**—S. R. Walton. **Chrmn Exec Comm**—D. D. Glass. **Pres & CEO**—H. L. Scott. **Sr Vice Chrmn**—D. G. Soderquist. **EVP & CFO**—T. M. Schoewe. **SVP & Secy**—R. K. Rhoads. **Dirs**—J. T. Chambers, S. Friedman, S. C. Gault, D. D. Glass, R. A. Hernandez, F. S. Humphries, E. S. Kroenke, J. P. Reason, E. A. Sanders, H. L. Scott Jr., J. Shewmaker, D. G. Soderquist, J. H. Villarreal, J. T. Walton, S. R. Walton. **Transfer Agent & Registrar**—First Chicago Trust Co. of NY, Jersey City, NJ. **Incorporated**—in Delaware in 1969. **Empl**— 1,244,000. **S&P Analyst:** Karen J. Sack, CFA

Part Two

Consumer Staples Stocks

STANDARD
&POOR'S
STOCK REPORTS

Anheuser-Busch

NYSE Symbol **BUD**
In S&P 500

18-AUG-01 **Industry:** Beverages (Alcoholic)

Summary: BUD, the parent company of the world's largest brewer, also has interests in entertainment operations.

S&P Opinion: Buy (★★★★★) Recent Price • 43 | 52 Wk Range • 49.87-36.75 | Yield • 1.7% | 12-Mo. P/E • 23.9

Quantitative Evaluations
Outlook
(1 Lowest—5 Highest)
• 2+
Fair Value
• 39.90
Risk
• Low
Earn./Div. Rank
• A

Technical Eval.
• **Neutral** since 7/01
Rel. Strength Rank
(1 Lowest—99 Highest)
• **58**
Insider Activity
• **Neutral**

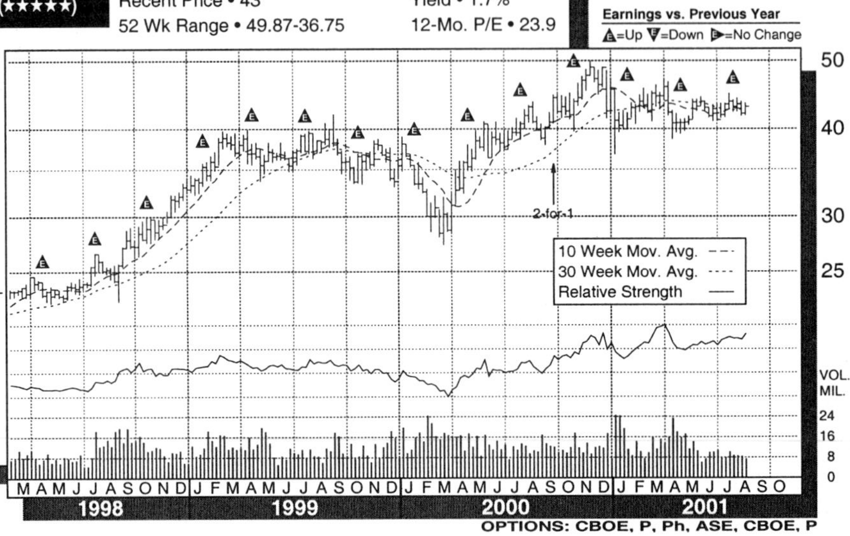

OPTIONS: CBOE, P, Ph, ASE, CBOE, P

Overview - 13-JUN-01

Net sales (after excise taxes) should rise 5% to 6% in 2001, reflecting 2% to 3% higher worldwide beer shipments and a 2.2% to 2.7% gain in net revenue per barrel. Domestic sales should continue to benefit from the strong growth in Bud Light and the rapid growth of new products such as Tequiza tequila flavored beer and Doc Otis hard lemonade. Introduced in 1999, Tequiza has become the third leading specialty/import beer in the U.S., following Corona and Heineken. Operating margins should widen, as improved operating efficiencies and lower brewing ingredient costs outweigh higher packaging and energy costs. With approximately 20% higher equity income from the company's stake in Grupo Modelo, Mexico's largest brewer, and improving profitability for international operations, net income should rise 10%. With about a 2% to 3% reduction in shares outstanding, EPS should reach $1.90 in 2001, up 12.4% from EPS of $1.69 in 2000. For 2002, a further rise to $2.15 is possible.

Valuation - 13-JUN-01

We continue our buy opinion on the shares, reflecting strong industry fundamentals and the company's solid volume and earnings momentum. With a favorable domestic beer pricing environment and expected gains in equity income, near-term earnings growth prospects should remain favorable for the foreseeable future. BUD is also benefiting from a favorable demographic shift (more 21- to 27-year olds, who typically consume the most beer), and from higher disposable incomes among consumers. At a recent P/E multiple of 22X our 2001 EPS estimate, the shares were trading in line with the P/E of the S&P 500 Index. In light of BUD's dominant and growing market position, increasing cash flows, and favorable domestic brewing industry fundamentals, we believe the shares warrant a premium to the P/E of the S&P 500.

Key Stock Statistics

S&P EPS Est. 2001	1.90	Tang. Bk. Value/Share	4.77
P/E on S&P Est. 2001	22.6	Beta	0.17
S&P EPS Est. 2002	2.15	Shareholders	60,100
Dividend Rate/Share	0.72	Market cap. (B)	$ 38.2
Shs. outstg. (M)	889.3	Inst. holdings	59%
Avg. daily vol. (M)	1.612		

Value of $10,000 invested 5 years ago: NA

Fiscal Year Ending Dec. 31

	2001	2000	1999	1998	1997	1996
Revenues (Million $)						
1Q	2,981	2,812	2,685	2,508	2,463	2,372
2Q	3,381	3,266	3,081	3,006	2,994	2,961
3Q	—	3,398	3,222	3,122	3,102	3,064
4Q	—	2,787	2,716	2,610	2,507	2,487
Yr.	—	12,262	11,704	11,246	11,066	10,884
Earnings Per Share ($)						
1Q	**0.43**	**0.38**	**0.33**	**0.27**	**0.26**	**0.27**
2Q	**0.58**	**0.52**	**0.45**	**0.40**	**0.38**	**0.35**
3Q	**E0.63**	**0.56**	**0.48**	**0.42**	**0.40**	**0.37**
4Q	**E0.26**	**0.23**	**0.20**	**0.17**	**0.15**	**0.15**
Yr.	**E1.90**	**1.69**	**1.47**	**1.26**	**1.18**	**1.14**

Next earnings report expected: late October

Dividend Data (Dividends have been paid since 1932.)

Amount ($)	Date Decl.	Ex-Div. Date	Stock of Record	Payment Date
0.165	Oct. 25	Nov. 07	Nov. 09	Dec. 11 '00
0.165	Jan. 16	Feb. 07	Feb. 09	Mar. 09 '01
0.165	Apr. 25	May. 07	May. 09	Jun. 11 '01
0.180	Jul. 25	Aug. 07	Aug. 09	Sep. 10 '01

A Division of The McGraw-Hill Companies

Anheuser-Busch Companies, Inc.

Business Summary - 13-JUN-01

Anheuser-Busch Cos. is the holding company parent of the largest U.S. brewer (Anheuser-Busch, Inc.), whose origins date back to 1875. The company has increased its focus on its brewing operations in recent years by divesting various non-beer businesses, including the St. Louis Cardinals baseball team; spinning off its food operations to shareholders as The Earthgrains Co. (NYSE: EGR); and divesting the assets of Eagle Snacks, Inc. The company retained its beer packaging and entertainment subsidiaries, and intends to support the growth of each.

Major beer brands include Budweiser, Bud Light, Bud Dry, Bud Ice, Michelob, Michelob Light, Michelob Dry, Michelob Golden Draft, Busch, Busch Light, Natural Light, Natural Pilsner, King Cobra, Red Wolf, and non-alcoholic malt beverages O'Doul's and Busch NA. During 1997, the company introduced the following brands: Hurricane Ice, Catalina Blonde, Michelob Honey Lager, Michelob Maple Brown, Michelob Pale Ale, Michelob Porter, Michelob Spiced Ale, and Tequiza.

BUD operates 12 breweries, strategically located across the country, to economically serve its distribution system. Worldwide sales of the company's beer brands in 2000 totaled 105.6 million barrels (up 2.6% from 102.9 million barrels in 1999). Domestic sales totaled 98.3 million barrels in 2000 (up 2.7%), or approximately 48.4% of U.S. industry sales. Through various subsidiaries, the company is involved in a number of beer-related operations that help insulate it from occasional rises in packaging and ingredient costs. These operations include can manufacturing, metalized paper printing, and barley malting.

Through the Busch Entertainment Corp. subsidiary, the company operates nine theme parks, including Busch Gardens in Florida and Virginia; Sea World parks in Florida, Texas and California; water parks in Florida and Virginia; and an educational play park in Pennsylvania; it also operates the Baseball City Sports Complex in Florida. Through a Spanish affiliate, BUD owns a 16.3% equity interest in Port Aventura S.A., a theme park near Barcelona, Spain. Busch Entertainment contributed 6.8% of total net sales and 4.6% of net income in 2000.

In September 1998, BUD purchased an additional 13.3% share in Diblo, Grupo Modelo's operating subsidiary, for $556 million. BUD currently holds a 50.2% direct and indirect interest in Modelo (Mexico's largest brewer) and its operating subsidiary, Diblo.

In the first quarter of 2001, BUD purchased approximately 18.5% of Chilean-based Compania Cerveccias Unidas S.A. (CCU), a diversified beverage company operating principally in Chile and Argentina. CCU is the leading brewer in Chile, holding a 90% domestic market share, and is also the second-largest Chilean soft-drink producer, the third-largest Chilean winery and the largest Chilean mineral water producer.

Per Share Data ($) **(Year Ended Dec. 31)**	**2000**	**1999**	**1998**	**1997**	**1996**	**1995**	**1994**	**1993**	**1992**	**1991**
Tangible Bk. Val.	4.11	3.79	3.96	3.69	3.61	3.93	3.82	3.52	3.69	3.44
Cash Flow	2.56	1.47	2.02	1.86	1.73	1.41	1.57	1.09	1.36	1.28
Earnings	1.69	1.47	1.26	1.18	1.14	0.62	0.98	0.54	0.87	0.81
Dividends	0.63	0.58	0.54	0.50	0.46	0.42	0.38	0.34	0.30	0.27
Payout Ratio	37%	39%	43%	42%	40%	67%	39%	63%	34%	32%
Prices - High	49.87	42.00	34.12	24.12	22.50	17.00	13.84	15.06	15.18	15.50
- Low	27.31	32.21	21.46	19.25	16.18	12.68	11.78	10.75	12.93	9.81
P/E Ratio - High	30	29	27	20	20	27	14	28	17	19
- Low	16	22	17	16	14	20	12	20	15	12
Income Statement Analysis (Million $)										
Revs.	12,262	11,704	11,245	11,066	10,884	10,341	12,054	11,505	11,394	10,996
Oper. Inc.	3,299	3,080	2,862	2,737	2,623	2,359	2,527	2,385	2,343	2,256
Depr.	804	NA	738	684	594	566	628	608	567	534
Int. Exp.	315	290	265	219	233	226	221	208	200	239
Pretax Inc.	2,380	2,165	1,937	1,883	1,893	1,462	1,707	1,050	1,615	1,521
Eff. Tax Rate	35%	35%	36%	37%	39%	39%	40%	43%	38%	38%
Net Inc.	1,552	1,402	1,233	1,179	1,156	887	1,032	595	994	940
Balance Sheet & Other Fin. Data (Million $)										
Cash	160	152	225	147	94.0	94.0	156	127	215	97.0
Curr. Assets	1,548	1,601	1,640	1,584	1,466	1,511	1,862	1,795	1,816	1,628
Total Assets	13,085	12,640	12,484	11,727	10,464	10,591	11,045	10,880	10,538	9,987
Curr. Liab.	1,676	1,987	1,730	1,501	1,431	1,242	1,669	1,816	1,460	1,403
LT Debt	5,375	4,881	4,719	4,366	3,271	3,270	3,078	3,032	2,643	2,645
Common Eqty.	4,128	3,921	4,216	4,042	4,029	4,434	4,415	4,255	4,620	4,438
Total Cap.	10,876	10,147	10,238	9,701	8,508	8,837	8,752	8,458	8,540	8,584
Cap. Exp.	1,075	856	818	1,199	1,085	953	785	777	737	703
Cash Flow	2,356	1,402	1,971	1,863	1,750	1,453	1,660	1,203	1,561	1,474
Curr. Ratio	0.9	0.8	0.9	1.1	1.0	1.2	1.1	1.0	1.2	1.2
% LT Debt of Cap.	49.4	48.1	46.1	45.0	21.4	37.0	35.2	35.8	30.9	30.8
% Net Inc.of Revs.	12.7	12.0	11.0	10.7	10.6	8.6	8.6	5.2	8.7	8.5
% Ret. on Assets	12.1	11.2	10.2	10.6	11.0	8.4	9.6	5.7	9.8	9.5
% Ret. on Equity	38.6	34.5	29.9	29.2	27.3	20.0	24.2	13.7	22.2	23.1

Data as orig reptd.; bef. results of disc opers/spec. items. Per share data adj. for stk. divs. Bold denotes diluted EPS (FASB 128)-prior periods restated. E-Estimated. NA-Not Available. NM-Not Meaningful. NR-Not Ranked.

Office—One Busch Place, St. Louis, MO 63118. **Tel**—(314) 577-2000. **Website**—http://www.budweiser.com **Chrmn & Pres**—A. A. Busch III. **SEVP**—P. T. Stokes. **VP & CFO**—W. R. Baker. **VP & Secy**—J. G. Brown. **Investor Contact**—David Sauerhoff. **Dirs**—A. A. Busch III, B. A. Edison, C. Fernandez G., J. E. Jacob, J. R. Jones, C. F. Knight, V. R. Loucks Jr., V. S. Martinez, J. B. Orthwein, W. P. Payne, J. M. Roche, P. T. Stokes, A. C. Taylor, D. A. Warner III, E. E. Whitacre Jr. **Transfer Agent & Registrar**—Mellon Investor Services, Ridgefield Park, NJ. **Incorporated**—in Missouri in 1925; reincorporated in Delaware in 1979. **Empl**— 23,725. **S&P Analyst:** Richard Joy

STANDARD
&POOR'S
STOCK REPORTS

Constellation Brands

NYSE Symbol **STZ**

In S&P SmallCap 600

23-AUG-01

Industry: Beverages (Alcoholic)

Summary: This leading U.S. producer and marketer of alcoholic beverages (formerly Canandaigua Brands) has grown rapidly in recent years, primarily through acquisitions.

S&P Opinion: Buy (★★★★★)

Recent Price • 45.15
52 Wk Range • 45.15-22.93
Yield • Nil
12-Mo. P/E • 16.8

Quantitative Evaluations

Outlook
(1 Lowest—5 Highest)
• **4−**

Fair Value
• **53.10**

Risk
• **Average**

Earn./Div. Rank
• **B+**

Technical Eval.
• **Bullish** since 5/01

Rel. Strength Rank
(1 Lowest—99 Highest)
• **89**

Insider Activity
• **Neutral**

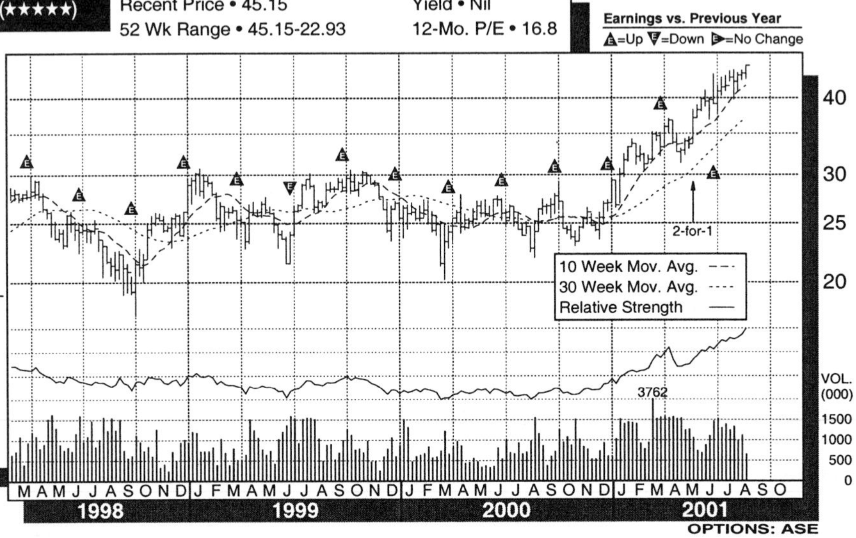

OPTIONS: ASE

Overview - 22-AUG-01

Net sales (after excise taxes) are projected to rise about 15% in FY 02 (Feb.), as contributions from the acquisition of Turner Road Vintners and Ravenswood Winery, solid unit volume growth, and higher prices for imported beers and premium wines outweigh potential negative foreign currency translations. Any strengthening of the U.S. dollar against the British pound would be positive. Most business segments are expected to post volume gains in FY 02, with the strongest organic growth coming from the beer and fine wine divisions. Cost structure improvements and increasing emphasis on more profitable premium wines should aid margins. Interest costs may decline modestly, benefiting from lower interest rates and continuing efforts to reduce debt levels. EPS should climb more than 17% in FY 02, to $3.06, from FY 01's $2.60 (as adjusted). For the longer term, EPS growth is seen at 15% to 20%.

Valuation - 22-AUG-01

We are maintaining our buy recommendation on the shares, reflecting expected strong volume and profit growth for the company's beer, wine and spirits businesses. Margins are benefiting from price increases, manufacturing efficiencies and an emphasis on higher margin premium and superpremium wines. The Turner Road Vintners and Ravenswood Winery acquisitions further strengthen the company's position as a major player in the fast growing, highly profitable premium wine segment. Accretive acquisitions remain a core feature of STZ's future growth, and the near-term focus will likely shift to niche brand acquisitions in the spirits area. We view the shares as undervalued, at a recent level of less than 13X our FY 03 EPS estimate of $3.55, a sharp discount to the P/E of the S&P SmallCap Index and STZ's peers, and to the company's expected long-term EPS growth rate of 15% or better.

Key Stock Statistics

S&P EPS Est. 2002	3.06	Tang. Bk. Value/Share	NM
P/E on S&P Est. 2002	14.8	Beta	0.65
S&P EPS Est. 2003	3.55	Shareholders	940
Dividend Rate/Share	Nil	Market cap. (B)	$ 1.6
Shs. outstg. (M)	42.1	Inst. holdings	69%
Avg. daily vol. (M)	0.220		

Value of $10,000 invested 5 years ago: $ 32,836

Fiscal Year Ending Feb. 28

	2002	2001	2000	1999	1998	1997
Revenues (Million $)						
1Q	642.1	585.6	530.2	312.9	306.0	276.5
2Q	—	637.5	621.6	349.4	301.5	279.2
3Q	—	629.6	661.5	375.6	322.7	317.7
4Q	—	544.0	527.2	459.4	282.6	261.6
Yr.	—	2,397	2,340	1,497	1,213	1,135
Earnings Per Share ($)						
1Q	**0.56**	**0.48**	**0.29**	**0.35**	**0.27**	**0.21**
2Q	**E0.82**	**0.70**	**0.57**	**0.41**	**0.33**	**0.13**
3Q	**E1.08**	**0.94**	**0.80**	**0.54**	**0.46**	**0.21**
4Q	**E0.60**	**0.48**	**0.42**	**0.33**	**0.27**	**0.15**
Yr.	**E3.06**	**2.60**	**2.09**	**1.65**	**1.31**	**0.71**

Next earnings report expected: late September

Dividend Data

Amount ($)	Date Decl.	Ex-Div. Date	Stock of Record	Payment Date
2-for-1	Apr. 18	May. 15	Apr. 30	May. 14 '01

A Division of The McGraw-Hill Companies

Constellation Brands, Inc.

Business Summary - 22-AUG-01

Through an aggressive acquisition policy over the past few years, Constellation Brands (formerly Canandaigua Brands) has become the second largest U.S. supplier of wines, the second largest importer of beers, and the fourth largest supplier of distilled spirits. The December 1998 acquisition of Matthew Clark plc established the company as a leading alcoholic beverage producer and wholesaler in the U.K. STZ markets more than 185 brands, including imported beers, wines, spirits, cider and bottled water.

The Canandaigua Wine division produces, bottles, imports and markets table wine, dessert wine, sparkling wine and brandy in the U.S. Leading brands include Inglenook, Almaden, Paul Masson, Arbor Mist, Manischewitz, Taylor, Marcus James, Estate Cellars, Vina Santa Carolina, Dunnwood, Mystic Cliffs, Cook's J. Roget, Richards Wild Irish Rose, and Paul Masson Grande Amber Brandy. Most of the wine is marketed in the popularly priced segment of the market. As a related part of its wine business, the company is one of the leading U.S. producers of grape juice concentrate.

The Barton division produces, bottles, imports and markets a diversified line of beer and distilled spirits. Barton distributes five of the 25 leading imported beer brands in the U.S.: Corona Extra, Modelo Especial, Corona Light, Pacifico, and St. Pauli Girl. Other imported beer brands include Negra Modelo, Tsingtao, Peroni, Double Diamond, and Tetleys English Ale. Principle distilled spirits brands include Black Velvet, Fleischmann's, Mr. Boston, Canadian LTD, Chi-Chi's prepared cocktails, Ten High, Montezuma, Barton, Inver House, and Monte Alban distilled spirits.

The company has grown in recent years through a combination of internal growth and acquisitions. The December 1998 acquisition of U.K.-based Matthew Clark plc provided a presence in the U.K., and a platform for growth in European markets. Matthew Clark brought several leading market positions in the U.K., including leading producer of branded boxed wine, leading branded producer of fortified British wine, leading branded bottler of sparkling water, and second leading producer of cider. In April 1999, furthering its expansion, STZ acquired several Canadian whiskey brands, including Black Velvet, from Diageo plc, for $185.5 million.

Beginning with the June 1999 acquisitions of Franciscan Vineyards, Inc. and Simi Winery, Inc., the company has positioned itself as a major player in the premium wine market. STZ further strengthened its premium wine portfolio with the March 2001 acquisition of Turner Road Vintners and the July 2001 acquisition of Ravenswood Winery.

Per Share Data ($)										
(Year Ended Feb. 28)	**2001**	**2000**	**1999**	**1998**	**1997**	**1996**	**1995**	**1994**	**1993**	**1992**
Tangible Bk. Val.	NM	NM	NM	4.64	9.66	9.09	8.98	6.38	4.96	4.11
Cash Flow	3.80	3.20	2.67	2.18	1.51	0.43	1.61	0.70	0.96	0.83
Earnings	2.60	2.15	1.65	1.31	0.70	0.09	1.07	0.37	0.65	0.54
Dividends	Nil	Nil	Nil	Nil	Nil	Nil	Nil	Nil	Nil	Nil
Payout Ratio	Nil	Nil	Nil	Nil	Nil	Nil	Nil	Nil	Nil	Nil
Cal. Yrs.	2000	1999	1998	1997	1996	1995	1994	1993	1992	1991
Prices - High	29.50	30.75	29.87	28.81	19.75	26.50	26.50	19.25	16.00	8.50
- Low	20.18	21.43	17.62	10.93	7.87	14.87	14.87	10.12	6.75	5.25
P/E Ratio - High	11	14	18	22	28	NM	25	52	25	16
- Low	8	10	11	8	11	NM	14	27	10	10
Income Statement Analysis (Million $)										
Revs.	2,397	2,340	1,497	1,213	1,135	535	907	630	306	245
Oper. Inc.	315	281	187	150	113	40.4	114	71.5	38.8	30.1
Depr.	44.6	40.9	38.6	33.2	31.9	14.0	20.7	10.5	7.4	6.1
Int. Exp.	109	106	41.5	32.2	34.1	17.4	25.1	18.4	6.3	6.5
Pretax Inc.	162	129	104	84.9	47.8	6.7	66.7	18.9	25.3	17.9
Eff. Tax Rate	40%	40%	59%	41%	42%	50%	39%	38%	38%	37%
Net Inc.	97.3	77.4	61.9	50.1	27.8	3.3	41.0	11.7	15.6	11.4
Balance Sheet & Other Fin. Data (Million $)										
Cash	146	34.3	27.6	1.2	10.0	3.3	4.2	1.5	3.7	2.2
Curr. Assets	1,191	996	856	564	501	518	402	454	244	134
Total Assets	2,512	2,349	1,794	1,073	1,020	1,055	786	827	355	218
Curr. Liab.	427	438	832	283	247	300	175	238	96.8	52.2
LT Debt	1,307	1,237	415	309	339	328	199	289	108	61.9
Common Eqty.	616	521	435	415	365	357	352	204	126	95.5
Total Cap.	2,056	1,874	1,355	783	765	742	600	537	255	165
Cap. Exp.	68.2	57.7	49.9	31.2	31.6	16.1	37.0	141	20.3	38.1
Cash Flow	142	118	101	83.2	59.7	17.3	61.7	22.3	23.0	17.4
Curr. Ratio	2.8	2.3	1.0	2.0	2.0	1.7	2.3	1.9	2.5	2.6
% LT Debt of Cap.	63.6	66.0	30.6	39.5	44.3	44.2	33.2	53.8	42.5	37.5
% Net Inc.of Revs.	4.1	3.3	4.1	4.1	2.4	0.6	4.6	1.9	5.1	4.6
% Ret. on Assets	4.0	3.7	4.3	4.8	2.7	NA	5.1	1.8	5.3	5.6
% Ret. on Equity	17.1	16.2	14.6	12.8	7.7	NA	14.8	6.5	13.5	14.0

Data as orig. reptd.; bef. results of disc. opers. and/or spec. items. Per share data adj. for stk. divs. as of ex-div. date. E-Estimated. NA-Not Available. NM-Not Meaningful. NR-Not Ranked. Yrs. ended Aug. 31 prior to 1996; FY 96 revs., EPS and inc. data are for six mos.

Office—235 N. Bloomfield Rd., Canandaigua, NY 14424. **Tel**—(716) 393-4130. **Fax**—(716) 394-6017. **Website**—http://www.cbrands.com **Chrmn, Pres & CEO**—Richard Sands. **EVP & Secy**—Robert Sands. **EVP & CFO**—T. Summer. **Dirs**—G. Bresler, J. K. Hauswald, J. A. Locke, T. C. McDermott, Richard Sands, Robert Sands, P. L. Smith. **Transfer Agent & Registrar**—Bank of Boston. **Incorporated**—in Delaware in 1972. **Empl**— 4,990. **S&P Analyst:** Richard Joy

STANDARD &POOR'S
STOCK REPORTS

Fleming Cos.

NYSE Symbol **FLM**
In S&P SmallCap 600

18-AUG-01

Industry: Distributors (Food & Health)

Summary: FLM, one of the largest U.S. wholesalers, supplies food and related products and services to about 3,000 supermarkets, 5,000 convenience stores, and 2,000 other format stores.

S&P Opinion: Buy (★★★★★)

Recent Price • 28.20
52 Wk Range • 37.89-10.31
Yield • 0.3%
12-Mo. P/E • NM

Quantitative Evaluations

Outlook (1 Lowest—5 Highest)
• **4**

Fair Value
• **39.40**

Risk
• **Average**

Earn./Div. Rank
• **B-**

Technical Eval.
• **Bearish** since 8/01

Rel. Strength Rank (1 Lowest—99 Highest)
• **21**

Insider Activity
• **Neutral**

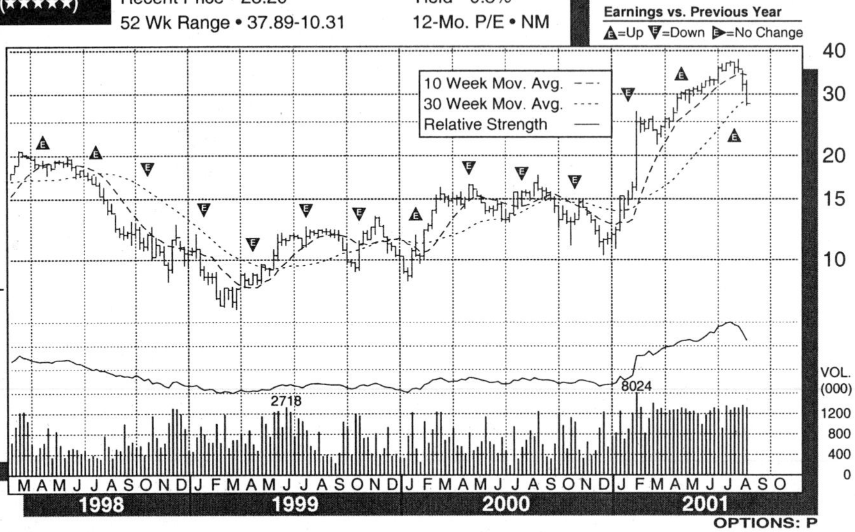

OPTIONS: P

Overview - 06-AUG-01

We expect wholesale revenues to climb about 20% in 2001, fueled by a recent distribution alliance with Kmart Corp. valued at about $4.5 billion, and more than $600 million in expected net incremental revenues from new customers. Meanwhile, retail sales will be down sharply, as the company recently completed the disposal of its high-cost conventional supermarkets in favor of its low-cost price-impact format. Operating margins should continue to widen, thanks to the disposition of underperforming retail units, warehouse productivity measures, the development of centralized procurement, and the consolidation of back-office operations. Excluding one-time charges, we expect 2001 EPS to climb 26% to $1.96, from $1.56 in 2000, and at least another 28% to $2.50 in 2002.

Valuation - 06-AUG-01

We believe the shares, recently trading at 18X our EPS estimate for 2001, remain undervalued, and, hence, retain our buy recommendation for them. Our favorable outlook is based on FLM's substantial progress in improving profitability and its growth opportunities. The company intends to reinvest $120 million of the $180 million in annual cost savings it expects to realize from the Kmart deal into top-line growth by passing that amount via lower prices for its goods and services to other clients. Meanwhile, talks are under way with Kmart to include health and beauty products, which could add another $2 billion in revenues. FLM also has a substantial growth opportunity in serving convenience stores, a $45 billion market at wholesale. It has around $1.5 billion in sales to this channel and looks to further penetrate that market in coming years.

Key Stock Statistics

S&P EPS Est. 2001	1.96	Tang. Bk. Value/Share	NM
P/E on S&P Est. 2001	14.4	Beta	-0.07
S&P EPS Est. 2002	2.50	Shareholders	14,900
Dividend Rate/Share	0.08	Market cap. (B)	$ 1.2
Shs. outstg. (M)	43.8	Inst. holdings	80%
Avg. daily vol. (M)	0.552		

Value of $10,000 invested 5 years ago: $ 22,881

Fiscal Year Ending Dec. 31

	2001	2000	1999	1998	1997	1996
Revenues (Million $)						
1Q	4,161	4,445	4,465	4,567	4,752	5,168
2Q	3,457	3,386	3,349	3,506	3,551	3,742
3Q	—	3,288	3,243	3,439	3,453	3,706
4Q	—	3,625	3,588	3,558	3,617	3,870
Yr.	—	14,444	14,646	15,069	15,373	16,487
Earnings Per Share ($)						
1Q	**0.37**	**-0.67**	**-0.64**	**0.40**	**0.14**	**0.16**
2Q	**-0.31**	**-0.35**	**-0.06**	**0.36**	**0.34**	**0.25**
3Q	—	**-1.17**	**-0.37**	**-0.06**	**0.26**	**0.03**
4Q	—	**-0.96**	**-0.10**	**-14.11**	**0.29**	**0.27**
Yr.	—	**-3.15**	**-1.17**	**-13.48**	**1.02**	**0.71**

Next earnings report expected: mid October

Dividend Data (Dividends have been paid since 1927.)

Amount ($)	Date Decl.	Ex-Div. Date	Stock of Record	Payment Date
0.020	Jan. 24	Feb. 15	Feb. 20	Mar. 09 '01
0.020	Feb. 28	May. 16	May. 18	Jun. 08 '01
0.020	May. 15	Aug. 16	Aug. 20	Sep. 10 '01
0.020	Aug. 14	Nov. 16	Nov. 20	Dec. 10 '01

Fleming Companies, Inc.

Business Summary - 06-AUG-01

From a humble start in 1915 as a small food wholesaler in Topeka, KS, Fleming Cos. has grown into one of the largest U.S. food and general merchandise distributors, supplying 3,000 supermarkets, 5,000 convenience stores, and over 2,000 supercenters, discount stores, limited assortment stores, drug stores, specialty stores and other stores across the U.S. In 2000, the distribution segment accounted for $14.4 billion, or 77%, of net sales. FLM's retail food division generated $3.3 billion, or 23%, of net sales. Of that amount, $1.9 billion was attributed to continuing chains.

After growing primarily through acquisitions, at the end of 1998, FLM announced a strategic restructuring plan, to be implemented through 2001. The plan focused on improving performance, increasing sales, and reducing costs. Key elements were the consolidation of 12 of its distribution centers, the centralization of its procurement process, and the centralization of back-office operations. In addition, FLM intended to develop new business, including gaining a greater share of business from existing customers, and attracting new customers.

As of the end of 2000, FLM distributed to approximately 2,500 companies that operate almost 7,000 retail locations under a wide variety of formats across the U.S. The top 10 customers accounted for approximately 17% of total net sales. Other than Kmart, which represented approximately 10% of net sales, no customer accounted for more than 2% of net sales. In February 2001, the company signed a 10-year exclusive distribution arrangement with Kmart valued at about $4.5 billion. FLM intends to reinvest $120 million of the $180 million in cost savings it expects to realize from the Kmart deal into top-line growth by passing that amount via lower prices for its goods and services to other clients. Meanwhile, talks are under way with Kmart to include health and beauty products, adding another $2 billion in revenues. FLM also has a substantial growth opportunity in serving convenience stores, a $35 billion market. The company had just over $1 billion in sales to this channel in 2000 and looks to gain another $3 to $4 billion annually in the next few years.

From 1998 to mid-2001, FLM will have sold or closed 238 of its conventional supermarkets, converted 10 to the price impact format, and will have adopted certain elements of the price impact format at the remaining 44 units. FLM plans to focus mainly on price impact supermarkets, which offer deep-discount, everyday low prices in a warehouse-style format and operate mostly under the Food4Less and Fresh4Less banners. Its typical price impact supermarket attracts weekly sales of $450,000 vs. $325,000 for a conventional supermarket. Its gross margin is narrower, owing to heavy discounting, but that is outweighed by lower SG&A costs as a percentage of sales. In 2000, FLM had 30 price impact stores; it looks to add 100 stores within three years.

Per Share Data ($) **(Year Ended Dec. 31)**	**2000**	**1999**	**1998**	**1997**	**1996**	**1995**	**1994**	**1993**	**1992**	**1991**
Tangible Bk. Val.	NM	NM	NM	3.29	2.10	1.65	2.42	15.93	16.19	14.44
Cash Flow	1.34	3.07	-8.58	5.79	5.66	5.87	5.42	3.77	5.33	4.22
Earnings	-3.15	-1.17	-13.48	1.02	0.71	1.12	1.51	1.02	3.33	2.06
Dividends	0.08	0.08	0.08	0.08	0.36	1.20	1.20	1.20	1.20	1.14
Payout Ratio	NM	NM	NM	8%	51%	107%	79%	118%	37%	58%
Prices - High	17.62	13.43	20.75	20.37	20.87	29.87	30.00	34.37	35.12	40.62
- Low	8.68	7.18	8.62	13.37	11.50	19.12	22.62	23.75	27.25	29.87
P/E Ratio - High	NM	NM	NM	20	29	27	20	34	11	20
- Low	NM	NM	NM	13	16	17	15	23	8	15
Income Statement Analysis (Million $)										
Revs.	14,444	14,646	15,069	15,373	16,487	17,502	15,753	13,092	12,938	12,902
Oper. Inc.	336	338	384	418	396	402	329	293	348	350
Depr.	174	162	185	181	188	181	146	101	71.8	72.7
Int. Exp.	175	165	161	163	163	176	121	78.0	81.1	93.5
Pretax Inc.	-201	-62.6	-599	83.0	54.6	85.9	112	72.0	195	117
Eff. Tax Rate	NM	NM	NM	53%	51%	51%	50%	48%	39%	38%
Net Inc.	-122	-44.7	-511	39.0	26.7	42.0	56.0	37.0	119	72.3
Balance Sheet & Other Fin. Data (Million $)										
Cash	30.4	6.7	6.0	30.0	63.7	4.4	28.4	1.6	4.7	21.1
Curr. Assets	1,623	1,729	1,588	1,495	1,564	1,651	1,820	1,361	1,403	1,343
Total Assets	3,403	3,573	3,491	3,924	4,055	4,297	4,608	3,103	3,118	2,956
Curr. Liab.	1,232	1,284	1,281	1,155	1,343	1,286	1,324	919	875	915
LT Debt	1,610	1,602	1,503	1,494	1,453	1,717	1,995	1,004	1,038	952
Common Eqty.	427	535	571	1,094	1,076	1,083	1,079	1,060	1,060	957
Total Cap.	2,037	2,137	2,073	2,649	2,567	2,840	3,125	2,092	2,138	1,935
Cap. Exp.	151	166	200	129	129	117	150	56.0	114	82.0
Cash Flow	52.0	118	-326	220	215	223	202	139	191	142
Curr. Ratio	1.3	1.3	1.2	1.3	1.2	1.3	1.4	1.5	1.6	1.5
% LT Debt of Cap.	79.0	75.0	72.5	56.4	56.6	60.5	63.8	48.0	48.6	49.2
% Net Inc.of Revs.	NM	NM	NM	0.3	0.2	0.2	0.4	0.3	0.9	0.6
% Ret. on Assets	NM	NM	NM	1.0	0.6	0.9	1.4	1.2	3.8	2.3
% Ret. on Equity	NM	NM	NM	3.6	2.5	3.9	5.2	3.5	11.6	7.5

Data as orig reptd.; bef. results of disc opers/spec. items. Per share data adj. for stk. divs. Bold denotes diluted EPS (FASB 128)-prior periods restated. E-Estimated. NA-Not Available. NM-Not Meaningful. NR-Not Ranked.

Office—1945 Lakepointe Drive, Box 299013, Lewisville, TX 75029. **Tel**—(972) 906-8000. **Website**—http://www.fleming.com **Chrmn & CEO**—M. S. Hansen. **EVP & CFO**—N. J. Rider. **Investor Contact**—Meredith C. Anderson. **SVP & Secy**—C. M. Hernandez. **Dirs**—H. M. Baum, K. M. Duberstein, A. R. Dykes, C. B. Hallett, R. S. Hamada, M. S. Hansen, E. C. Joullian, III, G. A. Osborn, A. M. Peterson. **Transfer Agent & Registrar**—First Chicago Trust Co., Jersey City, NJ. **Incorporated**—in Kansas in 1915; reincorporated in Oklahoma in 1981. **Empl**— 29,567. **S&P Analyst:** Phillip M. Seligman

STANDARD
&POOR'S
STOCK REPORTS

Hershey Foods

NYSE Symbol **HSY**

In S&P 500

18-AUG-01 **Industry:** Foods

Summary: Hershey is the leading U.S. producer of chocolate and confectionery products.

S&P Opinion: Buy (★★★★★)

Recent Price • 60.28
52 Wk Range • 70.15-41.56
Yield • 2.0%
12-Mo. P/E • 23.5

Quantitative Evaluations

Outlook
(1 Lowest—5 Highest)
• **2**

Fair Value
• **55.60**

Risk
• **Low**

Earn./Div. Rank
• **A**

Technical Eval.
• **Bearish** since 8/01

Rel. Strength Rank
(1 Lowest—99 Highest)
• **50**

Insider Activity
• **Neutral**

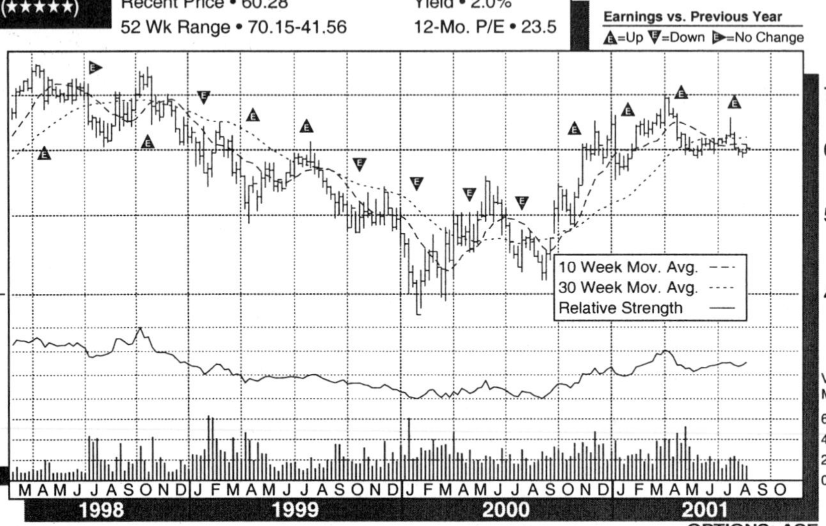

OPTIONS: ASE

Overview - 25-JUL-01

Sales are projected to rise 9% to 10% in 2001, as acquisition contributions, 2% to 3% domestic sales growth and strong gains for HSY's international export business outweigh approximately $100 million in SKU rationalizations. Additional marketing and promotional support for new products and to strengthen customer relationships may be a modest restraining factor. However, raw material prices should continue to be favorable, helping to dampen the effect of increased marketing spending. Logistics cost savings from a new distribution center and management information system and manufacturing efficiencies should continue to benefit operating margins. Net interest expense will likely decrease modestly due to lower interest rates. With a 0.5% to 1% reduction in shares outstanding, we expect EPS of $2.75 in 2001, up 15% from EPS before special items of $2.39 in 2000. Longer term, an 11% to 12% rate of annual EPS growth is seen.

Valuation - 25-JUL-01

We continue to rank the shares buy, reflecting strengthening retail sales trends for the company's products and expected strong earnings growth. In addition, a new East Coast distribution center should improve distribution efficiency and aid margins during 2001, while a new West Coast facility will benefit results in 2002. The December 2000 acquisition of Nabisco's intense and breath freshener mints and gum businesses is also expected to add to earnings in 2001. The shares were recently trading at a P/E multiple of 20X our 2002 EPS estimate, in line with the P/E multiple for the S&P 500 and a slight premium to that of HSY's food industry peers. In light of HSY's strengthening fundamentals and dominant position (about 30% of the total U.S. candy, mints and gum market) in the fast growing and relatively high-margin U.S. confectionery market, the shares are worth buying.

Key Stock Statistics

S&P EPS Est. 2001	2.75	Tang. Bk. Value/Share	5.17
P/E on S&P Est. 2001	21.9	Beta	-0.30
S&P EPS Est. 2002	3.05	Shareholders	41,482
Dividend Rate/Share	1.21	Market cap. (B)	$ 6.3
Shs. outstg. (M)	135.7	Inst. holdings	41%
Avg. daily vol. (M)	0.349		

Value of $10,000 invested 5 years ago: $ 14,829

Fiscal Year Ending Dec. 31

	2001	2000	1999	1998	1997	1996
Revenues (Million $)						
1Q	1,080	993.1	945.1	1,098	1,002	931.5
2Q	898.9	836.0	853.2	890.4	905.7	796.3
3Q	—	1,197	1,067	1,217	1,152	1,072
4Q	—	1,195	1,106	1,240	1,242	1,189
Yr.	—	4,221	3,971	4,436	4,302	3,989
Earnings Per Share ($)						
1Q	**0.57**	**0.51**	**1.57**	**0.52**	**0.45**	**0.38**
2Q	**0.38**	**0.29**	**0.35**	**0.33**	**0.33**	**0.26**
3Q	**E0.86**	**0.76**	**0.62**	**0.74**	**0.67**	**0.61**
4Q	**E0.94**	**0.84**	**0.70**	**0.76**	**0.80**	**0.51**
Yr.	**E2.75**	**2.42**	**3.26**	**2.34**	**2.23**	**1.75**

Next earnings report expected: late October

Dividend Data (Dividends have been paid since 1930.)

Amount ($)	Date Decl.	Ex-Div. Date	Stock of Record	Payment Date
0.280	Nov. 17	Nov. 20	Nov. 22	Dec. 15 '00
0.280	Feb. 07	Feb. 21	Feb. 23	Mar. 15 '01
0.280	Apr. 24	May. 23	May. 25	Jun. 15 '01
0.302	Aug. 07	Aug. 22	Aug. 24	Sep. 14 '01

A Division of The McGraw-Hill Companies

Hershey Foods Corporation

Business Summary - 25-JUL-01

Hershey Foods, primarily through its Hershey Chocolate U.S.A., Hershey International, and Hershey Pasta Group divisions, and its Hershey Canada Inc. subsidiary, produces and distributes a broad line of chocolate, confectionery and grocery products. Financial results have strengthened over the past few years, driven mainly by a rationalization of product lines that offered subpar investment returns, the integration of a number of complementary acquisitions, and an extraordinarily high rate of new product success.

The company makes chocolate and confectionery products in various packaged forms and markets them under more than 50 brands. Principal chocolate and confectionery products in the U.S. are: Hershey's, Hershey's with almonds, and Cookies 'N' Mint bars; Hugs and Kisses (both also with almonds) chocolates; Kit Kat wafer bars; Mr. Goodbar chocolate bars; Reese's Pieces candies; Rolo caramels in milk chocolate; Skor toffee bars; Y&S Twizzlers licorice; and Amazin' Fruit gummy bears fruit candy. HSY significantly increased its participation in the non-chocolate side of the confectionery industry through its late 1996 acquisition of Leaf North America, whose major brands include Jolly Rancher, Whoppers, Milk Duds, and Good & Plenty. Grocery products include Hershey's chocolate chips, cocoa and syrup; and Reese's peanut butter and peanut butter chips. Hershey's chocolate milk is produced and sold under license by independent dairies throughout the U.S., using a chocolate milk mix manufactured by HSY. The most significant raw material used in the production of the company's chocolate and confectionery products is cocoa beans.

In January 1999, Hershey completed the sale of 94% of its U.S. pasta business to New World Pasta, for $450 million in cash. The transaction resulted in an after-tax gain of approximately $1.17 a share in the 1999 first quarter. HSY had marketed its products on a regional basis under brand names that included San Giorgio, Ronzoni, Skinner, P&R, Light 'n Fluffy and American Beauty.

The company has various international arrangements, the investment in which changes from time to time, but which in the aggregate are not material to HSY.

In August 2000, the company announced a 7.7% increase in the dividend paid on the common stock, marking the 26th consecutive annual increase.

In December 2000, the company purchased the intense and breath freshener mints and gum businesses of Nabisco for $135 million. The acquired brands included Breath Savers mints, and Ice Breakers, Carefree, Stickfree, Bubble Yum and Fruit Stripe gums. The businesses had 1999 sales of approximately $270 million.

Per Share Data ($) (Year Ended Dec. 31)	2000	1999	1998	1997	1996	1995	1994	1993	1992	1991
Tangible Bk. Val.	5.14	4.68	3.58	2.11	3.89	4.24	5.70	5.36	5.91	5.07
Cash Flow	3.69	4.41	3.43	3.24	2.64	2.51	1.80	2.21	1.81	1.62
Earnings	2.42	3.26	2.34	2.23	1.77	1.70	1.06	1.66	1.34	1.22
Dividends	1.08	1.00	0.92	0.84	0.76	0.69	0.63	0.57	0.52	0.47
Payout Ratio	45%	31%	39%	38%	43%	40%	59%	34%	38%	39%
Prices - High	66.43	64.87	76.37	63.87	51.75	33.93	26.75	27.93	24.18	22.25
- Low	37.75	45.75	59.68	42.12	31.93	24.00	20.56	21.75	19.12	17.56
P/E Ratio - High	27	20	33	29	29	20	25	17	18	18
- Low	16	14	26	19	18	14	19	13	14	14
Income Statement Analysis (Million $)										
Revs.	4,221	3,971	4,436	4,302	3,989	3,691	3,606	3,488	3,220	2,899
Oper. Inc.	799	722	801	783	697	645	604	557	513	463
Depr.	176	163	158	153	133	134	129	100	84.4	72.7
Int. Exp.	81.0	77.3	88.6	79.1	53.6	50.0	40.3	34.9	41.8	39.7
Pretax Inc.	547	728	557	554	480	466	333	511	401	363
Eff. Tax Rate	39%	37%	39%	39%	43%	40%	45%	42%	40%	40%
Net Inc.	335	460	341	336	273	282	184	297	243	220
Balance Sheet & Other Fin. Data (Million $)										
Cash	32.0	118	39.0	54.2	61.4	32.0	27.0	16.0	203	71.0
Curr. Assets	1,295	1,280	1,134	1,035	986	922	949	889	940	744
Total Assets	3,448	3,347	3,404	3,291	3,185	2,831	2,891	2,855	2,673	2,342
Curr. Liab.	767	713	815	796	817	864	796	814	737	471
LT Debt	878	878	879	1,029	655	357	157	166	174	283
Common Eqty.	1,175	1,099	1,042	853	1,161	1,083	1,441	1,412	1,465	1,335
Total Cap.	2,353	2,303	2,243	2,149	2,040	1,632	1,792	1,751	1,843	1,790
Cap. Exp.	138	115	161	173	159	141	139	212	250	226
Cash Flow	511	624	499	489	407	416	313	397	327	292
Curr. Ratio	1.7	1.8	1.4	1.3	1.2	1.1	1.2	1.1	1.3	1.6
% LT Debt of Cap.	37.3	38.1	39.2	47.9	32.1	21.9	8.8	9.5	9.5	15.8
% Net Inc.of Revs.	7.9	11.6	7.7	7.8	6.9	7.6	5.1	8.5	7.5	7.6
% Ret. on Assets	9.8	13.6	10.2	10.4	9.1	9.9	6.4	10.9	9.7	9.9
% Ret. on Equity	29.4	43.0	36.0	33.4	24.4	22.3	13.0	21.0	17.3	17.0

Data as orig reptd.; bef. results of disc opers/spec. items. Per share data adj. for stk. divs. Bold denotes diluted EPS (FASB 128)-prior periods restated. E-Estimated. NA-Not Available. NM-Not Meaningful. NR-Not Ranked.

Office—100 Crystal A Drive, Hershey, PA 17033. **Tel**—(717) 534-6799. **Website**—http://www.hersheys.com **Chrmn**—K. L. Wolfe. **Pres & CEO**—R. H. Lenny. **EVP & COO**—W. F. Christ. **SVP & Secy**—R. M. Reese. **VP, CFO & Treas**—F. Cerminara. **Investor Contact**—James A. Edris (717-534-7556). **Dirs**—R. H. Campbell, C. McCollister Evarts, B. G. Hill, J. R. Hillier, J. C. Jamison, R. H. Lenny, M. J. McDonald, J. M. Pietruski, K. L. Wolfe. **Transfer Agent & Registrar**—Mellon Investor Services, Ridgefield Park, NJ. **Incorporated**—in Delaware in 1927. **Empl**— 14,300. **S&P Analyst:** Richard Joy

STANDARD
&POOR'S
STOCK REPORTS

PepsiCo

NYSE Symbol **PEP**

In S&P 500

18-AUG-01 **Industry:** Beverages (Non-Alcoholic)

Summary: PepsiCo is a major international producer of branded beverage and snack food products.

S&P Opinion: Buy (★★★★★)

Recent Price • 45.68 | Yield • 1.3%
52 Wk Range • 49.93-40.25 | 12-Mo. P/E • 28.9

Quantitative Evaluations

Outlook
(1 Lowest—5 Highest)
• **2**

Fair Value
• **42.80**

Risk
• **Low**

Earn./Div. Rank
• **A**

Technical Eval.
• **Neutral** since 8/01

Rel. Strength Rank
(1 Lowest—99 Highest)
• **62**

Insider Activity
• **Neutral**

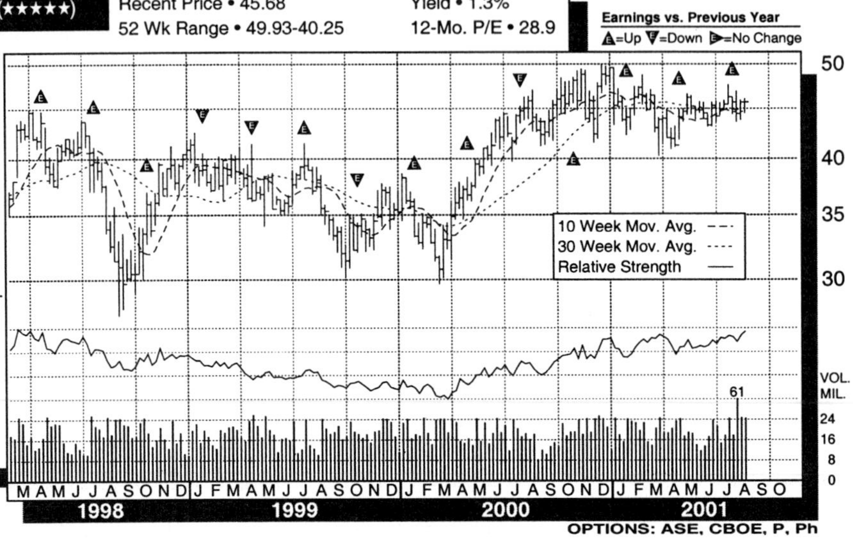

OPTIONS: ASE, CBOE, P, Ph

Overview - 23-JUL-01

PEP is currently seeking regulatory approval for the acquisition of Quaker Oats, maker of Gatorade brand sports drinks. Excluding contributions from this acquisition, profits for the beverage segment in 2001 are projected to rise a healthy 10%-11%, reflecting 3% volume growth in North America and a strong rebound for international operations. Beverage profits in North America should continue to benefit from a more favorable pricing environment. Snack food profits are expected to rise about 11%-12%, reflecting 2%-3% unit volume growth, 4%-5% higher prices and favorable raw material costs. Tropicana should continue to be a strong profit contributor in 2001, with a 7%-8% increase in profits anticipated. The equity income line could increase 18%-20%, due to continued strong results at the Pepsi Bottling Group. We expect EPS of $1.67 in 2001, up 15% from $1.45 in 2000.

Valuation - 23-JUL-01

We continue our buy recommendation on the shares, reflecting our expectation for enhanced profit growth, earnings consistency and accelerating free cash flow in light of the pending acquisition of the Quaker Oats Company. With this acquisition, we believe, PEP is poised to deliver 13%-14% annual EPS growth on a consistent basis. Taken together with its purchase of South Beach Beverage Co., these acquisitions provide PepsiCo with leading positions in several fast growing non-carbonated beverage categories. At a recent P/E multiple of 24X our 2002 EPS estimate of $1.90, the shares are valued at a discount to their beverage industry peers, but at a premium to the S&P 500 Index. Despite this premium valuation, the shares are attractive given the company's promising longer-term prospects from its large market positions in the growing worldwide packaged beverage and snack industries.

Key Stock Statistics

S&P EPS Est. 2001	1.67	Tang. Bk. Value/Share	1.91
P/E on S&P Est. 2001	27.4	Beta	0.85
S&P EPS Est. 2002	1.90	Shareholders	204,000
Dividend Rate/Share	0.58	Market cap. (B)	$ 80.8
Shs. outstg. (M)	1767.8	Inst. holdings	54%
Avg. daily vol. (M)	6.943		

Value of $10,000 invested 5 years ago: NA

Fiscal Year Ending Dec. 31

	2001	2000	1999	1998	1997	1996
Revenues (Million $)						
1Q	4,539	4,191	5,114	4,353	4,213	6,554
2Q	5,281	4,928	4,982	5,258	5,086	7,691
3Q	—	4,909	4,591	5,544	5,362	7,867
4Q	—	6,410	5,680	7,193	6,256	9,533
Yr.	—	20,438	20,367	22,348	20,917	31,645
Earnings Per Share ($)						
1Q	**0.34**	**0.29**	**0.22**	**0.24**	**0.20**	**0.18**
2Q	**0.44**	**0.38**	**0.49**	**0.33**	**0.11**	**0.27**
3Q	**E0.45**	**0.40**	**0.32**	**0.50**	**0.35**	**0.01**
4Q	**E0.44**	**0.41**	**0.33**	**0.24**	**0.29**	**0.13**
Yr.	**E1.67**	**1.48**	**1.37**	**1.31**	**0.95**	**0.59**

Next earnings report expected: early October

Dividend Data (Dividends have been paid since 1952.)

Amount ($)	Date Decl.	Ex-Div. Date	Stock of Record	Payment Date
0.140	Nov. 16	Dec. 06	Dec. 08	Jan. 02 '01
0.140	Feb. 01	Mar. 07	Mar. 09	Mar. 30 '01
0.145	May. 02	Jun. 06	Jun. 08	Jun. 29 '01
0.145	Jul. 26	Sep. 05	Sep. 07	Sep. 28 '01

PepsiCo, Inc.

Business Summary - 23-JUL-01

PepsiCo has undergone several transformations in recent years designed to reduce the capital intensiveness of its operations. In October 1997, the company spun off its restaurant division to shareholders (named TRICON Global Restaurants, Inc., and listed on the NYSE under the symbol YUM), and in March 1999 the majority of its company owned bottling operations was spun off (named Pepsi Bottling Group, and listed on the NYSE under the symbol PBG). The "new" PepsiCo is now focused on beverages and snack foods.

The soft drink business operates as the The Pepsi-Cola Company (25% of 2000 sales, 28% of operating profits), and primarily consists of the production and distribution (to licensed bottlers) of beverage concentrates. Pepsi-Cola bottlers are licensed by PepsiCo to manufacture, sell and distribute, within defined territories, beverages and syrups bearing the Pepsi-Cola beverage trademarks. Principal brands include Pepsi, Pepsi-Cola, Diet Pepsi, Pepsi One, Pepsi Max, Mountain Dew, Slice, Mug, Fruit Works, Sierra Mist, All-Sport, Aquafina and, within Canada, 7UP and Diet 7UP. The Pepsi/Lipton Tea Partnership joint venture sells tea concentrate to Pepsi-Cola bottlers under the Lipton trademark, including Lipton Brisk and Lipton's Iced Tea. A partnership with Starbucks Corporation develops ready-to-drink coffee products sold under the Frappucino trademark. Pepsi-Cola products are available in approximately 160 countries.

Tropicana Products, Inc. (12% of 2000 sales, 6% of operating profits) was purchased in August 1998 from The Seagram Company Ltd., for $3.3 billion cash. Tropicana is the world's largest marketer and producer of branded juices. In addition to Tropicana Pure Premium, Season's Best and Dole, Tropicana's portfolio includes Tropicana Pure Tropics 100% juice products and Tropicana Twister juice beverage products in the U.S., and Fruvita chilled juices, Looza nectars and juices, Copella fruit juices and Alvalle soups and fruit juices in Europe.

The snack food product business (63% of 2000 sales, 66% of operating profits) is operated as The Frito-Lay Company, which produces the best-selling line of snack foods in the U.S., including Fritos brand corn chips, Lay's and Ruffles brand potato chips, Doritos and Tostitos brand tortilla chips, Chee-tos brand cheese-flavored snacks, Rold Gold pretzels, and Sunchips brand multigrain snacks. Products are transported from Frito-Lay's manufacturing plants to major distribution centers, principally by company-owned trucks. Principal international markets include Australia, Brazil, France, Mexico, the Netherlands, Poland, Spain and the U.K. In October 1997, Frito-Lay acquired the Cracker Jack candy-coated popcorn and peanut snack business from Borden Foods.

Per Share Data ($) (Year Ended Dec. 31)	2000	1999	1998	1997	1996	1995	1994	1993	1992	1991
Tangible Bk. Val.	1.91	1.48	NM	0.72	NM	NM	-0.63	-0.99	-1.00	-0.24
Cash Flow	2.13	2.06	2.12	1.65	1.79	2.08	2.09	1.84	1.54	1.30
Earnings	1.48	1.37	1.31	0.95	0.72	1.00	1.11	0.98	0.81	0.68
Dividends	0.56	0.53	0.51	0.49	0.45	0.39	0.35	0.30	0.26	0.23
Payout Ratio	38%	39%	39%	52%	62%	39%	32%	31%	31%	34%
Prices - High	49.93	42.56	44.81	41.31	35.87	29.37	20.56	21.81	21.68	17.81
- Low	29.68	30.12	27.56	28.25	27.25	16.93	14.62	17.25	15.25	11.75
P/E Ratio - High	34	31	34	43	50	29	19	22	27	26
- Low	20	22	21	30	38	17	13	18	19	17
Income Statement Analysis (Million $)										
Revs.	20,438	20,367	22,348	20,917	31,645	30,421	28,472	25,021	21,970	19,608
Oper. Inc.	4,185	3,915	4,106	4,058	5,087	5,247	4,778	4,312	3,754	3,302
Depr.	960	1,032	1,234	1,106	1,719	1,740	1,577	1,405	1,189	1,009
Int. Exp.	221	363	395	478	600	682	645	573	586	616
Pretax Inc.	3,210	3,656	2,263	2,309	2,047	2,432	2,664	2,423	1,899	1,670
Eff. Tax Rate	32%	44%	12%	35%	44%	34%	33%	35%	31%	35%
Net Inc.	2,183	2,050	1,993	1,491	1,149	1,606	1,784	1,588	1,302	1,080
Balance Sheet & Other Fin. Data (Million $)										
Cash	864	964	311	2,883	786	1,498	1,488	1,856	2,058	2,036
Curr. Assets	4,604	4,173	4,362	6,251	5,139	5,546	5,072	5,164	4,842	4,566
Total Assets	18,339	17,551	22,660	20,101	24,512	25,432	24,792	23,706	20,951	18,775
Curr. Liab.	3,935	3,788	7,914	4,257	5,139	5,230	5,270	6,575	4,324	3,722
LT Debt	2,346	2,812	4,028	4,946	8,439	8,509	8,841	7,443	7,965	7,806
Common Eqty.	7,249	6,881	6,401	6,939	6,623	7,313	6,856	6,339	5,356	5,545
Total Cap.	10,956	10,902	12,432	13,582	16,840	17,707	17,669	15,789	15,003	14,422
Cap. Exp.	1,067	1,118	1,405	1,506	2,287	2,104	2,253	2,008	1,583	1,524
Cash Flow	3,143	3,082	3,227	2,597	2,868	3,346	3,361	2,993	2,491	2,089
Curr. Ratio	1.2	1.1	0.6	1.5	1.0	1.0	1.0	0.8	1.1	1.2
% LT Debt of Cap.	21.4	25.8	32.4	36.4	50.1	48.1	50.0	47.1	53.1	54.1
% Net Inc.of Revs.	10.7	10.1	8.9	7.1	3.6	5.3	6.3	6.3	5.9	5.5
% Ret. on Assets	12.2	10.2	9.3	7.1	4.6	6.4	7.4	7.1	6.5	6.0
% Ret. on Equity	30.9	30.9	29.9	22.0	16.5	22.7	27.2	27.2	22.0	20.7

Data as orig reptd.; bef. results of disc opers/spec. items. Per share data adj. for stk. divs. Bold denotes diluted EPS (FASB 128)-prior periods restated. E-Estimated. NA-Not Available. NM-Not Meaningful. NR-Not Ranked.

Office—700 Anderson Hill Rd., Purchase, NY 10577-1444. **Tel**—(914) 253-3035. **Fax**—(914) 253-2711. **Website**—http://www.pepsico.com **Chrmn & CEO**—S. S. Reinemund. **Vice Chrmn**—R. A. Enrico. **Pres & CFO**—I. K. Nooyi. **SVP & Treas**—M. M. McKenna. **SVP & Secy**—R. F. Sharpe, Jr. **VP & Investor Contact**—Susan Watson, CFA. **Dirs**—J. F. Akers, R. E. Allen, R. A. Enrico, P. Foy, R. L. Hunt, A. C. Martinez, J. J. Murphy, I. K. Nooyi, F. D. Raines, S. S. Reinemund, S. P. Rockefeller, F. A. Thomas, C. M. Trudell, S. D. Trujillo. **Transfer Agent**—Bank of Boston. **Incorporated**—in Delaware in 1919; reincorporated in North Carolina in 1986. **Empl**— 124,000. **S&P Analyst:** Richard Joy

STANDARD
&POOR'S
STOCK REPORTS

Hain Celestial Group

Nasdaq Symbol **HAIN**

In S&P SmallCap 600

22-AUG-01 **Industry:** Foods

Summary: This company sells natural and organic foods, specialty teas, medically directed foods, kosher foods, and weight management and portion control foods.

S&P Opinion: Accumulate (★★★★)

Recent Price • 24.30
52 Wk Range • 40.12-20.67
Yield • Nil
12-Mo. P/E • NM

Quantitative Evaluations

Outlook
(1 Lowest—5 Highest)
• 1-

Fair Value
• 21.90

Risk
• NA

Earn./Div. Rank
• NR

Technical Eval.
• Neutral since 7/01

Rel. Strength Rank
(1 Lowest—99 Highest)
• 51

Insider Activity
• Unfavorable

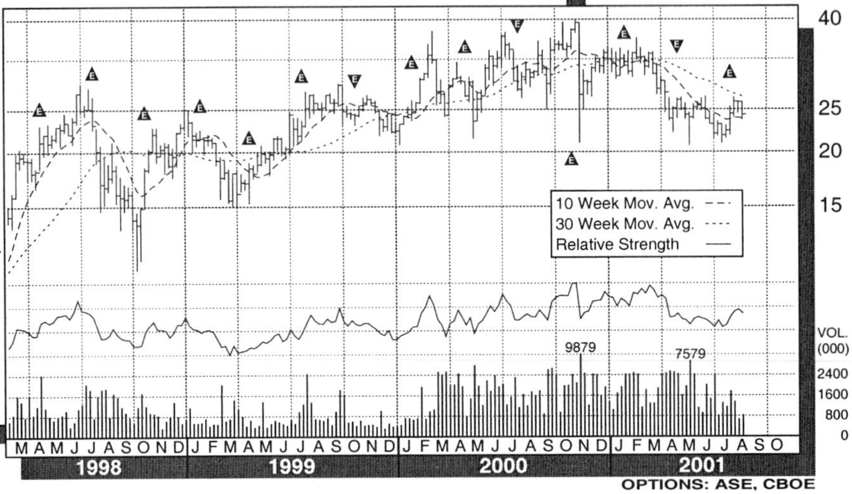

OPTIONS: ASE, CBOE

Overview - 22-AUG-01

Net sales growth in FY 02 (Jun.) should exceed 15%, reflecting strong growth in core natural food brands and acquisition contributions. HAIN recently acquired privately held Yves Veggie Cuisine, which could contribute more than $35 million to sales in FY 02. Margins should show some improvement over FY 01, reflecting moderating fuel and packaging costs and lower manufacturing costs from the opening of a new Terra Chip production facility. SG&A costs may increase on higher promotional spending to expand grocery distribution, especially for Westsoy. Longer term, we expect profitability to benefit from increased sales of higher-margin products and expanded distribution. Following lower net interest expense, we see EPS of $1.10 in FY 02, up 17.6% from an anticipated $0.73 in FY 01 before special items. Longer term, annual earnings growth of 15% to 20% is expected.

Valuation - 22-AUG-01

We continue to rank the shares accumulate, reflecting our expectation for continued strong volume and sales growth and a rebound in earnings in coming quarters. HAIN commands leading market positions in 13 of the top 15 natural and organic foods categories, among the fastest growing segments of the food industry. Results for the third quarter of FY 01 (Jun.) showed strong growth for its core soy beverages, Terra chips, Earth's Best baby food, Health Valley and Celestial teas product lines. The company should continue to benefit from increasing consumer interest in natural foods, new product introductions, enhanced distribution, acquisitions and international expansion. Recently trading at an enterprise value (market capitalization plus long-term debt minus cash) of less than 10 times our EBITDA estimate for FY 02, the shares are attractive given HAIN's strong balance sheet and brand momentum.

Key Stock Statistics

S&P EPS Est. 2001	0.73	Tang. Bk. Value/Share	3.84
P/E on S&P Est. 2001	33.3	Beta	0.87
S&P EPS Est. 2002	1.10	Shareholders	305
Dividend Rate/Share	Nil	Market cap. (B)	$0.723
Shs. outstg. (M)	33.6	Inst. holdings	62%
Avg. daily vol. (M)	0.318		

Value of $10,000 invested 5 years ago: $ 69,428

Fiscal Year Ending Jun. 30

	2001	2000	1999	1998	1997	1996
Revenues (Million $)						
1Q	93.65	87.94	43.50	16.34	15.44	13.53
2Q	116.0	116.7	50.60	28.68	17.12	18.12
3Q	103.9	111.9	50.83	28.21	13.62	17.22
4Q	—	87.01	61.04	31.03	19.18	19.74
Yr.	—	403.5	206.0	104.3	65.35	68.61
Earnings Per Share ($)						
1Q	**0.19**	**-0.05**	**0.12**	0.05	0.04	0.05
2Q	**0.30**	**0.28**	**0.17**	**0.11**	**0.05**	0.08
3Q	**0.12**	**0.28**	**0.21**	**0.11**	Nil	0.06
4Q	**E0.10**	**-0.93**	**0.23**	**0.13**	0.03	0.06
Yr.	**E0.73**	**-0.41**	**0.71**	**0.39**	**0.12**	**0.24**

Next earnings report expected: mid September

Dividend Data

No cash dividends have been paid. The company intends to retain its earnings for use in the development of its business and does not anticipate paying cash dividends in the foreseeable future.

The Hain Celestial Group, Inc.

Business Summary - 22-AUG-01

In May 2000, The Hain Food Group merged with Celestial Seasonings Inc. (CTEA), the specialty tea market leader. The new company was named The Hain Celestial Group. HAIN plans to leverage the distribution channels of both brands.

Hain products are divided into six categories: natural food and organic, tea and beverage, medically directed and weight management, specialty cooking oils, kosher, and snack foods. Distribution is focused on natural food stores, supermarkets, food service distributors, specialty groceries, mass merchandisers and drug stores.

HAIN distributes approximately 1,000 branded natural and organic food products that include non-dairy drinks (soy and rice milk), popcorn cakes, cookies, crackers, flour and baking mixes, hot and cold cereals, pasta, baby food, condiments, cooking oils, granolas, granola bars, cereal bars, canned and instant soups, chilis, packaged grain, nut butters and nutritional oils, as well as other food products. Specialty cooking oils feature the Hollywood brand line, which markets specialty cooking oils that are enhanced with vitamin E. Natural food products are defined as foods that are minimally processed, and largely free of artificial ingredients, preservatives and other non-naturally occurring chemicals.

The company's beverage and tea products consist of herb teas which are made from all natural ingredients and are offered in a wide variety of flavors. In FY 00 (Jun.), tea beverages accounted for approximately 24% of total net sales.

Medically directed and weight management products feature the Estee and Featherweight brands, which market a full line of sugar-free, fructose sweetened and low sodium products. These products are targeted at diabetic and health conscious consumers and those on medically directed diets.

Snack Foods include a variety of potato and vegetable chips, organic tortilla style chips, pretzels, and popcorn under the Terra Chips, Garden of Eatin', Little Bear, Boston Popcorn and Harry's Original brand names.

The company also offers a line of kosher frozen food products under the Kineret and Kosherific labels. Kosher food products are prepared according to Jewish dietary laws.

In FY 00, approximately 45% of the company's revenue was derived from products manufactured at independent co-packers using proprietary specifications controlled by the company. Product lines manufactured by co-packers include Estee, Garden of Eatin', Hain Pure Foods, Kineret, Little Bear Organic Foods, Terra Chips, Westbrae, and Westsoy product lines.

In September 1999, HAIN formed a strategic alliance with H. J. Heinz Co. for the global production of natural and organic foods and soy-based beverages. In connection with the alliance, Heinz acquired a 19.5% interest in the company, and HAIN acquired the Earth's Baby Food brand from Heinz.

Per Share Data ($) (Year Ended Jun. 30)	2000	1999	1998	1997	1996	1995	1994	1993	1992	1991
Tangible Bk. Val.	3.84	NM	NM	NM	NM	0.53	NA	NA	NA	NA
Cash Flow	0.01	1.01	0.52	0.22	0.33	0.35	-0.09	NA	NA	NA
Earnings	-0.41	0.71	0.39	0.12	0.24	0.28	-0.19	NA	NA	NA
Dividends	Nil	Nil	Nil	Nil	Nil	Nil	Nil	NA	NA	NA
Payout Ratio	Nil	Nil	Nil	Nil	Nil	Nil	Nil	NA	NA	NA
Prices - High	40.12	28.62	28.62	12.81	4.12	5.50	5.62	NA	NA	NA
- Low	20.75	14.93	9.00	3.37	2.87	2.75	2.50	NA	NA	NA
P/E Ratio - High	NM	40	73	93	17	19	NM	NA	NA	NA
- Low	NM	21	23	28	12	12	NM	NA	NA	NA
Income Statement Analysis (Million $)										
Revs.	404	206	104	65.4	68.6	58.1	15.0	NA	NA	NA
Oper. Inc.	33.4	29.3	12.1	4.9	6.8	6.5	1.2	NA	NA	NA
Depr.	11.8	4.6	1.6	0.9	0.8	0.6	0.3	NA	NA	NA
Int. Exp.	6.7	5.3	2.6	2.1	2.2	1.8	0.5	NA	NA	NA
Pretax Inc.	-7.5	19.5	7.9	1.9	3.8	4.1	-0.3	NA	NA	NA
Eff. Tax Rate	NM	43%	41%	42%	43%	43%	NA	NA	NA	NA
Net Inc.	-11.4	11.0	4.6	1.1	2.1	2.4	-0.5	NA	NA	NA
Balance Sheet & Other Fin. Data (Million $)										
Cash	38.3	0.5	0.5	0.2	0.3	0.2	0.7	NA	NA	NA
Curr. Assets	143	59.3	29.2	16.5	17.0	13.8	11.3	NA	NA	NA
Total Assets	416	282	88.3	48.9	47.4	34.9	31.7	NA	NA	NA
Curr. Liab.	53.1	40.5	14.7	12.0	10.5	4.9	6.8	NA	NA	NA
LT Debt	5.6	131	16.6	10.8	12.1	7.3	13.5	NA	NA	NA
Common Eqty.	352	110	53.2	25.1	24.4	22.3	11.5	NA	NA	NA
Total Cap.	363	241	71.0	35.9	36.5	30.0	25.0	NA	NA	NA
Cap. Exp.	4.3	0.9	0.6	0.1	0.2	0.4	NA	NA	NA	NA
Cash Flow	0.4	15.6	6.2	2.0	3.0	3.0	-0.2	NA	NA	NA
Curr. Ratio	2.7	1.5	2.0	1.4	1.6	2.8	1.7	NA	NA	NA
% LT Debt of Cap.	1.5	54.3	23.3	30.1	33.2	24.3	54.0	NA	NA	NA
% Net Inc.of Revs.	NM	5.4	4.4	1.6	3.1	4.1	NA	NA	NA	NA
% Ret. on Assets	NM	6.0	6.8	2.2	5.2	7.1	NA	NA	NA	NA
% Ret. on Equity	NM	13.5	11.8	4.3	9.1	14.0	NA	NA	NA	NA

Data as orig reptd.; bef. results of disc opers/spec. items. Per share data adj. for stk. divs. Bold denotes diluted EPS (FASB 128)-prior periods restated. E-Estimated. NA-Not Available. NM-Not Meaningful. NR-Not Ranked.

Office—50 Charles Lindbergh Blvd., Uniondale, NY 11553. **Tel**—(516) 237-6200. **Website**—www.hain-celestial.com **Chrmn, Pres & CEO**—I. D. Simon. **Vice Chrmn**—M. Siegel. **SVP & CFO**—G. M. Jacobs. **Dirs**—B. L. Bronner, N. Clare, K. J. Daley, J. Futterman, J. S. Gold, M. Hahn, A. R. Heyer, J. Jimenez, G. Ostrander, M. Siegel, I. D. Simon. **Transfer Agent & Registrar**—Continental Stock Transfer & Trust Co., NYC. **Incorporated**—in Delaware in 1993. **Empl**— 940. **S&P Analyst:** Richard Joy

STANDARD
&POOR'S
STOCK REPORTS

Kroger Co.

NYSE Symbol **KR**

In S&P 500

18-AUG-01

Industry:
Retail (Food Chains)

Summary: This leading operator of supermarkets and convenience stores merged with Fred Meyer, Inc., in May 1999, creating the largest U.S. supermarket company.

S&P Opinion: Accumulate (★★★★)

Recent Price • 25.52
52 Wk Range • 27.93-19.87
Yield • Nil
12-Mo. P/E • 19.9

Quantitative Evaluations

Outlook
(1 Lowest—5 Highest)
• 4+

Fair Value
• 29.70

Risk
• Low

Earn./Div. Rank
• B+

Technical Eval.
• Bullish since 7/01

Rel. Strength Rank
(1 Lowest—99 Highest)
• 62

Insider Activity
• Unfavorable

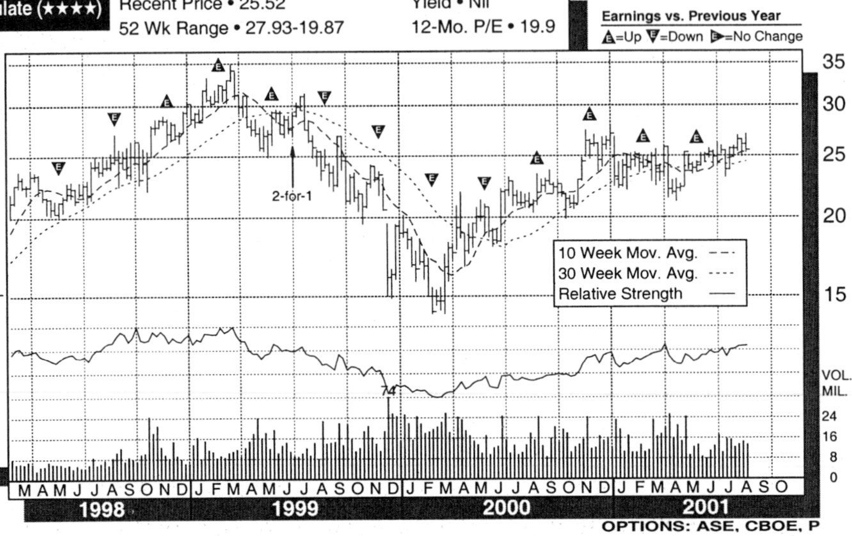

OPTIONS: ASE, CBOE, P

Overview - 25-MAY-01

We expect sales to grow 5% to 7% in FY 02 (Jan.), reflecting a 4.5% to 5.0% increase in square footage, and same-store sales gains of about 1.0% above the food inflation rate. Profitability will benefit from $380 million in annualized cost savings due to the May 1999 merger with Fred Meyer. Gross margins are likely to widen, reflecting greater purchasing leverage, improved manufacturing, and higher sales of private label products. Operating profitability should improve on lower overhead expenses, reflecting the elimination of redundant administrative functions and the consolidation of information systems at Fred Meyer. We expect operating EPS, excluding merger-related charges, to climb 19% in FY 02, to $1.60, from FY 01's $1.34.

Valuation - 25-MAY-01

We are maintaining an accumulate opinion on KR shares, reflecting the company's strong fundamentals and its attractiveness as a safe haven in an uncertain market. The shares were recently trading at only 14X our FY 02 EPS estimate, below the company's stated long-term annual EPS growth rate target of 15%. The shares have historically been penalized by the company's higher than average debt to capitalization level. KR's debt to capitalization ratio is 72%, versus an industry average of 40%, and we believe this has caused investor concern. However, these fears are likely to abate over the next few years, as KR uses free cash flow to lower debt levels. The company is also seeing positive earnings trends, as it realizes better than expected synergies from its merger with Fred Meyer. A $1 billion buyback program is an added plus. We believe the shares are an attractive portfolio addition for long-term investors.

Key Stock Statistics

S&P EPS Est. 2002	1.55	Tang. Bk. Value/Share	NM
P/E on S&P Est. 2002	16.5	Beta	0.18
S&P EPS Est. 2003	1.78	Shareholders	51,286
Dividend Rate/Share	Nil	Market cap. (B)	$ 20.5
Shs. outstg. (M)	804.0	Inst. holdings	71%
Avg. daily vol. (M)	2.653		

Value of $10,000 invested 5 years ago: $ 25,520

Fiscal Year Ending Jan. 31

	2002	2001	2000	1999	1998	1997
Revenues (Million $)						
1Q	15,102	14,329	13,493	6,389	6,139	5,784
2Q	—	11,017	10,289	6,442	6,232	5,844
3Q	—	10,962	10,329	8,024	7,687	7,343
4Q	—	12,692	11,240	7,349	6,510	6,199
Yr.	—	49,000	45,352	28,203	26,567	25,171
Earnings Per Share ($)						
1Q	**0.36**	**0.12**	**0.24**	**0.10**	0.17	0.15
2Q	**E0.32**	**0.26**	**0.06**	**0.18**	0.20	0.15
3Q	**E0.33**	**0.28**	**0.15**	**0.23**	0.18	0.14
4Q	**E0.52**	**0.44**	**0.29**	**0.34**	**0.28**	0.24
Yr.	**E1.55**	**1.04**	**0.77**	**0.85**	**0.84**	**0.68**

Next earnings report expected: mid September

Dividend Data

No cash dividends have been paid since 1988.

The Kroger Co.

Business Summary - 25-MAY-01

In May 1999, Kroger completed a merger with Fred Meyer, Inc., creating the largest U.S. supermarket chain. As a result of the merger, the company changed its fiscal year end from December 31 to January 31. As of February 3, 2001, KR operated 2,354 supermarkets, which operated under one of three operating formats: combination food and drug stores, multi-department stores, or price impact warehouse stores. In addition, KR operated 789 convenience stores, 77 supermarket fuel centers, and 398 jewelry stores. It also operated 42 manufacturing plants, consisting of 15 dairies, 12 deli or bakery plants, five grocery product plants, five ice cream or beverage plants, three meat plants, and two cheese plants.

KR's acquisition of Fred Meyer came after Fred Meyer itself acquired a number of supermarket chains. In 1998, Fred Meyer acquired Quality Food Centers, Inc., operating in the Seattle/Puget Sound region of Washington and in Southern California, and Food 4 Less Holdings, Inc., the operator of Ralphs and Food 4 Less stores, primarily located in Southern California. In 1997, it acquired Smith's, which operates in the Intermountain region and the Southwest; Hughes Markets, Inc., which operates in Southern California; and Keith Uddenberg, Inc., operating in the western and southern Puget Sound region.

KR's goals through FY 03 include increasing EPS 16% to 18% a year. It expects to achieve this growth through annual sales growth of at least 5% to 6% that will generate earnings per share growth of 10%-11%, margin improvements of 20 basis points per year that will produce 4% to 5% earnings per share growth, and deleveraging and stock repurchase that should add 2% growth to earnings per share. The company expects the 5% to 6% annual sales growth to be driven by a 1% increase in identical store sales above product cost inflation plus a 4% to 5% increase in retail square footage, excluding acquisitions. Identical store sales growth is expected to be achieved by rising pharmacy sales and the introduction of additional private label items. In FY 02, KR plans to open 110-120 supermarkets and complete approximately 180 remodels.

The major source of gross profit and operating, general and administrative expense improvement is the $380 million of projected annual synergies from the Fred Meyer integration expected to be delivered by FY 02. Operating margin expansion is also being driven by category management savings, increased private-label penetration, and manufacturing synergies. On March 1, 2001, directors authorized the repurchase of $1 billion of stock over the next two years. KR also set a goal of reducing net total debt from 2.3 times EBITDA, the level at the close of FY 01, to 2.0 times.

Per Share Data ($)

(Year Ended Jan. 31)	2001	2000	1999	1998	1997	1996	1995	1994	1993	1992
Tangible Bk. Val.	NM	NM	NM	NM	NM	NM	-4.97	-5.83	-7.53	-8.01
Cash Flow	2.11	1.86	1.66	1.57	1.33	1.10	1.20	0.99	0.94	0.93
Earnings	1.04	0.74	0.85	0.84	0.67	0.66	0.59	0.40	0.28	0.28
Dividends	Nil	Nil	Nil	Nil	Nil	Nil	Nil	Nil	Nil	Nil
Payout Ratio	Nil	Nil	Nil	Nil	Nil	Nil	Nil	Nil	Nil	Nil
Cal. Yrs.	2000	1999	1998	1997	1996	1995	1994	1993	1992	1991
Prices - High	27.93	34.90	18.65	11.87	9.43	6.71	5.43	5.28	6.12	4.25
- Low	14.06	14.87	11.34	8.37	5.84	4.84	3.50	2.81	3.15	2.65
P/E Ratio - High	27	47	22	18	14	11	14	19	22	18
- Low	14	20	13	12	9	8	9	10	11	11

Income Statement Analysis (Million $)

	2001	2000	1999	1998	1997	1996	1995	1994	1993	1992
Revs.	49,000	45,352	28,203	26,567	25,171	23,938	22,959	22,384	22,145	21,351
Oper. Inc.	3,397	3,125	1,410	1,377	1,212	1,134	1,027	954	889	934
Depr.	907	961	430	380	344	311	278	253	241	234
Int. Exp.	675	652	267	285	300	313	331	392	475	535
Pretax Inc.	1,508	1,129	713	712	568	510	421	284	173	169
Eff. Tax Rate	42%	43%	37%	38%	38%	37%	36%	40%	42%	40%
Net Inc.	880	638	450	444	353	319	269	171	101	101

Balance Sheet & Other Fin. Data (Million $)

	2001	2000	1999	1998	1997	1996	1995	1994	1993	1992
Cash	161	281	122	65.0	Nil	Nil	27.0	121	104	4.0
Curr. Assets	5,416	5,531	2,673	2,641	2,353	2,107	2,152	2,226	2,168	1,992
Total Assets	18,190	17,966	6,700	6,301	5,825	5,045	4,708	4,480	4,303	4,114
Curr. Liab.	5,591	5,728	3,192	2,944	2,713	2,565	2,395	2,251	2,174	2,087
LT Debt	8,210	8,045	3,229	3,493	3,479	3,490	3,889	4,135	4,473	4,408
Common Eqty.	3,089	2,683	-388	-784	-1,182	-1,603	-2,154	-2,460	-2,700	-2,749
Total Cap.	11,299	10,728	3,042	2,874	2,629	2,040	1,908	1,858	2,051	1,928
Cap. Exp.	1,623	1,701	923	612	734	726	534	395	245	226
Cash Flow	1,787	1,599	880	824	697	614	547	424	342	335
Curr. Ratio	1.0	1.0	0.8	0.9	0.9	0.8	0.9	1.0	1.0	1.0
% LT Debt of Cap.	72.7	75.0	106.1	121.5	103.2	171.1	203.8	222.5	218.1	228.6
% Net Inc.of Revs.	1.8	1.4	1.6	1.7	1.4	1.3	1.2	0.8	0.5	0.5
% Ret. on Assets	4.9	3.7	6.9	7.3	6.5	6.2	5.8	3.6	2.4	2.4
% Ret. on Equity	30.5	27.7	NM	NM	NM	NM	NM	NM	NM	NM

Data as orig reptd.; bef. results of disc opers/spec. items. Prior to 2000, yrs. ended Dec. 31 of the prior cal. yr. Per share data adj. for stk. divs. Bold denotes diluted EPS (FASB 128)-prior periods restated. E-Estimated. NA-Not Available. NM-Not Meaningful. NR-Not Ranked.

Office—1014 Vine St., Cincinnati, OH 45202. **Tel**—(513) 762-4000. **Website**—www.kroger.com **Chrmn & CEO**—J. A. Pichler. **Pres & COO**—D. B. Dillon. **Group VP & CFO**—J. M. Schlotman. **SVP & Secy**—P. W. Heldman. **VP & Treas**—L. Turner. **Investor Contact**—Kathy Kelly. **Dirs**—R. V. Anderson, R. D. Beyer, J. L. Clendenin, D. B. Dillon, C. J. Jenkins, B. Karatz, J. T. LaMacchia, E. M. Liddy, C. R. Moore, T. B. Morton Jr., T. H. O'Leary, K. D. Ortega, J. A. Pichler, S.R. Rogel, M. R. Seger, B. S. Shackouls, J. D. Woods. **Transfer Agent & Registrar**—Bank of New York, NYC. **Incorporated**—in Ohio in 1902. **Empl**— 312,000. **S&P Analyst:** Phillip M. Seligman

STANDARD &POOR'S
STOCK REPORTS

Pepsi Bottling Group

NYSE Symbol **PBG**

In S&P 500

18-AUG-01 **Industry:** Beverages (Non-Alcoholic)

Summary: This company is the world's largest manufacturer, seller and distributor of carbonated and non-carbonated Pepsi-Cola beverages.

S&P Opinion: Accumulate (★★★★) Recent Price • 42.81 | 52 Wk Range • 45.35-27.25 | Yield • 0.2% | 12-Mo. P/E • 23.9

Quantitative Evaluations

Outlook (1 Lowest—5 Highest) • **NA**

Fair Value • **NA**

Risk • **NA**

Earn./Div. Rank • **NR**

Technical Eval. • **Neutral** since 7/01

Rel. Strength Rank (1 Lowest—99 Highest) • **67**

Insider Activity • **Neutral**

OPTIONS: ASE, CBOE, P, Ph

Overview - 23-JUL-01

Sales in 2001 are expected to advance at a 6% to 7% rate, reflecting a 3% to 4% increase in unit case volumes and a 3% gain in net revenues per case. Volume comparisons should benefit from strong bottled water growth and the rollout of new juice drink products. Operating margins are expected to widen, as higher supermarket pricing and a product mix shift toward more profitable cold drink channel sales outweigh higher fuel prices and modestly higher aluminum and packaging costs. Cash operating profits (operating income before depreciation and amortization charges, or EBITDA) are seen rising about 12%, to nearly $1.2 billion. Share repurchases are expected to continue, reducing shares outstanding by 2% to 3%. EPS in 2001 should rise 22% to $1.87, from $1.53 per share in 2000. For 2002, a further rise to $2.21 is possible.

Valuation - 23-JUL-01

We continue to rank the shares accumulate, reflecting our expectation for strong EBITDA growth from improving volume trends and higher pricing for core beverage products. Continued pricing gains and more effective cost management should result in strong EBITDA growth of 10% to 12% a year for 2001-2003. We believe the shares are worth accumulating, given the company's accelerating free cash flows, expanding margins and improving returns on capital. Operating free cash flow should reach $275 million in 2001, and will continue to be used to fund acquisitions of new bottling businesses and share repurchases. Recently trading at an enterprise value (net total debt + market capitalization) of approximately 7.0X our 2002 cash operating profit estimate, PBG is attractively valued at a discount to many other consumer staples companies with less desirable growth attributes.

Key Stock Statistics

S&P EPS Est. 2001	1.87	Tang. Bk. Value/Share	NM
P/E on S&P Est. 2001	22.9	Beta	NA
S&P EPS Est. 2002	2.21	Shareholders	37,000
Dividend Rate/Share	0.08	Market cap. (B)	$ 6.1
Shs. outstg. (M)	142.6	Inst. holdings	62%
Avg. daily vol. (M)	0.549		

Value of $10,000 invested 5 years ago: NA

Fiscal Year Ending Dec. 31

	2001	2000	1999	1998	1997	1996
Revenues (Million $)						
1Q	1,647	1,545	1,452	—	—	—
2Q	2,060	1,913	1,831	—	—	—
3Q	—	2,125	2,036	—	—	—
4Q	—	2,399	2,186	—	—	—
Yr.	—	7,982	7,505	7,323	—	—
Earnings Per Share ($)						
1Q	**0.17**	**0.11**	**-0.02**	—	—	—
2Q	**0.78**	**0.58**	**0.14**	—	—	—
3Q	**E0.94**	**0.82**	**0.59**	—	—	—
4Q	**E0.08**	**0.02**	**-0.17**	—	—	—
Yr.	**E1.87**	**1.53**	**0.92**	**-0.77**	—	—

Next earnings report expected: early October

Dividend Data (Dividends have been paid since 1999.)

Amount ($)	Date Decl.	Ex-Div. Date	Stock of Record	Payment Date
0.020	Nov. 16	Dec. 06	Dec. 08	Jan. 02 '01
0.020	Feb. 13	Mar. 07	Mar. 09	Mar. 30 '01
0.020	May. 08	Jun. 06	Jun. 08	Jun. 29 '01
0.020	Aug. 07	Sep. 05	Sep. 07	Sep. 28 '01

A Division of The **McGraw-Hill** *Companies*

The Pepsi Bottling Group, Inc.

Business Summary - 23-JUL-01

The Pepsi Bottling Group, Inc. is the world's largest manufacturer, seller and distributor of carbonated and non-carbonated Pepsi-Cola beverages. Separated from PepsiCo in March 1999 through an initial public offering of stock, the company accounts for 55% of the Pepsi-Cola beverages sold in the United States and Canada, and 32% worldwide.

The company's brands are some of the most well recognized trademarks in the world and include Pepsi-Cola, Diet Pepsi, Mountain Dew, Lipton Brisk, Lipton's Iced Tea, 7UP outside the U.S., Pepsi Max, Pepsi One, Slice, Sierra Mist, Mug, Aquafina, Starbucks Frappaccino and Miranda, which are bottled under licenses from PepsiCo or PepsiCo joint ventures.

According to industry sources, Pepsi-Cola brands had an approximate 31.4% volume share of the U.S. carbonated soft drink market in 2000, compared to 44.1% for the brands of The Coca-Cola Company and 14.7% Cadbury Schweppes' Dr. Pepper and Seven Up brands. Globally, Pepsi-Cola brands also hold a number two position behind The Coca-Cola Company.

PBG has established an extensive production and distribution system to deliver products directly to stores without using wholesalers or middlemen. The company operates 67 soft drink production facilities worldwide, as well as 320 distribution facilities. The company also owns or leases and operates approximately 20,000 vehicles, and owns more than 1.1 million soft drink dispensing and vending machines.

The company's strategy includes a major push into the cold drink, or vending machine, distribution channel. In 2000, the company placed 140,000 pieces of incremental cold drink equipment into the North American market, down slightly from net placements of 142,000 in 1999. PBG expects a large part of the new capital investment it plans to make in 2001 to go towards continuing this push towards expanding vending machine distribution. Another key part of the company's strategy entails acquisitions and international markets. The company has been designated an anchor bottler by PepsiCo, providing it with the ability to make acquisitions of additional smaller Pepsi bottlers in territories in Pepsi's U.S. bottling system that represent about 14% of total system volume without getting specific prior approval from PepsiCo.

In December 1999, the company acquired The Pepsi-Cola Bottling Company of Bainbridge, GA, which serves a seven-county franchise area in southwestern Georgia. This deal marked the sixth acquisition for PBG in 1999.

Per Share Data ($) (Year Ended Dec. 31)	2000	1999	1998	1997	1996	1995	1994	1993	1992	1991
Tangible Bk. Val.	NM	NM	NM	NA	NA	NA	NA	NA	NA	NA
Cash Flow	4.46	4.87	5.93	NA	NA	NA	NA	NA	NA	NA
Earnings	1.53	0.92	-0.77	NA	NA	NA	NA	NA	NA	NA
Dividends	0.08	0.04	NA	NA	NA	NA	NA	NA	NA	NA
Payout Ratio	5%	4%	NA	NA	NA	NA	NA	NA	NA	NA
Prices - High	42.50	25.25	NA	NA	NA	NA	NA	NA	NA	NA
- Low	16.25	15.50	NA	NA	NA	NA	NA	NA	NA	NA
P/E Ratio - High	28	27	NA	NA	NA	NA	NA	NA	NA	NA
- Low	11	17	NA	NA	NA	NA	NA	NA	NA	NA
Income Statement Analysis (Million $)										
Revs.	7,982	7,505	7,041	NA	NA	NA	NA	NA	NA	NA
Oper. Inc.	1,025	901	749	NA	NA	NA	NA	NA	NA	NA
Depr.	435	505	472	NA	NA	NA	NA	NA	NA	NA
Int. Exp.	192	202	221	NA	NA	NA	NA	NA	NA	NA
Pretax Inc.	397	209	-192	NA	NA	NA	NA	NA	NA	NA
Eff. Tax Rate	34%	33%	NM	NA	NA	NA	NA	NA	NA	NA
Net Inc.	229	118	-146	NA	NA	NA	NA	NA	NA	NA
Balance Sheet & Other Fin. Data (Million $)										
Cash	318	190	36.0	NA	NA	NA	NA	NA	NA	NA
Curr. Assets	1,584	1,493	1,318	NA	NA	NA	NA	NA	NA	NA
Total Assets	7,736	7,619	7,322	NA	NA	NA	NA	NA	NA	NA
Curr. Liab.	967	947	1,025	NA	NA	NA	NA	NA	NA	NA
LT Debt	3,271	3,268	3,361	NA	NA	NA	NA	NA	NA	NA
Common Eqty.	1,646	1,563	-238	NA	NA	NA	NA	NA	NA	NA
Total Cap.	6,295	6,287	4,325	NA	NA	NA	NA	NA	NA	NA
Cap. Exp.	515	560	507	NA	NA	NA	NA	NA	NA	NA
Cash Flow	664	623	326	NA	NA	NA	NA	NA	NA	NA
Curr. Ratio	1.6	1.6	1.3	NA	NA	NA	NA	NA	NA	NA
% LT Debt of Cap.	52.0	51.9	77.7	NA	NA	NA	NA	NA	NA	NA
% Net Inc.of Revs.	2.9	1.6	NM	NA	NA	NA	NA	NA	NA	NA
% Ret. on Assets	3.0	1.6	NM	NA	NA	NA	NA	NA	NA	NA
% Ret. on Equity	14.3	17.8	NM	NA	NA	NA	NA	NA	NA	NA

Data as orig reptd.; bef. results of disc opers/spec. items. Per share data adj. for stk. divs. Bold denotes diluted EPS (FASB 128)-prior periods restated. E-Estimated. NA-Not Available. NM Not Meaningful. NR-Not Ranked.

Office—One Pepsi Way, Somers, NY 10589. **Tel**—(914) 767-6000. **Fax**—(914) 767-7761. **Website**—http://www.pbg.com **Chrmn & CEO**—C. E. Weatherup. **Pres & COO**—L. L. Nowell.**SVP & Secy**—P. C. McGuire. **VP & Treas**—C. S. Langhoff. **Dirs**—L. G. Alvarado, B. H. Beracha, J. T. Cahill, T. W. Jones, T. H. Kean, S. Kronick, M. D. Moore, R. F. Sharpe, Jr., C. E. Weatherup. **Transfer Agent & Registrar**—The Bank of New York, NYC. **Incorporated**—in Delaware in 1999. **Empl**— 35,700. **S&P Analyst:** Richard Joy

STANDARD &POOR'S STOCK REPORTS

Philip Morris

NYSE Symbol **MO**

In S&P 500

18-AUG-01 **Industry:** Tobacco

Summary: Philip Morris is the world's largest cigarette producer, the largest U.S. food processor (Kraft Foods), and the second largest U.S. brewer (Miller Brewing).

S&P Opinion: Accumulate (★★★★) Recent Price • 44.13 | 52 Wk Range • 53.88-26.06 | Yield • 4.8% | 12-Mo. P/E • 11.7

Quantitative Evaluations

Outlook (1 Lowest—5 Highest)
• **5+**

Fair Value
• **59.40**

Risk
• **Average**

Earn./Div. Rank
• **A**

Technical Eval.
• **Bearish** since 7/01

Rel. Strength Rank (1 Lowest—99 Highest)
• **40**

Insider Activity
• **Unfavorable**

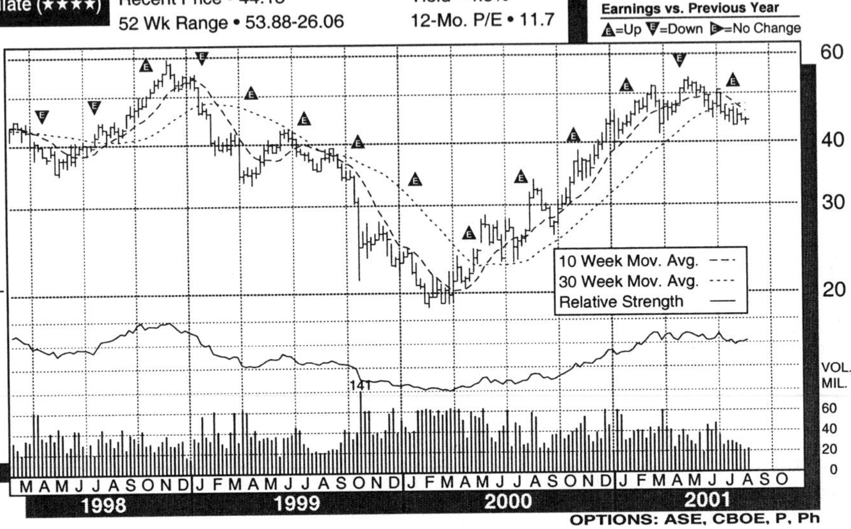

OPTIONS: ASE, CBOE, P, Ph

Overview - 11-JUN-01

Domestic tobacco operating profits are expected to rise 5% to 6% in 2001, as a slight decline in domestic cigarette volumes is outweighed by higher prices. International tobacco profits could gain 6% to 7%, reflecting a continued rebound in Eastern European and Asian markets. Food profits are expected to climb approximately 34%, on an improved business mix and acquisition contributions. Beer results could decline more than 12%, as inventory reductions outweigh the benefits of improved retail pricing. The financial services segment should continue its strong growth trend, with operating profits up over 14%. Higher interest expense and adverse foreign currency exchange translations could be a restraining factor, but more than $3.5 billion in share repurchases should let 2001 EPS gain 10.5% to $4.10, from EPS before special items of $3.71 in 2000. Longer-term, EPS growth of 13%-14% is expected.

Valuation - 11-JUN-01

We recently lowered our recommendation on the shares to accumulate, from buy, following a $3 billion verdict against the company awarded to a sick smoker in California. While this award is likely to be dismissed or reduced on appeal, the ruling may create some near-term volatility. Despite this, the shares remain attractive given the expected benefits of the December 2000 acquisition of Nabisco and the pending IPO of the combined food business, strong profit trends across business segments and a favorable regulatory environment. MO expects to garner more than $550 million in annual cost savings from the Nabisco acquisition by 2003. The IPO of the new Kraft/Nabisco food business will allow MO pay down debt and continue its share repurchase program. Recently trading at less than 12X our FY 01 EPS estimate, a sharp discount to the P/E multiple for the S&P 500 Index, we view the shares as attractive.

Key Stock Statistics

S&P EPS Est. 2001	4.05	Tang. Bk. Value/Share	NM
P/E on S&P Est. 2001	10.9	Beta	0.27
S&P EPS Est. 2002	4.60	Shareholders	139,700
Dividend Rate/Share	2.12	Market cap. (B)	$ 97.1
Shs. outstg. (M)	2199.7	Inst. holdings	62%
Avg. daily vol. (M)	4.663		

Value of $10,000 invested 5 years ago: $ 18,617

Fiscal Year Ending Dec. 31

	2001	2000	1999	1998	1997	1996
Revenues (Million $)						
1Q	17,982	15,590	15,134	14,156	14,093	13,734
2Q	23,188	16,423	15,567	14,786	14,290	13,760
3Q	—	15,757	15,492	14,371	13,991	13,688
4Q	—	15,506	15,558	14,500	13,740	13,371
Yr.	—	63,276	61,751	57,813	56,114	54,553
Earnings Per Share ($)						
1Q	**0.80**	**0.87**	**0.73**	**0.57**	**0.72**	**0.62**
2Q	**1.03**	**0.95**	**0.84**	**0.71**	**0.75**	**0.65**
3Q	**E1.08**	**1.03**	**0.84**	**0.81**	**0.58**	**0.67**
4Q	**E0.99**	**0.90**	**0.79**	**0.11**	**0.53**	**0.60**
Yr.	**E4.05**	**3.75**	**3.19**	**2.20**	**2.58**	**2.54**

Next earnings report expected: mid October

Dividend Data (Dividends have been paid since 1928.)

Amount ($)	Date Decl.	Ex-Div. Date	Stock of Record	Payment Date
0.530	Aug. 30	Sep. 13	Sep. 15	Oct. 10 '00
0.530	Nov. 10	Dec. 13	Dec. 15	Jan. 10 '01
0.530	Feb. 28	Mar. 13	Mar. 15	Apr. 10 '01
0.530	May. 30	Jun. 13	Jun. 15	Jul. 10 '01

Philip Morris Companies Inc.

18-AUG-01

Business Summary - 11-JUN-01

Philip Morris Cos. is a holding company. Its principal wholly owned subsidiaries are manufacturers and marketers of various consumer products, most notably Marlboro cigarettes, Kraft packaged foods, and Miller beer. The company's businesses have, in the aggregate, some 91 brands that generate annual revenues of over $100 million each, with 15 of those brands generating sales exceeding $1 billion each. Business segment contributions in 2000 were: tobacco (61% of revenues), food (33%), brewing (5.5%), and financial services (0.5%).

International operations accounted for 43% of sales and 40% of operating profits in 2000.

Philip Morris U.S.A. is the largest U.S. tobacco company, with total cigarette shipments in the U.S. amounting to 211.9 billion units in 2000 (up 1.8% from 1999 levels), accounting for 50.5% of total U.S. cigarette market shipments. PM U.S.A. contributed 28% of total company sales and 33% of operating profits in 2000. Major premium brands include Marlboro, Benson & Hedges, Merit, Virginia Slims and Parliament. Discount brands include Basic and Cambridge. The premium and discount segments accounted for 74% and 26%, respectively, of domestic cigarette industry volume. Philip Morris International's total cigarette shipments declined 0.1% in 2000, to 671.2 billion units. PM International contributed 33% of total company sales and 32% of operating profits in 2000.

Kraft Foods is the largest packaged food company in North America, and accounted for 23% of total company sales and 22% of operating profits in 2000. Kraft's principal products include Kraft cheese and cheese products; Nabisco cookie and cracker products; Oscar Mayer and Louis Rich processed meats; Maxwell House coffee; Claussen pickles, Post ready-to-eat cereals; Kraft salad dressings; and Kool-Aid, Tang, Capri Sun, Crystal Light and Country Time powdered and ready-to-drink beverages. Kraft Foods International (10% of 2000 sales, 7.5% of profits) produces a wide variety of coffee, confectionery, cheese and grocery and processed meat products in Europe, the Middle East, Africa and the Asia/Pacific region.

Miller Brewing (the second leading U.S. brewer) holds about 20.7% of the U.S. beer market based on volume. Brands include Miller Lite, Miller Genuine Draft, Miller Genuine Draft Light, Icehouse, Foster's, the Miller High Life franchise, Leinenkugel's, Olde English 800, Mickey's, Henry Weinhards, Milwaukee's Best, Red Dog, Hamm's and Magnum.

In December 2000, MO completed the acquisition of Nabisco Holdings Corp. for $19.2 billion, including the assumption of approximately $4.0 billion of existing Nabisco debt. The company is planning an initial public offering (IPO) for 15% of the combined Kraft/Nabisco food operation, with the proceeds slated for debt reduction. MO expects to complete the offering in June 2001.

Per Share Data ($) (Year Ended Dec. 31)	2000	1999	1998	1997	1996	1995	1994	1993	1992	1991
Tangible Bk. Val.	NM	NM	NM	NM	NM	-2.14	-2.73	-3.10	-2.24	-2.23
Cash Flow	4.50	3.90	2.89	3.28	3.25	2.83	2.44	1.97	2.36	1.93
Earnings	3.75	3.19	2.20	2.58	2.56	2.17	1.82	1.35	1.82	1.41
Dividends	2.02	1.80	1.64	1.60	1.47	1.22	1.01	0.87	0.78	0.64
Payout Ratio	54%	56%	75%	62%	57%	56%	56%	64%	43%	45%
Prices - High	45.93	55.56	59.50	48.12	39.66	31.45	21.50	25.87	28.87	27.25
- Low	18.68	21.25	34.75	36.00	28.54	18.58	15.75	15.00	23.16	16.08
P/E Ratio - High	12	17	27	19	15	14	12	19	16	19
- Low	5	7	16	14	11	9	9	11	13	11
Income Statement Analysis (Million $)										
Revs.	80,356	78,596	74,391	56,114	54,553	53,139	53,776	50,621	50,095	48,064
Oper. Inc.	16,396	15,192	15,048	14,820	13,460	12,192	11,080	9,939	11,550	10,515
Depr.	1,717	1,702	1,690	1,700	1,691	1,671	1,631	1,611	1,484	1,438
Int. Exp.	1,078	1,100	1,144	1,185	1,183	1,259	1,288	1,478	1,513	1,696
Pretax Inc.	13,960	12,695	9,087	10,611	10,683	9,347	8,216	6,196	8,608	6,971
Eff. Tax Rate	39%	40%	41%	41%	41%	41%	43%	42%	43%	44%
Net Inc.	8,510	7,675	5,372	6,310	6,303	5,478	4,725	3,568	4,939	3,927
Balance Sheet & Other Fin. Data (Million $)										
Cash	937	5,100	4,081	2,282	240	1,138	184	182	1,021	126
Curr. Assets	17,238	20,895	20,230	17,440	15,190	14,879	NA	NA	NA	NA
Total Assets	79,067	61,381	59,920	55,947	54,871	53,811	52,649	51,205	50,014	47,384
Curr. Liab.	25,949	18,017	16,379	15,071	14,867	14,273	NA	NA	NA	NA
LT Debt	19,154	12,226	12,615	11,585	11,827	13,107	14,975	15,021	14,265	14,200
Common Eqty.	15,005	15,305	16,197	14,920	14,218	13,985	12,786	11,627	12,563	12,512
Total Cap.	40,824	33,211	33,892	27,394	26,776	30,830	31,156	29,715	29,716	29,186
Cap. Exp.	1,682	1,749	1,804	1,874	1,782	1,621	1,726	1,592	1,573	1,562
Cash Flow	10,227	9,377	7,062	8,010	7,994	7,149	6,356	5,179	6,423	5,365
Curr. Ratio	0.7	1.2	1.2	1.2	1.0	1.4	NA	NA	NA	NA
% LT Debt of Cap.	46.9	36.8	37.2	42.3	44.2	42.6	48.1	50.6	48.0	48.7
% Net Inc.of Revs.	10.6	9.8	7.2	11.2	11.6	10.3	8.8	7.0	9.9	8.2
% Ret. on Assets	12.1	12.7	9.3	11.4	11.6	10.3	9.2	7.1	10.3	8.4
% Ret. on Equity	56.2	48.7	34.5	43.3	44.7	41.0	39.2	29.8	40.0	32.2

Data as orig reptd.; bef. results of disc opers/spec. items. Per share data adj. for stk. divs. Bold denotes diluted EPS (FASB 128)-prior periods restated. E-Estimated. NA-Not Available. NM-Not Meaningful. NR-Not Ranked.

Office—120 Park Ave., New York, NY 10017. **Tel**—(212) 880-5000. **Website**—http://www.philipmorris.com **Chrmn & CEO**—G. C. Bible. **COO**—W. H. Webb. **SVP & CFO**—L. C. Camilleri. **VP & Secy**—G. P. Holsenbeck. **Dirs**—E. E. Bailey, G. C. Bible, H. Brown, J. Evans, J. D. Fishburn, C. S. Helu, R. E. R. Huntley, B. J. King, R. Murdoch, J. D. Nichols, L. A. Noto, J. S. Reed, S. M. Wolf. **Transfer Agent & Registrar**—First Chicago Trust Co. of New York, NYC. **Incorporated**—in Virginia in 1919. **Empl**— 178,000. **S&P Analyst:** Richard Joy

STANDARD &POOR'S
STOCK REPORTS

Procter & Gamble

NYSE Symbol **PG**
In S&P 500

18-AUG-01 **Industry:** Household Products (Nondurables)

Summary: This leading consumer products company markets household and personal care products in more than 140 countries.

S&P Opinion: Accumulate (★★★★) Recent Price • 74.75 52 Wk Range • 79.31-55.96 Yield • 2.0% 12-Mo. P/E • 36.1

Quantitative Evaluations
Outlook (1 Lowest—5 Highest)
• 3+
Fair Value
• 73.50
Risk
• Low
Earn./Div. Rank
• A

Technical Eval.
• **Bullish** since 7/01
Rel. Strength Rank (1 Lowest—99 Highest)
• 89
Insider Activity
• Neutral

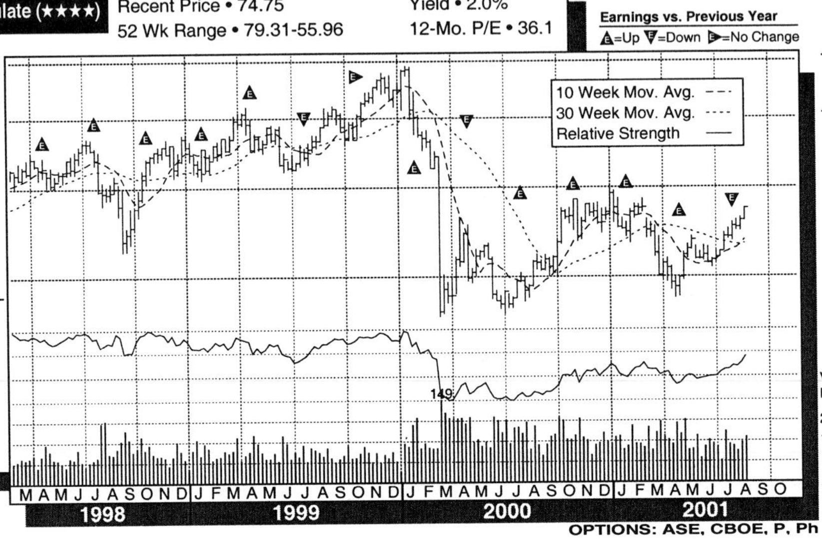

OPTIONS: ASE, CBOE, P, Ph

Overview - 15-AUG-01

We expect sales to rise about 2% in FY 02 (Jun.), reflecting greater volume growth, due to more competitive pricing, partly offset by a negative currency impact. The bulk of volume growth is likely to come from a greater focus on PG's 10 leading brands, and from new product introductions. We believe overall price increases will be difficult for the company to implement, due to severe competition in all of its industry segments. We expect a stabilization of raw material prices and better cost control to lead to improved gross margins. Operating margins should widen slightly, benefiting from a restructuring program that should streamline operations and improve new product flow. These gains are expected to be partially offset by higher marketing and advertisement expenses, related to new product launches. We are maintaining our FY 02 EPS estimate of $3.32.

Valuation - 15-AUG-01

We are maintaining our accumulate opinion on the shares, based on improving fundamentals and valuation. Results in the most recent quarters reveal a steady improvement in the company's margins. We attribute the gains to better pricing policies, and to cost cutting efforts. As P&G plans to shed most of its food and beverage division, we believe the company will soon be poised to better leverage its core operations to generate growth. Although the company still faces many competitive and cost pressures, we believe PG can return to more meaningful profit growth, with a lower cost structure. In light of the company's improved outlook, we believe the shares are attractively valued at 22X our FY 01 EPS estimate, a significant discount to their historic 20% to 30% premium to the P/E multiple of the S&P 500.

Key Stock Statistics

S&P EPS Est. 2002	3.32	Tang. Bk. Value/Share	1.35
P/E on S&P Est. 2002	22.5	Beta	0.34
Dividend Rate/Share	1.52	Shareholders	291,965
Shs. outstg. (M)	1295.1	Market cap. (B)	$ 96.8
Avg. daily vol. (M)	2.932	Inst. holdings	49%

Value of $10,000 invested 5 years ago: $ 17,698

Fiscal Year Ending Jun. 30

	2001	2000	1999	1998	1997	1996
Revenues (Million $)						
1Q	9,969	9,919	9,510	9,355	8,903	9,027
2Q	10,182	10,588	9,934	9,641	9,142	9,090
3Q	9,511	9,783	9,231	8,881	8,771	8,587
4Q	9,582	9,661	9,450	9,277	8,948	8,580
Yr.	39,244	39,951	38,125	37,154	35,764	35,284
Earnings Per Share ($)						
1Q	**0.82**	**0.80**	**0.80**	0.79	0.69	0.64
2Q	**0.84**	**0.78**	**0.72**	**0.71**	0.68	0.59
3Q	**0.63**	**0.52**	**0.72**	**0.65**	0.63	0.54
4Q	**-0.23**	**0.36**	**0.29**	**0.47**	0.43	0.39
Yr.	**2.07**	**2.47**	**2.59**	**2.56**	**2.28**	2.14

Next earnings report expected: NA

Dividend Data (Dividends have been paid since 1891.)

Amount ($)	Date Decl.	Ex-Div. Date	Stock of Record	Payment Date
0.350	Jan. 11	Jan. 17	Jan. 19	Feb. 15 '01
0.350	Apr. 10	Apr. 18	Apr. 20	May. 15 '01
0.380	Jul. 10	Jul. 18	Jul. 20	Aug. 15 '01
0.380	Jul. 10	Jul. 18	Jul. 20	Aug. 15 '01

The Procter & Gamble Company

Business Summary - 15-AUG-01

Procter & Gamble's goal is to create the most successful global brands in every category everywhere it competes. With brands like Crest toothpaste, Pampers disposable diapers and Tide detergent in its family of products, the company has amassed a portfolio of premier consumer brands in a variety of categories, manufacturing and marketing more than 300 brands of consumer products to nearly 5 billion consumers in more than 140 countries.

In June 1999, PG announced a sweeping restructuring program as part of its Organization 2005 project. The restructuring program will result in after-tax charges of $2.1 billion over six years, and lead to the elimination of 15,000 positions worldwide. PG recently lowered its projected long-term sales growth rate to 4% to 6%, from 6% to 8%. Projected net operating earnings growth was revised as well, to double digits, from 13% to 15% annually over the next five years. Part of the earnings growth will result from annual after-tax savings of approximately $1.2 billion by 2004.

By organizing itself into Global Business Units (GBUs), PG hopes to leverage its size by developing products and strategies globally. This should help the company increase innovation and let products be introduced more quickly than in the past. The GBUs will be supported by eight Market Development Organizations, which will act as the sales agents for all PG products in each local region. In addition, the Global Business Services unit will consolidate all accounting, benefits management, order management, and information technology services, effectively standardizing administrative functions.

The fabric and home care division, which sells cleaning detergents such as Tide, Cascade, and Downy contributed 30% of sales in FY 00 (Jun.). The paper division, which sells bathroom tissue and paper towels with brands such as Bounty and Charmin also accounted for 30% of sales. Beauty care, which sells personal care products under brands such as Cover Girl, Pantene, and Secret accounted for 19% of sales. Food and beverage, selling brands such as Pringles, Folgers, and Jif accounted for 12% of sales. Health care, selling brands such as Crest, Vicks, and Pepto-Bismol accounted for 10% of sales.

In FY 00, North America accounted for 54% of total sales, Europe, Middle East and Africa (28%); Asia (11%); Latin America (7%). In FY 00, the 30 leading customers provided nearly 45% of total volume, and the company expects them to account for over 50% of volume by 2005.

In FY 00, PG acquired The Iams Company, a producer of pet foods, for $2.2 billion in cash. Other acquisitions in FY 00 totaled $745 million, and consisted primarily of Recovery Engineering Inc., the manufacturer of Pu R water filtration products; and a joint venture ownership increase in China.

Per Share Data ($) (Year Ended Jun. 30)	2001	2000	1999	1998	1997	1996	1995	1994	1993	1992
Tangible Bk. Val.	NA	1.35	2.62	2.55	5.99	4.05	2.98	3.60	2.60	2.38
Cash Flow	NA	4.39	4.01	3.60	3.53	3.13	2.77	2.38	0.96	1.99
Earnings	2.07	2.47	2.59	2.56	2.43	2.15	1.85	1.54	0.13	1.31
Dividends	1.40	1.28	1.14	1.01	0.90	0.80	0.70	0.66	0.55	0.51
Payout Ratio	68%	52%	44%	39%	37%	37%	38%	43%	449%	39%
Prices - High	79.18	118.37	115.62	94.81	83.37	55.50	44.75	32.31	29.43	27.87
- Low	55.96	52.75	82.00	65.12	51.81	39.68	30.31	25.62	22.62	22.56
P/E Ratio - High	38	48	45	37	34	26	24	21	NM	21
- Low	27	21	32	25	21	19	16	17	NM	17
Income Statement Analysis (Million $)										
Revs.	NA	39,951	38,125	37,154	35,764	35,284	33,434	30,296	30,433	29,362
Oper. Inc.	NA	8,145	8,401	7,653	6,975	6,173	5,432	5,432	4,301	3,777
Depr.	NA	2,191	2,148	1,598	1,487	1,358	1,253	1,134	1,140	910
Int. Exp.	NA	722	650	548	457	484	488	482	577	535
Pretax Inc.	NA	5,536	5,838	5,708	5,249	4,669	4,000	3,346	349	349
Eff. Tax Rate	NA	36%	36%	34%	35%	35%	34%	34%	23%	35%
Net Inc.	NA	3,542	3,763	3,780	3,415	3,046	2,645	2,211	269	1,872
Balance Sheet & Other Fin. Data (Million $)										
Cash	NA	1,415	2,294	1,549	2,350	2,520	2,178	2,656	2,322	1,776
Curr. Assets	NA	10,069	11,358	10,577	10,786	10,807	10,842	9,988	9,975	9,366
Total Assets	NA	34,194	32,113	30,966	27,544	27,730	28,125	25,535	24,935	24,025
Curr. Liab.	NA	10,065	10,761	9,250	7,798	7,825	8,648	8,040	8,287	7,642
LT Debt	NA	8,916	6,231	5,765	4,143	4,670	5,161	4,980	5,174	5,223
Common Eqty.	NA	10,550	10,277	10,415	10,187	9,836	8,676	8,677	7,308	7,085
Total Cap.	NA	21,828	18,651	16,608	14,889	17,030	16,281	14,159	12,798	15,777
Cap. Exp.	NA	3,018	2,828	2,559	2,129	2,179	2,146	1,841	1,911	1,911
Cash Flow	NA	5,733	5,802	5,274	4,798	4,301	3,796	3,243	1,307	2,688
Curr. Ratio	NA	1.0	1.1	1.1	1.4	1.4	1.3	1.2	1.2	1.2
% LT Debt of Cap.	NA	40.8	33.4	34.7	27.8	27.4	31.7	35.2	40.4	33.1
% Net Inc.of Revs.	NA	8.9	9.9	10.2	9.5	8.6	7.9	7.3	0.9	6.4
% Ret. on Assets	NA	10.7	11.9	12.9	12.4	10.9	9.9	8.7	1.1	8.5
% Ret. on Equity	NA	34.0	35.3	35.7	33.1	31.8	32.7	26.3	2.0	27.7

Data as orig. reptd.; bef. results of disc. opers. and/or spec. items. Per share data adj. for stk. divs. as of ex-div. date. Bold denotes diluted EPS (FASB 128). E-Estimated. NA-Not Available. NM-Not Meaningful. NR-Not Ranked.

Office—1 Procter & Gamble Plaza, Cincinnati, OH 45202. **Registrar**—Chase Manhattan Trust Co, Cincinnati. **Transfer Agent**—Co. itself. **Tel**—(513) 983-1100. **Website**—www.pg.com **Chrmn**—J. E. Pepper. **Pres & CEO**—A. G. Lafley. **CFO**—C. C. Daley Jr. **VP & Treas**—G. W. Price. **Secy**—T. L. Overbey. **Investor Contact**—Tom Hills (513-983-2414). **Dirs**—N. R. Augustine, D. R. Beall, S. D. Cook, R. J. Ferris, J. T. Gorman, A. G. Lafley, C. R. Lee, L. M. Martin, J. E. Pepper, J. F. Smith Jr., R. Snyderman, R. D. Storey, M. v.N. Whitman. **Incorporated**—in Ohio in 1905. **Empl**— 110,000. **S&P Analyst:** Howard Choe

STANDARD
&POOR'S
STOCK REPORTS

Whole Foods Market

Nasdaq Symbol **WFMI**

In S&P SmallCap 600

18-AUG-01

Industry: Retail (Food Chains)

Summary: This company owns and operates the largest U.S. chain of natural foods supermarkets, with 123 stores as of July 2001.

S&P Opinion: Accumulate (★★★★)

Recent Price • 33.14
52 Wk Range • 35.13-19.46
Yield • Nil
12-Mo. P/E • NM

Quantitative Evaluations

Outlook
(1 Lowest—5 Highest)
• **2−**

Fair Value
• **31.10**

Risk
• **Average**

Earn./Div. Rank
• **B**

Technical Eval.
• **Bullish** since 7/01

Rel. Strength Rank
(1 Lowest—99 Highest)
• **93**

Insider Activity
• **Unfavorable**

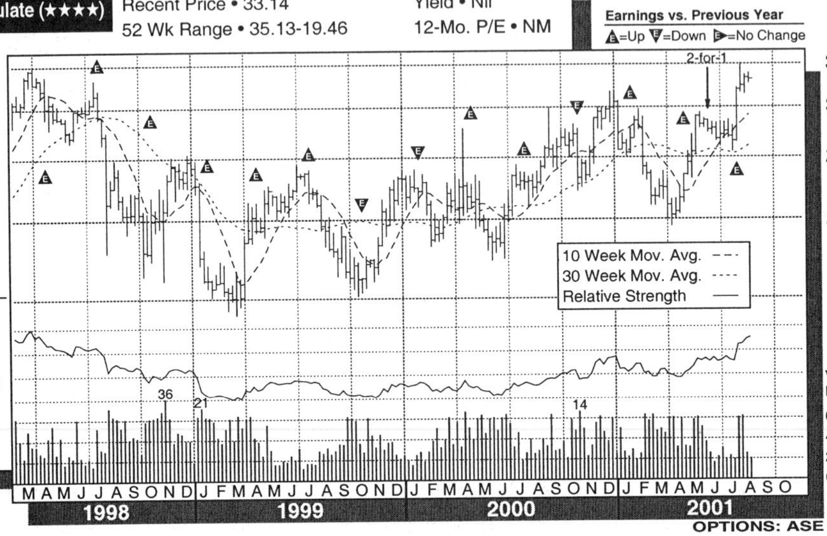

Overview - 30-JUL-01

We expect sales to grow about 20% in FY 01 (Sep.), fueled by the addition of 15 to 20 new stores and same-store sales gains of 8% to 10%. Gross margins should widen, on improved procurement, an improved business mix, and sales leverage. However, SG&A costs are likely to continue rising as a percentage of sales, as higher costs associated with new and acquired stores and greater wage expenses outweigh the benefits of other cost controls. With higher interest expense, related to new store growth, we expect FY 01 EPS to advance 11%, to $1.10, from FY 00's $0.99 (excluding charges). Going forward, WFMI plans to add 15 to 20 new stores per year over the next few years. At that rate, new units will account for a shrinking percentage of the store base, and as the stores mature, WFMI will be able to leverage its fixed costs over a larger base. Hence, in FY 02, assuming top-line growth of 20%, propelled in part by 8%-plus same-store growth, we look for EPS to rise 18% to $1.30.

Valuation - 30-JUL-01

We have raised our recommendation for WFMI shares to accumulate, from hold. WFMI posted better than expected same-store sales growth and EPS for FY 01's second and third quarters, suggesting that the slower economy so far has had little to no effect on demand for its offerings. Its impressive, recent 9%-10% sames-store sales growth is being contributed equally by a higher customer count and a larger average basket size. Demand for natural, organic, and health foods, which are priced at a premium to normal grocery items, is high. For example, the company is doing so well in San Fransisco, the home of an expanding, unemployed high-tech community, that it recently signed leases for four new stores there. All told, the stock looks attractive at 25X our FY 02 EPS estimate, given our long-term annual EPS growth projection of 19%.

Key Stock Statistics

S&P EPS Est. 2001	1.10	Tang. Bk. Value/Share	4.22
P/E on S&P Est. 2001	30.1	Beta	0.95
S&P EPS Est. 2002	1.30	Shareholders	1,520
Dividend Rate/Share	Nil	Market cap. (B)	$ 1.8
Shs. outstg. (M)	53.5	Inst. holdings	98%
Avg. daily vol. (M)	0.935		

Value of $10,000 invested 5 years ago: $ 19,739

Fiscal Year Ending Sep. 30

	2001	2000	1999	1998	1997	1996
Revenues (Million $)						
1Q	643.4	552.6	456.2	407.8	312.6	245.0
2Q	516.7	425.1	358.9	324.8	259.8	203.9
3Q	535.6	442.6	377.6	331.0	274.5	213.4
4Q	—	438.3	375.2	326.2	270.4	230.8
Yr.	—	1,839	1,568	1,390	1,117	892.0
Earnings Per Share ($)						
1Q	**0.27**	**0.22**	**0.23**	**0.22**	**0.12**	Nil
2Q	**0.27**	**0.23**	**0.21**	**0.20**	0.14	0.04
3Q	**0.29**	**0.24**	**0.22**	**0.20**	0.16	0.12
4Q	**E0.27**	**0.09**	**0.10**	**0.20**	0.10	-0.61
Yr.	**E1.10**	**0.53**	**0.77**	**0.82**	**0.53**	**-0.27**

Next earnings report expected: late November

Dividend Data

Amount ($)	Date Decl.	Ex-Div. Date	Stock of Record	Payment Date
2-for-1	May. 10	Jun. 05	May. 21	Jun. 04 '01

Whole Foods Market, Inc.

Business Summary - 30-JUL-01

Whole Foods Market, established in 1980, has quickly grown to become the largest U.S. retailer of natural foods, with $1.8 billion in sales in FY 00 (Sep.). Reflecting a series of store openings and aggressive acquisitions, the company has grown from a single Austin, TX, store in 1981 to a chain of 119 stores in 22 states and Washington, DC. WFMI's goal continues to be to provide the highest quality foods it can find, in terms of taste, appearance and nutrition. The company attributes its success to its ability to differentiate its stores from those of its competitors by tailoring its product mix, customer service attitude, and store environment to appeal to health conscious and gourmet customers.

Stores average about 27,000 sq. ft. and offer a selection of about 20,000 food and non-food products. Each store contributed approximately $17 million in annual sales, with sales per gross square foot an industry-leading $660. Products sold include organic and high quality produce; convenient and tasty prepared foods; high quality natural and conventional meats; a variety of wild and natural farm-raised seafood; a bakery featuring Whole Foods Market brand crusty breads; choice selections of specialty cheeses, beer, and wine; a mixture of natural, organic, gourmet and ethnic grocery products; numerous value priced items in the bulk department; and a nutrition area offering a complete alternative pharmacy with holistic remedies, herbs, vitamins and supplements as well as body care. WFMI covers every item sold in its stores with a 100% money-back guarantee.

The company opens or acquires stores in existing regions, and in metropolitan areas in which WFMI believes it can become the leading natural foods supermarket retailer. To this end, the company opened or acquired 20 stores in FY 00 (Sep.), and planned to open 15 to 20 units in FY 01. In developing new stores, WFMI seeks to open large format units of 25,000 sq. ft. to 45,000 sq. ft., located on premium sites, often in urban, highly populated areas.

Over the past few years, WFMI has developed three private label brands. During 1992, it introduced the Whole Foods label to promote premium and super premium products. WFMI targets artisan food producers, small batch production and hand-tested recipes for products under this label. In 1997, the company introduced the "365" label, used to sell everyday value products. Products in this line still meet WFMI's quality standards, but are an alternative to more expensive branded products. During 1999, the company introduced a product line that is targeted toward children under the Whole Kids label.

During the fourth quarter of FY 00, the company adopted a plan to discontinue operations at Amrion, its money losing vitamin and nutritional supplement manufacturing subsidiary. The company took a related charge of $49 million in the fourth quarter.

Per Share Data ($) (Year Ended Sep. 30)	2000	1999	1998	1997	1996	1995	1994	1993	1992	1991
Tangible Bk. Val.	4.22	4.70	4.33	3.24	2.68	2.23	2.27	1.60	2.14	0.53
Cash Flow	1.71	1.74	1.58	1.20	0.21	0.72	0.58	0.34	0.36	0.44
Earnings	0.84	0.77	0.82	0.53	-0.45	0.29	0.30	0.14	0.22	0.19
Dividends	Nil	Nil	Nil	Nil	Nil	Nil	Nil	Nil	Nil	Nil
Payout Ratio	Nil	Nil	Nil	Nil	Nil	Nil	Nil	Nil	Nil	Nil
Prices - High	31.87	24.81	35.06	25.68	18.56	8.12	12.87	11.68	8.50	NA
- Low	17.18	14.12	16.00	8.75	6.75	5.06	4.75	6.75	3.62	NA
P/E Ratio - High	38	32	43	49	NM	28	42	81	39	NA
- Low	20	18	20	17	NM	17	16	47	17	NA
Income Statement Analysis (Million $)										
Revs.	1,839	1,568	1,390	1,117	892	496	402	322	120	92.5
Oper. Inc.	181	144	125	89.5	50.0	29.7	22.8	16.4	6.7	5.1
Depr.	63.9	53.3	42.3	34.5	25.5	12.3	7.9	5.0	2.1	1.6
Int. Exp.	15.1	8.2	7.7	6.0	4.7	1.5	0.5	0.8	0.3	1.0
Pretax Inc.	63.5	69.1	72.1	39.4	-20.6	13.6	14.7	8.4	4.9	2.6
Eff. Tax Rate	54%	39%	37%	32%	NM	39%	41%	55%	38%	40%
Net Inc.	28.9	42.2	45.4	26.6	-17.2	8.2	8.6	3.8	3.1	1.6
Balance Sheet & Other Fin. Data (Million $)										
Cash	0.4	9.0	36.7	13.4	1.7	5.2	4.3	6.8	16.0	2.2
Curr. Assets	152	141	184	114	61.6	37.3	31.3	23.7	23.6	8.2
Total Assets	760	660	545	400	311	196	136	106	46.5	23.4
Curr. Liab.	143	121	91.0	77.3	56.7	35.8	26.0	22.7	7.9	8.3
LT Debt	298	209	159	92.7	84.3	47.0	7.2	3.2	0.3	9.3
Common Eqty.	307	311	277	205	146	106	97.7	75.5	36.3	5.0
Total Cap.	605	525	439	306	237	157	107	80.3	38.0	14.8
Cap. Exp.	111	75.0	41.2	31.1	18.2	16.0	28.9	27.8	6.7	2.8
Cash Flow	92.8	95.5	87.7	61.1	8.3	20.5	16.5	8.8	5.1	3.2
Curr. Ratio	1.1	1.2	2.0	1.5	1.1	1.0	1.2	1.0	3.0	1.0
% LT Debt of Cap.	49.2	39.8	36.2	30.3	35.6	30.0	6.7	4.0	0.9	62.9
% Net Inc.of Revs.	1.6	2.7	3.3	2.4	NM	1.7	2.2	1.2	2.6	1.7
% Ret. on Assets	4.1	7.0	9.6	7.5	NM	5.0	6.9	4.1	5.2	NA
% Ret. on Equity	9.4	14.3	18.8	15.1	NM	8.0	9.7	5.5	11.6	NA

Data as orig reptd.; bef. results of disc opers/spec. items. Per share data adj. for stk. divs. Bold denotes diluted EPS (FASB 128)-prior periods restated. E-Estimated. NA-Not Available. NM-Not Meaningful. NR-Not Ranked.

Office—601 N. Lamar, Suite 300, Austin, TX 78703. **Tel**—(512) 477-4455. **Website**—www.wholefoods.com **Chrmn & CEO**—J. Mackey. **Pres**—Chris Hitt. **VP, CFO, Secy & Investor Contact**—Glenda Flanagan. **Dirs**—D. W. Dupree, J. E. Elstrott, A. J. Goldberg, F. Lager, J. Mackey, R. Z. Sorenson. **Transfer Agent & Registrar**—Securities Transfer Corp., Dallas. **Incorporated**—in Texas in 1980. **Empl**— 16,600. **S&P Analyst:** Phillip M. Seligman

Part Three

Energy Stocks

STANDARD &POOR'S
STOCK REPORTS

BJ Services

NYSE Symbol **BJS**
In S&P MidCap 400

20-AUG-01 **Industry:** Oil & Gas (Drilling & Equipment)

Summary: This company provides pressure pumping and other oilfield services to the petroleum industry worldwide.

S&P Opinion: Buy (★★★★★)

Recent Price • 25.33
52 Wk Range • 43.10-21.18
Yield • Nil
12-Mo. P/E • 14.6

Quantitative Evaluations

Outlook
(1 Lowest—5 Highest)
• **3**

Fair Value
• **24.40**

Risk
• **Average**

Earn./Div. Rank
• **B**

Technical Eval.
• **Bearish** since 6/01

Rel. Strength Rank
(1 Lowest—99 Highest)
• **28**

Insider Activity
• **NA**

OPTIONS: ASE, CBOE

Overview - 20-AUG-01

Operating income should climb over 25% in FY 02 (Sep.), on continued strong industry fundamentals. Domestic pressure pumping services revenues should grow over 15%, on increased activity by independents (84% of FY 01 third quarter revenues), with emphasis on natural gas drilling (78%) and increased deep gas activity. Canadian sales will continue strong, on rate gains and increased activity. International pressure pumping services revenues should rise over 11%, on improved activity levels in the Middle East, Latin America, and Asia Pacific. We expect accelerating international markets to pick up the slack from any moderation in U.S. drilling on lower gas pricing. Margins should widen, on price increases, volume growth, and operational efficiencies, despite higher labor costs.

Valuation - 20-AUG-01

Over the past few months, the shares dropped sharply, in a sector sell-off reflecting investor concerns over slowing economies and greater than expected U.S. natural gas inventory builds. Although the price of U.S. natural gas has dropped to near $3 per million BTU, as demand for natural gas eased this summer (due to fuel switching by producers to residual fuel and coal, milder temperatures, and slower economies), the supply of U.S. natural gas continues to reflect limited resources and depletion issues; this should provide support for higher prices in the future. As a result, we view the stock's pullback as a buying opportunity. In July, BJS's directors approved a $150 increase in a share repurchase program, to $300 million. With international prospects improving, and the shares down over 40% from their 52-week high and trading at a discount to peer levels, at 9X our FY 02 EPS estimate, BJS is a solid buy.

Key Stock Statistics

S&P EPS Est. 2001	2.07	Tang. Bk. Value/Share	4.80
P/E on S&P Est. 2001	12.2	Beta	1.31
S&P EPS Est. 2002	2.59	Shareholders	2,028
Dividend Rate/Share	Nil	Market cap. (B)	$ 4.2
Shs. outstg. (M)	163.9	Inst. holdings	97%
Avg. daily vol. (M)	2.729		

Value of $10,000 invested 5 years ago: $ 27,570

Fiscal Year Ending Sep. 30

	2001	2000	1999	1998	1997	1996
Revenues (Million $)						
1Q	489.7	354.8	294.4	415.4	340.4	206.5
2Q	549.7	390.8	269.6	395.6	343.7	200.8
3Q	579.8	371.3	253.1	365.3	368.6	221.0
4Q	—	438.5	314.2	351.2	413.9	337.0
Yr.	—	1,555	1,131	1,527	1,467	965.3
Earnings Per Share ($)						
1Q	**0.38**	**0.13**	**-0.05**	**0.26**	0.12	0.09
2Q	**0.63**	**0.17**	**-0.08**	**0.23**	0.13	0.04
3Q	**0.63**	**0.15**	**-0.12**	**0.20**	0.17	0.08
4Q	**E0.60**	**0.25**	**0.03**	**0.01**	0.23	0.12
Yr.	**E2.07**	**0.70**	**-0.21**	**0.72**	**0.66**	0.32

Next earnings report expected: early November

Dividend Data

Amount ($)	Date Decl.	Ex-Div. Date	Stock of Record	Payment Date
2-for-1	Mar. 22	Jun. 01	May. 17	May. 31 '01

BJ Services Company

Business Summary - 20-AUG-01

BJ Services is a leading provider of pressure pumping and other oilfield services to the petroleum industry worldwide. Demand for its services depends on the number of oil and natural gas wells being drilled, the depth and drilling conditions of such wells, the number of well completions, and the level of workover activity worldwide.

BJS's principal customers consist of major and independent oil and natural gas producing companies. As of September 30, 2000, the company generated 52% of its revenues in the U.S., 14% in Canada, and 34% elsewhere.

The U.S. represents the largest single oilfield services market in the world. Due to aging oilfields and lower cost sources of oil internationally, as of FY 99, drilling activity in the U.S. had declined more than 75% from its peak in 1981. In order to operate in key U.S. markets in this environment, BJS believed a greater critical mass was needed, and consolidated its operations acquired from Western with those it had acquired from Nowsco.

The company operates in more than 40 countries in the major international oil and natural gas producing areas of Canada, Latin America, Europe, Africa, Southeast Asia, and the Middle East. With the June 1999 acquisition of Fracmaster Ltd. (1998 revenues of $209 million) for $78.4 million, Canada now represent the largest international segment. Other than Canada, the international market tends to be less volatile than the U.S. due to the size and complexity of investment, and projects tend to be managed with a longer-term perspective with regard to commodity prices. In addition, the international market is dominated by major oil and national oil companies, which tend to have different objectives and more operating stability than the typical independent producer in the U.S.

Pressure pumping services (86% of FY 00 revenues) are used in the completion of oil and gas wells, both onshore and offshore. Stimulation services (54%) are designed to improve the flow of oil and natural gas from producing formations using fracturing, acidizing, sand control, nitrogen, coiled tubing and and downhole tool services. Cementing (32%) is done between the casing pipe and the wellbore during the drilling and completion phase of a well. This is done to isolate fluids that could damage productivity, seal the casing from corrosive fluids and provide structural support for the casing string. Cementing services are also used when recompleting wells from one producing zone to another, and when plugging and abandoning wells.

BJS estimates that it holds a 25% dollar share of the pressure pumping market, with Halliburton's Energy Services (38%) and Schlumberger's Dowell (34%) as the other main participants.

Other oilfield services (14%) include product and equipment sales to customers in areas in which pressure pumping services are primarily provided by local service companies, such as Russia or China. Services include cementing and stimulation, tubular, process and pipeline, and specialty chemical.

Per Share Data ($) (Year Ended Sep. 30)	2000	1999	1998	1997	1996	1995	1994	1993	1992	1991
Tangible Bk. Val.	4.80	2.72	3.08	5.80	1.80	2.45	2.69	2.67	2.25	2.60
Cash Flow	1.30	0.50	1.28	2.40	0.85	0.61	0.57	0.61	0.22	0.75
Earnings	0.70	-0.21	0.72	0.66	0.32	0.12	0.17	0.23	-0.02	0.47
Dividends	Nil	Nil	Nil	Nil	Nil	Nil	Nil	Nil	Nil	Nil
Payout Ratio	Nil	Nil	Nil	Nil	Nil	Nil	Nil	Nil	Nil	Nil
Prices - High	38.37	21.71	21.90	22.68	13.12	6.84	5.62	7.90	4.50	7.40
- Low	19.06	6.71	5.93	9.56	6.28	3.87	4.06	3.40	2.50	3.31
P/E Ratio - High	53	NM	30	35	41	60	33	34	NM	16
- Low	26	NM	8	15	19	34	24	14	NM	7
Income Statement Analysis (Million $)										
Revs.	1,555	1,131	1,527	1,467	965	634	434	394	330	390
Oper. Inc.	297	125	316	273	148	79.6	44.8	43.7	26.2	44.8
Depr.	102	100	91.0	90.4	66.1	42.1	25.3	23.5	12.7	14.5
Int. Exp.	20.0	31.4	26.0	30.7	26.9	15.2	7.9	5.4	3.8	3.9
Pretax Inc.	175	-44.9	175	154	52.6	8.8	12.9	16.8	-4.2	31.1
Eff. Tax Rate	33%	NM	31%	30%	23%	NM	16%	9.50%	NM	17%
Net Inc.	118	-29.7	117	108	40.5	9.9	10.8	14.6	-1.1	24.4
Balance Sheet & Other Fin. Data (Million $)										
Cash	6.5	3.9	2.0	3.9	2.9	1.8	3.2	1.6	1.5	5.4
Curr. Assets	506	439	452	475	418	257	158	146	130	121
Total Assets	1,785	1,825	1,743	1,727	1,709	990	410	370	329	266
Curr. Liab.	337	445	513	385	292	204	121	90.0	129	86.0
LT Debt	142	423	242	299	523	260	74.7	84.5	55.5	31.0
Common Eqty.	1,170	877	900	960	842	467	190	187	135	135
Total Cap.	1,320	1,306	1,151	1,314	1,365	738	272	277	200	179
Cap. Exp.	80.5	111	168	102	54.2	31.0	39.3	37.4	26.2	34.6
Cash Flow	220	70.1	208	198	107	52.0	36.1	38.0	11.6	38.9
Curr. Ratio	1.5	1.0	0.9	1.2	1.4	1.3	1.3	1.6	1.0	1.4
% LT Debt of Cap.	10.8	32.4	21.0	22.7	38.3	35.2	27.5	30.6	27.8	17.3
% Net Inc.of Revs.	7.6	NM	7.7	7.4	4.2	1.6	2.5	3.7	NM	6.3
% Ret. on Assets	6.5	NM	6.7	6.3	3.0	1.4	2.8	3.8	NM	9.7
% Ret. on Equity	11.5	NM	12.6	12.0	6.2	3.0	5.7	8.4	NM	19.8

Data as orig reptd.; bef. results of disc opers/spec. items. Per share data adj. for stk. divs. Bold denotes diluted EPS (FASB 128)-prior periods restated. E-Estimated. NA-Not Available. NM-Not Meaningful. NR-Not Ranked.

Office—5500 Northwest Central Drive, Houston, TX 77092. **Tel**—(713) 462-4239. **Website:**—www.bjservices.com **Chrmn, CEO & Pres**—J. W. Stewart. **SVP, CFO & Investor Contact**—Michael McShane. **VP & Secy**—M. B. Shannon. **Dirs**—L. W. Heiligbrodt, J. R. Huff, D. D. Jordan, R. A. LeBlanc, M. McShane, M. E. Patrick, J. Payne, J. W. Stewart. **Transfer Agent & Registrar**—Bank of New York, NYC. **Incorporated**—in Delaware in 1990. **Empl**— 9,265. **S&P Analyst:** T. J. Vital

STANDARD
&POOR'S
STOCK REPORTS

Evergreen Resources

NYSE Symbol **EVG**

In S&P SmallCap 600

18-AUG-01

Industry:
Oil & Gas (Exploration & Production)

Summary: This independent energy company explores, develops, produces, operates and acquires oil & gas properties, primarily coal bed methane, in Colorado.

S&P Opinion: Buy (★★★★★)

Recent Price • 41.10
52 Wk Range • 50.99-26.75
Yield • Nil
12-Mo. P/E • 21.0

Quantitative Evaluations

Outlook
(1 Lowest—5 Highest)
• 2-

Fair Value
• 34.90

Risk
• Average

Earn./Div. Rank
• B-

Technical Eval.
• NA

Rel. Strength Rank
(1 Lowest—99 Highest)
• 84

Insider Activity
• NA

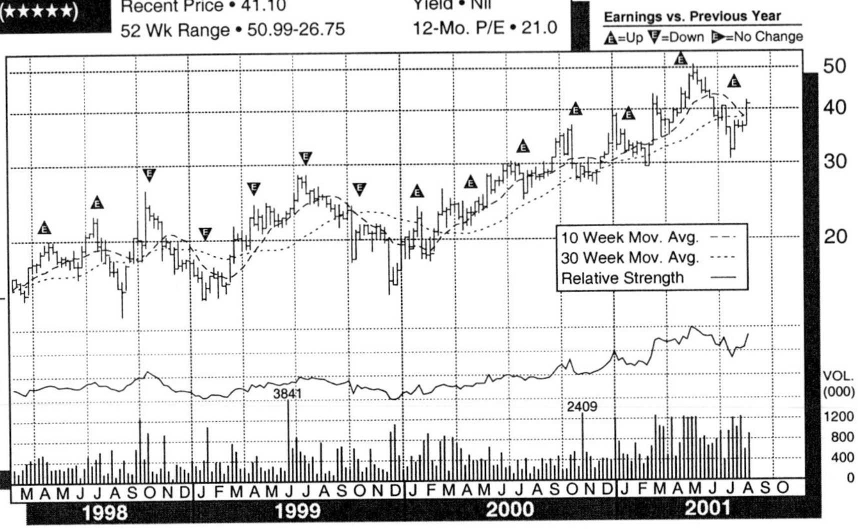

Overview - 06-AUG-01

Driven by favorable supply/demand dynamics for natural gas in the U.S., 2001 production should climb 56%, to nearly 31 Bcf. We see revenues more than doubling, on an average selling price of about $4.16 per Mcf, including hedges. All-in finding and development cost of $0.75 per Mcf in 2000, versus a historical average of $0.25, reflected acquired reserves, but surpassed the industry median of $0.95. Costs are likely to exceed $0.25 as production rates increase, but we expect costs to decrease as acquired operations are integrated. With favorable pricing, and as EVG drills about 135 new wells, margins should widen. The company sold 3 million common shares in November 2000; proceeds were used to redeem preferred stock. For 2001, we expect EPS to nearly triple, to $2.14, reflecting increasing production and relatively higher realized natural gas prices.

Valuation - 06-AUG-01

With growing demand for energy in the U.S., much of which is fueled by natural gas, we expect healthy exploration and production efforts to continue for three to five years. EVG's long-lived, proven and probable reserve base of about 2.0 Tcf (1 Tcf proven), excluding extensive reserve potential internationally, positions it well to capitalize on the cycle. The recent acquisitions of peers Barrett Resources and Pennaco provide evidence of interest in low cost, coal-bed methane producers. At 17.1X our EPS estimate for 2001, the stock was at a 47% discount to our five-year growth projection. Comparing EVG's price and enterprise value to reserve multiples, excluding U.K. interests, to the multiple offered for Barrett Resources, we value EVG at $69. Applying fundamental multiples of recently acquired peers, and considering various other valuation metrics, we have set a price target of $63 for the stock.

Key Stock Statistics

S&P EPS Est. 2001	2.14	Tang. Bk. Value/Share	16.35
P/E on S&P Est. 2001	19.2	Beta	0.32
S&P EPS Est. 2002	2.31	Shareholders	4,600
Dividend Rate/Share	Nil	Market cap. (B)	$0.762
Shs. outstg. (M)	18.5	Inst. holdings	92%
Avg. daily vol. (M)	0.202		

Value of $10,000 invested 5 years ago: $ 56,933

Fiscal Year Ending Dec. 31

	2001	2000	1999	1998	1997	1996
Revenues (Million $)						
1Q	37.94	7.44	4.62	4.46	2.66	0.76
2Q	32.78	8.38	5.20	4.62	2.74	0.78
3Q	—	12.29	5.86	5.67	3.70	1.36
4Q	—	27.86	7.25	5.05	4.27	2.09
Yr.	—	59.69	22.93	19.80	13.37	4.99
Earnings Per Share ($)						
1Q	**0.78**	**0.12**	**0.04**	**0.13**	**0.10**	-0.08
2Q	**0.57**	**0.14**	**0.07**	**0.12**	**0.08**	0.02
3Q	**E0.39**	**0.15**	**0.09**	**0.13**	**0.14**	-0.03
4Q	**E0.40**	**0.42**	**0.12**	**0.09**	**0.21**	-0.02
Yr.	**E2.14**	**0.87**	**0.34**	**0.47**	**0.51**	**0.10**

Next earnings report expected: mid October

Dividend Data

No cash dividends have been paid.

A Division of The **McGraw·Hill** *Companies*

Evergreen Resources, Inc.

Business Summary - 06-AUG-01

Evergreen Resources is a leading developer of coal bed methane gas, with approximately 258,000 gross acres of coal bed property in the Raton Basin in southern Colorado. The independent energy concern is engaged in development, production, operation, exploration and acquisition of oil and gas properties. In addition to its southern Colorado reserves, EVG holds exploration licenses on 470,000 acres in the U.K., working rights to an additional 1,085,000 acres in Ireland, an interest in a consortium exploring offshore in the Falkland Islands, an oil and gas exploration contract in Chile, and exploratory acreage in northwestern Colorado.

Coal bed methane accounts for about 7% of U.S. natural gas produced today, but burgeoning demand for the commodity has led to intensified efforts to tap the nation's wealth of embedded reserves. Methane is created in the coalification process. However, only recently has coal been discovered to be a reservoir rock, meaning that gas is trapped in the molecular structure of the coal itself; this uncovers an untapped resource. Coal bed methane is usually free of other hydrocarbons typically found in natural gas reserves, and thus, after water dehydration, is pipeline quality gas.

Some environmental organizations assert that there are risks associated with water removed from coal seams. Water quality may vary, and EVG says that in many cases it may meet federal drinking standards. In 2000, the company received a new five-year water discharge permit from the state of Colorado. As drilling activity expands and increases, new permits may be needed.

Natural gas accounts for all of EVG's estimated net proved reserves, (875 Bcf at year-end 2000). The company has a 100% working interest in the majority of its Raton Basin acreage and wells. As of May 2, 2001, EVG had 533 net producing gas wells, with daily sales of approximately 80 MMcf. This accounts for about 90% of the gas sold from the entire Raton Basin.

In 2000, EVG drilled 100 wells in the Raton Basin. The company has identified more than 750 additional drilling locations on its Raton acreage; 263 were included in proved reserves at year-end 2000. Reserves per well vary between the Vermejo formation (1.6 Bcf) and the Raton formation (0.8 Bcf), both of which are located in the Raton Basin. We estimate that additional probable reserves in the basin may approximate 1 Tcf.

In September 2000, EVG acquired interests in 24,000 gross acres of productive coal bed methane properties in the Raton Basin from an affiliate of KLT Gas, Inc. for approximately $182 million. At September 2000, the acquired properties were estimated to contain 153 Bcf of net proved gas reserves, and were generating daily net sales of 28 MMcf of gas from 151 wells.

In a November 2000 public offering, EVG sold 3 million shares, using net proceeds of $84 million to redeem preferred shares. In February 2001, EVG acquired a 100% working interest in 605,000 acres in Ireland; in April , it acquired 100% working interest in an additional 480,000 acres. The property is thought to hold 5 Tcf of natural gas.

Per Share Data ($) (Year Ended Dec. 31)	2000	1999	1998	1997	1996	1995	1994	1993	1992	1991
Tangible Bk. Val.	14.56	10.50	7.15	6.17	5.61	5.65	5.99	5.96	6.04	5.44
Cash Flow	1.73	0.65	0.81	0.79	-0.22	0.02	0.13	0.23	0.07	0.30
Earnings	0.87	0.34	0.47	0.51	0.10	-0.13	0.01	0.14	-0.08	0.13
Dividends	Nil	Nil	Nil	Nil	Nil	Nil	Nil	Nil	Nil	Nil
Payout Ratio	Nil	Nil	Nil	Nil	Nil	Nil	Nil	Nil	Nil	Nil
Prices - High	40.12	28.50	26.25	21.25	8.37	6.00	10.75	12.25	11.75	9.00
- Low	17.75	14.50	12.87	6.75	4.87	3.50	5.25	6.25	7.50	3.00
P/E Ratio - High	46	81	56	40	104	NM	NM	NM	78	NM
- Low	20	41	27	13	60	NM	NM	NM	50	NM
Income Statement Analysis (Million $)										
Revs.	59.1	22.9	19.1	12.9	2.2	2.8	3.5	2.5	3.0	3.8
Oper. Inc.	38.6	12.4	13.8	8.7	-0.3	-0.1	-0.2	-0.8	-0.2	1.0
Depr. Depl. & Amort.	8.2	4.8	4.2	2.8	0.6	0.7	0.7	0.4	0.6	0.7
Int. Exp.	3.3	1.9	1.9	0.8	0.0	0.0	0.0	0.0	0.1	0.1
Pretax Inc.	27.7	7.7	8.5	5.5	-0.1	-0.6	0.0	0.7	-0.3	0.3
Eff. Tax Rate	39%	39%	39%	Nil	Nil	Nil	Nil	Nil	Nil	Nil
Net Inc.	17.0	4.7	5.2	5.5	-0.1	-0.6	0.0	0.7	-0.3	0.3
Balance Sheet & Other Fin. Data (Million $)										
Cash	6.4	3.0	4.1	4.2	4.5	2.0	1.4	0.8	1.0	4.1
Curr. Assets	20.4	6.4	6.4	6.0	5.0	3.4	5.2	8.4	12.4	3.2
Total Assets	451	184	140	87.3	44.2	39.1	32.9	31.1	30.7	20.4
Curr. Liab.	13.5	6.5	6.8	6.2	2.5	1.5	2.0	0.8	1.3	1.1
LT Debt	150	15.5	47.0	Nil	1.2	Nil	Nil	Nil	NA	NA
Common Eqty.	267	154	79.7	64.2	31.6	32.2	30.4	30.0	29.1	17.6
Total Cap.	434	176	130	64.2	59.5	36.0	30.4	30.0	29.1	17.6
Cap. Exp.	130	43.2	47.0	18.6	8.3	6.8	6.3	5.9	3.4	1.7
Cash Flow	28.1	9.4	9.4	7.9	0.0	0.1	0.7	1.2	0.4	1.0
Curr. Ratio	1.5	1.0	0.9	1.0	2.0	2.2	2.6	10.4	9.7	3.0
% LT Debt of Cap.	34.5	8.8	36.2	Nil	2.0	Nil	Nil	Nil	NA	NA
% Ret. on Assets	5.4	2.9	4.6	7.0	1.0	-1.8	0.1	2.3	-0.9	1.6
% Ret. on Equity	9.5	4.0	7.2	8.7	1.3	-2.2	0.1	2.5	-0.9	1.8

Data as orig reptd.; bef. results of disc opers/spec. items. Per share data adj. for stk. divs. Bold denotes diluted EPS (FASB 128)-prior periods restated. E-Estimated. NA-Not Available. NM-Not Meaningful. NR-Not Ranked.

Office—1401 17th St., Suite 1200, Denver, CO 80202. **Tel**—(303) 298-8100. **Website**—http://www.evergreen-res.com **Chrmn, Pres & CEO**—M. S. Sexton. **SVP**—D. R. Carlton. **VP, CFO & Treas**—K. R. Collins. **Investor Contact**—John Kelso. **Dirs**—A. G. Blanchard, D. R. Carlton, L. D. Estridge, J. J. Ryan III, M. S. Sexton, S. D. Sheffield, A. L. Smith. **Transfer Agent & Registrar**—American Securities Transfer & Trust, Inc., Lakewood, CO. **Incorporated**—in Colorado. **Empl**— 132. **S&P Analyst:** Markos N. Kaminis

STANDARD &POOR'S STOCK REPORTS

Exxon Mobil

NYSE Symbol **XOM**

In S&P 500

18-AUG-01

Industry: Oil (International Integrated)

Summary: This company, formed through the merger of Exxon and Mobil in late 1999, is the world's largest publicly owned integrated oil company.

S&P Opinion: Buy (★★★★★)

Recent Price • 40.47
52 Wk Range • 47.71-37.60
Yield • 2.3%
12-Mo. P/E • 16.3

Quantitative Evaluations

Outlook (1 Lowest—5 Highest) • **1**

Fair Value • **36.50**

Risk • **Low**

Earn./Div. Rank • **A-**

Technical Eval. • **NA**

Rel. Strength Rank (1 Lowest—99 Highest) • **38**

Insider Activity • **Unfavorable**

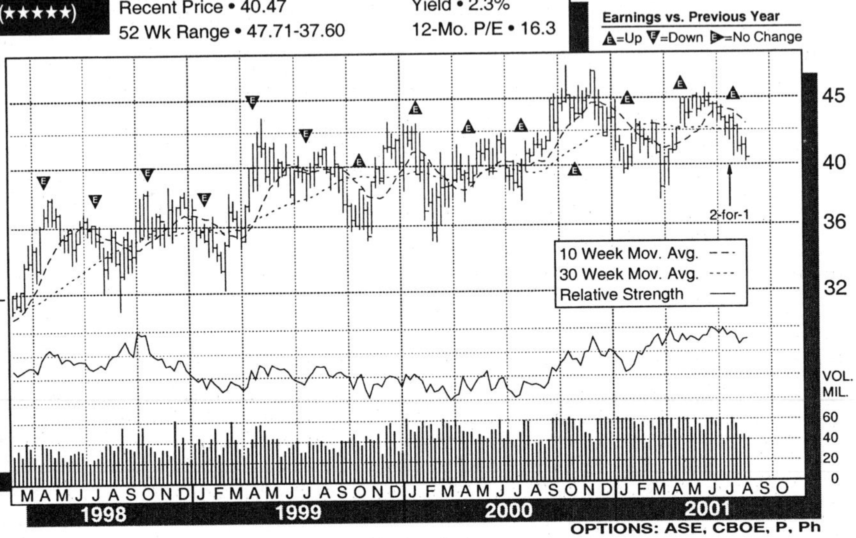

OPTIONS: ASE, CBOE, P, Ph

Overview - 06-AUG-01

In May 2001, XOM was awarded participation in a $25 billion Saudi Gas Initiative, which will free up more Saudi oil for export; XOM expects returns from this investment to exceed 15%. The company reported second quarter earnings of $4.4 billion, somewhat shy of its record 2000 fourth quarter earnings of $5.12 billion. We expect segment earnings to rise over 15% in 2001 on continued strong industry fundamentals. Margins in exploration and production (E&P) should widen, although earnings should drop slightly, reflecting an increase in oil and gas production of about 3%, albeit at reduced prices. Earnings from refining and marketing should rise over 40%, despite volatile margins, on continued demand and lower feedstock costs. Offsetting factors include weak chemical margins.

Valuation - 06-AUG-01

The shares have been lackluster performers thus far this year on investor concerns of soft demand stemming from a slowed U.S. economy. Recently, the company increased its synergy targets for its merger with Mobil to $7.0 billion, from $4.6 billion. In 2000, XOM replaced 112% of its production. BOE production totaled 1.6 billion barrels in 2000, up slightly from 1999. Capital and exploration spending for 2001 is projected to increase over 15% from 2000 levels of $11.14 billion. Future results should be aided by XOM's interest in the Gulf of Mexico Crazy Horse exploration unit, as well as its new Saudi natural gas project. XOM's share repurchase program continues, and during the second quarter, the company repurchased 34.8 million shares for $1.52 billion. The stock trades at 16X our 2002 EPS estimate, slightly above peers, but its top-of-the-class performance and balanced growth deserves a premium valuation.

Key Stock Statistics

S&P EPS Est. 2001	2.76	Tang. Bk. Value/Share	10.21
P/E on S&P Est. 2001	14.7	Beta	0.41
S&P EPS Est. 2002	2.70	Shareholders	715,020
Dividend Rate/Share	0.92	Market cap. (B)	$279.2
Shs. outstg. (M)	6899.8	Inst. holdings	49%
Avg. daily vol. (M)	9.144		

Value of $10,000 invested 5 years ago: $ 22,196

Fiscal Year Ending Dec. 31

	2001	2000	1999	1998	1997	1996
Revenues (Million $)						
1Q	57,278	54,081	26,884	26,211	29,556	30,474
2Q	56,456	55,956	29,422	25,525	28,673	31,625
3Q	—	58,568	33,072	25,384	28,765	32,938
4Q	—	64,132	55,961	29,663	33,275	32,120
Yr.	—	232,737	185,527	100,697	120,279	116,728
Earnings Per Share ($)						
1Q	0.71	0.43	0.21	0.37	0.43	0.38
2Q	0.65	0.56	0.24	0.33	0.39	0.31
3Q	E0.68	0.58	0.30	0.29	0.36	0.31
4Q	E0.71	0.74	0.33	0.31	0.50	0.50
Yr.	E2.76	2.27	1.13	1.30	1.69	1.50

Next earnings report expected: early November

Dividend Data (Dividends have been paid since 1882.)

Amount ($)	Date Decl.	Ex-Div. Date	Stock of Record	Payment Date
0.440	Jan. 31	Feb. 07	Feb. 09	Mar. 09 '01
0.440	Apr. 25	May. 10	May. 14	Jun. 11 '01
2-for-1	May. 30	Jul. 19	Jun. 20	Jul. 18 '01
0.230	Jul. 25	Aug. 09	Aug. 13	Sep. 10 '01

A Division of The McGraw-Hill Companies

Exxon Mobil Corporation

Business Summary - 06-AUG-01

In late 1999, in a corporate family reunion 88 years in the making, the FTC allowed Exxon and Mobil to reunite, in the largest merger in history. In 1911, the Supreme Court had ordered the break-up of John D. Rockefeller's Standard Oil Trust, resulting in a spin-off of 34 companies. Two of those companies were Standard Oil Co. of New Jersey (Exxon) and Standard Oil Co. of New York (Mobil).

Bringing the oil siblings together was not an easy task. It took a year of negotiations, and asset divestitures, to gain FTC approval in 1999. About $3 billion in assets were sold (2,431 gasoline stations, a refinery in California, and other U.S. and European assets). XOM estimates that the merger will generate about $7.0 billion in annual cost savings by 2002. Each Mobil share was exchanged for 1.32 Exxon shares. Following the exchange, former Exxon shareholders owned 70% of the combined company.

The day after the consummation of the merger, the company sold 1,740 retail gasoline and convenience outlets to Tosco Corp. for $860 million. The 160,000 barrel a day California refinery was sold to Valero Energy Corp. in May 2000, for slightly over $1 billion.

XOM serves customers in more than 200 countries worldwide, with 69% of 2000 sales conducted outside of the U.S. In May 2001, XOM was awarded lead participation in two Saudi natural gas projects. Company activities include oil and natural gas exploration and production (9% of 2000 sales; 70% of 2000 after-tax segment earnings); refining and marketing (82%; 19%); chemicals (8%; 7%); and other operations (less than 1%; 4%), such as electric power generation, coal and minerals.

In 2000, worldwide crude and natural gas liquids production averaged 2.553 million bbl. a day, up 1.4% from the 1999 level. Natural gas production averaged 10.343 billion cubic feet a day, up 0.3% from 1999. In February 2001, XOM reported the success of two wells (25% owned by XOM, 75% by BP Amoco) drilled during 2000 in the Crazy Horse Exploration Unit; results confirmed the discovery to be at least a billion barrels - the largest oil field development in the Gulf of Mexico.

As of year-end 2000, the company's proved oil and natural gas liquids (NGL) reserves totaled 11.561 billion bbl., and natural gas reserves totaled 55.866 trillion cubic feet.

XOM has an ownership interest in 46 refineries in 26 countries, with 6.2 million bbl. of distillation capacity a day. The company sells the gasoline produced at its refineries through more than 45,000 service stations in 118 countries. XOM markets under three brands: Exxon, Mobil and Esso.

XOM is also a major manufacturer and marketer of basic petrochemicals, including olefins, aromatics, polyethylene and polypropylene plastics and a wide variety of specialty products. Prime product sales totaled 25.6 million tonnes in 2000, up 4.5% from 1999.

Per Share Data ($) (Year Ended Dec. 31)	2000	1999	1998	1997	1996	1995	1994	1993	1992	1991
Tangible Bk. Val.	10.21	9.13	8.83	8.69	8.32	7.66	7.42	7.01	6.81	7.04
Cash Flow	3.43	2.30	2.38	2.81	2.58	2.38	2.03	2.01	1.97	2.10
Earnings	2.52	1.13	1.30	1.69	1.50	1.29	1.02	1.05	0.95	1.11
Dividends	0.88	0.83	0.82	0.81	0.78	0.75	0.73	0.72	0.71	0.67
Payout Ratio	35%	74%	63%	48%	52%	58%	71%	68%	74%	60%
Prices - High	47.71	43.62	38.65	33.62	25.31	21.50	16.84	17.25	16.37	15.46
- Low	34.93	32.15	28.31	24.12	19.40	15.03	14.03	14.43	13.43	12.40
P/E Ratio - High	19	39	30	20	17	17	17	16	17	14
- Low	14	29	22	14	13	12	14	14	14	11
Income Statement Analysis (Million $)										
Revs.	228,439	185,527	115,417	135,142	131,543	121,804	99,683	97,825	103,160	102,847
Oper. Inc.	33,309	42,565	12,326	16,993	15,387	14,584	11,942	12,063	11,928	13,006
Depr.	8,130	8,304	5,340	5,474	5,329	5,386	5,015	4,759	5,044	4,935
Int. Exp.	589	695	100	415	984	1,104	1,178	1,055	1,148	1,141
Pretax Inc.	27,493	11,295	9,241	13,204	11,916	10,442	8,037	8,302	7,534	8,685
Eff. Tax Rate	40%	29%	28%	33%	37%	38%	34%	33%	33%	34%
Net Inc.	15,990	7,910	6,440	8,460	7,510	6,470	5,100	5,280	4,810	5,600
Balance Sheet & Other Fin. Data (Million $)										
Cash	7,080	1,761	1,461	4,047	2,969	1,789	1,775	1,652	1,515	1,587
Curr. Assets	40,399	31,141	17,593	21,192	19,910	17,318	16,460	14,859	16,424	17,012
Total Assets	149,000	144,521	92,630	96,064	95,527	91,296	87,862	84,145	85,030	87,560
Curr. Liab.	38,191	38,733	19,412	19,654	19,505	18,736	19,493	18,590	19,663	20,854
LT Debt	7,280	8,402	4,530	7,050	7,236	7,778	8,831	8,506	8,637	8,582
Common Eqty.	70,757	63,466	43,645	43,470	43,239	39,982	36,861	34,840	33,824	34,974
Total Cap.	97,709	91,807	63,229	66,533	66,167	62,815	59,849	56,632	56,523	58,925
Cap. Exp.	8,446	10,849	8,359	7,393	7,209	7,128	6,643	6,919	7,225	7,262
Cash Flow	24,120	16,178	11,770	13,915	12,812	11,818	10,069	9,985	9,793	10,466
Curr. Ratio	1.1	0.8	0.9	1.1	2.1	0.9	0.8	0.8	0.8	0.8
% LT Debt of Cap.	7.5	9.2	7.2	10.6	10.9	12.4	14.8	15.0	15.3	14.6
% Net Inc.of Revs.	7.0	4.3	5.6	6.3	5.7	5.3	5.1	5.4	4.7	5.4
% Ret. on Assets	10.9	5.6	6.8	8.8	8.0	7.2	5.9	6.2	5.6	6.4
% Ret. on Equity	23.8	12.6	14.8	19.5	18.0	16.8	14.1	15.2	13.8	16.3

Data as orig reptd. for Exxon; bef. results of disc opers/spec. items. Per share data adj. for stk. divs. Bold denotes diluted EPS (FASB 128)-prior periods restated. E-Estimated. NA-Not Available. NM-Not Meaningful. NR-Not Ranked.

Office—5959 Las Colinas Blvd., Irving, TX 75039-2298. **Tel**—(972) 444-1000. **Website**—http://www.exxonmobil.com **Chrmn & CEO**—L. R. Raymond. **VP, Secy & Investor Contact**—T. P. Townsend. **VP & Treas**—F. A. Risch. **Dirs**—M. J. Boskin, R. Dahan, W. T. Esrey, D. V. Fites, C. A. Heimbold Jr., J. R. Houghton, W. R. Howell, H. L. Kaplan, R. C. King, P. E. Lippincott, H. J. Longwell, M. C. Nelson, L. R. Raymond, E. A. Renna, W. V. Shipley. **Transfer Agent**—EquiServe Trust Co., N.A., Providence, RI. **Incorporated**—in New Jersey in 1882. **Empl**— 119,000. **S&P Analyst:** T. J. Vital

STANDARD &POOR'S
STOCK REPORTS

Noble Drilling

NYSE Symbol **NE**
In S&P 500

18-AUG-01

Industry:
Oil & Gas (Drilling & Equipment)

Summary: This company principally provides contract drilling services for the oil and gas industry worldwide.

S&P Opinion: Buy (★★★★★)

Recent Price • 29.63
52 Wk Range • 54-25.50
Yield • Nil
12-Mo. P/E • 18.4

Quantitative Evaluations
Outlook
(1 Lowest—5 Highest)
• **4**
Fair Value
• **36.10**
Risk
• **High**
Earn./Div. Rank
• **B-**

Technical Eval.
• **Bearish** since 5/01
Rel. Strength Rank
(1 Lowest—99 Highest)
• **23**
Insider Activity
• **Neutral**

OPTIONS: CBOE, P, Ph

Overview - 17-AUG-01

Operating income should climb over 60% in 2002. During the 2001 second quarter, U.S. utilization rates were 98%, versus 99% in the first quarter; international rates were 87%, versus 79%. U.S. dayrates declined 2.6%, to $71,182, while international dayrates were up 11%, to $55,722. Although the fundamentals of NE's business remained intact, domestic earnings saw lower jackup rates in the Gulf of Mexico, which may spur the movement of some jackups to certain rebounding international areas. With over 60% of its fleet overseas, NE should benefit from these growing markets, particularly in the North Sea, Brazil, West Africa, Mexico, the Middle East and India. In July, the Noble Jimmy Puckett was damaged while under tow in Indian waters; the rig should be available for work in the 2002 first quarter. Results will be aided by higher international rates, and by Triton's shift in focus toward higher margin consulting services.

Valuation - 17-AUG-01

The shares have been lackluster performers thus far in 2001, on investor concerns over slowing global economies. However, stabilized oil prices at high levels and limited excess oil production capacity are boosting spending on exploration and production by at least 20% in 2001. NE has some exposure to the stalled shallow water Gulf of Mexico jackup market, but its focus on accelerating international markets should pick up the slack. Since the first quarter, NE had repurchased 2.1 million shares, for about $70.9 million. Debt was 30% of capitalization at June 30, 2001, and is expected to fall to 15% by the end of the year. With the shares down 44% from their 52-week highs, and trading below peer levels at 9X our 2002 EPS estimate, we see NE as a great buy, due to its compelling valuation and strong international growth potential.

Key Stock Statistics

S&P EPS Est. 2001	2.04	Tang. Bk. Value/Share	11.80
P/E on S&P Est. 2001	14.5	Beta	1.48
S&P EPS Est. 2002	3.44	Shareholders	1,815
Dividend Rate/Share	Nil	Market cap. (B)	$ 4.0
Shs. outstg. (M)	134.1	Inst. holdings	92%
Avg. daily vol. (M)	1.787		

Value of $10,000 invested 5 years ago: $ 19,294

Fiscal Year Ending Dec. 31

	2001	2000	1999	1998	1997	1996
Revenues (Million $)						
1Q	222.4	184.8	180.1	189.0	168.7	104.8
2Q	246.7	230.7	175.5	216.2	185.0	109.7
3Q	—	225.9	176.8	195.1	171.6	158.1
4Q	—	241.2	173.5	187.9	187.8	141.7
Yr.	—	882.6	705.9	788.2	713.2	514.3
Earnings Per Share ($)						
1Q	**0.40**	**0.19**	**0.20**	**0.35**	**0.17**	**0.10**
2Q	**0.50**	**0.32**	**0.21**	**0.38**	**1.20**	**0.16**
3Q	**E0.53**	**0.33**	**0.19**	**0.25**	**0.25**	**0.19**
4Q	**E0.61**	**0.38**	**0.12**	**0.25**	**0.34**	**0.20**
Yr.	**E2.04**	**1.22**	**0.72**	**1.23**	**1.98**	**0.67**

Next earnings report expected: late October

Dividend Data

No dividends have been paid on the common stock. Debt agreements prohibit payments. A stockholder rights plan was adopted in 1995.

Noble Drilling Corporation

Business Summary - 17-AUG-01

Noble Drilling provides contract drilling services in offshore markets worldwide. The company has a fleet of 49 offshore drilling rigs, including floating deepwater units (includes nine semisubmersibles and three dynamically positioned drillships, seven of which are designed to operate in depths greater than 5,000 ft.), 34 independent leg, cantilever jackup rigs (includes 21 premium units that operate in depths of 300 ft. or more, four that operate in depths of 360 ft. or more, and 11 that operate in water depths of 250 ft.), as well as three submersibles. Of these drilling units, nine can operate in harsh environments. In November 2000, NE purchased the remaining 30% equity interest in Ilion LLC (a Friede & Goldman 9500 Enhanced Pacesetter designed semisubmersible), for $12.8 million, and now owns 100% of the Ilion. Contract drilling operations (49% of 2000 contract drilling revenues originated outside the U.S.) accounted for 86% of total revenues in 2000; labor and turnkey contract drilling about 13%; and engineering, consulting and other approximately 2%.

Nearly 60% of NE's fleet was deployed in international markets at the end of 2000, including the North Sea, West Africa, Brazil, the Middle East, India, Venezuela and Mexico. Two customers (Royal Dutch/Shell and Petroleo Brasiliero S.A.) accounted for 13% of total revenues in 2000.

The company has focused on increasing the number of rigs in its fleet that can drill in deepwater offshore markets. NE believes demand for drilling in water depths greater than 5,000 ft. has increased substantially, due to a greater number of deepwater discoveries. Key to its deepwater strategy is the Noble EVA-4000 semisubmersible conversion program. The EVA-4000 is a proprietary design through which NE has converted submersible drilling rigs into ultra-deepwater semisubmersibles. The company believes the EVA-4000 program completes the conversion at a lower cost and on an accelerated delivery schedule versus new construction. Between December 1998 and December 1999, five EVA-4000 semisubmersibles were delivered with maximum water depth drilling capabilities ranging from 6,000 ft. to 8,900 ft..

The Triton Engineering Services Co. unit provides turnkey drilling services, involving drilling a well to a specified depth for a fixed price. Triton completed 20 wells in 2000, down from 26 in 1999. The company also provides engineering services, primarily related to design of drilling equipment for offshore development and production services, and to recertification of oilfield equipment.

The majority of NE's drilling contracts are awarded through competitive bidding. Payment is arranged on a dayrate basis, so that the company receives a fixed amount for each day that the drilling rig is operating.

In February 2001, NE acquired Maurer Engineering Inc., a privately held engineering firm that designs drilling products and drilling related software products.

Per Share Data ($) (Year Ended Dec. 31)	2000	1999	1998	1997	1996	1995	1994	1993	1992	1991
Tangible Bk. Val.	11.80	10.60	10.00	8.77	7.01	4.48	4.53	5.35	3.99	4.61
Cash Flow	2.04	1.39	1.77	2.56	1.19	0.34	0.62	0.85	0.08	0.17
Earnings	1.22	0.72	1.23	1.98	0.66	-0.08	0.11	0.32	-0.43	-0.42
Dividends	Nil	Nil	Nil	Nil	Nil	Nil	Nil	Nil	Nil	Nil
Payout Ratio	Nil	Nil	Nil	Nil	Nil	Nil	Nil	Nil	Nil	Nil
Prices - High	53.50	32.87	34.68	38.18	22.00	9.12	9.12	11.12	5.75	8.00
- Low	27.25	12.00	10.75	15.50	8.00	5.00	5.25	3.62	2.25	2.75
P/E Ratio - High	44	46	28	19	33	NM	83	35	NM	NM
- Low	22	17	9	8	12	NM	48	11	NM	NM
Income Statement Analysis (Million $)										
Revs.	883	706	788	713	514	328	352	195	140	177
Oper. Inc.	379	245	301	261	128	47.7	66.5	43.8	13.3	21.8
Depr.	111	89.0	72.0	77.9	52.2	36.5	39.5	20.4	17.7	19.9
Int. Exp.	54.6	33.1	5.2	12.9	18.8	12.2	12.4	5.4	7.8	14.5
Pretax Inc.	226	124	231	380	102	4.9	27.0	21.4	-5.8	-11.2
Eff. Tax Rate	27%	24%	30%	31%	22%	67%	21%	12%	NM	NM
Net Inc.	166	95.3	162	264	79.3	1.6	21.5	19.1	-8.1	-13.4
Balance Sheet & Other Fin. Data (Million $)										
Cash	177	137	217	66.4	174	64.5	145	44.1	27.5	56.1
Curr. Assets	379	291	438	265	388	188	240	117	80.0	118
Total Assets	2,596	2,432	2,179	1,506	1,367	741	740	500	310	377
Curr. Liab.	205	233	350	153	152	86.4	82.3	42.3	55.1	71.4
LT Debt	650	731	461	138	240	130	127	127	41.3	71.2
Common Eqty.	1,577	1,398	1,310	1,149	925	519	352	254	137	156
Total Cap.	2,372	2,197	1,828	1,351	1,216	654	655	456	253	302
Cap. Exp.	125	422	541	391	217	91.2	56.0	170	5.0	104
Cash Flow	276	184	234	342	132	30.9	48.3	32.8	2.9	5.8
Curr. Ratio	1.8	1.2	1.3	1.7	2.6	2.2	2.9	2.8	1.4	1.6
% LT Debt of Cap.	27.4	33.3	25.2	10.2	19.7	19.9	19.3	27.9	16.3	23.6
% Net Inc.of Revs.	18.8	13.5	20.6	37.0	15.4	0.5	6.1	9.8	NM	NM
% Ret. on Assets	6.6	4.1	8.8	18.4	7.5	0.2	2.8	4.1	NM	NM
% Ret. on Equity	11.1	7.0	13.2	25.5	10.9	NM	2.3	5.6	NM	NM

Data as orig reptd.; bef. results of disc opers/spec. items. Per share data adj. for stk. divs. Bold denotes diluted EPS (FASB 128)-prior periods restated. E-Estimated. NA-Not Available. NM-Not Meaningful. NR-Not Ranked.

Office—13135 South Dairy Ashford, Suite 800, Sugar Land, TX 77478. **Tel**—(281) 276-6100. **Website**—http://www.noblecorp.com **Chrmn & CEO**—J. C. Day. **Pres**—R. D. Campbell. **SVP-Fin & Treas**—M. A. Jackson. **SVP & Secy**—J. J. Robertson. **VP & Investor Contact**—John T. Rynd. **Dirs**—R. D. Campbell, M. A. Cawley, L. J. Chazen, J. C. Day, M. E. Leland, J. E. Little, W. A. Sears. **Transfer Agent & Registrar**—UMB Bank N.A., Kansas City, MO. **Incorporated**—in Delaware in 1939. **Empl**— 2,943. **S&P Analyst:** T. Vital

STANDARD &POOR'S
STOCK REPORTS

Santa Fe International

NYSE Symbol **SDC**

18-AUG-01

Industry: Oil & Gas (Drilling & Equipment)

Summary: This leading international offshore and land contract driller is also a leading provider of drilling related services to the petroleum industry worldwide.

S&P Opinion: Buy (★★★★★)

Recent Price • 29
52 Wk Range • 45.93-23
Yield • 0.4%
12-Mo. P/E • 21.5

Quantitative Evaluations

Outlook
(1 Lowest—5 Highest)
• **NA**

Fair Value
• **NA**

Risk
• **NA**

Earn./Div. Rank
• **NR**

Technical Eval.
• **Bearish** since 8/01

Rel. Strength Rank
(1 Lowest—99 Highest)
• **39**

Insider Activity
• **NA**

Earnings vs. Previous Year
▲=Up ▼=Down ▶=No Change

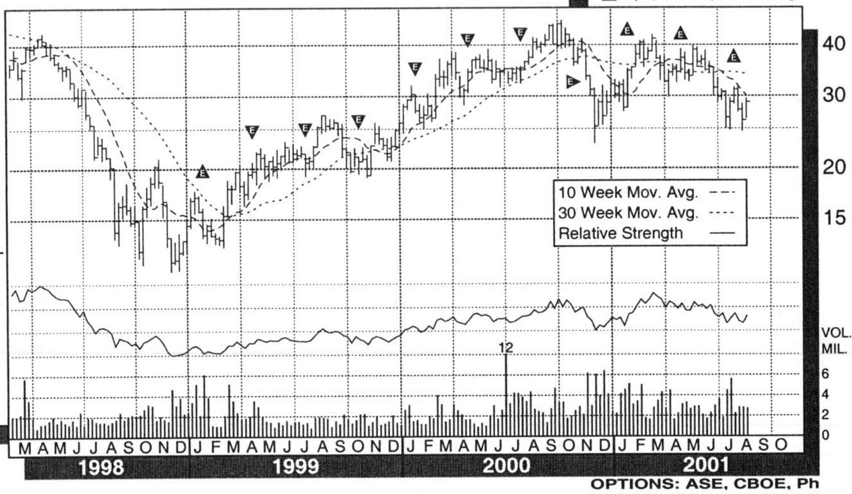

OPTIONS: ASE, CBOE, Ph

Overview - 19-JUL-01

Operating income should rise over 50% in 2001, as strong industry fundamentals continue to boost utilization rates and dayrates. In the second quarter, offshore rig utilization rates were 92.2% (vs. 93.8% in the first quarter), and dayrates rose 8.2% to an average $56,950. Land rig utilization rates rose to 80.1% (vs. 70.6%), and dayrates were up 2.3% to an average $15,687. Bidding activity was up across all markets worldwide, with Southeast Asia showing the greatest improvement, as drilling programs are firming up with existing customers. With SDC's use of high specification rigs in selected international markets that tend to show long-term stability, strong financial management, and uptrends in exploration and production spending of 20% or more in 2001, margins should benefit significantly over the next few years.

Valuation - 19-JUL-01

Over the past month, the shares dropped sharply, in a sector sell-off reflecting end of quarter window dressing and investor concerns over a slowed U.S. economy and a softening of domestic natural gas prices. However, SDC operations are focused on the oil-intensive international market, where contracts tend to be longer term in nature and projects are based on economics using cautious oil prices of $15-$18 per barrel. Earlier this year, SDC announced the construction of two high performance jackup rigs and two deepwater semisubmersibles. By building early in the market upswing, we expect SDC's newbuild program to provide cost savings and present market opportunities. With a strong balance sheet, and the shares trading at 9X our 2002 EPS estimate, at a premium to peers but at a discount to the broader market, we recommend buying the stock.

Key Stock Statistics

S&P EPS Est. 2001	1.70	Tang. Bk. Value/Share	13.57
P/E on S&P Est. 2001	17.1	Beta	NA
S&P EPS Est. 2002	2.92	Shareholders	460
Dividend Rate/Share	0.13	Market cap. (B)	$ 3.3
Shs. outstg. (M)	115.5	Inst. holdings	60%
Avg. daily vol. (M)	0.524		

Value of $10,000 invested 5 years ago: NA

Fiscal Year Ending Dec. 31

	2001	2000	1999	1998	1997	1996
Revenues (Million $)						
1Q	167.3	132.6	185.5	196.3	—	—
2Q	183.7	146.3	160.0	202.6	—	—
3Q	—	145.7	143.6	201.1	—	—
4Q	—	159.5	125.1	211.3	198.4	—
Yr.	—	584.0	614.2	811.4	375.2	470.9
Earnings Per Share ($)						
1Q	**0.29**	**0.16**	**0.51**	**0.59**	—	—
2Q	**0.52**	**0.23**	**0.37**	**0.56**	—	—
3Q	**E0.50**	**0.28**	**0.28**	**0.64**	—	—
4Q	**E0.55**	**0.29**	**0.14**	**0.72**	0.60	—
Yr.	**E1.70**	**0.92**	**1.30**	**2.50**	**1.12**	0.54

Next earnings report expected: mid October

Dividend Data (Dividends have been paid since 1997.)

Amount ($)	Date Decl.	Ex-Div. Date	Stock of Record	Payment Date
0.033	Sep. 18	Sep. 27	Sep. 29	Oct. 16 '00
0.033	Dec. 05	Dec. 27	Dec. 29	Jan. 15 '01
0.033	Mar. 11	Mar. 28	Mar. 30	Apr. 16 '01
0.033	Jun. 04	Jun. 27	Jun. 29	Jul. 16 '01

A Division of The McGraw-Hill Companies

Santa Fe International Corporation

Business Summary - 19-JUL-01

Most organizations become public companies only once, but Santa Fe International has made two IPOs. It started its drilling business with land rigs in California in 1946, and became a public company in 1960. In 1981, Kuwait Petroleum Corp. (KPC) acquired the company at the height of the drilling boom. In June 1997, SDC once again became a public company, with an offering of 40 million shares. In July 2000, KPC's ownership in SDC was reduced to 37.8%, from 65.1%, after a public offering.

At February 28, 2001, SDC owned 27 offshore drilling rigs and 33 land drilling rigs. As of January 31, 2001, the average age of SDC's entire offshore drilling fleet was 18.7 years. As of January 31, 2001, all of the company's rigs were located outside the U.S.

The company's offshore fleet consists of 23 jackup rigs, three semisubmersible rigs, and one platform rig. SDC classifies its jackup rigs in three categories: heavy duty harsh environment (HDHE), 300 ft. to 350 ft. premium cantilever, and 200 ft. to 250 ft. standard rigs. SDC owns one of the world's largest fleets of HDHE rigs (six of the 19 currently in service in the industry) that can withstand the harsh environment of the North Sea. The Galaxy I, II and III are Universe class rigs, capable of operating in water depths of up to 400 ft. The other three HDHE rigs are designed to operate in depths up to 350 ft. The company's 17 other jackup rigs can operate depths varying from 200 ft. to 350 ft. In February 2001, SDC announced the construction of two JU 2000 high performance jackup rigs (about $125 million each), plus options for additional units. In June 2001, SDC sold its jackup rig, Key Victoria, to Nabors Drilling International Ltd. for $27.5 million.

The three semisubmersible rigs are floating vessels that can be submerged so that a substantial portion of the lower hull is below the water surface during drilling operations. In April 2001, SDC announced the construction of two deepwater semisubmersibles (about $285 million each), plus options for two additional units.

The company owns one platform rig in the North Sea, consisting of a number of self-contained drilled equipment packages that, when assembled on a customer's offshore production platform, make a complete drilling rig.

At January 31, 2001, SDC had 33 land rigs in Kuwait, Venezuela, Egypt, Oman, the Neutral Zone, and Saudi Arabia.

In 2000, revenues for HDHE jackups increased 16%. Semisubmersible revenues declined 55%, on lower dayrates and utilization rates (70.6%, vs. 84.6%). Premium jackup sales dropped 10% on lower dayrates. Standard jackup revenues climbed 59%, reflecting higher utilization rates (83.7%, vs. 48.2%). Land rig revenues were down 9%, on lower utilization rates (65.9%, vs. 68.9%) and dayrates.

Per Share Data ($) (Year Ended Dec. 31)	2000	1999	1998	1997	1996	1995	1994	1993	1992	1991
Tangible Bk. Val.	12.79	11.88	10.69	8.31	6.94	NA	NA	NA	NA	NA
Cash Flow	1.63	1.92	2.99	1.34	1.22	NA	NA	NA	NA	NA
Earnings	0.92	1.30	2.50	1.12	0.54	NA	NA	NA	NA	NA
Dividends	0.13	0.13	0.13	0.07	NA	NA	NA	NA	NA	NA
Payout Ratio	14%	10%	5%	6%	NA	NA	NA	NA	NA	NA
Prices - High	45.93	27.00	42.93	57.00	NA	NA	NA	NA	NA	NA
- Low	23.00	12.81	11.18	28.50	NA	NA	NA	NA	NA	NA
P/E Ratio - High	50	21	17	51	NA	NA	NA	NA	NA	NA
- Low	25	10	4	25	NA	NA	NA	NA	NA	NA
Income Statement Analysis (Million $)										
Revs.	584	614	811	375	471	466	392	368	420	NA
Oper. Inc.	197	240	375	169	145	130	105	89.3	146	NA
Depr.	82.6	71.6	55.8	24.9	77.1	86.9	87.5	84.6	73.3	NA
Int. Exp.	Nil	Nil	Nil	Nil	0.4	5.1	8.5	7.6	4.0	NA
Pretax Inc.	130	178	327	145	77.8	49.3	18.5	-2.0	78.9	NA
Eff. Tax Rate	18%	16%	12%	11%	20%	10%	43%	NM	14%	NA
Net Inc.	107	150	287	129	62.0	44.3	10.5	-8.2	67.5	NA
Balance Sheet & Other Fin. Data (Million $)										
Cash	325	247	124	68.5	42.0	NA	NA	NA	NA	NA
Curr. Assets	522	409	352	294	NA	NA	NA	NA	NA	NA
Total Assets	1,694	1,564	1,454	1,161	1,000	NA	NA	NA	NA	NA
Curr. Liab.	178	149	182	172	NA	NA	NA	NA	NA	NA
LT Debt	Nil	Nil	Nil	Nil	Nil	NA	NA	NA	NA	NA
Common Eqty.	1,474	1,366	1,227	953	795	NA	NA	NA	NA	NA
Total Cap.	1,475	1,366	1,228	831	795	NA	NA	NA	NA	NA
Cap. Exp.	83.0	125	277	147	NA	NA	NA	NA	NA	NA
Cash Flow	190	221	343	153	NA	NA	NA	NA	NA	NA
Curr. Ratio	2.9	2.7	1.9	1.7	2.0	NA	NA	NA	NA	NA
% LT Debt of Cap.	Nil	Nil	Nil	Nil	Nil	NA	NA	NA	NA	NA
% Net Inc.of Revs.	18.4	24.4	35.4	34.3	13.2	NA	NA	NA	NA	NA
% Ret. on Assets	6.6	9.9	22.0	12.6	NA	NA	NA	NA	NA	NA
% Ret. on Equity	7.5	11.6	26.3	15.2	NA	NA	NA	NA	NA	NA

Data as orig. reptd.; bef. results of disc. opers. and/or spec. items. Per share data adj. for stk. divs. as of ex-div. date. Prior to 1997 (6 mos.), yrs. end. Jun. 30. Balance Sheet Data for 1996 pro forma as of Mar. 31, 1997. Bold denotes diluted EPS (FASB 128). E-Estimated. NA-Not Available. NM-Not Meaningful. NR-Not Ranked.

Office—Two Lincoln Centre, Suite 1100, 5420 LBJ Freeway, Dallas, TX 75240-2648. **Tel**—(972) 701-7300. **Website**—http://www.sfdrill.com **Chrmn**—G. M. Anderson. **Pres & CEO**—C. S. Garber Jr. **SVP & CFO**—S. M. McCarty. **VP & Secy**—C. A. Moomjian Jr. **VP & Investor Contact**—Richard Hoffman. **Dirs**—K. R. Al-Haroon, G. M. Anderson, F. A. Berger, C. S. Garber Jr., R. L. George, M. A. R. Razzuqi, S. J. Solarz, N. H. Sultan, R. E. Wycoff. **Transfer Agent & Registrar**—Mellon Investor Services L.L.C. **Incorporated**—in the Cayman Islands in 1990. **Empl**—5,500. **S&P Analyst:** T. J. Vital

STANDARD
&POOR'S
STOCK REPORTS

Seitel, Inc.

NYSE Symbol **SEI**

In S&P SmallCap 600

18-AUG-01 **Industry:** Oil & Gas (Drilling & Equipment)

Summary: This company owns what it believes to be the the largest nonproprietary seismic data library in North America.

S&P Opinion: Buy (★★★★★) | Recent Price • 12.12 | 52 Wk Range • 23.03-11.65 | Yield • Nil | 12-Mo. P/E • 12.2

Quantitative Evaluations

Outlook (1 Lowest—5 Highest) • **5**

Fair Value • **20.70**

Risk • **Average**

Earn./Div. Rank • **B**

Technical Eval. • **Bearish** since 8/01

Rel. Strength Rank (1 Lowest—99 Highest) • **20**

Insider Activity • **NA**

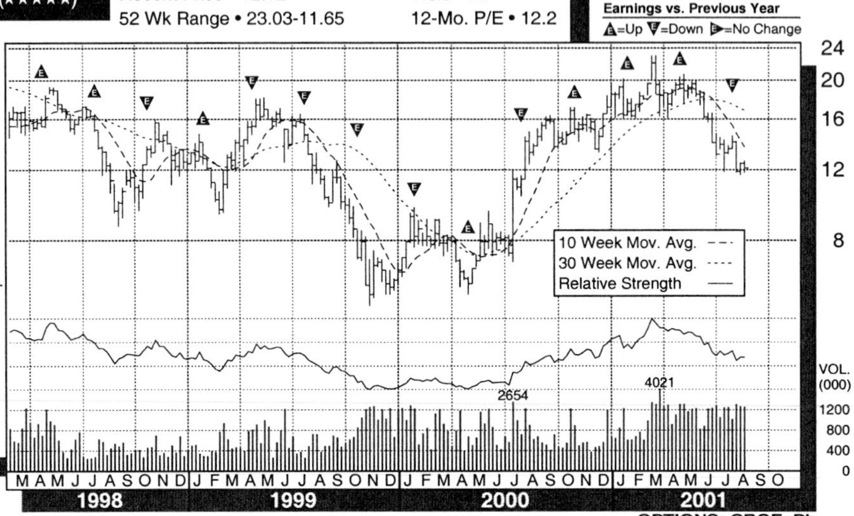

OPTIONS: CBOE, Ph

Overview - 19-JUN-01

Sustained profitable pricing trends for oil and natural gas have encouraged new exploration for those commodities. World oil supply is currently meeting demand, while U.S. domestic natural gas stores have been falling below average levels during high use periods. These trends bode well for SEI, as seismic data and analysis services can significantly improve drilling success rates. SEI is already seeing burgeoning demand for its services. Revenues should grow 29% in 2001, and continue strong well into the anticipated three to five year up cycle. Immediate demand is driving resales of library data, which nearly tripled year to year in the first quarter. The gross margin should widen slightly as resales of library data outweigh sales of newly created data and a greater contribution from DDD Energy. After soaring 67% in 2000, we see operating EPS climbing 29% in 2001, to $1.32.

Valuation - 19-JUN-01

In July 2000, the shares began a strong uptrend; the stock soared 173% in 2000, versus a 16% rise for the S&P Energy Index. Despite falling 13% thus far in 2001, we believe significant upside potential remains. At a recent multiple of 12X our EPS estimate for 2001, the shares were 52% discounted to our long-term growth projection of 25%. The shares were also discounted to the 24X P/E multiple of the company's closest seismic peers. The company has two operating segments, with approximately 16% of revenues derived from oil and gas exploration & production. In valuing SEI's segments separately, employing relative acquisition transaction multiples and peer mean values, we found a fair value 37% above market value. Our discounted free cash flow valuation model supports a value of $38. In comparing the various valuation metrics employed, we have set a 12-month price target of $28.

Key Stock Statistics

S&P EPS Est. 2001	1.22	Tang. Bk. Value/Share	11.20
P/E on S&P Est. 2001	9.9	Beta	0.85
S&P EPS Est. 2002	1.65	Shareholders	1,006
Dividend Rate/Share	Nil	Market cap. (B)	$0.304
Shs. outstg. (M)	25.1	Inst. holdings	70%
Avg. daily vol. (M)	0.346		

Value of $10,000 invested 5 years ago: NA

Fiscal Year Ending Dec. 31

	2001	2000	1999	1998	1997	1996
Revenues (Million $)						
1Q	48.98	28.43	37.88	30.93	27.22	20.27
2Q	43.42	40.07	34.13	36.98	34.67	27.18
3Q	—	44.83	24.62	38.33	30.79	30.31
4Q	—	50.49	32.08	38.62	34.87	28.25
Yr.	—	163.8	128.7	144.9	127.6	106.0
Earnings Per Share ($)						
1Q	0.29	0.11	0.03	0.21	0.19	0.14
2Q	0.03	0.08	0.20	0.28	0.25	0.20
3Q	—	0.30	0.03	0.28	0.98	0.22
4Q	—	0.35	0.12	0.29	0.02	0.28
Yr.	—	0.85	0.39	1.05	1.43	0.79

Next earnings report expected: early November

Dividend Data

Quarterly cash dividends were discontinued in 1992. A two-for-one stock split was effected in December 1997.

Business Summary - 19-JUN-01

Seitel provides proprietary seismic data and analysis services used in oil and natural gas exploration and production (E&P). The company owns and licenses what it believes to be the largest nonproprietary seismic data library in North America. The data library, which consists of both two-dimensional (2D) and three-dimensional (3D) data, is marketed to more than 400 oil and gas companies under license agreements. At year-end 2000, SEI owned about 1.1 million linear mi. of 2D and 19,200 sq. mi. of 3D seismic data, which it maintained in its library.

Three-dimensional seismic data provides a graphic geophysical depiction of the earth's subsurface from two horizontal dimensions and one vertical dimension, rendering a more detailed picture than 2D data, which present a cross-sectional view from one vertical and one horizontal dimension. As a result, 3D surveys enhance the interpreter's ability to predict the existence and location of subsurface hydrocarbons, increasing drilling success rates, reducing the occurrence of costly dry holes, and significantly lowering exploration and development finding costs. However, the cost to create 3D seismic data is substantially greater than that of creating 2D seismic data, particularly for onshore data. As a result, 2D is more economical for preliminary, broad scale exploration valuation, and in determining the location for 3D surveys.

Seitel has stated that it will not perform high-risk speculative data initiation because it believes that would put its shareholders at unnecessary financial risk. Instead, the company prefers the multi-client underwriting approach whereby at least 65%-75% of the cost of the survey is covered before the data initiation takes place. The company's customers may not transfer a seismic data license. Thus, if a new company would like to view the data, they must purchase a license, generating additional revenue for the company.

Through its DDD Energy subsidiary, the company employs its seismic expertise to participate directly in petroleum exploration, development, and ownership of hydrocarbon reserves via partnership relationships with more than 100 oil and gas companies. DDD Energy's E&P activities are focused on the onshore Gulf Coast areas of Texas, Louisiana, Alabama and Mississippi, as well as California and Arkansas. Proved reserves as of December 31, 2000, consisted of 41.6 Bcf of natural gas and 3.8 MMBbls of oil.

In September 2000, the company began an initiative to create a product that will enable its clients to access and interact, via the Internet, with the company's seismic data. During 2000, SEI made acquisitions of rights to certain software that will aid in the development of this product.

In May 1999, SEI formed an equally owned joint venture with Schlumberger, to perform seismic surveying work in the Gulf of Mexico in water depths up to 500 ft. In February 1999, SEI purchased Amoco Canada's seismic data covering Alberta, British Columb ia, Saskatchewan, and the Northwest Territory.

Per Share Data ($) **(Year Ended Dec. 31)**	**2000**	**1999**	**1998**	**1997**	**1996**	**1995**	**1994**	**1993**	**1992**	**1991**
Tangible Bk. Val.	11.20	10.29	10.05	9.27	8.24	6.38	5.74	3.48	2.98	2.83
Cash Flow	3.91	2.87	4.08	3.68	2.69	1.88	2.36	1.85	1.56	1.43
Earnings	0.85	0.39	1.05	1.43	0.79	0.52	0.61	0.46	0.38	0.57
Dividends	Nil	Nil	Nil	Nil	Nil	Nil	Nil	Nil	0.02	0.05
Payout Ratio	Nil	Nil	Nil	Nil	Nil	Nil	Nil	Nil	7%	9%
Prices - High	19.75	18.12	19.31	25.87	21.87	17.75	18.50	7.18	5.75	7.56
- Low	5.87	5.50	8.68	15.68	11.62	9.43	6.68	3.25	2.43	4.00
P/E Ratio - High	23	46	18	18	28	34	30	16	15	13
- Low	7	14	8	11	15	18	11	7	6	7
Income Statement Analysis (Million $)										
Revs.	164	129	145	128	106	74.4	73.8	43.5	31.2	27.8
Oper. Inc.	123	95.1	113	86.6	67.4	46.0	45.7	27.6	20.3	18.5
Depr.	73.7	59.6	69.9	49.7	39.2	26.9	27.2	19.9	13.5	9.2
Int. Exp.	13.2	11.8	6.0	4.6	4.1	3.4	3.5	2.3	1.6	0.9
Pretax Inc.	32.2	16.5	38.0	49.0	25.1	16.0	15.3	9.0	6.5	9.1
Eff. Tax Rate	37%	43%	36%	36%	35%	37%	37%	36%	33%	34%
Net Inc.	20.4	9.4	24.4	31.6	16.2	10.1	9.6	5.7	4.3	6.0
Balance Sheet & Other Fin. Data (Million $)										
Cash	10.2	5.2	3.2	4.9	3.3	6.2	1.5	1.8	3.5	1.1
Curr. Assets	NA	NA	NA	NA	NA	NA	NA	NA	NA	18.7
Total Assets	578	556	496	366	295	210	169	92.6	73.1	52.0
Curr. Liab.	NA	NA	NA	NA	NA	NA	45.6	18.4	10.5	8.0
LT Debt	207	225	151	90.0	84.0	57.6	14.6	30.7	26.2	11.5
Common Eqty.	276	243	238	208	159	120	101	41.6	35.6	31.4
Total Cap.	513	501	388	315	240	178	119	73.3	62.2	43.2
Cap. Exp.	2.3	138	161	141	106	82.4	52.6	22.9	22.0	20.0
Cash Flow	94.1	69.0	94.3	81.2	55.5	37.0	36.8	25.6	17.8	15.2
Curr. Ratio	NA	NA	NA	NA	NA	NA	NA	NA	NA	2.3
% LT Debt of Cap.	40.2	45.0	38.8	28.6	35.1	32.3	12.3	41.9	42.2	26.5
% Net Inc.of Revs.	12.5	7.3	16.8	24.7	15.3	13.6	13.0	13.2	14.4	22.0
% Ret. on Assets	3.6	1.8	5.7	9.6	6.4	5.4	6.3	6.9	6.7	12.4
% Ret. on Equity	7.9	3.9	10.9	17.2	11.5	9.1	11.8	14.8	12.5	21.0

Data as orig reptd.; bef. results of disc opers/spec. items. Per share data adj. for stk. divs. Bold denotes diluted EPS (FASB 128)-prior periods restated. E-Estimated. NA-Not Available. NM-Not Meaningful. NR-Not Ranked.

Office—50 Briar Hollow Lane, West Bldg., 7th Fl., Houston, TX 77027. **Tel**—(713) 881-8900. **Website**—http://www.seitel-inc.com **Chrmn**—H. M. Pearlman. **Pres & CEO**—P. A. Frame. **EVP-Fin, CFO, Treas & Secy**—D. D. Valice. **Investor Contact**—Russell Hoffman (203-629-0633). **Dirs**—W. M. Craig Jr., P. A. Frame, W. Lerner, H. M. Pearlman, J. E. Steiglitz, D. D. Valice, F. S. Zeidman. **Transfer Agent & Registrar**—American Stock Transfer & Trust Co., NYC. **Incorporated**—in Delaware in 1982. **Empl**— 128. **S&P Analyst:** Markos N. Kaminis

STANDARD
&POOR'S
STOCK REPORTS

Anadarko Petroleum

NYSE Symbol **APC**

In S&P 500

24-AUG-01

Industry: Oil & Gas (Exploration & Production)

Summary: Anadarko, one of the world's largest independent natural gas and crude oil production companies, acquired Union Pacific Resources (UPR) in July 2000.

S&P Opinion: Accumulate (★★★★)

Recent Price • 58.25
52 Wk Range • 75.95-46.52
Yield • 0.3%
12-Mo. P/E • 7.8

Quantitative Evaluations

Outlook (1 Lowest—5 Highest)
• **4−**

Fair Value
• **66.20**

Risk
• **Average**

Earn./Div. Rank
• **B+**

Technical Eval.
• **Bearish** since 8/01

Rel. Strength Rank (1 Lowest—99 Highest)
• **66**

Insider Activity
• **Favorable**

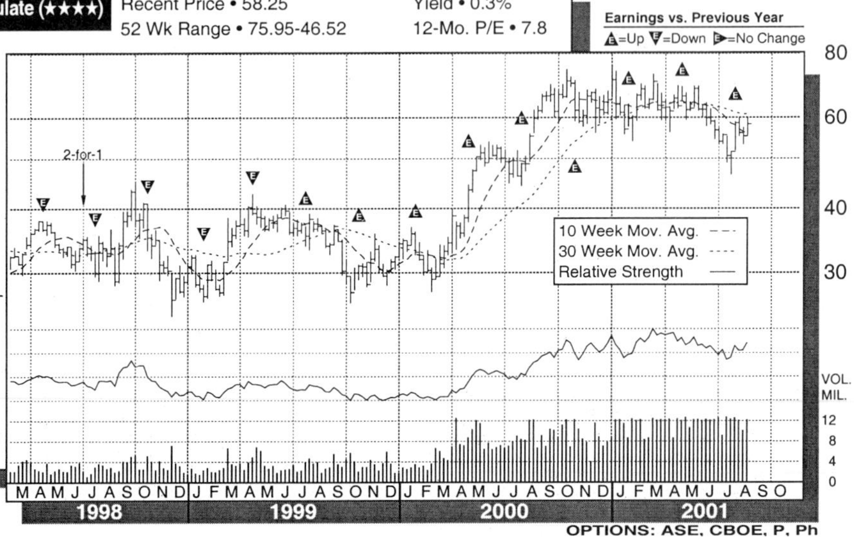

OPTIONS: ASE, CBOE, P, Ph

Overview - 24-AUG-01

We expect the company's total production to climb 82% in 2001, aided by a full year's inclusion of UPR. Key sources of production will include Hickory and Tanzanite (Gulf of Mexico), Bossier (East Texas/Louisiana), Alaska, Algeria and Venezuela. Furthermore, APC is establishing operations in the Middle East, following the the recent $137 million acquisition of Gulfstream Resources. For the longer term, we are especially bullish on the upside potential of APC's acreage positions in Alaska's North Slope and Foothills, and in Canada's Mackenzie Delta. Costs for drilling services should remain high, due to strong demand associated with relatively high commodity prices. APC is more exposed than its peers to such cost hikes, because a large percentage of its proved reserves is classified as undeveloped, implying significant expenditures to achieve commerciality. Overall, we look for discretionary cash flow per share (DCFPS) to advance about 30%, to $12.44.

Valuation - 24-AUG-01

Year to date, the shares were recently down 36%, compared with the peer group average decline of 12.5%, and were trading at 4.4X 2001 DCFPS, versus a group average of 3.5X. The relatively weak commodity environment as well as some profit-taking given last year's good performance, are the major reasons for the weak stock performance. However, over the longer term, APC can be expected to continue to deliver above average reserve replacement and production and cash flow growth, in part reflecting the company's significant exploration potential. With shares trading at $6.70 per barrel of oil equivalent on proven reserves, at a 90% discount of our DCF net asset value based on 2000 proven reserves, we reiterate our accumulate recommendation.

Key Stock Statistics

S&P EPS Est. 2001	5.56	Tang. Bk. Value/Share	25.08
P/E on S&P Est. 2001	10.5	Beta	0.70
S&P EPS Est. 2002	4.63	Shareholders	22,000
Dividend Rate/Share	0.20	Market cap. (B)	$ 13.5
Shs. outstg. (M)	250.8	Inst. holdings	79%
Avg. daily vol. (M)	2.596		

Value of $10,000 invested 5 years ago: $ 22,006

Fiscal Year Ending Dec. 31

	2001	2000	1999	1998	1997	1996
Revenues (Million $)						
1Q	3,051	661.0	136.4	146.4	170.5	135.7
2Q	2,264	748.0	161.5	137.6	138.9	135.1
3Q	—	1,871	179.9	140.2	158.3	128.6
4Q	—	2,406	223.3	135.5	205.5	169.7
Yr.	—	5,686	701.1	560.3	673.2	569.0
Earnings Per Share ($)						
1Q	**2.52**	**0.37**	**-0.19**	**0.06**	**0.28**	**0.17**
2Q	**1.50**	**0.48**	**0.06**	**0.02**	**0.12**	**0.15**
3Q	—	**1.03**	**0.15**	**-0.02**	**0.14**	**0.21**
4Q	—	**1.75**	**0.22**	**-0.47**	**0.35**	**0.32**
Yr.	—	**4.25**	**0.25**	**-0.41**	**0.89**	**0.84**

Next earnings report expected: NA

Dividend Data (Dividends have been paid since 1986.)

Amount ($)	Date Decl.	Ex-Div. Date	Stock of Record	Payment Date
0.050	Oct. 30	Dec. 11	Dec. 13	Dec. 27 '00
0.050	Feb. 01	Mar. 12	Mar. 14	Mar. 28 '01
0.050	Apr. 26	Jun. 11	Jun. 13	Jun. 27 '01
0.050	Jul. 30	Sep. 10	Sep. 12	Sep. 26 '01

A Division of The McGraw-Hill Companies

Anadarko Petroleum Corporation

Business Summary - 24-AUG-01

Anadarko Petroleum (APC) is one of the world's largest independent oil and gas exploration and production companies. In July 2000, the company acquired Union Pacific Resources (UPR), in exchange for approximately 115 million APC common shares. At the time the acquisition was announced, the companies stressed that the pending merger was not primarily intended to achieve cost savings, but to merge complementary skills and assets that could provide dramatic growth and profitability. APC's strengths were traditionally in exploration, while UPR's strengths were in drilling and completion technology. In addition, APC's reliance on production from Algeria, which has political risks, was reduced. The acquisition was accounted for using the purchase method of accounting.

At December 31, 2000 (1999), APC had 2,061 (991.0) million barrels of oil equivalent (MMBOEs), consisting of 51% (58%) oil, condensate and natural gas liquids (NGLs), and 49% (42%) natural gas. Approximately 56% of total reserves at the end of 2000 were located in the U.S. onshore, primarily in Texas, Louisiana, Alaska and the mid-continent and Rocky Mountain areas; the remaining reserves were in the Gulf of Mexico (9%), Canada (10%), Algeria (18%) and other international (7%). The company also owns and operates gas gathering systems in its U.S. core operating area, and participates in international exploration projects in Tunisia, the North Atlantic Ocean, and selected other areas.

During 2000 (1999), production totaled 112 (50) MMBOEs, comprised 32% of oil and condensate, 11% NGLs, and 57% natural gas. Average price realizations were $26.49 ($16.83) per bbl. of oil and condensate, $21.70 ($13.40) per bbl. of NGLs, and $4.13 ($2.08) per Mcf of gas.

During 2000 (1999), APC replaced 1,059% (213%) of total production with new reserves, mainly reflecting the effects of the UPR acquisition. The average worldwide finding costs in the five years ending with 2000 (1999) was $5.90 ($3.53) per BOE.

Capital spending, which totaled $1,708 million and $680 million in 2000 and 1999, respectively, has been set at $3,000 million for 2001. The budget is allocated to development (50%), exploration (29%), capitalized interest and overhead (12%), and gas gathering and other (9%).

In March 2001, Anadarko acquired Canada-based Berkley Petroleum for C$11.40 cash for each BKP share and the assumption of US$250 million of debt, outbidding two prior offers for Berkley by Hunt Oil Co. With reserves estimated at 95 MMBOE (70% gas), the acquisition accelerates APC's efforts to expand its Canadian presence.

In August 2001, Anadarko completed the acquisition of Gulfstream Resources for a total consideration of approximately $118 million plus the assumption of $10 million in debt. Gulfstream gives APC additional proven reserves (mainly in the Middle East) of approximately 70 million boe.

Per Share Data ($) (Year Ended Dec. 31)	2000	1999	1998	1997	1996	1995	1994	1993	1992	1991
Tangible Bk. Val.	20.99	10.30	8.65	25.10	8.38	7.58	7.64	7.37	5.94	5.81
Cash Flow	7.29	2.00	1.29	2.55	2.26	1.58	1.82	1.81	1.45	1.40
Earnings	4.25	0.25	-0.41	0.89	0.85	0.18	0.35	0.35	0.24	0.29
Dividends	0.20	0.20	0.19	0.15	0.15	0.15	0.15	0.15	0.15	0.15
Payout Ratio	5%	80%	NM	17%	18%	83%	43%	43%	61%	51%
Prices - High	75.95	42.75	44.87	38.37	34.43	27.06	29.25	25.87	16.43	16.56
- Low	27.56	26.25	24.75	25.37	23.37	17.81	18.50	12.81	9.25	10.75
P/E Ratio - High	18	NM	NM	43	41	NM	84	74	67	56
- Low	6	NM	NM	29	27	NM	53	37	38	36
Income Statement Analysis (Million $)										
Revs.	5,686	701	560	673	569	434	482	476	375	337
Oper. Inc.	2,190	421	267	402	349	232	267	272	201	194
Depr. Depl. & Amort.	593	218	204	199	167	165	173	168	133	121
Int. Exp.	Nil	74.1	57.7	41.0	56.0	53.0	41.6	38.0	36.6	36.8
Pretax Inc.	1,426	105	-65.1	164	158	29.3	64.7	77.4	40.0	48.0
Eff. Tax Rate	42%	59%	NM	35%	36%	28%	36%	48%	32%	33%
Net Inc.	824	42.6	-42.2	107	101	21.0	41.1	40.0	27.3	32.4
Balance Sheet & Other Fin. Data (Million $)										
Cash	199	44.8	17.0	8.9	15.0	17.0	6.5	17.8	14.8	15.0
Curr. Assets	1,894	356	230	219	270	163	139	141	139	107
Total Assets	16,590	4,098	3,633	2,992	2,584	2,267	2,142	2,023	1,905	1,676
Curr. Liab.	1,676	387	289	252	285	190	128	126	107	104
LT Debt	3,984	1,443	1,425	956	731	674	629	543	647	440
Common Eqty.	6,586	1,335	1,059	1,117	1,014	910	900	864	657	641
Total Cap.	10,770	3,555	3,208	2,620	2,244	2,034	1,968	1,831	1,783	1,556
Cap. Exp.	1,708	680	917	686	427	331	423	265	362	170
Cash Flow	1,406	250	155	306	268	186	214	208	160	154
Curr. Ratio	1.1	0.9	0.8	0.9	0.9	0.9	1.1	1.1	1.3	1.0
% LT Debt of Cap.	37.0	40.6	44.4	36.5	32.6	33.1	32.0	29.6	36.3	28.2
% Ret. on Assets	8.0	1.1	NM	3.8	4.2	1.0	2.0	2.0	1.5	1.9
% Ret. on Equity	20.5	2.6	NM	10.1	10.5	2.3	4.7	5.1	4.2	5.1

Data as orig reptd.; bef. results of disc opers/spec. items. Per share data adj. for stk. divs. Bold denotes diluted EPS (FASB 128)-prior periods restated. E-Estimated. NA-Not Available. NM-Not Meaningful. NR-Not Ranked.

Office—Anadarko Tower, 17001 Northchase Dr., P.O. Box 1330, Houston, TX 77060. **Tel**—(281) 875-1101. **Website**—www.anadarko.com **Chrmn & CEO**—R. J. Allison Jr. **Vice Chrmn**—G. Lindhal III. **Pres & COO**—J. N. Seitz. **SVP-Fin & CFO**—M. E. Rose. **VP & Treas**—A. L. Richey. **VP & Investor Contact**—A. Paul Taylor Jr. **Dirs**—C. P. Albert, R. J. Allison Jr., L. G. Barcus, R. Brown, J. L. Bryan, J. R. Butler Jr., P. M. Geren III, J. R. Gordon, L. M. Jones, G. Lindhal III, J. W. Poduska Sr., J. D. Sandefer, J. N. Seitz. **Transfer Agent & Registrar**—Mellon Investor Services, South Hackensack, NJ. **Incorporated**—in Delaware in 1985. **Empl**— 4,300. **S&P Analyst:** John Kartsonas

STANDARD & POOR'S
STOCK REPORTS

Apache

NYSE Symbol **APA**

In S&P 500

24-AUG-01

Industry: Oil & Gas (Exploration & Production)

Summary: This independent energy company explores for, produces and markets oil and natural gas.

S&P Opinion: Accumulate (★★★★)

Recent Price • 52.50
52 Wk Range • 74.18-44.30

Yield • 0.5%
12-Mo. P/E • 6.9

Quantitative Evaluations

Outlook
(1 Lowest—5 Highest)
• **5**

Fair Value
• **66.70**

Risk
• **Low**

Earn./Div. Rank
• **B+**

Technical Eval.
• **Bearish** since 8/01

Rel. Strength Rank
(1 Lowest—99 Highest)
• **54**

Insider Activity
• **Neutral**

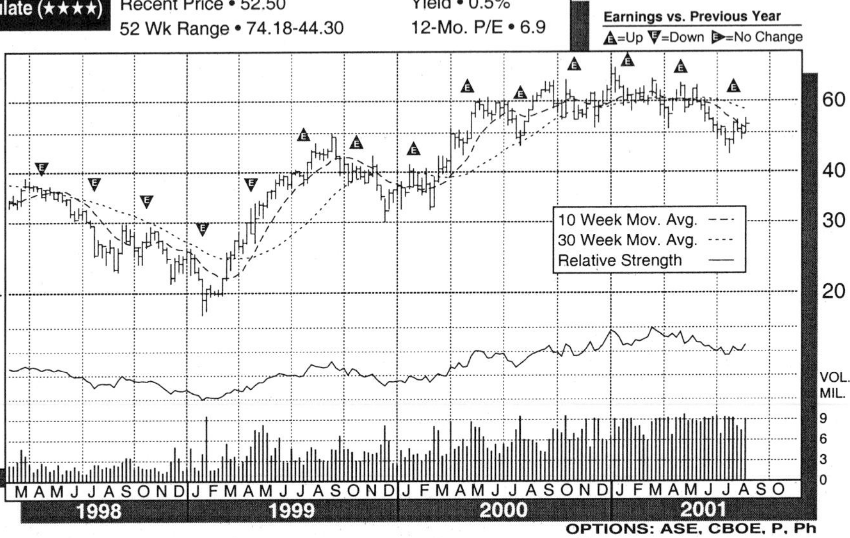

OPTIONS: ASE, CBOE, P, Ph

Overview - 24-AUG-01

Total production should climb 34% in 2001, mainly reflecting the recent closings of property acquisitions from Repsol YPF, Fletcher Challenge, and Phillips Petroleum, for a combined purchase price of approximately $1.5 billion. The volume growth, which should ease in 2002, will benefit from still relatively high commodity prices. Our 2001 EPS and discretionary cash flow per share (DCFPS) estimates of $6.74 and $16.13, reflect our pricing forecasts of $4.44 per MMBtu of Henry Hub natural gas, and $27.64 per barrel of West Texas Intermediate crude oil. As a result of the $410 million Repsol acquisition, APA increased its interest in the prolific Khalda/Khalda Offset Concession, located in Egypt, from 40% to 90%, and became the operator; the company has said the concession is the single-most valuable property in its worldwide portfolio. However, we believe it holds the highest risk/reward of all APA's assets.

Valuation - 24-AUG-01

The shares were recently down 28% in 2001, versus a 12.5% decrease for S&P's Exploration & Production index. The stock was trading at 3.1X DCFPS, versus APA's peer group average of 3.5X. APA is one of the few exploration and production companies that does well consistently in all key industry measures, including reserve life and reserve replacement ratios, production and all sources finding and development costs, and growth in earnings and cash flow. Despite its string of recent acquisitions, the company boasts one of the lowest debt/capitalization ratios in its peer group. Acquisition economics are typically locked in with hedges, and excess cash flow is used to reduce temporary debt hikes. With shares trading at 75% of our DCF net asset value based on 2000 proven reserves, we reiterate our accumulate recommendation.

Key Stock Statistics

S&P EPS Est. 2001	6.74	Tang. Bk. Value/Share	27.89
P/E on S&P Est. 2001	7.8	Beta	0.64
S&P EPS Est. 2002	7.00	Shareholders	55,000
Dividend Rate/Share	0.28	Market cap. (B)	$ 6.1
Shs. outstg. (M)	125.4	Inst. holdings	79%
Avg. daily vol. (M)	1.737		

Value of $10,000 invested 5 years ago: $ 17,731

Fiscal Year Ending Dec. 31

	2001	2000	1999	1998	1997	1996
Revenues (Million $)						
1Q	795.1	448.2	187.7	245.9	321.8	206.5
2Q	800.4	486.4	281.6	220.1	258.8	223.7
3Q	—	618.5	385.4	211.7	276.8	242.4
4Q	—	730.8	445.8	198.0	318.9	304.6
Yr.	—	2,284	1,301	875.7	1,176	977.1
Earnings Per Share ($)						
1Q	**2.15**	**0.96**	**-0.04**	**0.18**	**0.56**	**0.20**
2Q	**1.85**	**1.18**	**0.28**	**0.09**	**0.28**	**0.28**
3Q	—	**1.58**	**0.59**	**0.03**	**0.33**	**0.33**
4Q	—	**1.96**	**0.80**	**-1.64**	**0.48**	**0.54**
Yr.	—	**5.73**	**1.72**	**-1.34**	**1.65**	**1.38**

Next earnings report expected: late October

Dividend Data (Dividends have been paid since 1965.)

Amount ($)	Date Decl.	Ex-Div. Date	Stock of Record	Payment Date
0.140	Sep. 22	Nov. 13	Nov. 15	Dec. 15 '00

A Division of The McGraw·Hill Companies

Apache Corporation

Business Summary - 24-AUG-01

Apache Corp., an independent energy company that explores for, develops and produces natural gas, crude oil, and natural gas liquids, has grown recently through acquisitions. In North America, the company's exploration and production (E&P) operations focused on the Gulf of Mexico and Gulf Coast, and on the Anadarko, Permian, and Western Canadian Sedimentary Basins. Internationally, APA has E&P efforts offshore Western Australia and in Egypt. In addition, the company conducts exploration in Poland, and offshore The People's Republic of China.

At December 31, 2000 (1999), proved reserves totaled 1,086.4 (807.2) million barrels of oil equivalent (MMBOE). Oil and gas accounted for 48% (51%) and 52% (49%) of total reserves, respectively. Production in 2000 (1999) totaled 95.2 (74.6) MMBOE, and consisted of 53% (53%) gas, and 47% (47%) oil and natural gas liquids.

The company believes it is often more attractive to buy particular assets, rather than entire companies, due to cultural differences between boards of directors. APA's acquisition economics are often "locked in" via hedges. In May 1999, it bought from Shell Offshore its interest in 22 producing fields and 16 undeveloped blocks located in the Gulf of Mexico. The purchase price was $687.6 million in cash, plus 1 million common shares. The properties contained proved reserves of 123.2 million BOE. In December, APA purchased from Shell Canada (a separate entity) properties in western Canada that contained an estimated 87.5 MMBOE, for $517 million. The acquisition also included 300,000 net acres of undeveloped leaseholdings, a gas processing plant with 160 MMcf per day of capacity, and a substantial seismic database. The transaction, effective as of November 1, added daily production of 12.5 MBbls of oil and 64.8 MMcf of gas.

In January 2000, APA bought from Repsol properties located in western Oklahoma and the Texas Panhandle, with estimated proved reserves of 28.7 MMBOE, for $118.7 million. In June, it acquired from Collins & Ware properties located in the Permian Basin and South Texas, with estimated proved reserves of 83.7 MMBOE, for $320.7 million. In August, the company bought from Occidental Petroleum 32 producing fields located in the Gulf of Mexico, with estimated proved reserves of 53.1 MMBOE. The purchase price of $385 million was financed through a public equity offering of 9.2 million common shares. In December, APA acquired from Phillips Petroleum Co. assets located in Northwest Alberta, with estimated proved reserves of 70.0 MMBOE, for $490.3 million. Additional tactical acquisitions in 2000 totaled $104.0 million, containing estimated proved reserves of 18.3 MMBOE.

Per Share Data ($) (Year Ended Dec. 31)	2000	1999	1998	1997	1996	1995	1994	1993	1992	1991
Tangible Bk. Val.	27.89	20.71	17.42	18.53	16.86	14.11	13.28	12.86	10.12	9.39
Cash Flow	10.30	5.81	5.09	5.47	5.08	4.43	4.61	4.42	4.63	3.72
Earnings	5.73	1.72	-1.34	1.71	1.42	0.28	0.70	0.70	1.02	0.76
Dividends	0.21	0.28	0.28	0.28	0.28	0.28	0.28	0.28	0.28	0.28
Payout Ratio	4%	16%	NM	16%	20%	100%	40%	40%	27%	38%
Prices - High	74.18	49.93	38.75	45.06	37.87	31.00	29.25	33.50	22.12	20.75
- Low	32.12	17.62	21.06	30.12	24.37	22.25	22.25	17.62	12.00	12.00
P/E Ratio - High	13	29	NM	26	27	NM	42	48	22	27
- Low	6	10	NM	18	17	NM	32	25	12	16
Income Statement Analysis (Million $)										
Revs.	2,283	1,300	876	1,176	977	751	538	463	423	342
Oper. Inc.	1,310	870	509	712	577	411	327	281	244	201
Depr. Depl. & Amort.	584	443	630	388	315	297	240	199	169	136
Int. Exp.	109	84.6	70.4	68.7	89.8	88.1	36.0	32.0	39.2	32.7
Pretax Inc.	1,204	345	-187	259	200	38.1	64.0	58.0	70.0	44.0
Eff. Tax Rate	40%	42%	NM	40%	39%	39%	34%	36%	32%	22%
Net Inc.	721	201	-128	155	121	20.2	42.8	37.3	47.8	34.6
Balance Sheet & Other Fin. Data (Million $)										
Cash	37.2	13.2	14.5	9.7	13.2	13.6	15.1	17.1	26.1	6.4
Curr. Assets	630	343	227	348	268	208	135	123	114	91.0
Total Assets	7,482	5,503	3,996	4,139	3,432	2,681	1,879	1,592	1,219	1,209
Curr. Liab.	553	337	306	344	310	230	148	185	158	146
LT Debt	2,193	1,880	1,343	150	1,236	1,072	657	453	454	491
Common Eqty.	3,448	2,361	1,703	1,729	1,519	1,092	816	786	475	440
Total Cap.	5,948	4,549	3,416	3,586	3,010	2,345	1,630	1,367	1,013	996
Cap. Exp.	1,011	591	700	732	124	1,133	494	583	207	686
Cash Flow	1,284	629	499	543	436	318	283	237	217	170
Curr. Ratio	1.1	1.0	0.7	1.0	0.9	0.9	0.9	0.7	0.7	0.6
% LT Debt of Cap.	36.9	41.3	39.3	41.9	41.1	45.7	40.3	33.1	44.9	49.3
% Ret. on Assets	11.1	4.2	NM	4.1	3.9	0.9	2.5	2.3	3.9	3.3
% Ret. on Equity	24.1	9.2	NM	9.5	9.3	2.0	5.3	5.3	10.4	8.2

Data as orig reptd.; bef. results of disc opers/spec. items. Per share data adj. for stk. divs. Bold denotes diluted EPS (FASB 128)-prior periods restated. E-Estimated. NA-Not Available. NM-Not Meaningful. NR-Not Ranked.

Office—2000 Post Oak Blvd., Houston, TX 77056-4400. **Tel**—(713) 296-6000. **Website**—http://www.apachecorp.com **Chrmn & CEO**—Raymond Plank. **Pres & COO**—G. S. Farris. **EVP & CFO**—Roger B. Plank. **VP & Treas**—M. W. Dundrea. **Secy**—C. L. Peper. **VP & Investor Contact**—Robert Dye (713-296-6662). **Dirs**—F. M. Bohen, G. S. Farris, R. M. Ferlic, E. C. Fiedorek, A. D. Frazier Jr., J. A. Kocur, G. D. Lawrence Jr., M. R. Lowe, F. H. Merelli, R. D. Patton, Raymond Plank. C. J. Pitman. **Transfer Agent & Registrar**—Norwest Bank Minnesota, South St. Paul. **Incorporated**—in Delaware in 1954. **Empl**— 1,546. **S&P Analyst:** John Kartsonas

STANDARD
&POOR'S
STOCK REPORTS

ENSCO International

NYSE Symbol ESV
In S&P MidCap 400

18-AUG-01

Industry:
Oil & Gas (Drilling & Equipment)

Summary: This international contract drilling company also provides marine transportation services to the oil and gas industry.

S&P Opinion: Accumulate (★★★★)

Recent Price • 20.11
52 Wk Range • 44.49-18.33
Yield • 0.5%
12-Mo. P/E • 16.1

Quantitative Evaluations

Outlook
(1 Lowest—5 Highest)
• **4**

Fair Value
• **24.50**

Risk
• **High**

Earn./Div. Rank
• **B**

Technical Eval.
• **Bearish** since 5/01

Rel. Strength Rank
(1 Lowest—99 Highest)
• **18**

Insider Activity
• **NA**

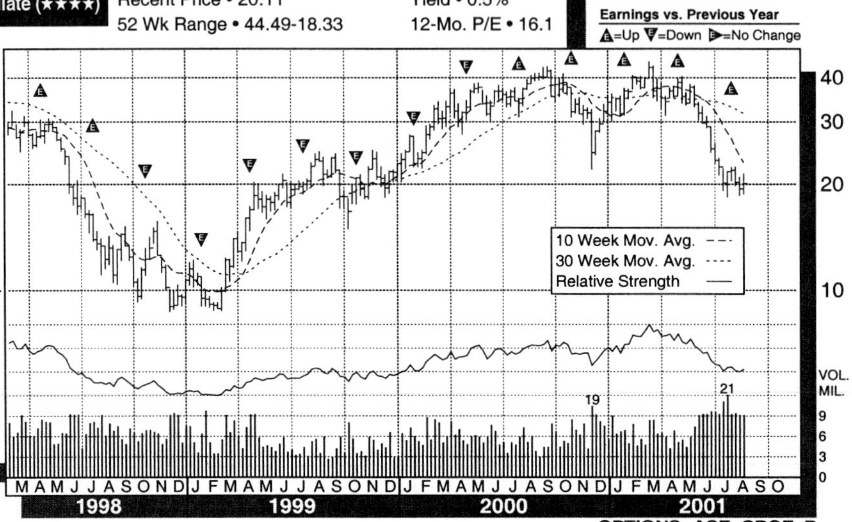

OPTIONS: ASE, CBOE, P

Overview - 18-JUL-01

We expect natural gas and oil prices to remain high throughout 2001, driving major oils and independents to raise exploration and production spending at least 20% this year. As a result, we see ESV's operating income climbing over 185% in 2001, reflecting accelerating international opportunities. During the second quarter, jackup utilization rates were 91%, versus 92% in the first quarter, while dayrates were up 11%, to $52,611; boat utilization rates were 84%, versus 77%, and dayrates rose 9% to $8,291. Margins should continue to widen in 2001, on rising international dayrates, a conservative cost structure, and as ESV's fixed assets are put back to work. In June, directors authorized the repurchase of up to 4.5 million common shares.

Valuation - 18-JUL-01

Over the past month, the shares dropped sharply, in a sector sell-off reflecting end of quarter window dressing and investor concern over slowing economies. In addition, the Gulf of Mexico jackup market is experiencing what we believe is temporary weakness in dayrates. With certain production targets met, budget approval is being sought for new projects, and certain large producers remain on the sidelines for the summer. Although domestic natural gas drilling may soften for a short period, we expect domestic oil drilling to pick up the slack. This activity is supplemented by increased international drilling activity. ESV should benefit from this mix, with a large jackup fleet serving the shallow water Gulf of Mexico, and expanded efforts in deeper water capabilities, such as the newly built ENSCO 7500 semisubmersible rig. With a fleet focused on the Gulf of Mexico, and with the shares trading at only 7X our 2002 EPS estimate, a discount to peer levels, we would accumulate the stock.

Key Stock Statistics

S&P EPS Est. 2001	1.79	Tang. Bk. Value/Share	10.28
P/E on S&P Est. 2001	11.2	Beta	1.32
S&P EPS Est. 2002	2.67	Shareholders	1,800
Dividend Rate/Share	0.10	Market cap. (B)	$ 2.8
Shs. outstg. (M)	138.0	Inst. holdings	82%
Avg. daily vol. (M)	2.156		

Value of $10,000 invested 5 years ago: $ 13,996

Fiscal Year Ending Dec. 31

	2001	2000	1999	1998	1997	1996
Revenues (Million $)						
1Q	195.3	96.20	127.7	246.4	161.6	84.55
2Q	215.5	116.6	79.40	234.0	195.4	97.25
3Q	—	149.8	76.40	179.8	223.2	134.6
4Q	—	171.2	80.20	153.0	234.8	152.4
Yr.	—	533.8	363.7	813.2	815.1	468.8
Earnings Per Share ($)						
1Q	**0.34**	**0.03**	**0.15**	**0.61**	**0.25**	**0.12**
2Q	**0.44**	**0.12**	**-0.07**	**0.57**	**0.37**	**0.17**
3Q	**E0.47**	**0.21**	**-0.08**	**0.42**	**0.47**	**0.19**
4Q	**E0.54**	**0.31**	**-0.05**	**0.20**	**0.55**	**0.22**
Yr.	**E1.79**	**0.61**	**-0.05**	**1.81**	**1.64**	**0.72**

Next earnings report expected: mid October

Dividend Data (Dividends have been paid since 1997.)

Amount ($)	Date Decl.	Ex-Div. Date	Stock of Record	Payment Date
0.025	Aug. 10	Aug. 31	Sep. 05	Sep. 19 '00
0.025	Nov. 15	Dec. 01	Dec. 05	Dec. 19 '00
0.025	Feb. 07	Feb. 27	Mar. 01	Mar. 15 '01
0.025	May. 17	Jun. 01	Jun. 05	Jun. 19 '01

ENSCO International Incorporated

Business Summary - 18-JUL-01

As an international offshore oil and gas contract drilling company, ENSCO International also provides marine transportation services to the energy industry. As of December 31, 2000, ESV's offshore drilling fleet (including rigs under construction) was comprised of 37 jackup rigs, nine barge rigs, seven platform rigs and one semisubmersible rig. The company's marine transportation fleet consists of 28 vessels, which are used to tow offshore rigs from location to location and ferry supplies and personnel from the mainland to offshore drilling sites.

ESV maintains a strategy of building its fleet of offshore drilling rigs through acquisitions and construction. During 2000, the company constructed the ENSCO 101, a harsh environment jackup rig (scheduled for delivery in the 2001 first quarter to repair leg damage sustained in August 2000 while moving to a drilling location in the U.K.), and the ENSCO 7500, a semisubmersible rig capable of drilling in water depths up to 8,000 ft. In the 2000 fourth quarter, ESV entered into a joint venture with Keppel FELS Ltd., through which it acquired a 25% interest in the KFELS MOD V, a new harsh environment rig under construction. The company has an option to purchase the remaining 75% interest in the new rig until two years after delivery.

Of the company's 37 jackup rigs, 22 are located in the Gulf of Mexico, eight are located in the North Sea, and seven are located in the Asia Pacific region. The company's nine barge rigs are all located in Venezuela, and the seven platform rigs are all located in the Gulf of Mexico. The semisubmersible rig ENSCO 7500 is under three year contract in the Gulf of Mexico. On March 1, 2001, the jackup rig ENSCO 51 was damaged as a result of a shallow gas blowout and subsequent fire.

The marine transportation business is conducted through a wholly owned subsidiary, ENSCO Marine Company. The fleet consists of five anchor handling tug supply (AHTS) vessels and 23 supply vessels.

During 2000, customers were served in the U.S. (66% of 2000 revenues), the Netherlands (2%), Venezuela (8%) and other countries (24%). Exxon Mobil Corp. and Chevron Corp. accounted for 18% and 11%, respectively, of ESV's 2000 revenues.

ESV's total jackup rig utilization rates rose to 86% in 2000, from 75% in 1999; average dayrates increased to $35,816 in 2000, from $24,286. Barge rig utilization rates were 33% in 2000, versus 31%; dayrates rose to $39,897 in 2000, from $35,113. Platform rig utilization rates were 57% in 2000, versus 51%; dayrates were $24,369, versus $23,204. The marine fleet posted utilization rates of 65% in 2000, up from 62%; while day rates for the vessels grew to $5,271, from $4,394. As of February 1, 2001, backlog was up 19% year to year, to $679.7 million.

Per Share Data ($) (Year Ended Dec. 31)	2000	1999	1998	1997	1996	1995	1994	1993	1992	1991
Tangible Bk. Val.	9.59	9.05	8.25	6.75	5.21	4.33	3.83	3.18	2.34	2.84
Cash Flow	1.32	0.76	2.40	2.41	1.33	0.82	0.77	0.52	-0.30	0.04
Earnings	0.61	-0.05	1.81	1.64	0.72	0.34	0.30	0.16	-0.56	-0.28
Dividends	0.10	0.10	0.10	0.05	Nil	Nil	Nil	Nil	Nil	Nil
Payout Ratio	16%	NM	6%	3%	Nil	Nil	Nil	Nil	Nil	Nil
Prices - High	43.12	25.00	33.56	47.00	25.06	11.50	9.62	8.12	4.00	6.50
- Low	20.25	8.75	8.68	20.25	10.00	5.62	5.37	1.75	2.00	2.50
P/E Ratio - High	71	NM	19	29	35	33	32	51	NM	NM
- Low	33	NM	5	12	14	16	18	11	NM	NM
Income Statement Analysis (Million $)										
Revs.	534	364	813	815	469	279	262	246	162	207
Oper. Inc.	230	102	469	494	231	114	106	66.3	Nil	10.3
Depr.	99	98.2	83.5	105	81.9	58.4	54.2	30.1	15.7	15.3
Int. Exp.	13.4	19.3	26.2	21.4	20.9	16.6	14.1	10.5	4.5	4.2
Pretax Inc.	125	5.2	383	376	143	47.3	43.9	29.6	-26.8	-8.0
Eff. Tax Rate	32%	NM	32%	37%	31%	7.20%	8.60%	20%	NM	NM
Net Inc.	85.4	6.7	254	235	95.4	41.8	37.2	16.7	-29.6	-8.7
Balance Sheet & Other Fin. Data (Million $)										
Cash	107	165	330	262	80.7	82.0	154	128	25.5	29.5
Curr. Assets	289	273	476	447	211	166	212	193	79.0	85.0
Total Assets	2,108	1,978	1,993	1,772	1,315	822	775	691	283	315
Curr. Liab.	117	135	159	131	104	86.8	88.2	65.9	40.1	44.9
LT Debt	422	371	376	401	259	159	162	126	23.6	31.0
Common Eqty.	1,329	1,241	1,245	1,077	846	531	488	384	143	165
Total Cap.	1,981	1,829	1,817	1,478	1,178	717	678	609	238	268
Cap. Exp.	256	248	331	282	176	143	153	384	4.0	44.6
Cash Flow	184	105	337	340	177	100	89.2	42.6	-18.2	2.0
Curr. Ratio	2.5	2.0	3.0	3.4	2.0	1.9	2.4	2.9	2.0	1.9
% LT Debt of Cap.	21.3	20.3	20.7	27.4	22.0	22.2	24.0	20.7	9.9	11.7
% Net Inc.of Revs.	16.0	1.8	31.2	28.8	20.3	15.0	14.2	6.8	NM	NM
% Ret. on Assets	4.2	0.3	13.5	15.2	8.9	6.0	4.9	2.8	NM	NM
% Ret. on Equity	6.7	0.5	21.9	24.4	13.9	9.4	7.7	3.8	NM	NM

Data as orig. reptd.; bef. results of disc. opers. and/or spec. items. Per share data adj. for stk. divs. as of ex-div. date. Bold denotes diluted EPS (FASB 128). E-Estimated. NA-Not Available. NM-Not Meaningful. NR-Not Ranked.

Office—2700 Fountain Place, 1445 Ross Ave., Dallas, TX 75202-2792. **Tel**—(214) 922-1500. **Website**—www.enscous.com **Chrmn, Pres & CEO**—C. F. Thorne. **SVP & COO**—R. A. Wilson. **VP-Fin & CFO**—C. C. Gaut. **Treas & Investor Contact**—Richard A. LeBlanc. **VP & Secy**—W. S. Chadwick Jr. **Dirs**—D. M. Carmichael, C. I. Fields, G. W. Haddock, T. L. Kelly II, M. H. Meyerson, D. W. Rabun, P. E. Rowsey III, C. F. Thorne, R. A. Wilson. **Transfer Agent & Registrar**—American Stock Transfer & Trust Co., NYC. **Incorporated**—in Texas in 1975; reincorporated in Delaware in 1987. **Empl**— 3,400. **S&P Analyst:** T. J. Vital

STANDARD & POOR'S STOCK REPORTS

Global Marine

NYSE Symbol **GLM**

In S&P MidCap 400

18-AUG-01

Industry: Oil & Gas (Drilling & Equipment)

Summary: This international offshore drilling contractor serves the oil and gas industry with a fleet of rigs, and provides offshore drilling management services.

S&P Opinion: Accumulate (★★★★)

Recent Price • 15.95
52 Wk Range • 34.25-15.05
Yield • Nil
12-Mo. P/E • 14.5

Quantitative Evaluations

Outlook (1 Lowest—5 Highest) • **4**

Fair Value • **19.70**

Risk • **High**

Earn./Div. Rank • **B-**

Technical Eval. • **Bearish** since 8/01

Rel. Strength Rank (1 Lowest—99 Highest) • **17**

Insider Activity • **NA**

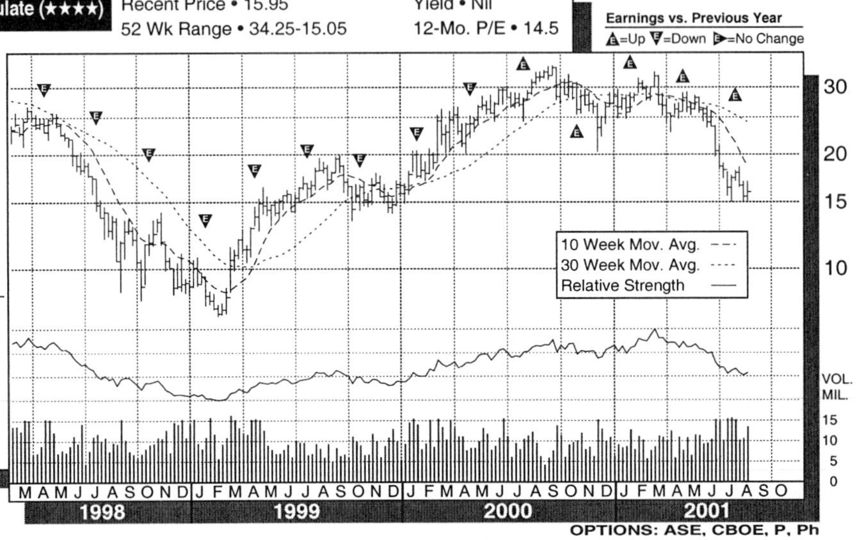

OPTIONS: ASE, CBOE, P, Ph

Overview - 18-JUL-01

Operating income should climb over 95% in 2001, boosted by increased contract drilling activity resulting from sustained high prices for oil and natural gas. Although most oil and gas being drilled today is from existing wells, production declines of more than 8% worldwide should drive development of new wells in the future. Utilization rates rose to 99% in the 2001 second quarter, from 89% in the first quarter; and average dayrates rose 6.2%, to $75,500. We expect rates to continue to increase, driven by accelerating international prospects, especially in the North Sea and West Africa. Results should also benefit from the new ultra-deepwater drillship additions of the Glomar Jack Ryan and the Glomar Robert F. Bauer. ADTI's performance may be marginal, due to its geographic mix, as well as competitive pressures.

Valuation - 18-JUL-01

Over the past month, the shares dropped sharply, in a sector sell-off reflecting end of quarter window dressing and investor concerns over slowing economies. In addition, the Gulf of Mexico jackup market is experiencing a temporary weakness in dayrates; with certain production targets met, budget approval is being sought for new projects, and certain large producers remain on the sidelines for the summer. Although domestic natural gas drilling may soften for a short period, we expect domestic oil drilling to pick up the slack. This activity is supplemented by accelerating international deepwater drilling activity. We expect worldwide exploration and production spending to increase over 20% in 2001, exceeding $110 billion. The shares were recently trading at 7X our 2002 EPS estimate, a discount to peer levels, but with rig fleet concentration in the Gulf of Mexico, we are maintaining our accumulate recommendation.

Key Stock Statistics

S&P EPS Est. 2001	1.49	Tang. Bk. Value/Share	7.96
P/E on S&P Est. 2001	10.7	Beta	1.16
S&P EPS Est. 2002	2.41	Shareholders	7,569
Dividend Rate/Share	Nil	Market cap. (B)	$ 2.8
Shs. outstg. (M)	176.6	Inst. holdings	78%
Avg. daily vol. (M)	2.451		

Value of $10,000 invested 5 years ago: $ 10,813

Fiscal Year Ending Dec. 31

	2001	2000	1999	1998	1997	1996
Revenues (Million $)						
1Q	274.8	204.1	228.0	275.1	210.3	123.0
2Q	376.4	231.3	195.7	356.0	233.1	159.9
3Q	—	272.0	168.6	272.2	304.4	177.9
4Q	—	332.4	198.7	258.9	319.3	219.9
Yr.	—	1,040	791.0	1,162	1,067	680.7
Earnings Per Share ($)						
1Q	**0.23**	**0.07**	**0.21**	**0.39**	**0.45**	**0.09**
2Q	**0.46**	**0.16**	**0.15**	**0.42**	**0.48**	**0.14**
3Q	**E0.37**	**0.18**	**0.08**	**0.27**	**0.53**	**0.18**
4Q	**E0.43**	**0.23**	**0.06**	**0.20**	**0.34**	0.63
Yr.	**E1.49**	**0.64**	**0.51**	**1.27**	**1.79**	**1.03**

Next earnings report expected: mid October

Dividend Data

No dividends have been paid since the 1989 reorganization. Dividends on the old common stock were omitted in 1985.

A Division of The McGraw-Hill Companies

Global Marine Inc.

Business Summary - 18-JUL-01

As a major international offshore oil and gas drilling contractor, Global Marine operates a premium fleet of drilling rigs, and is the largest provider of turnkey drilling management services in the Gulf of Mexico. In 2000, 59% of GLM's revenues were attributable to operations in the U.S., 18% in West Africa, and 12% in the North Sea.

As a holding company, GLM conducts its offshore contract drilling operations (56% of 2000 revenues; 84% of 2000 operating income) via subsidiaries: domestic operations by Global Marine Drilling Co.; and substantially all international operations by Global Marine International Drilling Corp.

As of January 15, 2001, the company had an active fleet of 33 mobile offshore rigs representing a balance between shallow-water and deepwater rigs, including 23 cantilevered jackups, five third-generation semisubmersibles, one fourth-generation semisubmersible, one moored drillship (Glomar Robert F. Bauer), one ultra-deepwater dynamically positioned drillship (Glomar Explorer), and two ultra-deepwater drillships (the Glomar C. R. Lugis, launched in the second quarter of 2000; and the Glomar Jack Ryan, launched in the third quarter of 2000). In addition, GLM had one inactive concrete island drilling system (CDIS), designed for Arctic operation. The average age of the fleet was 16.7 years.

A decline in oil prices in 1998 led major oil companies to curb their exploration spending in 1999, resulting in a decline in rig utilization and dayrates. Total fleet utilization averaged 84% in 2000, versus 76% in 1999. Utilization was 100% in the Gulf of Mexico, 77% in West Africa, and 62% in the North Sea, versus 1999 levels of 95% in the Gulf of Mexico, 48% in West Africa, and 81% in the North Sea. GLM's average dayrate was $59,000 in 2000, versus $59,600 in 1999.

Through its Applied Drilling Technology Inc. (ADTI, primarily in the Gulf of Mexico) unit and Global Marine Integrated Services - Europe (GMIS-E, other than the U.S. Gulf of Mexico), the company provides drilling management services (42%; 10%) on a completed project (turnkey) basis. For a guaranteed price, GLM assumes responsibility for the design and execution of specific offshore drilling programs and to deliver a logged or loggable hole to an agreed depth. Compensation is contingent on satisfactory completion of the drilling program. In 2000, the company completed 122 turnkey wells, up from 76 in 1999.

GLM conducts oil and gas exploration, development and production activities (2%; 6%) through its subsidiary, Challenger Minerals Inc. (CMI). These activities include participation in the development and operation of properties for oil and gas production.

At December 31, 2000, contract drilling backlog was $772 million, versus $1 billion a year earlier; drilling management backlog totaled $59 million, versus $53 million.

Per Share Data ($) (Year Ended Dec. 31)	2000	1999	1998	1997	1996	1995	1994	1993	1992	1991
Tangible Bk. Val.	7.22	6.51	6.00	4.68	2.71	1.62	1.29	1.26	1.10	0.39
Cash Flow	1.23	1.01	1.86	2.10	1.30	0.50	0.26	0.06	0.64	0.44
Earnings	0.64	0.51	1.27	1.79	1.06	0.31	0.03	-0.17	0.24	0.01
Dividends	Nil	Nil	Nil	Nil	Nil	Nil	Nil	Nil	Nil	Nil
Payout Ratio	Nil	Nil	Nil	Nil	Nil	Nil	Nil	Nil	Nil	Nil
Prices - High	34.25	19.87	26.75	36.81	21.75	8.87	5.00	5.62	3.00	5.25
- Low	14.87	7.50	8.25	17.25	7.62	3.37	3.50	2.12	1.12	1.62
P/E Ratio - High	54	39	21	21	21	29	NM	NM	13	NM
- Low	23	15	6	10	7	11	NM	NM	5	NM
Income Statement Analysis (Million $)										
Revs.	1,040	791	1,162	1,067	681	468	359	269	260	315
Oper. Inc.	301	232	414	360	182	91.3	63.5	39.1	52.0	96.0
Depr.	107	88.8	104	55.1	40.9	31.0	37.4	35.9	47.1	46.6
Int. Exp.	37.2	30.7	29.7	18.8	30.9	30.2	30.0	32.0	44.0	50.0
Pretax Inc.	155	115	284	294	120	55.1	5.0	-26.0	31.0	4.0
Eff. Tax Rate	27%	22%	21%	NM	NM	5.80%	11%	NM	10%	71%
Net Inc.	114	89.5	223	315	180	51.9	5.0	-27.0	28.0	1.0
Balance Sheet & Other Fin. Data (Million $)										
Cash	144	83.3	56.9	80.6	120	86.6	58.0	66.0	35.0	58.0
Curr. Assets	405	213	269	328	247	168	150	144	91.0	128
Total Assets	2,397	2,265	1,972	1,422	808	563	512	493	480	524
Curr. Liab.	183	150	152	184	87.6	52.1	56.0	37.0	61.0	40.0
LT Debt	919	955	768	417	242	225	225	225	225	386
Common Eqty.	1,271	1,135	1,040	806	459	269	212	205	155	45.0
Total Cap.	2,190	2,090	1,809	1,223	701	494	437	430	380	434
Cap. Exp.	178	448	638	580	118	73.5	75.9	64.0	21.0	23.0
Cash Flow	221	178	327	370	221	82.9	42.0	9.0	75.0	48.0
Curr. Ratio	2.2	1.4	1.8	1.8	2.8	3.2	2.7	3.9	1.5	3.2
% LT Debt of Cap.	42.0	45.7	42.5	51.7	34.5	45.5	51.5	52.3	59.3	89.0
% Net Inc.of Revs.	11.0	11.3	19.2	29.5	26.4	11.1	1.3	NM	10.6	0.3
% Ret. on Assets	4.9	4.2	13.2	28.3	26.3	9.7	1.0	NM	4.9	0.2
% Ret. on Equity	9.5	8.2	24.2	49.8	49.5	21.6	2.3	NM	26.2	4.4

Data as orig reptd.; bef. results of disc opers/spec. items. Per share data adj. for stk. divs. Bold denotes diluted EPS (FASB 128)-prior periods restated. E-Estimated. NA-Not Available. NM-Not Meaningful. NR-Not Ranked.

Office—777 North Eldridge Parkway, Houston, TX 77079-4493. **Tel**—(281) 596-5100. **Website**—http://www.glm.com **Chrmn, Pres & CEO**—R. E. Rose. **SVP, CFO & Treas**—W. M. Ralls. **Secy & Assist. GC**—A. A. Krezel. **VP & Investor Contact**—Michael R. Dawson (281-596-5813). **Dirs**—E. A. Blair, T. W. Cason, J. M. Galvin, C. R. Luigs, E. R. Muller, P. J. Powers, R. E. Rose, B. G. Streetman, C. W. Suggs, J. Whitmire. **Transfer Agent & Registrar**—Harris Trust & Savings Bank, Chicago. **Incorporated**—in Delaware in 1964. **Empl**— 2,700. **S&P Analyst:** T. J. Vital

STANDARD
&POOR'S
STOCK REPORTS

Halliburton Co.

NYSE Symbol **HAL**

In S&P 500

18-AUG-01

Industry:
Oil & Gas (Drilling & Equipment)

Summary: Halliburton provides services, equipment, maintenance, and engineering and construction to energy, industrial and governmental customers.

S&P Opinion: Accumulate (★★★★)

Recent Price • 31.92
52 Wk Range • 55.18-29.24
Yield • 1.6%
12-Mo. P/E • 21.3

Quantitative Evaluations

Outlook
(1 Lowest—5 Highest)
• 3+

Fair Value
• 31.90

Risk
• Average

Earn./Div. Rank
• B

Technical Eval.
• Bearish since 8/01

Rel. Strength Rank
(1 Lowest—99 Highest)
• 25

Insider Activity
• Neutral

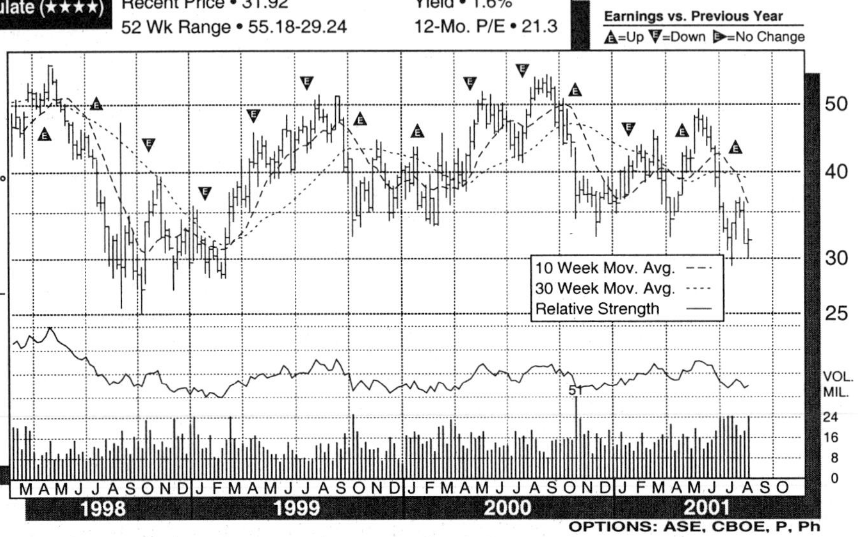

OPTIONS: ASE, CBOE, P, Ph

Overview - 09-AUG-01

Operating income should rise over 30% in 2002. Stable high oil and gas prices should drive increased exploration & production spending, boosting results for Energy Services and Landmark Graphics. Operating income surged 116% in the second quarter on greater than expected earnings from Energy Services. Although there is some uncertainty regarding the impact of increased U.S. natural gas storage levels on gas prices, going forward, we expect earnings in the Energy Services Group to remain strong for the remainder of the year, growing over 30% in 2002 on better pricing and increased international activity. Engineering & Construction should benefit from increased bid and proposal activity, as delayed projects are now being revitalized and new projects identified; however, we do not expect to see a significant impact on margins until 2002 or 2003.

Valuation - 09-AUG-01

In July 2001, we upgraded the shares to accumulate from hold on improved market opportunities. HAL has decided not to relieve Harbison-Walker Refractories Co. from its obligation to indemnify and defend Dresser from asbestos claims that Harbison assumed when spun off from Dresser in 1992. HAL believes its liability in this matter should be covered by a second quarter after-tax accrual under discontinued operations of $60 million, which was offset by a $300 million after-tax gain on the sale of Dresser Equipment. HAL's business units should show continued improvement. Energy Services Group should see a pick-up in international activity, and a restructured E&C unit should begin to see new contract awards in the second half of 2001. Although the shares trade above peers at 16X our 2002 EPS estimate, with the stock down 36% from 52-week highs and market opportunities improving, we would accumulate HAL.

Key Stock Statistics

S&P EPS Est. 2001	1.50	Tang. Bk. Value/Share	9.00
P/E on S&P Est. 2001	21.3	Beta	1.16
S&P EPS Est. 2002	2.17	Shareholders	25,800
Dividend Rate/Share	0.50	Market cap. (B)	$ 13.7
Shs. outstg. (M)	429.8	Inst. holdings	78%
Avg. daily vol. (M)	4.047		

Value of $10,000 invested 5 years ago: $ 12,740

Fiscal Year Ending Dec. 31

	2001	2000	1999	1998	1997	1996
Revenues (Million $)						
1Q	3,144	2,859	3,924	4,255	1,898	1,705
2Q	3,339	2,868	3,670	4,585	2,231	1,831
3Q	—	3,024	3,533	4,224	2,305	1,860
4Q	—	3,193	3,771	4,289	2,385	1,990
Yr.	—	11,944	14,898	17,353	8,819	7,385
Earnings Per Share ($)						
1Q	**0.20**	**0.06**	**0.18**	**0.46**	**0.32**	0.18
2Q	**0.33**	**0.12**	**0.19**	**0.55**	**0.40**	0.28
3Q	**E0.42**	**0.29**	**0.13**	**-1.20**	**0.47**	0.30
4Q	**E0.55**	**-0.05**	**0.17**	**0.15**	**0.56**	0.42
Yr.	**E1.50**	**0.42**	**0.67**	**-0.03**	**1.75**	**1.19**

Next earnings report expected: late October

Dividend Data (Dividends have been paid since 1947.)

Amount ($)	Date Decl.	Ex-Div. Date	Stock of Record	Payment Date
0.125	Oct. 26	Nov. 28	Nov. 30	Dec. 21 '00
0.125	Feb. 15	Feb. 27	Mar. 01	Mar. 22 '01
0.125	May. 15	Jun. 04	Jun. 06	Jun. 27 '01
0.125	Jul. 19	Sep. 04	Sep. 06	Sep. 27 '01

A Division of The McGraw-Hill Companies

Halliburton Company

Business Summary - 09-AUG-01

In September 1998, Halliburton and Dresser Industries merged to form the world's largest oilfield services company. About 66% of 2000 revenues were derived from international activities.

The Energy Services Group (66% of 2000 revenues; 97% of 2000 operating income) provides a wide range of products and services for the exploration, development and production of oil and gas. Halliburton Energy Services (HES) offers products and services used for drilling, completing, evaluating and producing oil and natural gas wells. Brown & Root Energy Services (BRES) supplies engineering and construction services to the upstream oil and gas industry. Landmark Graphics supplies information systems and software that help companies find and produce oil and gas. In September 2000, HES entered into an agreement with 4th Wave Imaging Corp. to offer 3D time-lapse vertical seismic profile services to oil and gas producing companies. In March 2001, HAL acquired PGS Data Management, a division of Petroleum Geo-Services ASA, for about $175 million. In April 2001, a joint venture between HAL and Shaw Industries, called Bredero-Shaw, acquired the Norwegian entity, Thermotite A/S; and HAL agreed to purchase Magic Earth, a 3-D visualization and interpretation technology company.

Engineering and Construction (E&C; 34%; 3%) consists of Kellogg Brown & Root, and Brown & Root Services. The group provides a wide range of services to energy and industrial customers and government entities worldwide. Kellogg Brown & Root is a global provider of technology-based engineering and construction services using proprietary processes including project development, technology licensing and development, consulting, project management, engineering, procurement, construction, operations and maintenance services. Brown & Root Services (BRS) is a global provider to the private (mainly non-energy) and government sectors offering planning, design, construction, operations, maintenance, asset management and decommissioning of infrastructure, facilities and installations. In August 2000, BRS was awarded a $238 million contract by the Defense Threat Reduction Agency to provide integrated project management support to eliminate Russian Inter-Continental Ballistic Missiles and their silos. In October 2000, HAL announced it would restructure its E&C unit, combining all of its units under Kellogg Brown & Root.

Historically, HAL's Dresser Equipment Group designed, manufactured and marketed highly engineered products and systems. The compression and pumping product line included two joint ventures: Dresser-Rand, and Ingersoll-Dresser Pump. Ingersoll-Dresser Pump was sold on December 30, 1999, for $515 million; Dresser-Rand was sold on February 2, 2000, for $579 million. In April 2001, HAL sold its remaining Dresser Equipment Group businesses to a group led by First Reserve and Odyssey Investment Partners for about $1.55 billion.

Per Share Data ($)										
(Year Ended Dec. 31)	**2000**	**1999**	**1998**	**1997**	**1996**	**1995**	**1994**	**1993**	**1992**	**1991**
Tangible Bk. Val.	7.80	7.96	7.48	8.63	7.70	6.76	7.58	7.29	8.30	9.49
Cash Flow	1.55	3.06	1.30	2.94	2.25	2.08	1.93	0.56	0.78	1.26
Earnings	0.42	0.67	-0.03	1.75	1.19	1.02	0.78	-0.71	-0.57	0.13
Dividends	0.50	0.50	0.50	0.50	0.50	0.50	0.50	0.50	0.50	0.50
Payout Ratio	119%	75%	NM	29%	42%	49%	64%	NM	NM	402%
Prices - High	55.18	51.75	57.25	63.25	31.81	25.43	18.62	22.00	18.43	27.62
- Low	32.25	28.12	25.00	29.68	22.37	16.43	13.93	12.87	10.87	12.75
P/E Ratio - High	NM	77	NM	36	27	25	24	NM	NM	NM
- Low	NM	42	NM	17	19	16	18	NM	NM	NM
Income Statement Analysis (Million $)										
Revs.	11,856	14,765	17,159	8,819	7,385	5,699	5,648	6,275	6,525	6,976
Oper. Inc.	789	1,069	1,769	1,117	772	627	446	448	412	296
Depr.	503	599	587	310	269	244	262	288	289	244
Int. Exp.	146	144	137	43.0	24.0	46.0	47.0	50.0	54.0	53.0
Pretax Inc.	335	1,012	278	766	404	367	291	-189	-131	93.0
Eff. Tax Rate	39%	21%	NM	39%	26%	36%	39%	NM	NM	69%
Net Inc.	188	755	-15.0	454	300	234	178	-161	-124	27.0
Balance Sheet & Other Fin. Data (Million $)										
Cash	231	466	203	221	214	175	507	133	256	331
Curr. Assets	5,568	6,022	6,083	2,972	2,398	2,050	NA	NA	NA	NA
Total Assets	10,103	10,728	11,112	5,603	4,437	3,647	5,268	5,403	4,736	5,017
Curr. Liab.	3,826	3,693	4,004	1,773	1,505	1,156	950	1,067	1,017	999
LT Debt	1,049	1,056	1,370	539	200	200	623	598	603	651
Common Eqty.	5,618	4,287	4,061	2,585	2,159	1,750	1,942	1,888	1,907	2,165
Total Cap.	6,705	5,496	5,601	3,144	2,359	1,950	2,570	2,489	2,522	2,875
Cap. Exp.	578	593	914	577	396	289	235	247	316	426
Cash Flow	691	1,354	572	764	568	478	439	127	166	270
Curr. Ratio	1.5	1.6	1.5	1.7	1.6	1.8	NA	NA	NA	NA
% LT Debt of Cap.	15.6	19.2	24.5	17.1	8.5	10.3	24.2	24.0	23.9	22.6
% Net Inc.of Revs.	1.6	5.1	NM	5.1	4.1	4.1	3.1	NM	NM	0.4
% Ret. on Assets	1.9	6.9	NM	9.0	7.3	6.1	3.3	NM	NM	0.6
% Ret. on Equity	3.7	18.1	NM	19.1	14.7	12.7	9.3	NM	NM	1.2

Data as orig. reptd.; bef. results of disc. opers. and/or spec. items. Per share data adj. for stk. divs. as of ex-div. date. Bold denotes diluted EPS (FASB 128). E-Estimated. NA-Not Available. NM-Not Meaningful. NR-Not Ranked.

Office—3600 Lincoln Plaza, 500 N. Akard Street, Dallas, TX 75201-3391. **Tel**—(214) 978-2600. **Website**—www.halliburton.com **Chrmn, Pres & CEO**—D. J. Lesar. **EVP & CFO**—D. L. Foshee. **VP & Investor Contact**—Guy T. Marcus (214-978-2691). **Dirs**—Lord Clitheroe, R. L. Crandall, K. T. Derr, C. J. DiBona, L. S. Eagleburger, W. R. Howell, R. L. Hunt, D. J. Lesar, A. B. Lewis, J. L. Martin, J. A. Precourt, D. L. Reed, C. J. Silas. **Transfer Agent & Registrar**—Mellon Investor Services, Ridgefield Park, NJ. **Incorporated**—in Delaware in 1924. **Empl**— 93,000. **S&P Analyst:** T. J. Vital

STANDARD
&POOR'S
STOCK REPORTS

Helmerich & Payne

NYSE Symbol **HP**

In S&P MidCap 400

18-AUG-01

Industry: Oil & Gas (Drilling & Equipment)

Summary: This leading contract driller in the U.S. and in Latin America is also engaged in the production of oil and natural gas.

S&P Opinion: Accumulate (★★★★) | Recent Price • 31.65 | 52 Wk Range • 58.73-28.10 | Yield • 0.9% | 12-Mo. P/E • 11.5

Quantitative Evaluations

Outlook (1 Lowest—5 Highest)
• **5**

Fair Value
• **39.20**

Risk
• **Average**

Earn./Div. Rank
• **B+**

Technical Eval.
• **Bearish** since 8/01

Rel. Strength Rank (1 Lowest—99 Highest)
• **34**

Insider Activity
• **NA**

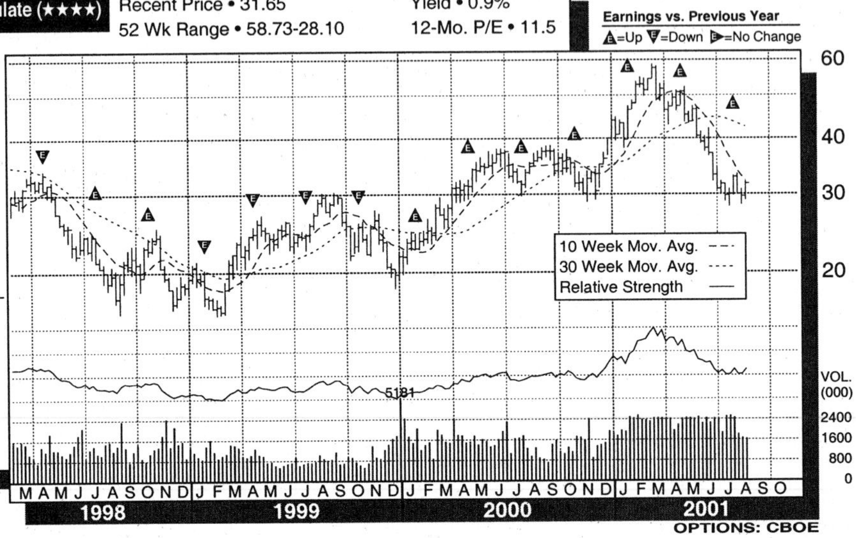

OPTIONS: CBOE

Overview - 23-JUL-01

After an anticipated climb of more than 100% in FY 01 (Sept.), operating income should be about flat in FY 02, as drilling activity moderates at high levels. Although natural gas prices have recently softened, on a temporary weakening in demand, they remain at historically high levels, and supply side challenges remain unchanged; this should provide opportunities for HP. In the FY 01 third quarter, HP's domestic land utilization rates rose to 98%, from 95% in the second quarter; and its U.S. offshore utilization rate remained at 100%. The company's international activities are concentrated in South America. Although markets in Venezuela are gaining strength, Bolivia and Argentina are neutral to slightly down, and Colombia is weakening. Latin American land drilling is expected to lag other foreign markets in FY 01, but should strengthen in FY 02. In the third quarter, international offshore utilization rates rose to 60%, from 49%.

Valuation - 23-JUL-01

Over the past month, the shares dropped sharply, in a sector sell-off reflecting end of quarter window dressing and investor concerns over slowing economies. Earlier in 2001, the company announced its FlexRig newbuild program; four rigs have been completed and are working, and three more were scheduled for completion during the fourth quarter. Another 20 FlexRigs will go into service by the end of FY 02, and 10 should be built in the first half of FY 03. With the domestic supply of land rigs tight, and HP's ability to obtain two- to three-year firm contracts for its newbuilds, we view the FlexRig program positively. In July, the company announced commitments to build two new platform rigs for work in the Gulf of Mexico, for Shell and BP. With the shares trading at 10X our FY 02 EPS estimate, in line with peer levels, we recommend accumulating the stock.

Key Stock Statistics

S&P EPS Est. 2001	2.91	Tang. Bk. Value/Share	19.12
P/E on S&P Est. 2001	10.9	Beta	0.89
S&P EPS Est. 2002	2.96	Shareholders	1,170
Dividend Rate/Share	0.30	Market cap. (B)	$ 1.6
Shs. outstg. (M)	50.6	Inst. holdings	80%
Avg. daily vol. (M)	0.395		

Value of $10,000 invested 5 years ago: $ 16,890

Fiscal Year Ending Sep. 30

	2001	2000	1999	1998	1997	1996
Revenues (Million $)						
1Q	192.6	139.3	143.9	151.8	118.3	88.43
2Q	221.6	151.8	155.4	142.4	132.5	95.21
3Q	217.2	152.0	131.8	177.1	129.8	101.4
4Q	—	177.7	133.3	165.3	137.3	108.3
Yr.	—	631.1	564.3	636.6	517.9	387.5
Earnings Per Share ($)						
1Q	**0.67**	**0.28**	**0.26**	**0.58**	0.41	0.19
2Q	**0.82**	**0.39**	**0.15**	**0.38**	0.45	0.20
3Q	**0.79**	**0.37**	**0.24**	**0.67**	0.47	0.26
4Q	**E0.66**	**0.48**	**0.21**	**0.38**	0.36	0.28
Yr.	**E2.91**	**1.64**	**0.86**	**2.00**	**1.67**	**0.91**

Next earnings report expected: mid November

Dividend Data (Dividends have been paid since 1959.)

Amount ($)	Date Decl.	Ex-Div. Date	Stock of Record	Payment Date
0.075	Sep. 06	Nov. 13	Nov. 15	Dec. 01 '00
0.075	Dec. 06	Feb. 13	Feb. 15	Mar. 01 '01
0.075	Mar. 07	May. 11	May. 15	Jun. 01 '01
0.075	Jun. 06	Aug. 13	Aug. 15	Sep. 04 '01

A Division of The McGraw-Hill Companies

Helmerich & Payne, Inc.

Business Summary - 23-JUL-01

Helmerich & Payne, a major land and offshore platform drilling contractor, also engages in exploration, production and sale of oil and natural gas, and in certain commercial real estate operations.

The company's contract drilling segment (56% of FY 00 (Sep.) revenues; 37% of FY 00 operating income) operates principally in North and South America, specializing in deep drilling in major gas producing basins of the U.S., and in drilling for oil and gas in remote international areas. At the end of FY 00, HP had 38 land rigs and 10 platform rigs operating in the U.S. (61% of drilling segment revenues), and had management contracts for four customer-owned rigs. Domestic contract drilling is conducted primarily in Oklahoma, Texas and Louisiana, and on offshore platforms in the Gulf of Mexico and offshore California. In FY 00, HP's average domestic rig utilization was 87%, up from 75% in FY 99. In July 2001, HP received commitments for two new self-moving platform rigs, from Shell Exploration & Production and BP.

The international drilling segment (39% of segment revenues) includes 40 land rigs, which operated at 47% utilization in FY 00, down from 53% in FY 99. Lower utilization reflected reduced demand due to a drop in worldwide oil prices. At the end of FY 00, HP owned and operated rigs in Venezuela (18 land drilling rigs), Colombia (7), Ecuador (6), Bolivia (6) and Argentina (3). In addition, it owns a 50% interest in an offshore platform rig currently stacked in Australia.

The company engages in the origination of prospects; the identification, acquisition, exploration and development of prospective and proved oil and gas properties; the production and sale of crude oil, condensate and natural gas; and the marketing of natural gas. HP considers itself a medium sized independent producer (38% of FY 00 revenues, 59% of operating income). Most exploration and drilling efforts are concentrated on Oklahoma, Kansas, Texas and Louisiana, but HP also explores in New Mexico, Alabama, Michigan, Mississippi, and the Rocky Mountains region. Proved reserves at the end of FY 00 were 6.3 billion bbl. of oil, versus 4.8 billion bbl. a year earlier, and 262 Bcf of natural gas (240 Bcf). In November 2000, HP said it was still interested in spinning off its exploration and production division, and was in engaged in discussions with several interested oil and gas companies.

Real estate operations (1%; 4%) are entirely in Tulsa, OK. The major holding is Utica Square Shopping Center, consisting of 15 buildings on about 30 acres; 14 buildings provide about 405,709 sq. ft. of net leasable retail sales and storage space (98% leased at the end of FY 00), and leasable general office space (99%).

HP holds a portfolio heavily weighted in energy stocks, with a market value of $383 million at the close of FY 00. The three largest positions, based on market value, were Atwood Oceanics, Inc. (43% of the shares outstanding); Schlumberger, Ltd. (21 %); and Occidental Petroleum Corp. (14%).

Per Share Data ($) (Year Ended Sep. 30)	2000	1999	1998	1997	1996	1995	1994	1993	1992	1991
Tangible Bk. Val.	19.12	17.09	16.06	15.60	12.98	11.36	10.61	10.33	10.04	10.03
Cash Flow	3.86	3.05	3.75	3.13	2.13	1.77	1.67	1.58	1.25	1.33
Earnings	1.64	0.86	2.00	1.69	0.92	0.20	0.43	0.51	0.23	0.44
Dividends	0.29	0.28	0.28	0.26	0.25	0.25	0.24	0.24	0.23	0.23
Payout Ratio	18%	33%	14%	15%	27%	125%	56%	48%	103%	53%
Prices - High	44.81	30.37	34.12	45.56	27.37	15.62	15.68	18.75	13.93	14.62
- Low	19.75	16.00	16.12	20.75	13.43	12.12	12.37	11.12	9.56	9.00
P/E Ratio - High	27	35	17	27	30	78	36	37	62	33
- Low	12	19	8	12	15	61	29	22	43	20
Income Statement Analysis (Million $)										
Revs.	599	557	592	506	387	315	323	306	230	190
Oper. Inc.	219	185	208	200	132	90.5	84.8	86.8	65.0	55.0
Depr.	111	109	88.3	71.7	59.4	77.1	60.4	52.6	49.6	43.1
Int. Exp.	3.1	6.5	0.9	4.2	0.7	0.4	0.4	0.9	0.6	0.4
Pretax Inc.	140	68.5	163	132	71.2	14.8	31.2	41.9	20.0	34.0
Eff. Tax Rate	41%	38%	35%	34%	36%	34%	33%	41%	44%	37%
Net Inc.	82.3	42.8	101	84.2	45.4	9.8	21.0	24.6	10.8	21.2
Balance Sheet & Other Fin. Data (Million $)										
Cash	108	21.8	24.5	28.0	17.9	28.7	38.0	71.0	51.0	70.0
Curr. Assets	265	161	184	158	114	115	123	150	133	142
Total Assets	1,259	1,110	1,090	1,034	822	710	625	611	586	575
Curr. Liab.	78.9	71.9	125	95.2	62.6	69.6	46.7	46.4	35.9	34.0
LT Debt	50.0	50.0	50.0	Nil	Nil	Nil	Nil	3.6	8.0	6.0
Common Eqty.	956	848	793	781	646	562	524	509	493	491
Total Cap.	1,162	1,015	946	922	744	628	569	557	541	539
Cap. Exp.	132	123	266	162	110	111	103	50.6	81.0	99
Cash Flow	193	152	190	156	105	86.9	81.4	77.1	60.5	64.0
Curr. Ratio	3.4	2.2	1.5	1.7	1.8	1.7	2.6	3.2	3.7	4.2
% LT Debt of Cap.	4.3	4.9	5.2	Nil	Nil	Nil	Nil	0.6	1.5	1.1
% Net Inc.of Revs.	13.7	7.7	17.1	16.6	11.7	3.1	6.5	8.0	4.7	11.2
% Ret. on Assets	6.9	3.9	9.5	9.1	5.9	1.5	3.4	4.1	1.9	3.7
% Ret. on Equity	9.1	5.2	12.9	11.8	7.5	1.8	4.1	4.9	2.2	4.4

Data as orig reptd.; bef. results of disc opers/spec. items. Per share data adj. for stk. divs. Bold denotes diluted EPS (FASB 128)-prior periods restated. E-Estimated. NA-Not Available. NM-Not Meaningful. NR-Not Ranked.

Office—Utica at 21st St., Tulsa, OK 74114. **Tel**—(918) 742-5531. **Website**—http://www.hpinc.com **Chrmn**—W. H. Helmerich III. **Pres & CEO**—H. Helmerich. **VP & Secy**—S. R. Mackey. **VP-Fin & Investor Contact**—Doug E. Fears (918-748-5208). **Dirs**—W. L. Armstrong, G. A. Cox, G. S. Dotson, H. Helmerich, W. H. Helmerich III, L. F. Rooney III, E. B. Rust Jr., G. A. Schaefer, J. D. Zeglis. **Transfer Agent & Registrar**—Liberty National Bank & Trust Co. of Oklahoma City. **Incorporated**—in Delaware in 1940. **Empl**— 2,312. **S&P Analyst:** T. J. Vital

STANDARD &POOR'S STOCK REPORTS

Mitchell Energy

NYSE Symbol **MND**

24-AUG-01

Industry: Natural Gas

Summary: This large independent producer of natural gas and natural gas liquids (NGLs) is being acquired by Devon Energy.

S&P Opinion: Accumulate (★★★★)

Recent Price • 60.55
52 Wk Range • 64-34.62
Yield • 0.9%
12-Mo. P/E • 8.3

Quantitative Evaluations

Outlook (1 Lowest—5 Highest) • 3−

Fair Value • 47

Risk • NA

Earn./Div. Rank • B

Technical Eval. • NA

Rel. Strength Rank (1 Lowest—99 Highest) • 97

Insider Activity • NA

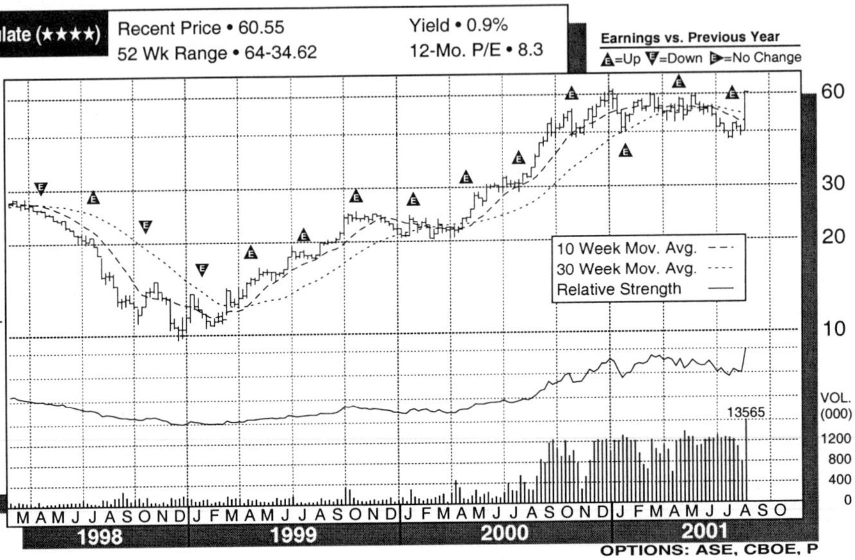

OPTIONS: ASE, CBOE, P

Overview - 24-AUG-01

Company-wide production of natural gas, which accounts for 91% of total volumes, is expected to climb more than 20% this year. With no hedges in place, revenues will be further boosted if, as we believe, natural gas prices remain strong this year. In June, MND announced the addition of 580 Bcf to the company's reserves, a 38% increase. Excluding the midstream assets, MND's market capitalization gives an in-ground reserve value of $5.05 per Mboe, which is below the industry average of $5.20 per Mboe. The company also has under lease another 110,000 acres where probable and possible reserves are estimated at 108 Mboe. Adding these reserves, MDU is trading at $4.00 per Mboe. Our EPS estimate of $6.10 assumes that gas prices will average $4.44 in 2001.

Valuation - 24-AUG-01

Following the August 14 cash and stock acquisition offer from Devon Energy (DVN), we downgraded MND to accumulate from buy, to reflect Devon's Stars ranking. Excluding the midstream assets, valued between $810-$850 million, DVN is paying $5.05 per barrel of oil equivalent for MND's proven reserves as of June 2001, at the low end compared with other recent mergers. The stock was recently trading at 5.2X our estimate of 2001 discretionary cash flow per share, above the peer group's average multiple. Nevertheless, we recently lowered our 2001 EPS estimate to $6.10 a share from $6.65 on lower forecasts for gas and oil prices. DRI-WEFA projects gas prices and oil prices to average $4.44 and $27.64 in 2001, respectively. With commodity price volatility likely to continue (and MND unhedged), the midstream business will continue to provide some earnings stability.

Key Stock Statistics

S&P EPS Est. 2001	6.10	Tang. Bk. Value/Share	16.26
P/E on S&P Est. 2001	9.9	Beta	0.31
S&P EPS Est. 2002	5.64	Shareholders	15,000
Dividend Rate/Share	0.53	Market cap. (B)	$ 2.9
Shs. outstg. (M)	49.9	Inst. holdings	34%
Avg. daily vol. (M)	0.988		

Value of $10,000 invested 5 years ago: $ 38,415

Fiscal Year Ending Dec. 31

	2001	2000	1999	1998	1997	1996
Revenues (Million $)						
1Q	655.1	315.8	162.6	172.4	206.9	237.3
2Q	486.1	402.8	207.6	180.7	175.6	241.1
3Q	—	446.1	265.5	175.3	224.1	245.4
4Q	—	550.8	258.7	172.9	221.0	381.0
Yr.	—	1,672	894.4	701.4	790.5	1,105
Earnings Per Share ($)						
1Q	**2.41**	**0.84**	**0.11**	**0.05**	**0.20**	**0.37**
2Q	**1.53**	**1.11**	**0.54**	**-0.09**	**-0.16**	**0.31**
3Q	—	**1.48**	**0.59**	**-0.08**	**0.35**	**0.20**
4Q	—	**1.88**	**0.71**	**-0.97**	**0.32**	**0.75**
Yr.	—	**5.13**	**1.95**	**-1.11**	**0.71**	**1.64**

Next earnings report expected: late August

Dividend Data (Dividends have been paid since 1976.)

Amount ($)	Date Decl.	Ex-Div. Date	Stock of Record	Payment Date
0.133	Dec. 13	Dec. 26	Dec. 28	Jan. 12 '01
0.133	Feb. 21	Mar. 09	Mar. 13	Apr. 02 '01
0.133	May. 09	Jun. 11	Jun. 13	Jul. 03 '01
0.133	Aug. 08	Sep. 07	Sep. 11	Oct. 02 '01

A Division of The **McGraw-Hill** *Companies*

Mitchell Energy & Development Corp.

Business Summary - 24-AUG-01

Mitchell Energy is the only independent U.S. producer of natural gas and natural gas liquids (NGLs) with a midstream business (natural gas gathering, processing and marketing) approximately equal in size to its upstream (exploration and production) business. The company believes this allows it to realize more total economic value from the raw materials produced from the wellhead.

MND's exploration and production operations are concentrated in North and East Texas, and along the Gulf Coast in Texas and Louisiana. The company's gas services division produces natural gas liquids and operates gas gathering systems.

Average daily production in 2000 (1999) was 305.5 (244.7) MMcf of natural gas, 49.8 (44.0) MBbls of NGLs, and 5.5 (5.9) MBbls of crude oil and condensate. Average price realizations were $4.23 ($2.42) per Mcf of gas, $21.97 ($14.20) per bbl. of NGLs, and $28.70 ($17.17) per bbl. of oil. Proved reserves at December 31, 2000 (1999), were estimated at 1,508 (1,106) Bcfe of natural gas and oil and 175 (179) MMBbls of NGLs.

In gas services, which includes gathering, processing and marketing, MND owns or has interests in six gas processing plants in Texas. The company has fractionating equipment at several of its processing plants, and has a 39% interest in a large fractionating plant. NGLs are fractionated into ethane, propane, butane and pentane. These byproducts are used by chemical companies in the production of plastics, paints, solvents, synthetic rubber, gasoline and a wide variety of other products. Propane is also widely used as a fuel in rural areas for cooking, home heating and crop drying. MND participates in the petrochemical business through its 33% interest in a plant that produces MTBE, an oxygenate used in the production of environmentally cleaner gasoline.

In February 1999, MND completed a downsizing, eliminating 235 positions. The work force reduction, which accounted for 21% of total employment, was the result of an industry downturn. In October, MND retained two investment banking firms to consider strategic alternatives, including the possible sale or merger of the company. In April 2000, MND announced that it would remain independent. The company added that it would increase its focus on upstream operations, combine its two classes of stock, repurchase up to 2.5 million common shares and reduce debt.

In June 2001, MND announced a 580 Bcfe addition to the company's gas and oil reserves. Proved reserves at June 30, 2001, were expected to be almost 2.1 Tcfe, or 38% higher than at the beginning of the year.

In August 2001, Devon Energy announced that it will acquire MND for $3.1 billion plus the assumption of $400 million in debt. Each MND shareholder will receive $31 in cash and 0.585 of a share of Devon stock. The transaction is expected to close in the fourth quarter of 2001.

Per Share Data ($) (Year Ended Dec. 31)	2000	1999	1998	1997	1996	1995	1994	1993	1992	1991
Tangible Bk. Val.	12.46	8.11	6.61	8.30	10.71	10.71	9.09	14.26	13.55	13.59
Cash Flow	8.02	9.40	5.16	6.32	4.00	3.76	3.54	3.50	3.61	3.68
Earnings	5.13	1.96	-1.11	0.71	1.99	0.71	0.87	0.49	0.77	0.95
Dividends	0.75	0.48	0.48	0.48	0.48	0.48	0.53	0.48	0.42	0.40
Payout Ratio	15%	24%	NM	68%	24%	68%	61%	98%	54%	42%
Prices - High	64.00	25.25	29.25	29.75	23.00	19.37	23.25	29.62	19.62	20.75
- Low	20.25	10.50	9.62	18.25	15.50	14.87	14.50	16.00	13.62	14.00
P/E Ratio - High	12	13	NM	42	12	27	27	60	25	22
- Low	4	5	NM	26	8	21	17	33	18	15

Income Statement Analysis (Million $)	2000	1999	1998	1997	1996	1995	1994	1993	1992	1991
Revs.	1,672	934	701	791	1,102	847	846	953	903	874
Oper. Inc.	525	285	175	202	295	244	210	240	246	244
Depr.	145	113	168	106	104	159	141	153	133	128
Int. Exp.	28.8	34.0	35.1	27.4	55.5	64.2	70.0	74.0	75.0	81.0
Pretax Inc.	358	147	-84.6	50.7	160	58.3	70.6	47.5	47.0	68.0
Eff. Tax Rate	28%	34%	NM	25%	35%	36%	35%	47%	23%	35%
Net Inc.	257	97.2	-53.0	37.8	103	37.1	45.8	25.1	36.3	44.3

Balance Sheet & Other Fin. Data (Million $)	2000	1999	1998	1997	1996	1995	1994	1993	1992	1991
Cash	23.5	16.0	20.3	105	79.6	21.3	12.0	21.8	28.1	51.4
Curr. Assets	268	75.4	79.6	268	349	244	184	189	202	210
Total Assets	1,520	1,168	1,146	1,252	1,853	1,843	1,856	2,415	2,272	2,252
Curr. Liab.	304	152	242	199	382	222	170	217	220	198
LT Debt	300	369	362	414	601	832	895	988	948	954
Common Eqty.	620	399	325	413	555	555	475	752	632	637
Total Cap.	1,124	929	817	995	1,403	1,507	1,571	2,080	1,911	1,921
Cap. Exp.	346	172	301	251	214	235	208	291	153	141
Cash Flow	402	210	-114	143	208	196	187	178	169	172
Curr. Ratio	0.9	0.5	0.3	1.4	0.9	1.1	1.1	0.9	0.9	1.1
% LT Debt of Cap.	26.7	39.7	44.3	41.6	42.8	55.2	57.0	47.5	49.6	49.7
% Net Inc.of Revs.	NA	NA	NA	NA	NA	4.4	5.4	2.6	4.0	5.1
% Ret. on Assets	19.2	8.4	NM	2.6	5.6	2.0	2.2	1.0	1.6	2.0
% Ret. on Equity	51.2	26.9	NM	44.2	20.0	7.8	7.5	3.4	5.7	7.1

Data as orig reptd.; bef. results of disc opers/spec. items. Prior to 2000, yrs. ended Jan. 31 of the fol. cal yr. Per share data adj. for stk. divs. Bold denotes diluted EPS (FASB 128)-prior periods restated. E-Estimated. NA-Not Available. NM-Not Meaningful. NR-Not Ranked.

Office—2001 Timberloch Place, The Woodlands, TX 77380. **Tel**—(713) 377-5500. **Website**—http://www.mitchellenergy.com **Chrmn & CEO**—G. P. Mitchell. **Pres & COO**—W. D. Stevens. **SVP & CFO**—P. S. Smith. **SVP & Secy**—T. P. Battle. **Investor Contact**—Dan Bach (713-377-5616). **Dirs**—R. W. Baldwin, B. F. Clark, W. D. Eberle, S. A. Khayatt, B. F. Love, G. P. Mitchell, J. T. Mitchell, M. K. Mitchell, W. D. Stevens. **Transfer Agent & Registrar**—Mellon Investor Services, L.L.C., Ridgefield Park, NJ. **Incorporated**—in Texas in 1946. **Empl**— 875. **S&P Analyst:** John Kartsonas

STANDARD &POOR'S
STOCK REPORTS

Murphy Oil

NYSE Symbol **MUR**
In S&P MidCap 400

20-AUG-01

Industry: Oil & Gas (Exploration & Production)

Summary: This integrated oil company has exploration, production, refining and marketing interests in the U.S. and worldwide.

S&P Opinion: Accumulate (★★★★)

Recent Price • 82.01
52 Wk Range • 87.85-53.37
Yield • 1.8%
12-Mo. P/E • 8.4

Quantitative Evaluations

Outlook (1 Lowest—5 Highest) • **1**

Fair Value • **70.40**

Risk • **Low**

Earn./Div. Rank • **B+**

Technical Eval. • **Neutral** since 7/01

Rel. Strength Rank (1 Lowest—99 Highest) • **85**

Insider Activity • **NA**

OPTIONS: ASE, CBOE, P

Overview - 20-AUG-01

While MUR's BOE production declined 2.5% last year due to field depletions and the timing of new projects, this trend should reverse in 2001, with production expected to rise over 10% to 115,000 BOE/d, and over 15% p.a. through 2005. Contributing to growth are low-cost, long-lived assets in Canada, the acquisition of high-potential natural gas reserves in western Canada and offshore Nova Scotia, recent acquisitions, and exploration success in the Gulf of Mexico and Canada. In June, MUR announced successful drilling results for its Front Runner South discovery, with reserves expected to exceed pre-drill estimates of 40 million to 60 million BOE. MUR has achieved stable earnings flow with its expanding retail marketing arrangement with Wal-Mart (current 339 sites should grow to 375 by year-end), through which it has been able to do a high volume business to support its U.S. refining operations.

Valuation - 20-AUG-01

In June, we upgraded the shares to accumulate, from hold, on recent exploration success in the deepwater Gulf of Mexico and Canada, which could add as much as 40,000 BOE/d to production over the next two years; and widened retail marketing margins that should aid MUR's expanding Wal-Mart retail gasoline operation. Capital spending will increase 28% in 2001, to $714 million, with E&P spending up 38%, to $540 million. R&M spending should rise 9%, to $168 million, reflecting the ongoing Wal-Mart program (100 to 125 stations slated for construction in 2001), and an upgrade of the Meraux refinery. Although MUR trades above peers at 10X our 2002 EPS estimate, with a strong balance sheet and production profile, and volume gains through its Wal-Mart retail gasoline venture, we would accumulate the stock.

Key Stock Statistics

S&P EPS Est. 2001	9.59	Tang. Bk. Value/Share	31.91
P/E on S&P Est. 2001	8.6	Beta	0.55
S&P EPS Est. 2002	8.11	Shareholders	3,185
Dividend Rate/Share	1.50	Market cap. (B)	$ 3.7
Shs. outstg. (M)	45.3	Inst. holdings	68%
Avg. daily vol. (M)	0.283		

Value of $10,000 invested 5 years ago: NA

Fiscal Year Ending Dec. 31

	2001	2000	1999	1998	1997	1996
Revenues (Million $)						
1Q	1,189	1,019	304.3	440.6	508.3	415.4
2Q	1,300	1,092	450.5	448.6	507.7	497.1
3Q	—	1,232	633.6	433.3	556.3	571.0
4Q	—	1,270	652.9	376.2	565.4	571.0
Yr.	—	4,639	2,041	1,699	2,138	2,009
Earnings Per Share ($)						
1Q	2.16	1.09	-0.15	0.35	0.68	0.45
2Q	3.56	1.61	0.35	0.49	0.61	0.55
3Q	E1.95	1.99	1.14	0.20	0.84	0.90
4Q	E1.92	2.06	1.32	-1.36	0.71	0.90
Yr.	E9.59	6.75	2.66	-0.32	2.94	2.80

Next earnings report expected: NA

Dividend Data (Dividends have been paid since 1961.)

Amount ($)	Date Decl.	Ex-Div. Date	Stock of Record	Payment Date
0.375	Oct. 04	Nov. 08	Nov. 10	Dec. 01 '00
0.375	Feb. 07	Feb. 09	Feb. 13	Mar. 01 '01
0.375	Apr. 04	May. 07	May. 09	Jun. 01 '01
0.375	Aug. 01	Aug. 09	Aug. 13	Sep. 01 '01

Murphy Oil Corporation

Business Summary - 20-AUG-01

As an integrated crude oil and natural gas company, Murphy Oil explores for oil and gas worldwide (16% of 2000 revenues; 82% of 2000 operating income), and has refining and marketing operations (84%; 18%) in the U.S. (66% of 2000 revenues) and the U.K. (15%), and crude oil transportation and trading operations in Canada (18%). About 25% of the common stock is owned by the Murphy family.

Exploration and production activities are conducted in the U.S. and Ecuador by Murphy Exploration & Production Co. (Murphy Expro), in western Canada and offshore eastern Canada by Murphy Oil Co. Ltd. (MOCL), and in the U.K. North Sea and the Atlantic Margin by Murphy Petroleum Ltd. In 2000, crude oil and liquids production declined 1%, to 65,259 barrels (bbl.) per day. Natural gas sales decreased 4.6%, to 229.4 million cubic feet (MMcf) per day. During 2000, MUR added over 79 million BOE, or 209% of hydrocarbon production. Proved oil, condensate and natural gas liquid reserves totaled 326.1 million bbl. at the end of 2000, up 7.9% from 1999. Natural gas proved reserves rose 18%, to 697.4 billion cubic feet (Bcf). In November 2000, MUR purchased independent Canadian exploration & production company Beau Canada Exploration Ltd. (adding probable reserves of about 48.2 million BOE, 74% of which is natural gas) for $255 million.

Murphy Oil USA, Inc. (MOUSA), owns and operates two U.S. refineries (a 100,000 bbl. per day facility at Meraux, LA, and a 35,000 bbl. per day refinery at Superior, WI), and a 30% stake in the U.K. Milford Haven refinery (108,000 bbl. per day capacity). Refined products are sold through a network of branded, unbranded and wholesale customers and retail gasoline stations in the southern and midwestern U.S. Branded wholesale customers use the name SPUR. MUR's retail stations are primarily located in parking areas of Wal-Mart stores, and use the brand name Murphy USA. At the end of 2000, MUR marketed through 276 Murphy USA stations and 436 SPUR stations (19 of which are owned or leased by MUR) in a 23-state area. MUR plans to add up to 125 new Murphy USA stations at Wal-Mart sites in the South and Midwest in 2001. Refined products were also distributed in the U.K. through 386 stations, under the brand names MURCO and EP.

MUR also owns a 20% interest in a 120-mile refined products pipeline (165,000 bbl. per day) that transports products from the Meraux refinery to two common carrier pipelines serving the southeastern U.S.; a 22% interest in a 312-mile crude oil pipeline in Montana and Wyoming (120,000 bbl. per day); and a 3.2% interest in LOOP LLC, which provides deepwater unloading accommodations off the Louisiana coast.

In March 2001, the company agreed to sell its Canadian pipeline and trucking operation for $163 million, including inventory.

Per Share Data ($) (Year Ended Dec. 31)	2000	1999	1998	1997	1996	1995	1994	1993	1992	1991
Tangible Bk. Val.	26.89	23.49	21.76	24.06	22.90	24.56	28.31	27.28	26.76	26.71
Cash Flow	11.48	7.20	4.19	7.60	6.86	2.39	7.24	6.13	5.44	4.63
Earnings	6.75	2.66	-0.32	2.94	2.80	-2.64	2.37	1.94	1.40	-0.24
Dividends	1.45	1.40	1.40	1.35	1.30	1.30	1.30	1.25	1.20	1.20
Payout Ratio	21%	53%	NM	46%	46%	NM	55%	64%	86%	NM
Prices - High	69.06	61.62	54.43	62.56	56.50	45.37	49.12	47.87	38.37	40.25
- Low	48.18	32.87	34.50	43.00	40.62	37.50	37.87	33.00	32.38	31.62
P/E Ratio - High	10	23	NM	21	20	NM	21	25	27	NM
- Low	7	12	NM	15	15	NM	16	17	23	NM
Income Statement Analysis (Million $)										
Revs.	4,639	2,037	1,694	2,132	2,008	1,691	1,738	1,637	1,631	1,601
Oper. Inc.	723	400	288	444	388	283	347	290	212	247
Depr.	213	204	203	209	182	226	218	188	182	192
Int. Exp.	16.3	20.3	10.5	0.6	13.1	14.7	12.4	7.6	17.1	31.0
Pretax Inc.	465	179	-8.3	212	216	-133	157	134	69.0	30.0
Eff. Tax Rate	34%	33%	NM	37%	42%	NM	32%	35%	9.50%	124%
Net Inc.	306	120	-14.4	132	126	-118	107	87.0	63.0	-10.0
Balance Sheet & Other Fin. Data (Million $)										
Cash	133	34.1	28.3	24.3	110	62.0	71.0	141	378	242
Curr. Assets	817	593	437	518	610	520	519	543	799	671
Total Assets	3,134	2,446	2,164	2,238	2,244	2,119	2,312	2,169	1,937	2,175
Curr. Liab.	745	488	381	469	554	416	440	413	427	515
LT Debt	525	393	333	206	202	194	172	109	25.0	193
Common Eqty.	1,260	1,057	978	1,079	1,027	1,101	1,271	1,222	1,200	1,201
Total Cap.	2,014	1,604	1,436	1,422	1,356	1,400	1,584	1,449	1,269	1,452
Cap. Exp.	512	387	389	468	418	296	414	570	191	185
Cash Flow	519	324	188	342	308	107	325	275	245	183
Curr. Ratio	1.1	1.2	1.1	1.1	1.1	1.3	1.2	1.3	1.9	1.3
% LT Debt of Cap.	26.1	24.5	23.2	14.5	14.9	7.2	10.9	7.5	2.0	13.3
% Net Inc.of Revs.	6.6	5.9	NM	6.2	6.3	NM	6.1	5.3	3.8	NM
% Ret. on Assets	11.0	5.2	NM	5.9	5.8	NM	4.8	4.2	3.1	NM
% Ret. on Equity	26.4	11.8	NM	12.6	11.8	NM	8.6	7.2	5.2	NM

Data as orig reptd.; bef. results of disc opers/spec. items. Per share data adj. for stk. divs. Bold denotes diluted EPS (FASB 128)-prior periods restated. E-Estimated. NA-Not Available. NM-Not Meaningful. NR-Not Ranked.

Office—200 Peach Street, Post Office Box 7000, El Dorado, AR 71731-7000. **Tel**—(870) 862-6411. **Fax**—(870) 862-9057. **Website**—www.murphyoilcorp.com **Chrmn**—R. M. Murphy. **Pres & CEO**—C. P. Deming. **Treas**—O. F. Vaughan. **Secy**—W. K. Compton. **Contr**—J. W. Eckart. **Investor Contact**—Kevin G. Fitzgerald (870-864-6272). **Dirs**—B. R. R. Butler, G. S. Dembroski, C. P. Deming, H. R. Hart, R. A. Hermes, M. W. Murphy, R. M. Murphy, W. C. Nolan Jr., W. L. Rosoff, D. J. H. Smith, C. G. Theus. **Transfer Agent & Registrar**—Computershare Investor Services, L.L.C., Chicago. **Incorporated**—in Delaware in 1963. **Empl**— 3,109. **S&P Analyst:** T. J. Vital

STANDARD & POOR'S
STOCK REPORTS

Nabors Industries

ASE Symbol **NBR**
In S&P 500

18-AUG-01

Industry: Oil & Gas (Drilling & Equipment)

Summary: This company is the world's largest oil and gas land drilling contractor.

S&P Opinion: Accumulate (★★★★) | Recent Price • 28.25 | 52 Wk Range • 63.12-25.31 | Yield • Nil | 12-Mo. P/E • 16.1

Quantitative Evaluations

Outlook (1 Lowest—5 Highest)
• **5**

Fair Value
• **37.70**

Risk
• **Average**

Earn./Div. Rank
• **B**

Technical Eval.
• **Bearish** since 5/01

Rel. Strength Rank (1 Lowest—99 Highest)
• **13**

Insider Activity
• **Neutral**

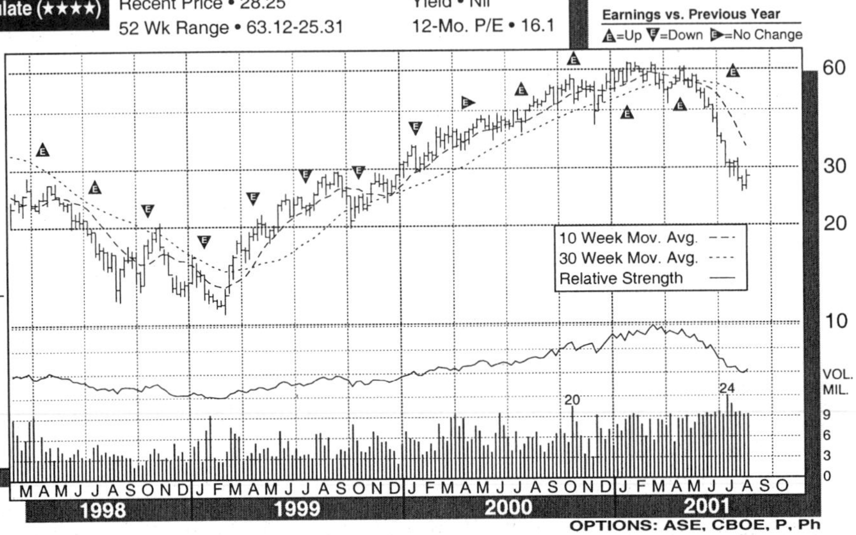

OPTIONS: ASE, CBOE, P, Ph

Overview - 07-AUG-01

Operating income should rise over 200% in 2001. During the second quarter, operating income rose 390%, reflecting strong lower 48 land drilling (with contributions from Alaska and international markets), which boosted the average margin per day 33%, to $5,450. While domestic natural gas prices have fallen recently, they remain at high levels supported by a U.S. natural gas shortfall and limited available land rigs. This U.S. shortfall is being supplemented by imports from Canada, whose capacity to export gas to the U.S. should be enhanced by the Alliance pipeline. Also, sustained high oil prices are leading to a rebound in international activity and in Alaska, which should accelerate. As NBR's fixed assets return to work, we see profitability improving dramatically. However, in light of the soft U.S. economy, we would expect pricing in North America to remain competitive - but we see no weakening in dayrates at this time.

Valuation - 07-AUG-01

Since June, the shares have dropped sharply, in a sector sell-off reflecting investor concerns over slowed economies. While the price of U.S. natural gas has dropped to near $3 per million BTU as the demand for natural gas has eased this summer (due to fuel switching by producers to residual fuel and coal, milder temperatures and slowed economies), the supply of U.S. natural gas continues to be plagued by limited resources and depletion issues which should provide support for higher natural gas prices going forward. Although the pullback in demand is viewed as temporary, NBR has suspended its refurbishment program until the domestic natural gas market strengthens. NBR is trading in line with peers at 9X our 2002 EPS estimate; with the shares down 56% from their 52-week high, and ROCE of about 23%, we would accumulate NBR.

Key Stock Statistics

S&P EPS Est. 2001	2.35	Tang. Bk. Value/Share	11.01
P/E on S&P Est. 2001	12.0	Beta	1.10
S&P EPS Est. 2002	2.95	Shareholders	2,297
Dividend Rate/Share	Nil	Market cap. (B)	$ 4.1
Shs. outstg. (M)	146.9	Inst. holdings	94%
Avg. daily vol. (M)	2.614		

Value of $10,000 invested 5 years ago: $ 17,560

Fiscal Year Ending Dec. 31

	2001	2000	1999	1998	1997	1996
Revenues (Million $)						
1Q	546.6	289.7	153.0	286.8	217.1	164.3
2Q	613.5	301.5	129.9	248.9	238.7	163.3
3Q	—	369.1	142.4	224.2	267.9	181.3
4Q	—	412.2	216.9	208.2	305.6	210.8
Yr.	—	1,409	642.3	968.2	1,029	719.7
Earnings Per Share ($)						
1Q	**0.51**	**0.12**	**0.12**	**0.36**	0.20	0.17
2Q	**0.63**	**0.16**	**0.03**	**0.33**	0.21	0.18
3Q	**E0.59**	**0.25**	**0.04**	**0.27**	0.30	0.20
4Q	**E0.62**	**0.35**	**0.06**	**0.20**	0.40	0.21
Yr.	**E2.35**	**0.89**	**0.23**	**1.16**	1.12	0.76

Next earnings report expected: late October

Dividend Data

Class A dividends were paid from 1973 until omission in July 1982.

Nabors Industries, Inc.

Business Summary - 07-AUG-01

As the world's largest land drilling contractor, with more than 500 actively marketed land rigs at the end of 2000, Nabors Industries is also one of the largest land well-servicing and workover contractors in the U.S., with about 740 land workover and well-servicing rigs. About 380 of the company's rigs (including 160 land rigs) are located in the U.S. lower 48 states. NBR has 35 rigs in Canada, and 21 Arctic drilling, workover and well-servicing rigs in Alaska. About 70 land drilling rigs, 40 workover/well-servicing rigs, two pulling units, one platform and two jackup drilling rigs are marketed internationally.

NBR operates in two segments: contract drilling (88% of 2000 revenues; 83% of 2000 operating income), and manufacturing and logistics (12%; 17%). Contract drilling provides drilling, workover, well-servicing and related services on land and offshore in the U.S. Lower 48 states, Canada, Alaska, and in international markets. Utilization rates for NBR's rigs rose to 46% in 2000, from 31% in 1999. The increase reflected improved demand for drilling services in response to higher crude oil and natural gas prices since the beginning of 1999.

In addition to its land drilling and workover rigs, NBR markets offshore drilling rigs, including 43 platform rigs, 13 jackup rigs, and three barge rigs in the Gulf of Mexico and internationally. To supplement its primary business, the company offers a number of ancillary wellsite services, such as oilfield management, engineering, transportation, construction, maintenance and well logging. The company also has a fleet of 30 marine transportation and support vessels in the Gulf of Mexico, providing transportation for supplies and crews for offshore rigs. A land transportation and hauling fleet consists of 240 rig and oilfield equipment hauling tractor-trailers, more than 300 fluid hauling trucks, about 950 fluid storage tanks, 12 salt water disposal wells and other equipment used in domestic drilling and well-servicing.

Manufacturing and logistics manufactures, leases and sells top drives, drilling instrumentation systems and rig reporting software domestically and internationally; and provides construction, logistics services and marine transportation and support services in Alaska and the U.S. lower 48 states.

NBR has grown from a land drilling business centered in Canada and Alaska to an international business with operations on land and offshore in many of the major markets in the world. In 1999, NBR acquired Bayard Drilling Technologies (adding 87 drilling rigs); and Pool Energy Services (790 land well servicing/workover rigs, 34 land rigs, and 25 offshore rigs). In 2000, NBR acquired one Arctic land rig and one ball mill unit from Parker Drilling; and seven offshore supply vessels from various sources. In June 2001, the company purchased two jackups, to be upgraded and deployed on long-term contracts in Saudi Arabia.

Per Share Data ($) (Year Ended Dec. 31)	2000	1999	1998	1997	1996	1995	1994	1993	1992	1991
Tangible Bk. Val.	11.01	9.51	8.61	7.23	5.26	4.38	3.91	3.84	3.15	2.52
Cash Flow	1.89	1.06	1.87	1.60	1.25	0.93	0.28	0.77	0.74	0.58
Earnings	0.89	0.23	1.16	1.12	0.76	0.58	0.01	0.50	0.52	0.44
Dividends	Nil	Nil	Nil	Nil	Nil	Nil	Nil	Nil	Nil	Nil
Payout Ratio	Nil	Nil	Nil	Nil	Nil	Nil	Nil	Nil	Nil	Nil
Prices - High	60.47	31.25	31.56	46.81	21.50	11.37	7.87	11.00	8.12	8.12
- Low	28.12	10.75	11.75	14.75	10.25	6.12	5.75	6.12	5.50	4.00
P/E Ratio - High	68	NM	27	42	28	20	NM	22	16	18
- Low	32	NM	10	13	13	11	NM	12	11	9
Income Statement Analysis (Million $)										
Revs.	1,327	639	968	1,029	720	573	423	352	286	240
Oper. Inc.	377	155	267	223	123	89.6	55.7	50.1	48.4	35.3
Depr.	152	100	84.9	66.4	46.1	31.0	19.6	18.5	14.4	8.5
Int. Exp.	35.4	30.4	15.5	16.5	11.9	7.6	7.2	8.0	5.6	5.2
Pretax Inc.	227	45.6	200	182	81.6	58.6	4.2	36.4	35.5	29.8
Eff. Tax Rate	40%	39%	38%	37%	14%	13%	85%	6.00%	4.90%	9.30%
Net Inc.	135	27.7	125	115	70.6	51.1	0.7	34.3	33.8	27.1
Balance Sheet & Other Fin. Data (Million $)										
Cash	551	112	47.3	3.9	104	15.2	45.1	63.1	14.8	16.4
Curr. Assets	1,018	461	266	306	329	183	160	188	102	83.0
Total Assets	3,137	2,398	1,450	1,234	871	584	419	427	309	263
Curr. Liab.	279	265	244	235	156	151	76.1	80.3	65.7	67.8
LT Debt	855	483	217	230	230	51.5	57.5	68.9	47.0	37.0
Common Eqty.	1,806	1,470	867	728	458	369	277	268	185	141
Total Cap.	2,759	2,046	1,157	986	706	424	335	337	234	180
Cap. Exp.	301	82.1	276	268	146	109	37.4	62.3	54.4	80.0
Cash Flow	288	128	210	181	117	82.1	20.3	52.7	48.2	35.5
Curr. Ratio	3.6	1.7	1.1	1.3	2.1	1.2	2.1	2.3	1.5	1.2
% LT Debt of Cap.	31.0	23.6	18.8	23.3	32.6	12.1	17.2	20.5	20.0	20.7
% Net Inc.of Revs.	10.2	4.3	12.9	11.2	9.8	8.9	0.2	9.7	11.8	11.3
% Ret. on Assets	4.9	1.4	9.3	10.9	9.7	10.2	0.2	8.6	11.6	11.3
% Ret. on Equity	8.3	2.4	15.7	19.4	17.1	15.8	0.2	14.1	20.3	21.8

Data as orig reptd.; bef. results of disc opers/spec. items. Per share data adj. for stk. divs. Bold denotes diluted EPS (FASB 128)-prior periods restated. E-Estimated. NA-Not Available. NM-Not Meaningful. NR-Not Ranked.

Office—515 West Greens Road, Suite 1200, Houston, TX 77067. **Tel**—(281) 874-0035. **Website**—http://www.nabors.com **Chrmn & CEO**—E. M. Isenberg. **Vice Chrmn**—R. A. Stratton. **Pres & COO**—A. G. Petrello. **VP-Fin**—B. P. Koch. **Secy**—D. McLachlin. **Investor Contact**—Dennis Smith (281-775-8038). **Dirs**—E. M. Isenberg, J. L. Payne, A. G. Petrello, H. W. Schmidt, M. M. Sheinfeld, R. A. Stratton, J. Wexler, M. J. Whitman. **Transfer Agent & Registrar**—First Chicago Trust Co. of New York, Jersey City, NJ. **Incorporated**—in Delaware in 1978. **Empl**— 17,980. **S&P Analyst:** T. J. Vital

STANDARD
&POOR'S
STOCK REPORTS

National-Oilwell

NYSE Symbol **NOI**

In S&P MidCap 400

18-AUG-01

Industry: Oil & Gas (Drilling & Equipment)

Summary: This company designs, manufactures and sells drilling machinery, motors and tools used in oil and gas drilling and production.

S&P Opinion: Accumulate (★★★★)

Recent Price • 18.25	Yield • Nil
52 Wk Range • 41.24-16	12-Mo. P/E • 23.1

Quantitative Evaluations

Outlook (1 Lowest—5 Highest)
• **4-**

Fair Value
• **20.40**

Risk
• **NA**

Earn./Div. Rank
• **NR**

Technical Eval.
• **Bearish** since 6/01

Rel. Strength Rank (1 Lowest—99 Highest)
• **12**

Insider Activity
• **NA**

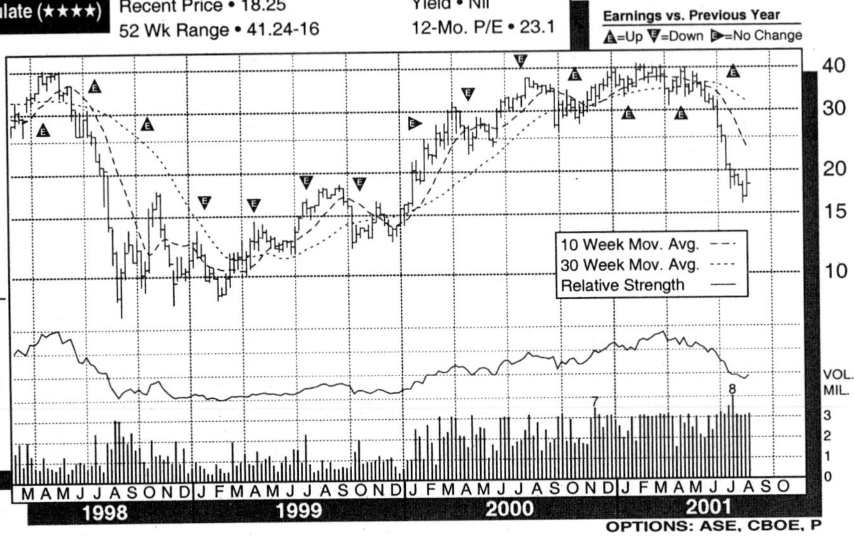

OPTIONS: ASE, CBOE, P

Overview - 07-AUG-01

Operating income should rise over 150% in 2001. NOI believes that excesses of readily usable equipment that have existed within the industry for the past 20 years are now essentially gone, and the company is well positioned to assist customers in their need for replacement parts for new and existing rigs. Growth within Products and Technology should be led by continued strong North American land drilling, aided by accelerating international opportunities. While some U.S. land refurbishments may be put on hold temporarily due to uncertain natural gas prices, U.S. offshore refurbishments appear unabated, and customers continue to modernizing their aging fleets. Distribution Services should benefit from recent investments in information technology and e-commerce.

Valuation - 07-AUG-01

Over the past month, the shares dropped sharply, in a sector sell-off reflecting investor concerns over slowed economies. While the price of U.S. natural gas has dropped to near $3 per million BTU as the demand for U.S. natural gas has eased this summer (due to fuel switching by producers to residual fuel oil and coal, milder temperatures and slowed economies), the supply of U.S. natural gas continues to be plagued by limited resources and depletion issues which should provide support for higher natural gas prices going forward. Therefore, NOI should benefit from continued strong drilling activity (U.S. rig counts up 29% and international rig counts up 16%, from last year) and the existence of a limited excess supply of usable drilling equipment. As of June 30, 2001, the capital equipment backlog was $441 million (60% related to land, 40% international), up 211% from a year earlier. With the shares trading at a deep discount to peers at 8.4X our 2002 EPS estimate, we would accumulate NOI.

Key Stock Statistics

S&P EPS Est. 2001	1.41	Tang. Bk. Value/Share	5.44
P/E on S&P Est. 2001	12.9	Beta	NA
S&P EPS Est. 2002	2.32	Shareholders	593
Dividend Rate/Share	Nil	Market cap. (B)	$ 1.5
Shs. outstg. (M)	80.9	Inst. holdings	83%
Avg. daily vol. (M)	0.790		

Value of $10,000 invested 5 years ago: NA

Fiscal Year Ending Dec. 31

	2001	2000	1999	1998	1997	1996
Revenues (Million $)						
1Q	360.3	229.4	185.2	301.9	206.7	141.1
2Q	434.6	270.3	159.1	294.8	234.0	153.5
3Q	—	286.3	168.2	306.5	265.0	173.5
4Q	—	329.4	198.3	268.9	299.8	180.5
Yr.	—	1,150	745.2	1,172	1,006	648.6
Earnings Per Share ($)						
1Q	0.26	0.05	0.07	0.40	0.19	0.12
2Q	0.31	-0.12	-0.01	0.46	0.21	0.04
3Q	E0.39	0.15	-0.03	0.40	0.17	0.18
4Q	E0.45	0.08	0.04	0.04	0.41	-0.15
Yr.	E1.41	0.16	0.03	1.30	0.99	0.25

Next earnings report expected: late October

Dividend Data

No cash dividends have been paid.

National-Oilwell, Inc.

Business Summary - 07-AUG-01

As a worldwide leader in the design, manufacture and sale of comprehensive systems and components used in oil and gas drilling and production, National-Oilwell also provides supply chain integration services to the upstream oil and gas industry. NOI estimates that more than 90% of the mobile offshore rig fleet and the majority of the world's larger land rigs (2,000 horsepower and greater) manufactured in the past 20 years utilize drawworks, mud pumps and other drilling components manufactured by NOI.

The company's strategy is to grow its market position by leveraging its installed base of higher capacity drilling machinery and equipment, expanding its downhole products, building its information technology, and making acquisitions to enhance its product line.

The Products and Technology segment (57% of 2000 revenues) designs, manufactures and sells drilling systems and components for both land and offshore drilling rigs, as well as complete land drilling and well servicing rigs. The major mechanical components include drawworks, mud pumps, power swivels, SCR houses, solids control equipment, traveling equipment and rotary tables. Many of these components are designed specifically for applications in offshore, extended reach and deep land drilling. This equipment is installed on new rigs and often replaced during the upgrade and refurbishment of existing rigs. With the February 2000 acquisition of Hitec ASA, NOI intends to expand its focus on technology. Hitec's core business is the design and production of control and data acquisition systems for drilling related operations, and automated and remotely controlled machinery for drilling rigs. In June 2000, NOI merged with IRI International Corp., a manufacturer focused on mobile well servicing and drilling rigs. In September 2000, NOI purchased Boots & Co.'s braking systems manufacturer, Baylor Co.; and Halliburton Co.'s Wheatley Gaso and Omega pump product lines. In January 2001, NOI purchased Aker Maritime ASA's coiled tubing manufacturer, Maritime Hydraulics (Canada) Ltd. Also in January 2001, NOI acquired Integrated Power Systems; in May, it purchased Tech Power Controls Co., a manufacturer of electrical control systems.

Distribution Services (43%) revenues result from the sale of maintenance, repair and operating supplies from NOI's network of over 130 distribution service centers. These distribution service centers stock and sell a variety of expendable items for oilfield applications and spare parts for NOI equipment. The company's e-commerce strategy incorporates interfacing directly with customers' systems, trading exchanges and development of its own system that will leverage its position in the upstream market. In January 2000, NOI purchased the U.S. operations of Republic Supply Co. (adding 20 distribution service centers); and in June, the company acquired Rye Supply (adding eight distribution service centers).

Per Share Data ($) (Year Ended Dec. 31)	2000	1999	1998	1997	1996	1995	1994	1993	1992	1991
Tangible Bk. Val.	5.44	3.79	4.31	4.91	2.85	2.29	NA	NA	NA	NA
Cash Flow	0.60	0.42	1.66	1.27	0.03	0.38	NA	NA	NA	NA
Earnings	0.16	0.03	1.30	0.99	0.01	0.27	NA	NA	NA	NA
Dividends	Nil	Nil	Nil	Nil	Nil	Nil	NA	NA	NA	NA
Payout Ratio	Nil	Nil	Nil	Nil	Nil	Nil	NA	NA	NA	NA
Prices - High	39.68	18.50	40.43	44.43	15.37	NA	NA	NA	NA	NA
- Low	14.00	8.50	7.62	14.00	8.50	NA	NA	NA	NA	NA
P/E Ratio - High	NM	NM	31	45	NM	NA	NA	NA	NA	NA
- Low	NM	NM	6	14	NM	NA	NA	NA	NA	NA
Income Statement Analysis (Million $)										
Revs.	1,150	745	1,172	1,006	649	546	NA	NA	NA	NA
Oper. Inc.	97.6	45.1	157	113	91.7	17.4	NA	NA	NA	NA
Depr.	35.0	23.2	19.2	14.7	0.4	3.6	NA	NA	NA	NA
Int. Exp.	Nil	Nil	12.5	6.2	12.1	5.6	NA	NA	NA	NA
Pretax Inc.	27.0	4.5	109	82.5	0.4	15.0	NA	NA	NA	NA
Eff. Tax Rate	51%	66%	37%	38%	38%	37%	NA	NA	NA	NA
Net Inc.	13.1	1.5	68.9	51.3	0.3	9.5	NA	NA	NA	NA
Balance Sheet & Other Fin. Data (Million $)										
Cash	42.5	12.4	11.4	19.8	4.3	4.5	NA	NA	NA	NA
Curr. Assets	743	478	558	464	233	220	NA	NA	NA	NA
Total Assets	1,279	782	818	568	267	259	NA	NA	NA	NA
Curr. Liab.	263	176	211	211	103	89.4	NA	NA	NA	NA
LT Debt	222	196	206	61.6	36.4	62.2	NA	NA	NA	NA
Common Eqty.	767	395	387	278	109	88.0	NA	NA	NA	NA
Total Cap.	1,006	597	597	342	145	150	NA	NA	NA	NA
Cap. Exp.	24.6	15.4	27.8	32.6	3.1	4.8	NA	NA	NA	NA
Cash Flow	48.2	24.8	88.1	66.0	0.7	13.1	NA	NA	NA	NA
Curr. Ratio	2.8	2.7	2.6	2.2	2.3	2.5	NA	NA	NA	NA
% LT Debt of Cap.	22.1	32.8	34.5	18.0	25.1	41.5	NA	NA	NA	NA
% Net Inc.of Revs.	1.1	0.2	5.9	5.1	NM	1.7	NA	NA	NA	NA
% Ret. on Assets	1.1	0.2	9.9	12.3	0.1	NA	NA	NA	NA	NA
% Ret. on Equity	1.9	0.4	20.7	26.5	0.2	NA	NA	NA	NA	NA

Data as orig. reptd.; bef. results of disc. opers. and/or spec. items. Per share data adj. for stk. divs. as of ex-div. date. Pro forma data for 1995. Bal. Sheet & Bk. Val. data for 1995 are as of Jun. 30, 1996. Bold denotes diluted EPS (FASB 128). E-Estimated. NA-Not Available. NM-Not Meaningful. NR-Not Ranked.

Office—10000 Richmond Avenue, 4th Floor, Houston, TX 77042-4200. **Tel**—(713) 346-7500. **Website**—www.natoil.com **Chrmn** —J. V. Staff. **Pres & CEO**—M. A. Miller Jr. **VP & CFO**—S. W. Krablin. **Secy & Investor Contact**—M. Gay Mather (713-346-7775). **Dirs**—H. Ansary, W. M. Dunwoody, B. A. Guill, J. Gjedebo, W. E. Macaulay, M. A. Miller Jr., F. W. Pheasey, J. V. Staff. **Transfer Agent & Registrar**—American Stock Transfer & Trust Co., NYC. **Incorporated**—in Delaware in 1996. **Empl**— 5,000. **S&P Analyst:** T. J. Vital

STANDARD
&POOR'S
STOCK REPORTS

Noble Affiliates

NYSE Symbol **NBL**

In S&P MidCap 400

18-AUG-01

Industry:
Oil & Gas (Exploration & Production)

Summary: This independent energy company explores for and develops crude oil and natural gas throughout the major basins in the U.S., the North Sea, and Africa.

S&P Opinion: Accumulate (★★★★)

Recent Price • 37.05
52 Wk Range • 51.09-30.85
Yield • 0.4%
12-Mo. P/E • 7.4

Quantitative Evaluations

Outlook
(1 Lowest—5 Highest)
• **2⁻**

Fair Value
• **34**

Risk
• **Average**

Earn./Div. Rank
• **B-**

Technical Eval.
• **Bearish** since 5/01

Rel. Strength Rank
(1 Lowest—99 Highest)
• **57**

Insider Activity
• **NA**

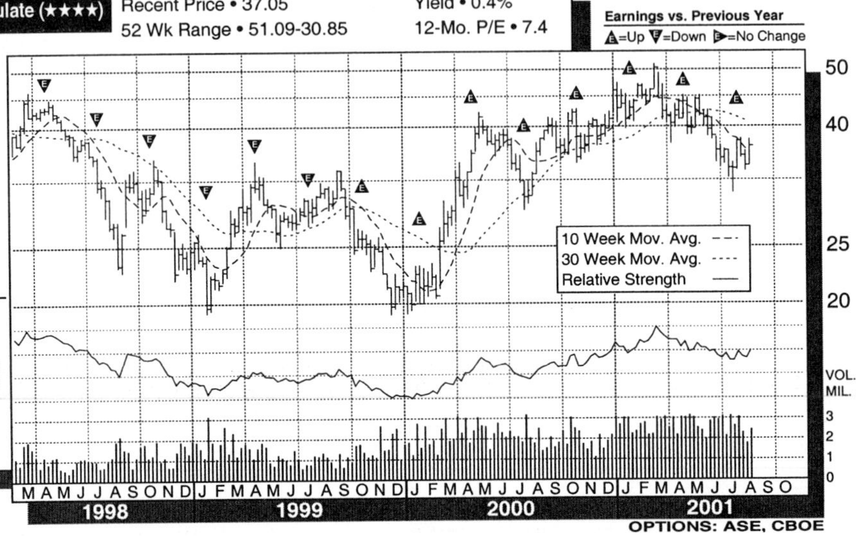

OPTIONS: ASE, CBOE

Overview - 11-JUL-01

Companywide production should rise 8.5% in 2001, reflecting a 20% increase in the exploration and development capital budget, acquisitions, and comparisons with dismal 2000 volumes. In May, NBL's methanol plant in Equatorial Guinea (45% interest) began production of commercial grade methanol. The methanol will be cheap to produce, with NBL's nearby Alba field providing natural gas feedstock; we project cash margin of $0.41 a gallon, making the plant among the world's most efficient. However, with recent weakening of natural prices, and with NBL's gas production unhedged, third quarter will decline. We recently cut our 2001 EPS estimate to $4.10, from $5.80, reflect weaker natural gas prices, and our 2002 estimate to $3.35, from $6.20.

Valuation - 11-JUL-01

The shares were recently down 32% in 2001, after reaching a 52-week high of $51.09, versus a 26% decline for NBL's peers, reflecting weak natural gas prices. Prices will remain low for the short term, but with new power capacity coming on line in the summer and the winter heating season approaching, the trend should reverse. NBL replaced 288% of worldwide 2000 production with new reserves, at an attractive cost of $5.22 per barrel of oil equivalent. The balance sheet shows long term debt at only 28% of capitalization. Finally, NBL is assured of long-term cash flow growth, due to recent discoveries in the Gulf of Mexico, Equatorial Guinea, and Israel. Nevertheless, the stock was recently trading at only 3.6X our 2001 estimate for discretionary cash flow per share, and 8.7X our EPS estimate, versus average multiples of 4.1X and 8.9X for shares of NBL's peers. We are maintaining our accumulate recommendation.

Key Stock Statistics

S&P EPS Est. 2001	4.10	Tang. Bk. Value/Share	15.15
P/E on S&P Est. 2001	9.0	Beta	0.84
S&P EPS Est. 2002	3.35	Shareholders	1,179
Dividend Rate/Share	0.16	Market cap. (B)	$ 2.1
Shs. outstg. (M)	56.6	Inst. holdings	85%
Avg. daily vol. (M)	0.494		

Value of $10,000 invested 5 years ago: $ 8,741

Fiscal Year Ending Dec. 31

	2001	2000	1999	1998	1997	1996
Revenues (Million $)						
1Q	561.0	271.8	177.9	248.1	322.5	170.4
2Q	413.5	306.6	218.6	247.4	236.7	183.6
3Q	—	360.9	255.5	212.3	234.3	257.2
4Q	—	454.3	257.9	203.8	323.1	276.0
Yr.	—	1,394	909.8	911.6	1,117	887.2
Earnings Per Share ($)						
1Q	**1.88**	**0.47**	**-0.16**	**0.24**	**0.67**	**0.43**
2Q	**0.91**	**0.65**	**0.16**	**0.21**	**0.23**	**0.32**
3Q	—	**1.01**	**0.49**	**-0.44**	**0.26**	**0.29**
4Q	—	**1.24**	**0.38**	**-2.89**	**0.57**	**0.51**
Yr.	—	**3.38**	**0.86**	**-2.88**	**1.73**	**1.55**

Next earnings report expected: late October

Dividend Data (Dividends have been paid since 1975.)

Amount ($)	Date Decl.	Ex-Div. Date	Stock of Record	Payment Date
0.040	Oct. 24	Nov. 02	Nov. 06	Nov. 20 '00
0.040	Jan. 30	Feb. 09	Feb. 13	Feb. 26 '01
0.040	Apr. 23	May. 03	May. 07	May. 21 '01
0.040	Jul. 24	Aug. 02	Aug. 06	Aug. 20 '01

A Division of The McGraw·Hill Companies

Noble Affiliates, Inc.

Business Summary - 11-JUL-01

Noble Affiliates (NBL) conducts exploration and production operations, primarily through its Samedan Oil Corp. subsidiary, throughout major basins in the U.S., including the Gulf of Mexico, the Gulf Coast, the Mid-Continent, and the Rocky Mountains. International operations focus on Argentina, China, Ecuador, Equatorial Guinea, the Mediterranean, and the North Sea.

In July 1996, Samedan Oil purchased Energy Development Corp. (EDC) for $768 million in cash. EDC had estimated proved reserves of 35.5 million bbl. of oil and 417.3 Bcf of natural gas. EDC's properties are located in the Gulf of Mexico, onshore the Gulf Coast of Louisiana and Texas, and in Argentina and the U.K. North Sea.

Noble Gas Marketing, Inc. (NGM), seeks opportunities to enhance the value of NBL's gas by marketing directly to end-users and accumulating gas to be sold to gas marketers and pipelines. During 1999, Samedan and EDC sold 59% of their production to NGM; all intercompany sales and expenses are eliminated in NBL's consolidated financial statements. NGM is also actively involved in the purchase and sale of gas from third-party producers. Through wholly owned Noble Gas Pipelines, Inc., NGM installs, purchases and operates gas gathering systems.

The company owns a 50% interest in Atlantic Methanol Capital Co., a joint venture that indirectly owns 90% of Atlantic Methanol Production Co. (AMPCO). AMPCO has been constructing a methanol plant on Bioko Island in Equatorial Guinea. The plant started commercial production in May 2001, and is designed to produce 2,500 metric tons of methanol per day, which equates to approximately 20 MBbls per day. At this level of production, the plant will use approximately 120 MMcf of gas per day from Samedan's 34%-owned Alba field as feedstock. The total cost of the project is estimated at about $425 million.

At December 31, 2000 (1999), NBL's total estimated proved reserves amounted to 149 (122) million bbl. of oil and 1.5 (1.3) trillion cubic feet of natural gas.

Daily production in 2000 (1999) averaged 25,805 (30,003) bbl. of oil and 406.3 (455.1) MMcf of gas a day. The company's average price per bbl. of oil was $24.37 ($16.29). Gas prices averaged $3.77 ($2.23) per Mcf.

Capital expenditures (excluding acquisitions) for 2001 have been budgeted at $700 million, a 40% increase from the approved 2000 budget of $498 million. Approximately 60% and 40% of the budget have been allocated to development and exploration, respectively.

In June 2001, NBL announced the completion and testing of a major natural gas and condensate well in the Alba Field of Equatorial Guinea, leading to a near doubling of the field's proven and probable reserves, which exceed 1 billion barrels of oil equivalent. NBL holds a 33.75% interest in the Alba field.

Per Share Data ($) (Year Ended Dec. 31)	2000	1999	1998	1997	1996	1995	1994	1993	1992	1991
Tangible Bk. Val.	15.15	11.98	11.27	14.20	12.66	8.19	8.24	8.32	6.83	5.99
Cash Flow	7.44	5.30	2.62	6.96	6.28	4.10	2.77	2.74	3.30	2.37
Earnings	3.42	0.87	-2.88	1.73	1.63	0.08	0.06	0.26	0.93	0.44
Dividends	0.16	0.16	0.16	0.16	0.16	0.16	0.16	0.16	0.16	0.16
Payout Ratio	5%	18%	NM	9%	10%	NM	NM	62%	17%	37%
Prices - High	48.37	35.00	46.18	50.00	49.00	30.50	32.25	31.00	20.25	17.75
- Low	19.18	19.12	21.93	32.18	26.87	21.25	22.50	15.75	11.62	12.50
P/E Ratio - High	14	40	NM	29	30	NM	NM	NM	22	40
- Low	6	22	NM	19	16	NM	NM	NM	13	28
Income Statement Analysis (Million $)										
Revs.	1,381	887	894	1,091	878	441	350	278	260	226
Oper. Inc.	550	352	315	479	397	181	150	147	142	117
Depr. Depl. & Amort.	231	255	313	300	234	201	135	119	105	85.0
Int. Exp.	31.6	43.0	43.8	46.8	38.5	21.9	24.7	20.4	20.5	21.0
Pretax Inc.	299	77.6	-247	158	136	8.0	5.0	21.0	61.0	29.0
Eff. Tax Rate	36%	36%	NM	37%	39%	49%	39%	39%	33%	33%
Net Inc.	192	49.5	-164	99	83.9	4.1	3.2	12.6	41.2	19.3
Balance Sheet & Other Fin. Data (Million $)										
Cash	23.2	2.9	19.1	55.1	94.8	12.0	22.0	176	119	1.8
Curr. Assets	271	148	188	259	317	118	104	257	189	78.0
Total Assets	1,879	1,450	1,686	1,875	1,957	989	934	1,068	626	590
Curr. Liab.	325	184	139	217	280	97.0	72.0	147	55.7	56.7
LT Debt	525	445	745	645	798	377	377	454	225	225
Common Eqty.	850	2,134	642	813	720	412	412	415	305	265
Total Cap.	1,492	2,662	1,494	1,602	1,627	858	815	914	563	524
Cap. Exp.	537	123	432	327	258	255	166	510	66.0	123
Cash Flow	422	304	149	400	317	205	138	132	146	104
Curr. Ratio	0.8	0.8	1.4	1.2	1.1	1.2	1.4	1.8	3.4	1.4
% LT Debt of Cap.	35.2	16.7	49.9	40.3	49.0	44.0	44.3	49.6	39.9	42.9
% Ret. on Assets	11.6	3.2	NM	5.2	5.7	0.5	0.3	1.4	6.8	3.3
% Ret. on Equity	25.0	2.2	NM	13.0	14.8	1.0	0.8	3.3	14.4	7.5

Data as orig reptd.; bef. results of disc opers/spec. items. Per share data adj. for stk. divs. Bold denotes diluted EPS (FASB 128)-prior periods restated. E-Estimated. NA-Not Available. NM-Not Meaningful. NR-Not Ranked.

Office—350 Glenborough Drive, Suite 100, Houston TX 77067. **Tel**—(281) 872-3100. **Chrmn, Pres & CEO**—C. D. Davidson. **VP, CFO & Treas**—J. L. McElvany. **SVP & Secy**—A. D. Hoppe. **Dirs**—C. D. Davidson, A. A. Baker, M. A. Cawley, E. F. Cox, D. P. Jones, T. D. Stacy. **Transfer Agent & Registrar**—First Chicago Trust Co., Jersey City, NJ. **Incorporated**—in Delaware in 1969. **Empl**— 556. **S&P Analyst:** John Kartsonas

STANDARD &POOR'S
STOCK REPORTS

Occidental Petroleum

NYSE Symbol **OXY**
In S&P 500

18-AUG-01

Industry:
Oil (Domestic Integrated)

Summary: This company has worldwide oil and natural gas operations, and a large chemicals division.

S&P Opinion: Accumulate (★★★★)

Recent Price • 28.05
52 Wk Range • 31.10-19.06

Yield • 3.6%
12-Mo. P/E • 6.1

Quantitative Evaluations
Outlook
(1 Lowest—5 Highest)
• **2**
Fair Value
• **27.40**
Risk
• **Low**
Earn./Div. Rank
• **B+**

Technical Eval.
• **Neutral** since 7/01
Rel. Strength Rank
(1 Lowest—99 Highest)
• **65**
Insider Activity
• **NA**

Earnings vs. Previous Year
▲=Up ▼=Down ▶=No Change

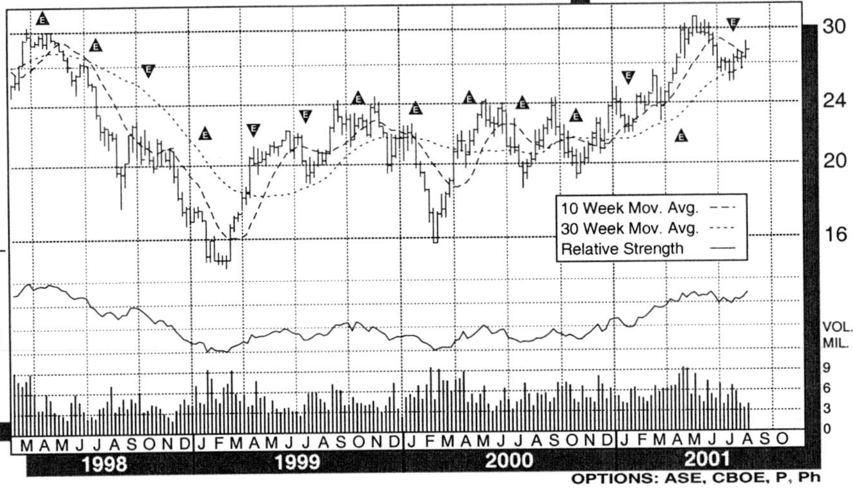

OPTIONS: ASE, CBOE, P, Ph

Overview - 23-JUL-01

In May, OXY won participation in the "Red Sea" Core Venture 2 project of the Saudi Natural Gas Initiative. The 1998 acquisition of the Elk Hills fields transformed OXY from a company with multiple businesses into an oil and gas concern with a large chemical division. Operating income should rise over 25% on increased BOE production, reflecting the April 2000 acquisition of Altura and THUMS. High oil and gas prices should continue to drive exploration and production profits. Operating costs per bbl. are expected to improve, and break-even costs have been reduced by $3 a bbl. over the past two years. Chemical margins will remain under pressure, reflecting lower operating rates, lower prices and volumes in chlorine and polyvinyl chloride, higher energy and feedstock costs, and lower ethylene dichloride earnings.

Valuation - 23-JUL-01

Over the past month, the shares have dropped sharply in a sector sell-off reflecting end of quarter window dressing and investor concerns over slowing economies. While domestic natural gas prices have recently softened on a temporary weaking in demand, they remain at historically high levels, and supply side challenges remain unchanged, which should provide opportunities for OXY going forward. Capital spending was $952 million in 2000, and should reach $1.1 billion (91% in exploration and production) in 2001. Sale of the Tangguh LNG project and OXY's interest in a Texas pipeline should yield $750 million in after-tax proceeds for debt reduction. Portions of OXY's non-U.S. assets remain exposed to political and economic risk, but with a strengthening balance sheet and the shares trading at only 6X our 2001 EPS estimate, a discount to peer levels, we recommend accumulating the stock.

Key Stock Statistics

S&P EPS Est. 2001	4.63	Tang. Bk. Value/Share	12.90
P/E on S&P Est. 2001	6.1	Beta	0.57
S&P EPS Est. 2002	4.01	Shareholders	74,175
Dividend Rate/Share	1.00	Market cap. (B)	$ 10.5
Shs. outstg. (M)	373.3	Inst. holdings	70%
Avg. daily vol. (M)	0.837		

Value of $10,000 invested 5 years ago: $ 14,485

Fiscal Year Ending Dec. 31

	2001	2000	1999	1998	1997	1996
Revenues (Million $)						
1Q	4,475	2,574	1,344	1,700	1,917	2,522
2Q	3,845	3,195	1,647	1,543	2,158	2,457
3Q	—	3,863	2,113	1,661	2,007	2,786
4Q	—	3,943	2,506	1,692	1,934	2,792
Yr.	—	13,575	7,610	6,596	8,016	10,557
Earnings Per Share ($)						
1Q	**1.37**	**0.74**	**-0.17**	**0.38**	**0.31**	0.44
2Q	**1.26**	**1.53**	**0.03**	**0.49**	**0.34**	0.49
3Q	**E1.03**	**1.09**	**0.35**	**0.10**	**0.31**	0.53
4Q	**E1.04**	**0.90**	**1.33**	**-0.12**	**-0.58**	0.41
Yr.	**E4.63**	**4.26**	**1.58**	**0.88**	**0.39**	**1.86**

Next earnings report expected: mid October

Dividend Data (Dividends have been paid since 1975.)

Amount ($)	Date Decl.	Ex-Div. Date	Stock of Record	Payment Date
0.250	Nov. 09	Dec. 06	Dec. 08	Jan. 15 '01
0.250	Feb. 08	Mar. 07	Mar. 09	Apr. 15 '01
0.250	Apr. 19	Jun. 06	Jun. 08	Jul. 15 '01
0.250	Jul. 12	Sep. 06	Sep. 10	Oct. 15 '01

A Division of The McGraw·Hill Companies

Occidental Petroleum Corporation

Business Summary - 23-JUL-01

Conducting business through subsidiaries, Occidental Petroleum is a leading global oil and gas exploration and production (E&P; 72% of 2000 revenues; 93% of segment earnings) and chemical (28%; 7%) company. Since 1997, OXY has completed several asset swaps (with Shell, Unocal, Enron Oil & Gas, BP Amoco, and EOG Resources), focusing on E&P growth opportunities, and on achieving cost savings. Domestic activities have been consolidated into five states, from 16; international activities have been consolidated into 10 countries, from 24.

The company has active E&P operations in the U.S. (including the Gulf of Mexico) and eight other countries. Since purchasing a 78% stake in the giant Elk Hills field in 1998, OXY has become the largest independent oil and gas producer in California. Production averaged 343,000 barrels per day (bbl./d) in 2000, up from 306,400 bbl./d in 1999. Natural gas production declined to 708 million cubic feet per day (MMcf/d) in 2000, from 714 MMcf/d. International operations accounted for 54% of OXY's oil production, while 93% of natural gas production came from the U.S. Oil reserves at the end of 2000 totaled 1.803 billion bbl. Natural gas reserves totaled 2.2 Tcf.

In April 2000, OXY sold its 29.2% stock interest in Canadian Occidental Petroleum Ltd., for about $700 million. Funds were used in part to pay for the April 2000 purchase of Altura Energy Ltd., which had proven reserves of 850 million bbl. of oil equivalent (BOE), for about $3.6 billion. Also in April, the company purchased ARCO Long Beach Inc. (the owner of the Long Beach Unit's operating contractor THUMS), for about $68 million, adding about 95 million bbl. of oil reserves and 25,000 bbl./d of oil production. In August 2000, OXY sold a partial interest in its Gulf of Mexico properties to Apache Corp., for $385 million.

The company's OxyChem subsidiary is a leading chemical manufacturer, with interests in basic chemicals (principally chlorine and caustic soda), vinyls, petrochemicals and specialty products. OxyChem also produces PVC, silicates, chrome and swimming pool chemicals. In recent few years, OXY has enhanced its position in core chemical product markets by entering into strategic alliances that offered cost-saving synergies. In 1998, the company became a partner in the Equistar alliance (with a 29.5% interest), a leading producer of ethylene and derivatives. In 1999, it combined its polyvinyl chloride (PVC) business with PolyOne Corp. (formerly The Geon Co.) to form the OxyVinyls, LP, alliance, the largest producer of PVC resins in North America. OXY is the operator, with a 76% interest. Also in 1999, the company formed a 10%-owned powder compounding partnership with Geon. In November 2000, OXY sold its Durez phenolic resins and compounding business to Sumitomo Bakelite Co., Ltd., for after tax proceeds of about $120 million.

Per Share Data ($) (Year Ended Dec. 31)	2000	1999	1998	1997	1996	1995	1994	1993	1992	1991
Tangible Bk. Val.	12.90	9.57	8.97	8.46	11.57	10.37	9.88	11.07	11.33	14.33
Cash Flow	6.69	3.84	3.26	2.78	5.00	4.21	2.48	2.99	3.24	3.95
Earnings	4.26	1.58	0.88	0.39	1.86	1.31	-0.36	0.12	0.41	1.25
Dividends	1.00	1.00	1.00	1.00	1.00	1.00	1.00	1.00	1.00	1.00
Payout Ratio	23%	63%	114%	NM	54%	76%	NM	833%	244%	81%
Prices - High	25.56	24.56	30.43	30.75	27.25	24.37	22.37	23.50	23.12	25.37
- Low	15.75	14.62	16.62	21.75	20.12	18.00	15.12	16.87	15.75	16.50
P/E Ratio - High	6	16	35	79	15	19	NM	NM	56	20
- Low	4	9	19	56	11	14	NM	NM	38	13
Income Statement Analysis (Million $)										
Revs.	13,574	7,610	6,596	8,016	10,557	10,423	9,236	8,116	8,494	10,096
Oper. Inc.	3,826	1,831	1,297	1,835	2,316	2,143	1,539	1,266	1,180	1,668
Depr.	901	805	835	822	921	922	882	878	856	806
Int. Exp.	518	498	559	434	484	579	589	591	659	902
Pretax Inc.	3,196	1,257	688	528	1,152	913	109	218	325	986
Eff. Tax Rate	45%	50%	53%	59%	39%	44%	131%	66%	60%	61%
Net Inc.	1,569	568	325	217	698	511	-36.0	74.0	126	379
Balance Sheet & Other Fin. Data (Million $)										
Cash	97.0	214	96.0	113	279	520	129	157	90.0	276
Curr. Assets	2,067	1,688	2,795	1,916	2,190	2,519	2,258	1,934	2,245	2,968
Total Assets	19,414	14,125	15,252	15,282	17,634	17,815	17,989	17,123	17,877	16,115
Curr. Liab.	2,740	1,967	2,931	1,870	2,470	2,657	2,201	2,048	2,290	2,778
LT Debt	5,658	4,854	5,367	4,925	4,511	4,819	6,114	6,047	5,806	5,925
Common Eqty.	4,774	3,523	3,120	2,304	3,809	3,305	3,132	3,383	3,440	4,300
Total Cap.	13,977	9,372	9,555	10,239	12,211	12,069	13,142	12,406	11,287	10,527
Cap. Exp.	952	601	1,074	1,549	1,185	979	1,103	1,007	765	954
Cash Flow	2,470	1,366	1,143	951	1,619	1,340	770	913	979	1,178
Curr. Ratio	0.8	0.9	1.0	1.0	0.9	0.9	1.0	0.9	1.0	1.1
% LT Debt of Cap.	40.5	51.8	56.2	48.1	36.9	40.0	46.5	48.7	51.4	56.3
% Net Inc.of Revs.	11.6	7.5	4.9	2.7	6.6	4.9	NM	0.9	1.5	3.8
% Ret. on Assets	9.4	3.9	2.1	1.3	3.9	2.9	NM	0.4	0.7	2.1
% Ret. on Equity	37.8	16.9	12.6	6.2	17.0	9.2	NM	1.0	3.2	8.8

Data as orig reptd.; bef. results of disc opers/spec. items. Per share data adj. for stk. divs. Bold denotes diluted EPS (FASB 128)-prior periods restated. E-Estimated. NA-Not Available. NM-Not Meaningful. NR-Not Ranked.

Office—10889 Wilshire Boulevard, Los Angeles, CA 90024. **Tel**—(310) 208-8800. **Website**—http://www.oxy.com **Chrmn & CEO**—R. R. Irani. **Pres**—D. R. Laurance. **EVP & CFO**—S. I. Chazen. **EVP & Secy**—D. P. de Brier. **VP & Treas**—J. A. Havert. **VP & Investor Contact**—Kenneth J. Huffman (212-603-8183). **Dirs**—R. W. Burkle, J. S. Chalsty, E. P. Djerejian, J. E. Feick, J. R. Hirl, R. R. Irani, D. R. Laurance, I. W. Maloney, R. Segovia, A. D. Syriani, R. Tomich. **Transfer Agents & Registrars**—Mellon Investor Services LLC, Ridgefield Park, NJ. **Incorporated**—in California in 1920; reincorporated in Delaware in 1986. **Empl**— 8,791. **S&P Analyst:** T. J. Vital

STANDARD &POOR'S STOCK REPORTS

Ocean Energy

NYSE Symbol **OEI**

In S&P MidCap 400

24-AUG-01

Industry: Oil & Gas (Exploration & Production)

Summary: This company explores for and produces natural gas and crude oil.

S&P Opinion: Accumulate (★★★★) Recent Price • 19.72 | 52 Wk Range • 21.72-12.59 | Yield • 0.8% | 12-Mo. P/E • 10.5

Quantitative Evaluations

Outlook (1 Lowest—5 Highest)
• **1⁻**

Fair Value
• **16.60**

Risk
• **Average**

Earn./Div. Rank
• **NR**

Technical Eval.
• **Bullish** since 7/01

Rel. Strength Rank (1 Lowest—99 Highest)
• **76**

Insider Activity
• **NA**

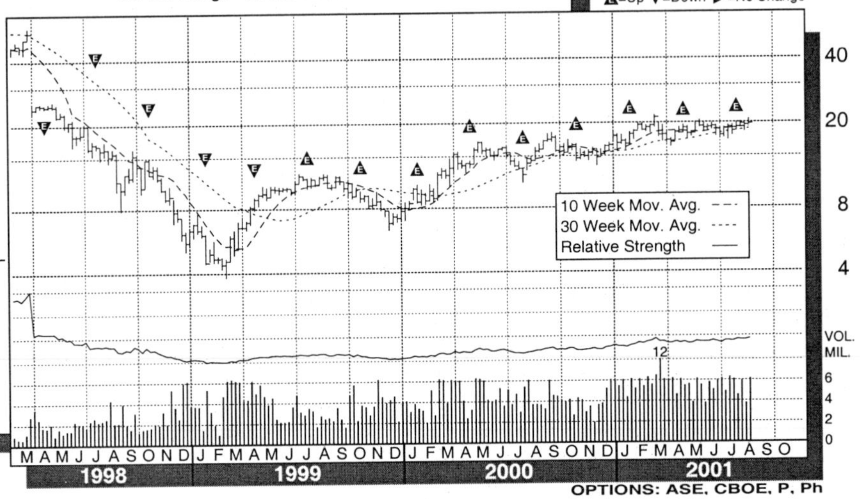

OPTIONS: ASE, CBOE, P, Ph

Overview - 24-AUG-01

Production in 2001 should rise 13%, partially reflecting the Texoil and Ensight acquisitions. In addition, volumes were off last year, on asset sales to reduce debt. With costs well maintained, discretionary cash flow per share (DCFPS) is expected to increase 29%, to $4.93, from $3.82. Longer term, we're especially bullish on the company's prospects in the deepwater Gulf of Mexico, where OEI and Kerr-McGee recently formed an exploration joint venture. Both companies have been developing the Nansen and Boomvang prospects in that area since 1999; production from the two fields is expected to begin in late 2001 and early 2002, respectively. Further debt reductions are unlikely, as the current long-term debt to total capitalization of 34% is only slightly higher than the peer group average. Our EPS estimate of $1.82 assumes average oil and gas prices for 2001 of $27.64 and $4.44, respectively.

Valuation - 24-AUG-01

Year to date, the shares were recently up 19%, versus the 12.5% decline for the S&P Exploration & Production (E&P) Index. The attractive OEI's assets combined with the current industry consolidation, are the main reasons for this performance. The stock was trading at 4.0X estimated 2001 DCFPS, versus a median of 3.5X for the company's peer group. However, OEI possesses some very attractive assets, and as a result, we continue to recommend accumulating the stock. In addition to its improving balance sheet, the company's five-year average finding and development costs were significantly lower last year. In the past few months, OEI instituted its first dividend program, and its debt ratings were upgraded to investment grade by several rating agencies. These events further demonstrate the company's strong cash position.

Key Stock Statistics

S&P EPS Est. 2001	1.82	Tang. Bk. Value/Share	8.11
P/E on S&P Est. 2001	10.8	Beta	0.71
S&P EPS Est. 2002	1.56	Shareholders	4,123
Dividend Rate/Share	0.16	Market cap. (B)	$ 3.4
Shs. outstg. (M)	171.3	Inst. holdings	74%
Avg. daily vol. (M)	1.052		

Value of $10,000 invested 5 years ago: $ 6,646

Fiscal Year Ending Dec. 31

	2001	2000	1999	1998	1997	1996
Revenues (Million $)						
1Q	403.3	246.1	105.7	141.9	64.48	36.83
2Q	355.8	236.4	196.2	133.2	65.59	32.25
3Q	—	261.1	214.4	124.0	74.33	47.59
4Q	—	312.4	219.2	124.2	87.78	71.78
Yr.	—	1,074	735.5	523.3	292.2	188.4
Earnings Per Share ($)						
1Q	**0.70**	**0.25**	**-0.79**	**-0.28**	**0.49**	0.12
2Q	**0.47**	**0.26**	**0.01**	**-1.34**	**0.30**	0.02
3Q	—	**0.33**	**0.16**	**-0.14**	**0.42**	0.26
4Q	—	**0.39**	**0.16**	**-2.27**	**0.57**	0.63
Yr.	—	**1.22**	**-0.16**	**-4.04**	**1.79**	**1.09**

Next earnings report expected: late October

Dividend Data (Dividends have been paid since 2001.)

Amount ($)	Date Decl.	Ex-Div. Date	Stock of Record	Payment Date
0.040	Dec. 18	Jan. 03	Jan. 05	Jan. 19 '01
0.040	Mar. 27	Apr. 04	Apr. 06	Apr. 20 '01
0.040	Jun. 26	Jul. 03	Jul. 06	Jul. 20 '01

Ocean Energy, Inc.

Business Summary - 24-AUG-01

On March 30, 1999, Ocean Energy merged into Seagull Energy Corp. The resulting corporation, renamed Ocean Energy, Inc., was among the largest oil and gas exploration and production companies in the U.S. in terms of production and reserves. The merger was accounted for under the purchase method. Following the merger, the company consolidated headquarters and operations and eliminated positions in order to realize cost savings. In addition, substantial assets were sold, with proceeds utilized to reduce debt.

In March 2001, the company completed its acquisition of Texoil, Inc. for $130 million cash. The acquisition expanded OEI's South Texas and Louisiana operations. Texoil had estimated proved reserves of 150 billion cubic feet of natural gas equivalent (Bcfe), of which 57% was natural gas. Also in March, Ocean agreed to acquire an estimated 104 Bcfe of reserves, of which 88% was gas, from Ensight Resources for $121 million. The assets are located in East Texas and North Louisiana.

OEI's North American operations focus on the shelf and deepwater areas of the Gulf of Mexico and the Permian Basin, Midcontinent, and Rocky Mountain regions. The company's domestic properties accounted for 62% of 2000 year-end reserves. Internationally, OEI explores for and produces oil and gas in West Africa (Equatorial Guinea, Cote d'Ivoire and Angola), Egypt, Russia, Pakistan and Indonesia.

As of December 31, 2000 (1999), proved reserves were estimated at 460 (415) million barrels of oil equivalent (MMBOE), with natural gas accounting for about 52% (56%) of the total. Average daily production during 2000 (1999) was 135.4 (144.4) MBOE; natural gas accounted for 50% (48%) of production.

The capital spending program for 2001 was budgeted at $700 million (excluding proved property acquisitions). Approximately 45%-55% will be utilized for exploratory spending. Capital expenditures in 2000 and 1999 totaled $565 million and $342 million, respectively.

In November 1999, the company sold its ENSTAR operations to SEMCO ENERGY, Inc., for about $290 million. ENSTAR engages in the intrastate transmission of natural gas in South-Central Alaska and the distribution of natural gas in Anchorage and other nearby communities in Alaska.

Per Share Data ($) (Year Ended Dec. 31)	2000	1999	1998	1997	1996	1995	1994	1993	1992	1991
Tangible Bk. Val.	6.89	5.52	3.39	12.88	4.82	0.99	0.27	NM	NA	NA
Cash Flow	2.98	1.94	-1.13	7.72	4.95	4.25	NM	NM	NA	NA
Earnings	1.22	-0.16	-0.04	1.79	1.07	0.66	NM	NM	NA	NA
Dividends	Nil	Nil	Nil	Nil	Nil	Nil	Nil	NM	NA	NA
Payout Ratio	Nil	Nil	Nil	Nil	Nil	Nil	Nil	Nil	NA	NA
Prices - High	18.12	11.81	57.50	70.56	54.37	15.25	10.50	NA	NA	NA
- Low	7.00	3.81	5.06	38.00	13.50	9.25	8.75	NA	NA	NA
P/E Ratio - High	15	NM	NM	39	51	23	NM	NA	NA	NA
- Low	6	NM	NM	21	13	14	NM	NA	NA	NA
Income Statement Analysis (Million $)										
Revs.	1,074	736	523	292	188	128	75.0	47.0	NA	NA
Oper. Inc.	788	497	319	208	127	77.3	35.1	23.4	NA	NA
Depr. Depl. & Amort.	311	317	294	124	76.2	54.8	36.8	20.3	NA	NA
Int. Exp.	119	147	46.2	45.5	47.4	53.7	52.1	37.7	18.5	19.6
Pretax Inc.	378	-21.6	-616	57.6	33.0	5.2	-22.2	2.2	NA	NA
Eff. Tax Rate	44%	NM	NM	35%	36%	NM	Nil	Nil	NA	NA
Net Inc.	213	-21.6	-406	37.5	21.0	9.9	-22.2	2.2	NA	NA
Balance Sheet & Other Fin. Data (Million $)										
Cash	23.0	64.9	10.7	8.5	12.1	0.2	0.6	NA	NA	NA
Curr. Assets	325	290	154	50.7	83.9	19.1	11.9	NA	NA	NA
Total Assets	2,890	2,783	2,007	823	461	216	182	132	NA	NA
Curr. Liab.	394	382	237	114	64.9	22.9	16.9	NA	NA	NA
LT Debt	1,033	1,333	1,372	390	284	157	144	13.0	NA	NA
Common Eqty.	1,153	948	377	305	105	20.0	9.7	-0.8	NA	NA
Total Cap.	2,185	2,281	1,757	707	395	177	154	13.0	NA	NA
Cap. Exp.	578	362	13.9	NA	291	75.5	39.4	113	NA	NA
Cash Flow	521	293	-112	162	97.1	64.0	-14.6	22.5	NA	NA
Curr. Ratio	0.8	0.8	0.6	0.4	1.3	0.8	0.7	NA	NA	NA
% LT Debt of Cap.	47.3	58.5	78.1	55.0	71.9	88.7	93.5	100.0	NA	NA
% Ret. on Assets	7.5	NM	NM	5.8	6.2	5.0	NM	2.6	NA	NA
% Ret. on Equity	20.0	NM	NM	18.2	33.5	66.5	NM	NM	NA	NA

Data as orig. reptd.; bef. results of disc. opers. and/or spec. items. Per share data adj. for stk. divs. as of ex-div. date. Bold denotes diluted EPS (FASB 128). E-Estimated. NA-Not Available. NM-Not Meaningful. NR-Not Ranked.

Office—1001 Fannin, Suite 1600, Houston, TX 77002-6714. **Tel**—(713) 265-6000. **Website**—www.oceanenergy.com **Chrmn, Pres & CEO**—J. T. Hackett. **EVP-Operations**—J. D. Schiller Jr. **EVP & CFO**—W. L. Transier. **EVP, Gen Counsel & Secy**—R. K. Reeves. **Investor Contact**—Bruce Busmire (713-265-6161). **Dirs**—J. E. Atwell, J. B. Brock, M. Carroll, T. D. Clark Jr., P. J. Fluor, B. J. Galt, J. T. Hackett, W. G. Henton, R. L. Howard, E. L. Mason, C. F. Mitchell, D. K. Newbigging, D. S. Osborne. **Transfer Agent & Registrar**—Boston EquiServe. **Incorporated**—in Texas in 1994. **Empl**— 1,051. **S&P Analyst:** John Kartsonas

STANDARD
&POOR'S
STOCK REPORTS

Patterson-UTI

Nasdaq Symbol **PTEN**

20-AUG-01

Industry: Oil & Gas (Drilling & Equipment)

Summary: This company provides domestic land drilling services to major and independent oil and gas companies. On May 8, 2001, Patterson Energy merged with UTI Energy.

S&P Opinion: Accumulate (★★★★)

Recent Price • 16.28
52 Wk Range • 41.37-14.05
Yield • Nil
12-Mo. P/E • 9.9

Quantitative Evaluations

Outlook
(1 Lowest—5 Highest)
• **4−**

Fair Value
• **19**

Risk
• **High**

Earn./Div. Rank
• **B-**

Technical Eval.
• **Bearish** since 8/01

Rel. Strength Rank
(1 Lowest—99 Highest)
• **15**

Insider Activity
• **NA**

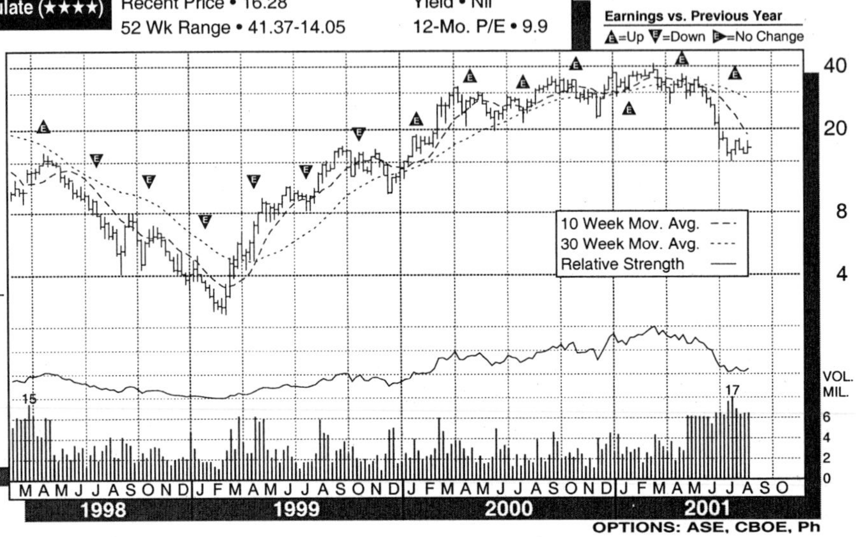

OPTIONS: ASE, CBOE, Ph

Overview - 20-AUG-01

In May, shareholders approved the merger of Patterson Energy and UTI Energy, creating the second largest U.S. land-based driller. As of the second quarter, utilization rates averaged 82% (versus 84% in the first quarter); dayrates were up 11%, to $10,950; and the cash margin per day was up 33%, to $4,850. Operating income should rise over 25% in 2002 on solid industry fundamentals. Drilling revenues should rise about 20%, as domestic land rig utilization rates and dayrates find support to remain high due to a limited supply of land rigs and limited North American natural resources, compounded by accelerating field depletion rates. Drilling fluids revenues should rise over 5%, and pressure pumping sales over 25% on continued strength in North American drilling.

Valuation - 20-AUG-01

In June, we downgraded PTEN to accumulate, from buy, as its smaller size compared to other contract drillers did not provide the shares with market stability to moderate a recent sell-off by investors reacting to a greater than expected seasonal natural gas inventory builds. However, consolidation in the land-based drilling industry in recent years has brought discipline to the sector (top three players are 60% of the market), and allowed margin expansion. We expect this trend to continue, as the market rewards larger drillers with higher multiples. The recent sell-off of natural gas based energy stocks appears to say that a lack of demand is overwhelming a lack of supply for natural gas. We believe such concerns are premature, given considerable field depletion issues in the U.S., despite increased drilling activity. With shares down over 55% from their 52-week highs and trading at a discount to those of PTEN's peers, at 5X our 2002 EPS estimate, we recommend accumulation.

Key Stock Statistics

S&P EPS Est. 2001	2.49	Tang. Bk. Value/Share	7.11
P/E on S&P Est. 2001	6.5	Beta	1.56
S&P EPS Est. 2002	3.18	Shareholders	8,357
Dividend Rate/Share	Nil	Market cap. (B)	$ 1.2
Shs. outstg. (M)	76.2	Inst. holdings	54%
Avg. daily vol. (M)	2.206		

Value of $10,000 invested 5 years ago: $ 38,305

Fiscal Year Ending Dec. 31

	2001	2000	1999	1998	1997	1996
Revenues (Million $)						
1Q	129.9	58.57	26.74	60.75	30.64	12.28
2Q	287.6	67.14	30.54	51.15	40.69	14.35
3Q	—	78.63	39.81	42.26	58.16	20.26
4Q	—	103.6	54.44	32.40	61.29	28.65
Yr.	—	307.9	151.5	186.6	190.8	83.71
Earnings Per Share ($)						
1Q	**0.52**	**0.03**	**-0.12**	**0.14**	0.06	0.13
2Q	**0.61**	**0.11**	**-0.10**	**0.05**	0.14	0.03
3Q	**E0.67**	**0.19**	**-0.07**	**-0.02**	0.26	-0.03
4Q	**E0.69**	**0.32**	**0.01**	**-0.19**	**0.27**	0.10
Yr.	**E2.49**	**0.66**	**-0.28**	**-0.01**	**0.75**	**0.21**

Next earnings report expected: late October

Dividend Data

No cash dividends have been paid.

Patterson-UTI Energy, Inc.

Business Summary - 20-AUG-01

On May 8, 2001, Patterson Energy merged with UTI Energy, creating Patterson-UTI Energy, North America's second largest operator of land-based oil and gas drilling rigs. Shareholders of UTI Energy received one PTEN share for each UTI common share. The combined company has 302 land-based drilling rigs, of which 286 are located in the U.S.; 16 rigs are in western Canada. PTEN is also engaged in pressure pumping; oil and gas exploration and production; and drilling and completion fluids services.

Patterson Energy markets contract drilling services (85% of 2000 revenues) to major oil companies and independent oil and natural gas producers. The company believes it has achieved a position as a leading provider of contract drilling services in its areas of operations by providing high quality services to customers at competitive rates. It has in-house capability to design, manufacture, repair and modify its drilling rigs. Of its Patterson's 152 drilling rigs, 140 are currently marketable. As of year-end 2000, 95 were capable of drilling to depths of 12,000 ft. or more, including 52 capable of drilling to 15,000 ft. or more. During 2000, Patterson Energy drilled 1,485 wells for 224 non-affiliated customers, maintaining an average utilization rate of 74%. Over the past six years, the company's operations expanded significantly through a series of acquisitions. In January 2001, it acquired Jones Drilling Corp. and affiliates, adding 21 contract drilling rigs, 14 of which were marketable, for about $36.2 million.

Oil and natural gas activities (5%) are designed to complement land drilling operations and diversify the overall business strategy. These activities primarily focus on mature producing regions in the Permian Basin and South Texas. At December 31, 2000, the company's proved developed reserves were approximately 1.8 million barrels of oil equivalent (BOE). Patterson Energy's strategy for its oil and natural gas operations is to increase its reserves primarily through developmental and exploratory drilling in producing areas. Although it will from time to time participate through a working interest in exploratory drilling, the focus of the company's drilling activities for the foreseeable future will be exploration and development drilling in the Permian Basin of West Texas, southeastern New Mexico, and South Texas.

Patterson Energy also provides contract drilling fluid services (10%) to a number of operators in the oil and natural gas industry. The company believes these services integrate well with its other core operating activities. Contract drilling fluids were added to operations in 1998, with the acquisition of Lone Star Mud, Inc., and Tejas Drilling Fluids, Inc., and further expanded with the acquisition of Ambar, Inc., in October 2000.

Per Share Data ($) (Year Ended Dec. 31)	2000	1999	1998	1997	1996	1995	1994	1993	1992	1991
Tangible Bk. Val.	7.11	3.40	3.50	3.95	2.20	1.59	1.37	1.05	0.65	NA
Cash Flow	1.59	0.60	1.02	1.29	0.75	0.57	0.62	0.41	0.41	NA
Earnings	0.66	-0.28	-0.01	0.75	0.21	0.16	0.25	0.24	0.09	NA
Dividends	Nil	Nil	Nil	Nil	Nil	Nil	Nil	Nil	NA	NA
Payout Ratio	Nil	Nil	Nil	Nil	Nil	Nil	Nil	Nil	NA	NA
Prices - High	39.50	16.75	20.00	32.62	7.56	3.65	1.96	1.93	NA	NA
- Low	11.62	2.59	3.43	5.50	2.81	1.50	1.50	1.62	NA	NA
P/E Ratio - High	60	NM	NM	43	35	21	7	8	NA	NA
- Low	18	NM	NM	7	13	8	5	6	NA	NA
Income Statement Analysis (Million $)										
Revs.	308	152	187	191	83.7	46.7	35.1	24.7	22.2	NA
Oper. Inc.	74.9	18.0	30.7	50.8	14.7	7.7	4.9	4.0	2.3	NA
Depr.	33.1	28.2	28.1	17.5	10.0	5.3	2.9	2.3	1.8	NA
Int. Exp.	5.0	4.1	4.5	1.0	1.6	1.1	0.4	0.3	0.4	NA
Pretax Inc.	38.0	-13.5	-0.2	35.1	2.0	1.8	2.3	1.7	0.9	NA
Eff. Tax Rate	37%	NM	NM	37%	NM	NM	NM	7.32%	41%	NA
Net Inc.	23.8	-9.1	-0.3	22.2	4.3	1.9	2.5	1.6	0.6	NA
Balance Sheet & Other Fin. Data (Million $)										
Cash	59.4	8.8	9.0	23.3	4.0	2.5	3.4	4.0	2.1	NA
Curr. Assets	168	58.8	53.5	77.0	35.5	16.8	16.4	10.6	7.2	NA
Total Assets	411	236	237	203	87.9	43.8	31.7	18.4	13.6	NA
Curr. Liab.	56.9	31.7	23.0	30.5	17.9	10.5	11.2	6.3	7.5	NA
LT Debt	19.9	50.0	47.1	21.8	25.7	12.9	6.0	2.1	2.3	NA
Common Eqty.	303	153	157	147	43.5	20.4	14.5	10.1	3.8	NA
Total Cap.	353	204	214	169	69.2	33.3	20.4	12.2	6.1	NA
Cap. Exp.	34.1	19.1	34.1	34.9	24.0	16.5	9.4	3.8	2.2	NA
Cash Flow	56.9	19.0	27.8	39.7	14.2	7.2	5.4	3.9	2.4	NA
Curr. Ratio	2.9	1.9	2.3	2.5	2.0	1.6	1.5	1.7	1.0	NA
% LT Debt of Cap.	5.7	24.5	22.1	12.9	37.2	38.8	29.2	17.3	37.8	NA
% Net Inc.of Revs.	7.7	NM	NM	11.7	5.1	4.1	7.2	6.3	4.6	NA
% Ret. on Assets	7.3	NM	NM	15.3	6.5	5.1	10.1	9.7	4.1	NA
% Ret. on Equity	10.4	NM	NM	23.4	13.4	11.0	20.6	22.5	14.8	NA

Data as orig reptd.; bef. results of disc opers/spec. items. Per share data adj. for stk. divs. Bold denotes diluted EPS (FASB 128)-prior periods restated. E-Estimated. NA-Not Available. NM-Not Meaningful. NR-Not Ranked.

Office—Post Office Box 1416, 4510 Lamesa Highway, Snyder, TX 79550. **Tel**—(915) 573-1104. **Website**—http://www.patenergy.com **Chairman**—M. S. Siegel. **CEO**—C. A. Talbott. **Pres & COO**—A. G. Patterson. **CFO and Investor Contact**—Jonathan D. Nelson (915-573-1104). **Dirs**—S. D. Armour III, S. DeGroat, R. C. Gist, A. G. Patterson, K. Peak, V. A. Rossi Jr., M. S. Siegel, C. A. Talbott. **Transfer Agent & Registrar**—Continental Stock Transfer & Trust Co. **Incorporated**—Formed in 1978; reincorporated in Delaware in 1993. **Empl**— 3,062. **S&P Analyst:** T. J. Vital

Rowan Companies

NYSE Symbol **RDC**

In S&P 500

18-AUG-01

Industry:
Oil & Gas (Drilling & Equipment)

Summary: This company performs contract oil and natural gas drilling, provides contract aviation services, and builds heavy equipment and offshore drilling rigs.

S&P Opinion: Accumulate (★★★★)

Recent Price • 17.20
52 Wk Range • 34.25-16.40
Yield • Nil
12-Mo. P/E • 14.0

Quantitative Evaluations

Outlook
(1 Lowest—5 Highest)
• **4**

Fair Value
• **21.80**

Risk
• **High**

Earn./Div. Rank
• **B-**

Technical Eval.
• **Bearish** since 6/01

Rel. Strength Rank
(1 Lowest—99 Highest)
• **14**

Insider Activity
• **Neutral**

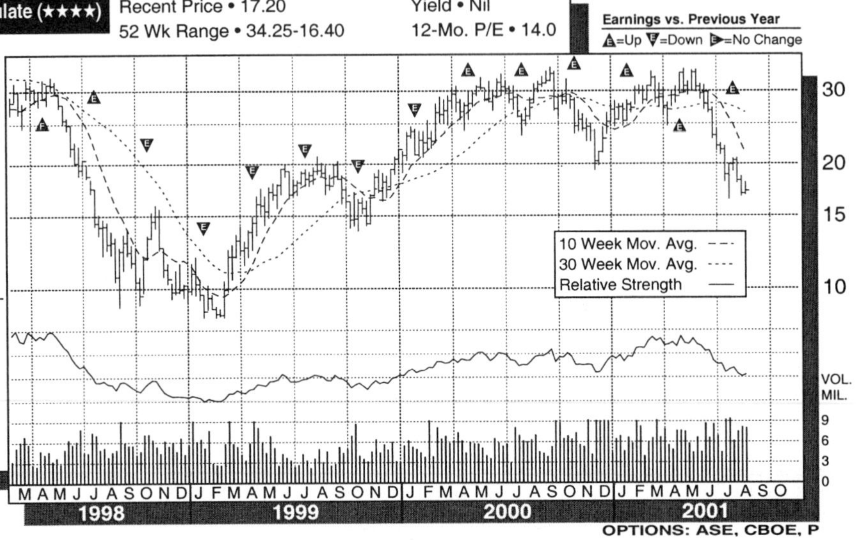

OPTIONS: ASE, CBOE, P

Overview - 16-JUL-01

Operating income should climb over 90% in 2001, on continued strong worldwide drilling activity, despite volatile domestic natural gas prices that may affect third quarter domestic revenues. In the second quarter, offshore utilization rates declined to 90%, from 97% in the first quarter, but dayrates rose 4.8%, to $61,100. Land rig utilization rates were 84% (76% in the first quarter), and dayrates were up 28%, to $14,300. Drilling revenues should benefit from price hikes driven by limited rig availability, demand for natural gas, and recovering international markets. RDC continues to keep contracts short, to benefit from new international opportunities. Manufacturing should show gains, on spare part and custom fabrication work. Aviation revenues will rise modestly. Margins should widen, as dayrates rise and fixed assets are put back to work; however, labor costs will rise.

Valuation - 16-JUL-01

Over the past month, the shares dropped sharply, in a sector sell-off reflecting end of quarter window dressing and investor concern over slowing economies. In June, we downgraded the shares to accumulate, from buy, on temporary weakness in dayrates in the Gulf of Mexico: with certain production targets met, budget approval is being sought for new projects, and some large producers remain on the sidelines for the summer. However, international deepwater drilling is accelerating. We expect upstream spending by producers to rise at least 20% in 2001. RDC should benefit from the favorable outlook for this sector. With the balance sheet is strong and the shares were recently trading at only 9X our 2002 EPS estimate, in line with peer levels, and with a fleet focused on the Gulf of Mexico, we recommend accumulation.

Key Stock Statistics

S&P EPS Est. 2001	1.43	Tang. Bk. Value/Share	11.17
P/E on S&P Est. 2001	12.0	Beta	1.53
S&P EPS Est. 2002	2.08	Shareholders	2,400
Dividend Rate/Share	Nil	Market cap. (B)	$ 1.6
Shs. outstg. (M)	94.3	Inst. holdings	80%
Avg. daily vol. (M)	1.481		

Value of $10,000 invested 5 years ago: $ 11,213

Fiscal Year Ending Dec. 31

	2001	2000	1999	1998	1997	1996
Revenues (Million $)						
1Q	193.5	127.7	100.0	183.9	144.8	126.8
2Q	210.4	143.2	119.2	204.2	164.8	137.2
3Q	—	190.8	119.9	183.5	195.5	154.7
4Q	—	184.2	121.4	134.7	190.3	152.5
Yr.	—	646.0	460.6	706.4	695.3	571.2
Earnings Per Share ($)						
1Q	**0.33**	**0.07**	**-0.12**	**0.48**	**0.09**	**0.03**
2Q	**0.36**	**0.12**	**-0.03**	**0.50**	**0.46**	**0.15**
3Q	**E0.41**	**0.27**	**0.01**	**0.37**	**0.61**	**0.26**
4Q	**E0.33**	**0.29**	**0.03**	**0.06**	**0.60**	**0.27**
Yr.	**E1.43**	**0.74**	**-0.12**	**1.43**	**1.76**	**0.70**

Next earnings report expected: mid October

Dividend Data

Common dividends, paid since 1964, were omitted in 1986.

Rowan Companies, Inc.

Business Summary - 16-JUL-01

Rowan Companies, a major provider of international and domestic contract drilling and aviation services, also operates a mini-steel mill, a manufacturing facility that produces heavy equipment, and a marine construction division.

As of year-end 2000, RDC owned a fleet of 23 offshore rigs, including 22 jackup rigs and one semisubmersible capable of drilling in water depths up to 1,200 ft. It also owns 14 land drilling rigs. Drilling operations (65% of 2000 revenues; 91% of operating profit) are conducted primarily in the Gulf of Mexico, the North Sea, and offshore eastern Canada.

The company's jackup rigs perform both exploratory and development drilling, and, in certain areas, well workover operations. Its larger, deepwater jackups can drill to depths of 20,000 ft. to 30,000 ft. in maximum water depths of 250 ft. to 550 ft. At December 31, 2000, RDC's offshore fleet included 15 cantilever jack-up rigs, with three harsh environment Gorilla Class rigs, two enhanced Super Gorilla class rigs, seven conventional jackup rigs (including four rigs with skid base capability), and one semisubmersible rig. The company operates two of the cantilever jackup rigs under sale/leaseback arrangements expiring in 2008. The Gorilla Class rigs (Gorillas II, III and IV) are heavier-duty rigs intended to drill up to 30,000 ft. in water depths up to 328 ft. in extreme hostile environments (winds up to 100 miles per hour and seas up to 90 ft.). During 1998, RDC launched the first of three Super Gorilla Class rigs, Rowan Gorilla V, an enhanced Gorilla Class rig and the world's largest bottom supported mobile offshore drilling unit; in June 2000 it launched Rowan Gorilla VI. Two additional Super Gorilla rigs, VII and VIII, are scheduled for completion at the end of 2001 and in the 2003 third quarter, respectively.

RDC's Gulf of Mexico rig utilization rate rose to 94% in 2000, from 69% in 1999; average dayrates increased 91%. The fleet grew from 17 to 22 units in 2000, following the relocation of two units from the North Sea (essentially withdrawing RDC from the North Sea market in March 2000) and offshore eastern Canada, and the delivery of Gorilla VI.

LeTourneau (16%; 6%) operates a mini-steel mill that recycles scrap and produces steel plate; a manufacturing facility that produces heavy equipment such as front-end loaders; and a marine group that has designed and/or built about 33% of all mobile offshore jackup drilling rigs, including all 22 operated by the company. The Gorilla and Super Gorilla offshore drilling rigs are made by the LeTourneau division.

Era Aviation (19%; 3%) provides contract and charter helicopter and fixed wing aviation services in Alaska, Louisiana, Texas, and the western U.S. Its fleet consisted of 94 helicopters and 19 fixed-wing aircraft as of March 30, 2001.

Per Share Data ($) (Year Ended Dec. 31)	2000	1999	1998	1997	1996	1995	1994	1993	1992	1991
Tangible Bk. Val.	11.17	8.69	8.77	7.53	5.80	5.06	5.25	5.49	5.13	6.11
Cash Flow	1.36	0.54	2.00	2.28	1.25	0.37	-0.33	0.49	-0.31	0.19
Earnings	0.74	-0.12	1.43	1.76	0.70	-0.22	-0.27	-0.17	-1.01	-0.53
Dividends	Nil	Nil	Nil	Nil	Nil	Nil	Nil	Nil	Nil	Nil
Payout Ratio	Nil	Nil	Nil	Nil	Nil	Nil	Nil	Nil	Nil	Nil
Prices - High	34.25	21.68	32.50	43.93	24.50	10.00	9.25	10.75	9.37	11.37
- Low	19.06	8.50	9.00	16.75	8.87	5.37	5.75	6.62	4.62	4.75
P/E Ratio - High	46	NM	23	25	35	NM	NM	NM	NM	NM
- Low	26	NM	6	10	13	NM	NM	NM	NM	NM
Income Statement Analysis (Million $)										
Revs.	646	461	706	695	571	471	438	353	250	272
Oper. Inc.	170	45.1	232	230	127	48.3	49.4	59.3	0.7	29.9
Depr.	58.9	54.7	49.7	47.1	47.9	50.6	50.8	51.9	51.4	52.7
Int. Exp.	12.1	11.5	1.2	16.2	27.5	27.7	27.5	25.4	26.3	21.4
Pretax Inc.	111	-14.5	194	173	60.5	-17.7	-22.5	-13.5	-73.3	-38.0
Eff. Tax Rate	37%	NM	36%	9.73%	NM	NM	NM	NM	NM	NM
Net Inc.	70.2	-9.7	124	156	61.3	-18.4	-23.0	-13.3	-73.8	-38.7
Balance Sheet & Other Fin. Data (Million $)										
Cash	193	87.1	149	108	97.2	90.0	111	117	30.0	235
Curr. Assets	483	325	366	412	317	273	254	216	103	303
Total Assets	1,678	1,356	1,249	1,122	899	802	805	765	684	896
Curr. Liab.	104	202	79.6	81.5	85.3	73.0	58.0	44.0	42.0	177
LT Debt	372	297	310	256	267	248	249	207	213	221
Common Eqty.	1,053	724	730	653	496	429	442	460	376	445
Total Cap.	1,516	1,099	1,116	984	765	681	695	672	594	671
Cap. Exp.	216	205	248	181	118	33.9	33.0	22.0	40.0	58.0
Cash Flow	129	45.0	174	204	109	32.1	27.8	38.7	-22.4	13.9
Curr. Ratio	4.6	1.6	4.6	5.1	3.7	3.8	4.4	4.9	2.5	1.7
% LT Debt of Cap.	24.5	27.0	27.8	26.0	34.9	36.4	35.7	30.8	35.9	32.9
% Net Inc.of Revs.	10.9	NM	17.6	22.5	10.8	NM	NM	NM	NM	NM
% Ret. on Assets	4.6	NM	10.5	15.5	7.2	NM	NM	NM	NM	NM
% Ret. on Equity	7.9	NM	18.0	27.2	13.3	NM	NM	NM	NM	NM

Data as orig reptd.; bef. results of disc opers/spec. items. Per share data adj. for stk. divs. Bold denotes diluted EPS (FASB 128)-prior periods restated. E-Estimated. NA-Not Available. NM-Not Meaningful. NR-Not Ranked.

Office—2800 Post Oak Blvd., Suite 5450, Houston, TX 77056-6127. **Tel**—(713) 621 7800. **Website**—http://www.rowancompanies.com **Chrmn, Pres & CEO**—C. R. Palmer. **SVP-Fin & Treas**—E. E. Thiele. **Secy**—M. H. Hay. **VP & Investor Contact**—William C. Provine (713-960-7575). **Dirs**—H. O. Boswell, H. M. Brinkhorst, R. G. Croyle, W. T. Fox III, F. R. Lausen, H. E. Lentz, D. F. McNease, C. B. Moynihan, C. R. Palmer. **Transfer Agent & Registrar**—ComputerShare Investor Services, LLC. **Incorporated**—in Delaware in 1947. **Empl**— 4,862. **S&P Analyst:** T. J. Vital

STANDARD
&POOR'S
STOCK REPORTS

Tidewater Inc.

NYSE Symbol **TDW**

In S&P MidCap 400

21-AUG-01

Industry:
Oil & Gas (Drilling & Equipment)

Summary: This company operates the largest fleet of vessels serving the international offshore energy business.

S&P Opinion: Accumulate (★★★★)

Recent Price • 34.24 | Yield • 1.8%

52 Wk Range • 52.95-31.60 | 12-Mo. P/E • 16.5

Quantitative Evaluations

Outlook (1 Lowest—5 Highest) • **4**

Fair Value • **40.10**

Risk • **Average**

Earn./Div. Rank • **B+**

Technical Eval. • **Bearish** since 6/01

Rel. Strength Rank (1 Lowest—99 Highest) • **28**

Insider Activity • **NA**

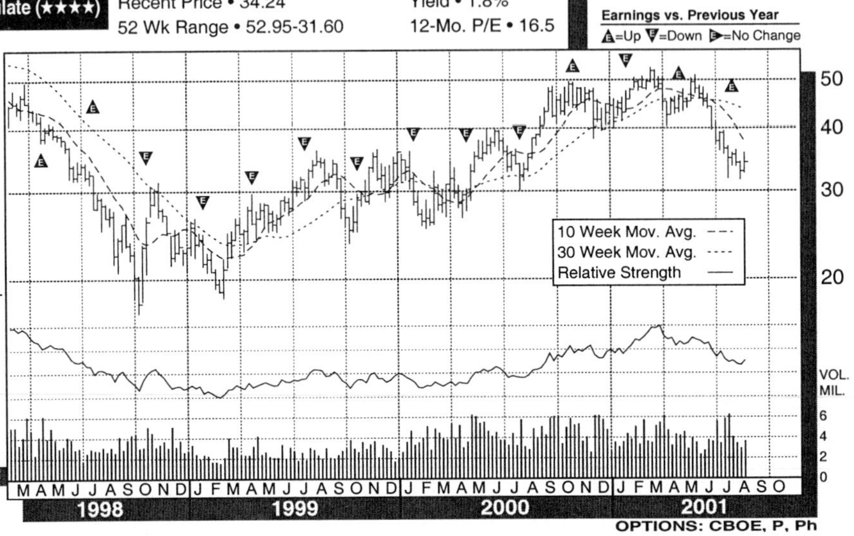

OPTIONS: CBOE, P, Ph

Overview - 20-AUG-01

Operating income should soar over 200% in FY 02 (Mar.), on rebounding international markets. The Gulf of Mexico jackup market is experiencing what we believe to be temporary weakness in dayrates. With certain production targets met, budget approval is being sought for new projects, and certain large producers remain on the sidelines for the summer. However, TDW's vessels have not been affected by the pullback in the Gulf of Mexico. In the first quarter, U.S. dayrates for TDW's boats rose 7.9%, to $6,437, and utilization rates were up to 66.7%, from 63.7% in FY 01. International dayrates rose 6.7%, to $5,163, and should accelerate, on the rollover of short-term contracts; utilization rates increased to 75.2%, from 74.8%. With demand for deepwater vessels running ahead of its newbuild program, TDW took delivery of two deepwater anchor handlers and one supply boat in the FY 01 fourth quarter.

Valuation - 20-AUG-01

The shares have been lackluster performers thus far in 2001, on investor concerns over TDW's newbuilds and fleet acquisitions in view of slowing economies. However, the boats fill a void in the market for deepwater vessels. With exploration and production (E&P) spending accelerating on new deepwater projects, we estimate that E&P spending will climb over 20% in 2001. In November 2000, the company strengthened its deepwater, high-end development exposure by purchasing eight vessels from Sanko for $160 million in cash. In addition, a $305 million new-build program should give TDW the largest platform supply vessels in the Gulf of Mexico. With no debt, the shares trading in line with peer levels at 11X our FY 02 EPS estimate, and the supply boat market heating up, we view TDW as attractive to accumulate.

Key Stock Statistics

S&P EPS Est. 2002	3.20	Tang. Bk. Value/Share	14.56
P/E on S&P Est. 2002	10.7	Beta	1.08
S&P EPS Est. 2003	3.37	Shareholders	2,137
Dividend Rate/Share	0.60	Market cap. (B)	$ 2.0
Shs. outstg. (M)	60.5	Inst. holdings	76%
Avg. daily vol. (M)	0.660		

Value of $10,000 invested 5 years ago: $ 10,084

Fiscal Year Ending Mar. 31

	2002	2001	2000	1999	1998	1997
Revenues (Million $)						
1Q	190.6	136.9	154.5	284.9	230.4	175.9
2Q	—	146.1	132.9	254.2	270.4	193.9
3Q	—	159.1	141.8	233.0	280.7	212.4
4Q	—	174.5	139.6	196.9	278.6	220.8
Yr.	—	616.7	574.8	969.0	1,060	803.0
Earnings Per Share ($)						
1Q	**0.69**	**0.15**	**0.30**	**1.05**	**0.80**	**0.36**
2Q	**E0.82**	**0.47**	**0.34**	**0.98**	**1.01**	**0.50**
3Q	**E0.87**	**0.38**	**0.40**	**0.71**	**1.15**	**0.66**
4Q	**E0.82**	**0.52**	**0.34**	**0.93**	**1.05**	**0.71**
Yr.	**E3.20**	**1.53**	**1.37**	**3.68**	**3.99**	**2.23**

Next earnings report expected: NA

Dividend Data (Dividends have been paid since 1992.)

Amount ($)	Date Decl.	Ex-Div. Date	Stock of Record	Payment Date
0.150	Nov. 28	Dec. 06	Dec. 08	Dec. 18 '00
0.150	Jan. 18	Jan. 25	Jan. 29	Feb. 07 '01
0.150	May. 31	Jun. 07	Jun. 11	Jun. 21 '01
0.150	Jul. 26	Aug. 02	Aug. 06	Aug. 16 '01

Tidewater Inc.

Business Summary - 20-AUG-01

As the world's largest operator of offshore service vessels, Tidewater provides equipment and services worldwide to the offshore oil and gas industry. The company has grown through acquisitions in recent years, and, as of FY 01 (Mar.), its fleet numbered about 570 vessels, which include towing-supply (78% of FY 01 vessel revenues), offshore tugs (10%), crew/utility (12%), and other major classes of vessels. With 66% of its FY 01 vessel revenues outside the U.S., TDW operates in the world's major offshore drilling regions, including the Gulf of Mexico, Australia, Brazil, Egypt, India, Indonesia, Malaysia, Mexico, Trinidad, Venezuela, West Africa, the North Sea, and the Persian Gulf.

Marine services and support functions include the towing and anchor-handling of mobile drilling rigs and equipment; transporting supplies and personnel necessary to sustain drilling, workover and production activities; and supporting pipelaying and construction activities. Wholly owned Quality Shipyards, Inc. operates two Houma, LA, shipyards that build, modify and repair drydock vessels. The majority of Quality's business in FY 01 was related to repairs and modifications of TDW's vessels.

Worldwide vessel utilization rates in FY 01 were 70% (65% in FY 00). The domestic fleet experienced 60% utilization (54%), while the international fleet utilization was at 76% (71%). Worldwide fleet average day rates were $4,539 ($4,160). Domestic fleet day rates averaged $4,803 ($3,558), while international rates averaged $4,415 ($4,423).

TDW has continued to build its presence in the deepwater, high-end development segment of the offshore vessel market. In January 2000, TDW announced a new-build program for 12 vessels for about $305 million. Delivery is expected in 2002, and includes five large anchor-handling vessels and seven large platform supply vessels capable of working in most deepwater markets in the world. In August 2000, the company purchased one platform supply vessel for $22.5 million from The Sanko Steamship Co. Ltd. (Sanko), and agreed to buy two 220 ft. UT755 platform supply vessels for $26.4 million. In October 2000, TDW sold its 40% interest in National Marine Service for $31 million, and agreed to purchase two 236 ft. UT755L platform supply vessels for about $30 million. The vessels are scheduled for delivery in 2000 and 2001. In November 2000, TDW purchased eight vessels (including four large anchor-handling, towing supply boats, and four large North Sea type platform supply vessels) from Sanko for $160 million. In December 2000, TDW sold four vessels (two offshore tugs, two crewboats) for about $17 million.

TDW's scrapping program has continued to bring down the average age of its vessels, which averaged 19 years as of the end of FY 01.

Per Share Data ($)

(Year Ended Mar. 31)	2001	2000	1999	1998	1997	1996	1995	1994	1993	1992
Tangible Bk. Val.	14.03	12.82	11.90	10.80	12.40	11.57	10.90	10.50	10.36	10.22
Cash Flow	2.94	2.85	5.33	5.49	3.67	2.55	2.42	2.25	2.03	2.01
Earnings	1.53	1.37	3.68	3.99	2.34	1.23	0.80	0.67	0.53	0.50
Dividends	0.60	0.60	0.60	0.60	0.57	0.47	0.40	0.40	0.33	Nil
Payout Ratio	39%	44%	16%	15%	25%	39%	50%	60%	43%	Nil
Cal. Yrs.	2000	1999	1998	1997	1996	1995	1994	1993	1992	1991
Prices - High	49.68	36.50	55.18	70.50	50.00	31.62	25.00	27.00	21.00	18.50
- Low	25.18	18.31	17.06	35.87	29.37	16.50	18.00	16.37	11.37	9.87
P/E Ratio - High	32	27	15	18	21	26	31	40	40	37
- Low	16	13	5	9	13	13	23	24	21	20

Income Statement Analysis (Million $)

	2001	2000	1999	1998	1997	1996	1995	1994	1993	1992
Revs.	617	575	969	1,060	803	643	539	522	476	547
Oper. Inc.	162	149	358	454	288	196	147	140	130	141
Depr.	79.5	82.5	94.8	91.4	82.3	82.4	86.6	83.7	79.9	79.6
Int. Exp.	1.2	0.7	2.4	24.7	1.0	5.9	4.7	7.9	12.3	18.6
Pretax Inc.	127	106	278	358	217	111	68.9	59.7	42.7	43.0
Eff. Tax Rate	32%	27%	24%	32%	33%	31%	36%	36%	29%	39%
Net Inc.	86.1	76.6	211	243	146	76.2	42.6	36.1	27.8	26.3

Balance Sheet & Other Fin. Data (Million $)

	2001	2000	1999	1998	1997	1996	1995	1994	1993	1992
Cash	95.2	227	10.4	25.0	41.1	28.8	15.0	107	109	113
Curr. Assets	289	404	281	319	269	209	201	286	297	289
Total Assets	1,505	1,432	1,394	1,493	1,039	978	902	810	839	846
Curr. Liab.	83.6	74.8	82.3	204	94.7	85.7	101	130	96.0	111
LT Debt	Nil	Nil	Nil	25.0	Nil	Nil	100	2.0	96.0	124
Common Eqty.	1,178	1,114	1,068	999	770	739	580	557	548	536
Total Cap.	1,334	1,259	1,197	1,183	865	815	738	615	699	718
Cap. Exp.	303	57.4	48.3	82.5	58.0	46.1	300	53.3	52.4	39.0
Cash Flow	166	159	306	334	228	159	129	120	108	106
Curr. Ratio	3.5	5.4	3.4	1.6	2.8	2.4	2.0	2.2	3.1	2.6
% LT Debt of Cap.	Nil	Nil	Nil	2.1	Nil	Nil	13.5	0.3	13.7	17.3
% Net Inc.of Revs.	14.0	13.3	21.7	22.9	18.2	11.8	7.9	6.9	0.8	4.8
% Ret. on Assets	5.9	5.4	14.6	19.2	14.5	7.5	5.0	4.4	3.3	3.4
% Ret. on Equity	7.5	7.0	20.4	27.5	19.4	10.7	7.5	6.5	5.1	5.2

Data as orig. reptd.; bef. results of disc. opers. and/or spec. items. Per share data adj. for stk. divs. as of ex-div. date. E-Estimated. NA-Not Available. NM-Not Meaningful. NR-Not Ranked.

Office—601 Poydras Street, Suite 1900, New Orleans, LA 70130. **Tel**—(504) 568-1010. **Website**—http://www.tdw.com **Chrmn, Pres & CEO**—W. C. O'Malley. **SVP, CFO & Investor Contact**—J. Keith Lousteau. **SVP & Secy**—C. F. Laborde. **Dirs**—R. H. Boh, D. T. Bollinger, A. R. Carlson, J. C. Madonna, P. W. Murrill, W. C. O'Malley, L. Pollack, J. H. Roff Jr., D. G. Russell. **Transfer Agent & Registrar**—First National Bank of Boston, c/o EquiServe, Boston. **Incorporated**—in Delaware in 1956. **Empl**— 6,400. **S&P Analyst:** T. J. Vital

STANDARD
&POOR'S
STOCK REPORTS

Valero Energy

NYSE Symbol **VLO**

In S&P MidCap 400

18-AUG-01

Industry:
Oil & Gas (Refining & Marketing)

Summary: This company is one of the largest independent U.S. petroleum refiners and marketers, and the largest on the Gulf Coast.

S&P Opinion: Accumulate (★★★★)

Recent Price • 35.84
52 Wk Range • 52.60-28.87
Yield • 0.9%
12-Mo. P/E • 3.6

Quantitative Evaluations

Outlook
(1 Lowest—5 Highest)
• 5

Fair Value
• 47.90

Risk
• Low

Earn./Div. Rank
• NR

Technical Eval.
• Neutral since 8/01

Rel. Strength Rank
(1 Lowest—99 Highest)
• 40

Insider Activity
• NA

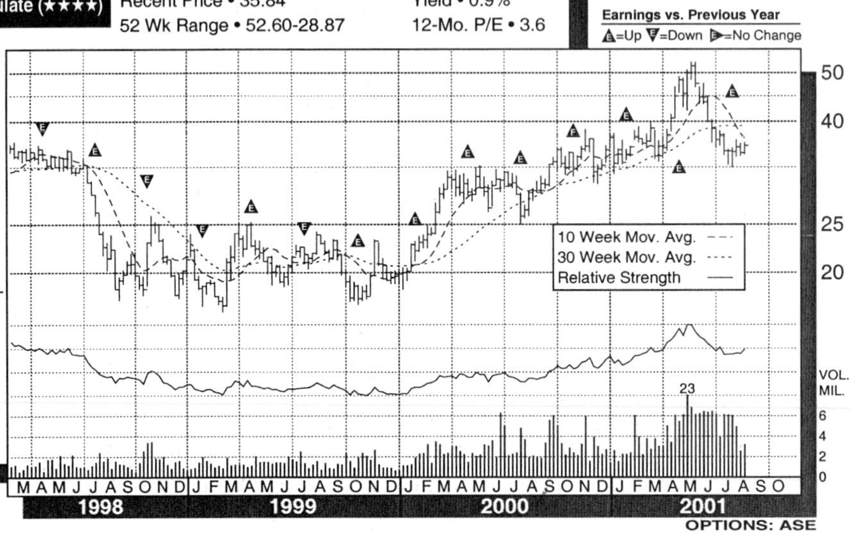

Overview - 18-APR-01

The proposed acquisition of Huntway Refining would expand the company's presence on the profitable West Coast, provide synergies with the adjacent Benicia refinery, add throughput, and be accretive to earnings. In addition, the $78 million acquisition, anticipated to close in June, would mark VLO's entry into the West Coast asphalt market, diversifying its product mix. Overall, we expect the company's throughput to increase 9.1%, aided by a full year of Benicia contributions and some small expansions. Despite demand reductions associated with an economic slowdown, industrywide margins should remain strong in 2001 and for the foreseeable future, as stringent regulations should continue to result in tight inventories. Results will be tempered by high prices for natural gas, a feedstock. Valero's interest expense should be lower, on reduced debt levels.

Valuation - 18-APR-01

The shares were recently up 21% in 2001, versus a 16% rise for S&P's Refining & Marketing (R&M) index. With the stock trading at only 6.4X estimated 2001 EPS, a discount to VLO's peer group average of 9.0X, we recently initiated coverage of the stock with an accumulate recommendation. The company is especially leveraged to the higher margin RFG Phase 2 and CARB gasolines. In addition, VLO's refineries are designed to use cheaper-grade crude feedstocks than other R&Ms. In general, we believe VLO's refineries are better equipped than those of its peers to deal with new regulations that require sulfur reductions in gasoline and diesel fuel over the next few years. As a result, the company will not be forced to spend substantial funds for upgrades. In addition to debt reductions, we expect free cash flow to be used for a dividend increase; the dividend yield was recently under 1%, versus a 2.8% average yield for VLO's peer group.

Key Stock Statistics

S&P EPS Est. 2001	8.06	Tang. Bk. Value/Share	25.10
P/E on S&P Est. 2001	4.4	Beta	1.20
S&P EPS Est. 2002	6.10	Shareholders	14,000
Dividend Rate/Share	0.32	Market cap. (B)	$ 2.2
Shs. outstg. (M)	61.2	Inst. holdings	94%
Avg. daily vol. (M)	0.832		

Value of $10,000 invested 5 years ago: NA

Fiscal Year Ending Dec. 31

	2001	2000	1999	1998	1997	1996
Revenues (Million $)						
1Q	3,769	2,929	1,337	1,362	821.8	—
2Q	4,499	3,373	1,825	1,448	1,363	—
3Q	—	4,249	2,162	1,339	1,976	—
4Q	—	4,121	2,638	1,390	1,596	—
Yr.	—	14,671	7,961	5,539	5,756	2,758
Earnings Per Share ($)						
1Q	**2.13**	**0.54**	**-0.05**	**-0.11**	0.45	—
2Q	**4.23**	**1.51**	**-0.39**	**0.70**	**0.50**	—
3Q	—	**2.01**	**0.40**	**0.08**	**0.91**	—
4Q	—	**1.47**	**0.29**	**-1.53**	**0.22**	—
Yr.	—	**5.60**	**0.25**	**-0.84**	**2.03**	0.51

Next earnings report expected: mid October

Dividend Data (Dividends have been paid since 1997.)

Amount ($)	Date Decl.	Ex-Div. Date	Stock of Record	Payment Date
0.080	Oct. 19	Nov. 13	Nov. 15	Dec. 13 '00
0.080	Jan. 18	Feb. 12	Feb. 14	Mar. 14 '01
0.080	May. 10	May. 24	May. 29	Jun. 13 '01
0.080	Jul. 19	Aug. 13	Aug. 15	Sep. 12 '01

A Division of The **McGraw·Hill** *Companies*

Business Summary - 18-APR-01

Valero Energy is one of the largest independent U.S. refining and marketing companies. It mainly produces premium, environmentally clean products such as reformulated gasoline, low-sulfur diesel and oxygenates. It also produces a substantial slate of middle distillates, jet fuel and petrochemicals. The company aims to remain a premier, independent refining and marketing company that focuses on innovative, efficient upgrading of low-cost feedstocks into higher-value products.

Revenue breakdown by product in 2000 was as follows: gasoline and blending components 53%; distillates 26%; petrochemicals 3%; lubes and asphalts 2%; and other 16%.

The company owns and operates six refineries, in Texas, California, Louisiana and New Jersey, with a combined throughput capacity of approximately 1,000,000 barrels per day (bpd) as of December 2000. The refineries are located in Corpus Christi, TX (capacity of 215,000 bpd); Texas City, TX (210,000); Paulsboro, NJ (185,000); Houston, TX (115,000); Krotz Springs, LA (85,000); and Benicia, CA (165,000).

VLO's strategy is to upgrade its refineries to increase both output and overall refining complexity and flexibility, enhancing its ability to process lower-cost feedstocks into value-added premium products. The company processes a wide range of feedstocks including sour crude oils, intermediates and residual fuel oils, or resid, which can typically be purchased at a discount to West Texas Intermediate, a benchmark crude oil. Approximately 75% of the company's feedstock is comprised of sour crudes, intermediates and resid.

Approximately 60% of the company's total gasoline production is premium-grade gasoline, reformulated gasoline, or RFG, and gasoline that meets the specifications of the California Air Resources Board, or CARB gasoline, all of which sell at a premium to conventional grades of gasoline. VLO can also produce up to 75% of its distillate slate as low-sulfur diesel and jet fuel, which sell for a premium over high-sulfur heating oil.

VLO sells refined products under spot and term contracts to bulk and truck rack customers at more than 200 locations in 34 states throughout the U.S., and in selected export markets in Latin America. The company also sells gasoline at retail service stations in California.

In 2000, the company made $304 million of capital investments, including $195 million for capital expenditures. In 2001, VLO expects to spend $390 million for capital investments, including $290 million for capital expenditures.

In the 2000 second quarter, VLO acquired ExxonMobil's Benicia refinery and California retail system, including 260 distribution arrangements with independently owned service stations, and 80 Exxon-branded service stations, for $895 million. The transaction was immediately accretive to earnings.

Per Share Data ($) (Year Ended Dec. 31)	2000	1999	1998	1997	1996	1995	1994	1993	1992	1991
Tangible Bk. Val.	25.10	19.35	19.40	20.64	NA	NA	NA	NA	NA	NA
Cash Flow	7.45	1.88	0.56	3.11	NA	NA	NA	NA	NA	NA
Earnings	5.79	0.25	-0.84	2.03	0.51	NA	NA	NA	NA	NA
Dividends	0.32	0.32	0.22	0.16	NA	NA	NA	NA	NA	NA
Payout Ratio	6%	128%	NM	8%	NA	NA	NA	NA	NA	NA
Prices - High	38.62	25.31	36.50	35.12	NA	NA	NA	NA	NA	NA
- Low	18.50	16.68	17.62	26.93	NA	NA	NA	NA	NA	NA
P/E Ratio - High	7	NM	NM	17	NA	NA	NA	NA	NA	NA
- Low	3	NM	NM	13	NA	NA	NA	NA	NA	NA
Income Statement Analysis (Million $)										
Revs.	14,671	7,961	5,539	5,756	2,758	NA	NA	NA	NA	NA
Oper. Inc.	723	162	198	276	145	NA	NA	NA	NA	NA
Depr. & Depl.	112	92.4	78.7	65.2	55.0	NA	NA	NA	NA	NA
Int. Exp.	83.0	55.4	32.5	42.5	41.4	NA	NA	NA	NA	NA
Pretax Inc.	528	20.2	-83.1	176	39.1	NA	NA	NA	NA	NA
Eff. Tax Rate	36%	29%	NM	36%	43%	NA	NA	NA	NA	NA
Net Inc.	339	14.3	-47.3	112	22.5	NA	NA	NA	NA	NA
Balance Sheet & Other Fin. Data (Million $)										
Cash	14.6	60.1	11.2	9.9	NA	NA	NA	NA	NA	NA
Curr. Assets	1,285	829	640	789	352	NA	NA	NA	NA	NA
Total Assets	4,308	2,979	2,726	2,493	1,986	NA	NA	NA	NA	NA
Curr. Liab.	1,039	719	498	597	301	NA	NA	NA	NA	NA
LT Debt	1,042	785	822	430	353	NA	NA	NA	NA	NA
Common Eqty.	1,527	1,085	1,085	1,159	1,076	NA	NA	NA	NA	NA
Total Cap.	3,149	2,146	2,117	1,846	1,655	NA	NA	NA	NA	NA
Cap. Exp.	195	101	166	69.2	NA	NA	NA	NA	NA	NA
Cash Flow	451	107	31.4	172	66.2	NA	NA	NA	NA	NA
Curr. Ratio	1.2	1.2	1.3	1.3	1.2	NA	NA	NA	NA	NA
% LT Debt of Cap.	33.0	36.5	NM	62.8	21.3	NA	NA	NA	NA	NA
% Ret. on Assets	9.3	0.5	NM	4.9	NA	NA	NA	NA	NA	NA
% Ret. on Equity	26.0	1.3	NM	10.0	NA	NA	NA	NA	NA	NA

Data as orig reptd.; bef. results of disc opers/spec. items. Per share data adj. for stk. divs. Bold denotes diluted EPS (FASB 128)-prior periods restated. E-Estimated. NA-Not Available. NM-Not Meaningful. NR-Not Ranked.

Office—One Valero Place, San Antonio, TX 78212. **Tel**—(210) 370-2000. **Website**—www.valero.com **Chrmn, Pres & CEO**—W. E. Greehey. **EVP & COO**—G. C. King. **EVP & CFO**—J. D. Gibbons. **Investor Contact**—Lee Bailey (210-370-2139). **Dirs**—R. K. Calgaard, D. M. Carlton, J. D. Choate, R. G. Dettmer, R. M. Escobedo, W. E. Greehey, L. H. Lebermann, S. K. Purcell, B. Richardson. **Transfer Agent & Registrar**—ComputerShare Investor Services, Chicago. **Incorporated**—in Delaware in 1981. **Empl**— 3,180. **S&P Analyst:** Ephraim Juskowicz

STANDARD & POOR'S
STOCK REPORTS

Vintage Petroleum

NYSE Symbol **VPI**

In S&P SmallCap 600

18-AUG-01

Industry:
Oil & Gas (Exploration & Production)

Summary: This independent oil and gas company acquires, explores and develops oil and gas properties.

S&P Opinion: Accumulate (★★★★)

Recent Price • 18.79
52 Wk Range • 27.93-15.20
Yield • 0.5%
12-Mo. P/E • 5.3

Quantitative Evaluations

Outlook
(1 Lowest—5 Highest)
• **4**

Fair Value
• **19.90**

Risk
• **Average**

Earn./Div. Rank
• **B+**

Technical Eval.
• **Bearish** since 6/01

Rel. Strength Rank
(1 Lowest—99 Highest)
• **57**

Insider Activity
• **NA**

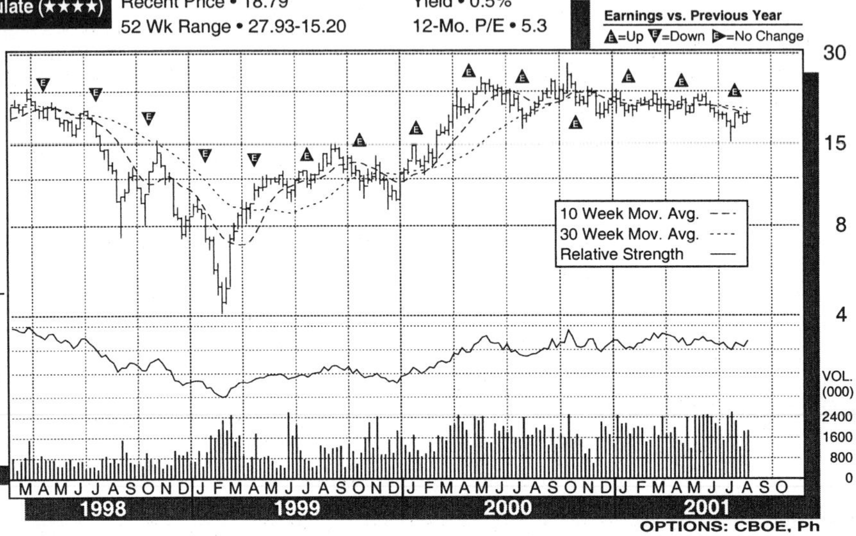

OPTIONS: CBOE, Ph

Overview - 16-JUL-01

Its recent Genesis and Cometra acquisitions give VPI exposure to the hot Canadian natural gas market. The Genesis properties are expected to significantly ramp up production; exploitation and exploration projects will focus on the West Central, Grouard and Sturgeon Lake areas of Alberta. In aggregate, we look for production in 2001 to advance 24%. However, with the recent weakening in commodity prices, we look for revenues from oil and gas to increase only 2.2%. In addition, interest expense will be substantially higher, reflecting debt associated with the acquisitions. Nevertheless, discretionary cash flow per share (DCFPS), a key industry measure, should increase 17%, to $5.94. Our EPS estimate of $3.23 assumes price forecasts of $4.87 per MMBtu for Henry Hub natural gas, and $27.66 for NYMEX WTI crude oil for 2001.

Valuation - 16-JUL-01

The shares were recently down 22% from their 2001 high reached in early June compared with a 31% drop for its peers. VPI and the S&P Exploration and Production (E&P) index were up 83% and 68%, respectively, in 2000. The group has been hurt by profit taking and lower oil and natural gas prices. Recently, we lowered our EPS estimate to $3.23 from $4.26 for 2001, and to $2.80 from $3.76 for 2002, to reflect the weak commodity environment. The stock was recently trading at $2.00 per BOE of proven reserves, a significant discount compared to an average of $5.20 for other E&Ps. This discount may be warranted, as the debt to capitalization ratio rose substantially, to 57%, following the Genesis acquisition. Nevertheless, VPI plans to immediately use free cash flow to reduce debt. Based on the industry's strong fundamentals and cash flow, we believe it is not imprudent to temporarily assume debt to add valuable assets.

Key Stock Statistics

S&P EPS Est. 2001	3.23	Tang. Bk. Value/Share	9.95
P/E on S&P Est. 2001	5.8	Beta	1.28
S&P EPS Est. 2002	2.80	Shareholders	10,000
Dividend Rate/Share	0.10	Market cap. (B)	$ 1.2
Shs. outstg. (M)	63.0	Inst. holdings	65%
Avg. daily vol. (M)	0.357		

Value of $10,000 invested 5 years ago: $ 14,942

Fiscal Year Ending Dec. 31

	2001	2000	1999	1998	1997	1996
Revenues (Million $)						
1Q	275.5	162.4	66.00	89.99	99.2	71.34
2Q	—	156.3	92.56	84.93	99.8	76.04
3Q	—	230.0	136.4	79.29	104.4	75.95
4Q	—	257.5	201.7	74.72	113.1	88.35
Yr.	—	806.2	496.7	328.9	416.6	311.7
Earnings Per Share ($)						
1Q	**1.10**	**0.62**	**-0.34**	**-0.03**	**0.41**	0.15
2Q	—	**0.42**	**0.09**	**-0.18**	**0.27**	0.20
3Q	—	**0.92**	**0.43**	**-0.19**	**0.29**	0.20
4Q	—	**1.12**	**0.92**	**-1.27**	**0.41**	0.29
Yr.	—	**3.08**	**1.24**	**-1.69**	**1.39**	**0.85**

Next earnings report expected: NA

Dividend Data (Dividends have been paid since 1992.)

Amount ($)	Date Decl.	Ex-Div. Date	Stock of Record	Payment Date
0.030	Sep. 18	Sep. 27	Sep. 29	Oct. 10 '00
0.030	Dec. 11	Dec. 20	Dec. 22	Jan. 04 '01
0.030	Mar. 15	Mar. 23	Mar. 27	Apr. 05 '01
0.035	Jun. 12	Jun. 19	Jun. 21	Jul. 03 '01

Vintage Petroleum, Inc.

Business Summary - 16-JUL-01

Vintage Petroleum is an independent oil and gas company that acquires, exploits and develops oil and gas properties. The company's domestic operations focus on the Gulf Coast, East Texas, Mid-Continent, and the West Coast. In December 2000, Vintage expanded its North American operations into Canada through the $46.2 million purchase of privately held Cometra Energy. Canadian activities were further expanded through the May 2001 acquisition of Genesis Exploration for $593 million. Other international core areas include Argentina, Bolivia and Ecuador. VPI is also involved in the gathering and marketing of natural gas and crude oil.

The company's goal is to maximize its value through profitable growth in its oil and gas reserves and production. VPI's strategy includes acquiring at favorable prices producing oil and gas properties with significant upside potential; focusing on exploitation, development and exploration activities to maximize production and ultimate reserve recovery on existing properties; exploring undeveloped properties; maintaining a low-cost operating structure; and maintaining financial flexibility. The company believes its primary strengths are its ability to add reserves at attractive prices, its technical expertise, and its low-cost operating structure.

As of December 31, 2000 (1999), proved reserves were estimated at 489.1 (468.0) million barrels of oil equivalent (MMBOE), with oil representing 65% (65%) of the total, and gas constituting the remaining 35% (35%). Based on year-end commodity prices, the present value of revenues associated with reserves was $3.0 ($2.3) billion.

Production in 2000 (1999) totaled 28.8 (24.9) MMBOE, of which 69% (68%) was oil, with the remainder gas. The average price realized, including the effects of hedging, was $25.55 ($16.62) per bbl. of oil and $3.22 ($1.89) per Mcf of gas. Production costs averaged $5.54 ($4.88) per BOE produced. Capital spending totaled $258.0 ($238.2) million. The 2001 capital budget has been set at $871 million, reflecting recent acquisitions.

Genesis was estimated to have 62.2 MMBOE of reserves, consisting of 46% oil and 54% natural gas. The acquired reserves are located in Alberta and Saskatchewan. The acquisition also provided significant exploration exposure in the Northwest Territories. In addition to reserves, Vintage acquired over 1 million net undeveloped acres, over 600 square miles of 3-D seismic, and over 15,000 miles of 2-D seismic. Net daily production associated with the Genesis properties (after royalties) was 17,800 boe, composed of 34% oil and 66% gas.

The Cometra assets consisted of 13 fields, primarily located in Alberta and British Columbia, with 2.7 MBOE of daily production. The acquisition also included processing and pipeline facilities and 146,000 net undeveloped acres.

Per Share Data ($)										
(Year Ended Dec. 31)	**2000**	**1999**	**1998**	**1997**	**1996**	**1995**	**1994**	**1993**	**1992**	**1991**
Tangible Bk. Val.	9.95	6.91	5.16	7.44	5.51	4.74	3.87	3.56	2.40	2.15
Cash Flow	4.65	3.05	0.41	3.29	2.27	1.50	1.41	1.20	0.77	0.58
Earnings	3.08	1.24	-1.69	1.39	0.84	0.27	0.33	0.41	0.26	0.20
Dividends	0.12	0.03	0.09	0.06	0.06	0.05	0.04	0.03	0.01	Nil
Payout Ratio	4%	2%	NM	4%	7%	17%	11%	6%	4%	Nil
Prices - High	27.93	15.12	23.12	25.87	17.37	11.25	11.37	13.05	7.00	4.56
- Low	11.18	4.06	7.25	12.50	9.50	8.00	7.37	6.15	2.80	2.75
P/E Ratio - High	9	12	NM	19	21	42	34	32	27	22
- Low	4	3	NM	9	11	30	22	15	11	13
Income Statement Analysis (Million $)										
Revs.	829	438	329	417	312	194	183	157	100	69.9
Oper. Inc.	477	209	92.3	225	157	86.8	77.8	65.8	34.5	24.0
Depr. Depl. & Amort.	100	108	109	99	70.1	52.3	45.8	33.2	17.4	12.8
Int. Exp.	48.4	58.7	43.7	36.8	30.1	20.2	12.0	6.9	4.5	4.2
Pretax Inc.	290	97.7	-131	89.6	56.6	15.6	22.4	28.5	13.7	10.9
Eff. Tax Rate	32%	25%	NM	19%	26%	33%	38%	41%	37%	38%
Net Inc.	197	73.4	-87.7	72.2	41.2	11.4	13.9	16.8	8.7	6.8
Balance Sheet & Other Fin. Data (Million $)										
Cash	19.5	42.7	5.2	5.8	2.8	2.5	0.4	0.6	0.6	0.3
Curr. Assets	186	154	84.1	89.7	84.7	59.1	39.3	36.6	27.1	16.4
Total Assets	1,338	1,168	1,014	990	814	648	408	384	260	144
Curr. Liab.	212	93.9	66.9	79.7	113	59.0	34.0	42.6	34.2	23.3
LT Debt	464	625	673	451	372	316	187	174	128	36.6
Common Eqty.	625	431	274	384	265	224	156	143	78.7	69.8
Total Cap.	1,122	1,072	946	907	697	585	374	342	226	121
Cap. Exp.	212	240	262	268	164	145	67.0	151	120	32.3
Cash Flow	297	181	21.3	171	111	63.6	59.7	49.9	26.0	19.6
Curr. Ratio	0.9	1.6	1.3	1.1	0.8	1.0	1.2	0.9	0.8	0.7
% LT Debt of Cap.	41.4	58.3	71.1	49.7	53.4	54.0	49.9	51.0	56.7	30.3
% Ret. on Assets	15.7	6.7	NM	8.0	5.7	2.2	3.5	4.8	4.3	5.1
% Ret. on Equity	37.4	20.8	NM	22.3	16.9	6.0	9.3	14.0	11.6	10.2

Data as orig reptd.; bef. results of disc opers/spec. items. Per share data adj. for stk. divs. Bold denotes diluted EPS (FASB 128)-prior periods restated. E-Estimated. NA-Not Available. NM-Not Meaningful. NR-Not Ranked.

Office—110 West 7th St., Tulsa, OK 74119. **Tel**—(918) 592-0101. **Website**—http://www.vintagepetroleum.com **Chrmn**—C. C. Stephenson Jr. **Pres & CEO**—S. C. George. **EVP, CFO, Secy & Treas**—W. C. Barnes. **VP & Investor Contact**—Robert E. Phaneuf. **Dirs**—W. L. Abernathy, W. C. Barnes, S. C. George, B. H. Lawrence, J. T. McNabb II, C. C. Stephenson Jr. **Transfer Agent & Registrar**—Mellon Investor Services, Ridgefield Park, NJ. **Incorporated**—in Delaware in 1983. **Empl**— 698. **S&P Analyst:** John Kartsonas

STANDARD
&POOR'S
STOCK REPORTS

XTO Energy

NYSE Symbol **XTO**
In S&P SmallCap 600

18-AUG-01

Industry:
Oil & Gas (Exploration & Production)

Summary: This oil and gas exploration and production company (formerly Cross Timbers Oil) has properties in Texas, Oklahoma, Kansas, New Mexico, Arkansas, Wyoming, Alaska and Louisiana.

S&P Opinion: Accumulate (★★★★)

Recent Price • 15.05
52 Wk Range • 21.73-10.66
Yield • 0.3%
12-Mo. P/E • 8.2

Quantitative Evaluations
Outlook
(1 Lowest—5 Highest)
• **4-**
Fair Value
• **17.20**
Risk
• **Average**
Earn./Div. Rank
• **NR**

Technical Eval.
• **Neutral** since 7/01
Rel. Strength Rank
(1 Lowest—99 Highest)
• **48**
Insider Activity
• **Neutral**

OPTIONS: Ph

Overview - 26-APR-01

Reserves grew strongly in 2000, with the company replacing 300% of production at just $2.41 per BOE. Nearly all of the reserve growth was internal, through extensions, discoveries and revisions. We are especially bullish on XTO's reserve base, as it primarily consists of natural gas, which has better prospects than oil. Primarily reflecting S&P's very bullish forecast for average 2001 Henry Hub natural gas prices ($5.92 per MMBtu), our EPS forecast for XTO is the highest on the Street. XTO has hedged a significant portion of production at attractive prices. The company will also gain from an anticipated 15% rise in production volumes, most of which will be derived internally, and well controlled costs. Interest expense will decline as free cash flow is utilized to reduce debt. We look for discretionary cash flow per share (DCFPS), an important industry measure, to rise 91% to $7.15.

Valuation - 26-APR-01

Year to date, the shares were recently up 2.8%, versus an 8.7% decline for the S&P Exploration and Production index. We recently initiated coverage of XTO with an accumulate recommendation. The stock was trading at 3.8X estimated 2001 DCFPS, a discount to the peer group's average multiple of 4.2X. We believe XTO's consistent track record of having the lowest five-year average finding and development costs in the E&P universe warrants a higher multiple than the group, despite XTO's very high long-term debt to capitalization ratio of 48%. As previously stated, we expect debt to continue being reduced with excess cash flow. The company is expected to grow cash flow by 21% into the foreseeable future. Consistent with that theme, S&P Ratings (a separate entity) recently upgraded its outlook on XTO from stable to positive. A 3-for-2 stock split was recently announced.

Key Stock Statistics

S&P EPS Est. 2001	2.12	Tang. Bk. Value/Share	4.04
P/E on S&P Est. 2001	7.1	Beta	0.91
S&P EPS Est. 2002	1.75	Shareholders	622
Dividend Rate/Share	0.04	Market cap. (B)	$ 1.8
Shs. outstg. (M)	122.7	Inst. holdings	81%
Avg. daily vol. (M)	0.965		

Value of $10,000 invested 5 years ago: $ 34,508

Fiscal Year Ending Dec. 31

	2001	2000	1999	1998	1997	1996
Revenues (Million $)						
1Q	249.2	113.3	69.42	50.62	53.49	36.08
2Q	209.0	121.7	65.55	67.53	45.97	36.74
3Q	—	160.5	95.33	67.04	44.09	39.20
4Q	—	205.4	111.0	70.82	57.12	49.37
Yr.	—	600.9	341.3	249.5	200.7	161.4
Earnings Per Share ($)						
1Q	**0.37**	**0.29**	**-0.02**	Nil	**0.12**	0.05
2Q	**0.73**	**0.01**	**0.27**	**0.01**	**0.04**	0.02
3Q	—	**0.29**	**0.12**	**-0.31**	**0.03**	0.05
4Q	—	**0.43**	**0.05**	**-0.40**	**0.07**	0.10
Yr.	—	**1.03**	**0.42**	**-0.73**	**0.26**	**0.21**

Next earnings report expected: NA

Dividend Data (Dividends have been paid since 1993.)

Amount ($)	Date Decl.	Ex-Div. Date	Stock of Record	Payment Date
3-for-2	Aug. 15	Sep. 19	Sep. 05	Sep. 18 '00
0.010	Nov. 21	Dec. 27	Dec. 29	Jan. 12 '01
0.010	Feb. 20	Mar. 28	Mar. 30	Apr. 17 '01
0.015	May. 15	Jun. 27	Jun. 29	Jul. 13 '01

Business Summary - 26-APR-01

XTO Energy (XTO; formerly Cross Timbers Oil) has grown primarily through acquisitions of proved oil and gas reserves. The company is engaged in the acquisition, development, exploitation and exploration of producing oil and gas properties, and in the production, processing, marketing and transportation of of oil and natural gas. Strategies include: acquiring long-lived, operated oil and gas properties; increasing production and reserves through aggressive management of operations and through development, exploitation and exploration activities; and retaining management and technical staff that have substantial experience in XTO's core areas. The present corporate title was adopted in June 2001.

The company's proved reserves are mainly located in relatively long-lived fields with well established production histories, concentrated in the East Texas Basin, the Arkoma Basin of Arkansas and Oklahoma, the San Juan Basin of northwestern New Mexico, the Hugoton Field of Oklahoma and Kansas, the Anadarko Basin of Oklahoma, the Green River Basin of Wyoming, the Permian Basin of West Texas and New Mexico, the Middle Ground Shoal Field of Alaska's Cook Inlet and the Colquitt and Oaks Fields of Louisiana.

At December 31, 2000 (1999), proved oil reserves consisted of 58.5 (61.6) MMBbls of oil, 1.8 (1.6) Tcf of natural gas, and 22.0 (17.9) MMBbls of natural gas liquids (NGLs). The standardized measure of after-tax discounted future cash flows associated with the reserves was $5,262.0 ($1,396.9) million.

Average daily production in 2000 (1999) was 12.9 (14.0) MBbls of oil, 343.9 (288.0) MMcf of natural gas, and 4.4 (3.6) MBbls of NGLs. The company received sales prices of $27.07 ($16.94) per bbl. of oil, $3.38 ($2.13) per Mcf of natural gas, and $19.61 ($11.80) per bbl. of NGLs. Production expense per Mcf of natural gas equivalent was $0.53 ($0.53).

During 2000, XTO drilled 229 gross (145.8 net) development wells, 220 (144.5) of which were productive, and 6 gross (3.8) exploratory well, 5 (3.3) of which were productive. At year end, the company had interests in 1,550,693 gross (945,586 net) developed acres, and in 69,122 gross (48,326) undeveloped acres.

In December 1998, XTO formed the Hugoton Royalty Trust by conveying an 80% net profits interest in principally gas-producing operated interests in the Hugoton area, Anadarko and Green River Basins. These net profits interests were conveyed to the trust in exchange for 40 million units of beneficial interest. Cross Timbers sold 17 million Hugoton Royalty Trust (HGT) common units in a 1999 initial public offering, followed by 1.3 million common units in 1999 and 2000. Sales of royalty trust units allow the company to more efficiently capitalize its mature, slower growth properties. The company may create and sell interests in additional royalty trusts in the future.

Per Share Data ($) (Year Ended Dec. 31)	2000	1999	1998	1997	1996	1995	1994	1993	1992	1991
Tangible Bk. Val.	4.04	2.27	1.48	1.60	1.32	1.40	1.41	1.43	1.45	NA
Cash Flow	3.51	1.42	0.12	0.79	0.64	0.30	0.43	0.28	0.38	NA
Earnings	1.03	0.42	-0.73	0.26	0.22	-0.13	0.04	-0.06	0.09	NA
Dividends	0.02	0.03	0.03	0.07	0.06	0.06	0.06	0.04	NA	NA
Payout Ratio	2%	7%	NM	25%	27%	NM	158%	NM	NA	NA
Prices - High	19.33	6.72	9.38	8.50	5.67	3.58	3.28	3.72	NA	NA
- Low	3.36	2.02	2.24	4.37	3.08	2.61	2.46	2.54	NA	NA
P/E Ratio - High	19	16	NM	32	26	NM	87	NM	NA	NA
- Low	3	5	NM	17	14	NM	66	NM	NA	NA
Income Statement Analysis (Million $)										
Revs.	601	341	249	201	161	113	96.0	78.1	107	NA
Oper. Inc.	398	208	124	114	85.9	52.7	44.2	29.7	39.4	NA
Depr. Depl. & Amort.	260	112	83.6	47.7	37.9	36.9	31.7	24.6	23.7	NA
Int. Exp.	78.9	64.2	52.1	26.7	17.2	12.9	8.3	5.6	4.7	NA
Pretax Inc.	176	70.6	-106	39.2	31.0	-0.2	4.8	-0.4	11.0	NA
Eff. Tax Rate	34%	34%	NM	34%	34%	NM	36%	NM	34%	NA
Net Inc.	117	46.7	-69.8	25.7	20.3	-11.2	3.0	-4.0	7.2	NA
Balance Sheet & Other Fin. Data (Million $)										
Cash	7.4	5.7	12.3	3.8	3.9	2.2	7.8	2.1	4.3	NA
Curr. Assets	193	113	138	52.2	51.8	32.7	26.9	22.8	21.8	NA
Total Assets	1,592	1,477	1,208	788	523	403	292	258	220	NA
Curr. Liab.	219	74.2	100	54.9	52.0	31.1	28.5	25.3	15.9	NA
LT Debt	769	991	921	539	315	238	143	112	79.9	NA
Common Eqty.	470	249	149	142	114	131	113	115	120	NA
Total Cap.	1,349	1,395	1,105	730	468	372	264	233	204	NA
Cap. Exp.	45.6	270	296	257	114	171	30.0	105	NA	NA
Cash Flow	375	157	12.0	71.6	57.6	25.7	34.8	20.6	31.0	NA
Curr. Ratio	0.9	1.5	1.4	1.0	1.0	1.1	0.9	0.9	1.4	NA
% LT Debt of Cap.	57.0	71.1	83.3	73.8	67.3	64.0	54.1	48.1	39.1	NA
% Ret. on Assets	7.6	3.5	NM	3.9	4.4	NM	1.1	NM	NA	NA
% Ret. on Equity	32.0	21.3	NM	18.7	16.2	NM	2.7	NM	NA	NA

Data as orig reptd.; bef. results of disc opers/spec. items. Per share data adj. for stk. divs. Bold denotes diluted EPS (FASB 128)-prior periods restated. E-Estimated. NA-Not Available. NM-Not Meaningful. NR-Not Ranked.

Office—810 Houston St., Suite 2000, Fort Worth, TX 76102. **Organized**—in Delaware in 1990. **Tel**—(817) 870-2800. **Website**—http://www.xtoenergy.com **Chrmn & CEO**—B. R. Simpson. **Vice Chrmn & Pres**—S. E. Palko. **EVP, CFO & Investor Contact**—Louis G. Baldwin. **Dirs**—W. H. Adams III, J. L. King Jr., S. E. Palko, J. P. Randall, S. G. Sherman, B. R. Simpson. **Transfer Agent & Registrar**—Mellon Investor Services, Dallas. **Incorporated**—in Delaware in 1990. **Empl**— 651. **S&P Analyst:** Ephraim Juskowicz

Part Four

Financials Stocks

Allstate Corp.

NYSE Symbol **ALL**

In S&P 500

18-AUG-01

Industry: Insurance (Property-Casualty)

Summary: Allstate, the second largest U.S. property-casualty insurer, is expanding into the life insurance and retirement savings arena.

S&P Opinion: Buy (★★★★★)

Recent Price • 33.81
52 Wk Range • 45.90-28.37
Yield • 2.2%
12-Mo. P/E • 13.4

Quantitative Evaluations

Outlook
(1 Lowest—5 Highest)
• **3+**

Fair Value
• **33.70**

Risk
• **Low**

Earn./Div. Rank
• **NR**

Technical Eval.
• **Bearish** since 7/01

Rel. Strength Rank
(1 Lowest—99 Highest)
• **24**

Insider Activity
• **Unfavorable**

OPTIONS: ASE, CBOE, P, Ph

Overview - 31-JUL-01

Revenues will grow about 6% in 2001, reflecting 5% to 6% higher property-casualty earned premiums, 7% to 8% higher financial services premiums and fees, and 6% to 7% higher net investment income. These estimates have been revised downward to reflect the negative impact that volatility in the equity markets is having on ALL's investment product sales. We have also lowered our premium growth assumptions in the property-casualty line. A decline in operating profits seen for 2001 is due to higher catastrophe and weather related losses, and lower than expected contributions from Allstate Financial. Excluding catastrophe losses of $402 million, versus $487 million, the year to date (through June 30) combined ratio inched upward, to 96.4%, from 93.1% in the 2000 interim. Long-term results will be aided by ALL's shifting business mix, and by cost cutting initiatives.

Valuation - 31-JUL-01

After strengthening considerably in 2000 and into 2001, the shares plunged in early July 2001 when ALL announced that second quarter results would fall below expectations. Although our near-term enthusiasm for the shares is tempered because of a rise in loss costs and difficult market environment at Allstate Financial, we nevertheless believe the shares are oversold in the wake of this correction. Many of the issues that are affecting ALL's results are macro in nature, and are affecting many of ALL's peers. ALL's underwriting results are superior to those of the overall industry. Moreover, the company has a well-positioned franchise with the personal lines property-casualty market, and is successfully leveraging that franchise and expanding into a broader-based financial services business model. This shift in business mix should lead to a higher P/E multiple for the stock.

Key Stock Statistics

S&P EPS Est. 2001	2.25	Tang. Bk. Value/Share	23.97
P/E on S&P Est. 2001	15.0	Beta	0.58
S&P EPS Est. 2002	3.10	Shareholders	172,064
Dividend Rate/Share	0.76	Market cap. (B)	$ 24.3
Shs. outstg. (M)	719.0	Inst. holdings	62%
Avg. daily vol. (M)	3.965		

Value of $10,000 invested 5 years ago: $ 15,777

Fiscal Year Ending Dec. 31

	2001	2000	1999	1998	1997	1996
Revenues (Million $)						
1Q	7,131	7,286	6,807	6,450	6,179	5,903
2Q	7,203	7,183	6,592	6,539	6,073	6,324
3Q	—	7,445	6,551	6,436	6,384	6,015
4Q	—	7,220	7,009	6,454	6,313	6,057
Yr.	—	29,134	26,959	25,879	24,949	24,299
Earnings Per Share ($)						
1Q	**0.69**	**0.73**	**1.27**	**1.10**	0.88	0.47
2Q	**0.23**	**0.61**	**0.95**	**1.05**	0.73	0.85
3Q	—	**0.87**	**0.62**	**0.86**	0.94	0.32
4Q	—	**0.74**	**0.54**	**0.93**	**1.01**	0.67
Yr.	—	**2.95**	**3.38**	**3.94**	**3.56**	**2.31**

Next earnings report expected: mid October

Dividend Data (Dividends have been paid since 1993.)

Amount ($)	Date Decl.	Ex-Div. Date	Stock of Record	Payment Date
0.170	Nov. 09	Nov. 28	Nov. 30	Jan. 02 '01
0.190	Feb. 15	Feb. 26	Feb. 28	Apr. 02 '01
0.190	May. 15	May. 29	May. 31	Jul. 02 '01
0.190	Jul. 10	Aug. 29	Aug. 31	Oct. 01 '01

The Allstate Corporation

Business Summary - 31-JUL-01

Established in 1931 by Sears, Roebuck & Co., Allstate (a.k.a. The Good Hands People) is the second largest U.S. personal lines property-casualty insurer, and one of the 20 largest life insurers. It writes business mainly through about 15,500 full-time Allstate agents in the U.S. and Canada. In late 1999, ALL unveiled a multi-access distribution model designed to allow customers to purchase company products through agents, over the Internet, and via telephone call centers. Implementation of the program, which began in the second quarter of 2000, is slated to be completed nationwide by the end of 2001. To fund this initiative, the company undertook a cost cutting plan. ALL became an independent company in June 1995, when Sears, Roebuck & Co. spun off its 80% interest.

The company's primary business is the sale of private passenger automobile and homeowners insurance, and it maintains national market shares of about 12% in each of these lines. ALL is licensed to write policies in all 50 states, the District of Columbia, Puerto Rico, and Canada. In 2000, property-casualty net written premiums equaled $21.9 billion, up 7.4% from the $20.4 billion in net written premiums recorded in 1999. The seemingly modest rate of written premium growth actually outpaced the 5.1% rate of written premium growth in 2000 for the entire property-casualty industry. Some of ALL's premium growth reflected contributions from the October 1999 acquisition of CNA Financial's personal lines unit for $1.2 billion. Of the $21.9 billion in 2000 net written premiums, standard automobile policies accounted for 57%, non-standard automobile policies for 15%, homeowners' coverage for 19%, and other lines for 6%. Property-casualty underwriting results during 2000 continued to be superior to those of the overall industry. The combined ratio in 2000 equaled 99.2%, versus 97.4% in 1999. The combined ratio for the entire personal lines sector equaled 109.8% in 2000. The combined ratio for the personal lines segment equaled 104.1% in 1999.

Allstate Financial (formerly Allstate Life) offers an array of life insurance, annuity, savings and investment and pension products through Allstate agents, financial institutions, independent agents and brokers, and direct marketing techniques. Premiums and deposits surged to $12.2 billion in 2000, up from $8.5 billion in 1999. Of the 2000 total, variable annuities comprised 33%, fixed annuities 31%, institutional investment products 20%, interest-sensitive life insurance 8%, and traditional and other life insurance 8%. In March 1999, ALL and Putnam Investments, a unit of Marsh & McLennan Cos. (NYSE: MMC), formed a joint venture to create and distribute a co-branded line of variable life insurance products.

Per Share Data ($) (Year Ended Dec. 31)	2000	1999	1998	1997	1996	1995	1994	1993	1992	1991
Tangible Bk. Val.	22.26	21.09	21.08	18.36	15.23	14.17	9.37	11.45	NA	NA
Oper. Earnings	NA	2.59	3.08	2.78	1.78	1.76	0.39	1.33	-0.70	NA
Earnings	2.95	3.38	3.94	3.56	2.31	2.12	0.54	1.50	-0.57	NA
Dividends	0.68	0.58	0.53	0.48	0.42	0.39	0.36	0.18	NA	NA
Relative Payout	23%	17%	13%	14%	18%	18%	67%	12%	NA	NA
Prices - High	44.75	41.00	52.37	47.18	30.43	21.18	14.93	17.12	NA	NA
- Low	17.18	22.87	36.06	28.12	18.68	11.75	11.31	13.50	NA	NA
P/E Ratio - High	15	12	13	13	13	10	28	11	NA	NA
- Low	6	7	9	8	8	6	21	9	NA	NA
Income Statement Analysis (Million $)										
Life Ins. In Force	NA	328,400	276,035	247,192	NA	NA	NA	138,423	124,040	NA
Prem. Inc.: Life A & H	21,871	1,623	1,519	1,502	1,336	1,368	1,053	1,079	1,128	1,197
Prem. Inc.: Cas./Prop.	2,205	20,112	19,307	18,604	18,366	17,540	16,807	16,323	15,738	15,147
Net Invest. Inc.	4,633	4,112	3,890	3,861	3,813	3,627	3,401	3,324	3,201	3,001
Total Revs.	29,134	26,959	25,879	24,949	24,299	22,793	21,464	20,946	20,228	19,350
Pretax Inc.	3,006	3,868	4,716	4,429	2,694	2,477	227	1,376	-1,425	539
Net Oper. Inc.	2,004	2,082	2,573	2,429	1,600	1,587	352	1,158	-607	719
Net Inc.	2,211	2,720	3,294	3,105	2,075	1,904	484	1,302	-500	723
Balance Sheet & Other Fin. Data (Million $)										
Cash & Equiv.	1,164	1,066	1,009	220	831	840	778	786	796	NA
Premiums Due	3,802	3,927	3,082	NA	2,691	2,935	2,316	1,964	1,875	NA
Invest. Assets: Bonds	60,758	55,286	53,560	50,860	47,095	45,272	38,041	38,888	32,144	NA
Invest. Assets: Stocks	6,086	6,738	6,421	6,765	5,561	6,150	4,852	4,555	3,837	NA
Invest. Assets: Loans	4,599	4,068	3,458	3,002	3,146	3,280	3,234	3,563	3,701	NA
Invest. Assets: Total	74,483	69,645	66,525	8,000	58,329	56,505	48,179	48,791	41,731	NA
Deferred Policy Costs	4,309	4,119	3,096	2,826	2,614	2,004	2,074	1,511	1,529	NA
Total Assets	104,808	98,119	87,691	80,918	74,508	70,029	61,369	59,358	52,098	NA
Debt	3,862	3,150	2,103	2,446	1,386	1,228	869	850	1,800	NA
Common Eqty.	17,451	16,601	17,240	15,610	13,452	12,680	8,426	10,300	5,383	NA
Comb. Loss-Exp. Ratio	99.2	97.4	93.2	94.0	100.5	100.4	111.0	103.0	120.8	107.5
% Return On Revs.	7.6	10.1	12.7	12.4	8.6	8.4	2.3	6.2	NM	3.7
% Ret. on Equity	13.0	16.1	20.1	21.4	12.3	18.0	5.2	16.6	NM	NM
% Invest. Yield	6.4	6.0	10.4	6.4	6.7	4.8	7.0	7.4	NA	NA

Data as orig reptd.; bef. results of disc opers/spec. items. Per share data adj. for stk. divs. Bold denotes diluted EPS (FASB 128)-prior periods restated. E-Estimated. NA-Not Available. NM-Not Meaningful. NR-Not Ranked.

Office—Allstate Plaza, 2775 Sanders Road, Northbrook, IL 60062. **Tel**—(847) 402-5000. **Website**—http://www.allstate.com **Chrmn, Pres & CEO**—E. M. Liddy. **VP & CFO**—J. L. Carl. **VP & Secy**—R. W. Pike. **Investor Contact**—Robert Block (800-416-8803). **Dirs**—F. D. Ackerman, J. G. Andress, W. L. Batts, E. A. Brennan, J. M. Denny, W. J. Farrell, R. T. LeMay, E. M. Liddy, M. A. Miles, H. J. Riley Jr., J. I. Smith, J. A. Sprieser M. A. Taylor. **Transfer Agent & Registrar**—First Chicago Trust Co. of New York, Jersey City, NJ. **Incorporated**—in Delaware in 1992. **Empl**— 40,834. **S&P Analyst:** Catherine A. Seifert

STANDARD &POOR'S
STOCK REPORTS

Ambac Financial Group

NYSE Symbol **ABK**

In S&P 500

18-AUG-01 **Industry:** Financial (Diversified)

Summary: The second largest municipal bond insurer, AMBAC has leveraged that strength and expanded into other types of financial guarantees.

S&P Opinion: Buy (★★★★★) | Recent Price • 59.35 | 52 Wk Range • 64-41.37 | Yield • 0.6% | 12-Mo. P/E • 16.4

Quantitative Evaluations

Outlook (1 Lowest—5 Highest) • **2-**

Fair Value • **56.20**

Risk • **Low**

Earn./Div. Rank • **A-**

Technical Eval. • **Bullish** since 8/01

Rel. Strength Rank (1 Lowest—99 Highest) • **71**

Insider Activity • **Neutral**

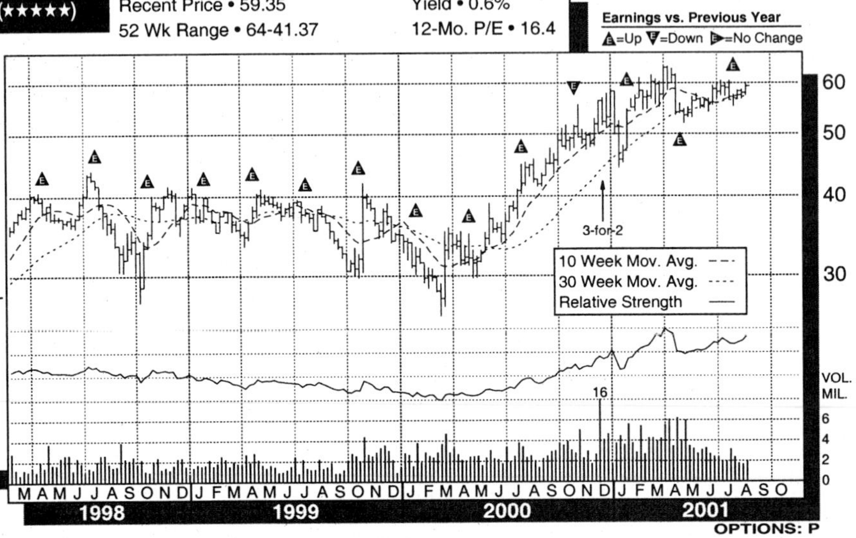

Overview - 19-JUL-01

Earned premium growth in 2001 is estimated to be around 17%, thanks to an interest rate-driven rebound in municipal finance activity (due in part to an increase in refundings), coupled with continued robust growth in the structured finance and asset-backed markets. Increased demand and improved pricing for municipal bond insurance will also aid results in this segment. Longer term growth prospects for international operations remain favorable, although year to year comparisons in 2001 could be difficult after a record 2000. New issue volume for the entire municipal bond industry exceeded $134 billion during the first six months of 2001, up more than 50% from new issue volume of almost $89 billion in the first half of 2000. The insured portion also increased during the first half of 2001, to 48.0%, from 40.4% in the 2000 interim. ABK's share of the insured market increased to 25.6% in the 2001 period, from 15.3% in the year ago interim.

Valuation - 19-JUL-01

After trending downward in early 2000, amid concerns over an interest rate driven slowdown in municipal finance activity, the shares have since recovered nicely. Much of the shares' recent strength reflects a sector rotation back into financial issues. Although there is still a degree of investor wariness regarding ABK's heightened foray into the structured finance market, the stock's relatively modest valuation already discounts much of this risk. Moreover, the company's P/E compared to its growth rate (its PEG ratio) is among the lowest in the financial services sector. In light of ABK's prospects for double-digit operating earnings growth, its superior ROE, and its franchise value, the shares are attractively valued, despite their recent strength.

Key Stock Statistics

S&P EPS Est. 2001	3.95	Tang. Bk. Value/Share	24.60
P/E on S&P Est. 2001	15.0	Beta	0.67
S&P EPS Est. 2002	4.50	Shareholders	75
Dividend Rate/Share	0.36	Market cap. (B)	$ 6.3
Shs. outstg. (M)	105.8	Inst. holdings	92%
Avg. daily vol. (M)	0.383		

Value of $10,000 invested 5 years ago: $ 35,455

Fiscal Year Ending Dec. 31

	2001	2000	1999	1998	1997	1996
Revenues (Million $)						
1Q	167.6	145.9	128.4	115.2	87.27	66.77
2Q	179.5	157.5	123.5	110.3	89.47	55.28
3Q	—	153.7	137.2	117.4	102.6	66.56
4Q	—	164.2	144.2	114.2	102.5	77.70
Yr.	—	621.3	533.3	414.3	381.8	266.3
Earnings Per Share ($)						
1Q	**0.90**	**0.80**	**0.69**	**0.61**	**0.47**	0.43
2Q	**0.99**	**0.87**	**0.67**	**0.57**	**0.50**	**1.28**
3Q	—	**0.84**	**0.85**	**0.61**	**0.57**	0.42
4Q	—	**0.89**	**0.79**	**0.58**	**0.55**	0.49
Yr.	—	**3.41**	**2.87**	**2.37**	**2.09**	2.63

Next earnings report expected: mid October

Dividend Data (Dividends have been paid since 1991.)

Amount ($)	Date Decl.	Ex-Div. Date	Stock of Record	Payment Date
3-for-2	Oct. 25	Dec. 13	Nov. 27	Dec. 12 '00
0.080	Jan. 24	Feb. 08	Feb. 12	Mar. 07 '01
0.080	May. 01	May. 08	May. 10	Jun. 06 '01
0.090	Jul. 18	Aug. 08	Aug. 10	Sep. 05 '01

A Division of The McGraw·Hill Companies

Ambac Financial Group, Inc.

Business Summary - 19-JUL-01

This holding company's main subsidiary, AMBAC Indemnity Corp., is the successor to the oldest municipal bond insurance company, which wrote the first municipal bond insurance policy in 1971. AMBAC is also the second largest municipal bond insurer (based on its nearly 22% share of the insured new issue market in 2000), and has leveraged that strength and market dominance into a diversification effort centered on other types of financial guarantees and investment management services. As of year-end 2000, the composition of the $65.3 billion net guaranteed portfolio was: structured finance 42% ($27.4 billion); municipal finance 29% ($18.9 billion); and international 29% ($19.0 billion).

The company guarantees payment when due of principal and interest on the bond insured. AMBAC primarily insures newly issued bonds, and the issuer normally pays a single premium to the company when the policy becomes effective. Premium rates are based on a percentage of the spread between a bond's intrinsic credit quality and a triple-A-rated bond. At year-end 2000, 49% of the insured portfolio had an internal credit rating of A, 30% was rated BBB, 14% was rated AA, 6% was rated AAA, and under 1% was rated below investment grade.

At year-end 2000, the $18.9 billion municipal insured portfolio was comprised of lease and tax backed bonds 41%; general obligation bonds 17%; utility revenue bonds 7%; and all other municipal obligations 35%.

The Specialized Finance division is a significant participant in the structured, asset-backed and mortgage-backed finance markets in the U.S. and abroad. At year-end 2000, the $27.4 billion domestic structured finance portfolio was comprised of mortgage-backed and home equity obligations 50%, asset-backed and conduits 39%, and other 11%. From late 1995 until early 2000, international structured finance activities were conducted through a joint venture with rival bond insurer MBIA Insurance Corp. (NYSE: MBI). At year-end 2000, ABK's $19.0 billion international portfolio was comprised of structured credit derivatives 70%, asset-backed and conduits 21%, and other 9%. The Financial Services division provides debt management, risk management and investment products to ABK's municipal and structured finance clients.

Per Share Data ($) **(Year Ended Dec. 31)**	**2000**	**1999**	**1998**	**1997**	**1996**	**1995**	**1994**	**1993**	**1992**	**1991**
Tangible Bk. Val.	24.60	19.23	19.98	17.85	15.34	13.35	9.83	10.38	8.14	7.11
Oper. Earnings	3.46	2.93	2.46	1.98	1.79	1.41	1.44	1.51	1.14	NA
Earnings	3.41	2.87	2.37	2.09	2.63	1.59	1.34	1.69	1.24	1.08
Dividends	0.31	0.28	0.25	0.23	0.20	0.18	0.17	0.15	0.14	0.03
Payout Ratio	9%	10%	11%	11%	8%	12%	12%	9%	11%	3%
Prices - High	58.31	42.00	43.95	31.70	23.16	15.95	15.00	16.58	15.08	11.66
- Low	25.91	29.79	27.25	20.66	15.16	12.16	10.08	12.66	10.00	6.70
P/E Ratio - High	17	15	19	15	9	10	11	10	12	11
- Low	8	10	11	10	6	8	8	7	8	6
Income Statement Analysis (Million $)										
Premium Inc.	311	383	311	154	137	112	117	152	103	80.0
Net Invest. Inc.	241	209	186	160	145	131	117	115	100	94.6
Oth. Revs.	380	324	-40.0	25.8	-15.3	5.8	37.1	61.1	37.8	12.4
Total Revs.	621	533	457	339	266	249	271	328	241	187
Pretax Inc.	482	405	329	286	376	214	180	247	171	147
Net Oper. Inc.	NA	313	263	212	188	148	152	158	NA	NA
Net Inc.	366	308	254	223	276	168	141	179	130	114
Balance Sheet & Other Fin. Data (Million $)										
Cash & Equiv.	20.5	142	134	9.3	73.7	42.0	54.4	44.2	27.4	25.5
Premiums Due	1.1	15.4	16.2	106	18.5	14.5	21.5	103	92.4	5.0
Invest. Assets: Bonds	8,065	8,738	8,622	6,774	5,088	4,265	3,626	3,024	1,681	1,222
Invest. Assets: Stocks	NA	Nil	Nil	Nil	Nil	Nil	Nil	Nil	Nil	Nil
Invest. Assets: Loans	NA	685	Nil	Nil	Nil	Nil	Nil	Nil	Nil	Nil
Invest. Assets: Total	8,324	8,963	9,698	7,281	5,201	4,442	3,764	3,133	1,769	1,297
Deferred Policy Costs	153	135	NA	106	94.2	82.6	71.8	51.0	44.0	42.7
Total Assets	10,120	11,345	11,212	8,250	5,876	5,310	4,293	3,807	2,075	1,432
Debt	424	424	424	224	224	224	224	224	149	149
Common Eqty.	2,729	2,018	2,096	1,872	1,615	1,404	1,033	1,100	861	747
Prop. & Cas. Loss Ratio	NA	NA	NA	NA	NA	3.0	2.2	0.9	2.1	12.2
Prop. & Cas. Expense Ratio	NA	NA	NA	NA	NA	20.9	28.0	14.9	14.7	22.9
Prop. & Cas. Combined Ratio	NA	NA	NA	NA	NA	23.9	30.2	15.8	16.8	35.1
% Return On Revs.	58.9	57.7	62.2	65.8	103.8	67.4	52.0	54.8	54.1	60.7
% Ret. on Equity	15.0	15.0	12.8	12.8	18.3	13.8	13.2	18.3	16.2	14.8

Data as orig reptd.; bef. results of disc opers/spec. items. Per share data adj. for stk. divs. Bold denotes diluted EPS (FASB 128)-prior periods restated. E-Estimated. NA-Not Available. NM-Not Meaningful. NR-Not Ranked.

Office—One State Street Plaza, New York, NY 10004. **Tel**—(212) 668-0340. **Fax**—(212) 509-9190. **Website**—http://www.ambac.com **Chrmn & CEO**—P. B. Lassiter. **Pres & COO**—R. J. Genader. **Vice Chrmn & CFO**—F. J. Bivona. **Gen Counsel**—K. J. Doyle. **Investor Contact**—Brian Moore (800-221-1854). **Dirs**—M. A. Callen, R. L. Caporali, J. M. Considine, R. Dulude, R. J. Genader, W. G. Gregory, P. B. Lassiter, C. R. O'Neil. **Transfer Agent & Registrar**—Citibank, NYC. **Incorporated**—in Delaware in 1991. **Empl**— 331. **S&P Analyst:** Catherine A. Seifert

STANDARD
&POOR'S
STOCK REPORTS

AmeriCredit Corp.

NYSE Symbol **ACF**

In S&P MidCap 400

21-AUG-01

Industry:
Consumer Finance

Summary: ACF is one of the largest mid-market U.S. finance companies specializing in purchasing, securitizing and servicing automobile loans.

S&P Opinion: Buy (★★★★★) | Recent Price • 52.60 | 52 Wk Range • 64.90-20.37 | Yield • Nil | 12-Mo. P/E • 20.2

Quantitative Evaluations

Outlook
(1 Lowest—5 Highest)
• **5**

Fair Value
• **74.60**

Risk
• **Average**

Earn./Div. Rank
• **B**

Technical Eval.
• **Neutral** since 8/01

Rel. Strength Rank
(1 Lowest—99 Highest)
• **39**

Insider Activity
• **NA**

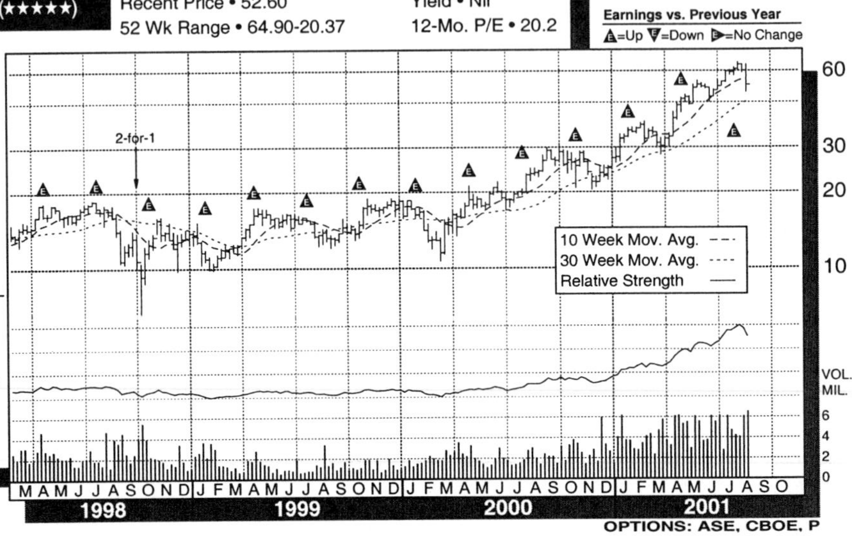

Overview - 21-AUG-01

We expect ACF's auto loan purchases to grow between 30% and 40% in FY 02 (Jun.), after rising 44% in FY 01 to $6.4 billion. Growth will be driven primarily by geographic expansion, aided by new branch openings, and by market share gains. Strategic alliances, such as one with Chase Auto, will also aid growth. In addition, GE Capital's recent exit from the subprime auto loan business has enhanced ACF's already dominant market position. The company raised rates in February 2000, and will likely keep the higher pricing structure in place. At the same time, declines in short-term interest rates have significantly reduced funding costs. In addition, operating expense ratios and costs of capital are declining, as ACF's size and reputation increase. Strong loss reserves, continued emphasis on selectivity, and a first-rate collections operation should help insulate profits from the effects of a slowing economy. We see EPS rising about 44% to $3.75 in FY 02.

Valuation - 21-AUG-01

The shares, which we recently upgraded to buy, from accumulate, are expected to significantly outperform the S&P 500 over the next six to 12 months. ACF is a focused, well run financial services company that has carved out a very profitable niche in the subprime auto loan business. We expect the company to generate 30% annual earnings growth over the next three to five years, driven by a combination of market share gains and geographic expansion. At recent levels, the stock was trading at a significant discount to ACF's projected long-term EPS growth rate, and to the S&P 500, based on our profit projections. We believe multiple expansion, driven by above-average earnings growth, will propel the shares higher.

Key Stock Statistics

S&P EPS Est. 2002	3.75	Tang. Bk. Value/Share	8.98
P/E on S&P Est. 2002	14.0	Beta	1.22
Dividend Rate/Share	Nil	Shareholders	280
Shs. outstg. (M)	82.8	Market cap. (B)	$ 4.3
Avg. daily vol. (M)	1.416	Inst. holdings	93%

Value of $10,000 invested 5 years ago: $ 73,824

Fiscal Year Ending Jun. 30

	2001	2000	1999	1998	1997	1996
Revenues (Million $)						
1Q	169.3	112.6	69.77	44.47	25.00	13.92
2Q	188.6	119.2	78.32	49.25	27.76	19.70
3Q	217.2	130.0	85.07	54.46	33.09	22.00
4Q	243.1	147.8	102.3	61.16	37.51	24.01
Yr.	818.2	509.7	335.5	209.3	123.4	79.63
Earnings Per Share ($)						
1Q	**0.51**	**0.35**	**0.23**	**0.16**	**0.10**	0.04
2Q	**0.57**	**0.36**	**0.26**	**0.18**	**0.11**	0.09
3Q	**0.70**	**0.41**	**0.29**	**0.20**	**0.13**	0.10
4Q	**0.81**	**0.48**	**0.33**	**0.21**	**0.14**	0.11
Yr.	**2.60**	**1.48**	**1.11**	**0.76**	**0.48**	**0.34**

Next earnings report expected: mid October

Dividend Data

No cash dividends have been paid. The shares were split two for one in 1998.

A Division of The McGraw·Hill Companies

Business Summary - 21-AUG-01

AmeriCredit Corp. is a consumer finance company specializing in servicing the subprime auto credit market, consisting of consumers who cannot obtain financing from traditional sources. Through its branch network, ACF purchases loans from automobile dealers and securitizes, sells, and services these loans. At June 30, 2000, it had 196 branch offices in 41 states and three Canadian provinces. In late 1999, the company closed its AMS mortgage lending operations.

ACF's main sources of revenue in FY 00 (Jun.) were gains on sales of securitized loans 41% (51% in FY 99), servicing fee income 33% (26%), and finance charge income from loans held for investment 24% (22%).

The company targets borrowers who have experienced prior credit difficulties or have limited credit histories. ACF works primarily with manufacturer franchised dealerships with used car operations, and prefers to finance later model, low mileage cars, and moderately priced new cars. It also works with selected independent dealers. In FY 00, the company purchased contracts from 14,076 dealers, versus 12,590 dealers in FY 99.

Average managed auto receivables increased 68% in FY 00, to $5.4 billion, on a 54% increase in loan purchases. Growth reflected a 25% increase in loan production at branch offices purchased before June 30, 1998, as well as volume from new branches. The increase in loan production showed ACF's strong (although non-exclusive) relationships with auto dealerships.

The company's most cost-effective source of funding results from the securitization and sale of its auto loans. In its securitizations, ACF transfers automobile receivables to newly formed trusts that then issue asset-backed securities. The securities are in turn sold to investors. The company uses net proceeds from the sale of these loans to pay down borrowings, thus increasing availability for future purchases. ACF must absorb the cost of higher than estimated future losses or prepayments on the securitized loans, but benefits from below estimate losses and prepayments. In FY 00, ACF sold $4.0 billion in receivables, versus $2.8 billion in FY 99.

ACF incorporates certain technologies to support its decision making process. Underwriters have on hand a credit scoring model that lets them quickly assess the credit risk of borrowers. Risk-based pricing tools help price loans for sale and statistically based behavioral assessment models aid collectors in focusing on the highest risk accounts.

As of June 30, 2000, the company's strategic alliance group had 15 partners, consisting of 11 auto dealers and four banks, including Chase Auto Finance. In the relationship with Chase, the two companies jointly market lending products to auto dealers, with Chase providing prime auto financing and ACF providing subprime financing.

ACF opened 20 branches in FY 00, versus 47 in FY 99.

Per Share Data ($) (Year Ended Jun. 30)	2001	2000	1999	1998	1997	1996	1995	1994	1993	1992
Tangible Bk. Val.	NA	8.98	6.07	4.58	3.57	2.86	2.56	2.08	2.11	2.35
Earnings	2.60	1.48	1.11	0.76	0.63	0.35	0.47	0.08	-0.33	-0.39
Dividends	Nil	Nil	Nil	Nil	Nil	Nil	Nil	Nil	Nil	Nil
Payout Ratio	Nil	Nil	Nil	Nil	Nil	Nil	Nil	Nil	Nil	Nil
Prices - High	64.90	31.12	18.93	18.65	17.18	10.00	5.75	4.06	2.37	2.37
- Low	26.00	10.62	9.81	6.62	5.93	5.18	2.62	2.56	1.06	1.06
P/E Ratio - High	25	21	17	25	27	28	12	51	NM	NM
- Low	10	7	9	9	9	15	6	32	NM	NM
Income Statement Analysis (Million $)										
Total Revs.	NA	510	335	209	138	81.0	33.1	15.9	24.9	74.2
Int. Exp.	NA	69.3	38.8	27.1	16.3	13.1	4.0	0.2	0.2	0.3
Exp./Op. Revs.	NA	57%	61%	58%	54%	58%	70%	68%	178%	131%
Pretax Inc.	NA	190	122	80.2	62.9	34.3	10.0	5.1	-19.4	-23.3
Eff. Tax Rate	NA	40%	38%	38%	39%	37%	NM	Nil	Nil	NM
Net Inc.	NA	115	74.8	49.3	38.7	21.6	28.9	5.1	-19.4	-24.2
Balance Sheet & Other Fin. Data (Million $)										
Cash & Secs.	NA	638	324	188	80.4	24.0	33.6	42.3	68.4	39.3
Loans	NA	878	456	343	267	251	222	72.2	43.9	69.5
Total Assets	NA	1,862	1,063	714	493	330	286	122	131	154
ST Debt	NA	507	133	171	16.6	30.4	70.5	0.2	0.4	0.5
Capitalization:										
Debt	NA	442	375	176	132	37.8	64.7	0.2	0.9	1.3
Equity	NA	689	400	288	217	163	147	120	123	147
Total	NA	1,223	849	495	349	201	212	120	124	149
Price Times Bk. Val.: High	NA	3.5	2.8	4.1	4.2	3.5	2.2	2.0	1.1	1.0
Price Times Bk. Val.: Low	NA	1.2	1.6	2.1	1.7	1.8	1.0	1.2	0.5	0.5
% Return On Revs.	NA	22.5	22.3	23.6	28.1	26.7	87.3	31.9	NM	NM
% Ret. on Assets	NA	7.8	8.4	8.2	9.4	7.0	14.2	4.0	NM	NM
% Ret. on Equity	NA	21.0	21.8	19.5	20.4	13.9	21.7	4.2	NM	NM
Loans/Equity	NA	126.6	114.1	122.9	136.2	152.2	110.2	47.9	42.0	57.9

Data as orig reptd.; bef. results of disc opers/spec. items. Per share data adj. for stk. divs. Bold denotes diluted EPS (FASB 128)-prior periods restated. E-Estimated. NA-Not Available. NM-Not Meaningful. NR-Not Ranked.

Office—801 Cherry St., Suite 3900, Fort Worth, TX 76102. **Tel**—(817) 302-7000. **Website**—http://www.americredit.com **Chrmn**—C. H. Morris Jr. **Vice Chrmn, Pres & CEO**—M. R. Barrington. **Vice Chrmn & CFO**—D. E. Berce. **EVP & Secy**—C. A. Choate. **Investor Contact**—Kim Pulliam (817-302-7009). **Dirs**—M. R. Barrington, D. E. Berce, A. R. Dike, E. H. Esstman, J. H. Greer, D. K. Higgins, K. H. Jones Jr., C. H. Morris Jr. **Transfer Agent & Registrar**—Mellon Investor Services, Dallas. **Incorporated**—in Texas in 1988. **Empl**— 3,048. **S&P Analyst:** R. McMillan

STANDARD
&POOR'S
STOCK REPORTS

Bank of America

NYSE Symbol **BAC**

In S&P 500

18-AUG-01

Industry: Banks (Money Center)

Summary: This banking company has offices in 21 states, and provides international corporate financial services.

S&P Opinion: Buy (★★★★★)

Recent Price • 62.69 | 52 Wk Range • 64.70-36.31 | Yield • 3.6% | 12-Mo. P/E • 14.4

Quantitative Evaluations

Outlook
(1 Lowest—5 Highest)
• 2+

Fair Value
• 62.10

Risk
• Average

Earn./Div. Rank
• A-

Technical Eval.
• Bullish since 4/01

Rel. Strength Rank
(1 Lowest—99 Highest)
• 72

Insider Activity
• Neutral

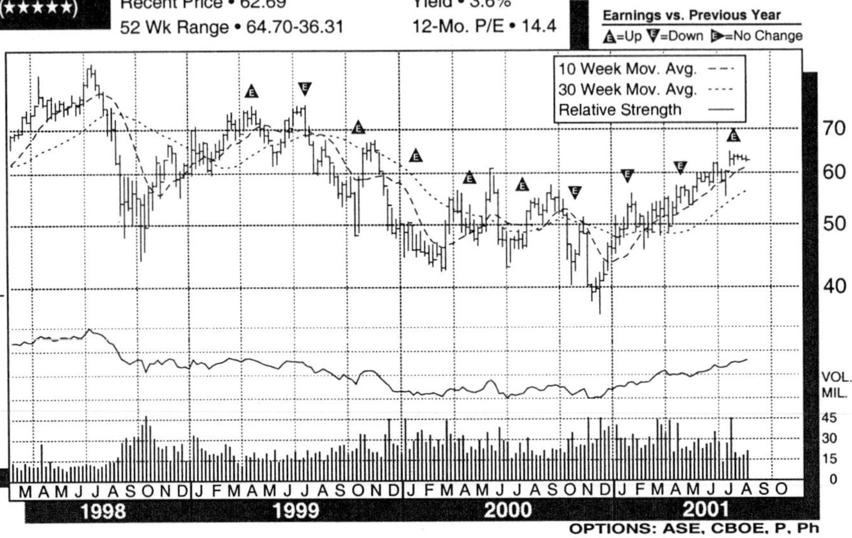

OPTIONS: ASE, CBOE, P, Ph

Overview - 31-JUL-01

Although only minimal loan growth of about 2% is expected for 2001, reflecting the impact of a slowing economy, a more favorable loan mix and lower funding costs resulting from a decline in short-term interest rates are expected to lead to mid-single digit net interest income growth. At $800 million, loss provisions were markedly higher in the second quarter of 2001 than in prior quarters, due to weakness in the commercial portfolio, and they are likely to remain high for the balance of the year. Fee revenues will remain the better growth story, with noticeable gains expected in service charges, mortgage banking, credit card income, and strong investment banking (aided by healthy fixed-income activities) and brokerage fees. Expense growth should remain in low single digits, as results benefit from some success on productivity initiatives. Overall, we see EPS of $4.95 in 2001, up from operating earnings of $4.72 in 2000, and project a further advance, to $5.40, in 2002.

Valuation - 31-JUL-01

The shares were recently up about 39% in 2001, substantially outperforming both the broader market and the shares of BAC's money center peers, in a rebound from a late 2000 slide that reflected investor concerns about credit quality and capital markets businesses. We believe the company will continue to recover from 2000 earnings concerns, as investors expect easier EPS comparisons in the second half. With the shares recently trading at 13X our 2001 EPS estimate of $4.95, a discount to the P/E multiple accorded the shares of money center peers, we believe BAC will be able to outperform the broader market in the year ahead, and recommend buying the stock.

Key Stock Statistics

S&P EPS Est. 2001	4.95	Tang. Bk. Value/Share	21.32
P/E on S&P Est. 2001	12.7	Beta	1.13
S&P EPS Est. 2002	5.40	Shareholders	256,883
Dividend Rate/Share	2.24	Market cap. (B)	$100.5
Shs. outstg. (M)	1602.9	Inst. holdings	56%
Avg. daily vol. (M)	3.730		

Value of $10,000 invested 5 years ago: $ 15,926

Fiscal Year Ending Dec. 31

	2001	2000	1999	1998	1997	1996
Revenues (Million $)						
1Q	14,021	14,132	12,554	13,411	—	—
2Q	13,666	14,237	12,780	13,393	—	—
3Q	—	14,910	13,066	12,293	—	—
4Q	—	14,468	13,232	12,697	—	—
Yr.	—	57,747	51,632	51,794	49,089	43,240
Earnings Per Share ($)						
1Q	**1.15**	**1.33**	**1.08**	**0.75**	—	—
2Q	**1.24**	**1.23**	**1.07**	**1.28**	—	—
3Q	**E1.26**	**1.10**	**1.23**	**0.21**	—	—
4Q	**E1.30**	**0.85**	**1.10**	**0.66**	—	—
Yr.	**E4.95**	**4.52**	**4.48**	**2.90**	**3.61**	**3.36**

Next earnings report expected: mid October

Dividend Data (Dividends have been paid since 1903.)

Amount ($)	Date Decl.	Ex-Div. Date	Stock of Record	Payment Date
0.560	Oct. 25	Nov. 29	Dec. 01	Dec. 20 '00
0.560	Jan. 24	Feb. 28	Mar. 02	Mar. 23 '01
0.560	Apr. 25	May. 30	Jun. 01	Jun. 22 '01
0.560	Jul. 25	Sep. 05	Sep. 07	Sep. 28 '01

A Division of The **McGraw·Hill** *Companies*

Bank of America Corporation

Business Summary - 31-JUL-01

Bank of America, formed through the September 1998 merger of North Carolina-based NationsBank Corp. and California-based BankAmerica Corp., is a bank holding company that provides a range of banking and financial services and products to 30 million households and 2 million businesses. Its primary market areas encompass the Mid-Atlantic, Midwest, Southeast, Southwest, Northwest and West, as well as select international markets. The company has leading deposit market share in California, Florida, Georgia, Maryland, North Carolina, Texas and Washington.

Consumer and commercial banking (60% of earnings in 2000) provides a wide range of products and services to individuals, small businesses and middle market companies through delivery channels that include 4,500 banking centers and 13,000 ATMs located in 21 states and the District of Columbia. This segment provides specialized services such as the origination and servicing of residential mortgage loans, issuance of credit cards, direct banking, student lending and certain insurance services.

Asset management (8%) includes the private bank (financial solutions for high net worth clients), capital management (equity, fixed income, cash and alternatives investments) and investment services (full-service and discount brokerage services). Global corporate and investment banking (26%) provides capital-raising products, trade finance, treasury management, capital markets, leasing and financial advisory services to domestic and international corporations, financial institutions and government entities. Equity investments (6%) includes principal investing, which is comprised of a portfolio of direct and indirect investments in companies at all stages of the business cycle.

In 2000, average earning assets, from which interest income is derived, amounted to $583.5 million and consisted mainly of loans and leases (67%) and investment securities (14%). Average sources of funds were interest-bearing deposits 39%, short-term borrowings 23%, noninterest-bearing deposits 14%, long-term debt 10%, shareholders' equity 7% and other 7%.

Nonperforming assets, consisting of nonperforming loans and foreclosed properties, totaled $5.5 billion (1.39% of loans and related assets) at December 31, 2000, up from $3.2 billion (0.86%) the year before. The allowance for loan losses, which is set aside for possible loan defaults, at 2000 year end was $6.8 billion (1.74% of loans and leases), equal to $6.8 billion (1.84%) a year earlier. Net chargeoffs were $2.4 billion (0.61% of average loans) in 2000, versus $2.0 billion (0.55%) in 1999.

Per Share Data ($) **(Year Ended Dec. 31)**	**2000**	**1999**	**1998**	**1997**	**1996**	**1995**	**1994**	**1993**	**1992**	**1991**
Tangible Bk. Val.	21.32	18.11	18.02	16.66	18.42	19.09	16.62	15.51	13.43	10.94
Earnings	4.52	4.48	2.90	4.17	4.00	3.56	3.06	2.50	2.30	0.38
Dividends	2.06	1.85	1.59	1.04	1.20	1.04	0.94	0.82	0.76	0.74
Payout Ratio	46%	41%	55%	25%	30%	29%	31%	33%	33%	195%
Prices - High	61.00	76.37	88.43	71.68	52.62	37.37	28.68	29.00	26.68	21.37
- Low	36.31	47.62	44.00	48.00	32.18	22.31	21.68	22.25	19.81	10.75
P/E Ratio - High	13	17	30	17	13	10	9	12	12	56
- Low	8	11	15	12	8	6	7	9	9	28
Income Statement Analysis (Million $)										
Net Int. Inc.	18,442	18,237	18,298	7,898	6,329	5,447	5,211	4,673	4,098	3,799
Tax Equiv. Adj.	322	215	128	116	94.0	113	94.0	86.0	92.0	141
Non Int. Inc.	14,489	14,069	12,189	6,351	3,646	3,078	2,597	2,101	1,913	1,742
Loan Loss Prov.	2,535	182	2,920	800	605	382	310	430	715	1,582
Exp./Op. Revs.	64%	57%	67%	52%	57%	60%	62%	65%	68%	76%
Pretax Inc.	11,788	12,215	8,048	4,796	3,634	2,991	2,555	1,991	1,396	109
Eff. Tax Rate	36%	35%	36%	36%	35%	35%	34%	35%	18%	NM
Net Inc.	7,517	7,882	5,165	3,077	2,452	1,950	1,690	1,301	1,145	202
% Net Int. Marg.	3.22	3.47	3.69	3.79	3.62	3.33	3.58	4.00	4.10	3.82
Balance Sheet & Other Fin. Data (Million $)										
Money Mkt. Assets	76,544	81,226	73,498	36,095	27,491	26,393	23,212	19,133	6,110	2,436
Inv. Securities	65,838	83,069	80,587	47,203	14,387	23,847	25,825	29,054	24,729	24,879
Com'l Loans	203,542	195,779	196,130	71,442	58,796	52,101	48,109	43,538	34,478	31,164
Other Loans	188,651	174,883	161,198	69,568	61,519	66,919	55,580	50,166	38,236	37,944
Total Assets	642,191	632,574	617,679	264,562	185,794	187,298	169,604	157,686	118,059	110,319
Demand Deposits	100,645	95,469	94,336	34,674	25,738	23,414	21,380	20,719	17,701	16,270
Time Deposits	263,599	251,804	262,974	103,520	80,760	77,277	79,090	70,394	65,026	71,805
LT Debt	72,502	60,441	50,842	27,204	22,985	17,775	8,488	7,648	3,066	2,876
Common Eqty.	47,556	44,355	45,855	21,243	13,538	12,699	10,900	9,771	7,695	6,145
% Ret. on Assets	1.2	1.3	0.9	1.4	13.0	1.1	1.0	0.9	1.0	0.2
% Ret. on Equity	16.3	17.5	11.5	17.6	18.0	16.5	16.3	14.8	15.9	2.7
% Loan Loss Resv.	-1.7	1.8	2.0	1.9	1.9	1.9	2.1	2.3	2.0	2.3
% Loans/Deposits	107.7	106.7	99.4	104.1	113.0	116.2	103.2	102.8	87.9	78.5
% Equity to Assets	7.2	7.2	7.6	7.7	7.0	6.6	6.2	6.3	6.1	5.4

Data as orig. reptd.; bef. results of disc opers. and/or spec. items. Data for 1997 and prior yrs. for NationsBank Corp. before merger with BankAmerica Corp. Per share data adj. for stk. divs. as of ex-div. date. Bold denotes diluted EPS (FASB 128). E-Estimated. NA-Not Available. NM-Not Meaningful. NR-Not Ranked.

Office—Bank of America Corporate Center, Charlotte, NC 28255. **Tel**—(888) 279-3457. **Website**—http://www.bankofamerica.com **Chrmn & CEO**—H. L. McColl Jr. **Vice Chrmn & CFO**—J. H. Hance Jr. **Pres & COO**—K. D. Lewis. **Investor Contacts**—Kevin Stitt, Susan Carr. **Dirs**—C. W. Coker, A. T. Dickson, F. Dowd IV, K. Feldstein, P. Fulton, D. E. Guinn, J. H. Hance Jr., C. R. Holman, W. W. Johnson, K. D. Lewis, W. E. Massey, H. L. McColl Jr., O. T. Sloan Jr., M. R. Spangler, R. Townsend, J. M. Ward, V. R. Williams. **Transfer Agent**—Mellon Investor Services. **Incorporated**—in North Carolina in 1968; reincorporated in Delaware in 1998. **Empl**— 144,287. **S&P Analyst:** Stephen R. Biggar

STANDARD &POOR'S STOCK REPORTS

Berkshire Hathaway

NYSE Symbol **BRK.A**

18-AUG-01

Industry: Insurance (Property-Casualty)

Summary: This holding company has interests in insurance, publishing, retailing and manufacturing. Its investment portfolio includes over $37 billion of marketable equity securities.

S&P Opinion: Buy (★★★★★)

Recent Price • 69200
52 Wk Range • 74600-53500
Yield • Nil
12-Mo. P/E • 33.7

Quantitative Evaluations

Outlook (1 Lowest—5 Highest) • **NA**

Fair Value • **NA**

Risk • **NA**

Earn./Div. Rank • **B**

Technical Eval. • **NA**

Rel. Strength Rank (1 Lowest—99 Highest) • **61**

Insider Activity • **Neutral**

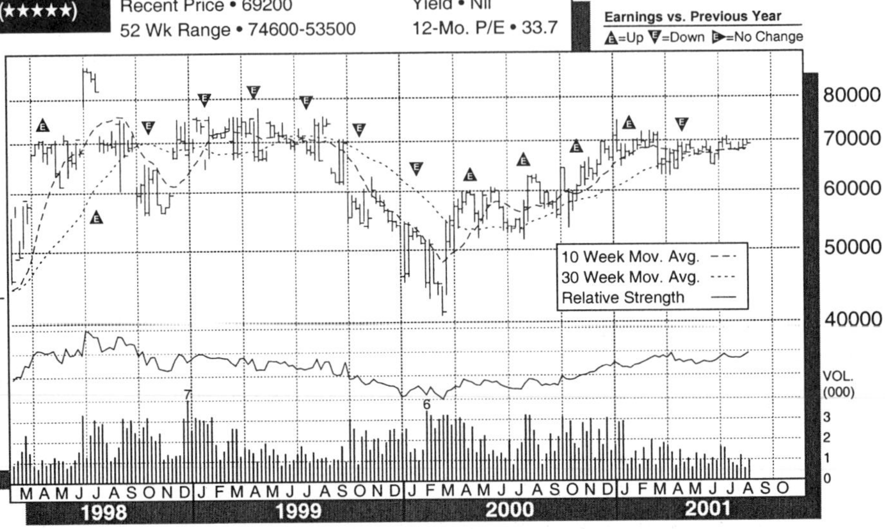

Overview - 31-MAY-01

The company's December 1998 acquisition of General Re increased Berkshire's reliance on property-casualty insurance. Underwriting losses at General Re held steady in 2000, while underwriting losses widened at GEICO. BRK is increasing premium rates at both units. The company has recently stepped up its pace of acquisitions. In August 2000, BRK purchased Justin Industries, a manufacturer of bricks and footwear, for $570 million cash. In January 2001, the company acquired an 87.3% stake in Shaw Industries, the world's largest carpet producer, for about $2 billion. Also in January, BRK completed the purchase of Benjamin Moore & Co., a leading paint manufacturer, for approximately $1 billion. In February, BRK completed a $2.8 billion tender offer for Johns Manville, a leading producer of building products.

Valuation - 31-MAY-01

Our recent upgrade of the shares to buy reflects improvement in underwriting results at General Re and GEICO. This improvement has driven down the cost of insurance float from over 6% to below 3%. The decline in first quarter net income reflected lower realized gains. Operating earnings for the quarter advanced 30%, to $303 a share, from $233 in 2000. Our recommendation is also based on the assumption that the company, through the efforts of its chairman, famed investor Warren Buffett, can continue to achieve investment returns that exceed those of the market. In 2000, the company largely dodged the bear market through its avoidance of technology issues. Our 2001 operating EPS estimate of $1,200 excludes expected realized gains. Reported EPS should approach $1,800 per Class A share.

Key Stock Statistics

S&P EPS Est. 2001	1100.00	Tang. Bk. Value/Share	28075.00
P/E on S&P Est. 2001	62.9	Beta	0.78
S&P EPS Est. 2002	1300.00	Shareholders	9,200
Dividend Rate/Share	Nil	Market cap. (B)	$ 92.9
Shs. outstg. (M)	1.5	Inst. holdings	17%
Avg. daily vol. (M)	0.000		

Value of $10,000 invested 5 years ago: $ 21,033

Fiscal Year Ending Dec. 31

	2001	2000	1999	1998	1997	1996
Revenues (Million $)						
1Q	8,135	6,474	5,446	3,325	2,075	4,140
2Q	—	6,553	5,461	3,936	2,338	1,915
3Q	—	8,426	7,051	2,909	2,373	2,015
4Q	—	12,523	6,070	3,662	3,644	2,431
Yr.	—	33,976	24,028	13,832	10,430	10,500
Earnings Per Share ($)						
1Q	397.00	531.00	356.00	582.00	230.80	1398.15
2Q	—	421.00	376.00	947.00	225.44	158.83
3Q	—	523.00	276.00	293.00	297.05	218.04
4Q	—	710.00	17.00	440.00	788.25	290.00
Yr.	—	2185.00	1025.00	2262.00	1542.00	2065.00

Next earnings report expected: NA

Dividend Data

No dividends have been paid since 1967.

A Division of The McGraw-Hill Companies

Berkshire Hathaway Inc.

Business Summary - 31-MAY-01

Berkshire Hathaway is a diversified company engaged in property and casualty insurance; aviation training; manufacture, import and distribution of footwear; publication of a daily newspaper in Buffalo, NY; manufacture and sale of candy; production of home cleaning products; publication of encyclopedias and other reference materials; retail sale of home furnishings; manufacture and distribution of uniforms; manufacture of building materials; and retail sale of fine jewelry.

In 2000, General Re contributed 30.2% of revenues (30.7% in 1999), GEICO Corp. 18.7% (21.1%), the Reinsurance group 15.7% (10.6%), the Direct Insurance group 1.1% (1.2%), interest and other investment income 9.4% (11.1%), flight services 7.6% (8.2%), retail businesses 6.2% (6.1%), Scott Fetzer 2.8% (4.5%), and other businesses 9.3% (7.7%).

The company has grown rapidly through acquisitions over the past 15 years. In 1986, it acquired Scott Fetzer Co., a diversified manufacturer with product lines including Kirby vacuum cleaners, Campbell Hausfeld air compressors and paint sprayers, and World Book encyclopedias. In July 1991, BRK acquired H. H. Brown Shoe Co., the leading U.S. producer of steel-toe safety work shoes; in November 1993, it purchased Dexter Shoe Co., a maker of casual shoes. During 1995, BRK acquired Helzberg's Diamond Shops, Inc., and R. C. Willey Home Furnishings. In early 1996, the company acquired GEICO Corp.; later in 1996, BRK purchased FlightSafety International, Inc., a provider of high technology training to operators of aircraft and ships. In 1997, it acquired Houston-based Star Furniture, a home furnishings retailer; in early 1998, it acquired International Dairy Queen.

In August 1998, BRK purchased Executive Jet, Inc., for $725 million. In December 1998, BRK acquired General Re Corp., the largest U.S.-based reinsurance group, in a stock transaction valued at about $22 billion. Acquisitions in 1999 included Jordan's Furniture, the largest furniture retailer in Massachusetts and New Hampshire, and a 75% stake in MidAmerican Energy Holdings, acquired for $2.05 billion. In 2000, BRK acquired Justin Industries, a maker of bricks and footwear for $570 million. In early 2001, the company acquired Benjamin Moore Paint for about $1 billion cash. It also purchased an 87.3% stake in Shaw Industries, the world's largest maker of carpet, for $2 billion; and acquired Johns Manville Corp. for $1.8 billion.

BRK's equity holdings had a market value of $37.6 billion at December 31, 2000. The largest holdings were The Coca-Cola Co. (market value $12.2 billion), The Gillette Co. ($3.5 billion), American Express Co. ($8.3 billion), Wells Fargo & Co. ($3.1 billion), and The Washington Post Co. ($1.1 billion).

Per Share Data ($) (Year Ended Dec. 31)	2000	1999	1998	1997	1996	1995	1994	1993	1992	1991
Tangible Bk. Val.	28075.06	25620.14	25654.11	23004.00	16490.00	13862.53	9697.00	8854.00	7745.00	6437.00
Oper. Earnings	614.00	442.00	1021.00	972.00	675.96	505.60	368.00	348.00	303.00	275.00
Earnings	2185.00	1025.00	2262.00	1542.00	2065.00	611.00	420.00	656.00	355.00	384.00
Dividends	Nil	Nil	Nil	Nil	Nil	Nil	Nil	Nil	Nil	Nil
Payout Ratio	Nil	Nil	Nil	Nil	Nil	Nil	Nil	Nil	Nil	Nil
Prices - High	71300	81100	88400	48600	38000	33400	21800	17800	11750	9125
- Low	40800	52000	45800	33000	29800	20250	15150	11450	8575	6550
P/E Ratio - High	33	79	39	32	18	55	52	27	33	24
- Low	19	51	20	21	14	33	36	17	24	17
Income Statement Analysis (Million $)										
Premium Inc.	19,343	14,306	5,481	4,761	4,118	958	923	656	664	776
Net Invest. Inc.	2,686	2,314	2,415	1,106	2,484	475	426	480	495	482
Oth. Revs.	11,947	7,408	4,887	4,563	3,898	3,055	2,498	2,517	1,870	1,848
Total Revs.	33,976	24,028	12,783	9,477	10,500	4,488	3,847	3,653	3,029	3,106
Pretax Inc.	5,587	2,450	4,314	2,828	3,710	1,009	662	1,190	551	593
Net Oper. Inc.	936	671	1,277	1,198	815	600	434	402	348	316
Net Inc.	3,328	1,557	2,830	1,902	2,489	725	495	759	407	440
Balance Sheet & Other Fin. Data (Million $)										
Cash & Equiv.	5,263	3,835	13,582	1,002	1,340	2,704	274	1,838	1,192	762
Premiums Due	11,764	8,558	7,224	1,712	1,523	719	581	525	691	904
Invest. Assets: Bonds	32,567	30,222	21,246	10,298	6,447	835	1,821	2,109	2,103	2,338
Invest. Assets: Stocks	37,619	39,508	39,761	36,248	27,751	22,823	16,260	12,540	11,653	9,183
Invest. Assets: Loans	Nil	Nil	Nil	Nil	Nil	Nil	Nil	Nil	Nil	Nil
Invest. Assets: Total	71,823	69,730	61,007	46,546	34,198	23,658	18,081	14,649	13,755	11,520
Deferred Policy Costs	NA	NA	NA	NA	NA	NA	NA	NA	NA	NA
Total Assets	135,792	131,416	122,237	56,111	43,410	29,929	21,338	19,520	16,945	14,462
Debt	1,392	1,943	2,088	2,267	1,944	1,062	811	972	1,300	1,255
Common Eqty.	61,724	57,761	57,403	31,455	23,427	17,217	11,875	10,428	8,896	7,380
Prop. & Cas. Loss Ratio	85.7	80.2	73.8	72.3	74.9	63.9	61.1	69.5	103.5	106.5
Prop. & Cas. Expense Ratio	18.3	19.3	19.5	18.9	18.0	31.7	25.0	22.8	11.6	8.6
Prop. & Cas. Combined Ratio	104.0	99.5	93.3	91.2	92.9	95.6	86.1	92.3	115.1	115.1
% Return On Revs.	9.8	6.5	22.1	20.1	23.7	16.2	12.9	20.8	13.4	14.2
% Ret. on Equity	5.6	2.7	6.4	6.9	12.4	5.0	4.4	7.9	5.0	6.9

Data as orig reptd.; bef. results of disc opers/spec. items. Per share data adj. for stk. divs. Bold denotes diluted EPS (FASB 128)-prior periods restated. E-Estimated. NA-Not Available. NM-Not Meaningful. NR-Not Ranked

Office—1440 Kiewit Plaza, Omaha, NE 68131. **Tel**—(402) 346-1400. **Website**—www.berkshirehathaway.com **Chrmn & CEO**—W. E. Buffett. **VP, Treas & Investor Contact**—Marc D. Hamburg. **Secy**—F. N. Krutter. **Dirs**—H. G. Buffett, S. T. Buffett, W. E. Buffett, M. G. Chace III, C. T. Munger, R. L. Olson, W. Scott Jr. **Transfer Agent & Registrar**—BankBoston. **Incorporated**—in Delaware in 1973; reincorporated in 1991. **Empl**— 112,000. **S&P Analyst:** David J. Braverman, CFA

STANDARD &POOR'S
STOCK REPORTS

Citigroup Inc.

NYSE Symbol **C**

In S&P 500

18-AUG-01

Industry: Financial (Diversified)

Summary: This diversified financial services company provides a wide range of financial services to consumer and corporate customers in more than 100 countries and territories.

S&P Opinion: Buy (★★★★★)

Recent Price • 46.60
52 Wk Range • 59.12-39
Yield • 1.4%
12-Mo. P/E • 17.7

Quantitative Evaluations

Outlook (1 Lowest—5 Highest)
• **3-**

Fair Value
• **49.90**

Risk
• **Low**

Earn./Div. Rank
• **A**

Technical Eval.
• **Neutral** since 8/01

Rel. Strength Rank (1 Lowest—99 Highest)
• **34**

Insider Activity
• **Neutral**

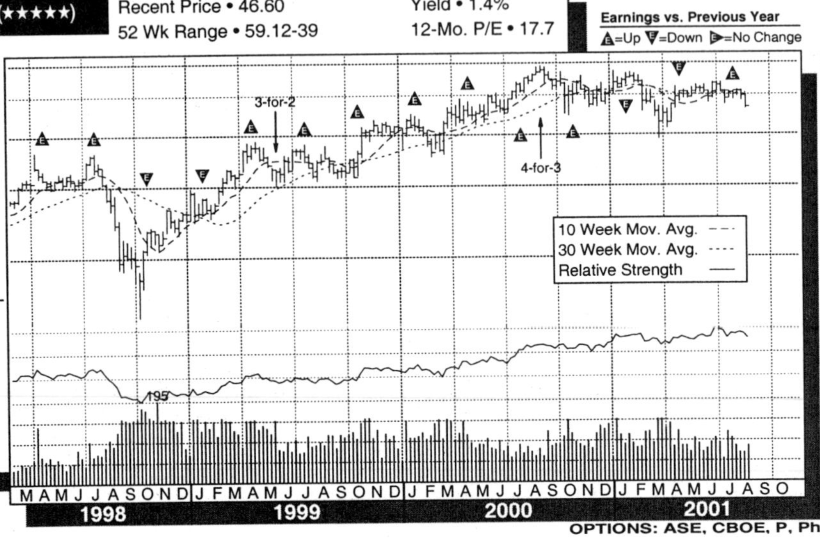

OPTIONS: ASE, CBOE, P, Ph

Overview - 14-AUG-01

Revenue growth, excluding foreign exchange, is expected to be in high single digits in 2001. Strength is expected in the global consumer segment, especially from CitiFinancial, which should continue to benefit from good receivables growth (particularly for real estate secured loans); and from credit cards, which will be aided by receivables gains in the U.S. and Japan. Cost savings related to the consolidation of Associates First Capital branches (acquired in late 2000), combined with lower cost of funds, should lead to a growth rate in the high teens for the global consumer segment. The global corporate segment will likely continue to experience revenue pressure resulting from a weak equity market environment, although strength from emerging markets and good expense controls should lead to low single digit income growth. Overall, we see EPS rising 9% in 2001, to $3.00, from $2.74 reported on an operating basis in 2000.

Valuation - 14-AUG-01

With a flat performance thus far in 2001, the shares have outperformed the broader market. We believe the shares have good upside potential, as investors recognize the company's unparalleled geographic and product diversity, which will allow it to maintain earnings momentum relative to its peers, particularly in light of expectations of a weaker economy. We continue to believe that investors will be willing to pay a premium valuation for the shares, in light of the company's solid proportion of revenues coming from stable growth businesses. With the stock trading at 14X our $3.50 EPS estimate for 2002, a 25% discount to the market multiple, we continue to recommend purchasing the shares for superior capital appreciation.

Key Stock Statistics

S&P EPS Est. 2001	3.00	Tang. Bk. Value/Share	12.84
P/E on S&P Est. 2001	15.5	Beta	1.48
S&P EPS Est. 2002	3.50	Shareholders	250,000
Dividend Rate/Share	0.64	Market cap. (B)	$234.3
Shs. outstg. (M)	5028.6	Inst. holdings	63%
Avg. daily vol. (M)	9.298		

Value of $10,000 invested 5 years ago: $ 43,206

Fiscal Year Ending Dec. 31

	2001	2000	1999	1998	1997	1996
Revenues (Million $)						
1Q	29,804	26,815	20,521	19,437	8,700	4,515
2Q	—	27,059	20,436	19,961	9,184	5,426
3Q	—	28,624	14,021	17,594	9,961	5,622
4Q	—	29,328	27,027	19,439	9,765	5,782
Yr.	—	111,826	82,005	76,431	37,609	21,345
Earnings Per Share ($)						
1Q	0.70	0.78	0.51	0.45	0.34	0.31
2Q	0.71	0.65	0.53	0.47	0.39	0.36
3Q	E0.75	0.67	0.53	0.15	0.42	0.28
4Q	E0.80	0.55	0.56	0.14	0.15	0.36
Yr.	E3.00	2.62	2.12	1.22	1.27	1.36

Next earnings report expected: mid October

Dividend Data (Dividends have been paid since 1986.)

Amount ($)	Date Decl.	Ex-Div. Date	Stock of Record	Payment Date
0.140	Oct. 17	Nov. 02	Nov. 06	Nov. 22 '00
0.140	Jan. 16	Feb. 01	Feb. 05	Feb. 23 '01
0.140	Apr. 17	May. 03	May. 07	May. 25 '01
0.160	Jul. 16	Aug. 02	Aug. 06	Aug. 24 '01

A Division of The **McGraw·Hill** *Companies*

Citigroup Inc.

Business Summary - 14-AUG-01

Citigroup Inc. was formed through the October 1998 combination of Citicorp and Travelers Group in one of the largest corporate mergers in history. Melding traditional banking and insurance businesses together on a scale never attempted, the company's goal is to serve the financial needs of the widest possible audience on a global scale.

The company's global consumer segment (35% of net income in 1999) includes Citibanking, which delivers banking, lending and investment services to customers through 367 branches; cards, which offers MasterCard, VISA and Diners Clubs products with 44 million accounts and $88 billion of managed receivables as of 2000 year end; CitiFinancial, which provides community-based lending such as real estate-secured loans, unsecured and secured personal loans through more than 1,200 offices in the U.S. and Canada; and insurance, which offers individual and group annuity and individual life insurance. An international unit provides banking, lending and investment services in Europe, Middle East and Africa, Japan, emerging markets of Asia, and Latin America.

The global corporate and investment bank segment (42%) provides investment advice, financial planning and retail brokerage services, banking and other financial services and commercial insurance products. The segment includes Salomon Smith Barney, which offers investment banking services such as underwriting of fixed income and equity securities. Salomon also provides capital raising, advisory, research and other brokerage services. In this segment, C is a major participant in foreign exchange and markets for derivative instruments including interest rate, equity and currency swaps, and various types of structured securities. The global relationship bank unit provides banking and financial services to multinational companies with core products including cash management, foreign exchange, structured products, securities custody, trade services and loan products. Through its commercial lines unit, the segment offers property and casualty insurance and insurance related services.

The Associates segment (9%), formed following the December 2000 acquisition of Associates First Capital, offers private label retail credit card and revolving programs; various credit-related and other insurance products; consumer finance and insurance products; and commercial finance and insurance products.

The global investment management and private banking segment (5%) offers a wide range of products and services to mutual funds, closed-end funds, managed accounts, unit investment trusts, variable annuities, pension administration and personalized wealth management services. The investment activities segment (9%) consists mainly of C's venture capital activities.

Per Share Data ($) (Year Ended Dec. 31)	2000	1999	1998	1997	1996	1995	1994	1993	1992	1991
Tangible Bk. Val.	12.84	10.64	8.95	6.99	4.97	4.08	3.07	3.24	1.91	1.44
Earnings	2.62	2.12	1.22	1.27	1.17	0.81	0.64	0.65	0.56	0.36
Dividends	0.52	0.41	0.28	0.20	0.15	0.13	0.10	0.08	0.06	0.04
Payout Ratio	20%	19%	23%	16%	13%	16%	15%	13%	11%	10%
Prices - High	59.12	43.68	36.75	28.68	15.83	10.64	7.18	8.25	4.15	3.34
- Low	35.34	24.50	14.25	14.58	9.41	5.39	5.06	4.02	2.97	1.82
P/E Ratio - High	23	21	30	23	14	11	11	13	7	9
- Low	13	12	12	11	8	7	8	6	5	5
Income Statement Analysis (Million $)										
Premium Inc.	12,429	10,441	9,850	8,995	7,633	4,977	7,590	1,480	1,694	1,783
Invest. Inc.	NA	NA	23,696	16,214	5,549	4,355	3,637	718	605	688
Oth. Revs.	NA	NA	42,885	12,400	8,163	7,251	7,238	4,599	2,826	4,138
Total Revs.	46,887	37,105	76,431	37,609	21,345	16,583	18,465	6,797	5,125	6,608
Int. Exp.	36,638	24,768	27,495	11,443	2,259	1,956	1,284	707	674	876
Exp./Op. Revs.	261%	183%	88%	87%	86%	85%	90%	78%	81%	89%
Pretax Inc.	21,143	15,948	9,269	5,012	3,398	2,521	2,149	1,523	1,188	791
Eff. Tax Rate	36%	36%	35%	34%	31%	35%	38%	36%	36%	36%
Net Inc.	13,519	9,994	5,807	3,104	2,300	1,628	1,326	951	756	479
Balance Sheet & Other Fin. Data (Million $)										
Receivables	36,237	32,677	21,413	16,549	12,174	10,123	12,256	10,477	3,220	3,263
Cash & Invest.	134,743	127,284	129,152	65,867	56,745	42,831	40,347	43,725	3,618	3,696
Loans	367,022	244,206	215,431	10,816	5,722	5,936	6,746	6,216	5,655	6,772
Total Assets	902,210	716,937	668,641	386,555	151,067	114,475	115,297	101,360	23,397	21,561
Capitalization:										
Debt	116,698	49,392	52,991	28,352	12,884	10,658	9,555	9,526	6,584	8,044
Equity	64,461	47,761	40,395	19,533	12,460	10,910	7,840	8,526	3,929	3,280
Total	182,904	99,078	95,839	51,906	25,294	21,568	18,333	18,052	10,813	11,323
Price Times Bk. Val.: High	4.6	4.1	4.1	4.1	3.2	2.6	2.3	2.5	2.1	2.3
Price Times Bk. Val.: Low	2.7	2.3	1.6	2.1	1.9	1.3	1.6	1.2	1.5	1.3
% Return On Revs.	28.8	26.9	7.6	8.3	10.8	9.8	7.2	14.0	14.8	7.2
% Ret. on Assets	1.6	1.4	1.1	1.2	1.7	1.4	1.2	1.5	3.4	2.3
% Ret. on Equity	22.2	22.3	14.2	18.6	18.9	16.4	15.2	15.5	20.8	15.6
Loans/Equity	5.6	5.3	516.9	51.7	50.0	54.4	0.8	1.0	1.6	1.8

Data as orig. reptd. (for Travelers prior to 1998); bef. results of disc. opers. and/or spec. items. Per share data adj. for stk. divs. as of ex-div. date. Bold denotes diluted EPS (FASB 128). E-Estimated. NA-Not Available. NM-Not Meaningful. NR-Not Ranked.

Office—388 Greenwich St., New York, NY 10013. **Tel**—(212) 816-8000. **Website**—http://www.citigroup.com **Chrmn & CEO**—S. I. Weill. **CFO**—T. Thomson. **Secy**—C. O. Prince III. **VP & Investor Contact**—Sheri Ptashek (212-559-4658). **Dirs**—C. M. Armstrong, A. J. P. Belda, K. J. Bialkin, K. T. Derr, J. M. Deutch, A. D. Jordan, R. I. Lipp, R. Mark, M. T. Masin, D. C. Mecum, R. D. Parsons, A. E. Pearson, R. E. Rubin, F. A. Thomas, S. I. Weill, A. Zankel. **Transfer Agent & Registrar**—Citibank Shareholder Services, Jersey City, NJ. **Incorporated**—in Delaware in 1968. **Empl**—230,000. **S&P Analyst:** Stephen R. Biggar

STANDARD & POOR'S STOCK REPORTS

Countrywide Credit Industries

NYSE Symbol **CCR**

In S&P 500

18-AUG-01

Industry: Consumer Finance

Summary: This leading mortgage banker originates, purchases, sells and services mortgage loans.

S&P Opinion: Buy (★★★★★)

Recent Price • 44.41

52 Wk Range • 52-31.50

Yield • 0.9%

12-Mo. P/E • 13.0

Quantitative Evaluations

Outlook (1 Lowest—5 Highest)
• **3−**

Fair Value
• **46.60**

Risk
• **Low**

Earn./Div. Rank
• **A**

Technical Eval.
• **Neutral** since 7/01

Rel. Strength Rank (1 Lowest—99 Highest)
• **68**

Insider Activity
• **Neutral**

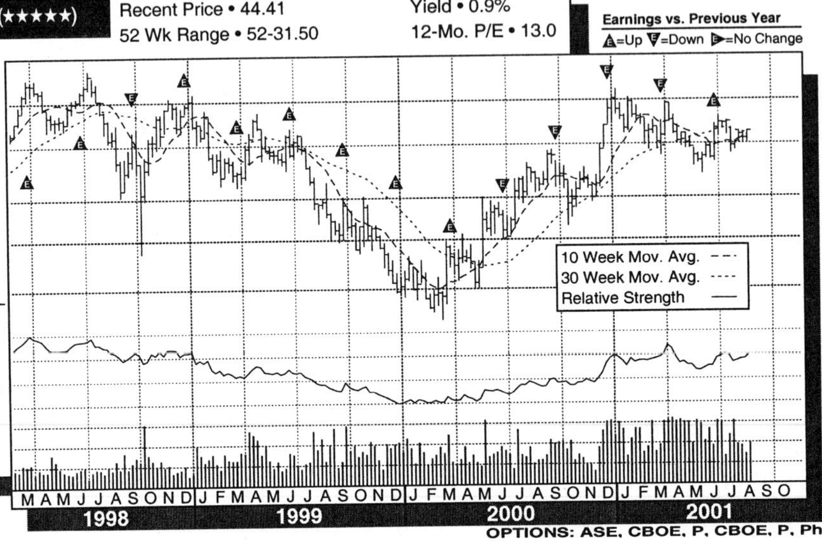

OPTIONS: ASE, CBOE, P, CBOE, P, Ph

Overview - 27-JUL-01

Mortgage rates fell steeply at the end of 2000, and have remained low, spurring home buying and refinancing, and aiding mortgage bankers like CCR. In the first quarter of FY 02 (Feb.), loan production revenue more than doubled, year to year. Aided by favorable comparisons and continued low mortgage rates, similar growth in loan production revenue is projected for the remainder of FY 02. A sharp increase in the amortization of loan servicing rights will partly offset these gains, however, with refinancing spurring mortgage prepayments. The company's non-consumer mortgage businesses, particularly its insurance carrier and loan closing services provider, should aid earnings growth in FY 02 and beyond. With total revenues advancing about 40%, and expenses rising at about the same rate, we are projecting a 38% increase in EPS in FY 02.

Valuation - 27-JUL-01

We recently upgraded the shares after first quarter results led us to adopt a more favorable outlook in two critical respects. First, CCR reported a record pipeline of loans in progress; coupled with recent dips in mortgage rates, this suggests that strong loan production revenue is sustainable over the next few quarters. Second, the company reported solid gains in its insurance, processing technology and mortgage-related capital markets and closing serving businesses. Combined, these sources contributed 32% of profits in the first quarter, up from 24% in the FY 01 period, despite the boom in mortgage originations. CCR's efforts to diversify its earnings base should serve it well when the inevitable downturn in the cyclical mortgage industry arrives. With the prospect of more consistent EPS in the future, we recommend buying the shares, trading at less than 10X our FY 02 estimate, a P/E multiple well below that of the broader market.

Key Stock Statistics

S&P EPS Est. 2002	4.33	Tang. Bk. Value/Share	30.17
P/E on S&P Est. 2002	10.3	Beta	0.81
S&P EPS Est. 2003	4.43	Shareholders	2,174
Dividend Rate/Share	0.40	Market cap. (B)	$ 5.3
Shs. outstg. (M)	119.1	Inst. holdings	89%
Avg. daily vol. (M)	0.712		

Value of $10,000 invested 5 years ago: $ 19,437

Fiscal Year Ending Feb. 28

	2002	2001	2000	1999	1998	1997
Revenues (Million $)						
1Q	684.5	528.2	537.0	450.3	318.6	263.3
2Q	—	512.3	537.0	482.2	405.2	270.8
3Q	—	520.6	491.8	514.2	375.1	281.5
4Q	—	548.8	452.9	532.4	410.0	296.8
Yr.	—	2,056	2,019	1,979	1,509	1,113
Earnings Per Share ($)						
1Q	**1.00**	**0.72**	**0.88**	**0.78**	0.64	0.58
2Q	—	**0.77**	**0.91**	**0.81**	0.99	**0.60**
3Q	—	**0.80**	**0.87**	**0.84**	0.71	0.62
4Q	—	**0.85**	**0.87**	**0.86**	**0.74**	0.63
Yr.	—	**3.14**	**3.52**	**3.29**	**3.09**	**2.44**

Next earnings report expected: early October

Dividend Data (Dividends have been paid since 1979.)

Amount ($)	Date Decl.	Ex-Div. Date	Stock of Record	Payment Date
0.100	Sep. 26	Oct. 11	Oct. 13	Oct. 31 '00
0.100	Dec. 27	Jan. 10	Jan. 12	Jan. 31 '01
0.100	Mar. 29	Apr. 09	Apr. 11	Apr. 30 '01
0.100	Jun. 21	Jul. 11	Jul. 13	Jul. 31 '01

Countrywide Credit Industries, Inc.

Business Summary - 27-JUL-01

Countrywide Credit Industries (CCR) is the largest independent U.S. residential mortgage lender and servicer. The company's primary business involves originating, purchasing, selling and servicing mortgage loans. CCR's other businesses include loan closing; insurance agency; mortgage-related investment banking and; property, liability and life insurance.

CCR's main sources of revenues are loan origination fees, gains from loan sales, interest earned on the mortgage loans during the period they are held for sale, loan servicing fees and interest derived from loans held in the company's servicing portfolio. In FY 01 (Feb.), loan production totaled $68.9 billion, up from $66.7 billion in FY 00.

In FY 01, loan origination fees accounted for 19% of total revenues. About 67% of the loans that CCR originated were conventional loans. Most conventional loans qualify for inclusion in guarantee programs sponsored by Fannie Mae or Freddie Mac. The remainder were non-conforming loans that either had original balances in excess of $275,000 or did not meet Fannie Mae or Freddie Mac guidelines. FHA/VA loans accounted for 19% of CCR's loan originations. These are loans that comply with the criteria established by these federal agencies. The remainder of CCR's loan originations included sub-prime loans (8%) and home equity loans (7%). As a mortgage banker, the company sells nearly all loans that it originates. Gains from loan sales accounted for 30% of FY 00 revenues.

The company services substantially all of the mortgage loans it originates. Servicing activities include collecting loans payments, responding to borrower inquiries, counseling delinquent borrowers and supervising foreclosures and property dispositions. Net revenues from servicing activities accounted for 28% of total revenues in FY 00.

CCR has a complex income statement. The most straightforward line item is the fees or points it charges borrowers when they take out a loan. Gain on sale refers to the appreciation a loan experiences between the time it is originated and then sold. Amortization and impairment/recovery of mortgage servicing rights refers to the noncash writedown or writeup the company makes to its loan servicing portfolio in response to such things as increased prepayments or "runoff." The servicing hedge gain or loss derives from price changes in the various financial instruments (options on treasury futures, CMO tranches, etc.) that CCR holds to offset changes in the value of its mortgage servicing portfolio.

In May 2001, the company acquired Treasury Bank, enabling it to offer depository products.

Per Share Data ($) (Year Ended Feb. 28)	2001	2000	1999	1998	1997	1996	1995	1994	1993	1992
Tangible Bk. Val.	30.23	25.45	22.37	19.12	15.19	12.91	10.32	9.67	8.29	7.00
Cash Flow	3.14	3.52	3.71	3.50	2.82	2.26	2.28	4.80	3.54	1.76
Earnings	3.14	4.08	3.29	3.09	2.44	1.95	0.96	1.97	1.65	0.88
Dividends	0.40	0.38	0.32	0.32	0.32	0.32	0.32	0.28	0.24	0.16
Payout Ratio	13%	11%	10%	10%	13%	16%	33%	14%	16%	18%
Cal. Yrs.	2000	1999	1998	1997	1996	1995	1994	1993	1992	1991
Prices - High	50.50	51.43	56.25	43.25	30.25	26.75	19.12	23.37	19.93	17.68
- Low	22.31	24.62	28.62	24.37	19.75	12.50	12.37	15.25	10.81	3.75
P/E Ratio - High	16	15	17	14	12	14	20	12	12	20
- Low	7	7	9	8	8	6	13	8	7	4
Income Statement Analysis (Million $)										
Loan Fees	1,600	1,599	1,647	1,209	967	632	471	518	342	150
Int. Inc.	1,341	999	999	440	350	354	343	376	212	115
Total Revs.	4,022	2,832	3,277	2,495	1,656	1,142	870	1,031	654	328
Int. Exp.	1,348	930	984	424	317	282	268	276	149	82.0
Exp./Op. Revs.	83%	132%	205%	119%	164%	72%	83%	71%	64%	69%
Pretax Inc.	586	631	632	566	422	326	147	299	234	100
Eff. Tax Rate	36%	35%	39%	39%	39%	40%	40%	40%	40%	40%
Net Inc.	374	410	385	345	257	196	88.4	179	140	60.2
Balance Sheet & Other Fin. Data (Million $)										
Net Prop.	397	411	312	226	274	141	146	146	95.0	54.0
Cash & Secs.	8,337	2,044	1,519	5,303	18.3	16.4	17.6	4.0	12.6	14.5
Loans	1,964	2,653	6,231	5,292	2,580	4,740	2,899	3,714	2,343	1,585
Total Assets	22,956	15,822	15,648	12,219	8,089	8,658	5,580	5,586	3,299	2,410
Capitalization:										
Debt	8,144	7,753	6,453	7,975	2,368	1,912	1,499	1,197	735	430
Equity	3,559	2,888	2,519	2,088	1,612	1,320	943	880	693	557
Total	13,273	10,641	8,972	6,284	3,980	3,145	2,442	2,077	1,428	1,026
Price Times Bk. Val.: High	1.7	2.0	2.5	2.3	2.0	2.1	1.9	2.0	2.8	2.8
Price Times Bk. Val.: Low	0.7	1.0	1.3	1.3	1.6	1.0	1.2	1.3	1.8	2.2
Cash Flow	374	476	435	390	298	227	210	437	300	120
% Return On Revs.	11.0	15.8	12.5	18.3	15.6	17.2	10.2	17.4	21.4	18.3
% Ret. on Assets	1.9	2.6	2.9	3.4	3.1	2.8	1.6	4.0	4.9	3.4
% Ret. on Equity	11.6	14.2	16.7	18.7	17.6	17.3	9.7	22.8	21.8	16.4

Data as orig reptd.; bef. results of disc opers/spec. items. Per share data adj. for stk. divs. Bold denotes diluted EPS (FASB 128)-prior periods restated. E-Estimated. NA-Not Available. NM-Not Meaningful. NR-Not Ranked.

Office—4500 Park Granada Blvd., Calabasas, CA 91302. **Tel**—(818) 225-3000. **Website**—http://www.countrywide.com **Chrmn, CEO & Pres**—A. R. Mozilo. **COO**—S. L. Kurland. **CFO**—C. M. Garcia. **Secy**—S. E. Samuels. **Investor Contact**—Eric Sieracki (818-225-3550). **Dirs**—H. G. Cisneros, J. M. Cunningham, R. J. Donato, M. E. Dougherty, B. M. Enis, E. Heller, S. L. Kurland, A. R. Mozilo, O. P. Robertson, H. W. Snyder. **Transfer Agent & Registrar**—Bank of New York, NYC. **Incorporated**—in New York in 1969; reincorporated in Delaware in 1987. **Empl**— 12,090. **S&P Analyst:** Erik J. Eisenstein

STANDARD & POOR'S
STOCK REPORTS

Eaton Vance

NYSE Symbol **EV**
In S&P MidCap 400

23-AUG-01

Industry: Investment Management

Summary: This Boston-based holding company is primarily engaged in investment management.

S&P Opinion: Buy (★★★★★)

Recent Price • 33.10
52 Wk Range • 39.22-21.43
Yield • 0.7%
12-Mo. P/E • 21.6

Quantitative Evaluations

Outlook
(1 Lowest—5 Highest)
• **1+**

Fair Value
• **32.10**

Risk
• **Average**

Earn./Div. Rank
• **A**

Technical Eval.
• **Neutral** since 8/01

Rel. Strength Rank
(1 Lowest—99 Highest)
• **43**

Insider Activity
• **NA**

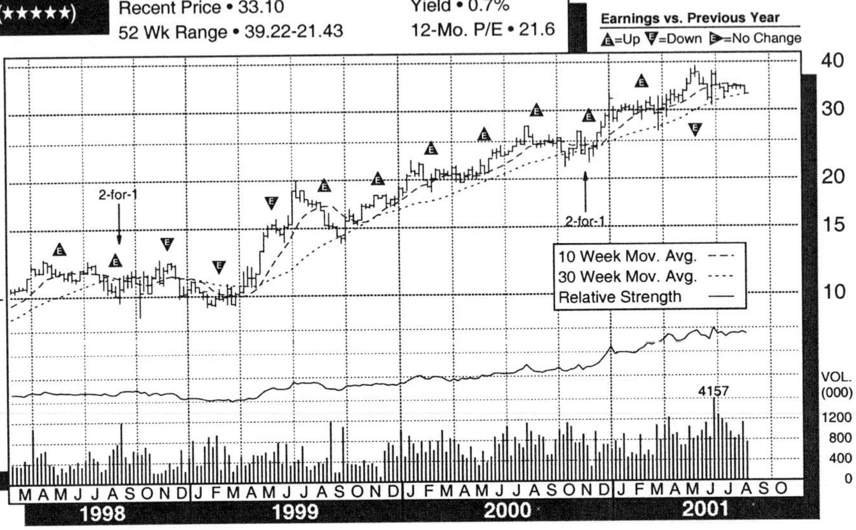

Overview - 23-AUG-01

After advancing 20% in FY 00 (Oct.), assets under management are expected to increase less than 10% in FY 01, driven by a combination of rising securities prices, fund sales and acquisitions. Assets under management at the end of the third quarter of FY 01 totaled $50.4 billion, up from $47.3 billion a year earlier. Net inflows in the first nine months of FY 01 increased 29% to $4.9 billion, from $3.8 billion last year. Revenues in FY 00 advanced 23%. For FY 01, we are projecting more modest growth. EV actively engages in share repurchases. In the first nine months of FY 01, EV bought back 1,055,000 common shares. We expect the company to repurchase about 2% of its common stock annually, and to hike the quarterly dividend in October 2001. We see operating EPS (excluding a loss of $0.12 a share relating to an impairment loss on investments) in FY 01 advancing 16%, to $1.78 in FY 01, aided by a sharply lower tax rate, and 12%, to $1.99 in FY 02.

Valuation - 23-AUG-01

The shares carry a buy recommendation, and are expected to outperform the S&P 500 over the next six to 12 months. On a P/E basis, the shares are trading at a discount to the P/E ratio of the S&P 500, and slightly above the P/Es of shares of the company's peers in the asset management group. However, we believe EV merits a premium valuation relative to its group, in light of its stellar growth in managed assets and operating cash flow. In addition, financial stocks in general should benefit in coming periods from a less aggressive policy stance on the part of the Federal Reserve. We expect the acquisition of a number of investment management companies in recent quarters to help refocus investor attention on small independent asset management companies such as EV. The company also boasts a strong balance sheet, with little debt.

Key Stock Statistics

S&P EPS Est. 2001	1.78	Tang. Bk. Value/Share	3.98
P/E on S&P Est. 2001	18.6	Beta	0.43
Dividend Rate/Share	0.24	Shareholders	950
Shs. outstg. (M)	69.1	Market cap. (B)	$ 2.3
Avg. daily vol. (M)	0.186	Inst. holdings	48%

Value of $10,000 invested 5 years ago: $ 73,842

Fiscal Year Ending Oct. 31

	2001	2000	1999	1998	1997	1996
Revenues (Million $)						
1Q	120.1	102.3	75.48	55.27	47.81	44.50
2Q	115.5	104.8	84.32	59.99	47.44	45.46
3Q	124.7	108.0	91.05	67.00	47.74	45.06
4Q	—	114.5	98.11	67.72	53.86	46.34
Yr.	—	429.6	348.9	250.0	200.9	181.4
Earnings Per Share ($)						
1Q	**0.44**	**0.38**	**-0.14**	**0.14**	0.13	0.13
2Q	**0.44**	**0.40**	**0.14**	**0.15**	0.12	0.12
3Q	—	**0.38**	**0.35**	**0.18**	0.14	0.12
4Q	—	**0.42**	**0.35**	**-0.08**	0.13	0.10
Yr.	—	**1.58**	**0.70**	**0.41**	**0.52**	**0.47**

Next earnings report expected: late November

Dividend Data (Dividends have been paid since 1976.)

Amount ($)	Date Decl.	Ex-Div. Date	Stock of Record	Payment Date
2-for-1	Oct. 11	Nov. 14	Oct. 31	Nov. 13 '00
0.060	Jan. 17	Jan. 29	Jan. 31	Feb. 12 '01
0.060	Apr. 18	Apr. 26	Apr. 30	May. 14 '01
0.060	Jul. 11	Jul. 27	Jul. 31	Aug. 13 '01

Business Summary - 23-AUG-01

Eaton Vance Corp. is a Boston-based investment advisory company. Historically, it has focused on offering products in the fixed-income sector, with particular emphasis on tax-free municipal bonds. However, with industry dynamics pushing an increasing number of investors into the stock market for superior investment returns, EV has targeted its equity business as a growth area. This was the primary driver in the 20% increase in total assets under management to $49.2 billion at the end of FY 00 (Oct.), from $40.9 billion at October 31, 1999.

Reflecting EV's strategy, the trend in recent years has been for equities to account for a higher percentage of fund assets, while non-taxable fixed income assets declined as a percentage of assets under management. Equities accounted for 52% of assets under management at October 31, 2000, versus 44% at the end of FY 99. At the end of FY 00, assets were divided as follows: equities 52%, bank loans 21%, non-taxable fixed income 13%, taxable fixed income 7%, separately managed accounts 7%, and money market less than 1%.

The company derives the vast majority of revenues from investment advisory and administration fees and distribution income received from more than 70 funds, and more than 800 separately managed accounts. Fees are calculated as a percentage of assets under management; as a result, operating results are largely dependent on EV's ability to attract and retain funds, and on the overall health of the securities markets.

EV employs two separate mutual fund sales teams that sell through the national, regional, and independent broker/dealer channels, and through banks and independent financial advisers. Funds are also offered to investors, without commissions or other transaction fees, through registered investment advisors via various institutional programs.

In addition to steadily increasing its cash dividend over the past decade, the company has used its significant cash reserves to repurchase stock. In FY 00, the company purchased nearly 2.4 million shares of its non-voting common stock. In FY 99, it purchased 1,254,000 shares of its non-voting common stock, and in FY 98, it bought back 2,099,000 shares.

At the beginning of the FY 99 third quarter, EV restructured certain of its bank loan funds, and received SEC approval to resume its historical practice of capitalizing and amortizing sales commissions. Reported earnings prior to this resumption had been significantly affected since mid-1998, when a new accounting rule was implemented that required commissions to be expensed as startup costs under the funds' previous structure.

EV has five funds funds based in Dublin, Ireland, for retail distribution in Europe. These funds are registered for retail sale in Germany and Switzerland. The company has also registered a number of its offshore funds in Hong Kong for sale there.

Per Share Data ($) (Year Ended Oct. 31)	2000	1999	1998	1997	1996	1995	1994	1993	1992	1991
Tangible Bk. Val.	3.63	2.73	2.96	3.02	2.77	2.58	2.25	1.95	1.26	0.97
Cash Flow	1.67	0.77	0.45	0.55	0.50	0.40	1.12	1.01	0.82	0.66
Earnings	1.58	0.70	0.41	0.52	0.47	0.36	0.38	0.39	0.31	0.22
Dividends	0.20	0.16	0.13	0.10	0.09	0.08	0.08	0.06	0.05	0.04
Payout Ratio	13%	23%	31%	20%	19%	22%	20%	16%	14%	17%
Prices - High	32.93	20.00	12.54	9.56	6.21	4.90	4.68	5.15	3.81	2.06
- Low	18.12	9.34	8.71	5.21	3.25	3.40	3.06	3.62	1.93	0.98
P/E Ratio - High	21	28	31	18	13	14	13	13	12	9
- Low	11	13	22	10	7	9	8	9	6	5
Income Statement Analysis (Million $)										
Commissions	226	199	152	118	100	85.4	85.8	75.2	69.5	61.5
Int. Inc.	5.7	3.6	5.6	3.6	3.7	2.6	4.9	4.6	3.7	3.7
Total Revs.	430	349	250	201	181	168	218	189	153	120
Int. Exp.	2.0	3.0	3.8	4.0	3.7	4.7	5.3	4.9	3.3	3.1
Pretax Inc.	187	85.9	50.0	67.5	59.9	46.1	47.7	47.0	33.1	21.1
Eff. Tax Rate	38%	39%	39%	40%	40%	38%	40%	42%	42%	40%
Net Inc.	116	52.4	30.5	40.2	35.8	30.4	28.5	27.3	19.3	12.7
Balance Sheet & Other Fin. Data (Million $)										
Total Assets	433	358	380	387	360	358	456	426	318	278
Cash Items	60.5	77.4	54.4	141	116	79.0	34.0	28.7	25.5	17.1
Receivables	15.4	14.9	11.2	13.1	7.7	1.6	13.1	11.6	10.5	7.2
Secs. Owned	NA	NA	NA	NA	NA	NA	88.3	80.2	64.0	50.8
Sec. Borrowed	NA	NA	NA	NA	NA	Nil	Nil	Nil	Nil	Nil
Due Brokers & Cust.	NA	NA	NA	NA	NA	Nil	Nil	Nil	Nil	Nil
Other Liabs.	35.9	23.5	2.1	121	125	138	226	205	162	153
Capitalization:										
Debt	21.4	28.6	53.0	50.9	54.5	56.1	60.3	73.2	78.4	64.0
Equity	255	194	212	226	211	195	166	145	77.5	59.6
Total	371	309	331	347	336	333	229	221	156	125
% Return On Revs.	27.0	34.9	12.2	20.0	19.8	16.1	13.1	14.5	12.6	10.6
% Ret. on Assets	29.3	14.2	8.0	10.8	10.0	6.6	6.5	7.4	6.4	5.1
% Ret. on Equity	51.7	25.8	13.9	18.4	17.7	15.0	18.3	24.7	28.0	23.5

Data as orig reptd.; bef. results of disc opers/spec. items. Per share data adj. for stk. divs. Bold denotes diluted EPS (FASB 128)-prior periods restated. E-Estimated. NA-Not Available. NM-Not Meaningful. NR-Not Ranked.

Office—255 State Street, Boston, MA 02109. **Tel**—(617) 482-8260. **Website**—http://www.eatonvance.com **Chrmn, Pres & CEO**—J. B. Hawkes. **VP & Secy**—A.R. Dynner. **VP, CFO & Investor Contact**—William M. Steul. **Dirs**—J. G. L. Cabot, J. B. Hawkes, L. I. Higdon, Jr., J. M. Nelson, V. M. O'Reilly, R. Z. Sorenson. **Transfer Agent & Registrar**—Boston EquiServe. **Incorporated**—in Maryland in 1959. **Empl**— 438. **S&P Analyst:** R. McMillan

STANDARD
&POOR'S
STOCK REPORTS

FleetBoston Financial

NYSE Symbol **FBF**

In S&P 500

24-AUG-01

Industry: Banks (Major Regional)

Summary: This bank holding company was formed via the October 1999 merger of Fleet Financial Group and BankBoston Corp.

S&P Opinion: Buy (★★★★★)

Recent Price • 37.24
52 Wk Range • 44.18-31.75
Yield • 3.5%
12-Mo. P/E • 15.3

Quantitative Evaluations

Outlook
(1 Lowest—5 Highest)
• **2−**

Fair Value
• **38**

Risk
• **NA**

Earn./Div. Rank
• **A-**

Technical Eval.
• **NA**

Rel. Strength Rank
(1 Lowest—99 Highest)
• **44**

Insider Activity
• **Neutral**

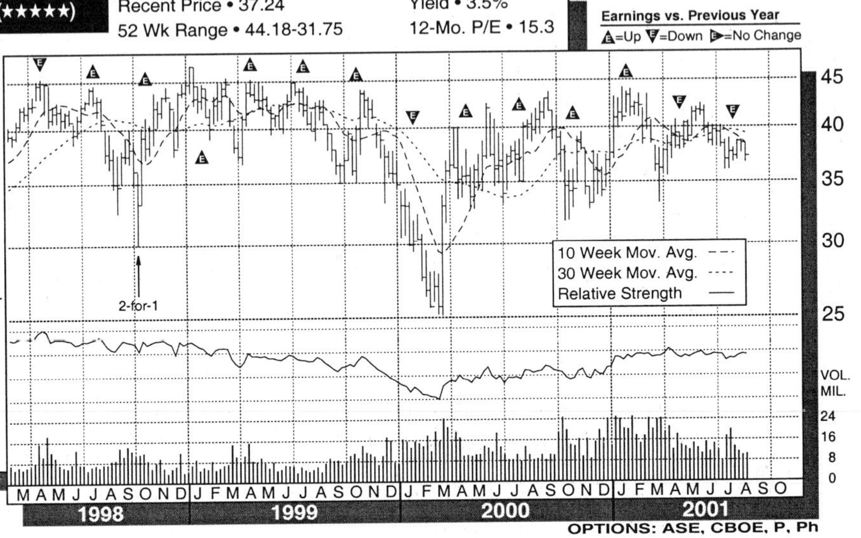

OPTIONS: ASE, CBOE, P, Ph

Overview - 24-AUG-01

Net interest income is expected to be modestly lower in 2001, as reduced lending volumes, particularly in the commercial lending segment, are offset by some net interest margin improvement from a declining interest rate environment. The sale of about $1 billion of troubled commercial loans late in 2000 has had a favorable effect on credit quality ratios, although modestly higher loan chargeoffs are expected through the end of 2001. Continued weakness is likely in capital markets businesses, reflecting less robust equity market fundamentals, although we expect most other fee-based businesses to maintain healthy momentum in noninterest income. The recent Summit Bancorp merger will give the company a leadership position in several New Jersey banking categories, and provides an attractive outlet for selling high margin products, including those related to asset management and capital markets.

Valuation - 24-AUG-01

The shares were recently up about 3% in 2001, outperforming our regional bank index, as well as the broader market. We believe FleetBoston will continue to attract investor attention, due to a more dynamic product mix than that of its peers. Although only minimal EPS growth is expected in 2001, mostly reflecting the impact of weak capital market conditions, a rebound is expected in 2002. The shares, recently trading at 11X our 2002 EPS estimate of $3.65, a discount to the valuation accorded the shares of major regional bank peers with similar business mixes, are expected to outperform the broader market in the coming year.

Key Stock Statistics

S&P EPS Est. 2001	2.80	Tang. Bk. Value/Share	13.33
P/E on S&P Est. 2001	13.3	Beta	1.31
S&P EPS Est. 2002	3.65	Shareholders	67,166
Dividend Rate/Share	1.32	Market cap. (B)	$ 41.4
Shs. outstg. (M)	1085.3	Inst. holdings	63%
Avg. daily vol. (M)	2.123		

Value of $10,000 invested 5 years ago: $ 19,846

Fiscal Year Ending Dec. 31

	2001	2000	1999	1998	1997	1996
Revenues (Million $)						
1Q	5,690	6,183	—	2,289	1,951	1,838
2Q	3,244	5,719	—	2,525	1,974	2,006
3Q	—	5,534	2,763	2,572	1,990	2,094
4Q	—	5,173	3,636	2,616	2,002	2,062
Yr.	—	22,608	13,748	10,002	8,095	8,000
Earnings Per Share ($)						
1Q	**0.12**	**1.03**	**0.69**	**0.53**	**0.55**	**0.47**
2Q	**0.48**	**0.91**	**0.72**	**0.65**	**0.59**	**0.48**
3Q	—	**0.90**	**0.72**	**0.66**	**0.60**	**0.51**
4Q	—	**0.84**	**-0.05**	**0.69**	**0.61**	**0.53**
Yr.	—	**3.68**	**2.10**	**2.52**	**2.37**	**1.99**

Next earnings report expected: mid October

Dividend Data (Dividends have been paid since 1791.)

Amount ($)	Date Decl.	Ex-Div. Date	Stock of Record	Payment Date
0.330	Oct. 17	Nov. 29	Dec. 03	Jan. 01 '01
0.330	Feb. 21	Feb. 28	Mar. 03	Apr. 01 '01
0.330	Apr. 17	May. 30	Jun. 03	Jul. 01 '01
0.330	Aug. 21	Aug. 29	Sep. 03	Oct. 01 '01

A Division of The McGraw-Hill Companies

FleetBoston Financial Corporation

Business Summary - 24-AUG-01

Now the seventh largest bank holding company in the U.S., FleetBoston Financial is the largest bank in New England, with about $180 billion in assets. FBF serves about 20 million customers. The company is managed along three business lines: global banking and financial services (52% of net income in 2000), commercial and retail banking (35%), and national financial services (13%).

Global banking and financial services includes corporate banking (specialized industry lending, institutional banking, investment banking and capital markets activities), international banking (in Brazil, Argentina and other Latin American countries), investment services (Quick & Reilly securities brokerage, specialized asset management and proprietary mutual funds), and principal investing (startup capital and debt financing to new ventures).

Commercial and retail banking includes domestic banking to consumer and small business customers, as well as domestic commercial banking operations such as middle market lending, asset-based lending, leasing, cash management, trade finance, and government banking services. Consumer retail products and services are distributed through a network of 1,250 branches

National financial services includes credit card services (FBF is the 10th largest bank credit card issuer in the U.S.), commercial real estate lending, mortgage banking (offices in 19 states), and student loan processing.

Total loans and leases of $109.4 billion at 2000 year end were divided: commercial and industrial 43%, consumer 22%, lease financing 12%, commercial real estate 8% and international 15%.

Nonperforming assets, those on which income recognition has either ceased or is limited, at December 31, 2000, were $925 million (0.85% of assets), up from $841 million (0.70%) a year earlier. The allowance for loan losses, held in anticipation of loan defaults, was $2.4 billion (2.20% of loans) at the end of 2000, down from $2.5 billion (2.10%) the year before. Net charge-offs in 2000 were $1.14 billion (0.99% of average loans), versus $896 million (0.76%) in 1999.

In March 2001, the company acquired New Jersey-based Summit Bancorp (NYSE: SUB) in a transaction valued at about $7 billion. Terms called for each SUB common share to be exchanged for 1.02 FBF shares. The transaction is expected to be accretive to operating earnings in 2001.

Per Share Data ($) (Year Ended Dec. 31)	2000	1999	1998	1997	1996	1995	1994	1993	1992	1991
Tangible Bk. Val.	12.79	12.16	9.88	9.97	9.09	9.23	6.78	10.13	6.03	6.67
Earnings	3.68	2.10	2.52	2.37	1.98	0.79	1.88	1.50	0.89	0.34
Dividends	1.23	1.08	0.98	0.92	0.87	0.80	0.70	0.51	0.41	0.40
Payout Ratio	33%	51%	39%	39%	44%	102%	37%	34%	46%	119%
Prices - High	43.75	46.81	45.37	37.59	28.12	21.62	20.68	18.93	16.93	13.18
- Low	25.12	33.25	30.00	24.37	18.81	14.93	14.93	14.12	12.12	4.81
P/E Ratio - High	12	22	18	16	14	28	11	13	19	39
- Low	7	16	12	10	10	19	8	9	14	14
Income Statement Analysis (Million $)										
Net Int. Inc.	6,521	6,742	3,869	3,627	3,043	3,020	1,982	2,051	1,954	1,404
Tax Equiv. Adj.	61.0	57.0	36.0	40.0	36.0	44.0	40.0	33.0	29.8	46.0
Non Int. Inc.	9,024	6,974	3,237	2,214	2,158	1,818	1,174	1,465	1,229	933
Loan Loss Prov.	1,196	933	470	322	213	101	62.0	271	486	509
Exp./Op. Revs.	55%	68%	58%	58%	66%	77%	65%	68%	74%	78%
Pretax Inc.	5,716	3,426	2,507	2,171	1,931	1,034	1,023	821	518	153
Eff. Tax Rate	40%	41%	39%	40%	41%	41%	39%	40%	44%	36%
Net Inc.	3,420	2,038	1,532	1,303	1,139	610	613	488	280	98.0
% Net Int. Marg.	4.24	4.23	4.63	5.21	4.81	4.12	4.65	5.02	4.81	4.05
Balance Sheet & Other Fin. Data (Million $)										
Money Mkt. Assets	9,039	10,202	103	498	1,772	61.0	NA	Nil	NM	463
Inv. Securities	25,797	26,456	14,752	9,362	8,680	19,331	11,244	14,123	12,660	10,624
Com'l Loans	69,308	74,984	41,372	35,614	31,889	25,474	12,675	12,333	12,517	12,199
Other Loans	40,064	44,716	28,004	25,565	26,955	26,051	15,355	13,977	16,217	16,751
Total Assets	179,519	190,692	104,382	85,535	85,518	84,432	48,757	47,923	46,939	45,445
Demand Deposits	25,676	26,305	13,400	13,148	17,903	12,305	6,890	6,473	6,483	6,517
Time Deposits	75,614	88,591	56,278	50,587	49,168	44,817	27,916	24,612	26,252	28,729
LT Debt	28,357	25,439	8,820	4,500	5,114	6,481	3,457	3,444	3,812	2,511
Common Eqty.	31,778	14,616	8,718	7,343	6,462	5,966	3,001	3,138	2,397	2,460
% Ret. on Assets	1.8	1.1	1.6	1.5	1.3	0.7	1.3	1.1	0.6	0.3
% Ret. on Equity	11.0	14.1	18.4	18.0	18.3	7.6	19.0	16.1	10.4	3.9
% Loan Loss Resv.	2.2	-2.1	2.2	2.3	2.5	2.6	3.4	3.8	3.6	3.6
% Loans/Deposits	108.0	104.2	99.6	200.7	85.5	90.2	80.5	84.6	87.8	80.2
% Equity to Assets	16.7	7.6	8.5	8.1	7.3	6.6	6.5	7.5	5.8	5.6

Data as orig reptd.; bef. results of disc opers/spec. items. Per share data adj. for stk. divs. Bold denotes diluted EPS (FASB 128)-prior periods restated. E-Estimated. NA-Not Available. NM-Not Meaningful. NR-Not Ranked.

Office—100 Federal St., Boston, MA 02110. **Tel**—(617) 434-2200. **Website**—http://www.fleet.com **Chrmn & CEO**—T. Murray. **Pres & COO**—C. K. Gifford. **Vice Chrmn & CFO**—E. M. McQuade. **Investor Contact**—John Kahwaty (617-434-3650). **Dirs**—J. B. Alvord, W. Barnet III, D. P. Burnham, P. J. Choquette, Jr., J. T. Collins, W. F. Connell, G. L. Countryman, T. J. D. Dunphy, A. F. Emerson, C. K. Gifford, M. L. Heard, R. J. Higgins, —R. M. Kavner, T. J. May, D. F. McHenry, H. de Campos Meirelles, T. Murray, M. B. Picotte, F. S. Rodgers, J. W. Rowe, T. M. Ryan, T. J. Semrod, P. R. Tregurtha. **Transfer Agent & Registrar**—EquiServe, First Chicago Trust Division, Jersey City, NJ. **Incorporated**—in Rhode Island in 1970. **Empl**—53,000. **S&P Analyst:** Stephen R. Biggar

STANDARD &POOR'S
STOCK REPORTS

IndyMac Bancorp

NYSE Symbol **NDE**

In S&P MidCap 400

18-AUG-01

Industry: Savings & Loan Companies

Summary: NDE is a savings and loan holding company for IndyMac Bank, an Internet-based diversified mortgage banking business.

S&P Opinion: Buy (★★★★★)

Recent Price • 27.73
52 Wk Range • 30.43-16.31
Yield • Nil
12-Mo. P/E • 17.9

Quantitative Evaluations

Outlook (1 Lowest—5 Highest)
• **2+**

Fair Value
• **26.80**

Risk
• **Low**

Earn./Div. Rank
• **B**

Technical Eval.
• **Bullish** since 8/01

Rel. Strength Rank (1 Lowest—99 Highest)
• **82**

Insider Activity
• **NA**

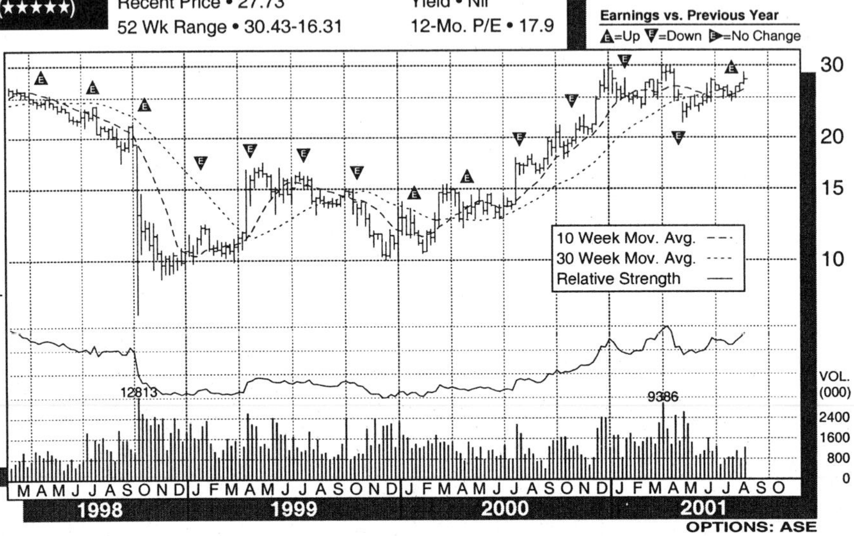

Overview - 31-JUL-01

With mortgage rates falling at the end of 2000, and remaining low thus far in 2001, home lending is enjoying a banner year. Aided by this surge in mortgage originations, and the strength of NDE's Internet platform, we expect loan growth of over 50%. Following this advance, and a wider net interest margin, we anticipate net interest income to be up over 20%. Provisioning should rise, but credit quality is not a major concern. Noninterest income should climb 40%, benefiting from higher gains on loan sales following an increased pipeline of fixed-rate mortgages. Servicing fees should be down, with higher prepayment rates associated with refinancing. Our forecast calls for efficiency in the low fifties. We expect operating EPS to increase about 43% in 2001, to $1.89. In 2002, we are projecting a 26% gain in operating EPS, to $2.39.

Valuation - 31-JUL-01

NDE is successfully leveraging its on-line origination capabilities to build scale in the highly fragmented mortgage banking industry. Mortgage loan production more than doubled in the second quarter of 2001, year to year, bolstered by an excellent operating environment. Although mortgage rates will begin to rise as the economy improves, we see NDE continuing to generate strong loan growth and at least approaching its goal of becoming a top 10 mortgage lender nationwide by 2003, aided by rising use of the Internet by brokers, consumers and realtors to streamline the mortgage origination process. We also expect NDE to have a cost advantage over competitors in years to come, with a mostly branchless infrastructure. With NDE recently at about 2.1 times book value, about average for an S&L, we see market expansion following continued execution, and recommend investors buy the stock for its compelling growth potential.

Key Stock Statistics

S&P EPS Est. 2001	1.89	Tang. Bk. Value/Share	11.08
P/E on S&P Est. 2001	14.7	Beta	-0.04
S&P EPS Est. 2002	2.39	Shareholders	4,358
Dividend Rate/Share	Nil	Market cap. (B)	$ 1.7
Shs. outstg. (M)	61.0	Inst. holdings	71%
Avg. daily vol. (M)	0.196		

Value of $10,000 invested 5 years ago: $ 20,768

Fiscal Year Ending Dec. 31

	2001	2000	1999	1998	1997	1996
Revenues (Million $)						
1Q	201.1	132.6	92.90	124.5	75.22	59.22
2Q	212.6	145.5	82.69	146.1	89.49	61.76
3Q	—	169.0	87.50	156.1	94.05	67.23
4Q	—	188.7	96.56	107.2	107.8	72.55
Yr.	—	636.4	359.6	528.8	360.9	260.8
Earnings Per Share ($)						
1Q	**0.39**	**0.69**	**0.30**	**0.50**	**0.41**	**0.35**
2Q	**0.48**	**0.31**	**0.36**	**0.53**	**0.42**	**0.36**
3Q	—	**0.31**	**0.39**	**0.54**	**-0.83**	**0.39**
4Q	—	**0.36**	**0.41**	**-0.98**	**0.47**	**0.40**
Yr.	—	**1.69**	**1.48**	**0.48**	**0.43**	1.51

Next earnings report expected: mid October

Dividend Data

No dividends have been paid since the company terminated its REIT status in January, 2000.

IndyMac Bancorp

Business Summary - 31-JUL-01

In January 2000, IndyMac Bancorp (formerly IndyMac Mortgage Holdings) terminated its REIT status, as part of a strategy to become a taxable, growth oriented, technology-driven consumer bank.

In July 2000, NDE acquired SGV Bancorp, Inc. (SGV), a savings and loan operating in Southern California, for $59.5 million. NDE contributed its operations and assets to the thrift, now called IndyMac Bank, which is regulated as a savings and loan. SGV had nine branches and assets of $491 million at the time of the merger date. NDE planned to continue develop its existing mortgage and consumer lending business, and to increase the bank's existing deposit base (a stable source of loan funding) over the next several years to 30% to 50% of NDE's total liabilities.

IndyMac conducts a diversified mortgage banking business, manages an investment portfolio, and offers commercial lending and retail banking products.

The company's core Mortgage Banking Group employs several distinct loan-production channels. A business-to-business channel (B2B), with mortgage brokers, small mortgage bankers and community financial institutions, effectively provides the company with access to a variable-cost, nationwide branch network. IndyMac also employs a branchless, technology-driven, business-to-consumer (B2C) channel. A business-to-realtor channel (B2R), LoanWorks.com, extends the company's technology to real estate professionals involved in the mortgage loan process on behalf of their home-buying customers. IndyMac uses its proprietary loan approval and pricing system, e-MITS, across its B2B, B2C and B2R channels.

Other operations include Construction Lending Corp. of America, which offers residential construction loan programs for builders and developers.

IndyMac produced $10.1 billion in loans in 2000, a 45% increase over 1999. Internet production accounted for 69% of that total, compared to 34% in the prior year. The core Mortgage Banking Group produced $9.2 billion in mortgages in 2000, up 48%.

NDE offers a full array of consumer banking products with a primary focus on gathering certificates of deposit. IndyMac increased deposits to $798 million at December 31, 2000, from $354 million at the time of the SGV acquisition.

In the 2000 third quarter, NDE acquired for cash certain mortgage loans and other assets of PNB mortgage, a wholesale loan originator that specializes in FHA and VA mortgage lending. With the acquisition, NDE projected FHA/VA production at about $1 billion for 2001.

In December 2000, NDE suspended its repurchase activities, after having repurchased 18.5 million shares, or 23% of shares outstanding since the inception of its buyback program. In the first half of 2001, IndyMac repurchased an additional 2.8 million shares.

Per Share Data ($) (Year Ended Dec. 31)	2000	1999	1998	1997	1996	1995	1994	1993	1992	1991
Tangible Bk. Val.	11.08	11.02	10.85	11.11	9.82	8.56	7.93	7.83	7.42	7.13
Earnings	1.69	1.48	0.48	0.43	1.51	1.25	0.86	0.13	0.36	0.78
Dividends	Nil	1.74	1.89	1.71	1.47	1.17	0.72	0.48	0.48	0.78
Payout Ratio	Nil	118%	NM	NM	97%	94%	84%	NM	133%	100%
Prices - High	30.43	17.43	27.18	26.12	21.87	17.25	11.75	11.37	6.87	7.37
- Low	10.37	9.81	7.37	19.37	14.75	8.50	7.00	5.25	4.50	4.37
P/E Ratio - High	18	12	57	61	14	14	14	88	19	9
- Low	6	7	15	45	10	7	8	40	13	6
Income Statement Analysis (Million $)										
Net Int. Inc.	155	161	173	119	83.0	NA	NA	NA	NA	NA
Non Int. Inc.	193	6.1	-55.4	25.7	22.9	NA	NA	NA	NA	NA
Loan Loss Prov.	16.0	16.4	35.9	18.6	13.0	NA	NA	NA	NA	NA
Non Int. Exp.	196	34.6	29.3	102	23.0	NA	NA	NA	NA	NA
Exp./Op. Revs.	56%	21%	35%	71%	22%	NA	NA	NA	NA	NA
Pretax Inc.	141	116	33.8	24.0	69.0	NA	NA	NA	NA	NA
Eff. Tax Rate	16%	Nil	Nil	Nil	Nil	NA	NA	NA	NA	NA
Net Inc.	118	116	33.8	24.0	69.0	NA	NA	NA	NA	NA
% Net Int. Marg.	NA	NA	NA	NA	NA	NA	NA	NA	NA	NA
Balance Sheet & Other Fin. Data (Million $)										
Money Mkt. Assets	NA	Nil	Nil	Nil	Nil	NA	NA	NA	NA	NA
Inv. Securities	1,218	471	235	558	NA	NA	NA	NA	NA	NA
Tot. Loans	4,041	2,954	4,115	2,389	NA	NA	NA	NA	NA	NA
Total Assets	5,740	3,727	4,851	5,849	3,370	NA	NA	NA	NA	NA
Demand Deposits	NA	Nil	Nil	Nil	Nil	NA	NA	NA	NA	NA
Time Deposits	758	Nil	Nil	Nil	Nil	NA	NA	NA	NA	NA
LT Debt	987	143	140	221	264	NA	NA	NA	NA	NA
Common Eqty.	728	828	822	704	493	NA	NA	NA	NA	NA
% Ret. on Assets	2.5	2.7	0.6	0.5	2.3	NA	NA	NA	NA	NA
% Ret. on Equity	15.2	14.1	4.4	4.0	16.1	NA	NA	NA	NA	NA
% Loan Loss Resv.	1.5	NA	NA	NA	NA	NA	NA	NA	NA	NA
% Loans/Deposits	506.4	NM	NM	NM	NM	NA	NA	NA	NA	NA
% Loans/Assets	75.4	82.4	60.8	70.5	NA	NA	NA	NA	NA	NA
% Equity to Assets	16.4	19.2	14.3	13.0	14.2	NA	NA	NA	NA	NA

Data as orig reptd.; bef. results of disc opers/spec. items. Per share data adj. for stk. divs. Bold denotes diluted EPS (FASB 128)-prior periods restated. E-Estimated. NA-Not Available. NM-Not Meaningful. NR-Not Ranked.

Office—155 North Lake Ave., Passadena, CA 91101-7211. **Tel**—(800) 669-2300. **Website**—http://www.indymacbank.com **Chrmn**—D. S. Loeb. **CEO & Vice Chrmn**—M. W. Perry. **EVP & CFO**—C. L. Grahn. **EVP & Secy**—R. L. Sommers. **Investor Contact**—Pamela Marsh (626-535-8465). **Dirs**—L. E. Gramley, H. M. Grant, P.C. Haden, T. J. Kearns, D. S. Loeb, F. J. Napolitano, M. W. Perry, J. R. Ukropina. **Transfer Agent**—Bank of New York, NYC. **Incorporated**—in Delaware in 1987; originally incorporated in Maryland in 1985.**Empl**— 1,746. **S&P Analyst:** Erik J. Eisenstein

STANDARD &POOR'S STOCK REPORTS

J.P. Morgan Chase

NYSE Symbol **JPM**

In S&P 500

18-AUG-01

Industry: Financial (Diversified)

Summary: This bank holding company, which offers a wide range of domestic and international financial services, was formed on the merger of Chase Manhattan and J.P. Morgan.

S&P Opinion: Buy (★★★★★)

Recent Price • 41.48
52 Wk Range • 58.37-32.37
Yield • 3.3%
12-Mo. P/E • 23.2

Quantitative Evaluations

Outlook (1 Lowest—5 Highest) • **2−**

Fair Value • **41.10**

Risk • **NA**

Earn./Div. Rank • **B+**

Technical Eval. • **Bearish** since 6/01

Rel. Strength Rank (1 Lowest—99 Highest) • **36**

Insider Activity • **Neutral**

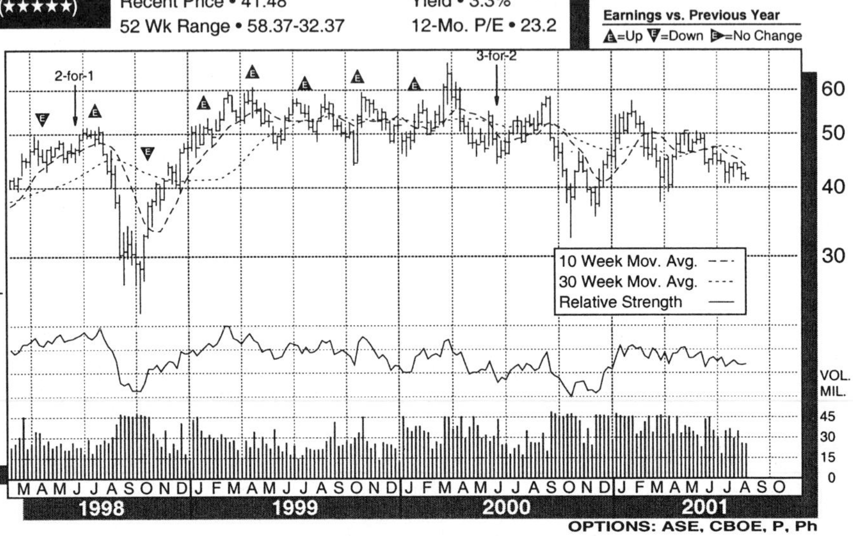

OPTIONS: ASE, CBOE, P, Ph

Overview - 04-MAY-01

Operating revenues in the first quarter of 2001 rose in all major segments not related to capital markets businesses, while cash operating expenses were down or at most flat with the prior year quarter. Although we do not expect a quick turnaround in capital markets units, operating revenues are expected to advance 10% in 2001, given a reasonable equity market environment and no major upsets to the economy. We believe recent results have highlighted the capabilities of the combined company, namely better diversification of capital market income sources and market share gains in areas such as merger and acquisition advisory. Merger cost savings will be a primary earnings driver, with some 30% of the merger's overall $1.5 billion in savings expected in 2001. Financial goals remain annual revenue growth of 10%-12% and cash EPS growth of 15%.

Valuation - 04-MAY-01

The shares are up about 8% thus far in 2001, easily outpacing the broader market. We believe that investors are becoming more comfortable with the combined J.P. Morgan/Chase Manhattan and that revenue and cost synergies could be better than initial estimates. Accordingly, fears of earnings dilution from the premium paid for J.P. Morgan's shares are subsiding. We also believe that investors will continue to overlook recent weakness in capital markets operations, given the Federal Reserve's more accommodative policy on interest rates and the likelihood of a soft landing. With the transaction expected to deliver earnings momentum in the key growth areas of asset management, equity underwriting and global merger advisory activities, we think the shares will outperform the broader market in the year ahead.

Key Stock Statistics

S&P EPS Est. 2001	2.55	Tang. Bk. Value/Share	12.95
P/E on S&P Est. 2001	16.3	Beta	1.53
S&P EPS Est. 2002	3.60	Shareholders	83,472
Dividend Rate/Share	1.36	Market cap. (B)	$ 82.3
Shs. outstg. (M)	1985.2	Inst. holdings	60%
Avg. daily vol. (M)	5.683		

Value of $10,000 invested 5 years ago: $ 18,354

Fiscal Year Ending Dec. 31

	2001	2000	1999	1998	1997	1996
Revenues (Million $)						
1Q	15,015	—	7,967	8,258	7,224	6,932
2Q	6,871	—	8,344	8,352	7,491	6,720
3Q	—	—	8,017	7,627	7,858	6,774
4Q	—	16,004	9,382	8,431	7,808	6,995
Yr.	—	60,065	33,710	32,379	30,381	27,421
Earnings Per Share ($)						
1Q	**0.59**	—	**0.88**	**0.53**	**0.66**	**-0.11**
2Q	**0.18**	—	**1.07**	**0.80**	**0.67**	**0.60**
3Q	—	—	**0.91**	**0.63**	**0.72**	**0.59**
4Q	—	**0.34**	**1.32**	**0.87**	**0.65**	**0.06**
Yr.	—	**2.86**	**4.18**	**2.83**	**2.68**	**1.65**

Next earnings report expected: mid October

Dividend Data (Dividends have been paid since 1827.)

Amount ($)	Date Decl.	Ex-Div. Date	Stock of Record	Payment Date
0.320	Sep. 19	Oct. 04	Oct. 06	Oct. 31 '00
0.320	Dec. 13	Jan. 03	Jan. 05	Jan. 31 '01
0.340	Mar. 20	Apr. 04	Apr. 06	Apr. 30 '01
0.340	Jun. 19	Jul. 03	Jul. 06	Jul. 31 '01

J.P. Morgan Chase & Co.

Business Summary - 04-MAY-01

Formed through the December 2000 merger between J.P. Morgan and Chase Manhattan, J.P. Morgan Chase & Co. is now the second largest U.S. bank holding company.

Operations are divided into five major business lines. Investment bank (47% of revenues in 2000) advises on corporate strategy and structure, raises capital, makes markets in financial instruments and offers risk management services. The company is the U.S. leader in syndicated lending and second largest in U.S. investment grade bond underwriting. Retail and middle markets financial services (30%) includes cardmember services (fifth largest credit card issuer in U.S.), regional banking (serving consumers and small businesses in New York, New Jersey, Connecticut and Texas), home finance (mortgages and related products), diversified consumer services (auto loans and leases and student loans), and middle markets (corporate finance, cash management and international finance to middle market companies). Investment management and private banking (10%) offers traditional cash management and equity and fixed income investments as well as alternative asset classes such as private equity and real estate, and also offers customized solutions from banking and planning to structuring and investments for high net worth individuals. Treasury and securities services (11%) include cash management services, custodian services, institutional trust services and related transaction management services. JPMorgan Partners (2%) provides principal and mezzanine capital financing to companies throughout the business development life cycle.

In 2000, average earning assets, from which interest income is derived, amounted to $513.4 billion and consisted mainly of loans (41%) and investment securities (57%). Average sources of funds included interest-bearing deposits (32%), noninterest-bearing deposits (8%), short-term borrowings (31%), long-term debt (7%), shareholders' equity (5%) and other (17%).

At year-end 2000, nonperforming assets, consisting primarily of nonaccrual loans, were $1.92 billion (0.91% of net loans), up from $1.87 billion (0.94%) a year earlier. The allowance for loan losses, which is set aside for possible loan defaults, was $3.67 billion (1.70% of loans), versus $3.74 billion (1.84%) a year earlier. Net chargeoffs, or the amount of loans actually written off as uncollectible, were $1.40 billion (0.71% of average loans) in 2000, versus $1.75 billion (0.87%) in 1999.

The J.P. Morgan/Chase Manhattan merger called for each J.P. Morgan share to be exchanged for 3.7 Chase Manhattan shares. The merger is expected to result in $1.9 billion in financial synergies, including $1.5 billion in cost savings and $400 million of incremental revenues, by the end of 2002.

Per Share Data ($) (Year Ended Dec. 31)	2000	1999	1998	1997	1996	1995	1994	1993	1992	1991
Tangible Bk. Val.	12.95	18.59	17.93	15.84	14.16	13.94	12.63	12.54	10.81	10.33
Earnings	2.86	4.18	2.83	2.68	1.67	2.08	1.55	1.88	1.30	0.04
Dividends	1.55	1.06	0.93	0.81	0.73	0.63	0.55	0.46	0.40	0.35
Payout Ratio	54%	25%	33%	30%	43%	30%	35%	24%	31%	NM
Prices - High	67.16	60.75	51.70	42.18	31.95	21.58	14.04	15.45	13.16	10.04
- Low	32.37	43.87	23.70	28.20	17.37	11.91	11.20	11.66	7.29	3.50
P/E Ratio - High	23	15	18	16	19	10	9	8	10	NM
- Low	11	10	8	11	10	6	7	6	6	NM
Income Statement Analysis (Million $)										
Net Int. Inc.	9,512	8,744	8,566	8,158	8,340	8,202	4,674	4,636	4,598	4,113
Tax Equiv. Adj.	NA	NA	NA	NA	NA	45.0	24.0	21.0	31.0	47.0
Non Int. Inc.	23,193	13,372	9,692	8,313	7,377	6,626	35.3	3,882	2,973	2,736
Loan Loss Prov.	1,377	1,621	1,343	804	897	758	550	1,259	1,365	1,345
Exp./Op. Revs.	70%	55%	64%	61%	59%	63%	67%	62%	65%	77%
Pretax Inc.	8,733	8,375	5,930	NA	3,811	4,812	2,212	2,108	1,329	290
Eff. Tax Rate	34%	35%	36%	NA	35%	38%	42%	26%	18%	47%
Net Inc.	5,727	5,446	3,782	NA	2,461	2,970	1,294	1,604	1,086	154
% Net Int. Marg.	NA	2.98	2.89	2.86	3.21	3.37	3.61	3.73	3.82	3.33
Balance Sheet & Other Fin. Data (Million $)										
Money Mkt. Assets	293,429	115,168	83,391	106,207	97,266	77,966	29,539	28,265	14,009	16,849
Inv. Securities	117,494	61,513	64,490	52,738	48,546	41,769	26,997	25,948	23,426	19,763
Com'l Loans	119,460	88,120	88,056	88,906	70,245	38,738	24,972	33,620	28,015	31,929
Other Loans	96,590	88,039	83,756	79,548	84,847	112,542	54,255	42,238	54,647	52,908
Total Assets	715,348	406,105	365,875	NA	336,099	303,989	171,423	149,888	139,655	138,930
Demand Deposits	62,713	55,529	51,623	49,808	47,057	39,116	21,399	23,443	22,813	18,025
Time Deposits	216,652	186,216	160,814	143,880	133,864	132,418	75,107	74,834	71,360	74,925
LT Debt	47,788	20,690	18,375	NA	13,314	12,825	6,753	8,192	6,798	5,738
Common Eqty.	40,818	22,689	22,810	NA	20,444	18,186	9,262	9,510	8,003	5,683
% Ret. on Assets	0.8	1.4	1.0	1.1	0.8	1.0	0.8	1.1	0.8	0.1
% Ret. on Equity	15.2	23.6	17.2	18.4	12.3	16.0	14.8	16.1	16.0	0.4
% Loan Loss Resv.	1.7	2.0	2.1	2.2	2.3	2.5	3.1	4.0	3.7	3.9
% Loans/Deposits	77.3	72.9	84.0	87.0	85.7	87.6	81.6	76.7	87.1	90.6
% Equity to Assets	5.4	5.9	5.9	5.5	5.7	5.8	4.7	7.3	4.2	3.4

Data as orig reptd.; bef. results of disc opers/spec. items. Per share data adj. for stk. divs. Bold denotes diluted EPS (FASB 128)-prior periods restated. E-Estimated. NA-Not Available. NM-Not Meaningful. NR-Not Ranked.

Office—270 Park Ave., New York, NY 10017. **Tel**—(212) 270-6000. **Website**—http://www.jpmorganchase.com **Chrmn**—D. A. Warner III. **Pres & CEO**—W. B. Harrison, Jr. **Investor Contact**—John Borden (212-270-7318). **Dirs**—H. W. Becherer, R. P. Bechtel, F. A. Bennack Jr., L. A. Bossidy, M. A. Burns, H. L. Fuller, E. V. Futter, W. H. Gray III, W. B. Harrison, Jr., H. L. Kaplan, L. R. Raymond, J. R. Stafford, L. D. Ward, D. A. Warner III, M. v.N. Whitman. **Transfer Agent & Registrar**—Mellon Investor Services. **Incorporated**—in Delaware in 1968. **Empl**— 90,000. **S&P Analyst:** Stephen R. Biggar

STANDARD
&POOR'S
STOCK REPORTS

Lehman Brothers Holdings

NYSE Symbol **LEH**

In S&P 500

18-AUG-01

Industry: Investment Banking/ Brokerage

Summary: This major global investment bank serves institutional, corporate and government clients and high net worth individuals.

S&P Opinion: Buy (★★★★★)

Recent Price • 64
52 Wk Range • 86.20-47

Yield • 0.4%
12-Mo. P/E • 10.8

Quantitative Evaluations

Outlook
(1 Lowest—5 Highest)
• **1−**

Fair Value
• **45.10**

Risk
• **Average**

Earn./Div. Rank
• **NR**

Technical Eval.
• **Bearish** since 8/01

Rel. Strength Rank
(1 Lowest—99 Highest)
• **26**

Insider Activity
• **Neutral**

Earnings vs. Previous Year
▲=Up ▼=Down ▶=No Change

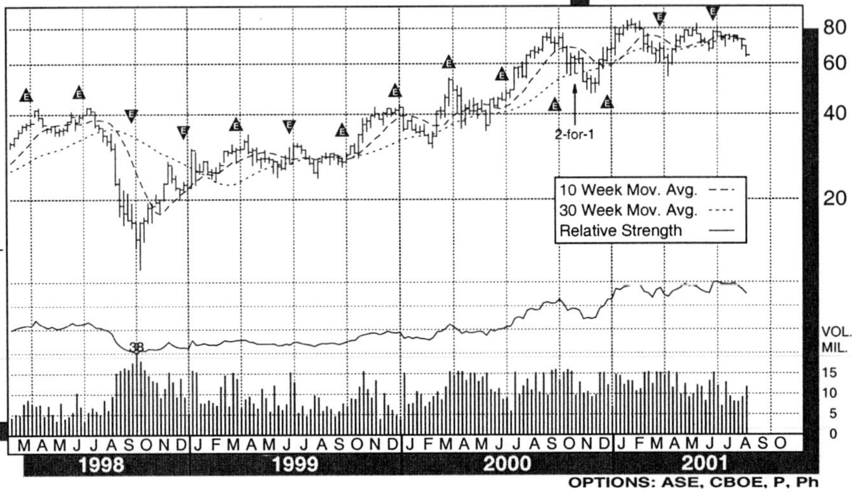

OPTIONS: ASE, CBOE, P, Ph

Overview - 21-JUN-01

Revenues and earnings of investment banks and brokerage firms are notoriously difficult to predict, due to their dependence on the level and health of both the equity and debt markets. After a very strong FY 00 (Nov.), in which net revenues advanced 44% and EPS soared 56%, we expect net revenues and earnings to decline slightly this year, reflecting a weak business environment. Despite a strong debt underwriting and capital markets environment, less equity underwriting and merger and acquisition activity, as well as declining securities prices, have hurt results in recent periods. Nevertheless, we expect business conditions to improve later this year, spurring a revenue and earnings rebound in the second half of 2001 that will continue into 2002. Longer term, the company's efforts to boost revenues in higher margin businesses such as investment banking, equities, and high net worth retail should lead to a more diverse and profitable revenue stream.

Valuation - 21-JUN-01

The shares carry a buy recommendation. Price to book value has historically been the most common measure used to value the shares of securities brokers, because their balance sheets can be marked to market to arrive at a meaningful value of shareholders' equity. Nevertheless, valuations comparing P/E ratios have gained greater acceptance recently, as companies have taken steps to diversify their businesses. LEH's shares are trading at a discount to those of most of the company's larger peers, both on a price to book value and on a P/E basis. This discount, coupled with an improved business environment later this year, should boost the stock in coming periods. In addition, UBS AG's generous bid for PaineWebber last year has caused investors to speculate whether Lehman is the next takeover target.

Key Stock Statistics

S&P EPS Est. 2001	6.00	Tang. Bk. Value/Share	29.10
P/E on S&P Est. 2001	10.7	Beta	2.35
S&P EPS Est. 2002	6.40	Shareholders	22,580
Dividend Rate/Share	0.28	Market cap. (B)	$ 15.4
Shs. outstg. (M)	240.9	Inst. holdings	58%
Avg. daily vol. (M)	1.835		

Value of $10,000 invested 5 years ago: $ 59,192

Fiscal Year Ending Nov. 30

	2001	2000	1999	1998	1997	1996
Revenues (Million $)						
1Q	6,752	6,340	4,591	4,580	3,999	3,386
2Q	6,284	6,334	4,932	5,554	3,806	3,476
3Q	—	7,359	4,765	5,963	4,469	3,585
4Q	—	6,414	4,701	3,797	4,609	3,813
Yr.	—	26,447	18,989	19,894	16,883	14,260
Earnings Per Share ($)						
1Q	**1.39**	**1.84**	**0.79**	**0.72**	0.58	0.40
2Q	**1.38**	**1.39**	**1.04**	**1.06**	0.47	0.45
3Q	**E1.54**	**1.69**	**1.10**	**0.55**	0.65	0.30
4Q	**E1.69**	**1.46**	**1.14**	**0.26**	0.65	0.48
Yr.	**E6.00**	**6.38**	**4.08**	**2.60**	**2.36**	**1.62**

Next earnings report expected: late September

Dividend Data (Dividends have been paid since 1994.)

Amount ($)	Date Decl.	Ex-Div. Date	Stock of Record	Payment Date
0.055	Nov. 03	Nov. 13	Nov. 15	Nov. 30 '00
0.070	Jan. 29	Feb. 08	Feb. 12	Feb. 28 '01
0.070	May. 03	May. 11	May. 15	May. 31 '01
0.070	Aug. 01	Aug. 13	Aug. 15	Aug. 31 '01

A Division of The McGraw-Hill Companies

Lehman Brothers Holdings Inc.

Business Summary - 21-JUN-01

In FY 00 (Nov.), Lehman Brothers generated nearly 42% of its revenues outside the U.S., making it one of the most global of U.S. investment banks. The company serves institutional, corporate, government, and high net worth individual clients and customers through its worldwide headquarters in New York, and regional headquarters in London and Tokyo. These offices are augmented by other offices in the U.S., Canada, Europe, the Middle East, Latin America and the Caribbean, and the Asia/Pacific region.

Lehman divides its operations into three segments: Investment Banking; Capital Markets; and Client Services. In FY 00, Investment Banking accounted for 28% of net revenues and 19% of pretax earnings, Capital Markets accounted for 61% of net revenues and 70% of pretax income, while Client Services accounted for 11% of both net revenue and pretax earnings. In FY 99, Investment Banking accounted for 31% of both net revenues and pretax earnings, Capital markets accounted for 58% of net revenues and 60% of pretax income, while Client Services accounted for 11% of net revenue and 9% of pretax earnings.

As an investment banker, Lehman raises debt or equity capital for corporations, governments and other organizations, typically earning a fee representing the difference between what the company buys the offering for from the issuer, and what it sells the securities for in the open market. In 2000, LEH was involved in 191 equity issuance transactions worth a total of $88 billion. LEH was the lead manager of $155.0 billion in global debt offerings in 2000. Investment banking revenues also include fees the company receives for advising companies on mergers and acquisitions, divestitures and other restructuring moves. In 2000, Lehman was again among the leaders in global mergers and acquisitions, serving as financial adviser on 223 completed mergers and acquisitions totaling $340 billion.

The Capital Markets segment combines the efforts of LEH's sales, trading and research professionals. Results in the Capital Markets segment reflect institutional flow activities and secondary trading and financing activities related to a broad spectrum of equity and fixed income products.

The Client Services segment encompasses LEH's Private Client Services Group and LEH's Private Equity Division. The Private Client Services Group includes 450 professionals who serve the investment needs of high net worth individuals and 2,200 mid-sized institutional accounts worldwide. The Private Equity Division has over $4.5 billion in assets under management in four areas: Merchant Banking, Venture Capital, Communications and Real Estate.

American Express and Nippon Life Insurance are entitled to receive an annual non-cumulative preferred dividend equal to 50% of LEH's net income that exceeds $400 million for the full fiscal year through 2002. The amount American Express and Nippon Life are allowed to receive is capped at $50 million a year.

Per Share Data ($) (Year Ended Nov. 30)	2000	1999	1998	1997	1996	1995	1994	1993	1992	1991
Tangible Bk. Val.	29.19	25.63	19.10	16.51	15.81	13.44	11.96	10.96	NA	NA
Cash Flow	7.08	4.02	2.96	2.72	NA	NA	NA	NA	NA	NA
Earnings	6.38	4.08	2.60	2.36	1.62	0.88	0.41	1.54	NA	NA
Dividends	0.22	0.18	0.15	0.12	0.10	0.10	0.09	NA	NA	NA
Payout Ratio	3%	4%	6%	5%	6%	11%	22%	NA	NA	NA
Prices - High	80.12	42.78	42.50	28.25	16.25	12.31	10.43	NA	NA	NA
- Low	30.31	21.90	11.31	14.25	10.31	7.25	6.87	NA	NA	NA
P/E Ratio - High	13	10	16	12	10	14	26	NA	NA	NA
- Low	5	5	4	6	6	8	17	NA	NA	NA
Income Statement Analysis (Million $)										
Commissions	944	651	513	423	362	450	445	488	NA	NA
Int. Inc.	19,440	14,251	16,542	13,635	11,298	10,788	6,761	5,679	NA	NA
Total Revs.	26,447	18,989	19,894	16,883	14,260	13,476	9,190	8,692	NA	NA
Int. Exp.	18,796	13,691	15,781	13,010	10,816	10,405	6,452	5,203	NA	NA
Pretax Inc.	2,523	1,589	1,052	937	637	369	193	587	NA	NA
Eff. Tax Rate	30%	29%	30%	31%	35%	34%	35%	37%	NA	NA
Net Inc.	1,775	1,132	736	647	416	242	126	368	NA	NA
Balance Sheet & Other Fin. Data (Million $)										
Total Assets	224,720	192,244	153,890	151,705	128,596	115,303	109,947	80,474	NA	NA
Cash Items	7,594	7,175	4,238	2,834	2,837	1,819	2,384	2,406	NA	NA
Receivables	10,382	12,360	11,965	12,838	9,944	60,694	58,597	40,816	NA	NA
Secs. Owned	105	89,059	77,000	76,862	61,453	51,322	47,473	35,699	NA	NA
Sec. Borrowed	7,242	127,693	96,533	93,284	82,483	67,236	69,853	50,319	NA	NA
Due Brokers & Cust.	13,559	16,723	13,690	21,703	14,882	8,824	5,657	5,515	NA	NA
Other Liabs.	8,735	10,144	10,913	11,934	11,435	22,780	19,721	11,439	NA	NA
Capitalization:										
Debt	36,093	31,401	27,341	20,261	15,922	12,765	11,321	9,899	NA	NA
Equity	14,862	5,595	4,505	4,015	3,366	2,990	2,687	2,594	NA	NA
Total	51,655	37,684	32,754	24,276	19,796	16,463	14,716	13,201	NA	NA
% Return On Revs.	29.3	27.7	3.7	4.3	3.0	1.8	1.4	4.2	NA	NA
% Ret. on Assets	0.9	0.7	0.5	0.5	0.3	0.2	NA	NA	NA	NA
% Ret. on Equity	12.6	20.5	15.2	15.5	11.9	7.0	NA	NA	NA	NA

Data as orig. reptd.; bef. results of disc. opers. and/or spec. items. Per share data adj. for stk. divs. as of ex-div. date. Yr. ended Dec. 31 in 1993. Pro forma pr. to 1995. Bold denotes diluted EPS (FASB 128). E-Estimated. NA-Not Available. NM-Not Meaningful. NR-Not Ranked.

Office—3 World Financial Center, New York, NY 10285. **Tel**—(212) 526-7000. **Website**—http://www.lehman.com **Chrmn & CEO**—R. S. Fuld Jr. **CFO**—J. L. Cecil. **Investor Contact**—Shaun Butler (212-526-8381). **Dirs**—M. L. Ainslie, J. F. Akers, R. S. Berlind, T. H. Cruikshank, R. S. Fuld Jr., H. Kaufman, J. D. Macomber, D. Merrill. **Transfer Agent & Registrar**—Bank of New York, NYC. **Incorporated**—in Delaware in 1983. **Empl**—11,300. **S&P Analyst:** Michael Schneider, CFA

STANDARD
&POOR'S
STOCK REPORTS

MBNA Corp.

NYSE Symbol **KRB**

In S&P 500

18-AUG-01

Industry: Consumer Finance

Summary: MBNA, one of the largest U.S. lenders through bank credit cards and a leading issuer of affinity cards, also provides retail deposit and financial transaction processing services.

S&P Opinion: Buy (★★★★★)

Recent Price • 35.85 | 52 Wk Range • 40.12-27.30 | Yield • 1.0% | 12-Mo. P/E • 21.2

Quantitative Evaluations

Outlook (1 Lowest—5 Highest)
• **4-**

Fair Value
• **42.90**

Risk
• **Average**

Earn./Div. Rank
• **A+**

Technical Eval.
• **Bullish** since 7/01

Rel. Strength Rank (1 Lowest—99 Highest)
• **62**

Insider Activity
• **Unfavorable**

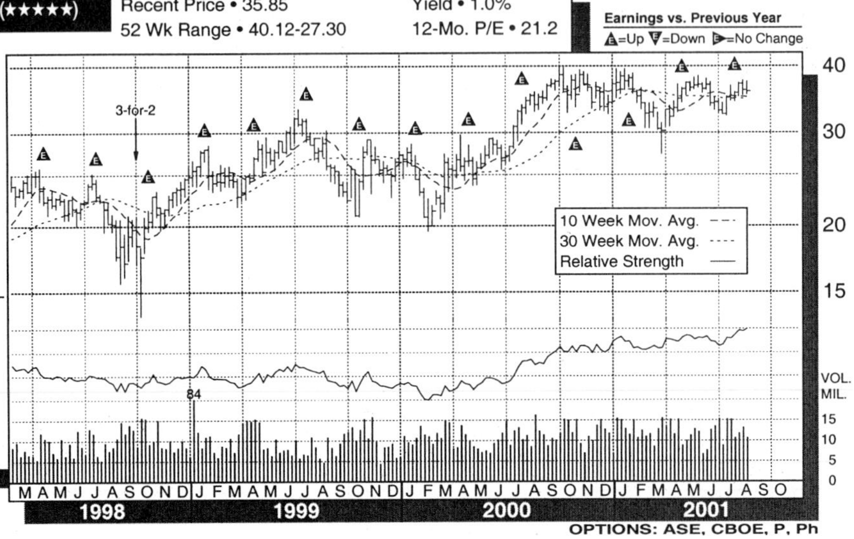

OPTIONS: ASE, CBOE, P, Ph

Overview - 16-JUL-01

Managed loans advanced 23% in 2000, to $88.8 billion. We expect KRB's managed loan portfolio to grow over 20% in 2001, aided by increases in new accounts, and new endorsements from organizations. We expect the Internet to be a rich source of new account growth over the next 12 months. The company uses a unique marketing strategy targeting individual membership organizations, and developing co-branding relationships with commercial concerns. This innovative strategy has let KRB develop a customer base that generates spending rates above the industry average, and credit losses below the average. Provisions for credit losses are likely to significantly rise this year, and credit quality is expected to deteriorate slightly. Nevertheless, we expect credit losses to remain well within manageable levels. We project an EPS advance of over 23% in 2001, to $1.89.

Valuation - 16-JUL-01

We expect the shares to outperform the S&P 500 over the next six to 12 months. KRB is a well run company, with a focused business strategy and a history of solid financial performance. Profits should continue to be driven by a combination of exceptional credit card receivables growth, aided by successful marketing strategies and expanding market share, good control of credit costs, and greater operating efficiency. At recent levels, KRB was trading at a discount to its expected three- to five-year EPS growth rate of about 22%, based on our profit projections. The shares were also trading at a discount to the level of the S&P 500, despite KRB's above average growth prospects. Although further earnings multiple expansion is unlikely, we expect above average earnings growth will lead to strong capital appreciation in the coming year.

Key Stock Statistics

S&P EPS Est. 2001	1.89	Tang. Bk. Value/Share	4.55
P/E on S&P Est. 2001	19.0	Beta	1.54
S&P EPS Est. 2002	2.27	Shareholders	3,079
Dividend Rate/Share	0.36	Market cap. (B)	$ 30.5
Shs. outstg. (M)	851.8	Inst. holdings	71%
Avg. daily vol. (M)	2.298		

Value of $10,000 invested 5 years ago: $ 39,655

Fiscal Year Ending Dec. 31

	2001	2000	1999	1998	1997	1996
Revenues (Million $)						
1Q	2,221	1,778	1,445	1,165	1,048	719.9
2Q	—	1,861	1,615	1,224	1,130	765.8
3Q	—	2,035	1,663	1,347	1,129	824.2
4Q	—	2,195	1,747	1,459	1,217	969.3
Yr.	—	7,869	6,470	5,195	4,524	3,279
Earnings Per Share ($)						
1Q	**0.35**	**0.28**	**0.22**	**0.19**	**0.15**	**0.11**
2Q	**0.43**	**0.34**	**0.27**	**0.21**	**0.17**	**0.13**
3Q	**E0.49**	**0.43**	**0.34**	**0.27**	**0.21**	**0.16**
4Q	**E0.61**	**0.48**	**0.38**	**0.30**	**0.23**	**0.19**
Yr.	**E1.89**	**1.53**	**1.21**	**0.97**	**0.77**	**0.59**

Next earnings report expected: mid October

Dividend Data (Dividends have been paid since 1991.)

Amount ($)	Date Decl.	Ex-Div. Date	Stock of Record	Payment Date
0.080	Oct. 11	Dec. 13	Dec. 15	Jan. 01 '01
0.090	Jan. 10	Mar. 13	Mar. 15	Apr. 01 '01
0.090	Apr. 11	Jun. 13	Jun. 15	Jul. 01 '01
0.090	Jul. 12	Sep. 12	Sep. 15	Oct. 01 '01

A Division of The McGraw·Hill Companies

MBNA Corporation

Business Summary - 16-JUL-01

MBNA is the world's largest independant credit card lender, as well as the leading issuer of affinity credit cards. Affinity credit cards are marketed to members of associations and customers of financial institutions. In addition to credit card lending, the company makes other types of consumer loans and offers insurance and deposit products. With a motto of "Getting the right customers and keeping them," KRB has rapidly increased both the number of card accounts and receivable balances in recent years. At the end of 2000, managed loans totaled $88.8 billion, up 23% from the level a year earlier. In 2000, the company added 13.7 million new accounts, including 5.6 million new international accounts, and acquired the endorsement of almost 460 new groups, including the United States Tennis Association, National Audubon Society, and Atlanta Braves.

KRB offers two general types of credit cards -- premium (gold) and standard -- issued under either the MasterCard or Visa name. The company markets standard and premium cards to new customers and premium cards to qualifying standard card customers. Premium card usage and average account balances are usually higher than those of standard card customers.

The company's other consumer loan products include unsecured lines of credit accessed by check, unsecured installment loans, and secured loans to individuals including home equity loans and airplane loans. It also offers money market deposit accounts and certificates of deposit. Insurance products include credit insurance offered to credit card customers, as well as automobile insurance and life insurance.

To attract new customers and gain new endorsements, KRB conducts extensive marketing campaigns. The company uses a combination of direct mail, telemarketing, person-to-person and Internet marketing to market its credit cards. It has an in-house advertising agency, and 18 telemarketing facilities in nine states.

As a lender, credit quality is of the utmost importance to the company. Decisions to extend credit are made using sophisticated technology such as credit scoring models, as well as the insight of a credit analyst. Fewer than 50% of applications received in 2000 were approved.

Delinquency rates on the managed loan portfolio totaled 4.49% in 2000, versus 4.49% in 1999. Accounts are deemed delinquent if the minimum payment is not received by the date specified on the statement. Net credit losses are accounts that are 180 days overdue, and are generally considered uncollectible. Net credit losses amounted to 4.39% of the managed loan portfolio in 2000, versus 4.33% in 1999.

Per Share Data ($) (Year Ended Dec. 31)	2000	1999	1998	1997	1996	1995	1994	1993	1992	1991
Tangible Bk. Val.	4.55	3.24	2.29	2.13	1.98	1.61	1.16	0.95	0.81	0.73
Earnings	1.53	1.21	0.97	0.77	0.59	0.46	0.35	0.27	0.23	0.20
Dividends	0.32	0.27	0.24	0.21	0.19	0.16	0.14	0.13	0.12	0.11
Payout Ratio	21%	22%	25%	28%	32%	36%	41%	46%	51%	53%
Prices - High	40.12	33.25	25.87	20.38	12.96	8.61	5.40	4.98	3.30	2.66
- Low	19.50	20.81	13.50	11.94	6.71	4.41	3.80	2.81	2.33	1.50
P/E Ratio - High	26	27	27	27	22	19	15	18	14	14
- Low	13	17	14	16	11	10	11	10	10	8
Income Statement Analysis (Million $)										
Net Int. Inc.	1,084	934	742	692	640	544	532	474	358	240
Tax Equiv. Adj.	2.4	1.9	1.9	1.9	1.8	1.8	1.6	1.6	1.5	1.3
Non Int. Inc.	811	4,208	3,229	2,813	1,896	1,425	1,014	740	577	540
Loan Loss Prov.	409	409	310	260	178	138	108	99	97.5	86.7
Exp./Op. Revs.	192%	205%	61%	63%	62%	63%	64%	64%	60%	59%
Pretax Inc.	2,120	1,655	1,254	1,022	731	585	441	190	272	235
Eff. Tax Rate	38%	38%	38%	39%	35%	40%	40%	NM	37%	36%
Net Inc.	1,313	1,024	776	623	474	353	267	208	173	149
% Net Int. Marg.	4.76	4.63	4.42	4.86	5.52	5.74	7.61	8.76	7.20	5.20
Balance Sheet & Other Fin. Data (Million $)										
Money Mkt. Assets	700	2,014	1,526	2,086	877	574	268	31.0	81.0	475
Inv. Securities	3,050	3,046	1,880	2,509	2,318	2,096	2,002	1,409	1,265	1,293
Com'l Loans	NA	Nil	Nil	Nil	Nil	Nil	Nil	Nil	Nil	Nil
Other Loans	NA	7,971	11,776	11,162	10,129	8,135	5,707	3,726	3,979	3,486
Total Assets	38,678	30,859	25,806	21,306	17,035	13,229	9,672	7,320	6,455	6,009
Demand Deposits	5,815	568	498	312	234	170	101	71.0	70.0	65.0
Time Deposits	18,529	18,147	14,909	9,123	9,918	8,439	6,531	5,171	4,498	5,029
LT Debt	5,736	5,709	5,939	5,479	3,950	2,658	1,564	780	471	Nil
Common Eqty.	6,627	4,199	2,391	1,970	1,704	1,265	920	769	661	592
% Ret. on Assets	3.8	3.6	3.3	3.2	3.1	3.1	3.2	3.1	3.0	2.8
% Ret. on Equity	24.0	30.7	34.9	33.0	32.0	35.5	32.7	30.0	28.6	37.0
% Loan Loss Resv.	1.9	-2.0	1.8	2.0	1.5	2.2	1.8	2.6	2.5	2.8
% Loans/Deposits	82.0	94.4	76.4	64.0	74.3	94.5	86.0	71.1	87.1	68.4
% Equity to Assets	15.6	11.6	9.3	9.6	9.8	9.6	9.7	10.5	10.4	7.6

Data as orig reptd.; bef. results of disc opers/spec. items. Per share data adj. for stk. divs. Bold denotes diluted EPS (FASB 128)-prior periods restated. E-Estimated. NA-Not Available. NM-Not Meaningful. NR-Not Ranked.

Office—1100 North King St., Wilmington, DE 19884. **Tel**—(800) 362-6255. **Website**—http://www.mbna.com **Chrmn & CEO**—A. Lerner. **Pres**—C. M. Cawley. **EVP, CFO & Treas**—M. S. Kaufman. **Investor Contact**—Brian D. Dalphon (302-432-1251). **Dirs**—J. H. Berick, C. M. Cawley, B. R. Civiletti, B. P. Healy, W. L. Jews, M.D., A. Lerner, R. D. Lerner, S. L. Markowitz, M. Rosenthal. **Transfer Agent & Registrar**—National City Bank, Cleveland. **Incorporated**—in Maryland in 1990. **Empl**— 25,000. **S&P Analyst:** Michael Schneider, CFA

STANDARD
&POOR'S
STOCK REPORTS

Moody's Corp.

NYSE Symbol **MCO**

In S&P 500

20-AUG-01 **Industry:** Financial (Diversified)

Summary: This company, which was separated from Dun & Bradstreet Corp. on September 30, 2000, is a leading global credit rating, research and risk analysis concern.

S&P Opinion: Buy (★★★★★)

Recent Price • 34.11
52 Wk Range • 36.18-22.62
Yield • 0.5%
12-Mo. P/E • 30.2

Quantitative Evaluations

Outlook
(1 Lowest—5 Highest)
• **4+**

Fair Value
• **38.70**

Risk
• **High**

Earn./Div. Rank
• **B-**

Technical Eval.
• **NA**

Rel. Strength Rank
(1 Lowest—99 Highest)
• **76**

Insider Activity
• **Neutral**

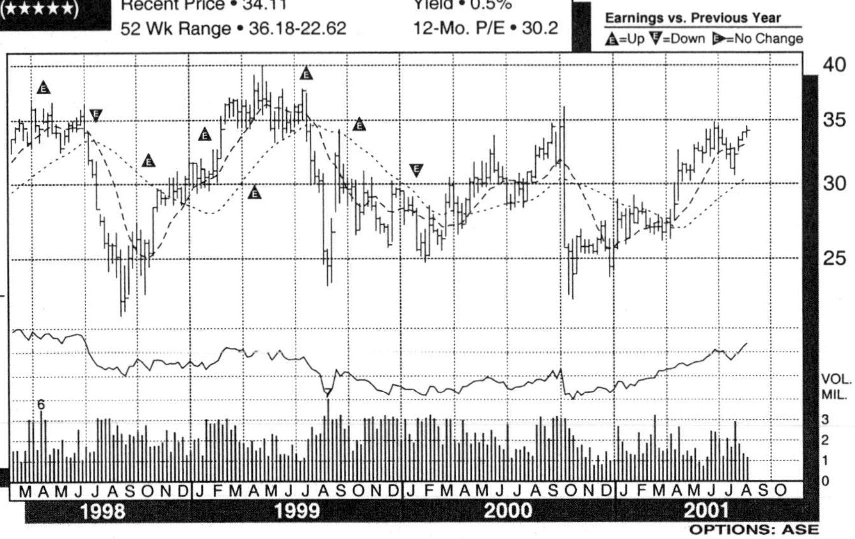

Overview - 20-AUG-01

We see revenue gains of about 21% overall in 2001, with U.S. revenue advancing about 21%, helped by a favorable U.S. debt capital market. International is expected to advance 20%, largely due to continued healthy capital markets in Western Europe. Structured finance, which increased 16% in 2000 and now accounts for 38% of MCO's business, should see continued strong growth. Corporate finance ratings, which climbed sharply in the first half, are expected to grow at a slower pace over the remainder of the second half. Even though corporate treasurers are taking advantage of declining interest rates, the high-yield bond market will probably continue to languish. Operating margins should widen to 50.4%, from 47.8%, helped by cost control efforts and the greater volume. We are projecting a nearly 28% rise in 2001 EPS, to $1.24. We are tentatively forecasting an 8% revenue rise in 2002, with EPS advancing to $1.37.

Valuation - 20-AUG-01

Although the shares climbed 33% in 2001 through mid-August, we still consider MCO a timely investment, in light of S&P's forecast of a favorable interest rate environment in coming months. Positive factors also include strong growth prospects in international markets, a high level of cash flow generation, and very wide operating profit margins that consistently range between 47% and 51%. The stock's appeal is also heightened by MCO's position as the only pure-play publicly held credit rating concern. We are reasonably confident that management will meet its longer term targets of low-teens revenue and operating income growth, and mid-teens EPS advances. Based on these factors, we believe MCO continues to merit a premium P/E ratio relative to that of the S&P 500 as well as other service companies, and recommend buying the stock.

Key Stock Statistics

S&P EPS Est. 2001	1.24	Tang. Bk. Value/Share	NM
P/E on S&P Est. 2001	27.5	Beta	NA
S&P EPS Est. 2002	1.37	Shareholders	8,332
Dividend Rate/Share	0.18	Market cap. (B)	$ 5.4
Shs. outstg. (M)	157.5	Inst. holdings	81%
Avg. daily vol. (M)	0.357		

Value of $10,000 invested 5 years ago: NA

Fiscal Year Ending Dec. 31

	2001	2000	1999	1998	1997	1996
Revenues (Million $)						
1Q	180.2	—	491.0	471.1	436.4	450.4
2Q	205.2	—	497.0	484.0	440.9	505.1
3Q	—	152.5	474.0	459.6	447.8	509.8
4Q	—	161.1	510.0	519.8	485.9	693.9
Yr.	—	602.3	1,972	1,935	1,811	2,159
Earnings Per Share ($)						
1Q	**0.30**	—	**0.36**	**0.30**	0.21	0.13
2Q	**0.34**	—	**0.40**	**0.23**	0.28	-0.26
3Q	**E0.28**	**0.25**	**0.41**	**0.40**	0.31	0.14
4Q	**E0.32**	**0.25**	**0.39**	**0.52**	**0.46**	-0.17
Yr.	**E1.24**	**0.97**	**1.56**	**1.44**	**1.27**	**-0.16**

Next earnings report expected: mid October

Dividend Data (Dividends have been paid since 1934.)

Amount ($)	Date Decl.	Ex-Div. Date	Stock of Record	Payment Date
0.045	Dec. 20	Feb. 22	Feb. 26	Mar. 10 '01
0.045	Oct. 18	Feb. 22	Feb. 26	Mar. 10 '01
0.045	Apr. 23	May. 16	May. 20	Jun. 10 '01
0.045	Jul. 23	Aug. 16	Aug. 20	Sep. 10 '01

A Division of The McGraw-Hill Companies

Moody's Corporation

Business Summary - 20-AUG-01

Moody's Investors Service and the Dun & Bradstreet operating company were separated into stand-alone entities on September 30, 2000. Each holder of "old" Dun & Bradstreet Corp. (DNB) was distributed one share of "new" DNB for every two shares of "old" DNB held as of September 20, 2000. "Old" DNB changed its name to Moody's Corp. (MCO), and "new" DNB assumed the name Dun & Bradstreet Corp. A holder of two shares of Dun & Bradstreet stock on the record date now holds one share of "new" DNB and two shares of Moody's stock. Both companies are listed on the NYSE (as DNB and MCO, respectively).

Moody's Investors Service is a leading global provider of financial analysis, opinion, research and information. Moody's publishes credit opinions, research, and ratings on fixed-income securities, issuers of securities and other credit obligations. The company also provides a broad range of business and financial information in print or electronic formats. Founded in 1900, Moody's employs more than 700 analysts based in 14 countries. It provides ratings and information on governmental and commercial entities in more than 100 countries. The international markets provide strong growth opportunities. In 2000, Moody's revenues from international operations were $173.4 million, or 28% of total revenues, versus 25% in 1999, 20% in 1998, and 18% in 1997.

Credit ratings help investors analyze the credit risks associated with fixed-income securities. Ratings also create efficiencies in fixed-income markets by providing reliable, credible and independent assessments of credit risk. For issuers, Moody's services increase market liquidity and may reduce transaction costs.

Ratings fees paid by issuers account for most of Moody's revenues. Thus, a substantial portion of revenues is dependent upon the volume of debt securities issued in the global capital markets. Moody's is therefore affected by the performance of, and the prospects for, the major world economies and by the fiscal and monetary policies pursued by their governments. However, annual fee arrangements with frequent debt issuers and annual fees from commercial paper and medium-term note programs, bank and insurance company financial strength rating, mutual fund ratings and other areas are less dependent on, or independent of, the volume of debt securities issued in the global capital markets.

Moody's expects to begin a share repurchase program to offset the dilutive effect of shares issued under employee benefit plans, and as a way to return free cash flow to shareholders. The current board of directors is comprised of directors who served on the Dun & Bradstreet board. In coming months, the company plans to add new outside directors.

Per Share Data ($) (Year Ended Dec. 31)	2000	1999	1998	1997	1996	1995	1994	1993	1992	1991
Tangible Bk. Val.	NM	NM	NM	NM	NM	NM	NM	NM	6.14	5.79
Cash Flow	1.07	2.42	2.26	2.03	0.15	4.68	5.61	4.01	4.72	4.35
Earnings	0.97	1.56	1.44	1.27	-0.69	1.89	3.70	2.42	3.10	2.85
Dividends	0.56	0.74	0.81	0.88	1.82	2.63	2.56	2.40	2.25	2.15
Payout Ratio	57%	47%	56%	69%	NM	139%	69%	99%	73%	75%
Prices - High	36.18	40.00	36.68	31.25	69.00	65.50	64.00	68.50	59.12	58.00
- Low	22.62	23.37	21.75	23.12	19.25	48.50	51.87	55.75	50.62	39.12
P/E Ratio - High	37	26	25	36	NM	35	17	28	19	20
- Low	23	15	15	18	NM	26	14	23	16	14
Income Statement Analysis (Million $)										
Revs.	602	1,972	1,935	1,811	1,783	5,415	4,896	4,710	4,751	4,643
Oper. Inc.	305	621	591	536	198	876	1,249	1,111	1,075	1,020
Depr.	16.6	141	142	132	141	475	324	282	289	268
Int. Exp.	3.6	5.0	12.0	53.0	37.0	53.0	39.0	24.7	32.8	52.7
Pretax Inc.	284	457	400	332	-14.0	444	879	588	795	731
Eff. Tax Rate	44%	39%	39%	34%	NM	28%	28%	27%	30%	30%
Net Inc.	159	256	246	219	-115	321	630	429	554	509
Balance Sheet & Other Fin. Data (Million $)										
Cash	119	113	91.0	82.0	128	439	362	669	540	311
Curr. Assets	278	785	764	806	760	2,299	1,981	2,122	1,930	1,767
Total Assets	398	1,786	1,789	2,225	2,294	5,516	5,464	5,170	4,915	4,777
Curr. Liab.	253	1,415	1,353	1,497	2,008	2,834	2,187	2,044	1,645	1,527
LT Debt	300	Nil	Nil	Nil	Nil	Nil	Nil	Nil	Nil	Nil
Common Eqty.	-282	-416	-370	-489	-454	1,183	1,319	1,111	2,156	2,161
Total Cap.	17.5	-114	-70.0	-187	-454	1,351	1,528	1,197	2,156	2,161
Cap. Exp.	12.3	44.1	55.0	51.0	58.0	286	273	236	197	226
Cash Flow	175	397	388	351	25.0	796	953	710	842	776
Curr. Ratio	1.1	0.6	0.6	0.5	0.4	0.8	0.9	1.0	1.2	1.2
% LT Debt of Cap.	1714.3	Nil	Nil	Nil	Nil	Nil	Nil	Nil	Nil	Nil
% Net Inc.of Revs.	26.3	13.0	12.7	12.1	NM	6.0	12.9	9.1	11.7	11.0
% Ret. on Assets	47.1	14.3	NA	10.2	NM	5.9	11.9	8.7	11.4	10.7
% Ret. on Equity	NM	NM	NM	NM	NM	25.7	51.9	27.0	25.7	24.0

Data as orig reptd.; bef. results of disc opers/spec. items. Per share data adj. for stk. divs. Certain data for 1997 and 1996 restated. Bold denotes diluted EPS (FASB 128)-prior periods restated. E-Estimated. NA-Not Available. NM-Not Meaningful. NR-Not Ranked.

Office—99 Church Street, NYC, NY 10007. **Tel**—(212) 553-0300. **Website**—www.moodys.com **Chrmn** —C. L. Alexander Jr. **Pres & CEO** —J. Rutherfurd Jr. **SVP & CFO**—Jeanne M. Dering. **Treas**—R. Roy.**Secy**—J. Clark. **Investor Contact**—Robert Becton (212-553-4102). **Dirs**—H. Adams Jr., C. L. Alexander Jr., M. J. Evans, R. R. Glauber, H. A. McKinnell, J. Rutherfurd Jr. **Transfer Agent & Registrar**—First Chicago Trust Co., Jersey City, NJ. **Incorporated**—in Delaware in 1930. **Empl**— 1,400. **S&P Analyst:** William H. Donald

STANDARD
&POOR'S
STOCK REPORTS

PNC Financial Services

NYSE Symbol **PNC**

In S&P 500

18-AUG-01

Industry:
Banks (Major Regional)

Summary: This bank holding company (formerly PNC Bank Corp.) conducts regional banking, wholesale banking and asset management businesses.

S&P Opinion: Buy (★★★★★)

Recent Price • 67.60
52 Wk Range • 75.81-54.87

Yield • 2.8%
12-Mo. P/E • 15.9

Quantitative Evaluations

Outlook
(1 Lowest—5 Highest)
• **2+**

Fair Value
• **66.60**

Risk
• **Low**

Earn./Div. Rank
• **A-**

Technical Eval.
• **Bullish** since 8/01

Rel. Strength Rank
(1 Lowest—99 Highest)
• **66**

Insider Activity
• **NA**

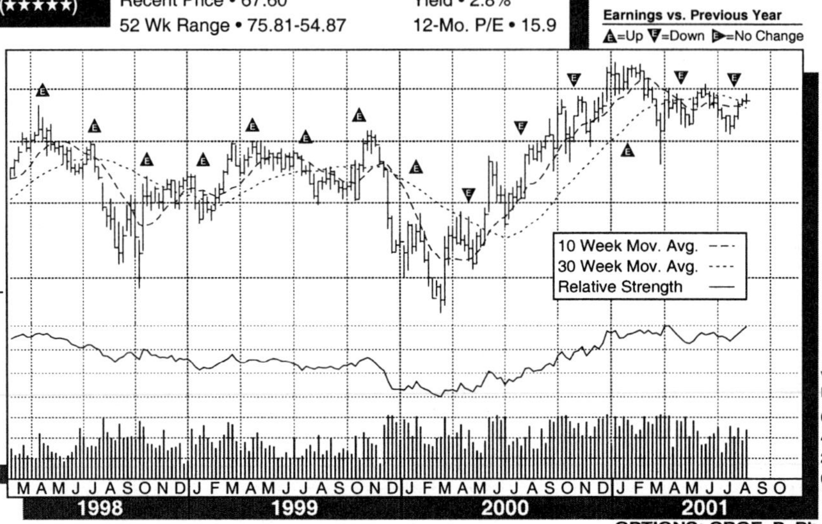

OPTIONS: CBOE, P, Ph

Overview - 23-MAY-01

The company should continue to experience good growth in core lending categories in 2001, following a downsizing of certain portfolios, the sale of the credit card portfolio, and loan securitizations that led to a lower level of earning assets in 2000. After narrowing in 2000, on the sale of higher yielding credit card loans, the net interest margin is expected to be relatively stable in 2001, helped by a lower interest rate environment. Non-interest income remains the preferred source of growth. In particular, gains are seen in the asset management and fund servicing lines, the two largest components of non-interest income. Proceeds from the January 2001 sale of the mortgage banking business will be reinvested in businesses that will provide less cyclical profit growth. The company's internal financial goals for 2001 include EPS growth of 11% to 13%.

Valuation - 23-MAY-01

After a strong run in 2000, the shares were recently down about 6% in 2001, about equal to the decline in our major regional bank index. We believe investors are becoming increasingly comfortable with the company's shifting business mix, which relies more on revenues from noninterest income sources. This minimizes exposure to interest rate and credit quality cycles, and should result in a higher P/E multiple being accorded the shares. The recent sale of certain businesses has also reduced PNC's risk profile, and has freed up resources that can be re-directed to fee-based business lines. We regard the shares, trading at 15X our 2001 EPS estimate of $4.45, as having superior appreciation potential in the coming year, and recommend buying the stock.

Key Stock Statistics

S&P EPS Est. 2001	4.40	Tang. Bk. Value/Share	13.37
P/E on S&P Est. 2001	15.4	Beta	0.76
S&P EPS Est. 2002	4.95	Shareholders	56,976
Dividend Rate/Share	1.92	Market cap. (B)	$ 19.5
Shs. outstg. (M)	289.0	Inst. holdings	57%
Avg. daily vol. (M)	0.873		

Value of $10,000 invested 5 years ago: $ 24,974

Fiscal Year Ending Dec. 31

	2001	2000	1999	1998	1997	1996
Revenues (Million $)						
1Q	1,873	1,889	2,021	1,830	1,667	1,576
2Q	1,289	1,908	1,868	1,924	1,691	1,580
3Q	—	1,901	1,863	2,030	1,717	1,566
4Q	—	1,925	1,914	2,151	1,785	1,611
Yr.	—	7,623	7,666	7,936	6,859	6,333
Earnings Per Share ($)						
1Q	**0.89**	**1.01**	**1.05**	**0.87**	**0.80**	**0.69**
2Q	**1.00**	**1.01**	**1.03**	**0.90**	**0.81**	**0.72**
3Q	—	**1.01**	**1.06**	**0.91**	**0.83**	**0.58**
4Q	—	**1.06**	**1.01**	**0.92**	**0.85**	**0.79**
Yr.	—	**4.09**	**4.15**	**3.60**	**3.28**	**2.88**

Next earnings report expected: mid October

Dividend Data (Dividends have been paid since 1865.)

Amount ($)	Date Decl.	Ex-Div. Date	Stock of Record	Payment Date
0.480	Oct. 05	Oct. 11	Oct. 13	Oct. 24 '00
0.480	Jan. 04	Jan. 10	Jan. 12	Jan. 24 '01
0.480	Apr. 05	Apr. 10	Apr. 13	Apr. 24 '01
0.480	Jul. 05	Jul. 11	Jul. 13	Jul. 24 '01

A Division of The McGraw-Hill Companies

The PNC Financial Services Group, Inc.

Business Summary - 23-MAY-01

PNC Financial Services Group (formerly PNC Bank Corp.) is a bank holding company that operates retail banking, asset management and wholesale banking businesses nationally and in its primary market area of Pennsylvania, New Jersey, Delaware, Ohio and Kentucky. Activities have recently focused on greater diversity of earnings, with increased contributions from asset management and processing businesses; and greater consistency of earnings, with decreased reliance on lending activities and greater contributions from fee-based revenues.

Operations are currently divided into seven lines of business. Community banking (46% of total income in 2000) provides credit, deposit, branch-based brokerage and electronic banking products and services to retail customers, as well as credit, treasury management and capital markets products to small businesses. Corporate banking (19%) provides credit, equipment leasing, capital markets and treasury management products and services to corporations, institutions and government entities. PNC Real Estate Finance (6%) provides credit, capital markets, treasury management, commercial mortgage loan servicing and other products to developers, owners and investors in commercial real estate. PNC Business Credit (4%) provides asset-based lending, capital markets and treasury management products and services to middle market customers nationally. PNC Advisors (14%) offers customized investment products and services, including full-service brokerage, to affluent customers. BlackRock (7%), which is 70%-owned, manages assets for institutions and individuals through a variety of fixed income, liquidity, equity and alternative investment products, including the proprietary BlackRock family of funds. PFPC (4%), the company's global fund services subsidiary, provides a range of processing services to the investment management industry.

In 2000, average earning assets, from which interest income is derived, amounted to $59.9 billion, and consisted mainly of loans (84%) and investment securities (10%). Average sources of funds included interest-bearing deposits (54%), noninterest-bearing deposits (12%), short-term borrowings (10%), long-term debt (10%), shareholders' equity (9%) and other (5%).

At December 31, 000, nonperforming assets, mainly non-accrual loans and foreclosed assets, were $372 million (0.71% of loans and related assets), versus $325 million (0.61%) a year earlier. The allowance for loan losses, which is set aside for possible loan defaults, was $675 million (1.33% of loans), versus $674 million (1.36%) a year earlier. Net chargeoffs (loans written off as uncollectible) were $135 million (0.27% of average loans) in 2000, versus $161 million (0.31%).

Per Share Data ($) (Year Ended Dec. 31)	2000	1999	1998	1997	1996	1995	1994	1993	1992	1991
Tangible Bk. Val.	13.37	12.07	11.49	12.47	13.08	13.21	15.80	18.34	15.96	15.27
Earnings	4.09	4.15	3.60	3.28	2.90	1.19	2.57	3.14	2.36	1.98
Dividends	1.83	1.68	1.58	1.50	1.42	1.40	1.31	1.18	1.06	1.06
Payout Ratio	45%	40%	44%	46%	49%	118%	51%	37%	45%	54%
Prices - High	75.00	62.00	66.75	58.75	39.75	32.37	31.62	36.37	29.25	24.12
- Low	36.00	43.00	38.75	36.50	27.50	21.12	20.00	27.00	23.12	9.43
P/E Ratio - High	18	15	19	18	14	27	12	12	12	12
- Low	9	10	11	11	9	18	8	9	10	5
Income Statement Analysis (Million $)										
Net Int. Inc.	2,164	2,433	2,573	2,495	2,444	2,142	1,936	1,829	1,657	1,435
Tax Equiv. Adj.	18.0	22.0	49.0	99	35.0	46.6	33.5	39.5	42.8	59.0
Non Int. Inc.	2,871	2,723	2,503	1,759	1,373	1,240	931	945	673	742
Loan Loss Prov.	136	163	225	70.0	Nil	6.0	60.1	204	324	428
Exp./Op. Revs.	61%	60%	64%	61%	60%	72%	61%	55%	61%	57%
Pretax Inc.	1,848	1,891	1,710	1,618	1,527	627	902	1,117	778	548
Eff. Tax Rate	34%	33%	35%	35%	35%	35%	32%	33%	32%	29%
Net Inc.	1,214	1,264	1,115	1,052	992	408	610	745	529	390
% Net Int. Marg.	3.64	3.68	3.85	3.94	3.83	3.15	3.40	3.95	4.03	3.73
Balance Sheet & Other Fin. Data (Million $)										
Money Mkt. Assets	NA	1,148	1,014	1,526	774	1,611	809	856	1,165	1,868
Inv. Securities	7,053	8,759	8,088	8,522	11,917	15,839	20,921	23,060	20,742	14,173
Com'l Loans	28,635	24,198	25,182	19,989	18,062	16,812	12,445	12,463	11,751	12,211
Other Loans	21,966	26,572	32,468	34,668	33,736	32,244	23,689	20,845	14,358	13,936
Total Assets	69,844	75,413	77,207	75,120	73,260	73,404	64,145	62,080	51,380	44,892
Demand Deposits	8,490	8,441	9,943	10,158	10,937	10,707	6,992	7,057	5,889	5,095
Time Deposits	39,174	38,227	37,553	37,491	34,739	36,192	28,019	26,058	23,580	24,924
LT Debt	7,266	9,395	10,994	11,523	11,744	10,398	11,754	2,585	1,018	1,287
Common Eqty.	6,649	5,939	6,036	5,377	5,862	5,767	4,375	4,305	3,712	3,280
% Ret. on Assets	1.7	1.7	1.5	1.4	1.4	0.5	1.0	1.5	1.2	0.9
% Ret. on Equity	19.0	20.8	19.2	18.4	17.0	7.1	14.1	18.8	15.5	14.0
% Loan Loss Resv.	1.3	1.2	1.3	1.8	2.3	2.5	2.8	2.9	3.5	3.1
% Loans/Deposits	109.6	119.7	121.4	111.8	113.4	105.2	102.5	100.6	87.6	84.8
% Equity to Assets	9.0	7.8	7.5	7.6	7.9	7.6	7.1	7.9	7.6	6.4

Data as orig reptd.; bef. results of disc opers/spec. items. Per share data adj. for stk. divs. Bold denotes diluted EPS (FASB 128)-prior periods restated. E-Estimated. NA-Not Available. NM-Not Meaningful. NR-Not Ranked.

Office—One PNC Plaza, 249 Fifth Ave., Pittsburgh, PA 15222. **Tel**—(412) 762-1553. **Website**—http://www.pncbank.com **Chrmn**—T. H. O'Brien. **Pres & CEO**—J. E. Rohr. **Vice-Chrmn**—W. E. Gregg Jr. **SVP & CFO**—R. L. Haunschild. **VP & Investor Contact**—William H. Callihan. **Dirs**—P. W. Chellgren, R. N. Clay, G. A. Davidson Jr., D. F. Girard-diCarlo, W. E. Gregg Jr., W. R. Johnson, B. C. Lindsay, W. C. McClelland, T. H. O'Brien, J. G. Pepper, J. E. Rohr, L. K. Steffes, T. J. Usher, M. A. Washington, H. H. Wehmeier. **Transfer Agent & Registrar**—Chase Manhattan Bank, Ridgefield Park, NJ. **Empl**— 25,300. **S&P Analyst:** Stephen R. Biggar

STANDARD & POOR'S
STOCK REPORTS

St. Paul Companies

NYSE Symbol **SPC**

In S&P 500

20-AUG-01

Industry: Insurance (Property-Casualty)

Summary: This company, which owns St. Paul Fire & Marine Insurance and 78% of John Nuveen & Co., has divested its personal lines unit and is selling its life insurance unit.

S&P Opinion: Buy (★★★★★)

Recent Price • 44.11
52 Wk Range • 57-39.57
Yield • 2.5%
12-Mo. P/E • 14.0

Quantitative Evaluations

Outlook (1 Lowest—5 Highest)
• **2**

Fair Value
• **40.70**

Risk
• **Low**

Earn./Div. Rank
• **A-**

Technical Eval.
• **Bearish** since 7/01

Rel. Strength Rank (1 Lowest—99 Highest)
• **42**

Insider Activity
• **Unfavorable**

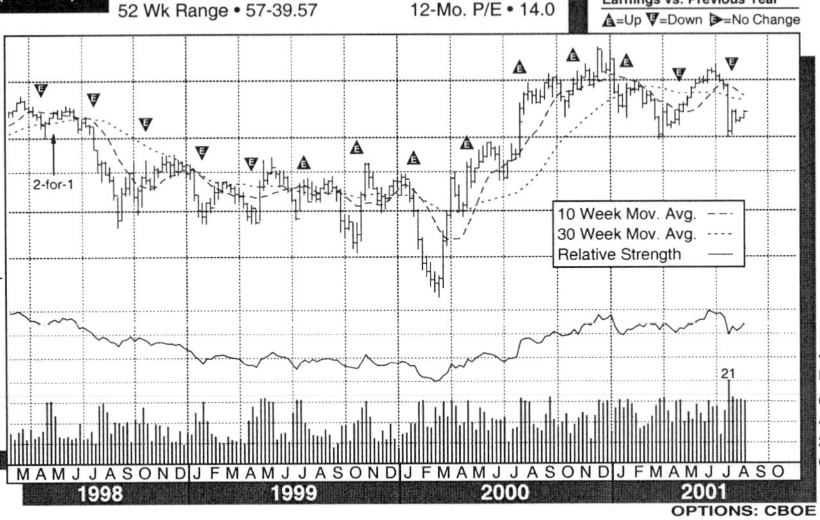

OPTIONS: CBOE

Overview - 20-AUG-01

Net written premium growth in 2001 could top 15%, versus growth of about 7% seen for the industry as a whole. SPC's strategy of narrowing its scope around a select number of specialty commercial property-casualty lines should aid long term results. To that end, SPC announced in April 2001 that it was selling Fidelity and Guaranty Life Insurance Co. to London-based Old Mutual plc. That transaction frees up $675 million that SPC can redeploy into its core operations. Operating earnings in 2002 will be aided by the robust level of written premiums recorded in 2001, and by the absence of a $107 million pretax second quarter 2001 charge taken to boost reserves for prior year claims in the health care line. Profitability will also be aided by positive effects of numerous cost savings initiatives. Share results will be aided by stock buybacks. During 2000, 17.9 million shares were reacquired. Another 8.3 million shares were reacquired in the first six months of 2001.

Valuation - 20-AUG-01

The shares of this property-casualty (p-c) insurer corrected in mid-2001 after SPC reported disappointing Q2 operating earnings due to adverse claim trends in the health care line. The shares' strong performance in 2000 was sparked by a sector rotation back into "value-oriented" financial stocks, and by the market's enthusiasm for the group's improved fundamentals. We recommend investors use any near term weakness as a buying opportunity. SPC shares still trade at a discount to their peer group. Moreover, SPC is on track to produce top line growth that outpaces that of the industry, without sacrificing its underwriting standards. SPC's ability to achieve double digit premium growth, while cutting costs, could produce powerful results over the next 12 to 18 months, and should yield an expansion in the P/E multiple.

Key Stock Statistics

S&P EPS Est. 2001	2.60	Tang. Bk. Value/Share	30.54
P/E on S&P Est. 2001	17.0	Beta	0.78
S&P EPS Est. 2002	3.50	Shareholders	22,603
Dividend Rate/Share	1.12	Market cap. (B)	$ 9.5
Shs. outstg. (M)	214.4	Inst. holdings	80%
Avg. daily vol. (M)	1.597		

Value of $10,000 invested 5 years ago: $ 19,397

Fiscal Year Ending Dec. 31

	2001	2000	1999	1998	1997	1996
Revenues (Million $)						
1Q	2,355	2,253	2,244	2,324	1,557	1,330
2Q	2,166	2,105	1,998	2,380	1,621	1,364
3Q	—	2,031	1,856	2,211	1,497	1,476
4Q	—	2,219	1,942	2,193	1,544	1,564
Yr.	—	8,608	7,569	9,108	6,219	5,734
Earnings Per Share ($)						
1Q	**0.90**	**1.53**	**0.79**	**0.86**	**1.05**	**0.79**
2Q	**0.41**	**0.95**	**0.91**	**-1.18**	**1.25**	**0.74**
3Q	—	**0.98**	**0.58**	**0.27**	**0.89**	**0.63**
4Q	—	**0.86**	**0.57**	**0.40**	**1.01**	**0.90**
Yr.	—	**4.32**	**3.19**	**0.32**	**4.20**	**3.06**

Next earnings report expected: early November

Dividend Data (Dividends have been paid since 1872.)

Amount ($)	Date Decl.	Ex-Div. Date	Stock of Record	Payment Date
0.270	Nov. 09	Dec. 27	Dec. 29	Jan. 17 '01
0.280	Feb. 06	Mar. 28	Mar. 30	Apr. 17 '01
0.280	May. 01	Jun. 27	Jun. 29	Jul. 17 '01
0.280	Aug. 07	Sep. 26	Sep. 28	Oct. 17 '01

The St. Paul Companies, Inc.

Business Summary - 20-AUG-01

Founded in Saint Paul, MN, in 1853, the St. Paul Companies is Minnesota's oldest business corporation. The principal operating subsidiary is St. Paul Fire & Marine Insurance Co., a leading property-casualty insurer. St. Paul is also a leading surety underwriter and one of the largest medical liability insurers in the U.S. St. Paul International underwrites property-casualty insurance overseas. St. Paul Re underwrites and sells reinsurance worldwide. SPC also has a 78% ownership interest in John Nuveen & Co., a municipal bond underwriter that traces its roots back to the 19th century. Life insurance operations are being sold.

Segment contributions to pretax earnings in 2000 (before parent company expenses) were: property-casualty insurance 89%, asset management 8%, and life insurance 3%.

The company writes most lines of property-casualty insurance. Net written premiums totaled $5.9 billion in 2000, versus $5.1 billion in 1999. During 2000, commercial lines accounted for 28% of net written premiums, specialty commercial lines 27%, reinsurance 20%, global health care 10%, surety 7%, and international 8%. Recently, SPC has undertaken a series of strategic initiatives aimed at refocusing its resources on the commercial property-casualty insurance marketplace. In October 1999, the company sold its personal lines division to Metropolitan Life Insurance Co. (NYSE; MET) for about $600 million. In May 2000, SPC sold its nonstandard auto insurance line to The Prudential Insurance Company of America for about $200 million. To enhance its commercial lines offerings, SPC has also made some acquisitions, including the purchase, in April 2000, of MMI Companies Inc., a health care risk concern, for $206 million in cash and the assumption of $165 million of MMI debt and capital securities. SPC also completed the integration of USF&G Corp. into its operations during 1999, realizing $260 million in pretax annual expense savings. SPC acquired USF&G Corp. in 1998 for $3.5 billion in stock and the assumption of debt.

Fidelity & Guaranty Life Insurance Co. (F&G Life) underwrites and sells annuity and life insurance products. On April 26, 2001 SPC announced plans to sell F&G Life to U.K.-based Old Mutual plc for $635 million in cash and stock. F&G Life also returned $40 million in capital to SPC.

John Nuveen & Co., 78%-owned as of year-end 2000, underwrites and trades municipal bonds and tax-exempt unit investment trusts and markets tax-exempt open-end and closed-end bond funds. At year-end 2000, assets under management totaled $62.0 billion.

Per Share Data ($) (Year Ended Dec. 31)	2000	1999	1998	1997	1996	1995	1994	1993	1992	1991
Tangible Bk. Val.	30.54	26.40	25.76	25.10	22.96	20.27	14.57	16.06	12.37	12.05
Oper. Earnings	2.66	2.61	1.61	2.88	2.27	2.67	2.39	2.22	-1.64	2.19
Earnings	4.32	3.19	0.32	4.20	3.25	3.00	2.56	2.46	-1.42	2.34
Dividends	1.08	1.03	0.98	0.94	0.88	0.80	0.75	0.70	0.68	0.65
Payout Ratio	25%	32%	309%	22%	27%	27%	29%	28%	NM	28%
Prices - High	57.00	37.06	47.18	42.75	30.37	29.68	22.75	24.50	20.18	18.56
- Low	21.31	25.37	28.06	28.81	25.06	21.75	18.84	18.75	16.62	14.25
P/E Ratio - High	13	12	NM	10	13	10	9	10	NM	8
- Low	5	8	NM	7	11	7	7	8	NM	6
Income Statement Analysis (Million $)										
Premium Inc.	5,898	5,298	6,945	4,616	4,448	3,971	3,412	3,178	3,143	3,146
Net Invest. Inc.	1,616	1,557	1,585	886	807	772	695	661	666	676
Oth. Revs.	1,094	722	578	717	479	667	595	621	690	530
Total Revs.	8,608	7,569	9,108	6,219	5,734	5,410	4,701	4,460	4,499	4,352
Pretax Inc.	1,453	1,017	-47.0	1,019	699	656	564	523	-224	528
Net Oper. Inc.	626	636	249	531	415	465	414	387	-256	381
Net Inc.	1,013	779	89.0	773	558	521	443	428	-232	405
Balance Sheet & Other Fin. Data (Million $)										
Cash & Equiv.	897	165	229	23.0	181	232	230	200	195	189
Premiums Due	3,493	2,922	2,152	1,503	1,559	1,969	2,000	1,813	1,759	1,761
Invest. Assets: Bonds	20,470	19,329	21,056	12,450	11,944	10,373	8,829	9,148	8,361	7,833
Invest. Assets: Stocks	1,466	1,618	1,259	2,991	1,394	1,100	861	847	725	687
Invest. Assets: Loans	1,249	1,504	1,507	Nil	Nil	Nil	Nil	Nil	Nil	Nil
Invest. Assets: Total	27,099	26,207	27,116	15,036	14,366	13,067	11,163	11,256	9,577	8,973
Deferred Policy Costs	1,088	959	878	404	402	372	324	295	280	293
Total Assets	41,075	38,873	38,323	21,501	20,681	19,657	17,496	17,149	13,597	12,982
Debt	2,033	1,915	1,779	869	689	704	623	640	567	487
Common Eqty.	7,178	6,448	6,622	4,611	3,988	3,719	2,733	3,005	2,202	2,533
Prop. & Cas. Loss Ratio	70.0	72.9	82.1	70.9	74.6	72.1	72.1	72.5	85.6	75.2
Prop. & Cas. Expense Ratio	34.8	35.0	34.1	33.8	30.9	29.7	30.2	32.0	32.2	29.4
Prop. & Cas. Combined Ratio	104.8	107.9	116.2	104.7	105.5	101.8	102.3	104.5	117.8	104.6
% Return On Revs.	11.8	10.3	1.0	14.5	9.7	9.6	9.4	9.6	NM	9.3
% Ret. on Equity	14.8	11.8	1.4	17.8	14.3	15.9	15.4	16.4	NM	16.9

Data as orig reptd.; bef. results of disc opers/spec. items. Per share data adj. for stk. divs. Bold denotes diluted EPS (FASB 128)-prior periods restated. E-Estimated. NA-Not Available. NM-Not Meaningful. NR-Not Ranked.

Office—385 Washington St., St. Paul, MN 55102. **Tel**—(651) 310-7911. **Website**—www.stpaul.com **Chrmn & CEO**—D. W. Leatherdale. **CFO**—T. A. Bradley. **SVP & Secy**—B. A. Backberg. **Investor Contact**—Laura Gagnon (651-310-7696). **Dirs**—C. H. Baldwin, H. F. Baldwin, J. H. Dasburg, J. Dolan, K. M. Duberstein, P. M. Grieve, T. R. Hodgson, D. G. John, W. H. Kling, D. W. Leatherdale, B. K. MacLaury, G. D. Nelson, G. M. Sprenger. **Transfer Agent & Registrar**—Wells Fargo Shareholder Services, Saint Paul, MN. **Incorporated**—in Minnesota in 1853; reincorporated in 1968. **Empl**— 10,500. **S&P Analyst:** Catherine A. Seifert

AFLAC Inc.

NYSE Symbol **AFL**

In S&P 500

23-AUG-01

Industry: Insurance (Life & Health)

Summary: AFLAC offers supplemental cancer insurance and other individual health coverages. Nearly 75% of segment operating profits in 2000 were derived from business in Japan.

S&P Opinion: Accumulate (★★★★)

Recent Price • 27.77
52 Wk Range • 37.46-23.38
Yield • 0.7%
12-Mo. P/E • 22.9

Quantitative Evaluations

Outlook
(1 Lowest—5 Highest)
• **2+**

Fair Value
• **27.20**

Risk
• **Low**

Earn./Div. Rank
• **A+**

Technical Eval.
• **Bearish** since 7/01

Rel. Strength Rank
(1 Lowest—99 Highest)
• **32**

Insider Activity
• **Unfavorable**

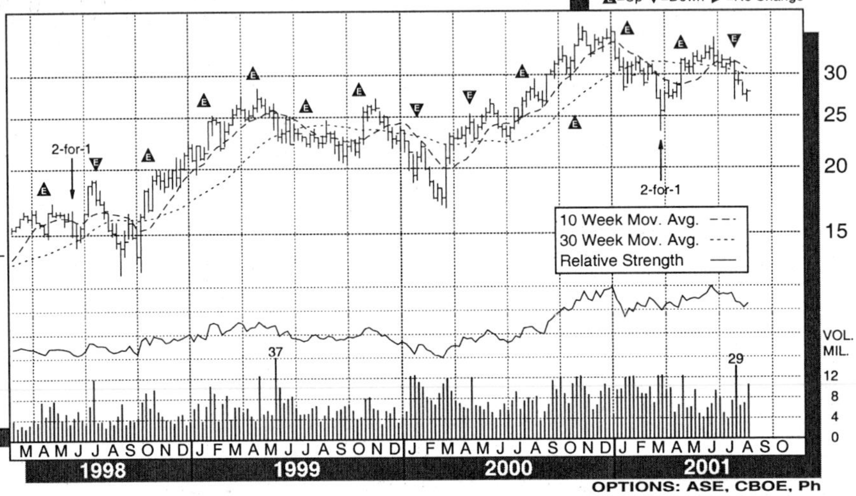

OPTIONS: ASE, CBOE, Ph

Overview - 23-AUG-01

A weakening Japanese yen (in relation to the U.S. dollar) may mask otherwise positive underlying results in coming periods. Aside from this, our forecast of higher earnings is based on AFL's ability to ride out economic turmoil and financial services deregulation in Japan. AFL is the dominant underwriter of supplemental cancer insurance in Japan, and has capitalized on that strength and on its low-cost producer status, to exploit new market and product niches. In the U.S., a product expansion program away from solely cancer coverage, combined with increased marketing, aids the long-term premium growth outlook. Investment income growth has benefited from repatriation of funds from Japan. EPS comparisons will continue to be aided by an aggressive stock repurchase program.

Valuation - 23-AUG-01

After trending downward in early 2001, the shares recovered after AFL reaffirmed its positive earnings guidance during the second quarter earnings conference call. However, renewed concerns over the negative impact from a weaker yen (compared with the U.S. dollar), combined with worries over the health of the U.S. and Japanese economies, have pressured the shares. We view any near term weakness as an opportunity to accumulate the shares. AFL's double-digit sales and operating earnings growth lend credibility to the belief AFL can continue to thrive despite Japan's fragile economy. In addition, AFL's projection of 15% to 17% operating EPS growth (before currency effects) for 2002 through 2003 will continue to fuel stock price gains, as will aggressive stock buybacks. During the first six months of 2001, AFL reacquired 6.7 million shares. Although the stock trades at a slight premium to its peer group, in light of AFL's franchise value, market dominance and growth prospects, the premium is merited.

Key Stock Statistics

S&P EPS Est. 2001	1.33	Tang. Bk. Value/Share	10.36
P/E on S&P Est. 2001	20.9	Beta	1.08
S&P EPS Est. 2002	1.55	Shareholders	143,400
Dividend Rate/Share	0.20	Market cap. (B)	$ 14.6
Shs. outstg. (M)	524.7	Inst. holdings	53%
Avg. daily vol. (M)	1.762		

Value of $10,000 invested 5 years ago: $ 33,203

Fiscal Year Ending Dec. 31

	2001	2000	1999	1998	1997	1996
Revenues (Million $)						
1Q	2,421	2,398	2,048	1,757	1,708	1,730
2Q	2,348	2,358	2,032	1,704	2,009	1,742
3Q	—	2,475	2,196	1,700	1,790	1,776
4Q	—	2,488	2,365	1,944	1,745	1,853
Yr.	—	9,720	8,640	7,104	7,251	7,100
Earnings Per Share ($)						
1Q	**0.33**	**0.28**	**0.35**	**0.29**	**0.16**	**0.15**
2Q	**0.28**	**0.37**	**0.23**	**0.18**	**0.54**	**0.15**
3Q	—	**0.30**	**0.26**	**0.20**	**0.17**	**0.15**
4Q	—	**0.30**	**0.18**	**0.21**	**0.17**	**0.23**
Yr.	—	**1.26**	**1.03**	**0.88**	**1.04**	**0.68**

Next earnings report expected: late October

Dividend Data (Dividends have been paid since 1973.)

Amount ($)	Date Decl.	Ex-Div. Date	Stock of Record	Payment Date
0.085	Oct. 24	Nov. 14	Nov. 16	Dec. 01 '00
0.085	Jan. 29	Feb. 13	Feb. 15	Mar. 01 '01
2-for-1	Feb. 13	Mar. 19	Feb. 27	Mar. 16 '01
0.050	Jul. 24	Aug. 14	Aug. 16	Sep. 04 '01

AFLAC Incorporated

Business Summary - 23-AUG-01

AFLAC Inc. (AFL) is the leading marketer of supplemental insurance products at the work site in the U.S. and Japan. From its origins in the mid-1950s as a provider of cancer expense insurance, the company has expanded its product offerings to include an array of supplemental health insurance products designed to help pay out-of-pocket expenses not covered by primary insurance.

Foreign insurance operations consist primarily of the underwriting and sale of cancer insurance in Japan. AFL's policies pay cash directly to policyholders to help defray certain out-of-pocket expenses incurred in the treatment of cancer. The majority of new cancer policy sales are made on a payroll-deduction basis, through corporate-sponsored agencies. AFL dominates the large-company market: 95% of companies listed on the Tokyo Stock Exchange offer AFL's products to their employees. In recent years, the company has sought to expand both its product line and its distribution system. Although cancer policies accounted for 40% of policy sales in 2000, AFL's sales mix in Japan is shifting to include sales of living benefit life products and long-term care products. In January 1998, the company began offering Rider MAX, a new product that offers accident and medical/sickness benefits, and that is sold as a rider to AFL's core cancer policy. During 2000, the company sold more than 1.5 million of these riders, accounting for 41% of new premium sales. AFL has also been expanding its distribution capabilities. A new Internet venture, aflacdirect.com, is being developed, making AFL the first insurance company to sell insurance in Japan exclusively via the Internet. In September 2000, AFL announced that Dai-ichi Mutual Life Insurance Co. will begin marketing AFL products in 2001. Because Japan is such an important market for AFL (accounting for 81% of revenues in 2000), fluctuations in the yen/dollar exchange rate can greatly affect results. Although the yen weakened in late 2000, for the full year, a strengthening of the yen relative to the U.S. dollar boosted operating earnings by $0.06 a share (versus a $0.12 a share gain in 1999).

In the U.S., AFL has expanded its product line away from solely cancer insurance (although this remains a core offering) to include an array of supplemental health insurance products, including hospital intensive care, home health care, accident and disability, Medicare supplemental and long-term care protection. As a result, the company has become one of the leading marketers of individual accident insurance in the U.S. During 2000, accident/disability coverage accounted for more than 50% of new sales. To better focus on its core insurance business, in April 1997 the company sold its broadcast properties (which consisted of seven network-affiliated TV stations) to Raycom Media Inc. for $485 million.

Per Share Data ($) (Year Ended Dec. 31)	2000	1999	1998	1997	1996	1995	1994	1993	1992	1991
Tangible Bk. Val.	8.87	7.28	7.09	6.44	3.74	3.58	2.75	2.02	1.56	1.31
Oper. Earnings	1.21	1.00	0.78	0.67	0.60	0.58	0.47	0.38	0.30	0.24
Earnings	1.26	1.03	0.88	1.04	0.68	0.58	0.47	0.39	0.30	0.24
Dividends	0.17	0.14	0.13	0.11	0.10	0.08	0.07	0.06	0.06	0.05
Payout Ratio	13%	14%	14%	11%	14%	14%	16%	17%	19%	20%
Prices - High	37.46	28.37	22.65	14.46	11.00	7.45	6.02	5.66	4.64	4.14
- Low	16.78	19.50	11.34	9.37	7.06	5.31	4.20	4.12	3.19	2.38
P/E Ratio - High	30	27	26	14	16	13	13	15	16	17
- Low	13	19	13	9	10	9	9	11	11	10
Income Statement Analysis (Million $)										
Life Ins. In Force	51,476	44,993	28,182	19,310	15,913	NA	NA	NA	10,553	9,839
Prem. Inc.: Life	716	625	508	474	206	NA	NA	NA	16.7	17.0
Prem. Inc.: A & H	7,523	6,639	5,435	5,400	5,704	6,071	5,181	4,225	3,353	2,748
Net Invest. Inc.	1,550	1,369	1,138	1,078	1,022	1,025	839	689	533	431
Total Revs.	9,720	8,640	7,104	6,983	7,100	7,191	6,111	5,001	3,986	3,283
Pretax Inc.	1,012	778	551	865	650	601	504	428	325	265
Net Oper. Inc.	657	550	429	374	347	349	293	242	183	148
Net Inc.	687	571	487	585	394	349	293	244	183	149
Balance Sheet & Other Fin. Data (Million $)										
Cash & Equiv.	989	985	690	265	254	261	238	208	185	184
Premiums Due	301	270	229	216	227	321	304	232	180	160
Invest. Assets: Bonds	31,305	31,175	26,424	22,584	20,589	19,907	15,862	12,304	9,267	7,861
Invest. Assets: Stocks	236	215	177	146	136	108	84.4	82.1	68.0	61.0
Invest. Assets: Loans	Nil	Nil	9.0	Nil	17.8	22.2	25.1	57.5	89.9	88.6
Invest. Assets: Total	31,558	31,408	26,620	22,644	20,747	20,041	15,976	12,446	9,425	8,010
Deferred Policy Costs	3,685	3,692	3,067	2,582	2,583	2,565	2,403	1,953	1,614	1,407
Total Assets	37,232	37,041	31,183	29,454	25,023	25,338	20,287	15,443	11,901	10,145
Debt	956	931	596	523	354	327	185	122	126	139
Common Eqty.	4,694	3,868	3,770	3,430	2,126	2,134	1,752	1,366	1,082	923
% Return On Revs.	7.1	6.6	6.9	8.4	5.6	4.9	4.8	4.9	4.6	4.5
% Ret. on Assets	1.8	1.7	1.6	2.1	1.6	1.5	1.6	1.8	1.7	1.6
% Ret. on Equity	16.0	15.0	13.5	21.1	18.5	18.0	18.8	19.9	18.3	17.3
% Invest. Yield	4.9	4.7	4.6	4.9	5.0	5.7	5.9	6.3	6.1	6.1

Data as orig reptd.; bef. results of disc opers/spec. items. Per share data adj. for stk. divs. Bold denotes diluted EPS (FASB 128)-prior periods restated. E-Estimated. NA-Not Available. NM-Not Meaningful. NR-Not Ranked.

Office—1932 Wynnton Rd., Columbus, GA 31999. **Tel**—(706) 323-3431; (800) 235-2667. **Website**—www.aflac.com **Chrmn & CEO**—D. P. Amos. **Pres**—K. Cloninger III. **SVP & Secy**—J. M. Loudermilk. **SVP & Investor Contact**—Kenneth S. Janke Jr. **Dirs**—D. P. Amos, J. S. Amos II, M. H. Armacost, K. Cloninger III, M. D. Edwards, J. F. Harris, E. J. Hudson, K. S. Janke Sr., C. B. Knapp, H. Kobayashi, T. Murai, Y. Otake, E. S. Purdom, B. K. Rimer, M. R. Schuster, H. C. Schwob, J. K. Spencer, G. Vaughn Jr., R. L. Wright. **Transfer Agent**—Co.'s office. **Registrar**—Columbus Bank & Trust Co. **Incorporated**—in Georgia in 1955; reincorporated in 1973. **Empl**—5,278. **S&P Analyst:** Catherine A. Seifert

STANDARD
&POOR'S
STOCK REPORTS

American Express

NYSE Symbol **AXP**

In S&P 500

18-AUG-01 **Industry:** Financial (Diversified)

Summary: This company, a leader in travel-related services, is also active in investment services, expense management services, and international banking.

S&P Opinion: Accumulate (★★★★) Recent Price • 37.50 | 52 Wk Range • 63-34 | Yield • 0.9% | 12-Mo. P/E • 23.9

Quantitative Evaluations

Outlook (1 Lowest—5 Highest)
• **1+**

Fair Value
• **30**

Risk
• **Low**

Earn./Div. Rank
• **A-**

Technical Eval.
• **Neutral** since 8/01

Rel. Strength Rank (1 Lowest—99 Highest)
• **35**

Insider Activity
• **NA**

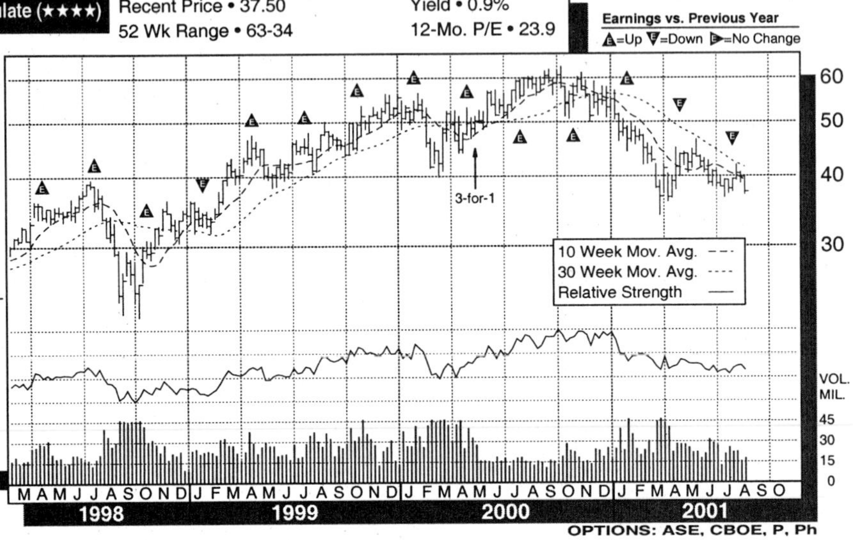

OPTIONS: ASE, CBOE, P, Ph

Overview - 07-AUG-01

Managed net revenues advanced 13% in 2000. In 2001, we expect managed net revenues to fall slightly, as the slowing economy and weak financial markets cause AXP to miss its stated financial target of 8% annual revenue growth. Despite the slowing economy, AXP is positioning itself to benefit from an eventual market turnaround by expanding its international presence, strengthening its charge card network, broadening its product offerings and aggressively reducing costs. We think the weak economy will cause the growth in cards in force and billed business to slow this year. The number of cards in force rose 12% in 2000 while billed business advanced nearly 17%. In addition to 8% annual revenue growth, internal financial targets remain 12% to 15% annual earnings growth, and 18% to 20% return on equity. We see 2001 EPS falling to $1.46, on high yield investment losses in the financial advisory business, before rising to $2.29 in 2002.

Valuation - 07-AUG-01

The shares carry an accumulate recommendation, and are expected to outperform the S&P 500 over the next six to 12 months. On a P/E basis, AXP is trading near the high end of its historical range and roughly in line with the broader market. We believe the stock warrants its current valuation, in light of its premier franchise, strong brand name, and history of solid financial performance. However, we think continued P/E multiple expansion will be modest at best. Future increases in share price should therefore be driven by gains in EPS, which we expect to be fueled by AXP's strategy of expanding its international presence, strengthening its charge card network, and broadening its product offerings. Though we expect lower EPS this year, a resumption of EPS growth in 2002 should propel the shares higher in coming months.

Key Stock Statistics

S&P EPS Est. 2001	1.46	Tang. Bk. Value/Share	8.81
P/E on S&P Est. 2001	25.7	Beta	1.13
S&P EPS Est. 2002	2.29	Shareholders	53,884
Dividend Rate/Share	0.32	Market cap. (B)	$ 49.6
Shs. outstg. (M)	1323.1	Inst. holdings	67%
Avg. daily vol. (M)	3.842		

Value of $10,000 invested 5 years ago: $ 27,406

Fiscal Year Ending Dec. 31

	2001	2000	1999	1998	1997	1996
Revenues (Million $)						
1Q	5,719	5,657	4,971	5,062	4,164	4,257
2Q	4,910	5,970	5,298	4,787	4,422	4,056
3Q	—	5,981	5,311	4,761	4,500	4,044
4Q	—	6,067	5,699	4,521	4,674	3,882
Yr.	—	23,675	21,278	19,132	17,760	16,237
Earnings Per Share ($)						
1Q	**0.40**	**0.48**	**0.42**	**0.39**	**0.31**	**0.27**
2Q	**0.13**	**0.54**	**0.47**	**0.42**	**0.36**	**0.31**
3Q	**E0.42**	**0.54**	**0.47**	**0.41**	**0.37**	**0.32**
4Q	**E0.51**	**0.50**	**0.44**	**0.33**	**0.35**	**0.41**
Yr.	**E1.46**	**2.07**	**1.81**	**1.54**	**1.38**	1.30

Next earnings report expected: late October

Dividend Data (Dividends have been paid since 1870.)

Amount ($)	Date Decl.	Ex-Div. Date	Stock of Record	Payment Date
0.080	Sep. 25	Oct. 04	Oct. 06	Nov. 10 '00
0.080	Nov. 27	Jan. 03	Jan. 05	Feb. 09 '01
0.080	Mar. 26	Apr. 04	Apr. 06	May. 10 '01
0.080	May. 23	Jul. 03	Jul. 06	Aug. 10 '01

American Express Company

Business Summary - 07-AUG-01

American Express, probably best known for its flagship charge card and travelers cheque products, also offers travel related services, financial advisory services, and international banking services. The company's growth strategy focuses on three principal themes: expanding international presence, strengthening the charge card network, and broadening financial services offerings. Contributions by principal operating segment in 2000 were: Travel Related Services 72% of revenues; Financial Advisors 26%; and American Express Bank 2%.

Travel Related Services (TRS) markets travelers cheques and the American Express Card, including the Gold Card, the Platinum Card, the Corporate Card, and the Optima Card. At year-end 2000, cards in force worldwide aggregated 51.7 million, up 12.3% from the level a year earlier. Growth was driven by greater card acquisition activities, growth in proprietary products and the addition of a substantial number of new network cards internationally. Card charge volume in 2000 was $296.7 billion, up 16.7%. Managed charge card receivables totaled $29.0 billion at the end of 2000, up from $27.0 billion a year earlier. TRS also offers business expense management products and services, corporate and consumer travel products, tax preparation and business planning services, magazine publishing, and merchant transaction processing.

Over the past few years, TRS has introduced several new revolving credit card products and features designed to meet the needs of specific customer segments, and to increase consumer loans outstanding. TRS has also expanded its Membership Rewards program to include a broader range of travel rewards and retail merchandise and gourmet gifts. The program remains an important part of TRS's strategy to increase cardmember spending and loyalty.

Financial Advisors provides financial products including financial planning and advice, insurance and annuities, investment products such as certificates, mutual funds and limited partnerships, investment advisory services, trust and employee plan administration services, personal auto and homeowner's insurance, and retail securities brokerage services. At year-end 2000, AXP had a sales force of over 12,000 financial planners. At the end of 2000, managed and administered assets totaled $275.0 billion, up from $270.0 billion a year earlier.

American Express Bank Ltd. offers products designed to meet the financial service needs of corporations, financial institutions, affluent individuals and retail customers. This segment's business activities are conducted outside the United States. Primary business lines are personal financial services, private banking and corporate banking.

Per Share Data ($) (Year Ended Dec. 31)	2000	1999	1998	1997	1996	1995	1994	1993	1992	1991
Tangible Bk. Val.	8.81	7.53	7.18	6.84	6.01	5.53	4.19	5.60	4.86	4.81
Earnings	2.07	1.81	1.54	1.38	1.30	1.04	0.89	1.06	0.28	0.53
Dividends	0.32	0.30	0.30	0.30	0.38	0.30	0.31	0.33	0.33	0.32
Payout Ratio	15%	17%	19%	22%	29%	29%	35%	32%	120%	60%
Prices - High	63.00	56.29	39.54	30.50	20.12	15.04	11.04	12.20	8.45	10.12
- Low	39.83	31.62	22.33	17.87	12.87	9.66	8.33	7.45	6.66	6.00
P/E Ratio - High	30	31	26	22	15	15	12	12	31	19
- Low	19	18	14	13	10	9	9	7	24	11
Income Statement Analysis (Million $)										
Cards in Force	51.7	46.0	42.7	42.7	41.5	37.8	36.3	35.4	34.7	36.6
Card Chg Volume	297	254,100	227,500	209,200	184,000	163,000	141,000	124,000	118,000	111,000
Premium Inc.	575	517	469	424	395	735	783	702	776	711
Commissions	16,407	3,626	3,304	4,386	2,540	2,542	8,591	7,818	13,188	12,006
Int & Div.	4,277	4,679	4,631	2,750	4,357	4,531	4,120	4,914	11,380	11,490
Total Revs.	23,675	16,599	14,501	17,760	16,237	15,841	14,282	14,173	26,961	25,763
Net Bef. Taxes	3,908	3,438	2,925	2,750	2,664	2,183	1,891	2,326	775	759
Net Inc.	2,810	2,475	2,141	1,991	1,901	1,564	1,380	1,605	436	789
Balance Sheet & Other Fin. Data (Million $)										
Total Assets	154,423	148,517	126,933	120,003	108,512	107,405	97,006	94,132	175,752	146,441
Cash Items	8,487	7,471	4,092	4,179	2,677	3,200	3,433	3,312	5,395	4,876
Investment Asset:										
Bonds	NA	Nil	Nil	Nil	Nil	36,772	23,026	23,026	63,778	49,597
Stocks	NA	Nil	Nil	Nil	Nil	Nil	Nil	Nil	1,693	1,982
Loans	26,884	24,332	21,861	20,816	18,518	21,595	29,830	29,904	22,782	24,047
Total	43,747	43,052	41,299	59,757	56,857	58,652	54,830	52,930	88,543	76,476
Accounts Receivable	30,543	26,467	22,224	21,774	20,491	19,914	17,147	16,142	32,785	29,882
Cust. Deposits	13,870	12,197	10,398	9,444	9,555	9,885	10,013	11,131	21,360	24,778
Travel Cheques Outst	NA	6,213	5,823	5,634	5,838	5,697	5,271	4,800	4,729	4,375
Debt	5,211	6,495	7,519	7,873	6,552	7,570	7,162	8,561	15,122	13,292
Common Eqty.	11,466	10,095	9,698	9,574	8,528	8,020	6,233	8,234	6,999	6,815
% Ret. on Assets	1.9	1.8	1.7	1.7	1.8	1.5	1.4	1.7	0.3	0.6
% Ret. on Equity	26.6	25.0	22.2	22.0	22.9	21.3	18.6	20.5	5.7	11.6

Data as orig reptd.; bef. results of disc opers/spec. items. Per share data adj. for stk. divs. Bold denotes diluted EPS (FASB 128)-prior periods restated. E-Estimated. NA-Not Available. NM-Not Meaningful. NR-Not Ranked.

Office—World Financial Center, 200 Vesey St., New York, NY 10285. **Tel**—(212) 640-2000. **Website**—http://www.americanexpress.com **Chrmn & CEO**—K. I. Chenault. **CFO**—G. Crittenden. **Vice Chrmn**—J. S. Linen. **Dirs**—D. F. Akerson, E. L. Artzt, W. G. Bowen, K. I. Chenault, B. S. Greenough, F. R. Johnson, V. E. Jordan Jr., J. Leschly, R. A. McGinn, F. P. Popoff. **Transfer Agent & Registrar**—Mellon Investor Services LLC, Ridgefield Park, NJ. **Incorporated**—in New York in 1965; predecessor organized in 1868. **Empl**— 88,850. **S&P Analyst:** R. McMillan

STANDARD
&POOR'S
STOCK REPORTS

AmSouth Bancorporation

NYSE Symbol **ASO**

In S&P 500

18-AUG-01

Industry:
Banks (Major Regional)

Summary: This bank holding company, with about $38 billion in assets, operates approximately 600 banking offices in six southeastern states.

S&P Opinion: Accumulate (★★★★)

Recent Price • 19.73
52 Wk Range • 20.24-11.68
Yield • 4.3%
12-Mo. P/E • 20.8

Quantitative Evaluations

Outlook
(1 Lowest—5 Highest)
• 2+

Fair Value
• 20.10

Risk
• Low

Earn./Div. Rank
• A-

Technical Eval.
• Bullish since 4/01

Rel. Strength Rank
(1 Lowest—99 Highest)
• 74

Insider Activity
• NA

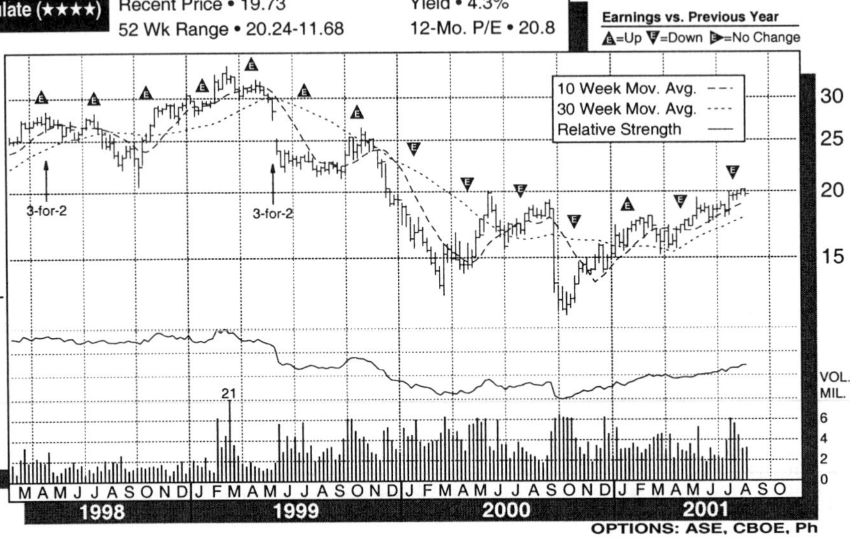

OPTIONS: ASE, CBOE, Ph

Overview - 14-AUG-01

A financial restructuring in the 2000 third quarter left ASO with a reduced level of interest-earning assets. In addition, loan growth should be sluggish in 2001, as the bank focuses on expanding its consumer and small business loan portfolio, while de-emphasizing riskier commercial and industrial loans. As a result, we expect net interest income to be flat, despite a wider net interest margin. However, we believe 2000's loan sales, coupled with tighter underwriting, have set the stage for credit quality improvement toward the end of 2001, and for somewhat lower loss provisioning. Non-interest income should be down 12%, reflecting the sale of IFC Holdings in the 2000 third quarter. Even with an improvement in efficiency, we are projecting a 2% decline in 2001 operating EPS, to $1.43. For 2002, we see a 15% increase in operating EPS, to $1.64, as ASO begins to reap the benefits of expanded market share in the Southeast resulting from the October 1999 First American merger.

Valuation - 14-AUG-01

The shares have trended significantly upward since October 2000, most likely as a result of the bank's low relative valuation in an improving interest rate environment. The trend in interest rates continues to be favorable, and we expect ASO's stock to rise further, as the company benefits from lower rates in terms of higher interest margins, increased loan demand, and improved credit quality. Although we project lower EPS in 2001, the stock carries a P/E ratio below that of ASO's peers, and provides a generous dividend yield. We continue to recommend accumulating the shares, based on ASO's low relative valuation and long-term growth prospects, and on an improving environment.

Key Stock Statistics

S&P EPS Est. 2001	1.43	Tang. Bk. Value/Share	7.52
P/E on S&P Est. 2001	13.8	Beta	0.73
S&P EPS Est. 2002	1.64	Shareholders	27,992
Dividend Rate/Share	0.84	Market cap. (B)	$ 7.3
Shs. outstg. (M)	370.4	Inst. holdings	34%
Avg. daily vol. (M)	0.809		

Value of $10,000 invested 5 years ago: $ 21,077

Fiscal Year Ending Dec. 31

	2001	2000	1999	1998	1997	1996
Revenues (Million $)						
1Q	882.1	1,003	444.2	431.3	400.4	386.5
2Q	531.0	1,004	455.6	476.7	412.4	395.8
3Q	—	—	474.4	450.1	411.8	403.8
4Q	—	1,365	240.6	451.1	419.2	402.9
Yr.	—	3,740	3,780	1,809	1,644	1,589
Earnings Per Share ($)						
1Q	**0.34**	**0.35**	**0.39**	**0.34**	**0.29**	0.24
2Q	**0.36**	**0.41**	**0.42**	**0.36**	**0.30**	0.25
3Q	—	**-0.10**	**0.44**	**0.37**	**0.31**	0.18
4Q	—	**0.34**	**-0.16**	**0.38**	**0.32**	0.28
Yr.	—	**0.86**	**0.86**	**1.45**	**1.21**	**0.95**

Next earnings report expected: mid October

Dividend Data (Dividends have been paid since 1943.)

Amount ($)	Date Decl.	Ex-Div. Date	Stock of Record	Payment Date
0.210	Oct. 18	Dec. 11	Dec. 13	Jan. 02 '01
0.210	Jan. 22	Mar. 15	Mar. 19	Apr. 02 '01
0.210	Apr. 24	Jun. 14	Jun. 18	Jul. 02 '01
0.210	Jul. 19	Sep. 13	Sep. 17	Oct. 01 '01

AmSouth Bancorporation

Business Summary - —

On October 1, 1999, AmSouth Bancorporation acquired First American Corp., a financial services company based in Nashville, TN, in a stock transaction valued at about $6.3 billion. In May 2000, ASO completed the integration of First American. At December 31, 2000, the bank, operated approximately 600 banking offices, in Alabama, Florida, Georgia, Louisiana, Mississippi and Tennessee, with $38.9 million in assets. Operations are divided into three segments: Consumer Banking, Commercial Banking, and Wealth Management (which offers fiduciary, retirement and investment management services for both institutional and individual clients).

Over the next two to three years, ASO plans to boost growth by targeting small business and consumer banking and trust and investment services (with an emphasis on cross-selling products and services), as well as increasing its penetration of high-growth areas in Florida.

In the third quarter of 2000, the bank completed a financial restructuring to reduce interest rate sensitivity, mitigate the effects of steep interest rate increases, and address emerging credit quality issues. In connection with the restructuring the bank recorded pretax charges of $259.7 million, and sold $5 billion in lower-yielding investment securities, selected auto loans, and certain syndicated loans. In addition, ASO increased reserves associated with syndicated loans remaining on its portfolio. Also in the third quarter, the bank sold IFC Holdings, a provider of insurance and investment products, in keeping with its focus on southeastern markets.

Poor asset quality can have a significant impact on bank earnings and profitability. Banks reserve for existing and potential nonperforming assets on a regular basis. At December 31, 2000, the allowance for loan losses covered 1.55% of net loans, versus 1.35% a year earlier. Asset quality declined in 2000; nonperforming assets rose to 0.80% of loans, from 0.61%.

A majority of the bank's income is derived from interest on loans. During 2000, net loans were down 6.3%, to $24.6 billion. Loans (by type) at the end of 2000 were divided as follows: consumer 43% (44% in 1999), commercial 37% (38%), commercial real estate 20% (18%).

Lending profitability, commonly measured by the net yield on a bank's average earning assets, or the net interest margin, is affected by changes in the volume and mix of assets and liabilities, and changes in interest rates. ASO's net interest margin declined 27 basis points, to 3.75%, in 2000.

The company has set goals of annual EPS growth of 12% to 15%, and return on equity of 20% to 22%.

Per Share Data ($) (Year Ended Dec. 31)	2000	1999	1998	1997	1996	1995	1994	1993	1992	1991
Tangible Bk. Val.	7.52	7.56	8.05	7.65	7.38	7.16	4.90	5.55	5.77	5.34
Earnings	0.86	0.86	1.45	1.21	0.96	0.89	0.67	0.92	0.76	0.64
Dividends	0.81	0.67	0.53	0.51	0.48	0.46	0.42	0.36	0.32	0.29
Payout Ratio	94%	78%	37%	42%	50%	51%	64%	39%	42%	45%
Prices - High	20.06	34.58	30.41	25.36	15.07	12.25	10.33	10.62	9.66	6.57
- Low	11.68	18.75	20.45	14.00	10.18	7.62	7.51	8.11	6.33	3.64
P/E Ratio - High	23	40	21	21	16	14	15	12	13	10
- Low	14	22	14	12	11	9	11	9	8	6
Income Statement Analysis (Million $)										
Net Int. Inc.	1,379	1,508	699	676	652	596	567	462	376	319
Tax Equiv. Adj.	62.7	4.8	5.6	7.0	9.4	12.4	14.6	17.4	19.0	22.0
Non Int. Inc.	669	848	347	266	235	232	205	193	150	138
Loan Loss Prov.	228	166	58.1	67.4	65.2	40.1	30.1	19.0	37.0	42.0
Exp./Op. Revs.	65%	70%	55%	56%	60%	61%	66%	63%	65%	68%
Pretax Inc.	455	541	405	349	288	275	193	217	142	107
Eff. Tax Rate	28%	37%	35%	35%	37%	36%	34%	33%	28%	25%
Net Inc.	329	340	263	226	183	175	127	146	102	80.0
% Net Int. Marg.	3.75	4.02	3.92	4.09	3.93	3.88	4.14	4.55	4.73	4.26
Balance Sheet & Other Fin. Data (Million $)										
Money Mkt. Assets	2,226	205	39.0	20.4	18.9	4.8	159	229	126	306
Inv. Securities	8,559	13,015	5,176	4,780	4,935	4,647	3,720	2,907	2,526	2,577
Com'l Loans	13,918	14,715	3,693	3,854	3,668	3,112	2,699	2,373	2,263	2,258
Other Loans	11,170	11,551	9,177	8,384	8,412	8,708	8,927	5,963	4,028	3,516
Total Assets	38,936	43,407	19,902	18,622	18,407	17,739	16,778	12,548	9,751	9,459
Demand Deposits	4,934	4,739	2,216	2,063	1,952	1,835	1,902	1,619	1,323	1,169
Time Deposits	21,689	23,173	11,068	10,882	10,516	11,574	11,165	7,949	5,105	6,204
LT Debt	5,883	5,603	3,240	1,633	1,436	448	386	163	136	139
Common Eqty.	2,813	2,959	1,428	1,385	1,396	1,383	1,310	1,090	783	716
% Ret. on Assets	0.8	0.8	1.4	1.2	1.0	1.0	0.8	1.3	1.1	0.9
% Ret. on Equity	11.4	11.0	18.7	16.3	13.1	13.0	10.2	14.9	13.6	12.5
% Loan Loss Resv.	1.5	1.4	1.4	1.5	1.5	1.5	1.5	1.4	1.4	1.5
% Loans/Deposits	92.8	94.7	96.9	95.7	96.9	87.6	88.5	86.4	83.8	77.2
% Equity to Assets	7.0	7.3	7.3	7.5	7.7	7.8	8.2	8.5	8.2	7.3

Data as orig. reptd.; bef. results of disc opers. and/or spec. items. Per share data adj. for stk. divs. as of ex-div. date. Bold denotes diluted EPS (FASB 128). E-Estimated. NA-Not Available. NM-Not Meaningful. NR-Not Ranked.

Office—AmSouth Sonat Tower, 1900 Fifth Ave. North, Birmingham, AL 35203. **Tel**—(205) 320-7151. **Website**—www.amsouth.com **Chrmn, Pres & CEO**—C. D. Ritter. **Vice Chrmn & CFO**—S. D. Gibson. **Investor Contact**—M. List Underwood (205-801-0265). **Dirs**—J. H. Chandler, J. E. Dalton Jr., E. W. Deavenport Jr., R. C. Gilbert, E. B. Harris, M. R. Ingram, V. B. Jackson, R. L. Kuehn Jr., J. R. Malone, C. B. Nielsen, J. N. Palmer, B. F. Payton, C. D. Ritter. **Transfer Agent & Registrar**—Bank of New York, NYC. **Incorporated**—in Delaware in 1970; bank chartered in 1872 under the National Bank Act. **Empl**— 12,300. **S&P Analyst:** Erik J. Eisenstein

STANDARD
&POOR'S
STOCK REPORTS

Aon Corp.

NYSE Symbol **AOC**

In S&P 500

18-AUG-01

Industry: Insurance Brokers

Summary: This leading insurance broker plans to spin off its insurance underwriting unit to shareholders.

S&P Opinion: Accumulate (★★★★)

Recent Price • 38.17 | Yield • 2.4%
52 Wk Range • 42.31-28.12 | 12-Mo. P/E • 26.9

Quantitative Evaluations

Outlook
(1 Lowest—5 Highest)
• **1–**

Fair Value
• **32.80**

Risk
• **Low**

Earn./Div. Rank
• **B+**

Technical Eval.
• **Bullish** since 7/01

Rel. Strength Rank
(1 Lowest—99 Highest)
• **84**

Insider Activity
• **NA**

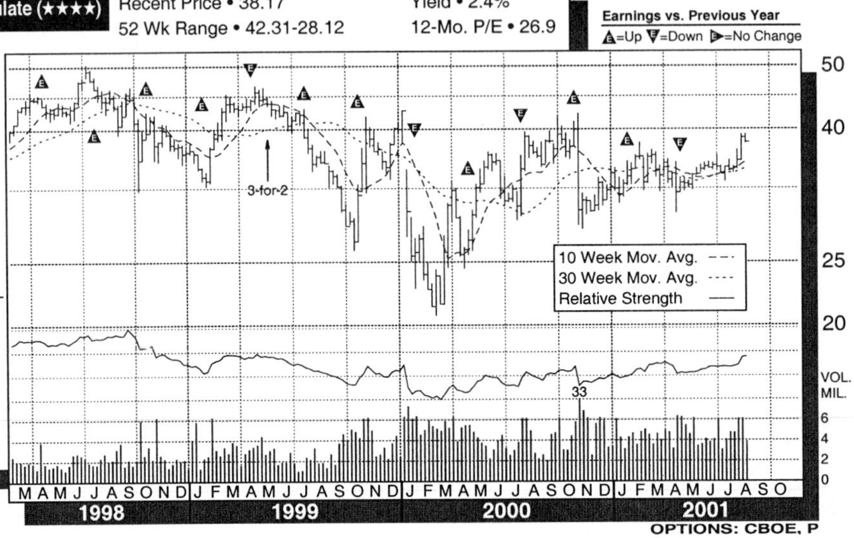

OPTIONS: CBOE, P

Overview - 10-AUG-01

Revenues will likely rise between 6% and 8% in 2001 amid improved pricing for most lines of commercial insurance. This compares to revenue growth of 4% in 2000. Revenue growth of 13% in 1998 was aided by the January 1997 acquisition of Alexander & Alexander Services (AAL). The acquisition of AAL greatly expanded AOC's presence in the insurance brokerage market. Earnings growth in 2001 and beyond is predicated on AOC's ability to improve brokerage margins. Comparisons in 2002 will be aided by the absence of $0.49 a share of net restructuring charges taken in the first half of 2001. This followed a similar charge of $0.19 a share taken in 2000. Pretax charges of $0.74 a share were recorded in 1999 to settle certain Unicover charges, and to restructure the brokerage unit. We view the pending spinoff of the underwriting unit positively, as it will allow AOC's core insurance brokerage business to garner a higher price/earnings multiple.

Valuation - 10-AUG-01

After a sharp correction in early 2000 that was sparked by concerns about AOC's integration of its acquisitions, and its exposure to Unicover-related claims, the shares recovered. After trading in a narrow range thus far in 2001, the shares have recently strengthened, reflecting a rotation back into financial stocks and positive investor response to a firming of commercial insurance rates and AOC's restructuring and planned spinoff of its insurance unit. Despite their recent strength, we believe the shares have some additional upside. At current levels, the stock's P/E multiple is approximately three-quarters that accorded the shares of AOC's rival, Marsh & McLennan Companies (NYSE: MMC). As AOC takes steps to become more of a "pure" insurance brokerage and consulting firm, its shares will likely be rewarded with an expansion of their P/E multiple.

Key Stock Statistics

S&P EPS Est. 2001	2.30	Tang. Bk. Value/Share	NM
P/E on S&P Est. 2001	16.6	Beta	1.04
S&P EPS Est. 2002	2.55	Shareholders	13,650
Dividend Rate/Share	0.90	Market cap. (B)	$ 10.0
Shs. outstg. (M)	261.9	Inst. holdings	60%
Avg. daily vol. (M)	1.081		

Value of $10,000 invested 5 years ago: $ 20,177

Fiscal Year Ending Dec. 31

	2001	2000	1999	1998	1997	1996
Revenues (Million $)						
1Q	1,811	1,810	1,699	1,562	1,354	942.1
2Q	—	1,819	1,723	1,623	1,425	932.4
3Q	—	1,785	1,770	1,607	1,451	944.3
4Q	—	1,961	1,878	1,702	1,521	1,069
Yr.	—	7,375	7,070	6,493	5,751	3,888
Earnings Per Share ($)						
1Q	**0.07**	**0.47**	**0.19**	**0.53**	**-0.01**	0.37
2Q	—	**0.49**	**0.57**	**0.54**	**0.32**	0.24
3Q	—	**0.53**	**0.52**	**0.47**	**0.38**	0.32
4Q	—	**0.33**	**0.05**	**0.53**	**0.43**	0.17
Yr.	—	**1.82**	**1.33**	**2.07**	**1.12**	**1.09**

Next earnings report expected: NA

Dividend Data (Dividends have been paid since 1950.)

Amount ($)	Date Decl.	Ex-Div. Date	Stock of Record	Payment Date
0.220	Oct. 13	Oct. 31	Nov. 02	Nov. 15 '00
0.220	Jan. 19	Feb. 06	Feb. 08	Feb. 21 '01
0.225	Apr. 20	May. 01	May. 03	May. 16 '01
0.225	Jul. 13	Jul. 31	Aug. 02	Aug. 15 '01

Aon Corporation

Business Summary - 10-AUG-01

Aon Corp. has transformed itself from a multiline insurer with a relatively modest presence in the insurance brokerage arena into the second largest insurance broker in the world. The company accomplished this through an aggressive acquisition plan that included the January 1997 purchase of a beleaguered rival, Alexander & Alexander Services. While AOC's relatively lofty P/E multiple is like that of an insurance broker, the company still underwrites an array of insurance products. During 2000, insurance brokerage and other related activities accounted for 67% of revenues, insurance premiums and other revenue for 26%, and investment income for 7%. In April 2001, AOC announced plans to spin off its underwriting division to shareholders via a tax-free stock dividend expected to occur by the end of 2001.

At the end of 2000, AOC was the second largest retail insurance broker and the largest reinsurance broker globally. Through a number of subsidiaries, the company offers risk management services, including insurance placement, claims management, loss control, and administrative services. It has also developed specialties in certain lines of business, including marine, aviation, directors and officers liability, financial institutions, construction, energy, media and entertainment. The unit's operations were greatly expanded following the January 1997 acquisition of Alexander & Alexander Services, Inc., for about $1.2 billion. AOC has also made subsequent, smaller acquisitions. During 1999, AOC incurred $313 million in pretax charges. Of that amount, $120 million covered a restructuring of the brokerage operations. The remaining $193 million was earmarked to make redress payments to certain clients of the consulting group that purchased private pension plans in the U.K., and to cover losses and litigation expenses from the failed Unicover workers' compensation reinsurance pool.

Insurance underwriting provides accident and health coverage, traditional life insurance, and extended warranties through distribution networks owned by other AOC subsidiaries. The consulting group provides an array of consulting services in the areas of employee benefits, human resources and compensation.

In November 2000 AOC announced a "business transformation plan" aimed at improving operating efficiencies and profitability. Pretax charges of $300 million were taken in the fourth quarter of 2000 ($82 million, or $0.19 a share after taxes); and in the first six months of 2001 ($218 million, or $0.49 a share after taxes) to cover associated costs. Annual expense savings from this restructuring are estimated at between $150 million and $200 million and will begin to be realized in the fourth quarter of 2001.

Per Share Data ($) (Year Ended Dec. 31)	2000	1999	1998	1997	1996	1995	1994	1993	1992	1991
Tangible Bk. Val.	NM	NM	NM	NM	4.93	5.99	2.88	3.26	6.05	5.94
Oper. Earnings	NA	NA	NA	1.53	1.09	1.13	1.38	1.20	0.84	1.08
Earnings	1.82	1.33	2.07	1.12	1.10	1.14	1.40	1.25	0.86	1.10
Dividends	0.87	0.81	0.73	0.68	0.63	0.60	0.56	0.52	0.49	0.47
Relative Payout	48%	61%	35%	61%	57%	52%	40%	42%	57%	43%
Prices - High	42.75	46.66	50.37	39.25	28.77	22.61	15.88	17.33	16.00	12.37
- Low	20.68	26.06	32.16	26.77	21.11	13.94	13.00	13.70	11.59	8.81
P/E Ratio - High	23	35	24	35	26	20	11	14	19	11
- Low	11	20	16	24	19	12	9	11	14	8
Income Statement Analysis (Million $)										
Life Ins. In Force	18,803	14,444	10,653	10,438	10,997	NA	75,222	72,161	71,851	71,900
Prem. Inc.: Life A & H	1,233	1,137	1,084	1,081	1,105	1,254	1,684	1,562	1,548	1,487
Prem. Inc.: Cas./Prop.	673	671	589	528	421	173	250	261	278	247
Net Invest. Inc.	508	577	590	494	384	329	760	745	737	713
Total Revs.	7,375	7,070	6,493	5,751	3,888	3,466	4,157	3,845	3,337	2,931
Pretax Inc.	854	635	931	542	446	458	538	479	291	332
Net Oper. Inc.	NA	NA	NA	402	283	301	NA	312	203	239
Net Inc.	481	352	541	299	292	304	360	324	206	242
Balance Sheet & Other Fin. Data (Million $)										
Cash & Equiv.	1,118	837	786	1,085	479	268	642	292	229	183
Premiums Due	1,278	1,116	1,120	863	989	580	2,520	2,101	1,720	822
Invest. Assets: Bonds	2,337	2,497	3,103	4,841	4,092	7,687	7,927	7,858	7,366	6,774
Invest. Assets: Stocks	492	574	768	806	879	1,006	939	933	830	610
Invest. Assets: Loans	Nil	NA	Nil	Nil	87.2	858	782	767	797	852
Invest. Assets: Total	6,019	6,184	6,452	5,922	5,213	10,639	9,783	9,652	9,088	8,360
Deferred Policy Costs	656	636	573	549	599	1,262	1,182	1,005	948	911
Total Assets	22,251	21,132	19,688	18,691	13,723	19,736	17,922	16,279	14,290	11,633
Debt	1,848	1,811	1,380	2,201	475	498	496	521	478	418
Common Eqty.	3,388	3,051	3,017	2,822	2,827	2,666	2,246	2,274	2,089	1,771
Comb. Loss-Exp. Ratio	NA	NA	NA	NA	NA	NA	NA	NA	NA	NA
% Return On Revs.	6.5	5.0	8.3	5.2	7.6	8.8	8.7	8.4	6.2	8.3
% Ret. on Equity	14.8	11.5	18.4	10.1	11.5	11.4	14.5	14.8	9.9	15.0
% Invest. Yield	8.3	9.1	9.5	8.9	4.9	3.6	7.8	8.0	8.4	8.9

Data as orig reptd.; bef. results of disc opers/spec. items. Per share data adj. for stk. divs. Bold denotes diluted EPS (FASB 128)-prior periods restated. E-Estimated. NA-Not Available. NM-Not Meaningful. NR-Not Ranked.

Office—200 East Randolph Drive, Chicago, IL 60602. **Tel**—(312) 701-3000. **Website**—http://www.aon.com **Chrmn & CEO**—P. G. Ryan. **Pres**—M. D. O'Halleran. **EVP & CFO**—H. N. Medvin. **Treas**—D. Aigotti. **Investor Contact**—Sean O' Neill. **Dirs**— F. A. Cole, E. D. Jannotta, L. B. Knight, P. J. Lewis, A. J. McKenna, R. S. Morrison, R. C. Notebaert, M. D. O'Halleran, D. S. Perkins, J. W. Rogers Jr., P. G. Ryan, G. A. Schaefer, R. I. Skilling, F. L. Turner, A. R. Weber, C. Y. Woo. **Transfer Agent & Registrar**—EquiServe, Jersey City, NJ. **Incorporated**—in Illinois in 1949; reincorporated in Delaware in 1980. **Empl**— 51,000. **S&P Analyst:** Catherine A. Seifert

STANDARD &POOR'S
STOCK REPORTS

Bear Stearns

NYSE Symbol **BSC**
In S&P 500

20-AUG-01

Industry: Investment Banking/ Brokerage

Summary: This company's Bear, Stearns & Co. unit is a leading investment bank and broker, and is ranked as one of the largest NYSE member firms.

S&P Opinion: Accumulate (★★★★)

Recent Price • 53.75
52 Wk Range • 72.50-40.65
Yield • 1.1%
12-Mo. P/E • 10.9

Quantitative Evaluations

Outlook
(1 Lowest—5 Highest)
• **2+**

Fair Value
• **54.60**

Risk
• **Average**

Earn./Div. Rank
• **A**

Technical Eval.
• **Bullish** since 6/01

Rel. Strength Rank
(1 Lowest—99 Highest)
• **38**

Insider Activity
• **Unfavorable**

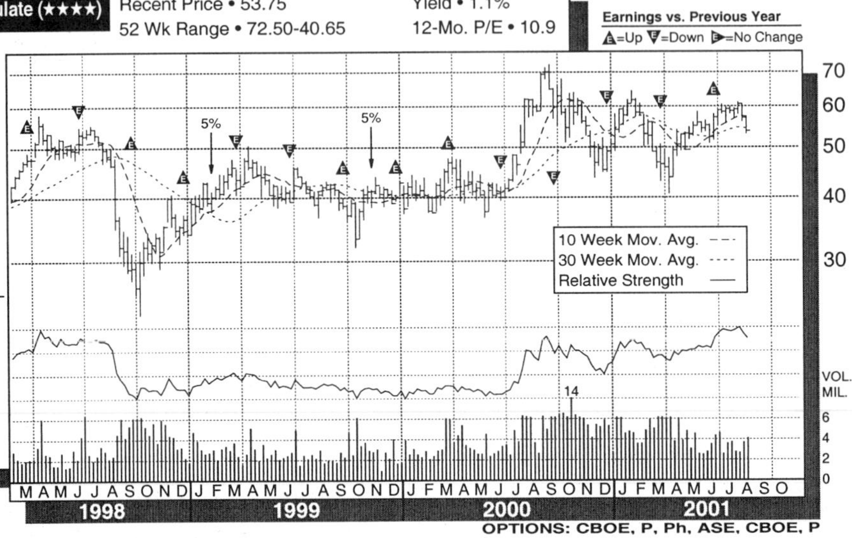

OPTIONS: CBOE, P, Ph, ASE, CBOE, P

Overview - 20-AUG-01

The revenues and earnings of investment banking concerns are difficult to predict, due to their dependence on the health of the equity and debt markets and the level and direction of interest rates, among other factors. Net revenues in FY 00 (Nov.) rose 7%. We expect net revenues this year to be essentially flat. Results early this year were negatively impacted by a weak underwriting market, as falling securities prices tempered the demand for new equity issues, less merger and acquisition activity, and lower customer margin balances. Still, we expect business to improve as the year progresses, as falling interest rates spur debt underwriting and trading. We think the equity markets will stabilize, resulting in increased equity underwriting and M&A activity. Despite the current tough business conditions, competition for employees will result in higher costs. We look for EPS this year of $4.68, versus the $5.98 a share in operating EPS earned in FY 00 (excluding a $0.63 litigation charge). In FY 02, we expect EPS to rise about 9.4%, to $5.12.

Valuation - 20-AUG-01

While price to book value has historically been the preferred method for valuing shares of securities brokers, P/E ratio analysis has become more popular as securities firms have worked to limit the volatility of their earnings streams. At recent levels, the shares were trading at a discount to those of BSC's peers, on both a price to book and a P/E basis. Though earnings in recent periods have been weak, we expect recent cuts in the fed funds rate to lead to a turnaround later this year. BSC is frequently the subject of takeover speculation. Nevertheless, we do not believe it is in any serious takeover discussions, and see any buyout as a long way off.

Key Stock Statistics

S&P EPS Est. 2001	4.68	Tang. Bk. Value/Share	45.49
P/E on S&P Est. 2001	11.5	Beta	1.72
Dividend Rate/Share	0.60	Shareholders	2,462
Shs. outstg. (M)	101.2	Market cap. (B)	$ 5.4
Avg. daily vol. (M)	0.655	Inst. holdings	65%

Value of $10,000 invested 5 years ago: $ 32,151

Fiscal Year Ending Nov. 30

	2001	2000	1999	1998	1997	1996
Revenues (Million $)						
1Q	2,146	2,688	1,724	1,813	1,236	1,074
2Q	2,449	2,504	2,003	1,993	1,557	1,190
3Q	—	2,416	1,805	1,928	1,511	1,296
4Q	—	2,669	2,351	2,246	1,773	1,403
Yr.	—	10,277	7,882	7,980	6,077	4,964
Earnings Per Share ($)						
1Q	**1.10**	**1.89**	**0.36**	1.01	0.65	0.54
2Q	**1.18**	**0.77**	**0.80**	**1.01**	1.10	0.63
3Q	**E1.18**	**1.32**	**1.35**	**1.04**	1.03	0.78
4Q	**E1.22**	**1.36**	**1.76**	**1.12**	1.04	1.02
Yr.	**E4.68**	**5.35**	**4.27**	**4.17**	**3.81**	**2.96**

Next earnings report expected: mid September

Dividend Data (Dividends have been paid since 1986.)

Amount ($)	Date Decl.	Ex-Div. Date	Stock of Record	Payment Date
0.150	Sep. 14	Oct. 13	Oct. 17	Oct. 31 '00
0.150	Jan. 04	Jan. 12	Jan. 17	Jan. 31 '01
0.150	Mar. 30	Apr. 11	Apr. 16	Apr. 30 '01
0.150	Jun. 20	Jul. 13	Jul. 17	Jul. 31 '01

A Division of The McGraw·Hill Companies

The Bear Stearns Companies Inc.

Business Summary - 20-AUG-01

The Bear Stearns Companies Inc. is one of the best known concerns on Wall Street. It is a leading worldwide investment banking and securities trading firm serving corporate, government, institutional and individual clients around the globe. BSC operates offices in various cities across the U.S. and in international business centers such as London and Hong Kong, to name a few. The company operates in three segments: Capital Markets, Global Clearing Services and Wealth Management.

The Capital Markets segment encompasses BSC's sales, trading and research efforts surrounding equity, debt, derivatives and many other types of securities. Capital Markets also includes Bear's investment banking activities. As an investment banker, BSC provides two main services to clients. The company generates merger and acquisition (M&A) fees by advising corporations on strategic acquisitions, mergers, corporate takeovers and defenses and the like. As an underwriter, Bear helps corporations issue debt and equity. Investment banking operations are supported by its large research department. BSC's institutional equity staff, for instance, covers more than 1,200 companies in 100 industry sectors. The Capital Markets division accounted for 64% of net revenues in FY 00 (Nov.) and 77% of pretax income.

BSC's international equities business accounted for 41% of Capital Markets net revenues in FY 00, while fixed income accounted for 31% and investment banking accounted for 28%. In the twelve months ended November 1999, institutional equities accounted for 31% of net revenues, fixed income accounted for 40% and investment banking accounted for 30%.

The Global Clearing Services segment provides clearing, margin lending and securities borrowing to facilitate customer short sales to roughly 2,900 clients worldwide. These clients include hedge funds, short sellers, arbitrageurs and other professional investors as well as companies engaged in the institutional or retail brokerage business. BSC processed approximately 251,000 trades per day in FY 00, compared to 172,000 a year earlier. In FY 00, Global Clearing Services accounted for 20% a net revenues and 40% of pretax income.

BSC's Wealth Management segment includes Private Client Services and Asset Management. Private Client Services provides high-net-worth individuals with sophisticated financial advice. The Asset Management division had $19.5 billion in assets under management at November 30, 2000, versus $13.0 billion a year earlier. Wealth Management accounted for 13% of net revenues in FY 00 and 11% of pretax profits.

Per Share Data ($) (Year Ended Nov. 30)	2000	1999	1998	1997	1996	1995	1994	1993	1992	1991
Tangible Bk. Val.	45.49	33.90	27.84	22.69	17.57	14.03	12.17	10.54	8.61	6.35
Cash Flow	4.89	4.64	4.47	4.16	3.27	1.69	2.50	2.47	2.01	1.04
Earnings	5.35	4.27	4.17	3.81	2.96	1.40	2.26	2.24	1.83	0.84
Dividends	0.55	0.55	0.54	0.53	0.52	0.49	0.44	0.42	0.41	0.33
Payout Ratio	10%	13%	13%	14%	17%	35%	20%	19%	22%	39%
Prices - High	72.50	50.47	58.05	43.99	24.51	19.23	18.46	13.37	13.41	11.37
- Low	36.50	31.90	23.58	23.21	15.73	11.94	12.53	9.56	9.59	5.50
P/E Ratio - High	14	12	14	12	8	14	8	6	7	12
- Low	7	7	6	6	5	9	6	4	5	6
Income Statement Analysis (Million $)										
Commissions	1,207	1,014	903	732	687	547	483	421	375	339
Int. Inc.	5,642	4,009	4,286	3,058	2,393	1,970	1,304	902	997	1,279
Total Revs.	10,277	7,882	7,980	6,077	4,964	3,754	3,441	2,857	2,677	2,380
Int. Exp.	4,801	3,380	3,639	2,551	1,981	1,679	1,020	710	835	1,141
Pretax Inc.	1,172	1,064	1,063	1,014	835	388	643	614	508	230
Eff. Tax Rate	34%	37%	38%	40%	41%	38%	40%	41%	42%	38%
Net Inc.	773	673	660	613	491	241	387	362	295	143
Balance Sheet & Other Fin. Data (Million $)										
Total Assets	171,166	153,894	154,496	121,434	92,085	74,597	67,392	57,440	45,768	39,285
Cash Items	6,093	5,020	3,357	2,698	1,830	2,010	3,285	2,610	2,280	2,331
Receivables	19,305	18,065	90,537	79,258	63,221	50,372	49,014	38,840	30,292	27,317
Secs. Owned	61,760	41,943	44,620	38,437	26,222	21,509	14,444	15,215	12,162	8,792
Sec. Borrowed	21,541	64,819	59,960	53,848	43,222	38,155	34,847	28,743	24,630	24,077
Due Brokers & Cust.	51,236	43,019	47,175	32,730	23,753	17,404	17,098	14,634	11,338	9,011
Other Liabs.	3,104	25,954	29,423	23,109	16,171	12,475	9,722	10,404	7,483	4,443
Capitalization:										
Debt	17,243	15,147	13,296	8,120	6,044	4,060	3,408	1,883	1,040	682
Equity	4,958	4,156	3,499	2,941	2,307	2,000	1,729	1,439	1,127	1,001
Total	22,898	20,103	17,938	11,746	8,789	6,562	5,725	3,660	2,167	1,754
% Return On Revs.	8.5	9.8	8.3	10.1	9.9	6.4	11.2	12.7	11.0	6.0
% Ret. on Assets	0.5	0.4	0.5	0.6	0.6	0.3	0.6	0.7	0.7	0.4
% Ret. on Equity	16.2	16.6	19.5	22.1	25.6	11.3	22.9	27.7	28.1	13.9

Data as orig reptd.; bef. results of disc opers/spec. items. Per share data adj. for stk. divs. Bold denotes diluted EPS (FASB 128)-prior periods restated. Prior to 2000, yrs. ended Jun. 30. E-Estimated. NA-Not Available. NM-Not Meaningful. NR-Not Ranked.

Office—245 Park Ave., New York, NY 10167. **Tel**—(212) 272-2000. **Website**—http://www.bearstearns.com **Chrmn**—A. C. Greenberg. **Pres & CEO**—J. E. Cayne. **Secy**—K. L. Edlow. **Treas**—M. Minikes. **SVP-Fin & CFO**—S. L. Molinaro Jr. **Investor Contact**—Rebecca Haas (212-272-8188). **Dirs**—J. E. Cayne, C. D. Glickman, A. C. Greenberg, D. J. Harrington, W. L. Mack, F. T. Nickell, F. V. Salerno, A. D. Schwartz, W. J. Spector, V. Tese, F. Wilpon. **Transfer Agent & Registrar**—Mellon Shareholder Services, Ridgefield Park, NJ. **Incorporated**—in Delaware in 1985. **Empl**— 11,201. **S&P Analyst:** Michael Schneider, CFA

STANDARD &POOR'S
STOCK REPORTS

Capital One Financial

NYSE Symbol **COF**

In S&P 500

18-AUG-01 **Industry:** Consumer Finance

Summary: This company is one of the largest issuers of Visa and MasterCard credit cards, with 33.8 million cardholders.

S&P Opinion: Accumulate (★★★★)

Recent Price • 61.01
52 Wk Range • 73.25-45.87
Yield • 0.2%
12-Mo. P/E • 23.9

Quantitative Evaluations

Outlook (1 Lowest—5 Highest) • **4−**

Fair Value • **79.40**

Risk • **Average**

Earn./Div. Rank • **NR**

Technical Eval. • **Neutral** since 7/01

Rel. Strength Rank (1 Lowest—99 Highest) • **44**

Insider Activity • **Unfavorable**

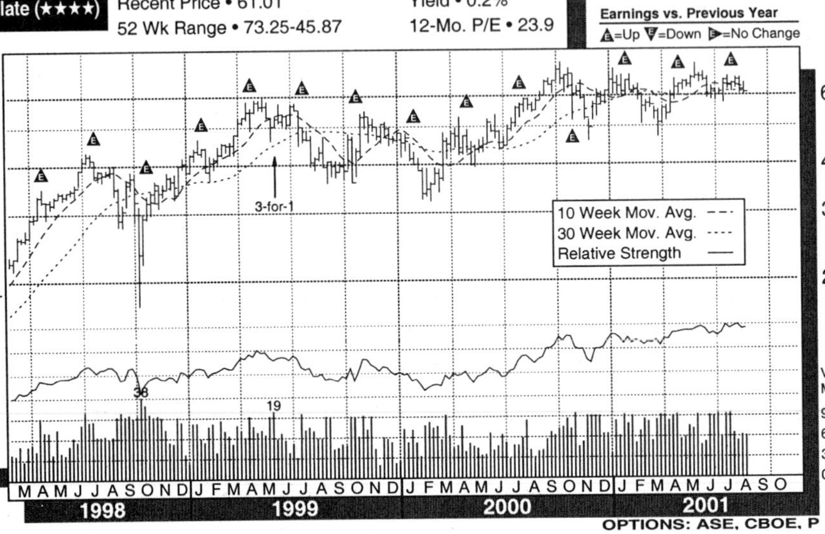

OPTIONS: ASE, CBOE, P

Overview - 20-JUL-01

Managed loans advanced 46% in 2000, to $29.5 billion. We expect 25% growth in 2001 to be driven by solid, albeit slowing, consumer spending, and rapid new account growth, especially in the second half of the year. The Internet, in particular, will be a major source of new account growth in 2001. COF generated 1.4 million new accounts over the Internet alone in 2000, easily surpassing its 1.0 million account goal. The company's information-based strategy, designed to differentiate among its customers, and to match client characteristics with product offerings, will continue to play a large part in COF's growth. The company continues to spend heavily on marketing, in an effort to expand its customer franchise. Marketing expenses in 2000 totaled $906 million, up 24% from the level of 1999. We expect credit quality to deteriorate slightly in 2001, driven by the impact of a slowing economy, higher unemployment levels and seasoning in some product portfolios. We see EPS in 2001 advancing 30%, to $2.91.

Valuation - 20-JUL-01

The shares are expected to outperform the S&P 500 over the next six to 12 months. We expect COF to boost earnings at a rate of 25% or more a year for the next three to five years. The company's above average growth should be driven by steady consumer spending patterns and an expanding customer base. Although credit quality may deteriorate slightly in 2001, we expect losses to remain well within manageable bounds. The shares were recently trading at a slight discount to COF's projected EPS growth rate, and about in line with the market P/E, based on our 2001 EPS estimates. Although we do not anticipate further earnings multiple expansion, in light of the company's above average earnings growth prospects, the shares have strong capital appreciation potential.

Key Stock Statistics

S&P EPS Est. 2001	2.91	Tang. Bk. Value/Share	9.94
P/E on S&P Est. 2001	21.0	Beta	1.33
S&P EPS Est. 2002	3.64	Shareholders	10,019
Dividend Rate/Share	0.11	Market cap. (B)	$ 12.7
Shs. outstg. (M)	208.4	Inst. holdings	68%
Avg. daily vol. (M)	1.200		

Value of $10,000 invested 5 years ago: $ 58,938

Fiscal Year Ending Dec. 31

	2001	2000	1999	1998	1997	1996
Revenues (Million $)						
1Q	1,675	1,171	877.7	573.9	411.6	304.3
2Q	1,731	1,247	949.8	600.4	395.9	308.4
3Q	—	1,428	1,033	670.1	459.9	394.9
4Q	—	1,578	1,105	755.4	519.6	416.3
Yr.	—	5,424	3,966	2,600	1,787	1,424
Earnings Per Share ($)						
1Q	0.66	0.51	0.39	0.32	0.21	0.19
2Q	0.70	0.54	0.41	0.32	0.19	0.19
3Q	E0.75	0.58	0.45	0.33	0.24	0.19
4Q	E0.80	0.61	0.47	0.35	0.29	0.20
Yr.	E2.91	2.24	1.72	1.32	0.93	0.77

Next earnings report expected: mid October

Dividend Data (Dividends have been paid since 1995.)

Amount ($)	Date Decl.	Ex-Div. Date	Stock of Record	Payment Date
0.027	Oct. 17	Nov. 06	Nov. 08	Nov. 20 '00
0.027	Jan. 18	Feb. 06	Feb. 08	Feb. 20 '01
0.027	Apr. 26	May. 07	May. 09	May. 21 '01
0.027	Aug. 01	Aug. 06	Aug. 08	Aug. 20 '01

Capital One Financial Corporation

Business Summary - 20-JUL-01

Capital One Financial (COF) is one of the 10 leading U.S. issuers of Visa and MasterCard credit cards. At the end of 2000, COF had 33.8 million customer accounts and $29.5 billion in managed consumer loans outstanding, versus 23.7 million customer accounts and $20.2 billion in managed receivables a year earlier. Since 1996, managed loans have grown at a compound annual rate of over 23%, while total accounts have grown at a compound annual rate of over 40%. COF attributes this rapid growth not only to the favorable dynamics of the credit card industry, but also to the company's information-based strategy (IBS), which it initiated in 1988. Prior to its November 1994 IPO, COF was a wholly owned subsidiary of Signet Banking Corp., which was acquired by First Union Corp. in late 1997.

COF uses IBS to differentiate among customers based on credit risk, card usage and other characteristics. IBS is also used to match customer characteristics with appropriate product offerings. This helps ensure successful and profitable product launches. COF continuously seeks to apply IBS to other financial products and services. In July 1998, the company acquired Summit Acceptance Corp., an automobile finance lender that offers loans throughout the U.S. secured by automobiles and marketed mainly through dealer networks. COF is using Summit as a platform to test IBS in the auto loan market.

COF's credit card products are offered throughout the U.S., as well as internationally, including the U.K. and Canada. Credit card products are designed to apply to different consumer preferences and needs by combining different product features such as annual percentage rates, fees and charges, and reward programs. To continue its international growth, the company opened a new operations center in England in 1998.

Marketing is a very important part of COF's operations. Since 1988, the company has steadily increased its marketing efforts. In 2000, the company spent over $906 million on marketing, compared to nearly $732 million in 1999. Most of the company's accounts are generated through direct mail and telemarketing solicitations, although the company is increasing its efforts to generate accounts through Internet, newspaper, magazine, radio, and television advertising.

At year-end 2000, 5.23% of total managed loans were 30 days or more past due, compared with 5.23% in 1999 and 4.70% in 1998. Net chargeoffs include the principal amount of losses less any current period recoveries. Loans that are 180 days past due are charged off. In 2000, net chargeoffs were equal to 3.90% of average managed loans outstanding, versus 3.85% in 1999 and 5.33% in 1998.

Per Share Data ($) (Year Ended Dec. 31)	2000	1999	1998	1997	1996	1995	1994	1993	1992	1991
Tangible Bk. Val.	9.94	7.69	6.45	4.55	3.72	3.02	2.39	2.32	NA	NA
Earnings	2.24	1.72	1.32	0.93	0.77	0.63	0.48	0.46	NA	NA
Dividends	0.11	0.11	0.11	0.11	0.11	0.08	Nil	NA	NA	NA
Payout Ratio	5%	6%	8%	11%	14%	13%	Nil	NA	NA	NA
Prices - High	73.25	60.25	43.31	18.10	12.29	9.87	5.54	NA	NA	NA
- Low	32.06	35.81	16.85	10.16	7.25	5.12	4.62	NA	NA	NA
P/E Ratio - High	33	35	33	19	16	16	12	NA	NA	NA
- Low	14	21	13	11	9	8	10	NA	NA	NA
Income Statement Analysis (Million $)										
Net Int. Inc.	1,589	1,053	695	383	365	208	165	166	NA	NA
Non Int. Inc.	3,034	2,372	1,488	1,069	763	553	397	197	NA	NA
Loan Loss Prov.	718	383	267	263	167	65.9	30.7	34.0	NA	NA
Non Int. Exp.	3,148	2,465	1,472	884	713	497	384	189	NA	NA
Exp./Op. Revs.	68%	72%	67%	61%	63%	65%	68%	52%	NA	NA
Pretax Inc.	757	577	444	305	248	198	147	140	NA	NA
Eff. Tax Rate	38%	37%	38%	38%	38%	36%	35%	35%	NA	NA
Net Inc.	470	363	275	189	155	129	95.3	90.4	NA	NA
% Net Int. Marg.	12	11	9.95	8.86	8.16	6.28	6.90	NA	NA	NA
Balance Sheet & Other Fin. Data (Million $)										
Money Mkt. Assets	162	112	284	174	450	465	300	Nil	NA	NA
Inv. Securities	1,697	1,856	1,797	1,243	895	769	113	785	NA	NA
Tot. Loans	14,059	9,914	6,157	4,862	4,225	2,450	2,160	1,790	NA	NA
Total Assets	18,889	13,336	9,419	7,078	6,467	4,759	3,092	3,052	NA	NA
Demand Deposits	Nil	Nil	Nil	Nil	Nil	Nil	Nil	Nil	Nil	Nil
Time Deposits	8,379	3,784	2,000	1,314	943	696	452	Nil	NA	NA
LT Debt	4,051	4,181	3,038	3,633	3,994	2,592	1,376	Nil	NA	NA
Common Eqty.	1,963	1,518	1,270	893	740	599	475	460	NA	NA
% Ret. on Assets	2.9	3.2	3.3	2.8	2.8	2.9	3.6	NA	NA	NA
% Ret. on Equity	27.0	26.0	25.4	23.2	22.9	23.3	39.8	NA	NA	NA
% Loan Loss Resv.	3.7	3.5	3.8	3.8	2.7	2.9	3.1	3.5	NA	NA
% Loans/Deposits	167.8	262.0	307.9	370.1	NM	NM	NM	NM	NA	NA
% Loans/Assets	72.3	70.6	66.8	68.0	77.4	64.3	69.8	58.7	NA	NA
% Equity to Assets	10.8	12.3	13.1	12.1	15.7	12.6	15.4	15.1	NA	NA

Data as orig reptd.; bef. results of disc opers/spec. items. Per share data adj. for stk. divs. Bold denotes diluted EPS (FASB 128)-prior periods restated. E-Estimated. NA-Not Available. NM-Not Meaningful. NR-Not Ranked.

Office—2980 Fairview Park Dr., Falls Church, VA 22042. **Tel**—(703) 205-1000. **Website**—http://www.capitalone.com **Chrmn & CEO**—R. D. Fairbank. **Pres & COO**—N. W. Morris. **CFO**—D. M. Willey. **SVP & Secy**—J. G. Finneran Jr. **Investor Contact** —Paul Paquin (703) 205-1039. **Dirs**—W. R. Dietz, R. D. Fairbank, J. A. Flick Jr., P. W. Gross, J. V. Kimsey, N. W. Morris, S. I. Westreich. **Transfer Agent & Registrar**—First Chicago Trust Co. of New York, Jersey City, NJ. **Incorporated**—in Delaware in 1994. **Empl**— 19,247. **S&P Analyst:** Michael Schneider-CFA

STANDARD
&POOR'S
STOCK REPORTS

Charter One Financial

NYSE Symbol **CF**

In S&P 500

18-AUG-01

Industry: Savings & Loan Companies

Summary: This company is one of the the 30 largest U.S. bank holding companies, with assets of approximately $36 billion.

S&P Opinion: Accumulate (★★★★)

Recent Price • 31
52 Wk Range • 32.98-19.87
Yield • 2.6%
12-Mo. P/E • 14.5

Quantitative Evaluations

Outlook
(1 Lowest—5 Highest)
• 2+

Fair Value
• 30.70

Risk
• Low

Earn./Div. Rank
• B+

Technical Eval.
• NA

Rel. Strength Rank
(1 Lowest—99 Highest)
• 56

Insider Activity
• Unfavorable

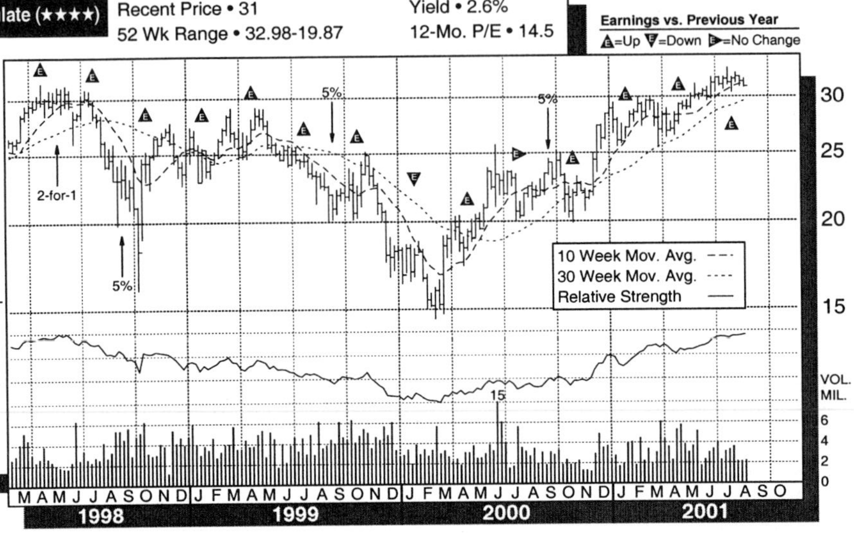

Overview - 15-AUG-01

In 2001, we expect CF to continue to strategically shift its asset base toward higher-yielding consumer and commercial loans, and away from the single-family residential mortgage product. Although the resulting organic loan growth should be modest, we expect a 10% advance in net interest income, following the acquisition of Alliance Bancorp and some widening of the net interest margin. Although credit quality is not a major concern, we do expect provisioning to be up in 2001, reflecting a higher risk loan portfolio and slower economic growth. Noninterest income should post an 18% increase, fueled by retail banking, and aided by a greater contribution from mortgage banking in the second half. With continued efficiency in the low to mid-40% area, we project that operating EPS will increase 13%. In 2002, we expect operating EPS to advance 12%, to $2.66.

Valuation - 15-AUG-01

The 1999 acquisition of St. Paul Bancorp, and its subsequent integration, established the company as a leading player in the attractive Chicago market. In July 2001, CF strengthened its foothold by acquiring Alliance Bancorp, a move we view positively. The company also continues to move toward a more bank-like, and profitable, balance sheet. By June 30, 2001, low yielding one- to four-family loans accounted for only 39% of CF's loan portfolio, down from 50% a year earlier. With its proven ability to increase core deposits, a culture geared towards cross-selling, a strong retail banking franchise, and a solid track record of integrating acquisitions, we expect CF's EPS over the next few years to grow faster that those of its peer group. Although the shares were recently trading at 13X our 2001 EPS estimate, average for a thrift, we are maintaining our accumulate recommendation.

Key Stock Statistics

S&P EPS Est. 2001	2.37	Tang. Bk. Value/Share	11.60
P/E on S&P Est. 2001	13.1	Beta	0.92
S&P EPS Est. 2002	2.66	Shareholders	20,100
Dividend Rate/Share	0.80	Market cap. (B)	$ 6.6
Shs. outstg. (M)	214.2	Inst. holdings	60%
Avg. daily vol. (M)	0.497		

Value of $10,000 invested 5 years ago: $ 27,535

Fiscal Year Ending Dec. 31

	2001	2000	1999	1998	1997	1996
Revenues (Million $)						
1Q	693.3	616.7	483.0	402.5	360.7	254.9
2Q	696.6	644.5	—	409.3	372.6	492.2
3Q	—	677.3	504.9	410.0	382.6	269.3
4Q	—	701.5	553.5	492.9	372.6	275.2
Yr.	—	2,640	2,359	1,972	1,489	1,062
Earnings Per Share ($)						
1Q	**0.54**	**0.50**	**0.45**	**0.39**	**0.35**	**0.31**
2Q	**0.57**	**0.47**	**0.47**	**0.42**	**0.37**	**0.32**
3Q	—	**0.51**	**0.47**	**0.43**	**0.36**	**0.11**
4Q	—	**0.52**	**0.09**	**0.24**	**-0.06**	**0.35**
Yr.	—	**2.00**	**1.46**	**1.47**	**1.00**	**1.08**

Next earnings report expected: mid October

Dividend Data (Dividends have been paid since 1988.)

Amount ($)	Date Decl.	Ex-Div. Date	Stock of Record	Payment Date
0.180	Oct. 19	Nov. 01	Nov. 03	Nov. 20 '00
0.180	Jan. 23	Feb. 02	Feb. 06	Feb. 20 '01
0.200	Apr. 18	May. 03	May. 07	May. 21 '01
0.200	Jul. 18	Aug. 02	Aug. 06	Aug. 20 '01

A Division of The McGraw-Hill Companies

Charter One Financial, Inc.

Business Summary - 15-AUG-01

Cleveland headquartered Charter One Financial is the parent company of Charter One Bank, a federally chartered savings bank, and Charter One Commercial. It is one of the 30 largest U.S. bank holding companies, with assets of nearly $33 billion at December 31, 2000, and an extensive network of more than 420 branches stretching from Michigan to Illinois, Ohio, New York, and into Massachusetts and Vermont. CF also operates a mortgage banking subsidiary that has loan production offices in 11 states; and an indirect auto finance subsidiary operating in 11 states.

Acquisitions have played an integral part in CF's growth since its 1989 IPO. Significant acquisitions in recent years included St. Paul Bancorp (October 1999), with $6.2 billion in assets, and 58 branches in the Chicago market; ALBANK Financial Corp. (November 1998), which had $4 billion in assets, and 109 offices in upstate New York, Massachusetts and Vermont; and RCSB Financial (October 1997), which had $4 billion in assets, and 38 offices in Rochester and Buffalo.

The company's primary objective is to increase its portfolios of "energized" assets and "energized" liabilities. Energized assets include second mortgages, marine and recreational vehicle loans, corporate loans to small and medium-size businesses, and commercial mortgages and leases. At year-end 2000, CF's portfolio of high-yielding loans totaled $13.3 billion, up 24%, year to year. "Energized" liabilities are core, low cost deposits used to fund loan growth. At December 31, 2000, these deposits, made up of checking accounts, savings accounts, and money market accounts, totaled $9.4 billion, up from $8.6 billion at year earlier.

At year-end 2000, CF's loan and lease portfolio totaled $24.3 billion, and consisted of real estate mortgage loans (54%), retail consumer loans (19%), auto loans (13%), leases (7%), consumer finance (4%) and corporate banking (3%). At year-end 1999, CF's $22.5 billion loan and lease portfolio was made up of real estate mortgage loans (62%), retail consumer loans (17%), auto loans (11%), leases (5%), consumer finance (3%) and corporate banking (3%).

The company's long-term performance goals include EPS growth of 13% to 16% a year, return on assets of 1.6%, and return on equity of 20% or better.

In July 2001, CF acquired Chicago-based Alliance Bancorp. (ABCL), with $2.0 billion in assets, by exchanging $5.25 and 0.72 of a CF share for each ABCL share. The acquisition increased CF's branch network to 436.

In July 2000, directors authorized the repurchase of up to 20 million common shares (10%, of the shares outstanding). Through June 2001, CF had bought back 8.6 million shares.

Per Share Data ($) (Year Ended Dec. 31)	2000	1999	1998	1997	1996	1995	1994	1993	1992	1991
Tangible Bk. Val.	10.97	10.06	9.41	8.70	7.66	7.26	6.41	6.43	5.23	4.67
Earnings	2.00	1.46	1.47	1.01	1.10	0.29	1.14	1.05	0.86	0.81
Dividends	0.68	0.57	0.35	0.40	0.37	0.25	0.23	0.16	0.12	0.11
Payout Ratio	34%	39%	24%	42%	33%	88%	20%	15%	14%	14%
Prices - High	30.00	29.13	31.63	27.64	18.40	13.07	9.40	9.79	7.83	5.58
- Low	14.52	16.66	15.98	16.91	11.06	7.39	6.95	6.66	4.43	2.18
P/E Ratio - High	15	20	22	27	17	45	8	9	9	7
- Low	7	11	11	17	10	26	6	6	5	3
Income Statement Analysis (Million $)										
Net Int. Inc.	903	934	729	527	383	318	178	170	136	88.0
Loan Loss Prov.	54.2	35.2	29.5	40.9	4.0	1.0	2.8	5.2	6.5	6.4
Non Int. Inc.	384	288	16.1	-3.2	57.0	-47.8	28.1	26.2	25.7	31.9
Non Int. Exp.	604	633	667	488	244	216	102	97.9	88.7	61.2
Pretax Inc.	638	496	419	223	0.9	53.2	101	93.4	66.5	52.5
Eff. Tax Rate	32%	32%	34%	32%	34%	36%	33%	34%	35%	36%
Net Inc.	434	336	277	151	128	34.0	67.6	61.4	43.3	33.5
% Net Int. Marg.	3.02	3.19	3.14	2.93	2.92	2.24	3.23	3.53	3.32	2.83
Balance Sheet & Other Fin. Data (Million $)										
Total Assets	32,971	31,819	24,467	19,760	13,905	13,579	6,130	5,215	4,262	3,666
Loans	23,950	22,277	17,503	12,360	8,100	6,678	5,581	4,715	3,772	3,239
Deposits	19,606	19,074	15,165	10,219	7,841	7,012	4,368	4,179	3,643	3,187
Capitalization:										
Debt	6,226	5,111	6,316	5,600	3,405	3,372	1,319	604	305	221
Equity	2,411	2,398	1,875	1,377	929	844	369	370	253	188
Total	8,637	7,509	24,467	6,977	4,334	4,216	1,688	974	558	409
% Ret. on Assets	1.3	1.1	53.5	0.9	0.9	0.2	1.2	1.3	1.0	1.0
% Ret. on Equity	18.0	14.0	17.0	13.1	14.4	3.9	17.9	18.1	18.7	19.4
% Loan Loss Resv.	0.8	0.8	0.8	0.0	0.8	1.0	0.7	0.7	0.8	0.7
% Risk Based Capital	10.3	11.2	10.9	10.0	10.6	14.3	13.4	14.4	12.1	9.5
Price Times Book Value:										
Hi	2.7	2.9	3.4	3.2	2.4	1.8	1.5	1.5	1.5	1.2
Low	1.3	1.7	1.7	1.9	1.4	1.0	1.1	1.0	0.8	0.5

Data as orig reptd.; bef. results of disc opers/spec. items. Per share data adj. for stk. divs. Bold denotes diluted EPS (FASB 128)-prior periods restated. E-Estimated. NA-Not Available. NM-Not Meaningful. NR-Not Ranked.

Office—1215 Superior Ave., Cleveland, OH 44114. **Tel**—(216) 566-5300. **Website**—http://www.charterone.com **Chrmn, Pres & CEO**—C. J. Koch. **EVP & CFO**—R. W. Neu. **Investor Contact**—Ellen L. Batkie (800-262-6301). **Dirs**—P. J. Agnew, H. G. Chorbajian, P. W. Fisher, D. M. Fugo, M. D. Grossi, C. M. Heidel, K. R. Hitchcock, J. D. Koch, M. P.Morley, R. W. Neu, H. R. Nolte Jr., R. F. Poe, V. A. Ptak, M. J. Rachal, J. L. Schostak, J. C. Scully, M. Shaevsky, L. S. Simon, J. P. Tierney, E. R. Williams. **Transfer Agent & Registrar**—Equiserve, Providence, RI. **Incorporated**—in Delaware in 1987. **Empl**— 6,573. **S&P Analyst:** Erik J. Eisenstein

STANDARD
&POOR'S
STOCK REPORTS

Chubb Corp.

NYSE Symbol **CB**

In S&P 500

18-AUG-01

Industry: Insurance (Property-Casualty)

Summary: This large, broadly based property-casualty insurance organization has divested its interests in life and health insurance and real estate development.

S&P Opinion: Accumulate (★★★★)

Recent Price • 68.94
52 Wk Range • 90.25-63.30
Yield • 2.0%
12-Mo. P/E • 17.6

Quantitative Evaluations

Outlook
(1 Lowest—5 Highest)
• **3**

Fair Value
• **69.80**

Risk
• **Low**

Earn./Div. Rank
• **B+**

Technical Eval.
• **Bearish** since 7/01

Rel. Strength Rank
(1 Lowest—99 Highest)
• **42**

Insider Activity
• **Neutral**

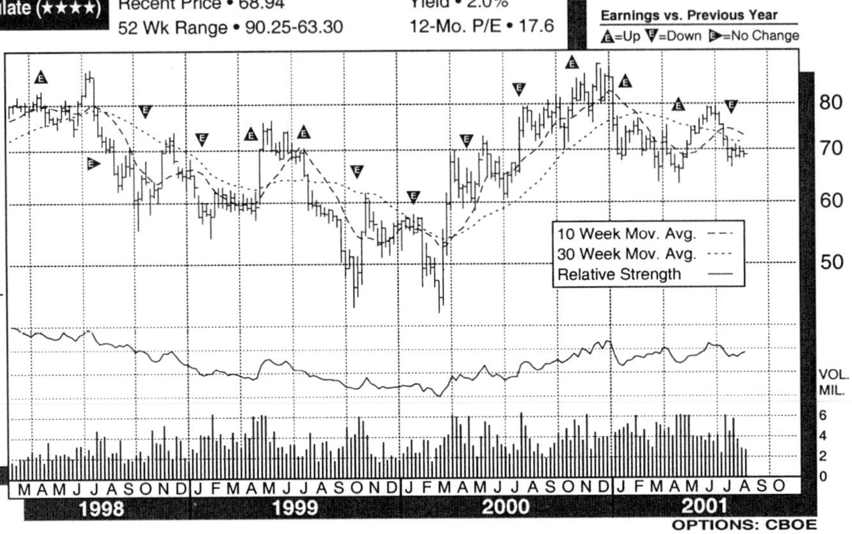

OPTIONS: CBOE

Overview - 03-AUG-01

Written premium growth in 2001 will likely be about 10% to 12%, particularly if pricing strength that has begun to emerge continues. Standard commercial lines pricing remains competitive, but this is being offset by a more favorable outlook for specialty commercial lines and personal lines pricing. Year-to-year operating profit growth in 2001 is also predicated on CB's ability to manage its exposure to catastrophe and weather-related losses, particularly in its growing personal lines unit. Catastrophe losses totaled $91.8 million in the first half of 2001, up from $54.6 million in the first half of 2000 and $71.6 million for all of 2000. However, unlike some of its competitors, CB's conservative reserving policy leaves the company well positioned. For the longer term, margins should be aided by a cost cutting initiative. Investment income growth will likely be about 6% to 7% in 2001. Per share results will be aided by an ongoing stock repurchase plan. About 3.9 million shares were acquired during the first half of 2001.

Valuation - 03-AUG-01

After bottoming in early 2000, together with many other financial stocks, the shares of this property-casualty insurer have rebounded. Their recent strength was tied to favorable comments about the outlook for property-casualty insurance pricing made by CB management. Despite their recent strength, the shares trade at a P/E multiple that is about in line with the company's peer group average. However, in light of CB's prowess as an underwriter, coupled with its growing specialty lines franchise, the shares should see a modest expansion of their current P/E multiple. At these levels, additional upside exists. In addition, as the financial services industry consolidates, CB could become an attractive takeover target, further boosting the shares.

Key Stock Statistics

S&P EPS Est. 2001	4.00	Tang. Bk. Value/Share	37.15
P/E on S&P Est. 2001	17.2	Beta	0.66
S&P EPS Est. 2002	5.00	Shareholders	7,225
Dividend Rate/Share	1.36	Market cap. (B)	$ 12.1
Shs. outstg. (M)	175.2	Inst. holdings	71%
Avg. daily vol. (M)	0.744		

Value of $10,000 invested 5 years ago: $ 16,483

Fiscal Year Ending Dec. 31

	2001	2000	1999	1998	1997	1996
Revenues (Million $)						
1Q	—	1,767	1,630	1,587	1,577	1,482
2Q	—	1,774	1,687	1,598	1,510	1,382
3Q	—	1,859	1,709	1,593	1,569	1,357
4Q	—	1,852	1,443	1,572	2,009	1,460
Yr.	—	7,252	5,652	6,350	6,664	5,681
Earnings Per Share ($)						
1Q	0.97	0.87	1.14	1.12	1.08	—
2Q	0.83	1.02	1.18	1.08	1.08	—
3Q	—	1.17	0.44	1.04	1.10	—
4Q	—	0.95	0.93	0.95	1.13	—
Yr.	—	4.01	3.66	4.19	4.39	2.75

Next earnings report expected: late October

Dividend Data (Dividends have been paid since 1902.)

Amount ($)	Date Decl.	Ex-Div. Date	Stock of Record	Payment Date
0.330	Sep. 08	Sep. 20	Sep. 22	Oct. 10 '00
0.330	Dec. 01	Dec. 13	Dec. 15	Jan. 03 '01
0.340	Mar. 02	Mar. 20	Mar. 22	Apr. 05 '01
0.340	Jun. 01	Jun. 13	Jun. 15	Jul. 03 '01

The Chubb Corporation

Business Summary - 03-AUG-01

Chubb sold its life insurance and real estate operations in 1997 to better focus on its core property-casualty insurance business. During 1998 and 1999, CB focused its efforts on addressing the issue of inadequate pricing of many of its commercial insurance products. The company's chairman said that "fixing the pricing problem . . . in standard commercial lines is our number one priority...." Turning away inadequately priced business is one way to address this issue. Another way is to shift CB's business mix to areas with more favorable pricing and growth prospects, such as specialty commercial and personal lines. The July 1999 acquisition of Executive Risk, Inc., for about $850 million in stock was also part of this plan. Executive Risk underwrites an array of specialty lines coverage, including directors and officers liability and errors and omissions coverage.

Chubb's property-casualty operations, as a group, constitute the 13th largest U.S. property-casualty (p-c) insurer, based on 1999 net written premiums (latest available). In 2000, Chubb wrote $6.33 billion in net property-casualty premiums (up from $5.70 billion in 1999), of which commercial lines accounted for 73%, and personal lines constituted 27%. Written premiums were divided: executive protection 21%, commercial casualty 12%, commercial multi-peril 11%, homeowners 15%, commercial property & marine 8%, financial institutions 8%, workers' compensation 5%, personal auto 6%, other personal lines 6%, and other commercial lines 8%.

During 2000, property-casualty written premiums rose 11%, as a robust 13% increase in personal lines written premiums and a 21% acquisition-aided surge in specialty commercial lines were partly offset by a 3% decline in standard commercial lines premiums. Chubb's underwriting results (as measured by the combined ratio) have typically exceeded industry averages. During 2000, CB's combined ratio was 100.4%, versus an estimated combined ratio of 106% for the entire p-c industry. A combined ratio of under 100% indicates an underwriting profit, while one in excess of 100% points to an underwriting loss. The p-c group operates in the U.S. and abroad through about 4,000 independent agents and 525 insurance brokers.

In 1997, most of the commercial real estate assets of Bellemead Development Corp., CB's real estate development unit, were sold for $737 million. In May 1997, the company sold its life and health insurance unit to Jefferson-Pilot Corp. (NYSE: JP) for $875 million in cash.

Per Share Data ($) (Year Ended Dec. 31)	2000	1999	1998	1997	1996	1995	1994	1993	1992	1991
Tangible Bk. Val.	37.15	32.85	34.84	33.47	31.24	29.71	24.05	23.92	22.18	19.94
Oper. Earnings	NA	3.33	3.65	4.00	3.58	3.45	2.75	1.12	2.79	2.92
Earnings	4.01	3.66	4.19	4.39	2.75	3.92	2.98	1.96	3.48	3.16
Dividends	1.32	1.27	1.22	1.16	1.08	0.98	0.92	0.86	0.80	0.74
Relative Payout	33%	35%	29%	26%	39%	25%	31%	44%	23%	23%
Prices - High	90.25	76.37	88.81	78.50	56.25	50.31	41.56	48.18	45.50	39.00
- Low	43.25	44.00	55.37	51.12	40.87	38.06	34.31	38.00	31.18	25.00
P/E Ratio - High	23	21	21	18	20	13	14	25	13	12
- Low	11	12	13	12	15	10	12	19	9	8
Income Statement Analysis (Million $)										
Life Ins. In Force	NA	NA	NA	NA	NA	66,661	61,701	54,283	46,455	41,502
Prem. Inc.: Life A & H	NA	NA	NA	NA	NA	623	836	801	689	634
Prem. Inc.: Cas./Prop.	NA	5,652	5,304	5,157	4,569	4,147	3,776	3,505	3,163	3,037
Net Invest. Inc.	957	893	822	785	712	901	829	800	751	701
Total Revs.	7,252	6,730	6,350	6,664	5,681	6,089	5,710	5,500	4,941	4,513
Pretax Inc.	851	710	850	973	547	900	639	344	748	684
Net Oper. Inc.	NA	565	615	701	434	614	487	193	493	509
Net Inc.	715	621	707	770	486	697	528	344	617	552
Balance Sheet & Other Fin. Data (Million $)										
Cash & Equiv.	720	735	229	12.0	200	257	221	210	207	199
Premiums Due	3,263	1,235	1,199	1,144	985	873	787	720	625	632
Invest. Assets: Bonds	15,564	14,519	13,319	12,454	11,158	12,603	10,722	10,718	10,000	8,660
Invest. Assets: Stocks	831	769	1,092	871	646	588	642	930	738	1,143
Invest. Assets: Loans	NA	NA	NA	Nil	Nil	212	203	194	193	187
Invest. Assets: Total	17,001	16,019	14,755	14,049	1,281	13,887	12,378	11,842	10,932	9,990
Deferred Policy Costs	842	780	729	677	601	1,171	1,136	1,012	929	886
Total Assets	25,027	23,537	20,746	19,616	19,939	22,997	20,723	19,437	15,019	13,775
Debt	754	759	608	399	1,071	1,344	1,439	1,369	1,361	1,280
Common Eqty.	6,982	6,272	5,644	5,657	5,463	5,263	4,247	4,196	3,954	3,542
Comb. Loss-Exp. Ratio	100.4	102.8	96.1	96.9	98.3	96.8	99.5	114.8	101.1	99.5
% Return On Revs.	9.9	9.2	11.1	11.6	8.6	11.4	9.3	5.9	12.5	12.2
% Ret. on Equity	10.8	10.4	12.5	13.8	9.1	14.7	12.5	8.4	16.5	17.2
% Invest. Yield	5.8	5.8	5.7	6.0	6.2	6.9	6.8	7.0	7.1	7.3

Data as orig reptd.; bef. results of disc opers/spec. items. Per share data adj. for stk. divs. Bold denotes diluted EPS (FASB 128)-prior periods restated. E-Estimated. NA-Not Available. NM-Not Meaningful. NR-Not Ranked.

Office—15 Mountain View Rd., Warren, NJ 07061-1615. **Tel**—(908) 903-2000. **Website**—www.chubb.com **Chrmn & CEO**—D. R. O'Hare. **Pres**—J. J. Degnan. **VP & Secy**—H. G. Gulick. **VP & Treas**—P. J. Sempier. **SVP-CFO & Investor Contact**—Weston M. Hicks (908-903-4334). **Dirs**—Z. E. Baird, J. C. Beck, S. P. Burke, J. I. Cash Jr., P. Chubb III, J. J. Cohen, J. M. Cornelius, D. H. Hoag, D. R. O'Hare, W. B. Rudman, Sir David Scholey, R. G. H. Seitz, L. M. Small, K. H. Williams, J. M. Zimmerman, A. W. Zollar. **Transfer Agent & Registrar**—First Chicago Trust Co. of New York. **Incorporated**—in New Jersey in 1967. **Empl**— 12,000. **S&P Analyst:** Catherine A. Seifert

STANDARD & POOR'S STOCK REPORTS

Federal Home Loan Mortgage

NYSE Symbol **FRE**

In S&P 500

18-AUG-01

Industry: Financial (Diversified)

Summary: Federal Home Loan Mortgage (Freddie Mac), a U.S. government-sponsored enterprise (GSE), buys mortgages from lenders in order to increase the supply of funds for housing.

S&P Opinion: Accumulate (★★★★)

Recent Price • 69
52 Wk Range • 70.40-40.62
Yield • 1.2%
12-Mo. P/E • 16.6

Quantitative Evaluations

Outlook (1 Lowest—5 Highest)
• **3**

Fair Value
• **69.80**

Risk
• **Average**

Earn./Div. Rank
• **A+**

Technical Eval.
• **Bullish** since 5/01

Rel. Strength Rank (1 Lowest—99 Highest)
• **68**

Insider Activity
• **NA**

Earnings vs. Previous Year
E=Up E=Down E=No Change

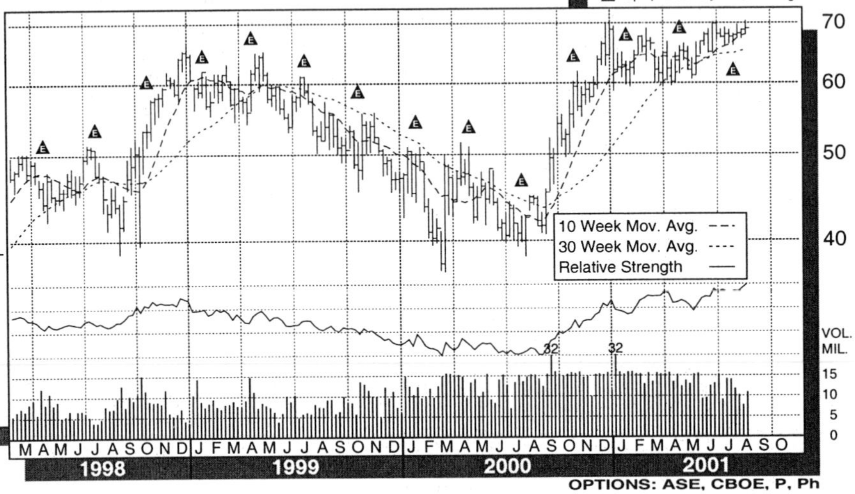

OPTIONS: ASE, CBOE, P, Ph

Overview - 15-AUG-01

FRE's retained mortgage portfolio grew at a 32% compound annual rate in the first half of 2001, to $444 billion. Although we see that growth rate slowing for the remainder of the year as the refinancing boom draws to a close, we anticipate a 27% increase in 2001. With the net interest yield slightly wider, net interest income should advance over 28%. The company's securitization business should benefit from continued strength in the fixed-rate mortgage origination market, increased issuance of mortgage-backed securities, and deeper market penetration. Credit-related expenses should remain low by historical standards, continuing to benefit from a strong housing market and low unemployment levels. We project that operating EPS in 2001 will advance 23%, to $4.17. In 2002, we see operating EPS up 13%, to $4.70, reflecting more difficult comparisons.

Valuation - 15-AUG-01

We continue to look for 14% to 16% annual gains in EPS for the next few years beyond 2002, aided by growth in total mortgage debt outstanding, favorable trends in credit quality, and the company's access to low-cost financing by virtue of its quasi-agency status. Not all wish to see this competitive advantage perpetuate, though, giving rise to political risk. In the near term, this risk was diminished when the Democratic Party gained control of the U.S. Senate. Longer term, however, we expect efforts to either heighten regulation or authorize additional GSEs to place some pressure on the stock. Still, we do not currently believe these efforts will pose a serious threat to FRE, which enjoys considerable political support. The shares were recently trading at a discount to the P/E of the S&P 500, based on our 2001 EPS estimate, despite above average EPS growth prospects. We therefore anticipate some future multiple expansion.

Key Stock Statistics

S&P EPS Est. 2001	4.17	Tang. Bk. Value/Share	16.80
P/E on S&P Est. 2001	16.5	Beta	0.61
S&P EPS Est. 2002	4.70	Shareholders	2,403
Dividend Rate/Share	0.80	Market cap. (B)	$ 47.8
Shs. outstg. (M)	692.6	Inst. holdings	86%
Avg. daily vol. (M)	2.006		

Value of $10,000 invested 5 years ago: $ 32,180

Fiscal Year Ending Dec. 31

	2001	2000	1999	1998	1997	1996
Revenues (Million $)						
1Q	1,421	6,930	5,627	3,985	3,411	2,749
2Q	1,601	7,323	5,818	4,318	3,604	2,995
3Q	—	7,652	6,269	4,502	3,589	3,137
4Q	—	8,064	6,554	5,243	3,795	3,235
Yr.	—	29,969	24,268	18,048	14,399	12,116
Earnings Per Share ($)						
1Q	**1.12**	**0.81**	**0.69**	**0.54**	0.44	0.40
2Q	**1.29**	**0.83**	**0.74**	**0.56**	0.46	0.43
3Q	—	**0.86**	**0.74**	**0.58**	0.49	0.41
4Q	—	**0.89**	**0.79**	**0.62**	**0.51**	0.43
Yr.	—	**3.39**	**2.95**	**2.31**	**1.88**	**1.65**

Next earnings report expected: mid October

Dividend Data (Dividends have been paid since 1989.)

Amount ($)	Date Decl.	Ex-Div. Date	Stock of Record	Payment Date
0.170	Sep. 08	Sep. 14	Sep. 18	Sep. 29 '00
0.170	Dec. 01	Dec. 07	Dec. 11	Dec. 29 '00
0.200	Mar. 02	Mar. 08	Mar. 12	Mar. 30 '01
0.200	Jun. 01	Jun. 07	Jun. 11	Jun. 29 '01

Federal Home Loan Mortgage Corporation

Business Summary - 15-AUG-01

The Federal Home Loan Mortgage Corp., better known as Freddie Mac, is one of two public government-sponsored enterprises (the other being rival Fannie Mae) formed to promote home ownership by increasing the availability of mortgage financing. The company was originally part of the Federal Home Loan Bank Board, which was dismantled under the S&L bailout law of 1989. Of its 18 directors, 13 are elected by stockholders and five are picked by the President of the U.S. Freddie Mac has two principal business segments.

In its portfolio business, Freddie Mac functions in a manner similar to a savings and loan, which originates home mortgage loans to hold for its own account. The major differences are: (1) Freddie Mac uses capital market borrowings to finance its mortgage purchases, whereas the thrift uses retail savings; and (2) Freddie Mac purchases mortgages from various lenders, while a thrift actually issues the homebuyer a mortgage.

The term "retained mortgage portfolio" is intended to indicate that these mortgages are "warehoused" (i.e. held) as a long-term investment for their valuable interest income. This business is quite profitable for Freddie Mac, because its cost of funds is in one sense subsidized by its quasi-agency status. The retained portfolio business generates the majority of the company's profits. At December 31, 2000, Freddie Mac's retained mortgage portfolio totaled $385.1 billion, up from $322.6 billion a year earlier.

The company's mortgage backed securities (MBS) operation is best illustrated by an example. Typically, a bank or thrift will decide it prefers to hold MBSs as opposed to originated loans. The institution then turns over the loan, or more often a pool of loans, to Freddie Mac, which gives the lender MBSs in return. Both parties win. Freddie Mac receives a fee of about one-fifth of 1% to guarantee the principal and interest on the MBSs. Meanwhile, the lender has a nearly risk-free instrument on which it receives principal and interest payments. Freddie Mac makes money in this business because its loss rate is very low: people will default on all sorts of bills, but the basic need for shelter provides a powerful incentive to keep the mortgage more or less current.

Nonperforming single-family loans amounted to 0.50% of the total portfolio at December 31, 2000, up from 0.43% a year earlier. Apartment delinquencies and foreclosures were 0.04% of the total portfolio, based on principal balances, versus 0.14% a year earlier.

In April 2001, Freddie Mac completed implementation of the six voluntary commitments made in October 2000 to enhance its risk management, capital and disclosure practices.

Per Share Data ($) (Year Ended Dec. 31)	2000	1999	1998	1997	1996	1995	1994	1993	1992	1991
Tangible Bk. Val.	16.80	11.99	11.55	8.74	9.63	7.38	6.45	4.95	4.17	3.56
Earnings	3.39	2.96	2.31	1.88	1.67	1.42	1.33	1.02	0.82	0.77
Dividends	0.68	0.60	0.48	0.40	0.35	0.30	0.26	0.22	0.19	0.17
Payout Ratio	20%	20%	21%	21%	21%	21%	20%	22%	23%	22%
Prices - High	70.12	65.25	66.37	44.56	29.25	20.90	15.71	14.18	12.31	11.57
- Low	36.87	45.37	38.68	26.68	19.06	12.46	11.75	11.31	8.43	3.68
P/E Ratio - High	21	22	29	24	18	15	12	14	15	15
- Low	11	15	17	14	11	9	9	11	10	5
Income Statement Analysis (Million $)										
Interest On: Mtges.	23,989	19,714	14,269	11,030	9,038	6,505	4,528	3,296	2,608	2,332
Interest On: Invest.	4,361	3,039	2,369	1,971	1,745	1,888	1,287	1,127	917	1,095
Int. Exp.	25,512	20,213	14,711	11,119	8,241	6,997	4,703	3,571	2,830	2,744
Guaranty Fees	0.0	0.0	0.0	0.0	1,249	1,087	1,108	1,033	936	792
Loan Loss Prov.	40.0	60.0	190	310	320	255	200	300	473	431
Admin. Exp.	883	655	578	495	440	395	379	361	329	287
Pretax Inc.	3,534	3,161	2,356	2,215	1,797	1,586	1,482	1,128	901	800
Eff. Tax Rate	28%	30%	28%	26%	30%	31%	31%	30%	31%	31%
Net Inc.	2,539	2,218	1,700	1,395	1,243	1,091	1,027	786	622	555
Balance Sheet & Other Fin. Data (Million $)										
Mtges.	385,117	322,569	255,348	164,250	137,520	107,411	72,295	55,732	33,523	26,537
Invest.	40,718	31,747	44,753	13,402	16,331	13,962	17,808	18,223	12,542	9,956
Cash & Equiv.	366	5,144	2,565	438	9,141	7,483	11,442	3,216	6,453	7,987
Total Assets	459,297	386,684	321,421	194,597	173,866	137,181	106,199	83,880	59,502	46,860
ST Debt	183,576	175,525	193,871	85,128	80,105	62,141	47,303	17,999	12,854	17,239
LT Debt	243,178	185,056	Nil	83,446	76,386	57,820	48,984	31,994	16,777	13,023
Equity	11,642	8,330	8,028	5,934	6,685	5,000	4,300	3,574	3,008	2,566
% Ret. on Assets	0.6	0.6	0.7	0.8	0.8	0.9	1.1	1.1	1.2	1.3
% Ret. on Equity	23.6	25.2	22.6	20.6	18.5	22.1	24.4	21.4	21.2	23.6
Equity/Assets Ratio	42.4	43.3	37.0	3.1	4.0	3.8	4.2	4.6	5.2	5.4
Price Times Book Value:										
Hi	4.2	5.4	5.7	5.1	3.0	2.8	2.4	2.9	2.5	3.3
Low	2.2	3.8	3.3	4.1	2.0	1.7	1.8	2.3	1.7	1.0

Data as orig reptd.; bef. results of disc opers/spec. items. Per share data adj. for stk. divs. Bold denotes diluted EPS (FASB 128)-prior periods restated. E-Estimated. NA-Not Available. NM-Not Meaningful. NR-Not Ranked.

Office—8200 Jones Branch Dr., McLean, VA 22102-3100. **Tel**—(703) 903-2000 **Website**—http://www.freddiemac.com **Chrmn & CEO**—L. C. Brendsel. **Vice Chrmn & Pres**—D. W. Glenn. **EVP & Secy**—M. Mater. **EVP & CFO**—V. A. Clarke. **VP-Fin & Investor Contact**—Joseph E. Amato (703-903-2798). **Dirs**—L. C. Brendsel, C. B. Cabrera, M. Engler, D. W. Glenn, G. D. Gould, D. J. Gribbin III, T. W. Jones, H. Kaufman, M. Mater, J. B. McCoy, J. F. Montgomery, R. F. Poe, W. D. Powers, S. A. Ross, D. J. Schuenke, C. Seix, C. Stepp, W. J. Turner. **Transfer Agent & Registrar**—First Chicago Trust Co. of New York, Jersey City, NJ. **Incorporated**—under the laws of the United States in 1970. **Empl**— 3,500. **S&P Analyst:** Erik J. Eisenstein

STANDARD &POOR'S STOCK REPORTS

Federal National Mortgage Assoc.

NYSE Symbol **FNM**

In S&P 500

18-AUG-01

Industry: Financial (Diversified)

Summary: FNM (Fannie Mae), a U.S. government-sponsored enterprise (GSE), uses mostly borrowed funds to buy a variety of mortgages, thereby creating a secondary market for mortgage lenders.

S&P Opinion: Accumulate (★★★★)

Recent Price • 84.35
52 Wk Range • 89.37-52.06
Yield • 1.4%
12-Mo. P/E • 17.6

Quantitative Evaluations

Outlook (1 Lowest—5 Highest) • **2+**

Fair Value • **84.30**

Risk • **Low**

Earn./Div. Rank • **A+**

Technical Eval. • **Bullish** since 8/01

Rel. Strength Rank (1 Lowest—99 Highest) • **62**

Insider Activity • **NA**

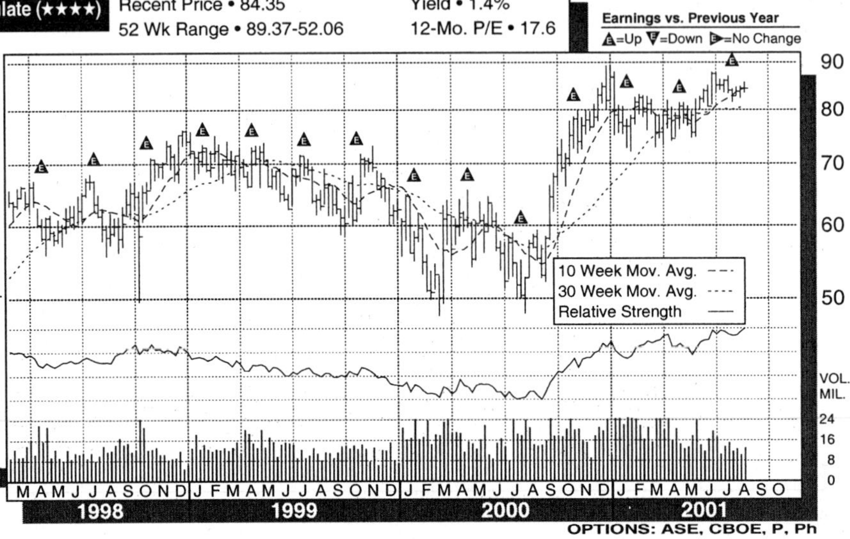

OPTIONS: ASE, CBOE, P, Ph

Overview - 14-AUG-01

FNM's net mortgage portfolio grew at a 15% compound annual rate in the second quarter of 2001, to $663 billion. Although we see the sequential rate of growth slowing in coming quarters, as the refinancing boom draws to a close, we are projecting a mid-teen increase for 2001. We also expect the net interest margin to increase. Higher fees should boost the bottom line, as FNM's technology services continue to grow in popularity. Credit-related expenses will likely be flat or modestly down in 2001, despite current economic weakness, reflecting continued strength in the housing market and historically low unemployment levels. We look for operating EPS to advance 21% in 2001, to $5.17. In 2002, we expect a 10% rise in operating EPS, to $5.68, with slower growth reflecting a more typical home lending market.

Valuation - 14-AUG-01

FNM continues to enjoy very favorable long-term growth prospects, reflecting projected increases in mortgage debt outstanding, continued gains in securitization activities, new housing initiatives, and increasing use of its technology services. FNM's access to low-cost financing, by virtue of its quasi-agency status, remains a sizable competitive advantage. In the past, however, this advantage has attracted political scrutiny. Recently the near-term political risk was diminished when the Democratic Party gained control of the U.S. Senate. Longer term, however, we expect efforts to either heighten regulation or authorize additional GSEs to place some pressure on the stock. Still, we do not presently believe these efforts will pose a serious threat to FNM, which enjoys considerable political support. We recommend accumulating the shares, recently trading at a significant discount to the P/E of the S&P 500, based on our 2001 EPS estimate.

Key Stock Statistics

S&P EPS Est. 2001	5.17	Tang. Bk. Value/Share	18.58
P/E on S&P Est. 2001	16.3	Beta	0.40
S&P EPS Est. 2002	5.68	Shareholders	376,000
Dividend Rate/Share	1.20	Market cap. (B)	$ 84.3
Shs. outstg. (M)	999.0	Inst. holdings	83%
Avg. daily vol. (M)	2.335		

Value of $10,000 invested 5 years ago: $ 27,874

Fiscal Year Ending Dec. 31

	2001	2000	1999	1998	1997	1996
Revenues (Million $)						
1Q	12,366	10,306	8,658	7,401	6,672	6,065
2Q	—	10,658	8,938	7,754	6,862	6,146
3Q	—	11,204	9,433	8,117	7,004	6,317
4Q	—	11,921	9,939	8,227	7,237	6,526
Yr.	—	44,088	36,968	31,499	27,777	25,054
Earnings Per Share ($)						
1Q	**1.14**	**1.02**	**0.88**	**0.78**	0.67	0.61
2Q	**1.45**	**1.02**	**0.92**	**0.80**	0.69	0.61
3Q	—	**1.09**	**0.94**	**0.82**	0.72	0.63
4Q	—	**1.13**	**0.99**	**0.85**	**0.75**	0.65
Yr.	—	**4.26**	**3.73**	**3.26**	**2.84**	**2.50**

Next earnings report expected: mid October

Dividend Data (Dividends have been paid since 1956.)

Amount ($)	Date Decl.	Ex-Div. Date	Stock of Record	Payment Date
0.280	Oct. 17	Oct. 27	Oct. 31	Nov. 25 '00
0.300	Jan. 16	Jan. 29	Jan. 31	Feb. 25 '01
0.300	Apr. 17	Apr. 26	Apr. 30	May. 25 '01
0.300	Jul. 17	Jul. 27	Jul. 31	Aug. 25 '01

The Federal National Mortgage Association

Business Summary - 14-AUG-01

The Federal National Mortgage Association (known as Fannie Mae) is a government-sponsored enterprise, chartered by Congress to increase the availability of mortgage credit for homebuyers. Its mission is essentially to increase the rate of home ownership, making American society more stable. The company's predecessor was formed during the Great Depression, to make home ownership possible in a time when it was nearly impossible for people in certain parts of the U.S. to obtain a mortgage. FNM basically operates in two business segments.

In its retained mortgage portfolio business, which accounts for most of the company's profits, FNM buys mortgages from lenders such as thrifts, banks and mortgage bankers, and holds them on account. It funds mortgages purchases with debt of various maturities, earning a spread on the difference between the yield on the mortgages and the cost of the debt. In 2000, FNM purchased $154 billion of mortgages, versus $195 billion in 1999 and $188 billion in 1998.

In its securitization operations, which account for much of FNM's remaining profits, the company swaps mortgage-backed securities (MBSs) for mortgages with various lending institutions, and in the process earns a fee of about 0.19%. One reason that lenders swap loans for MBSs is that the latter add to liquidity. FNM functions as a mortgage insurer in that it accepts the risk of default on the mortgage in exchange for a fee or a premium. In 2000, it issued $212 billion of MBSs, versus $301 billion in 1999.

Finally, the company earns a small amount for guaranteeing complex mortgage-backed securities that are put together by Wall Street concerns.

Earnings in 2000 benefited from a steep decline in credit related expenses, which include the provision for losses and foreclosed property expenses. Credit related expenses totaled $94 million in 2000, down from $127 million in 1999 and $261 million in 1998. The decrease was driven by the strong national housing market, aggressive loss mitigation efforts and greater amounts of insurance coverage on loans that entered foreclosure.

Although FNM is highly profitable in a variety of interest rate environments, Congress is constantly concerned about its risk exposure on the $1 trillion plus of mortgages and mortgage-backed securities outstanding, since the U.S. government might ultimately have to make good on large-scale defaults. Congress has therefore established capital standards, which the company meets.

In October 2000, FNM agreed to a number of voluntary measures to enhance disclosure, capital and market discipline. The company put these initiatives into place in the first quarter of 2001.

FNM has a stated goal of doubling its 1998 EPS by the end of 2003.

Per Share Data ($) (Year Ended Dec. 31)	2000	1999	1998	1997	1996	1995	1994	1993	1992	1991
Tangible Bk. Val.	18.58	16.03	13.95	12.34	11.10	10.04	8.74	7.39	6.20	5.08
Earnings	4.26	3.73	3.26	2.84	2.50	1.94	1.95	1.86	1.50	1.33
Dividends	1.12	1.08	0.96	0.84	0.76	0.68	0.60	0.46	0.34	0.26
Payout Ratio	26%	29%	29%	30%	30%	35%	31%	25%	23%	20%
Prices - High	89.37	75.87	76.18	57.31	41.62	31.50	22.59	21.53	19.31	17.40
- Low	47.87	58.56	49.56	36.12	27.50	17.18	17.03	18.21	13.78	8.09
P/E Ratio - High	21	20	23	20	17	16	12	12	13	13
- Low	11	16	15	13	11	9	9	10	9	6
Income Statement Analysis (Million $)										
Interest On: Mtges.	39,403	32,672	25,676	22,716	20,560	18,154	15,851	13,957	12,651	11,603
Interest On: Invest.	3,378	2,823	4,319	3,662	3,212	2,917	1,496	876	884	990
Int. Exp.	37,107	30,601	25,885	22,429	20,180	18,024	14,524	12,300	11,476	10,815
Guaranty Fees	NA	0.0	0.0	0.0	1,196	0.0	1,083	961	834	675
Loan Loss Prov.	Nil	-120	50.0	100	195	140	155	175	320	370
Admin. Exp.	905	800	708	636	560	546	525	443	381	319
Pretax Inc.	5,982	5,440	4,645	4,337	3,905	2,995	3,146	3,005	2,382	2,081
Eff. Tax Rate	26%	28%	26%	29%	30%	28%	32%	32%	31%	30%
Net Inc.	4,416	3,921	3,444	3,068	2,754	2,155	2,141	2,042	1,649	1,455
Balance Sheet & Other Fin. Data (Million $)										
Mtges.	607,399	522,780	415,223	313,316	286,259	252,588	220,525	189,892	156,021	126,486
Invest.	54,968	39,751	58,213	64,596	56,606	57,273	46,335	21,396	14,786	10,999
Cash & Equiv.	617	2,099	743	2,205	850	318	231	977	5,193	3,194
Total Assets	675,072	575,167	485,014	391,673	351,041	316,550	272,508	216,979	180,978	147,072
ST Debt	280,322	226,582	205,413	175,400	159,900	146,153	112,602	71,950	56,404	34,608
LT Debt	362,360	321,037	254,878	194,374	171,370	153,021	144,628	129,162	109,896	99,329
Equity	18,560	16,329	14,303	12,793	12,773	10,959	9,541	8,052	6,774	5,547
% Ret. on Assets	0.7	0.7	0.8	0.8	0.8	0.7	0.9	1.0	1.0	1.0
% Ret. on Equity	24.6	25.1	25.4	24.4	23.9	21.0	24.3	27.5	26.8	30.7
Equity/Assets Ratio	35.8	2.9	3.1	3.6	3.4	3.5	3.6	3.7	3.8	3.4
Price Times Book Value:										
Hi	4.8	4.7	5.5	4.6	3.8	3.1	2.6	2.9	3.1	3.4
Low	2.6	3.7	3.6	2.9	2.5	1.7	1.9	2.5	2.2	1.6

Data as orig reptd.; bef. results of disc opers/spec. items. Per share data adj. for stk. divs. Bold denotes diluted EPS (FASB 128)-prior periods restated. E-Estimated. NA-Not Available. NM-Not Meaningful. NR-Not Ranked.

Office—3900 Wisconsin Ave. N.W., Washington, DC 20016-2892. **Tel**—(202) 752-7000. **Website**—http://www.fanniemae.com **Chrmn & CEO**—F. D. Raines. **Vice Chrmn & COO**—D. H. Mudd. **EVP & CFO**—J. T. Howard. **Controller**—L. G. Spencer. **Investor Contact**—Jayne Shontell (202-752-7115). **Dirs**—V. Ashe, S. B. Ashley, M. H. Bordonado, K. M. Duberstein, S. Friedman, T. P. Gerrity, J. S. Gorelick, W. R. Harvey, A. McLaughlin Korologos, V. A. Mai, D. B. Marron, D. H. Mudd, A. M. Mulchahy, J. K. Pickett, F. D. Raines, T. C. Segue III, H. P. Swygert. **Transfer Agent & Registrar**—EquiServe, Jersey City, NJ. **Incorporated**—under the laws of the United States in 1938. **Empl**— 4,100. **S&P Analyst:** Erik Eisenstein

STANDARD
&POOR'S
STOCK REPORTS

Golden State Bancorp

NYSE Symbol **GSB**

In S&P MidCap 400

18-AUG-01

Industry: Savings & Loan Companies

Summary: Golden State, with $61 billion in assets, is the parent company of California Federal Bank (Cal Fed), which operates 356 branches in California and Nevada.

S&P Opinion: Accumulate (★★★★)

Recent Price • 34.68
52 Wk Range • 35.43-18.50
Yield • 1.2%
12-Mo. P/E • 13.2

Quantitative Evaluations

Outlook
(1 Lowest—5 Highest)
• **2−**

Fair Value
• **33.50**

Risk
• **Average**

Earn./Div. Rank
• **NR**

Technical Eval.
• **Bullish** since 6/01

Rel. Strength Rank
(1 Lowest—99 Highest)
• **87**

Insider Activity
• **NA**

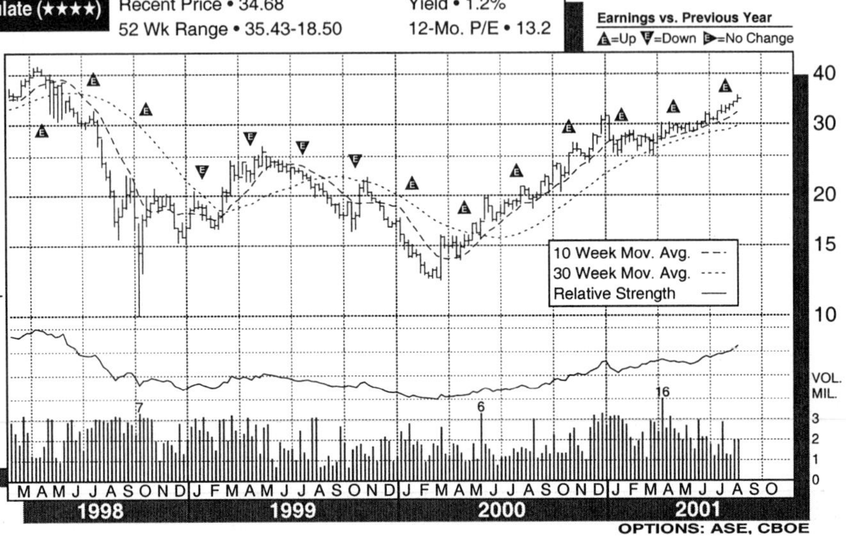

OPTIONS: ASE, CBOE

Overview - 16-AUG-01

We expect GSB to sell, rather than hold, the predominately fixed rate mortgages originated in this lower interest rate environment. As a result, we are projecting essentially flat interest earning assets in the current year. However we still expect net interest income to advance in the high teens in 2001, fueled by a greater proportion of higher yielding loans, a lower cost deposit base, and a normal yield curve. Loan loss provisions will probably remain low, not only because of the healthy California housing market, but also because of GSB's ample reserve levels. We expect a slight reduction in noninterest income, despite higher retail banking fees and gains on loan sales, reflecting lower net loan servicing fees mortgage on increased prepayments. With efficiency in the high 50% area, operating EPS should advance 16% in 2001, to $2.82. For 2002, we project a 12% gain in operating EPS, to $3.17, with the aid of a FASB accounting change regarding goodwill amortization.

Valuation - 16-AUG-01

We expect the shares to outperform their peers for the remainder of 2001. GSB continues to improve its lending margins with a greater proportion of non-single family residential loans and non-interest-bearing deposits. In addition, conservative lending practices have resulted in strong credit quality, enabling the company to better withstand current economic weakness. At June 30, 2001, nonperforming assets were equal to 0.21% of total assets, down from 0.26% a year earlier. We also believe the thrift may become an acquisition target, reflecting attractive West Coast markets served. We recommend that investors accumulate the shares, recently trading at about 12X our 2001 EPS estimate, below peer levels.

Key Stock Statistics

S&P EPS Est. 2001	2.82	Tang. Bk. Value/Share	12.87
P/E on S&P Est. 2001	12.3	Beta	NA
S&P EPS Est. 2002	3.17	Shareholders	6,168
Dividend Rate/Share	0.40	Market cap. (B)	$ 4.7
Shs. outstg. (M)	135.7	Inst. holdings	47%
Avg. daily vol. (M)	0.321		

Value of $10,000 invested 5 years ago: $ 20,103

Fiscal Year Ending Dec. 31

	2001	2000	1999	1998	1997	1996
Revenues (Million $)						
1Q	1,118	1,076	998.0	623.2	316.2	281.7
2Q	1,137	1,130	1,011	638.5	311.2	288.8
3Q	—	1,171	1,020	816.7	300.9	291.1
4Q	—	1,177	1,041	947.4	334.5	300.3
Yr.	—	4,547	4,071	3,026	1,267	1,162
Earnings Per Share ($)						
1Q	**0.65**	**0.59**	**0.50**	**0.84**	0.40	-0.50
2Q	**0.73**	**0.60**	**0.59**	**5.07**	**0.41**	0.31
3Q	—	**0.62**	**0.59**	**0.65**	**0.45**	0.34
4Q	—	**0.63**	**0.61**	**0.11**	**0.51**	0.37
Yr.	—	**2.44**	**2.29**	**4.88**	**1.78**	**0.64**

Next earnings report expected: mid October

Dividend Data (Dividends have been paid since 2000.)

Amount ($)	Date Decl.	Ex-Div. Date	Stock of Record	Payment Date
0.100	Jul. 20	Jul. 27	Jul. 31	Sep. 01 '00
0.100	Oct. 23	Nov. 01	Nov. 03	Dec. 01 '00
0.100	Apr. 23	May. 03	May. 07	Jun. 01 '01
0.100	Jul. 17	Aug. 02	Aug. 06	Sep. 04 '01

Golden State Bancorp Inc.

Business Summary - 16-AUG-01

Golden State Bancorp (GSB), the second largest U.S. thrift, is the holding company for California Federal Bank (Cal Fed). At year-end 2000, the bank had about $61 billion in assets and $23 billion in deposits. It serves its customers through 354 branches and 511 automated teller machines in California and Nevada. Cal Fed's subsidiary, First Nationwide Mortgage Corp., is one of the 10 largest U.S. mortgage loan servicers, and one of the 20 leading mortgage loan originators. The bank's primary business consists of attracting checking and savings deposits from the public and purchasing and origination loans secured by mortgages on residential real estate, to be sold to various investors in the secondary market, or retained in its own portfolio. GSB also originates and/or purchases commercial real estate, commercial and consumer loans for investment.

The bank derives its income primarily from the interest it receives on real estate, business and consumer loans, and to a lesser extent, from interest on investment securities, fees received in connection with loans, loan servicing and deposit services, as well as other services. Its major expenses are the interest it pays on deposits and on borrowings and general operating expenses. The difference between interest income and interest expense is called net interest income. This is a thrift's most important revenue source, because it represents what the institution earns from its basic business of making loans funded by savings deposits.

At year-end 2000, 77% of the loan portfolio consisted of one-to-four unit residential mortgage loans, down from 79% a year earlier. The company offers both fixed and variable rate loans. Borrowers generally prefer fixed rate mortgages, but for the right price they will take out an adjustable. GSB also offers multi-family real estate, or apartment loans (9% of the loan portfolio at year end 2000), commercial real estate loans (6%), auto loans (4%), commercial loans (1%), home equity loans (1%), and other (1%). To improve profitability, the bank intends to focus on increasing its mix of non-single family residential loans.

Passbook accounts accounted for 13% of GSB's deposit base at year-end 2000, interest bearing checking accounts 9%, noninterest bearing checking accounts 11%, money market accounts 13%, and CDs 54%.

Non-performing assets, which consist of non-performing loans, foreclosed real estate and repossessed assets, accounted for 0.23% of total assets at December 31, 2000, versus 0.35% a year earlier.

In September 1998, GSB merged with California Federal (Cal Fed) through an exchange of shares. Cal Fed is the surviving merged bank, and Golden State is the surviving holding company.

In November 2000, directors authorized the repurchase in 2001 of up to $250 million of issued securities.

Per Share Data ($) (Year Ended Dec. 31)	2000	1999	1998	1997	1996	1995	1994	1993	1992	1991
Tangible Bk. Val.	10.87	6.07	5.12	16.99	15.83	16.11	16.63	14.82	12.80	NA
Earnings	2.44	2.29	4.88	1.78	0.63	0.36	1.28	-6.48	-4.27	-3.69
Dividends	0.20	Nil	Nil	Nil	Nil	Nil	Nil	Nil	NA	NA
Payout Ratio	8%	Nil	Nil	Nil	Nil	Nil	Nil	Nil	NA	NA
Prices - High	31.87	26.56	42.06	42.06	37.75	23.87	18.00	13.50	NA	NA
- Low	12.25	16.25	10.00	19.75	22.25	15.50	8.75	5.12	NA	NA
P/E Ratio - High	13	12	9	24	60	66	14	NM	NA	NA
- Low	5	7	2	11	35	43	7	NM	NA	NA
Income Statement Analysis (Million $)										
Net Int. Inc.	1,147	1,186	729	440	379	333	318	311	363	508
Loan Loss Prov.	NA	10.0	40.0	NM	25.2	40.4	66.0	140	251	314
Non Int. Inc.	441	419	477	109	88.7	34.4	134	60.3	11.1	-8.2
Non Int. Exp.	913	925	764	328	356	264	261	465	298	308
Pretax Inc.	674	669	402	222	86.6	63.4	125	-233	-175	-123
Eff. Tax Rate	20%	28%	NM	42%	42%	34%	42%	NM	NM	NM
Net Inc.	347	321	398	129	50.4	42.1	73.0	-223	-135	-117
% Net Int. Marg.	2.05	2.27	2.07	2.89	2.68	2.29	2.02	1.86	2.19	NA
Balance Sheet & Other Fin. Data (Million $)										
Total Assets	60,517	57,019	54,869	18,117	16,218	14,457	16,044	16,803	18,301	NA
Loans	39,593	33,953	30,281	13,932	14,185	12,969	14,623	14,960	14,638	NA
Deposits	23,430	23,036	24,620	10,698	9,357	8,724	8,735	10,920	11,616	NA
Capitalization:										
Debt	19,659	14,399	14,358	5,677	4,799	3,849	3,524	2,540	2,286	NA
Equity	2,151	1,562	1,582	1,124	897	812	741	651	1,090	NA
Total	22,310	16,460	16,533	6,916	5,696	4,806	4,466	3,418	3,382	NA
% Ret. on Assets	0.6	0.6	0.9	0.8	0.3	0.3	0.4	NM	NM	NA
% Ret. on Equity	18.7	20.4	40.8	12.8	3.6	2.1	8.0	NM	NM	NA
% Loan Loss Resv.	Nil	1.6	1.9	1.1	1.4	1.4	1.4	2.1	2.3	NA
% Risk Based Capital	13.1	12.9	11.7	11.5	11.2	11.9	11.2	9.6	9.6	NA
Price Times Book Value:										
Hi	2.9	4.4	8.2	2.5	2.0	1.2	0.9	0.9	NA	NA
Low	1.1	2.7	2.0	1.2	1.4	1.0	0.6	0.3	NA	NA

Data as orig. reptd.; bef. results of disc. opers. and/or spec. items. Prior to 1998, yrs. ended Jun. 30 of the fol. cal. yr. Per share data adj. for stk. divs. as of ex-div. date. Bold denotes diluted EPS (FASB 128). Data pr. to 1994 pro forma. E-Estimated. NA-Not Available. NM-Not Meaningful. NR-Not Ranked.

Office—135 Main Street, San Francisco, CA 94105. **Tel**—(415) 904-1100. **Website**—http://www.goldenstate.com **Chrmn & CEO**—G. J. Ford. **Pres & COO**—C. B. Webb. **Secy**—V. L. Washington. **Investor Contact**—Fred Cannon (415-904-1451). **Dirs**—P. M. Bass Jr., G. W. Bramblett Jr., B. P. Dempsey, G. J. Ford, H. Gittis, J. F. King, J. F. Kooken, G. K. McDonald, J. A. Moran, R. O. Perelman, B. M. Rankin Jr., T. S. Sayles, R. Setrakian, C. M. Tellez, C. B. Webb. **Transfer Agent & Registrar**—Mellon Investor Services, Ridgefield Park, NJ. **Incorporated**—in Delaware in 1997; bank was chartered in 1934 and converted to federal stock association in 1983. **Empl**— 8,446. **S&P Analyst:** Erik J. Eisenstein

STANDARD &POOR'S

STOCK REPORTS

Golden West Financial

NYSE Symbol **GDW**

In S&P 500

18-AUG-01

Industry: Savings & Loan Companies

Summary: Golden West is the holding company for World Savings & Loan, one of the largest U.S. savings and loan associations.

S&P Opinion: Accumulate (★★★★)

Recent Price • 64.49 | 52 Wk Range • 70.90-45.06 | Yield • 0.4% | 12-Mo. P/E • 17.3

Quantitative Evaluations

Outlook (1 Lowest—5 Highest)
• **2**

Fair Value
• **60.70**

Risk
• **Low**

Earn./Div. Rank
• **A-**

Technical Eval.
• **Bearish** since 8/01

Rel. Strength Rank (1 Lowest—99 Highest)
• **60**

Insider Activity
• **Unfavorable**

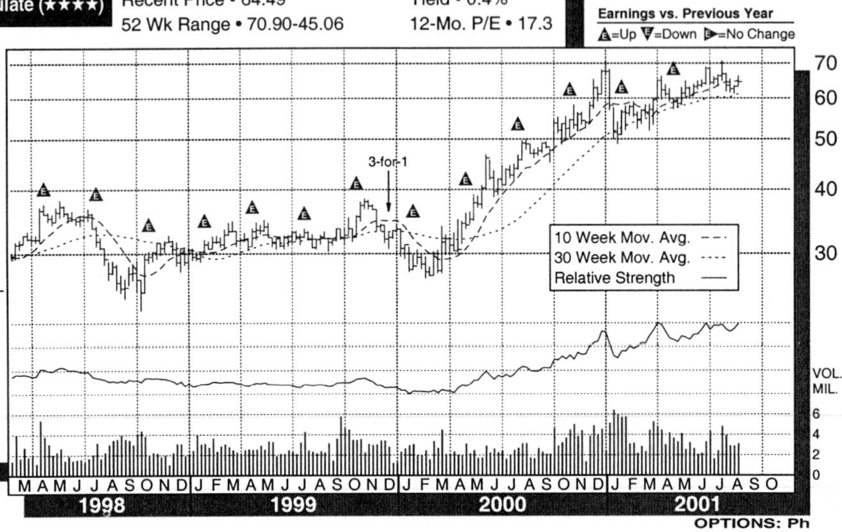

OPTIONS: Ph

Overview - 26-JUL-01

Lower mortgage rates tend to reduce the popularity of Golden West's specialty, the adjustable rate mortgage (ARM), and encourage homeowners with ARMs to prepay and refinance with fixed rate mortgages. Nonetheless, despite low mortgage rates in the first half of 2001, GDW registered respectable 5% annualized loan growth. With the refinance boom likely to slow towards year-end, we expect interest earning assets to advance about 16% in 2001. Aided by a widening of the net interest margin, reflecting continued strong deposit gathering, we expect net interest income to increase 31%. With a weaker California economy, we project a mild increase in provisioning, although credit quality is not a concern. Non-interest income should grow 19%, benefiting from fees garnered on a larger deposit base, greater gains on loan sales and higher prepayment fees. Cost containment remains a key focus for GDW; we see well contained expenses through 2001. Overall, we expect operating EPS to increase 38% in 2001. In 2002, we project operating EPS advancing 9%, after borrowing costs stabilize and the net interest margin snaps back to a more normal level.

Valuation - 26-JUL-01

The shares were recently down 3.5% in 2001, versus an 11% decline for the broader market. GDW is a very well managed thrift, with one of the lowest cost structures in the industry. This is an important advantage, in light of the commodity-like nature of the thrift business. On a P/E basis, the shares were recently trading at a well deserved premium to those of GDW's peers, reflecting the company's superior management and low cost structure. At a recent level of about 14X our 2001 EPS estimate of $4.71, and 2.6X book value, we recommend accumulating the shares.

Key Stock Statistics

S&P EPS Est. 2001	4.71	Tang. Bk. Value/Share	23.28
P/E on S&P Est. 2001	13.7	Beta	0.41
S&P EPS Est. 2002	5.12	Shareholders	1,358
Dividend Rate/Share	0.25	Market cap. (B)	$ 10.2
Shs. outstg. (M)	158.7	Inst. holdings	67%
Avg. daily vol. (M)	0.630		

Value of $10,000 invested 5 years ago: $ 34,420

Fiscal Year Ending Dec. 31

	2001	2000	1999	1998	1997	1996
Revenues (Million $)						
1Q	1,178	826.0	730.3	781.2	693.5	655.9
2Q	—	932.3	727.9	783.7	710.0	646.3
3Q	—	1,056	733.7	775.3	738.6	664.3
4Q	—	1,143	777.4	760.0	771.6	684.6
Yr.	—	3,957	2,969	3,100	2,914	2,656
Earnings Per Share ($)						
1Q	**1.10**	**0.78**	**0.70**	**0.63**	**0.48**	**0.48**
2Q	—	**0.84**	**0.72**	**0.67**	**0.50**	**0.50**
3Q	—	**0.86**	**0.71**	**0.62**	**0.52**	**0.52**
4Q	—	**0.93**	**0.73**	**0.65**	**0.54**	**0.54**
Yr.	—	**3.41**	**2.87**	**2.58**	**2.04**	**2.10**

Next earnings report expected: NA

Dividend Data (Dividends have been paid since 1977.)

Amount ($)	Date Decl.	Ex-Div. Date	Stock of Record	Payment Date
0.063	Nov. 01	Nov. 13	Nov. 15	Dec. 11 '00
0.063	Feb. 06	Feb. 13	Feb. 15	Mar. 12 '01
0.063	May. 01	May. 11	May. 15	Jun. 11 '01
0.063	Jul. 30	Aug. 13	Aug. 15	Sep. 10 '01

Golden West Financial Corporation

Business Summary - 26-JUL-01

Golden West Financial (GDW) is a savings and loan holding company that had 414 offices in 32 states at December 31, 2000. The company is essentially a plain-vanilla thrift that focuses on the traditional thrift activity of collecting deposits from the public, typically in the form of savings accounts, and investing these funds in one- to four-family mortgage loans and mortgage backed securities (MBSs). GDW ranks as one of the largest thrifts in the U.S., based on total assets of approximately $56 billion. Branch operations are concentrated in California. The company is run by the husband and wife team of Herbert and Marion Sandler, who own over 20% of the shares outstanding shares, and who are known as astute and somewhat tight-fisted business people.

Management's strategy is three-pronged: to keep costs as low as possible; to lend only to the most creditworthy homebuyers; and to capture the high-end saver's dollar. As an indication of the company's operating efficiency, overhead costs are less than 1% of its assets, much lower than the industry average. GDW's low cost structure was achieved through the following: a spare branch office design; reliance on part-time branch personnel, who for the most part do not receive benefits; a high degree of automation; and a light support staff at headquarters. Visitors to headquarters will find no receptionist. They must use a telephone to announce themselves.

The company typically generates a high volume of new loans through a combination of frequent media advertising, aggressive pricing, and high-level marketing to realtors' associations. GDW basically offers one loan product: a monthly adjustable-rate mortgage (ARM) indexed to thrift cost of funds in California, Arizona and Nevada (the Federal Home Loan Bank's 11th District). Although not perfect, this instrument helps smooth out earnings fluctuations across interest rate environments. New loans originated in 2000 totaled $19.8 billion, up 56% from the former record high of $12.7 billion in 1999. Despite the high volume, credit losses have historically been low. GDW keeps losses down by requiring downpayments slightly higher than average, and by using outside appraisers, who assess a property's marketability in addition to its value based on comparable sales.

In gathering deposits, GDW competes with other thrifts, banks, mutual funds, insurance companies and credit unions for the saver's dollar. GDW's average savings customer maintains far larger balances than typical, and also receives a higher interest rate. Management believes this focus on the well-to-do saver, when properly executed, leads to improved operating efficiencies, which partially compensate for the higher rate that the company pays out to attract the funds. In 2000, deposits grew 8.4%, to $30.0 billion, from $27.7 billion in 1999.

Per Share Data ($) (Year Ended Dec. 31)	2000	1999	1998	1997	1996	1995	1994	1993	1992	1991
Tangible Bk. Val.	23.28	19.80	18.30	15.73	13.63	12.07	10.60	10.06	8.15	6.63
Earnings	3.41	2.87	2.58	2.04	2.11	1.33	1.24	1.43	1.49	1.25
Dividends	0.22	0.19	0.17	0.15	0.13	0.12	0.10	0.09	0.08	0.06
Payout Ratio	6%	7%	7%	7%	6%	9%	8%	6%	5%	5%
Prices - High	70.50	38.41	38.16	32.64	22.91	19.16	15.33	16.79	15.41	14.75
- Low	26.87	28.91	23.27	19.62	16.33	11.58	11.41	12.37	11.83	7.41
P/E Ratio - High	21	13	15	16	11	14	12	12	10	12
- Low	8	10	9	10	8	9	9	9	8	6
Income Statement Analysis (Million $)										
Net Int. Inc.	1,151	1,006	967	890	831	723	721	733	717	632
Loan Loss Prov.	9.2	-2.1	11.3	57.6	84.3	61.0	63.0	65.8	43.2	30.2
Non Int. Inc.	150	121	99	73.1	74.9	43.0	37.5	62.0	41.1	26.9
Non Int. Exp.	425	386	355	327	453	319	303	273	252	242
Pretax Inc.	878	763	739	587	368	385	390	457	464	387
Eff. Tax Rate	38%	37%	40%	40%	NM	39%	41%	40%	39%	38%
Net Inc.	546	480	447	354	370	235	230	274	284	239
% Net Int. Marg.	2.31	2.48	2.46	2.32	2.39	2.13	2.43	2.61	2.83	2.66
Balance Sheet & Other Fin. Data (Million $)										
Total Assets	55,704	42,142	38,469	39,590	37,731	35,118	31,684	28,829	25,890	24,298
Loans	33,763	27,920	25,721	33,261	34,179	34,380	28,265	25,435	23,760	22,088
Deposits	30,048	27,715	26,219	24,110	22,100	20,848	19,219	17,422	16,486	16,819
Capitalization:										
Debt	15,898	7,213	7,713	9,737	10,712	9,367	8,874	8,178	6,515	4,973
Equity	3,687	3,195	3,124	2,698	2,350	2,278	2,000	2,066	1,727	1,449
Total	19,585	10,408	10,838	12,435	13,062	11,645	10,874	10,244	8,242	6,422
% Ret. on Assets	1.1	1.2	1.1	0.9	1.1	0.7	0.8	1.0	1.1	1.0
% Ret. on Equity	15.9	15.2	15.4	14.0	16.0	11.0	11.1	14.4	17.9	17.9
% Loan Loss Resv.	0.7	0.8	0.9	0.7	0.1	0.1	0.4	0.4	0.3	0.2
% Risk Based Capital	12.4	11.9	12.9	12.8	10.0	13.4	13.5	17.4	16.3	15.0
Price Times Book Value:										
Hi	NA	1.9	2.1	2.1	1.7	1.6	1.4	1.7	1.9	2.2
Low	NA	1.5	1.3	1.2	1.2	1.0	1.1	1.2	1.5	1.1

Data as orig reptd.; bef. results of disc opers/spec. items. Per share data adj. for stk. divs. Bold denotes diluted EPS (FASB 128)-prior periods restated. E-Estimated. NA-Not Available. NM-Not Meaningful. NR-Not Ranked.

Office—1901 Harrison St., Oakland, CA 94612. **Tel**—(510) 446-3420. **Co-Chrmn & Co-CEO**—H. M. Sandler. **Co-Chrmn & Co-CEO**—M. O. Sandler. **Pres, Treas & CFO**—R. W. Kettell. **EVP & Secy**—M. Roster. **Group SVP & Investor Contact**—William C. Nunan (510-446-3614). **Dirs**—L. J. Galen, A. Hernandez, M. Cattani Herringer, P. A. King, B. A. Osher, K. T. Rosen, H. M. Sandler, M. O. Sandler. L. Tang Schilling. **Transfer Agent & Registrar**—Mellon Investor Services, LLC, SF. **Incorporated**—in Delaware in 1959. **Empl**— 6,103. **S&P Analyst:** Erik J. Eisenstein

STANDARD
&POOR'S
STOCK REPORTS

Goldman Sachs Group

NYSE Symbol **GS**

18-AUG-01

Industry: Investment Banking/ Brokerage

Summary: Goldman Sachs is one of the world's leading investment banking and securities companies.

S&P Opinion: Accumulate (★★★★)

Recent Price • 77.25
52 Wk Range • 133.62-77

Yield • 0.6%
12-Mo. P/E • 14.8

Quantitative Evaluations

Outlook
(1 Lowest—5 Highest)
• 1⁻

Fair Value
• **69.40**

Risk
• **NA**

Earn./Div. Rank
• **NR**

Technical Eval.
• **Bearish** since 8/01

Rel. Strength Rank
(1 Lowest—99 Highest)
• **27**

Insider Activity
• **Unfavorable**

Earnings vs. Previous Year
A=Up V=Down >=No Change

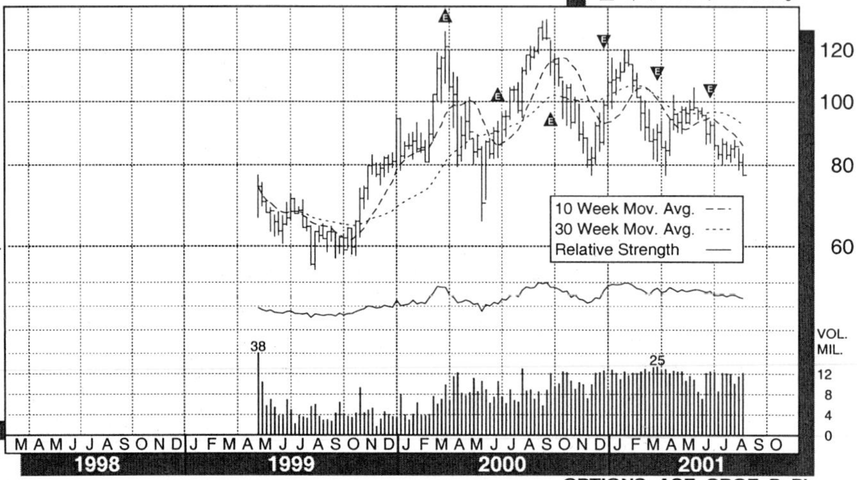

OPTIONS: ASE, CBOE, P, Ph

Overview - 21-JUN-01

Revenues and earnings for investment banking and brokerage companies are notoriously difficult to predict, as they depend on the health and level of the equity and debt markets, among other factors. Although net revenues are expected to increase in FY 01 (Nov.), we look for EPS to fall, reflecting more shares outstanding. Recent results have been mixed, as a weak equity IPO market, reduced merger and acquisition activity, and declining securities prices have hurt results in recent periods. Nevertheless, debt underwriting, fixed income trading, and asset management results have been strong. Secular trends also remain very favorable. As a world leader in the underwriting and M&A advisory business, GS stands to profit handsomely from the global trend of industry consolidation. The company is also a leader in securities trading and market making, so that growth of the global capital markets will also bolster profits.

Valuation - 21-JUN-01

The shares are expected to outperform the S&P 500 over the next six to 12 months. Goldman is one of the blue chip names in the investment banking industry, with leading positions in the global underwriting and M&A advisory businesses. We believe the company's focus on the faster growing, higher margin segments of both the investment banking and asset management businesses will enable GS to post EPS gains of 12% to 15% a year, and return on equity of at least 20%, over the course of the business cycle. For FY 01, we look for GS to post EPS of $5.75. On a P/E basis, the shares were recently trading at a discount to the level of the S&P 500. This discount, coupled with prospects for improved business conditions later this year, suggests that the shares have room for further appreciation.

Key Stock Statistics

S&P EPS Est. 2001	5.75	Tang. Bk. Value/Share	37.54
P/E on S&P Est. 2001	13.4	Beta	NA
S&P EPS Est. 2002	6.45	Shareholders	1,917
Dividend Rate/Share	0.48	Market cap. (B)	$ 37.5
Shs. outstg. (M)	485.6	Inst. holdings	29%
Avg. daily vol. (M)	2.356		

Value of $10,000 invested 5 years ago: NA

Fiscal Year Ending Nov. 30

	2001	2000	1999	1998	1997	1996
Revenues (Million $)						
1Q	9,502	7,964	5,856	—	—	—
2Q	8,158	8,196	6,355	—	—	—
3Q	—	8,851	6,440	—	—	—
4Q	—	7,989	6,712	—	—	—
Yr.	—	33,000	25,363	22,478	—	—
Earnings Per Share ($)						
1Q	**1.40**	**1.76**	**0.06**	—	—	—
2Q	**1.06**	**1.48**	**0.69**	—	—	—
3Q	**E1.63**	**1.62**	**1.31**	—	—	—
4Q	**E1.66**	**1.16**	**1.54**	—	—	—
Yr.	**E5.75**	**6.00**	**5.27**	**2.62**	—	—

Next earnings report expected: mid September

Dividend Data (Dividends have been paid since 1999.)

Amount ($)	Date Decl.	Ex-Div. Date	Stock of Record	Payment Date
0.120	Sep. 19	Oct. 19	Oct. 23	Nov. 20 '00
0.120	Dec. 19	Jan. 18	Jan. 22	Feb. 22 '01
0.120	Mar. 20	Apr. 20	Apr. 24	May. 24 '01
0.120	Jun. 19	Jul. 27	Jul. 31	Aug. 30 '01

The Goldman Sachs Group, Inc.

Business Summary - 21-JUN-01

Goldman Sachs is one of the world's leading investment banking and securities companies. Its business lines include investment banking, trading and principal investments, and asset management and securities services. GS's goal is to be the adviser of choice for its clients, and to be a leading participant in global financial markets. Clients include corporations, financial institutions, governments, and high net worth individuals. The company went public in May 1999, in what was one of the most anticipated initial public offerings (IPOs) of all time. Employees, including former partners, own about 55% of the stock.

As an investment bank, GS helps clients raise capital by issuing various debt and equity securities. The company is one of the global leaders in the underwriting business. In 2000, GS ranked first in equity offerings worldwide, and second in U.S. high-yield debt offerings. In the financial advisory business, the company advises clients on corporate takeovers, defenses, mergers and acquisitions, and the like. GS is also a global leader in the financial advisory business, with the leading market share in worldwide mergers and acquisitions advisory services from 1994 through 2000. Investment banking revenues accounted for 32% and 33% of net revenues in FY 00 (Nov.) and FY 99, respectively.

Trading and principal investments accounted for 40% of net revenues in FY 00 and 43% of net revenues in FY 99. Goldman makes markets in equity and fixed income products, currencies and commodities. The company also enters into derivative transactions like swaps, and engages in proprietary trading and arbitrage. In its principal investments business, Goldman invests in private equity deals as well as real estate. Merchant banking activities account for most of the net revenues in principal investments.

Goldman's asset management and securities services business accounted for 28% and 24% of net revenues in FY 00 and FY 99, respectively. This segment consists of three different businesses. The asset management business generates fees by providing investment strategies and advice to Goldman's institutional and individual clients. Securities services provides prime brokerage, financial services and securities lending to hedge funds, pension funds and high net worth individuals. Commissions include fees earned on agency transactions for Goldman's institutional and high net worth clients.

Assets under management, which include mutual funds, separate accounts managed for institutional and individual investors, merchant banking funds, and other alternative investment funds, grew from $94 billion in FY 96 to $294 billion in FY 00. Other client assets, which include assets in brokerage accounts of high net worth individuals, grew from $77 billion in FY 96 to $198 billion in FY 00.

Per Share Data ($) (Year Ended Nov. 30)	2000	1999	1998	1997	1996	1995	1994	1993	1992	1991
Tangible Bk. Val.	34.15	22.65	NA	NA	NA	NA	NA	NA	NA	NA
Cash Flow	6.94	6.27	NA	NA	NA	NA	NA	NA	NA	NA
Earnings	6.00	5.27	2.62	NA	NA	NA	NA	NA	NA	NA
Dividends	0.48	0.24	NA	NA	NA	NA	NA	NA	NA	NA
Payout Ratio	8%	4%	NA	NA	NA	NA	NA	NA	NA	NA
Prices - High	133.62	94.81	NA	NA	NA	NA	NA	NA	NA	NA
- Low	65.50	53.00	NA	NA	NA	NA	NA	NA	NA	NA
P/E Ratio - High	22	17	NA	NA	NA	NA	NA	NA	NA	NA
- Low	11	10	NA	NA	NA	NA	NA	NA	NA	NA
Income Statement Analysis (Million $)										
Commissions	Nil	Nil	NA	NA	NA	NA	NA	NA	NA	NA
Int. Inc.	17,396	12,722	NA	NA	NA	NA	NA	NA	NA	NA
Total Revs.	33,000	25,363	22,478	NA	NA	NA	NA	NA	NA	NA
Int. Exp.	16,410	12,018	13,986	NA	NA	NA	NA	NA	NA	NA
Pretax Inc.	5,020	1,992	2,129	NA	NA	NA	NA	NA	NA	NA
Eff. Tax Rate	39%	NM	41%	NA	NA	NA	NA	NA	NA	NA
Net Inc.	3,067	2,708	1,256	NA	NA	NA	NA	NA	NA	NA
Balance Sheet & Other Fin. Data (Million $)										
Total Assets	289,760	250,491	231,796	NA	NA	NA	NA	NA	NA	NA
Cash Items	21,002	12,190	2,702	NA	NA	NA	NA	NA	NA	NA
Receivables	39,286	150,154	NA	NA	NA	NA	NA	NA	NA	NA
Secs. Owned	95,260	81,809	NA	NA	NA	NA	NA	NA	NA	NA
Sec. Borrowed	9,215	49,352	NA	NA	NA	NA	NA	NA	NA	NA
Due Brokers & Cust.	3,871	59,534	NA	NA	NA	NA	NA	NA	NA	NA
Other Liabs.	11,116	110,508	NA	NA	NA	NA	NA	NA	NA	NA
Capitalization:										
Debt	31,395	20,952	20,776	NA	NA	NA	NA	NA	NA	NA
Equity	16,530	10,145	7,627	NA	NA	NA	NA	NA	NA	NA
Total	47,925	31,097	28,403	NA	NA	NA	NA	NA	NA	NA
% Return On Revs.	9.3	10.7	5.6	NA	NA	NA	NA	NA	NA	NA
% Ret. on Assets	1.1	1.2	NA	NA	NA	NA	NA	NA	NA	NA
% Ret. on Equity	23.0	30.4	NA	NA	NA	NA	NA	NA	NA	NA

Data as orig reptd.; bef. results of disc opers/spec. items. Pro forma data in 1998. Per share data adj. for stk. divs. Bold denotes diluted EPS (FASB 128)-prior periods restated. E-Estimated. NA-Not Available. NM-Not Meaningful. NR-Not Ranked.

Office—85 Broad Street, New York, NY 10004. **Tel**—(212) 902-1000. **Website**—http://www.gs.com **Chrmn & CEO**—H. M. Paulson Jr. **Vice Chrmn**—R. J. Hurst. **Pres & Co-COO**—J. A. Thain. **General Counsel**—G. K. Palm. **CIO**—L. M. Tortora. **CFO**—D. A. Viniar. **Dirs**—Sir J. Browne, J. H. Bryan, R. J. Hurst, J. A. Johnson, H. M. Paulson Jr., Dr. R. J. Simmons, J. A. Thain, J. L. Thornton, J. L. Weinberg. **Transfer Agent & Registrar**—Mellon Investor Services LLC, Ridgefield Park, NJ. **Incorporated**—in Delaware in 1999. **Empl**— 22,627. **S&P Analyst:** Michael Schneider-CFA

STANDARD &POOR'S

STOCK REPORTS

GreenPoint Financial

NYSE Symbol **GPT**

In S&P MidCap 400

18-AUG-01

Industry: Savings & Loan Companies

Summary: This company owns GreenPoint Bank, a New York State-chartered thrift, as well as a number of specialty mortgage banking subsidiaries.

S&P Opinion: Accumulate (★★★★)

Recent Price • 43.40 | Yield • 2.3%

52 Wk Range • 44.19-24.50 | 12-Mo. P/E • 16.9

Quantitative Evaluations

Outlook (1 Lowest—5 Highest)
• 3+

Fair Value
• 45.20

Risk
• Average

Earn./Div. Rank
• NR

Technical Eval.
• Bullish since 7/01

Rel. Strength Rank (1 Lowest—99 Highest)
• 87

Insider Activity
• NA

Earnings vs. Previous Year

E=Up E=Down E=No Change

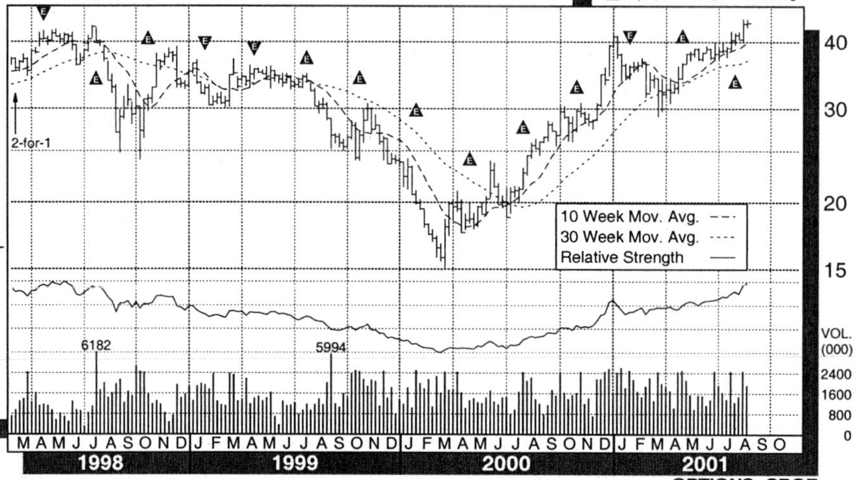

OPTIONS: CBOE

Overview - 17-AUG-01

Net interest income should advance 10% in 2001, due to increased mortgage and consumer loan originations, partly offset by the impact of lagging growth in core deposits. After high set asides for manufactured housing loans in 2000, loss provisioning should decline. In the fourth quarter of 2000, GPT recorded a pretax charge of $94 million, related to the valuation of its retained interests in manufactured housing securitizations. Comparisons will benefit from the absence of this charge, and from increased gains on loan sales in a more favorable interest rate environment; noninterest income should advance over 60%. Efficiency should improve in the coming year, reflecting the scaling down of the operations of Greenpoint Credit. We expect operating EPS to surge 59% in 2001, to $3.76. In 2002, we see an 18% gain in operating EPS, to $4.45, as more difficult comparisons are partly offset by an FASB accounting change with regard to goodwill amortization.

Valuation - 17-AUG-01

As a result of excess inventory in the manufactured housing market, Greenpoint Credit was a drag on earnings in 2000. GPT reacted by tightening underwriting standards, revaluing the retained interests in its manufacture housing securitizations, and generally reducing the scope of the troubled subsidiary's operations. Although these already devalued assets remain at risk, we continue to believe GPT's remedial efforts will take hold, and that the worst is over for Greenpoint Credit. The shares recently traded at about 12X our 2001 operating EPS estimate, and at 1.8X book value, both well below peer levels. With a presence in the desirable New York retail banking market and several relatively high margin businesses, GPT remains attractive both to investors and to potential acquirers.

Key Stock Statistics

S&P EPS Est. 2001	3.76	Tang. Bk. Value/Share	13.18
P/E on S&P Est. 2001	11.5	Beta	1.02
S&P EPS Est. 2002	4.45	Shareholders	3,935
Dividend Rate/Share	1.00	Market cap. (B)	$ 4.4
Shs. outstg. (M)	101.0	Inst. holdings	58%
Avg. daily vol. (M)	0.385		

Value of $10,000 invested 5 years ago: $ 27,393

Fiscal Year Ending Dec. 31

	2001	2000	1999	1998	1997	1996
Revenues (Million $)						
1Q	435.0	375.6	266.4	257.9	257.6	262.6
2Q	—	395.4	359.7	257.6	252.8	269.9
3Q	—	408.8	371.7	262.2	260.3	250.2
4Q	—	330.9	390.6	284.3	258.2	248.2
Yr.	—	1,511	1,483	1,062	1,029	1,031
Earnings Per Share ($)						
1Q	**0.86**	**0.63**	**0.36**	**0.45**	0.47	0.30
2Q	—	**0.71**	**0.61**	**0.54**	0.43	0.41
3Q	—	**0.74**	**0.63**	**0.54**	0.47	0.39
4Q	—	**0.24**	**0.62**	**0.40**	**0.49**	0.40
Yr.	—	**2.34**	**2.23**	**1.92**	**1.86**	1.51

Next earnings report expected: NA

Dividend Data (Dividends have been paid since 1994.)

Amount ($)	Date Decl.	Ex-Div. Date	Stock of Record	Payment Date
0.250	Nov. 14	Nov. 21	Nov. 24	Dec. 06 '00
0.250	Feb. 13	Feb. 21	Feb. 23	Mar. 09 '01
0.250	May. 08	May. 16	May. 18	Jun. 05 '01
0.250	Jul. 10	Jul. 18	Jul. 20	Sep. 05 '01

A Division of The McGraw-Hill Companies

GreenPoint Financial Corp.

Business Summary - 17-AUG-01

GreenPoint Financial owns GreenPoint Bank, a New York State-chartered savings bank founded in 1869. At the end of 2000, GreenPoint Bank had $11.2 billion in deposits; 74 branches were serving more than 400,000 households in the Greater New York City area. GPT also owns GreenPoint Mortgage Corp., a national mortgage banking company, and GreenPoint Credit Corp., the second largest U.S. manufactured housing lender.

GPT's primary source of income is interest earned on its loan portfolio and investment securities. At year-end 2000, residential one- to four-family home loans accounted for 81% of the loan portfolio (80% at year-end 1999), residential multifamily loans 4% (5%), commercial property loans 7% (7%), manufactured housing loans 6% (6%), home equity loans 1% (1%), and other loans 1% (1%).

GPT funds its loan portfolio primarily with deposits, but also with loan sales and securitizations. Deposits of $11.2 billion at year-end 2000 were divided as follows: savings and club accounts 11%, checking and NOW accounts 5%, variable rate savings 17%, money market 6%, and CDs 62%.

GreenPoint Mortgage Corp. specializes in No Doc loans. These loans receive fairly expedient processing because they require less income and asset information than loans underwritten in compliance with Fannie Mae standards. In return, No Doc borrowers pay a premium, in the form of higher interest rates and loan fees, and provide larger down payments. No Doc loans carry higher yields than traditional conforming loans, so that GPT typically posts above average net interest margins. However, such loans also experience higher levels of delinquencies; as a result, the company's level of nonperforming assets is also above average.

Although GPT's nonperforming asset ratios are higher than average, they decreased steadily over the past five years. At the end of 2000, nonperforming assets were equal to 1.33% of total assets, down from 1.47% at the end of 1999, 1.98% at the end of 1998 and 2.74% at year-end 1997.

In 1998, GPT significantly expanded its lending capabilities by acquiring BankAmerica Housing Services (now called GreenPoint Credit). The company originates both fixed and variable rate manufactured homes loans. It then pools and securitizes these loans. The company retains the servicing on the loans, collecting payments from the borrower and remitting principal and interest rate payments to the holder of the securities.

On March 30, 1999, GPT acquired Headlands Mortgage (renamed and merged into GreenPoint Mortgage), a leading mortgage banking company that specializes in "Alt A" lending. Alt A borrowers do not conform to government agency guidelines.

In February 2001, directors authorized the repurchase program of up 5 million common shares (about 5% of the shares outstanding).

Per Share Data ($) (Year Ended Dec. 31)	2000	1999	1998	1997	1996	1995	1994	1993	1992	1991
Tangible Bk. Val.	13.18	10.03	8.26	8.34	8.85	8.44	13.86	13.01	NA	NA
Earnings	2.34	2.23	1.92	1.86	1.51	1.15	1.10	0.83	NA	NA
Dividends	1.00	0.88	0.64	0.50	0.40	0.40	0.30	Nil	NA	NA
Payout Ratio	43%	39%	33%	27%	26%	35%	27%	Nil	NA	NA
Prices - High	41.31	37.12	42.87	36.75	25.12	14.87	12.62	NA	NA	NA
- Low	15.00	23.31	24.00	22.75	11.75	10.18	8.75	NA	NA	NA
P/E Ratio - High	18	17	22	20	17	13	11	NA	NA	NA
- Low	6	10	12	12	8	9	7	NA	NA	NA
Income Statement Analysis (Million $)										
Net Int. Inc.	573	540	484	475	447	351	338	303	NA	NA
Loan Loss Prov.	-36.9	-14.2	13.8	18.9	15.7	9.5	32.3	43.6	NA	NA
Non Int. Inc.	322	394	72.5	54.5	56.9	35.8	27.1	13.0	NA	NA
Non Int. Exp.	509	550	303	271	217	160	121	100	NA	NA
Pretax Inc.	354	371	242	242	244	198	211	173	NA	NA
Eff. Tax Rate	40%	42%	38%	39%	41%	46%	47%	48%	NA	NA
Net Inc.	213	216	150	148	133	108	113	89.8	NA	NA
% Net Int. Marg.	4.17	4.02	3.99	3.93	3.51	4.05	4.92	5.07	NA	NA
Balance Sheet & Other Fin. Data (Million $)										
Total Assets	15,765	15,401	13,970	13,084	13,326	14,671	6,955	6,445	NA	NA
Loans	8,574	9,180	9,273	8,796	7,294	5,859	5,623	5,201	NA	NA
Deposits	11,176	11,560	11,173	10,973	11,452	12,898	5,224	5,543	NA	NA
Capitalization:										
Debt	1,487	1,080	400	200	Nil	Nil	Nil	Nil	NA	NA
Equity	2,050	2,092	1,796	1,270	1,459	1,551	1,521	1,395	NA	NA
Total	3,537	3,172	2,196	1,669	1,459	1,551	1,521	1,395	NA	NA
% Ret. on Assets	1.4	1.4	1.1	1.1	0.9	1.2	1.6	1.4	NA	NA
% Ret. on Equity	10.6	10.4	9.8	10.8	8.8	7.0	7.9	6.4	NA	NA
% Loan Loss Resv.	1.1	1.1	1.2	1.2	1.2	1.8	1.8	2.5	NA	NA
% Risk Based Capital	10.9	11.8	12.2	15.3	16.4	8.0	30.3	17.0	NA	NA
Price Times Book Value:										
Hi	3.1	3.7	5.2	4.4	2.8	1.8	0.9	NA	NA	NA
Low	1.1	2.3	2.9	2.7	1.3	1.2	0.6	NA	NA	NA

Data as orig reptd.; bef. results of disc opers/spec. items. Per share data adj. for stk. divs. Bold denotes diluted EPS (FASB 128)-prior periods restated. E-Estimated. NA-Not Available. NM-Not Meaningful. NR-Not Ranked.

Office—90 Park Ave., New York, NY 10016. **Tel**—(212) 834-1000. **Website**—http://www.greenpoint.com **Chrmn & CEO**—T. S. Johnson. **Pres & COO**—B. B. Bhatt. **EVP & CFO**—J. R. Leeds. **EVP & Gen Counsel**—H. Bluver. **Investor Contact**—Richard Humphrey (212-834-1201). **Dirs**—B. B. Bhatt, D. F. Huebner, W. M. Jackson, T. S. Johnson, R. M. McLane, C. B. McQuade, P. T. Paul, A. N. Puryear, R. P. Quinn, E. C. Schmults, R. F. Vizza. **Transfer Agent**—Mellon Investor Services, LLC, South Hackensack, NJ. **Incorporated**—in Delaware in 1993; bank organized in New York in 1868. **Empl**— 3,909. **S&P Analyst:** Erik J. Eisenstein

STANDARD
&POOR'S
STOCK REPORTS

Hartford Financial Services Group

NYSE Symbol **HIG**

In S&P 500

18-AUG-01

Industry:
Insurance (Multi-Line)

Summary: HIG is one of the largest U.S. multi-line insurance holding companies, and the leading writer of individual variable annuities in the U.S.

S&P Opinion: Accumulate (★★★★)

Recent Price • 64.50
52 Wk Range • 80-53.50
Yield • 1.6%
12-Mo. P/E • 15.2

Quantitative Evaluations

Outlook
(1 Lowest—5 Highest)
• **2−**

Fair Value
• **63.40**

Risk
• **Low**

Earn./Div. Rank
• **NR**

Technical Eval.
• **Neutral** since 7/01

Rel. Strength Rank
(1 Lowest—99 Highest)
• **49**

Insider Activity
• **Unfavorable**

Earnings vs. Previous Year
▲=Up ▼=Down ▶=No Change

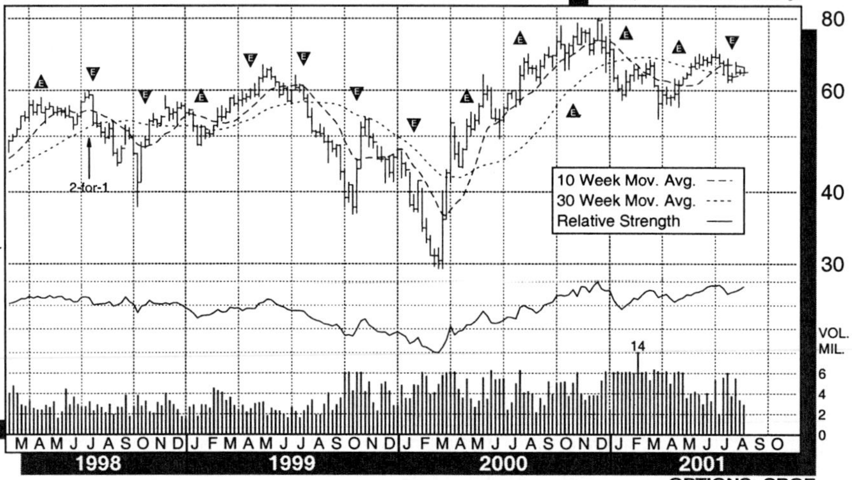

OPTIONS: CBOE

Overview - 03-AUG-01

Operating earnings growth in 2001 and beyond will be driven by gains at Hartford Life (HLI), reflecting strong sales of annuities and investment products. Although robust growth seen here could be hard to sustain for the long term, HIG will retain its position as the leading writer of variable annuities. Profit growth will also be aided by the company's increased ownership of HLI. In June 2000, HLI became a wholly owned subsidiary of HIG, after HIG acquired the 18.5% of HLI shares that it did not already own, for $50.50 each (about $1.3 billion). The $1.1 billion acquisition of Fortis, Inc.'s individual life, annuity and mutual fund units will likely be accretive to earnings in 2002. Property-casualty written premiums will likely rise 8% to 10% in 2001, versus industrywide premium growth of about 5% to 7%. Expanded distribution efforts and modestly-improved pricing will drive results here. Anticipated year to year gains in property-casualty earnings in 2001 are also predicated on continued favorable claim trends.

Valuation - 03-AUG-01

After bottoming in early 2000, the shares have staged a very strong comeback, as investors have focused on HIG's attractive franchises in the variable annuity and property casualty segments of the insurance marketplace. Despite their recent strength, the shares remain undervalued relative to their peer group. Prospects for earnings growth are being aided by HIG's success at identifying opportunities for growth and then successfully capitalizing on them. The company has also increased its credibility in the investment community by establishing, and then meeting, a number of ambitious goals, such as double digit increases in core earnings, and ROE of 15%. In addition, upside from HIG's potential as a takeover target is not fully reflected in the stock's current valuation.

Key Stock Statistics

S&P EPS Est. 2001	4.55	Tang. Bk. Value/Share	32.88
P/E on S&P Est. 2001	14.2	Beta	1.19
S&P EPS Est. 2002	5.15	Shareholders	160,000
Dividend Rate/Share	1.00	Market cap. (B)	$ 15.3
Shs. outstg. (M)	236.9	Inst. holdings	74%
Avg. daily vol. (M)	0.768		

Value of $10,000 invested 5 years ago: $ 26,333

Fiscal Year Ending Dec. 31

	2001	2000	1999	1998	1997	1996
Revenues (Million $)						
1Q	3,722	3,499	3,299	3,728	3,118	3,278
2Q	3,847	3,514	3,349	3,493	3,142	3,026
3Q	—	3,791	3,444	3,640	3,306	2,836
4Q	—	3,899	3,436	4,161	3,739	3,333
Yr.	—	14,703	13,528	15,022	13,305	12,473
Earnings Per Share ($)						
1Q	**1.12**	**1.10**	**1.04**	**1.10**	**0.85**	**0.41**
2Q	**0.94**	**0.97**	**0.93**	**0.99**	**2.40**	**0.60**
3Q	—	**1.09**	**0.82**	**0.91**	**1.25**	**-2.31**
4Q	—	**1.12**	**1.00**	**1.30**	**1.07**	**0.86**
Yr.	—	**4.36**	**3.79**	**4.30**	**5.58**	**-0.42**

Next earnings report expected: NA

Dividend Data (Dividends have been paid since 1996.)

Amount ($)	Date Decl.	Ex-Div. Date	Stock of Record	Payment Date
0.250	Oct. 19	Nov. 29	Dec. 01	Jan. 02 '01
0.250	Feb. 22	Mar. 01	Mar. 05	Apr. 02 '01
0.250	May. 17	May. 30	Jun. 01	Jul. 02 '01
0.250	Jul. 19	Aug. 30	Sep. 04	Oct. 01 '01

The Hartford Financial Services Group

Business Summary - 03-AUG-01

Hartford Financial Services Group was a subsidiary of ITT Corp. until its December 1995 spinoff. From its founding in 1810 as a local fire insurance company, HIG has grown to become one of the 10 largest insurers in both the property-casualty and life insurance industries. In 2000, revenues totaled $14.7 billion, with worldwide life insurance operations accounting for 41% and worldwide property and casualty insurance for 59%. Life insurance accounted for 60% of operating profits of $1.1 billion in 2000 (before corporate and other allocations) and property-casualty accounted for 40%.

Worldwide property-casualty operations provide a wide range of commercial, personal, specialty and reinsurance coverages. This unit is the ninth largest property-casualty insurance organization in the U.S., and is the endorsed provider of automobile and homeowners coverages to members of the American Association of Retired Persons. Written premiums exceeded $7.2 billion in 2000, of which commercial lines accounted for 48%, personal lines 36%, reinsurance 11%, and international and other lines for 5%. HIG's combined ratio improved a bit in 2000 to 102.4%, from 103.3% in 1999. HIG also offers an array of insurance products primarily in Europe, but has been selling off these divisions.

HIG's life insurance operations are conducted primarily by Hartford Life, Inc. (wholly owned as of June 27, 2000), the third largest life insurer in the U.S. This unit sells variable annuities, mutual funds, and individual and corporate-owned life insurance (COLI), and an array of employee benefits products. This unit has established a very effective distribution strategy that utilizes a myriad of distribution channels, including broker-dealers, other financial institutions (like banks), and insurance agents and brokers. Growth here has been fueled to a large degree by robust sales of variable annuities. Indeed, Hartford Life was the leading writer of individual variable annuities during 2000. Core after-tax operating profits totaled $632 million in 2000 (up 35% from $467 million in 1999), of which investment products (annuities and mutual funds) accounted for 67%, individual life insurance for 13%, and employee benefits, corporate-owned life insurance and other for 20%. HIG also plans to expand this business through acquisitions, including the April 2001 purchase of Fortis, Inc.'s life, annuity and mutual fund division for $1.1 billion. To help fund this transaction, HIG sold publicly 10 million shares at $64 each, for net proceeds of $615 million.

Per Share Data ($) (Year Ended Dec. 31)	2000	1999	1998	1997	1996	1995	1994	1993	1992	1991
Tangible Bk. Val.	32.88	25.07	28.17	25.79	19.23	20.07	13.38	16.86	NA	NA
Oper. Earnings	NA	3.68	3.45	4.70	-1.35	3.17	2.90	2.68	NA	NA
Earnings	4.36	3.79	4.30	5.58	-0.42	2.38	2.65	2.25	-1.15	1.81
Dividends	0.97	0.90	0.85	0.80	0.80	Nil	NA	NA	NA	NA
Relative Payout	22%	24%	20%	14%	NM	Nil	NA	NA	NA	NA
Prices - High	80.00	66.43	60.00	47.25	34.93	25.06	NA	NA	NA	NA
- Low	29.37	36.50	37.62	32.43	22.25	23.68	NA	NA	NA	NA
P/E Ratio - High	18	18	14	8	NM	11	NA	NA	NA	NA
- Low	7	10	9	6	NM	10	NA	NA	NA	NA
Income Statement Analysis (Million $)										
Life Ins. In Force	585,582	527,285	528,608	407,860	312,176	339,291	246,138	182,784	126,447	NA
Prem. Inc.: Life A & H	8,941	4,069	4,371	3,323	3,185	2,738	2,173	1,812	1,340	NA
Prem. Inc.: Cas./Prop.	NA	6,488	7,245	7,000	6,891	6,890	6,580	6,338	6,094	NA
Net Invest. Inc.	2,674	2,627	3,102	2,655	2,523	2,420	2,259	2,033	1,985	NA
Total Revs.	14,703	13,528	15,022	13,305	12,473	12,150	11,102	10,338	9,862	9,242
Pretax Inc.	1,418	1,235	1,475	1,703	-318	742	852	687	-501	NA
Net Oper. Inc.	962	837	816	1,117	-318	742	691	638	NA	NA
Net Inc.	974	862	1,015	1,332	-99	559	632	537	-274	431
Balance Sheet & Other Fin. Data (Million $)										
Cash & Equiv.	227	182	123	140	112	95.0	55.0	61.0	NA	NA
Premiums Due	6,874	2,071	1,833	1,873	1,797	1,890	2,000	1,788	NA	NA
Invest. Assets: Bonds	34,492	32,875	35,331	35,053	31,449	31,168	27,418	26,870	NA	NA
Invest. Assets: Stocks	1,056	1,286	1,066	1,922	1,865	1,342	1,350	1,302	NA	NA
Invest. Assets: Loans	3,610	4,222	6,687	3,759	3,839	3,380	2,614	1,402	NA	NA
Invest. Assets: Total	40,669	39,141	43,696	37,363	33,800	36,675	32,453	30,582	NA	NA
Deferred Policy Costs	5,305	5,038	4,579	4,181	3,535	2,945	2,525	2,024	NA	NA
Total Assets	171,532	167,051	150,632	131,743	108,840	93,855	76,765	66,179	54,180	37,771
Debt	3,105	2,798	2,798	1,773	1,532	1,022	596	579	576	594
Common Eqty.	7,464	5,466	6,423	6,085	4,520	4,702	3,184	4,012	3,679	3,816
Comb. Loss-Exp. Ratio	102.4	103.3	102.9	102.3	105.2	104.5	102.8	105.9	114.8	111.3
% Return On Revs.	6.6	6.4	6.8	10.0	NM	4.6	5.7	5.2	NM	4.7
% Ret. on Equity	15.1	14.5	16.2	25.1	NM	14.2	15.4	14.2	NM	NA
% Invest. Yield	6.7	6.3	7.7	6.7	6.8	7.0	7.0	7.0	7.6	NA

Data as orig reptd.; bef. results of disc opers/spec. items. Per share data adj. for stk. divs. Bold denotes diluted EPS (FASB 128)-prior periods restated. E-Estimated. NA-Not Available. NM-Not Meaningful. NR-Not Ranked.

Office—690 Asylum Ave., Hartford, CT 06115. **Tel**—(860) 547-5000. **Website**—http://www.thehartford.com **Chrmn, CEO & Pres**—R. Ayer. **Vice Chrmn**—L. A. Smith. **EVP & CFO**—D. K. Zwiener. **EVP & Chief Investment Officer**—B. J. Furlong. **VP & Secy**—K. V. Trumbull. **Investor Contact**—Stuart Carlisle (860-547-8418). **Dirs**— R. V. Araskog, R. Ayer, D. Dublon, D. R. Frahm, P. G. Kirk, R. W. Selander, L. A. Smith, H. P. Swygert, G. I. Ulmer, D. K. Zwiener. **Transfer Agent**—Bank of New York, NYC. **Incorporated**—in Delaware in 1995. **Empl**— 266,000. **S&P Analyst:** Catherine A. Seifert

STANDARD
&POOR'S
STOCK REPORTS

Hibernia Corp.

NYSE Symbol **HIB**

In S&P MidCap 400

18-AUG-01

Industry: Banks (Regional)

Summary: This bank holding company operates over 260 branches throughout Louisiana and East Texas and also in Mississippi.

S&P Opinion: Accumulate (★★★★)

Recent Price • 19
52 Wk Range • 19.11-10.75

Yield • 2.7%
12-Mo. P/E • 17.6

Earnings vs. Previous Year
E=Up E=Down E=No Change

Quantitative Evaluations

Outlook
(1 Lowest—5 Highest)
• **1+**

Fair Value
• **17.20**

Risk
• **Low**

Earn./Div. Rank
• **B**

Technical Eval.
• **Bullish** since 4/01

Rel. Strength Rank
(1 Lowest—99 Highest)
• **85**

Insider Activity
• **Neutral**

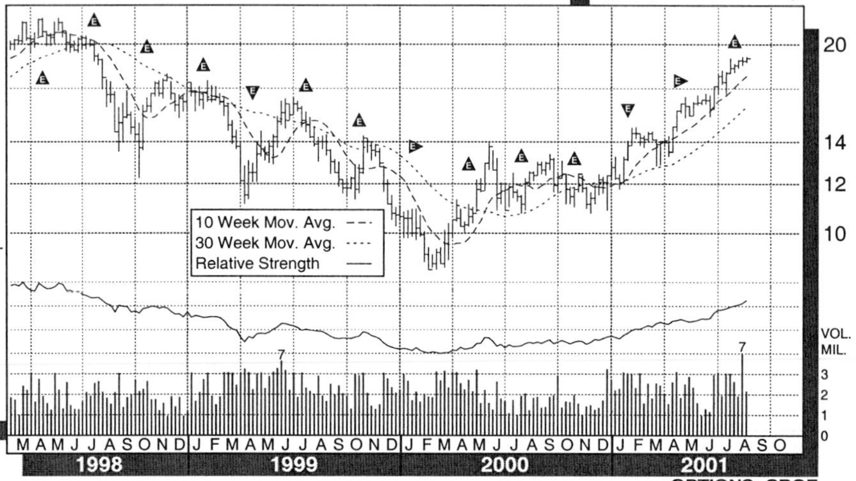

OPTIONS: CBOE

Overview - 15-AUG-01

We expect net interest income to be up 10% in 2001, driven by growth in consumer and small business loans. In the fourth quarter of 2000, the company appointed a new CEO and charged off $55 million of loans, increasing loss reserves by $70 million. By the end of the second quarter, non-performing assets declined to 0.61% of total loans (from 0.73% at year-end 2000 and 0.98% at September 30, 2000). Reserve coverage of non-performing loans increased to 292%, from 218% and 154%. With this improvement in credit quality, we project that provisioning will fall 25% from 2000's unusually high level. Noninterest income should advance 19%, on higher deposit service charges and mortgage fees, and increased contributions from recently acquired insurance and investment banking groups. With efficiency in the mid-fifties, EPS should grow 30% in 2001, to $1.35. In 2002, we see EPS up an additional 11%, to $1.50.

Valuation - 15-AUG-01

The shares are up moderately from lows in March 2000, but are still significantly below highs set in mid-1998. Decreased interest rates and the likelihood that the worst of credit quality problems have passed should further boost the valuation of HIB shares. In addition, Hibernia's recent moves into insurance and investment banking add to the attractiveness of its stock by helping to diversify revenue sources. In the second quarter of 2001, noninterest income excluding securities transactions increased to 31% of total revenues, from 29% in the year ago quarter. The shares currently sell at about 14 times our 2001 EPS estimate, below their regional banking peers. They also sell at only 2 times book value, and offer a respectable yield. The shares remain attractive for investors seeking long-term price appreciation and income.

Key Stock Statistics

S&P EPS Est. 2001	1.35	Tang. Bk. Value/Share	7.27
P/E on S&P Est. 2001	14.1	Beta	0.89
S&P EPS Est. 2002	1.50	Shareholders	16,708
Dividend Rate/Share	0.52	Market cap. (B)	$ 3.0
Shs. outstg. (M)	158.2	Inst. holdings	40%
Avg. daily vol. (M)	0.691		

Value of $10,000 invested 5 years ago: $ 20,452

Fiscal Year Ending Dec. 31

	2001	2000	1999	1998	1997	1996
Revenues (Million $)						
1Q	383.1	342.5	302.3	271.6	208.8	175.2
2Q	381.5	361.9	309.3	283.3	220.2	179.5
3Q	—	376.9	326.3	289.1	227.2	178.3
4Q	—	384.6	332.2	294.8	252.4	203.1
Yr.	—	1,466	1,270	1,139	895.5	736.0
Earnings Per Share ($)						
1Q	**0.31**	**0.31**	**0.18**	**0.25**	**0.22**	**0.21**
2Q	**0.34**	**0.31**	**0.29**	**0.27**	**0.23**	**0.22**
3Q	—	**0.33**	**0.30**	**0.29**	**0.25**	**0.19**
4Q	—	**0.10**	**0.30**	**0.30**	**0.27**	**0.23**
Yr.	—	**1.04**	**1.06**	**1.10**	**0.98**	**0.84**

Next earnings report expected: mid October

Dividend Data (Dividends have been paid since 1993.)

Amount ($)	Date Decl.	Ex-Div. Date	Stock of Record	Payment Date
0.130	Oct. 25	Nov. 02	Nov. 06	Nov. 20 '00
0.130	Jan. 24	Feb. 01	Feb. 05	Feb. 20 '01
0.130	Apr. 17	Apr. 25	Apr. 27	May. 21 '01
0.130	Jul. 25	Aug. 02	Aug. 06	Aug. 20 '01

Hibernia Corporation

Business Summary - 15-AUG-01

With its expansion throughout East Texas and Louisiana, Hibernia has become the largest bank holding company headquartered in Louisiana. Its two principal banking subsidiaries are Hibernia National Bank (originally chartered in 1933) and Hibernia National Bank of Texas (formerly Texarkana National Bank, originally chartered in 1887). Recent mergers have boosted HIB's assets to $16.7 billion at December 31, 2000. The company operated 263 locations in 34 Louisiana parishes, 16 Texas counties, and two Mississippi counties. HIB's statewide share of deposits in Louisiana was 23.3%, as of December 2000, ranking it first in the state. The company also ranked in the top three in deposit share in 31 Louisiana parishes and seven Texas counties. Hibernia's Louisiana markets represent approximately 82% of the state's population and 86% of its deposits.

Hibernia's principal operating goal is to be the first or second largest bank in each community in which it operates, with market share of at least 15% in each community. The company's strategy is based on a well established link between market share and profitability in banking. Acquisitions in 1999 included MarTex Bancshares (TX), assets $312 million, completed in March 1999; in May 1999, HIB acquired the Beaumont operations of Chase Bank of Texas ($465 million in deposits). In April 2000, HIB acquired Southcoast Capital, significantly expanding its investment banking capabilities and providing noninterest revenue growth. In June 2000, Hibernia purchased three East Texas offices, with deposits of $115 million and loans of $39 million, from Alabama-based Compass Bank. HIB managers believe more bank acquisition opportunities exist, and expect to continue this strategy.

In May 2000, Hibernia purchased the Rosenthal Agency, the largest independent insurance broker in Louisiana. As of the date of the announcement, the agency generated $90 million in annual premiums and served commercial and retail clients in Hibernia's Louisiana and East Texas markets. The acquisition significantly expands HIB's insurance operations.

At year-end 2000, the bulk of HIB's earning assets were financing loans; its loan portfolio had grown to $12.1 billion, from $10.9 billion a year earlier. Consumer loans were up 30%, to $6.2 billion from 1999, and small business loans rose 1.4% to $2.4 billion. Commercial loans totaled $3.5 billion, down 5.2%. Total deposits at December 31, 2000, were $12.7 billion, a 7.1% increase from $11.9 billion a year earlier. The net interest margin was 4.21% for 2000, down from 4.38% in 1999.

Per Share Data ($) (Year Ended Dec. 31)	2000	1999	1998	1997	1996	1995	1994	1993	1992	1991
Tangible Bk. Val.	7.27	6.54	6.84	6.83	5.32	5.85	4.88	4.65	3.86	5.09
Earnings	1.04	1.06	1.10	0.98	0.85	1.05	0.78	0.58	-0.27	-5.12
Dividends	0.49	0.43	0.39	0.33	0.29	0.25	0.19	0.03	Nil	0.15
Payout Ratio	47%	41%	35%	34%	34%	24%	24%	5%	Nil	NM
Prices - High	13.93	17.50	22.00	19.62	13.62	11.00	9.12	9.12	7.00	8.25
- Low	8.75	10.25	12.25	12.37	9.50	6.87	7.25	5.87	2.50	2.00
P/E Ratio - High	13	17	20	20	16	10	12	16	NM	NM
- Low	8	10	11	13	11	7	9	10	NM	NM
Income Statement Analysis (Million $)										
Net Int. Inc.	611	585	531	428	366	300	260	196	197	235
Tax Equiv. Adj.	10.5	11.3	11.0	8.9	6.5	5.4	4.6	4.0	6.0	12.0
Non Int. Inc.	253	214	179	145	116	97.6	85.7	67.0	69.0	91.0
Loan Loss Prov.	121	88.0	26.0	0.6	NM	Nil	-17.2	6.0	66.0	178
Exp./Op. Revs.	54%	81%	58%	63%	65%	66%	77%	82%	83%	91%
Pretax Inc.	263	271	273	211	169	133	88.0	49.6	-8.0	-143
Eff. Tax Rate	35%	35%	35%	35%	35%	7.06%	3.76%	3.40%	Nil	NM
Net Inc.	171	175	179	137	110	124	84.7	48.0	-8.0	-144
% Net Int. Marg.	4.21	4.38	4.51	4.75	4.89	4.70	4.55	4.60	4.38	3.99
Balance Sheet & Other Fin. Data (Million $)										
Money Mkt. Assets	NA	Nil	349	393	158	85.2	186	220	578	290
Inv. Securities	3,049	2,961	2,676	2,147	2,179	2,098	2,274	1,921	1,450	1,225
Com'l Loans	4,257	4,517	3,880	3,092	2,334	1,855	NA	532	685	1,028
Other Loans	7,867	6,340	6,126	4,381	3,703	2,614	3,376	1,633	1,675	2,774
Total Assets	16,698	15,314	14,012	11,023	9,307	7,196	6,336	4,796	4,734	6,018
Demand Deposits	2,243	2,085	2,026	1,621	1,541	1,167	1,063	813	760	829
Time Deposits	10,450	9,771	8,577	7,013	6,281	4,918	4,443	3,273	3,277	4,473
LT Debt	1,044	744	806	507	51.3	8.7	5.7	Nil	8.0	8.0
Common Eqty.	1,393	1,276	1,218	950	836	717	557	429	369	199
% Ret. on Assets	1.1	1.2	1.4	1.3	1.3	1.8	1.4	1.0	NM	NM
% Ret. on Equity	12.3	13.5	15.8	15.2	13.5	18.9	15.6	11.0	NM	NM
% Loan Loss Resv.	1.5	1.4	1.3	1.4	2.1	3.3	4.4	6.8	7.8	5.6
% Loans/Deposits	96.5	92.4	94.4	87.8	75.6	73.4	61.3	57.0	58.5	70.6
% Equity to Assets	8.3	8.5	8.7	8.8	9.4	9.4	8.7	8.4	4.2	4.1

Data as orig reptd.; bef. results of disc opers/spec. items. Per share data adj. for stk. divs. Bold denotes diluted EPS (FASB 128)-prior periods restated. E-Estimated. NA-Not Available. NM-Not Meaningful. NR-Not Ranked.

Office—313 Carondelet St., New Orleans, LA 70130. **Tel**—(504) 533-3333. **Website**—http://www.hiberniabank.com **Chrmn**—R. H. Boh. **Pres & CEO**—J. H. Boydstun. **Investor Contact**—Trisha Voltz (504-533-2180). **Dirs**—R. H. Boh, J. H. Boydstun, E. R. Campbell, R. W. Freeman Jr., D. H. Hearin, R. T. Holleman, R. E. Howard, E. R. King, S. W. Lassen, D. J. Nalty, R. B. Nesbitt, W. C. O'Malley, J.R. Peltier, R. T. Ratcliff, J. M. Tucker. **Transfer Agent & Registrar**—Mellon Investor Services, Ridgefield Park, NJ. **Incorporated**—in Louisiana in 1972; bank chartered under National Banking Act in 1933. **Empl**— 5,366. **S&P Analyst:** Erik J. Eisenstein

STANDARD &POOR'S
STOCK REPORTS

Household International

NYSE Symbol **HI**

In S&P 500

18-AUG-01 **Industry:** Consumer Finance

Summary: This company is a major provider of consumer financial services in the U.S., Canada and the U.K.

S&P Opinion: Accumulate (★★★★) Recent Price • 65.99 52 Wk Range • 69.98-43.87 Yield • 1.3% 12-Mo. P/E • 17.3

Quantitative Evaluations

Outlook (1 Lowest—5 Highest) • **2+**

Fair Value • **65**

Risk • **Low**

Earn./Div. Rank • **A**

Technical Eval. • **Bullish** since 8/01

Rel. Strength Rank (1 Lowest—99 Highest) • **56**

Insider Activity • **Neutral**

OPTIONS: ASE, CBOE, P

Overview - 20-JUL-01

Managed receivables increased over 22% in 2000, to $87.6 billion. In 2001, we expect managed receivables to rise over 13%, led by strength in the consumer finance and credit card segments. The managed net interest margin, which stood at 8.10% at the end of 2000, should increase in 2001, reflecting improvement in the business mix. We expect credit quality to deteriorate slightly in 2001, reflecting the slowing economy and expected increases in unemployment rates. Net charge-offs were 3.71% of average managed consumer receivables at June 30, 2001, compared to 3.56% at March 31, 2001. Expenses, which advanced 18% in 2000, should increase at a slower pace in 2001, resulting in an improved efficiency ratio. Share repurchases, particularly in the first half of the year, should aid EPS comparisons. We expect EPS for 2001 to advance over 15%, to $4.10.

Valuation - 20-JUL-01

The shares carry an accumulate recommendation, and are expected to outperform the S&P 500 over the next 6 to 12 months. We view HI as being in a considerably stronger position since the Beneficial merger, and therefore a winner in the long-term trend of consolidation in the diversified financial services industry. Good receivables growth, healthy margins, and efficiency improvements are expected to allow for continued earnings momentum. The shares were recently trading at a slight premium to HI's projected long-term EPS growth rate of 15%, but at a discount to the S&P 500, based on our EPS estimates. We think HI deserves a P/E multiple closer to that of the S&P 500. In light of the potential for P/E multiple expansion, the shares have strong capital appreciation potential. In our view, Citigroup's generous bid for Associates First Capital in September 2000 has cast a spotlight on Household as the next potential takeover target.

Key Stock Statistics

S&P EPS Est. 2001	4.10	Tang. Bk. Value/Share	13.55
P/E on S&P Est. 2001	16.1	Beta	0.92
S&P EPS Est. 2002	4.65	Shareholders	19,468
Dividend Rate/Share	0.88	Market cap. (B)	$ 30.5
Shs. outstg. (M)	461.7	Inst. holdings	83%
Avg. daily vol. (M)	1.771		

Value of $10,000 invested 5 years ago: $ 26,394

Fiscal Year Ending Dec. 31

	2001	2000	1999	1998	1997	1996
Revenues (Million $)						
1Q	3,437	2,760	2,256	2,332	1,336	1,175
2Q	3,331	2,841	2,234	2,119	1,293	1,307
3Q	—	3,087	2,424	2,191	1,423	1,242
4Q	—	3,273	2,568	2,255	1,451	1,335
Yr.	—	11,961	9,499	8,898	5,503	5,059
Earnings Per Share ($)						
1Q	**0.91**	**0.78**	**0.65**	**0.71**	**0.43**	**0.36**
2Q	**0.93**	**0.80**	**0.67**	**-1.03**	**0.49**	**0.41**
3Q	**E1.07**	**0.94**	**0.83**	**0.63**	**0.57**	**0.49**
4Q	**E1.19**	**1.03**	**0.92**	**0.71**	**0.66**	**0.54**
Yr.	**E4.10**	**3.55**	**3.07**	**1.03**	**2.17**	**1.77**

Next earnings report expected: mid October

Dividend Data (Dividends have been paid since 1926.)

Amount ($)	Date Decl.	Ex-Div. Date	Stock of Record	Payment Date
0.190	Sep. 12	Sep. 27	Sep. 29	Oct. 15 '00
0.190	Nov. 14	Dec. 27	Dec. 29	Jan. 15 '01
0.190	Mar. 13	Mar. 28	Mar. 30	Apr. 15 '01
0.220	May. 09	Jun. 27	Jun. 29	Jul. 15 '01

A Division of The McGraw-Hill Companies

Household International, Inc.

Business Summary - 20-JUL-01

Household International (HI) traces its roots back to 1878, when founder Frank Mackey wrote a personal cash loan from a Minneapolis jewelry store. Today, HI is one of the leading consumer finance companies in the U.S. Operations were significantly expanded in June 1998, when HI acquired Beneficial Corp., a consumer finance company based in Wilmington, DE. The company's primary products include home equity loans, auto finance loans, MasterCard and Visa credit cards, private label credit cards, tax refund anticipation loans and other types of secured loans. HI also offers credit and specialty insurance in the U.S., the U.K., and Canada. The company divides its operations into three reported segments: Consumer, Credit Card Services, and International.

The Consumer segment includes branch-based and correspondent consumer finance, private label credit card and auto finance businesses in the U.S. HI is the second largest U.S. subprime home equity lender, with over 1,400 branches in 46 states. It is also the second largest provider of third party private label credit cards in the U.S., with 8.5 million customer accounts. In addition, the company is one of the largest U.S. non-captive non-prime automobile lenders. The company generates auto loan volume primarily through dealer relationships.

The company's Credit Card segment encompasses HI's MasterCard and Visa credit card businesses in the U.S, including the company's GM Card and Union Privilege credit cards. HI's credit card business is generated mostly through direct mail, telemarketing, Internet applications, application displays and promotional activity associated with the company's co-branding relationships. The company's largest credit card account base is in California.

The International segment consists of HI's operations in the U.K. and Canada. The company offers secured and unsecured lines of credit, insurance and credit card products in the U.K. Loans in the U.K. are marketed through HI's 181 branches, merchants, and direct mail. The Canadian consumer finance business offers consumer loans, mortgages, revolving credit and retail finance products. It also accepts deposits. Products are offered through 99 branch offices, direct mail and telemarketing.

At year-end 2000, managed receivables totaled $87.6 billion, compared to $71.7 billion at year-end 1999. At December 31, 2000, home equity loans accounted for 42% of managed receivables, MasterCard/Visa 20%, private label credit cards 14%, auto finance 5%, other unsecured 19%, and commercial 1%.

Net chargeoffs amounted to 3.64% of managed receivables in 2000, versus 4.13% in 1999. Delinquencies at year-end 2000 totaled 4.20% of managed receivables, versus 4.66% a year earlier. Credit loss reserves are used to cover losses of both principal and interest in the company's loan portfolios. At year-end 2000, credit loss reserves amounted to 3.65% of managed receivables, versus 3.72% a year earlier.

Per Share Data ($) (Year Ended Dec. 31)	2000	1999	1998	1997	1996	1995	1994	1993	1992	1991
Tangible Bk. Val.	13.26	10.38	9.36	8.58	6.74	7.23	5.12	5.59	4.51	4.24
Earnings	3.55	3.07	1.03	2.17	1.77	1.44	1.17	0.97	0.66	0.53
Dividends	0.74	0.66	0.59	0.54	0.49	0.44	0.41	0.39	0.38	0.37
Payout Ratio	21%	21%	57%	25%	28%	30%	35%	40%	58%	71%
Prices - High	57.43	52.31	53.68	43.33	32.70	22.79	13.25	13.50	10.08	10.50
- Low	29.50	35.81	23.00	26.20	17.33	11.95	9.50	9.00	6.91	4.58
P/E Ratio - High	16	17	52	20	19	16	11	14	15	20
- Low	8	12	22	12	10	8	8	9	11	9
Income Statement Analysis (Million $)										
Total Revs.	11,558	9,107	8,898	5,503	5,058	5,144	4,603	4,455	4,181	4,594
Int. Exp.	3,929	2,777	2,517	1,503	1,521	1,557	1,243	1,150	1,420	1,887
Exp./Op. Revs.	63%	41%	61%	60%	55%	58%	66%	67%	93%	96%
Pretax Inc.	2,611	2,221	953	1,029	822	754	528	451	278	200
Eff. Tax Rate	35%	33%	45%	33%	35%	40%	30%	34%	31%	25%
Net Inc.	1,701	1,486	524	687	539	453	368	299	191	150
Balance Sheet & Other Fin. Data (Million $)										
Cash & Secs.	3,749	3,399	3,660	2,566	2,521	4,909	9,546	9,113	7,646	6,710
Loans	NA	52,158	43,948	23,811	24,067	21,732	20,556	19,563	18,961	18,987
Total Assets	76,706	60,749	52,893	30,303	29,595	29,219	34,338	32,961	31,128	29,982
ST Debt	NA	17,349	9,918	6,081	6,428	6,659	4,372	5,642	5,253	4,142
Capitalization:										
Debt	45,728	28,691	30,814	20,930	14,802	11,228	10,274	9,114	9,015	9,595
Equity	7,951	6,451	6,221	4,691	2,941	2,691	2,200	2,078	1,608	1,525
Total	53,844	35,306	37,199	19,690	17,538	14,124	13,117	11,531	10,959	11,624
Price Times Bk. Val.: High	4.3	5.0	5.7	5.0	4.9	3.2	2.6	2.4	2.2	2.5
Price Times Bk. Val.: Low	2.2	3.5	2.5	3.0	2.6	1.7	1.9	1.6	1.5	1.1
% Return On Revs.	14.7	16.3	5.9	12.5	10.6	8.8	8.0	6.7	4.6	3.3
% Ret. on Assets	2.5	2.6	1.1	2.3	1.8	1.4	1.1	0.9	0.6	0.5
% Ret. on Equity	23.5	23.3	8.2	17.3	19.1	17.5	16.0	14.2	10.6	9.0
Loans/Equity	NA	7.6	6.6	6.4	12.2	11.6	9.4	10.5	11.8	14.2

Data as orig reptd.; bef. results of disc opers/spec. items. Per share data adj. for stk. divs. Bold denotes diluted EPS (FASB 128)-prior periods restated. E-Estimated. NA-Not Available. NM-Not Meaningful. NR-Not Ranked.

Office—2700 Sanders Rd., Prospect Heights, IL 60070-2799. **Tel**—(847) 564-5000. **Website**—http://www.household.com **Chrmn & CEO**—W F Aldinger. **EVP & CFO**—D. A. Schoenholz. **Investor Contact**—Celeste M. Murphy (847-564-7568). **Dirs**—W. F. Aldinger, R. J. Darnall, G. G. Dillon, J. A. Edwardson, M. J. Evans, J. D. Fishburn, C. F. Freidheim Jr., J. H. Gilliam Jr., L. E. Levy, G. A. Lorch, J. D. Nichols, J. B. Pitblado, S. J. Stewart, L. W. Sullivan. **Transfer Agent & Registrar**—ComputerShare Investor Services LLC, Chicago. **Incorporated**—in Delaware in 1925. **Empl**—28,800. **S&P Analyst:** Michael Schneider, CFA

STANDARD
&POOR'S
STOCK REPORTS

Lincoln National Corp.

NYSE Symbol **LNC**

In S&P 500

21-AUG-01

Industry: Insurance (Life & Health)

Summary: LNC offers annuities, life insurance, mutual funds, asset management and related advisory services to affluent individuals.

S&P Opinion: Accumulate (★★★★)

Recent Price • 50.20
52 Wk Range • 56.37-38

Yield • 2.4%
12-Mo. P/E • 16.1

Quantitative Evaluations

Outlook
(1 Lowest—5 Highest)
• **2+**

Fair Value
• **47.80**

Risk
• **Low**

Earn./Div. Rank
• **A-**

Technical Eval.
• **Bullish** since 8/01

Rel. Strength Rank
(1 Lowest—99 Highest)
• **63**

Insider Activity
• **Neutral**

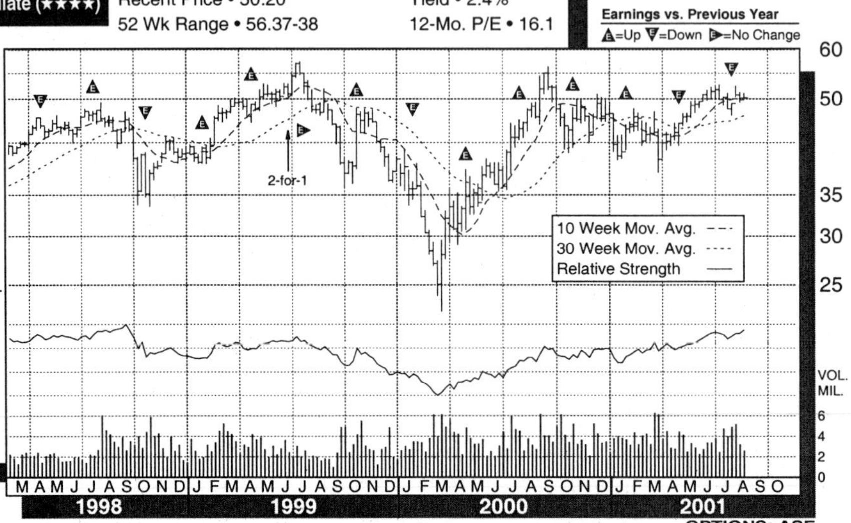

OPTIONS: ASE

Overview - 21-AUG-01

Operating earnings growth (before restructuring charges) in 2001 will likely be driven by growth in the core life insurance and annuity segments. Although the rate of year-to-year profit growth may slow from the acquisition-driven surge in 1999 operating profits, the benefits of a cost-cutting initiative will aid margins. However, in 2000, the annuities segment continued to experience net cash outflows, as had occurred in 1999. Although LNC is addressing this issue, it continues to temper our outlook. The pending sale of the reinsurance unit is positive, since it frees up capital LNC can redeploy into its core life insurance/annuity/asset management businesses. LNC's ability to turn around the investment management unit is predicated on its ability to stem the cash outflows in this area, and to increase assets under management. In September 2000, LNC said it planned to cease writing new business in the U.K., and incurred net restructuring charges of $37 million in the fourth quarter of 2000 to cover the associated costs.

Valuation - 21-AUG-01

After a strong recovery in the latter half of 2000 -- sparked by a sector rotation back into financial stocks amid hopes that interest rates have peaked -- the shares have recently plateaued. At current levels, the shares are trading at a slight discount to the life insurance peer group average. However, in light of LNC's above-average long-term growth prospects, and its favorable business mix, the shares merit an expansion in their P/E ratio. Although we believe the shares are undervalued, the uncertainty surrounding the potential repeal of the estate tax will likely keep the shares under pressure. Also, positive asset inflows into the annuity and investment management units are necessary for the shares to stage a sustained recovery.

Key Stock Statistics

S&P EPS Est. 2001	3.70	Tang. Bk. Value/Share	12.29
P/E on S&P Est. 2001	13.6	Beta	0.82
S&P EPS Est. 2002	4.10	Shareholders	11,102
Dividend Rate/Share	1.22	Market cap. (B)	$ 9.5
Shs. outstg. (M)	188.1	Inst. holdings	80%
Avg. daily vol. (M)	0.748		

Value of $10,000 invested 5 years ago: $ 25,747

Fiscal Year Ending Dec. 31

	2001	2000	1999	1998	1997	1996
Revenues (Million $)						
1Q	1,699	1,669	1,675	1,448	1,701	1,641
2Q	1,599	1,693	1,678	1,507	1,128	1,644
3Q	—	1,716	1,642	1,418	1,267	1,685
4Q	—	1,774	1,808	1,714	1,305	1,752
Yr.	—	6,852	6,804	6,087	4,898	6,721
Earnings Per Share ($)						
1Q	**0.85**	**0.87**	**0.71**	**0.60**	0.64	0.67
2Q	**0.80**	**0.84**	**0.73**	**0.73**	-0.23	0.54
3Q	—	**0.71**	**0.66**	**0.56**	0.61	0.57
4Q	—	**0.76**	**0.18**	**0.62**	**-0.67**	0.69
Yr.	—	**3.19**	**2.30**	**2.51**	**0.10**	**1.69**

Next earnings report expected: late October

Dividend Data (Dividends have been paid since 1920.)

Amount ($)	Date Decl.	Ex-Div. Date	Stock of Record	Payment Date
0.305	Nov. 09	Jan. 08	Jan. 10	Feb. 01 '01
q.305	Mar. 08	Apr. 06	Apr. 10	May. 01 '01
0.305	May. 10	Jul. 06	Jul. 10	Aug. 01 '01
0.305	Aug. 09	Oct. 05	Oct. 10	Nov. 01 '01

Lincoln National Corporation

Business Summary - 21-AUG-01

By focusing on life insurance, annuities, investment management and life reinsurance, Lincoln National has transformed itself from a staid, slow growing multiline insurance company into a leading provider of financial services to the affluent. Contributions to operating profits (before corporate and other charges) in 2000 were: life insurance 34%, annuities 42%, Lincoln UK 7%, reinsurance 15%, investment management 2%.

The life insurance segment underwrites and sells universal life, variable universal life, interest-sensitive whole life and corporate owned life insurance. Term life insurance and tax deferred fixed annuities are also offered. At year-end 2000, life insurance and annuity account values equaled $12.7 billion, of which universal life accounted for 54%, annuities for 15%, variable universal life for 14%, and interest-sensitive whole life for 17%. Life insurance in force at year-end 2000 totaled $216 billion, of which universal and other life accounted for 54% and term life insurance for 46%. Through a broad based distribution network, the Annuities segment offers an array of annuity products to indivduals and employer-sponsored groups. Annuity account values totaled $53 billion at year-end 2000 (down from $56.3 billion at year-end 1999), of which variable annuities accounted for 74% and fixed annuities for 26%. LNC has increased its presence in the annuity and life insurance market through a series of acquisitions. On January 2, 1998, LNC acquired CIGNA Corp.'s individual life insurance and annuity division for $1.4 billion. On October 1, 1998, LNC acquired Aetna, Inc.'s domestic individual life insurance business for $1.0 billion.

Investment management activities consist of institutional investment management (including pension accounts and LNC's internal investment adviser business, which were moved to this unit as part of a reorganization in 1999); and retail mutual funds (mostly through the Delaware family of retail mutual funds). At year-end 2000, external assets under management totaled $52.9 billion, of which retail accounted equaled 52% and institutional accounts equaled 48%.

Lincoln UK offers life insurance, investment and retirement planning products. At 2000 year end, individual life insurance in force totaled $24.3 billion, and unit-linked assets under management (similar to variable life insurance) equaled $6.4 billion. In late September 2000, LNC decided to stop writing new business in the U.K., and is reviewing options for this unit.

LNC's reinsurance unit, Lincoln Re, is a leading life/health reinsurer, offering life, accident and disability programs to insurance companies, HMOs and self-funded employer-sponsored plans worldwide. On July 29, 2001, LNC announced plans to sell this unit to Swiss Re for $2 billion. Property-casualty insurance operations were sold in October 1997 to SAFECO Corp. for $2.82 billion.

Per Share Data ($) (Year Ended Dec. 31)	2000	1999	1998	1997	1996	1995	1994	1993	1992	1991
Tangible Bk. Val.	11.06	5.59	10.16	19.34	15.96	16.23	13.67	18.74	14.11	12.65
Oper. Earnings	3.69	3.12	2.61	-0.24	2.08	1.48	1.88	1.68	1.31	0.94
Earnings	3.19	2.30	2.51	0.10	2.46	2.31	1.69	2.03	1.95	1.15
Dividends	1.16	1.10	1.30	0.98	0.92	0.86	0.82	0.76	0.73	0.68
Relative Payout	36%	48%	52%	NM	37%	37%	49%	37%	37%	59%
Prices - High	56.37	57.50	49.43	39.06	28.50	26.87	22.18	24.12	19.03	13.81
- Low	22.62	36.00	33.50	24.50	20.37	17.31	17.31	17.34	12.62	9.50
P/E Ratio - High	18	25	20	NM	12	12	13	12	10	12
- Low	7	16	13	NM	8	7	10	9	6	8
Income Statement Analysis (Million $)										
Life Ins. In Force	637,100	345,500	292,700	212,500	218,900	194,400	NA	233,766	217,985	255,557
Prem. Inc.: Life A & H	1,813	1,882	1,621	1,329	2,193	2,098	NA	3,515	3,216	4,488
Prem. Inc.: Cas./Prop.	NA	Nil	Nil	832	1,617	1,679	NA	1,841	2,083	2,242
Net Invest. Inc.	2,747	2,808	2,681	2,251	2,366	2,286	2,011	2,147	1,987	1,799
Total Revs.	6,852	6,798	6,087	4,898	6,721	6,633	6,984	8,289	8,034	9,169
Pretax Inc.	836	570	697	34.0	712	627	376	588	425	199
Net Oper. Inc.	NA	NA	NA	257	434	307	390	344	241	NA
Net Inc.	621	460	510	21.0	514	482	350	415	363	208
Balance Sheet & Other Fin. Data (Million $)										
Cash & Equiv.	2,474	2,429	2,433	3,795	1,715	2,036	1,471	1,123	1,452	972
Premiums Due	297	260	775	621	651	538	565	602	792	926
Invest. Assets: Bonds	27,450	27,689	30,233	24,066	27,906	25,834	21,644	23,964	20,331	17,849
Invest. Assets: Stocks	550	604	543	660	993	1,165	1,039	1,080	923	1,025
Invest. Assets: Loans	6,624	6,628	6,233	4,051	4,031	3,790	3,406	3,896	3,699	3,675
Invest. Assets: Total	35,369	35,578	37,929	25,212	34,045	31,936	26,971	29,732	25,525	22,987
Deferred Policy Costs	3,071	2,800	1,964	1,624	1,892	1,437	2,444	2,011	2,118	1,972
Total Assets	99,844	103,096	99,836	77,175	71,713	63,258	49,330	48,380	39,672	34,095
Debt	1,457	1,457	712	808	626	659	420	335	423	253
Common Eqty.	4,953	4,264	5,388	4,983	4,467	4,375	2,730	3,761	2,636	2,461
Comb. Loss-Exp. Ratio	NA	NM	NM	NM	105.8	104.9	105.7	107.5	112.7	111.9
% Return On Revs.	9.1	6.8	28.6	0.7	7.6	7.3	5.0	5.0	4.5	2.3
% Ret. on Equity	13.5	0.4	9.8	0.4	11.6	13.3	10.3	13.0	13.6	8.3
% Invest. Yield	7.7	7.6	7.9	7.5	7.2	7.3	7.1	7.8	8.2	8.5

Data as orig reptd.; bef. results of disc opers/spec. items. Per share data adj. for stk. divs. Bold denotes diluted EPS (FASB 128)-prior periods restated. E-Estimated. NA-Not Available. NM-Not Meaningful. NR-Not Ranked.

Office—Centre Square, West Tower, 1500 Market St., Suite 3900, Philadelphia, PA 19102-2112. **Tel**—(215) 448-1400. **Website**—www.lfg.com **Chrmn & CEO**—J. A. Boscia. **EVP & CFO**—R. C. Vaughan. **Secy**—C. S. Womack. **VP & Investor Contact**—Priscilla Brown (215-448-1422; pbrown@lnc.com). **Dirs**—J. P. Barrett, T. D. Bell Jr., J. A. Boscia, J. K. Britell, J. G. Drosdick, E. G. Johnson, M. L. Lachman, M. F. Mee, J. M. Pietruski, R. J. Ponder, J. S. Ruckelshaus, G. R. Whitaker Jr. **Transfer Agent & Registrar**—EquiServe/First Chicago Division. **Incorporated**—in Indiana in 1905; reincorporated in 1968. **Empl**— 7,820. **S&P Analyst:** C. Seifert

STANDARD
&POOR'S
STOCK REPORTS

MBIA Inc.

NYSE Symbol **MBI**

In S&P 500

18-AUG-01

Industry: Insurance (Property-Casualty)

Summary: This leading financial guarantee company is also the leading insurer of municipal bonds, based on its 28% share of the new issue, long-term municipal bond market in 2000.

S&P Opinion: Accumulate (★★★★)

Recent Price • 57.11
52 Wk Range • 57.49-40.04

Yield • 1.1%
12-Mo. P/E • 16.2

Quantitative Evaluations

Outlook (1 Lowest—5 Highest) • **2**

Fair Value • **55.90**

Risk • **Low**

Earn./Div. Rank • **A**

Technical Eval. • **Bullish** since 5/01

Rel. Strength Rank (1 Lowest—99 Highest) • **77**

Insider Activity • **Unfavorable**

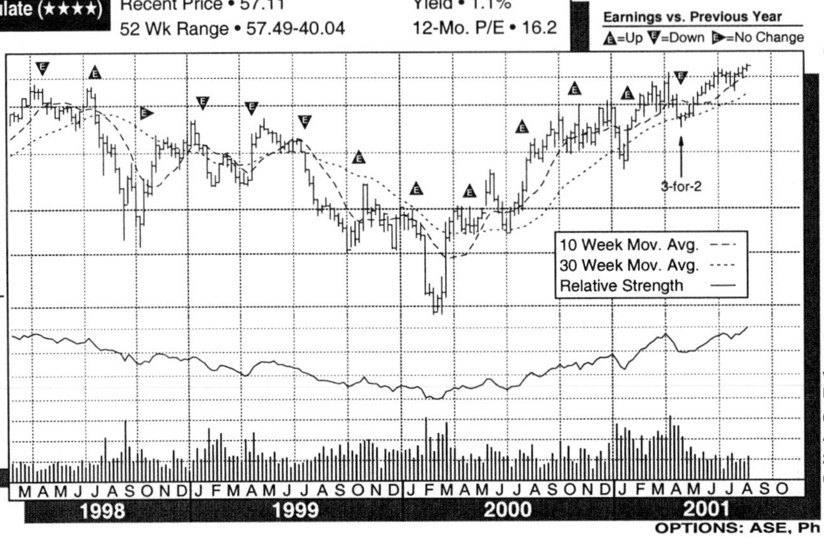

OPTIONS: ASE, Ph

Overview - 13-AUG-01

Earned premiums will likely rise 10% to 13% in 2001. This estimated rate of growth assumes that an interest rate driven surge in refundings helps boost overall new issue volume. Partly offsetting this boost is an expectation that pricing in certain areas of the municipal bond market continue to be competitive. In the first six months of 2001, new issue volume surged 42%, year to year, to $119.7 billion. The insured portion of the new issue volume was 53.5%, up from 44.4% in the year-earlier period. MBI's share of the insured market also slipped, to 23.2% from 28.4%. Though MBI maintained its lead, its share has been slipping in recent years -- from a high of 42.4% in 1997 to a low of 18.4% in the 2001 first quarter. Partially offsetting this slowdown is MBI's foray into international and structured finance markets, which helped fuel a 26% rise in net written premiums in the first six months of 2001.

Valuation - 13-AUG-01

After bottoming in early 2000, the shares have trended steadily upward, as investors shrugged off MBI's more than $1 billion (net par value) exposure to two troubled California utilities and instead focused on the positive effects of a lower interest rate environment on MBI's core municipal bond insurance business. We are encouraged by the resumption of MBI's solid top line growth trends and the likelihood that expense savings will aid margins in 2001 and beyond. Although our outlook is tempered somewhat by MBI's more than $1 billion (net par value) exposure to Pacific Gas & Electric and Southern California Edison, we continue to view MBI as a top notch, well managed "franchise" company with solid longer term growth prospects.

Key Stock Statistics

S&P EPS Est. 2001	3.75	Tang. Bk. Value/Share	27.86
P/E on S&P Est. 2001	15.2	Beta	0.85
S&P EPS Est. 2002	4.20	Shareholders	945
Dividend Rate/Share	0.60	Market cap. (B)	$ 8.5
Shs. outstg. (M)	148.2	Inst. holdings	89%
Avg. daily vol. (M)	0.380		

Value of $10,000 invested 5 years ago: $ 22,735

Fiscal Year Ending Dec. 31

	2001	2000	1999	1998	1997	1996
Revenues (Million $)						
1Q	229.0	254.4	236.8	218.5	153.9	130.2
2Q	—	262.5	235.4	218.0	153.0	135.0
3Q	—	266.2	215.1	236.0	166.7	140.0
4Q	—	274.3	216.1	214.2	180.4	140.3
Yr.	—	1,057	853.8	812.4	654.0	545.5
Earnings Per Share ($)						
1Q	**0.87**	**0.89**	**0.06**	**0.67**	**0.69**	**0.60**
2Q	—	**0.87**	**0.37**	**0.78**	**0.68**	**0.61**
3Q	—	**0.88**	**0.85**	**0.72**	**0.72**	**0.64**
4Q	—	**0.92**	**0.85**	**0.69**	**0.72**	**0.62**
Yr.	—	**3.55**	**2.12**	**2.88**	**2.81**	**2.48**

Next earnings report expected: NA

Dividend Data (Dividends have been paid since 1987.)

Amount ($)	Date Decl.	Ex-Div. Date	Stock of Record	Payment Date
0.205	Dec. 07	Dec. 18	Dec. 20	Jan. 15 '01
0.225	Mar. 15	Mar. 22	Mar. 26	Apr. 16 '01
3-for-2	Mar. 15	Apr. 23	Apr. 02	Apr. 20 '01
0.150	Jun. 18	Jun. 21	Jun. 25	Jul. 16 '01

Business Summary - 13-AUG-01

MBIA, a dominant force in the municipal bond insurance market (based on its 23.2% share of the new issue market through the first six months of 2001), is leveraging its strength and expanding into the structured finance market and into selected international markets. It is also expanding asset management operations. At year-end 2000, assets under management totaled $36.6 billion, up from $30.1 billion at year-end 1999. MBI is the successor to the Municipal Bond Insurance Association, a voluntary association formed in 1974 by five multi-line insurance companies to insure municipal bonds. The association was reorganized in 1986, with four of the original five members participating. MBI's principal business in insuring municipal bonds unconditionally and irrevocably guarantees payment of principal and interest when due on insured municipal bonds.

At December 31, 2000, net insurance in force equaled $680.9 billion ($635.9 billion in 1999), of which general obligation municipal bonds accounted for 23%, utility bonds 11%, health care bonds 10%, special revenue bonds 9%, transportation bonds 7%, other municipal bonds 13%, structured finance obligations (asset/mortgage backed) 20%, and international and other bonds 7%. Of the $680.9 billion of in-force insurance at December 31, 2000, 12% had been issued by California, 10% by New York, 5% by Florida, and approximately 4% each by Texas, New Jersey and Pennsylvania.

MBI offers insurance for new issues of municipal bonds, and for bonds traded in the secondary market, including bonds held in unit investment trusts and mutual funds. The economic value of municipal bond insurance to the governmental unit or agency offering bonds is a saving in interest costs reflecting the difference in yield on an insured bond from that on the same bond if uninsured. MBI's guarantee also increases market acceptance for complex financings, and for municipal bonds of issuers that are not well known.

MBI has expanded its presence in the structured finance (or asset-backed) and the international financial guarantee markets. However, growth in these areas has been somewhat disappointing. In 2000, MBI insured $48 billion (par value) of domestic structured finance securities, unchanged from a year ago. International volume (including international structured finance) totaled $18 billion in 2000, up sharply from $8 billion in 1999. From late 1995 until early 2000, international structured finance activities were conducted through a joint venture with rival bond insurer Ambac Financial Group, Inc. (NYSE: ABK).

Per Share Data ($) (Year Ended Dec. 31)	2000	1999	1998	1997	1996	1995	1994	1993	1992	1991
Tangible Bk. Val.	27.86	23.01	24.59	21.81	18.27	16.88	12.76	11.80	10.02	8.09
Oper. Earnings	3.41	3.15	3.05	2.71	2.41	2.09	2.01	1.88	1.49	NA
Earnings	3.55	2.13	2.88	2.81	2.48	2.14	2.06	1.93	1.54	1.25
Dividends	0.55	0.53	0.52	0.51	0.48	0.44	0.38	0.31	0.25	0.21
Payout Ratio	15%	25%	18%	18%	20%	20%	18%	16%	16%	17%
Prices - High	50.79	47.91	53.95	44.91	34.87	25.83	21.75	27.08	22.16	16.45
- Low	24.20	30.08	30.70	30.29	23.33	18.45	15.75	18.41	14.41	7.58
P/E Ratio - High	14	23	19	16	14	12	11	14	14	13
- Low	7	14	11	11	9	9	8	10	9	6
Income Statement Analysis (Million $)										
Premium Inc.	446	443	425	297	252	215	218	231	163	132
Net Invest. Inc.	394	359	332	281	248	220	194	179	150	130
Oth. Revs.	217	605	156	75.1	46.0	27.0	27.4	18.8	14.5	5.1
Total Revs.	1,057	964	912	654	546	462	440	429	328	269
Pretax Inc.	715	388	565	480	408	345	329	324	244	190
Net Oper. Inc.	NA	NA	NA	364	313	265	254	240	NA	NA
Net Inc.	529	321	433	374	322	271	260	246	189	145
Balance Sheet & Other Fin. Data (Million $)										
Cash & Equiv.	246	229	148	23.2	112	110	76.4	57.3	58.8	42.1
Premiums Due	NA	NA	NA	13.4	1.0	6.1	0.9	31.9	2.1	2.4
Invest. Assets: Bonds	11,737	10,274	9,562	4,867	4,150	3,653	3,052	2,797	2,346	1,842
Invest. Assets: Stocks	Nil	Nil	Nil	Nil	Nil	Nil	Nil	Nil	Nil	Nil
Invest. Assets: Loans	Nil	Nil	Nil	Nil	205	212	139	105	60.8	26.0
Invest. Assets: Total	12,233	10,694	10,080	8,470	7,648	6,607	4,867	3,544	2,527	1,961
Deferred Policy Costs	274	252	230	154	148	140	133	120	110	97.0
Total Assets	13,894	12,264	11,797	9,811	8,562	7,267	5,456	4,106	2,885	2,278
Debt	795	689	689	474	374	374	299	299	299	199
Common Eqty.	4,223	3,513	3,792	3,048	2,480	2,234	1,705	1,596	1,382	1,063
Prop. & Cas. Loss Ratio	6.2	12.3	8.0	6.3	6.1	4.9	3.7	3.4	3.4	13.0
Prop. & Cas. Expense Ratio	22.1	23.6	16.8	26.2	28.3	29.3	28.8	27.4	33.2	32.9
Prop. & Cas. Combined Ratio	28.3	35.9	24.8	32.5	34.4	34.2	32.5	30.8	36.6	45.9
% Return On Revs.	50.0	33.2	47.5	57.2	59.1	58.7	59.2	57.4	57.5	53.8
% Ret. on Equity	13.7	8.8	12.7	13.5	13.7	13.8	15.8	17.4	15.4	14.5

Data as orig reptd.; bef. results of disc opers/spec. items. Per share data adj. for stk. divs. Bold denotes diluted EPS (FASB 128)-prior periods restated. E-Estimated. NA-Not Available. NM-Not Meaningful. NR-Not Ranked.

Office—113 King St., Armonk, NY 10504. **Tel**—(914) 273-4545. **Fax**—(914) 765-3163. **Website**—http://www.mbia.com **Chrmn & CEO**—J. W. Brown Jr. **Pres & COO**—G. C. Dunton. **VP-CFO**—N. G. Budnick. **VP- Secy**—R. L. Weill. **VP-Treas**— J. L. Sevely. **Investor Contact**—Judith Radasch (914-765-3860). **Dirs**—J. W. Brown Jr., D. C. Clapp, G. C. Dunton, D. H. Elliott, C. L. Gaudiani, W. H. Gray III, F. S. Johnson, D. P. Kearney, J. A. Lebenthal, J. A. Rolls, R. L. Weill. **Transfer Agent & Registrar**—Mellon Investor Services, Ridgefield Park, NJ. **Incorporated**—in Connecticut in 1986. **Empl**— 745. **S&P Analyst:** Catherine A. Seifert

STANDARD &POOR'S STOCK REPORTS

Morgan Stanley Dean Witter & Co.

NYSE Symbol **MWD**

In S&P 500

18-AUG-01

Industry: Financial (Diversified)

Summary: Morgan Stanley Dean Witter & Co. is a leading securities concern, with worldwide operations.

S&P Opinion: Accumulate (★★★★)

Recent Price • 51.20 | 52 Wk Range • 110-44.10 | Yield • 1.8% | 12-Mo. P/E • 13.2

Quantitative Evaluations

Outlook (1 Lowest—5 Highest) • **1**

Fair Value • **41.20**

Risk • **Average**

Earn./Div. Rank • **NR**

Technical Eval. • **Bearish** since 7/01

Rel. Strength Rank (1 Lowest—99 Highest) • **20**

Insider Activity • **NA**

OPTIONS: ASE, CBOE, P, Ph

Overview - 22-JUN-01

The revenues and earnings of investment banks are difficult to predict, since they depend on the health of both the equity and debt markets, and movements in interest rates, among other things. We expect MWD's net revenues and earnings to decline in FY 01 (Nov.), reflecting less investment activity by individual and institutional investors, a weak equity underwriting market and a fall-off in global merger and acquisition advisory deals. Nevertheless, we think recent interest rate cuts, a rebound in corporate earnings, and stabilizing equity markets will lead to a revenue and earnings rebound later this year that will continue into 2002. Long term growth will be aided by the secular trends of worldwide industry consolidation and privatization, increased global demand for asset management products and services, and growth in the global capital markets. We expect declining credit quality to adversely impact results in the credit card segment this year.

Valuation - 22-JUN-01

The shares are expected to outperform the S&P 500 over the coming six to 12 months. In FY 00, 12% of MWD's net income was derived from its credit services business, while 14% came from asset management operations. Although investment banks and brokerage companies have traditionally been valued on the basis of price to book value, MWD's relatively diversified earnings stream and leading global franchise argues for a P/E-based approach. Based on our profit projections, the shares were recently trading at a discount to the P/E of the S&P 500. Given their discount to the broader markets, as well as the prospects for improved business conditions over the next 18 months, the shares have room for further capital appreciation.

Key Stock Statistics

S&P EPS Est. 2001	3.75	Tang. Bk. Value/Share	17.54
P/E on S&P Est. 2001	13.7	Beta	2.10
S&P EPS Est. 2002	4.56	Shareholders	196,884
Dividend Rate/Share	0.92	Market cap. (B)	$ 56.8
Shs. outstg. (M)	1108.7	Inst. holdings	62%
Avg. daily vol. (M)	3.738		

Value of $10,000 invested 5 years ago: $ 41,985

Fiscal Year Ending Nov. 30

	2001	2000	1999	1998	1997	1996
Revenues (Million $)						
1Q	12,777	11,614	8,405	7,585	6,562	—
2Q	12,692	11,692	8,529	8,428	6,376	—
3Q	—	11,711	8,370	7,498	7,257	—
4Q	—	10,444	8,624	7,620	6,939	—
Yr.	—	45,413	33,928	31,131	27,132	22,172
Earnings Per Share ($)						
1Q	**0.94**	**1.34**	**0.88**	**0.55**	0.47	0.35
2Q	**0.82**	**1.26**	**0.97**	**0.69**	0.42	0.35
3Q	**E0.96**	**1.09**	**0.82**	**0.51**	0.56	0.35
4Q	**E1.02**	**1.06**	**1.42**	**1.03**	0.67	0.34
Yr.	**E3.75**	**4.73**	**4.10**	**2.76**	**1.06**	1.40

Next earnings report expected: late September

Dividend Data (Dividends have been paid since 1993.)

Amount ($)	Date Decl.	Ex-Div. Date	Stock of Record	Payment Date
0.200	Sep. 21	Oct. 04	Oct. 06	Oct. 27 '00
0.230	Dec. 19	Jan. 10	Jan. 12	Jan. 30 '01
0.230	Mar. 20	Apr. 04	Apr. 06	Apr. 27 '01
0.230	Jun. 21	Jul. 03	Jul. 06	Jul. 27 '01

Morgan Stanley Dean Witter & Co.

Business Summary - 22-JUN-01

Financial services giant Morgan Stanley Dean Witter & Co. was formed via the May 1997 merger of Dean Witter, Discover & Co. and Morgan Stanley Group. MWD, combining Morgan Stanley's strengths in investment banking and institutional sales and trading with Dean Witter's skill in providing investment and global asset management services and profitable Discover Card franchise, has emerged as a true financial services powerhouse, with a diverse revenue stream spread across a number of businesses.

In FY 00 (Nov.), after-tax profits in MWD's securities business totaled $4.0 billion; in the asset management business $683 million; and in the credit services business $726 million. In FY 99, after-tax profits in MWD's securities business totaled $3.7 billion; in the asset management business $448 million; and in the credit services business $662 million.

The company's worldwide securities business includes investment banking, institutional sales and trading, full and online brokerage services, and principal investing activities. At the end of FY 00, MWD's financial advisers served more than 5.4 million client accounts in the U.S., with assets of $659 billion. The company has the second largest U.S. financial adviser network. As an investment banker, MWD helps raise capital for corporate clients through equity and debt offerings, and advises corporate clients on matters such as takeover defenses, acquisitions and restructurings. In FY 00, it advised on over $1.0 trillion of announced M&A deals. In its sales and trading operations, the company advises major buy-side institutions such as mutual funds and pension funds on developments affecting their securities holdings, receiving either a commission or positive spread when the client places a buy or sell order. In its retail operations, registered representatives or stockbrokers give financial advice to individuals, typically suggesting stocks, bonds or mutual funds that they believe to be attractive.

MWD is one of the world's 10 largest asset managers. At November 30, 2000, it had $502 million in assets under management or supervision. The company's asset management group offers a wide range of domestic and international equity, bond and multi-class funds for both individual and institutional investors. Money management is a highly profitable business, partly because fees are computed on assets that run into billions of dollars, while costs amount to little more than paying portfolio managers and renting office space.

Credit services include the Discover Card, the Discover Platinum Card and the Morgan Stanley Dean Witter Card. Managed consumer loans totaled $47.1 billion at November 30, 2000, up from $38.0 billion a year earlier.

Per Share Data ($) (Year Ended Nov. 30)	2000	1999	1998	1997	1996	1995	1994	1993	1992	1991
Tangible Bk. Val.	16.91	14.79	11.88	10.99	8.69	6.91	5.84	4.84	3.77	NA
Earnings	4.73	4.10	2.76	2.13	1.40	1.22	1.09	0.92	0.66	NA
Dividends	0.80	0.48	0.40	0.28	0.22	0.16	0.13	0.08	NA	NA
Payout Ratio	17%	12%	14%	13%	16%	13%	11%	8%	NA	NA
Prices - High	110.00	71.43	48.75	29.75	17.25	14.56	10.78	11.62	NA	NA
- Low	58.62	35.40	18.25	16.37	11.25	8.37	7.87	6.75	NA	NA
P/E Ratio - High	23	17	18	14	12	12	10	13	NA	NA
- Low	12	9	7	8	8	7	7	7	NA	NA
Income Statement Analysis (Million $)										
Net Int. Inc.	3,058	2,365	2,922	2,777	2,021	1,804	1,459	1,094	1,009	965
Non Int. Inc.	24,179	20,110	14,656	13,549	5,441	4,615	4,095	3,912	484	2,835
Loan Loss Prov.	810	529	1,173	1,493	1,232	744	548	458	NA	453
Non Int. Exp.	18,746	14,281	15,530	12,052	5,917	4,280	3,791	3,553	3,063	2,791
Exp./Op. Revs.	66%	63%	67%	NA	63%	67%	82%	83%	87%	89%
Pretax Inc.	8,526	7,728	5,385	4,274	1,545	1,396	1,215	996	703	556
Eff. Tax Rate	36%	38%	37%	39%	38%	39%	39%	39%	38%	38%
Net Inc.	5,456	4,791	3,393	2,586	951	856	741	604	439	345
% Net Int. Marg.	6.08	8.47	9.00	8.45	8.16	8.47	9.05	8.22	8.27	8.29
Balance Sheet & Other Fin. Data (Million $)										
Money Mkt. Assets	50,992	70,366	90,101	6,890	4,044	3,391	2,828	22.0	2,447	1,800
Inv. Securities	130,818	112,042	41,689	35,801	4,477	5,421	5,215	5,472	4,542	5,060
Tot. Loans	21,870	20,229	22,388	24,499	23,177	21,557	15,608	11,711	9,459	9,525
Total Assets	426,794	366,967	317,590	302,287	42,414	38,208	31,859	27,662	23,822	22,751
Demand Deposits	1,589	1,458	1,355	1,210	1,716	1,552	1,166	1,157	1,362	1,264
Time Deposits	10,341	8,939	6,842	7,783	5,497	4,639	4,043	3,731	3,495	3,811
LT Debt	36,830	28,604	27,435	18,627	8,144	6,732	5,293	3,140	Nil	1,039
Common Eqty.	18,796	16,344	13,445	14,079	5,165	4,834	4,108	3,477	2,673	2,096
% Ret. on Assets	1.4	1.4	NA	1.5	2.4	2.4	2.5	2.3	1.8	1.6
% Ret. on Equity	30.3	30.3	25.2	26.2	19.0	19.2	19.5	19.6	17.6	17.5
% Loan Loss Resv.	3.6	3.7	NA	NA	3.5	3.3	3.5	3.5	3.4	3.5
% Loans/Deposits	183.3	229.2	272.8	294.2	322.4	348.2	300.0	240.0	195.0	188.0
% Loans/Assets	5.4	6.2	7.5	13.8	53.6	53.9	49.0	42.3	39.7	41.9
% Equity to Assets	4.5	4.4	4.3	5.6	12.4	12.8	12.9	12.6	11.2	9.2

Data as orig. reptd. in annual tables for Dean Witter, Discover & Co.; bef. results of disc. opers. and/or spec. items. Per share data adj. for stk. divs. as of ex-div. date. Prior to 1997, fis. yrs. ended Dec. 31.Bold denotes diluted EPS (FASB 128). E-Estimated. NA-Not Available. NM-Not Meaningful. NR-Not Ranked.

Office—1585 Broadway, New York, NY 10036. **Tel**—(212) 761-4000. **Website**—http://www.morganstanley.com **Chrmn & CEO**—P. J. Purcell. **Pres & COO**—R. G. Scott. **EVP & CFO**—S. S. Crawford. **EVP & Chief Legal Officer**—D. G. Kempf. **Investor Contact**—William Pike (212-761-0008). **Dirs**—R. P. Bauman, E. A. Brennan, C. R. Kidder, C. F. Knight, J. J. Mack, J. W. Madigan, M. L. Marsh, M. A. Miles, P. J. Purcell, C. B. Rogers Jr., L. D. Tyson. **Transfer Agent & Registrar**—Morgan Stanley Trust FSB, Jersey City, NJ. **Incorporated**—in Delaware in 1981. **Empl**— 62,679. **S&P Analyst:** Michael Schneider, CFA

STANDARD
&POOR'S
STOCK REPORTS

Providian Financial

NYSE Symbol **PVN**

In S&P 500

18-AUG-01

Industry:
Consumer Finance

Summary: This diversified consumer lender offers a broad range of lending products, including credit cards, revolving lines of credit and home equity loans.

S&P Opinion: Accumulate (★★★★)

Recent Price • 45.09
52 Wk Range • 67-39.71

Yield • 0.3%
12-Mo. P/E • 15.1

Quantitative Evaluations

Outlook
(1 Lowest—5 Highest)
• **3**

Fair Value
• **48.40**

Risk
• **NA**

Earn./Div. Rank
• **NR**

Technical Eval.
• **Bearish** since 7/01

Rel. Strength Rank
(1 Lowest—99 Highest)
• **24**

Insider Activity
• **Neutral**

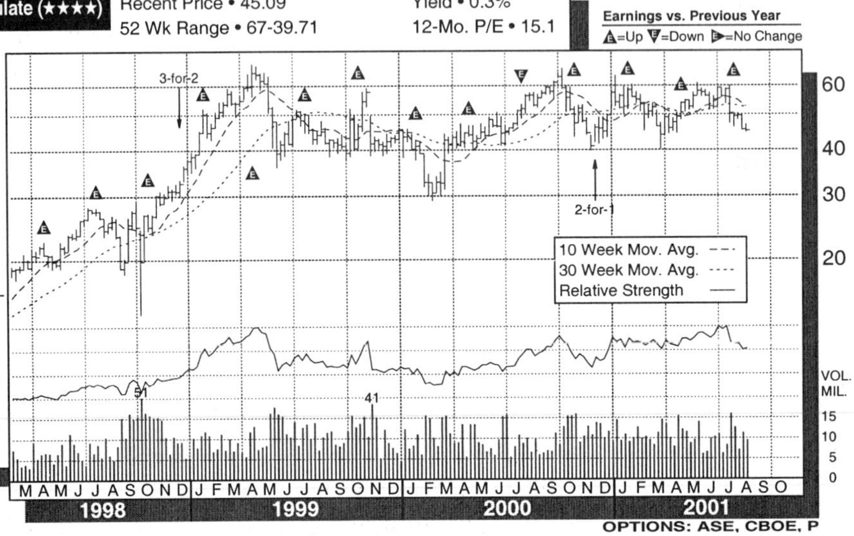

OPTIONS: ASE, CBOE, P

Overview - 25-JUL-01

Managed credit card loans climbed 42% in 2000, to $27 billion. We expect managed credit card loans to advance 32% in 2001, as the company's proven marketing strategies, particularly in the unbanked credit card segment, result in solid account expansion. We expect PVN to add 3 million net new accounts this year. The net interest margin, which widened sharply on a sequential basis in the second quarter, should stabilize as the year progresses. We expect PVN's efficiency ratio to improve this year, driven by a higher base of earning assets and disciplined expense growth. Credit quality has deteriorated so far this year, due to the slowing economy, increased bankruptcies, and seasoning in some product portfolios. We anticipate net credit losses this year of nearly 10%, compared to net credit losses last year of 7.7%. We expect EPS to advance nearly 21% in 2001, to $3.30, from the $2.73 operating EPS of 2000.

Valuation - 25-JUL-01

We expect the shares to outperform the S&P 500 over the next six to 12 months. EPS should climb more than 20% annually over the next three to five years, driven by ongoing product development, strong account growth, a focus on efficiency and asset quality, and healthy net interest margins. The shares were recently trading at a significant discount to PVN's expected long-term EPS growth rate, and to the S&P 500, based on our 2001 EPS projections. With above average earnings growth prospects, and the potential for some P/E multiple expansion, the stock has strong appeal. Last year, PVN resolved certain class action lawsuits and inquiries by state and local governments regarding some of its more aggressive business practices. With these issues seemingly out of the way, PVN will now be able to focus completely on its business plan.

Key Stock Statistics

S&P EPS Est. 2001	3.30	Tang. Bk. Value/Share	7.11
P/E on S&P Est. 2001	13.7	Beta	NA
S&P EPS Est. 2002	4.10	Shareholders	9,358
Dividend Rate/Share	0.12	Market cap. (B)	$ 12.9
Shs. outstg. (M)	285.5	Inst. holdings	84%
Avg. daily vol. (M)	2.000		

Value of $10,000 invested 5 years ago: NA

Fiscal Year Ending Dec. 31

	2001	2000	1999	1998	1997	1996
Revenues (Million $)						
1Q	1,606	1,355	768.9	387.3	280.3	—
2Q	1,621	1,477	944.4	472.2	274.8	—
3Q	—	1,441	1,090	575.5	322.1	—
4Q	—	1,674	1,233	673.7	335.1	—
Yr.	—	5,948	4,037	2,109	1,217	1,008
Earnings Per Share ($)						
1Q	**0.78**	**0.60**	**0.39**	**0.19**	**0.15**	—
2Q	**0.79**	**0.21**	**0.43**	**0.22**	**0.16**	—
3Q	**E0.85**	**0.68**	**0.52**	**0.28**	**0.17**	—
4Q	**E0.89**	**0.73**	**0.55**	**0.33**	**0.19**	—
Yr.	**E3.30**	**2.23**	**1.90**	**1.02**	**0.67**	**0.54**

Next earnings report expected: mid October

Dividend Data (Dividends have been paid since 1997.)

Amount ($)	Date Decl.	Ex-Div. Date	Stock of Record	Payment Date
2-for-1	Oct. 19	Dec. 01	Nov. 15	Nov. 30 '00
0.030	Feb. 14	Feb. 27	Mar. 01	Mar. 15 '01
0.030	May. 09	May. 30	Jun. 01	Jun. 15 '01
0.030	Aug. 08	Aug. 29	Sep. 03	Sep. 17 '01

Providian Financial Corporation

Business Summary - 25-JUL-01

Providian Financial provides lending and deposit products to customers in the United States and the United Kingdom, and offers credit cards in Argentina. PVN was a wholly owned subsidiary of Providian Corp. until its June 1997 spin-off. At December 31, 2000, managed loans totaled $27.1 billion, compared to $21.0 billion a year earlier. Substantially all managed loans at year-end 2000 were credit card loans. At year-end 1999, 9% of managed loans were home loans. During 2000, PVN stopped issuing home loans and sold nearly all of its home loan portfolio. Total accounts at December 31, 2000, amounted to 16.3 million, up from 12.4 million a year earlier.

Credit card loans are generated mostly through Visa and MasterCard credit cards. PVN products target a wide range of individuals. Platinum credit card holders may be offered credit lines of $5,000 or more. Gold, classic and secured credit cards are designed to service individuals in the middle market and those who have limited access to credit due to past credit problems or little or no credit history. PVN uses proprietary credit scoring models that it believes enable it to target customers in this market segment who will have lower default rates than the segment average. Credit card products are marketed primarily through direct mail and telemarketing channels, but PVN also uses television and the Internet to market to consumers.

PVN offers a number of cardholder service products to enhance the customers' use of their credit cards. These products generally offer a package of benefits and services the company develops internally or assembles from third party vendors. Some of the benefits offered include health related credit and prescription discounts, auto and other travel related benefits, a shopping and discount service, and a program that offers nonaccrual of interest and deferral of payment on credit card loans payable to the company in case of unemployment, disability or hospitalization.

PVN's global e-commerce business consists of www.aria.com, a credit card website that enables consumers to apply and receive a credit decision online; www.providian.com, which offers certificates of deposit and money market accounts; and getsmart.com, an online marketplace designed to match individual consumers seeking a specific product with lenders offering those products.

An account is deemed delinquent when the minimum payment is not received by the next billing date. Total 30-day or more delinquencies amounted to 7.52% of managed loans in 2000, versus 5.66% in 1999. Net credit losses represent the principal amount of losses from customers who have not paid their existing loan balances, less any recoveries in the current period. In 2000, net credit losses amounted to 7.71% of average managed loans, down from 6.94% in 1999.

Per Share Data ($) (Year Ended Dec. 31)	2000	1999	1998	1997	1996	1995	1994	1993	1992	1991
Tangible Bk. Val.	7.11	4.72	2.86	2.09	1.49	NA	NA	NA	NA	NA
Earnings	2.23	1.89	1.02	0.67	0.54	NA	NA	NA	NA	NA
Dividends	0.13	0.10	0.08	0.03	NA	NA	NA	NA	NA	NA
Payout Ratio	6%	5%	7%	5%	NA	NA	NA	NA	NA	NA
Prices - High	67.00	69.00	37.84	15.60	NA	NA	NA	NA	NA	NA
- Low	29.06	34.75	14.18	9.70	NA	NA	NA	NA	NA	NA
P/E Ratio - High	30	37	37	23	NA	NA	NA	NA	NA	NA
- Low	13	18	14	15	NA	NA	NA	NA	NA	NA
Income Statement Analysis (Million $)										
Net Int. Inc.	1,825	1,175	595	399	408	NA	NA	NA	NA	NA
Tax Equiv. Adj.	NA	NA	NA	NA	NA	NA	NA	NA	NA	NA
Non Int. Inc.	3,248	2,412	1,266	635	412	NA	NA	NA	NA	NA
Loan Loss Prov.	1,515	1,099	546	149	127	NA	NA	NA	NA	NA
Exp./Op. Revs.	49%	74%	44%	55%	53%	NA	NA	NA	NA	NA
Pretax Inc.	1,086	917	491	311	262	NA	NA	NA	NA	NA
Eff. Tax Rate	40%	40%	40%	38%	38%	NA	NA	NA	NA	NA
Net Inc.	652	550	296	191	162	NA	NA	NA	NA	NA
% Net Int. Marg.	11	12	11	NA	NA	NA	NA	NA	NA	NA
Balance Sheet & Other Fin. Data (Million $)										
Money Mkt. Assets	307	1,298	298	115	172	NA	NA	NA	NA	NA
Inv. Securities	2,572	581	434	173	7.2	NA	NA	NA	NA	NA
Com'l Loans	NA	Nil	Nil	Nil	Nil	NA	NA	NA	NA	NA
Other Loans	13,770	11,610	5,741	2,961	2,950	NA	NA	NA	NA	NA
Total Assets	18,055	14,341	7,231	4,449	4,381	NA	NA	NA	NA	NA
Demand Deposits	79.8	63.9	48.2	32.1	28.3	NA	NA	NA	NA	NA
Time Deposits	13,034	10,474	4,624	3,181	3,362	NA	NA	NA	NA	NA
LT Debt	1,113	1,118	560	82.0	165	NA	NA	NA	NA	NA
Common Eqty.	2,032	1,099	803	595	420	NA	NA	NA	NA	NA
% Ret. on Assets	4.0	5.1	5.1	4.4	NA	NA	NA	NA	NA	NA
% Ret. on Equity	38.7	51.5	42.4	35.5	NA	NA	NA	NA	NA	NA
% Loan Loss Resv.	10.5	8.9	7.9	4.9	3.1	NA	NA	NA	NA	NA
% Loans/Deposits	105.0	109.8	122.9	NA	120.9	NA	NA	NA	NA	NA
% Equity to Assets	10.4	9.9	12.0	12.3	NA	NA	NA	NA	NA	NA

Data as orig reptd.; bef. results of disc opers/spec. items. Per share data adj. for stk. divs. Bold denotes diluted EPS (FASB 128)-prior periods restated. E-Estimated. NA-Not Available. NM-Not Meaningful. NR-Not Ranked.

Office—201 Mission St., San Francisco, CA 94105. **Tel**—(415) 543-0404. **Website**—http://www.providian.com **Chrmn, Pres & CEO**—S. J. Mehta. **EVP, CFO & Treas**—D. J. Petrini. **Investor Contact**—Nancy Murphy (415-278-4483). **Dirs**—C. L. Darwall, J. V. Elliot, L. Everingham, J. D. Grissom, F. W. McFarlan, S. J. Mehta, R. M. Owades, L. D. Schaeffer, L. D. Thompson, J. L. Weinberg. **Transfer Agent & Registrar**—First Chicago Trust Co. of New York, Jersey City, NJ. **Incorporated**—in Delaware in 1997. **Empl**— 12,449. **S&P Analyst:** Michael Schneider-CFA

STANDARD &POOR'S
STOCK REPORTS

Stilwell Financial

NYSE Symbol **SV**

In S&P 500

18-AUG-01

Industry: Investment Management

Summary: Through Janus Capital Corp. and other subsidiaries, SV is one of the largest investment management companies in the U.S.

S&P Opinion: Accumulate (★★★★)

Recent Price • 28.26
52 Wk Range • 54.50-23.27
Yield • 0.1%
12-Mo. P/E • 12.4

Quantitative Evaluations

Outlook (1 Lowest—5 Highest)
• **NA**

Fair Value
• **NA**

Risk
• **NA**

Earn./Div. Rank
• **NR**

Technical Eval.
• **NA**

Rel. Strength Rank (1 Lowest—99 Highest)
• **31**

Insider Activity
• **Neutral**

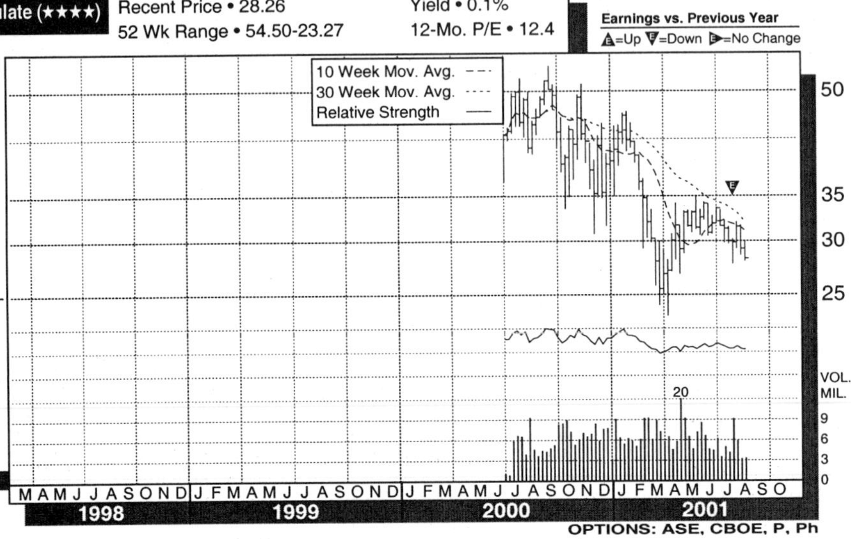

OPTIONS: ASE, CBOE, P, Ph

Overview - 17-AUG-01

The assets under management of SV's subsidiaries are primarily invested in growth-oriented equity securities. Therefore, the revenues and earnings of SV largely reflect the performance of the domestic equity markets. We expect revenues this year to decline about 20%, reflecting a decline in average assets under management. Assets under management at June 30, 2001, totaled $220 billion, down from $313 billion a year earlier. Declines in assets under management reflect the declines in the broader equity markets. Though operating expenses are expected to decline this year, led by lower compensation costs, they are unlikely to completely offset the declines in revenue. Share repurchases should aid EPS comparisons in coming periods. We look for EPS in 2001 of $1.88, compared to the $2.67 of operating EPS posted in 2000.

Valuation - 17-AUG-01

The shares carry an accumulate recommendation, and are expected to outperform the S&P 500 over the next six to 12 months. Though recent declines in the broader equity markets have hurt assets under management and caused the stock to decline, we are optimistic that the shares will rebound in the second half of this year. We think recent and future reductions in the Fed funds rate by the Federal Reserve will drive equity prices higher, causing assets under management, revenues and EPS to rebound in the second half of 2001. In addition, SV is trading at a discount to the broader market and its asset management company peers, which provides it with some downside protection, in our view. We also think that favorable demographic trends, such as the continuing need to save for retirement on the part of the baby boom generation, will fuel growth longer term.

Key Stock Statistics

S&P EPS Est. 2001	1.88	Tang. Bk. Value/Share	3.50
P/E on S&P Est. 2001	15.0	Beta	NA
S&P EPS Est. 2002	2.12	Shareholders	6,000
Dividend Rate/Share	0.04	Market cap. (B)	$ 6.2
Shs. outstg. (M)	219.3	Inst. holdings	74%
Avg. daily vol. (M)	1.087		

Value of $10,000 invested 5 years ago: NA

Fiscal Year Ending Dec. 31

	2001	2000	1999	1998	1997	1996
Revenues (Million $)						
1Q	448.5	—	—	—	—	—
2Q	412.0	563.0	—	—	—	—
3Q	—	609.5	—	—	—	—
4Q	—	530.5	—	—	—	—
Yr.	—	2,248	1,212	671.0	485.0	—
Earnings Per Share ($)						
1Q	**0.48**	—	—	—	—	—
2Q	**0.39**	**0.67**	—	—	—	—
3Q	**E0.49**	**0.73**	—	—	—	—
4Q	**E0.50**	**0.66**	—	—	—	—
Yr.	**E1.88**	**2.90**	**1.31**	—	—	—

Next earnings report expected: late October

Dividend Data (Dividends have been paid since 2000.)

Amount ($)	Date Decl.	Ex-Div. Date	Stock of Record	Payment Date
0.010	Dec. 07	Jan. 01	Jan. 15	Jan. 31 '01
0.010	Apr. 10	Apr. 11	Apr. 16	Apr. 30 '01
0.010	Apr. 10	Apr. 11	Apr. 16	Apr. 30 '01
0.010	May. 10	Jul. 12	Jul. 16	Jul. 31 '01

Business Summary - 17-AUG-01

Stilwell Financial Inc. (SV) was spun off from Kansas City Southern Industries, Inc., in July 2000. SV is a financial services holding company whose subsidiaries include Janus Capital Corporation, Berger LLC and Nelson Money Managers. SV also has a 33% equity investment in DST Systems. The businesses that make up SV's subsidiaries offer a variety of asset management and related financial services to registered investment companies, retail investors, institutions and individuals. Janus is SV's principal subsidiary, accounting for 96% of revenues and 89% of net income, excluding certain one-time gains, in 2000. At December 31, 2000, SV's subsidiaries had assets under management totaling $257.8 billion.

Janus and its adviser subsidiaries are investment advisers registered with the U.S. Securities and Exchange Commission (the SEC) or other regulatory bodies, and are the investment advisers of the Janus Investment Fund, Janus Aspen Series, Janus World Funds Plc and Janus Universal Funds (collectively, the Janus Advised Funds). In addition, Janus is the adviser or sub-adviser to other investment companies and institutional and individual private accounts, including pension, profit-sharing and other employee-benefit plans, trusts, charitable organizations, endowments, foundations and others (collectively, Janus Sub-Advised Funds and Private Accounts). At December 31, 2000, Janus had total assets under management of $248.8 billion, of which $202.5 billion are in the Janus Advised Funds and the remainder are in Janus Sub-Advised Funds and Private Accounts. Janus primarily offers equity portfolios to its investors, which comprised approximately 94% of total assets under management for Janus and its affiliates at December 31, 2000. At that date, funds advised by Janus had approximately 6.0 million shareowner accounts.

Berger, an investment adviser registered with the SEC, serves as an investment adviser to a group of registered investment companies known as the Berger Advised Funds. Berger is also the sub-adviser to a group of registered investment companies and separate accounts known as the Berger Sub-Advised Funds and Private Accounts. Berger also owned an 80% interest in Berger/Bay Isle LLC, which acts as an investment adviser to privately managed separate accounts. At December 31, 2000, Berger had total assets under management of $7.6 billion.

Nelson Money Managers provides investment advice and money management services in the United Kingdom, primarily to individuals who are either retired or contemplating retirement.

DST provides information processing, printing and mailing and computer software services and products to mutual funds, investment managers, communications industries and other service industries.

Per Share Data ($) (Year Ended Dec. 31)	2000	1999	1998	1997	1996	1995	1994	1993	1992	1991
Tangible Bk. Val.	3.50	NA	NA	NA	NA	NA	NA	NA	NA	NA
Cash Flow	3.30	1.51	NA	NA	NA	NA	NA	NA	NA	NA
Earnings	2.90	1.31	NA	NA	NA	NA	NA	NA	NA	NA
Dividends	0.01	NA	NA	NA	NA	NA	NA	NA	NA	NA
Payout Ratio	NM	NA	NA	NA	NA	NA	NA	NA	NA	NA
Prices - High	54.50	NA	NA	NA	NA	NA	NA	NA	NA	NA
- Low	30.75	NA	NA	NA	NA	NA	NA	NA	NA	NA
P/E Ratio - High	19	NA	NA	NA	NA	NA	NA	NA	NA	NA
- Low	11	NA	NA	NA	NA	NA	NA	NA	NA	NA
Income Statement Analysis (Million $)										
Revs.	2,248	1,212	671	485	NA	NA	NA	NA	NA	NA
Oper. Inc.	1,118	554	297	212	NA	NA	NA	NA	NA	NA
Depr.	81.2	35.4	16.8	13.1	NA	NA	NA	NA	NA	NA
Int. Exp.	7.7	5.9	6.5	10.4	NA	NA	NA	NA	NA	NA
Pretax Inc.	1,202	587	289	230	NA	NA	NA	NA	NA	NA
Eff. Tax Rate	36%	37%	36%	38%	NA	NA	NA	NA	NA	NA
Net Inc.	664	313	152	118	NA	NA	NA	NA	NA	NA
Balance Sheet & Other Fin. Data (Million $)										
Cash	364	324	139	NA	NA	NA	NA	NA	NA	NA
Curr. Assets	641	525	259	NA	NA	NA	NA	NA	NA	NA
Total Assets	1,581	1,232	823	NA	NA	NA	NA	NA	NA	NA
Curr. Liab.	196	163	71.1	NA	NA	NA	NA	NA	NA	NA
LT Debt	Nil	Nil	16.6	NA	NA	NA	NA	NA	NA	NA
Common Eqty.	1,058	815	540	NA	NA	NA	NA	NA	NA	NA
Total Cap.	1,342	1,024	710	NA	NA	NA	NA	NA	NA	NA
Cap. Exp.	107	50.5	35.0	NA	NA	NA	NA	NA	NA	NA
Cash Flow	745	348	169	NA	NA	NA	NA	NA	NA	NA
Curr. Ratio	3.3	3.2	3.6	NA	NA	NA	NA	NA	NA	NA
% LT Debt of Cap.	Nil	Nil	2.3	NA	NA	NA	NA	NA	NA	NA
% Net Inc.of Revs.	29.5	25.8	22.7	NA	NA	NA	NA	NA	NA	NA
% Ret. on Assets	47.2	30.5	NA	NA	NA	NA	NA	NA	NA	NA
% Ret. on Equity	70.9	46.2	NA	NA	NA	NA	NA	NA	NA	NA

Data as orig reptd.; bef. results of disc opers/spec. items. Per share data adj. for stk. divs. Bold denotes diluted EPS (FASB 128)-prior periods restated. E-Estimated. NA-Not Available. NM-Not Meaningful. NR-Not Ranked.

Organized—in Delaware in 2000. **Office**—920 Main Street, Kansas City, MO 64105. **Tel**—(816) 218-2400. **Website**—http://www.stilwellfinancial.com **Chrmn, Pres & CEO**—L. H. Rowland. **COO**—J. D. Monello. **Dirs**—J. E. Barnes, P. F. Balser, L. H. Rowland, R. Skidelsky, M. I. Sosland. **Transfer Agent & Registrar**—UMB Bank, Kansas City, MO. **Empl**— 3,472. **S&P Analyst:** R. McMillan

Torchmark Corp.

NYSE Symbol **TMK**

In S&P 500

21-AUG-01

Industry: Insurance (Life & Health)

Summary: This financial services company derives most of its earnings from life and health insurance operations.

S&P Opinion: Accumulate (★★★★) Recent Price • 42.50 52 Wk Range • 42.74-26.31 Yield • 0.8% 12-Mo. P/E • 14.4

Quantitative Evaluations

Outlook (1 Lowest—5 Highest) • **1+**

Fair Value • **38.10**

Risk • **High**

Earn./Div. Rank • **A**

Technical Eval. • **Bullish** since 5/01

Rel. Strength Rank (1 Lowest—99 Highest) • **81**

Insider Activity • **Neutral**

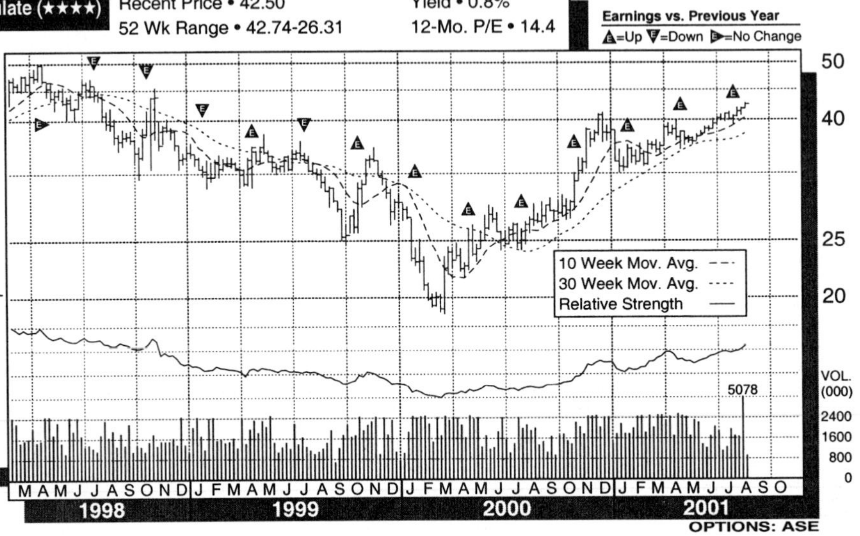

OPTIONS: ASE

Overview - 21-AUG-01

Revenue growth in 2001 could top 15%, if the positive sales trends currently underway continue. Sales of health insurance products increased 31% in 2000, driven by sharply higher sales of Medicare supplement products. Life insurance sales rose 13% in 2000, thanks mainly to a greater contribution from direct response sales. Life insurance margins should be aided by steps taken to enhance agent productivity and increase persistency rates. (Improved policy persistency rates lower policy acquisition costs.) Health insurance margins will remain under pressure from rising claim costs and competitive pressures in the Medicare supplement business. Per share results will be aided by stock buybacks, including the 5.8 million shares repurchased at a cost of $135 million during 2000. Another 1.55 million shares were reacquired at a cost of $54 million in the first half of 2001.

Valuation - 21-AUG-01

The shares of this life/health insurer have strengthened recently, reflecting a general rotation back into the financial sector. This sector rotation is driven by investors seeking a "value oriented" safe haven amid the sell-off in growth/technology stocks. Despite their recent strength, TMK shares still have additional upside, particularly if the recent improvement in margins continues. Though our outlook is tempered a bit by concerns over the potential for some future margin compression in the health insurance area, this is offset by the economies of scale and margin improvement seen in the life insurance segment. Despite their recent strength, TMK shares trade at a discount to their peer group. We believe that a slight expansion from the current P/E multiple is warranted, in light of TMK's improved growth trends.

Key Stock Statistics

S&P EPS Est. 2001	3.12	Tang. Bk. Value/Share	14.34
P/E on S&P Est. 2001	13.6	Beta	0.64
S&P EPS Est. 2002	3.46	Shareholders	5,991
Dividend Rate/Share	0.36	Market cap. (B)	$ 5.3
Shs. outstg. (M)	125.5	Inst. holdings	67%
Avg. daily vol. (M)	0.457		

Value of $10,000 invested 5 years ago: NA

Fiscal Year Ending Dec. 31

	2001	2000	1999	1998	1997	1996
Revenues (Million $)						
1Q	674.8	619.0	567.5	550.0	557.1	550.8
2Q	—	615.1	507.2	556.0	554.2	552.0
3Q	—	640.5	565.8	511.3	584.1	550.4
4Q	—	641.2	586.4	540.5	589.9	552.6
Yr.	—	2,516	2,227	2,158	2,282	2,206
Earnings Per Share ($)						
1Q	**0.79**	**0.68**	**0.61**	**0.55**	**0.55**	**0.53**
2Q	**0.78**	**0.65**	**0.26**	**0.34**	**0.53**	**0.55**
3Q	—	**0.77**	**0.55**	**0.38**	**0.66**	**0.51**
4Q	—	**0.73**	**0.56**	**0.36**	**0.66**	**0.58**
Yr.	—	**2.82**	**1.93**	**1.81**	**2.39**	**2.22**

Next earnings report expected: late October

Dividend Data (Dividends have been paid since 1933.)

Amount ($)	Date Decl.	Ex-Div. Date	Stock of Record	Payment Date
0.090	Oct. 24	Jan. 05	Jan. 09	Feb. 01 '01
0.090	Mar. 08	Apr. 04	Apr. 06	May. 01 '01
0.090	Apr. 27	Jul. 03	Jul. 06	Aug. 01 '01
0.090	Jul. 26	Oct. 03	Oct. 05	Nov. 01 '01

Torchmark Corporation

Business Summary - 21-AUG-01

Torchmark's principal operating subsidiaries are Liberty National Life Insurance Co., Globe Life and Accident Insurance Co., United American Insurance Co., American Income Life Insurance Co., United Investors Life Insurance Co., and American Income Life Insurance Co. The subsidiaries are licensed to sell insurance in all 50 states, the District of Columbia, Puerto Rico, Guam, the Virgin Islands, New Zealand and Canada. Distribution is through direct solicitation, independent agents and exclusive agents.

TMK's subsidiaries offer a full line of nonparticipating ordinary individual life products and health insurance (primarily Medicare supplemental coverage). Fixed and variable annuities are also offered. During 2000, life insurance premiums accounted for 43% of total operating revenues premiums (versus 44% in 1999); health insurance premiums 36% (35% in 1999); other premiums 2% (2%); and investment and other income 19% (19% in 1999).

Annualized life and health insurance premiums in force at year-end 2000 exceeded $2.2 billion, of which Medicare supplemental accounted for 33%, traditional whole life 30%, term life 17%, interest-sensitive life 7%, cancer 8%, and other life and health policies 6%. Annuity deposits at year-end 2000 were more than $4.2 billion, of which 16% were fixed and 84% variable.

During 2000 annualized life insurance premium issued totaled $290.7 million (up 13% from $257.2 million in 1999), of which 39% was distributed via direct response channels, 39% through the exclusive agent channel, and 22% via independent agents. Health insurance premiums issued during 2000 totaled $252.5 million (up 31% from $192.8 million in 1999). Exclusive agents accounted for 65% of this volume, while independent agents accounted for 34% and direct response channels for 1%.

As part of a long term plan to enhance shareholder value and narrow its scope of focus, in early 1998, Torchmark (TMK) sold 36% of Waddell & Reed (W&R), its mutual fund/asset management unit, in an initial public offering. TMK shareholders then received the remaining 64% of W&R in a tax-free spinoff completed in November 1998. TMK shareholders received three W&R shares for every 10 TMK shares held. The spinoff reduced TMK shareholders' equity by about $174 million. TMK's share of W&R's earnings equaled $48 million during 1998. As a result of the spinoff, TMK incurred $54 million of expenses, mostly federal income taxes. The Waddell & Reed sales force continues to market TMK products under a general agents' contract.

Per Share Data ($) (Year Ended Dec. 31)	2000	1999	1998	1997	1996	1995	1994	1993	1992	1991
Tangible Bk. Val.	14.34	12.05	13.48	10.05	7.81	7.21	4.70	8.38	7.24	6.74
Oper. Earnings	2.85	2.45	2.29	NA	2.21	1.97	1.91	1.84	1.79	1.55
Earnings	2.82	1.93	1.81	2.56	2.23	1.90	1.86	1.88	1.79	1.56
Dividends	0.36	0.36	0.58	0.59	0.58	0.56	0.56	0.54	0.53	0.50
Payout Ratio	13%	19%	32%	23%	26%	30%	30%	29%	30%	32%
Prices - High	41.18	38.00	49.81	42.81	26.06	22.62	24.75	32.37	29.18	19.75
- Low	18.75	24.56	31.81	25.00	20.12	17.12	16.18	20.56	18.00	15.43
P/E Ratio - High	15	20	28	17	12	12	13	17	16	13
- Low	7	13	18	10	9	9	9	11	10	10
Income Statement Analysis (Million $)										
Life Ins. In Force	108,319	101,846	96,339	91,870	86,948	80,391	74,835	61,367	58,306	56,111
Prem. Inc.: Life	2,046	1,018	960	910	855	772	602	556	544	524
Prem. Inc.: A & H	NA	825	760	739	733	751	768	800	798	770
Net Invest. Inc.	472	447	460	434	405	382	330	372	383	364
Total Revs.	2,516	2,220	2,158	1,849	2,206	2,067	1,923	2,177	2,046	1,932
Pretax Inc.	553	393	410	516	495	428	387	441	418	381
Net Oper. Inc.	365	328	324	336	316	281	275	272	266	243
Net Inc.	362	259	256	338	319	272	269	280	265	246
Balance Sheet & Other Fin. Data (Million $)										
Cash & Equiv.	154	127	104	126	110	95.2	70.0	110	68.9	63.9
Premiums Due	75.0	53.5	130	127	112	122	224	153	131	95.0
Invest. Assets: Bonds	5,950	5,680	5,768	5,860	5,328	5,210	4,505	4,762	4,193	3,889
Invest. Assets: Stocks	0.5	29.0	10.0	12.0	8.9	10.6	32.0	41.0	54.0	38.0
Invest. Assets: Loans	374	245	358	301	271	246	202	154	152	151
Invest. Assets: Total	6,471	6,399	6,413	6,538	5,940	5,779	5,236	5,441	4,926	4,542
Deferred Policy Costs	1,942	1,742	1,503	1,371	1,254	1,121	1,017	902	904	1,028
Total Assets	12,963	12,132	11,249	10,967	9,801	9,364	8,404	7,646	6,770	6,161
Debt	366	372	383	564	792	792	793	792	498	667
Common Eqty.	2,202	1,993	2,260	1,933	1,629	1,589	1,243	1,416	1,115	1,078
% Return On Revs.	14.4	11.7	11.9	18.3	14.4	13.2	14.0	12.8	13.0	12.8
% Ret. on Assets	2.9	2.2	2.3	3.3	3.3	3.1	3.4	3.9	4.1	4.2
% Ret. on Equity	17.2	12.2	12.2	19.0	19.8	19.2	20.2	21.8	23.9	23.8
% Invest. Yield	7.5	6.8	7.1	7.0	6.9	7.1	7.1	7.2	8.1	8.4

Data as orig reptd.; bef. results of disc opers/spec. items. Per share data adj. for stk. divs. Bold denotes diluted EPS (FASB 128)-prior periods restated. E-Estimated. NA-Not Available. NM-Not Meaningful. NR-Not Ranked.

Office—2001 Third Avenue South, Birmingham, AL 35233. **Tel**—(205) 325-4200. **Website**—www.torchmarkcorp.com **Chrmn & CEO**—C. B. Hudson. **EVP & CFO**—G. L. Coleman. **VP & Investor Contact**—Joyce Lane. **Dirs**—D. L. Boren, J. M. Farley, L. T. Hagopian, C. B. Hudson, J. L. Lanier Jr., M. S. McAndrew, H. T. McCormick, G. J. Records, R. K. Richey, L. Smith. **Transfer Agent & Registrar**—First Chicago Trust Co. of New York, Jersey City, NJ.**Incorporated**—in Alabama in 1929; reincorporated in Delaware in 1979. **Empl**— 4,458. **S&P Analyst:** Catherine A. Seifert

STANDARD
&POOR'S
STOCK REPORTS

Washington Mutual

NYSE Symbol **WM**

In S&P 500

18-AUG-01

Industry: Savings & Loan Companies

Summary: Washington Mutual is the largest U.S. savings institution, with about $229 billion in assets.

S&P Opinion: Accumulate (★★★★)

Recent Price • 42.08
52 Wk Range • 42.99-21.08
Yield • 2.2%
12-Mo. P/E • 14.7

Quantitative Evaluations

Outlook
(1 Lowest—5 Highest)
• **2-**

Fair Value
• **40.90**

Risk
• **Average**

Earn./Div. Rank
• **B+**

Technical Eval.
• **Bullish** since 5/01

Rel. Strength Rank
(1 Lowest—99 Highest)
• **85**

Insider Activity
• **Neutral**

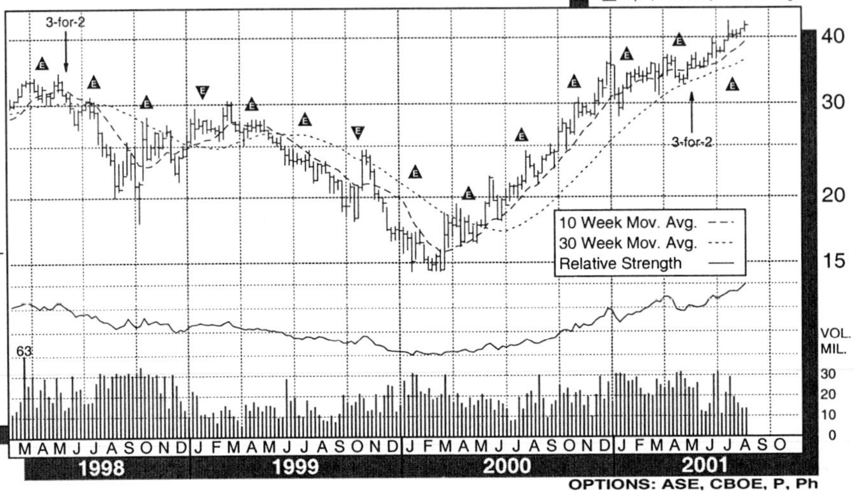

OPTIONS: ASE, CBOE, P, Ph

Overview - 09-AUG-01

Despite higher rates of mortgage prepayment associated with lower interest rates, we project interest earning asset growth in the mid-teens in 2001, fueled by acquisitions completed in the first half. A wider net interest margin will drive an increase of over 50% in net interest income. In the 2001 second quarter, the net interest margin widened to 3.21%, from 2.65% in the first quarter. We expect provisioning to rise significantly, with a slower growing economy and a more bank-like balance sheet. Noninterest income should climb more than 60%, bolstered by higher mortgage banking revenues resulting from refinancing activity. After an improvement in efficiency, we anticipate that EPS will advance 51% in 2001, to $3.56. In 2002, we expect the Dime Bancorp (DME) acquisition to have little overall effect on EPS, which should increase 11%, to $3.95.

Valuation - 09-AUG-01

With its ability to act both as a portfolio lender and as a mortgage banker, Washington Mutual can generate income growth in a variety of interest rate environments, making it one of the most attractive franchises in the S&L industry. Recently announced acquisitions have made WM even more attractive by enhancing its geographic reach and its ability to hedge against interest rate cycles. We also expect the S&L's low-cost Occasio retail financial store concept, which it plans to implement in the attractive New York retail banking market, and its decreasing dependence on spread-based income, to drive future EPS advances. Although the shares were recently trading at 11X our 2001 EPS estimate of $3.56, about average among the company's peers, with targets of return on equity in excess of 20%, and a long-term growth rate higher than that of most S&Ls, the shares remain attractive for accumulation.

Key Stock Statistics

S&P EPS Est. 2001	3.56	Tang. Bk. Value/Share	11.21
P/E on S&P Est. 2001	11.8	Beta	0.72
S&P EPS Est. 2002	3.95	Shareholders	35,207
Dividend Rate/Share	0.92	Market cap. (B)	$ 36.9
Shs. outstg. (M)	877.6	Inst. holdings	75%
Avg. daily vol. (M)	3.082		

Value of $10,000 invested 5 years ago: $ 29,279

Fiscal Year Ending Dec. 31

	2001	2000	1999	1998	1997	1996
Revenues (Million $)						
1Q	4,664	3,727	3,206	2,992	1,804	821.6
2Q	4,741	3,862	3,324	3,172	1,858	834.9
3Q	—	3,996	3,429	3,423	1,840	865.9
4Q	—	4,181	3,612	3,159	2,023	886.1
Yr.	—	15,767	13,571	12,746	7,524	3,409
Earnings Per Share ($)						
1Q	**0.77**	**0.55**	**0.51**	**0.43**	**0.32**	**0.28**
2Q	**0.91**	**0.61**	**0.52**	**0.45**	**0.33**	**0.32**
3Q	—	**0.57**	**0.55**	**0.64**	**-0.24**	**-0.07**
4Q	—	**0.63**	**0.53**	**0.18**	**0.42**	**-0.17**
Yr.	—	**2.36**	**2.11**	**1.71**	**0.83**	**0.36**

Next earnings report expected: mid October

Dividend Data (Dividends have been paid since 1986.)

Amount ($)	Date Decl.	Ex-Div. Date	Stock of Record	Payment Date
0.300	Oct. 17	Oct. 27	Oct. 31	Nov. 15 '00
0.310	Jan. 16	Jan. 29	Jan. 31	Feb. 15 '01
3-for-2	Apr. 17	May. 16	Apr. 30	May. 15 '01
0.230	Jul. 17	Jul. 27	Jul. 31	Aug. 15 '01

A Division of The **McGraw·Hill** *Companies*

Washington Mutual, Inc.

Business Summary - 09-AUG-01

Washington Mutual aims to become one of the premier U.S. financial services organizations, by delivering exceptional customer service, expanding fee-based businesses, maintaining a high quality balance sheet, improving efficiency, and effectively managing interest rate risk. With assets of $194.7 billion and over 2,000 offices at year-end 2000, WM was the largest U.S. savings institution. The company's subsidiaries provide a wide range of products and services to individuals and small and mid-sized businesses including mortgage banking, consumer and commercial banking, consumer finance, full-service securities brokerage, mutual fund management and property/casualty and life insurance.

At year-end 2000, single-family residential loans accounted for 69% of WM's loan portfolio (71% at year-end 1999), commercial business and real estate loans 17% (17%), consumer loans 9% (7%), and specialty finance loans 6% (4%).

Single-family residential real estate loans basically consist of mortgages extended to homebuyers for the purchase of a 1-4 family house. Both 30-year and 15-year fixed rate mortgages are offered, as are a variety of adjustable rate products. Mortgages can also be issued to refinance an existing debt. Commercial real estate loans are mortgages extended to individuals or corporations to buy or refinance properties such as apartments, office buildings, warehouses, etc. Second mortgages are loans made primarily for debt consolidation purposes to individuals with substantial equity in their home. In the event of a default, a second mortgage has a lower claim than a first mortgage.

Savings products offered include checking accounts, certificates of deposit of various maturities and regular savings accounts. The company is attempting to build up its checking account base as a means to lower its cost of funds and generate fee income. In addition, checking accounts, which are viewed as constituting the primary customer relationship with the bank, can be used to cross-sell other products. Deposits in checking accounts comprised 18% of total deposits at year-end 2000 (17% at year-end 1999), savings accounts and money market deposit accounts 39% (37%), and time deposit accounts 43% (46%).

In January 2001, WM completed the acquisition of the residential mortgage business of The PNC Financial Services Group, Inc. In February, the company acquired Houston-based Bank United Corp. (BNKU), with assets of $18.3 billion. In June 2001, the company acquired Fleet Mortgage Corp., making WM the nation's largest mortgage lender and servicer. Also in June, WM agreed to acquire Dime Bancorp (DME), with $14 billion in deposits and 123 branches in the New York area. The transaction, valued at $5.2 billion in cash and stock, with an exchange ratio of 1.05 WM shares for each DME share, is expected to close early in the first quarter of 2002, subject to shareholder and regulatory approval.

Per Share Data ($) (Year Ended Dec. 31)	2000	1999	1998	1997	1996	1995	1994	1993	1992	1991
Tangible Bk. Val.	11.21	9.16	9.37	9.09	7.98	9.60	7.98	7.19	5.36	5.29
Earnings	2.36	2.11	1.71	0.83	0.38	1.19	1.13	1.22	0.97	0.75
Dividends	0.76	0.65	0.55	0.47	0.40	0.34	0.31	0.22	0.15	0.11
Payout Ratio	32%	31%	37%	57%	106%	29%	28%	18%	15%	14%
Prices - High	37.29	30.50	34.44	32.27	20.38	13.11	11.11	12.61	10.00	7.11
- Low	14.41	16.45	17.83	18.77	11.61	7.38	7.00	7.96	5.22	2.29
P/E Ratio - High	16	14	20	39	54	11	10	10	10	10
- Low	6	8	10	23	31	6	6	7	5	3
Income Statement Analysis (Million $)										
Net Int. Inc.	4,311	4,452	4,292	2,656	1,191	578	571	529	295	205
Loan Loss Prov.	185	167	162	207	202	10.0	20.0	35.0	13.5	20.5
Non Int. Inc.	1,985	1,509	1,524	751	259	107	108	144	88.5	92.9
Non Int. Exp.	3,126	2,910	3,284	2,300	1,025	382	384	369	217	174
Pretax Inc.	2,984	2,884	2,369	901	223	292	275	269	153	103
Eff. Tax Rate	36%	37%	37%	47%	43%	35%	37%	35%	35%	35%
Net Inc.	1,899	1,817	1,487	482	114	191	172	175	100	67.5
% Net Int. Marg.	2.38	2.63	2.88	3.03	2.89	3.05	3.60	4.12	3.97	3.17
Balance Sheet & Other Fin. Data (Million $)										
Total Assets	194,716	186,514	165,493	96,981	44,552	21,633	18,458	15,827	8,980	7,118
Loans	118,612	113,497	108,371	67,140	30,467	12,536	12,555	13,868	8,065	6,302
Deposits	79,574	81,130	85,492	50,986	24,080	10,597	9,778	9,351	5,383	4,802
Capitalization:										
Debt	29,951	28,313	45,198	23,791	7,918	3,936	3,817	2,164	964	498
Equity	10,166	9,053	9,344	5,191	2,398	1,592	1,305	1,190	877	558
Total	40,117	37,366	54,542	29,100	10,316	5,527	5,122	3,359	1,841	1,056
% Ret. on Assets	1.0	1.0	1.0	0.5	0.3	1.0	1.0	1.4	1.2	1.0
% Ret. on Equity	19.8	19.8	20.2	9.3	3.9	11.9	13.7	14.8	13.9	13.1
% Loan Loss Resv.	-0.8	0.9	1.0	1.0	1.2	1.1	1.0	0.8	0.6	0.8
% Risk Based Capital	11.4	11.2	12.1	NA	NA	11.5	14.9	10.6	16.5	14.2
Price Times Book Value:										
Hi	3.3	3.3	3.7	3.9	2.6	1.4	1.4	1.8	1.9	1.3
Low	1.3	1.8	1.9	2.3	1.5	0.8	0.9	1.1	1.0	0.4

Data as orig reptd.; bef. results of disc opers/spec. items. Per share data adj. for stk. divs. Bold denotes diluted EPS (FASB 128)-prior periods restated. E-Estimated. NA-Not Available. NM-Not Meaningful. NR-Not Ranked.

Office—1201 Third Ave., Seattle, WA 98101. **Tel**—(206) 461-2000. **Website**—www.wamu.com **Chrmn, Pres & CEO**—K. K. Killinger. **CFO**—W. A. Longbrake. **Investor Contact**—JoAnn DeGrande (206-461-3186). **Dirs**—D. P. Beighle, D. Bonderman, J. T. Crandall, R. H. Eigsti, J. W. Ellis, A. V. Farrell, S. E. Frank, W. P. Gerberding, E. Hernandez Jr., K. K. Killinger, P. D. Matthews, M. K. Murphy, M. E. Pugh, W. G. Reed Jr., E. A. Sanders, W. D. Schulte, J. H. Stever, W. B. Wood Jr. **Transfer Agent & Registrar**—Mellon Investor Services LLC, Ridgefield, NJ. **Incorporated**—in Washington in 1983. **Empl**— 28,798. **S&P Analyst:** Erik J. Eisenstein

Part Five

Health Care Stocks

STANDARD &POOR'S STOCK REPORTS

AmeriPath Inc.

Nasdaq Symbol **PATH**

18-AUG-01

Industry: Health Care (Specialized Services)

Summary: This leading integrated physician group practice and laboratory management company focuses on the provision of anatomic pathology diagnostic services.

S&P Opinion: Buy (★★★★★)

Recent Price • 33.22 | 52 Wk Range • 37.16-10.25 | Yield • Nil | 12-Mo. P/E • 52.7

Quantitative Evaluations

Outlook (1 Lowest—5 Highest)
• **3-**

Fair Value
• **33.50**

Risk
• **NA**

Earn./Div. Rank
• **NR**

Technical Eval.
• **Bullish** since 6/01

Rel. Strength Rank (1 Lowest—99 Highest)
• **91**

Insider Activity
• **Unfavorable**

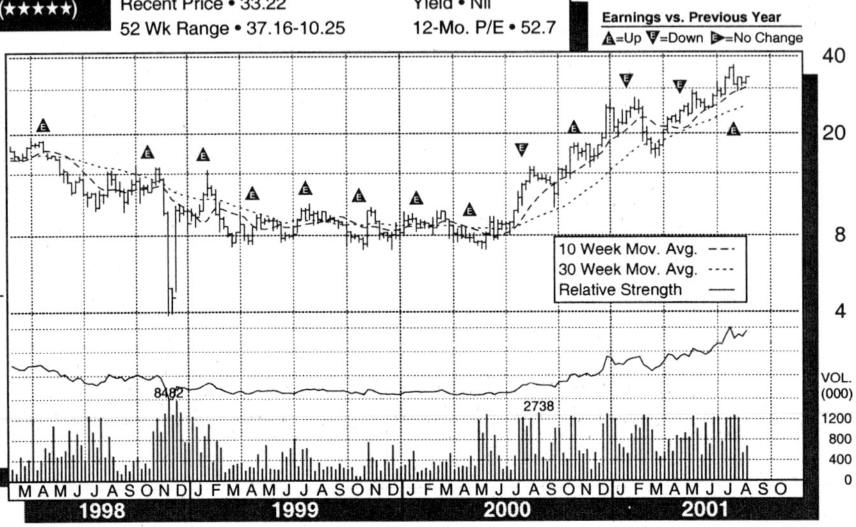

Overview - 01-AUG-01

AmeriPath has grown largely through acquisitions, with revenues rising at an average annual rate of 46% over the past three years. Revenues should rise 29% in 2001, driven by 15% same-practice growth and acquisitions. Same-practice revenues will benefit from increasing dermatopathology, urology and gastroenterology revenues, and from the rollout of advanced testing from PATH's Center for Advanced Diagnostics. Revenues will also benefit from the expansion of acquired practices' geographical reach and operational capability. Margins will be pressured in 2001 by the acquisition of Inform DX, a less profitable practice. However, increased leverage on the cost structure offset the effect in the second quarter. As PATH grows, it will gain economies of scale and scope, and margins should widen. Following a 15% rise in 2000, we see EPS growing 23% in 2001.

Valuation - 01-AUG-01

After more than tripling in 2000, the shares were recently up 20% in 2001, compared to a 13.4% decline in the S&P Health Care Index. We believe the stock possesses recession-resistant characteristics. The domestic market for outpatient and inpatient pathology is approximately $3.2 billion. The American Cancer Society estimates that 13 million Americans have had or still have cancer, and this is likely to increase as the population ages. As a consolidator of a fragmented industry, containing an estimated 3,300 pathology practices operating outpatient laboratories, PATH stands to benefit from economies of scale. In addition, as the study of cells and DNA expands, PATH's extensive inventory of tissue samples and its database of information should prove valuable. With a P/E of 18.7X our EPS estimate for the forward twelve months, the shares are well discounted to peers and 36% below our expectation for 29% growth through the period.

Key Stock Statistics

S&P EPS Est. 2001	1.42	Tang. Bk. Value/Share	NM
P/E on S&P Est. 2001	23.4	Beta	NA
S&P EPS Est. 2002	1.76	Shareholders	222
Dividend Rate/Share	Nil	Market cap. (B)	$0.836
Shs. outstg. (M)	25.2	Inst. holdings	55%
Avg. daily vol. (M)	0.224		

Value of $10,000 invested 5 years ago: NA

Fiscal Year Ending Dec. 31

	2001	2000	1999	1998	1997	1996
Revenues (Million $)						
1Q	98.75	68.17	52.34	37.99	22.06	—
2Q	105.0	73.68	55.41	40.83	23.26	—
3Q	—	74.92	59.87	47.01	27.81	—
4Q	—	87.60	65.15	51.48	35.28	—
Yr.	—	330.1	108.2	177.3	108.4	42.56
Earnings Per Share ($)						
1Q	**0.12**	**0.28**	**0.24**	**0.19**	**0.12**	—
2Q	**0.35**	**0.13**	**0.26**	**0.22**	—	—
3Q	—	**0.32**	**0.27**	**0.23**	**0.08**	—
4Q	—	**-0.13**	**0.28**	**0.25**	**0.18**	—
Yr.	—	**0.47**	**1.05**	**0.89**	**0.53**	**0.22**

Next earnings report expected: NA

Dividend Data

No dividends have been paid.

Business Summary - 01-AUG-01

If you have had a skin, prostate or other type of biopsy excised, or a pap smear taken, chances are it was examined and diagnosed by an AmeriPath pathologist. AmeriPath, Inc. is the leading integrated physician group practice and laboratory management company in the U.S. focused on providing anatomic pathology, cancer diagnostic, genomics, and health care information services.

Pathologists are medical doctors who specialize in the science of pathology, or the study of disease. The 425 pathologists employed by the company provide medical diagnostic services in outpatient laboratories owned and operated by the company, and in hospitals and outpatient ambulatory surgery centers.

The company's pathologists serve a large addressable market. Based on a study prepared for PATH in 1995, the company believes the domestic market for non-hospital outpatient pathology services to be approximately $2.1 billion, and the market for inpatient pathology services in hospitals with 400 or fewer beds at roughly $1.1 billion. The American Cancer Society estimates that approximately 13 million Americans alive today have had, or still have, a form of cancer.

Since its inception, PATH has grown largely through acquisition, having acquired or affiliated with 49 physician practices located in 21 states. In 2000, PATH acquired eight practices in 14 states, including eight new states. The anatomic pathology industry is highly fragmented, with the majority of services being provided by relatively small practices. The company estimates that there are over 3,300 practices operating outpatient laboratories in the U.S.

PATH adds value to practices by spurring internal growth through its professional sales and marketing program. The program is designed to: increase relationships with physicians over a broader geographic region; expand contracts with national clinical laboratories that subcontract for anatomic pathology services; and capitalize on existing managed care relationships. The company believes its regional business model offers national clinical laboratories and managed care organizations a convenient single source for anatomic pathology services.

AmeriPath believes its focus on anatomic pathology provides it with a competitive advantage in the management of such practices, by furnishing its pathologists with an internal network for consultations and by offering specialized services and testing to their clients. The company's Center for Advanced Diagnostics (CAD) focuses on the detection and diagnosis of cancers by employing a full array of diagnostics including molecular genetics, flow cytometry, cytogenetics, specialized immunohistochemistry, and minimal residual disease detection. With diagnostic sciences advancing to the tiny universe of cells and DNA, the company plans to use its vast database of statistical information and store of physical samples to add further value by performing developmental work for diagnostic manufacturers, clinic al research organizations and pharmaceutical companies.

Per Share Data ($) (Year Ended Dec. 31)	2000	1999	1998	1997	1996	1995	1994	1993	1992	1991
Tangible Bk. Val.	NM	NM	NM	NM	NM	NM	NA	NA	NA	NA
Cash Flow	1.42	1.77	1.44	0.75	1.13	1.47	NA	NA	NA	NA
Earnings	0.47	1.05	0.89	0.53	0.22	0.13	NA	NA	NA	NA
Dividends	Nil	Nil	Nil	Nil	Nil	Nil	NA	NA	NA	NA
Payout Ratio	Nil	Nil	Nil	Nil	Nil	Nil	NA	NA	NA	NA
Prices - High	27.12	14.50	19.12	20.25	NA	NA	NA	NA	NA	NA
- Low	7.00	7.00	3.87	15.62	NA	NA	NA	NA	NA	NA
P/E Ratio - High	58	14	21	38	NA	NA	NA	NA	NA	NA
- Low	15	7	4	29	NA	NA	NA	NA	NA	NA
Income Statement Analysis (Million $)										
Revs.	330	233	177	108	42.6	16.0	NA	NA	NA	NA
Oper. Inc.	79.4	65.0	53.0	30.6	11.3	4.2	NA	NA	NA	NA
Depr.	21.3	15.7	12.1	7.6	2.8	1.2	NA	NA	NA	NA
Int. Exp.	15.4	9.3	8.2	8.8	3.5	1.5	NA	NA	NA	NA
Pretax Inc.	27.2	40.1	32.8	12.8	3.6	1.5	NA	NA	NA	NA
Eff. Tax Rate	52%	43%	43%	43%	43%	39%	NA	NA	NA	NA
Net Inc.	13.1	23.0	18.6	7.3	2.0	0.9	NA	NA	NA	NA
Balance Sheet & Other Fin. Data (Million $)										
Cash	2.4	0.6	0.5	0.4	2.3	0.1	NA	NA	NA	NA
Curr. Assets	86.2	54.2	46.0	26.7	18.2	2.5	NA	NA	NA	NA
Total Assets	562	450	362	269	158	20.0	NA	NA	NA	NA
Curr. Liab.	45.9	19.0	17.4	14.6	13.0	1.0	NA	NA	NA	NA
LT Debt	201	164	122	72.4	95.5	15.1	NA	NA	NA	NA
Common Eqty.	238	204	178	145	12.7	-2.2	NA	NA	NA	NA
Total Cap.	503	431	345	217	127	19.0	NA	NA	NA	NA
Cap. Exp.	9.2	8.1	3.6	3.2	1.0	0.5	NA	NA	NA	NA
Cash Flow	34.4	38.7	30.7	13.6	4.8	2.1	NA	NA	NA	NA
Curr. Ratio	1.9	2.8	2.6	1.8	1.4	2.4	NA	NA	NA	NA
% LT Debt of Cap.	39.9	38.1	35.5	33.3	75.4	79.7	NA	NA	NA	NA
% Net Inc.of Revs.	4.0	9.9	10.5	6.8	4.8	5.6	NA	NA	NA	NA
% Ret. on Assets	2.5	5.7	5.9	2.6	1.0	2.8	NA	NA	NA	NA
% Ret. on Equity	5.9	12.0	11.6	4.8	13.0	NM	NA	NA	NA	NA

Data as orig reptd.; bef. results of disc opers/spec. items. Per share data adj. for stk. divs. Bold denotes diluted EPS (FASB 128)-prior periods restated. E-Estimated. NA-Not Available. NM-Not Meaningful. NR-Not Ranked.

Office—7289 Garden Rd., Suite 200, Riviera Beach, FL 33404. **Tel**—(561) 845-1850. **Website**—www.ameripath.com **Chrmn & CEO**—J. C. New. **Pres**—B. C. Carr. **VP, CFO & Secy**—G. A. Marsh. **COO**—A. Levin. **Investor Contact**—Michelle Getty (561-712-6260). **Dirs**—B. C. Carr, M. Gibson, J. C. New, A. Levin, E. R. Stamps IV, C. A. Renschler. **Transfer Agent & Registrar**—American Stock Transfer & Trust Co., NYC. **Incorporated**—In Delaware. **Empl**— 2,325. **S&P Analyst:** Markos N. Kaminis

Andrx Group

Nasdaq Symbol **ADRX**

18-AUG-01

Industry: Health Care (Drugs - Generic & Other)

Summary: Andrx produces generic versions of controlled-release drugs utilizing its proprietary drug delivery technologies. It also distributes generic drugs made by others.

S&P Opinion: Buy (★★★★★)

Recent Price • 64.92
52 Wk Range • 95.87-38.50

Yield • Nil
12-Mo. P/E • 69.8

Quantitative Evaluations

Outlook (1 Lowest—5 Highest)
• **5**

Fair Value
• **102.30**

Risk
• **High**

Earn./Div. Rank
• **NR**

Technical Eval.
• **Bearish** since 8/01

Rel. Strength Rank (1 Lowest—99 Highest)
• **49**

Insider Activity
• **Unfavorable**

OPTIONS: ASE, CBOE, P

Overview - 14-JUN-01

Revenues are projected to grow 15% in 2001. The gains should be fueled by new generic versions of Biovail's Tiazac anti-hypertensive, Schering-Plough's K-Dur potassium supplement, and AstraZeneca's Prilosec antiulcer treatment (subject to FDA approval and resolution of legal hurdles initiated by makers of the branded products). Revenues should also be augmented by higher sales of distributed products, as well as by the recent acquisitions of Armstrong Pharmaceuticals and CTEX Pharmaceuticals. However, margins are likely to remain under pressure from sharp increases in SG&A costs, R&D spending and interest charges. EPS are projected at $1.10. Boosted by new drugs, especially from generic Prilosec, EPS could reach $2.80 in 2002.

Valuation - 14-JUN-01

The shares moved higher in recent months, boosted by strength in the specialty/generic drug sector; ADRX's filing for an extended- release version of Merck's Mevacor cholesterol-lowering drug; and a recent favorable court ruling concerning Prilosec. ADRX is engaged in a major legal battle with AstraZeneca (AZN) over ADRX's planned generic version of AZN's Prilosec antiulcer drug (U.S. sales of $4.2 billion in 2000). In late May 2001, a court ruled in ADRX's favor in the active metabolite Prilosec patent case. While there are still other patent issues yet to be decided, we believe that ADRX will probably prevail in those cases as well, and its generic Prilosec should be launched by late 2001 or early 2002 with 180 days of first-to-file marketing exclusivity. ADRX has has applications for 15 generic drugs under FDA review, with 25 others in varying stages of development. The speculative shares are recommended for superior appreciation.

Key Stock Statistics

S&P EPS Est. 2001	1.30	Tang. Bk. Value/Share	6.62
P/E on S&P Est. 2001	49.9	Beta	0.41
S&P EPS Est. 2002	3.20	Shareholders	30,000
Dividend Rate/Share	Nil	Market cap. (B)	$ 4.5
Shs. outstg. (M)	69.8	Inst. holdings	55%
Avg. daily vol. (M)	1.077		

Value of $10,000 invested 5 years ago: $ 179,089

Fiscal Year Ending Dec. 31

	2001	2000	1999	1998	1997	1996
Revenues (Million $)						
1Q	157.3	—	77.92	50.70	31.06	18.92
2Q	178.4	—	164.6	55.96	32.85	20.41
3Q	—	132.3	111.4	67.27	43.06	23.60
4Q	—	143.7	122.1	73.14	43.82	26.05
Yr.	—	520.0	476.0	247.1	149.7	88.98
Earnings Per Share ($)						
1Q	**0.27**	—	**0.11**	**-0.02**	**-0.03**	**-0.02**
2Q	**0.34**	—	**0.76**	**-0.03**	**-0.04**	**-0.03**
3Q	**E0.34**	**0.22**	**0.28**	**0.08**	**-0.05**	**-0.02**
4Q	**E0.35**	**0.25**	**0.32**	**0.10**	**-0.02**	**-0.02**
Yr.	**E1.30**	**0.95**	**1.45**	**0.13**	**-0.14**	**-0.08**

Next earnings report expected: NA

Dividend Data

The company has never paid any cash dividends on its common stock and does not intend to pay cash dividends for the foreseeable future.

Andrx Group

Business Summary - 14-JUN-01

Andrx Group specializes in the formulation and marketing of controlled-release generic and proprietary oral pharmaceuticals using its own in-house developed drug delivery technologies. The company also distributes generic drugs manufactured by third parties to independent pharmacies, pharmacy chains and others. In September 2000, Andrx Corp. was reorganized into two tracking stocks -- Andrx Group (ADRX), which conducts pharmaceutical businesses; and Cybear, Inc. (CYBA), an information technology company providing Internet-based communications products to the health care industry.

Distributed products accounted for about 63% of total revenues in 2000, manufactured products for 34%, and licensing fees and other income for 3%.

The company has nine proprietary patented or patent pending drug delivery technologies that have the ability to be modified to fit a variety of pharmaceutical products and therapeutic needs. These technologies utilize various polymers and other materials to encapsulate or entrap active drug compounds and release them at varying rates at predetermined locations in the gastrointestinal tract. Drugs incorporating new delivery technologies typically offer advantages such as less frequent dosing, reduced side effects, and improved patient compliance.

The Andrx Pharmaceuticals division currently manufactures and markets four sustained release products -- Cartia XT, a bioequivalent version of Aventis's Cardizem CD drug used to treat hypertension and angina; Diltia XT, a bioequivalent of Aventis's Dilacor XR treatment for hypertension and angina; Pentoxifylline ER, a generic version of Aventis's Trental vasodilator; and Ketoprofen ER, a generic version of American Home Products' Oruvail nonsteroidal anti-inflammatory drug.

Andrx's generic pipeline includes some 15 abbreviated new drug applications for new generics filed with the FDA, which have an aggregate branded sales market estimated at about $11 billion. These include generic versions of Prilosec treatment for gastrointestinal disorders, Tiazac for hypertension and angina, Naprelan anti-inflammatory, Wellbutrin antidepressant, Zyban smoking cessation agent, K-Dur potassium supplement, Claritin D-24 allergy treatment, Depakote epilepsy drug, and Lodine XL treatment for arthritis.

Anda (the company's distribution business) purchases generic drugs directly from manufacturers and wholesalers, and markets them through its in-house telemarketing staff and sales representatives to independent pharmacies and regional pharmacy chains that do not maintain their own central warehousing facilities. Anda offers this customer group competitive pricing, quality products and responsive customer service. Aura Laboratories uses the drug delivery technologies developed by Andrx Pharmaceuticals to develop brand name controlled-release products across a broad spectrum of therapeutic applications.

Per Share Data ($) (Year Ended Dec. 31)	2000	1999	1998	1997	1996	1995	1994	1993	1992	1991
Tangible Bk. Val.	6.62	3.51	1.20	1.02	0.80	0.43	NA	NA	NA	NA
Cash Flow	0.97	1.56	0.19	-0.09	-0.06	-0.10	NA	NA	NA	NA
Earnings	0.95	1.45	0.13	-0.14	-0.08	-0.14	NA	NA	NA	NA
Dividends	Nil	Nil	Nil	Nil	Nil	NA	NA	NA	NA	NA
Payout Ratio	Nil	Nil	Nil	Nil	Nil	NA	NA	NA	NA	NA
Prices - High	95.87	39.00	12.92	11.75	4.40	NA	NA	NA	NA	NA
- Low	20.12	11.12	6.12	3.81	2.75	NA	NA	NA	NA	NA
P/E Ratio - High	NM	27	98	NM	NM	NA	NA	NA	NA	NA
- Low	NM	8	46	NM	NM	NA	NA	NA	NA	NA
Income Statement Analysis (Million $)										
Revs.	520	476	247	150	89.0	53.2	NA	NA	NA	NA
Oper. Inc.	93.7	150	11.2	-5.0	-1.4	-2.1	NA	NA	NA	NA
Depr.	9.6	4.5	3.0	2.0	1.0	0.9	NA	NA	NA	NA
Int. Exp.	0.8	1.7	0.4	0.5	0.8	0.6	NA	NA	NA	NA
Pretax Inc.	94.3	148	8.7	-7.6	-4.0	-5.2	NA	NA	NA	NA
Eff. Tax Rate	42%	38%	3.82%	NM	NM	NM	NA	NA	NA	NA
Net Inc.	58.5	94.1	8.4	-7.6	-4.0	-5.2	NA	NA	NA	NA
Balance Sheet & Other Fin. Data (Million $)										
Cash	116	32.6	17.5	6.6	3.4	13.8	NA	NA	NA	NA
Curr. Assets	561	304	100	75.1	56.8	32.2	NA	NA	NA	NA
Total Assets	668	358	121	90.8	66.6	36.1	NA	NA	NA	NA
Curr. Liab.	108	123	48.6	29.9	23.9	17.8	NA	NA	NA	NA
LT Debt	Nil	Nil	Nil	Nil	Nil	NA	NA	NA	NA	NA
Common Eqty.	560	221	72.6	60.9	42.8	18.3	NA	NA	NA	NA
Total Cap.	560	234	72.6	60.9	42.8	18.3	NA	NA	NA	NA
Cap. Exp.	44.5	22.2	8.0	7.7	6.9	1.5	NA	NA	NA	NA
Cash Flow	68.1	99	11.4	-5.6	-3.0	-4.3	NA	NA	NA	NA
Curr. Ratio	5.2	2.5	2.1	2.5	2.4	1.8	NA	NA	NA	NA
% LT Debt of Cap.	Nil	Nil	Nil	Nil	Nil	NA	NA	NA	NA	NA
% Net Inc.of Revs.	11.3	19.8	3.4	NM	NM	NM	NA	NA	NA	NA
% Ret. on Assets	11.4	39.3	7.9	NM	NM	NM	NA	NA	NA	NA
% Ret. on Equity	15.0	64.1	12.6	NM	NM	NM	NA	NA	NA	NA

Data as orig reptd.; bef. results of disc opers/spec. items. Per share data adj. for stk. divs. Bold denotes diluted EPS (FASB 128)-prior periods restated. E-Estimated. NA-Not Available. NM-Not Meaningful. NR-Not Ranked.

Office—4001 Southwest 47th Avenue, Fort Lauderdale, FL 33314. **Tel**—(954) 584-0300. **Website**—http://www.andrx.com **Co-Chrmn & CEO**—A. P. Cohen. **Co-Chrmn** —C. J. Chen. **Pres**—E. F. Hahn. **Secy**—S. Lodin. **CFO & Investor Contact**—A. C. Malahias. **Dirs**—T. A. Baum, A. P. Cohen, C. J. Chen, L. J. DuBow, I. C. Gerson, E. F. Hahn, M, A. Schwartz. **Transfer Agent & Registrar**—American Stock Transfer & Trust, NYC. **Incorporated**—in Delaware in 1992. **Empl**— 970. **S&P Analyst:** H. B. Saftlas

STANDARD
&POOR'S
STOCK REPORTS

Biovail Corp.

NYSE Symbol **BVF**

18-AUG-01

Industry:
Health Care (Drugs - Generic & Other)

Summary: This company is engaged in formulation, clinical testing, registration, and manufacture of drug products using advanced drug delivery technologies.

S&P Opinion: Buy (★★★★★)

Recent Price • 45.16
52 Wk Range • 48.45-29.03

Yield • Nil
12-Mo. P/E • NM

Quantitative Evaluations

Outlook
(1 Lowest—5 Highest)
• **NA**

Fair Value
• **NA**

Risk
• **Average**

Earn./Div. Rank
• **B**

Technical Eval.
• **Bullish** since 5/01

Rel. Strength Rank
(1 Lowest—99 Highest)
• **78**

Insider Activity
• **NA**

OPTIONS: ASE, CBOE, Ph, ASE, CBOE, P

Overview - 13-AUG-01

Revenues are expected to climb 90% in 2001, to $590 million, largely reflecting the December 2000 purchase of the Cardizem cardiovascular line from Aventis, and the October 2000 acquisition of DJ Pharma (now called Biovail Pharma). Sales of Cardizem antihypertensives should add over $160 million to revenues. Volume will also be boosted by gains for Tiazac anti-hypertensive agent, and higher generic drug sales. Sales in the important Procardia XL and Adalat CC cardiovascular lines will benefit from additional dosage strengths. Top line growth should also be spurred by an enlarged sales force. Royalty and licensing income will also increase, but research and development revenues are expected to decline sharply, reflecting the termination of a research and development agreement with Intelligent Polymers Ltd. EPS are projected at $1.30, with a gain to $1.70 seen for 2002.

Valuation - 13-AUG-01

The shares moved higher in recent months, buoyed by strength in the specialty/generic drug sector, better than expected second quarter earnings, and the company's raised EPS guidance for the 2001 (now projected at $1.25 to $1.33). The R&D pipeline includes 16 products based on BVF's controlled release technologies. The most significant pipeline drug is Cardizem XL, a unique formulation that, when dosed at bedtime, reduces blood pressure in the morning when the risk of heart attack and stroke are highest. Once-daily formulations are also under development for Wellbutrin for attention deficit disorder, Glucophage diabetes treatment, Buspar anti-anxiety, and Ultram for chronic pain. The shares, valued in line with the overall specialty/generic group, are recommended for superior long-term appreciation.

Key Stock Statistics

S&P EPS Est. 2001	1.30	Tang. Bk. Value/Share	NM
P/E on S&P Est. 2001	34.7	Beta	0.65
S&P EPS Est. 2002	1.70	Shareholders	586
Dividend Rate/Share	Nil	Market cap. (B)	$ 5.9
Shs. outstg. (M)	131.5	Inst. holdings	43%
Avg. daily vol. (M)	0.889		

Value of $10,000 invested 5 years ago: $ 72,256

Fiscal Year Ending Dec. 31

	2001	2000	1999	1998	1997	1996
Revenues (Million $)						
1Q	119.2	46.86	28.23	21.89	16.39	16.89
2Q	133.5	60.44	36.16	25.26	18.45	18.30
3Q	—	88.69	45.61	28.99	21.23	17.84
4Q	—	99.8	66.49	36.70	27.31	13.92
Yr.	—	309.2	176.5	112.8	82.38	66.43
Earnings Per Share ($)						
1Q	**0.20**	**0.10**	**0.09**	**0.07**	0.06	0.05
2Q	**0.30**	**0.15**	**0.12**	**0.09**	0.07	0.06
3Q	**E0.35**	**-0.79**	**0.17**	**0.12**	0.09	0.06
4Q	**E0.45**	**-0.18**	**0.21**	**0.14**	**0.13**	0.07
Yr.	**E1.30**	**-0.66**	**0.61**	**0.41**	**0.34**	**0.23**

Next earnings report expected: late October

Dividend Data

Amount ($)	Date Decl.	Ex-Div. Date	Stock of Record	Payment Date
2-for-1	Sep. 28	Oct. 16	Oct. 10	Oct. 13 '00

A Division of The McGraw-Hill Companies

Biovail Corporation

Business Summary - 13-AUG-01

Biovail specializes in the development of pharmaceuticals that incorporate advanced oral controlled release delivery technologies. These drugs generally offer important advantages over conventional branded products in terms of dosing convenience and cost. Products are developed for the branded and generic market segments, and manufactured by the company, or by others under license. Product sales accounted for 73% of total revenues in 2000, research and development revenues for 22%, and royalty and licensing income for 5%.

Controlled release (CR) products are formulations that release active drug compounds in the body gradually and predictably over a 12- to 24-hour period, and that therefore need be taken only once or twice daily. Benefits of controlled release formulations over immediate release drugs include greater effectiveness in the treatment of chronic conditions, reduced side effects, greater convenience, and greater patient compliance.

The company's principal product, Tiazac, which accounted for an estimated 25% of revenues in 2000, belongs to a class of drugs for the treatment of hypertension and angina called calcium channel blockers. Tiazac, a once-daily controlled release formulation of diltiazem, is made by BVF and marketed by its licensees in the U.S. and Europe, and by wholly owned Crystaal Corp. in Canada. In December 2000, BVF purchased the Cardizem cardiovascular line from Aventis, for $410 million. Cardizem, a treatment for hypertension and angina, is expected to add over $160 million to 2001 sales. In October 2000, Biovail acquired DJ Pharma, a marketer of drugs for respiratory, allergy and dermatological conditions, for $213 million in cash and assumed debt.

BVF has developed or is currently developing 16 controlled release products (mostly for off-patent drugs), of which 12 have been licensed to Teva Pharmaceuticals under a 1997 agreement. These drugs include controlled release versions of Trental, Procardia XL, Adalat CC, Verelan, Dilacor, Cardizem CD and Cardizem SR cardiovasculars; and Voltaren anti-inflammatory agent. Under the Teva agreement, BVF manufactures certain drugs, and receives 50% to 60% of the profits, after deducting cost of goods manufactured and an allowance for selling and distribution expenses. The company has also developed and licensed to other drugmakers controlled release versions of other treatments for heart disease, inflammation, respiratory ailments, obesity, and other conditions.

R&D spending totaled $52.7 million in 2000, equal to 17% of total revenues. Key pipeline products include branded Cardizem XL; control release versions of Glucophage anti-diabetes drug, Buspar anti-anxiety, Wellbutrin for attention deficit hyperactivity disorder, and Ultram analgesic; and FlashDose rapid dissolving versions of Paxil antidepressant and Ambien sleeping aid.

Per Share Data ($) (Year Ended Dec. 31)	2000	1999	1998	1997	1996	1995	1994	1993	1992	1991
Tangible Bk. Val.	NM	3.15	0.23	0.65	0.29	0.08	0.05	-0.19	NA	NA
Cash Flow	-0.44	0.71	0.47	0.37	0.24	0.07	0.12	-0.06	NA	NA
Earnings	-0.66	0.61	0.41	0.34	0.23	0.06	0.11	-0.07	NA	NA
Dividends	Nil	Nil	Nil	Nil	Nil	Nil	Nil	Nil	NA	NA
Payout Ratio	Nil	Nil	Nil	Nil	Nil	Nil	Nil	Nil	NA	NA
Prices - High	45.37	23.65	12.37	9.92	10.00	6.45	0.85	NA	NA	NA
- Low	19.12	8.09	5.10	5.09	2.20	0.57	0.35	NA	NA	NA
P/E Ratio - High	NM	39	30	29	43	NM	8	NA	NA	NA
- Low	NM	13	13	15	10	NM	3	NA	NA	NA
Income Statement Analysis (Million $)										
Revs.	309	176	113	82.4	66.4	20.6	17.3	11.1	NA	NA
Oper. Inc.	152	85.7	54.1	40.7	25.6	3.6	3.6	-0.9	NA	NA
Depr.	21.5	10.1	5.0	3.2	2.0	1.3	0.8	0.6	NA	NA
Int. Exp.	Nil	9.2	1.7	0.4	0.6	0.7	0.7	0.8	NA	NA
Pretax Inc.	-75.1	66.7	47.4	37.2	23.9	6.1	9.9	-2.2	NA	NA
Eff. Tax Rate	NM	6.32%	4.27%	5.22%	2.90%	3.30%	4.30%	NM	NA	NA
Net Inc.	-84.4	62.5	45.4	35.2	23.3	5.9	9.4	-3.2	NA	NA
Balance Sheet & Other Fin. Data (Million $)										
Cash	125	178	78.3	8.3	4.5	24.3	2.8	2.9	NA	NA
Curr. Assets	260	340	138	63.0	26.6	34.7	8.7	6.8	NA	NA
Total Assets	1,107	635	200	93.7	58.6	60.8	25.6	23.2	NA	NA
Curr. Liab.	286	74.4	22.5	15.3	17.0	34.0	8.2	4.5	NA	NA
LT Debt	556	125	126	3.0	4.7	8.0	9.8	21.4	NA	NA
Common Eqty.	237	435	51.2	75.5	36.9	14.6	7.7	-8.4	NA	NA
Total Cap.	794	561	177	78.4	41.6	22.6	17.5	18.8	NA	NA
Cap. Exp.	15.8	7.8	3.7	2.7	6.7	2.6	1.2	0.3	NA	NA
Cash Flow	-62.9	72.6	50.4	38.4	25.3	7.2	10.3	-3.0	NA	NA
Curr. Ratio	0.9	4.6	6.1	4.1	1.6	1.0	1.1	1.5	NA	NA
% LT Debt of Cap.	70.1	22.4	71.1	3.8	11.3	35.2	56.0	113.8	NA	NA
% Net Inc.of Revs.	NM	35.4	40.3	42.8	35.1	28.5	54.7	NM	NA	NA
% Ret. on Assets	NM	15.0	30.9	46.3	39.0	13.6	26.5	NA	NA	NA
% Ret. on Equity	NM	25.7	71.7	62.7	90.5	52.7	NM	NA	NA	NA

Data as orig reptd.; bef. results of disc opers/spec. items. Per share data adj. for stk. divs. Bold denotes diluted EPS (FASB 128)-prior periods restated. E-Estimated. NA-Not Available. NM-Not Meaningful. NR-Not Ranked.

Organized—in Ontario in 1994. **Office**—2488 Dunwin Dr., Mississauga, ON, Canada L5L 1J9. **Tel**—(416) 285-6000. **Website**—http://www.biovail.com **Chrmn**—E. N. Melnyk. **CEO**—B. Brydon. **CFO**—B. H. Crombie.**Secy**—K. C. Cancellara. **Dirs**—W. G. Bristow, B. Brydon, P. Haddy, E. N. Melnyk, R. A. Podruzny, R. Reininghaus, R. Rowan, R. Vujea. **Transfer Agents & Registrars**—R-M Trust Co., Toronto; Mellon Securities Trust Co., NYC. **Empl**— 1,200. **S&P Analyst:** Herman Saftlas

STANDARD &POOR'S STOCK REPORTS

Genzyme Corp.-Gen'l Division

Nasdaq Symbol **GENZ**

In S&P MidCap 400

18-AUG-01

Industry: Biotechnology

Summary: This company (formerly Genzyme Corp.) makes therapeutic and diagnostic products, and offers genetic diagnostic services. Its lead product is Cerezyme, a drug for Gaucher disease.

S&P Opinion: Buy (★★★★★)

Recent Price • 52.14
52 Wk Range • 64-28.43

Yield • Nil
12-Mo. P/E • NM

Quantitative Evaluations

Outlook
(1 Lowest—5 Highest)
• **1−**

Fair Value
• **49**

Risk
• **Average**

Earn./Div. Rank
• **B-**

Technical Eval.
• **Bullish** since 8/01

Rel. Strength Rank
(1 Lowest—99 Highest)
• **41**

Insider Activity
• **Neutral**

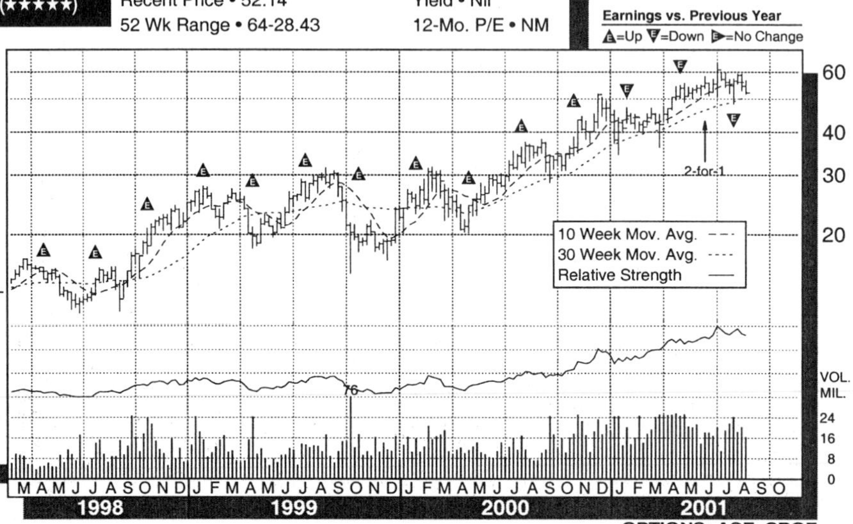

OPTIONS: ASE, CBOE

Overview - 03-AUG-01

In August, GENZ's Fabrazyme and a competing candidate (Replagal) from Transkaryotic received approval in Europe. The products are also under FDA review, although there is uncertainty regarding U.S. approval, as the FDA has requested additional data. We believe GENZ has an edge, due to its established sales infrastructure and experience in selling Cerezyme. Second quarter Renagel sales of $40.4 million were $8 million higher than our projection. Excluding amortization, EPS of $0.30 exceeded our $0.28 estimate. We expect Renagel sales to grow rapidly, on market penetration, the reintroduction of an 800 mg dose, and studies supporting use in its target population. We have increased our 2001 projection for Renagel sales to $165 million, from $133 million. We estimate 2002 sales at $259 million, and 2003 sales at $327 million. Excluding amortization, we estimate 2001 EPS of $1.19, 2002 EPS of $1.47, and 2003 EPS of $1.96.

Valuation - 03-AUG-01

We are maintaining our buy recommendation on GENZ, and expect strong revenue and earnings gains, and positive news. The stock has outperformed the biotech sector since late 2000, and we expect this to continue through 2002. Outperformance should result from fundamental factors, including attractive valuation relative to peer levels, strong growth, good pipeline prospects, and a diverse line of approved products. Renagel will continue to be the main growth driver; we also see strength in diagnostic sales. Fabrazyme and Aldurazyme should support growth in 2002 and 2003, although there is some uncertainty regarding FDA approval for Fabrazyme. Based on our net present value analysis of GENZ's therapeutics, diagnostics, and pipeline, we view the stock as clearly undervalued.

Key Stock Statistics

S&P EPS Est. 2001	1.16	Tang. Bk. Value/Share	2.15
P/E on S&P Est. 2001	44.9	Beta	0.52
S&P EPS Est. 2002	1.47	Shareholders	2,175
Dividend Rate/Share	Nil	Market cap. (B)	$ 10.1
Shs. outstg. (M)	193.7	Inst. holdings	64%
Avg. daily vol. (M)	3.983		

Value of $10,000 invested 5 years ago: NA

Fiscal Year Ending Dec. 31

	2001	2000	1999	1998	1997	1996
Revenues (Million $)						
1Q	278.3	170.6	150.8	154.1	144.6	111.8
2Q	239.0	186.7	154.2	169.0	147.6	114.0
3Q	—	192.2	157.7	167.1	148.8	142.9
4Q	—	203.0	272.9	183.1	156.1	144.7
Yr.	—	752.5	762.9	688.5	597.2	511.4
Earnings Per Share ($)						
1Q	**0.18**	**0.28**	**0.24**	**0.15**	0.14	0.13
2Q	**0.17**	**0.36**	**0.23**	**0.20**	0.15	0.14
3Q	**E0.27**	**0.32**	**0.21**	**0.20**	0.15	-0.05
4Q	**E0.30**	**-0.34**	**0.36**	**0.20**	**0.06**	-0.46
Yr.	**E1.16**	**0.67**	**1.00**	**0.74**	**0.49**	**-0.23**

Next earnings report expected: NA

Dividend Data

Amount ($)	Date Decl.	Ex-Div. Date	Stock of Record	Payment Date
2-for-1	Apr. 25	Jun. 04	May. 24	Jun. 01 '01

Genzyme Corporation-General Division

Business Summary - 03-AUG-01

Genzyme Corp.-General Division is a leading biotechnology company. It develops and markets therapeutic and diagnostic products, and genetic diagnostic services.

GENZ's lead therapeutic product is Cerezyme, a treatment for Gaucher disease. Cerezyme sales totaled $537 million in 2000 (up from $479 million in 1999). An injectable drug, Cerezyme is a recombinant form of the enzyme glucocerbrosidase made in mammalian cell culture. Gaucher disease is a debilitating genetic disease that causes fatigue, anemia and bone erosion. About 2,500 patients worldwide are treated with Ceredase.

In December 2000, the company acquired GelTex Pharmaceuticals in a transaction valued at about $1 billion. GelTex was GENZ's co-marketing partner for Renagel, a drug used to reduce elevated serum phosphorus in patients on kidney dialysis. Sales in 2000 were $56 million ($19.5 million). In addition to Renagel, GENZ acquired WelChol, an LDL cholesterol lowering drug marketed by Sankyo Pharma in the U.S. GENZ has marketing rights outside the U.S.

Thyrogen, to treat thyroid cancer, had sales of $23 million in 2000 ($8.3 million). GENZ also produces active drug substances, intermediates, synthetic phospholipids and other items sold to lie sciences firms. Under an agreement with Biogen, GENZ plans to market Biogen's Avonex treatment for multiple sclerosis in Japan (subject to regulatory approval).

Diagnostic products include diagnostic components (enzymes, substrates, antibodies and antigens); bulk reagents and devices (including test kits for infectious diseases, cholesterol, pregnancy, etc.); and related items. Genetic diagnostic services include prenatal, postnatal and cancer cytogenetics, fluorescence in situ hybridization, flow cytometry and molecular (DNA) analysis. Principal customers include physicians, hospitals and clinical laboratories.

R&D spending totaled $112.8 million in 2000 (15% of operating revenues). Compounds in the pipeline include Fabrazyme (approved in Europe in August 2001, and under FDA review for approval), a treatment for Fabry disease; Aldurazyme (Phase III), to treat MPS-I, a lysosomal storage disorder; an enzyme replacement therapy for Pompe disease, expected to begin Phase III testing in 2001; a treatment for clostridium difficile colitis (Phase II); and DX88 (Phase II) to treat hereditary angiodema. The pipeline also includes diagnostic tests for infectious diseases, diabetes, and cardiovascular conditions.

Genzyme Transgenics (26% owned) is developing transgenic animals that yield human proteins in their milk. In June 1999, Genzyme Surgical Products (GZSP) was spun off to GENZ shareholders. In December 2000, GZSP merged with Biomatrix Inc. and Genzyme Tissue Repair to form Genzyme Biosurgery (GZBX).

In May 2001, GENZ acquired privately held Wyntek Diagnostics Inc., for $65 million in cash, expanding GENZ's presence in the point-of-care diagnostic test market.

Per Share Data ($) (Year Ended Dec. 31)	2000	1999	1998	1997	1996	1995	1994	1993	1992	1991
Tangible Bk. Val.	4.31	3.91	3.89	3.65	3.69	5.04	2.78	3.14	2.88	2.98
Cash Flow	-0.71	0.76	0.74	0.41	-0.31	0.55	0.25	0.05	-0.26	0.19
Earnings	0.68	1.00	0.74	0.49	-0.23	0.36	0.30	-0.06	-0.35	0.13
Dividends	Nil	Nil	0.01	Nil	Nil	Nil	Nil	Nil	Nil	Nil
Payout Ratio	Nil	Nil	1%	Nil	Nil	Nil	Nil	NM	NM	Nil
Prices - High	51.87	31.56	25.00	16.50	19.25	17.51	9.56	11.55	16.60	14.68
- Low	19.84	15.37	11.75	10.37	9.87	6.81	6.00	6.30	8.10	5.84
P/E Ratio - High	77	32	34	34	NM	48	31	NM	NM	NM
- Low	29	15	16	21	NM	19	20	NM	NM	NM
Income Statement Analysis (Million $)										
Revs.	753	772	709	609	519	379	311	270	219	109
Oper. Inc.	-185	193	150	-8.8	-43.7	81.2	58.8	54.9	47.9	11.6
Depr.	41.2	70.7	58.9	10.4	30.0	22.0	13.5	10.9	8.0	5.6
Int. Exp.	14.2	21.8	22.6	1.7	7.0	1.1	10.6	7.2	7.8	1.8
Pretax Inc.	-179	122	98.2	-20.7	-76.0	65.3	29.1	-22.4	-13.2	20.6
Eff. Tax Rate	52%	39%	41%	44%	NM	33%	50%	NM	NM	57%
Net Inc.	-85.9	71.0	62.6	-19.6	-30.5	43.7	16.3	-6.1	-30.8	11.2
Balance Sheet & Other Fin. Data (Million $)										
Cash	136	130	119	15.0	150	209	77.0	58.0	116	107
Curr. Assets	605	730	638	20.9	510	371	207	156	203	159
Total Assets	2,499	1,787	1,691	53.8	1,271	855	658	542	481	391
Curr. Liab.	167	138	223	9.5	114	62.6	103	56.8	36.6	23.3
LT Debt	454	291	287	170	242	124	127	145	105	101
Common Eqty.	1,750	1,356	1,173	13.5	902	659	419	334	323	260
Total Cap.	2,329	1,647	1,460	1,182	1,144	784	548	485	440	366
Cap. Exp.	72.6	57.7	39.5	29.3	63.8	48.7	102	119	61.0	8.0
Cash Flow	-127	142	121	-9.2	-42.6	65.7	29.8	4.8	-22.8	16.8
Curr. Ratio	3.6	5.3	2.9	2.2	4.5	5.9	2.0	2.8	5.5	6.8
% LT Debt of Cap.	19.5	17.6	19.7	14.3	21.2	15.9	23.1	29.8	23.9	27.6
% Net Inc.of Revs.	11.4	9.2	8.8	2.2	NM	11.5	5.2	NM	NM	10.2
% Ret. on Assets	4.0	4.1	4.2	1.1	NM	5.9	2.3	NM	NM	4.1
% Ret. on Equity	5.5	5.6	5.7	1.4	NM	8.3	3.6	NM	NM	5.9

Data as orig reptd.; bef. results of disc opers/spec. items. Per share data adj. for stk. divs. Bold denotes diluted EPS (FASB 128)-prior periods restated. E-Estimated. NA-Not Available. NM-Not Meaningful. NR-Not Ranked.

Office—One Kendall Sq., Cambridge, MA 02139. **Tel**—(617) 252-7500. **Website**—http://www.genzyme.com **Chrmn, Pres & CEO**—H. A. Termeer. **CFO**—M. S. Wyzga. **Investor Contact**—Sally Curley (617-591-7140). **Dirs**—C. E. Anagnostopoulos, D. A. Berthiaume, H. E. Blair, R. J. Carpenter, C. L. Cooney, H. A. Termeer. **Transfer Agent & Registrar**—American Stock Transfer & Trust Co., NYC. **Incorporated**—in Delaware in 1981; reincorporated in Massachusetts in 1991. **Empl**— 4,000. **S&P Analyst:** Frank DiLorenzo

STANDARD
&POOR'S
STOCK REPORTS

HCA Inc.

NYSE Symbol **HCA**

In S&P 500

18-AUG-01

Industry:
Health Care (Hospital Management)

Summary: This company (formerly HCA-The Healthcare Company) owns and operates the largest U.S. chain of acute care hospitals, and some outpatient surgery centers and psychiatric facilities.

S&P Opinion: Buy (★★★★★)

Recent Price • 46.10
52 Wk Range • 47-32.31

Yield • 0.2%
12-Mo. P/E • 32.5

Quantitative Evaluations

Outlook
(1 Lowest—5 Highest)
• 2

Fair Value
• 44.50

Risk
• Average

Earn./Div. Rank
• B

Technical Eval.
• NA

Rel. Strength Rank
(1 Lowest—99 Highest)
• 80

Insider Activity
• Unfavorable

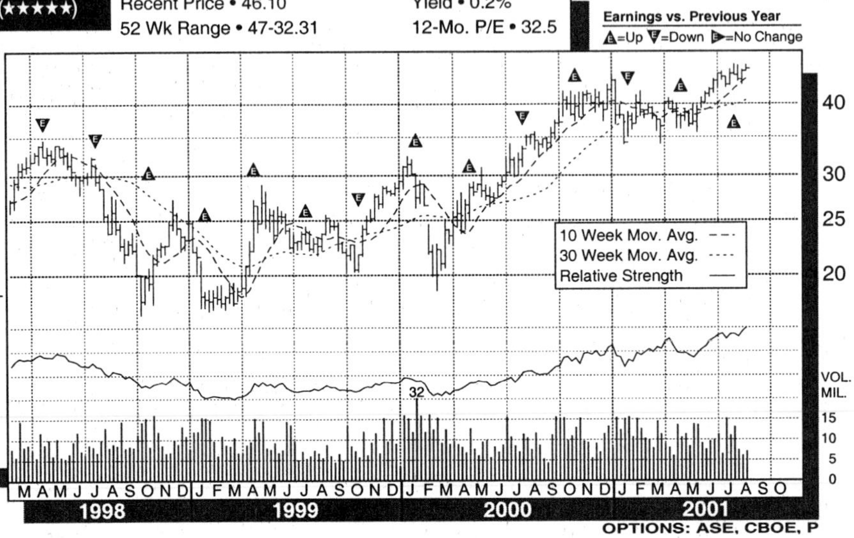

OPTIONS: ASE, CBOE, P

Overview - 23-JUL-01

We see 2001 revenue growth of 7%, as inpatient admissions growth of about 4% to 5% joins with HMO price increases and significantly higher Medicare inpatient reimbursement rates. Management believes that the latest round of Medicare funding increases will boost 2001 Medicare reimbursements by about 2%. Nursing labor costs continue to pose a challenge; salaries and benefits could consume about 40% of revenues in 2001, although productivity gains have limited the negative impact in recent quarters. HCA continues to tightly manage the supply line, and EBITDA margins should widen to 19.5% in 2001, versus 19.1% in 2000. We look for 2001 cash flow to reach $2.2 billion ($4.00 per share). Given the continued strength in both pricing and volume, we recently raised our 2001 operating EPS estimate by $0.13 to $1.95, and our 2002 estimate by $0.15 to $2.25.

Valuation - 23-JUL-01

The company posted exceptional results in the first half of 2001, and we believe the strong operating trends now evident will continue through 2003, reflecting favorable demographics, improved pricing and operating margin expansion. Hospital operators such as HCA have been able to dramatically improve their cash flow generation over the past few years by combining the benefits of rising inpatient admissions, higher patient acuity levels and increased private and Medicare pricing with tightly managed operating cost structures and more aggressive collection efforts. We believe that HCA remains in the early stages of a multi-year upswing in revenue, cash flow and EPS growth, and have upgraded the stock to buy from hold in order to reflect our bullish outlook. Trading at 8.5x our forward sales estimate and 20 times our 2002 EPS forecast, the stock ranks among our least expensive hospital names.

Key Stock Statistics

S&P EPS Est. 2001	1.95	Tang. Bk. Value/Share	4.14
P/E on S&P Est. 2001	23.6	Beta	0.57
S&P EPS Est. 2002	2.25	Shareholders	17,081
Dividend Rate/Share	0.08	Market cap. (B)	$ 23.8
Shs. outstg. (M)	537.5	Inst. holdings	72%
Avg. daily vol. (M)	1.660		

Value of $10,000 invested 5 years ago: NA

Fiscal Year Ending Dec. 31

	2001	2000	1999	1998	1997	1996
Revenues (Million $)						
1Q	4,501	4,271	4,655	4,901	4,988	4,951
2Q	4,476	4,133	4,161	4,781	4,845	4,933
3Q	—	4,093	3,899	4,579	14,445	4,887
4Q	—	4,173	3,942	4,420	4,374	5,138
Yr.	—	16,670	16,657	18,681	18,819	19,909
Earnings Per Share ($)						
1Q	**0.59**	**0.52**	**0.43**	**0.34**	**0.66**	**0.59**
2Q	**0.48**	**-0.49**	**0.31**	**0.27**	**0.58**	**0.54**
3Q	—	**0.31**	**0.24**	**0.25**	**0.15**	**0.44**
4Q	—	**0.04**	**0.16**	**-0.04**	**-1.16**	**0.58**
Yr.	—	**0.39**	**1.11**	**0.82**	**0.27**	**2.15**

Next earnings report expected: late October

Dividend Data (Dividends have been paid since 1993.)

Amount ($)	Date Decl.	Ex-Div. Date	Stock of Record	Payment Date
0.020	Nov. 30	Jan. 30	Feb. 01	Mar. 01 '01
0.020	Jan. 26	Apr. 27	May. 01	Jun. 01 '01
0.020	May. 24	Jul. 30	Aug. 01	Sep. 01 '01
0.020	Jul. 26	Oct. 30	Nov. 01	Dec. 01 '01

A Division of The McGraw-Hill Companies

HCA Inc.

Business Summary - 23-JUL-01

HCA Inc. (formerly HCA-The Healthcare Company; and before that, Columbia/HCA) operates the largest chain of acute care hospitals in the U.S., along with an expansive network of outpatient surgery centers and some psychiatric hospitals. At the end of 2000, HCA owned and/or operated 196 hospitals, including 179 general acute care facilities, eight psychiatric hospitals and nine hospitals included in joint ventures. In addition, HCA operated 78 freestanding surgery centers. The facilities are located in the U.S., England (6) and Switzerland (2).

Most of HCA's acute care hospitals provide a full range of medical and surgical services, including inpatient care, intensive care, cardiac care, diagnostic services and emergency services. They also provide outpatient services such as surgery, laboratory, radiology, respiratory therapy, cardiology and physical therapy.

At the end of 2000, HCA owned 187 hospitals with 41,009 licensed beds (down from 195 and 42,484, respectively, at the end of 1999). On a "same-store" basis to include those facilities in operation for the full year, admissions rose 2.8%, equivalent admissions advanced 2.6%, and revenue per equivalent admission gained 3.6%. The average length of stay held steady at 4.9 days; the occupancy rate climbed to 50.3% from 47.5%; and outpatient revenue as a percentage of total patient revenues was 37.4% versus 38.8%.

HCA's eight psychiatric hospitals, containing 904 licensed beds, provide therapeutic programs including child, adolescent and adult psychiatric care, as well as adult and adolescent alcohol and drug abuse treatment and counseling.

Patient revenues in 2000 were generated from managed care (40%), Medicare (28%), Medicaid (7%) and other (25%) sources.

In May 2000, HCA reached an understanding with the Department of Justice under which it agreed to settle, subject to certain conditions, civil claims against the company concerning DRG (diagnosis related group) coding, outpatient laboratory billing and home health care issues. The understanding includes a payment to the government of $745 million ($498 million after tax), plus 6.5% interest, which began accruing on May 18, 2000. There remain two areas of civil claims still outstanding, along with several criminal charges including allegations that the company intentionally submitted fraudulent bills to Medicare.

In March 2000, directors authorized the buyback of up to $1.0 billion of HCA common stock. Certain financial organizations purchased about 19.4 million HCA shares for $535 million during 2000, utilizing forward purchase contracts. During 2000, HCA settled forward purchase contracts representing approximately 11.7 million shares at a cost to the company of about $300 million. In accordance with terms of the contracts, about 7.7 million shares, at a cost of $235 million, remain outstanding until settled by the company.

Per Share Data ($) (Year Ended Dec. 31)	2000	1999	1998	1997	1996	1995	1994	1993	1992	1991
Tangible Bk. Val.	4.14	5.85	7.26	5.81	7.30	5.43	5.07	4.43	6.83	4.27
Cash Flow	2.20	2.96	2.75	2.14	3.92	3.03	2.58	2.22	1.66	1.35
Earnings	0.39	1.11	0.82	0.27	2.22	1.58	1.42	1.13	0.79	0.61
Dividends	0.08	0.08	0.08	0.07	0.08	0.08	0.06	0.04	Nil	Nil
Payout Ratio	21%	7%	10%	26%	4%	5%	4%	4%	Nil	Nil
Prices - High	45.25	29.43	34.62	44.87	41.87	36.00	30.16	22.58	14.66	12.50
- Low	18.75	17.25	17.00	25.75	31.66	23.58	22.16	10.83	9.16	6.50
P/E Ratio - High	NM	27	42	NM	19	23	21	20	19	20
- Low	NM	16	21	NM	14	15	16	10	12	11
Income Statement Analysis (Million $)										
Revs.	16,670	16,657	18,681	18,819	19,909	17,695	11,132	10,252	807	499
Oper. Inc.	3,051	2,798	2,756	2,783	4,136	3,620	2,214	1,938	115	77.0
Depr.	1,033	1,094	1,247	1,238	1,155	981	609	554	28.7	18.4
Int. Exp.	559	471	561	493	498	460	260	333	49.1	23.9
Pretax Inc.	600	1,284	1,151	538	2,656	1,892	12.6	978	52.5	34.3
Eff. Tax Rate	50%	44%	48%	38%	38%	38%	39%	40%	32%	28%
Net Inc.	219	657	532	182	1,505	1,064	745	575	25.9	15.2
Balance Sheet & Other Fin. Data (Million $)										
Cash	314	190	297	110	113	232	13.0	224	76.1	29.4
Curr. Assets	4,453	3,597	3,863	4,423	4,413	4,200	2,550	2,488	338	166
Total Assets	17,568	16,885	19,429	22,022	21,272	19,892	12,339	10,216	1,072	485
Curr. Liab.	4,141	3,332	3,559	2,773	2,946	2,738	1,767	1,915	203	98.0
LT Debt	5,631	5,284	5,685	9,276	6,781	7,137	3,853	3,335	539	230
Common Eqty.	4,405	5,617	7,581	7,250	8,609	7,129	5,022	3,471	265	118
Total Cap.	10,608	11,664	14,031	17,362	17,490	16,247	9,612	7,420	851	380
Cap. Exp.	1,155	1,287	1,255	1,422	1,400	1,527	975	1,042	344	96.0
Cash Flow	1,252	1,751	1,779	1,420	2,660	2,045	1,354	1,129	54.6	33.6
Curr. Ratio	1.1	1.1	1.1	1.6	1.5	1.5	1.4	1.3	1.7	1.7
% LT Debt of Cap.	53.1	45.3	40.5	53.4	38.8	43.9	40.1	44.9	63.3	60.5
% Net Inc.of Revs.	1.3	3.9	2.8	1.0	7.6	6.0	6.7	5.6	3.2	3.0
% Ret. on Assets	1.3	3.6	2.6	0.8	7.3	5.9	6.4	4.8	3.0	3.4
% Ret. on Equity	4.4	10.0	7.2	2.3	19.0	16.1	17.0	16.6	12.0	17.6

Data as orig. reptd.; bef. results of disc. opers. and/or spec. items. Per share data adj. for stk. divs. as of ex-div. date. E-Estimated. NA-Not Available. NM-Not Meaningful. NR-Not Ranked.

Office—One Park Plaza, Nashville, TN 37203. **Tel**—(615) 344-9551. **Website**—http://www.hcahealthcare.com **Chrmn**—T. F. Frist Jr. **Pres & CEO**—J. O. Bovander Jr. **SVP-Fin & Treas**—D. G. Anderson. **SVP-Contr**—R. M. Johnson. **Investor Contact**—W. Mark Kimbrough (615-344-1199). **Dirs**—M. Averhoff, J. O. Bovander, J. M. Cook, M. Feldstein, T. F. Frist Jr., F. W. Gluck, G. A. Hatchett, T. M. Long, J. H. McArthur, T. S. Murphy, K. C. Nelson, C. E. Reichardt, F. S. Royal. **Transfer Agent & Registrar**—National City Bank, Cleveland. **Incorporated**—in Nevada in 1990. **Empl**— 164,000. **S&P Analyst:** Robert M. Gold

STANDARD &POOR'S
STOCK REPORTS

HEALTHSOUTH Corp.

NYSE Symbol **HRC**

In S&P 500

18-AUG-01

Industry: Health Care (Specialized Services)

Summary: HEALTHSOUTH is the largest U.S. provider of outpatient surgery and rehabilitation services.

S&P Opinion: Buy (★★★★★)

Recent Price • 17.15 | 52 Wk Range • 18-5.62 | Yield • Nil | 12-Mo. P/E • 33.0

Quantitative Evaluations

Outlook (1 Lowest—5 Highest) • **4-**

Fair Value • **20.70**

Risk • **Average**

Earn./Div. Rank • **B**

Technical Eval. • **Bullish** since 6/01

Rel. Strength Rank (1 Lowest—99 Highest) • **87**

Insider Activity • **Neutral**

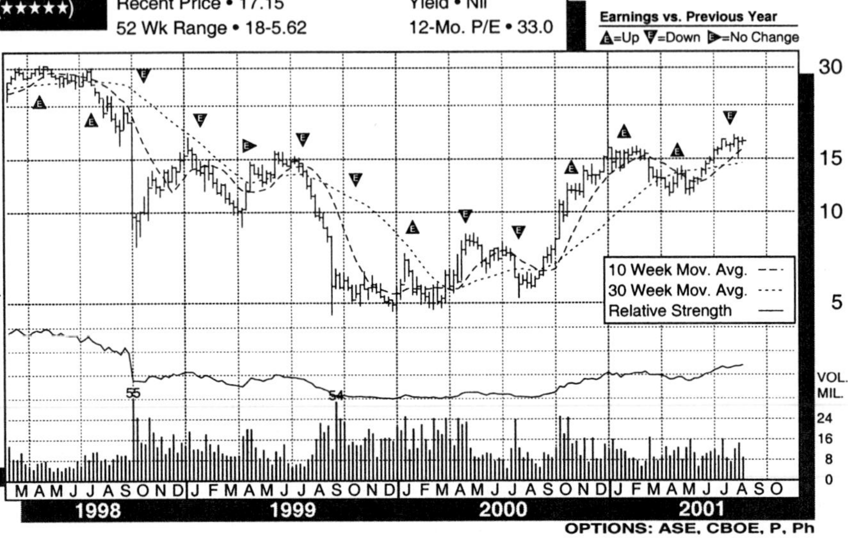

OPTIONS: ASE, CBOE, P, Ph

Overview - 03-AUG-01

Revenue growth of 4% to 5% is expected in 2001, aided by improved commercial pricing, volume growth in the outpatient and inpatient rehabilitation and outpatient surgery areas, and expansion of the diagnostic imaging segment. In the commercial business, rate increases should average 3.5% in 2001. Operating margins should continue to benefit from unit operating cost disciplines, moderating therapist wage inflation, and more aggressive collection efforts; EBITDA margins are seen at 28% to 29%. We assume that the adoption of new Medicare inpatient rehabilitation reimbursement rates will have a positive impact on 2002 results. We currently see 2001 EPS rising 17%, to $0.81, and maintain a conservative 2002 estimate of $0.95, until we have greater visibility on 2002 Medicare rate settings.

Valuation - 03-AUG-01

The stock has risen well above its 2001 lows, aided by investor rotation into the healthcare provider sector, and, more recently, by a solid second quarter earnings report and indications that Medicare is nearing a decision on full implementation of new inpatient rehabilitation rates. The Medicare issue has served to restrict meaningful upside momentum for HRC for several months, and we believe the removal of this overhang will let the stock be valued more in line with the acute care hospital group. On average, we believe Medicare PPS rates for inpatient rehabilitation should be $11,500 per discharge, and there are some indications that rates could range as high as $11,900 per discharge, while Healthsouth's average cost per discharge is $9,600. The new rates could boost annual EPS by over $0.15. The shares are trading at a sizable discount to the levels accorded the hospital group, both on a price-to-EBITDA and P/E basis.

Key Stock Statistics

S&P EPS Est. 2001	0.83	Tang. Bk. Value/Share	2.18
P/E on S&P Est. 2001	20.7	Beta	0.65
S&P EPS Est. 2002	0.95	Shareholders	6,852
Dividend Rate/Share	Nil	Market cap. (B)	$ 6.7
Shs. outstg. (M)	391.3	Inst. holdings	75%
Avg. daily vol. (M)	2.092		

Value of $10,000 invested 5 years ago: $ 10,014

Fiscal Year Ending Dec. 31

	2001	2000	1999	1998	1997	1996
Revenues (Million $)						
1Q	1,090	1,021	1,031	939.0	691.6	581.2
2Q	1,099	1,036	1,048	979.0	723.0	595.6
3Q	—	1,060	993.3	1,047	748.4	616.9
4Q	—	1,077	1,001	1,041	854.3	642.8
Yr.	—	4,195	4,072	4,006	3,017	2,437
Earnings Per Share ($)						
1Q	**0.19**	**0.17**	**0.26**	**0.26**	0.19	0.12
2Q	**-0.05**	**0.17**	**0.27**	**0.28**	0.23	0.18
3Q	**E0.21**	**0.18**	**-0.01**	**0.01**	0.24	0.18
4Q	**E0.22**	**0.19**	**-0.37**	**-0.46**	**0.25**	0.19
Yr.	**E0.83**	**0.71**	**0.18**	**0.11**	**0.91**	**0.55**

Next earnings report expected: late October

Dividend Data

No cash dividends have been paid. A two-for-one stock split was effected in March 1997.

HEALTHSOUTH Corporation

Business Summary - 03-AUG-01

Healthsouth Corp. (HRC) began operations in 1984, with a focus on providing outpatient orthopaedic and musculoskeletal rehabilitation services. Through acquisitions and organic growth, HRC has become the largest U.S. provider of outpatient surgery and rehabilitative health care services, with more than 2,000 locations in 50 states, Puerto Rico, the U.K., Canada and Australia at the end of 2000.

HRC operates the largest group of affiliated proprietary outpatient rehabilitation facilities in the U.S.; at December 31, 2000, it provided outpatient rehabilitative services through about 1,407 locations in all 50 states and the U.K., including freestanding centers, outpatient satellites of inpatient facilities and outpatient facilities managed under contract. These centers offer a range of services including physical and occupational therapy, with a primary focus on orthopedic, sports-related, work-related and hand and spine injuries, and various neurological/neuromuscular conditions.

Healthsouth also operates the largest network of outpatient surgery centers in the U.S., with 222 freestanding surgery centers in 40 states at 2000 year-end. More than 80% of facilities are located in markets served by the company's outpatient and rehabilitative service facilities, allowing HRC to generate significant cross-selling opportunities and to centralize administrative functions. These centers provide the facilities and medical support staff necessary for physicians to perform non-emergency surgical procedures. The typical center has two to six fully equipped operating and procedure rooms and ancillary areas for reception, preparation, recovery and administration. Each of these facilities is available for use only by licensed physicians, oral surgeons, and podiatrists.

The company is the largest operator of outpatient diagnostic centers in the U.S., with 142 centers in 31 states and the U.K. These facilities provide services such as magnetic resonance imaging (MRI), computed tomography (CT), X-ray, ultrasound, mammography, nuclear medicine, and fluoroscopy.

HRC also operates the largest network of affiliated proprietary inpatient rehabilitation facilities in the U.S., with 120 facilities containing 7,696 licensed beds in the continental U.S., plus two rehabilitation hospitals located in Australia and Puerto Rico. These facilities provide medical, nursing, therapy and ancillary services to patients suffering significant physical disabilities due to conditions such as head injury, spinal cord injury, stroke, certain orthopedic problems, and neuromuscular disease.

The company operates five medical centers, with 1,125 licensed beds, in four geographic markets, including one facility managed under contract, providing general and specialty medical and surgical healthcare services emphasizing orthopaedics, sports medicine, and rehabilitation.

Per Share Data ($) (Year Ended Dec. 31)	2000	1999	1998	1997	1996	1995	1994	1993	1992	1991
Tangible Bk. Val.	1.76	0.98	1.10	2.31	1.46	1.03	3.12	2.54	2.52	2.49
Cash Flow	1.64	1.09	0.90	1.59	1.26	0.80	0.85	0.36	0.41	0.32
Earnings	0.71	0.18	0.11	0.91	0.67	0.41	0.35	0.06	0.25	0.21
Dividends	Nil	Nil	Nil	Nil	Nil	Nil	Nil	Nil	Nil	Nil
Payout Ratio	Nil	Nil	Nil	Nil	Nil	Nil	Nil	Nil	Nil	Nil
Prices - High	17.50	17.75	30.81	28.93	19.87	16.18	9.84	6.59	9.31	8.78
- Low	4.75	4.56	7.68	17.75	13.50	8.18	5.84	3.03	3.81	3.65
P/E Ratio - High	25	99	NM	32	30	39	28	NM	37	41
- Low	7	25	NM	20	20	20	17	NM	15	17
Income Statement Analysis (Million $)										
Revs.	4,195	4,072	4,006	3,017	2,437	1,557	1,127	482	407	225
Oper. Inc.	1,133	1,608	1,289	975	730	537	234	107	75.6	50.3
Depr.	361	374	345	250	189	143	75.6	36.5	18.9	10.5
Int. Exp.	222	177	148	112	97.3	102	59.0	15.1	12.8	11.9
Pretax Inc.	559	230	267	602	270	212	87.3	10.9	46.5	35.4
Eff. Tax Rate	33%	29%	54%	34%	34%	36%	39%	37%	33%	33%
Net Inc.	278	76.5	46.6	331	221	92.5	53.2	6.7	29.7	22.4
Balance Sheet & Other Fin. Data (Million $)										
Cash	180	133	143	148	152	156	83.0	62.0	86.0	107
Curr. Assets	1,431	1,271	1,347	1,083	848	704	396	262	213	185
Total Assets	7,380	6,832	6,773	5,401	3,372	2,230	1,552	1,168	642	472
Curr. Liab.	383	418	401	516	304	297	177	90.1	42.4	19.9
LT Debt	3,169	3,077	2,781	1,555	1,451	1,356	930	780	300	164
Common Eqty.	3,526	3,206	3,423	3,157	1,516	1,186	426	295	290	279
Total Cap.	6,993	6,410	6,360	4,883	3,065	2,624	1,362	1,078	599	444
Cap. Exp.	584	474	714	346	173	172	124	111	133	104
Cash Flow	639	451	391	581	410	236	129	43.2	48.7	32.8
Curr. Ratio	3.7	3.0	3.4	2.1	2.8	2.0	2.2	2.9	5.0	9.3
% LT Debt of Cap.	45.3	48.0	43.7	31.9	47.3	51.7	68.3	72.3	50.0	37.0
% Net Inc.of Revs.	6.6	1.9	1.2	11.0	9.1	4.6	4.7	1.4	7.3	9.9
% Ret. on Assets	3.9	1.1	0.8	7.5	7.0	3.6	3.6	0.7	5.3	4.9
% Ret. on Equity	8.3	2.3	1.4	14.1	16.3	9.5	13.8	2.3	10.3	9.6

Data as orig reptd.; bef. results of disc opers/spec. items. Per share data adj. for stk. divs. Bold denotes diluted EPS (FASB 128)-prior periods restated. E-Estimated. NA-Not Available. NM-Not Meaningful. NR-Not Ranked.

Office—One Healthsouth Pkwy., Birmingham, AL 35243. **Tel**—(205) 967-7116. **Website**—http://www.healthsouth.com **Chrmn & CEO**—R. M. Scrushy. **EVP & CFO**—W. T. Owens. **Dirs**—J. C. Chamberlin, C. S. Givens, J. C. Gordon, C. W. Newhall III, W. T. Owens, R. M. Scrushy, L. D. Striplin Jr., G. H. Strong, P. C. Watkins. **Transfer Agent & Registrar**—Mellon Investor Services, Ridgefield Park, NJ. **Incorporated**—in Delaware in 1984. **Empl**— 53,216. **S&P Analyst:** Robert M. Gold

STANDARD & POOR'S STOCK REPORTS

IDEC Pharmaceuticals

Nasdaq Symbol **IDPH**

In S&P MidCap 400

18-AUG-01 **Industry:** Biotechnology

Summary: This biopharmaceutical concern develops targeted therapies to treat cancer and autoimmune diseases.

S&P Opinion: Buy (★★★★★) | Recent Price • 50.31 | 52 Wk Range • 77.64-32.62 | Yield • Nil | 12-Mo. P/E • NM

Quantitative Evaluations

Outlook (1 Lowest—5 Highest)
• **1-**

Fair Value
• **43.40**

Risk
• **High**

Earn./Div. Rank
• **B-**

Technical Eval.
• **Bearish** since 7/01

Rel. Strength Rank (1 Lowest—99 Highest)
• **29**

Insider Activity
• **Unfavorable**

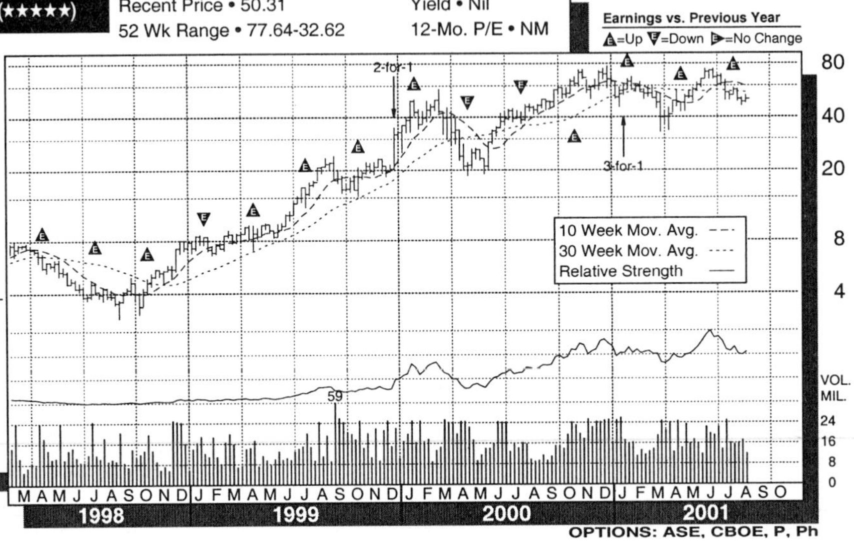

OPTIONS: ASE, CBOE, P, Ph

Overview - 25-JUL-01

In July, IDPH said Zevalin would be reviewed by an FDA advisory committee on September 11. Earlier in 2001, the FDA requested additional data on Zevalin before evaluating it for approval; IDPH submitted supplemental information in July. If Zevalin gains a positive review, we believe it could be approved by late 2001. Zevalin will likely be used with Rituxan to treat late-stage lymphoma patients not responding to current therapies. By the first half of 2002, IDPH may start clinical trials of Rituxan to treat cutaneous lymphocytic leukemia, with a goal of gaining expanded FDA approval for this indication. IDPH reported second quarter U.S. sales of Rituxan of $180 million, $3 million above our estimate. EPS of $0.15 were $0.02 higher than we expected. We project 2002 Zevalin sales of $36 million, with $96 million for 2003. Our projections for U.S. Rituxan sales are $730 million in 2001 and $833 million in 2002. We estimate 2001 EPS at $0.60, with 2002 EPS of $0.79 and 2003 EPS of $1.13.

Valuation - 25-JUL-01

In late July, we upgraded the shares to buy, from accumulate, speculating that Zevalin will receive a positive recommendation in September. In our view, Rituxan will remain the primary growth driver through 2002. If Zevalin is approved, we believe it could drive significant earnings gains in 2002 and 2003, since IDPH will directly market the product, whereas it only receives a percentage of revenues from partner Genentech on Rituxan sales. Sales gains for Rituxan should be fueled by growing off-label use in combination with CHOP chemotherapy, increased maintenance therapy, expanded approval (including bulky disease and additional infusions), and growing off-label use. We believe annual Rituxan sales will exceed $1 billion by 2004. Based on our valuation models, we believe the volatile shares could strongly outpace the market.

Key Stock Statistics

S&P EPS Est. 2001	0.60	Tang. Bk. Value/Share	4.63
P/E on S&P Est. 2001	83.9	Beta	1.42
S&P EPS Est. 2002	0.79	Shareholders	335
Dividend Rate/Share	Nil	Market cap. (B)	$ 7.5
Shs. outstg. (M)	149.2	Inst. holdings	83%
Avg. daily vol. (M)	2.995		

Value of $10,000 invested 5 years ago: $ 151,879

Fiscal Year Ending Dec. 31

	2001	2000	1999	1998	1997	1996
Revenues (Million $)						
1Q	56.54	25.40	20.51	18.13	6.66	9.94
2Q	64.85	37.39	35.29	24.06	5.40	7.07
3Q	—	41.18	30.19	17.01	6.43	2.90
4Q	—	45.84	32.01	27.75	26.11	10.10
Yr.	—	154.7	118.0	86.96	44.61	30.01
Earnings Per Share ($)						
1Q	**0.12**	**0.02**	**0.03**	**0.03**	-0.02	0.02
2Q	**0.15**	**0.09**	**0.13**	**0.07**	-0.10	-0.04
3Q	**E0.16**	**0.10**	**0.07**	**0.01**	-0.09	-0.04
4Q	**E0.17**	**0.12**	**0.05**	**0.04**	**0.06**	0.01
Yr.	**E0.60**	**0.36**	**0.29**	**0.15**	**-0.14**	**-0.06**

Next earnings report expected: mid October

Dividend Data

Amount ($)	Date Decl.	Ex-Div. Date	Stock of Record	Payment Date
3-for-1	Nov. 30	Jan. 18	Dec. 26	Jan. 17 '01

A Division of The McGraw-Hill Companies

IDEC Pharmaceuticals Corporation

Business Summary - 25-JUL-01

IDEC Pharmaceuticals researches, develops and markets therapeutics to treat cancer and autoimmune diseases. It emphasizes full or partial commercialization rights for drugs it develops, positioning it to gain a greater share of income from marketed therapeutics than via royalty-based arrangements.

IDPH's sole commercial drug is Rituxan, a single-agent treatment for relapsed or refractory, low grade or follicular B-cell non-Hodgkin's lymphomas. There are about 275,000 U.S. patients with various forms of this disease. Approved in the U.S. in November 1997, Rituxan is the first monoclonal antibody to receive FDA approval to treat cancer. Rituxan is also used off-label, primarily to treat cutaneous lymphocytic leukemia.

Rituxan is being marketed and sold in the U.S. under a co-promotion agreement with Genentech; IDPH receives joint business revenues on a percentage of sales. F. Hoffman-La Roche has marketing rights (under the name MabThera) outside the U.S., with IDPH receiving a low single-digit royalty on sales. MabThera received marketing approval in the European Union in June 1998 and in Japan in June 2001.

Rituxan is in a Phase III trial to treat intermediate and high-grade lymphoma in combo with CHOP (a chemotherapy regimen consisting of cyclophosphamide, doxorubicin, vincristine and prednisone).

IDPH's next potential product is Zevalin, a radioimmunotherapy for use in combination with Rituxan in a regimen intended for patients with advanced forms of lymphoma who have not adequately responded to standard treatments. In January 2001, the FDA accepted an application for approval (submitted in November 2000). In April, IDPH said the FDA had requested more data to evaluate Zevalin for potential approval. Additional data was submitted in July, with a scheduled review by an FDA advisory committee set for September 11, 2001.

IDPH has exclusive U.S. rights to Zevalin, which will allow the firm to book all sales proceeds from the product. Outside the U.S., Schering AG has exclusive marketing rights, with the company to receive milestone payments and royalties.

In January 2001, IDPH began a Phase II study on IDEC-114 (primatized anti-B7 antibody) to treat psoriasis. IDEC-151 (primatized anti-CD 4 antibody), a treatment for rheumatoid arthritis, began a Phase II study in combination with methotrexate in the third quarter of 2000. IDPH is also developing IDEC-152 (primatized anti-CD23 antibody) to treat allergic asthma, with a Phase I/II trial likely to start in 2001.

Also in January 2001, IDPH began a Phase II trial of IDEC-131 (anti-CD40L antibody) to treat patients with chronic, refractory ITP (immune thrombocytopenic purpura). ITP is a rare blood disorder. IDEC-131 is also in Phase II studies to treat psoriasis. In June 2000, IDPH and Taisho Pharmaceuticals of Japan announced a collaboration to develop therapies to combat macrophage migration inhibitory factor, implicated in some inflammatory and autoimmune diseases.

Per Share Data ($) (Year Ended Dec. 31)	2000	1999	1998	1997	1996	1995	1994	1993	1992	1991
Tangible Bk. Val.	4.63	1.11	0.88	0.53	0.61	0.19	0.34	0.63	0.79	1.01
Cash Flow	0.39	0.31	0.18	-0.10	-0.02	-0.17	-0.24	-0.15	NA	NA
Earnings	0.36	0.29	0.15	-0.14	-0.06	-0.20	-0.28	-0.16	-0.23	-0.15
Dividends	Nil	Nil	Nil	Nil	Nil	Nil	Nil	Nil	NA	NA
Payout Ratio	Nil	Nil	Nil	Nil	Nil	Nil	Nil	Nil	NA	NA
Prices - High	77.64	35.00	8.03	7.70	5.43	3.93	1.12	1.54	3.37	3.54
- Low	18.54	6.60	2.87	2.62	2.31	0.35	0.35	0.62	0.95	1.83
P/E Ratio - High	NM	NM	52	NM	NM	NM	NM	NM	NM	NM
- Low	NM	NM	19	NM	NM	NM	NM	NM	NM	NM
Income Statement Analysis (Million $)										
Revs.	155	118	87.0	44.6	30.0	23.6	7.4	12.7	5.2	5.2
Oper. Inc.	60.6	45.8	23.2	-14.0	-2.8	-2.6	-16.1	-9.6	NA	-7.4
Depr.	4.7	4.4	4.3	4.0	2.6	2.4	2.4	0.7	NA	0.5
Int. Exp.	7.1	6.1	0.6	0.9	2.7	2.3	0.5	0.4	NA	0.1
Pretax Inc.	69.3	45.6	21.9	-15.5	-5.0	-17.3	-18.0	-8.9	-12.7	-5.8
Eff. Tax Rate	17%	5.37%	1.93%	NM	NM	NM	NM	NM	NM	NM
Net Inc.	57.4	43.2	21.5	-15.5	-5.0	-17.3	-18.0	-8.9	-12.7	-5.8
Balance Sheet & Other Fin. Data (Million $)										
Cash	401	61.4	73.5	34.8	25.3	18.8	13.7	9.7	NA	12.0
Curr. Assets	631	279	101	79.2	91.6	27.4	22.6	22.7	NA	41.8
Total Assets	856	307	125	106	114	47.6	45.5	50.7	52.6	58.4
Curr. Liab.	23.0	15.6	14.5	19.4	13.7	8.7	9.4	11.2	NA	1.8
LT Debt	129	123	2.1	2.0	5.0	6.6	7.4	3.6	0.2	NA
Common Eqty.	695	160	106	80.7	66.0	17.1	27.9	35.7	43.8	54.9
Total Cap.	824	283	109	84.4	71.0	23.7	35.3	39.3	43.9	NA
Cap. Exp.	31.4	4.3	1.7	5.9	6.3	1.3	1.6	NA	NA	NA
Cash Flow	62.1	47.5	25.8	-11.5	-2.3	-14.9	-15.6	-8.2	NA	-5.3
Curr. Ratio	27.4	17.8	7.0	4.1	6.7	3.1	2.4	2.0	NA	22.7
% LT Debt of Cap.	15.7	43.4	1.9	2.4	7.0	27.9	20.9	9.2	Nil	NA
% Net Inc.of Revs.	37.1	36.6	24.7	NM	NM	NM	NM	NM	NM	NM
% Ret. on Assets	9.9	20.0	18.6	NM	NM	NM	NM	NM	NM	NM
% Ret. on Equity	13.4	32.4	23.0	NM	NM	NM	NM	NM	NM	NM

Data as orig reptd.; bef. results of disc opers/spec. items. Per share data adj. for stk. divs. Bold denotes diluted EPS (FASB 128)-prior periods restated. E-Estimated. NA-Not Available. NM-Not Meaningful. NR-Not Ranked.

Office—11011 Torreyana Rd., San Diego, CA 92121. **Tel**—(858) 431-8500. **Website**—http://www.idecpharm.com **Chrmn, Pres & CEO**—W. H. Rastetter. **CFO**—P. M. Schneider. **Secy**—K. J. Woolcott. **Investor Contact**—Connie Matsui (858-550-8634). **Dirs**—C. C. Edwards, A. B. Glassberg, K. Hashimoto, F. P. Johnson, R. W. Pangia, W. H. Rastetter, B. R. Ross, L. Schenk, W. D. Young. **Transfer Agent & Registrar**—Mellon Investor Services. **Incorporated**—in Delaware in 1985; reincorporated in Delaware in 1997. **Empl**— 493. **S&P Analyst:** Frank DiLorenzo

STANDARD
&POOR'S
STOCK REPORTS

Immunex Corp.

Nasdaq Symbol **IMNX**

18-AUG-01 **Industry:** Biotechnology

Summary: This biopharmaceutical concern produces therapeutics for the treatment of rheumatoid arthritis, cancer-related conditions, and multiple sclerosis.

S&P Opinion: Buy (★★★★★)

Recent Price • 15.95
52 Wk Range • 51.75-10.75
Yield • Nil
12-Mo. P/E • 53.2

Quantitative Evaluations

Outlook
(1 Lowest—5 Highest)
• **4⁻**

Fair Value
• **17.50**

Risk
• **High**

Earn./Div. Rank
• **B-**

Technical Eval.
• **Neutral** since 8/01

Rel. Strength Rank
(1 Lowest—99 Highest)
• **50**

Insider Activity
• **NA**

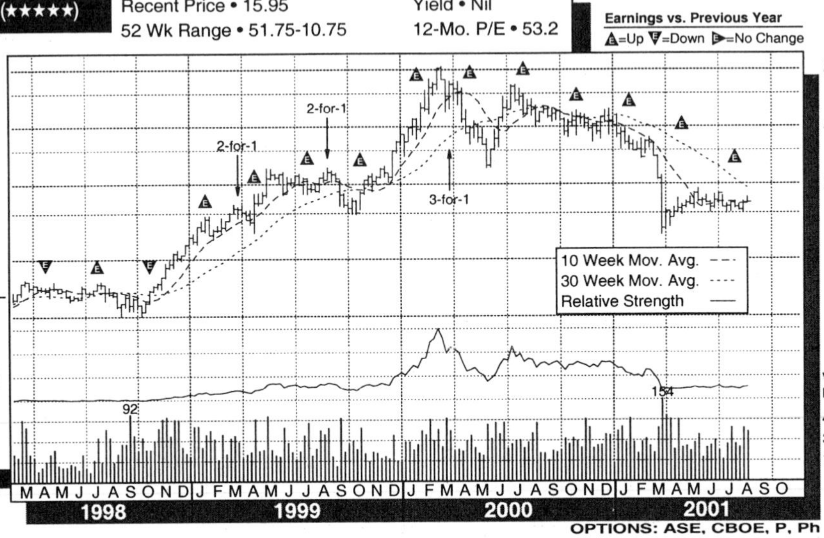

OPTIONS: ASE, CBOE, P, Ph

Overview - 25-JUL-01

Second quarter revenues of $238 million were $6 million above our estimate. Enbrel sales of $183 million were $3 million below our projection. According to IMNX, Enbrel sales should reach $750 million in 2001. We project Enbrel sales of $739 million in 2001 and $1 billion in 2002, assuming a new manufacturing plant in Rhode Island is ready for commercial production by mid-2002. In July, IMNX filed a supplemental application for approval of Enbrel for the treatment of psoriatic arthritis. If IMNX is granted priority review, approval could occur by early 2002. This indication could add about 250,000 patients to Enbrel's target market. We have increased our EPS estimates to $0.31, from $0.26, for 2001, and to $0.37, from $0.35, for 2002. We see a jump to EPS of $0.55 in 2003 as new manufacturing capacity should be fully on-line.

Valuation - 25-JUL-01

IMNX shares have been trending higher since a sharp sell-off in March, which resulted from disappointing trial results for Enbrel to treat CHF and Nuvance for asthma. With bad news behind it, we feel positive developments will occur over the next several months. Enbrel should resume solid growth in 2002 and IMNX could make solid progress on its pipeline over the next year. ABX-EGF recently began Phase II testing to treat kidney cancer and trials in other indications are possible. IMNX should release Phase II data on Enbrel for treating psoriasis by the end of 2001. Positive results would lead to Phase III trials in the first half of 2002. IMNX also plans to start a Phase I trial on IL-1 receptor type II to treat inflammatory conditions. Based on a net present value analysis of IMNX's products and pipeline, plus net cash, we continue to feel IMNX is the cheapest stock in our biotech universe and should outperform the market over the next twelve months.

Key Stock Statistics

S&P EPS Est. 2001	0.31	Tang. Bk. Value/Share	3.34
P/E on S&P Est. 2001	51.5	Beta	1.75
S&P EPS Est. 2002	0.37	Shareholders	1,723
Dividend Rate/Share	Nil	Market cap. (B)	$ 8.6
Shs. outstg. (M)	542.2	Inst. holdings	36%
Avg. daily vol. (M)	6.330		

Value of $10,000 invested 5 years ago: $ 154,666

Fiscal Year Ending Dec. 31

	2001	2000	1999	1998	1997	1996
Revenues (Million $)						
1Q	217.8	179.0	98.18	41.87	39.45	41.75
2Q	228.3	213.2	128.5	64.16	43.01	41.62
3Q	—	219.0	152.4	49.18	55.96	33.36
4Q	—	250.7	162.7	88.25	46.88	34.47
Yr.	—	861.8	541.7	243.4	185.3	151.2
Earnings Per Share ($)						
1Q	**0.07**	**0.06**	Nil	**-0.02**	-0.02	-0.01
2Q	**0.09**	**0.08**	**0.01**	Nil	-0.02	-0.01
3Q	**E0.07**	**0.06**	**0.04**	**-0.01**	0.01	-0.02
4Q	**E0.08**	**0.09**	**0.03**	**0.03**	**-0.01**	-0.06
Yr.	**E0.31**	**0.28**	**0.08**	**0.01**	**-0.03**	**-0.11**

Next earnings report expected: mid October

Dividend Data

Cash dividends have never been paid on the common shares. A shareholder rights plan was adopted in 1991. A distribution of $21 a share was paid in 1993 in connection with the merger with Lederle Oncology.

Immunex Corporation

Business Summary - 25-JUL-01

Immunex is a biotech firm that develops and markets human therapeutics to treat rheumatoid arthritis, cancer, and multiple sclerosis. Its revenues and R&D programs were substantially enlarged through a 1993 combination with Lederle Oncology Corp., a unit of American Cyanamid Co. (now part of American Home Products). American Home owns 41% of IMNX's stock.

The company's principal product is Enbrel, a breakthrough treatment for rheumatoid arthritis (RA) approved by the FDA in November 1998. A soluble tumor necrosis factor receptor fusion protein, Enbrel acts by binding tumor necrosis factor (TNF), one of the dominant cytokines or proteins that plays a key role in the inflammatory process associated with RA. Reflecting a label expansion granted by the FDA in June 2000, Enbrel is currently indicated as a first-line therapy for reducing symptoms and delaying structural damage in patients with moderately to severely active rheumatoid arthritis, including earlier stages of the disease.

At the end of 2000, there were about 70,000 RA patients on Enbrel therapy. Enbrel had sales of $652.4 million in 2000, up from $367 million in 1999. As of mid-2001, IMNX was working on a new manufacturing facility to potentially double Enbrel's capacity, which was limited to about $800 million in annual sales. In March 2001, IMNX announced positive Phase III results for Enbrel to treat psoriatic arthritis, as well as disappointing Phase II/III results for treating congestive heart failure. The company filed for expanded approval to treat psoriatic arthritis with the FDA in July 2001. Enbrel is also in Phase II studies for treating psoriasis.

IMNX's first major product was Leukine. A granulocyte-macrophage colony stimulating factor, Leukine is used to facilitate bone marrow transplant engraftment and to treat bone marrow transplant graft failure. Leukine is also used for acute myelogenous leukemia, allogenic bone marrow transplantation and peripheral blood cell procedures. The drug is also being studied for other conditions in which the stimulation of granulocytes and macrophages may be of benefit.

IMNX's Novantrone is used in combination with corticosteroids to treat pain related to advanced hormone refractory prostate cancer. Novantrone is also indicated in combination with other drugs for the initial treatment of acute nonlymphocytic leukemia in adults. In October 2000, Novantrone received FDA approval as a treatment for worsening forms of multiple sclerosis.

Through a collaboration with Abgenix, IMNX is also developing ABX-EGF, a fully human monoclonal antibody, to treat cancer by blocking the epidermal growth factor receptor. A Phase II trial was initiated in kidney cancer in May 2001. Phase II trials in other cancer indications are possible by early 2002. In the third quarter of 2001, IMNX should initiate a Phase I trial on IL-1 receptor type II as a potential treatment for inflammatory disorders. In partnership with Genentech, Trail/Apo2 L for cancer may begin Phase I trials by the end of 2001. In March 2001, IMNX announced disappointing Phase II results on Nuvance to treat asthma.

Per Share Data ($) (Year Ended Dec. 31)	**2000**	**1999**	**1998**	**1997**	**1996**	**1995**	**1994**	**1993**	**1992**	**1991**
Tangible Bk. Val.	3.34	0.63	0.47	0.32	0.24	0.23	0.17	0.30	0.73	1.19
Cash Flow	0.32	0.12	0.04	0.00	-0.08	0.01	-0.04	NA	-0.40	0.03
Earnings	0.28	0.08	0.00	-0.03	-0.11	-0.02	-0.07	-0.80	-0.43	0.00
Dividends	Nil	Nil	Nil	Nil	Nil	Nil	Nil	1.75	Nil	Nil
Payout Ratio	Nil	Nil	Nil	Nil	Nil	Nil	Nil	NM	Nil	Nil
Prices - High	83.60	40.16	10.53	6.69	1.64	1.54	1.64	4.54	5.66	5.12
- Low	24.18	9.58	3.92	1.57	0.92	0.81	0.89	1.14	1.87	2.77
P/E Ratio - High	NM	NM	NM	NM	NM	NM	NM	NM	NM	NM
- Low	NM	NM	NM	NM	NM	NM	NM	NM	NM	NM
Income Statement Analysis (Million $)										
Revs.	862	542	243	185	151	157	144	123	61.8	52.7
Oper. Inc.	129	59.1	14.6	-2.9	-21.1	5.2	-12.9	-31.5	-17.1	-4.7
Depr.	21.8	20.1	18.1	16.9	15.2	15.9	14.6	10.2	5.3	4.1
Int. Exp.	10.7	8.7	0.4	0.6	0.3	1.1	2.5	1.6	1.8	1.4
Pretax Inc.	157	56.8	3.2	-15.6	-53.5	-11.1	-31.0	-429	-77.6	0.8
Eff. Tax Rate	1.47%	22%	69%	NM	NM	NM	NM	NM	Nil	Nil
Net Inc.	154	44.3	1.0	-15.8	-53.6	-11.3	-33.0	-430	-77.6	0.8
Balance Sheet & Other Fin. Data (Million $)										
Cash	553	261	145	66.2	23.9	20.4	25.0	13.0	100	145
Curr. Assets	1,756	791	202	117	54.7	50.4	57.0	52.0	119	164
Total Assets	2,039	941	325	227	178	174	193	204	236	254
Curr. Liab.	200	135	75.5	45.5	31.5	32.8	41.7	49.7	78.1	15.5
LT Debt	Nil	451	NA	Nil	5.6	4.6	33.7	10.8	17.6	24.2
Common Eqty.	1,838	355	247	176	138	137	112	138	134	212
Total Cap.	1,838	806	247	176	147	141	146	149	155	239
Cap. Exp.	80.7	35.6	29.4	7.4	4.7	5.3	7.8	11.2	29.2	41.0
Cash Flow	176	64.4	19.1	1.2	-38.4	4.6	-19.0	-420	-72.3	4.9
Curr. Ratio	8.8	5.9	2.7	2.6	1.7	1.5	1.4	1.0	1.5	10.6
% LT Debt of Cap.	Nil	55.9	NA	Nil	5.8	3.3	23.2	7.3	11.3	10.1
% Net Inc.of Revs.	17.9	8.2	0.4	NM	NM	NM	NM	NM	NM	1.5
% Ret. on Assets	10.4	7.0	0.4	NM	NM	NM	NM	NM	NM	0.4
% Ret. on Equity	14.1	14.7	0.5	NM	NM	NM	NM	NM	NM	0.5

Data as orig reptd.; bef. results of disc opers/spec. items. Per share data adj. for stk. divs. Bold denotes diluted EPS (FASB 128)-prior periods restated. E-Estimated. NA-Not Available. NM-Not Meaningful. NR-Not Ranked.

Reincorporated—in Washington in 1987. **Office**—51 University St., Seattle, WA 98101. **Tel**—(206) 587-0430. **Fax**—(206) 587-0606. **Website**—http://www.immunex.com **Chrmn & CEO**—E. V. Fritzky. **VP-Fin**—D. A. Mann. **VP & Secy**—S. G. Hallquist. **Investor Contact**—Mark R. Leahy (206-389-4363). **Dirs**—K. L. Cramer, E. V. Fritzky, R. J. Herbold, J. E. Lyons, J. M. Mahady, E. W. Martin, P. V. Phillips, L. V. Stein, D. E. Williams. **Transfer Agent & Registrar**—Mellon Investor Services, NYC. **Empl**— 1,425. **S&P Analyst:** Frank DiLorenzo

STANDARD
&POOR'S
STOCK REPORTS

Myriad Genetics

Nasdaq Symbol **MYGN**

23-AUG-01

Industry:
Biotechnology

Summary: This emerging biotech company focuses on developing novel therapeutic and diagnostic products derived from its proprietary genomic and proteomic technologies.

S&P Opinion: Buy (★★★★★)

Recent Price • 38.31
52 Wk Range • 138-29.50
Yield • Nil
12-Mo. P/E • NM

Quantitative Evaluations

Outlook
(1 Lowest—5 Highest)
• **NA**

Fair Value
• **NA**

Risk
• **High**

Earn./Div. Rank
• **C**

Technical Eval.
• **Bearish** since 7/01

Rel. Strength Rank
(1 Lowest—99 Highest)
• **12**

Insider Activity
• **Unfavorable**

OPTIONS: CBOE, Ph

Overview - 23-AUG-01

MYGN's fourth quarter FY 01 (Jun.) loss per share of $0.09 was a penny wider than our estimate. Predictive medicine sales of $5 million were in line with our view. The company continues to file patent applications on its gene discoveries on a regular basis and in June, MYGN announced it discovered a gene (CHD2) that may contribute to high cholesterol. MYGN should introduce Prolaris, a prostate cancer test, by the end of 2001. Melaris, a melanoma cancer test, may be launched by the end of 2002. MYGN plans to leverage its gene discovery acumen with additional diagnostic products in the future. Pivotal trials of MPC-7869 to treat prostate cancer may begin by early 2002. We project predictive medicine sales of $28 million in FY 02 and $42 million in FY 03. We expect losses per share of $0.31 in FY 02, and $0.24 in FY 03.

Valuation - 23-AUG-01

The shares remain well off their highs for 2001 and have been considerably more volatile than the overall biotech sector. Although risky, we feel the shares have the potential to revisit their 2001 highs over the next twelve months due to a number of factors. We believe MYGN has the potential to become the leader in predictive diagnostic testing. In our view, MYGN is also building a dominant position in population genetics. This data can be used to discover novel genes that can be turned into products. By 2003, we believe MYGN will have up to five compounds in clinical testing for the treatment of cancer, cardiovascular disorders, and HIV. Based on fairly conservative assumptions that S&P has used for its discounted cash flow calculations and NPV analysis of MYGN's products and pipeline, we feel the shares are undervalued.

Key Stock Statistics

S&P EPS Est. 2002	-0.31	Tang. Bk. Value/Share	3.55
P/E on S&P Est. 2002	NM	Beta	0.52
S&P EPS Est. 2003	-0.24	Shareholders	2,500
Dividend Rate/Share	Nil	Market cap. (B)	$0.940
Shs. outstg. (M)	23.3	Inst. holdings	66%
Avg. daily vol. (M)	0.501		

Value of $10,000 invested 5 years ago: $ 33,313

Fiscal Year Ending Jun. 30

	2001	2000	1999	1998	1997	1996
Revenues (Million $)						
1Q	10.82	6.86	5.56	5.92	2.20	1.01
2Q	11.95	8.28	5.75	5.09	2.75	1.67
3Q	11.57	9.72	7.06	5.69	2.74	1.91
4Q	10.82	9.16	6.94	6.51	—	2.20
Yr.	45.16	34.01	25.31	23.21	15.24	6.63
Earnings Per Share ($)						
1Q	**-0.09**	**-0.12**	**-0.14**	-0.10	-0.16	-0.16
2Q	**-0.05**	**-0.10**	**-0.15**	**-0.12**	**-0.20**	-0.04
3Q	**-0.07**	**-0.10**	**-0.12**	**-0.14**	-0.18	-0.10
4Q	**-0.09**	**-0.12**	**-0.12**	**-0.17**	—	—
Yr.	**-0.31**	**-0.43**	**-0.53**	**-0.53**	**-0.52**	-0.39

Next earnings report expected: early November

Dividend Data

Amount ($)	Date Decl.	Ex-Div. Date	Stock of Record	Payment Date
2-for-1	Aug. 16	Sep. 12	Aug. 28	Sep. 11 '00

Myriad Genetics, Inc.

Business Summary - 23-AUG-01

Myriad Genetics, Inc. is committed to being a leader in the emerging field of proteomics. This discipline has the potential to revolutionize medicine by allowing researchers to identify the specific set of protein-based drug targets that will be most valuable in the prevention and treatment of disease. MYGN's strategy is to understand the relationship between protein function and particular diseases, which is the essence of proteomics, in order to develop the next generation of therapeutic and molecular diagnostic products.

MYGN has used its proprietary proteomic technology, ProNet, to generate thousands of disease pathway proteins both for itself and its drug company collaborators. ProNet allows the company and its collaborators to identify proteins involved in critical interactions along the pathway, and to select high-quality drug discovery targets from disease pathways.

MYGN's drug development partners include Bayer, Eli Lilly, Hoffmann-LaRoche, Pharmacia, Novartis, Schering-Plough, and Schering AG. The majority of these collaborations provide MYGN's partners with rights to its intellectual property. In exchange, MYGN will receive payments, milestones, and royalties on product sales. The company's deal with Schering AG provides for an equal profit split on future sales.

As of mid-2001, the company had identified approximately 55 drug targets, of which 13 have been licensed to strategic partners for further development. MYGN's in-house drug discovery efforts are the responsibility of Myriad Pharmaceuticals. This subsidiary targets a number of disease areas, with a current emphasis on cancer and infectious disease. In April 2001, the company released encouraging Phase II data on its lead compound, MPC-7869. Of 23 prostate cancer patients, 39% had stable Prostate Specific Antigen levels following treatment of 7869.

MYGN is also involved in population genetics, whereby the firm compiles medical records, DNA samples, genealogy data, and other health information from a specific population. The company's current data mining efforts are centered around distinct populations from Utah, Quebec, and Sardinia. MYGN uses this information to discover disease causing genes based on inherited genetic mutations within these populations.

Myriad Genetic Labs develops and sells products used for predictive and personalized medicine. It has commercialized BRACAnalysis, a molecular diagnostic test for analyzing susceptibility to breast and ovarian cancer, and CardiaRisk, a test that is used in the therapeutic management of hypertensive patients. In September 2000, MYGN launched COLARIS, a predictive medicine test for hereditary colon cancer and uterine cancer.

In April 2001, MYGN, Hitachi, and Oracle formed Myriad Proteomics Inc., a joint venture to map the human proteome in three years and commercialize a database based on this information. MYGN has a 50% ownership in the venture. In addition to future database product opportunities, MYGN will use data culled from this project in its drug discovery efforts.

Per Share Data ($) (Year Ended Jun. 30)	2001	2000	1999	1998	1997	1996	1995	1994	1993	1992
Tangible Bk. Val.	NA	3.55	2.56	3.08	3.59	4.03	-0.61	NA	NA	NA
Cash Flow	NA	-0.27	-0.36	-0.35	-0.36	-0.25	-0.69	NA	NA	NA
Earnings	-0.31	-0.43	-0.53	-0.53	-0.52	-0.39	-0.59	NA	NA	NA
Dividends	Nil	Nil	Nil	Nil	Nil	Nil	NA	NA	NA	NA
Payout Ratio	Nil	Nil	Nil	Nil	Nil	Nil	Nil	NA	NA	NA
Prices - High	81.75	138.00	25.37	12.81	23.00	18.12	Nil	NA	NA	NA
- Low	29.50	19.00	4.25	2.87	10.37	8.25	9.00	NA	NA	NA
P/E Ratio - High	NM	NM	NM	NM	NM	NM	NM	NA	NA	NA
- Low	NM	NM	NM	NM	NM	NM	NM	NA	NA	NA
Income Statement Analysis (Million $)										
Revs.	NA	34.0	25.3	23.2	15.2	6.6	1.3	NA	NA	NA
Oper. Inc.	NA	-8.3	-9.1	-9.7	-9.9	-7.3	-5.3	NA	NA	NA
Depr.	NA	3.3	3.2	3.3	2.5	1.6	0.4	NA	NA	NA
Int. Exp.	NA	Nil	0.0	0.0	0.1	0.1	0.1	NA	NA	NA
Pretax Inc.	NA	-8.7	-10.0	-9.8	-9.2	-5.9	-5.3	NA	NA	NA
Eff. Tax Rate	NA	NM	NM	NM	NM	NM	NM	NA	NA	NA
Net Inc.	NA	-8.7	-10.0	-9.8	-9.2	-5.9	-5.3	NA	NA	NA
Balance Sheet & Other Fin. Data (Million $)										
Cash	NA	56.2	9.9	30.9	15.7	13.2	16.1	NA	NA	NA
Curr. Assets	NA	85.9	13.7	31.7	48.6	50.6	16.5	NA	NA	NA
Total Assets	NA	106	53.6	67.4	76.1	79.6	19.7	NA	NA	NA
Curr. Liab.	NA	28.7	5.3	9.9	9.8	8.9	2.7	NA	NA	NA
LT Debt	NA	Nil	NA	Nil	0.1	0.5	0.8	NA	NA	NA
Common Eqty.	NA	77.7	48.2	57.5	66.2	70.2	16.2	NA	NA	NA
Total Cap.	NA	77.7	48.2	57.5	66.3	70.7	17.0	NA	NA	NA
Cap. Exp.	NA	4.6	4.0	3.2	4.7	6.4	2.5	NA	NA	NA
Cash Flow	NA	-5.4	-6.8	-6.5	-6.7	-4.3	-4.9	NA	NA	NA
Curr. Ratio	NA	3.0	2.6	3.2	5.0	5.7	6.1	NA	NA	NA
% LT Debt of Cap.	NA	Nil	Nil	Nil	0.2	0.7	4.6	NA	NA	NA
% Net Inc.of Revs.	NA	NM	NM	NM	NM	NM	NM	NA	NA	NA
% Ret. on Assets	NA	NM	NM	NM	NM	NM	NM	NA	NA	NA
% Ret. on Equity	NA	NM	NM	NM	NM	NM	NM	NA	NA	NA

Data as orig reptd.; bef. results of disc opers/spec. items. Per share data adj. for stk. divs. Bold denotes diluted EPS (FASB 128)-prior periods restated. E-Estimated. NA-Not Available. NM-Not Meaningful. NR-Not Ranked.

Office—320 Wakara Way, Salt Lake City, UT 84108. **Tel**—(801) 584-3600. **Website**—http://www.myriad.com **Chrmn**—J. J. Horan. **Vice Chrmn**—W. Gilbert. **Pres & CEO**—P. D. Meldrum. **VP & CFO**—J. M. Moyes. **Dirs**—M. J. Berendt, W. Gilbert, A. H. Hayes, J. J. Horan, A. J. Main, P. D. Meldrum, M. H. Skolnick, D. A. Stringfellow, L. S. Wilson. **Transfer Agent & Registrar**—Mellon Investor Services, East Hartford, CT. **Incorporated**—in Delaware. **Empl**— 425. **S&P Analyst:** Frank DiLorenzo

STANDARD
&POOR'S
STOCK REPORTS

Oxford Health Plans

NYSE Symbol **OHP**

In S&P MidCap 400

18-AUG-01

Industry:
Health Care (Managed Care)

Summary: Oxford Health operates managed health care plans with a geographic focus on New York, New Jersey and Connecticut.

S&P Opinion: Buy (★★★★★)

Recent Price • 28.51
52 Wk Range • 42.75-23.12

Yield • Nil
12-Mo. P/E • 10.1

Quantitative Evaluations

Outlook
(1 Lowest—5 Highest)
• **5**

Fair Value
• **43.80**

Risk
• **Average**

Earn./Div. Rank
• **B-**

Technical Eval.
• **NA**

Rel. Strength Rank
(1 Lowest—99 Highest)
• **72**

Insider Activity
• **Neutral**

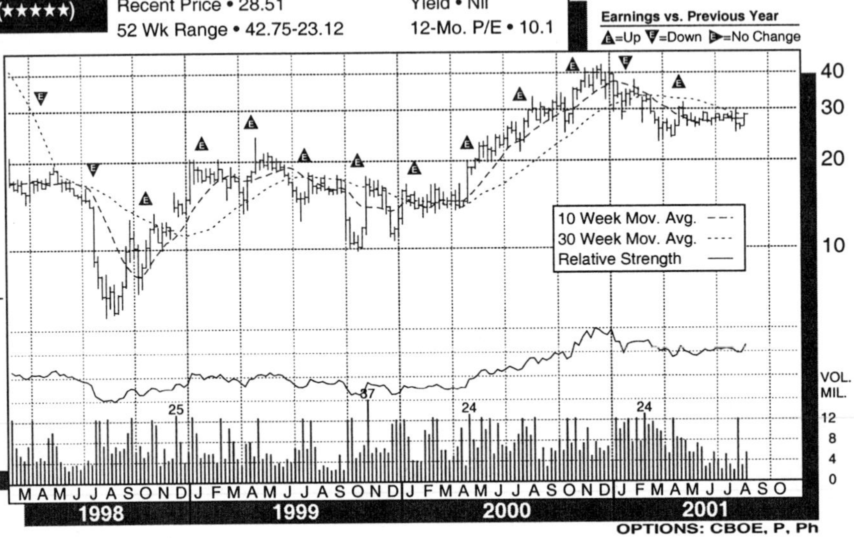

OPTIONS: CBOE, P, Ph

Overview - 08-AUG-01

Second quarter results exceeded our expectations. In 2001, we see premium revenues rising 7%, to $4.4 billion, on 9% higher premium rates and 4% commercial enrollment growth, partly offset by market exits. In the second quarter, the commercial medical loss ratio (MLR) improved to 81.7% vs. 82.4%, on higher premiums, exit from unprofitable markets, and cost containment initiatives. The administrative cost ratio (ACR) fell to 10.8% from 12.1%. We expect the MLR will remain stable at 80.0% in 2001, on 9%-10% medical cost inflation. The ACR will likely decline to 10.6%. For 2002, we estimate premium rates will climb 12%-13%, before benefit buydowns, with 3%-4% higher enrollment. The MLR could deteriorate 50-100 basis points in 2002, offset by ACR improvements. Excluding one-time items and adjustments, we project EPS growth of 44% in 2001, to $2.80, and to $3.25 in 2002.

Valuation - 08-AUG-01

We are maintaining our buy on OHP, reflecting its superior margins and renewed focus on enrollment growth and geographical expansion. OHP delivered a third sequential quarter of enrollment growth, adding 10,000 new fully insured members, in the second quarter. We believe OHP is gaining members at the expense of Aetna. The company continues to deliver industry leading margins, a testament to its cost reduction initiatives and its exit from underperforming markets. In early 2001, OHP capped its turnaround by refinancing its debt on more favorable terms, and converting preferred stock and warrants issued into common stock. In addition, Oxford is often talked about as an acquisition target due to its well known brand name and strong New York market position. Trading at 8.0X our 2002 EPS estimate of $3.25, well below its HMO peer group average of 14X, the shares are undervalued.

Key Stock Statistics

S&P EPS Est. 2001	2.78	Tang. Bk. Value/Share	6.25
P/E on S&P Est. 2001	10.3	Beta	0.98
S&P EPS Est. 2002	3.25	Shareholders	1,117
Dividend Rate/Share	Nil	Market cap. (B)	$ 2.8
Shs. outstg. (M)	99.3	Inst. holdings	82%
Avg. daily vol. (M)	1.133		

Value of $10,000 invested 5 years ago: $ 5,718

Fiscal Year Ending Dec. 31

	2001	2000	1999	1998	1997	1996
Revenues (Million $)						
1Q	1,078	1,022	1,060	1,230	987.3	658.1
2Q	1,110	1,013	1,051	1,191	1,062	725.3
3Q	—	1,038	1,052	1,172	1,064	811.3
4Q	—	1,039	1,034	1,128	1,127	880.3
Yr.	—	4,112	4,198	4,722	4,240	3,075
Earnings Per Share ($)						
1Q	0.65	0.34	0.04	-0.57	0.42	0.25
2Q	—	0.45	-0.16	-6.41	0.45	0.28
3Q	—	0.81	0.34	-0.58	-0.99	0.33
4Q	—	0.59	3.05	-0.23	-3.58	0.39
Yr.	—	2.24	3.26	-7.79	-3.70	1.25

Next earnings report expected: NA

Dividend Data

The company has never paid cash dividends on its common stock. Two-for-one stock splits were effected in 1995 and 1996.

A Division of The **McGraw-Hill** *Companies*

Oxford Health Plans, Inc.

Business Summary - 08-AUG-01

Oxford Health Plans offers a wide range of benefit plan options to about 1.5 million members, primarily in New York, New Jersey and Connecticut. In 1997, widely publicized computer conversion problems seriously disrupted billing and collection functions.

In 1998, new management implemented a turnaround plan aimed at restoring profitability by focusing on core commercial operations and disposing of or restructuring non-core commercial businesses, reducing administrative and health care costs, exiting all Medicaid markets, and trimming exposure in unprofitable Medicare markets. During 1999 and 2000, OHP withdrew from Florida, New Hampshire and nearly all Pennsylvania markets, and exited the Medicaid business and Medicare business in Pennsylvania and several counties in the New York metropolitan area. Improved profitability in 2000 allowed OHP to restructure debt assumed during the early stages of its turnaround.

The Freedom Plan (73% of membership enrollment at December 31, 2000) is a point-of-service managed care option that combines the benefits of OHP's HMOs with those of conventional fee-for-service health insurance. The Freedom Plan lets members use the company's HMO plan or choose unaffiliated physicians. Small to medium-size employers (10 to 1,500 employees) are targeted for the product. New York Freedom Plan membership accounts for a majority Freedom Plan enrollment, which totaled 1,151,900 at June 30, 2001, up from 1,115,900 a year earlier.

The company's HMOs (15%) offer plans in each state in which it operates. More than 650 employers offer OHP's HMO programs. At June 30, 2001, commercial HMO membership was 219,000, versus 223,000 at June 30, 2000.

The New York, New Jersey and Connecticut HMOs provide Medicare (6%) plans to eligible individuals. At June 30, 2001, Medicare membership had been reduced to 85,200, from 90,100 a year earlier.

OHP also offers health plans under which employers self-insure health care expenses and pay for health claims only as they are incurred. The company earns fees to provide claims processing and health care cost containment services through its provider network and utilization management programs. Self-funded enrollment was 55,900 at June 30, 2001, down from 62,600 a year earlier.

The company has a network of 55,000 physicians in New York (32,000), New Jersey (15,000) and Connecticut (8,000). The majority of physicians have contracted individually with OHP.

Having completed its capital restructuring in late 2000, OHP's strategy for 2001 is to increase membership through additional market penetration in the Tri-State area and geographic expansion, and to continue to increase administration efficiencies by, among other things, added Internet functionality.

Per Share Data ($) (Year Ended Dec. 31)	2000	1999	1998	1997	1996	1995	1994	1993	1992	1991
Tangible Bk. Val.	4.67	1.21	NM	4.39	7.73	3.20	2.00	1.46	0.13	NA
Cash Flow	2.60	3.91	-6.96	-2.75	1.41	1.03	0.51	0.27	0.15	NA
Earnings	2.24	3.26	-7.79	-3.70	1.24	0.71	0.41	0.23	0.13	0.08
Dividends	Nil	Nil	Nil	Nil	Nil	Nil	Nil	Nil	Nil	Nil
Payout Ratio	Nil	Nil	Nil	Nil	Nil	Nil	Nil	Nil	Nil	Nil
Prices - High	42.75	24.25	22.00	89.00	62.25	41.87	20.87	14.00	NA	NA
- Low	12.06	9.75	5.81	13.75	27.68	19.25	9.87	3.93	NA	NA
P/E Ratio - High	19	7	NM	NM	50	59	52	62	NA	NA
- Low	5	3	NM	NM	22	27	24	18	NA	NA
Income Statement Analysis (Million $)										
Revs.	4,112	4,198	4,719	4,240	3,075	1,765	714	306	151	NA
Oper. Inc.	553	288	-307	-339	190	118	51.4	22.7	10.7	NA
Depr.	34.2	54.5	67.1	75.3	13.2	23.0	7.1	2.9	1.3	NA
Int. Exp.	34.3	49.6	57.1	Nil	Nil	Nil	Nil	Nil	Nil	NA
Pretax Inc.	485	164	-615	-432	172	91.4	49.5	26.1	13.8	NA
Eff. Tax Rate	41%	NM	NM	NM	42%	43%	44%	43%	42%	NA
Net Inc.	285	320	-597	-291	100	52.4	27.9	14.9	8.0	NA
Balance Sheet & Other Fin. Data (Million $)										
Cash	199	333	238	4.1	72.2	369	191	110	NA	NA
Curr. Assets	1,256	1,331	1,361	1,130	1,201	492	255	135	NA	NA
Total Assets	1,445	1,687	1,638	1,398	1,347	609	315	166	106	NA
Curr. Liab.	957	888	1,151	1,049	749	389	188	75.0	NA	NA
LT Debt	28.0	356	369	Nil	Nil	Nil	Nil	Nil	Nil	NA
Common Eqty.	459	99	-181	349	598	220	127	91.0	66.0	NA
Total Cap.	487	799	487	349	598	220	127	91.0	66.0	NA
Cap. Exp.	12.8	9.0	40.0	102	48.3	83.9	30.8	11.7	2.9	NA
Cash Flow	246	329	-557	-216	113	75.4	35.0	17.8	9.3	NA
Curr. Ratio	1.3	1.5	1.2	1.1	1.6	1.3	1.4	1.8	NA	NA
% LT Debt of Cap.	5.7	44.5	75.8	Nil	Nil	Nil	Nil	Nil	0.3	NA
% Net Inc.of Revs.	6.9	7.6	NM	NM	3.2	3.0	3.9	4.9	5.3	NA
% Ret. on Assets	18.2	19.2	NM	NM	10.2	11.2	11.6	11.0	9.6	NA
% Ret. on Equity	75.9	NM	NM	NM	24.4	29.7	25.6	19.0	14.5	NA

Data as orig reptd.; bef. results of disc opers/spec. items. Per share data adj. for stk. divs. Bold denotes diluted EPS (FASB 128)-prior periods restated. E-Estimated. NA-Not Available. NM-Not Meaningful. NR-Not Ranked.

Office—48 Monroe Turnpike, Trumbull, CT 06611. **Tel**—(203) 459-6000. **Website**—www.oxhp.com **Chrmn & CEO**—N. C. Payson. **Pres & COO**—C. M. Schneider. **EVP & CFO**—K. B. Thompson. **EVP & Secy** —Daniel N. Gregoire. **Investor Contact** —Deborah Abraham. **Dirs**—D. Bonderman, J. W. Brown Jr., J. J. Coslet, J. G. Coulter, R. B. Milligan Jr., F. F. Nazem, N. C. Payson, B. H. Safirstein, T. A. Scully, K. J. Thiry. **Transfer Agent**—State Street Bank (c/o EquiServe), Boston, MA. **Incorporated**—in Delaware in 1984. **Empl**— 3,400. **S&P Analyst:** John A. Massey

STANDARD &POOR'S
STOCK REPORTS

Techne Corp.

Nasdaq Symbol **TECH**

In S&P SmallCap 600

18-AUG-01 **Industry:** Biotechnology

Summary: This company is a specialty manufacturer and distributor of biological products.

S&P Opinion: Buy (★★★★★) Recent Price • 32.67 52 Wk Range • 66.43-19.37 Yield • Nil 12-Mo. P/E • 40.8

Quantitative Evaluations

Outlook
(1 Lowest—5 Highest)
• **3⁻**

Fair Value
• **30.40**

Risk
• **NA**

Earn./Div. Rank
• **NR**

Technical Eval.
• **Bearish** since 8/01

Rel. Strength Rank
(1 Lowest—99 Highest)
• **81**

Insider Activity
• **NA**

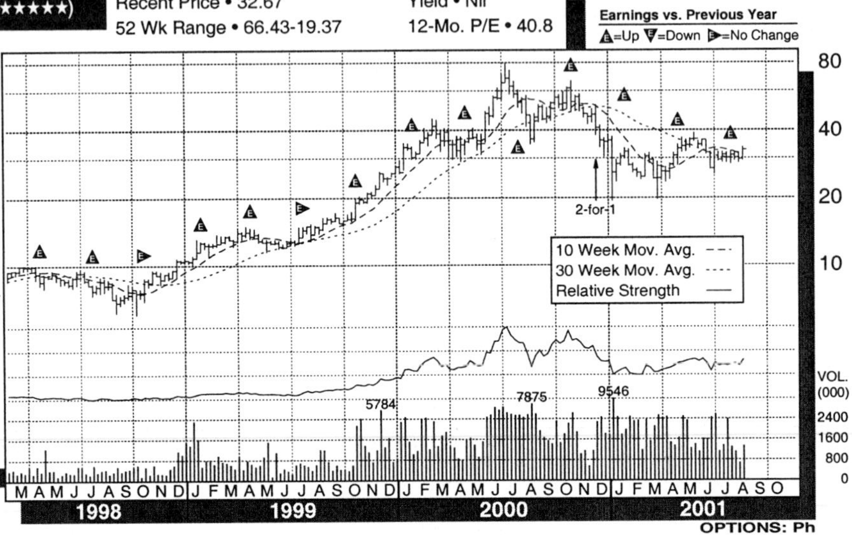

OPTIONS: Ph

Overview - 18-JUL-01

TECH's R & D Systems Europe subsidiary's sales are being adversely affected by the strong dollar. In the nine months ended March 31, 2001, its sales increased 3% at existing exchange rates; adjusting for steady currencies, sales would have risen 15%. The Biotechnology and Hematology divisions reported 14% and 10% sales increases, respectively, during the period. For FY 01 (Jun.), S&P estimates that consolidated revenues will increase 11%. Margins have widened in FY 01, as higher cost inventory acquired in FY 99 was absorbed, and profit sharing, printing and promotion expenses were somewhat lower. EPS are expected to rise 24%, to $0.78. In FY 02, we expect less of a currency impact on sales, which we forecast to increase 16%. With lower intangible amortization charges and increases in selling and R&D at a slower pace than sales growth, margins are expected to widen, leading to a 22% increase in EPS in FY 02, to $0.95.

Valuation - 18-JUL-01

S&P is raising its opinion on Techne Corp. from hold to buy. The stock is down 18% since the beginning of 2001, and is 24% below its 2001 high, reached in May. We attribute the decline to concerns that TECH's customers in the biotechnology area would be constrained from obtaining needed capital in the depressed equity and high-yield fixed income markets, and that initial euphoria over the completion of the mapping of the human genome would not quickly be followed up by major commercial product success. However, Techne has a proven track record of sales and earnings growth over the past 10 years (compound annual growth of 21% for sales and 33% for EPS). Based on a discounted free cash flow analysis that assumes 20% growth in FY 02, dropping over a multi-year period to 5% in perpetuity, our 12-month target price range is $38 to $40.

Key Stock Statistics

S&P EPS Est. 2002	0.93	Tang. Bk. Value/Share	2.54
P/E on S&P Est. 2002	35.1	Beta	0.71
Dividend Rate/Share	Nil	Shareholders	14,500
Shs. outstg. (M)	41.4	Market cap. (B)	$ 1.4
Avg. daily vol. (M)	0.216	Inst. holdings	75%

Value of $10,000 invested 5 years ago: $ 41,670

Fiscal Year Ending Jun. 30

	2001	2000	1999	1998	1997	1996
Revenues (Million $)						
1Q	27.72	24.62	21.34	15.54	14.03	12.79
2Q	26.69	25.13	21.46	15.47	14.41	12.51
3Q	30.24	26.78	23.79	17.70	16.25	14.71
4Q	30.71	27.31	24.31	18.58	16.24	14.57
Yr.	115.4	103.8	90.90	67.29	60.92	54.59
Earnings Per Share ($)						
1Q	**0.17**	**0.12**	**0.09**	**0.09**	0.06	0.05
2Q	**0.16**	**0.13**	**0.09**	**0.08**	0.06	0.04
3Q	**0.24**	**0.18**	**0.11**	**0.10**	0.08	0.07
4Q	**0.22**	**0.20**	**0.12**	**0.12**	0.09	0.07
Yr.	**0.80**	**0.63**	**0.41**	**0.39**	**0.28**	**0.22**

Next earnings report expected: NA

Dividend Data

Amount ($)	Date Decl.	Ex-Div. Date	Stock of Record	Payment Date
2-for-1	Nov. 09	Dec. 04	Nov. 24	Dec. 01 '00

Techne Corporation

18-AUG-01

Business Summary - 18-JUL-01

Techne Corp. believes it is the leading worldwide supplier of cytokine related products in the research marketplace. Through its Research and Diagnostic Systems, Inc., subsidiary, the company is engaged domestically in the development and manufacture of biotechnology products and hematology calibrators and controls. Through its wholly owned English subsidiary, R & D Systems Europe Ltd., TECH distributes biotechnology products throughout Europe.

In FY 00 (Jun.), 62% of consolidated revenue came from the biotechnology segment, 13% from hematology, and 25% from R & D Systems Europe.

R & D Systems is the world's leading supplier of cytokines and cytokine-related reagents to the biotechnology research community. These valuable proteins exist in minute amounts in different types of cells, and can be extracted from these cells or made through recombinant DNA technology. The company also sells antibodies for specific cytokines, cytokine assay kits, clinical diagnostic kits, kits for cytokine receptor binding studies and related research reagents.

Cytokines are intercellular messengers. They act as signals by interacting with specific receptors on the affected cells, carrying vital signals to the cell's genetic machinery that can trigger events that can lead to significant changes in a cell, tissue or organism.

Hematology controls and calibrators are products made up of the various cellular components of blood. Proper diagnosis of many illnesses requires a thorough and accurate analysis of the patient's blood cells, which is usually done with automatic or semiautomatic hematology instruments. Controls and calibrators ensure that these instruments are performing accurately and reliably. The linearity control product provides a means of assessing the linearity of hematology analyzers for white blood cells, red blood cells, hemoglobin and platelets.

Original equipment manufacturer agreements represent the largest market for hematology controls and calibrators made by R & D Systems. In FY 00, OEM contracts accounted for 46% of hematology revenues, and 6% of consolidated revenues.

R & D Systems released new cytokines, antibodies, and cytokine assay kits in FY 00. All of these products are for research purposes only, and do not require FDA clearance. The hematology division developed several new control products in recent years, and is continually working on product improvements and enhancements. Research and development outlays were $11.2 million, $12.0 million and $10.6 million in FY 00, FY 99 and FY 98, respectively.

TECH holds a 49% voting stake in ChemoCentryx, Inc., a new technology and drug development concern that works in the area of chemokines. Chemokines are cytokines that regulate the traffic patterns of leukocytes, the effector cells of the human immune system.

Per Share Data ($) **(Year Ended Jun. 30)**	**2001**	**2000**	**1999**	**1998**	**1997**	**1996**	**1995**	**1994**	**1993**	**1992**
Tangible Bk. Val.	NA	2.54	1.27	1.69	2.52	0.99	0.75	0.58	0.58	NA
Cash Flow	NA	0.93	0.69	0.45	0.69	0.29	0.23	0.20	0.17	0.09
Earnings	0.80	0.63	0.41	0.39	0.28	0.22	0.17	0.14	0.12	0.06
Dividends	Nil	Nil	Nil	Nil	Nil	Nil	Nil	Nil	Nil	NA
Payout Ratio	Nil	Nil	Nil	Nil	Nil	Nil	Nil	Nil	Nil	Nil
Prices - High	38.84	79.90	27.93	10.75	10.09	Nil	6.06	3.25	4.62	4.43
- Low	19.37	25.56	10.06	6.00	5.53	4.43	2.43	2.18	2.31	2.12
P/E Ratio - High	49	NM	69	28	28	37	26	24	40	81
- Low	24	NM	25	16	19	20	13	16	20	39
Income Statement Analysis (Million $)										
Revs.	NA	104	90.9	67.3	60.9	54.6	47.7	40.3	28.7	22.3
Oper. Inc.	NA	52.0	37.0	23.6	17.9	14.1	11.1	9.5	8.3	5.1
Depr.	NA	12.7	11.9	2.4	2.6	2.1	1.9	2.4	1.9	1.5
Int. Exp.	NA	1.4	Nil	Nil	0.0	0.0	0.0	0.0	0.1	0.2
Pretax Inc.	NA	39.4	26.1	22.4	16.0	12.6	9.6	7.2	6.5	3.3
Eff. Tax Rate	NA	33%	36%	32%	32%	31%	30%	29%	32%	40%
Net Inc.	NA	26.6	16.7	15.2	10.9	8.6	6.7	5.1	4.4	2.0
Balance Sheet & Other Fin. Data (Million $)										
Cash	NA	17.4	12.8	27.4	8.6	7.4	5.3	5.9	4.0	4.5
Curr. Assets	NA	86.3	50.9	58.5	39.8	33.3	27.8	20.9	15.0	11.6
Total Assets	NA	180	124	72.9	53.9	44.4	34.1	26.8	20.4	15.7
Curr. Liab.	NA	12.6	13.5	7.4	4.9	5.0	4.1	3.6	2.4	2.4
LT Debt	NA	18.9	Nil	Nil	Nil	Nil	Nil	Nil	NM	NA
Common Eqty.	NA	141	96.8	63.8	48.1	38.9	29.5	23.0	17.8	11.2
Total Cap.	NA	160	96.8	63.8	48.0	38.9	29.5	23.0	17.8	NA
Cap. Exp.	NA	30.4	5.6	2.8	4.2	NA	NA	NA	NA	NA
Cash Flow	NA	39.2	28.5	17.6	13.4	10.7	8.7	7.5	6.3	3.5
Curr. Ratio	NA	6.9	3.8	7.9	8.1	6.6	6.8	5.9	6.3	4.8
% LT Debt of Cap.	NA	11.8	Nil	Nil	Nil	Nil	Nil	Nil	0.2	NA
% Net Inc.of Revs.	NA	25.6	18.3	22.6	17.9	15.8	14.1	12.6	15.2	8.8
% Ret. on Assets	NA	17.5	16.9	23.9	22.1	22.0	22.0	21.6	24.3	15.6
% Ret. on Equity	NA	22.3	20.7	27.1	25.0	25.3	25.6	25.0	30.3	22.6

Data as orig reptd.; bef. results of disc opers/spec. items. Per share data adj. for stk. divs. Bold denotes diluted EPS (FASB 128)-prior periods restated. E-Estimated. NA-Not Available. NM-Not Meaningful. NR-Not Ranked.

Office—614 McKinley Place N.E., Minneapolis, MN 55413. **Tel**—(612) 379-8854. **Website**—www.rndsystems.com **Chrmn, Pres & Treas**—T. E. Oland. **VP & Secy**—T. M. Heaney. **VPs**—M. Tsang, M. Veronneau. **Dirs**—T. M. Heaney, C. S. Henney, G. A. Herbert, R. C. Lucas, H. V. O'Connell, T. E. Oland, L. E. Sears, R. C. Steer. **Transfer Agent & Registrar**—Mellon Investor Services, Ridgefield Park, NJ. **Incorporated**— in Minnesota in 1976. **Empl**— 486. **S&P Analyst:** Mark S. Basham

STANDARD
&POOR'S
STOCK REPORTS

Tenet Healthcare

NYSE Symbol **THC**

In S&P 500

18-AUG-01

Industry:
Health Care (Hospital Management)

Summary: The second largest for-profit hospital manager, with 111 acute care facilities in 17 states, Tenet also operates other health care facilities and related businesses.

S&P Opinion: Buy (★★★★★)

Recent Price • 54.38

52 Wk Range • 57-28.06

Yield • Nil

12-Mo. P/E • 26.1

Quantitative Evaluations

Outlook
(1 Lowest—5 Highest)
• **4-**

Fair Value
• **68**

Risk
• **Low**

Earn./Div. Rank
• **B**

Technical Eval.
• **Bullish** since 5/01

Rel. Strength Rank
(1 Lowest—99 Highest)
• **78**

Insider Activity
• **Neutral**

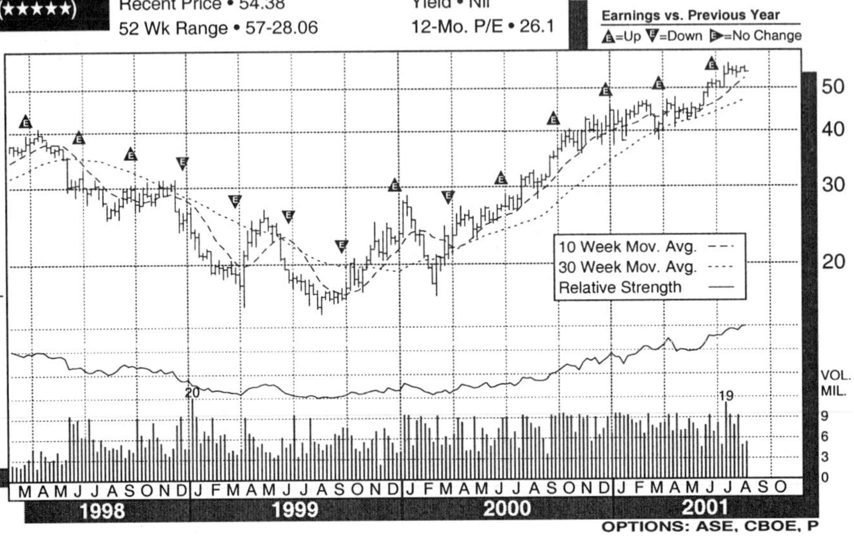

OPTIONS: ASE, CBOE, P

Overview - 18-JUL-01

We anticipate that FY 02 (May) revenues will advance approximately 6% to 8%, on same-store admissions growth of 3% to 4%, improved Medicare and managed care pricing, and rising patient acuity levels. Strategic acquisitions of non-profit hospitals may provide some incremental growth opportunities. The company continues to reap the benefits of its labor outsourcing initiatives, and supply costs remain among the lowest in the industry as a percentage of revenues. Assuming that rising unit labor costs are offset by productivity gains and SG&A reductions, EBITDA margins could approach 20% in FY 02, up from 18.6% in FY 01. Cash flows should benefit from widening operating margins, lower bad debt costs, and reduced interest expense; we see free cash flow (after capital expenditures) of about $1.7 billion in FY 02. After taxes at an expected rate of 41%, we look for FY 02 EPS of $2.75, and have initiated a FY 03 estimate of $3.25.

Valuation - 18-JUL-01

We are maintaining our buy recommendation on the shares, and believe the company's operating strategies will allow for three-year earnings growth in excess of 16% annually. Positive operating trends include surging patient admissions, rising occupancy levels, increased private and government pricing, operating cost disciplines, and falling bad debt levels. During FY 01, free cash flow more than doubled, to $1.2 billion, and we look for an approximate 40% gain in FY 02, to $1.7 billion. Based on our free cash flow projections over the coming 10 years, we believe the shares are priced at an approximate 40% discount to their intrinsic value of $90. In addition, the P/E multiple remains below that of the S&P 500, as well as that of Tenet's hospital peers. We recommend that investors continue to purchase the stock for superior capital appreciation.

Key Stock Statistics

S&P EPS Est. 2002	2.75	Tang. Bk. Value/Share	NM
P/E on S&P Est. 2002	19.8	Beta	0.49
S&P EPS Est. 2003	3.25	Shareholders	11,700
Dividend Rate/Share	Nil	Market cap. (B)	$ 17.6
Shs. outstg. (M)	324.2	Inst. holdings	92%
Avg. daily vol. (M)	1.481		

Value of $10,000 invested 5 years ago: $ 26,393

Fiscal Year Ending May 31

	2001	2000	1999	1998	1997	1996
Revenues (Million $)						
1Q	2,893	2,873	2,553	2,331	1,439	1,284
2Q	2,915	2,780	2,563	2,429	1,476	1,371
3Q	3,036	2,850	2,822	2,564	2,237	1,432
4Q	3,209	2,911	2,942	2,571	2,351	1,472
Yr.	12,053	11,414	10,880	9,895	8,691	5,559
Earnings Per Share ($)						
1Q	**0.48**	**0.41**	**0.44**	0.38	0.33	0.59
2Q	**0.54**	**0.43**	**0.40**	0.44	0.35	0.90
3Q	**0.60**	**0.12**	**0.40**	**0.47**	**-0.21**	0.33
4Q	**0.46**	**0.12**	**-0.44**	**-0.08**	-0.67	0.12
Yr.	**2.08**	**1.08**	**0.79**	**1.22**	**-0.24**	1.90

Next earnings report expected: early October

Dividend Data (Dividends have been paid since 2000.)

Dividends, initiated in 1973, were omitted in 1993. A special dividend of $0.01 a share was paid in March 2000.

Tenet Healthcare Corporation

Business Summary - 18-JUL-01

Tenet ranks as the second largest U.S. for-profit hospital manager, owning or operating a total of 111 acute care hospitals with about 27,000 licensed beds as of early January 2001. The largest concentrations of hospital beds are in California (38%), Texas (14%) and Florida (12%). The hospitals offer acute care services, and most offer operating and recovery rooms, radiology services, intensive care and coronary care nursing units, pharmacies, clinical labs, respiratory and physical therapy services and outpatient facilities. Several hospitals also offer services such as open-heart surgery, neonatal intensive care, neurosciences, orthopedic services, and oncology services.

Tenet also owns and operates a small number of rehabilitation hospitals, specialty hospitals, long-term care facilities, and psychiatric facilities, as well as certain ancillary health care businesses, including outpatient surgery centers, home health care programs, ambulatory, occupational and rural health care clinics, a health maintenance organization (HMO), a preferred provider organization (PPO), and a managed care insurance company.

Hospital net patient revenues in FY 01 (May) were derived from Medicare (31%), managed care (43%), Medicaid (8%) and indemnity/other (18%) sources.

On a same-facility basis (under THC management for at least one year), admissions rose 3.6% in FY 01 (934,276 versus 901,540), net inpatient revenue per patient day surged 6.9% ($1,558 versus $1,458), and net inpatient revenue per admission was up 7.7% ($8,194 versus $7,608). The average length of stay edged up to 5.3 days versus 5.2 days, while the number of outpatient visits rose 1.1% (8,975,730 from 8,881,950).

In the first nine months of FY 00, the company sold 17 general hospitals, three skilled nursing facilities, and certain other assets, for a total of $643 million in cash and $9 million in notes; a related gain of $63 million was recorded.

In November 1998, Tenet purchased from the Allegheny Health and Education Foundation eight general hospitals and certain other assets, including several physician practices in the Philadelphia area that were involved bankruptcy proceedings. The transaction diluted FY 99 EPS by $0.05.

In February 2000, the company and Ventro Corp. (formerly Chemdex Corp.) formed Broadlane Inc., a new business-to-business e-commerce company intended to provide an extensive marketplace for the high-volume hospital and medical supply market.

Per Share Data ($) (Year Ended May 31)	2001	2000	1999	1998	1997	1996	1995	1994	1993	1992
Tangible Bk. Val.	NA	2.35	1.51	0.47	0.26	0.07	9.93	7.95	10.56	10.03
Cash Flow	NA	2.77	2.57	2.68	1.21	3.43	2.20	2.15	1.97	1.68
Earnings	2.08	1.08	0.79	1.22	-0.24	1.90	1.10	1.29	0.96	0.77
Dividends	Nil	0.01	Nil	Nil	Nil	Nil	Nil	0.12	0.48	0.46
Payout Ratio	Nil	1%	Nil	Nil	Nil	Nil	Nil	9%	50%	60%
Cal. Yrs.	2000	1999	1998	1997	1996	1995	1994	1993	1992	1991
Prices - High	45.75	27.18	40.93	34.87	23.75	20.75	19.50	14.37	18.12	25.87
- Low	16.93	15.37	23.75	21.37	18.12	13.37	12.50	6.50	9.62	12.62
P/E Ratio - High	22	25	52	29	NM	11	18	11	19	34
- Low	8	14	30	18	NM	7	11	5	10	16
Income Statement Analysis (Million $)										
Revs.	NA	11,414	10,880	9,895	8,691	5,559	3,318	2,967	3,762	3,951
Oper. Inc.	NA	1,935	1,858	1,809	1,597	1,099	623	534	581	644
Depr.	NA	533	556	460	443	321	195	143	168	156
Int. Exp.	NA	479	485	464	417	312	138	74.0	88.0	105
Pretax Inc.	NA	639	481	669	-21.0	746	338	360	272	239
Eff. Tax Rate	NA	44%	47%	40%	NM	47%	40%	40%	36%	41%
Net Inc.	NA	340	249	378	-73.0	-73.0	194	216	160	133
Balance Sheet & Other Fin. Data (Million $)										
Cash	NA	135	29.0	155	151	201	294	373	239	200
Curr. Assets	NA	3,594	3,962	2,890	2,391	1,545	1,624	1,444	1,068	1,097
Total Assets	NA	13,161	13,771	12,833	11,705	8,332	7,918	3,697	4,173	4,236
Curr. Liab.	NA	1,912	2,022	1,767	1,869	1,134	1,356	1,640	913	874
LT Debt	NA	5,668	6,391	5,829	5,022	3,191	3,273	223	892	1,066
Common Eqty.	NA	4,066	3,870	3,558	3,224	2,636	1,986	1,320	1,752	1,674
Total Cap.	NA	10,225	10,701	9,810	8,678	6,221	5,560	1,668	2,961	3,072
Cap. Exp.	NA	619	592	534	406	370	264	185	306	509
Cash Flow	NA	873	805	838	370	719	389	359	328	289
Curr. Ratio	NA	1.9	2.0	1.6	1.3	1.4	1.2	0.9	1.2	1.3
% LT Debt of Cap.	NA	55.4	59.7	59.4	57.9	51.3	58.9	13.4	30.1	34.7
% Net Inc.of Revs.	NA	3.0	2.3	3.8	NM	7.2	5.9	7.3	4.3	3.4
% Ret. on Assets	NA	2.5	1.9	3.1	NM	4.9	3.4	5.5	3.8	3.3
% Ret. on Equity	NA	8.6	6.7	11.1	NM	17.3	11.8	14.1	9.4	7.9

Data as orig reptd.; bef. results of disc opers/spec. items. Per share data adj. for stk. divs. Bold denotes diluted EPS (FASB 128)-prior periods restated. E-Estimated. NA-Not Available. NM-Not Meaningful. NR-Not Ranked.

Office—3820 State St., Santa Barbara, CA 93105. **Tel**—(805) 563-7000. **Website**—http://www.tenethealth.com **Chrmn & CEO**—J. C. Barbakow. **Vice Chrmn & CFO**—D. L. Dennis. **COO**—T. B. Mackey. **SVP-Fin & Treas**—S. D. Farber. **Pres & COO**—T. B. Mackey. **SVP & Investor Contact**—Paul J. Russell (805-563-7188). **Dirs**—J. C. Barbakow, L. Biondi, B. B. Bratter, S. Cloud Jr., D. L. Dennis, M. J. DeWald, M. H. Focht Sr., R. A. Hay, V. B. Honeycutt, L. P. Korn, F. D. Loop, R. S. Schweiker. **Transfer Agent & Registrar**—Bank of New York, NYC. **Incorporated**—in California in 1968; reincorporated in Nevada in 1976. **Empl**— 104,000. **S&P Analyst:** Robert M. Gold

STANDARD
&POOR'S
STOCK REPORTS

Andrx Group

Nasdaq Symbol **ADRX**

18-AUG-01

Industry:
Health Care (Drugs - Generic & Other)

Summary: Andrx produces generic versions of controlled-release drugs utilizing its proprietary drug delivery technologies. It also distributes generic drugs made by others.

S&P Opinion: Buy (★★★★★)	Recent Price • 64.92	Yield • Nil
	52 Wk Range • 95.87-38.50	12-Mo. P/E • 69.8

Quantitative Evaluations

Outlook
(1 Lowest—5 Highest)
• **5**

Fair Value
• **102.30**

Risk
• **High**

Earn./Div. Rank
• **NR**

Technical Eval.
• **Bearish** since 8/01

Rel. Strength Rank
(1 Lowest—99 Highest)
• **49**

Insider Activity
• **Unfavorable**

Earnings vs. Previous Year
E=Up E=Down E=No Change

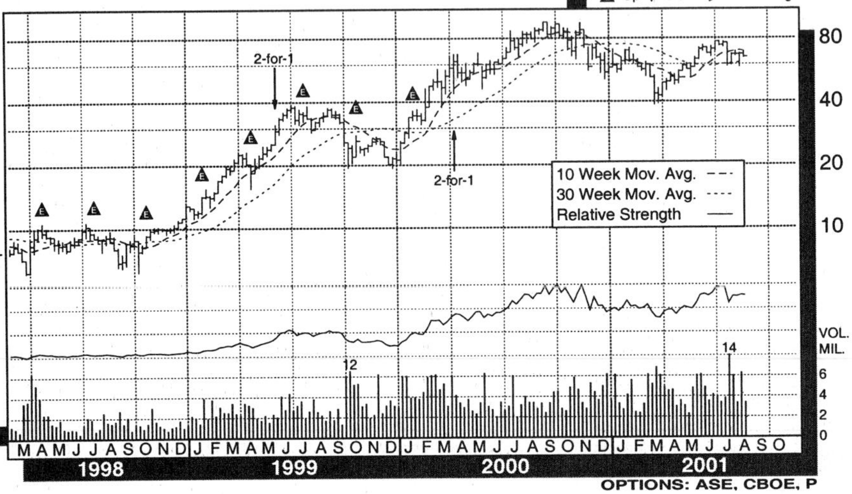

OPTIONS: ASE, CBOE, P

Overview - 14-JUN-01

Revenues are projected to grow 15% in 2001. The gains should be fueled by new generic versions of Biovail's Tiazac anti-hypertensive, Schering-Plough's K-Dur potassium supplement, and AstraZeneca's Prilosec antiulcer treatment (subject to FDA approval and resolution of legal hurdles initiated by makers of the branded products). Revenues should also be augmented by higher sales of distributed products, as well as by the recent acquisitions of Armstrong Pharmaceuticals and CTEX Pharmaceuticals. However, margins are likely to remain under pressure from sharp increases in SG&A costs, R&D spending and interest charges. EPS are projected at $1.10. Boosted by new drugs, especially from generic Prilosec, EPS could reach $2.80 in 2002.

Valuation - 14-JUN-01

The shares moved higher in recent months, boosted by strength in the specialty/generic drug sector; ADRX's filing for an extended- release version of Merck's Mevacor cholesterol-lowering drug; and a recent favorable court ruling concerning Prilosec. ADRX is engaged in a major legal battle with AstraZeneca (AZN) over ADRX's planned generic version of AZN's Prilosec antiulcer drug (U.S. sales of $4.2 billion in 2000). In late May 2001, a court ruled in ADRX's favor in the active metabolite Prilosec patent case. While there are still other patent issues yet to be decided, we believe that ADRX will probably prevail in those cases as well, and its generic Prilosec should be launched by late 2001 or early 2002 with 180 days of first-to-file marketing exclusivity. ADRX has has applications for 15 generic drugs under FDA review, with 25 others in varying stages of development. The speculative shares are recommended for superior appreciation.

Key Stock Statistics

S&P EPS Est. 2001	1.30	Tang. Bk. Value/Share	6.62
P/E on S&P Est. 2001	49.9	Beta	0.41
S&P EPS Est. 2002	3.20	Shareholders	30,000
Dividend Rate/Share	Nil	Market cap. (B)	$ 4.5
Shs. outstg. (M)	69.8	Inst. holdings	55%
Avg. daily vol. (M)	1.077		

Value of $10,000 invested 5 years ago: $ 179,089

Fiscal Year Ending Dec. 31

	2001	2000	1999	1998	1997	1996
Revenues (Million $)						
1Q	157.3	—	77.92	50.70	31.06	18.92
2Q	178.4	—	164.6	55.96	32.85	20.41
3Q	—	132.3	111.4	67.27	43.06	23.60
4Q	—	143.7	122.1	73.14	43.82	26.05
Yr.	—	520.0	476.0	247.1	149.7	88.98
Earnings Per Share ($)						
1Q	0.27	—	0.11	-0.02	-0.03	-0.02
2Q	0.34	—	0.76	-0.03	-0.04	-0.03
3Q	E0.34	0.22	0.28	0.08	-0.05	-0.02
4Q	E0.35	0.25	0.32	0.10	-0.02	-0.02
Yr.	E1.30	0.95	1.45	0.13	-0.14	-0.08

Next earnings report expected: NA

Dividend Data

The company has never paid any cash dividends on its common stock and does not intend to pay cash dividends for the foreseeable future.

A Division of The McGraw-Hill Companies

Andrx Group

Business Summary - 14-JUN-01

Andrx Group specializes in the formulation and marketing of controlled-release generic and proprietary oral pharmaceuticals using its own in-house developed drug delivery technologies. The company also distributes generic drugs manufactured by third parties to independent pharmacies, pharmacy chains and others. In September 2000, Andrx Corp. was reorganized into two tracking stocks -- Andrx Group (ADRX), which conducts pharmaceutical businesses; and Cybear, Inc. (CYBA), an information technology company providing Internet-based communications products to the health care industry.

Distributed products accounted for about 63% of total revenues in 2000, manufactured products for 34%, and licensing fees and other income for 3%.

The company has nine proprietary patented or patent pending drug delivery technologies that have the ability to be modified to fit a variety of pharmaceutical products and therapeutic needs. These technologies utilize various polymers and other materials to encapsulate or entrap active drug compounds and release them at varying rates at predetermined locations in the gastrointestinal tract. Drugs incorporating new delivery technologies typically offer advantages such as less frequent dosing, reduced side effects, and improved patient compliance.

The Andrx Pharmaceuticals division currently manufactures and markets four sustained release products -- Cartia XT, a bioequivalent version of Aventis's Cardizem CD drug used to treat hypertension and angina; Diltia XT, a bioequivalent of Aventis's Dilacor XR treatment for hypertension and angina; Pentoxifylline ER, a generic version of Aventis's Trental vasodilator; and Ketoprofen ER, a generic version of American Home Products' Oruvail nonsteroidal anti-inflammatory drug.

Andrx's generic pipeline includes some 15 abbreviated new drug applications for new generics filed with the FDA, which have an aggregate branded sales market estimated at about $11 billion. These include generic versions of Prilosec treatment for gastrointestinal disorders, Tiazac for hypertension and angina, Naprelan anti-inflammatory, Wellbutrin antidepressant, Zyban smoking cessation agent, K-Dur potassium supplement, Claritin D-24 allergy treatment, Depakote epilepsy drug, and Lodine XL treatment for arthritis.

Anda (the company's distribution business) purchases generic drugs directly from manufacturers and wholesalers, and markets them through its in-house telemarketing staff and sales representatives to independent pharmacies and regional pharmacy chains that do not maintain their own central warehousing facilities. Anda offers this customer group competitive pricing, quality products and responsive customer service. Aura Laboratories uses the drug delivery technologies developed by Andrx Pharmaceuticals to develop brand name controlled-release products across a broad spectrum of therapeutic applications.

Per Share Data ($) (Year Ended Dec. 31)	2000	1999	1998	1997	1996	1995	1994	1993	1992	1991
Tangible Bk. Val.	6.62	3.51	1.20	1.02	0.80	0.43	NA	NA	NA	NA
Cash Flow	0.97	1.56	0.19	-0.09	-0.06	-0.10	NA	NA	NA	NA
Earnings	0.95	1.45	0.13	-0.14	-0.08	-0.14	NA	NA	NA	NA
Dividends	Nil	Nil	Nil	Nil	Nil	NA	NA	NA	NA	NA
Payout Ratio	Nil	Nil	Nil	Nil	Nil	NA	NA	NA	NA	NA
Prices - High	95.87	39.00	12.92	11.75	4.40	NA	NA	NA	NA	NA
- Low	20.12	11.12	6.12	3.81	2.75	NA	NA	NA	NA	NA
P/E Ratio - High	NM	27	98	NM	NM	NA	NA	NA	NA	NA
- Low	NM	8	46	NM	NM	NA	NA	NA	NA	NA
Income Statement Analysis (Million $)										
Revs.	520	476	247	150	89.0	53.2	NA	NA	NA	NA
Oper. Inc.	93.7	150	11.2	-5.0	-1.4	-2.1	NA	NA	NA	NA
Depr.	9.6	4.5	3.0	2.0	1.0	0.9	NA	NA	NA	NA
Int. Exp.	0.8	1.7	0.4	0.5	0.8	0.6	NA	NA	NA	NA
Pretax Inc.	94.3	148	8.7	-7.6	-4.0	-5.2	NA	NA	NA	NA
Eff. Tax Rate	42%	38%	3.82%	NM	NM	NM	NA	NA	NA	NA
Net Inc.	58.5	94.1	8.4	-7.6	-4.0	-5.2	NA	NA	NA	NA
Balance Sheet & Other Fin. Data (Million $)										
Cash	116	32.6	17.5	6.6	3.4	13.8	NA	NA	NA	NA
Curr. Assets	561	304	100	75.1	56.8	32.2	NA	NA	NA	NA
Total Assets	668	358	121	90.8	66.6	36.1	NA	NA	NA	NA
Curr. Liab.	108	123	48.6	29.9	23.9	17.8	NA	NA	NA	NA
LT Debt	Nil	Nil	Nil	Nil	Nil	NA	NA	NA	NA	NA
Common Eqty.	560	221	72.6	60.9	42.8	18.3	NA	NA	NA	NA
Total Cap.	560	234	72.6	60.9	42.8	18.3	NA	NA	NA	NA
Cap. Exp.	44.5	22.2	8.0	7.7	6.9	1.5	NA	NA	NA	NA
Cash Flow	68.1	99	11.4	-5.6	-3.0	-4.3	NA	NA	NA	NA
Curr. Ratio	5.2	2.5	2.1	2.5	2.4	1.8	NA	NA	NA	NA
% LT Debt of Cap.	Nil	Nil	Nil	Nil	Nil	NA	NA	NA	NA	NA
% Net Inc.of Revs.	11.3	19.8	3.4	NM	NM	NM	NA	NA	NA	NA
% Ret. on Assets	11.4	39.3	7.9	NM	NM	NM	NA	NA	NA	NA
% Ret. on Equity	15.0	64.1	12.6	NM	NM	NM	NA	NA	NA	NA

Data as orig reptd.; bef. results of disc opers/spec. items. Per share data adj. for stk. divs. Bold denotes diluted EPS (FASB 128)-prior periods restated. E-Estimated. NA-Not Available. NM-Not Meaningful. NR-Not Ranked.

Office—4001 Southwest 47th Avenue, Fort Lauderdale, FL 33314. **Tel**—(954) 584-0300. **Website**—http://www.andrx.com **Co-Chrmn & CEO**—A. P. Cohen. **Co-Chrmn** —C. J. Chen. **Pres**—E. F. Hahn. **Secy**—S. Lodin. **CFO & Investor Contact**—A. C. Malahias. **Dirs**—T. A. Baum, A. P. Cohen, C. J. Chen, L. J. DuBow, I. C. Gerson, E. F. Hahn, M, A. Schwartz. **Transfer Agent & Registrar**—American Stock Transfer & Trust, NYC. **Incorporated**—in Delaware in 1992. **Empl**— 970. **S&P Analyst:** H. B. Saftlas

STANDARD & POOR'S
STOCK REPORTS

ArthroCare Corp.

Nasdaq Symbol **ARTC**

In S&P SmallCap 600

18-AUG-01

Industry: Health Care (Medical Products & Supplies)

Summary: This specialized medical device company supplies minimally invasive surgical systems for arthroscopic and other surgical applications.

S&P Opinion: Accumulate (★★★★) Recent Price • 31.67 | 52 Wk Range • 45.75-11.87 | Yield • Nil | 12-Mo. P/E • 52.8

Quantitative Evaluations

Outlook (1 Lowest—5 Highest) • **5**

Fair Value • **40.40**

Risk • **High**

Earn./Div. Rank • **NR**

Technical Eval. • **Bullish** since 7/01

Rel. Strength Rank (1 Lowest—99 Highest) • **96**

Insider Activity • **Unfavorable**

Overview - 25-JUL-01

We expect product sales to increase 30% in 2001, exceeding $80 million, on further penetration of the arthroscopic surgery market, and a full-year contribution from new rapidly growing non-arthroscopic markets. Despite the slower than anticipated ramp-up of new non-arthroscopic product sales in the second half of 2000, reflecting a sales force transition and a seasonal slowdown in cosmetic surgery, we believe these new businesses are poised to deliver substantial growth for the remainder of 2001. ARTC converted most of its domestic spinal and ear, nose and throat (ENT) market's distribution network to direct sales, which disrupted sales and resulted in high product returns in 2000. International sales should benefit from regulatory approvals in various countries. Strong revenue growth should drive substantial operating profit margin improvements, despite higher SG&A and R&D expenses.

Valuation - 25-JUL-01

We are maintaining our accumulate opinion on ARTC, reflecting its leading position in the arthroscopic surgery market, and product line extensions into new high-growth areas. Despite the slower than anticipated acceptance of new non-arthroscopic surgical procedures, a transition from distributor to direct sales in spinal and ENT markets, and a seasonal slowdown in elective procedures, the core arthroscopic surgery business continues to deliver strong, stable revenue growth. Moreover, we expect non-arthroscopic application sales growth to improve in late 2001 and early 2002, due to more favorable market opportunities. Despite the costs, the conversion to direct sales should have a beneficial long term impact. With 30% revenue growth through 2002, 50% EPS growth in 2002, and about 40% long-term EPS growth, we think ARTC is undervalued and will outperform the broader market.

Key Stock Statistics

S&P EPS Est. 2001	0.52	Tang. Bk. Value/Share	5.68
P/E on S&P Est. 2001	60.9	Beta	0.94
S&P EPS Est. 2002	0.70	Shareholders	201
Dividend Rate/Share	Nil	Market cap. (B)	$0.705
Shs. outstg. (M)	22.3	Inst. holdings	93%
Avg. daily vol. (M)	0.419		

Value of $10,000 invested 5 years ago: $ 48,723

Fiscal Year Ending Dec. 31

	2001	2000	1999	1998	1997	1996
Revenues (Million $)						
1Q	19.09	17.76	9.70	4.87	2.26	1.16
2Q	23.58	18.37	12.23	5.67	2.83	1.41
3Q	—	15.51	12.30	6.72	3.37	1.57
4Q	—	17.00	14.50	7.36	4.34	1.88
Yr.	—	67.63	48.73	24.62	12.80	6.02
Earnings Per Share ($)						
1Q	0.09	0.18	0.02	0.02	-0.13	-0.15
2Q	0.14	0.18	0.07	-0.06	-0.12	-0.10
3Q	—	0.29	0.06	-0.06	-0.11	-0.11
4Q	—	0.08	0.13	-0.01	-0.09	-0.13
Yr.	—	0.68	0.29	-0.12	-0.43	-0.47

Next earnings report expected: mid October

Dividend Data

No cash dividends have been paid.

A Division of The McGraw-Hill Companies

ArthroCare Corporation

Business Summary - 25-JUL-01

ArthroCare specializes in minimally invasive coblation technology, which enables surgeons to ablate (disintegrate), shrink, sculpt and suction soft tissue, and seal small bleeding vessels. Its multi-purpose system can replace surgical tools traditionally used in soft-tissue surgical procedures, including arthroscopy; cosmetic surgery; ear, nose and throat (ENT); spinal; neurosurgery; and some cardiology applications.

In 2000, about 3 million arthroscopic procedures were performed in the U.S. to remove torn cartilage and ligament tears, and loose or degenerative tissue. Historically, joint injuries (knee, shoulder, elbow, ankle, wrist and hip) were treated using open surgery in a hospital setting. Arthroscopic surgery, introduced in the 1980s, is performed through several small incisions, usually in an outpatient setting at lower cost, and with a shorter recovery period. ARTC introduced its arthroscopic surgery system in late 1995. As of December 31, 2000, it had shipped more than 10,500 systems and more than 1 million disposable devices, for various indications. Arthroscopic surgery products account for 80% to 85% of total product sales. ARTC believes it has penetrated 30% to 35% of U.S. hospitals performing arthroscopic procedures.

The spinal surgery market, estimated at over $1 billion in 2000, is growing over 20% annually. Chronic back pain affects 9 million people in the U.S., and is the leading reason for health care expenses. The main cause of persistent back pain is inflammation of the disc or instability of the disc wall. Herniated discs can often be treated by non-surgical means. In more severe cases, a disc is removed and surrounding vertebrae fused together (spinal fusion). ARTC's system targets patients for whom non-surgical treatment has been unsuccessful, but who do not want to undergo spinal fusion. Its spinal system removes some of the inner "jelly-like" part of the disc, relieving pressure on the spinal column. It entered the spinal surgery market in September 1999.

The company has expanded the use of its arthroscopic system to applications in neurologocial, ENT and cosmetic procedures. About 110,000 metastic brain tumors are diagnosed annually in the U.S. ARTC believes its system offers minimally invasive access to ablate tumors. It aims to use its system to treat ENT disorders, such as sleep apnea and snoring, by ablating excess tissue obstructing passages. In 2000, 1.5 million ENT procedures were performed. ARTC's cosmetic system removes facial tissue in an attempt to reduce wrinkles and treat imperfections. About 325,000 laser resurfacing procedures are performed annually in the U.S.. ARTC is also exploring the use of coblation in certain cardiology procedures via an agreement with Boston Scientific.

ARTC's arthroscopic, spinal surgery, ENT and cosmetic surgery products are sold through more than 141 independent distributors in the U.S. In 2000, international sales accounted for 14% of total sales.

Per Share Data ($) (Year Ended Dec. 31)	2000	1999	1998	1997	1996	1995	1994	1993	1992	1991
Tangible Bk. Val.	5.68	9.62	1.25	1.32	1.75	2.05	NA	NA	NA	NA
Cash Flow	0.86	0.78	-0.07	-0.40	-0.45	NA	NA	NA	NA	NA
Earnings	0.68	0.27	-0.12	-0.43	-0.47	NA	NA	NA	NA	NA
Dividends	Nil	Nil	Nil	Nil	NA	NA	NA	NA	NA	NA
Payout Ratio	Nil	Nil	Nil	Nil	NA	NA	NA	NA	NA	NA
Prices - High	79.25	40.00	11.50	7.37	13.25	NA	NA	NA	NA	NA
- Low	12.25	6.37	5.09	2.62	2.87	NA	NA	NA	NA	NA
P/E Ratio - High	NM	NM	NM	NM	d	NA	NA	NA	NA	NA
- Low	NM	NM	NM	NM	d	NA	NA	NA	NA	NA
Income Statement Analysis (Million $)										
Revs.	67.6	48.7	27.9	12.8	6.0	NA	NA	NA	NA	NA
Oper. Inc.	11.6	7.1	-2.1	-8.5	-8.8	NA	NA	NA	NA	NA
Depr.	4.1	2.4	1.0	0.6	0.4	NA	NA	NA	NA	NA
Int. Exp.	Nil	Nil	Nil	NA	NA	NA	NA	NA	NA	NA
Pretax Inc.	12.4	5.8	-2.1	-7.7	-7.7	NA	NA	NA	NA	NA
Eff. Tax Rate	NM	4.00%	NM	NA	NA	NA	NA	NA	NA	NA
Net Inc.	15.8	5.5	-2.1	-7.7	-7.7	NA	NA	NA	NA	NA
Balance Sheet & Other Fin. Data (Million $)										
Cash	86.8	79.6	2.8	8.2	11.4	NA	NA	NA	NA	NA
Curr. Assets	109	92.1	22.1	23.3	25.8	NA	NA	NA	NA	NA
Total Assets	140	110	27.8	26.7	33.3	NA	NA	NA	NA	NA
Curr. Liab.	9.4	6.9	5.2	3.0	2.3	NA	NA	NA	NA	NA
LT Debt	0.0	0.1	0.2	NA	NA	NA	NA	NA	NA	NA
Common Eqty.	126	103	22.3	23.5	30.8	NA	NA	NA	NA	NA
Total Cap.	126	103	22.5	NA	NA	NA	NA	NA	NA	NA
Cap. Exp.	6.2	5.3	3.9	NA	NA	NA	NA	NA	NA	NA
Cash Flow	20.0	8.0	-1.2	-7.1	-7.3	NA	NA	NA	NA	NA
Curr. Ratio	11.7	13.3	4.3	7.8	11.0	NA	NA	NA	NA	NA
% LT Debt of Cap.	0.0	0.1	0.7	NA	NA	NA	NA	NA	NA	NA
% Net Inc.of Revs.	23.4	11.4	NM	NA	NA	NA	NA	NA	NA	NA
% Ret. on Assets	12.7	8.0	NM	NA	NA	NA	NA	NA	NA	NA
% Ret. on Equity	13.8	8.9	NM	NA	NA	NA	NA	NA	NA	NA

Data as orig reptd.; bef. results of disc opers/spec. items. Per share data adj. for stk. divs. Bold denotes diluted EPS (FASB 128)-prior periods restated. E-Estimated. NA-Not Available. NM-Not Meaningful. NR-Not Ranked.

Office—595 North Pastoria Ave., Sunnyvale, CA 94086. **Tel**—(408) 736-0224. **Website**—www.arthrocare.com **Pres & CEO**—M. Baker. **VP-Fin & CFO**—C. Hanni. **Dirs**—M. Baker, A. J. Campbell-White, C. R. Larkin, T. Lendau, J. S. Lewis, R. R. Momsen, H. V. Thapliyal, P. L. Wilson. **Transfer Agent & Registrar**—Norwest Bank Minnesota, N.A. **Incorporated**—in California in 1993. **Empl**— 272. **S&P Analyst:** John A. Massey

STANDARD
&POOR'S
STOCK REPORTS

Aventis

NYSE Symbol **AVE**

18-AUG-01

Industry:
Health Care (Drugs - Major Pharmaceuticals)

Summary: AVE, formed via the 1999 merger of Rhone-Poulenc S.A. and Hoechst AG, is a global life sciences company with operations in pharmaceuticals, agriculture and animal health.

S&P Opinion: Accumulate (★★★★)

Recent Price • 73.90
52 Wk Range • 87.50-66.62

Yield • 0.4%
12-Mo. P/E • NM

Earnings vs. Previous Year
▲=Up ▼=Down ▶=No Change

Quantitative Evaluations

Outlook
(1 Lowest—5 Highest)
• **1**

Fair Value
• **54.60**

Risk
• **Average**

Earn./Div. Rank
• **NR**

Technical Eval.
• **NA**

Rel. Strength Rank
(1 Lowest—99 Highest)
• **46**

Insider Activity
• **NA**

OPTIONS: ASE, CBOE

Overview - 19-JUN-01

Revenues in 2001 are expected to rise 11%, led by strong gains in Allegra/Telfast antihistamine, Lovenox/Clexane low-molecular weight heparin, Taxotere anticancer therapy, Arava anti-arthritic, and Amaryl diabetes treatment. New products such as Lantus for diabetes, Actonel for osteoporosis, and Ketek antibiotic for resistant infections should also augment volume. However, sales of older respiratory and anti-infective drugs are expected to decline. Vaccine sales should remain robust, but only modest growth is seen for therapeutic proteins and crop protection products (the latter business is being divested). Margins should widen on the better volume, merger synergies and an improved product mix. EPS are estimated at $1.70, with further progress to $2.20 forecast for 2002.

Valuation - 19-JUN-01

The shares moved sideways in recent months, largely reflecting sluggishness in major international pharmaceutical stocks (especially in companies with premium P/E multiples such as AVE). Formed through the 1999 combination of Rhone Poulenc and Hoechst, Aventis ranks among the world's largest drugmakers, as well as in the top tier in terms of profit growth. AVE has projected annual earnings growth of 25%-30% over the next three years, driven by new product launches, expansion in gross margins and merger-related cost savings (to total about $700 million by the end 2002). Promising new products include Actonel for osteoporosis, Lantus for diabetes, and Ketek anti-infective. Profitability should also benefit from the divestiture of lower-margined agricultural and chemical lines. AVE's premium P/E is warranted by its strong EPS growth prospects. The shares merit accumulation.

Key Stock Statistics

S&P EPS Est. 2001	1.70	Tang. Bk. Value/Share	NM
P/E on S&P Est. 2001	43.5	Beta	0.39
S&P EPS Est. 2002	2.20	Shareholders	NA
Dividend Rate/Share	0.33	Market cap. (B)	$ 58.1
Shs. outstg. (M)	786.0	Inst. holdings	3%
Avg. daily vol. (M)	0.100		

Value of $10,000 invested 5 years ago: $ 30,375

Fiscal Year Ending Dec. 31

	2000	1999	1998	1997	1996	1995
Revenues (Million $)						
1Q	5,044	3,572	3,550	—	4,201	4,030
2Q	—	—	3,698	—	4,301	4,080
3Q	—	—	3,671	—	4,021	4,790
4Q	—	—	3,898	—	4,310	4,476
Yr.	21,020	12,684	15,623	15,430	16,391	17,376
Earnings Per ADR ($)						
1Q	**0.21**	—	**0.39**	—	0.37	0.43
2Q	—	—	**1.19**	—	0.47	0.33
3Q	—	—	**-0.19**	—	0.46	0.50
4Q	—	—	**-0.21**	—	0.34	0.11
Yr.	**-0.18**	**-2.51**	**2.03**	-2.55	**1.63**	1.37

Next earnings report expected: NA

Dividend Data (Dividends have been paid since 1993.)

Amount ($)	Date Decl.	Ex-Div. Date	Stock of Record	Payment Date
0.328	—	May. 18	May. 22	Jul. 02 '01

Aventis S.A.

Business Summary - 19-JUN-01

Aventis, headquartered in France, is a global life sciences company that was created via the union of France's Rhone Poulenc S.A. and Germany's Hoechst AG in December 1999. The company operates through two major divisions: Aventis Pharma and Aventis Agriculture. AVE is divesting its non-core crop protection and industrial chemicals units in order to focus on higher-margin life sciences businesses.

Total sales in 2000 were divided by business segment as follows: Aventis Pharma prescription drugs 62%, Aventis Pasteur vaccines 5%, Behring therapeutic proteins 5%, Aventis Crop Science 18%, Aventis Animal Nutrition 3%, and Messer industrial chemicals 7%.

Aventis Pharma's drugs are concentrated primarily in cardiology/thrombosis, oncology, respiratory, arthritis/bone, metabolism, anti-infectives, and central nervous system sectors. Key drugs include Allegra for treating hay fever; Lovenox, a treatment for deep-vein thrombosis and unstable angina; Delix, a drug for hypertension and congestive heart failure; Taxotere, a treatment for breast cancer and lung cancer; Amaryl, a drug for non-insulin dependent or Type 2 diabetes; and Arava, a treatment for rheumatoid arthritis. The U.S. represented 33% of Pharma sales in 2000, Europe 33%, Latin America 8%, Japan 7%, and all other areas 19%.

Aventis Pasteur offers vaccines in the areas of infectious diseases and cancers. Accounting for nearly one-third of the global vaccine market, this division immunizes more than 400 million people. Vaccines are provided against a wide range of diseases, including diphtheria, yellow fever, influenza, pneumonia, hepatitis A & B, measles, meningitis, polio, tuberculosis and typhoid fever.

Aventis Behring (formerly Centeon) is a global leader in the therapeutic protein industry, producing nearly one-fifth of the world's plasma-based therapies. Behring's products include coagulation therapies for hemophilia; wound-healing agents; blood clot inhibiting agents; immunoglobulins for immune disorders; and plasma expanders to treat shock, burns and circulatory disorders. Aventis Bio-Services collects, stores and tests plasma used in Behring's products.

Aventis Agriculture includes Aventis Crop Science, a leading producer of crop protection products such as herbicides, insecticides and fungicides sold under the Puma, Temik and Rovral names; Aventis Animal Nutrition, a producer of nutritional feed additives for animals and poultry; and Merial (50%-owned), a maker of veterinary drugs and vaccines.

Pharmaceutical R&D spending totaled $2.5 billion in 2000, equal to 16.8% of Aventis Pharma sales. Key products in development include Actonel for osteoporosis; Lantus for diabetes; Ketek anti-infective; inhaled insulin; and treatments for cancer, meningitis, hemophilia and other conditions.

Per ADR Data ($) (Year Ended Dec. 31)	2000	1999	1998	1997	1996	1995	1994	1993	1992	1991
Tangible Bk. Val.	NM	NM	NM	NM	2.09	NM	2.48	-0.64	-8.83	-10.88
Cash Flow	2.75	2.10	5.71	3.46	5.48	4.95	4.73	4.31	12.82	12.41
Earnings	-0.18	-2.51	2.03	-2.55	1.61	1.37	1.20	0.65	2.41	1.45
Dividends	0.33	0.48	0.47	0.45	0.43	0.44	0.44	0.50	1.18	0.99
Payout Ratio	NM	NM	23%	NM	27%	32%	38%	78%	49%	68%
Prices - High	87.50	68.56	58.62	47.00	35.00	25.62	27.62	29.00	28.00	20.12
- Low	45.50	43.37	35.81	29.62	20.50	19.37	21.00	22.62	19.50	9.75
P/E Ratio - High	NM	NM	29	NM	22	19	23	45	12	14
- Low	NM	NM	18	NM	13	14	17	35	8	7
Income Statement Analysis (Million $)										
Revs.	21,020	12,684	15,623	15,439	16,391	17,376	16,147	13,607	14,781	16,135
Oper. Inc.	3,644	1,707	2,785	2,455	2,757	2,761	2,568	2,120	2,439	2,550
Depr.	2,286	1,796	1,373	2,019	1,253	1,132	1,057	923	1,184	1,247
Int. Exp.	1,259	848	958	756	787	919	946	953	1,049	1,154
Pretax Inc.	-23.6	-829	1,343	-479	1,182	959	847	764	838	852
Eff. Tax Rate	NM	NM	30%	NM	26%	13%	9.80%	26%	25%	31%
Net Inc.	-27.3	-857	928	-668	739	680	568	258	376	248
Balance Sheet & Other Fin. Data (Million $)										
Cash	1,065	500	1,135	482	791	886	813	1,111	653	835
Curr. Assets	13,205	14,225	9,346	8,489	8,961	9,293	8,589	7,062	7,430	8,228
Total Assets	39,754	41,863	28,713	27,659	27,091	27,748	22,946	19,336	20,324	21,809
Curr. Liab.	14,241	17,158	9,792	7,824	7,496	8,220	6,746	5,319	6,197	7,842
LT Debt	7,743	6,481	4,566	6,722	5,146	5,426	3,706	3,655	4,576	4,095
Common Eqty.	9,621	29,317	8,852	7,045	8,255	6,776	6,080	4,328	3,494	3,555
Total Cap.	19,900	38,532	16,141	17,513	13,511	16,851	14,285	12,275	12,702	12,426
Cap. Exp.	2,358	1,388	916	1,099	1,883	1,861	1,608	1,507	1,255	1,395
Cash Flow	2,148	820	2,134	1,163	1,776	1,569	1,416	1,085	1,459	1,412
Curr. Ratio	0.9	0.8	1.0	1.1	1.2	1.1	1.3	1.3	1.2	1.0
% LT Debt of Cap.	38.9	16.8	28.3	38.4	38.1	32.2	25.9	29.8	36.0	33.0
% Net Inc.of Revs.	NM	NM	5.9	NM	4.5	3.9	3.5	1.9	2.5	1.5
% Ret. on Assets	NM	NM	3.2	NM	2.8	2.6	2.4	0.8	1.8	1.1
% Ret. on Equity	NM	NM	8.6	NM	6.7	6.4	6.2	2.7	7.8	4.9

Data as orig reptd.; bef. results of disc opers/spec. items. Per share data adj. for stk. divs. Bold denotes diluted EPS (FASB 128)-prior periods restated. Data prior to 1999 for Rhone-Poulenc S.A. E-Estimated. NA-Not Available. NM-Not Meaningful. NR-Not Ranked.

Office—Espace-Europeen de l'Enterprise, 16 ave de l'Europe, Schiltigheim, France, F 67300. **Tel**—33 3 88 99 11 00. **Website**—http://www.aventis.com **U.S. Office**—Rte. 202-206, Bridgewater, NJ 08807. **Chrmn**—J. Dormann. **CFO**—P. Langlois. **U.S. Investor Contact**—Norma Hunt-Allen (212-251-8077). **Management Board**—J. Dormann, J.-R. Fourtou, I. Landau, H. Waesche. **Supervisor Board**—J.-M. Bruel, M. Fruhauf, S. Kampf, H. Markl, G. Metz, D. Pineau-Valencienne, S. Razzouqi, M. Renault, H.-J. Schinzler, M. Vienot. **Despositary for ADRs**—Citibank, NYC. **Incorporated**—in France in 1999. **Empl**— 90,000. **S&P Analyst:** H. B. Saftlas.

STANDARD
&POOR'S
STOCK REPORTS

Caremark Rx

NYSE Symbol **CMX**

18-AUG-01

Industry: Health Care (Specialized Services)

Summary: This manager of pharmacy benefits has divested its physician practice division and other non-core operating assets.

S&P Opinion: Accumulate (★★★★)

Recent Price • 17.25 | Yield • Nil
52 Wk Range • 18.50-8.06 | 12-Mo. P/E • 57.5

Quantitative Evaluations

Outlook
(1 Lowest—5 Highest)
• **3⁻**

Fair Value
• **18**

Risk
• **Average**

Earn./Div. Rank
• **NR**

Technical Eval.
• **Bullish** since 6/01

Rel. Strength Rank
(1 Lowest—99 Highest)
• **79**

Insider Activity
• **Neutral**

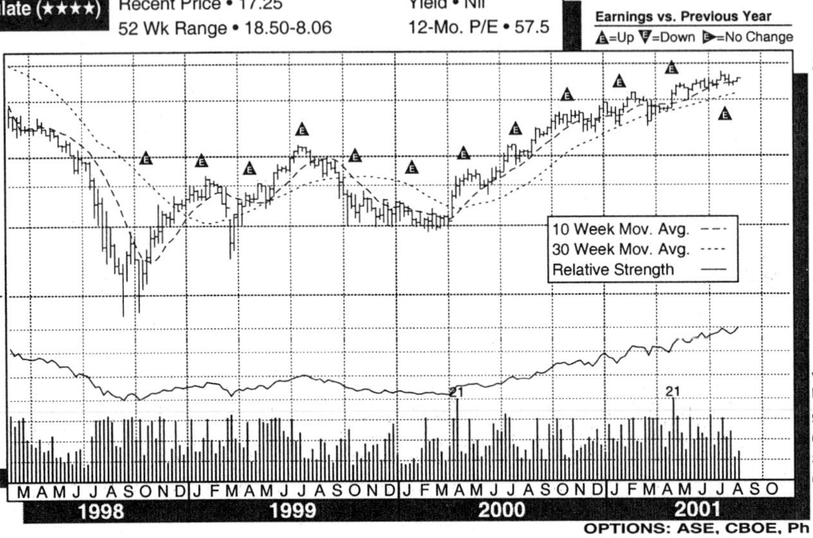

OPTIONS: ASE, CBOE, Ph

Overview - 14-AUG-01

As a result of slowing retail prescription processing volumes as well as slowing retail drug price inflation, we have reduced our 2001 revenue growth forecast to 27%, somewhat below the company's 28% to 30% guidance. Revenues from the pharmacy benefits management (PBM) and specialty services businesses should climb about 28% in 2001, reflecting the inclusion of new contracts, continued pharmaceutical price inflation (expected to run about 13%), increased service usage by the existing customer base, and new service offerings. Operating margins should continue to benefit from strength in the mail order business, although there are some pressures from constraints in obtaining recombinant hemophilia factor VIII from supplier Baxter International. Operating cash flow should be about $220 million. We see 2001 operating EPS growth from continuing operations of 58%, to $0.68, with a 25% advance, to $0.85, projected for 2002.

Valuation - 14-AUG-01

Although the company's 2001 revenue growth may fall below our original 30% expectation, operating margin expansion should help drive significant cash flow and net income gains. In fact, we recently boosted our 2001 EPS estimate by $0.03, to account for sequential gross margin per prescription improvement, distribution efficiencies, and lower debt levels. The stock continues to trade at under 1X forward sales, about in line with its PBM/drug distribution peer group, and at a modest 1.1X our three-year growth rate projection of 19%. The company also has significant operating loss carryforward credits that are likely to be utilized in next few years. Participating in a growing segment of the healthcare sector, with good visibility on earnings growth exceeding 20% over the next two years, we believe CMX offers further upside.

Key Stock Statistics

S&P EPS Est. 2001	0.68	Tang. Bk. Value/Share	NM
P/E on S&P Est. 2001	25.4	Beta	0.92
S&P EPS Est. 2002	0.85	Shareholders	27,299
Dividend Rate/Share	Nil	Market cap. (B)	$ 4.0
Shs. outstg. (M)	230.8	Inst. holdings	89%
Avg. daily vol. (M)	1.041		

Value of $10,000 invested 5 years ago: $ 8,571

Fiscal Year Ending Dec. 31

	2001	2000	1999	1998	1997	1996
Revenues (Million $)						
1Q	1,374	1,053	785.1	620.2	--	1,150
2Q	1,373	1,084	796.2	639.5	--	1,196
3Q	—	1,089	813.0	660.6	4,642	1,200
4Q	—	1,204	913.5	713.7	1,689	1,268
Yr.	—	4,430	3,308	2,634	6,331	4,814
Earnings Per Share ($)						
1Q	**0.15**	**0.09**	**0.06**	**0.03**	--	0.02
2Q	**0.16**	**0.09**	**0.06**	**0.01**	--	0.22
3Q	**E0.18**	**0.11**	**0.07**	**0.06**	0.05	-1.00
4Q	**E0.19**	**0.14**	**0.10**	**0.06**	-4.47	0.17
Yr.	**E0.68**	**0.43**	**-0.74**	**0.16**	**-4.25**	**-0.45**

Next earnings report expected: early November

Dividend Data

No dividends have been paid, and the company does not intend to pay any in the foreseeable future.

A Division of The McGraw-Hill Companies

Business Summary - 14-AUG-01

CaremarkRx (formerly MedPartners Inc.) provides pharmacy benefit management services and therapeutic pharmaceutical services that assist employers, insurance companies, unions, government employee group, HMOs and other sponsors of health benefit plans and individuals throughout the U.S. in delivering prescription drugs in a cost-effective manner. During 2000, CMX managed more than 68 million prescriptions for individuals from more than 1,200 organizations.

Pharmacy benefits management involves the design and administration of programs aimed at reducing the costs and improving the safety, effectiveness and convenience of prescription drug use. CMX dispenses prescription drugs to patients through a network of more than 50,000 third party retail pharmacies (about 96% of all retail pharmacies in the U.S.) and through three of its own mail service pharmacies. In 2000, the company processed about 53.8 million retail prescriptions (up from 38.5 million in 1999), and filled 14.6 million (12.2 million) mail order prescriptions.

In 2001, CMX planned to transfer the operations of its Lincolnshire, IL, automated mail service pharmacy to a larger facility in nearby Mount Prospect, IL. In addition, it planned to begin development of a fourth automated mail service pharmacy, to meet projected demand.

Through its Caremark Therapeutic Services (CTS) unit, the company offers therapeutic pharmaceutical services and associated disease management programs to improve outcomes and lower the cost of treating chronic illnesses. Therapies and services are provided to patients with conditions such as hemophilia, growth disorders, immune deficiencies, cystic fibrosis, multiple sclerosis, and respiratory difficulties. Services generally include provision of injectable bio-pharmaceutical drugs and supplies and associated patient support services. Drugs are distributed by a national network of 23 specialty pharmacies and one retail pharmacy. CTS programs currently serve more than 34,000 patients, delivering over 322,000 specialized prescriptions per year.

In July 1999, the company launched RxRequest.com, a fully secure customer Internet website that provides expanded services, including on-line prescription refill order capabilities for CMX's prescription drug plan participants. RXRequest.com also lets users check the status of their prescription refill orders, print order and claim forms, and locate the most appropriate participating retail pharmacies.

During 1998, CMX began several initiatives intended to refocus its operations on the PBM division, including a sweeping asset divestiture program. In 1999, the company sold its contract services operations, all of its California physician practice management (PPM) operations, and all but four of the clinics in its non-California PPM operations. The remaining four clinics were sold during 2000.

Per Share Data ($) **(Year Ended Dec. 31)**	**2000**	**1999**	**1998**	**1997**	**1996**	**1995**	**1994**	**1993**	**1992**	**1991**
Tangible Bk. Val.	NM	NM	NM	NA	0.49	1.49	NA	NA	NA	NA
Cash Flow	0.55	-0.62	0.29	-3.09	-0.05	0.68	0.51	0.44	NA	NA
Earnings	0.43	-0.74	0.16	-4.25	-0.58	Nil	-0.08	-0.05	NA	NA
Dividends	Nil	Nil	Nil	Nil	Nil	Nil	NA	NA	NA	NA
Payout Ratio	Nil	Nil	Nil	Nil	Nil	Nil	NA	NA	NA	NA
Prices - High	13.93	9.00	22.37	32.00	36.00	34.50	NA	NA	NA	NA
- Low	3.75	2.87	1.62	17.87	16.37	13.00	NA	NA	NA	NA
P/E Ratio - High	32	NM	NM	NM	NM	NM	NA	NA	NA	NA
- Low	9	NM	NM	NM	NM	NM	NA	NA	NA	NA
Income Statement Analysis (Million $)										
Revs.	4,430	3,308	2,634	6,331	4,813	1,137	802	541	NA	NA
Oper. Inc.	236	201	163	110	318	103	34.0	26.0	NA	NA
Depr.	25.4	22.1	24.7	120	81.9	29.1	21.9	14.1	NA	NA
Int. Exp.	110	120	78.8	55.7	23.9	8.4	6.0	3.3	NA	NA
Pretax Inc.	100	-138	49.6	-772	-95.1	-25.5	4.3	8.3	NA	NA
Eff. Tax Rate	8.49%	NM	38%	NM	NM	NM	NM	NM	NA	NA
Net Inc.	91.4	-143	30.8	-694	-89.8	-0.2	-3.1	-1.5	NA	NA
Balance Sheet & Other Fin. Data (Million $)										
Cash	2.4	6.8	23.1	216	124	90.9	NA	NA	NA	NA
Curr. Assets	453	535	1,186	1,313	947	269	NA	NA	NA	NA
Total Assets	686	771	1,862	2,891	2,266	579	NA	NA	NA	NA
Curr. Liab.	635	563	1,100	1,237	777	210	NA	NA	NA	NA
LT Debt	933	1,430	1,735	1,471	716	201	NA	NA	NA	NA
Common Eqty.	-969	-1,281	-1,144	90.9	739	184	NA	NA	NA	NA
Total Cap.	-35.7	149	591	1,562	1,455	385	NA	NA	NA	NA
Cap. Exp.	23.2	20.4	28.7	123	122	NA	NA	NA	NA	NA
Cash Flow	117	-121	55.5	-573	-7.9	28.9	18.8	12.6	NA	NA
Curr. Ratio	0.7	0.9	1.1	1.1	1.2	1.3	NA	NA	NA	NA
% LT Debt of Cap.	NM	962.7	293.6	94.1	49.2	52.2	NA	NA	NA	NA
% Net Inc.of Revs.	2.1	NM	1.2	NM	NM	NM	NM	NM	NA	NA
% Ret. on Assets	12.6	NM	1.3	NM	NM	NM	NA	NA	NA	NA
% Ret. on Equity	NM	NM	NA	NM	NM	NM	NA	NA	NA	NA

Data as orig. reptd. (pro forma prior to 1996); bef. results of disc. opers. and/or spec. items. Per share data adj. for stk. divs. as of ex-div. date. Bold denotes diluted EPS (FASB 128). E-Estimated. NA-Not Available. NM-Not Meaningful. NR-Not Ranked.

Office—3000 Galleria Tower, Suite 1000, Birmingham, AL 35244. **Tel**—(205) 733-8996. **Website**—http://www.caremark.com **Chrmn & CEO**—E. M. Crawford. **Pres & COO**—J. H. Dickerson Jr. **EVP-CFO**—H. A. McLure. **Investor Contact**—P. Clemens. **Dirs**—C. D. Brown, C. Conway-Welch, E. M. Crawford, H. Diamond, J. H. Dickerson Jr., K. E. Gibney, E. L. Hardin Jr., T. H. McCourtney Jr., C. A. Piccolo. **Transfer Agent & Registrar**—Mellon Investor Services, Ridgefield Park, NJ. **Incorporated**—in Delaware in 1995. **Empl**— 3,474. **S&P Analyst:** Robert M. Gold

STANDARD
&POOR'S
STOCK REPORTS

CIGNA Corp.

NYSE Symbol **CI**

In S&P 500

18-AUG-01

Industry:
Health Care (Managed Care)

Summary: The July 1999 sale of its property-casualty insurance unit completed CI's transformation from a multi-line insurer to an employee benefits company.

S&P Opinion: Accumulate (★★★★)

Recent Price • 90.17
52 Wk Range • 136.75-86.48
Yield • 1.4%
12-Mo. P/E • 13.0

Quantitative Evaluations

Outlook
(1 Lowest—5 Highest)
• **4+**

Fair Value
• **99.70**

Risk
• **Low**

Earn./Div. Rank
• **B+**

Technical Eval.
• **Bearish** since 8/01

Rel. Strength Rank
(1 Lowest—99 Highest)
• **38**

Insider Activity
• **NA**

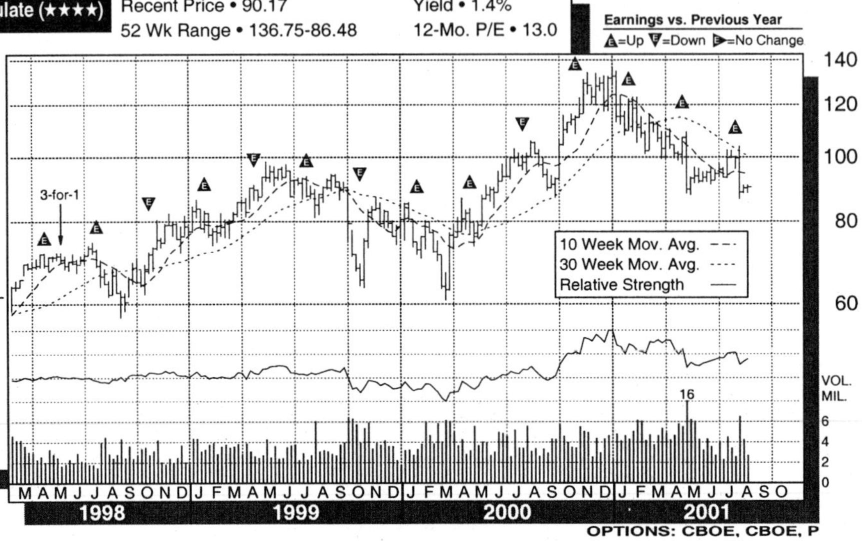

OPTIONS: CBOE, CBOE, P

Overview - 03-AUG-01

Second quarter results were disappointing, reflecting higher than anticipated medical cost trends in the HMO unit and lower fee income from the retirement unit due to stock market volatility. For 2001, we project revenue of about $19.5 billion, on higher premiums, partly offset by slightly lower enrollment in the Health Care unit. Health Care operations (two-thirds of operating profit) should post modest earnings gains, on 12% premium rate hikes, partly offset by lower enrollment. We see medical cost trends at 12%-13%, and expect the commercial medical loss ratio (MLR) to deteriorate. SG&A expenses will likely rise slightly as a percentage of sales, on higher technology and e-commerce spending. Retirement Benefits' results should decline, as stock market volatility hurts returns. CI repurchased 1.7 million shares in the second quarter, with $484 million still authorized at August 1.

Valuation - 03-AUG-01

We reiterate our accumulate opinion on CI, reflecting its diverse operations and large percentage of non-risk health care business. In the second quarter, medical cost trends of 12%-13% were higher than expected, partly offset by 12% premium rate hikes. The risk-based MLR rose 110 basis points, to 85.7%, from 84.6% in 2000. Through early August, the stock has fallen about 30%, reflecting the disappointing first half results. However, we continue to view CI as one of the most attractive managed care companies, due to its diverse business mix, strong balance sheet, and consistent earnings performance. Long term, we think CI will continue to offset rising medical costs with disciplined premium pricing and mid single-digit member growth. Despite weak health care results, which will continue in the second half of 2001, trading at 10.5X our 2002 EPS estimate, a discount to a peer group, CI is undervalued.

Key Stock Statistics

S&P EPS Est. 2001	7.16	Tang. Bk. Value/Share	23.26
P/E on S&P Est. 2001	12.6	Beta	0.60
S&P EPS Est. 2002	8.25	Shareholders	10,947
Dividend Rate/Share	1.28	Market cap. (B)	$ 13.4
Shs. outstg. (M)	148.1	Inst. holdings	79%
Avg. daily vol. (M)	1.045		

Value of $10,000 invested 5 years ago: $ 24,471

Fiscal Year Ending Dec. 31

	2001	2000	1999	1998	1997	1996
Revenues (Million $)						
1Q	4,732	4,891	5,400	5,411	4,645	4,645
2Q	4,663	4,971	4,697	5,321	4,719	4,731
3Q	—	5,026	4,689	5,226	5,182	4,685
4Q	—	5,106	4,898	5,479	5,492	4,889
Yr.	—	19,994	18,781	21,437	20,038	18,950
Earnings Per Share ($)						
1Q	1.78	1.60	1.34	2.27	1.30	1.05
2Q	1.66	0.99	1.48	1.42	1.25	1.01
3Q	—	1.74	-0.68	1.19	1.25	1.24
4Q	—	1.76	1.63	1.14	1.09	1.36
Yr.	—	6.08	3.54	6.05	4.88	4.64

Next earnings report expected: early November

Dividend Data (Dividends have been paid since 1867.)

Amount ($)	Date Decl.	Ex-Div. Date	Stock of Record	Payment Date
0.310	Dec. 11	Dec. 20	Dec. 22	Jan. 10 '01
0.320	Feb. 28	Mar. 09	Mar. 13	Apr. 10 '01
0.320	Apr. 25	Jun. 08	Jun. 12	Jul. 10 '01
0.320	Jul. 25	Sep. 10	Sep. 12	Oct. 10 '01

A Division of The McGraw-Hill Companies

CIGNA Corporation

Business Summary - 03-AUG-01

CIGNA Corp. is one of the largest investor-owned employee benefits organizations in the U.S. The company provides health care products and services, group life, accident and disability insurance, retirement products and services, and investment management.

Segment contributions to operating income in recent years were: Employee Health Care, Life and Disability $762 million in 2000 and $728 million in 1999; Employee Retirement and Investment Management $257 million and $265 million; International $48 million and $16 million; and other $101 million and $137 million.

CIGNA Healthcare offers a complete range of group medical, dental and life insurance products, and designs benefit plans to meet the needs of employers of all sizes and their employees. CIGNA Healthcare is one of the leading providers of employee benefits, with programs in all 50 states, the District of Columbia, and Puerto Rico. Medical covered lives at June 30, 2001, totaled 14.3 million, consisting of 6.9 million HMO members and 7.4 million medical indemnity lives. At year-end 2000, the company's HMO networks included 288,000 physicians and 3,600 hospitals. On January 1, 2001, CIGNA exited all but two Medicare markets. The company also offers dental, behavioral health, and employee assistance services.

CIGNA Group Insurance provides a full spectrum of employer-paid and voluntary life, accident and disability products, and designs disability management services to meet specific company needs. Based on earned premiums, it is a leading U.S. provider of group accident insurance and among the largest providers of group long-term disability insurance. At December 31, 2001, CI held group life insurance policies covering 17.6 million lives.

CIGNA Retirement and Investment Services businesses provide investment products, including its proprietary Charter Funds, and professional services primarily to sponsors of qualified pension, profit sharing and retirement savings plans. It also offers corporate life insurance, principally to Fortune 1000 companies. At June 30, 2001, assets under management totaled $54.7 billion, down from $56.6 billion a year earlier.

The CIGNA International Life, Health and Employee Benefits unit operates in selected markets outside the U.S. and provides individual and group life, accident and health, health care and pension products. In 1999 and January, 2001, the company sold 29% and 21%, respectively, of its Japanese Life Operation to Yasuda Fire & Marine Insurance Co., reducing its ownership stake to 40%. CI is considering selling its remaining ownership interest in the Japanese Life Operation to Yasuda.

In April 2001, directors increased the stock repurchase authorization by $500 million; at August 1, 2001, the current authorization stood at $484 million.

Per Share Data ($) (Year Ended Dec. 31)	2000	1999	1998	1997	1996	1995	1994	1993	1992	1991
Tangible Bk. Val.	23.26	24.67	28.07	24.95	27.66	26.49	21.44	24.59	20.26	20.38
Oper. Earnings	NA	3.52	4.63	4.72	4.38	0.23	2.42	0.05	0.67	1.87
Earnings	6.08	3.54	6.05	4.88	4.62	0.95	2.55	1.08	1.57	2.11
Dividends	1.24	1.19	1.14	1.11	1.07	1.01	1.01	1.01	1.01	1.01
Relative Payout	20%	34%	19%	23%	23%	106%	40%	94%	65%	48%
Prices - High	136.75	98.62	82.37	66.91	47.79	38.33	24.66	22.79	20.29	20.58
- Low	60.75	63.43	56.00	44.70	33.58	20.75	19.00	18.83	15.70	12.00
P/E Ratio - High	22	28	14	14	10	40	10	21	13	10
- Low	10	18	9	9	7	22	7	17	10	6
Income Statement Analysis (Million $)										
Life Ins. In Force	58,903	662,693	670,667	695,272	NA	NA	NA	NA	574,318	508,756
Prem. Inc.: Life A & H	16,328	15,079	13,913	12,251	9,518	9,272	8,869	8,516	9,127	9,019
Prem. Inc.: Cas./Prop.	NA	Nil	2,500	2,684	4,398	4,640	5,043	5,136	4,797	5,276
Net Invest. Inc.	2,942	2,959	3,705	4,245	4,333	4,296	3,946	3,902	3,914	3,860
Total Revs.	19,994	18,781	21,437	20,038	18,950	18,955	18,392	18,402	18,582	18,750
Pretax Inc.	1,497	1,219	2,010	1,650	1,601	251	805	165	179	584
Net Oper. Inc.	983	695	1,190	971	1,000	50.0	526	NA	145	401
Net Inc.	987	699	1,292	1,086	1,056	211	554	234	337	453
Balance Sheet & Other Fin. Data (Million $)										
Cash & Equiv.	2,739	2,732	3,797	2,625	2,177	2,467	2,528	1,975	1,745	2,561
Premiums Due	2,814	2,475	4,469	4,265	4,229	4,268	3,986	4,065	3,564	3,931
Invest. Assets: Bonds	24,776	22,944	32,634	36,358	36,253	37,354	31,670	33,112	28,228	26,296
Invest. Assets: Stocks	569	585	1,043	854	701	661	1,860	1,849	2,321	2,140
Invest. Assets: Loans	12,755	12,816	15,784	18,112	18,223	18,117	15,325	13,684	12,975	13,024
Invest. Assets: Total	41,516	38,295	50,707	37,697	56,534	57,710	50,919	50,728	45,082	42,597
Deferred Policy Costs	1,052	927	1,069	1,542	1,230	1,109	1,128	1,085	1,061	1,056
Total Assets	95,088	95,333	114,612	108,199	98,932	95,903	86,102	84,975	69,827	66,737
Debt	1,163	1,359	1,431	2,155	1,021	1,066	1,389	1,235	929	848
Common Eqty.	5,634	6,149	8,277	7,932	7,208	7,157	5,811	6,575	5,744	5,863
Comb. Loss-Exp. Ratio	NA	NA	107.1	NA	132.0	144.5	123.9	137.4	131.3	117.3
% Return On Revs.	4.9	3.7	6.0	5.4	5.6	1.1	3.0	1.3	1.8	2.4
% Ret. on Equity	16.5	9.1	15.9	14.3	14.7	3.3	8.9	3.8	5.8	8.2
% Invest. Yield	7.1	7.4	8.4	7.5	7.6	15.2	7.8	8.1	8.9	9.4

Data as orig reptd.; bef. results of disc opers/spec. items. Per share data adj. for stk. divs. Bold denotes diluted EPS (FASB 128)-prior periods restated. E-Estimated. NA-Not Available. NM-Not Meaningful. NR-Not Ranked.

Office—One Liberty Place, Philadelphia, PA 19192. **Inc.**—in Delaware in 1981. **Tel**—(215) 761-1000. **Website**—www.cigna.com **Chrmn, Pres & CEO**—H. E. Hanway. **EVP & CFO**—J. G. Stewart. **Secy**—C. J. Ward. **Investor Contact**—Ted Detrick (215-761-6130). **Dirs**—R. P. Bauman, R. H. Campbell, A. C. DeCrane Jr., H. E. Hanway, P. N. Larson, J. Neubauer, C. R. Shoemate, L. W. Sullivan, H. A. Wagner, C. C. Wait, M. Ware. **Transfer Agent & Registrar**—First Chicago Trust Co. of New York, Jersey City, NJ. **Incorporated**—in Delaware in 1981. **Empl**— 43,200. **S&P Analyst:** John A. Massey

STANDARD & POOR'S
STOCK REPORTS

Cytyc Corp.

Nasdaq Symbol **CYTC**

18-AUG-01

Industry: Health Care (Medical Products & Supplies)

Summary: This company is the leading provider of automated cervical cancer screening processors and tests (ThinPrep) that replace the traditional Pap smear.

S&P Opinion: Accumulate (★★★★)

Recent Price • 25.70
52 Wk Range • 27.01-11.25
Yield • Nil
12-Mo. P/E • 54.7

Quantitative Evaluations

Outlook (1 Lowest—5 Highest)
• 5
Fair Value
• 37
Risk
• High
Earn./Div. Rank
• B-

Technical Eval.
• Bullish since 4/01
Rel. Strength Rank (1 Lowest—99 Highest)
• 83
Insider Activity
• Neutral

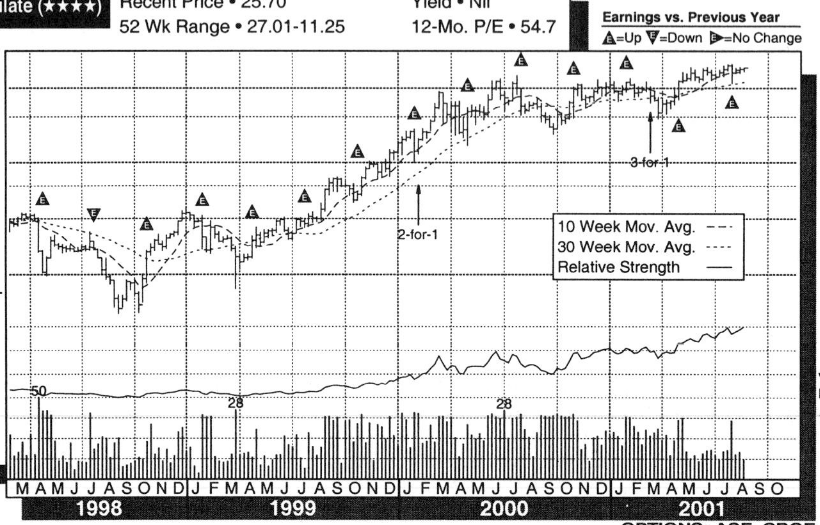

OPTIONS: ASE, CBOE

Overview - 27-JUL-01

Second quarter results exceeded our estimate. In 2001, revenue should increase more than 50%, to about $215 million, as adoption of ThinPrep accelerates, aided by an aggressive direct-to-consumer advertising campaign. With increased awareness and education about its advantages, market share should reach 53% by year-end. The addition of new payors boosted U.S. covered lives to over 200 million; exclusive lab agreements should drive further gains. Labs that process ThinPrep handle over 80% of the estimated 50 million to 55 million U.S. Pap smears processed annually. Shipments of the new high-volume ThinPrep 3000 processor should ramp up in the second half of 2001. We expect CYTC to file a pre-market application (PMA) for its new imaging system by year-end, with U.S. sales to start by mid-2002. With high-margin consumables accounting for 80%-85% of sales, sales growth will drive margin gains. Operating margins should be 38.5%.

Valuation - 27-JUL-01

We are maintaining our accumulate opinion on CYTC, reflecting the strong ThinPrep market penetration, international expansion plans and the launch of its imaging system in 2002. Cervical cancer, the second most common cancer among women, remains the largest non-automated diagnostic test. In clinical trials, ThinPrep improved detection 65% and cut the need for repeat testing of inadequate samples over 50%. With U.S. penetration at 46%, a huge opportunity exists for the dominant player in a $500 million market. Worldwide, 110 million to 120 million pap tests are conducted annually (50 million to 55 million in the U.S.). ThinPrep continues to gain market share rapidly; we expect it to reach 53% of U.S. tests by year-end. Trading at 34X our 2002 EPS estimate of $0.71, with strong momentum, CYTC should outperform.

Key Stock Statistics

S&P EPS Est. 2001	0.45	Tang. Bk. Value/Share	1.80
P/E on S&P Est. 2001	57.1	Beta	1.99
S&P EPS Est. 2002	0.71	Shareholders	303
Dividend Rate/Share	Nil	Market cap. (B)	$ 3.0
Shs. outstg. (M)	115.6	Inst. holdings	90%
Avg. daily vol. (M)	1.268		

Value of $10,000 invested 5 years ago: $ 82,240

Fiscal Year Ending Dec. 31

	2001	2000	1999	1998	1997	1996
Revenues (Million $)						
1Q	47.47	28.78	16.21	8.06	3.44	1.11
2Q	53.00	33.53	18.83	9.23	5.16	1.68
3Q	—	37.21	21.33	12.35	7.01	2.69
4Q	—	42.55	24.73	14.63	10.74	2.71
Yr.	—	142.1	81.10	44.26	26.35	8.20
Earnings Per Share ($)						
1Q	**0.13**	**0.05**	**0.01**	**-0.06**	-0.07	-0.04
2Q	**0.13**	**0.06**	**0.01**	**-0.07**	-0.07	-0.03
3Q	—	**0.09**	**0.01**	**-0.01**	-0.06	-0.03
4Q	—	**0.12**	**0.05**	**0.03**	**-0.02**	-0.05
Yr.	—	**0.32**	**0.05**	**-0.11**	**-0.22**	**-0.15**

Next earnings report expected: NA

Dividend Data

No cash dividends have been paid. The stock was split two for one in 2000 and three for one in 2001.

A Division of The McGraw-Hill Companies

Cytyc Corporation

Business Summary - 27-JUL-01

Cytyc manufactures sample preparation systems for medical diagnostic applications, specifically cervical cancer. The company's ThinPrep System allows for the automated preparation of cervical cell specimens on microscope slides.

Since the late 1940s, cervical cancer screening has been conducted using the Pap smear. Widespread use in the U.S. has reduced mortality rates from cervical cancer over 70%. However, despite its success, the Pap smear test has some deficiencies, including inadequacies in sample collection and slide preparation, slide interpretation errors, and inability to use the specimen for additional tests. These limitations result in a substantial number of inaccurate or inconclusive test results that too often result in false negative diagnosis, which can lead to significantly higher treatment costs and retesting. A study by the U.S. Department of Health and Human Services concluded that the false negative rate using the conventional Pap smear is about 49%.

The ThinPrep system, originally cleared by the FDA in 1996, improves accuracy via better slide preparation and simplified sample preparation process, allows for multiple tests to be conducted from a single sample, and improves productivity. With ThinPrep, the cervical sample device is deposited in a vial filled with CYTC's PreserveCyt solution, which separates the contents into groups; the vial is then forwarded to the lab. At the lab, the vial is inserted into a ThinPrep processor that removes the blood and mucus and homogenizes the cell population. The cells are spread in a thin layer, transferred onto a glass slide, and treated with a preservative solution. As an indication of ThinPrep's effectiveness, the FDA allows CYTC to claim that ThinPrep is significantly more effective in detecting low grade squamous intraepithelial lesions and more severe lesions than the conventional Pap smear method.

In clinical trials, ThinPrep improved disease detection by 65% in screening centers, and reduced the need for repeat testing of inadequate samples by over 50%.

In late 2000, the company began shipping its next-generation high-volume ThinPrep 3000 system, which can process up to 80 sample vials simultaneously. In December 2000, CYTC's ThinPrep Imaging System, which partially automates cervical cancer screening, began clinical trials in the U.S. The imaging systems was launched internationally in the 2001 second quarter. In late 2001, CYTC plans to file for FDA approval, with a U.S. launch planned by mid 2002.

In October 2000, CYTC entered into an agreement with Roche Diagnostics to co-promote the benefits of testing for chlamydia and gonorrhea directly from the ThinPrep collection vial. In January 2001, it entered into a similar agreement with Digene Corp. for human papillomavirus (HPV) .

Currently, about 350 health insurance companies, representing over 200 million lives, provide coverage for ThinPrep testing. The company has installed more than 1,400 T hinPrep processors to date.

Per Share Data ($) (Year Ended Dec. 31)	2000	1999	1998	1997	1996	1995	1994	1993	1992	1991
Tangible Bk. Val.	1.30	0.88	0.80	0.92	0.56	0.66	NA	NA	NA	NA
Cash Flow	0.35	0.07	-0.10	-0.21	-0.15	NA	NA	NA	NA	NA
Earnings	0.32	0.06	-0.11	-0.22	-0.15	NA	NA	NA	NA	NA
Dividends	Nil	Nil	Nil	Nil	Nil	NA	NA	NA	NA	NA
Payout Ratio	Nil	Nil	Nil	Nil	Nil	NA	NA	NA	NA	NA
Prices - High	23.47	10.38	4.64	5.25	5.75	NA	NA	NA	NA	NA
- Low	7.93	1.66	1.22	2.41	1.95	NA	NA	NA	NA	NA
P/E Ratio - High	73	NM	NM	NM	NM	NA	NA	NA	NA	NA
- Low	25	NM	NM	NM	NM	NA	NA	NA	NA	NA
Income Statement Analysis (Million $)										
Revs.	142	81.1	44.3	26.3	8.2	NA	NA	NA	NA	NA
Oper. Inc.	37.8	3.1	-17.5	-26.1	-13.6	NA	NA	NA	NA	NA
Depr.	3.5	2.0	1.6	1.1	0.5	NA	NA	NA	NA	NA
Int. Exp.	Nil	Nil	Nil	Nil	Nil	NA	NA	NA	NA	NA
Pretax Inc.	39.0	5.8	-11.7	-22.1	-11.9	NA	NA	NA	NA	NA
Eff. Tax Rate	2.19%	2.25%	NM	NA	NA	NA	NA	NA	NA	NA
Net Inc.	38.2	5.6	-11.7	-22.1	-11.9	NA	NA	NA	NA	NA
Balance Sheet & Other Fin. Data (Million $)										
Cash	61.6	29.7	33.6	47.2	27.6	NA	NA	NA	NA	NA
Curr. Assets	141	99	87.1	100	44.0	NA	NA	NA	NA	NA
Total Assets	171	112	97.7	108	50.2	NA	NA	NA	NA	NA
Curr. Liab.	23.8	17.3	11.9	12.2	3.5	NA	NA	NA	NA	NA
LT Debt	Nil	Nil	Nil	Nil	Nil	NA	NA	NA	NA	NA
Common Eqty.	147	95.0	85.8	96.2	46.7	NA	NA	NA	NA	NA
Total Cap.	147	95.0	85.8	96.2	46.7	NA	NA	NA	NA	NA
Cap. Exp.	10.8	3.8	4.6	NA	NA	NA	NA	NA	NA	NA
Cash Flow	41.6	7.6	-10.1	-21.0	-11.4	NA	NA	NA	NA	NA
Curr. Ratio	5.9	5.7	7.3	8.2	12.6	NA	NA	NA	NA	NA
% LT Debt of Cap.	Nil	Nil	Nil	Nil	Nil	NA	NA	NA	NA	NA
% Net Inc.of Revs.	26.9	7.0	NM	NM	NM	NA	NA	NA	NA	NA
% Ret. on Assets	26.9	5.4	NM	NM	NM	NA	NA	NA	NA	NA
% Ret. on Equity	31.5	6.2	NM	NM	NM	NA	NA	NA	NA	NA

Data as orig reptd.; bef. results of disc opers/spec. items. Per share data adj. for stk. divs. Bold denotes diluted EPS (FASB 128)-prior periods restated. E-Estimated. NA-Not Available. NM-Not Meaningful. NR-Not Ranked.

Office—85 Swanson Road, Boxborough, MA 01719. **Tel**—(978) 263-8000. **Website**—www.cytyc.com **Chmn**—M. E. Trout. **Pres & CEO**—P. J. Sullivan. **VP & CFO**—R. Bowen. **Investor Contact**—Anne Rivers (978-266-3010). **VP & Secy**—A. S. Meszner-Eltrich. **Dirs**—A. J. Battaglia, W. E. Boomer, S. W. Crawford, W. G. Little, W. H. Longfield, C. W. McDaniel, A. S. Richo, P. J. Sullivan, M. E. Trout. **Transfer Agent & Registrar**—Fleet Bank, c/o EquiServe. **Incorporated**—in Massachusetts in 1987. **Empl**— 457. **S&P Analyst:** John Massey

STANDARD
&POOR'S
STOCK REPORTS

Elan Corporation, plc

NYSE Symbol **ELN**

18-AUG-01

Industry:
Health Care (Drugs - Generic & Other)

Summary: This leading worldwide drug delivery and specialty pharmaceutical company derives its revenues from licensed and proprietary products.

S&P Opinion: Accumulate (★★★★)

Recent Price • 54.98
52 Wk Range • 65-42.75

Yield • Nil
12-Mo. P/E • 29.7

Quantitative Evaluations

Outlook
(1 Lowest—5 Highest)
• **5**

Fair Value
• **72.30**

Risk
• **NA**

Earn./Div. Rank
• **NR**

Technical Eval.
• **Bearlish** since 8/01

Rel. Strength Rank
(1 Lowest—99 Highest)
• **42**

Insider Activity
• **NA**

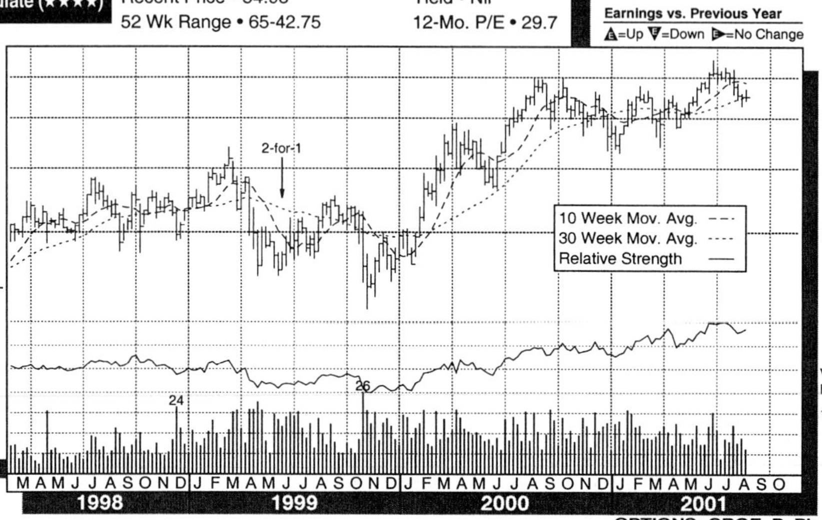

OPTIONS: CBOE, P, Ph

Overview - 04-MAY-01

Revenues should advance 20% in 2001. The rise should reflect strength in Zanaflex anti-spasticity, Skelaxin pain treatment and other established drugs, as well as new drugs such as Abelcet antifungal, Myobloc for cervical dystonia, Zonegran anti-epileptic, Frovelan anti-migraine and Ziconotide for severe pain. These gains should more than outweigh expected slowing in sales of Naprelan antiarthritic, Permax Parkinson's disease treatment and Ceclor CD anti-allergy. Modest growth is projected for contract revenues and sales from diagnostic products. Margins should benefit from a more profitable sales mix and synergies from recently acquired Dura Pharmaceuticals. EPS from operations should reach $1.89, with further progress to $2.24 seen for 2002.

Valuation - 04-MAY-01

These shares moved in an erratic pattern over the past nine months, mirroring volatility in the specialty drug sector, weakness in certain Elan product lines and initial dilution from Dura Pharmaceuticals (acquired in November 2000 for about 31 million ELN shares). However, Dura should be accretive to Elan's EPS for the full 2001, supported by synergies and cost economies estimated at about $100 million this year. Last year, the FDA approved Myobloc for cervical dystonia, Abelcet antifungal agent and Zonegran anti-epileptic. Important new drug launches anticipated in 2001 include Frovelan migraine treatment and Ziconotide for chronic severe pain. Other acquisitions completed in 2000 included Liposome, a leader in the field of lipid-based drugs; and Quadrant Healthcare, a drug delivery firm specializing in proteins and peptides. Conservatively valued at a modest discount to the specialty drug group average P/E, the shares merit accumulation.

Key Stock Statistics

S&P EPS Est. 2001	1.90	Tang. Bk. Value/Share	1.77
P/E on S&P Est. 2001	28.9	Beta	0.39
S&P EPS Est. 2002	2.34	Shareholders	3,800
Dividend Rate/Share	Nil	Market cap. (B)	$ 17.7
Shs. outstg. (M)	322.5	Inst. holdings	54%
Avg. daily vol. (M)	1.381		

Value of $10,000 invested 5 years ago: $ 34,977

Fiscal Year Ending Dec. 31

	2001	2000	1999	1998	1997	1996
Revenues (Million $)						
1Q	429.4	—	233.1	—	—	—
2Q	461.2	—	234.4	—	—	—
3Q	—	—	253.4	104.9	—	—
4Q	—	—	283.4	214.9	—	—
Yr.	—	1,302	1,008	676.7	389.0	236.0
Earnings Per ADS ($)						
1Q	**0.22**	—	**0.27**	—	—	—
2Q	**0.37**	—	**0.29**	—	—	—
3Q	—	—	**0.32**	**0.23**	—	—
4Q	—	—	**0.06**	**-0.21**	—	—
Yr.	—	**1.10**	**1.19**	**0.56**	0.91	-0.01

Next earnings report expected: mid October

Dividend Data

No cash dividends have been paid in recent years. The shares were split two for one in May 1999.

Elan Corporation, plc

Business Summary - 04-MAY-01

Elan has established itself as a worldwide leader in drug delivery technology through the discovery of new technologies, the development of a broad-based portfolio of drugs, and strategic alliances. Revenues are derived from products manufactured and marketed by the company; royalties from Elan-developed products; fees from manufacturing and distributing licensed products; and contract research. Product revenues accounted for 69% of total revenues in 2000, with contract revenues accounting for the balance. Over 90% of revenues are derived from the U.S.

Elan's controlled-release (CD) drug products are based on controlled-absorption drug delivery systems, which allow active ingredients to be absorbed at a slower pace than conventional drugs. These formulations permit lower dosing and are associated with fewer side effects. CD drugs also allow for extended patent lives and enhanced commercial prospects for existing drugs.

Neurological drugs represent Elan's largest single therapeutic class, accounting for about 30% of product revenues in 2000. Elan's neurological base was significantly expanded through the acquisitions of Athena Neurosciences, Carnick and Neurex. Key neurological products include Zanaflex for the management of increased muscle tone associated with spasticity, Zonegran anti-epileptic, Skelaxin for the relief of acute painful musculoskeletal conditions, Permax treatment for Parkinson's disease, Naprelan treatment for osteoarthritis and rheumatoid arthritis, Diastat for epileptic cluster seizures, Mysoline treatment of epilepsy and seizure disorders, and Myobloc for cervical dystonia. Elan also offers over 50 diagnostic neurological testing services including peripheral neuropathies, movement disorders, neuromuscular disorders, and stroke.

Through Dura Pharmaceuticals (acquired in November 2000), ELN also offers drugs to treat infectious diseases and respiratory conditions. Key Dura drugs include Ceclor CD oral antibiotic, Maxipime and Azactam injectable antibiotics, and Nasarel inhaled corticosteroid. Other acquisitions completed in recent years include Liposome, a leader in the field of lipsome and lipid-based drugs; and Sano, a producer of controlled release drugs.

R&D spending totaled $322 million in 2000, equal to about 21% of total revenues. The R&D pipeline includes Ziconotide for chronic severe pain, Frovelan anti-migraine, Zelapar for Parkinson's disease, Antegren for multiple sclerosis and Crohn's disease, Corlopam for heart ailments and renal failure, nicotine/mecamylamine for smoking cessation, buspirone for various central nervous system conditions, Morphelan analgesic, and beta-secretase for Alzheimer's disease. In late 1999 and early 2000, the company repurchased two of its contract research vehicles -- Axogen and Neuralab (the latter is working on new Alzheimer's treatments).

Per ADS Data ($) (Year Ended Dec. 31)	2000	1999	1998	1997	1996	1995	1994	1993	1992	1991
Tangible Bk. Val.	1.77	1.26	2.44	2.86	1.44	2.71	1.82	1.28	1.41	1.17
Cash Flow	1.68	1.37	0.64	0.97	0.10	0.70	0.56	-0.45	0.33	0.23
Earnings	1.10	1.19	0.56	0.91	-0.01	0.59	0.47	-0.52	0.25	0.17
Dividends	Nil	Nil	Nil	Nil	Nil	Nil	Nil	Nil	Nil	Nil
Payout Ratio	Nil	Nil	Nil	Nil	Nil	Nil	Nil	Nil	Nil	Nil
Prices - High	60.12	43.93	38.37	28.43	16.93	12.75	11.96	11.03	9.03	8.03
- Low	26.00	21.25	24.06	15.00	11.50	8.22	7.53	6.40	5.40	3.31
P/E Ratio - High	55	37	NM	31	NM	NM	25	NM	36	46
- Low	24	18	NM	17	NM	NM	16	NM	21	19
Income Statement Analysis (Million $)										
Revs.	1,302	1,008	677	389	236	223	193	154	136	101
Oper. Inc.	443	339	237	153	24.7	92.2	75.7	51.6	39.6	24.4
Depr.	141	29.6	21.5	12.5	17.7	15.5	12.4	9.8	9.7	7.4
Int. Exp.	133	88.6	25.2	5.8	6.7	6.7	9.4	8.3	3.6	0.7
Pretax Inc.	351	343	150	181	-0.4	89.6	68.2	-73.5	33.7	21.9
Eff. Tax Rate	2.56%	2.12%	2.60%	0.70%	NM	NM	1.00%	NM	5.10%	2.80%
Net Inc.	342	336	146	180	-0.8	88.7	67.5	-72.4	32.3	21.3
Balance Sheet & Other Fin. Data (Million $)										
Cash	984	744	820	317	71.5	228	179	214	241	65.6
Curr. Assets	1,565	1,189	1,185	617	311	458	247	264	282	109
Total Assets	8,097	4,674	3,799	1,153	715	688	490	395	388	196
Curr. Liab.	620	436	233	63.3	66.7	28.7	28.0	26.0	30.7	18.3
LT Debt	2,162	1,551	1,235	319	134	162	159	150	145	0.1
Common Eqty.	5,315	2,688	2,332	770	464	494	299	215	208	172
Total Cap.	7,477	4,239	3,567	1,090	599	657	458	365	353	172
Cap. Exp.	64.4	76.7	65.5	37.7	20.0	21.9	23.7	22.3	14.3	5.4
Cash Flow	483	365	168	193	16.9	104	79.9	-62.6	42.1	28.7
Curr. Ratio	2.5	2.7	5.1	9.7	4.7	16.0	8.8	10.1	9.2	6.0
% LT Debt of Cap.	28.9	36.6	34.6	29.3	22.4	24.7	34.8	41.2	41.0	0.1
% Net Inc.of Revs.	26.3	33.3	21.6	46.3	NM	NM	35.1	NM	23.8	21.1
% Ret. on Assets	5.4	7.9	5.9	19.3	NM	NM	23.4	NM	11.0	12.2
% Ret. on Equity	8.5	13.4	9.4	29.2	NM	NM	40.5	NM	16.9	15.8

Data as orig. reptd.; bef. results of disc. opers. and/or spec. items. Per share data adj. for stk. divs. as of ex-div. date. Yrs. ended Mar. 31 of fol. cal. yr. prior to 1996 (9 mos.). Each ADR represents one ord. share. Bold denotes diluted EPS (FASB 128). E-Estimated. NA-Not Available. NM-Not Meaningful. NR-Not Ranked.

Offices—Lincoln House, Lincoln Place, Dublin 2, Republic of Ireland. **Tel**—011-353-902-95000. **Website**—http://www.elan.ie **Chrmn & CEO**—D. J. Geaney. **EVP & CFO**—T. G. Lynch. **U.S. Investor Contact**—Mary Ansaldi (212-755-3218). **Dirs**—G. H. Armen, B. Boushel, L. G. Crowley, D. J. Geaney, A. R. Gillespie, J. Groom, T. Lynch, K. McGowan, K. McIntyre, K. McLaughlin, D. J. Selkoe, R. Thornburgh, D. P. Tully. **ADR Transfer Agent**—Bank of New York, NYC. **Incorporated**—in Ireland in 1969. **Empl**— 1,600. **S&P Analyst:** Herman Saftlas

STANDARD
&POOR'S
STOCK REPORTS

Forest Laboratories

NYSE Symbol **FRX**

In S&P 500

18-AUG-01

Industry:
Health Care (Drugs - Major Pharmaceuticals)

Summary: This company develops and makes branded and generic ethical drug products, sold primarily in the U.S., Puerto Rico, and Western and Eastern Europe.

S&P Opinion: Accumulate (★★★★)

Recent Price • 78.49
52 Wk Range • 82.33-46.46
Yield • Nil
12-Mo. P/E • 55.3

Quantitative Evaluations

Outlook
(1 Lowest—5 Highest)
• **3−**

Fair Value
• **81.70**

Risk
• **Average**

Earn./Div. Rank
• **B+**

Technical Eval.
• **Bullish** since 5/01

Rel. Strength Rank
(1 Lowest—99 Highest)
• **80**

Insider Activity
• **Unfavorable**

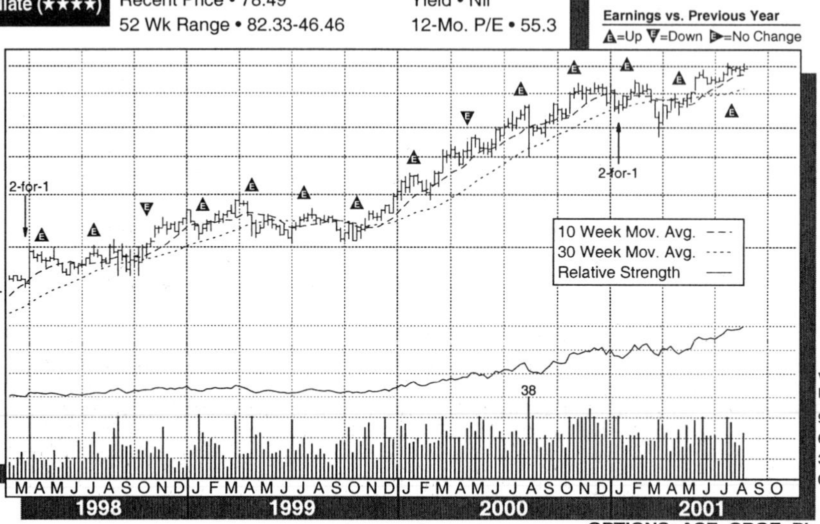

OPTIONS: ASE, CBOE, Ph

Overview - 24-JUL-01

Revenues are expected to advance over 25% in FY 02 (Mar.). By far Forest's most important product, Celexa selective serotonin reuptake inhibitor (SSRI) antidepressant should post a 45% advance in sales, to close to $1.1 billion. The product's outstanding success reflects its proven potency, fast onset of action, favorable side effects profile and fewer interactions with other prescription drugs. Sales growth is also being augmented by an expanded sales force. However, sales prospects for Tiazac antihypertensive are likely to be impacted by anticipated generic competition in that line. Despite sharply higher R&D expenses and increased SG&A costs (largely due to the larger sales force), margins should widen on the higher Celexa sales. Earnings are projected to rise 40%, to $1.65 a share. Bolstered by new products, further EPS progress to $2.00 is seen for FY 03.

Valuation - 24-JUL-01

The shares were robust performers in recent months, buoyed by strength in the overall specialty pharmaceutical sector, market share growth in the principal Celexa antidepressant line, and positive new product developments. Celexa presently accounts for 15.7% of all new U.S. SSRI antidepressant prescriptions, up from about 12% in July 2000. FRX recently submitted a New Drug Application with the FDA for escitalopram, an advanced formulation of Celexa. Escitalopram is expected to eventually replace Celexa, which loses marketing exclusivity in 2004. The R&D pipeline also includes memantine for Alzheimer's disease; flunisolide HFA for asthma; lercanidipine for hypertension; and treatments for osteoarthritis, irritable bowel syndrome and other conditions. The stock's premium valuation to the specialty drug group is justified by FRX's strong EPS growth prospects. The shares merit accumulation.

Key Stock Statistics

S&P EPS Est. 2002	1.65	Tang. Bk. Value/Share	5.19
P/E on S&P Est. 2002	47.6	Beta	0.63
S&P EPS Est. 2003	2.08	Shareholders	2,095
Dividend Rate/Share	Nil	Market cap. (B)	$ 13.9
Shs. outstg. (M)	177.0	Inst. holdings	80%
Avg. daily vol. (M)	1.269		

Value of $10,000 invested 5 years ago: $ 85,630

Fiscal Year Ending Mar. 31

	2002	2001	2000	1999	1998	1997
Revenues (Million $)						
1Q	359.1	265.9	186.9	127.8	90.33	113.9
2Q	—	287.6	206.3	149.4	111.4	92.19
3Q	—	317.7	240.8	137.5	115.9	40.60
4Q	—	333.9	265.3	192.2	142.9	62.46
Yr.	—	1,205	899.3	546.3	474.7	309.1
Earnings Per Share ($)						
1Q	**0.40**	**0.16**	**0.14**	**0.04**	0.01	0.12
2Q	—	**0.28**	**0.16**	**0.06**	0.09	0.03
3Q	—	**0.36**	**0.18**	**0.13**	**0.12**	-0.19
4Q	—	**0.38**	**0.15**	**0.23**	**0.01**	-0.11
Yr.	—	**1.18**	**0.64**	**0.45**	**0.22**	**-0.14**

Next earnings report expected: mid October

Dividend Data

Amount ($)	Date Decl.	Ex-Div. Date	Stock of Record	Payment Date
2-for-1	Dec. 18	Jan. 12	Dec. 26	Jan. 11 '01

A Division of The **McGraw-Hill** *Companies*

Forest Laboratories, Inc.

Business Summary - 24-JUL-01

Forest Laboratories produces niche-oriented branded and generic prescription pharmaceuticals, as well as a line of nonprescription or over-the-counter (OTC) medications. Most of the company's key products were developed in collaboration with licensing partners. The most important product is Celexa antidepressant, which accounted for about 61% of total revenues in FY 01 (Mar.).

Approved by the FDA in July 1998, Celexa (generically known as citalopram HBr) is a selective serotonin reuptake inhibitor (SSRI) drug used to treat depression. Sales of this drug rose from $92 million in FY 99 to $714 million in FY 01, boosted by its proven efficacy; fast onset of action; and reduced side effects and drug interactions compared with older antidepressants. Celexa accounted for 15.7% of new SSRI prescriptions in the U.S. in mid-July 2001, up from 12% in July 2000. Forest licenses the U.S. rights to Celexa from H. Lundbeck A/S, a privately held drug company based in Copenhagen, Denmark. Effective April 30, 2000, FRX terminated its Celexa co-marketing pact with Warner-Lambert due to the latter's merger with Pfizer (which markets a competing antidepressant drug).

Other products include Tiazac, a once daily diltiazem calcium channel blocker for the treatment of hypertension (about 15% of revenues); Aerobid, a metered-dose inhaled steroid to treat asthma (5%); the Lorcet line of potent analgesics; Aerochamber, a spacer device used to improve the delivery of aerosol products; Levothroid, a thyroid product; Flumadine for Influenza A; Infasurf, a treatment for respiratory distress syndrome in premature infants; Cervidil, used to aid in cervical dilation and labor induction; and Monurol, a single dose antibiotic used to treat uncomplicated urinary tract infections. FRX also receives royalties from Climara, a transdermal estrogen patch marketed by Berlex Laboratories.

The generic product line, marketed in the U.S. by the Inwood Laboratories unit, specializes in controlled-release pharmaceuticals. These include Propranolol E.R., a beta blocker used to treat hypertension; Indomethacin E.R., an antiarthritic; and Theochron, an asthma drug. Forest's U.K. and Ireland subsidiaries offer various prescription and over-the-counter drugs.

R&D spending totaled $105.7 million in FY 01, equal to 8.8% of total revenues. Key pipeline drugs include escitalopram, an advanced, single enantiomer form of Celexa (licensed from H. Lundbeck); memantine, a treatment for Alzheimer's disease and neuropathic pain (licensed from Merz & Co.); flunisolide HFA for asthma; lercanidipine for hypertension; and various other treatments for osteoarthritis, central nervous system disorders, irritable bowel syndrome, anxietyand migraine headache.

Per Share Data ($) **(Year Ended Mar. 31)**	**2001**	**2000**	**1999**	**1998**	**1997**	**1996**	**1995**	**1994**	**1993**	**1992**
Tangible Bk. Val.	5.19	3.58	3.20	2.49	2.45	3.16	2.87	2.38	1.95	1.42
Cash Flow	1.41	0.87	0.57	0.34	-0.03	0.64	0.61	0.49	0.41	0.34
Earnings	1.18	0.64	0.45	0.22	-0.14	0.56	0.54	0.44	0.35	0.28
Dividends	Nil	Nil	Nil	Nil	Nil	Nil	Nil	Nil	Nil	Nil
Payout Ratio	Nil	Nil	Nil	Nil	Nil	Nil	Nil	Nil	Nil	Nil
Cal. Yrs.	2000	1999	1998	1997	1996	1995	1994	1993	1992	1991
Prices - High	70.65	30.87	26.62	12.32	13.93	13.06	13.12	11.96	11.21	10.90
- Low	28.68	20.62	12.15	7.90	7.06	10.09	10.00	6.87	7.50	5.56
P/E Ratio - High	60	48	59	56	NM	24	24	27	32	39
- Low	24	32	27	36	NM	18	19	16	21	20
Income Statement Analysis (Million $)										
Revs.	1,181	882	546	427	281	447	393	352	285	240
Oper. Inc.	318	181	54.3	27.2	-48.1	164	159	126	102	83.5
Depr.	43.3	40.6	21.3	20.1	19.2	16.5	14.1	10.7	10.5	10.3
Int. Exp.	Nil	Nil	Nil	Nil	Nil	Nil	Nil	Nil	2.0	3.7
Pretax Inc.	299	157	111	54.8	-39.0	162	156	125	101	77.5
Eff. Tax Rate	28%	28%	30%	33%	NM	36%	36%	36%	36%	36%
Net Inc.	215	113	77.2	36.7	-23.5	104	100	80.2	64.3	49.6
Balance Sheet & Other Fin. Data (Million $)										
Cash	506	355	279	150	172	124	142	181	172	133
Curr. Assets	884	645	502	372	360	471	349	348	315	244
Total Assets	1,447	1,098	875	744	700	899	757	619	521	431
Curr. Liab.	224	211	130	130	73.5	89.5	57.6	52.2	41.1	55.9
LT Debt	Nil	Nil	Nil	Nil	Nil	Nil	Nil	Nil	Nil	Nil
Common Eqty.	1,222	885	744	614	626	810	699	567	479	373
Total Cap.	1,223	887	745	614	626	810	700	700	479	375
Cap. Exp.	30.9	35.3	17.2	6.9	9.7	11.6	22.2	27.1	6.3	3.6
Cash Flow	258	153	98.4	56.8	-4.4	121	114	90.9	74.8	59.9
Curr. Ratio	4.0	3.1	3.9	2.9	4.9	5.3	6.1	6.7	7.6	4.4
% LT Debt of Cap.	Nil	Nil	Nil	Nil	Nil	Nil	Nil	Nil	Nil	Nil
% Net Inc.of Revs.	18.2	12.8	14.1	8.6	NM	23.3	25.5	22.8	22.5	20.6
% Ret. on Assets	16.7	11.4	9.5	5.1	NM	12.6	14.3	14.0	13.3	12.6
% Ret. on Equity	20.4	13.8	11.4	5.9	NM	13.8	15.6	15.2	14.9	15.1

Data as orig reptd.; bef. results of disc opers/spec. items. Per share data adj. for stk. divs. Bold denotes diluted EPS (FASB 128)-prior periods restated. E-Estimated. NA-Not Available. NM-Not Meaningful. NR-Not Ranked.

Office—909 Third Ave., New York, NY 10022-4731. **Tel**—(212) 421-7850. **Website**—http://www.frx.com **Chrmn & CEO**—H. Solomon. **Pres & COO**—K. E. Goodman. **CFO & Investor Contact**—J. H. Eggers. **Secy**—W. J. Candee III. **Dirs**—W. J. Candee III, G. S. Cohan, D. L. Goldwasser, K. E. Goodman, L. B. Salans, P. N. Satow, H. Solomon. **Transfer Agent**—ChaseMellon Shareholder Services, Ridgefield Park, NJ. **Incorporated**—in Delaware in 1956. **Empl**— 2,826. **S&P Analyst:** H. B. Saftlas

STANDARD
&POOR'S
STOCK REPORTS

Health Management Associates

NYSE Symbol **HMA**

In S&P MidCap 400

18-AUG-01

Industry:
Health Care (Hospital Management)

Summary: This company operates a rapidly growing network of general acute-care hospitals located primarily in nonurban areas in the Southeast and Southwest.

S&P Opinion: Accumulate (★★★★)

Recent Price • 19.76 | Yield • Nil
52 Wk Range • 22.75-13.42 | 12-Mo. P/E • 27.8

Quantitative Evaluations

Outlook
(1 Lowest—5 Highest)
• **4+**

Fair Value
• **23**

Risk
• **Average**

Earn./Div. Rank
• **B+**

Technical Eval.
• **Neutral** since 8/01

Rel. Strength Rank
(1 Lowest—99 Highest)
• **69**

Insider Activity
• **NA**

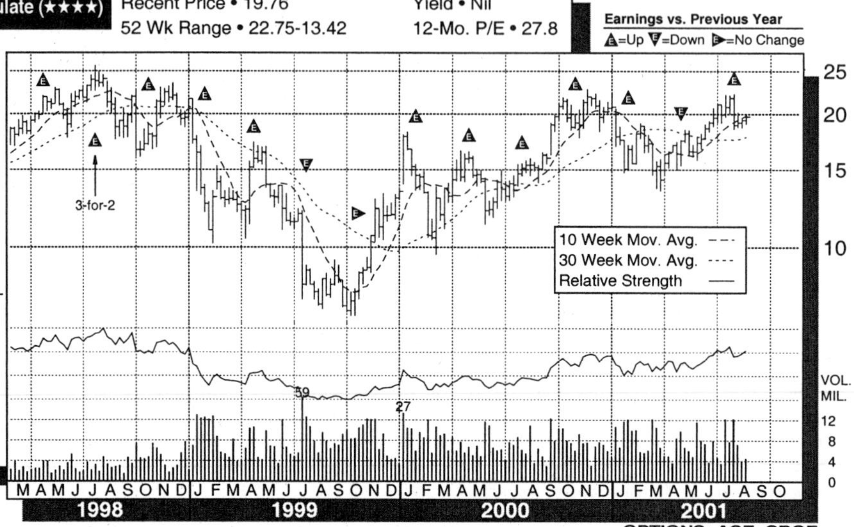

OPTIONS: ASE, CBOE

Overview - 25-JUL-01

The company should continue to generate 16% to 18% revenue growth through FY 02 (Sep.), as inpatient admissions gains of 14% to 16% (3% to 5% on a same-store basis) combine with some selected hospital acquisitions and improved private pay and government pricing trends. Recently enacted revisions to Medicare hospital payment rates are expected to meaningfully contributed to positive revenue comparisons through the first half of FY 02. Wage inflation remains a problem area, and is particularly high at newly acquired facilities. However, same-store salaries are rising more modestly. Assuming slightly higher supply expenses, EBITDA margins should approximate 24% in FY 01 and FY 02, and we expect full-year cash flow in the current fiscal year to approximate $78 million. Per share operating earnings in FY 01 are expected to rise nearly 18%, to $0.80, and we see a 14% advance, to $0.91, in FY 02.

Valuation - 25-JUL-01

The stock moved sharply above its 2001 lows in recent months, reflecting a broad recovery in the hospital sector amid rapidly improving fundamentals and investor rotation into the healthcare facilities group. Although we expect that the company will continue to execute well in coming quarters, we recently downgraded the stock from strong buy to accumulate in order to reflect that the recent run has brought the valuation closer to our 12 month price target of $24. HMA was recently trading at 3.0X sales, and at 22X our FY 02 EPS estimate, versus 1.9X sales and 21X earnings for its peers. We believe this premium is warranted by the company's industry-leading operating margins and rural market focus, but believe material P/E expansion will be more difficult in the coming months.

Key Stock Statistics

S&P EPS Est. 2001	0.80	Tang. Bk. Value/Share	3.42
P/E on S&P Est. 2001	24.7	Beta	0.88
S&P EPS Est. 2002	0.91	Shareholders	1,724
Dividend Rate/Share	Nil	Market cap. (B)	$ 4.8
Shs. outstg. (M)	245.1	Inst. holdings	88%
Avg. daily vol. (M)	1.437		

Value of $10,000 invested 5 years ago: $ 19,225

Fiscal Year Ending Sep. 30

	2001	2000	1999	1998	1997	1996
Revenues (Million $)						
1Q	434.2	370.1	305.5	234.6	199.2	151.9
2Q	481.1	408.7	339.8	302.9	237.8	184.8
3Q	473.2	391.1	352.5	302.1	232.7	184.4
4Q	—	407.9	358.0	299.2	225.8	193.2
Yr.	—	1,578	1,356	1,139	895.5	714.3
Earnings Per Share ($)						
1Q	**0.16**	**0.14**	**0.12**	**0.10**	0.08	0.06
2Q	**0.19**	**0.21**	**0.18**	**0.16**	0.13	0.10
3Q	**0.21**	**0.18**	**0.13**	**0.15**	0.12	0.10
4Q	—	**0.16**	**0.13**	**0.13**	0.10	0.08
Yr.	—	**0.68**	**0.59**	**0.54**	**0.43**	**0.34**

Next earnings report expected: mid October

Dividend Data

No cash dividends have been paid.

Business Summary - 25-JUL-01

Health Management Associates (HMA) has emerged as the leading operator of acute care hospitals in nonurban and rural areas of the U.S., with a primary focus on markets in the Southeast and Southwest. As of July 2001, HMA operated 37 general acute care hospitals containing 5,224 licensed beds, and three psychiatric hospitals with 186 licensed beds. About 96% of net patient service revenues in FY 00 (Sep.) were generated from the acute care hospitals.

HMA seeks to efficiently and profitably operate its existing chain of hospitals, while acquiring underperforming hospitals with 100 to 300 beds, in high-growth, nonurban areas with populations of 40,000 to 400,000, and with established physician bases. Many of these facilities are unprofitable at the time of acquisition, and the company immediately employs an executive director and controller, implements its proprietary management information system, recruits physicians, induces strict cost control measures with respect to hospital staffing and volume purchasing, and spends the required capital to upgrade the facility and equipment. HMA operates each acquired hospital to maximize operating margins and return on capital within the first 24 to 36 months of operation, a time-period that it believes to be sufficient to fully implement the plan of improvement.

The company's acute care hospitals offer a broad range of medical and surgical services, including inpatient care, intensive and cardiac care, diagnostic services and emergency services that are physician-staffed 24 hours a day, seven days a week. HMA also provides outpatient services such as one-day surgery, laboratory, X-ray, respiratory therapy, cardiology and physical therapy. Some of the hospitals provide specialty services such as oncology, radiation therapy, CT scanning, MRI imaging, lithotripsy and full-service obstetrics. The company seeks to provide at least 90% of the acute-care needs of each community in its service areas, thereby reducing out-migration of potential patients to hospitals in larger urban areas.

HMA's psychiatric hospitals, which accounted for 1% of FY 00 net patient service revenues, focus mainly on child/adolescent residential treatment programs.

In FY 00, the company's acute care hospitals (37 at September 30, 2000, versus 36 a year earlier) generated total admissions of 161,895 (143,078 in FY 99); patient days reached 791,617 (718,035). Average length of an acute care hospital stay was 4.5 days in each year; the average length of a psychiatric stay was 117.1 days (47.5). The hospital occupancy rate was 46% (47%).

Patient service revenues in FY 00 were generated from Medicare (48%), Medicaid (12%), and private pay and other sources (40%).

During FY 99, the company repurchased 7.5 million common shares, completing a share buyback plan authorized by directors in February 1998. In September 1999, directors authorized the purchase of up to 25 million Class A common shares.

Per Share Data ($) (Year Ended Sep. 30)	2000	1999	1998	1997	1996	1995	1994	1993	1992	1991
Tangible Bk. Val.	3.44	2.98	2.82	2.29	1.76	1.36	1.09	0.85	0.63	0.40
Cash Flow	0.98	0.83	0.73	0.58	0.45	0.34	0.27	0.20	0.16	0.13
Earnings	0.68	0.60	0.54	0.43	0.34	0.26	0.21	0.14	0.10	0.07
Dividends	Nil	Nil	Nil	Nil	Nil	Nil	Nil	Nil	Nil	Nil
Payout Ratio	Nil	Nil	Nil	Nil	Nil	Nil	Nil	Nil	Nil	Nil
Prices - High	22.75	21.62	25.75	17.66	11.11	6.93	5.26	3.85	2.51	2.33
- Low	9.62	7.00	14.91	9.50	7.44	4.64	3.55	1.38	1.64	0.95
P/E Ratio - High	33	36	48	41	33	27	26	27	25	34
- Low	14	12	28	22	22	18	17	10	16	14
Income Statement Analysis (Million $)										
Revs.	1,578	1,356	1,139	895	714	531	438	347	278	226
Oper. Inc.	376	316	280	219	169	128	102	74.1	58.2	46.8
Depr.	74.5	61.3	50.4	36.6	27.2	20.6	16.2	12.8	12.6	10.9
Int. Exp.	25.4	8.4	4.8	3.7	3.5	3.6	4.3	4.8	7.2	14.1
Pretax Inc.	276	247	225	178	138	104	81.7	56.4	38.4	21.8
Eff. Tax Rate	39%	39%	39%	39%	39%	39%	40%	43%	43%	45%
Net Inc.	168	150	137	108	84.1	63.3	49.1	32.2	21.9	12.0
Balance Sheet & Other Fin. Data (Million $)										
Cash	16.5	12.9	12.7	67.4	31.2	75.3	109	74.4	25.2	0.2
Curr. Assets	487	425	309	236	178	173	178	119	57.9	41.3
Total Assets	1,772	1,517	1,112	728	592	467	399	326	243	229
Curr. Liab.	170	175	121	82.9	70.9	50.6	39.6	43.2	35.3	32.7
LT Debt	520	402	177	49.7	68.7	67.7	76.0	78.0	63.0	112
Common Eqty.	1,030	891	757	560	418	318	253	193	135	76.0
Total Cap.	1,585	1,325	974	629	505	404	348	273	201	191
Cap. Exp.	121	159	237	111	41.2	22.9	40.6	34.3	14.5	23.0
Cash Flow	242	211	187	145	111	83.9	65.3	45.1	34.5	22.9
Curr. Ratio	2.9	2.4	2.6	2.8	2.5	3.4	4.5	2.7	1.6	1.3
% LT Debt of Cap.	32.8	30.3	18.2	7.9	13.6	16.8	21.8	28.5	31.4	58.9
% Net Inc.of Revs.	10.6	11.1	12.0	12.1	11.8	11.9	11.2	9.3	7.9	5.3
% Ret. on Assets	10.2	11.4	14.9	16.4	15.9	14.6	13.4	11.1	8.7	4.6
% Ret. on Equity	17.5	18.2	20.8	22.2	22.9	22.2	21.8	19.2	19.8	23.0

Data as orig reptd.; bef. results of disc opers/spec. items. Per share data adj. for stk. divs. Bold denotes diluted EPS (FASB 128)-prior periods restated. E-Estimated. NA-Not Available. NM-Not Meaningful. NR-Not Ranked.

Office—5811 Pelican Bay Blvd., Suite 500, Naples, FL 34108. **Tel**—(941) 598-3131. **Website**—http://www.hma-corp.com **Chrmn**—W. J. Schoen. **Pres & CEO**—J. V. Vumbacco. **EVP-Fin & CFO**—S. M. Ray. **Investor Contact**—John C. Merriwether (941-598-3104). **Dirs**—K. P. Dauten, D. E. Kiernan, R. A. Knox, C. R. Lees, K. D. Lewis, W. E. Mayberry, W. J. Schoen, J. V. Vumbacco, R. Westerfield. **Transfer Agent & Registrar**—First Union National Bank of North Carolina, Charlotte. **Incorporated**—in Delaware in 1979. **Empl**— 19,000. **S&P Analyst:** Robert M. Gold

Health Net

NYSE Symbol **HNT**

In S&P MidCap 400

18-AUG-01

Industry:
Health Care (Managed Care)

Summary: HNT (formerly Foundation Health Systems), formed via the April 1997 merger of Foundation Health Corp. and Health Systems International, is one of the largest for-profit U.S. HMOs.

S&P Opinion: Accumulate (★★★★)

Recent Price • 18.27
52 Wk Range • 26.93-15.56
Yield • Nil
12-Mo. P/E • 13.1

Quantitative Evaluations

Outlook
(1 Lowest—5 Highest)
• 4

Fair Value
• 19.40

Risk
• Average

Earn./Div. Rank
• NR

Technical Eval.
• NA

Rel. Strength Rank
(1 Lowest—99 Highest)
• 57

Insider Activity
• NA

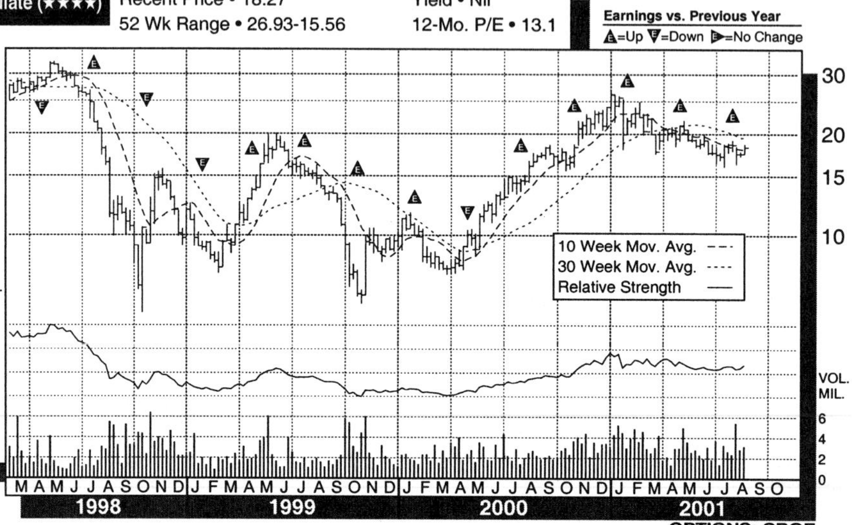

OPTIONS: CBOE

Overview - 31-JUL-01

For 2001, we estimate commercial premiums will increase 11.5%, to over \$9.9 billion, on 10.0%-10.5% premium rate hikes and slightly higher enrollment, despite the company's exit from underperforming markets and sale of its Florida health plan. HNT withdrew from 18 Medicare counties on January 1, cutting 19,000 members. However, strong commercial enrollment in California, reflecting recently launched flexible (POS, PPO and indemnity) plans, offset Medicare withdrawals. With medical cost trends averaging 9.5%-10.0%, the medical loss ratio should remain stable at about 85.0% in 2001. Arizona plans continue to show improvement, with pricing on major account renewals of 20%-plus. The SG&A ratio should decline modestly, to about 13.5%, reflecting the sale and improvement in underperforming plans, partly offset by higher spending on Internet initiatives. In 2002, we see 9.6% higher commercial premiums and modest margin improvement.

Valuation - 31-JUL-01

We are maintaining our accumulate opinion on HNT, reflecting its ongoing turnaround and valuation relative to its earnings growth rate. We are encouraged by the ongoing turnaround of Arizona health plans; HNT is raising premium rates by over 20% to correct previous underpricing on select large group accounts. HNT continues to use free cash flow to reduce debt, resulting in a debt-to-capital ratio of 36%. With the company's new plan offerings, and the expected launch of a "value" and Latino-oriented plan, we believe it is ready to begin delivering solid enrollment growth. In addition, HNT has identified cost reduction opportunities that should result in a 1-3 percentage point reduction in SG&A over the next few years. At 10X our 2002 EPS estimate of \$1.85, a significant discount to its peer group, and with a 15% long-term EPS growth rate, HNT is undervalued.

Key Stock Statistics

S&P EPS Est. 2001	1.58	Tang. Bk. Value/Share	1.61
P/E on S&P Est. 2001	11.6	Beta	0.63
S&P EPS Est. 2002	1.85	Shareholders	2,000
Dividend Rate/Share	Nil	Market cap. (B)	$ 2.2
Shs. outstg. (M)	123.0	Inst. holdings	90%
Avg. daily vol. (M)	0.678		

Value of \$10,000 invested 5 years ago: \$ 7,163

Fiscal Year Ending Dec. 31

	2001	2000	1999	1998	1997	1996
Revenues (Million $)						
1Q	2,488	2,199	2,219	2,175	1,770	801.4
2Q	—	2,230	2,126	2,237	1,774	798.0
3Q	—	2,288	2,164	2,214	1,793	802.8
4Q	—	2,360	2,197	2,270	1,898	802.0
Yr.	—	9,077	8,706	8,896	7,235	3,204
Earnings Per Share ($)						
1Q	**0.34**	**0.28**	**0.39**	**0.22**	**0.38**	0.54
2Q	—	**0.32**	**0.23**	**0.01**	**-1.64**	0.51
3Q	—	**0.36**	**0.29**	**-0.73**	**0.49**	0.52
4Q	—	**0.37**	**0.31**	**-0.85**	0.25	-0.05
Yr.	—	**1.33**	**1.21**	**-1.35**	**-0.55**	1.52

Next earnings report expected: NA

Dividend Data

No dividends have been paid.

Health Net, Inc.

Business Summary - 31-JUL-01

Health Net, Inc. (formerly Foundation Health Systems, Inc.), formed through the 1997 merger of Health Systems International and Foundation Health Corp., is one of the largest for-profit U.S. managed care companies, with annual revenues of over $9 billion, and health benefits membership of approximately 5.4 million provided throughout 16 states.

In 2000, HNT decided to withdrawal from the Ohio, West Virginia and Western Pennsylvania markets. As of February 2001, the company no longer had any members in these markets. In January 2001, HNT agreed to sell its underperforming Florida health plan, subject to regulatory approvals.

The company's core operations include Health Plan Services and Government Contracts/Specialty Services. The Government Contracts/Specialty Services group provides supplemental benefits, including prescription drug program, behavioral health, vision and dental services; and government operations (the provision of managed health care services to beneficiaries of the Department of Defense's TRICARE program (formerly CHAMPUS) in eleven states.

HNT provides a comprehensive range of health care services through its HMO networks, marketed to employer groups, and Medicare and Medicaid beneficiaries. Services provided to commercial and individual members include primary and specialty physician care, ambulatory, hospital care, laboratory and radiology services, prescription drugs, dental and vision care, skilled nursing care, physical therapy and mental health. The company's HMO service network includes approximately 50,500 primary care physicians and 109,000 specialists. In addition, HNT provides third-party administrative services (ASO) to large employer groups in Arizona, Connecticut, New Jersey, New York and Pennsylvania

At June 30, 2001, excluding non-core health plans, Health Net's enrollment was 5,424,000, up from 5,217,000 at December 31, 2000. Membership consisted of commercial group and individual members (3,001,000, versus 2,763,000), Medicare (223,000, versus 224,000) and Medicaid (737,000, versus 580,000). The company also serves beneficiaries of the federal government's TRICARE program; TRICARE HMO enrollment totaled 906,000, up from 871,000, while TRICARE PPO/Indemnity enrollment was 558,000, down from 624,000.

Open enrollment in the company's health plans for January 2001 saw enrollment gains, reflecting appropriate price increases due to medical cost inflation, despite Medicare+Choice market withdrawals.

In late 2000, HNT launched Questium, one of the first consumer websites to link members directly with personal health benefit information. Among its features, Questium allows members to view their own benefit plans, co-payment information and out-of-pocket maximums online.

Per Share Data ($) (Year Ended Dec. 31)	2000	1999	1998	1997	1996	1995	1994	1993	1992	1991
Tangible Bk. Val.	1.61	NM	NM	NM	0.75	-1.05	0.84	NM	NM	NA
Cash Flow	2.18	2.12	-0.30	0.25	2.61	2.82	2.57	1.17	1.48	NA
Earnings	1.33	1.21	-1.35	-0.55	1.52	1.83	1.77	0.48	0.81	NA
Dividends	Nil	Nil	Nil	Nil	Nil	Nil	Nil	Nil	Nil	NA
Payout Ratio	Nil	Nil	Nil	Nil	Nil	Nil	Nil	Nil	Nil	NA
Prices - High	26.93	20.06	32.62	33.93	37.12	34.25	36.75	NA	NA	NA
- Low	7.62	6.25	5.87	22.06	19.37	24.87	20.00	NA	NA	NA
P/E Ratio - High	20	17	NM	NM	24	19	21	NA	NA	NA
- Low	6	5	NM	NM	13	14	11	NA	NA	NA
Income Statement Analysis (Million $)										
Revs.	8,974	8,561	8,797	7,121	3,204	2,732	2,306	1,957	1,538	NA
Oper. Inc.	355	306	142	354	208	211	186	116	101	NA
Depr.	106	112	128	98.4	52.6	48.1	39.7	34.2	32.7	NA
Int. Exp.	87.9	83.8	92.2	63.6	24.5	19.7	14.6	18.7	16.9	NA
Pretax Inc.	263	244	-254	-89.2	125	157	151	52.2	68.0	NA
Eff. Tax Rate	38%	39%	NM	NM	41%	43%	42%	54%	41%	NA
Net Inc.	164	148	-165	-67.8	73.6	89.6	88.1	23.8	40.3	NA
Balance Sheet & Other Fin. Data (Million $)										
Cash	1,047	1,011	764	559	590	593	512	466	351	NA
Curr. Assets	2,400	2,348	2,240	2,410	753	737	630	556	419	NA
Total Assets	3,670	3,696	3,930	4,076	1,212	1,214	894	835	772	NA
Curr. Liab.	1,811	1,730	1,825	1,765	478	568	478	421	381	NA
LT Debt	766	1,039	1,254	1,309	362	354	158	220	224	NA
Common Eqty.	1,061	891	744	896	365	286	224	154	127	NA
Total Cap.	1,836	1,936	1,998	2,205	727	640	411	410	387	NA
Cap. Exp.	86.9	36.6	148	132	37.6	35.6	28.9	24.6	22.2	NA
Cash Flow	270	260	-37.1	30.5	126	138	128	58.0	73.0	NA
Curr. Ratio	1.3	1.4	1.2	1.4	1.6	1.3	1.3	1.3	1.1	NA
% LT Debt of Cap.	41.7	53.7	62.8	59.4	49.8	55.4	38.6	53.7	57.9	NA
% Net Inc.of Revs.	1.8	1.7	NM	NM	2.3	3.3	3.8	1.2	2.6	NA
% Ret. on Assets	4.4	3.9	NM	NM	6.1	8.5	10.2	3.0	NA	NA
% Ret. on Equity	16.8	18.1	NM	NM	22.6	35.2	46.7	16.9	NA	NA

Data as orig reptd.; bef. results of disc opers/spec. items. Per share data adj. for stk. divs. Bold denotes diluted EPS (FASB 128)-prior periods restated. E-Estimated. NA-Not Available. NM-Not Meaningful. NR-Not Ranked.

Office—21650 Oxnard St., Woodland Hills, CA 91367. **Tel**—(818) 676-6000. **Website**—http://www.health.net **Chrmn**—R.W. Hanselman. **Pres & CEO**—J. M. Gellert. **EVP & CFO**—S. P. Erwin.**SVP & Secy**—B. C. Westen. **Investor Contact**—David Olson (818-676-6978).**Dirs**—J. T. Bouchard, G. Deukmejian, T. T. Farley, G. S. Fitzgerald, P. Foley, J. M. Gellert, R. F. Greaves, R. W. Hanselman, R. J. Stegemeier, R. S. Troubh, B. G. Willison. **Transfer Agent & Registrar**—ComputerShare Investor Services, Chicago. **Incorporated**—in Delaware in 1990. **Empl**— 11,000. **S&P Analyst:** John A. Massey

STANDARD &POOR'S
STOCK REPORTS

Johnson & Johnson

NYSE Symbol **JNJ**

In S&P 500

18-AUG-01

Industry: Health Care (Diversified)

Summary: The world's largest and most comprehensive health care company, J&J offers a broad line of drugs, consumer products and other medical and dental items.

S&P Opinion: Accumulate (★★★★) Recent Price • 53.75 52 Wk Range • 57.60-40.25 Yield • 1.3% 12-Mo. P/E • 29.9

Quantitative Evaluations

Outlook (1 Lowest—5 Highest) **• 2**

Fair Value **• 53.50**

Risk **• Low**

Earn./Div. Rank **• A+**

Technical Eval. **• Neutral** since 7/01

Rel. Strength Rank (1 Lowest—99 Highest) **• 68**

Insider Activity **• Unfavorable**

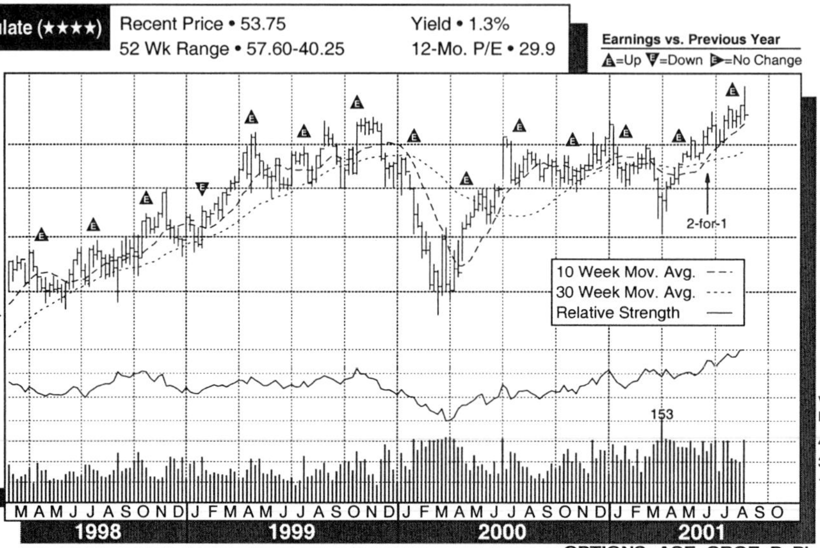

OPTIONS: ASE, CBOE, P, Ph

Overview - 19-JUL-01

Sales are expected to rise 10% in 2001. Drug sales should be augmented by strong gains in Procrit treatment for anemia, Duragesic transdermal patch for chronic pain, and Remicade anti-inflammatory agent. Greater contributions are also seen from new drugs such Aciphex antiulcer, Topamax antiepileptic, and Reminyl for Alzheimer's disease. We also see higher sales from recently acquired ALZA Corp. Solid sales gains are projected for professional products, led by continued strength in cardiac stents, orthopedic products, and glucose monitoring devices. However, more modest growth is seen for consumer product lines. Despite anticipated dilution from ALZA, margins should benefit from the greater volume and cost efficiencies. EPS are projected at $1.88 for 2001, with further progress, to $2.18, seen for 2002.

Valuation - 19-JUL-01

The shares moved sharply higher in recent months, significantly outperforming the big pharmaceutical sector, which has been in the doldrums. JNJ's strength mirrored robust earnings showings in recent quarters, and investor enthusiasm for the recent acquisition of ALZA Corp. and new product prospects. Despite estimated initial dilution of $0.07 a share in 2001, ALZA should rejuvenate JNJ's higher-margin pharmaceuticals business with new drugs and drug delivery technologies, and also provide cost synergies. Although sales and EPS growth in 2001 are expected to trend below historical norms, JNJ should resume robust growth in coming years, boosted by new drugs such as Remicade anti-inflammatory agent and Reminyl Alzheimer's treatment, and by new devices such as drug-coated coronary stents. Valued in line with other leading drug/medical companies, the shares (split two for one in June) merit accumulation for above average total return.

Key Stock Statistics

S&P EPS Est. 2001	1.88	Tang. Bk. Value/Share	4.15
P/E on S&P Est. 2001	28.6	Beta	0.58
S&P EPS Est. 2002	2.18	Shareholders	165,900
Dividend Rate/Share	0.72	Market cap. (B)	$162.8
Shs. outstg. (M)	3028.1	Inst. holdings	55%
Avg. daily vol. (M)	7.431		

Value of $10,000 invested 5 years ago: $ 22,263

Fiscal Year Ending Dec. 31

	2001	2000	1999	1998	1997	1996
Revenues (Million $)						
1Q	7,791	7,319	6,638	5,783	5,715	5,334
2Q	8,342	7,508	6,854	5,783	5,698	5,382
3Q	—	7,204	6,749	5,724	5,586	5,402
4Q	—	7,108	6,877	6,367	5,630	5,502
Yr.	—	29,139	27,471	23,657	22,629	21,620
Earnings Per Share ($)						
1Q	**0.53**	**0.47**	**0.41**	**0.36**	**0.33**	**0.29**
2Q	**0.48**	**0.47**	**0.42**	**0.37**	**0.34**	**0.29**
3Q	—	**0.45**	**0.40**	**0.35**	**0.32**	**0.28**
4Q	—	**0.32**	**0.27**	**0.03**	**0.23**	**0.20**
Yr.	—	**1.70**	**1.47**	**1.11**	**1.21**	**1.06**

Next earnings report expected: mid October

Dividend Data (Dividends have been paid since 1944.)

Amount ($)	Date Decl.	Ex-Div. Date	Stock of Record	Payment Date
0.320	Jan. 02	Feb. 15	Feb. 20	Jan. 13 '01
0.360	Apr. 26	May. 18	May. 22	Jun. 12 '01
2-for-1	Apr. 26	Jun. 13	May. 22	Jun. 12 '01
0.180	Jul. 16	Aug. 17	Aug. 21	Sep. 11 '01

A Division of The McGraw-Hill Companies

Johnson & Johnson

Business Summary - 19-JUL-01

Well known for household names like Tylenol and Band-Aid adhesive bandages, Johnson & Johnson ranks as the largest and most diversified health care company in the world. The company traces its roots to James Johnson and Edward Mead Johnson, who formed the JNJ more than 110 years ago. Today, it offers an impressive list of blockbuster prescription drugs, medical instruments and the broadest line of health-related consumer products.

Pharmaceuticals accounted for 41% of sales and 62% of operating profits in 2000; professional products for 35% and 25%; and consumer products for 24% and 13%. J&J is one of the most geographically diversified health care companies, with operations outside of the U.S. representing 42% of 2000 sales.

Despite its immense size, JNJ continues to generate robust earnings growth. While helped by an expanding health care marketplace, Its outstanding success also reflects proficient management, which directed the company's growth through well planned, strategic acquisitions, aggressive R&D spending and a policy of decentralized management. Over the past 10 years, the company acquired 42 businesses, many of which have become important sources of growth. R&D outlays totaled $2.9 billion in 2000, equal to 10% of sales.

Some of the more noteworthy fast-growing product lines developed or acquired in recent years include Remicade anti-inflammatory, Risperdal anti-psychotic and Procrit anti-anemia drugs, the LifeScan home glucose monitoring system and the BX Velocity coronary stent used after angioplasty procedures. These and similar products enabled JNJ to chalk up compound EPS growth (excluding nonrecurring items) of about 13% in the 10 years through 2000.

Although usually thought of as a medical products and hospital supplies firm, the company derives over 60% of its profits from a growing list of drugs. More than 90 different prescription drug, contraceptive and veterinary products are sold, many of which generate sales in the hundreds of millions. JNJ expanded its position in biotechnology with the October 1999 acquisition of Centocor, a leader in monoclonal antibody technology, acute vascular care and immunology.

Leading positions are also maintained in growing professional and consumer products lines. Professional items include older items such as sutures, wound closure products, surgical accessories and orthopedic products, as well as newer products such as coronary stents, angioplasty catheters and disposable contact lenses. The orthopedic business was significantly enlarged in 1998 with the purchase of DePuy, a leading maker of spinal implants. Albeit slower growing, a long list of consumer products such as Tylenol, bandages and toiletries provides a solid base of stability and cash flow.

Per Share Data ($) (Year Ended Dec. 31)	2000	1999	1998	1997	1996	1995	1994	1993	1992	1991
Tangible Bk. Val.	4.15	3.11	2.38	3.38	2.90	2.35	1.83	1.80	1.70	1.83
Cash Flow	2.23	1.98	1.57	1.59	1.47	1.26	1.06	0.92	0.83	0.73
Earnings	1.70	1.47	1.11	1.24	1.08	0.93	0.78	0.69	0.61	0.55
Dividends	0.62	0.55	0.48	0.42	0.37	0.32	0.28	0.25	0.22	0.19
Payout Ratio	36%	37%	43%	35%	34%	34%	36%	37%	36%	35%
Prices - High	52.96	53.43	44.87	33.65	27.00	23.09	14.12	12.59	14.68	14.68
- Low	33.06	38.50	31.68	24.31	20.78	13.40	9.00	8.90	10.75	8.17
P/E Ratio - High	31	36	40	27	25	25	18	18	24	26
- Low	19	26	28	20	19	14	12	13	17	15
Income Statement Analysis (Million $)										
Revs.	29,139	27,471	23,657	22,629	21,620	18,842	15,734	14,138	13,753	12,447
Oper. Inc.	7,992	7,370	6,291	5,689	5,312	6,002	3,531	3,011	2,837	2,657
Depr.	1,515	1,444	1,246	1,067	1,009	857	724	617	560	493
Int. Exp.	146	197	110	120	180	213	186	174	177	175
Pretax Inc.	6,622	5,753	4,269	4,576	4,033	3,317	2,681	2,332	2,207	2,038
Eff. Tax Rate	28%	28%	28%	28%	28%	28%	25%	23%	26%	28%
Net Inc.	4,800	4,167	3,059	3,303	2,887	2,403	2,006	1,787	1,625	1,461
Balance Sheet & Other Fin. Data (Million $)										
Cash	6,013	4,320	2,994	2,753	2,136	1,364	704	476	878	792
Curr. Assets	15,450	13,200	11,132	10,563	9,370	7,938	6,680	5,217	5,423	4,933
Total Assets	31,321	29,163	26,211	21,453	20,010	17,873	15,668	12,242	11,884	10,513
Curr. Liab.	7,140	7,454	8,162	5,283	5,184	4,388	4,266	3,212	3,427	2,689
LT Debt	2,037	2,450	1,269	1,126	1,410	2,107	2,199	1,493	1,365	1,301
Common Eqty.	18,808	16,213	13,590	12,359	10,836	9,045	7,122	5,568	5,171	5,626
Total Cap.	21,100	18,950	15,437	13,660	12,416	11,308	9,451	7,183	6,627	6,927
Cap. Exp.	1,646	1,728	1,460	1,391	1,373	1,256	937	975	1,103	987
Cash Flow	6,315	5,611	4,305	4,370	3,896	3,260	2,730	2,404	2,185	1,954
Curr. Ratio	2.2	1.8	1.4	2.0	1.8	1.8	1.6	1.6	1.6	1.8
% LT Debt of Cap.	9.7	12.9	8.2	8.2	11.4	18.6	23.3	20.8	20.6	18.8
% Net Inc.of Revs.	16.5	15.2	12.9	14.6	13.3	12.8	12.7	12.6	11.8	11.7
% Ret. on Assets	15.9	14.8	12.8	15.9	15.2	14.3	14.4	15.0	14.6	14.6
% Ret. on Equity	27.4	27.5	23.6	28.5	29.0	29.7	31.6	33.6	30.4	27.8

Data as orig reptd.; bef. results of disc opers/spec. items. Per share data adj. for stk. divs. Bold denotes diluted EPS (FASB 128)-prior periods restated. E-Estimated. NA-Not Available. NM-Not Meaningful. NR-Not Ranked.

Office—One Johnson & Johnson Plaza, New Brunswick, NJ 08933. **Tel**—(732) 524-0400. **Website**—http://www.jnj.com **Chrmn & CEO**—R. S. Larsen. **Sr Vice Chrmn**—R. N. Wilson. **Vice Chrmn**—J. T. Lenehan, W. C. Weldon. **VP-Fin & CFO**—R. J. Darretta. **Secy**—M. H. Ullmann. **Treas**—J. A. Papa. **Investor Contact**—Helen E. Short (800-950-5089). **Dirs**—G. N. Burrow, J. G. Cooney, J. G. Cullen, M. J. Folkman, A. D. Jordan, A. G. Langbo, R. S. Larsen, J. T. Lenehan, J. S. Mayo, L. F. Mullin, H. B. Schacht, M. F. Singer, J. W. Snow, W. C. Weldon, R. N. Wilson. **Transfer Agent & Registrar**—EquiServe Trust Co., Jersey City, NJ. **Incorporated**—in New Jersey in 1887. **Empl**— 98,500. **S&P Analyst:** H. B. Saftlas

STANDARD
&POOR'S
STOCK REPORTS

Laboratory Corp. of America

NYSE Symbol **LH**

18-AUG-01

Industry: Health Care (Specialized Services)

Summary: This clinical laboratory organization offers more than 4,000 different clinical laboratory tests through a national network of laboratories.

S&P Opinion: Accumulate (★★★★)

Recent Price • 81.65
52 Wk Range • 91.50-49.75

Yield • Nil
12-Mo. P/E • 38.5

Quantitative Evaluations

Outlook
(1 Lowest—5 Highest)
• **2−**

Fair Value
• **76.70**

Risk
• **High**

Earn./Div. Rank
• **B-**

Technical Eval.
• **Bullish** since 5/01

Rel. Strength Rank
(1 Lowest—99 Highest)
• **67**

Insider Activity
• **NA**

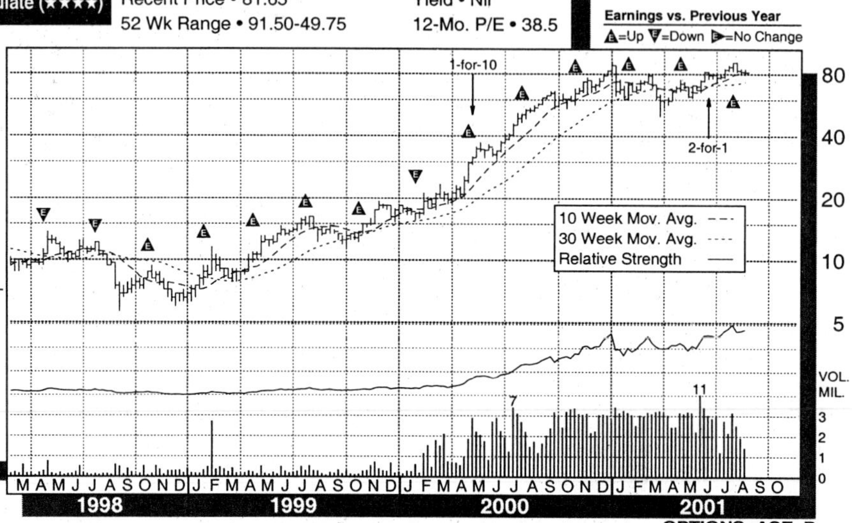

OPTIONS: ASE, P

Overview - 24-JUL-01

Second quarter results easily exceeded our expectations, on better than expected pricing and margins. We estimate that 2001 revenues will increase 13.0%, to about $2.2 billion, on 6.5% to 7.0% testing volume growth and 6.0% to 6.5% higher pricing. Volume gains will reflect new customers as well as higher managed care and hospital testing volumes, resulting in part from an outsourcing trend due to a shortage of lab technicians. We expect LH to process more than 277,000 tests a day in 2001, up from 2000's 260,000. Pricing is benefiting from a larger percentage of high cost specialty (esoteric) testing, aided by the acquisition of National Genetics Institute, and from price hikes. We see EBITDA margins widening by 320 basis points, to 21.0%, on better pricing, lower bad debt expense, leverage over fixed costs, and higher capacity utilization. We project 2001 EPS at $2.54, with 2002 at $3.25.

Valuation - 24-JUL-01

We are maintaining our accumulate opinion on LH, reflecting accelerating revenue and earnings growth exceeding strong industry trends. We expect continued low double-digit revenue growth, with margin improvements driving substantially higher earnings gains through 2002. Profitability gains reflect rapid growth of high margin esoteric and molecular testing, and revenue driven leverage over fixed costs. With volume growth exceeding industry levels, LH continues to gain market share. In the second quarter, it achieved its goal of reducing days sales outstanding, to 64, from 68 in the first quarter. Second quarter operating cash flow was $74 million; $33 million was used to reduce debt. The stock, recently trading at 33X our 2001 EPS estimate, versus a projected three-year compound annual EPS growth rate of 25%, is undervalued in light of positive industry fundamentals.

Key Stock Statistics

S&P EPS Est. 2001	2.54	Tang. Bk. Value/Share	0.45
P/E on S&P Est. 2001	32.1	Beta	0.36
S&P EPS Est. 2002	3.25	Shareholders	713
Dividend Rate/Share	Nil	Market cap. (B)	$ 5.7
Shs. outstg. (M)	70.1	Inst. holdings	64%
Avg. daily vol. (M)	0.514		

Value of $10,000 invested 5 years ago: $ 40,825

Fiscal Year Ending Dec. 31

	2001	2000	1999	1998	1997	1996
Revenues (Million $)						
1Q	525.4	462.7	417.9	387.7	391.5	403.9
2Q	549.7	482.4	429.5	402.4	389.6	410.0
3Q	—	448.1	428.6	414.7	376.5	402.6
4Q	—	486.1	422.7	407.8	361.4	391.2
Yr.	—	1,919	1,699	1,613	1,519	1,608
Earnings Per Share ($)						
1Q	0.62	0.38	0.12	-0.05	0.10	0.25
2Q	0.74	0.47	0.28	0.05	0.10	-0.60
3Q	—	0.47	0.16	Nil	-0.25	-5.95
4Q	—	0.30	0.03	0.55	-5.30	0.05
Yr.	—	1.61	0.58	1.00	-5.30	-6.25

Next earnings report expected: late October

Dividend Data

Amount ($)	Date Decl.	Ex-Div. Date	Stock of Record	Payment Date
2-for-1	May. 18	Jun. 12	Jun. 04	Jun. 11 '01

Laboratory Corporation of America Holdings

Business Summary - 24-JUL-01

For many Americans, a visit to the doctor's office is often followed by a short wait for test results. Since 1971, Laboratory Corp. of America Holdings has played an integral role in this process by providing a broad range of testing services used by the medical profession. The company has grown into the largest independent U.S. clinical laboratory. At December 31, 2000, it had more than 200,000 clients nationwide.

The company's laboratory services, which involve the testing of both bodily fluids and human tissue, are generally used by independent physicians, hospitals and managed care groups. LH has 24 major laboratories, and approximately 1,200 service sites consisting of branches, patient service centers and STAT laboratories that have the ability to perform certain routine tests quickly and report results to the physician immediately.

LH offers more than 4,000 different tests, of which the most frequently administered include blood chemistry analyses, urinalysis, blood cell counts, pap smears, AIDS tests and substance-abuse test. An average of 260,000 specimens were processed per day in 2000, with routine testing results generally available within 24 hours. The company also provides specialty and niche testing such as more reliable information regarding HIV, genetic diseases, cancer and many other viral and bacterial diseases.

The primary client groups served by LH include independent physicians and physician groups, hospitals, HMOs and other managed care groups, and other institutions. No client accounted for over 2% of LH's 2000 net sales. Commercial clients accounted for 40.9% of accession volume and $22.42 revenue per accession; managed care clients 40.2% and $29.25; Medicare, Medicaid and Insurance 15.6% and $29.80; and private patients 3.3% and $102.87.

The clinical laboratory industry has shifted from traditional, fee-for-service medicine to managed-cost health care. The growth of the managed care sector presents challenges to LH and other independent clinical laboratories. Managed care organizations typically contract with a limited number of clinical laboratories, and negotiate discounts. These discounts have resulted in price erosion, and have restricted LH's operating margins. In 2000, such contracts accounted for $101.9 million of net sales (5%).

One of LH's primary growth strategies is to continue to expand its specialty (esoteric and molecular) testing capabilities, generally more profitable than routine tests. As part of this strategy, in August 2000, the company acquired National Genetics Institute, a leader in the development of PCR assays for Hepatitis C. Another growth target is to continue to develop hospital alliances. Hospitals, facing increasing pressure from lower reimbursement rates, are outsourcing lab testing functions. In 2000, LH added 43 new hospital, physician group, and health care provider agreements, representing $25 million in annual sales.

Per Share Data ($) (Year Ended Dec. 31)	2000	1999	1998	1997	1996	1995	1994	1993	1992	1991
Tangible Bk. Val.	0.17	NM	NM	NM	-25.75	-20.55	-22.75	-8.30	1.35	6.95
Cash Flow	3.49	0.39	4.35	-1.78	-2.80	3.10	4.40	8.10	3.55	6.35
Earnings	1.61	0.58	1.00	-5.30	-6.25	-0.15	1.80	6.30	2.15	5.25
Dividends	Nil	Nil	Nil	Nil	Nil	Nil	0.40	1.60	1.55	1.35
Payout Ratio	Nil	Nil	Nil	Nil	Nil	Nil	22%	25%	72%	26%
Prices - High	91.50	19.37	13.75	20.00	46.87	77.50	78.75	97.50	146.25	154.37
- Low	15.62	6.25	5.62	6.56	11.87	40.62	53.12	60.00	78.12	44.37
P/E Ratio - High	57	33	14	NM	NM	NM	44	15	68	29
- Low	10	11	6	NM	NM	NM	30	10	36	8
Income Statement Analysis (Million $)										
Revs.	1,919	1,699	1,613	1,519	1,608	1,432	873	761	721	604
Oper. Inc.	340	234	212	17.5	174	215	158	218	227	188
Depr.	89.6	84.5	84.2	86.8	84.5	72.4	44.4	32.2	26.9	22.0
Int. Exp.	38.5	41.6	48.7	71.7	71.7	65.5	34.5	10.9	4.2	Nil
Pretax Inc.	208	106	81.5	-161	-188	3.0	55.0	191	62.0	169
Eff. Tax Rate	46%	38%	16%	NM	NM	NM	46%	41%	35%	39%
Net Inc.	112	65.4	68.8	-107	-154	-4.0	30.0	113	41.0	104
Balance Sheet & Other Fin. Data (Million $)										
Cash	48.8	40.3	22.7	23.3	29.3	16.4	26.8	12.3	33.4	51.3
Curr. Assets	512	500	519	528	722	600	293	183	180	135
Total Assets	1,667	1,590	1,641	1,659	1,917	1,837	1,013	586	477	411
Curr. Liab.	312	246	251	197	253	351	203	121	148	71.1
LT Debt	354	483	576	650	704	940	564	288	84.6	Nil
Common Eqty.	877	176	154	129	258	412	166	141	213	331
Total Cap.	1,231	1,217	1,257	779	962	1,352	750	432	297	337
Cap. Exp.	55.5	69.4	58.7	34.5	54.1	75.4	48.9	33.6	34.9	25.4
Cash Flow	167	100	109	-44.0	-69.0	68.4	75.0	145	68.0	126
Curr. Ratio	1.6	2.0	2.1	2.7	2.9	1.7	1.4	1.5	1.2	1.9
% LT Debt of Cap.	28.7	39.7	45.8	83.4	73.2	69.6	75.1	66.7	28.5	Nil
% Net Inc.of Revs.	5.8	3.9	4.3	NM	NM	NM	3.4	14.8	5.6	17.2
% Ret. on Assets	6.9	4.0	4.2	NM	NM	NM	3.8	22.2	9.6	26.4
% Ret. on Equity	14.8	9.1	17.2	NM	NM	NM	19.6	67.9	15.9	35.4

Data as orig. reptd.; bef. results of disc. opers. and/or spec. items. Per share data adj. for stk. divs. as of ex-div. date. Prior to 1995, data for National Health Laboratories only. E-Estimated. NA-Not Available. NM-Not Meaningful. NR-Not Ranked.

Office—358 South Main Street, Burlington, NC 27215. **Tel**—(336) 229-1127. **Website**—www.labcorp.com **Chrmn, Pres & CEO**—T. P. MacMahon. **EVP, CFO & Treas**—W. R. Elingburg. **EVP & COO**—R. L. Novak. **EVP & Secy**—B. T. Smith. **Dirs**—J. L. Belingard, W. E. Lane, T. P. MacMahon, R. E. Mittelstaedt, J. B. Powell, D. B. Skinner, A. G. Wallace. **Transfer Agent & Registrar**—American Stock Transfer & Trust Co., NYC. **Incorporated**—in Delaware in 1971. **Empl**— 18,850. **S&P Analyst:** John Massey

STANDARD & POOR'S STOCK REPORTS

Manor Care

NYSE Symbol **HCR**

In S&P 500

24-AUG-01

Industry: Health Care (Long-Term Care)

Summary: This provider of long-term health care services was formed through the 1998 merger of Health Care and Retirement Corp. and Manor Care Inc.

S&P Opinion: Accumulate (★★★★)

Recent Price • 29.17
52 Wk Range • 34.50-11.93
Yield • Nil
12-Mo. P/E • 30.7

Quantitative Evaluations

Outlook (1 Lowest—5 Highest)
• **2**

Fair Value
• **29.50**

Risk
• **Low**

Earn./Div. Rank
• **NR**

Technical Eval.
• **Bullish** since 5/01

Rel. Strength Rank (1 Lowest—99 Highest)
• **56**

Insider Activity
• **Neutral**

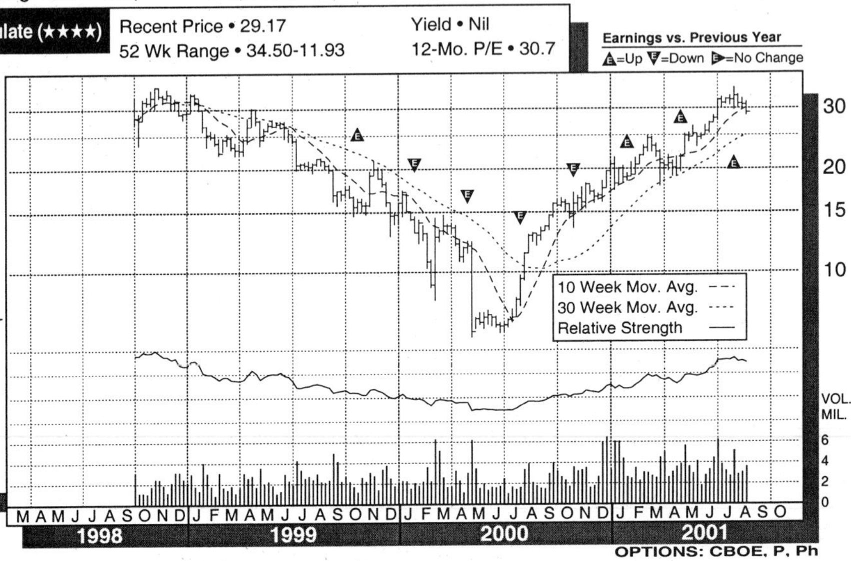

OPTIONS: CBOE, P, Ph

Overview - 24-AUG-01

Revenue growth of 13% to 14% is seen for 2001, aided by increased Medicare and Medicaid reimbursement rates, further improvements in the private pay rate environment, slight gains in the skilled nursing occupancy levels, and contributions from In Home Health. Strategic acquisitions in the home health care and outpatient rehabilitation areas are possible. The primary risk to operating margins is labor cost inflation; patient liability costs in Florida are also troublesome. However, the strengthening revenue line should allow for EBITDA (earnings before interest, taxes, depreciation and amortization) margins of 15% in 2001, and rising levels of operating cash flow are allowing for debt paydowns and reduced interest costs. Assuming that the assisted living and transcription businesses are earnings neutral in the second half, we look for 2001 EPS of $1.13, and $1.35 in 2002.

Valuation - 24-AUG-01

The stock has been one of the best performers in our healthcare provider universe in 2001, benefiting from dramatically improved long term care industry fundamentals. These include rising private and governmental reimbursement rates, steadily improving occupancy levels and rising operating margins. Typically, health care services stocks rally when pricing is on the mend, and we believe the long-term care sector will continue to generate strong revenue comparisons through the middle of 2002. We view HCR as the premier investment in the group, and would continue to add to holdings despite a year-to-date gain that has taken away the stock's valuation discount relative to the S&P 500. However, the stock's valuation has reached levels at which any signs of weakness could result in significant downward pressure. For now, we would continue to accumulate the stock.

Key Stock Statistics

S&P EPS Est. 2001	1.13	Tang. Bk. Value/Share	9.32
P/E on S&P Est. 2001	25.8	Beta	1.02
S&P EPS Est. 2002	1.35	Shareholders	3,777
Dividend Rate/Share	Nil	Market cap. (B)	$ 3.2
Shs. outstg. (M)	103.1	Inst. holdings	100%
Avg. daily vol. (M)	0.665		

Value of $10,000 invested 5 years ago: NA

Fiscal Year Ending Dec. 31

	2001	2000	1999	1998	1997	1996
Revenues (Million $)						
1Q	584.6	545.7	531.9	—	—	—
2Q	663.3	581.3	530.5	—	—	—
3Q	—	604.5	536.7	577.2	—	—
4Q	—	624.9	536.3	555.2	—	—
Yr.	—	2,381	2,135	2,209	2,229	1,924
Earnings Per Share ($)						
1Q	**0.24**	**-0.01**	**0.37**	—	—	—
2Q	**0.30**	**-0.03**	**0.30**	—	—	—
3Q	**E0.29**	**0.20**	**0.31**	**-0.73**	—	—
4Q	**E0.30**	**0.22**	**-1.59**	**0.25**	—	—
Yr.	**E1.13**	**0.38**	**-0.51**	**-0.42**	**1.40**	**1.02**

Next earnings report expected: early November

Dividend Data

No cash dividends have been paid.

A Division of The McGraw-Hill Companies

Manor Care, Inc.

Business Summary - 24-AUG-01

Manor Care, created through the September 1998 merger of Health Care and Retirement and the original Manor Care Inc., is a provider of a range of health care services, including skilled nursing care, assisted living, subacute medical and rehabilitation care, rehabilitation therapy, home health care, hospice care and management services for subacute care and rehabilitation therapy.

The most significant portion of the company's business relates to skilled nursing care and assisted living. At December 31, 2000, it operated 298 skilled nursing facilities and 56 assisted living facilities in 32 states, with more than 60% located in Ohio, Michigan, Illinois, Pennsylvania and Florida. Within some of its centers, there are medical specialty units which provide subacute medical and rehabilitation care, and/or Alzheimer's care programs. Some of the company's assisted living facilities operate under the brand names "Arden Courts" and "Springhouse." The Arden Courts facilities are specifically focused on providing care to persons suffering from early to middle-stage Alzheimer's disease and related memory impairment, while the Springhouse facilities serve the general assisted living population of frail elderly. These facilities provide housing, personalized support and health care services in a non-institutional setting designed to address the needs of the elderly or Alzheimer's afflicted.

The home health care business specializes in all levels of home health, hospice care and rehabilitation therapy from 78 offices located in 18 states, including the acquisition of In Home Health Inc. in 2000.

Manor Care provides rehabilitation therapy in its long term care centers, other skilled nursing centers, hospitals, and the company's 87 outpatient therapy clinics serving the Midwestern and Mid-Atlantic states, Texas and Florida. The company provides program management services for subacute care and acute rehabilitation programs in hospitals and skilled nursing centers. HCR owns and operates a general media/surgical acute care hospital with 172 licensed beds in Texas. It has long term management contracts with physician practices in the Midwestern states, specializing in vision care and refractive eye surgery. The company also owns about 96% of a start-up medical transcription business, which converts medical dictation into electronically formatted patient records.

In 2000, revenues in the skilled nursing, assisted living and rehabilitation operations were generated from Medicaid (33%), Medicare (24%), and private pay and other (43%) sources.

HCR formed a strategic alliance with Alterra Healthcare Corp. in 1998 to develop a broad-based network primarily dedicated to the care of patients suffering from Alzheimer's disease. However, the venture was suspended during 2000 and plans regarding future development activities have been terminated.

Per Share Data ($) (Year Ended Dec. 31)	2000	1999	1998	1997	1996	1995	1994	1993	1992	1991
Tangible Bk. Val.	8.87	8.72	10.35	6.78	NA	NA	NA	NA	NA	NA
Cash Flow	1.55	0.57	0.67	2.32	NA	NA	NA	NA	NA	NA
Earnings	0.38	-0.51	-0.42	NA	NA	NA	NA	NA	NA	NA
Dividends	Nil	Nil	Nil	NA	NA	NA	NA	NA	NA	NA
Payout Ratio	Nil	Nil	Nil	NA	NA	NA	NA	NA	NA	NA
Prices - High	21.18	33.50	35.00	NA	NA	NA	NA	NA	NA	NA
- Low	6.43	12.75	23.50	NA	NA	NA	NA	NA	NA	NA
P/E Ratio - High	56	NM	NM	NA	NA	NA	NA	NA	NA	NA
- Low	17	NM	NM	NA	NA	NA	NA	NA	NA	NA
Income Statement Analysis (Million $)										
Revs.	2,381	2,135	2,209	892	NA	NA	NA	NA	NA	NA
Oper. Inc.	260	362	397	151	NA	NA	NA	NA	NA	NA
Depr.	121	116	119	37.7	NA	NA	NA	NA	NA	NA
Int. Exp.	60.7	54.0	46.6	17.2	NA	NA	NA	NA	NA	NA
Pretax Inc.	61.7	-101	-24.1	101	NA	NA	NA	NA	NA	NA
Eff. Tax Rate	35%	NM	NM	31%	NA	NA	NA	NA	NA	NA
Net Inc.	39.1	-55.2	-46.2	70.1	NA	NA	NA	NA	NA	NA
Balance Sheet & Other Fin. Data (Million $)										
Cash	24.9	12.0	33.7	7.5	NA	NA	NA	NA	NA	NA
Curr. Assets	505	431	418	171	NA	NA	NA	NA	NA	NA
Total Assets	2,358	2,281	2,715	936	NA	NA	NA	NA	NA	NA
Curr. Liab.	473	409	504	121	NA	NA	NA	NA	NA	NA
LT Debt	644	688	693	NA	NA	NA	NA	NA	NA	NA
Common Eqty.	1,013	980	1,557	434	NA	NA	NA	NA	NA	NA
Total Cap.	1,766	1,795	2,496	NA	NA	NA	NA	NA	NA	NA
Cap. Exp.	117	166	296	NA	NA	NA	NA	NA	NA	NA
Cash Flow	160	60.8	73.1	108	NA	NA	NA	NA	NA	NA
Curr. Ratio	1.1	1.1	0.8	1.4	NA	NA	NA	NA	NA	NA
% LT Debt of Cap.	36.5	38.3	27.8	NA	NA	NA	NA	NA	NA	NA
% Net Inc.of Revs.	1.6	NM	NM	7.9	NA	NA	NA	NA	NA	NA
% Ret. on Assets	1.7	NM	NM	8.1	NA	NA	NA	NA	NA	NA
% Ret. on Equity	3.9	NM	NM	17.0	NA	NA	NA	NA	NA	NA

Data as orig reptd.; bef. results of disc opers/spec. items. Per share data adj. for stk. divs. Bold denotes diluted EPS (FASB 128)-prior periods restated. E-Estimated. NA-Not Available. NM-Not Meaningful. NR-Not Ranked.

Office—333 N. Summit St., Toledo, OH 43604-2617. **Tel**—(419) 252-5500. **Website**—http://www.hcr-manorcare.com **Chrmn**—S. Bainum Jr. **Pres & CEO**—P. A. Ormond. **Sr. EVP & COO**—M. K. Weikel. **EVP, CFO & Treas**—G. G. Meyers. **Dirs**—S. Bainum, S. Bainum Jr., J. H. Lemieux, W. H. Longfield, F. V. Malek, P. A. Ormond, J. T. Schwieters, R. G. Siefers, M. K. Weikel, G. R. Wilensky, T. L. Young. **Transfer Agent**—ComputerShare Investor Services, Chicago. **Empl**— 54,000. **S&P Analyst:** Robert M. Gold

STANDARD
&POOR'S
STOCK REPORTS

McKesson Corp.

NYSE Symbol **MCK**

In S&P 500

22-AUG-01

Industry: Distributors (Food & Health)

Summary: This company (formerly McKesson HBOC) provides pharmaceutical supply management and information technologies to a broad range of health care customers.

S&P Opinion: Accumulate (★★★★)

Recent Price • 40.44
52 Wk Range • 41.50-23.40
Yield • 0.6%
12-Mo. P/E • NM

Quantitative Evaluations

Outlook (1 Lowest—5 Highest)
• **2**

Fair Value
• **38**

Risk
• **Low**

Earn./Div. Rank
• **NR**

Technical Eval.
• **Bullish** since 4/01

Rel. Strength Rank (1 Lowest—99 Highest)
• **89**

Insider Activity
• **Neutral**

OPTIONS: ASE, CBOE, P, Ph

Overview - 22-AUG-01

Revenue growth of 12% to 14% is seen in FY 02 (Mar.), largely reflecting gains within the core supply management business. This would be about in line with the overall growth within the U.S. medical supply industry. Positive operating trends in the supply management unit include increased pharmaceutical utilization and increasing emphasis on generic drug substitutions, particularly as a large number of branded pharmaceuticals lose patent protection. Information technology revenue growth of 10% is expected in FY 02, as software demand begins to improve. EBITDA (earnings before interest, taxes, depreciation and amortization) in FY 02 should approximate $900 million, or 3% of sales. Assuming flat interest expense and taxes at 39.0%, we see FY 02 EPS of $1.44 (including special gains of $0.05 recorded in Q1), and look for 18% growth to $1.70 in FY 03.

Valuation - 22-AUG-01

Moving up with its health care distribution peers, the stock has significantly outperformed the S&P 500 year-to-date in 2001. After a few years of operational struggles, we are now seeing strong trends in the core supply management business, and the company has obtained several new contracts, and extended relationships with companies such as Caremark, Safeway and Costco. There now appears to be sufficient strength in the distribution area to allow for 16% to 18% earnings growth over the coming three years, a notable characteristic in a generally recessionary economic environment. Although no longer cheap on a P/E basis, the stock continues to trade at a steep discount to its peer group at only 0.3 times forward sales. With an accelerating top-line and margin expansion opportunities, we believe there is room for additional appreciation.

Key Stock Statistics

S&P EPS Est. 2002	1.44	Tang. Bk. Value/Share	8.94
P/E on S&P Est. 2002	28.1	Beta	0.28
S&P EPS Est. 2003	1.70	Shareholders	17,000
Dividend Rate/Share	0.24	Market cap. (B)	$ 11.3
Shs. outstg. (M)	285.5	Inst. holdings	67%
Avg. daily vol. (M)	1.841		

Value of $10,000 invested 5 years ago: $ 19,691

Fiscal Year Ending Mar. 31

	2002	2001	2000	1999	1998	1997
Revenues (Million $)						
1Q	11,654	9,729	8,697	6,283	—	2,671
2Q	—	9,874	9,050	7,337	—	2,731
3Q	—	11,029	9,891	8,367	—	3,487
4Q	—	11,409	9,305	8,395	—	3,999
Yr.	—	42,010	36,734	30,382	16,835	12,887
Earnings Per Share ($)						
1Q	**0.36**	**0.22**	**0.25**	**0.25**	—	-0.24
2Q	—	**0.22**	**0.21**	**0.10**	—	0.29
3Q	—	**0.03**	**0.56**	**0.18**	—	-0.41
4Q	—	**-0.62**	**-0.31**	**-0.22**	—	0.41
Yr.	—	**-0.15**	**0.66**	**0.31**	**0.40**	**0.06**

Next earnings report expected: late October

Dividend Data (Dividends have been paid since 1995.)

Amount ($)	Date Decl.	Ex-Div. Date	Stock of Record	Payment Date
0.060	Oct. 25	Nov. 29	Dec. 01	Jan. 02 '01
0.060	Jan. 31	Feb. 27	Mar. 01	Apr. 02 '01
0.060	May. 25	May. 31	Jun. 04	Jul. 02 '01
0.060	Jul. 25	Aug. 29	Sep. 03	Oct. 01 '01

STANDARD & POOR'S
STOCK REPORTS

McKesson Corporation

22-AUG-01

Business Summary - 22-AUG-01

McKesson Corp. (formerly McKesson HBOC) is a leading distributor of medical products and supplies and health care information technology products and services. MCK seeks to become the world leader in health care supply and comprehensive pharmaceutical management across the entire supply chain, from manufacturer to patient.

The Health Care Supply Management segment, which accounted for 96% of FY 01 (Mar.) revenues, primarily distributes ethical and proprietary drugs, medical-surgical supplies and health and beauty care products in North America. The business focuses on three primary customer segments: retail chains (pharmacies, food stores and mass merchandisers); retail independent pharmacies; and institutional providers in all 50 states. These customer categories accounted for 42%, 25% and 33%, respectively, of this group's revenues in FY 01.

The Medical Group provides medical-surgical supplies, equipment, logistics and related services to the continuum of health care providers: hospitals, physicians' offices, long-term care and home care. It also makes and markets automated pharmacy systems to hospitals and retail pharmacies. Key products include the ROBOT-Rx robotic pharmacy dispensing and utilization tracking system; AcuDose-Rx unit-based cabinets that automate storage, dispensing and tracking of commonly used drugs in patient areas; and AcuScan-Rx, which records, automates and streamlines drug administration and medication information requirements through bedside bar code scanning.

The Information Technology (IT, formerly HBO & Co.; 4%) unit provides patient care, clinical, financial, managed care and strategic management software solutions to the health care industry. Products and services are sold to integrated delivery networks, hospitals, physicians' offices, home health providers, pharmacies, reference labs and HMOs. IT products are designed to help automate individual hospital departments; provide care management services and medical call center management, data analysis and sharing and computer telephony and Internet links; document patient information for physicians and other clinicians; provide enterprise services such as UNIX support; and for practice management applications.

MCK has formed an Internet-based company with AmeriSource Health, Cardinal Health, Fisher Scientific International and Owens & Minor to provide commercially neutral product information focused on streamlining the process of identifying, buying and distributing pharmaceuticals, medical and surgical supplies, devices and other lab products and services.

Per Share Data ($)										
(Year Ended Mar. 31)	**2001**	**2000**	**1999**	**1998**	**1997**	**1996**	**1995**	**1994**	**1993**	**1992**
Tangible Bk. Val.	8.55	8.40	5.89	7.11	5.74	9.38	9.01	2.48	2.17	1.17
Cash Flow	0.72	1.37	0.98	2.39	0.85	2.22	-1.46	2.83	2.31	1.47
Earnings	-0.15	0.66	0.31	1.59	0.06	1.45	-2.25	1.84	1.34	0.42
Dividends	0.24	0.30	0.50	0.50	0.50	0.50	0.76	0.83	0.80	0.80
Payout Ratio	NM	46%	161%	31%	NM	34%	NM	45%	60%	65%
Cal. Yrs.	2000	1999	1998	1997	1996	1995	1994	1993	1992	1991
Prices - High	37.00	89.75	96.25	56.87	28.50	26.62	54.62	28.62	22.12	20.06
- Low	16.00	18.56	47.87	25.87	19.50	15.93	15.06	19.25	15.12	15.18
P/E Ratio - High	NM	NM	NM	36	NM	18	NM	16	16	48
- Low	NM	NM	NM	16	NM	11	NM	10	11	36
Income Statement Analysis (Million $)										
Revs.	42,010	36,734	30,382	20,857	12,887	13,716	13,171	12,428	11,669	10,313
Oper. Inc.	454	359	531	449	165	345	305	360	324	304
Depr.	246	201	199	86.0	72.0	71.3	69.8	80.7	77.4	81.5
Int. Exp.	118	120	124	103	56.0	46.7	46.0	41.4	49.5	57.7
Pretax Inc.	9.6	307	202	254	36.4	227	-71.0	275	197	82.0
Eff. Tax Rate	NM	40%	58%	39%	86%	39%	NM	40%	40%	49%
Net Inc.	-42.7	185	85.0	155	5.0	135	-192	157	115	40.0
Balance Sheet & Other Fin. Data (Million $)										
Cash	446	606	269	36.0	230	477	693	96.0	120	161
Curr. Assets	9,164	7,966	6,500	4,106	3,761	2,665	2,699	2,186	1,898	1,814
Total Assets	11,530	10,373	9,082	5,608	5,173	3,504	3,479	3,193	2,800	2,757
Curr. Liab.	6,550	5,122	4,800	2,578	2,637	1,723	1,738	1,784	1,615	1,493
LT Debt	1,232	1,440	1,142	1,194	825	443	459	463	347	490
Common Eqty.	3,493	4,213	2,882	1,523	1,261	1,065	1,014	553	493	426
Total Cap.	4,724	5,653	4,024	2,796	1,541	1,564	1,532	1,193	986	1,061
Cap. Exp.	159	145	251	130	76.9	77.3	82.0	100	70.0	73.0
Cash Flow	203	386	284	241	77.0	207	-126	231	185	114
Curr. Ratio	1.4	1.6	1.4	1.6	1.4	1.5	1.6	1.2	1.2	1.2
% LT Debt of Cap.	26.1	25.5	28.4	42.7	53.5	28.3	29.9	38.8	35.2	46.2
% Net Inc.of Revs.	NM	0.5	0.3	0.7	Nil	1.0	NM	1.3	1.0	0.4
% Ret. on Assets	NM	1.9	1.2	2.9	0.1	3.9	NM	5.2	4.0	1.5
% Ret. on Equity	NM	4.8	3.9	10.7	0.4	13.0	NM	28.7	23.0	6.6

Data as orig. reptd.; pr. to 1995 for predecessor co. (Old McKesson); bef. results of disc. opers. and/or spec. items. Per share data adj. for stk. divs. as of ex-div. date. Bold denotes diluted EPS (FASB 128). E-Estimated. NA-Not Available. NM-Not Meaningful. NR-Not Ranked.

Office—One Post St., San Francisco, CA 94104. **Tel**—(415) 983-8300. **Website**—http://www.mckhboc.com **Chrmn**—A. Seelenfreund. **Pres & CEO**—J. H. Hammergren. **SVP & CFO**—W. R. Graber. **SVP & Secy**—I. D. Meyerson. **Investor Contact**—Ana Schrank (415-983-7153). **Dirs**—A. C. Eckert III, T. M. Friedman, J. H. Hammergren, A. F. Irby III, M. C. Jacobs, M. M. Koffel, G. E. Mayo, J. V. Napier, D. S. Pottruck, C. E. Reichardt, A. Seelenfreund, J. E. Shaw. **Transfer Agent & Registrar**—First Chicago Trust Co. of New York, Jersey City, NJ. **Incorporated**—in Delaware in 1994. **Empl**— 23,000. **S&P Analyst:** Robert M. Gold

STANDARD
&POOR'S
STOCK REPORTS

MedImmune

Nasdaq Symbol **MEDI**

In S&P 500

18-AUG-01

Industry:
Biotechnology

Summary: This biotech concern develops, manufactures and markets therapeutics and vaccines to treat and prevent certain infectious diseases and cancer.

S&P Opinion: Accumulate (★★★★)

Recent Price • 36.55
52 Wk Range • 86.12-27.62
Yield • Nil
12-Mo. P/E • 50.8

Quantitative Evaluations

Outlook
(1 Lowest—5 Highest)
• **2⁻**

Fair Value
• **32.50**

Risk
• **High**

Earn./Div. Rank
• **B-**

Technical Eval.
• **Bearish** since 7/01

Rel. Strength Rank
(1 Lowest—99 Highest)
• **30**

Insider Activity
• **Neutral**

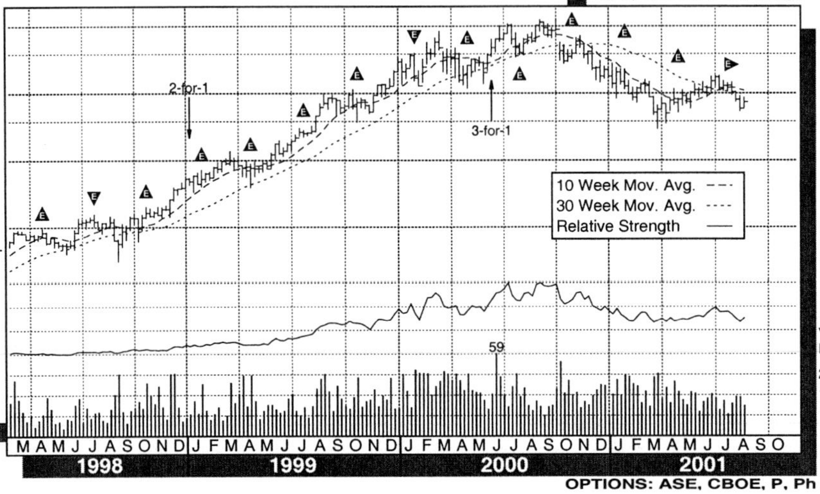

OPTIONS: ASE, CBOE, P, Ph

Overview - 27-JUL-01

Second quarter sales of Synagis (an antibody to prevent respiratory syncytial virus (RSV) disease, primarily in premature babies) totaled $15 million, meeting our expectations. A loss per share of $0.04 was a penny wider than our estimate. We are maintaining our 2001 Synagis sales projection at $544 million, raising our 2002 sales view to $652 million (from $640 million), and estimating $739 million in 2003 sales. Positive trends for Synagis sales include potential approvals in Canada and Japan by the end of the year, higher levels of retreatment in the following RSV season, and increased dosing per season. MEDI has also improved its manufacturing process, resulting in higher gross margins. A Phase I trial of Numax, a potential next generation RSV drug, should start by the end of 2001. We estimate 2001 EPS of $0.82, 2002 at $1.06, and 2003 at $1.29.

Valuation - 27-JUL-01

As of late July, the shares were down about 20% in 2001. MEDI's first half results have been in line with estimates, but there have not been any significant events to drive expectations higher. In 2002, pending Phase II results, we still feel MEDI could have three new compounds in Phase III testing, for psoriasis, cervical cancer, and urinary tract infections, respectively. Additionally, we speculate the firm may file for expanded approval of Synagis to include congenital heart disease in infants by the end of 2002 or 2003. In April 2002, rights to the chemoprotectant Ethoyl will revert back to MEDI from ALZA (recently acquired by J&J). While sales of this product have been slow, MEDI will have an opportunity to reinvigorate them with its own direct salesforce. On overlooked prospects and a P/E discount to its peers, we consider MEDI shares undervalued with less risk than the overall biotech sector.

Key Stock Statistics

S&P EPS Est. 2001	0.82	Tang. Bk. Value/Share	4.41
P/E on S&P Est. 2001	44.6	Beta	1.20
S&P EPS Est. 2002	1.06	Shareholders	1,723
Dividend Rate/Share	Nil	Market cap. (B)	$ 7.8
Shs. outstg. (M)	213.7	Inst. holdings	71%
Avg. daily vol. (M)	2.721		

Value of $10,000 invested 5 years ago: $ 146,200

Fiscal Year Ending Dec. 31

	2001	2000	1999	1998	1997	1996
Revenues (Million $)						
1Q	245.2	198.3	128.7	59.34	10.14	11.43
2Q	33.37	29.50	10.24	24.59	6.41	6.93
3Q	—	57.36	48.91	23.84	10.66	4.78
4Q	—	238.2	173.7	92.94	53.76	17.96
Yr.	—	540.5	383.4	200.7	80.96	41.10
Earnings Per Share ($)						
1Q	**0.36**	**0.27**	**0.15**	**0.07**	-0.11	-0.01
2Q	**-0.04**	**-0.04**	**-0.06**	**-0.12**	-0.09	-0.06
3Q	**E0.05**	**0.03**	**0.03**	**-0.07**	-0.10	-0.08
4Q	**E0.46**	**0.36**	**0.16**	**0.38**	**0.03**	-0.08
Yr.	**E0.82**	**0.66**	**0.44**	**0.30**	**-0.26**	—

Next earnings report expected: mid October

Dividend Data

Cash dividends have never been paid.

A Division of The **McGraw·Hill** *Companies*

MedImmune, Inc.

Business Summary - 27-JUL-01

MedImmune, founded in 1988, is a rapidly growing biotechnology company that focuses on using advances in immunology and related biological sciences to develop new compounds for infectious diseases, autoimmune disorders and cancer. Its principal product is Synagis, a treatment for respiratory syncytial virus (RSV). In November 1999, the company acquired U.S. Bioscience, a maker of treatments for cancer and AIDS, in exchange for about $530 million in common stock.

MEDI's principal product, Synagis, is an injectable humanized monoclonal antibody that is effective in neutralizing respiratory syncytial virus (RSV) infection. RSV, an ailment that typically breaks out in the fall, winter and early spring, is the most common cause of lower respiratory infections such as pneumonia and bronchiolitis in infants and toddlers. More than 90,000 infants are hospitalized with severe RSV disease in the U.S. annually, with about 300,000 infants in the U.S. and a similar number outside the U.S. at risk of acquiring severe RSV each year. Synagis has a monopoly in its market, as it is the only drug with FDA clearance to treat RSV. Patent protection extends to 2015.

The company co-markets Synagis with Abbott Laboratories in the U.S. Overseas, Abbott has exclusive marketing rights to Synagis, which it purchases from MEDI; the company records all sales. Synagis sales totaled $427 million in 2000, up from $293 million in 1999. Sales in Europe began in 1999. Synagis is also being studied to treat RSV in pediatric congenital heart disease, pediatric cystic fibrosis patients, and bone marrow transplants. MEDI is also developing an inhaled formulation of Synagis to treat RSV-related ailments in the elderly.

MEDI plans to start Phase I trials of Numax, a next generation version of Synagis, in 2001. In addition, it is researching fully human monoclonal antibodies that may be useful against RSV.

Other marketed products include CytoGam, an intravenous immune globulin product enriched in antibodies against cytomegalvirus (CMV), and used to prevent CMV disease associated with organ transplants; and Ethyol, a drug to alleviate certain negative side effects associated with chemotherapy. ALZA (a division of J&J) has rights to market Ethoyl in the U.S., with MEDI copromoting the product. In April 2002, however, MEDI will regain marketing rights to the drug and likely increase its efforts to improve sales of the product.

Clinical candidate MEDI-507 (anti-CD2 humanized monoclonal antibody) is in Phase II trials to treat psoriasis. The drug is also being developed as a treatment for graft-versus-host disease. In partnership with GlaxoSmithKline, a vaccine for human papillomaviruses, responsible for genital warts and cervical cancer, is undergoing Phase II testing. In addition, a Phase II trial on a vaccine for urinary tract infections is being conducted. MEDI is also developing Vitaxin as a potential treatment for certain cancers, with a Phase I/II trial init iated with colorectal cancer patients in July 2001.

Per Share Data ($) (Year Ended Dec. 31)	2000	1999	1998	1997	1996	1995	1994	1993	1992	1991
Tangible Bk. Val.	3.99	2.63	1.28	0.28	0.56	0.41	0.39	0.60	0.58	0.69
Cash Flow	0.69	0.46	0.31	-0.25	-0.22	-0.22	-0.20	-0.15	-0.08	0.02
Earnings	0.66	0.44	0.30	-0.27	-0.23	-0.23	-0.21	-0.16	-0.09	0.02
Dividends	Nil	Nil	Nil	Nil	Nil	Nil	Nil	Nil	Nil	Nil
Payout Ratio	Nil	Nil	Nil	Nil	Nil	Nil	Nil	Nil	Nil	Nil
Prices - High	86.12	58.60	16.89	7.25	3.35	3.58	2.20	5.43	8.41	9.16
- Low	42.00	14.33	6.47	1.89	1.89	0.58	0.56	1.66	2.08	1.66
P/E Ratio - High	NM	NM	56	NM	NM	NM	NM	NM	NM	NM
- Low	NM	NM	21	NM	NM	NM	NM	NM	NM	NA
Income Statement Analysis (Million $)										
Revs.	540	383	201	81.0	41.1	27.4	18.9	15.1	13.1	14.0
Oper. Inc.	188	81.8	9.6	-34.7	-31.1	-22.5	-18.5	-13.9	-3.9	0.8
Depr.	7.3	5.0	3.5	2.7	1.8	1.6	1.5	1.1	0.7	0.4
Int. Exp.	0.5	3.2	4.0	3.5	2.3	0.3	0.3	0.3	0.3	0.1
Pretax Inc.	209	86.3	8.8	-36.9	-29.5	-22.7	-18.8	-13.2	-8.4	1.7
Eff. Tax Rate	31%	NM	NM	NM	NM	NM	NM	NM	NM	2.20%
Net Inc.	145	93.4	56.2	-36.9	-29.5	-22.7	-18.8	-13.2	-8.5	1.6
Balance Sheet & Other Fin. Data (Million $)										
Cash	526	270	135	30.0	115	38.0	22.5	44.4	46.9	55.8
Curr. Assets	688	402	216	100	133	49.0	32.3	51.9	52.6	59.6
Total Assets	1,007	648	353	170	164	57.3	44.7	61.2	60.2	65.3
Curr. Liab.	151	99	58.0	43.7	20.0	11.0	7.8	5.7	11.1	7.9
LT Debt	9.6	10.4	83.2	85.3	70.9	2.0	2.1	2.2	2.2	2.2
Common Eqty.	844	537	210	40.5	72.9	43.8	34.2	53.0	46.8	55.1
Total Cap.	853	547	293	126	144	45.8	36.3	55.2	48.9	57.3
Cap. Exp.	8.3	12.2	10.1	36.7	22.7	1.1	1.4	3.8	2.2	4.2
Cash Flow	152	98.4	59.7	-34.1	-27.7	-21.1	-17.3	-12.2	-7.7	1.9
Curr. Ratio	4.5	4.1	3.7	2.3	6.7	4.4	4.1	9.2	4.7	7.5
% LT Debt of Cap.	1.1	1.9	28.4	67.7	49.3	4.3	5.8	4.0	4.4	3.8
% Net Inc.of Revs.	26.8	24.4	28.0	NM	NM	NM	NM	NM	NM	11.6
% Ret. on Assets	17.5	17.7	21.5	NM	NM	NM	NM	NM	NM	1.6
% Ret. on Equity	21.0	23.8	44.9	NM	NM	NM	NM	NM	NM	NM

Data as orig reptd.; bef. results of disc opers/spec. items. Per share data adj. for stk. divs. Bold denotes diluted EPS (FASB 128)-prior periods restated. E-Estimated. NA-Not Available. NM-Not Meaningful. NR-Not Ranked.

Office—35 W. Watkins Mill Rd., Gaithersburg, MD 20878. **Tel**—(301) 417-0770. **Website**—http://www.medimmune.com **CEO & Vice Chrmn**—D. M. Mott. **Pres & COO**—M. D. Booth. **CFO**—G. S. Patrick. **Chrmn**—W. T. Hockmeyer. **Investor Contact**—Lori Weiman. **Dirs**—M. J. Barrett, M. D. Booth, J. H. Cavanaugh, B. H. Franklin, W. T. Hockmeyer, L. C. Hoff, G. S. Macklin, D. M. Mott, F. H. Top Jr.**Transfer Agent & Registrar**—American Stock Transfer & Trust Co., NYC. **Incorporated**—in Delaware in 1987. **Empl**— 790. **S&P Analyst:** Frank DiLorenzo

STANDARD & POOR'S STOCK REPORTS

Merck & Co.

NYSE Symbol **MRK**

In S&P 500

24-AUG-01

Industry: Health Care (Drugs - Major Pharmaceuticals)

Summary: Merck is one of the world's largest prescription pharmaceuticals concerns. Its Medco unit is a leading U.S. pharmacy benefits management company.

S&P Opinion: Accumulate (★★★★)

Recent Price • 69.15 | 52 Wk Range • 96.68-60.35 | Yield • 2.0% | 12-Mo. P/E • 22.9

Quantitative Evaluations

Outlook (1 Lowest—5 Highest)
• **2+**

Fair Value
• **65.10**

Risk
• **Low**

Earn./Div. Rank
• **A+**

Technical Eval.
• **Neutral** since 8/01

Rel. Strength Rank (1 Lowest—99 Highest)
• **55**

Insider Activity
• **NA**

Earnings vs. Previous Year
E=Up E=Down E=No Change

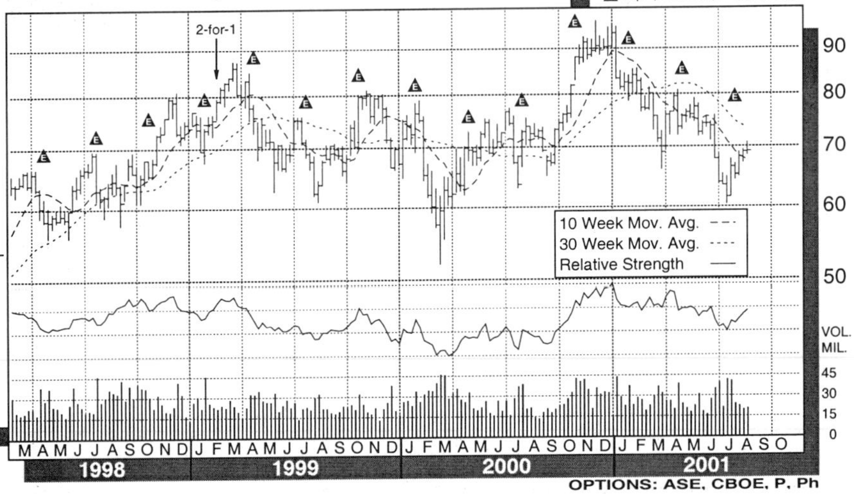

OPTIONS: ASE, CBOE, P, Ph

Overview - 24-AUG-01

Total revenues are expected to increase 18% in 2001, boosted by gains in both prescription pharmaceutical sales and Merck-Medco revenues. Drugs expected to post robust growth include Vioxx antiarthritic (up 43% in the first half of 2001), Zocor cholesterol-lowering agent (+17%), Fosamax for osteoporosis (+40%), and Prinivil/ Prinzide and Cozaar/Hyzaar antihypertensives. These gains should more than offset steep reductions in off-patent drugs such as Vasotec antihypertensive and Pepcid antiulcer. Merck-Medco managed care revenues should rise 30%, boosted by a broadened client base. Gross margins are expected to narrow to about 40%, from 44.4% in 2000, reflecting a less favorable product mix. EPS are projected at $3.15, with further progress to $3.45 seen for 2002.

Valuation - 24-AUG-01

The shares are down sharply to date in 2001, mirroring weakness in the overall pharmaceutical sector, studies showing adverse cardiac effects with Vioxx, and patent expirations on key Merck drugs. Combined sales of patent-expired drugs, including Vasotec, Pepcid and Mevacor, are expected to drop 40% in 2001. However, MRK should still be able to post 9%-11% EPS growth over the next few years, powered by continued robust growth in newer lines such as Vioxx, Zocor, Fosamax, Cozaar/Hyzaar, and Singulair. Addressing the Vioxx safety issue, Merck has released data from a large study showing Vioxx's incidence of cardiovascular events were similar to placebo and those of widely prescribed anti-inflammatory agents. The R&D pipeline includes treatments for infection, depression, heart conditions and pain. The shares, valued at a steep discount to the drug group's average P/E multiple, merit accumulation.

Key Stock Statistics

S&P EPS Est. 2001	3.15	Tang. Bk. Value/Share	3.32
P/E on S&P Est. 2001	22.0	Beta	0.55
S&P EPS Est. 2002	3.45	Shareholders	231,300
Dividend Rate/Share	1.40	Market cap. (B)	$156.8
Shs. outstg. (M)	2289.4	Inst. holdings	56%
Avg. daily vol. (M)	4.543		

Value of $10,000 invested 5 years ago: $ 21,732

Fiscal Year Ending Dec. 31

	2001	2000	1999	1998	1997	1996
Revenues (Million $)						
1Q	11,345	8,851	7,537	6,059	5,568	4,530
2Q	11,893	9,477	8,018	6,470	5,909	4,909
3Q	—	10,568	8,196	6,839	5,928	4,983
4Q	—	11,467	8,963	7,531	6,232	5,406
Yr.	—	40,363	32,714	26,898	23,637	19,829
Earnings Per Share ($)						
1Q	0.71	0.62	0.54	0.47	0.41	0.34
2Q	0.78	0.73	0.61	0.54	0.47	0.39
3Q	E0.84	0.78	0.64	0.56	0.48	0.41
4Q	E0.80	0.75	0.66	0.58	0.51	0.42
Yr.	E3.15	2.90	2.45	2.15	1.87	1.56

Next earnings report expected: mid October

Dividend Data (Dividends have been paid since 1935.)

Amount ($)	Date Decl.	Ex-Div. Date	Stock of Record	Payment Date
0.340	Nov. 28	Dec. 06	Dec. 08	Jan. 02 '01
0.340	Feb. 27	Mar. 07	Mar. 09	Apr. 02 '01
0.340	May. 22	May. 31	Jun. 04	Jul. 02 '01
0.350	Jul. 24	Aug. 30	Sep. 04	Oct. 01 '01

Merck & Co., Inc.

Business Summary - 24-AUG-01

Merck ranks among the world's largest pharmaceutical companies, manufacturing and marketing a wide range of prescription drugs in many therapeutic classes both in the U.S. and abroad. Foreign business is important, with subsidiaries outside of the U.S. representing about 36% of total pharmaceutical and vaccine sales in 2000. The company was originally founded in 1887 as a U.S. branch of E. Merck of Germany and grew significantly in subsequent years through aggressive new drug development and acquisition programs.

The company is a leader in the vast market for high-margin cardiovascular drugs, with five drugs generating aggregate sales of over $12 billion in 2000. Key products include Vioxx ($2.2 billion), a COX-2 inhibtor for arthritis and pain; cholesterol-lowering agents such as Zocor (sales of $5.3 billion) and Mevacor ($520 million); and treatments for high blood pressure and congestive heart failure like Cozaar/Hyzaar ($1.8 billion), Vasotec/Vaseretic ($1.8 billion), and Prinivil/Prinzide ($1.1 billion). As of April 2001, Vioxx had about a 23% prescription share of the U.S. antiarthritic market, Zocor had a 20% share of the cholesterol reduction market, and Cozaar/Hyzaar accounted for about 38% of the angiotensin II antagonist hypertension-angina market.

Other key prescription pharmaceuticals include Fosamax for osteoporosis (a bone-thinning disease that affects postmenopausal women); Primaxin, an intravenous antibiotic; Crixivan, a protease inhibitor AIDS drug, which in combination with other agents has been able to decrease HIV in the bloodstream to undetectable levels; Proscar, a treatment for enlarged prostates that is also benefiting from new indications; and Singulair, an asthma treatment. Other important drugs include Pepcid antiulcer agent, Timoptic and Trusoft anti-glaucoma medicines, and Aggrastat for unstable angina. Merck is also a leading maker of vaccines.

The huge success of Merck's drugs has enabled it to support a $2.3 billion R&D program (equal to 20% of product sales in 2000), which promises to spawn an ongoing stream of blockbuster drugs in the years ahead. Key products in late-stage clinical trials include treatments for unstable angina, depression, diabetes and infections.

Over-the-counter medications such as Pepcid AC are offered through a venture with Johnson & Johnson. Merial, a leading animal health products company, is owned jointly by Merck and Rhone-Poulenc SA. Through a venture with Astra AB of Sweden, Merck books sales of Prilosec antiulcer agent and other Astra drugs. Merck-Medco Managed Care provides mail-order drug and related services to some 65 million people. Merck-Medco represents about half of Merck's total 2000 revenues, but a relatively small percentage of profits.

Per Share Data ($) (Year Ended Dec. 31)	2000	1999	1998	1997	1996	1995	1994	1993	1992	1991
Tangible Bk. Val.	3.23	2.43	1.91	2.44	2.17	2.00	1.57	1.34	2.12	2.03
Cash Flow	3.44	3.02	2.67	2.29	1.90	1.62	1.46	1.10	1.19	1.02
Earnings	2.90	2.45	2.15	1.87	1.60	1.35	1.19	0.94	1.06	0.92
Dividends	1.26	1.10	0.94	0.87	0.74	0.64	0.58	0.53	0.48	0.40
Payout Ratio	43%	45%	44%	47%	46%	47%	49%	57%	45%	43%
Prices - High	96.68	87.37	80.87	54.09	42.12	33.62	19.75	22.06	28.31	27.84
- Low	52.00	60.93	50.68	39.00	28.25	18.18	14.06	14.31	20.25	13.65
P/E Ratio - High	33	36	38	29	26	25	17	24	27	30
- Low	18	25	24	21	18	13	12	15	19	15
Income Statement Analysis (Million $)										
Revs.	40,363	32,714	26,898	23,637	19,829	16,681	14,970	10,498	9,663	8,603
Oper. Inc.	10,686	9,056	7,655	6,701	5,912	5,262	5,075	4,262	3,782	3,352
Depr.	1,277	1,145	1,279	1,034	731	667	670	377	290	243
Int. Exp.	484	317	206	130	139	99	124	84.7	72.7	68.7
Pretax Inc.	10,133	8,842	8,295	6,594	5,685	4,889	4,509	3,153	3,596	3,192
Eff. Tax Rate	30%	31%	35%	28%	29%	30%	32%	30%	31%	33%
Net Inc.	6,822	5,891	5,248	4,614	3,881	3,335	2,997	2,166	2,447	2,122
Balance Sheet & Other Fin. Data (Million $)										
Cash	2,537	2,022	2,606	1,125	2,181	3,349	2,270	1,542	1,094	1,412
Curr. Assets	13,353	11,259	10,229	8,213	7,727	8,618	6,922	5,735	4,400	4,311
Total Assets	39,910	35,633	31,853	25,812	24,293	23,832	21,857	19,928	11,086	9,499
Curr. Liab.	9,710	8,759	6,069	5,569	4,829	5,690	5,449	5,896	3,617	2,814
LT Debt	3,601	3,144	3,221	1,347	1,156	1,373	1,146	1,121	496	494
Common Eqty.	14,832	45,571	12,802	12,613	11,971	11,736	11,139	10,022	5,003	4,916
Total Cap.	23,454	52,175	21,491	16,645	15,437	13,109	14,735	12,650	6,215	6,296
Cap. Exp.	2,728	2,561	1,973	1,449	1,197	1,006	1,009	1,013	1,067	1,042
Cash Flow	8,099	7,035	6,527	5,648	4,612	4,002	3,667	2,543	2,737	2,364
Curr. Ratio	1.4	1.3	1.7	1.5	1.6	1.5	1.3	1.0	1.2	1.5
% LT Debt of Cap.	15.4	6.0	15.0	8.1	7.5	10.5	7.8	8.9	8.0	7.8
% Net Inc.of Revs.	16.9	18.0	19.5	19.5	19.6	20.0	20.0	20.6	25.3	24.7
% Ret. on Assets	18.1	17.4	18.2	18.4	16.1	14.6	14.4	13.5	23.9	24.2
% Ret. on Equity	48.6	20.1	41.3	37.5	33.1	29.2	28.4	27.9	49.6	48.5

Data as orig reptd.; bef. results of disc opers/spec. items. Per share data adj. for stk. divs. Bold denotes diluted EPS (FASB 128)-prior periods restated. E-Estimated. NA-Not Available. NM-Not Meaningful. NR-Not Ranked.

Office—One Merck Drive, P.O. Box 100, Whitehouse Station, NJ 08889. **Tel**—(908) 423-1000. **Website**—http://www.merck.com **Chrmn, Pres & CEO**—R. V. Gilmartin. **EVP & CFO**—J. C. Lewent. **Secy**—C. A. Colbert. **Treas**—C. Dorsa. **Investor Contact**—Laura Jordan (908-423-5185). **Dirs**—L. A. Bossidy, W. G. Bowen, E. B. Bowles, J. B. Cole, N. FitzGerald, R. V. Gilmartin, W. B. Harrison, W. N. Kelley, H. G. Miller, E. M. Scolnick, T. E. Shenk, A. M. Tatlock, S. O. Thier. **Transfer Agent & Registrar**—Wells Fargo Bank Minnesota, N.A., South St. Paul, MN. **Incorporated**—in New Jersey in 1934. **Empl**— 69,300. **S&P Analyst:** H. B. Saftlas

STANDARD
&POOR'S
STOCK REPORTS

Mylan Laboratories

NYSE Symbol **MYL**

In S&P MidCap 400

24-AUG-01

Industry:
Health Care (Drugs - Generic & Other)

Summary: This leading manufacturer of generic pharmaceuticals produces a broad range of generic drugs in varying strengths, and also sells several proprietary drugs.

S&P Opinion: Accumulate (★★★★)

Recent Price • 34.60
52 Wk Range • 34.60-20.15
Yield • 0.5%
12-Mo. P/E • 27.0

Quantitative Evaluations

Outlook
(1 Lowest—5 Highest)
• **4+**

Fair Value
• **38.40**

Risk
• **Average**

Earn./Div. Rank
• **A-**

Technical Eval.
• **Bullish** since 7/01

Rel. Strength Rank
(1 Lowest—99 Highest)
• **93**

Insider Activity
• **NA**

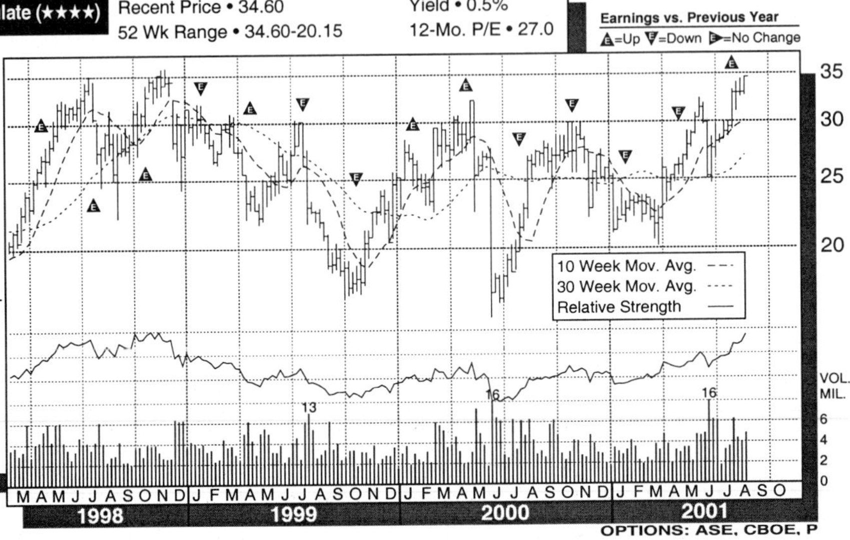

OPTIONS: ASE, CBOE, P

Overview - 24-AUG-01

Revenues are expected to advance about 20%, to over $1 billion in FY 02 (Mar.), supported by firming trends in certain generic markets, and by contributions from new products. Mylan received FDA approval for about 20 new generic products over the past 18 months, including generic versions of Taxol anticancer therapy, Buspar anti-anxiety; Mevacor cholesterol-lowering agent; Pepcid antiulcer; Wellbutrin antidepressant; Luvox treatment for obsessive compulsive disorder; and Cardura, Ziac and Vasotec antihypertensives. Sales of proprietary products should also rise, aided by projected gains in Mentax topical antifungal cream, Avita acne treatment, and Nitrek nitroglycerin patch, as well as new products such as an extended release version of phenytoin antiepileptic agent. EPS from operations are projected at $1.60, with further progress, to $1.75, seen for FY 03.

Valuation - 24-AUG-01

The shares moved sharply higher in recent months, buoyed by greater than expected first quarter FY 02 (Mar.) EPS and positive new product developments. Revenues in the first quarter advanced 42%, bolstered by the recent launch of a generic version of Buspar anti-anxiety agent (MYL has 180 days of first-to-file marketing exclusivity on this drug). Unexpected investment income also boosted Q1 EPS by $0.06. In mid-July, the FDA approved Mylan's generic equivalent of Bristol-Myers Squibb's injectable Taxol treatment for ovarian and breast cancer. Other key anticipated launches include generic versions of Glucophage diabetes drug and Accutane acne treatment. In total, MYL's pipeline consists of about 22 new generic products, as well as several promising proprietary products. The shares, trading at a modest discount to the average P/E multiple for generics equities, merit accumulation.

Key Stock Statistics

S&P EPS Est. 2002	1.60	Tang. Bk. Value/Share	6.69
P/E on S&P Est. 2002	21.6	Beta	0.64
S&P EPS Est. 2003	1.75	Shareholders	99,112
Dividend Rate/Share	0.16	Market cap. (B)	$ 4.6
Shs. outstg. (M)	130.9	Inst. holdings	60%
Avg. daily vol. (M)	0.935		

Value of $10,000 invested 5 years ago: $ 23,916

Fiscal Year Ending Mar. 31

	2002	2001	2000	1999	1998	1997
Revenues (Million $)						
1Q	273.9	167.3	177.1	166.7	109.2	98.54
2Q	—	207.6	194.5	177.6	154.0	109.0
3Q	—	223.2	203.9	186.2	129.5	114.0
4Q	—	248.7	214.7	190.6	162.8	118.7
Yr.	—	846.7	790.1	721.1	555.4	440.2
Earnings Per Share ($)						
1Q	0.40	-0.59	0.25	0.28	0.13	0.11
2Q	E0.42	0.27	0.28	0.30	0.25	0.14
3Q	E0.36	0.30	0.31	0.06	0.18	0.15
4Q	E0.41	0.33	0.34	0.27	0.26	0.11
Yr.	E1.60	0.29	1.18	0.91	0.82	0.51

Next earnings report expected: late October

Dividend Data (Dividends have been paid since 1983.)

Amount ($)	Date Decl.	Ex-Div. Date	Stock of Record	Payment Date
0.040	Sep. 14	Sep. 27	Sep. 30	Oct. 15 '00
0.040	Dec. 15	Dec. 27	Dec. 31	Jan. 15 '01
0.040	Mar. 15	Mar. 28	Mar. 30	Apr. 16 '01
0.040	Jun. 18	Jun. 27	Jun. 30	Jul. 16 '01

STANDARD
&POOR'S
STOCK REPORTS

Mylan Laboratories Inc.

24-AUG-01

Business Summary - 24-AUG-01

Mylan Laboratories (MYL) is a leading manufacturer of generic pharmaceutical products in finished tablet, capsule, and powder dosage forms, for resale by others. Mylan began operations in 1961 as a privately owned company founded by Milan Puskar and an associate in White Sulphur Springs, WV. Generic drugs are typically sold at prices significantly below those of comparable branded products. The company produces more than 115 generic drugs, in more than 410 sizes and/or dosage strengths. Generic drugs accounted for 83% of FY 01 (Mar.) sales, with branded proprietary products providing the balance.

Generic drugs are the chemical equivalents of branded drugs, and are marketed after patent expirations on the primary products. Mylan's generic drugs encompass 33 different therapeutic classes, including analgesics, antianginals, antianxiety agents, antibiotics, antidepressants, antidiabetics, antidiarrheals, an antigout drug, an antihistamine, antihypertensives, anti-inflammatories, antipsychotics, anxiolytics, a bronchial dilator, diuretics, hypnotic agents, a muscle relaxant and a uricosuric. UDL Laboratories supplies unit dose generic drugs for the institutional and long-term care markets.

Through its Bertek Pharmaceuticals unit, the company markets several proprietary products. These include Maxzide, a diuretic used to treat hypertension; Nitrek, a nitroglycerin transdermal patch; Clorpres, an anti-hypertensive agent; Acticin, a topical scabicidal agent; Sulfamylon, a topical antimicrobial cream used to treat patients with second and third degree burns; Zagam, a treatment for bronchitis; Digitek, a treatment for moderate heart failure; and several wound care products. Through a venture with Penederm, Bertek co-promotes Mentax topical antifungal and Avita topical retinoic acid product. Bertek's goal is to eventually expand Mylan's branded business to 50% of total revenues. with new products focusing on neurology, dermatology and cardiology.

Eldepryl, a treatment for Parkinson's disease, is marketed by Somerset Pharmaceuticals, jointly owned by the company and Watson Pharmaceuticals. Eldepryl is also sold by Novartis under an agreement with Somerset. Mylan incurred a loss of $1.5 million on its investment in Somerset in FY 01, down from a loss of $4.2 million in FY 00. In May 2001, Somerset filed a new drug application with the FDA for EMSAM, a new selegiline patch for treatment of depression.

R&D spending amounted to $64.4 million in FY 01 (equal to 7.6% of sales). Mylan has about 18 Abbreviated New Drug Applications (ANDAs) under review at the FDA, including generic versions of Taxol anticancer and Glucophage treatment for type 2 diabetes. The branded pipeline includes new treatments for epilepsy, severe acne, and other conditions.

Per Share Data ($)										
(Year Ended Mar. 31)	**2001**	**2000**	**1999**	**1998**	**1997**	**1996**	**1995**	**1994**	**1993**	**1992**
Tangible Bk. Val.	6.69	6.74	5.61	5.04	4.28	4.45	3.81	2.92	2.20	1.67
Cash Flow	0.63	1.46	1.12	1.00	0.66	0.97	1.12	0.71	0.65	0.39
Earnings	0.29	1.18	0.96	0.82	0.52	0.86	1.01	0.62	0.61	0.35
Dividends	0.16	0.16	0.16	0.16	0.16	0.17	0.22	0.10	0.08	0.07
Payout Ratio	55%	14%	17%	20%	31%	20%	22%	16%	13%	19%
Cal. Yrs.	2000	1999	1998	1997	1996	1995	1994	1993	1992	1991
Prices - High	32.25	32.00	35.93	25.31	23.37	24.50	19.91	25.08	21.25	14.16
- Low	16.00	17.06	17.06	11.50	14.00	16.50	10.41	13.08	10.50	5.66
P/E Ratio - High	NM	27	37	31	45	28	20	40	35	41
- Low	NM	14	18	14	27	19	10	21	17	16
Income Statement Analysis (Million $)										
Revs.	847	790	721	555	440	393	396	252	212	132
Oper. Inc.	209	259	224	146	75.3	114	151	69.7	77.5	32.1
Depr.	42.4	35.7	26.9	21.7	17.3	13.5	12.7	11.2	5.1	5.1
Int. Exp.	Nil	Nil	Nil	Nil	Nil	NA	NA	0.0	0.1	0.3
Pretax Inc.	58.0	243	192	148	87.2	142	171	87.1	97.3	50.1
Eff. Tax Rate	36%	36%	40%	32%	28%	28%	30%	16%	27%	20%
Net Inc.	37.1	154	115	101	63.1	102	121	73.1	70.6	40.1
Balance Sheet & Other Fin. Data (Million $)										
Cash	285	303	260	104	140	189	180	88.5	98.2	60.3
Curr. Assets	879	687	583	430	379	379	331	210	180	120
Total Assets	1,466	1,341	1,207	848	778	778	546	403	351	227
Curr. Liab.	291	87.8	96.4	71.3	78.7	48.6	56.4	17.9	26.5	17.9
LT Debt	23.3	30.6	26.8	26.2	22.8	7.9	Nil	Nil	Nil	Nil
Common Eqty.	1,133	1,204	1,060	744	660	616	483	380	296	203
Total Cap.	1,175	1,253	1,110	776	689	633	483	381	298	205
Cap. Exp.	24.7	28.8	16.7	28.9	26.9	31.4	17.5	20.2	12.3	10.0
Cash Flow	79.5	190	142	122	80.5	116	134	84.2	75.7	45.2
Curr. Ratio	3.0	7.8	6.0	6.0	4.8	7.8	5.9	11.7	6.8	6.7
% LT Debt of Cap.	2.0	2.4	2.4	3.4	3.3	1.2	Nil	Nil	Nil	Nil
% Net Inc.of Revs.	4.4	19.5	16.0	18.1	14.4	26.0	30.5	29.0	33.3	30.4
% Ret. on Assets	2.6	12.1	11.2	12.4	8.6	16.5	25.4	19.3	24.3	19.7
% Ret. on Equity	3.2	13.6	12.8	14.4	9.9	18.6	28.0	21.5	28.1	21.9

Data as orig reptd.; bef. results of disc opers/spec. items. Per share data adj. for stk. divs. Bold denotes diluted EPS (FASB 128)-prior periods restated. E-Estimated. NA-Not Available. NM-Not Meaningful. NR-Not Ranked.

Office—1030 Century Building, Pittsburgh, PA 15222. **Tel**—(412) 232-0100. **Website**—http://www.mylan.com **Chrmn & CEO**—M. Puskar. **Pres & COO**—C. B. Todd. **VP & CFO**—G. Sphar. **Secy**—R. W. Smiley. **VP & Investor Contact**—Patricia A. Sunseri. **Dirs**—D. G. Barnett, L. S. DeLynn, L. Daniels, J. C. Gaisford, D. J. Leech, M. Puskar, P. A. Sunseri, C. B. Todd, S. Williams. **Transfer Agent & Registrar**—American Stock Transfer & Trust Co., NYC. **Incorporated**—in Pennsylvania in 1970. **Empl**— 2,300. **S&P Analyst:** H. B. Saftlas

STANDARD
&POOR'S
STOCK REPORTS

Omnicare, Inc.

NYSE Symbol **OCR**

In S&P MidCap 400

18-AUG-01

Industry:
Health Care (Specialized Services)

Summary: This company provides pharmacy management and related consulting services to skilled nursing, assisted living and other institutional health care providers.

S&P Opinion: Accumulate (★★★★)

Recent Price • 24.17
52 Wk Range • 26-11.75
Yield • 0.4%
12-Mo. P/E • 36.6

Quantitative Evaluations

Outlook
(1 Lowest—5 Highest)
• **4⁻**

Fair Value
• **31.30**

Risk
• **Average**

Earn./Div. Rank
• **A-**

Technical Eval.
• **Bullish** since 7/01

Rel. Strength Rank
(1 Lowest—99 Highest)
• **81**

Insider Activity
• **Neutral**

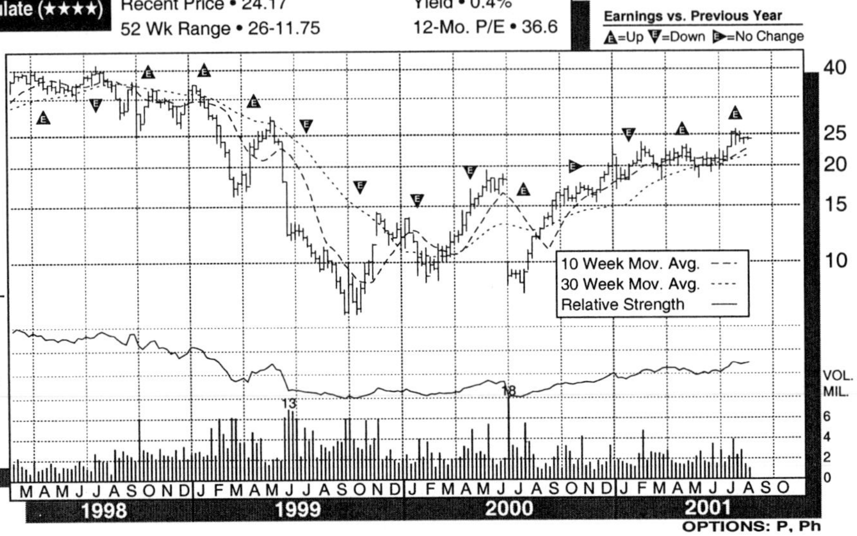

OPTIONS: P, Ph

Overview - 10-AUG-01

Operating revenues are expected to increase by 10% in 2001, as improving demand for institutional pharmacy services, partially reflecting improved financial stability within the core nursing home customer base, is joined by a recovery in the contract research organization unit. Demand for infusion therapy and other ancillary service offerings continues to benefit from improved Medicare-reimbursed nursing home census levels. Gross margins should improve to 27.5% of revenues from 26.7% in 2000. OCR continues to reduce operating costs through productivity enhancements, asset sales, consolidations and work force cuts. This is expected to save $46 million annually. We look for a 40% advance in 2001 operating EPS to $0.98, and see 2002 EPS reaching $1.15.

Valuation - 10-AUG-01

We maintain a bullish stance on the shares, and believe that strengthening trends in the nursing home industry will continue to drive higher demand for the company's institutional pharmacy services business. Medicare skilled nursing rates were boosted 4% in October 2000, and more rate hikes were effected on April 1, 2001. Coupled with operating cost disciplines put into place by OCR over the past year, Omnicare is expected to generate solid earnings and cash flow expansion through 2001 and into 2002. We maintain an accumulate opinion in the belief that there is a good chance for upside to our present revenue and EPS estimates. Recently priced at less than 1.0 time forward sales and 22 times our 2002 EPS estimate, OCR appears modestly valued relative to the S&P 500 despite the company's superior growth prospects over the coming four quarters.

Key Stock Statistics

S&P EPS Est. 2001	0.98	Tang. Bk. Value/Share	NM
P/E on S&P Est. 2001	24.7	Beta	0.74
S&P EPS Est. 2002	1.15	Shareholders	2,553
Dividend Rate/Share	0.09	Market cap. (B)	$ 2.3
Shs. outstg. (M)	93.1	Inst. holdings	83%
Avg. daily vol. (M)	0.376		

Value of $10,000 invested 5 years ago: $ 9,863

Fiscal Year Ending Dec. 31

	2001	2000	1999	1998	1997	1996
Revenues (Million $)						
1Q	523.6	493.0	445.7	340.3	181.6	117.2
2Q	530.1	480.5	454.6	358.2	203.1	121.8
3Q	—	491.3	474.0	383.6	228.1	140.7
4Q	—	506.6	487.6	435.3	285.0	156.8
Yr.	—	1,971	1,862	1,517	897.7	536.6
Earnings Per Share ($)						
1Q	**0.19**	**0.16**	**0.31**	**0.23**	**0.17**	**0.13**
2Q	**0.21**	**0.12**	**0.05**	**0.09**	**0.19**	**0.14**
3Q	**E0.27**	**0.15**	**0.15**	**0.29**	**0.13**	**0.16**
4Q	**E0.31**	**0.11**	**0.12**	**0.29**	**0.20**	**17.00**
Yr.	**E0.98**	**0.53**	**0.63**	**0.90**	**0.69**	**0.61**

Next earnings report expected: early November

Dividend Data (Dividends have been paid since 1989.)

Amount ($)	Date Decl.	Ex-Div. Date	Stock of Record	Payment Date
0.023	Nov. 01	Nov. 22	Nov. 27	Dec. 11 '00
0.023	Feb. 07	Feb. 26	Feb. 28	Mar. 14 '01
0.023	May. 21	May. 30	Jun. 01	Jun. 12 '01
0.023	Aug. 01	Aug. 24	Aug. 28	Sep. 11 '01

A Division of The **McGraw·Hill** *Companies*

Omnicare, Inc.

Business Summary - 10-AUG-01

Omnicare is a leading provider of pharmacy management services to long term care institutions such as nursing homes, assisted living facilities and other institutional healthcare facilities. The company also offers consultant pharmacist services and ancillary services, and operates a contract research organization. At the end of 2000, OCR's pharmacy services unit served 636,500 residents in about 8,400 long term care and other settings.

The institutional pharmacy segment purchases, repackages, and dispenses prescription and nonprescription medication in accordance with physician orders, and delivers such prescriptions at least daily to nursing facilities for administration to patients by the facility's nursing staff. OCR typically serves nursing homes in a 150-mile radius of its pharmacies. A 24-hour a day, 365-day a year on-call pharmacist service is provided for emergency dispensing and delivery, or for consultation with the facility's staff or attending physician.

Integral to the company's drug distribution system is its computerized medical records and documentation system. OCR provides the facility with computerized medical administration records and physicians' order sheets and treatment records for each patient. Data extracted from these records is formulated into monthly management reports on patient care and quality assurance. When combined with OCR's unit dose drug delivery system, the computerized system allows greater efficiency in nursing time, improved control, reduced drug waste, and lower error rates both in dispensing and in administration; this can improve drug efficacy and reduce drug-related hospitalizations.

OCR also provides consultant pharmacist services to help clients comply with federal and state regulations related to the quality and standardization of nursing home care. Services include comprehensive, monthly drug regimen reviews for each resident; monthly inspection of medication carts and storage rooms; monitoring and monthly reporting on facility-wide drug usage and drug administration systems and practices; and development and maintenance of pharmaceutical policy and procedures manuals.

The company's Omnicare Guidelines, introduced in 1994, are believed to be the first clinically based formulary for the elderly residing in long-term care institutions.

Ancillary offerings provided to nursing facilities include infusion therapy; dialysis services; distribution of disposable medical supplies, including urological, ostomy, nutritional support and wound care products and other disposables needed in nursing homes; and direct Medicare billing services for certain product lines for patients eligible under the Medicare Part B program.

The Contract Research Organization unit provides comprehensive product development services to companies in the pharmaceutical, biotechnology, medical device and diagnostics industries.

Per Share Data ($) (Year Ended Dec. 31)	2000	1999	1998	1997	1996	1995	1994	1993	1992	1991
Tangible Bk. Val.	NM	NM	NM	0.99	4.87	1.08	1.21	0.18	0.55	1.19
Cash Flow	1.33	1.39	1.43	1.01	0.87	0.69	0.47	0.35	0.17	0.20
Earnings	0.53	0.63	0.90	0.69	0.64	0.47	0.30	0.23	0.10	0.13
Dividends	0.09	0.09	0.08	0.07	0.06	0.05	0.05	0.04	0.04	0.03
Payout Ratio	17%	14%	9%	10%	9%	11%	15%	17%	38%	24%
Prices - High	23.00	36.18	41.56	34.56	32.50	22.68	11.31	8.03	7.87	5.62
- Low	8.00	6.87	25.00	22.37	19.12	10.21	6.71	3.31	4.06	1.87
P/E Ratio - High	43	57	46	50	51	48	37	34	83	45
- Low	15	11	28	32	30	22	22	14	43	15
Income Statement Analysis (Million $)										
Revs.	1,971	1,862	1,517	896	537	400	276	160	103	116
Oper. Inc.	232	241	223	133	80.6	56.0	36.5	19.7	11.8	8.7
Depr.	74.0	69.4	47.6	25.7	15.4	11.1	7.4	4.4	2.8	2.8
Int. Exp.	55.1	46.2	23.6	5.6	3.6	6.0	5.8	2.1	2.0	0.5
Pretax Inc.	77.5	91.7	136	96.8	72.1	41.2	22.5	13.9	6.6	6.8
Eff. Tax Rate	37%	37%	41%	42%	40%	40%	40%	37%	48%	35%
Net Inc.	48.8	57.7	80.4	55.7	43.5	24.8	13.4	8.7	3.4	4.4
Balance Sheet & Other Fin. Data (Million $)										
Cash	114	97.3	54.3	131	217	40.1	79.6	63.3	13.3	3.4
Curr. Assets	818	752	603	472	391	161	162	111	52.2	51.7
Total Assets	2,210	2,168	1,904	1,290	722	361	306	219	131	108
Curr. Liab.	257	322	234	128	61.7	54.7	37.2	34.2	31.6	19.4
LT Debt	781	737	652	353	2.0	83.0	83.0	83.5	3.4	6.5
Common Eqty.	1,068	1,028	963	774	634	215	179	96.6	88.7	74.6
Total Cap.	1,913	1,803	1,631	1,137	641	300	263	180	95.0	84.0
Cap. Exp.	32.4	58.7	53.2	30.5	26.7	13.6	8.6	3.4	2.2	3.6
Cash Flow	123	127	128	81.4	58.9	35.9	20.8	13.1	6.3	7.2
Curr. Ratio	3.2	2.3	2.6	3.7	6.3	2.9	4.4	3.3	1.6	2.7
% LT Debt of Cap.	40.8	40.9	39.9	31.0	0.4	27.6	31.5	46.3	3.5	7.8
% Net Inc.of Revs.	2.5	3.1	5.3	6.2	8.1	6.2	4.9	5.5	3.3	3.8
% Ret. on Assets	2.2	2.8	5.0	5.5	8.1	7.3	4.4	5.0	2.8	4.4
% Ret. on Equity	4.7	5.8	9.3	7.9	10.3	12.5	8.7	9.4	4.2	6.1

Data as orig reptd.; bef. results of disc opers/spec. items. Per share data adj. for stk. divs. Bold denotes diluted EPS (FASB 128)-prior periods restated. E-Estimated. NA-Not Available. NM-Not Meaningful. NR-Not Ranked.

Office—100 E. RiverCenter Blvd., Covington, KY 41011. **Tel**—(859) 392-3300. **Website**—http://www.omnicare.com **Chrmn**—E. L. Hutton. **Pres**—J. F. Gemunder. **SVP & CFO**—D. W. Froesel Jr. **SVP, Secy & Investor Contact**—Cheryl D. Hodges. **Dirs**—C. H. Erhart Jr., M. Fox, D. W. Froesel Jr., J. F. Gemunder, C. D. Hodges, E. L. Hutton, T. C. Hutton, P. E. Keefe, S. E. Laney, A. R. Lindell, S. Margen, K. J. McNamara, J. H. Timoney. **Transfer Agent & Registrar**—ChaseMellon Shareholder Services, Ridgefield Park, NJ. **Incorporated**—in Delaware in 1981. **Empl**— 9,300. **S&P Analyst:** Robert M. Gold

STANDARD
&POOR'S
STOCK REPORTS

Orthodontic Centers of America

NYSE Symbol **OCA**

In S&P SmallCap 600

18-AUG-01

Industry:
Health Care (Specialized Services)

Summary: This company develops and manages orthodontic practices on a national basis pursuant to long-term agreements.

S&P Opinion: Accumulate (★★★★)

Recent Price • 28.57 | Yield • Nil
52 Wk Range • 35.31-16.80 | 12-Mo. P/E • 30.7

Quantitative Evaluations

Outlook
(1 Lowest—5 Highest)
• **5**

Fair Value
• **38.70**

Risk
• **NA**

Earn./Div. Rank
• **NR**

Technical Eval.
• **Bearish** since 8/01

Rel. Strength Rank
(1 Lowest—99 Highest)
• **48**

Insider Activity
• **NA**

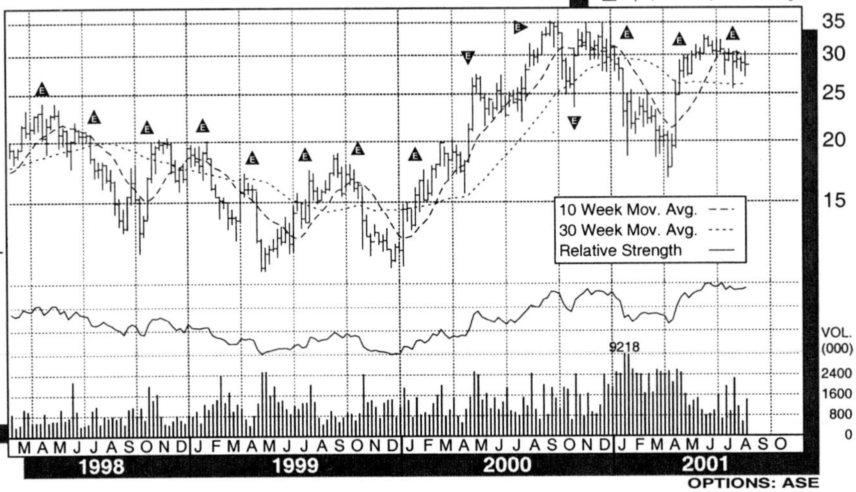

OPTIONS: ASE

Overview - 27-JUL-01

Under recently adopted revenue recognition practices, OCA will no longer book 24% of a new contract's value upfront, but will amortize the value of the contract over the typical 26 month course of treatment. On that basis, and using the restated 2000 revenue number of $269 million, we anticipate that OCA will generate 25% top-line expansion in 2001 as solid same-facility volume gains join with higher pricing, new center openings and expanded orthodontist affiliations. Incremental growth opportunities lie in offerings such as teeth whitening and "invisible" braces for adult patients, and from penetration into new U.S. and international markets. Operating cash flow is expected to approximate $45 million to $50 million in 2001. Based on the revised 2000 EPS of $0.96, we look for 2001 EPS of $1.20, and see 2002 EPS of $1.40.

Valuation - 27-JUL-01

The stock continues to trade at a modest P/E to growth (PEG) ratio under 1.0, with the 2002 P/E recently at 19 and our three-year EPS growth expectation at 22%. OCA also appears reasonable at under 4.0 times forward sales, given the prospect for 25% revenue growth through 2002. Based on this reasonable valuation, we are maintaining our accumulate opinion on the stock; however, OCA could struggle a bit ahead of the upcoming acquisition of rival orthodontic practice manager OrthAlliance (NASDAQ; ticker ORAL), since terms of the deal are partially based on the number of affiliated orthodontists who agree to amend their existing employment agreements. The deal is expected to close in the third quarter of 2001, but its ultimate financial impact remains uncertain. We continue to look for 2001 EPS of $1.20, representing an approximate 25% advance over 2000.

Key Stock Statistics

S&P EPS Est. 2001	1.20	Tang. Bk. Value/Share	1.91
P/E on S&P Est. 2001	23.8	Beta	0.67
S&P EPS Est. 2002	1.50	Shareholders	326
Dividend Rate/Share	Nil	Market cap. (B)	$ 1.4
Shs. outstg. (M)	49.2	Inst. holdings	85%
Avg. daily vol. (M)	0.266		

Value of $10,000 invested 5 years ago: $ 17,356

Fiscal Year Ending Dec. 31

	2001	2000	1999	1998	1997	1996
Revenues (Million $)						
1Q	77.48	59.28	49.05	37.69	24.90	13.72
2Q	82.23	65.84	55.40	41.53	27.48	15.51
3Q	—	69.72	59.77	44.70	31.44	18.88
4Q	—	73.99	62.07	47.38	33.51	23.16
Yr.	—	268.8	226.3	171.3	117.3	71.27
Earnings Per Share ($)						
1Q	**0.28**	**0.20**	**0.21**	**0.16**	**0.11**	**0.07**
2Q	**0.30**	**0.24**	**0.24**	**0.17**	**0.12**	**0.07**
3Q	**E0.27**	**0.23**	**0.25**	**0.18**	**0.13**	**0.09**
4Q	**E0.36**	**0.29**	**0.26**	**0.19**	**0.14**	**0.10**
Yr.	**E1.20**	**0.96**	**0.96**	**0.70**	**0.50**	**0.33**

Next earnings report expected: late October

Dividend Data

No cash dividends have been paid.

Orthodontic Centers of America, Inc.

Business Summary - 27-JUL-01

Orthodontic Centers of America Inc. (OCA) develops, acquires and manages orthodontic practices on a national basis pursuant to long-term agreements. Since inception in 1985, OCA has grown to manage 592 orthodontic centers located in 43 states, Puerto Rico, Japan and Mexico, with 346 affiliated orthodontists at the end of 2000. Of these centers, 306 were developed internally and 361 were practices acquired by the company (net of 75 consolidated centers).

The company generally manages all operations of its orthodontic centers, other than the provision of orthodontic services. It provides financial, accounting, billing and collection services and employs the orthodontic center's business personnel. OCA provides advertising and marketing services, personnel recruiting and training services, management and financial information systems, and purchasing and distribution services. During 2000, OCA spent an average of about $66,439 per affiliated orthodontist on direct marketing and advertising activities.

Comprehensive management and marketing services are provided to affiliated orthodontists pursuant to service or consulting agreements. Under these agreements, OCA manages the business and marketing sides of orthodontic centers, provides capital, facilities and equipment (including utilities, maintenance and rental), implements marketing programs, prepares budgets and financial statements, orders and purchases inventory and supplies, provides patient scheduling systems and staff, bills and collects patient fees, maintains files and records, and arranges for certain legal and accounting services.

The orthodontic centers are generally located either in shopping centers or in professional office buildings, and substantially all include private treatment rooms and large patient waiting areas, allowing the centers to locate in a broader range of office space than a traditional orthodontic practice. The centers typically include up to six treatment rooms, and range in size from about 2,000 sq. ft. to 2,500 sq. ft.

OCA believes the average cost of developing a new orthodontic center is about $255,000, including the cost of equipment, leasehold improvements, working capital and funding of losses with the initial operation of the orthodontic center.

During 2000, OCA affiliated orthodontists initiated treatment of about 160,639 patients, up 27% from 1999, representing initial new patient contract balances of $494.1 million for 2000, up about 34% over 1999. At 2000 year-end, these orthodontists were treating a total of 343,373 patients, up 28% from 267,965 patients at the end of 1999.

The company has an agreement with BrightSmile Inc., a developer and manufacturer of light activated teeth whitening technology and related products, whereby BrightSmile's teeth whitening systems are being installed at some of the company's orthodontic centers. At December 31, 2000, about 17.7% of OCA affiliated centers were offering teeth whitening ser vices.

Per Share Data ($) (Year Ended Dec. 31)	2000	1999	1998	1997	1996	1995	1994	1993	1992	1991
Tangible Bk. Val.	1.91	2.31	1.65	1.91	1.42	1.71	0.78	NA	NA	NA
Cash Flow	1.26	1.21	0.89	0.62	0.41	0.27	0.12	NA	NA	NA
Earnings	0.96	0.96	0.70	0.50	0.34	0.24	0.11	NA	NA	NA
Dividends	Nil	Nil	Nil	Nil	Nil	Nil	Nil	NA	NA	NA
Payout Ratio	Nil	Nil	Nil	Nil	Nil	Nil	Nil	NA	NA	NA
Prices - High	35.31	20.12	24.06	20.25	22.62	12.06	3.12	NA	NA	NA
- Low	11.06	10.81	11.75	11.00	10.37	2.90	2.75	NA	NA	NA
P/E Ratio - High	37	21	34	40	67	50	28	NA	NA	NA
- Low	12	11	17	22	31	12	25	NA	NA	NA

Income Statement Analysis (Million $)	2000	1999	1998	1997	1996	1995	1994	1993	1992	1991
Revs.	269	226	171	117	71.3	41.6	25.4	18.8	14.5	NA
Oper. Inc.	95.2	89.2	63.4	41.6	24.5	13.7	9.7	7.8	6.4	NA
Depr.	15.2	12.2	9.1	5.6	2.8	1.4	0.9	1.1	1.2	NA
Int. Exp.	4.6	2.6	0.3	0.2	0.4	0.5	0.3	0.2	0.2	NA
Pretax Inc.	76.3	74.7	54.6	37.1	23.6	14.2	4.7	6.4	5.1	NA
Eff. Tax Rate	37%	38%	38%	39%	39%	36%	57%	5.10%	11%	NA
Net Inc.	47.7	46.5	33.8	22.6	14.4	9.0	2.0	6.1	4.5	NA

Balance Sheet & Other Fin. Data (Million $)	2000	1999	1998	1997	1996	1995	1994	1993	1992	1991
Cash	4.7	5.8	1.6	9.9	24.4	33.6	17.1	1.5	0.8	NA
Curr. Assets	61.7	121	87.0	84.9	56.1	54.4	28.9	9.3	5.7	NA
Total Assets	368	367	297	229	145	92.6	37.5	12.5	7.2	NA
Curr. Liab.	22.2	18.8	27.4	16.7	15.9	10.7	8.0	3.4	2.6	NA
LT Debt	58.6	52.8	22.7	6.5	2.5	3.4	3.7	1.5	1.2	NA
Common Eqty.	287	279	231	191	115	77.3	25.7	7.6	3.4	NA
Total Cap.	346	348	269	212	129	81.9	29.5	9.1	4.6	NA
Cap. Exp.	20.3	22.5	17.6	15.0	12.3	8.2	4.7	1.8	0.3	NA
Cash Flow	62.9	58.8	42.9	28.3	17.2	10.5	3.0	7.2	5.7	NA
Curr. Ratio	2.8	6.4	3.2	5.1	3.5	5.1	3.6	2.7	2.2	NA
% LT Debt of Cap.	16.9	15.2	8.4	3.1	1.9	4.1	12.6	16.1	26.2	NA
% Net Inc.of Revs.	17.7	20.6	19.7	19.3	20.2	21.7	8.0	32.5	31.1	NA
% Ret. on Assets	13.1	14.0	12.9	12.1	12.1	13.9	8.1	62.1	NA	NA
% Ret. on Equity	16.9	18.3	16.0	14.8	15.0	17.5	12.2	111.0	NA	NA

Data as orig reptd.; bef. results of disc opers/spec. items. Per share data adj. for stk. divs. Bold denotes diluted EPS (FASB 128)-prior periods restated. E-Estimated. NA-Not Available. NM-Not Meaningful. NR-Not Ranked.

Office—5000 Sawgrass Village, Suite 25, Ponte Vedra Beach, FL 32082. **Tel**—(904) 280-6285. **Website**—http://www.4braces.com **Chrmn, Pres, CEO & Treas**—B. F. Palmisano Sr. **CFO & Secy**—B. F. Palmisano Jr. **VP & Investor Contact**—John Glover. **Dirs**—G. L. Faux, M. C. Johnsen, B. F. Palmisano Sr., A. J. Ryan Jr., A. G. Tunstall, E. J. Walters Jr. **Transfer Agent**—First Union National Bank of North Carolina, Charlotte. **Incorporated**—in Delaware in 1994. **Empl**— 2,381. **S&P Analyst:** Robert M. Gold

STANDARD &POOR'S STOCK REPORTS

Pharmaceutical Product Development

Nasdaq Symbol **PPDI**

In S&P SmallCap 600

18-AUG-01

Industry: Health Care (Specialized Services)

Summary: PPDI provides contract and consulting research and development services for pharmaceutical and biotechnology companies.

S&P Opinion: Accumulate (★★★★) | Recent Price • 32.88 | 52 Wk Range • 38.36-10 | Yield • Nil | 12-Mo. P/E • 38.7

Quantitative Evaluations

Outlook (1 Lowest—5 Highest)
• **2-**

Fair Value
• **30.10**

Risk
• **High**

Earn./Div. Rank
• **NR**

Technical Eval.
• **Neutral** since 8/01

Rel. Strength Rank (1 Lowest—99 Highest)
• **60**

Insider Activity
• **Unfavorable**

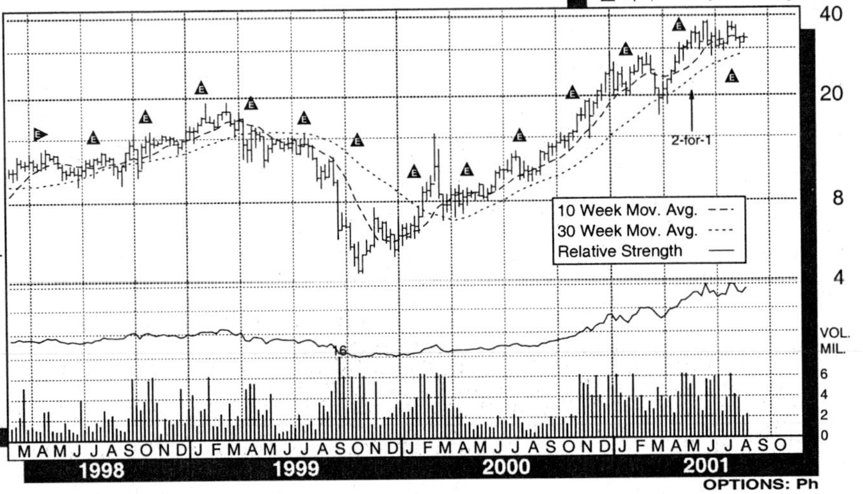

Overview - 25-JUL-01

Revenues are expected to advance over 20% in 2001. The gain should reflect projected increases in the size and number of contracts in the Life Sciences contract research organization (CRO) division, higher laboratory services volume, and brisk demand for PPD Discovery's functional genomics services. Revenues in the first half were also boosted by milestone payments from Johnson & Johnson's ALZA subsidiary, which has licensed PPDI's dapoxetine treatment for premature ejaculation. Margins should widen, aided by the higher volume, a more favorable product mix, and benefits of cost economies. EPS are projected at $0.89, with further progress to $1.02 seen for 2002.

Valuation - 25-JUL-01

The shares moved higher in recent months, buoyed by strength in the overall CRO sector and PPDI's better-than-expected EPS showings during the first and second quarters. New authorizations for the second quarter were a record $182 million, up from $165 million during the first quarter, representing an annualized growth rate of 40%. The order backlog at mid-year totaled $567 million, up 37%, year to year. Rising demand for PPDI's services reflects its unique capabilities in the CRO industry. These include expertise in the areas of functional genomics and pharmaceutical chemistry; a strategy of partnering with clients to share in the profits of new drugs; and the discovery of dapoxetine, an experimental drug for premature ejaculation. Phase III clinical trials on dapoxetine, which has been licensed to Johnson & Johnson's ALZA unit, are expected to commence in early 2002. Valued at a lower P/E multiple than other CRO stocks, the shares merit accumulation.

Key Stock Statistics

S&P EPS Est. 2001	0.89	Tang. Bk. Value/Share	5.13
P/E on S&P Est. 2001	36.9	Beta	0.08
S&P EPS Est. 2002	1.02	Shareholders	10,500
Dividend Rate/Share	Nil	Market cap. (B)	$ 1.7
Shs. outstg. (M)	51.9	Inst. holdings	63%
Avg. daily vol. (M)	0.597		

Value of $10,000 invested 5 years ago: $ 20,629

Fiscal Year Ending Dec. 31

	2001	2000	1999	1998	1997	1996
Revenues (Million $)						
1Q	107.0	81.76	69.61	52.15	57.67	47.08
2Q	102.0	84.05	76.25	57.47	60.07	49.47
3Q	—	89.27	79.36	61.45	58.27	49.50
4Q	—	90.24	77.31	64.48	59.20	51.75
Yr.	—	345.3	302.5	235.6	235.3	197.8
Earnings Per Share ($)						
1Q	0.28	0.14	0.13	0.08	0.08	0.05
2Q	0.20	0.14	0.14	0.06	-0.03	0.06
3Q	E0.20	0.17	0.15	0.10	0.09	-0.28
4Q	E0.21	0.20	0.17	0.12	0.08	0.09
Yr.	E0.89	0.64	0.58	0.33	0.21	-0.09

Next earnings report expected: mid October

Dividend Data

Amount ($)	Date Decl.	Ex-Div. Date	Stock of Record	Payment Date
2-for-1	Apr. 17	May. 14	Apr. 27	May. 11 '01

Pharmaceutical Product Development, Inc.

Business Summary - 25-JUL-01

Pharmaceutical Product Development provides a broad range of research and development and consulting services in the life and discovery sciences. PPDI believes it is the world's third largest contract research organization (CRO), providing integrated product development resources on a global basis to complement the research and development activities of companies in the pharmaceutical and biotechnology industries. The company's discovery sciences subsidiary, PPD Discovery, focuses on the discovery segment of the research and development outsourcing market. PPDI also engages in partnering with its CRO clients, to share in the profits of potential new drug compounds.

The Life Sciences Group, operating through PPD Development, provides worldwide clinical research and development of pharmaceutical products and medical devices, biostatistical analysis and analytical laboratory services. The PPD Informatics division provides software development and system integration services to the pharmaceutical and biotechnology industries. PPD ATP (acquired March 1999) provides customized inbound and outbound telecommunications programs targeting consumers and health care providers.

The company's CRO services are designed to allow its clients to reduce drug development times, which means they are able to get products into the market faster, and maximize the periods of marketing exclusivity and economic returns from those products. In addition, PPDI's integrated services also offer clients a variable cost alternative to the fixed costs associated with internal drug development.

PPD Discovery was established in June 1997, when PPDI acquired SARCO, Inc., a combinational chemistry company, and the GSX System, a functional genomics platform technology. PPD Discovery focuses on the discovery research segment of the research and development outsourcing market. PPD Virtual provides consultant and management services for product portfolio management, strategic development and commercial product assessment.

The company's 10 largest clients accounted for 53% of total revenues in 2000. Clients located outside of the U.S. provided 33% of 2000 revenues.

In December 2000, the company's PPD GenuPro R&D unit licensed development and marketing rights to its dapoxetine experimental treatment for premature ejaculation to ALZA Corp. (a unit of Johnson & Johnson). In return, PPDI received an undisclosed up-front payment, as well as rights to future milestone payments and royalties. Eli Lilly & Co. will also be entitled to a share of the dapoxetine earnings, under a 1998 agreement through which PPDI first acquired rights to dapoxetine from Eli Lilly. The company's order backlog totaled $567 million at the end of June 2001, up from $498 million at the end of 2000.

Per Share Data ($)										
(Year Ended Dec. 31)	**2000**	**1999**	**1998**	**1997**	**1996**	**1995**	**1994**	**1993**	**1992**	**1991**
Tangible Bk. Val.	4.44	3.71	3.00	2.38	2.24	0.47	NA	NA	NA	NA
Cash Flow	0.98	0.88	0.63	0.48	0.16	0.42	NA	NA	NA	NA
Earnings	0.64	0.58	0.33	0.21	-0.09	0.17	NA	NA	NA	NA
Dividends	Nil	Nil	Nil	Nil	Nil	NA	NA	NA	NA	NA
Payout Ratio	Nil	Nil	Nil	Nil	Nil	NA	NA	NA	NA	NA
Prices - High	29.37	19.25	15.34	15.00	23.87	NA	NA	NA	NA	NA
- Low	5.43	4.28	6.50	6.12	7.25	NA	NA	NA	NA	NA
P/E Ratio - High	46	33	47	71	NM	NA	NA	NA	NA	NA
- Low	8	7	20	29	NM	NA	NA	NA	NA	NA
Income Statement Analysis (Million $)										
Revs.	345	303	236	235	198	54.4	NA	NA	NA	NA
Oper. Inc.	60.8	88.7	38.4	36.3	25.4	5.6	NA	NA	NA	NA
Depr.	17.2	15.0	14.2	12.4	10.4	1.5	NA	NA	NA	NA
Int. Exp.	0.5	0.4	0.4	0.5	0.4	NA	NA	NA	NA	NA
Pretax Inc.	50.8	41.0	24.6	15.7	0.6	4.3	NA	NA	NA	NA
Eff. Tax Rate	36%	30%	38%	39%	659%	NA	NA	NA	NA	NA
Net Inc.	32.3	28.9	15.2	9.6	-3.5	4.3	NA	NA	NA	NA
Balance Sheet & Other Fin. Data (Million $)										
Cash	76.4	61.3	34.1	15.9	36.0	2.3	NA	NA	NA	NA
Curr. Assets	214	201	173	136	128	19.1	NA	NA	NA	NA
Total Assets	345	289	237	197	181	27.5	NA	NA	NA	NA
Curr. Liab.	107	93.9	79.0	66.5	61.7	15.2	NA	NA	NA	NA
LT Debt	1.4	0.4	0.2	0.3	1.4	NA	NA	NA	NA	NA
Common Eqty.	234	192	155	128	115	9.4	NA	NA	NA	NA
Total Cap.	235	193	155	128	117	NA	NA	NA	NA	NA
Cap. Exp.	21.5	23.2	19.3	13.6	11.2	NA	NA	NA	NA	NA
Cash Flow	49.5	43.9	29.4	22.0	6.9	5.8	NA	NA	NA	NA
Curr. Ratio	2.0	2.1	2.2	2.1	2.1	1.3	NA	NA	NA	NA
% LT Debt of Cap.	0.6	0.2	0.1	0.3	0.1	NA	NA	NA	NA	NA
% Net Inc.of Revs.	9.4	9.5	6.4	4.1	NM	7.9	NA	NA	NA	NA
% Ret. on Assets	10.2	11.0	7.0	5.1	NM	17.7	NA	NA	NA	NA
% Ret. on Equity	15.2	16.6	10.7	7.9	NM	57.8	NA	NA	NA	NA

Data as orig reptd.; bef. results of disc opers/spec. items. Per share data adj. for stk. divs. Bold denotes diluted EPS (FASB 128)-prior periods restated. E-Estimated. NA-Not Available. NM-Not Meaningful. NR-Not Ranked.

Office—3151 South Seventeenth Street, Wilmington, NC 28412. **Tel**—(910) 251-0081. **Website**—http://www.ppdi.com **Chrmn**—E. Mario. **Vice Chrmn & CEO**—F. N. Eshelman. **VP & Secy**—F. B. Davenport Jr. **CFO**—P. Maitre. **Dirs**—S. Bondurant, A. E. Cohen, F. N. Eshelman, F. Frank, C. M. Klema, T. Magnuson, E. Mario, J. A. McNeill Jr, P. J. Rizzo. **Transfer Agent & Registrar**—Wachovia Bank of North Carolina, Winston-Salem. **Incorporated**—in North Carolina in 1989. **Empl**— 3,700. **S&P Analyst:** Herman Saftlas

STANDARD
&POOR'S
STOCK REPORTS

Quest Diagnostics

NYSE Symbol **DGX**

In S&P MidCap 400

18-AUG-01

Industry:
Health Care (Specialized Services)

Summary: This company provides diagnostic testing, information and services to physicians, hospitals, managed care organizations, employers and government agencies.

S&P Opinion: Accumulate (★★★★) | Recent Price • 61.45 | 52 Wk Range • 75.75-36.60 | Yield • Nil | 12-Mo. P/E • 42.7

Quantitative Evaluations

Outlook
(1 Lowest—5 Highest)
• **5**

Fair Value
• **83.90**

Risk
• **NA**

Earn./Div. Rank
• **NR**

Technical Eval.
• **Bearish** since 8/01

Rel. Strength Rank
(1 Lowest—99 Highest)
• **37**

Insider Activity
• **Neutral**

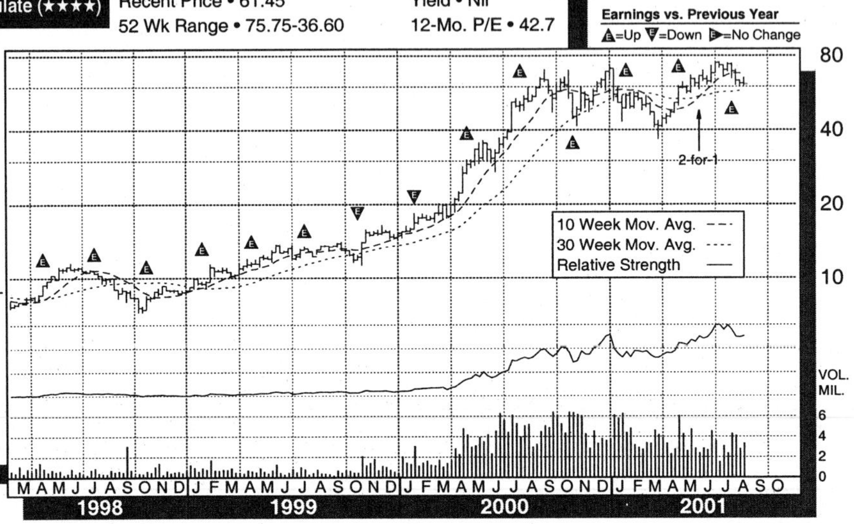

Overview - 24-JUL-01

Second quarter results exceeded our expectations, benefiting from higher than anticipated average revenue per test. In 2001, we expect revenues to increase 7.5%, to over $3.6 billion, on 5.0%-5.5% higher pricing and 2.0%-2.5% volume increases. Average revenue per test has been rising, as a result of renegotiated contracts with private payors, a larger percent of fee-for-service testing, and an increasing percent of higher cost specialized (esoteric) tests. High margin esoteric testing now accounts for nearly 20% of total revenue. Annual integration synergies from the Smithkline (SKB) acquisition should exceed $150 million by year end; in the second quarter, DGX achieved an annual $120 million run rate. Revenue growth and SKB synergies should reduce the cost of goods sold and SG&A expenses as a percentage of revenues, leading to a 200 basis point widening of EBITDA, to 15.2% of revenue.

Valuation - 24-JUL-01

We are maintaining our accumulate opinion on DGX, reflecting expected strong earnings growth, driven primarily by margin improvement. Revenue growth is likely to moderate in 2001, due to the loss of certain customers with which DGX was unable to negotiate satisfactory rate increases. However, the elimination of low margin customers, combined with further integration savings from SKB should fuel significant margin gains. Despite the stock's volatility year-to-date, following last year's outstanding performance, we believe DGX should resume its upward trend. Long term, the company aims for double-digit revenue growth, bad-debt expense of 4%, EBITDA margin over 20%, and annual EPS growth exceeding 30%. We expect DGX to continue to use free cash flow, estimated at $210 million in 2001, to reduce debt. Trading at 39X our 2001 EPS estimate of $1.88, DGX should outperform.

Key Stock Statistics

S&P EPS Est. 2000	NA	Tang. Bk. Value/Share	NM
P/E on S&P Est. 2000	NA	Beta	NA
S&P EPS Est. 2001	1.88	Shareholders	6,800
Dividend Rate/Share	Nil	Market cap. (B)	$ 5.8
Shs. outstg. (M)	94.0	Inst. holdings	52%
Avg. daily vol. (M)	0.718		

Value of $10,000 invested 5 years ago: NA

Fiscal Year Ending Dec. 31

	2001	2000	1999	1998	1997	1996
Revenues (Million $)						
1Q	882.5	857.5	381.8	367.9	388.1	401.4
2Q	931.5	877.1	394.0	366.7	401.5	424.5
3Q	—	850.2	614.8	360.7	373.7	405.4
4Q	—	836.4	814.5	363.3	365.4	385.0
Yr.	—	3,421	2,205	1,459	1,529	1,616
Earnings Per Share ($)						
1Q	**0.37**	**0.20**	**0.12**	**0.11**	0.07	--
2Q	**0.48**	**0.32**	**0.21**	**0.14**	**0.14**	—
3Q	—	**0.30**	**-0.10**	**0.10**	**0.05**	—
4Q	—	**0.29**	**-0.17**	**0.09**	**-0.65**	—
Yr.	—	**1.11**	**-0.02**	**0.45**	**-0.39**	NA

Next earnings report expected: mid October

Dividend Data

Amount ($)	Date Decl.	Ex-Div. Date	Stock of Record	Payment Date
2-for-1	Feb. 22	Jun. 01	May. 16	May. 31 '01

Quest Diagnostics Incorporated

Business Summary - 24-JUL-01

Quest Diagnostics is the largest independent U.S. clinical lab provider. The company offers a broad range of clinical laboratory testing services used by physicians in the detection, diagnosis, evaluation, monitoring and treatment of diseases and other medical conditions. Tests range from routine (such as blood cholesterol tests) to highly complex (such as molecular diagnostics testing).

The company processes more than 100 million requisitions (order forms completed by physicians indicating tests to be performed) annually. Customers include physician practices, managed care organizations, hospitals, employers and institutions, and other independent clinical laboratories.

At the end of 2000, DGX had a network of major laboratories in 30 major metropolitan areas throughout the U.S., several joint venture and branch laboratories, 150 smaller "rapid response" laboratories, and about 1,300 patient service centers. It also has an esoteric testing laboratory and research and development facility, Nichols Institute, and facilities in Mexico City and near London. DGX expects to realize cost savings of $150 million annually beginning in mid 2002, from its 1999 SmithKline Beecham Clinical Laboratories acquisition.

DGX aims to be recognized by customers, employees and competitors as the best provider of comprehensive and innovative clinical testing, information and services. It expects its strategy to produce annual earnings growth (before integration charges) of at least 30% over the next several years.

DGX's laboratory testing business consists of routine, esoteric and clinical trial testing. Routine testing generated 83% of net revenues in 2000, esoteric testing 12%, and clinical trials 3%. The balance of revenues came from the manufacture and sale of diagnostic test systems and the provision of information derived from clinical laboratory data to customers such as managed care organizations and pharmaceutical companies.

Routine tests measure important health parameters such as the function of the kidney, heart, liver, thyroid and other organs. Commonly ordered tests include blood cholesterol level tests; complete blood cell counts; pap smears; HIV-related tests; urinalyses; pregnancy tests; and alcohol and other substance-abuse tests.

Nichols Institute performs esoteric clinical testing. Esoteric tests are performed less frequently than routine tests, and/or require more sophisticated equipment and materials, professional hands-on attention and more highly skilled personnel. As a result, they are generally priced substantially higher than routine tests. Because it is not cost effective for most clinical laboratories to perform low volume esoteric tests in-house, they generally refer a significant portion of such tests to esoteric clinical testing laboratories.

Per Share Data ($) (Year Ended Dec. 31)	2000	1999	1998	1997	1996	1995	1994	1993	1992	1991
Tangible Bk. Val.	NM	NM	1.20	0.45	NA	0.48	NA	NA	NA	NA
Cash Flow	2.54	1.28	1.58	0.90	NA	1.19	NA	NA	NA	NA
Earnings	1.11	-0.02	0.45	-0.39	NA	-0.39	NA	NA	NA	NA
Dividends	Nil	Nil	Nil	Nil	Nil	NA	NA	NA	NA	NA
Payout Ratio	Nil	Nil	Nil	Nil	Nil	NA	NA	NA	NA	NA
Prices - High	73.12	16.46	11.53	10.43	7.87	NA	NA	NA	NA	NA
- Low	14.56	8.87	7.25	7.12	6.62	NA	NA	NA	NA	NA
P/E Ratio - High	66	NM	26	NM	NA	NA	NA	NA	NA	NA
- Low	13	NM	16	NM	NA	NA	NA	NA	NA	NA
Income Statement Analysis (Million $)										
Revs.	3,421	2,205	1,459	1,529	1,616	1,629	NA	NA	NA	NA
Oper. Inc.	452	243	163	151	166	183	NA	NA	NA	NA
Depr.	134	90.8	68.8	76.4	99	90.9	NA	NA	NA	NA
Int. Exp.	120	69.8	44.0	46.0	74.9	50.7	NA	NA	NA	NA
Pretax Inc.	210	19.8	53.9	-19.1	-676	-15.7	NA	NA	NA	NA
Eff. Tax Rate	46%	NM	50%	NM	NM	NM	NA	NA	NA	NA
Net Inc.	105	-1.3	26.9	-22.3	-626	-22.5	NA	NA	NA	NA
Balance Sheet & Other Fin. Data (Million $)										
Cash	171	27.3	203	162	42.0	40.0	NA	NA	NA	NA
Curr. Assets	981	873	578	572	511	700	NA	NA	NA	NA
Total Assets	2,865	2,878	1,360	1,401	1,395	1,612	NA	NA	NA	NA
Curr. Liab.	955	701	309	295	249	394	NA	NA	NA	NA
LT Debt	761	1,171	413	482	515	515	NA	NA	NA	NA
Common Eqty.	1,031	862	567	541	538	604	NA	NA	NA	NA
Total Cap.	1,793	2,046	2,034	1,024	1,054	1,119	NA	NA	NA	NA
Cap. Exp.	116	76.0	39.6	30.8	70.4	93.1	NA	NA	NA	NA
Cash Flow	239	89.6	95.7	54.1	-527	68.4	NA	NA	NA	NA
Curr. Ratio	1.0	1.2	1.9	1.9	2.1	1.8	NA	NA	NA	NA
% LT Debt of Cap.	42.4	57.6	42.1	47.1	48.9	46.0	NA	NA	NA	NA
% Net Inc.of Revs.	3.1	NM	1.8	NM	NM	NM	NA	NA	NA	NA
% Ret. on Assets	3.7	NM	1.9	NM	NM	NA	NA	NA	NA	NA
% Ret. on Equity	11.1	NM	4.9	NM	NM	NA	NA	NA	NA	NA

Data as orig. reptd.; bef. results of disc. opers. and/or spec. items. Per share data adj. for stk. divs. as of ex-div. date. Balance Sheet Data and Book Value for 1995 are pro forma as of Sep. 30, 1996. Bold denotes diluted EPS (FASB 128). E-Estimated. NA-Not Available. NM-Not Meaningful. NR-Not Ranked.

Office—One Malcolm Ave., Teterboro, NJ 07608. **Tel**—(201) 393-5000. **Website**—www.questdiagnostics.com **Chrmn & CEO**—K. W. Freeman. **Pres & COO**—S. Mohapatra. **VP & CFO**—R. A. Hagemann. **VP & Secy**—L. C. Farrenkopf Jr. **Dirs**—K. D. Brody, W. F. Buehler, V. C. Campbell, M. A. Cirillo, K. W. Freeman, W. R. Grant, D. C. Stanzione, G. R. Wilensky, J. B. Ziegler. **Transfer Agent & Registrar**—ComputerShare Investor Services, Chicago. **Incorporated**—in Delaware. **Empl**— 27,000. **S&P Analyst:** John Massey

STANDARD
&POOR'S
STOCK REPORTS

Renal Care Group

Nasdaq Symbol **RCGI**

In S&P SmallCap 600

18-AUG-01

Industry:
Health Care (Specialized Services)

Summary: This nephrology services company provides care to 17,000 patients with kidney disease, including patients suffering from chronic kidney failure.

S&P Opinion: Accumulate (★★★★)

Recent Price • 31.25
52 Wk Range • 32.89-14.50
Yield • Nil
12-Mo. P/E • 25.4

Quantitative Evaluations

Outlook (1 Lowest—5 Highest)
• **4-**

Fair Value
• **34.10**

Risk
• **NA**

Earn./Div. Rank
• **NR**

Technical Eval.
• **Bearish** since 8/01

Rel. Strength Rank (1 Lowest—99 Highest)
• **82**

Insider Activity
• **Unfavorable**

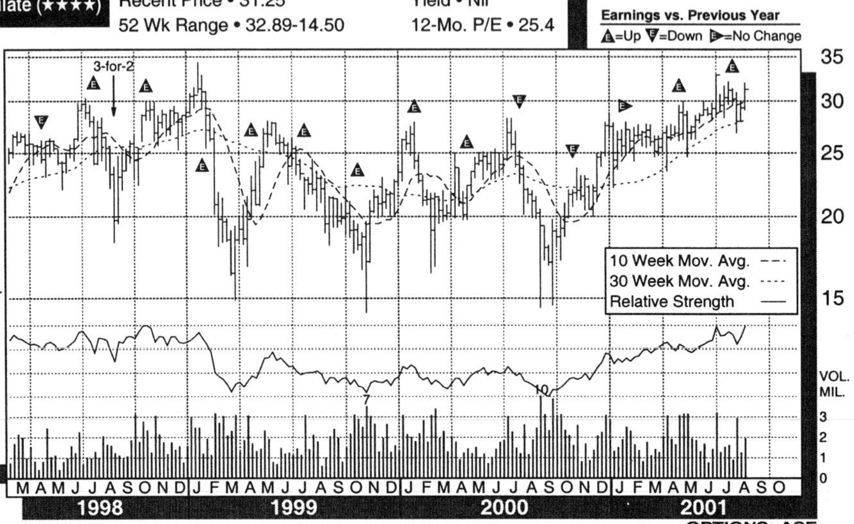

OPTIONS: ASE

Overview - 08-AUG-01

In 2001, we expect revenue to increase about 16%, to nearly $725 million, on 8%-9% private payor rate hikes, a 2.4% Medicare increase, 6%-7% higher patient treatment volume, development of new dialysis centers, and acquisitions. As an alternative to acquisitions, which have become increasingly expensive, RCGI plans to build 15-20 new centers in 2001, with 10 opening in the second half of the year. RCGI has already acquired 600 patients this year, and with a solid pipeline of prospects, we believe it will make more acquisitions. Treatment costs should rise 5%-6%, while Epogen pricing remains stable. However, Amgen announced a price increase that will impact 2002 Epogen costs. Gross margins should hold steady, as efficiency improvements and rate hikes offset 5.5% higher labor costs. EBITDA should rise to 24.1%, aided by the divestiture of the wound care business in early 2001. We see 2002 revenue up 9%, to $790 million, with slightly wider margins.

Valuation - 08-AUG-01

We are maintaining our accumulate opinion on RCGI, as we believe its predictable and recurring revenue stream will support a higher valuation as investors seek a safe haven in a slowing economy. Medicare legislation enacted in late 2000 should lead to annual rate hikes, which the renal care industry has not received from Medicare since 1991. Longer patient life expectancies, higher incidence rates of kidney failure, and a renewed focus on home-based dialysis should drive mid single-digit organic treatment growth. In addition, RCGI continues to add patients through acquisitions. Second quarter operating cash flow was $31 million, while the debt/capital ratio fell to 5%. Days sales outstanding (receivables) stood at 63. Trading at 17X our 2002 EPS estimate, with 15%-20% long-term EPS growth, RCGI should outperform.

Key Stock Statistics

S&P EPS Est. 2000	1.32	Tang. Bk. Value/Share	3.62
P/E on S&P Est. 2000	23.7	Beta	0.86
S&P EPS Est. 2001	1.51	Shareholders	8,500
Dividend Rate/Share	Nil	Market cap. (B)	$ 1.5
Shs. outstg. (M)	47.4	Inst. holdings	79%
Avg. daily vol. (M)	0.347		

Value of $10,000 invested 5 years ago: $ 18,061

Fiscal Year Ending Dec. 31

	2001	2000	1999	1998	1997	1996
Revenues (Million $)						
1Q	174.8	144.3	120.9	80.46	46.11	24.53
2Q	183.5	154.2	128.5	89.51	51.67	31.83
3Q	—	156.5	133.5	96.81	54.04	34.63
4Q	—	164.2	137.8	102.6	62.20	38.53
Yr.	—	624.6	520.6	369.4	214.0	129.5
Earnings Per Share ($)						
1Q	**0.36**	**0.32**	**0.17**	**0.17**	0.17	0.11
2Q	**0.37**	**0.25**	**0.29**	**0.19**	0.13	0.09
3Q	—	**0.20**	**0.30**	**0.22**	0.15	0.05
4Q	—	**0.31**	**0.31**	**0.24**	**0.16**	0.11
Yr.	—	**1.07**	**1.04**	**0.83**	**0.56**	0.37

Next earnings report expected: early November

Dividend Data

No cash dividends have been paid.

A Division of The McGraw-Hill Companies

Renal Care Group, Inc.

Business Summary - 08-AUG-01

Renal Care Group, a nephrology services company, has grown substantially since it began operations in February 1996 with an aggregate of 41 dialysis centers serving about 2,663 patients in eight states. As of June 30, 2001, the company was providing dialysis and ancillary services to about 17,200 patients, through 223 owned and managed outpatient dialysis centers in 25 states, in addition to providing acute dialysis services in 115 hospitals.

RCGI provides nephrology services, the specialized practice of medicine dedicated to providing care to patients with end-stage renal disease (ESRD) and other kidney-specific ailments. An essential part of the nephrologist's practice is the dialysis facility, where ESRD patients receive treatments three times a week in a technologically advanced outpatient setting. ESRD is the state of advanced renal impairment that is irreversible and imminently lethal. Patients with ESRD eventually require dialysis or kidney transplantation to sustain life. According to industry data, the number of patients receiving chronic dialysis services in the U.S. grew from 66,000 in 1982 to about 233,000 in 1998. It is estimated that the number of ESRD patients will more than double from the 1998 level, reaching 660,000 by 2010.

In addition to its dialysis business, the company offers practice management and administrative services to physician practices. RCGI also operated a business that provides wound care and diabetic services. Because of the chronic nature of ESRD, and the fact that many ESRD patients are also diabetic, many patients also require wound care services. However, in early 2001, the company closed its wound care business, to focus exclusively on providing dialysis services.

RCGI believes an integrated network of nephrologist and dialysis centers, combined with its clinical expertise, management experience and access to capital, will provide significant advantages to patients and third-party payors by improving the quality of care while reducing the overall costs associated with treating patients with all forms of kidney disease, including those with ESRD.

The dialysis industry is highly fragmented, and very competitive. According to industry experts, there were more than 3,800 dialysis centers in the U.S. at the end of 1999. The company believes about 55% were owned by multi-center dialysis companies, 20% to 25% were owned by independent physicians, and 20% to 25% were affiliated with hospitals.

In 2000, Medicare accounted for 53% of net patient revenues, Medicaid for 5%, commercial and other payors 36%, and hospital inpatient dialysis services 6%.

In December 2000, RCGI settled for $1.98 million claims arising from alleged inadequacies in physician documentation related to laboratory tests performed by its RenaLab subsidiary.

In October 2000, directors authorized the repurchase of up to $50 million of common stock.

Per Share Data ($) (Year Ended Dec. 31)	2000	1999	1998	1997	1996	1995	1994	1993	1992	1991
Tangible Bk. Val.	3.62	2.59	1.32	1.52	2.49	0.69	NA	NA	NA	NA
Cash Flow	1.75	1.61	1.26	0.81	0.53	NA	NA	NA	NA	NA
Earnings	1.07	1.04	0.83	0.56	0.37	NA	NA	NA	NA	NA
Dividends	Nil	Nil	Nil	Nil	Nil	NA	NA	NA	NA	NA
Payout Ratio	Nil	Nil	Nil	Nil	Nil	NA	NA	NA	NA	NA
Prices - High	28.62	34.37	30.33	24.33	17.33	NA	NA	NA	NA	NA
- Low	14.50	14.25	18.00	13.22	8.00	NA	NA	NA	NA	NA
P/E Ratio - High	27	33	37	43	31	NA	NA	NA	NA	NA
- Low	14	14	22	24	14	NA	NA	NA	NA	NA
Income Statement Analysis (Million $)										
Revs.	623	521	369	214	130	43.0	41.6	18.1	8.7	NA
Oper. Inc.	163	137	81.8	41.5	23.6	5.0	6.5	0.9	0.6	NA
Depr.	32.3	26.4	18.4	9.0	4.5	1.6	1.5	0.6	0.1	NA
Int. Exp.	5.0	5.0	3.1	-0.6	NM	0.5	0.4	0.1	0.0	NA
Pretax Inc.	96.2	87.3	59.3	32.7	17.7	3.0	4.6	0.3	0.5	NA
Eff. Tax Rate	36%	36%	35%	36%	39%	Nil	Nil	50%	9.70%	NA
Net Inc.	51.5	48.5	35.2	20.0	10.7	3.0	4.6	0.1	0.4	NA
Balance Sheet & Other Fin. Data (Million $)										
Cash	29.9	14.5	19.9	9.1	53.4	1.3	NA	NA	NA	NA
Curr. Assets	216	160	110	65.8	86.5	11.1	NA	NA	NA	NA
Total Assets	585	482	377	248	132	20.8	17.3	14.4	2.6	NA
Curr. Liab.	101	74.4	56.7	41.3	37.0	12.5	NA	NA	NA	NA
LT Debt	58.3	76.1	62.6	15.5	Nil	3.7	NA	NA	NA	NA
Common Eqty.	394	310	229	175	93.3	4.6	5.9	4.9	1.5	NA
Total Cap.	484	408	320	207	94.8	8.2	NA	NA	NA	NA
Cap. Exp.	45.7	44.1	28.8	27.4	11.4	4.8	2.4	NA	NA	NA
Cash Flow	83.8	74.9	53.6	29.0	15.3	4.6	6.1	0.7	0.6	NA
Curr. Ratio	2.2	2.2	1.9	1.6	2.3	0.9	NA	NA	NA	NA
% LT Debt of Cap.	12.0	18.7	19.6	7.5	Nil	44.5	NA	NA	NA	NA
% Net Inc.of Revs.	8.3	9.3	9.5	9.3	8.3	6.9	11.1	0.7	4.7	NA
% Ret. on Assets	9.5	10.8	11.3	10.5	14.1	15.6	29.3	1.5	NA	NA
% Ret. on Equity	14.6	17.4	17.4	14.9	22.0	56.7	85.7	4.1	NA	NA

Data as orig reptd.; bef. results of disc opers/spec. items. Per share data adj. for stk. divs. Bold denotes diluted EPS (FASB 128)-prior periods restated. E-Estimated. NA-Not Available. NM-Not Meaningful. NR-Not Ranked.

Office—2100 West End Ave., Suite 800, Nashville, TN 37203. **Tel**—(615) 345-5500. **Website**—www.renalcaregroup.com **Chrmn, Pres & CEO**—S. A. Brooks Jr. **EVP, CFO & Treas**—R. D. Allison. **Secy**—D. B. Chappell. **Dirs**—J. D. Bower, S. A. Brooks Jr., J. C. Hutts, H. R. Jacobson, K. Johnson, W. Lapham, T. A. Lowrey, S. D. McMurray, T. Meredith. **Transfer Agent & Registrar**—First Union National Bank of North Carolina, Charlotte. **Incorporated**—in Delaware in 1995. **Empl**— 4,815. **S&P Analyst:** John A. Massey

STANDARD &POOR'S
STOCK REPORTS

Syncor International

Nasdaq Symbol **SCOR**

In S&P SmallCap 600

18-AUG-01

Industry: Health Care (Medical Products & Supplies)

Summary: This distributor of radiopharmaceuticals operates an international network of nuclear pharmacy centers serving hospitals, clinics and physicians.

S&P Opinion: Accumulate (★★★★)

Recent Price • 34.20
52 Wk Range • 45.18-22.75
Yield • Nil
12-Mo. P/E • 27.4

Quantitative Evaluations

Outlook (1 Lowest—5 Highest)
• **4-**

Fair Value
• **42.60**

Risk
• **High**

Earn./Div. Rank
• **B**

Technical Eval.
• **Bullish** since 8/01

Rel. Strength Rank (1 Lowest—99 Highest)
• **88**

Insider Activity
• **NA**

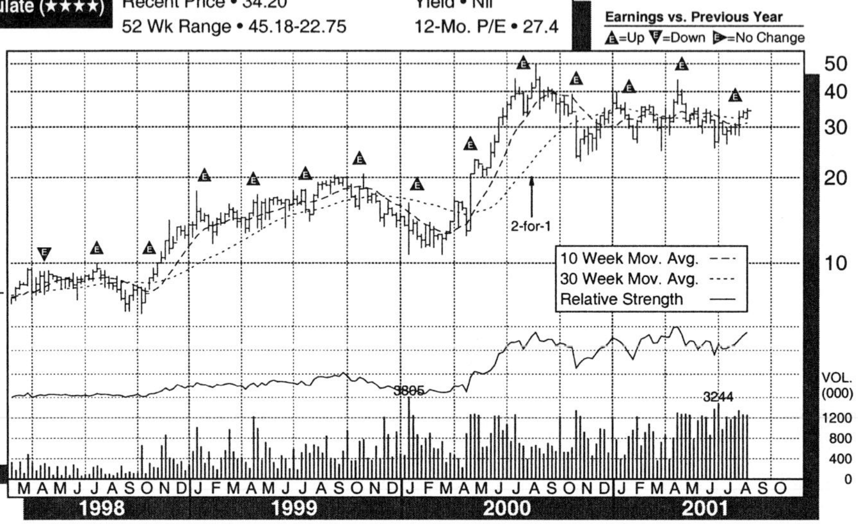

Overview - 15-AUG-01

Revenue growth in 2001 is seen at 20% to 22%, as gains in the core radiopharmaceutical business join with increased contributions from medical imaging. In pharmacy services. Looking into 2002, we estimate that revenues will advance at a 19% pace. For now, sales of the cardiac imaging agent Cardiolite still represent the most critical revenue stream, but SCOR and Dupont have decided to not automatically extend their existing Cardiolite distribution agreement beyond 2003. Within the imaging division, same-store growth should approximate 14% to 16%. Despite increased expenditures related to information technology and initiatives in the oncology business, together with increased outlays tied to support functions, we see 2001 EPS growth of 23%, to $1.39, and look for 2002 EPS of $1.70.

Valuation - 15-AUG-01

The stock gained positive momentum following the announcement that the company entered into an agreement to distribute Eli Lilly's Zigris, a biotechnology compound for the treatment of severe sepsis that is under priority review by the Food and Drug Administration. Although there remain some concerns about the possible removal of Cardiolite from the revenue stream after 2003, the long term outlook for the radiopharmaceutical distribution business remains solid. This area should continue to grow rapidly, aided by technological innovations within the medical imaging industry and the associated increase in utilization of imaging procedures. We would also note that Cardiolite contributions are on the decline as the revenue stream becomes more diversified; Cardiolite sales in 2001 will account for about 30% of total sales, down from over 40% in 2000. Recently trading at 19 times our 2002 EPS estimate and less than 1.0 times estimated 2002 sales, the stock ranks among our least expensive medical distribution names.

Key Stock Statistics

S&P EPS Est. 2001	1.40	Tang. Bk. Value/Share	3.17
P/E on S&P Est. 2001	24.4	Beta	0.63
S&P EPS Est. 2002	1.70	Shareholders	738
Dividend Rate/Share	Nil	Market cap. (B)	$0.836
Shs. outstg. (M)	24.4	Inst. holdings	67%
Avg. daily vol. (M)	0.386		

Value of $10,000 invested 5 years ago: $ 62,665

Fiscal Year Ending Dec. 31

	2001	2000	1999	1998	1997	1996
Revenues (Million $)						
1Q	181.4	149.0	123.9	102.7	93.08	92.02
2Q	187.7	154.4	130.3	113.3	98.19	93.30
3Q	—	155.5	131.5	114.1	94.49	90.25
4Q	—	170.6	134.6	119.0	94.80	90.88
Yr.	—	629.4	520.3	449.0	380.6	366.4
Earnings Per Share ($)						
1Q	**0.38**	**0.30**	**0.20**	**0.15**	**0.16**	**0.09**
2Q	**0.41**	**0.34**	**0.25**	**0.20**	**0.17**	**0.13**
3Q	**E0.29**	**0.23**	**0.13**	**0.12**	**0.09**	**0.07**
4Q	**E0.32**	**0.25**	**0.18**	**0.14**	**0.08**	**0.05**
Yr.	**E1.40**	**1.11**	**0.76**	**0.61**	**0.49**	**0.33**

Next earnings report expected: late October

Dividend Data

No cash has been paid on the common shares.

A Division of The McGraw-Hill Companies

Syncor International Corporation

Business Summary - 15-AUG-01

Syncor International is a leading provider of radiopharmacy services, engaged in compounding, dispensing, and distributing radiopharmaceutical products and services through an international network of nuclear pharmacy service centers. The company is also pursuing a leadership position through its Comprehensive Medical Imaging, Inc. (CMI) unit, which provides medical imaging services.

SCOR's nuclear pharmacy network (78% of 2000 revenues) services more than 7,000 hospitals and outpatient clinics in 48 U.S. states and 14 foreign countries. As of late July 2001, radiopharmaceuticals were distributed through 128 domestic and 19 international nuclear pharmacies. Radiopharmaceuticals dispensed through this network are used by physicians for diagnostic imaging of physiological functions and organ systems, and for the monitoring and treatment of diseases. Historically, most of the radiopharmaceuticals dispensed and distributed by the company have been used in diagnosing cardiovascular disease and other heart problems. SCOR has preferred distribution rights, under an agreement set to expire in 2003, to DuPont Corp.'s Cardiolite, the world's best selling cardiac imaging agent. Cardiolite accounted for 45% of total company sales in 2000.

During 2000, the company began two initiatives for the production and distribution of radiopharmaceuticals used in other diagnostic and therapeutic procedures. One product is F-18 Flourodeoxyglucose (FDG) , the most common radiopharmaceutical used in positive emission tomography (PET) procedures. PET is a clinically proven, safe method for imaging lung, esophageal and colorectal cancers, lymphoma, melanoma, head and neck cancers, myocardial viability and refractory seizures. SCOR will open eight to 10 cyclotron sites for the production of FDG during 2001. The other product is Palladium-103 brachytherapy seeds, radioactive implants that are used in about one-third of the prostate cancer bracchytherapy procedures in the U.S.

SCOR has three types of radiopharmacy customers. Corporate account customers representing regional or national networks of hospitals accounted for 28% of net sales in 2000.

Through its CMI subsidiary (16%), SCOR continues to expand its role in medical imaging services. As of late July 2001, the company owned or partly owned 63 domestic (including 13 acquired from U.S. Diagnostics Inc.) and 13 international medical imaging centers that offer magnetic resonance imaging (MRI) and other medical imaging modalities, including computed tomography (CT), nuclear imaging, mammography, ultrasound, X-ray and flouroscopy. In selected geographic markets, SCOR intends to offer PET imaging technology in some of its centers; in June 2000, the company opened its first PET imaging center in Rancho Mirage, CA.

Per Share Data ($) (Year Ended Dec. 31)	2000	1999	1998	1997	1996	1995	1994	1993	1992	1991
Tangible Bk. Val.	3.17	5.46	1.75	3.63	3.15	3.08	2.98	2.75	2.58	1.95
Cash Flow	2.10	3.04	1.29	0.97	0.81	0.74	0.54	0.32	0.81	0.56
Earnings	1.11	0.76	0.61	0.49	0.32	0.23	0.06	0.08	0.47	0.32
Dividends	Nil	Nil	Nil	Nil	Nil	Nil	Nil	Nil	Nil	Nil
Payout Ratio	Nil	Nil	Nil	Nil	Nil	Nil	Nil	Nil	Nil	Nil
Prices - High	50.00	20.62	14.18	8.81	8.31	6.06	12.37	13.25	17.25	13.62
- Low	10.68	11.68	6.62	3.56	3.06	3.06	3.25	7.12	7.50	4.56
P/E Ratio - High	45	27	23	18	26	27	NM	NM	36	43
- Low	10	15	11	7	9	14	NM	NM	16	14
Income Statement Analysis (Million $)										
Revs.	629	520	449	381	366	332	320	142	231	210
Oper. Inc.	82.6	59.0	39.8	23.0	19.0	17.8	12.2	7.7	23.4	16.7
Depr.	26.3	19.5	15.3	9.9	10.4	10.8	10.6	5.3	7.2	5.4
Int. Exp.	10.2	7.0	5.3	1.2	0.8	0.7	0.8	0.3	0.6	0.8
Pretax Inc.	49.2	33.9	24.2	17.0	11.3	7.8	2.1	2.8	16.9	11.6
Eff. Tax Rate	40%	43%	42%	41%	39%	40%	42%	39%	40%	41%
Net Inc.	29.5	19.2	13.9	10.0	6.9	4.7	1.2	1.7	10.2	6.9
Balance Sheet & Other Fin. Data (Million $)										
Cash	24.3	13.4	13.8	25.5	25.2	23.0	18.0	18.7	20.9	10.0
Curr. Assets	224	148	119	92.6	93.0	83.6	76.3	63.7	60.7	52.0
Total Assets	471	313	257	165	146	134	129	115	104	90.8
Curr. Liab.	143	91.6	74.6	57.9	57.0	49.4	49.7	36.6	33.3	31.8
LT Debt	138	76.3	70.3	17.3	7.6	5.2	5.2	6.8	4.5	6.0
Common Eqty.	186	140	111	89.3	78.5	78.3	73.9	71.2	65.8	52.4
Total Cap.	327	221	182	107	86.1	83.5	79.0	78.0	70.7	59.7
Cap. Exp.	31.4	24.5	16.0	10.9	8.1	3.9	9.2	5.5	10.6	10.5
Cash Flow	55.8	38.7	29.2	20.0	17.3	15.5	11.8	6.9	17.3	12.3
Curr. Ratio	1.6	1.6	1.6	1.6	1.6	1.7	1.5	1.7	1.8	1.6
% LT Debt of Cap.	42.2	34.5	38.7	16.2	8.8	6.2	6.5	8.8	6.4	10.2
% Net Inc.of Revs.	4.7	3.7	3.1	2.6	1.9	14.0	0.4	1.2	4.4	3.3
% Ret. on Assets	7.5	6.8	6.6	6.5	4.9	3.6	1.0	NA	10.4	8.3
% Ret. on Equity	18.1	15.3	13.9	11.8	8.8	6.1	1.7	NA	17.1	14.4

Data as orig. reptd.; bef. results of disc. opers. and/or spec. items. Per share data adj. for stk. divs. as of ex-div. date. Bold denotes diluted EPS (FASB 128). E-Estimated. NA-Not Available. NM-Not Meaningful. NR-Not Ranked.

Office—6464 Canoga Ave., Woodland Hills, CA 91367. **Tel**—(818) 737-4000. **Website**—http://www.syncor.com **Chrmn**—M. Fu. **Pres & CEO**—R. G. Funari. **SVP, Treas & CFO**—W. P. Forster. **SVP & Secy**—H. Bagerdjian. **Investor Contact**—Tim Guttman (818-737-4507). **Dirs**—M. Fu, R. G. Funari, S. B. Gerber, G. S. Oki, B. Puckett, A. E. Spangler, H. N. Wagner Jr., G. R. Wilensky, R. Williams. **Transfer Agent & Registrar**—American Stock Transfer & Trust Co., NYC. **Incorporated**—in New Mexico in 1974; reincorporated in Delaware in 1985. **Empl**— 3,600. **S&P Analyst:** Robert M. Gold

STANDARD
&POOR'S
STOCK REPORTS

Trigon Healthcare

NYSE Symbol **TGH**

In S&P MidCap 400

18-AUG-01

Industry: Health Care (Managed Care)

Summary: TGH, the largest managed health care company in Virginia, markets its products under the Blue Cross/Blue Shield name.

S&P Opinion: Accumulate (★★★★)

Recent Price • 65.99
52 Wk Range • 81.50-46.90
Yield • Nil
12-Mo. P/E • 22.1

Quantitative Evaluations

Outlook
(1 Lowest—5 Highest)
• **4+**

Fair Value
• **81.30**

Risk
• **Low**

Earn./Div. Rank
• **NR**

Technical Eval.
• **Bullish** since 6/01

Rel. Strength Rank
(1 Lowest—99 Highest)
• **73**

Insider Activity
• **Neutral**

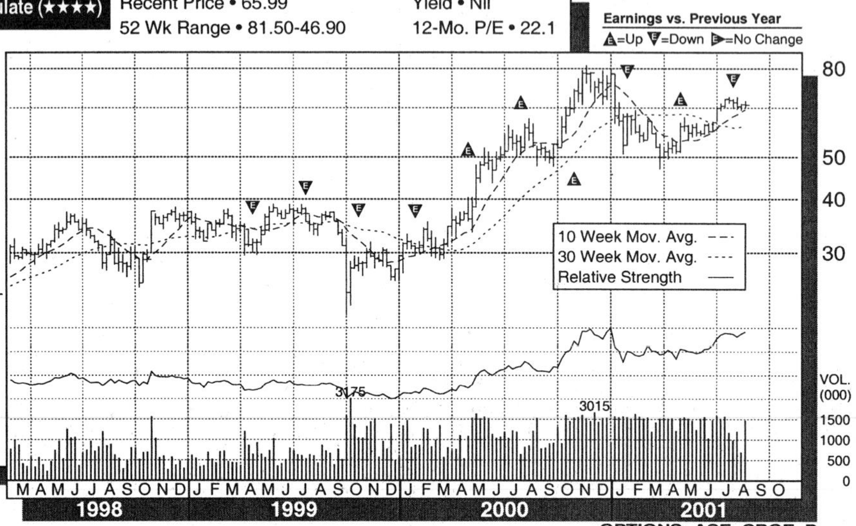

OPTIONS: ASE, CBOE, P

Overview - 15-AUG-01

Second quarter results beat our expectations. We see 2001 revenues growing 14%, to about $3 billion, on 6% to 8% commercial and 8% to 10% self-funded enrollment growth, and 9% premium rate hikes. Enrollment will benefit from further penetration of the Virginia market and launch of four low-cost health plans. Second quarter commercial enrollment rose 5.0%, aided by a 15% gain in PPO members. We expect 8% to 9% commercial medical cost inflation, among the lowest in TGH's peer group. The commercial medical loss ratio (MLR) deteriorated to 81.4%, from 81.1% in 2000, on higher than anticipated utilization. We project MLR of 80.6%, flat with 2000. Despite higher spending on Internet initiatives, the SG&A cost ratio should improve, on utilization of new technology. For 2002, we see revenue up 13%, modest enrollment growth and slight margin improvement.

Valuation - 15-AUG-01

We are maintaining our accumulate opinion on TGH, reflecting its consistent earnings growth, strong market position, and focus on Virginia. In an environment of accelerating medical cost inflation, we believe TGH's cost controls and narrow focus on an economically vibrant market will continue to deliver consistent EPS growth. Focus on commercial accounts and flexible plan offerings have led to member retention of over 95% in the large group segment. TGH continues to use excess cash flow to repurchase stock, but is seeking to acquire a neighboring Blue Cross plan. Through mid-August, the shares were down about 10% in 2001, versus 15% for TGH's peer group. We project 2001 EPS growth of 30%, above TGH's historical trend. With 35% penetration of Virginia, TGH has room for growth. At 14X our 2002 EPS estimate, in line with peer levels, TGH should outperform.

Key Stock Statistics

S&P EPS Est. 2001	4.08	Tang. Bk. Value/Share	26.63
P/E on S&P Est. 2001	16.2	Beta	NA
S&P EPS Est. 2002	4.80	Shareholders	76,708
Dividend Rate/Share	Nil	Market cap. (B)	$ 2.4
Shs. outstg. (M)	36.4	Inst. holdings	69%
Avg. daily vol. (M)	0.216		

Value of $10,000 invested 5 years ago: NA

Fiscal Year Ending Dec. 31

	2001	2000	1999	1998	1997	1996
Revenues (Million $)						
1Q	728.2	629.2	556.5	551.8	511.8	—
2Q	722.7	645.2	587.9	542.3	510.0	—
3Q	—	666.5	590.4	544.9	524.1	1,318
4Q	—	670.7	611.6	597.3	517.7	545.1
Yr.	—	2,612	2,346	2,236	2,064	1,863
Earnings Per Share ($)						
1Q	**0.84**	**0.73**	**0.28**	**0.80**	—	—
2Q	**0.71**	**0.75**	**0.43**	**0.48**	—	—
3Q	—	**0.88**	**-0.91**	**0.47**	—	1.46
4Q	—	**0.54**	**0.70**	**1.13**	—	1.30
Yr.	—	**2.90**	**0.49**	**2.88**	**1.86**	**2.73**

Next earnings report expected: early November

Dividend Data

The company has not paid cash dividends on its common stock. TGH anticipates that all earnings for the foreseeable future will be retained to finance the continuing development of its business. A preferred stock purchase rights plan was adopted in July 1997.

Trigon Healthcare, Inc.

Business Summary - 15-AUG-01

Trigon Healthcare is the largest managed health care company in Virginia, serving approximately 2.1 million members primarily through statewide and regional provider networks. The company's membership represents about 28% of the Virginia population (34% of the population in those areas in which TGH has the exclusive right to use the Blue Cross and Blue Shield service marks and trade names).

The company divides its business into four segments: health insurance, government programs, investments and other. The health insurance segment provides a comprehensive spectrum of managed care products primarily through three network systems with a range of utilization and cost containment controls. Within the network product offerings, employer groups may choose various funding options, ranging from fully insured to partly or fully self-funded financial arrangements.

At June 30, 2001, fully insured (also referred to as commercial) products made up 53% of total enrollment. Components include HMO networks (285,246 members), the company's most tightly managed and cost efficient networks; preferred provider organization (PPO) networks (509,011 members), which offer greater choice of providers than HMO networks; and the participating provider (PAR) network (126,692 members), the company's broadest and most flexible network. Commercial products also include Medicare supplement plans (120,562 members) and the Medicaid/Medicare HMO plans (58,465 members).

Self-funded enrollment as of June 30, 2001, was 754,317 members (36% of total enrollment). Self-funded arrangements are available to groups with more than 100 employees, and are typically used by groups with more than 1,000 employees. TGH charges self-funded groups an administrative fee based on the number of members in the group, or on the group's claims experience. In addition, most self-funded groups purchase aggregate and/or claim specific stop loss coverage.

The government segment, which includes the Federal Employee Program (FEP) and claims processing for Medicare, provides health benefits to 222,425 federal employees as of June 30, 2001.

TGH is targeting the densely populated eastern and northern regions of Virginia, where its market share is lowest, for much of its new growth in that state. In addition, the company is looking to expand outside of Virginia.

In May 2000, the company sold Mid-South Insurance Co. to World Insurance Co. Mid-South provides health care coverage for about 25,000 people in several southeastern states, including North Carolina, South Carolina and Georgia.

TGH plans to transfer the administration services provided by its Employee Benefits unit of Trigon Administrators to Ceridian Benefits Services by August 2001.

Per Share Data ($)										
(Year Ended Dec. 31)	**2000**	**1999**	**1998**	**1997**	**1996**	**1995**	**1994**	**1993**	**1992**	**1991**
Tangible Bk. Val.	26.63	24.15	23.84	21.05	18.62	17.16	NA	NA	NA	NA
Cash Flow	3.29	0.49	2.89	2.25	5.06	1.12	NA	NA	NA	NA
Earnings	2.90	0.49	2.88	1.86	2.73	0.86	NA	NA	NA	NA
Dividends	Nil	Nil	Nil	Nil	Nil	Nil	NA	NA	NA	NA
Payout Ratio	Nil	Nil	Nil	Nil	Nil	Nil	NA	NA	NA	NA
Prices - High	81.50	39.00	38.37	27.25	NA	NA	NA	NA	NA	NA
- Low	26.87	21.50	23.50	15.37	NA	NA	NA	NA	NA	NA
P/E Ratio - High	28	80	13	15	NA	NA	NA	NA	NA	NA
- Low	9	44	8	8	NA	NA	NA	NA	NA	NA
Income Statement Analysis (Million $)										
Revs.	2,612	2,346	2,236	2,064	1,863	1,571	NA	NA	NA	NA
Oper. Inc.	198	39.9	195	150	78.3	71.0	NA	NA	NA	NA
Depr.	15.3	NA	NA	NA	17.1	11.0	NA	NA	NA	NA
Int. Exp.	17.2	8.4	5.3	4.6	18.9	5.3	NA	NA	NA	NA
Pretax Inc.	166	31.5	187	145	183	54.7	NA	NA	NA	NA
Eff. Tax Rate	30%	26%	34%	34%	NM	35%	NA	NA	NA	NA
Net Inc.	112	20.5	124	95.1	197	35.6	NA	NA	NA	NA
Balance Sheet & Other Fin. Data (Million $)										
Cash	6.3	2.5	7.5	7.0	1,214	1,158	NA	NA	NA	NA
Curr. Assets	2,300	2,169	1,979	1,739	1,632	1,556	NA	NA	NA	NA
Total Assets	2,448	2,314	2,174	1,929	1,833	1,769	NA	NA	NA	NA
Curr. Liab.	1,026	1,004	875	748	891	772	NA	NA	NA	NA
LT Debt	275	248	89.3	216	85.0	92.4	NA	NA	NA	NA
Common Eqty.	1,015	937	1,071	959	864	808	NA	NA	NA	NA
Total Cap.	1,303	1,195	1,169	1,181	953	905	NA	NA	NA	NA
Cap. Exp.	35.5	17.8	16.9	8.2	14.1	13.3	NA	NA	NA	NA
Cash Flow	127	20.5	124	95.1	214	46.5	NA	NA	NA	NA
Curr. Ratio	2.2	2.2	2.3	2.3	1.8	2.0	NA	NA	NA	NA
% LT Debt of Cap.	21.1	20.7	7.6	18.3	8.9	10.2	NA	NA	NA	NA
% Net Inc.of Revs.	NA	3.5	19.9	4.6	10.6	NA	NA	NA	NA	NA
% Ret. on Assets	4.7	0.9	6.0	5.1	10.9	NA	NA	NA	NA	NA
% Ret. on Equity	11.5	2.0	12.2	11.2	23.5	NA	NA	NA	NA	NA

Data as orig. reptd.; bef. results of disc. opers. and/or spec. items. Per share data adj. for stk. divs. as of ex-div. date. Bold denotes diluted EPS (FASB 128). E-Estimated. NA-Not Available. NM-Not Meaningful. NR-Not Ranked.

Office—2015 Staples Mill Rd., Richmond, VA 23230 (Mailing Address: P.O. Box 27401, Richmond, VA 23279). **Tel**—(804) 354-7000. **Website**—www.trigon.com **Chrmn & CEO**—T. G. Snead Jr. **Pres & COO**—J. W. Coyle. **SVP & CFO**—T. R. Byrd. **SVP & Secy**—J. C. Wiltshire. **Investor Contact**—Chris Drake (804-354-3463). **Dirs**—L. D. Baker Jr., A. H. Ewing III, R. M. Freeman, W. R. Harvey, G. A. Jobson, J. S. Mallory, D. B. Nolan, W. N. Powell, J. Sherman Jr., R. G. Smith, T. G. Snead Jr., H. R. Stallard, J. M. Ward. **Transfer Agent & Registrar**—Bank of New York. **Incorporated**—in Virginia in 1996. **Empl**— 3,917. **S&P Analyst:** John A. Massey

STANDARD
&POOR'S
STOCK REPORTS

Universal Health Services

NYSE Symbol **UHS**

In S&P SmallCap 600

18-AUG-01

Industry:
Health Care (Hospital Management)

Summary: This company owns and operates acute care medical/surgical/psychiatric hospitals, as well as outpatient surgery and radiation therapy centers nationwide.

S&P Opinion: Accumulate (★★★★)

Recent Price • 48.80 | Yield • Nil
52 Wk Range • 56.46-31.62 | 12-Mo. P/E • 28.0

Quantitative Evaluations

Outlook
(1 Lowest—5 Highest)
• **3+**

Fair Value
• **51**

Risk
• **Low**

Earn./Div. Rank
• **B+**

Technical Eval.
• **Bullish** since 6/01

Rel. Strength Rank
(1 Lowest—99 Highest)
• **74**

Insider Activity
• **Unfavorable**

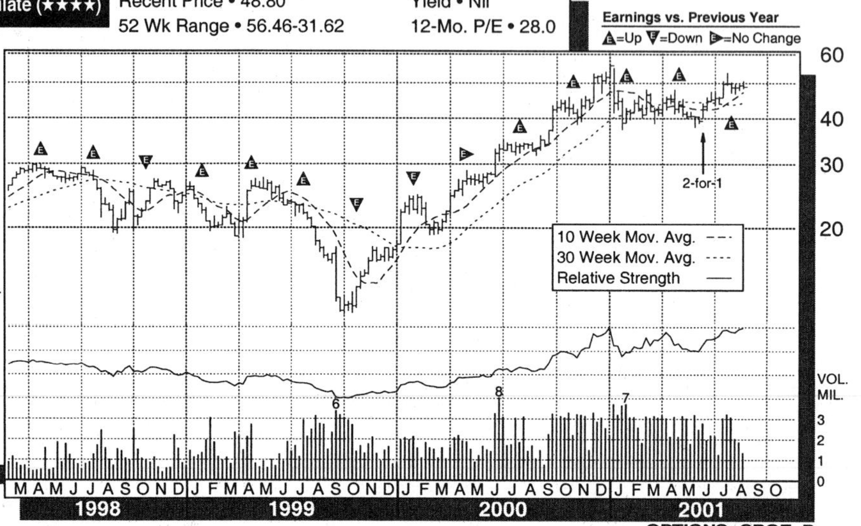

OPTIONS: CBOE, P

Overview - 14-AUG-01

We look for revenue growth of about 16% in 2001, as same-store acute care admissions growth of 2% to 3% combines with strong performance in the behavioral care division and improved private pay and Medicare pricing. Within the behavioral care unit, revenue growth should continue to be bolstered by acquisitions, while same-store pricing and admission trends stay robust; these operations (20% of net revenues) are an important driver of growth. Acquisitions are likely to be part of the company-wide growth strategy. On the margin front, UHS is experiencing significant inflation in both labor and pharmaceutical costs which, along with increased bad debt provisions, should eliminate any significant margin growth opportunities. As adjusted for a recent 2-for-1 split, we look for 2001 EPS of $1.97 and envision a 14% advance to $2.25 in 2002.

Valuation - 14-AUG-01

The stock has weakened in 2001, much in contrast with the majority of the hospital management sector, but we believe that UHS should ultimately benefit from the protracted investor rotation into the healthcare provider group, and the hospital group in particular. While the company's operating margins remain at the low end of the for-profit hospital peer group average, largely reflecting certain acquisitions, there is a good opportunity for UHS to generate margin expansion as these facilities are absorbed into the company's hospital network. The company maintains an attractive portfolio of hospitals in its asset base, with about 80% of these facilities ranked number one or two in their respective markets. Recently trading at only 22X our 2002 EPS estimate, and only 1.3X projected 2002 sales, UHS is selling at a sizable discount to its hospital peers.

Key Stock Statistics

S&P EPS Est. 2001	1.97	Tang. Bk. Value/Share	6.68
P/E on S&P Est. 2001	24.8	Beta	0.59
S&P EPS Est. 2002	2.25	Shareholders	528
Dividend Rate/Share	Nil	Market cap. (B)	$ 2.7
Shs. outstg. (M)	60.0	Inst. holdings	0%
Avg. daily vol. (M)	0.442		

Value of $10,000 invested 5 years ago: $ 38,330

Fiscal Year Ending Dec. 31

	2001	2000	1999	1998	1997	1996
Revenues (Million $)						
1Q	677.0	541.0	520.1	463.1	340.2	271.6
2Q	718.6	524.8	513.1	474.6	343.8	287.0
3Q	—	561.8	489.8	456.1	362.4	303.5
4Q	—	614.8	519.4	480.7	396.3	328.1
Yr.	—	2,242	2,042	1,874	1,443	1,190
Earnings Per Share ($)						
1Q	**0.57**	**0.46**	**0.46**	**0.39**	**0.33**	**0.27**
2Q	**0.51**	**0.38**	**0.35**	**0.30**	**0.26**	**0.21**
3Q	**E0.44**	**0.36**	**0.17**	**0.20**	**0.21**	**0.17**
4Q	**E0.45**	**0.31**	**0.23**	**0.30**	**0.23**	**0.18**
Yr.	**E1.97**	**1.50**	**1.22**	**1.20**	**1.01**	**0.82**

Next earnings report expected: mid October

Dividend Data

Amount ($)	Date Decl.	Ex-Div. Date	Stock of Record	Payment Date
2-for-1	Apr. 27	Jun. 04	May. 16	Jun. 01 '01

Universal Health Services, Inc.

Business Summary - 14-AUG-01

Universal Health Services (UHS) is one of the largest investor-owned hospital chains in the U.S., with 2000 revenues of $2.2 billion. At 2000 year end, UHS operated 23 acute care hospitals, 35 behavioral care centers, 25 ambulatory surgery and radiation oncology centers, and a specialized women's center in Arkansas, California, Delaware, the District of Columbia, Florida, Georgia, Illinois, Indiana, Kentucky, Louisiana, Massachusetts, Michigan, Mississippi, Missouri, Nevada, New Jersey, Oklahoma, Pennsylvania, Puerto Rico, South Carolina, Tennessee, Texas, Utah and Washington.

Services provided by the acute care hospitals include general surgery, internal medicine, obstetrics, emergency room care, radiology, oncology, diagnostic care, coronary care, pediatric services and psychiatric services. UHS provides capital resources as well as various management services to its facilities, including central purchasing, data processing, finance and control systems, facilities planning, physician recruitment services, administrative personnel management, marketing, and public relations.

During 2000, net patient revenues came from Medicare (32%), Medicaid (11%), managed care (35%) and other sources (22%).

UHS selectively seeks opportunities to expand its operations by acquiring, constructing or leasing additional hospital facilities. In addition, it aims to increase the operating revenues and profitability of its hospitals by introducing new services, improving existing services, physician recruitment, and the application of financial and operational controls. UHS will also dispose of facilities that do not have the potential to contribute to its growth or operating strategy.

In August 2000, UHS acquired 12 behavioral health facilities from bankrupt Charter Behavioral Health Systems, together with the associated real estate, and one additional behavioral health facility from Crescent Real Estate Funding VII L.P., for about $105 million.

During 2000, acute care hospitals operated by the company had an average of 4,980 licensed beds (4,806 in 1999), while admissions rose 5.0% to 214,771. The average length of stay held firm at 4.7 days, patient days totaled 1,017,646 (963,842), and the average occupancy rate per licensed bed was 56% (55%). At the behavioral care centers, licensed beds averaged 2,612 (1,976), admissions totaled 49,971 (37,810), average length of stay was 12.2 days (11.8), patient days reached 608,423 (444,632), and average occupancy rate per licensed bed was 64% (62%).

During 2000, the company purchased or agreed to purchase three acute care hospitals and 15 behavioral care centers with combined annual revenues of $310 million. Total consideration for these facilities will approximate $215 million.

The company acts as adviser to Universal Health Realty Income Trust (NYSE: UHT), which leases to UHS the real property of six UHS facilities. UHS receives an advisory service fee and owns 8.5% of UHT's shares.

Per Share Data ($) (Year Ended Dec. 31)	2000	1999	1998	1997	1996	1995	1994	1993	1992	1991
Tangible Bk. Val.	6.68	5.79	5.40	5.81	4.70	2.89	4.02	3.46	3.10	2.59
Cash Flow	3.18	2.91	2.78	2.24	1.99	1.54	1.24	1.07	0.93	0.92
Earnings	1.50	1.22	1.20	1.01	0.82	0.63	0.51	0.43	0.36	0.36
Dividends	Nil	Nil	Nil	Nil	Nil	Nil	Nil	Nil	Nil	Nil
Payout Ratio	Nil	Nil	Nil	Nil	Nil	Nil	Nil	Nil	Nil	Nil
Prices - High	56.46	27.56	29.87	25.40	15.37	11.12	7.40	5.30	3.93	4.59
- Low	18.06	11.56	19.21	13.87	10.81	5.62	4.78	3.12	2.78	2.03
P/E Ratio - High	38	23	25	25	19	18	15	12	11	13
- Low	12	10	16	14	13	9	9	7	8	6
Income Statement Analysis (Million $)										
Revs.	2,242	2,042	1,874	1,443	1,190	931	781	747	699	686
Oper. Inc.	359	485	404	315	177	127	104	81.0	69.0	68.0
Depr.	113	108	105	80.7	71.9	51.4	42.4	39.6	35.6	35.0
Int. Exp.	29.9	26.9	29.7	19.4	21.4	11.8	6.5	9.1	11.9	10.3
Pretax Inc.	160	129	132	106	80.0	53.0	46.9	35.1	41.0	30.3
Eff. Tax Rate	33%	35%	33%	36%	37%	33%	39%	32%	51%	33%
Net Inc.	93.4	77.8	79.6	67.3	50.7	35.5	28.7	24.0	20.0	20.3
Balance Sheet & Other Fin. Data (Million $)										
Cash	10.5	6.2	1.3	0.3	0.3	0.0	0.8	0.6	6.7	22.7
Curr. Assets	476	403	320	230	194	157	118	102	119	141
Total Assets	1,742	1,498	1,448	1,085	966	749	521	460	472	501
Curr. Liab.	249	217	170	160	140	135	104	86.0	85.0	127
LT Debt	548	419	418	272	276	237	85.0	75.0	115	127
Common Eqty.	717	642	627	527	453	298	261	224	203	184
Total Cap.	1,422	1,207	1,198	799	729	535	346	303	327	326
Cap. Exp.	114	67.6	96.8	129	106	60.7	59.0	59.0	44.0	55.0
Cash Flow	206	186	185	148	123	86.9	71.1	63.6	55.6	55.3
Curr. Ratio	1.9	1.9	1.9	1.4	1.4	1.2	1.1	1.2	1.4	1.1
% LT Debt of Cap.	38.5	34.7	34.9	34.0	37.8	44.3	24.6	24.7	35.2	39.0
% Net Inc.of Revs.	4.2	3.8	4.2	4.7	4.3	3.8	3.7	3.2	2.9	3.0
% Ret. on Assets	5.8	5.3	6.3	6.6	5.9	5.6	5.8	5.2	4.1	3.9
% Ret. on Equity	13.7	12.3	13.8	13.7	13.5	12.7	11.7	11.3	10.4	11.5

Data as orig reptd.; bef. results of disc opers/spec. items. Per share data adj. for stk. divs. Bold denotes diluted EPS (FASB 128)-prior periods restated. E-Estimated. NA-Not Available. NM-Not Meaningful. NR-Not Ranked.

Office—367 South Gulph Rd., P.O. Box 61558, King of Prussia, PA 19406-0958. **Tel**—(610) 768-3300. **Website**—http://www.uhsinc.com **Chrmn, Pres & CEO**—A. B. Miller. **SVP, CFO & Investor Contact**—Kirk E. Gorman. **VP, Contr & Secy**—S.G. Filton. **Dirs**—J. H. Herrell, R. H. Hotz, L. Ducat, A. B. Miller, S. Miller, A. Pantaleoni, J. T. Sabastianelli, J. F. Williams Jr. **Transfer Agent & Registrar**—Mellon Investor Services, Ridgefield Park, NJ. **Incorporated**—in Delaware in 1978. **Empl**— 25,600. **S&P Analyst:** Robert M. Gold

STANDARD &POOR'S
STOCK REPORTS

WellPoint Health Networks

NYSE Symbol **WLP**

In S&P 500

18-AUG-01

Industry: Health Care (Managed Care)

Summary: WellPoint operates a managed care network serving more than 9.8 million medical and more than 40.0 million specialty members.

S&P Opinion: Accumulate (★★★★) Recent Price • 103.12 | 52 Wk Range • 121.50-79.50 | Yield • Nil | 12-Mo. P/E • 17.9

Quantitative Evaluations

Outlook (1 Lowest—5 Highest)
• **4-**

Fair Value
• **114.50**

Risk
• **Average**

Earn./Div. Rank
• **B+**

Technical Eval.
• **Neutral** since 8/01

Rel. Strength Rank (1 Lowest—99 Highest)
• **79**

Insider Activity
• **NA**

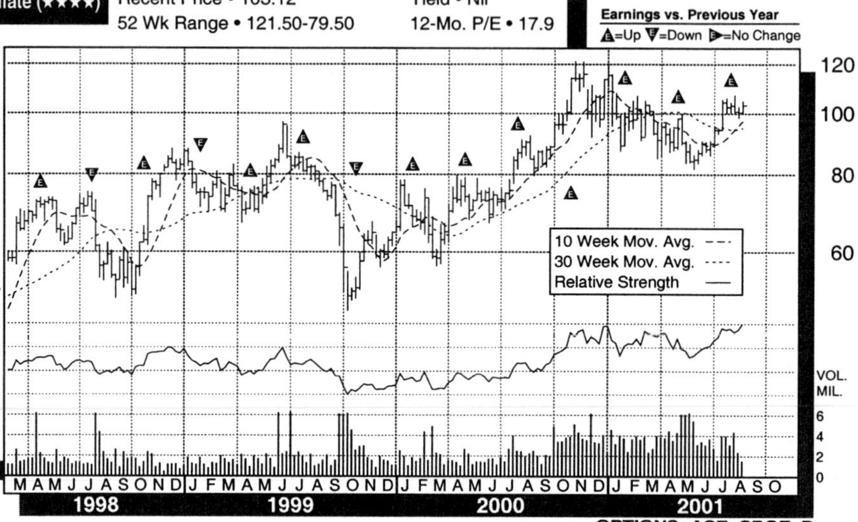

OPTIONS: ASE, CBOE, P

Overview - 30-JUL-01

Second quarter results exceeded our expectations, driven by higher than projected enrollment growth. For 2001, we see revenues climbing over 30%, from the full-year benefit of Rush Prudential Health Plans, acquisition of Cerulean, mid-single-digit organic enrollment growth, and commercial rate hikes of 8.5% in California and 10%-12% elsewhere. The Cerulean acquisition was completed March 15. Enrollment should benefit from the introduction of new "value" plans this summer, which will be targeted toward cost conscious members and the uninsured. In addition, WLP is developing a novel multi-tier copayment plan for health care providers with different contract terms, similar to a pharmacy three-tier co-payment plan. Despite medical cost inflation of 7.5%-8.0% in 2001, we expect the consolidated medical loss ratio to deteriorate modestly, reflecting Rush Prudential's and Cerulean's higher loss ratios.

Valuation - 30-JUL-01

We are maintaining our accumulate opinion on WLP. We view WLP as one of the best positioned managed care companies, in part due to its consistent, high quality earnings, but we think the slowing economy could lower enrollment growth. Furthermore, the acquisition of Cerulean, with its lower profit margins, adds an element of risk. However, WLP's flexible plan offerings and stable rate hikes should drive market share gains at the expense of weak competitors. WLP continues to navigate the litigious and legislative landscape by focusing on expanding small group commercial membership. With only a slight contribution from government funded programs, stable earnings, and a healthy balance sheet, WLP remains a strong performer. Based on its industry leading margins, we believe the stock can command a premium P/E multiple. Trading at 14.5X our 2002 EPS estimate, WLP should outperform.

Key Stock Statistics

S&P EPS Est. 2001	6.21	Tang. Bk. Value/Share	16.89
P/E on S&P Est. 2001	16.6	Beta	0.53
S&P EPS Est. 2002	7.10	Shareholders	555
Dividend Rate/Share	Nil	Market cap. (B)	$ 6.5
Shs. outstg. (M)	63.3	Inst. holdings	93%
Avg. daily vol. (M)	0.557		

Value of $10,000 invested 5 years ago: $ 37,920

Fiscal Year Ending Dec. 31

	2001	2000	1999	1998	1997	1996
Revenues (Million $)						
1Q	2,615	2,145	1,771	1,584	1,272	817.6
2Q	3,145	2,289	1,857	1,562	1,486	1,065
3Q	—	2,353	1,892	1,629	1,512	1,131
4Q	—	2,442	1,966	1,704	1,558	1,156
Yr.	—	9,229	7,485	6,479	5,826	4,170
Earnings Per Share ($)						
1Q	**1.48**	**1.23**	**1.04**	**0.95**	0.76	**0.91**
2Q	**1.53**	**1.30**	**1.03**	**0.45**	**0.70**	**0.75**
3Q	**E1.63**	**1.38**	**1.11**	**2.16**	**0.79**	**0.68**
4Q	**E1.57**	**1.37**	**1.20**	**0.99**	**1.02**	**0.71**
Yr.	**E6.21**	**5.29**	**4.38**	**4.55**	**3.27**	**3.04**

Next earnings report expected: NA

Dividend Data

Regular cash dividends have never been paid. A special dividend of $10 a share was paid in May 1996.

A Division of The McGraw-Hill Companies

WellPoint Health Networks Inc.

Business Summary - 30-JUL-01

WellPoint Health Networks, the former not-for-profit California Blue Cross health plan, has become one of the largest investor-owned managed care companies in the U.S. Principal products are the health maintenance organization (HMO), preferred provider organization (PPO) and Point-of-Service (POS) health plans. WLP also offers a range of specialty health care products, marketed either as separate plans or incorporated into broader medical plans. At June 31, 2001, WLP had total medical membership of 9.8 million, up from 7.6 million a year earlier. By geographic markets, members were located in California (58%), Georgia (19%), Illinois (5.3%), Texas (3.7%), and other states (13%). Specialty services are provided to more than 42 million individuals.

The company's HMO plans are marketed primarily in California under the Blue Cross banner and outside of California principally under the UNICARE name. WLP provides health care services through a network of about 31,000 primary care and specialist physicians, and about 427 hospitals in California. Outside of California, the company provides services through a network of 92,700 primary care and specialist physicians and 870 hospitals. The networks include both multi-specialty medical group practices and individual practice associations. Substantially all network physician services are reimbursed on a capitated basis specifying fixed per member per month payments to providers.

About 61% of California members are in WLP's PPO plan. WLP's PPO provider network includes about 48,000 physicians and 440 hospitals. PPO plans are similar to HMO plans, in that they provide for health care delivery at lower costs than traditional health insurance, but members have the option to receive care from providers who are not part of the network, typically at substantial out-of-pocket costs.

Through its specialty care networks, WLP provides pharmacy (29 million members at December 31, 2000), dental (2.2 million), utilization management (2.1 million), as well as life insurance (2.0 million) and products to individuals covered through disability insurance (569,000) and behavioral health (4.4 million).

WLP also offers Medicare supplemental plans, which typically pay the difference between the health care cost incurred and the amount paid by Medicare while utilizing the PPO and HMO provider networks.

In March 2001, WLP acquired Cerulean Companies Inc., which, through its Blue Cross Blue Shield of Georgia subsidiary, offers insured and administrative service products primarily in Georgia, for $700 million in cash. As of December 31, 2000, Cerulean served 1.8 million medical members.

In March 2000, the company acquired Chicago-based Rush Prudential Health Plans, for approximately $200 million. At December 31, 1999, Rush served 300,000 medical members, primarily in the Chicago area.

Per Share Data ($) (Year Ended Dec. 31)	2000	1999	1998	1997	1996	1995	1994	1993	1992	1991
Tangible Bk. Val.	16.89	14.28	13.19	7.52	4.78	15.53	12.83	12.39	NA	9.41
Cash Flow	6.42	5.75	5.34	4.09	3.61	2.02	2.30	1.91	1.78	1.47
Earnings	5.29	4.38	4.55	3.27	3.04	1.81	2.14	1.88	1.76	1.45
Dividends	Nil	Nil	Nil	Nil	10.00	Nil	Nil	Nil	Nil	NA
Payout Ratio	Nil	Nil	Nil	Nil	NM	Nil	Nil	Nil	Nil	NA
Prices - High	121.50	97.00	87.87	61.12	39.12	37.00	37.00	39.75	NA	NA
- Low	56.93	48.25	42.06	32.50	23.37	27.00	24.25	23.00	NA	NA
P/E Ratio - High	23	22	19	19	13	20	17	21	NA	NA
- Low	11	11	9	10	8	15	11	12	NA	NA
Income Statement Analysis (Million $)										
Revs.	9,229	7,485	6,478	5,826	4,170	3,107	2,792	2,449	2,275	1,927
Oper. Inc.	710	617	501	525	434	395	375	320	294	230
Depr.	75.4	68.8	55.0	57.1	37.7	22.0	15.2	3.8	2.1	2.4
Int. Exp.	24.0	20.2	26.9	36.7	36.6	Nil	Nil	Nil	Nil	Nil
Pretax Inc.	564	487	392	382	340	303	352	313	289	225
Eff. Tax Rate	39%	39%	19%	41%	41%	41%	39%	40%	40%	38%
Net Inc.	342	297	320	227	202	180	213	187	175	140
Balance Sheet & Other Fin. Data (Million $)										
Cash	567	505	411	284	313	1,070	371	112	78.0	NA
Curr. Assets	4,500	3,816	3,434	3,506	2,538	2,463	586	321	224	NA
Total Assets	5,505	4,593	4,226	4,533	3,406	2,679	2,386	1,927	1,156	1,556
Curr. Liab.	3,073	2,527	2,183	2,344	1,545	840	875	655	648	NA
LT Debt	401	348	300	388	625	Nil	Nil	Nil	Nil	Nil
Common Eqty.	2,220	1,885	1,315	1,223	870	1,670	1,419	1,233	507	913
Total Cap.	2,621	2,233	1,615	1,611	1,495	1,670	1,419	1,233	507	913
Cap. Exp.	46.9	39.0	78.0	58.4	43.3	25.2	22.1	13.1	5.1	2.4
Cash Flow	418	366	375	284	240	202	228	190	177	143
Curr. Ratio	1.5	1.5	1.6	1.5	1.6	2.9	0.7	0.5	0.3	NA
% LT Debt of Cap.	15.3	15.6	18.6	24.1	41.8	Nil	Nil	Nil	Nil	Nil
% Net Inc.of Revs.	3.7	4.0	4.9	3.9	4.9	5.8	7.6	7.6	7.7	7.3
% Ret. on Assets	6.8	6.7	7.3	5.7	6.7	7.0	9.9	NA	NA	NA
% Ret. on Equity	16.7	15.5	25.2	21.7	15.9	11.6	16.1	NA	NA	NA

Data as orig. reptd.; bef. results of disc. opers. and/or spec. items. Per share data adj. for stk. divs. as of ex-div. date. Bold denotes diluted EPS (FASB 128). E-Estimated. NA-Not Available. NM-Not Meaningful. NR-Not Ranked.

Office—1 Wellpoint Way, Thousand Oaks, CA 91362. **Tel**—(805) 557-6789. **Website**—www.wellpoint.com **Chrmn & CEO**—L. D. Schaeffer. **EVP & CFO**—D. C. Colby. **EVP & Secy**—T. C. Geiser. **VP & Investor Contact**—John Cygul (805-557-6789). **Dirs**—W. T. Besson, R. E. Birk, S. Burke, S. L. Davenport, J. A. Hill, W. Y. Jobe, E. A. Sanders, L. D. Schaeffer. **Transfer Agent & Registrar**—Mellon Investor Services, Ridgefield Park, NJ. **Incorporated**—in Delaware in 1992. **Empl**— 10,900. **S&P Analyst:** John A. Massey

Part Six

Industrials Stocks

STANDARD
&POOR'S
STOCK REPORTS

Canadian National Railway

NYSE Symbol **CNI**

18-AUG-01 **Industry:** Railroads

Summary: CNI operates Canada's largest railroad. In January 2001, it agreed to acquire Wisconsin Central Transportation Co. for $1.2 billion.

S&P Opinion: Buy (★★★★★)

Recent Price • 43.54 | Yield • 1.2%
52 Wk Range • 46.44-26.87 | 12-Mo. P/E • NM

Quantitative Evaluations

Outlook
(1 Lowest—5 Highest)
• **NA**

Fair Value
• **NA**

Risk
• **NA**

Earn./Div. Rank
• **NR**

Technical Eval.
• **Bullish** since 7/01

Rel. Strength Rank
(1 Lowest—99 Highest)
• **68**

Insider Activity
• **NA**

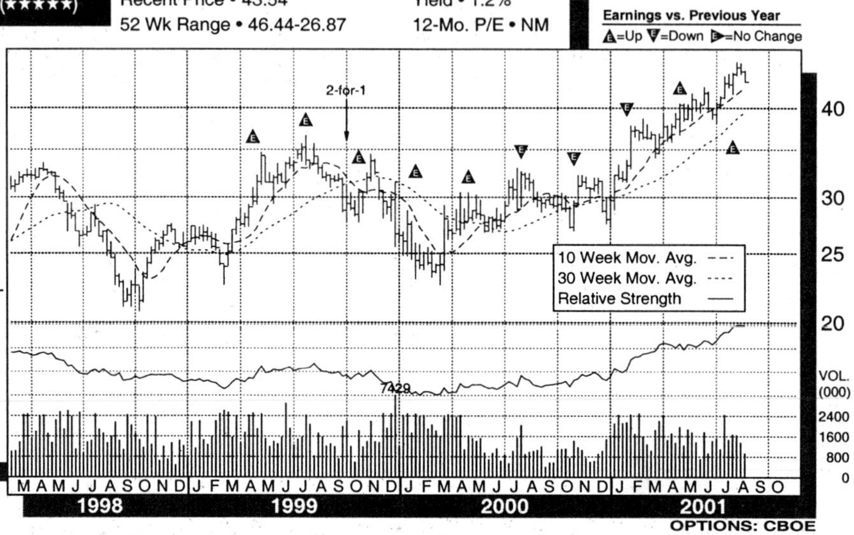

OPTIONS: CBOE

Overview - 07-AUG-01

Revenues (in Canadian dollars) may increase 6.0% in 2002, up from the 4% estimated for 2001. Continued strength is seen for intermodal shipments, reflecting growing international trade and market share gains. CNI should also benefit from increased demand for coal, as power producers look to offset high natural gas prices. Other areas that may yield positive results include metals and minerals, and grains and fertilizers. CNI's operating margin will improve in 2002. The railroad's high on-time performance is boosting asset and labor productivity. Margins will also benefit from lower operating taxes and moderating fuel prices. We see 2002 EPS of C$5.80, up from 2001's C$4.96 estimate ($3.79 and $3.24, respectively, using the August 3, 2001, exchange rate of $0.6537/C$1.00). The 2001 total excludes special items that would add C$0.26 to EPS.

Valuation - 07-AUG-01

The shares of this Canadian railroad rallied following the announcement in July 2000 that it had ditched a proposed merger with Burlington Northern Santa Fe (BNI). We liked the transaction, but investors pummeled the shares when the deal was announced in late 1999, because of the poor track record of rail mergers. In January 2001, the company agreed to acquire Wisconsin Central Transportation for $1.2 billion. The acquisition, which is subject to regulatory approval, would give CNI greater access to the Chicago market, expand its market share lead in the transport of forest products, and let it improve asset utilization. The shares carry P/E and price to growth ratios well below the average for the company's peer group. With CNI enjoying the widest profit margins in the industry, we believe the stock is undervalued, and recommend purchase.

Key Stock Statistics

S&P EPS Est. 2001	4.96	Tang. Bk. Value/Share	28.12
P/E on S&P Est. 2001	NA	Beta	0.73
S&P EPS Est. 2002	5.80	Shareholders	35,000
Dividend Rate/Share	0.78	Market cap. (B)	$ 8.3
Shs. outstg. (M)	190.6	Inst. holdings	62%
Avg. daily vol. (M)	0.277		

Value of $10,000 invested 5 years ago: $ 50,874

Fiscal Year Ending Dec. 31

	2001	2000	1999	1998	1997	1996
Revenues (Million Can. $)						
1Q	1,398	1,379	1,018	1,059	1,033	1,015
2Q	1,392	1,337	1,055	1,030	1,126	1,064
3Q	—	1,334	1,284	967.0	1,068	1,000
4Q	—	1,396	1,387	1,065	1,125	1,080
Yr.	—	5,446	5,261	4,121	4,352	4,159
Earnings Per Share (Can. $)						
1Q	**1.39**	**1.20**	**0.71**	**0.60**	—	0.48
2Q	**1.10**	**0.92**	**1.00**	**0.80**	—	0.73
3Q	**E1.30**	**0.80**	**0.96**	**-1.07**	—	0.59
4Q	**E1.42**	**0.87**	**1.03**	**0.94**	—	-1.08
Yr.	**E4.96**	**3.81**	**3.02**	**1.21**	**2.48**	0.73

Next earnings report expected: late October

Dividend Data (Dividends have been paid since 1996.)

Amount (Can. $)	Date Decl.	Ex-Div. Date	Stock of Record	Payment Date
0.175	Oct. 23	Dec. 06	Dec. 08	Dec. 29 '00
0.195	Jan. 23	Mar. 06	Mar. 08	Mar. 29 '01
0.195	Apr. 23	Jun. 05	Jun. 07	Jun. 28 '01
0.195	Jul. 23	Sep. 05	Sep. 07	Sep. 28 '01

A Division of The McGraw-Hill Companies

Canadian National Railway Company

Business Summary - 07-AUG-01

Canadian National Railway, which was controlled by the Canadian government until November 1995, operates the largest Canadian railroad. In December 1999, CNI and Burlington Northern Santa Fe Corp. agreed to merge their railroads. However, as a result of regulatory obstacles, the transaction was terminated by mutual agreement in July 2000. The acquisition of Illinois Central in 1999 established CNI as the only rail system to offer service throughout North America. Unlike other railroads, CNI has been operating with scheduled train service since 1998.

In December 1999, CNI agreed to merge with Burlington Northern Santa Fe Corp. (BNI), operator of a major western U.S. railroad. The merger would have created North America's largest railroad, a 50,000 mile system spanning from the Pacific to the Atlantic coasts and extend south through the U.S. Midwest and Gulf of Mexico. Because of significant regulatory obstacles, Canadian National and BNI terminated the agreement in July 2000. CNI said it would continue to strengthen its ties with BNI, and to capture system improvements and efficiencies, while the two remain separate entities. In November 2000, a marketing agreement was announced under which both railroads will be able to price and market traffic in the western U.S. and Canada.

In 1999, CNI acquired Illinois Central Railroad creating a combined system spanning 15,777 miles, linking the Pacific, Atlantic and Gulf Coasts. Service to Mexico is provided through an alliance with Kansas City Southern Railway. The combination with Illinois Central, which operates a 3,450 mile rail network running south from Chicago to the Gulf of Mexico, facilitates the movement of cross-border traffic.

The combined CNI/IC rail system moved 3,796,000 carloads of traffic in 2000. Grain and fertilizers generated 22% of revenues while forest products accounted for 19%, petroleum and chemicals (17%) and intermodal shipments (18%).

Since late 1998, CNI has been offering scheduled train service. Typically, railroads hold up trains until enough cars accumulate. With a time schedule, CNI may run shorter trains, but has realized greater operating efficiency since the peaks and valleys of service are smoothed out. In 2000, 90% of the company's trains met their scheduled time of arrival. CNI's 30.4% operating margin in 2000 was the highest of any major North American railroad.

Approximately 80% of CNI's work force is comprised of unionized employees. As of February 2001, about 70% of these employees had bargaining agreements that had already expired or would expire in 2001.

Per Share Data (U.S. $) (Year Ended Dec. 31)	2000	1999	1998	1997	1996	1995	1994	1993	1992	1991
Tangible Bk. Val.	18.84	17.44	14.54	13.96	10.23	7.23	7.36	NA	NA	NA
Cash Flow	3.87	3.17	1.18	2.63	1.89	-3.89	2.63	NA	NA	NA
Earnings	2.10	1.87	0.81	1.78	0.54	-4.95	1.50	NA	NA	NA
Dividends	0.31	0.47	0.35	0.33	0.29	Nil	NA	NA	NA	NA
Payout Ratio	15%	25%	44%	19%	55%	Nil	NA	NA	NA	NA
Prices - High	33.00	36.62	33.56	28.43	21.18	7.87	NA	NA	NA	NA
- Low	22.56	22.56	20.68	16.93	7.50	7.25	NA	NA	NA	NA
P/E Ratio - High	16	20	41	12	40	NM	NA	NA	NA	NA
- Low	11	12	26	7	14	NM	NA	NA	NA	NA
Income Statement Analysis (Million Can. $)										
($) Per Canadian $	0.00	0.62	0.67	0.72	0.73	0.73	0.74	0.00	0.00	0.00
Revs.	5,446	5,261	4,144	4,352	4,159	4,098	4,305	NA	NA	NA
Oper. Inc.	1,797	1,640	1,050	1,005	806	-779	713	NA	NA	NA
Depr.	412	407	213	202	196	234	253	NA	NA	NA
Int. Exp.	295	308	261	124	117	218	107	NA	NA	NA
Pretax Inc.	1,214	971	115	746	135	-1,109	343	NA	NA	NA
Eff. Tax Rate	36%	38%	5.22%	44%	8.10%	NM	2.60%	NA	NA	NA
Net Inc.	772	602	109	421	124	-1,091	334	NA	NA	NA
Balance Sheet & Other Fin. Data (Million Can. $)										
($) Per Canadian $	0.00	0.68	0.65	0.70	0.73	0.73	0.74	0.00	0.00	0.00
Cash	19.0	307	263	365	106	119	70.0	NA	NA	NA
Curr. Assets	1,125	1,527	1,050	1,549	1,161	1,329	1,229	NA	NA	NA
Total Assets	15,196	14,757	10,864	7,075	6,236	6,198	6,133	NA	NA	NA
Curr. Liab.	1,903	1,777	1,392	1,205	1,337	1,603	1,540	NA	NA	NA
LT Debt	3,886	3,961	4,009	1,640	1,499	1,313	1,301	NA	NA	NA
Common Eqty.	5,371	5,179	4,291	3,417	2,380	2,306	2,216	NA	NA	NA
Total Cap.	12,100	11,720	8,300	5,057	3,879	3,619	3,517	NA	NA	NA
Cap. Exp.	607	629	494	577	496	326	NA	NA	NA	NA
Cash Flow	1,173	1,000	322	623	320	-857	587	NA	NA	NA
Curr. Ratio	0.6	0.9	0.8	1.3	0.9	0.8	0.8	NA	NA	NA
% LT Debt of Cap.	32.1	33.8	48.3	32.4	38.6	36.3	37.0	NA	NA	NA
% Net Inc.of Revs.	14.2	11.4	2.6	9.7	3.0	NM	7.8	NA	NA	NA
% Ret. on Assets	5.2	4.7	1.2	6.3	2.0	NM	NA	NA	NA	NA
% Ret. on Equity	14.4	12.5	2.8	14.5	5.3	NM	NA	NA	NA	NA

Data as orig reptd.; bef. results of disc opers/spec. items. Per share data adj. for stk. divs. Bold denotes diluted EPS (FASB 128)-prior periods restated. Quarterly data based on US GAAP after 1997. E-Estimated. NA-Not Available. NM-Not Meaningful. NR-Not Ranked.

Office—935 de La Gauchetiere St., West, Montreal, QC, Canada H3B 2M9. **Tel**—(514) 399-4743. **Website**—http://www.cn.ca **Chrmn**—D. G. A. McLean. **Pres & CEO**—P. M. Tellier. **SVP & Secy**—S. Finn. **EVP & CFO**—C. Mongeu. **VP & Investor Contact**—Robert E. Noorigan (514-399-0052). **Dirs**—M. R. Armellino, P. Crawford, J. V. R. Cyr, V. M. Kempston Darkes, J. K. Gray, E. H. Harrison, R. H. Kroft, G. H. Lamphere, D. Losier, E. C. Lumley, A. P. Lynch, D. G. A. McLean, R. Pace, C. E. Ritchie, P. M. Tellier. **Transfer Agents & Registrars**—Computershare Trust Co. of Canada, Montreal, Toronto, Calgary, Vancouver; Computershare Trust Co. of New York, NYC. **Incorporated**—in Canada in 1922. **Empl**—22,457. **S&P Analyst:** Richard N. Stice

STANDARD
&POOR'S
STOCK REPORTS

Ecolab Inc.

NYSE Symbol **ECL**

In S&P 500

18-AUG-01

Industry:
Chemicals (Specialty)

Summary: Ecolab is the leading worldwide marketer of cleaning, sanitizing and maintenance products and services for the hospitality, institutional and industrial markets.

S&P Opinion: Buy (★★★★★)

Recent Price • 40.73
52 Wk Range • 45.68-33.25
Yield • 1.3%
12-Mo. P/E • 25.3

Quantitative Evaluations

Outlook
(1 Lowest—5 Highest)
• 2

Fair Value
• 39.60

Risk
• Low

Earn./Div. Rank
• A-

Technical Eval.
• Bearish since 7/01

Rel. Strength Rank
(1 Lowest—99 Highest)
• 62

Insider Activity
• Unfavorable

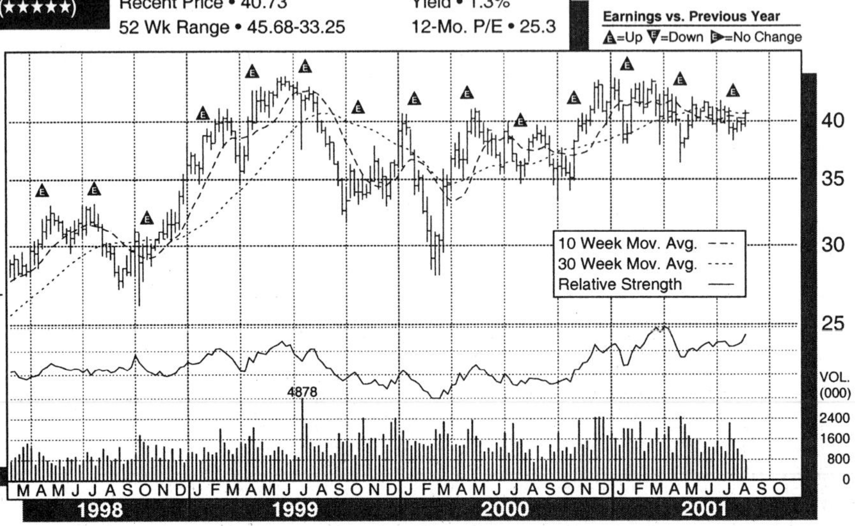

Overview - 20-JUN-01

S&P projects continued good sales growth in 2001, aided by new customers, as well as sales force and product line expansions. The domestic institutional, Kay, food & beverage, and pest elimination units will continue to grow well, and the weak janitorial business should rebound; newer businesses such as kitchen equipment repair and water care will also grow. International sales will be boosted by gains in most parts of the world; Asia should show better growth comparisons. Acquisitions will also contribute to sales gains. Profitability will likely be maintained, through continued product introductions, as well as volume gains, although fuel and raw material costs will again be modestly higher. Interest expense may be slightly greater. ECL's European joint venture contribution may be similar to that of 2000, as modest sales growth is offset by higher expenses and a weaker euro. An expanded stock buyback program should aid EPS comparisons.

Valuation - 20-JUN-01

After a sluggish performance from mid-1999 through late 2000, the stock reached a record high, as investors sought refuge in companies with stable earnings growth. In mid-March, we upgraded the shares to buy, from accumulate, reflecting ECL's attractive long-term growth prospects and strong cash flow, despite the stock's modest premium to the P/E multiple of the overall market. Domestic hospitality, lodging, and food service markets are generally healthy, and a modestly positive pricing environment will help offset higher raw material costs in 2001. An agreement to buy the remaining 50% interest in the European joint venture in early 2002 should be viewed positively. The dividend, raised in early 2001 for the ninth consecutive year, should continue to be boosted regularly.

Key Stock Statistics

S&P EPS Est. 2001	1.64	Tang. Bk. Value/Share	6.39
P/E on S&P Est. 2001	24.8	Beta	0.71
S&P EPS Est. 2002	1.80	Shareholders	5,388
Dividend Rate/Share	0.52	Market cap. (B)	$ 5.2
Shs. outstg. (M)	127.9	Inst. holdings	53%
Avg. daily vol. (M)	0.223		

Value of $10,000 invested 5 years ago: $ 28,628

Fiscal Year Ending Dec. 31

	2001	2000	1999	1998	1997	1996
Revenues (Million $)						
1Q	580.9	526.3	489.3	436.4	373.8	333.7
2Q	595.8	570.7	520.4	468.5	411.8	373.2
3Q	—	600.7	554.5	500.0	432.9	392.1
4Q	—	566.7	515.8	483.4	421.9	391.0
Yr.	—	2,264	2,080	1,888	1,640	1,490
Earnings Per Share ($)						
1Q	**0.34**	**0.32**	**0.26**	**0.23**	**0.20**	**0.15**
2Q	**0.37**	**0.36**	**0.32**	**0.28**	**0.25**	**0.21**
3Q	**E0.48**	**0.46**	**0.41**	**0.35**	**0.30**	**0.27**
4Q	**E0.45**	**0.44**	**0.32**	**0.29**	**0.26**	**0.23**
Yr.	**E1.64**	**1.58**	**1.31**	**1.15**	**1.00**	**0.85**

Next earnings report expected: NA

Dividend Data (Dividends have been paid since 1936.)

Amount ($)	Date Decl.	Ex-Div. Date	Stock of Record	Payment Date
0.120	Aug. 18	Sep. 15	Sep. 19	Oct. 16 '00
0.130	Dec. 07	Dec. 15	Dec. 19	Jan. 16 '01
0.130	Feb. 23	Mar. 16	Mar. 20	Apr. 16 '01
0.130	May. 11	Jun. 15	Jun. 19	Jul. 16 '01

A Division of The McGraw·Hill Companies

Business Summary - 20-JUN-01

Using its "Circle the Customer-Circle the Globe" strategy, this leading global supplier of cleaning, sanitizing and maintenance products and services for hospitality, institutional and industrial markets has been successful in leveraging its customer base by providing all the services and products to meet their needs and in expanding its products and services worldwide. Ecolab (ECL) achieved record sales, net income and share earnings for the ninth consecutive year in 2000.

In the U.S. cleaning and sanitizing business (67% of 2000 sales, 76% of profits), the institutional division (40% of 2000 total sales) is the leading provider of cleaners and sanitizers for warewashing, laundry, kitchen cleaning and general housekeeping, product dispensing equipment and dishwashing racks and related kitchen sundries to the foodservice, lodging and health care industries. It also provides products and services for pool and spa treatment. The Kay division (6%) is the largest supplier of cleaning and sanitizing products for the quick-service restaurant, convenience store and food retail markets. The Food and Beverage division (12%) offers cleaning and sanitizing products and services to farms, dairy plants, food and beverage processors, and pharmaceutical plants. ECL also supplies janitorial products (detergents, floor care, disinfectants, odor control, and hand care products; 4%), under the Airkem and Huntington brand names; textile care products (3%) for large institutional and commercial laundries; vehicle care products for rental, fleet and retail car washes (2%); and water treatment products (1%) for commercial, institutional and industrial markets.

Other U.S. services (11% and 8%) includes institutional and commercial pest elimination and prevention services (7%) and the GCS commercial kitchen equipment repair services (4%); the dishwashing machine manufacturing unit was sold in late 2000.

ECL's international business (22% and 16%) provides similar services to those in the U.S. to Canada and about 40 countries in Latin America, Africa, and the Asia/Pacific region.

In 1998, as part of a strategy to boost growth through acquisitions, ECL bought GCS Service, Inc., a provider of commercial kitchen equipment repair services. ECL has added to this business through small acquisitions. In February 1999, it acquired Blue Coral Systems, the leading marketer of branded vehicle cleaning and specialty products to the commercial vehicle wash industry (annual sales of $30 million); this completed national coverage for ECL's vehicle wash offerings.

The 50%-owned Henkel-Ecolab joint venture provides cleaning and sanitizing services for European institutional and industrial markets. Sales declined 7% in 2000, to $870 million; equity income in the venture was a record $19.5 million, versus $18.3 million in 1999, aided by higher sales in local currency and tight cost controls. Henkel KGaA owns 25% of ECL.

Per Share Data ($) (Year Ended Dec. 31)	2000	1999	1998	1997	1996	1995	1994	1993	1992	1991
Tangible Bk. Val.	3.54	3.96	3.51	2.59	3.27	3.13	3.13	2.67	2.51	2.12
Cash Flow	2.71	2.31	2.06	1.75	1.57	1.33	1.12	1.00	0.89	0.88
Earnings	1.58	1.31	1.15	1.00	0.88	0.75	0.63	0.60	0.52	0.48
Dividends	0.49	0.42	0.38	0.34	0.29	0.26	0.23	0.20	0.18	0.17
Payout Ratio	31%	32%	33%	34%	33%	34%	36%	33%	35%	42%
Prices - High	45.68	44.43	38.00	28.00	19.75	15.87	11.75	11.90	9.56	8.37
- Low	28.00	31.68	26.12	18.12	14.56	10.00	9.62	9.06	6.65	4.87
P/E Ratio - High	29	34	33	28	23	21	19	20	19	18
- Low	18	24	23	18	17	13	15	15	13	10
Income Statement Analysis (Million $)										
Revs.	2,264	2,080	1,888	1,640	1,490	1,341	1,208	1,042	1,005	918
Oper. Inc.	471	714	384	319	275	239	212	172	165	154
Depr.	148	135	122	101	89.5	76.3	66.9	50.2	47.7	43.6
Int. Exp.	24.6	22.7	25.0	12.6	14.4	11.5	16.2	25.2	39.7	36.2
Pretax Inc.	338	286	256	219	184	159	135	109	91.6	84.7
Eff. Tax Rate	38%	38%	40%	39%	39%	38%	37%	31%	30%	34%
Net Inc.	209	176	155	134	113	99	84.6	75.9	64.3	55.7
Balance Sheet & Other Fin. Data (Million $)										
Cash	44.0	47.7	28.4	61.2	69.3	24.7	98.0	48.0	36.0	78.0
Curr. Assets	601	577	504	510	436	358	401	298	254	284
Total Assets	1,714	1,586	1,471	1,416	1,208	1,061	1,020	863	832	922
Curr. Liab.	532	471	400	404	328	311	254	196	188	238
LT Debt	234	169	227	259	149	89.4	105	126	208	319
Common Eqty.	757	929	691	552	520	457	462	374	344	298
Total Cap.	991	1,098	918	811	669	546	567	500	552	617
Cap. Exp.	150	146	148	122	112	110	88.0	68.0	57.0	53.0
Cash Flow	357	310	276	235	203	175	151	126	112	95.0
Curr. Ratio	1.1	1.2	1.3	1.3	1.3	1.1	1.6	1.5	1.4	1.2
% LT Debt of Cap.	23.6	15.4	24.7	31.9	22.2	16.4	18.6	25.1	37.8	51.7
% Net Inc.of Revs.	9.2	8.5	8.2	8.2	7.6	7.4	7.0	7.3	6.4	6.1
% Ret. on Assets	12.6	11.5	10.7	10.2	10.0	9.6	8.7	9.0	7.3	5.2
% Ret. on Equity	27.5	18.9	24.9	25.0	23.2	21.6	19.6	21.1	19.9	13.7

Data as orig reptd.; bef. results of disc opers/spec. items. Per share data adj. for stk. divs. Bold denotes diluted EPS (FASB 128)-prior periods restated. E-Estimated. NA-Not Available. NM-Not Meaningful. NR-Not Ranked.

Office—Ecolab Center, St. Paul, MN 55102. **Tel**—(612) 293-2233. **E-Mail**—ecolab@shareholder.com **Website**—http://www.ecolab.com **Chrmn & CEO**—A. L. Schuman. **Pres & COO**—B. Deschamps. **VP & Secy**—K. A. Iverson. **EVP & CFO**—L. W. Mattews III. **VP & Investor Contact**—Michael J. Monahan. **Dirs**—L. S. Biller, J. A. Grundhofer, S. Hamelmann, J. J. Howard, W. L. Jews, J. W. Johnson, U. Lehner, J. W. Levin, R. L. Lumpkins, L. W. Mattews III, A. L. Schuman, H. Uytherhoeven. **Transfer Agent & Registrar**—First Chicago Trust Co. of New York, Jersey City, NJ. **Incorporated**—in Delaware in 1924. **Empl**— 14,250. **S&P Analyst:** Richard O'Reilly, CFA

STANDARD &POOR'S
STOCK REPORTS

Jacobs Engineering Group

NYSE Symbol **JEC**

In S&P MidCap 400

18-AUG-01

Industry: Engineering & Construction

Summary: This company provides engineering, construction and maintenance services to both private industry and federal government agencies on a worldwide basis.

S&P Opinion: Buy (★★★★★)

Recent Price • 60.50
52 Wk Range • 75.67-36.31
Yield • Nil
12-Mo. P/E • 19.5

Quantitative Evaluations

Outlook (1 Lowest—5 Highest) • **3⁻**

Fair Value • **61.80**

Risk • **Low**

Earn./Div. Rank • **B+**

Technical Eval. • **Bearish** since 7/01

Rel. Strength Rank (1 Lowest—99 Highest) • **45**

Insider Activity • **Unfavorable**

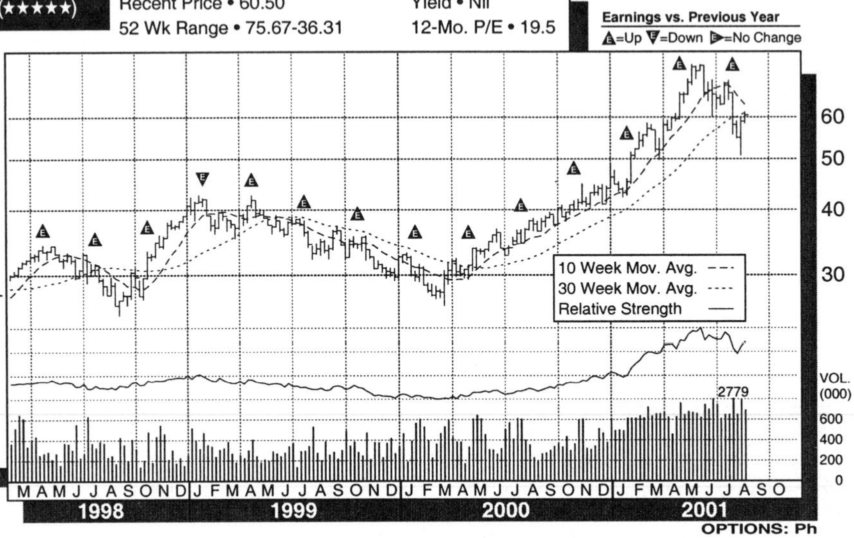

Overview - 23-JUL-01

Revenues should grow in the mid- to high teens through FY 02 (Sep.), on strong bookings for technical professional services (44% of a recent $5.9 billion backlog), and strength in refining, pharmaceuticals and biotechnology, and publicly funded infrastructure projects. Bookings should take 16 to 18 months to translate into revenues. Gross margins should exceed 12.5%, on higher selling prices, due to the significant amount of work available. Operating margins will benefit from synergies related to Sverdrup and Stork, cost reductions, and more client relationships (74% of third quarter bookings). After capital spending ($27 million) and depreciation and amortization ($40 million), free cash flow should reach $4.10 a share in FY 02, up 15% from the FY 01 level. With more market diversity and cost controls, we see FY 01 EPS up 14%, to $3.21, with a gain of 15% in FY 02, to $3.70.

Valuation - 23-JUL-01

With positive industry prospects for the next two to three years, and FY 01 third quarter earnings in line with expectations, we are maintaining our buy recommendation. We believe JEC is better positioned to offset weak global economies than it was in the 1994 downturn, as it has more publicly funded projects (35%) and a more diversified geographic and customer mix. In addition, with more long-term preferred contracts, risk is reduced and the earnings stream is more consistent. We expect strong cash flow to be used mostly for debt reduction (debt was 26% of capital at June 30) and niche acquisitions (recently GIBB). A possible rebound in the chemicals sector, and a major U.K. rail system upgrade expected over the next 10 years, should aid bookings. Despite a projected P/E of 18X our FY 02 EPS estimate, on a par with that of the market, with positive trends, we see potential for further gains.

Key Stock Statistics

S&P EPS Est. 2001	3.21	Tang. Bk. Value/Share	8.58
P/E on S&P Est. 2001	18.8	Beta	0.66
S&P EPS Est. 2002	3.70	Shareholders	1,115
Dividend Rate/Share	Nil	Market cap. (B)	$ 1.6
Shs. outstg. (M)	26.8	Inst. holdings	72%
Avg. daily vol. (M)	0.413		

Value of $10,000 invested 5 years ago: $ 28,304

Fiscal Year Ending Sep. 30

	2001	2000	1999	1998	1997	1996
Revenues (Million $)						
1Q	929.2	809.1	555.2	506.4	433.6	471.1
2Q	1,010	881.8	779.9	524.8	437.7	487.0
3Q	1,041	857.8	771.9	525.0	430.2	436.8
4Q	—	870.2	768.1	545.0	479.1	404.0
Yr.	—	3,419	2,875	2,101	1,781	1,799
Earnings Per Share ($)						
1Q	**0.75**	**-0.22**	**-0.58**	**0.49**	**0.42**	0.37
2Q	**0.79**	**0.69**	**0.61**	**0.51**	0.44	0.38
3Q	**0.82**	**0.72**	**0.63**	**0.54**	0.46	0.40
4Q	**E0.85**	**0.75**	**0.65**	**0.55**	**0.49**	0.41
Yr.	**E3.21**	**1.93**	**2.47**	**2.08**	**1.80**	1.56

Next earnings report expected: early November

Dividend Data

Cash dividends were omitted in 1984. A poison pill stock purchase rights plan was adopted in 1990.

Jacobs Engineering Group Inc.

Business Summary - 23-JUL-01

Jacobs Engineering aims to avoid the risk and expense associated with developing its own technology. Instead, it plans to offer more relationship-based technical services to major clients (70% of business preferred relationship based), while building its international presence; international business provided over 16% of revenues in FY 00 (Sep.).

Over the past several years, the company has expanded through internal initiatives and strategic acquisitions. Acquisitions have let JEC expand and enhance its range of services, increase its client base, and obtain access to new geographic areas.

In early 1999, JEC acquired St. Louis-based Sverdrup Corp. ($1 billion in sales), a privately held engineering and construction firm, for $229 million. In February 2000, JEC acquired a 40% stake in Stork Engineering Group, a unit of Stork N.V. of the Netherlands, for $25 million. In February 2001, JEC acquired Stork's engineering and contracting business.

FY 00 revenues by sector were: chemical and petrochemicals (20%); buildings (16%); federal programs (18%); pharmaceutical & biotech (14%); petroleum (8%); infrastructure (8%); technology and manufacturing (9%); and pulp & paper (7%).

Professional services include project services (engineering, design, architectural and other); process, scientific and systems consulting; operations and maintenance; and construction.

Project services (53%) include the engineering and design of process plants and high-technology facilities, as well as remedial engineering and design for major environmental and hazardous waste programs.

Construction services (28%) offers traditional field services to private and public sector clients.

Process, scientific and systems consulting (3.5%) includes performing pricing studies, market analyses and financial projections to determine the feasibility of a project; and gasoline reformulation modeling.

Operations and maintenance services (15%) include all tasks required to keep a process plant in day-to-day operation, including the repair and replacement of pumps, piping, heat exchangers and other equipment.

In FY 00, revenues directly or indirectly derived from agencies of the U.S. government accounted for 18% of the total. Total federal contracts (nearly 40%) are expected to gradually rise to about 50% of JEC's business.

FY 00 EPS of $2.82 exclude a first quarter litigation charge of $0.89.

As of July 2001, JEC had repurchased more than 1.6 million shares under a 3 million share authorization, including 126,000 shares through the first nine months of FY 01.

In May 2001, the company acquired LawGibb Group's international business ($100 million in revenues), which provides engineering consulting.

Per Share Data ($) (Year Ended Sep. 30)	2000	1999	1998	1997	1996	1995	1994	1993	1992	1991
Tangible Bk. Val.	8.58	7.78	11.49	9.65	9.46	7.72	6.44	6.42	5.33	4.18
Cash Flow	3.44	3.66	2.97	2.56	2.26	1.87	1.22	1.50	1.43	1.15
Earnings	1.93	2.47	2.08	1.80	1.56	1.27	0.75	1.15	1.11	0.86
Dividends	Nil	Nil	Nil	Nil	Nil	Nil	Nil	Nil	Nil	Nil
Payout Ratio	Nil	Nil	Nil	Nil	Nil	Nil	Nil	Nil	Nil	Nil
Prices - High	49.18	42.75	40.75	32.56	29.37	25.75	26.87	29.87	36.50	28.87
- Low	26.18	29.25	24.75	23.25	19.62	17.25	16.87	20.00	21.62	10.12
P/E Ratio - High	25	17	20	18	19	20	36	26	33	34
- Low	14	12	12	13	13	14	23	17	19	12
Income Statement Analysis (Million $)										
Revs.	3,419	2,875	2,101	1,781	1,799	1,723	1,166	1,143	1,106	1,036
Oper. Inc.	165	140	110	93.2	82.7	67.7	43.8	54.9	46.2	39.2
Depr.	40.1	31.6	23.2	19.6	18.1	15.0	12.0	8.8	7.7	6.9
Int. Exp.	11.4	8.8	2.4	3.0	2.8	2.2	0.8	0.8	0.3	0.6
Pretax Inc.	81.3	105	88.8	77.4	66.8	53.4	31.4	49.3	45.9	35.1
Eff. Tax Rate	37%	37%	39%	39%	40%	40%	40%	42%	42%	42%
Net Inc.	51.0	65.4	54.4	46.9	40.4	32.2	18.8	28.7	26.6	20.4
Balance Sheet & Other Fin. Data (Million $)										
Cash	65.8	53.5	101	56.0	65.6	39.1	48.5	40.6	35.1	34.1
Curr. Assets	851	730	566	504	384	369	367	265	258	207
Total Assets	1,384	1,220	807	744	573	534	504	351	317	260
Curr. Liab.	684	585	368	326	228	255	261	164	171	146
LT Debt	147	135	26.2	54.1	36.3	17.8	25.0	Nil	Nil	Nil
Common Eqty.	496	449	371	324	283	239	200	174	140	107
Total Cap.	648	590	404	384	320	258	225	174	141	109
Cap. Exp.	44.4	39.0	46.3	28.0	16.7	35.0	24.3	9.9	12.1	8.5
Cash Flow	91.1	97.0	77.6	66.5	58.5	47.2	30.7	37.5	34.3	27.3
Curr. Ratio	1.2	1.2	1.5	1.5	1.7	1.4	1.4	1.6	1.5	1.4
% LT Debt of Cap.	22.7	22.9	6.5	14.1	11.4	6.9	11.1	Nil	Nil	Nil
% Net Inc.of Revs.	1.5	2.3	2.6	2.6	2.2	1.9	1.6	2.5	2.4	2.0
% Ret. on Assets	3.9	6.5	7.0	7.1	7.3	6.0	4.4	8.4	9.2	7.8
% Ret. on Equity	10.8	16.0	15.6	15.4	15.5	12.5	10.0	17.9	21.4	21.1

Data as orig reptd.; bef. results of disc opers/spec. items. Per share data adj. for stk. divs. Bold denotes diluted EPS (FASB 128)-prior periods restated. E-Estimated. NA-Not Available. NM-Not Meaningful. NR-Not Ranked.

Office—1111 S. Arroyo Pkwy., Pasadena, CA 91105. **Tel**—(626) 578-3500. **Website**—http://www.jacobs.com **Chrmn**—J. J. Jacobs. **Vice Chrmn**—R. E. Beumer. **Pres & CEO**—N. G. Watson. **VP & Secy**—W. C. Markley III. **SVP-Fin, Treas & Investor Contact**—John W. Prosser Jr. **Dirs**—R. E. Beumer, P. H. Dailey, R. C. Davidson Jr., R. B. Gwyn, J. J. Jacobs, L. K. Jacobs, J. C. LaForce, D. R. Laurance, L. F. Levinson, B. F. Montoya, D. M. Petrone, J. Rainey Jr., N. G. Watson. **Transfer Agent & Registrar**—Mellon Investor Services, LA. **Incorporated**—in California in 1957; reincorporated in Delaware in 1987. **Empl**— 29,000. **S&P Analyst:** Stewart Scharf

STANDARD &POOR'S
STOCK REPORTS

Kaydon Corp.

NYSE Symbol **KDN**

In S&P MidCap 400

21-AUG-01

Industry: Machinery (Diversified)

Summary: This company makes custom bearings and other sophisticated components for everything from earthmoving machinery to industrial robots to medical and semiconductor equipment.

S&P Opinion: Buy (★★★★★)

Recent Price • 24.13
52 Wk Range • 28.25-20.06
Yield • 2.0%
12-Mo. P/E • 19.5

Quantitative Evaluations

Outlook (1 Lowest—5 Highest)
• **2**

Fair Value
• **23.70**

Risk
• **Low**

Earn./Div. Rank
• **A**

Technical Eval.
• **Bearish** since 6/01

Rel. Strength Rank (1 Lowest—99 Highest)
• **43**

Insider Activity
• **NA**

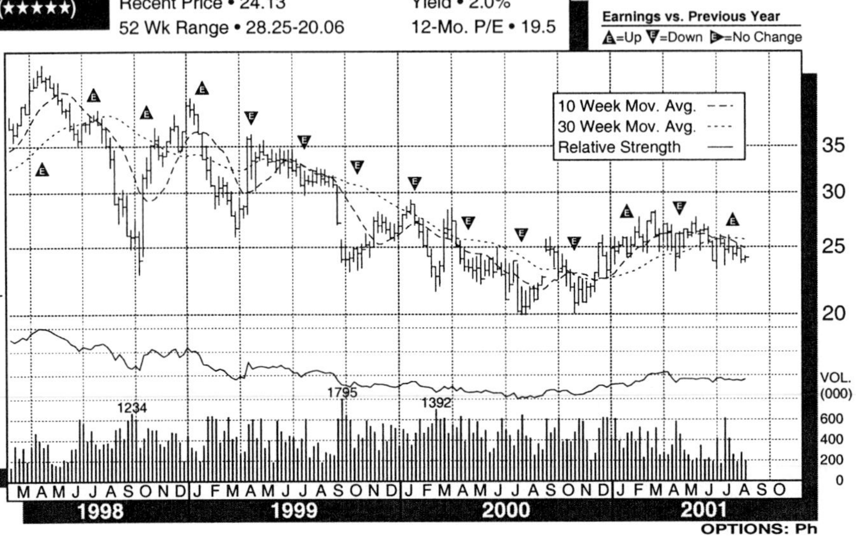

OPTIONS: Ph

Overview - 21-AUG-01

Revenues should rise about 5% in 2001, as a 20% jump in acquisition-related sales should more than offset a 15% drop in organic revenues. We believe that weakening global economies will continue to take a toll on KDN's biggest markets: the heavy construction, automated machinery and electronics industries. The drop in volume sales should materially hike underabsorption of fixed operating costs, which in turn should cause operating profit margins to fall to 15%+, well below KDN's 25% historical average. As a result, we believe EPS will plunge about 25% in 2001. However, we're more sanguine about KDN's long-term prospects, due to its continued focus on high-margin proprietary components, migration into faster-growing health care and electronics markets, and ongoing productivity improvements. Thus, we believe probabilities are high that over the next five to 10 years, KDN will be able post average annual cash EPS growth of 15% and return on equity (ROE) of 20%-25%.

Valuation - 21-AUG-01

We're maintaining our strong buy opinion on KDN, as we believe the stock is trading at a material discount to its intrinsic value (defined as the present value of KDN's long-term cash earnings power). Our cash flow models (which value KDN by adding the sum of estimated long-term cash earnings growing at a projected 15% average rate) indicate KDN is trading at a 25%-45% discount, even after applying a 25% margin of safety cushion. Another "stand-alone" valuation model also suggests the stock is undervalued. This model, which incorporates, in part, our projections of sustainable average ROE of 23%, 10-year treasury bond yields of 7%, and estimated 2001 per-share net worth of $12, values the stock at about $30 a share.

Key Stock Statistics

S&P EPS Est. 2001	1.00	Tang. Bk. Value/Share	12.95
P/E on S&P Est. 2001	24.1	Beta	0.90
S&P EPS Est. 2002	1.10	Shareholders	1,132
Dividend Rate/Share	0.48	Market cap. (B)	$0.723
Shs. outstg. (M)	29.9	Inst. holdings	78%
Avg. daily vol. (M)	0.045		

Value of $10,000 invested 5 years ago: $ 10,649

Fiscal Year Ending Dec. 31

	2001	2000	1999	1998	1997	1996
Revenues (Million $)						
1Q	91.35	84.92	88.12	99.1	76.53	73.40
2Q	89.60	86.07	85.52	99.5	84.45	76.13
3Q	—	81.29	73.73	92.80	83.38	69.84
4Q	—	86.97	78.33	84.71	84.67	71.31
Yr.	—	339.3	325.7	376.2	329.0	290.7
Earnings Per Share ($)						
1Q	**0.35**	**0.44**	**0.50**	**0.55**	0.42	0.37
2Q	**0.22**	**0.19**	**0.50**	**0.57**	0.48	0.40
3Q	**E0.20**	**0.24**	**0.41**	**0.54**	0.47	0.38
4Q	**E0.23**	**0.45**	**0.44**	**0.51**	**0.49**	0.39
Yr.	**E1.00**	**1.30**	**1.85**	**2.17**	**1.86**	**1.53**

Next earnings report expected: late October

Dividend Data (Dividends have been paid since 1986.)

Amount ($)	Date Decl.	Ex-Div. Date	Stock of Record	Payment Date
0.110	Aug. 23	Sep. 07	Sep. 11	Oct. 02 '00
0.120	Nov. 10	Dec. 07	Dec. 11	Jan. 02 '01
0.120	Feb. 15	Mar. 08	Mar. 12	Apr. 02 '01
0.120	May. 03	Jun. 07	Jun. 11	Jul. 02 '01

Kaydon Corporation

Business Summary - 21-AUG-01

Although KDN's bearings, hydraulic cylinders, slip rings and industrial filters aren't particularly glamorous, KDN's profit margins and returns on equity (ROE) are nevertheless very impressive. Over the past 10 years, operating and net profit margins averaged about 25% and 15%, respectively, putting KDN in the same league as Coca-Cola, Pfizer and Cisco Systems. During the same period, ROE averaged almost 25%, without the aid of high debt levels.

KDN's superlative margins and returns can be primarily attributed to the company's highly engineered, proprietary products. Most of KDN's components are used to perform critical functions, where there's zero tolerance for error. Thus, customers are often willing to pay full price for KDN's products. In addition, KDN's proprietary components help keep competition at bay, which allows KDN to maintain pricing power.

Currently, the company serves cyclical and relatively slow-growing markets. KDN derives about 40% of revenues from sales to earthmoving equipment makers, 18%-20% from commercial aircraft/military hardware manufacturers, 5%-8% from oil & gas producers and 5% from certain export markets. However, KDN is carefully expanding into the electronics and medical diagnostics equipment markets (10%-12% sales), as well as certain highly profitable, hi-tech factory automation sectors 12%-15%.

Over the past several years, EPS growth and ROE fell well below historical averages, primarily due to ripple effects from the Asian financial crisis, which took a heavy toll on the construction, mining and energy industries, big KDN end-markets. Unrelated downturns in the civil and military aerospace industries, another major KDN end-market, also took a toll on profitability. To compound the problem, KDN's former management, which had become complacent, was slow in cutting production levels and streamlining operations. Subsequently, in 2000, the company also posted $13.7 million ($0.46 per share) in one-time litigation charges.

Brian Campbell, who became KDN's CEO in late 1998, has been shaking up the company. In the past several years, Campbell has been replacing underperforming managers, investing in lean manufacturing systems, and implementing long-term employee incentive plans. Moreover, Campbell is also using an aggressive but judicious acquisition strategy to expand the scope of Kaydon's end-markets and product lines.

Acquisition candidates must meet strict standards. KDN looks for those companies that make proprietary products, possess dominant positions in niche markets, aren't capital-intensive, generate 15%-20% operating profit margins and strong cash flows, and contribute immediately to the bottom line.

In 1993, KDN was named as a defendant by the creditors of KDN's former parent, Keene Corp., alleging KDN was spun off at less than market value. Earlier in 1993, Keene filed for bankruptcy, due to mounting asbestos liability claims. KDN believes it has very strong defenses, but maintains that a worst-case scenario would not materially hurt its financial position.

Per Share Data ($) (Year Ended Dec. 31)	2000	1999	1998	1997	1996	1995	1994	1993	1992	1991
Tangible Bk. Val.	7.22	7.78	7.68	6.57	5.42	4.21	5.00	4.31	3.92	3.97
Cash Flow	1.88	2.34	2.59	2.24	1.88	1.36	1.25	1.09	1.02	0.99
Earnings	1.30	1.85	2.17	1.86	1.52	1.14	0.94	0.80	0.73	0.73
Dividends	0.45	0.40	0.37	0.30	0.25	0.23	0.20	0.18	0.16	0.13
Payout Ratio	35%	22%	17%	16%	16%	20%	22%	23%	21%	18%
Prices - High	29.31	41.06	45.93	34.93	24.75	15.81	12.62	16.00	13.31	11.93
- Low	19.93	23.00	22.81	20.87	14.43	11.37	9.87	8.75	9.75	8.00
P/E Ratio - High	23	22	21	19	16	14	14	20	18	16
- Low	15	12	11	11	9	10	11	11	13	11
Income Statement Analysis (Million $)										
Revs.	339	326	376	329	291	230	205	184	184	161
Oper. Inc.	96.2	105	124	108	91.0	70.0	60.4	54.6	52.5	48.7
Depr.	17.4	15.6	14.0	12.8	11.7	11.2	10.6	10.3	10.0	8.8
Int. Exp.	1.2	0.0	0.0	0.2	0.3	0.3	0.3	0.3	1.8	1.6
Pretax Inc.	62.1	94.0	115	99	81.6	61.8	50.4	44.5	40.8	39.4
Eff. Tax Rate	37%	37%	38%	38%	38%	38%	38%	38%	37%	36%
Net Inc.	39.3	58.8	71.2	61.7	50.5	38.2	31.2	27.7	25.6	25.5
Balance Sheet & Other Fin. Data (Million $)										
Cash	115	89.7	96.2	74.7	83.2	4.8	39.7	24.5	13.7	7.9
Curr. Assets	241	212	230	215	186	135	12.7	107	97.5	96.3
Total Assets	476	407	414	384	332	268	244	217	211	217
Curr. Liab.	60.0	54.2	71.2	71.0	66.8	44.0	40.9	34.7	40.8	37.1
LT Debt	47.5	Nil	Nil	Nil	4.0	8.0	8.0	13.7	8.0	33.7
Common Eqty.	322	317	312	284	232	188	167	144	136	138
Total Cap.	370	317	312	284	236	196	175	158	144	180
Cap. Exp.	11.8	11.6	25.4	12.7	9.3	7.3	6.7	5.1	6.1	15.4
Cash Flow	56.7	74.4	85.2	74.4	62.2	45.5	41.9	38.0	35.6	34.3
Curr. Ratio	4.0	3.9	3.2	3.0	2.8	3.1	3.1	3.1	2.4	2.6
% LT Debt of Cap.	12.8	Nil	Nil	Nil	1.7	4.1	4.6	8.7	5.6	18.7
% Net Inc.of Revs.	11.6	18.0	18.9	18.7	17.3	16.7	15.3	15.0	13.9	15.8
% Ret. on Assets	8.9	14.3	17.8	17.2	16.8	14.9	13.6	13.2	11.9	12.9
% Ret. on Equity	12.3	18.7	23.9	23.9	24.0	21.4	20.1	20.2	18.7	20.2

Data as orig reptd.; bef. results of disc opers/spec. items. Per share data adj. for stk. divs. Bold denotes diluted EPS (FASB 128)-prior periods restated. E-Estimated. NA-Not Available. NM-Not Meaningful. NR-Not Ranked.

Office—315 E. Eisenhower Pkwy., Suite 300, Ann Arbor, MI 48108-3330. **Tel**—(734) 747-7025. **Website**—http://www.kaydon.com **Chrmn, CEO & Pres**—B. P. Campbell. **CFO**—K. W. Crawford. **Secy**—J. F. Brocci. **Dirs**—G. J. Breen, B. P. Campbell, T. C. Sullivan, B. J. White. **Transfer Agent & Registrar**—Bank of New York, NYC. **Incorporated**—in Delaware in 1983. **Empl**— 2,500. **S&P Analyst:** Robert E. Friedman, CPA

Landstar System

Nasdaq Symbol **LSTR**

In S&P SmallCap 600

21-AUG-01

Industry: Truckers

Summary: This company operates a family of truckload carriers using independent drivers and commission sales agents.

S&P Opinion: Buy (★★★★★)

Recent Price • 76.91 | Yield • Nil
52 Wk Range • 81.14-37.62 | 12-Mo. P/E • 14.5

Quantitative Evaluations

Outlook
(1 Lowest—5 Highest)
• 3+

Fair Value
• 79.10

Risk
• **Average**

Earn./Div. Rank
• **NR**

Technical Eval.
• **Bullish** since 6/01

Rel. Strength Rank
(1 Lowest—99 Highest)
• 83

Insider Activity
• **Neutral**

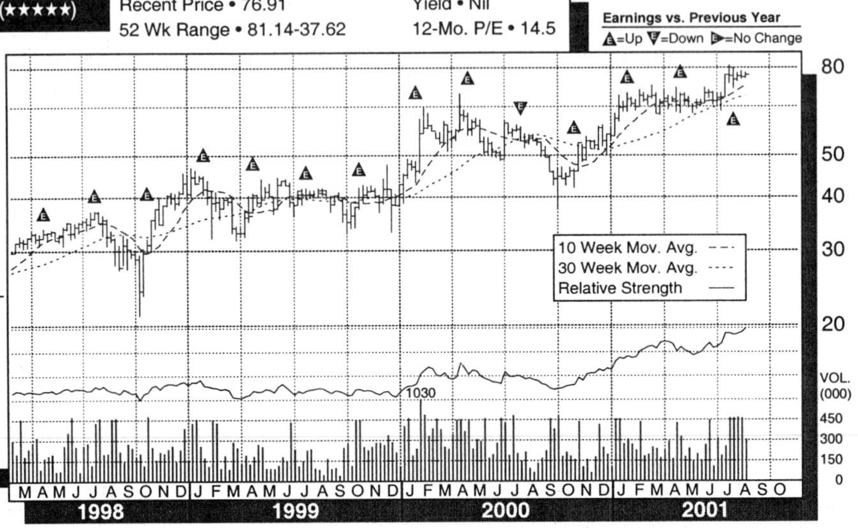

Overview - 21-AUG-01

We forecast revenue growth of 5% in 2002, after a slight minimal increase estimated for 2001, on higher carrier and multimodal revenue growth, driven by rising shipping demand in the wake of a more favorable economic climate. Investment income should produce solid results. Margins should widen, based on our expectations of a decline in commission payments and a modest increase for insurance and claims expenses. We expect the price per mile to rise, and see a good likelihood of market share gains. Growth in the company's truck count should resume in 2002, following a drop in early 2001, due to defections among independent drivers. Interest expense should remain stable, and the effective tax rate should remain at 38.5%. We are forecasting 2002 EPS of $6.40, up 16% from 2001's estimated $5.52. Comparisons should be aided by ongoing share repurchases.

Valuation - 21-AUG-01

We recently upgraded the shares to buy, from accumulate. Our discounted cash flow model shows the stock trading below fair value. In addition, the company has the lowest PE/G ratio and the highest sales per share among the trucking companies that we follow. The shares have run up sharply since the 2000 fourth quarter, as investors have shifted to trucking companies in anticipation of a strengthening economy and a peak in fuel prices. We expect a continued rotation into these stocks, and see LSTR as the cream of the trucking crop. We like the company's unique model of using independent drivers and commissioned sales agents; this allows it to operate with sharply wider margins, and with reduced capital requirements. As a result, LSTR generates excellent cash flow from operations; it has been using this increasingly to buy back stock. We expect the shares to continue to outperform the overall market over the next six to 12 months.

Key Stock Statistics

S&P EPS Est. 2001	5.60	Tang. Bk. Value/Share	10.53
P/E on S&P Est. 2001	13.7	Beta	0.34
S&P EPS Est. 2002	6.75	Shareholders	75
Dividend Rate/Share	Nil	Market cap. (B)	$0.655
Shs. outstg. (M)	8.4	Inst. holdings	93%
Avg. daily vol. (M)	0.093		

Value of $10,000 invested 5 years ago: $ 31,715

Fiscal Year Ending Dec. 31

	2001	2000	1999	1998	1997	1996
Revenues (Million $)						
1Q	331.3	327.0	311.4	298.2	305.6	295.5
2Q	358.0	358.6	345.1	327.5	333.7	329.1
3Q	—	352.4	351.5	324.0	326.3	330.2
4Q	—	380.6	380.1	333.9	347.1	329.0
Yr.	—	1,418	1,388	1,284	1,313	1,284
Earnings Per Share ($)						
1Q	**0.96**	**0.89**	**0.71**	**0.42**	**0.24**	**0.25**
2Q	**1.26**	**1.04**	**1.05**	**0.79**	**0.51**	**0.54**
3Q	**E1.50**	**1.30**	**1.20**	**0.85**	**0.60**	**0.60**
4Q	**E1.88**	**1.85**	**1.63**	**1.07**	**0.62**	**0.08**
Yr.	**E5.60**	**5.03**	**4.55**	**3.10**	**1.96**	**1.47**

Next earnings report expected: mid October

Dividend Data

The company has not paid cash dividends on the common stock and does not intend to pay any for the foreseeable future.

Landstar System, Inc.

Business Summary - 21-AUG-01

Landstar System operates a family of truckload carriers, collectively one of the largest in North America. Truckload carriers transport large shipments from origin to destination. It also provides logistics, intermodal services and expedited land and air delivery of time-critical freight.

The company's operating strategy is to limit investment in fixed assets by harnessing the services of independent owner-operator drivers and commission sales agents. LSTR compensates its independent contractors with 60% to 70% of the revenues generated per load, if they supply the tractor, and with 75% to 79% of revenues if they supply both a tractor and trailer. By using contractors, the company minimizes investment in rolling stock. Approximately 70% of the trailers available to the carrier segment are provided by independent contractors or are leased by LSTR at rental rates that vary with the revenue generated by the trailer. LSTR's 850 independent commission sales agents earn between 5% and 8% of the gross revenue on a shipment.

LSTR provides drivers and sales agents with various services, including safety training, strategic planning, technology, legal, financial and information services. It leverages its purchasing power to obtain for drivers lower costs for equipment, fuel, tires, parts, and mobile communications equipment.

The company's carrier group (79% of 2000 revenues) consists of Landstar Ranger, Landstar Inway, Landstar Ligon, and Landstar Gemini. The carrier group provides truckload services ranging from the movement of packaged goods to bulk goods and perishable commodities. In early 2000, Landstar Gemini was moved into the carrier group, from the multi-modal group. In June 2000, Landstar Ligon's headquarters was relocated to the company's main corporate headquarters in Jacksonville, FL. A related net charge of $1,815,000 ($0.20 a share) was recorded in the 2000 second quarter, to cover costs associated with the relocation. In January 2000, the Department of Transportation (DOT) said it would not revoke Landstar Ligon's satisfactory safety rating. A DOT audit of Ligon in November 1999 uncovered several safety discrepancies. As a result of the audit, a large fleet of independent drivers at Ligon was disqualified, and the unit's president was replaced.

The multimodal group (20%) consists of Landstar Logistics and Landstar Express America. Landstar Logistics provides a single source solution for large customers for all of their transportation and distribution needs. Intermodal services involves the arrangement of transportation (both rail and truck) to provide door to door coverage. Landstar Express provides emergency and expedited air and ground transportation services throughout the U.S. and parts of Canada and Mexico.

Signature Insurance Co., established in 1997 (2%), provides risk and claims management services for LSTR's operating companies and offers property, casualty and occupational accident coverage for its contractors.

Per Share Data ($) (Year Ended Dec. 31)	2000	1999	1998	1997	1996	1995	1994	1993	1992	1991
Tangible Bk. Val.	8.88	7.99	7.38	8.21	7.28	5.58	5.66	3.69	NM	NA
Cash Flow	6.48	5.71	4.01	3.63	3.36	3.58	2.95	2.22	0.98	NA
Earnings	5.03	4.55	3.10	1.96	1.48	1.95	1.90	1.14	0.67	0.22
Dividends	Nil	Nil	Nil	Nil	Nil	Nil	Nil	Nil	Nil	Nil
Payout Ratio	Nil	Nil	Nil	Nil	Nil	Nil	Nil	Nil	Nil	Nil
Prices - High	69.75	47.62	45.62	29.00	30.62	37.75	36.00	22.12	NA	NA
- Low	37.62	31.68	21.06	21.75	21.50	21.25	19.75	12.25	NA	NA
P/E Ratio - High	14	10	15	15	21	19	19	19	NA	NA
- Low	7	7	7	11	15	11	10	11	NA	NA
Income Statement Analysis (Million $)										
Revs.	1,418	1,388	1,284	1,313	1,284	1,205	984	781	672	NA
Oper. Inc.	96.6	121	69.9	71.3	71.2	70.8	59.3	43.0	34.7	NA
Depr.	13.0	11.7	10.2	20.9	24.0	20.8	13.5	12.8	11.8	NA
Int. Exp.	9.1	4.5	3.5	4.6	7.5	17.5	4.1	5.7	9.7	NA
Pretax Inc.	73.5	77.2	58.0	42.6	32.4	42.5	41.6	24.5	13.2	NA
Eff. Tax Rate	38%	41%	40%	42%	41%	41%	41%	45%	52%	NA
Net Inc.	45.2	45.9	34.5	24.7	19.0	25.0	24.4	13.6	6.4	NA
Balance Sheet & Other Fin. Data (Million $)										
Cash	32.9	23.7	26.7	18.0	4.2	3.4	17.8	15.1	NA	NA
Curr. Assets	249	252	219	218	201	179	155	124	NA	NA
Total Assets	370	365	314	357	371	353	267	219	NA	NA
Curr. Liab.	154	171	143	139	130	127	113	87.0	NA	NA
LT Debt	84.9	Nil	29.7	36.2	67.2	73.2	30.5	36.4	NA	NA
Common Eqty.	-107	107	112	152	148	128	105	81.0	NA	NA
Total Cap.	-22.6	107	142	190	215	202	136	117	NA	NA
Cap. Exp.	7.3	12.7	7.2	9.8	12.8	7.3	7.5	6.7	3.5	NA
Cash Flow	58.2	57.6	44.6	45.6	42.9	45.8	37.9	26.3	18.2	NA
Curr. Ratio	1.6	1.5	1.5	1.6	1.5	1.4	1.2	1.4	NA	NA
% LT Debt of Cap.	-375.0	Nil	21.0	19.1	31.3	36.3	22.5	31.2	NA	NA
% Net Inc.of Revs.	3.2	3.3	2.7	1.9	1.5	2.1	2.5	1.7	0.9	NA
% Ret. on Assets	12.3	13.5	10.3	6.8	5.2	8.1	10.1	6.8	NA	NA
% Ret. on Equity	NA	42.0	26.2	16.5	13.7	21.4	26.2	24.2	NA	NA

Data as orig reptd.; bef. results of disc opers/spec. items. Per share data adj. for stk. divs. Bold denotes diluted EPS (FASB 128)-prior periods restated. E-Estimated. NA-Not Available. NM-Not Meaningful. NR-Not Ranked.

Office—13410 Sutton Park Drive South, Jacksonville, FL 32224. **Tel**—(904) 398-9400. **Website**—http://www.landstar.com **Chrmn, Pres & CEO**—J. C. Crowe. **EVP & CFO**—H. H. Gerkens. **VP & Secy**—M. L. Harvey. **Investor Contact**—Stacey L. Taylor (904-390-1530). **Dirs**—D. G. Bannister, J. C. Crowe, R. W. Drucker, W. S. Elston, H. H. Gerkens, M. J. Mott, D. M. Murphy. **Transfer Agent**—Mellon investor Services, NYC. **Incorporated**—in Delaware in 1991. **Empl**— 1,266. **S&P Analyst:** Jim Corridore

STANDARD &POOR'S
STOCK REPORTS

Sensormatic Electronics

NYSE Symbol **SRM**

In S&P MidCap 400

18-AUG-01

Industry: Electrical Equipment

Summary: This company makes and services electronic and video surveillance equipment used to deter theft in retail stores and other environments.

S&P Opinion: Buy (★★★★★)

Recent Price • 23.21
52 Wk Range • 23.50-12
Yield • Nil
12-Mo. P/E • 47.4

Quantitative Evaluations

Outlook
(1 Lowest—5 Highest)
• **3-**

Fair Value
• **24.40**

Risk
• **Average**

Earn./Div. Rank
• **B-**

Technical Eval.
• **Bullish** since 8/01

Rel. Strength Rank
(1 Lowest—99 Highest)
• **98**

Insider Activity
• **NA**

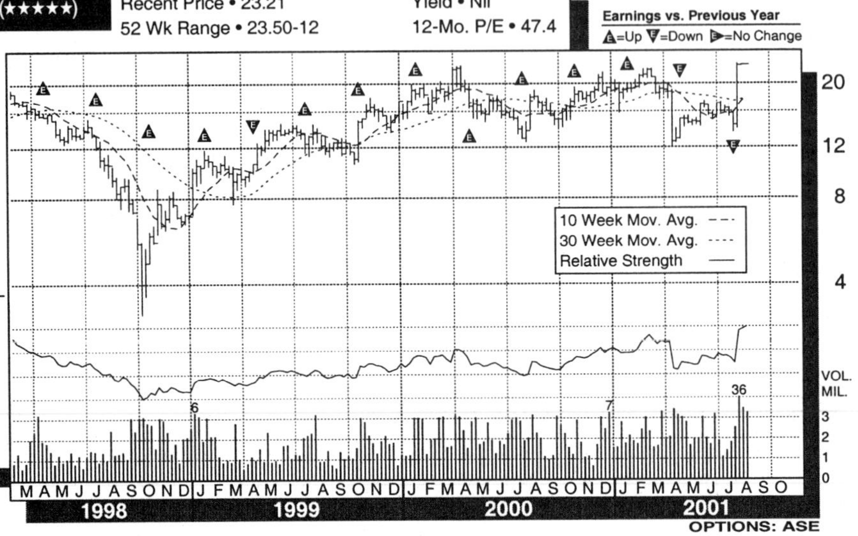

OPTIONS: ASE

Overview - 10-MAY-01

Looking to FY 02 (Jun.), we expect SRM to be impacted by the harsh economic climate. With retail customers concerned with matters other than security, and analog video sales seeing weak demand, we expect revenues to rise only 5%-7%. Source tagging, which has lost some steam early on in calendar 2001, should reaccelerate when the economy improves. Digital video growth should remain strong, partially offsetting weak analog demand. Gross margins should be impacted by price actions on analog video as well as strong growth in the services area, which carries lower margins than the corporate average. SRM has instituted a number of actions designed to cut operating costs, including plant consolidations, employee reductions and shared services initiatives. We forecast operating expenses to decline to about 31.5% of revenues, from our FY 01 target of 33.4%.

Valuation - 10-MAY-01

The shares dropped sharply after SRM announced that it would miss revenue and earnings targets in the third quarter of FY 01. The company is being impacted by matters largely beyond its own control, and we believe that revenue momentum will return when the overall economy improves. The company has reacted aggressively, seeking to drive down operating costs and taking actions to improve sales momentum. We are disappointed with the pace of action in the analog video side of the business, but SRM is now taking steps to improve this segment. The company has added several impressive new customers in recent months, which should help to partly offset the tough environment. Trading at about 17X our FY 02 EPS estimate of $0.85, the shares are attractively valued at a below-market P/E multiple that does not reflect SRM's strong industry position.

Key Stock Statistics

S&P EPS Est. 2002	0.85	Tang. Bk. Value/Share	5.25
P/E on S&P Est. 2002	27.3	Beta	0.95
Dividend Rate/Share	Nil	Shareholders	32,000
Shs. outstg. (M)	79.4	Market cap. (B)	$ 1.8
Avg. daily vol. (M)	2.987	Inst. holdings	95%

Value of $10,000 invested 5 years ago: $ 13,812

Fiscal Year Ending Jun. 30

	2001	2000	1999	1998	1997	1996
Revenues (Million $)						
1Q	263.5	254.6	227.2	245.4	246.0	267.2
2Q	281.6	270.4	250.4	243.7	256.6	244.6
3Q	256.9	261.1	245.5	237.0	250.1	225.3
4Q	288.6	313.9	294.4	260.8	273.0	257.5
Yr.	1,097	1,100	1,018	986.9	1,026	994.6
Earnings Per Share ($)						
1Q	**0.12**	**0.06**	**-0.02**	**-0.89**	0.03	0.23
2Q	**0.21**	**0.17**	**0.10**	**0.07**	0.08	-0.88
3Q	**0.07**	**0.22**	**0.12**	**0.17**	0.08	-0.68
4Q	**0.10**	**0.34**	**0.26**	**0.14**	-0.48	0.01
Yr.	**0.49**	**0.78**	**0.35**	**-0.50**	**-0.29**	**-1.33**

Next earnings report expected: mid October

Dividend Data

Cash dividends were suspended in August 1997.

Sensormatic Electronics Corporation

18-AUG-01

Business Summary - 10-MAY-01

Back in 1966, after a supermarket store manager named Ron Assaf unsuccessfully chased a shoplifter, he decided that there had to be a better way. More than 30 years and billions of dollars of sales later, the company he founded, Sensormatic Electronics (SRM), is a world leader in electronic security systems. The company designs, makes, markets and services electronic article surveillance (EAS) and electronic asset protection (EAP) systems, closed-circuit television (CCTV) systems, and access control systems.

Sensormatic's EAS and CCTV systems are used by both soft goods and hard goods retailers to deter shoplifting and internal theft, and its CCTV, access control and EAP security systems are used by retail and commercial/industrial customers to protect assets, information and people. The company markets its products through an extensive worldwide sales and service organization, complemented by a broad network of business partners, independent distributors and dealers.

The EAS system consists of electronic detection units, housed in pedestals, overhead units, walls, ceilings or floors and placed at exits of stores, departments or at checkout aisles. These units are used in conjunction with sensitized reusable tags and disposable labels that are attached to merchandise and then removed using a detaching or deactivator device when the item is purchased. If an item is taken through the controlled exit with the label attached, an alarm is activated.

CCTV video surveillance systems are used by a variety of businesses, industries and government agencies to protect against inventory shrinkage in retail businesses and for the protection and monitoring of personnel and assets in office and manufacturing complexes, hospitals, casinos, nuclear facilities, warehouses, correctional facilities, airports and numerous other facilities. SRM's CCTV systems can be used alone, or in conjunction with EAS, access control and asset management systems.

Access control systems are designed to monitor, control and appropriately authorize passage (pedestrian, asset or vehicular) into and out of designated areas. In a typical situation, each individual is issued a badge and inserts or swipes the badge at a door reader to gain access to buildings, rooms, or other enclosures. Access control systems can be integrated with CCTV and alarm management systems to provide additional security and protection.

The company's customer list reads like a who's-who of the retailing industry. Major customers include Wal-Mart, K mart, Home Depot, Sports Authority, MusicLand, CVS, Food Lion, Federated Department Stores, Sears, Dayton Hudson, J. C. Penney, Montgomery Ward, and 7-Eleven. In fact, millions of shoppers see SRM's products every day, most without noticing them.

Per Share Data ($) (Year Ended Jun. 30)	2001	2000	1999	1998	1997	1996	1995	1994	1993	1992
Tangible Bk. Val.	NA	5.25	3.83	3.65	4.00	4.66	6.25	5.71	8.43	4.78
Cash Flow	NA	1.75	1.36	0.37	0.61	-0.52	1.56	1.70	1.47	1.07
Earnings	0.49	0.78	0.35	-0.50	-0.29	-1.32	0.97	1.16	0.96	0.73
Dividends	Nil	Nil	Nil	Nil	0.22	0.22	0.22	0.21	0.20	0.20
Payout Ratio	Nil	Nil	Nil	Nil	NM	NM	23%	18%	21%	27%
Prices - High	23.50	23.18	17.93	20.00	18.00	23.75	38.25	39.25	35.00	20.34
- Low	12.00	12.50	7.00	3.12	11.75	13.62	20.12	26.00	20.00	9.25
P/E Ratio - High	48	30	51	NM	NM	NM	39	34	36	28
- Low	24	16	20	NM	NM	NM	21	22	21	13
Income Statement Analysis (Million $)										
Revs.	NA	1,100	1,018	987	1,026	995	889	656	487	310
Oper. Inc.	NA	191	146	126	95.1	10.0	139	138	99	58.1
Depr.	NA	63.4	64.5	64.3	66.2	59.2	41.3	32.8	28.4	14.5
Int. Exp.	NA	40.3	44.1	50.8	47.9	38.4	29.0	22.7	18.7	11.4
Pretax Inc.	NA	108	55.5	-54.1	-30.3	-160	89.0	96.0	72.0	41.0
Eff. Tax Rate	NA	33%	31%	NM	NM	NM	22%	25%	25%	23%
Net Inc.	NA	72.2	38.1	-37.1	-21.4	-97.7	70.0	72.1	54.1	31.5
Balance Sheet & Other Fin. Data (Million $)										
Cash	NA	224	209	127	21.7	117	70.3	55.0	118	63.0
Curr. Assets	NA	798	769	737	610	634	NA	NA	NA	NA
Total Assets	NA	1,763	1,776	1,802	1,644	1,630	1,571	1,156	927	462
Curr. Liab.	NA	384	403	344	329	259	NA	NA	NA	NA
LT Debt	NA	371	428	515	502	492	327	151	264	134
Common Eqty.	NA	780	723	731	773	832	953	728	490	256
Total Cap.	NA	1,379	1,317	1,246	1,274	1,323	1,279	878	754	390
Cap. Exp.	NA	46.0	29.1	29.3	38.4	49.8	0.1	NA	NA	39.0
Cash Flow	NA	136	103	27.2	44.8	-38.5	111	105	82.5	46.1
Curr. Ratio	NA	2.1	1.9	2.1	1.9	2.4	NA	NA	NA	NA
% LT Debt of Cap.	NA	26.9	32.5	41.3	39.4	37.2	25.5	17.2	35.1	34.4
% Net Inc.of Revs.	NA	6.6	3.7	NM	NM	NM	7.9	11.0	11.1	10.2
% Ret. on Assets	NA	4.1	2.1	NM	NM	NM	5.1	6.5	NA	7.0
% Ret. on Equity	NA	9.6	5.2	NM	NM	NM	8.3	11.1	NA	13.0

Data as orig reptd.; bef. results of disc opers/spec. items. Per share data adj. for stk. divs. Bold denotes diluted EPS (FASB 128)-prior periods restated. E-Estimated. NA-Not Available. NM-Not Meaningful. NR-Not Ranked.

Office—951 Yamato Rd., Boca Raton, FL 33431-0700. **Tel**—(561) 989-7000. **Website**—http://www.sensormatic.com **Chrmn**—R. G. Assaf. **Pres & CEO**—P. Loof. **SVP & CFO**—G. C. Thompson. **VP & Secy**—W. A. Engdahl. **Investor Contact**—David A. Hogan (561-989-7538). **Dirs**—P. L. Aker, R. G. Assaf, T. V. Buffet, F. A. Breidenbach, T. P. Hartman, J. E. Lineberger, J. R. Munro, P. Loof, J. T. Ray Jr. **Transfer Agent & Registrar**—Fleet National Bank c/o Equiserve L.P. **Incorporated**—in Delaware in 1968. **Empl**— 5,500. **S&P Analyst:** Jim Corridore

STANDARD
&POOR'S
STOCK REPORTS

Tyco International Ltd.

NYSE Symbol **TYC**

In S&P 500

18-AUG-01

Industry: Manufacturing (Diversified)

Summary: Tyco's businesses include electronic components, fire protection and electronic security, disposable medical products, undersea communications and commercial finance.

S&P Opinion: Buy (★★★★★)

Recent Price • 52.66
52 Wk Range • 63.21-40.15

Yield • 0.1%
12-Mo. P/E • 17.5

Quantitative Evaluations

Outlook
(1 Lowest—5 Highest)
• **4-**

Fair Value
• **67**

Risk
• **Low**

Earn./Div. Rank
• **B+**

Technical Eval.
• **Neutral** since 8/01

Rel. Strength Rank
(1 Lowest—99 Highest)
• **50**

Insider Activity
• **Neutral**

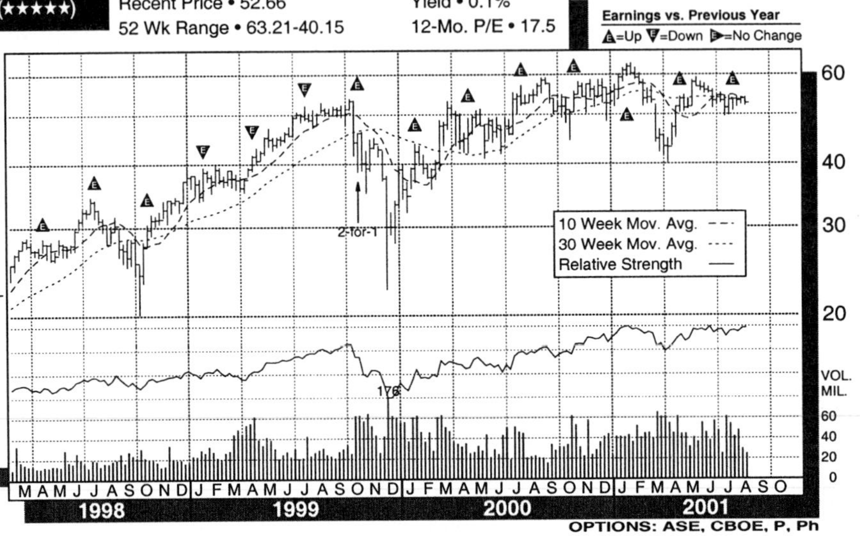

OPTIONS: ASE, CBOE, P, Ph

Overview - 14-AUG-01

Strong sales gains should go on through FY 02 (Sep.), on solid internal growth and the inclusion of non-pooled acquisitions (including CIT Group). The fire and security segment should be aided by a large base of recurring revenues and customer additions, while further growth seems likely in healthcare. Electronics sales will likely be higher in FY 01, but the big downturn seen in communications markets should bring a high-single-digit drop in FY 02. The telecommunications sector will likely see lower FY 01 sales, as it transitions to an owner and supplier of undersea capacity. Yet, with the network's first phase operational as of mid-2001, we expect a modest sales gain in FY 02. Margins should widen, on production efficiencies and TYC's aggressive integration of recent takeovers. Planned acquisitions have not been included in our forecast, but should be modestly additive to EPS upon completion. FY 00 EPS totaled $2.18 before one-time items.

Valuation - 14-AUG-01

Tyco's strong earnings performance during the current U.S. economic malaise has been a testament to its business model, which stresses recurring and service revenues. We were surprised by TYC's decision to move outside its core business areas through the June 2001, purchase of CIT Group, a commercial finance company, but the deal will likely be a success. TYC's exhaustive due diligence brought some very successful takeovers in the past decade, and we also favor TYC's plan to use CIT's financial capabilities across the full breadth of its operations. The shares have recently traded at a P/E multiple below that of the S&P 500, but our very positive outlook on Tyco makes us feel that a premium valuation is warranted. S&P's discounted cash flow analysis, which determines an intrinsic value of $90 to $100, further supports our recommendation.

Key Stock Statistics

S&P EPS Est. 2001	2.80	Tang. Bk. Value/Share	0.42
P/E on S&P Est. 2001	18.8	Beta	1.18
S&P EPS Est. 2002	3.45	Shareholders	7,700
Dividend Rate/Share	0.05	Market cap. (B)	$ 99.6
Shs. outstg. (M)	1892.0	Inst. holdings	73%
Avg. daily vol. (M)	7.096		

Value of $10,000 invested 5 years ago: $ 49,907

Fiscal Year Ending Sep. 30

	2001	2000	1999	1998	1997	1996
Revenues (Million $)						
1Q	8,020	6,639	5,214	2,688	2,290	1,216
2Q	8,898	7,070	5,239	2,852	2,333	1,244
3Q	9,225	7,418	5,820	3,235	2,548	1,258
4Q	—	7,805	6,225	3,537	2,709	1,372
Yr.	—	28,932	22,497	12,311	—	5,090
Earnings Per Share ($)						
1Q	**0.57**	**0.46**	**-0.07**	**0.21**	0.15	0.11
2Q	**0.65**	**0.50**	**0.07**	**0.24**	0.15	0.12
3Q	**0.66**	**0.58**	**0.12**	**0.27**	0.18	0.13
4Q	**E0.85**	**1.12**	**0.46**	**0.28**	0.19	0.15
Yr.	**E2.80**	**2.64**	**0.62**	**1.01**	—	0.51

Next earnings report expected: late October

Dividend Data (Dividends have been paid since 1975.)

Amount ($)	Date Decl.	Ex-Div. Date	Stock of Record	Payment Date
0.013	Sep. 27	Sep. 29	Oct. 03	Nov. 01 '00
0.013	Dec. 15	Dec. 28	Jan. 02	Feb. 02 '01
0.013	Mar. 15	Mar. 29	Apr. 02	May. 02 '01
0.013	Jun. 15	Jun. 28	Jul. 02	Aug. 01 '01

Tyco International Ltd.

Business Summary - 14-AUG-01

Tyco International operates in the areas of electronics (34% of sales and 39% of operating profits in FY 00--Sep.--all totals exclude one-time items); telecommunications (9% and 9%, respectively); healthcare and specialty products (22%, 24%); fire and safety services (21%, 16%); and flow control (14%, 12%); TYC later reclassified flow control into its fire and safety and electronics divisions. In June 2001, Tyco moved outside of its core business areas to purchase CIT Group, the largest independent commercial finance company, for a total of $10 billion in TYC shares and cash. Tyco also reached agreements in May 2001, to acquire C.R. Bard ($1.1 billion of 2001 revenues), a medical devices maker, for $3.2 billion (mostly stock); and August 2001, to buy Sensormatic Electronics ($1.1 billion of revenues in latest fiscal year), a supplier of electronic security solutions, for $2.3 billion (mostly stock). TYC derived 36% of sales outside of the Americas in FY 00.

TYC's recent takeovers continue a very aggressive program conducted over much of the past decade. Other recent deals included the Power Systems business of Lucent Technologies (January 2001), for $2.5 billion in cash; and Mallinckrodt Inc. (October 2000), for a total of $4.2 billion in stock and assumed debt. To be considered for purchase, a company must be able to make an immediate positive earnings contribution, and strategically strengthen a core business.

In fire and safety, TYC is the world's largest contractor for the design and installation of fire detection, suppression and sprinkler systems, and for the servicing of such systems. Systems are placed in buildings and other installations. The division is also the world's leading provider of electronic security services.

Flow control products consist of pipe, fittings, valves, meters and related products, which are used to transport, control and measure the flow of liquids and gases.

The electronics sector makes electrical and electronic components. TYC expanded the division through the purchases of Lucent Technologies' Power Systems unit, which provides energy solutions and power products; and AMP (bought in April 1999), the world's leading electrical and electronic connection devices maker.

The TyCom telecommunications unit designs, makes, installs, operates and services undersea cable communications systems. In early 2000, TYC started to build its own global undersea fiber optic communications network, which would be the world's largest upon completion. The first phase became operational in mid-2001.

The healthcare and specialty products segment produces medical supplies and instruments, adhesive products and tapes, and other products. The purchase of Mallinckrodt (annual revenues of $2.6 billion), a maker of respiratory care, diagnostic imaging, and analgesic pharmaceutical products, made Tyco Healthcare the world's second largest producer of medical devices.

Per Share Data ($) (Year Ended Sep. 30)	2000	1999	1998	1997	1996	1995	1994	1993	1992	1991
Tangible Bk. Val.	0.42	0.10	NM	1.30	1.15	1.04	0.58	0.23	0.30	0.12
Cash Flow	3.60	1.40	1.49	0.84	0.64	0.58	0.52	0.37	0.44	0.50
Earnings	2.64	0.62	1.01	0.65	0.51	0.36	0.34	0.20	0.26	0.32
Dividends	0.05	0.05	0.05	0.05	0.05	0.05	0.06	0.04	0.06	0.04
Payout Ratio	2%	8%	5%	8%	10%	14%	19%	19%	22%	14%
Prices - High	59.18	53.87	39.09	22.75	14.00	8.90	6.90	6.46	5.29	6.53
- Low	32.00	22.50	20.12	12.93	8.09	5.81	5.35	4.67	3.82	1.00
P/E Ratio - High	22	87	39	35	28	18	20	33	21	20
- Low	12	36	20	20	16	11	16	24	15	11
Income Statement Analysis (Million $)										
Revs.	28,932	22,497	12,311	6,598	5,090	4,535	3,263	3,115	3,066	3,108
Oper. Inc.	7,393	4,977	2,490	899	666	618	312	282	261	328
Depr.	1,644	1,322	566	120	83.0	133	66.2	63.1	66.5	64.8
Int. Exp.	845	547	236	90.8	62.0	63.0	45.0	50.5	63.3	73.9
Pretax Inc.	6,465	1,651	1,718	688	524	385	201	129	131	189
Eff. Tax Rate	30%	38%	32%	39%	41%	44%	38%	44%	28%	38%
Net Inc.	4,520	1,031	1,177	419	310	217	125	72.0	95.0	117
Balance Sheet & Other Fin. Data (Million $)										
Cash	1,265	1,762	820	171	69.4	66.0	6.2	32.9	32.1	22.7
Curr. Assets	12,816	11,163	5,743	2,447	1,696	1,452	1,048	1,133	1,107	1,098
Total Assets	40,404	32,362	16,527	5,888	3,954	3,381	2,416	2,459	2,452	2,393
Curr. Liab.	11,679	9,179	5,048	1,735	1,292	1,085	811	869	833	855
LT Debt	9,462	9,109	4,652	919	512	506	413	562	535	609
Common Eqty.	17,033	12,333	6,137	3,052	1,938	1,635	1,079	920	1,041	905
Total Cap.	27,630	21,946	10,847	3,996	2,469	2,151	1,506	1,490	1,602	1,538
Cap. Exp.	1,704	1,633	781	199	123	119	73.0	80.0	68.0	67.0
Cash Flow	6,165	2,353	1,743	539	393	350	191	135	162	182
Curr. Ratio	1.1	1.2	1.1	1.4	1.3	1.3	1.3	1.3	1.3	1.3
% LT Debt of Cap.	34.2	41.5	42.9	23.0	20.7	23.5	27.4	37.7	33.4	39.6
% Net Inc.of Revs.	15.6	4.6	9.6	6.4	6.1	4.8	3.8	2.3	3.1	3.8
% Ret. on Assets	12.4	3.7	8.7	8.5	8.5	6.6	5.1	3.0	3.9	NA
% Ret. on Equity	30.7	9.3	24.6	16.8	17.4	14.4	12.5	7.4	9.8	NA

Data as orig. reptd.; bef. results of disc. opers. and/or spec. items. Per share data adj. for stk. divs. as of ex-div. date. Yrs. ended Jun. 30 prior to 1997 on Rev. and EPS tables, and through 1997 on Per Share Data, Income Statement and Balance Sheet tables; 1997 Rev. and EPS tables restated for pooling-of-int. acqs. Bold denotes diluted EPS (FASB 128). E-Estimated. NA-Not Available. NM-Not Meaningful.

Office—The Zurich Centre, 90 Pitts Bay Rd., Pembroke HM 08, Bermuda. **Tel**—(441) 292-8674. **Website**—http://www.tyco.com **Chrmn, Pres & CEO**—L. D. Kozlowski. **SVP & Investor Contact**—R. Jackson Blackstock (212) 424-1344. **Dirs**—M. A. Ashcroft, J. M. Berman, R. S. Bodman, J. F. Fort, III, S. W. Foss, L. D. Kozlowski, W. E. Lane, J. S. Pasman Jr., W. P. Slusser, F. E. Walsh Jr. **Transfer Agents & Registrars**—AS&K Services Ltd., Hamilton, Bermuda; Mellon Investor Services, Ridgefield Park, NJ. **Incorporated**—in Bermuda in 1984. **Empl**— 215,000. **S&P Analyst:** Michael W. Jaffe

STANDARD &POOR'S
STOCK REPORTS

URS Corp.

NYSE Symbol **URS**

In S&P SmallCap 600

18-AUG-01

Industry: Engineering & Construction

Summary: URS is a worldwide provider of architectural and engineering services to public and private sector clients.

S&P Opinion: Buy (★★★★★)

Recent Price • 24.41
52 Wk Range • 27.94-10.75
Yield • Nil
12-Mo. P/E • 10.5

Quantitative Evaluations

Outlook (1 Lowest—5 Highest)
• **5**

Fair Value
• **44.60**

Risk
• **Average**

Earn./Div. Rank
• **B+**

Technical Eval.
• **Bearish** since 8/01

Rel. Strength Rank (1 Lowest—99 Highest)
• **55**

Insider Activity
• **NA**

Earnings vs. Previous Year
▲=Up ▼=Down ▶=No Change

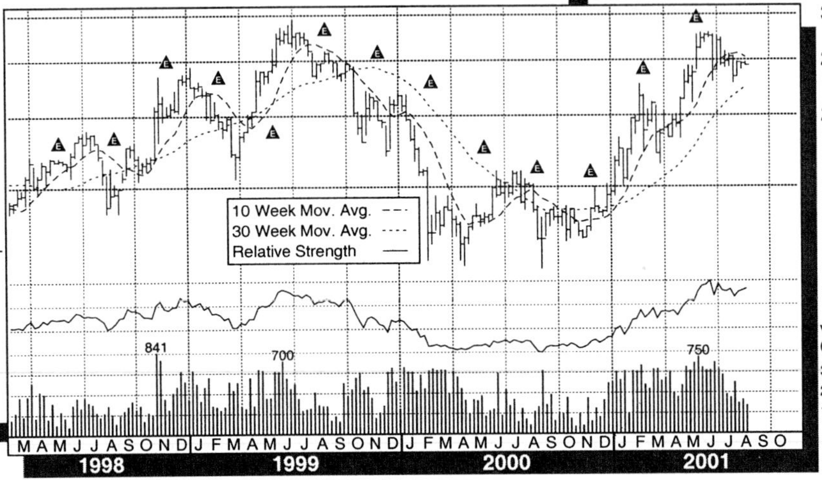

Overview - 29-JUN-01

Revenues are expected to advance 2% to 3% in FY 01 (Oct.), with some improvement likely in FY 02, as growth in public infrastructure projects is offset by soft economic conditions, a tight market for engineers, and weak foreign currencies. However, operating (EBITDA) margins should widen by at least 100 basis points, on improved operating efficiencies, as synergies from acquisitions, including a further consolidation of offices, lead to lower overhead. In addition, URS should benefit from the integration and consolidation of a new accounting and billing system, which will likely improve accounts receivables levels. We expect in excess of $11 million in free cash flow to be used for debt reduction, leading to a decline in interest expense and increased profitability. After taxes as 45%, and after preferred dividends, we project EPS at $2.45 for FY 01, with a 12% gain, to $2.75, for FY 02.

Valuation - 29-JUN-01

We recently initiated coverage of URS with a buy recommendation. We expect the company to benefit from increased transportation infrastructure spending, and from more water and energy-related projects. Although URS's attractive valuation reflects its high debt level and risk profile, the company is focusing on improving its operating strategy. We anticipate that strong cash generation will let URS bring the debt down to about 55% of capital by late FY 02, from a recent 68%, while return on equity remains in the high teens. The shares have been trading at nearly a 40% discount to those of URS's peers, and 50% below the projected P/E for the S&P SmallCap 600; we see potential for capital gains with the stock at only 10X our FY 01 EPS estimate, and 5.4X enterprise value-to-EBITDA. In addition, with a PEG ratio (P/E-to-EPS growth) of only 0.75 for FY 02, prospects are very positive.

Key Stock Statistics

S&P EPS Est. 2001	2.45	Tang. Bk. Value/Share	NM
P/E on S&P Est. 2001	10.0	Beta	0.85
S&P EPS Est. 2002	2.75	Shareholders	4,591
Dividend Rate/Share	Nil	Market cap. (B)	$0.417
Shs. outstg. (M)	17.1	Inst. holdings	75%
Avg. daily vol. (M)	0.034		

Value of $10,000 invested 5 years ago: $ 33,903

Fiscal Year Ending Oct. 31

	2001	2000	1999	1998	1997	1996
Revenues (Million $)						
1Q	515.6	512.9	199.1	186.2	95.54	48.50
2Q	546.0	535.4	222.2	195.2	99.8	64.86
3Q	—	558.5	428.5	207.5	100.2	89.73
4Q	—	598.8	568.8	217.1	111.0	102.4
Yr.	—	2,206	1,419	806.0	406.4	305.5
Earnings Per Share ($)						
1Q	**0.42**	**0.40**	**0.35**	**0.27**	**0.22**	0.11
2Q	**0.55**	**0.51**	**0.42**	**0.31**	0.24	0.18
3Q	**E0.71**	**0.64**	**0.53**	**0.40**	0.28	0.22
4Q	**E0.77**	**0.72**	**0.68**	**0.45**	0.32	0.29
Yr.	**E2.45**	**2.27**	**1.98**	**1.43**	**1.08**	**0.81**

Next earnings report expected: NA

Dividend Data

Cash dividends, which have not been paid since 1986, are restricted by terms of debt agreements.

URS Corporation

Business Summary - 29-JUN-01

URS Corp. (URS) is a leading architecture and engineering services company. Its strategy is to focus on infrastructure markets, including surface, air, and rail systems; industrial process/petrochemical; facilities projects; and environmental projects. Headquartered in San Francisco, URS competes to obtain regional contracts or large national or multi-national contracts.

The company provides three main services: planning, design, and program and construction management services. URS provides services in seven markets: surface transportation, air transportation, railroads/mass transit, industrial process/petrochemical, general building and facilities, water/wastewater and hazardous waste. Services are offered to state, local, and federal government agencies, and to clients in the chemical, pharmaceutical, manufacturing, forest products, energy, oil, gas, mining, healthcare, water supply, retail and commercial development, telecommunications, and utilities industries. Revenues were derived as follows in FY 00 (Oct.): local and state agencies 33%, federal agencies 16%, private businesses 39%, and international 11%.

In planning services, URS provides a broad range of projects ranging from design and technical and economic feasibility studies to community involvement programs and archaeological investigations. The company uses the planning process to develop a project blueprint. URS uses planning analyses and reports to identify and evaluate alternatives, estimate usage levels, determine financial feasibility, assess available technology, ascertain economic and environmental impacts, and recommend optimal courses of action.

In design and design-related services, projects include architectural and interior design and civil, structural, mechanical, electrical, sanitary, environmental, water resources, geotechnical/underground, dam, mining and seismic engineering design. For each project, URS identifies project requirements and integrates and coordinates the various design elements. The result is a set of contract documents that include plans, specifications, and cost estimates used to build a project, and details design characteristics, lists material the contractor should use, and provides the schedule for construction.

Program and construction management services include master scheduling of both the design and construction phases, construction and life-cycle cost estimating, cash flow analysis, value engineering, constructability reviews, environmental and specialized engineering, and construction and bid management. URS also oversees and coordinates the activities of construction contractors. This involves acting as the owner's representative for on-site supervision and inspection of the work.

In June 2000, URS sold DecisionQuest, its litigation support services subsidiary, to a group led by DecisionQuest management, for $20 million.

Per Share Data ($) (Year Ended Oct. 31)	2000	1999	1998	1997	1996	1995	1994	1993	1992	1991
Tangible Bk. Val.	NM	NM	2.42	3.23	1.48	3.89	4.16	3.45	3.21	2.48
Cash Flow	3.79	3.63	2.36	1.79	1.58	0.95	0.82	0.61	0.81	0.63
Earnings	2.27	1.98	1.43	1.06	0.80	0.68	0.60	0.18	0.55	0.40
Dividends	Nil	Nil	Nil	Nil	Nil	Nil	Nil	Nil	Nil	Nil
Payout Ratio	Nil	Nil	Nil	Nil	Nil	Nil	Nil	Nil	Nil	Nil
Prices - High	21.81	29.56	23.68	19.06	9.87	7.37	8.00	10.12	11.12	12.50
- Low	10.75	15.50	11.31	9.00	6.25	5.12	4.75	4.37	6.50	3.12
P/E Ratio - High	10	15	17	18	12	11	13	56	20	31
- Low	5	8	8	8	8	8	8	24	12	8
Income Statement Analysis (Million $)										
Revs.	2,206	1,419	806	406	305	180	164	146	137	123
Oper. Inc.	205	135	64.8	31.9	20.2	10.8	8.7	7.6	8.3	6.8
Depr.	41.8	33.8	14.6	7.9	5.3	3.1	2.6	3.0	2.4	2.0
Int. Exp.	71.9	34.6	8.8	4.8	3.9	1.4	1.2	1.2	1.2	2.3
Pretax Inc.	91.6	66.3	41.5	19.2	12.1	6.4	4.9	1.4	4.7	2.5
Eff. Tax Rate	46%	45%	45%	40%	39%	21%	9.20%	9.80%	9.70%	9.80%
Net Inc.	49.9	36.6	22.7	11.5	7.4	5.1	4.4	1.3	4.3	2.3
Balance Sheet & Other Fin. Data (Million $)										
Cash	23.7	45.7	36.5	22.1	22.4	8.8	9.5	6.6	5.7	5.2
Curr. Assets	777	746	286	149	128	59.7	54.3	46.5	43.8	37.8
Total Assets	1,427	1,437	452	213	186	74.1	65.2	58.1	54.9	49.8
Curr. Liab.	382	387	95.0	86.2	70.3	23.4	20.6	18.8	17.0	15.9
LT Debt	603	649	95.0	41.4	55.4	10.0	9.3	8.3	8.7	8.3
Common Eqty.	258	207	166	77.2	56.7	39.5	34.0	29.4	27.9	23.3
Total Cap.	1,005	975	267	119	112	49.5	43.2	37.7	36.6	31.6
Cap. Exp.	15.9	20.2	12.2	5.1	3.0	1.6	2.1	1.9	1.2	1.0
Cash Flow	83.4	67.0	37.3	19.4	12.7	8.2	7.0	4.3	6.7	4.3
Curr. Ratio	2.0	1.9	3.0	1.7	1.8	2.6	2.6	2.5	2.6	2.4
% LT Debt of Cap.	60.0	66.6	35.6	34.8	49.4	20.2	21.4	22.0	23.8	26.4
% Net Inc.of Revs.	2.3	2.6	2.8	2.8	2.4	2.9	2.7	0.9	3.1	1.9
% Ret. on Assets	3.5	3.9	6.8	5.8	5.6	7.3	7.2	2.3	8.1	3.3
% Ret. on Equity	17.9	17.8	18.7	17.2	15.4	13.8	14.0	4.5	16.6	18.1

Data as orig reptd.; bef. results of disc opers/spec. items. Per share data adj. for stk. divs. Bold denotes diluted EPS (FASB 128)-prior periods restated. E-Estimated. NA-Not Available. NM-Not Meaningful. NR-Not Ranked.

Office—100 California St., Suite 500, San Francisco, CA 94111-4529. **Tel**—(415) 774-2700. **Website**—http://www.urscorp.com **Chrmn, Pres & CEO**—M. M. Koffel. **EVP, CFO & Secy**—K. P. Ainsworth. **VP, Treas & Investor Contact**—David C. Nelson. **Dirs**—K. P. Ainsworth, R. C. Blum, S. R. Foley Jr., M. L. Knowles, M. M. Koffel, R. B. Madden, A. Der Marderosian, J. Y. Perez, R. Q. Praeger, I. L. Rosenstein, W. D. Walsh. **Transfer Agent & Registrar**—Mellon Investor Services, SF. **Incorporated**—in California in 1957; reincorporated in Delaware in 1976. **Empl**— 15,900. **S&P Analyst:** Stewart Scharf

STANDARD
&POOR'S
STOCK REPORTS

Vishay Intertechnology

NYSE Symbol **VSH**

In S&P MidCap 400

23-AUG-01

Industry:
Electrical Equipment

Summary: This company is a leading manufacturer and supplier of a wide range of passive electronic components and discrete semiconductors.

S&P Opinion: Buy (★★★★★)

Recent Price • 21.75
52 Wk Range • 42.18-13.75

Yield • Nil
12-Mo. P/E • 7.4

Quantitative Evaluations

Outlook
(1 Lowest—5 Highest)
• **4-**

Fair Value
• **28.40**

Risk
• **Average**

Earn./Div. Rank
• **B**

Technical Eval.
• **Neutral** since 8/01

Rel. Strength Rank
(1 Lowest—99 Highest)
• **44**

Insider Activity
• **NA**

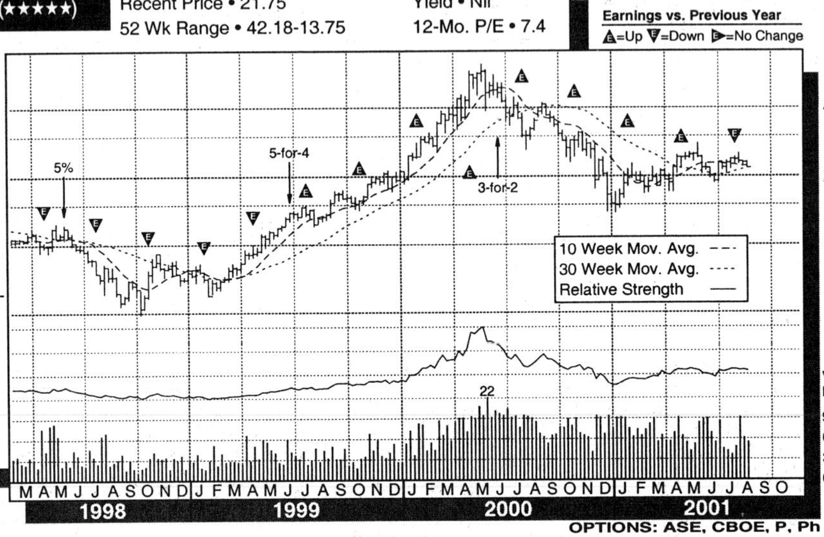

OPTIONS: ASE, CBOE, P, Ph

Overview - 08-AUG-01

We expect revenues to be down 35% in 2001 as the electronics industry finishes out a cyclical downturn. We expect average prices for VSH's components to be weak into mid-2002. Gross margins are at cycle-low levels. A $29 million restructuring charge for plant closures and a $20 million charge for marking inventories of the key raw material tantalum down to market prices were taken in the second quarter of 2001. About 4,000 employees have been let go in 2001, as factories run at low utilization rates. On August 1, 2001, VSH announced the acquisition of General Semiconductor Inc., of Melville, NY, in a stock transaction valued at $539 million plus $229 million of assumed debt; the deal adds a line of power management chips. We estimate 2001 EPS at $1.20 (excluding $0.29 in one-time items), 2002 EPS at $1.25, and 2003 EPS at $2.00 as a recovery unfolds.

Valuation - 08-AUG-01

The shares have started to recover from lows set near year-end 2000 as investors begin to anticipate the next industry upturn. In the present economic slowdown, the company's capacitor and discrete semiconductors businesses will be constrained. However, over the next few years, growth in wireless phone sales offers great opportunities for the company, as each unit could potentially use over $13 in products of the types made by VSH and Siliconix; next generation 3G phones could use $25 worth. VSH is making its product mix richer through acquisitions. The company has little debt. The shares recently traded at 2.1X tangible book value, which is near cycle-low levels, and at 18X our 2002 EPS estimate of $1.25, which is near VSH's estimated long-term growth rate of 16%. Given an attractive valuation and good long-term opportunities, we recommend purchase of the shares.

Key Stock Statistics

S&P EPS Est. 2001	1.20	Tang. Bk. Value/Share	11.15
P/E on S&P Est. 2001	18.1	Beta	1.26
S&P EPS Est. 2002	1.25	Shareholders	2,067
Dividend Rate/Share	Nil	Market cap. (B)	$ 2.8
Shs. outstg. (M)	137.9	Inst. holdings	54%
Avg. daily vol. (M)	1.308		

Value of $10,000 invested 5 years ago: $ 23,230

Fiscal Year Ending Dec. 31

	2001	2000	1999	1998	1997	1996
Revenues (Million $)						
1Q	558.5	538.9	423.1	348.7	273.3	310.7
2Q	383.4	612.8	425.3	412.8	272.7	273.5
3Q	—	669.8	443.7	399.5	285.4	259.9
4Q	—	643.6	46.00	411.7	293.9	253.9
Yr.	—	2,465	1,760	1,573	1,125	1,098
Earnings Per Share ($)						
1Q	**0.65**	**0.56**	**0.01**	**0.13**	**0.16**	**0.22**
2Q	**0.02**	**0.96**	**0.16**	**0.13**	**0.16**	**0.03**
3Q	—	**1.22**	**0.20**	**0.10**	**0.16**	**0.12**
4Q	—	**1.01**	**0.28**	**-0.29**	**-0.06**	**0.05**
Yr.	—	**3.77**	**0.65**	**0.07**	**0.42**	**0.42**

Next earnings report expected: NA

Dividend Data

No cash dividends have been paid.

A Division of The McGraw·Hill Companies

Vishay Intertechnology, Inc.

Business Summary - 08-AUG-01

Vishay Intertechnology is a leading global manufacturer of discrete passive electronic components including resistors, capacitors and inductors, and discrete active electronic components such as diodes and transistors.

Unlike integrated circuits, which combine many electronic functions in one chip, discrete electronic components perform a single function per device. Passive components adjust and regulate electric current, or store energy and filter frequencies. They are passive in the sense that they do not amplify DC current or voltage. Active components generate, control, regulate, amplify or switch electronic signals or energy. VSH's sales in 2000 were 66% from passive components and 34% from active components.

The company's products are used in virtually every type of product containing electronic circuitry, including computer related products, telecommunications, measuring instruments, industrial equipment, military/aerospace equipment, and automotive applications. International sales, primarily to Europe and Asia, accounted for 56% of the 2000 total.

VSH's broad line of electronic components offers customers one-stop shopping for the primary elements of electronic circuitry. Products include fixed resistors, tantalum capacitors, multi-layer ceramic chip capacitors (MLCCs), film capacitors, power MOSFETs, power integrated circuits, signal processing switches, optocouplers, diodes and transistors. Products are sold primarily to original equipment manufacturers (OEMs), OEM subcontractors that assemble printed circuit boards, and independent distributors that maintain large inventories of electronic goods for resale to OEMs.

An aggressive acquisition strategy has been a major element of the company's growth in the past, and should continue to be in the future. In March 1998, VSH purchased an 80% interest in Siliconix, a publicly traded power and analog chip company, and 100% of TEMIC Semiconductor GmbH, a discrete active electronic component company. The integrated circuit division of TEMIC was later sold to Atmel Inc. In February 2001, VSH proposed to purchase the remaining 20% interest in Siliconix, but the offer was refused. In June 2001, VSH closed its acquisition of the infrared components operations of Infineon Technologies AG, of Munich. In August 2001, the company announced an agreement to purchase component maker General Semiconductor Corp. in an all-stock transaction valued at about $539 million in stock plus $229 million in assumed debt.

An important part of VSH's strategy includes achieving production cost savings through the transfer and expansion of manufacturing operations to lower cost areas, such as Israel, Mexico, the Czech Republic, Taiwan and China. At year-end 2000, about 33% of the company's identifiable assets were located in the U.S., 29% were in Europe, 24% were in Israel, and 14% in Asia.

Per Share Data ($) (Year Ended Dec. 31)	2000	1999	1998	1997	1996	1995	1994	1993	1992	1991
Tangible Bk. Val.	11.15	4.83	4.49	5.31	5.87	4.99	3.09	3.71	2.67	1.77
Cash Flow	4.79	1.74	1.17	1.12	1.07	1.43	1.08	0.88	0.69	0.58
Earnings	3.77	0.65	0.06	0.42	0.42	0.79	0.55	0.42	0.36	0.26
Dividends	Nil	Nil	Nil	Nil	Nil	Nil	Nil	Nil	Nil	Nil
Payout Ratio	Nil	Nil	Nil	Nil	Nil	Nil	Nil	Nil	Nil	Nil
Prices - High	62.66	21.33	12.50	16.19	15.77	20.44	11.49	7.88	7.41	4.30
- Low	13.87	5.93	4.89	9.36	8.40	10.58	6.86	5.32	3.08	2.21
P/E Ratio - High	17	33	NM	38	38	26	21	19	21	16
- Low	4	9	NM	14	20	13	12	13	9	8
Income Statement Analysis (Million $)										
Revs.	2,465	1,760	1,573	1,125	1,098	1,224	988	856	664	442
Oper. Inc.	837	333	277	212	208	233	154	118	85.9	71.9
Depr.	141	140	140	89.1	77.2	69.5	55.9	46.8	33.4	25.4
Int. Exp.	25.2	53.3	49.0	18.8	17.4	29.4	24.8	20.6	19.1	15.2
Pretax Inc.	690	135	42.6	89.6	70.3	123	74.1	50.9	37.9	27.3
Eff. Tax Rate	21%	27%	72%	38%	25%	25%	21%	16%	20%	23%
Net Inc.	518	83.2	8.2	53.3	52.6	92.7	58.9	42.6	30.4	20.9
Balance Sheet & Other Fin. Data (Million $)										
Cash	337	105	114	55.3	20.9	19.6	26.9	10.9	16.0	14.2
Curr. Assets	1,475	927	957	646	623	640	561	394	288	207
Total Assets	2,784	2,324	2,463	1,720	1,556	1,543	1,334	948	662	449
Curr. Liab.	418	345	317	191	189	229	232	188	142	78.0
LT Debt	140	657	815	347	230	229	402	267	140	128
Common Eqty.	1,835	1,015	1,003	960	945	908	565	377	347	201
Total Cap.	2,118	1,796	1,938	1,349	1,208	1,178	1,007	670	496	340
Cap. Exp.	230	120	152	75.9	124	166	83.0	190	144	31.0
Cash Flow	659	223	148	142	136	169	115	89.4	63.8	46.3
Curr. Ratio	3.5	2.7	3.0	3.4	3.3	2.8	2.4	2.1	2.0	2.6
% LT Debt of Cap.	6.6	36.6	42.0	25.8	19.0	19.4	39.9	39.9	28.1	37.6
% Net Inc.of Revs.	21.0	4.7	0.5	4.7	4.8	7.6	6.0	5.0	4.6	4.7
% Ret. on Assets	20.3	3.5	0.4	3.3	3.4	6.5	5.0	5.3	4.9	4.7
% Ret. on Equity	36.3	8.2	0.8	5.6	5.7	12.6	12.1	11.8	10.1	11.0

Data as orig reptd.; bef. results of disc opers/spec. items. Per share data adj. for stk. divs. Bold denotes diluted EPS (FASB 128)-prior periods restated. E-Estimated. NA-Not Available. NM-Not Meaningful. NR-Not Ranked.

Office—63 Lincoln Highway, Malvern, PA 19355-2120. **Tel**—(610) 644-1300. **Website**—http://www.vishay.com **Chrmn & CEO**—F. Zandman. **EVP, Treas & CFO**—R. N. Grubb. **Investor Contact**—Robert A. Freece. **VP & Secy**—W. J. Spires. **Dirs**—A. D. Eden, R. A. Freece, R. N. Grubb, E. Hurvitz, G. Paul, E. B. Shils, Z. Shoshani, L. B. Slaner, M. I. Solomon, J.-C. Tine, F. Zandman, M. Zandman, R. Zandman. **Transfer Agent & Registrar**—American Stock Transfer & Trust Co., NYC. **Incorporated**—in Delaware in 1962. **Empl**— 18,400. **S&P Analyst:** T. W. Smith, CFA

STANDARD & POOR'S
STOCK REPORTS

American Standard

NYSE Symbol **ASD**

In S&P MidCap 400

18-AUG-01

Industry: Manufacturing (Diversified)

Summary: This company is a leading worldwide manufacturer of air conditioning systems and bathroom and kitchen fixtures, and a major European producer of commercial vehicle braking systems.

S&P Opinion: Accumulate (★★★★)

Recent Price • 68.33 | Yield • Nil
52 Wk Range • 70.25-38.50 | 12-Mo. P/E • 14.9

Quantitative Evaluations

Outlook (1 Lowest—5 Highest)
• **1–**

Fair Value
• **59.40**

Risk
• **Average**

Earn./Div. Rank
• **NR**

Technical Eval.
• **Bullish** since 7/01

Rel. Strength Rank (1 Lowest—99 Highest)
• **79**

Insider Activity
• **Unfavorable**

OPTIONS: CBOE

Overview - 14-JUN-01

Sales should be flat to very slightly higher in 2001, with a likely small gain in the air conditioning sector offset by weaker plumbing and vehicle control sales. Moderation of the domestic economy and a weak euro currency will likely limit air conditioning sales, but market share gains should lift the division's performance. We also see that division's unitary products business being aided by still solid demand for replacement and renovation projects, driven by the booming housing market of recent years. We expect the weak euro to cause a small drop in plumbing product sales, based on the sector's big presence in Europe. We also think sales of vehicle control systems will fall about 10%-15%, hurt by difficult European macroeconomic conditions and much slower U.S. truck production. Margins should be somewhat wider, on operating efficiencies, materials management efforts and initial savings from a late 2000 restructuring plan.

Valuation - 14-JUN-01

The shares have surged since December 2000, as investors started to anticipate the eventual benefits of the Fed Funds easing program that was initiated in early 2001. The shares had also been helped by the belief that the euro currency might be less of a drag on profits in 2001, but that will not likely occur in the near-term. We have been impressed by American Standard's ability to record profit gains throughout 2000 and into 2001, when facing a slowing domestic economy and the negative impact of a very weak euro. ASD's strong brand names, aggressive marketing effort and extensive attention to operating efficiencies should enable it to record ongoing solid profit gains in 2001. In light of that outlook, the shares seem undervalued in their recent trading area of about 13 times our 2001 EPS forecast, and should be a good holding for a likely economic recovery in late 2001.

Key Stock Statistics

S&P EPS Est. 2001	4.90	Tang. Bk. Value/Share	NM
P/E on S&P Est. 2001	13.9	Beta	0.60
S&P EPS Est. 2002	5.65	Shareholders	951
Dividend Rate/Share	Nil	Market cap. (B)	$ 4.9
Shs. outstg. (M)	71.9	Inst. holdings	73%
Avg. daily vol. (M)	0.350		

Value of $10,000 invested 5 years ago: $ 21,544

Fiscal Year Ending Dec. 31

	2001	2000	1999	1998	1997	1996
Revenues (Million $)						
1Q	1,791	1,822	1,649	1,493	1,361	1,364
2Q	2,039	2,046	1,911	1,795	1,589	1,519
3Q	—	1,961	1,876	1,728	1,519	1,485
4Q	—	1,769	1,754	1,638	1,539	1,437
Yr.	—	7,598	7,190	6,654	6,008	5,805
Earnings Per Share ($)						
1Q	0.90	0.82	0.68	0.49	0.43	-2.66
2Q	1.63	1.48	1.28	1.04	0.96	0.74
3Q	E1.42	1.23	1.07	0.49	-0.46	0.70
4Q	E0.95	0.82	0.62	-1.66	0.62	0.56
Yr.	E4.90	4.36	3.63	0.46	1.57	-0.60

Next earnings report expected: mid October

Dividend Data

No cash dividends have been paid, and the company has said it does not currently intend to pay any.

A Division of The McGraw-Hill Companies

American Standard Companies Inc.

Business Summary - 14-JUN-01

American Standard Companies is a major worldwide maker of air conditioning systems, bathroom and kitchen fixtures and fittings, and commercial vehicle control systems. In November 2000, ASD sold the last piece of its small Medical Systems Group, which pursued initiatives in medical diagnostics.

ASD derived 62% of sales and 63% of operating profits in 2000 from its air conditioning business; 24% and 19% from plumbing products; and 14% and 18% from vehicle control systems.

Brands include Trane and American Standard for air conditioning; American Standard, Ideal Standard, Porcher, Armitage Shanks and Dolomite for plumbing products; and Wabco for vehicle control systems.

Operations in Europe accounted for 28% of sales and 25% of operating profits in 2000. Other foreign operations contributed 16% and 8%, respectively.

The company is a leading U.S. maker of air conditioning systems for domestic and export sales, and also produces air conditioning systems outside the U.S. ASD makes unitary systems, which are factory-assembled central air conditioning systems; and applied systems, which are custom-engineered for commercial use. The company focuses on the growing and higher-margin replacement, repair and servicing businesses, which generated 65% of its air conditioning sales in 2000.

ASD is a leading maker in Europe, the U.S. and several other nations of bathroom and kitchen fixtures and fittings. It supplies these products to residential and commercial construction markets and retail sales channels. Markets for these products include replacement and remodeling, and new construction. About 65% of plumbing segment sales in 2000 were from non-U.S. operations. The company expanded its foreign plumbing business through the February 1999 acquisition of Blue Circle Industries PLC's bathrooms division, which included its Armitage Shanks and Ceramica Dolomite operations, for $427 million.

The company is a leading producer, mainly in Europe and Brazil, of braking and control systems for the commercial and utility vehicle industry.

During 2000's fourth quarter, ASD recorded $75 million of one-time pretax charges related to productivity initiatives announced in December 2000. American targeted the program at eliminating redundant work, enhancing productivity and improving profitability. It planned to reduce its workforce by about 1,200 positions and expected the overall program to generate about $50 million in annualized cost savings, with initial benefits expected in late 2001. Also in the quarter, ASD recorded a $57 million pretax gain on the $68 million sale of a water heater business to Grupo Industrial Saltillo. After recording a $5 million reversal of prior year restructuring charges, the company's combined net one-time charges in the quarter amounted to $0.01 a share.

Per Share Data ($) (Year Ended Dec. 31)	2000	1999	1998	1997	1996	1995	1994	1993	1992	1991
Tangible Bk. Val.	NM	NM	NM	NM	NM	NM	NA	NA	NA	NA
Cash Flow	7.32	6.42	3.04	3.73	1.27	3.81	NA	NA	NA	NA
Earnings	4.36	3.63	0.46	1.57	-0.60	1.90	NA	NA	NA	NA
Dividends	Nil	Nil	Nil	Nil	Nil	Nil	NA	NA	NA	NA
Payout Ratio	Nil	Nil	Nil	Nil	Nil	Nil	NA	NA	NA	NA
Prices - High	49.75	49.43	49.25	51.62	39.75	32.00	NA	NA	NA	NA
- Low	34.31	31.12	21.62	34.62	25.50	19.62	NA	NA	NA	NA
P/E Ratio - High	11	14	NM	33	NM	17	NA	NA	NA	NA
- Low	8	9	NM	22	NM	10	NA	NA	NA	NA
Income Statement Analysis (Million $)										
Revs.	7,598	7,190	6,654	6,008	5,805	5,221	NA	NA	NA	NA
Oper. Inc.	916	839	748	711	665	624	NA	NA	NA	NA
Depr.	213	202	190	164	146	143	NA	NA	NA	NA
Int. Exp.	199	188	188	192	202	217	NA	NA	NA	NA
Pretax Inc.	509	452	167	247	57.6	239	NA	NA	NA	NA
Eff. Tax Rate	38%	42%	79%	47%	181%	36%	NA	NA	NA	NA
Net Inc.	315	264	33.6	120	-46.7	142	NA	NA	NA	NA
Balance Sheet & Other Fin. Data (Million $)										
Cash	85.4	61.2	64.8	28.8	59.7	89.0	NA	NA	NA	NA
Curr. Assets	1,878	1,726	1,591	1,394	1,386	1,295	NA	NA	NA	NA
Total Assets	4,745	4,686	4,156	3,669	3,520	3,520	NA	NA	NA	NA
Curr. Liab.	1,807	2,287	2,351	1,841	1,237	1,307	NA	NA	NA	NA
LT Debt	2,376	1,887	1,528	1,551	1,742	1,770	NA	NA	NA	NA
Common Eqty.	-393	-497	-701	-610	-380	-390	NA	NA	NA	NA
Total Cap.	2,028	1,445	875	941	1,430	1,425	NA	NA	NA	NA
Cap. Exp.	219	274	255	245	212	164	NA	NA	NA	NA
Cash Flow	529	466	224	284	99	285	NA	NA	NA	NA
Curr. Ratio	1.0	0.8	0.7	0.8	1.1	1.0	NA	NA	NA	NA
% LT Debt of Cap.	117.1	130.5	174.6	165.0	121.0	124.2	NA	NA	NA	NA
% Net Inc.of Revs.	4.1	3.7	0.5	2.0	NM	2.7	NA	NA	NA	NA
% Ret. on Assets	6.7	6.0	0.9	3.3	NM	4.3	NA	NA	NA	NA
% Ret. on Equity	NM	NM	NM	NM	NM	NM	NA	NA	NA	NA

Data as orig reptd.; bef. results of disc opers/spec. items. Per share data adj. for stk. divs. Bold denotes diluted EPS (FASB 128)-prior periods restated. E-Estimated. NA-Not Available. NM-Not Meaningful. NR-Not Ranked.

Office—One Centennial Ave., P.O. Box 6820, Piscataway, NJ 08855-6820. **Tel**—(732) 980-6000. **Website**—http://www.americanstandard.com **Chrmn & CEO**—F. M. Poses. **SVP & CFO**—G. P. D'Aloia. **SVP & Secy**—J. P. McGrath. **VP & Investor Contact**—Bruce Fisher (732-980-6095). **Dirs**—S. E. Anderson, J. L. Cohon, E. E. Hagenlocker, J. F. Hardymon, R. W. Parsons, F. M. Poses, J. D. Quayle, D. M. Roderick. **Transfer Agent & Registrar**—Citibank, NYC. **Incorporated**—in Delaware in 1988. **Empl**— 61,000. **S&P Analyst:** Michael W. Jaffe

STANDARD &POOR'S
STOCK REPORTS

Automatic Data Processing

NYSE Symbol **ADP**

In S&P 500

18-AUG-01

Industry: Services (Data Processing)

Summary: This company is one of the largest independent computing services firms in the world, providing a broad range of data processing services.

S&P Opinion: Accumulate (★★★★)

Recent Price • 49.60
52 Wk Range • 69.31-46.84
Yield • 0.8%
12-Mo. P/E • 34.4

Quantitative Evaluations

Outlook (1 Lowest—5 Highest) • **1**

Fair Value • **39.70**

Risk • **Low**

Earn./Div. Rank • **A+**

Technical Eval. • **Bearish** since 6/01

Rel. Strength Rank (1 Lowest—99 Highest) • **42**

Insider Activity • **Unfavorable**

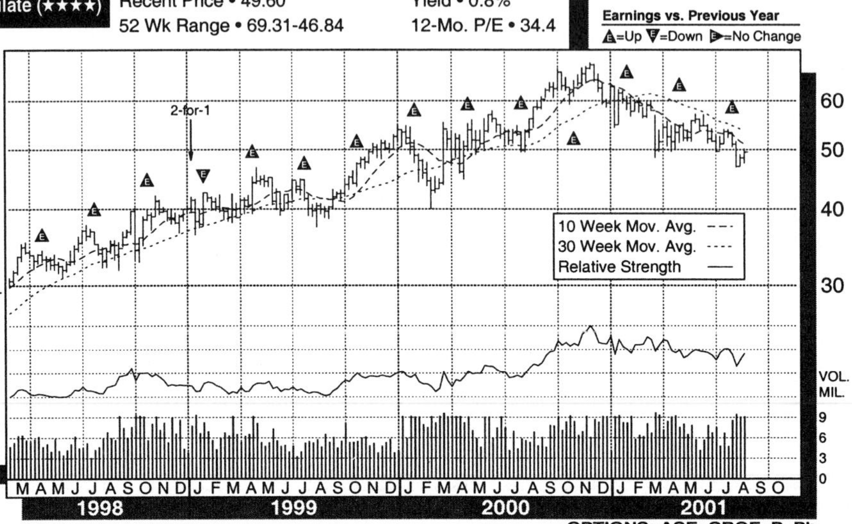

OPTIONS: ASE, CBOE, P, Ph

Overview - 15-AUG-01

Revenues should grow approximately 10% in FY 02 (Jun.), aided by gains in each of the company's four major business segments: employer, brokerage, dealer and claims services. The employer services segment should continue to see growth in the mid-teens, aided by robust sales activity. This segment also continues to benefit from strong customer retention rates. Brokerage services revenue growth should remain strong, aided by higher trading volume. Dealer and claims services revenues should also improve. Operating margins should widen slightly in FY 02, due to recent cost cutting initiatives, but the tax rate will likely be higher due to a change in the mix of ADP's investment portfolio; we estimate an increase in operating EPS of about 18% in FY 02, to $1.80.

Valuation - 15-AUG-01

ADP should generate annual earnings growth in the mid-teens over the next several years, driven by continued gains in its four major businesses. Strategic acquisitions should continue to add to the company's business and strengthen its competitive position. We expect growth in payroll services to continue at 17% to 18%. Despite its huge base of over 450,000 clients, the market for payroll outsourcing is still relatively untapped. We also see huge opportunities from the Internet, as all core products are becoming Internet-enabled. The stock merits its premium valuation in light of the company's record of predictable earnings growth, helped by a strong client retention rate. ADP has posted an unprecedented 160 consecutive quarters of record sales and earnings, and 40 straight years of double-digit earnings per share growth. At 27 times our FY 02 EPS estimate of $1.80, the shares are attractively valued and should outperform the market in the months ahead.

Key Stock Statistics

S&P EPS Est. 2002	1.80	Tang. Bk. Value/Share	4.71
P/E on S&P Est. 2002	27.6	Beta	0.72
Dividend Rate/Share	0.41	Shareholders	33,985
Shs. outstg. (M)	624.2	Market cap. (B)	$ 31.0
Avg. daily vol. (M)	2.087	Inst. holdings	71%

Value of $10,000 invested 5 years ago: $ 24,918

Fiscal Year Ending Jun. 30

	2001	2000	1999	1998	1997	1996
Revenues (Million $)						
1Q	1,587	1,351	1,245	1,039	910.7	747.1
2Q	1,684	1,492	1,310	1,148	995.6	819.7
3Q	1,894	1,720	1,514	1,309	1,126	1,032
4Q	1,853	1,724	1,471	1,302	1,080	967.9
Yr.	7,018	6,288	5,540	4,798	4,112	3,567
Earnings Per Share ($)						
1Q	**0.27**	**0.23**	**0.20**	**0.17**	**0.15**	**0.14**
2Q	**0.32**	**0.31**	**0.24**	**0.24**	**0.21**	**0.18**
3Q	**0.45**	**0.42**	**0.36**	**0.31**	**0.28**	**0.24**
4Q	**0.40**	**0.36**	**0.30**	**0.26**	**0.21**	**0.20**
Yr.	**1.44**	**1.31**	**1.10**	**0.99**	**0.85**	**0.77**

Next earnings report expected: NA

Dividend Data (Dividends have been paid since 1974.)

Amount ($)	Date Decl.	Ex-Div. Date	Stock of Record	Payment Date
0.102	Nov. 14	Dec. 07	Dec. 11	Jan. 01 '01
0.102	Jan. 23	Mar. 07	Mar. 09	Apr. 01 '01
0.102	May. 15	Jun. 06	Jun. 08	Jul. 01 '01
0.102	Aug. 13	Sep. 12	Sep. 14	Oct. 01 '01

Automatic Data Processing, Inc.

Business Summary - 15-AUG-01

Automatic Data Processing provides a broad range of data processing services in four business segments: employer, brokerage, dealer and claims. The company is the largest independent computing services company in the U.S.

Employer services, accounting for 58% of revenues in FY 00 (Jun.), provides payroll, human resource, benefits administration, time and attendance, and tax filing and reporting services to over 450,000 clients in the U.S., Canada, Europe and Latin America. The company processes the paychecks of more than 29 million workers. ADP is the second largest professional employer organization (PEO) in the U.S. A PEO provides a comprehensive outsourcing solution, including payroll, human resources, benefits and workers' compensation.

Brokerage services (24% of revenues) includes securities processing, desktop productivity applications, and investor communications services to the financial services industry. The company is the largest provider of securities processing services in North America. ADP handled an average of 1.2 million trades per day, up over 50% from FY 99. The company also processed over 680 million shareholder mailings.

Dealer services (12% of revenues) is the world's largest provider of transaction systems, data products, and professional services to automobile and truck dealers and manufacturers worldwide. Over 18,000 auto and truck dealer clients and over 30 vehicle manufacturers use the company's on-site systems and communications networks to manage sales and operations.

Claims services (6% of revenues) offers a broad line of products to help clients accurately estimate auto damage, bodily injury and property claims. Clients include most of the major property and casualty insurance carriers and many of the independent adjusting companies, nearly 14,000 collision repair centers, and more than 3,000 auto parts recycling facilities. In FY 00, ADP processed about 13 million claims estimates.

Revenue growth in FY 00 was as follows: 11% in employer services, 29% in brokerage services, flat in dealer services, and 17% in claims services and other. Excluding the impact of acquisitions and dispositions, revenues would have grown 31% in brokerage services.

In FY 00, cash flow from operations was approximately $1.1 billion. The company repurchased 4.6 million shares of its common stock. ADP also acquired several businesses for an aggregate total of $200 million in cash, following acquisitions totaling $107 million in FY 99 and $351 million in FY 98. Capital expenditures totaled $166 million in FY 00.

Per Share Data ($) (Year Ended Jun. 30)	2001	2000	1999	1998	1997	1996	1995	1994	1993	1992
Tangible Bk. Val.	NA	4.71	3.97	2.90	2.30	1.85	2.41	1.92	1.63	1.32
Cash Flow	NA	1.74	1.52	1.37	1.26	1.14	0.99	0.85	0.77	0.67
Earnings	1.44	1.31	1.10	0.99	0.88	0.79	0.69	0.59	0.52	0.46
Dividends	0.40	0.26	0.30	0.26	0.22	0.20	0.15	0.14	0.12	0.10
Payout Ratio	27%	20%	21%	26%	25%	25%	22%	23%	23%	23%
Prices - High	63.56	69.31	54.81	42.15	31.29	21.68	20.56	14.93	14.21	13.90
- Low	46.84	40.00	36.25	28.78	19.75	17.81	14.37	11.90	11.71	9.68
P/E Ratio - High	44	53	50	43	36	28	30	25	27	30
- Low	33	31	33	29	22	23	21	20	23	21
Income Statement Analysis (Million $)										
Revs.	NA	6,288	5,540	4,798	4,112	3,567	2,894	2,469	2,223	1,941
Oper. Inc.	NA	1,904	1,376	1,153	1,005	867	731	615	547	470
Depr.	NA	284	273	245	223	202	173	148	140	116
Int. Exp.	NA	13.1	19.1	24.0	27.8	29.7	24.3	20.8	19.8	12.3
Pretax Inc.	NA	1,290	1,085	884	724	635	534	446	387	342
Eff. Tax Rate	NA	35%	36%	32%	29%	28%	26%	25%	24%	25%
Net Inc.	NA	841	697	605	514	455	395	334	294	256
Balance Sheet & Other Fin. Data (Million $)										
Cash	NA	1,824	1,092	752	1,025	636	698	591	368	414
Curr. Assets	NA	3,064	2,194	1,829	1,805	1,454	1,211	985	771	734
Total Assets	NA	16,851	5,825	5,175	4,383	3,840	3,201	2,706	2,439	2,169
Curr. Liab.	NA	1,297	1,286	1,221	1,020	836	543	478	416	367
LT Debt	NA	132	146	192	401	404	390	373	348	333
Common Eqty.	NA	4,583	4,062	3,406	2,661	2,315	2,097	1,691	1,494	1,297
Total Cap.	NA	4,866	4,346	3,745	3,165	2,832	2,506	2,098	1,917	1,693
Cap. Exp.	NA	166	178	199	175	164	118	111	87.0	56.0
Cash Flow	NA	1,125	970	850	737	656	567	482	434	372
Curr. Ratio	NA	2.4	1.7	1.5	1.8	1.7	2.2	2.1	1.9	2.0
% LT Debt of Cap.	NA	2.7	3.4	5.1	12.7	14.3	15.6	17.8	18.1	19.7
% Net Inc.of Revs.	NA	13.4	12.6	12.6	12.5	12.7	13.6	13.5	13.2	13.2
% Ret. on Assets	NA	5.7	12.6	12.7	12.5	12.9	13.4	13.0	12.7	13.6
% Ret. on Equity	NA	19.6	17.9	20.0	20.6	20.6	20.8	21.0	21.0	21.7

Data as orig reptd.; bef. results of disc opers/spec. items. Per share data adj. for stk. divs. Bold denotes diluted EPS (FASB 128)-prior periods restated. E-Estimated. NA-Not Available. NM-Not Meaningful. NR-Not Ranked.

Office—One ADP Blvd., Roseland, NJ 07068-1728. **Tel**—(973) 994-5000. **Website**—www.adp.com **Chrmn & CEO**—A. F. Weinbach. **Pres & COO**—G. C. Butler. **CFO**—R. J. Haviland. **Dirs**—G. C. Butler, J. A. Califano Jr., L. G. Cooperman, G. H. Heilmeier, A. D. Jordan, H. M. Krueger, F. V. Malek, H. Taub, L. A. Tisch, A. F. Weinbach, J. S. Weston. **Transfer Agent**—Mellon Investor Services, Ridgefield Park, NJ. **Incorporated**—in Delaware in 1961. **Empl**— 40,000. **S&P Analyst:** Jonathan Rudy

STANDARD
&POOR'S
STOCK REPORTS

Canadian Pacific

NYSE Symbol **CP**

18-AUG-01 **Industry:** Railroads

Summary: This Canadian company is in the process of spinning off four of its business units. It plans to retain hotel opertations as its primary business.

S&P Opinion: Accumulate (★★★★) Recent Price • 37.80 | 52 Wk Range • 43.63-25.50 | Yield • 1.0% | 12-Mo. P/E • NM

Quantitative Evaluations

Outlook (1 Lowest—5 Highest) • **4**

Fair Value • **46.40**

Risk • **Low**

Earn./Div. Rank • **B**

Technical Eval. • **Neutral** since 8/01

Rel. Strength Rank (1 Lowest—99 Highest) • **48**

Insider Activity • **NA**

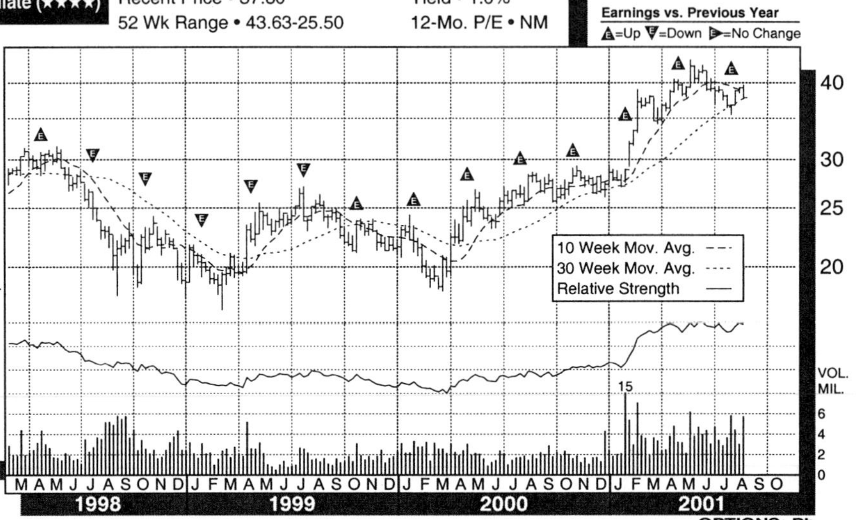

OPTIONS: Ph

Overview - 02-AUG-01

Revenues may climb 30% in 2002, after an estimated 34% gain in 2001. The advance will be driven by natural gas prices, which should remain above historical norms, and production increases at CP's petroleum unit. Rail traffic growth is likely to rebound as the economy improves. Margins may narrow slightly, as natural gas prices fall from peak levels, outweighing better labor and asset utilization. Shipping volume growth should rise as the economic environment improves. Coal profits will continue to be a bright spot, due to higher output, a better mix of coal quality, and rising prices. Hotel income will rise, as an expanded portfolio and higher average room rates outweigh lower occupancy rates. We project 2002 EPS of C$7.60, up about 13% from 2001's estimated C$6.70 ($4.94 and $4.36, respectively, using an August 1, 2001, exchange rate of $0.6504/C$1.00).

Valuation - 02-AUG-01

The stock has risen steadily since the second quarter of 2000, as investors finally recognized that CP has been reaping huge profits as a result of rising oil and gas prices. In February, CP announced its intention to split into five separate publicly traded companies, with shareholders receiving a stake in each. We believe the distribution, scheduled to occur in early fall, is beneficial, as it will unlock the value of each individual business, and attract new investors. The company has excess cash flow that it is using to buy back shares. In August 2000, directors authorized the repurchase of another 5% of the stock, after CP acquired 5% over the previous 12 months. With the stock recently trading at P/E, price to sales, and price to EBITDA ratios all at discounts to those of other railroad equities, the shares offer uncommon value.

Key Stock Statistics

S&P EPS Est. 2001	6.70	Tang. Bk. Value/Share	26.23
P/E on S&P Est. 2001	NA	Beta	0.66
S&P EPS Est. 2002	7.60	Shareholders	34,210
Dividend Rate/Share	0.56	Market cap. (B)	$ 11.9
Shs. outstg. (M)	314.0	Inst. holdings	46%
Avg. daily vol. (M)	0.941		

Value of $10,000 invested 5 years ago: $ 18,308

Fiscal Year Ending Dec. 31

	2001	2000	1999	1998	1997	1996
Revenues (Million Can. $)						
1Q	5,368	3,488	2,562	2,370	2,185	2,100
2Q	—	3,674	2,634	2,422	2,279	2,047
3Q	—	4,121	3,424	2,504	2,354	2,062
4Q	—	4,819	3,271	2,855	2,742	2,475
Yr.	—	16,102	11,367	10,151	9,560	8,684
Earnings Per Share (Can. $)						
1Q	**1.68**	**0.93**	**0.35**	**0.48**	**0.46**	0.42
2Q	**E1.50**	**1.19**	**-0.32**	**0.51**	**0.72**	0.53
3Q	**E1.70**	**1.47**	**0.81**	**0.61**	**0.75**	0.73
4Q	**E1.82**	**1.92**	**0.93**	**0.79**	**0.81**	0.74
Yr.	**E6.70**	**5.52**	**1.76**	**2.39**	**2.74**	**2.44**

Next earnings report expected: NA

Dividend Data (Dividends have been paid since 1944.)

Amount (Can. $)	Date Decl.	Ex-Div. Date	Stock of Record	Payment Date
0.140	Dec. 11	Dec. 22	Dec. 27	Jan. 29 '01
0.140	Mar. 12	Mar. 23	Mar. 27	Apr. 30 '01
0.140	Jun. 11	Jun. 25	Jun. 27	Jul. 30 '01
0.140	Jul. 30	Aug. 23	Aug. 27	Sep. 28 '01

Business Summary - 02-AUG-01

Canadian Pacific has restructured its operations over the past few decades. It now concentrates on transportation, energy and hotels. Its focus in recent years has been to slim down its rail unit, expand its shipping business through acquisitions, and convert and expand its hotel management business, while limiting its ownership of properties.

Canadian Pacific Railway (22% of total revenues in 2000) provides services via a 14,000 mile railroad system running from Montreal to Vancouver and stretching into the U.S. Midwest and Northeast. In 2000, CP entered into several strategic agreements, including a comprehensive shared access arrangement with Norfolk Southern; joint commercial, routing and switching with Union Pacific and co-production agreements with Canadian National. In 2000, intermodal shipments accounted for 23% of freight revenues; grain shipments 22%; and coal, sulphur and fertilizers together 23%.

CP Ships (24% of revenues) has aggressively expanded its shipping operations over the past few years. Thanks to acquisitions, including Ivaran Lines and Australia-New Zealand Direct Line (ANZDL) in 1998, CP's container loads have climbed 58% since 1998. The CP Ships family moved 1,833,000 containers in 2000, using some 80 vessels. In March 2000, CP bought out the stake of its 50% partner in Americana Ships, Transportacion Maritima Mexicana, for C$106 million.

Accounting for 44% of total revenues in 2000, PanCanadian Petroleum is a leading North American energy company active in the exploration, development, production and marketing of natural gas, crude oil and natural gas liquids. At The end of 2000, it had reserves totaling 1.04 billion bbl. of oil and equivalents. Since 1994, it has increased its land position 210%. PanCanadian is currently diversifying its geographic properties holdings. As part of this strategy, in October 2000, PanCanadian bought Montana Power Co.'s oil and gas properties, for C$689 million.

Fording Coal (5% of revenues) produced 15.1 million metric tons of coal in 2000 (mostly metallurgical grade used in steel consumption). Operations include three British Columbia metallurgical coal mines that export principally to Pacific Rim countries.

Hotel operations (5% of revenues) were significantly expanded with the 1999 formation of Fairmont Hotels & Resorts (67% owned), which manages 36 landmark and luxury properties; and the 1998 acquisition of Delta Hotels, which manages 35 lower-priced urban properties. In the first quarter of 2001, CP sold two of its Fairmont Hotels to Legacy Hotels REIT for C$305 million. CP holds a 34% stake in Legacy.

Per Share Data (U.S. $) (Year Ended Dec. 31)	2000	1999	1998	1997	1996	1995	1994	1993	1992	1991
Tangible Bk. Val.	17.57	14.95	13.83	14.59	13.17	12.12	14.16	14.18	15.38	17.86
Cash Flow	6.48	3.20	3.76	3.99	3.80	0.70	2.57	1.68	1.08	-0.01
Earnings	3.70	1.09	1.60	1.97	1.77	-1.33	0.86	-0.07	-1.18	-2.48
Dividends	0.38	0.35	0.35	0.34	0.35	0.26	0.23	0.25	0.26	0.55
Payout Ratio	10%	32%	22%	18%	20%	NM	27%	NM	NM	NM
Prices - High	29.31	27.12	31.56	31.68	8.75	18.87	18.50	17.50	16.50	20.00
- Low	18.25	17.00	17.87	22.62	4.56	13.37	14.00	12.40	10.40	14.37
P/E Ratio - High	8	25	20	17	16	NM	22	NM	NM	NM
- Low	5	16	11	12	10	NM	16	NM	NM	NM
Income Statement Analysis (Million Can. $)										
($) Per Canadian $	0.00	0.62	0.67	0.72	0.73	0.73	0.73	0.78	0.00	0.00
Revs.	16,102	11,367	10,151	9,560	8,684	5,790	5,028	4,963	7,050	8,713
Oper. Inc.	4,497	2,328	2,526	2,728	2,336	314	1,371	1,258	1,090	1,133
Depr.	1,320	1,123	1,084	963	971	694	574	557	720	789
Int. Exp.	372	314	300	271	294	356	363	439	600	640
Pretax Inc.	2,734	886	1,114	1,547	1,133	-736	441	44.0	-640	-1,135
Eff. Tax Rate	30%	28%	26%	36%	25%	NM	27%	90%	NM	NM
Net Inc.	1,767	594	801	947	834	-452	292	-21.0	-376	-791
Balance Sheet & Other Fin. Data (Million Can. $)										
($) Per Canadian $	0.00	0.68	0.65	0.70	0.73	0.73	0.72	0.75	0.00	0.00
Cash	904	561	613	599	981	817	992	1,258	1,091	1,387
Curr. Assets	3,800	2,745	2,636	3,217	2,671	1,782	1,867	2,029	2,430	3,537
Total Assets	24,166	20,318	19,669	17,332	11,072	11,825	12,055	12,926	15,906	17,812
Curr. Liab.	5,028	3,618	4,074	3,151	3,077	2,064	1,541	2,250	2,221	2,487
LT Debt	4,032	3,491	3,300	2,686	2,655	3,087	3,384	3,673	5,658	6,044
Common Eqty.	9,335	8,049	7,998	7,573	6,405	4,259	4,847	4,538	4,932	5,796
Total Cap.	17,782	14,945	14,072	12,713	10,759	8,661	9,795	9,816	12,819	14,574
Cap. Exp.	2,587	1,977	2,337	2,465	1,531	1,437	990	857	1,099	1,463
Cash Flow	3,075	1,707	1,885	1,910	1,805	241	866	536	343	-2.0
Curr. Ratio	0.8	0.8	0.6	1.0	0.9	0.9	1.2	0.9	1.1	1.4
% LT Debt of Cap.	22.7	23.4	23.5	21.1	24.7	35.6	34.5	37.4	44.1	41.5
% Net Inc.of Revs.	11.0	5.2	7.9	9.9	9.6	NM	58.0	NM	NM	NM
% Ret. on Assets	8.0	3.0	4.3	5.8	5.3	NM	2.3	NM	NM	NM
% Ret. on Equity	20.2	7.3	10.3	13.6	13.6	NM	6.0	NM	NM	NM

Data as orig. reptd.; bef. results of disc. opers. and/or spec. items. Per share data adj. for stk. divs. as of ex-div. date. Prior to 1996, data in Inc. & Bal. Sheet tables in US$. Bold denotes diluted EPS (FASB 128). E-Estimated. NA-Not Available. NM-Not Meaningful. NR-Not Ranked.

Office—1800 Bankers Hall East, 855 2nd St. S.W., Calgary, AB, Canada T2P 4Z5. **Tel**—(403) 218 8000. **Website**—http://www.cp.ca **Chrmn, Pres & CEO**—D. P. O'Brien. **EVP & CFO**—M. A. Grandin. **VP & Secy**— A. T. Love. **Investor Contact**—Sheila McIntosh (403-218-8060). **Dirs**—S. E. Bachand, D. Cohen, A. A. MacNaughton, J. D. McNeil, J. E. Newall, D. P. O'Brien. M. E. J. Phelps, R. Phillips, R. D. Southern, A. R. Taylor, C. Taylor, The Rt. Hon.Viscount Weir. **Transfer Agents**—Bank of Montreal Trust Co., NYC; Montreal Trust Co., Montreal. **Incorporated**—in Canada in 1881. **Empl**— 45,421. **S&P Analyst:** Richard N. Stice

STANDARD
&POOR'S
STOCK REPORTS

Cendant Corp.

NYSE Symbol **CD**

In S&P 500

18-AUG-01

Industry: Services (Commercial & Consumer)

Summary: This major provider of consumer and business services was known as CUC International prior to a December 1997 stock-swap merger with HFS Inc.

S&P Opinion: Accumulate (★★★★)

Recent Price • 20.04 | 52 Wk Range • 21.53-8.12 | Yield • Nil | 12-Mo. P/E • 18.9

Quantitative Evaluations

Outlook (1 Lowest—5 Highest) • **4⁻**

Fair Value • **23.50**

Risk • **NA**

Earn./Div. Rank • **B**

Technical Eval. • **Bearish** since 8/01

Rel. Strength Rank (1 Lowest—99 Highest) • **72**

Insider Activity • **NA**

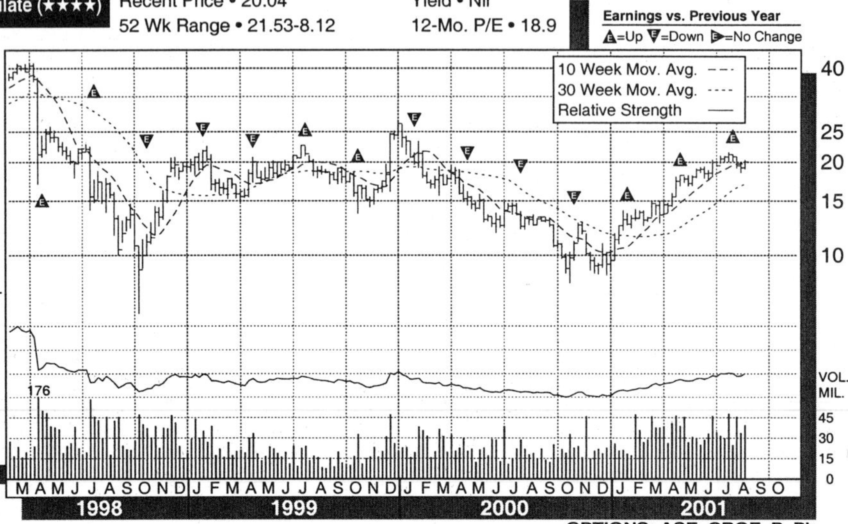

OPTIONS: ASE, CBOE, P, Ph

Overview - 14-AUG-01

We expect revenues from continuing operations to advance sharply in 2001, primarily due to acquisitions. Since March 2001, CD has acquired rental car company Avis Group Holdings, Inc., and Fairfield Communities, Inc., which sells vacation ownership interests. In June, CD agreed to acquire Galileo International, Inc., a leading provider of electronic global distribution services for the travel industry, in a stock-and-cash transaction valued at about $2.9 billion, and in August it agreed to buy Cheap Tickets, Inc., an online seller of discount airline tickets, for $425 million cash. In 2001, CD is expected to have higher interest costs related to a $2.85 billion litigation settlement, Excluding unusual items and some Internet-related businesses, we look for CD's EPS in 2001 to be $1.10, followed by an increase to $1.40 in 2002. A portion of the rise in 2002 is projected to come from a change in how companies account for acquisition-related goodwill.

Valuation - 14-AUG-01

As of early August 2001, the shares had sharply outperformed the S&P 500 year to date, following significant underperformance in 2000. We generally like recent moves by the company to reshape itself via acquisitions, outsourcing and licensing, and an asset sale. We expect the company, under the leadership of CEO Henry Silverman, to be looking for further accretive acquisitions in the travel or real estate areas. Also, we expect that a cloud over CD from accounting and lawsuit problems is lessening, with investors increasingly focusing on prospects that the company will generate a large amount of free cash flow, and that it will put this cash to good use. Based partly on expected cash generation and a P/E of about 14X estimated 2002 EPS, we recommend accumulating the stock for capital gains.

Key Stock Statistics

S&P EPS Est. 2001	1.10	Tang. Bk. Value/Share	NM
P/E on S&P Est. 2001	18.2	Beta	1.79
S&P EPS Est. 2002	1.40	Shareholders	9,598
Dividend Rate/Share	Nil	Market cap. (B)	$ 17.1
Shs. outstg. (M)	851.8	Inst. holdings	68%
Avg. daily vol. (M)	7.319		

Value of $10,000 invested 5 years ago: $ 8,650

Fiscal Year Ending Dec. 31

	2001	2000	1999	1998	1997	1996
Revenues (Million $)						
1Q	1,303	945.0	1,318	1,129	953.7	660.9
2Q	2,403	973.0	1,391	1,278	1,000	775.3
3Q	—	1,044	1,410	1,458	1,187	953.6
4Q	—	968.0	1,283	1,419	1,100	847.9
Yr.	—	3,930	5,402	5,284	4,240	3,238
Earnings Per Share ($)						
1Q	**0.28**	**0.15**	**0.20**	**0.21**	**0.13**	0.07
2Q	**0.27**	**0.21**	**1.06**	**0.18**	**-0.09**	0.11
3Q	—	**0.25**	**0.27**	**0.14**	**0.24**	0.08
4Q	—	**0.17**	**-2.08**	**-0.36**	**-0.22**	0.13
Yr.	—	**0.78**	**-0.30**	**0.18**	**0.08**	0.39

Next earnings report expected: mid October

Dividend Data

In June 1989, CD paid special dividends of $1.48 a share (not adjusted) in cash and $2.07 face amount ($0.93 discount amount) of zero coupon notes due 1996, as part of a recapitalization plan.

Cendant Corporation

18-AUG-01

Business Summary - 14-AUG-01

Cendant Corp. (CD), a large consumer and business services company, is being reshaped through acquisitions and other transactions. The company, which has also disposed of various businesses in recent years, was formed through the 1997 merger of CUC International (renamed Cendant Corp.) and HFS Inc. Accounting irregularities and errors were disclosed in 1998, and some past earnings were restated downward. In the 2000 third quarter, CD began to accrue interest expense on a $2.85 billion settlement obligation related to shareholder litigation.

In June 2001, CD agreed to acquire Galileo International (GLC), a leading provider of electronic global distribution services for the travel industry, for a stock-and-cash transaction valued at about $2.9 billion. In 2000, GLC had revenue of $1.6 billion, and net income, before special items, of $170.5 million. In August, CD agreed to buy Cheap Tickets, Inc., an online seller of discount airline tickets, for $425 million cash. Earlier, in April, CD acquired Fairfield Communities, Inc. (FFD), which operates a business through which vacation ownership interests are sold, for about $690 million in cash. For 2000, FFD reported revenues of $587 million, and income, before merger-related expenses and a special gain, of about $64 million. In March 2001, CD acquired, in a transaction valued at about $937 million, all of the shares of rental car company Avis Group Holdings, Inc. (AVI), that it did not already own. For 2000, AVI reported revenue of $4.2 billion, exceeding CD's total revenues of $3.9 billion from continuing operations in 2000. AVI's net income in 2000, after preferred stock dividends, was $102 million.

In July 2001, CD said it had entered into agreements to outsource and license its indvidual membership and loyalty business. In February, CD's Move.com real estate unit was acquired by Homestore.com (HOMS). As a result of the transaction, CD owned about 21.5 million HOMS common shares.

Cendant is the world's largest hotel franchisor, including properties operating under the Days Inn, Ramada (in the U.S.) and Super 8 brands. It is also a large franchisor of residential real estate brokerage offices, operating under the Century 21, Coldwell Banker and ERA names; provides corporate relocation services; and originates residential mortgage loans. Other businesses include the Avis vehicle rental franchise system; insurance; a private car park operator in the U.K.; and the Jackson Hewitt tax preparation business.

CD paid $250 million to a stockholder litigation settlement trust in 2001's second quarter, reducing the net outstanding principal obligation associated with a class action litigation settlement at June 30, 2001, to $2 billion.

Per Share Data ($) (Year Ended Dec. 31)	2000	1999	1998	1997	1996	1995	1994	1993	1992	1991
Tangible Bk. Val.	NM	NM	NM	NM	2.28	1.60	1.60	0.42	-0.12	-0.31
Cash Flow	1.33	0.19	0.55	0.36	0.49	0.49	0.53	0.43	0.32	0.18
Earnings	0.78	-0.28	0.18	0.08	0.39	0.28	0.44	0.34	0.25	0.12
Dividends	Nil	Nil	Nil	Nil	Nil	Nil	Nil	Nil	Nil	Nil
Payout Ratio	Nil	Nil	Nil	Nil	Nil	Nil	Nil	Nil	Nil	Nil
Prices - High	26.31	26.93	41.68	34.37	27.50	26.16	15.94	17.66	8.58	6.52
- Low	8.12	13.62	6.50	19.25	18.33	14.50	11.11	7.38	5.11	2.58
P/E Ratio - High	34	NM	NM	NM	71	93	36	52	34	59
- Low	10	NM	NM	NM	47	52	25	22	21	24
Income Statement Analysis (Million $)										
Revs.	4,659	5,402	5,284	4,240	2,348	1,415	1,039	875	739	641
Oper. Inc.	1,725	1,919	1,590	1,250	479	286	209	166	122	99
Depr.	352	371	323	238	32.5	15.4	23.3	22.3	17.3	15.7
Int. Exp.	148	199	149	51.0	Nil	Nil	NA	4.8	8.7	16.0
Pretax Inc.	1,106	-574	315	257	276	266	191	142	96.1	45.1
Eff. Tax Rate	33%	NM	33%	74%	41%	39%	38%	39%	39%	44%
Net Inc.	660	-229	160	66.0	164	163	118	87.4	58.8	25.1
Balance Sheet & Other Fin. Data (Million $)										
Cash	944	1,164	1,009	67.0	553	270	181	117	28.6	14.4
Curr. Assets	2,728	4,592	4,547	2,590	1,430	768	504	377	243	205
Total Assets	15,072	15,149	20,217	14,073	2,473	1,141	768	613	479	322
Curr. Liab.	2,466	5,610	2,872	2,534	481	150	109	123	127	133
LT Debt	6,046	6,238	4,835	5,603	23.5	14.0	15.0	22.0	37.0	69.0
Common Eqty.	2,774	2,206	4,836	3,922	1,255	727	443	285	150	-1.0
Total Cap.	9,296	8,754	10,089	9,891	1,279	741	458	307	187	68.0
Cap. Exp.	246	277	355	155	59.7	30.2	17.6	9.1	4.6	6.7
Cash Flow	1,012	142	483	304	197	179	141	110	76.1	40.8
Curr. Ratio	1.1	0.8	1.6	1.0	3.0	5.1	4.6	3.1	1.9	1.5
% LT Debt of Cap.	65.0	71.3	47.9	56.6	1.8	1.9	3.3	7.2	19.9	101.4
% Net Inc.of Revs.	14.2	NM	3.0	1.6	7.0	11.5	11.3	10.0	8.0	3.9
% Ret. on Assets	4.4	NM	0.9	0.9	9.1	16.2	16.9	15.8	14.1	7.8
% Ret. on Equity	26.5	NM	3.7	2.8	16.6	27.1	32.0	39.7	NM	NM

Data bef. results of disc. opers. and/or spec. items. Some data reflect restatements in Sep. 1998. Also, some years likely reflect different fiscal year ends. Per share data adj. for stk. divs. as of ex-div. date. Bold denotes diluted EPS (FASB 128). E-Estimated. NA-Not Available. NM-Not Meaningful. NR-Not Ranked.

Office—9 West 57th St., New York, NY 10019. **Tel**—(212) 413-1800. **Website**—www.cendant.com **Chrmn, Pres & CEO**—H. R. Silverman. **SEVP & CFO**—K. M. Sheehan. **Secy**—E. J. Bock. **SVP & Investor Contact**—Samuel J. Levenson. **VP & Investor Contact**—Denise L. Gillen. **Dirs**—M. J. Biblowit, J. E. Buckman, W. S. Cohen, L. S. Coleman, M. Edelman, S. P. Holmes, J. C. Malone, C. D. Mills, B. Mulroney, R. E. Nederlander, R. W. Pittman, S. Z. Rosenberg, H. R. Silverman, R. F. Smith. **Transfer Agent & Registrar**—Mellon Investor Services, South Hackensack, NJ. **Incorporated**—in Delaware in 1974. **Empl**— 28,000. **S&P Analyst:** Tom Graves, CFA

STANDARD
&POOR'S
STOCK REPORTS

Convergys Corporation

NYSE Symbol **CVG**

In S&P 500

18-AUG-01

Industry:
Services (Commercial & Consumer)

Summary: This company is a leading provider of outsourced billing and customer management solutions.

S&P Opinion: Accumulate (★★★★) Recent Price • 27.55 | 52 Wk Range • 52.25-25.14 | Yield • Nil | 12-Mo. P/E • 23.8

Quantitative Evaluations

Outlook
(1 Lowest—5 Highest)
• 2⁻

Fair Value
• 29

Risk
• NA

Earn./Div. Rank
• NR

Technical Eval.
• Bearish since 8/01

Rel. Strength Rank
(1 Lowest—99 Highest)
• 21

Insider Activity
• Neutral

Earnings vs. Previous Year
▲=Up ▼=Down ▶=No Change

OPTIONS: ASE, CBOE

Overview - 13-AUG-01

We project top line growth of about 20% for 2001, reflecting gains for both the IMG and CMG groups, as well as the recent acquisition of Geneva Technologies Ltd., which enhances CVG's international presence. Convergys is capitalizing on a trend toward outsourcing of non-core business activities. The company has signed contracts with many leading players in the global wireless industry. Costs to integrate Geneva and expansion initiatives such as online billing should impact operating margins somewhat, partly offset by tight cost controls. The acquisition of Geneva is expected to reduce 2001 EPS by $0.15 a share. This dilution will be partly offset by a change in FASB rules on accounting for goodwill, which will increase 2001 EPS by about $0.08. We forecast $1.35 EPS for 2001, 10% higher than reported 2000 EPS. After 2001, our annual growth targets over the next five years are 15% for revenues, and 25% for EPS.

Valuation - 13-AUG-01

We view CVG as a pioneer in an era of communications consolidation, addressing the growing outsourcing needs of the telecom industry and other sectors. Investors should be drawn to the company's air-tight cost structure, and to its use of proprietary software. We do not foresee any risk from CVG's dependence on industry leader AT&T, which currently accounts for over 40% of total revenue. A major contract between the companies runs until 2006. The stock has recently reversed a long-term uptrend reflecting investor concerns about the impact of the slowing economy on the company. We see the shares as attractive at their recent level of 22X our 2001 EPS estimate of $1.35, an unwarranted discount to CVG's long term growth rate, in light of the company's industry position, consistency, and revenue and EPS visibility.

Key Stock Statistics

S&P EPS Est. 2001	1.35	Tang. Bk. Value/Share	2.41
P/E on S&P Est. 2001	20.4	Beta	NA
S&P EPS Est. 2002	1.60	Shareholders	18,849
Dividend Rate/Share	Nil	Market cap. (B)	$ 4.7
Shs. outstg. (M)	170.9	Inst. holdings	55%
Avg. daily vol. (M)	0.984		

Value of $10,000 invested 5 years ago: NA

Fiscal Year Ending Dec. 31

	2001	2000	1999	1998	1997	1996
Revenues (Million $)						
1Q	577.8	513.6	399.8	—	—	—
2Q	571.2	521.9	426.2	—	—	—
3Q	—	544.5	450.2	—	—	—
4Q	—	582.5	486.7	404.7	—	—
Yr.	—	2,163	1,763	1,447	1,390	—
Earnings Per Share ($)						
1Q	**0.34**	**0.28**	**0.21**	—	—	—
2Q	**0.16**	**0.29**	**0.21**	—	—	—
3Q	**E0.34**	**0.32**	**0.26**	—	—	—
4Q	**E0.36**	**0.34**	**0.21**	**0.22**	—	—
Yr.	**E1.35**	**1.23**	**0.89**	**0.57**	0.54	—

Next earnings report expected: late October

Dividend Data

No cash dividends have been paid, and no payments are expected in the foreseeable future.

Convergys Corporation

Business Summary - 13-AUG-01

Convergys is a leading provider of outsourced billing and customer management solutions, through its Information Management Group (IMG) and Customer Management Group (CMG). By providing value-added billing and customer management solutions for its clients, generally pursuant to long-term relationships, the company has developed a large base of recurring revenues. A contract with industry powerhouse AT&T currently accounts for about 40% of revenues, and does not expire until 2006. The company also has agreements with Verizon, Ameritech and Sprint, and with such non-telecom companies as Comcast, Cox Communications, DirecTV, Hallmark, Palm and Time Warner.

IMG is a leading outsourced provider of billing and information services to all segments of the communications industry, including wireless, wireline, cable, broadband, direct broadcast satellite and Internet services. The unit's software and data center capabilities enable it to activate services, capture usage information, calculate billing charges, consolidate billing for multiple services or equipment and enable clients to use such data to target customers for new or expanded product or service offerings. During 2000, over 63% of IMG's revenues came from data processing services from recurring monthly payments from its clients. Professional and consulting services accounted for 20% of IMG's revenues, and its remaining revenues were primarily from software license arrangements and other services.

CMG is the largest provider of outsourced customer management solutions, serving leading companies in the communications, technology, financial services and consumer products industries. In 2000, approximately 91% of CMG's revenues were related to providing value-added (dedicated) customer service, technical support, and sales account management, primarily through personnel dedicated to a specific client. The remaining 9% of CMG's 2000 revenues were derived from traditional campaign-based inbound/outbound teleservices.

CVG has a 45% limited partnership interest in the Cellular Partnership, which operates a cellular telecommunications business in central and southwestern Ohio and northern Kentucky. In 2000, the company's equity in earnings of the Cellular Partnership was $20.5 million.

The company's strategy includes leveraging its industry leadership position in billing solutions for the communications industry; pursuing international growth; increasing its sales and marketing efforts to realize its market potential; and pursuing strategic acquisitions and alliances that expand its client base, add new capabilities or enable it to accelerate product development efforts or geographic expansion. In April 2001, the company acquired Geneva Technology Ltd., a U.K.-based provider of billing solutions with more than 40 clients in 17 countries, for about 17.6 million common shares.

Per Share Data ($) (Year Ended Dec. 31)	2000	1999	1998	1997	1996	1995	1994	1993	1992	1991
Tangible Bk. Val.	2.41	1.13	0.29	-0.09	NA	NA	NA	NA	NA	NA
Cash Flow	2.25	1.73	1.28	1.07	NA	NA	NA	NA	NA	NA
Earnings	1.23	0.89	0.57	0.54	NA	NA	NA	NA	NA	NA
Dividends	Nil	Nil	Nil	NA	NA	NA	NA	NA	NA	NA
Payout Ratio	Nil	Nil	Nil	NA	NA	NA	NA	NA	NA	NA
Prices - High	55.43	31.75	23.75	NA	NA	NA	NA	NA	NA	NA
- Low	26.62	14.50	9.62	NA	NA	NA	NA	NA	NA	NA
P/E Ratio - High	45	36	42	NA	NA	NA	NA	NA	NA	NA
- Low	22	16	17	NA	NA	NA	NA	NA	NA	NA
Income Statement Analysis (Million $)										
Revs.	2,163	1,763	1,447	988	NA	NA	NA	NA	NA	NA
Oper. Inc.	489	388	313	220	NA	NA	NA	NA	NA	NA
Depr.	161	130	101	61.0	NA	NA	NA	NA	NA	NA
Int. Exp.	32.9	32.5	33.9	5.4	NA	NA	NA	NA	NA	NA
Pretax Inc.	317	223	131	131	NA	NA	NA	NA	NA	NA
Eff. Tax Rate	39%	38%	38%	34%	NA	NA	NA	NA	NA	NA
Net Inc.	195	137	81.0	86.6	NA	NA	NA	NA	NA	NA
Balance Sheet & Other Fin. Data (Million $)										
Cash	28.2	30.8	3.8	2.1	NA	NA	NA	NA	NA	NA
Curr. Assets	481	298	361	266	NA	NA	NA	NA	NA	NA
Total Assets	1,780	1,580	1,451	654	NA	NA	NA	NA	NA	NA
Curr. Liab.	359	387	698	217	NA	NA	NA	NA	NA	NA
LT Debt	291	250	Nil	430	NA	NA	NA	NA	NA	NA
Common Eqty.	1,113	927	732	431	NA	NA	NA	NA	NA	NA
Total Cap.	1,403	1,178	732	NA	NA	NA	NA	NA	NA	NA
Cap. Exp.	175	155	93.5	NA	NA	NA	NA	NA	NA	NA
Cash Flow	356	267	182	148	NA	NA	NA	NA	NA	NA
Curr. Ratio	1.3	0.8	0.5	1.2	NA	NA	NA	NA	NA	NA
% LT Debt of Cap.	20.7	21.3	Nil	NA	NA	NA	NA	NA	NA	NA
% Net Inc.of Revs.	9.0	7.8	5.6	8.8	NA	NA	NA	NA	NA	NA
% Ret. on Assets	11.6	9.0	7.7	NA	NA	NA	NA	NA	NA	NA
% Ret. on Equity	19.1	16.5	13.9	NA	NA	NA	NA	NA	NA	NA

Data as orig reptd.; bef. results of disc opers/spec. items. Per share data adj. for stk. divs. Bold denotes diluted EPS (FASB 128)-prior periods restated. E-Estimated. NA-Not Available. NM-Not Meaningful. NR-Not Ranked.

Office—201 E. Fourth St., Cincinnati, OH 45202. **Tel**—(513) 397-5364. **Website**—http://www.convergys.com **Chrmn, Pres & CEO**—J. F. Orr. **CFO**—S. G. Rolls. **Secy**—W. B. Baskett, III. **Dirs**—J. F. Barrett, J. G. Boynton, G. C. Butler, D. B. Dillon, E. C. Fast, R. L. Howe, S. C. Mason, P. A. Odeen, J. F. Orr, B. H. Rowe, J. M. Zimmerman. **Transfer Agent & Registrar**—Fifth Third Bank, Cincinnati. **Incorporated**—in Ohio in 1873; reincorporated in Ohio in 1983. **Empl**— 41,000. **S&P Analyst:** Jim Corridore

STANDARD
&POOR'S
STOCK REPORTS

Fastenal Co.

Nasdaq Symbol **FAST**

In S&P MidCap 400

18-AUG-01 **Industry:** Retail (Building Supplies)

Summary: This company distributes fasteners and other industrial and construction supplies through nearly 1,000 stores throughout the U.S. and in Canada.

S&P Opinion: Accumulate (★★★★) Recent Price • 63.55 | 52 Wk Range • 73-45.12 | Yield • 0.1% | 12-Mo. P/E • 30.3

Quantitative Evaluations

Outlook (1 Lowest—5 Highest)
• **4**

Fair Value
• **74.60**

Risk
• **Average**

Earn./Div. Rank
• **A+**

Technical Eval.
• **Neutral** since 8/01

Rel. Strength Rank (1 Lowest—99 Highest)
• **59**

Insider Activity
• **Neutral**

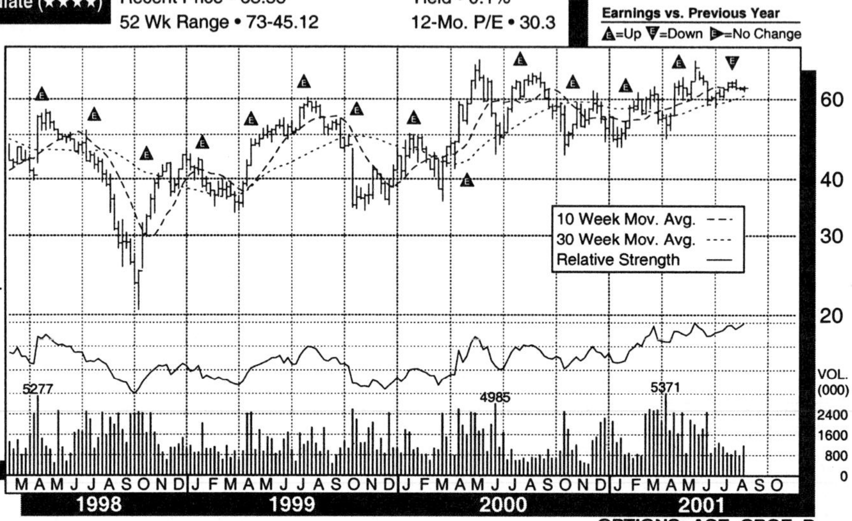

OPTIONS: ASE, CBOE, P

Overview - 15-AUG-01

Sales should grow about 10% in 2001, followed by an increase in the upper teens in 2002. We see growth in both years generated through new store openings, the maturation of store sites, market share gains, and an ongoing expansion of FAST's product offerings. A less robust economy will likely keep sales growth below historical levels in 2001, but we believe a better interest rate environment will let the company's business pick up as we move into 2002. Margins should narrow in 2001, limited by the challenging sales environment and higher fuel costs. A pick-up in new store openings could also hurt margins, as startup costs and the time necessary to generate a customer base typically cause new sites to operate at a loss for the first nine to 12 months. However, margins should widen in 2002, as the expected recovery of sales trends outweighs the impact of ongoing store opening costs.

Valuation - 15-AUG-01

The shares have shown little direction since the spring of 2000, with worries about economic moderation pulling them one way, and optimism stemming from lower interest rates pulling them in the opposite direction. We think the current Fed funds easing program will firm up the economy in late 2001 and boost FAST's performance. We also believe FAST's good operating strategy and top management team will let it continue its long history of solid EPS growth for an extended period (despite an expected slight downturn in 2001). With the shares recently trading at a forward P/E multiple of about 1.5 times the 20% long-term EPS growth rate that we project, we think the stock is undervalued. We base our accumulate recommendation on our view that Fastenal's PEG ratio (P/E to growth rate) should be at a premium to that of the broad market, rather than a discount (the S&P 500 has a PEG of about 2.0).

Key Stock Statistics

S&P EPS Est. 2001	2.10	Tang. Bk. Value/Share	10.43
P/E on S&P Est. 2001	30.3	Beta	0.72
S&P EPS Est. 2002	2.60	Shareholders	2,400
Dividend Rate/Share	0.09	Market cap. (B)	$ 2.4
Shs. outstg. (M)	37.9	Inst. holdings	61%
Avg. daily vol. (M)	0.187		

Value of $10,000 invested 5 years ago: $ 14,787

Fiscal Year Ending Dec. 31

	2001	2000	1999	1998	1997	1996
Revenues (Million $)						
1Q	201.0	176.3	140.6	116.7	87.10	63.06
2Q	204.9	188.6	153.9	126.4	98.23	70.85
3Q	—	192.9	159.4	131.3	105.5	76.21
4Q	—	188.0	155.3	128.6	107.1	77.57
Yr.	—	745.7	609.2	503.1	398.0	287.7
Earnings Per Share ($)						
1Q	**0.55**	**0.53**	**0.41**	**0.33**	**0.23**	**0.20**
2Q	**0.50**	**0.55**	**0.45**	**0.37**	**0.28**	**0.22**
3Q	**E0.53**	**0.55**	**0.45**	**0.37**	**0.30**	**0.23**
4Q	**E0.52**	**0.50**	**0.42**	**0.33**	**0.27**	**0.21**
Yr.	**E2.10**	**2.13**	**1.73**	**1.40**	**1.08**	**0.86**

Next earnings report expected: mid October

Dividend Data (Dividends have been paid since 1991.)

Amount ($)	Date Decl.	Ex-Div. Date	Stock of Record	Payment Date
0.090	Jan. 16	Feb. 21	Feb. 23	Mar. 09 '01

Fastenal Company

Business Summary - 15-AUG-01

Fastenal began operations 34 years ago, with a strategy to be a supplier of threaded fasteners in small to medium-size cities. The company opened its first store in Winona, MN, and at 2000 year end, had 897 stores in the lower 48 states, Puerto Rico and Canada, up from 809 sites a year earlier (991 sites at June 30, 2001); in August 2001, FAST announced its first branch openings in Alaska and Hawaii. As of 2000 year end, FAST had closed only four store sites in its history. More than 80% of the company's stores were opened in the past decade, and Texas, with 56 sites at the end of 2000, had the most stores of any state. FAST distributes products to its store sites from 11 distribution centers located throughout the U.S. Threaded fasteners accounted for 51% of sales in both 2000 and 1999.

One of the company's goals is to expand its stores through improved customer service. Fastenal boosted its store opening pace to about 90 new sites in 2000, from 44 in the prior year, when it slowed its new store growth. It also increased its site personnel by 19% in 2000 (21% during 1999). The company sees new store growth of 10% to 15% in coming years. Fastenal also began selling directly from its website on July 1, 1999.

FAST has two types of stores: stand-alone stores and satellite stores. Stand-alone stores are typically located in cities with populations of more than 8,000. The company believes there are about 1,000 such markets in the U.S. and Canada, including markets in which it already has stores. A satellite store is usually located within 30 miles of a stand-alone store, and is managed by personnel from the stand-alone store. Fastenal has satellite stores in communities with as few as 2,000 people, and believes it could eventually open 500 satellite stores. At the end of 2000, 828 of the stores were operating as traditional Fastenal stores and 69 as satellite stores. FAST has also started to open in-plant stores for large customers, but does not count them as stores because they are not open to the general public.

The company offered nine product lines at 2000 year end, and plans to add additional lines in the future. Its original product line now consists of about 68,000 different types of threaded fasteners and supplies. Other product lines offered include 51,000 different types of tools; 24,000 different metal cutting tool blades; 23,000 types of fluid transfer components and accessories for hydraulic and pneumatic power; 8,000 types of material handling and storage products; 4,000 kinds of janitorial and paper products; 7,000 types of electrical supply items; 7,000 welding supply items; and 3,000 different safety supplies. FAST sells mostly to customers in the construction industry; and the manufacturing market, for both original equipment manufacturers and maintenance and repair operations.

The vast majority of products sold are manufactured by other companies. No supplier accounted for over 5% of the company's purchases in 2000.

In August 2001, Fastenal agreed to acquire the retail fastener and related hardware businesses of two units of Textron Inc. (annual sales of about $40 million), for an undisclosed amount.

Per Share Data ($) (Year Ended Dec. 31)	2000	1999	1998	1997	1996	1995	1994	1993	1992	1991
Tangible Bk. Val.	9.47	7.43	5.74	4.37	3.32	2.49	1.78	1.31	1.01	NA
Cash Flow	2.44	2.04	1.69	1.32	1.05	0.87	0.59	0.38	0.28	NA
Earnings	2.13	1.73	1.40	1.08	0.86	0.72	0.49	0.31	0.23	0.17
Dividends	0.08	0.04	0.02	0.02	0.02	0.02	0.02	0.01	0.01	NA
Payout Ratio	4%	2%	1%	2%	2%	3%	4%	3%	4%	NA
Prices - High	73.31	60.56	56.87	60.50	50.00	43.00	23.00	15.87	11.00	NA
- Low	35.68	33.62	20.50	30.75	28.75	19.87	14.50	9.50	7.00	NA
P/E Ratio - High	34	35	41	56	58	60	47	51	48	NA
- Low	17	19	15	28	33	28	30	31	30	NA
Income Statement Analysis (Million $)										
Revs.	746	609	503	398	288	223	162	110	81.0	62.3
Oper. Inc.	141	117	98.1	76.6	60.8	50.9	34.6	22.5	16.3	NA
Depr.	11.8	11.8	11.0	9.4	7.3	5.4	3.6	2.6	1.9	NA
Int. Exp.	Nil	0.1	1.1	0.9	0.1	0.1	Nil	Nil	Nil	NA
Pretax Inc.	131	106	86.1	67.3	54.4	46.2	31.4	20.1	14.7	10.7
Eff. Tax Rate	39%	39%	39%	39%	40%	41%	41%	41%	40%	39%
Net Inc.	80.7	65.5	53.0	40.8	32.5	27.4	18.7	11.9	8.8	6.6
Balance Sheet & Other Fin. Data (Million $)										
Cash	32.7	28.1	2.4	0.4	0.4	6.6	3.1	2.0	NA	NA
Curr. Assets	293	227	173	144	103	81.1	59.5	41.0	NA	NA
Total Assets	402	319	251	205	152	109	81.8	57.5	NA	34.1
Curr. Liab.	36.6	33.7	30.8	37.6	25.0	15.0	14.1	7.7	NA	NA
LT Debt	Nil	Nil	Nil	Nil	Nil	Nil	Nil	Nil	NA	Nil
Common Eqty.	359	282	218	166	126	94.3	67.6	49.8	NA	30.2
Total Cap.	366	285	220	168	127	94.3	67.6	49.8	NA	30.2
Cap. Exp.	36.7	39.2	37.2	28.7	26.2	16.7	8.1	5.5	5.4	NA
Cash Flow	92.5	77.2	64.0	50.2	39.9	32.8	22.3	14.5	10.7	NA
Curr. Ratio	8.0	6.8	5.6	3.8	4.1	5.4	4.2	5.4	NA	NA
% LT Debt of Cap.	Nil	Nil	Nil	Nil	Nil	Nil	Nil	Nil	NA	Nil
% Net Inc.of Revs.	10.8	10.7	10.5	10.3	11.2	12.3	11.5	10.8	10.9	10.6
% Ret. on Assets	22.4	23.0	23.2	22.9	24.9	28.7	26.8	22.0	NA	20.9
% Ret. on Equity	25.2	26.2	27.6	28.0	29.5	33.8	31.9	27.0	NA	24.5

Data as orig reptd.; bef. results of disc opers/spec. items. Per share data adj. for stk. divs. Bold denotes diluted EPS (FASB 128)-prior periods restated. E-Estimated. NA-Not Available. NM-Not Meaningful. NR-Not Ranked.

Office—2001 Theurer Blvd., Winona, MN 55987. **Tel**—(507) 454-5374. **Website**—http://www.fastenal.com **Chrmn & CEO**—R. A. Kierlin. **Pres**—W. D. Oberton. **Dirs**—M. J. Dolan, M. M. Gostomski, R. A. Hansen, R. A. Kierlin, H. K. McConnon, W. D. Oberton, J. D. Remick, S. M. Slaggie, R. K. Wisecup. **Transfer Agent**—Norwest Bank, Minneapolis. **Incorporated**—in Minnesota in 1968. **Empl**— 6,477. **S&P Analyst:** Michael W. Jaffe

STANDARD &POOR'S
STOCK REPORTS

FedEx Corp.

NYSE Symbol **FDX**

In S&P 500

18-AUG-01

Industry: Air Freight

Summary: This company provides guaranteed domestic and international air express, residential and business ground package delivery, heavy freight and logistics services.

S&P Opinion: Accumulate (★★★★) Recent Price • 40.14 | 52 Wk Range • 49.85-35.50 | Yield • Nil | 12-Mo. P/E • 20.2

Quantitative Evaluations
Outlook (1 Lowest—5 Highest) • **4-**
Fair Value • **43.90**
Risk • **Low**
Earn./Div. Rank • **B**

Technical Eval. • **Neutral** since 8/01
Rel. Strength Rank (1 Lowest—99 Highest) • **53**
Insider Activity • **NA**

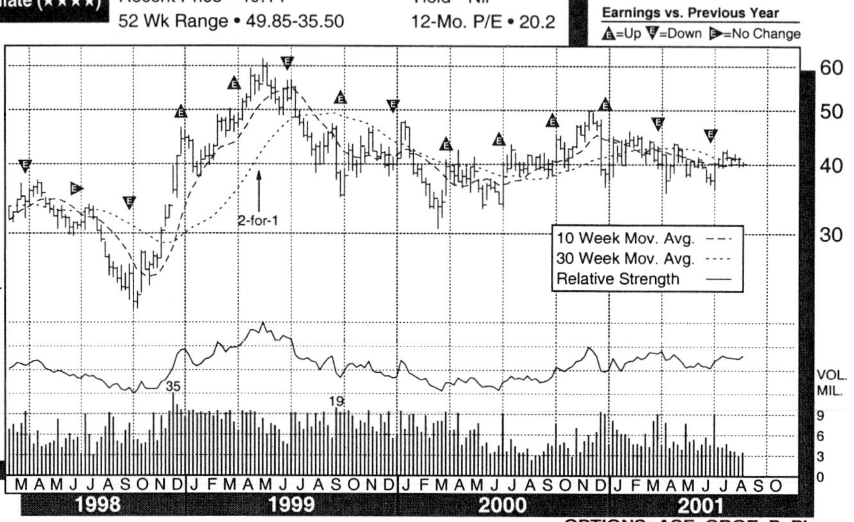

OPTIONS: ASE, CBOE, P, Ph

Overview - 29-JUN-01

Revenues are expected to increase slightly in FY 02 (May), versus a 7.5% rise in FY 01, as the ongoing economic weakness will continue to hinder growth until at least the latter part of 2001. We see solid revenue growth resuming in the fourth quarter of FY 02, as benefits from interest rate cuts, the expansion of FDX's home delivery facilities, and the company's U.S. Postal Service agreement are realized. Domestic volumes should improve from their weak showing in FY 01. Solid gains are projected on the international side, reflecting strength in Asia, as well as FDX's return to the intra-European market. FedEx Ground is seen growing at a 12% pace, up from 10% in FY 01. Margins will be aided by aggressive spending controls. The company's new seven-year agreement with the U.S. Postal Service is expected to generate $7 billion in revenue for FDX, subject to regulatory approval, and will be accretive beginning in FY 02.

Valuation - 29-JUN-01

The shares are down modestly so far in 2001, as investors have become concerned about the slowing economy. FDX has done an excellent job controlling costs, particularly in its Express segment, and is well positioned for a potential economic turnaround in the fourth quarter of 2001. The company's home delivery service is being aggressively expanded, and will reach 100% saturation of the U.S. by September 2002. The service is expected to lose $50 million in FY 01 and FY 02. FDX's agreement with the U.S. Postal Service will broaden its customer base, as it will have an option to place a self-service drop box in every U.S. postal location. We see the stock as undervalued, with price to sales and price to EBITDA ratios at discounts to those of FDX's peers, and believe it will outperform the broader market over the next six to 12 months.

Key Stock Statistics

S&P EPS Est. 2002	2.45	Tang. Bk. Value/Share	15.68
P/E on S&P Est. 2002	16.4	Beta	0.97
Dividend Rate/Share	Nil	Shareholders	16,293
Shs. outstg. (M)	307.0	Market cap. (B)	$ 12.3
Avg. daily vol. (M)	0.677	Inst. holdings	58%

Value of $10,000 invested 5 years ago: $ 21,479

Fiscal Year Ending May 31

	2001	2000	1999	1998	1997	1996
Revenues (Million $)						
1Q	4,779	4,320	4,082	3,866	2,692	2,453
2Q	4,895	4,570	4,209	3,942	2,852	2,547
3Q	4,839	4,518	4,098	3,986	2,907	2,535
4Q	5,117	4,849	4,384	4,078	3,068	2,738
Yr.	19,629	18,257	16,773	15,873	11,520	10,274
Earnings Per Share ($)						
1Q	**0.58**	**0.52**	**0.50**	**0.56**	0.27	0.33
2Q	**0.67**	**0.57**	**0.61**	**0.50**	0.45	0.39
3Q	**0.37**	**0.39**	**0.26**	**0.06**	0.27	0.12
4Q	**0.38**	**0.85**	**0.39**	**0.57**	0.57	0.50
Yr.	**1.99**	**2.32**	**2.10**	**1.68**	**0.48**	**1.37**

Next earnings report expected: mid September

Dividend Data

No dividends have been paid on the common stock.

A Division of The McGraw-Hill Companies

FedEx Corporation

Business Summary - 29-JUN-01

FedEx Corp. (formerly FDX Corp.) provides global time-definite air express services for packages, documents and freight, ground-based deferred delivery of small packages in North America, expedited critical shipment delivery, customs brokerage and trade facilitation solutions, less-than-truckload (LTL) freight transportation in the western U.S., and customized logistics solutions. In early 2000, FDX undertook a $100 million rebranding program designed to provide a more integrated approach to its service offerings. In March 2000, it began a major roll-out of a new residential delivery service aimed at capturing Internet-based retail transactions. FDX expected the rebranding program and startup costs for its home delivery services to depress operating profits by $160 million in FY 01 (May).

Federal Express Corp. (dba FedEx Express) is the company's original business. Formed in 1973, FedEx Express is the world's leading provider of guaranteed, express delivery services. In FY 99, it provided 82.5% of total revenue. It provides same-day, overnight and deferred delivery services for documents, packages and freight, using a network of 49,000 ground vehicles, 663 aircraft, and 46,000 drop off boxes.

About 70% of FedEx Express's revenues are from domestic services, with about 72% of express and 23% lower yielding deferred delivery. The remaining 5% of revenues come from transportation of heavy freight in the U.S.

International business (27% of FedEx Express revenues) is growing faster than domestic side. FDX has a strong position in Asian markets, and is one of only four U.S. air carriers with rights to serve China. In 1999, FedEx Express began to rebuild its European position, launching its EuroOne service. EuroOne is limited to high-yielding, intra-Europe overnight shipments to 38 business centers. About 3% of FedEx Express revenues are derived from the sale of hush kits.

FedEx Ground (11.1% of total revenue) is North America's second largest ground package delivery company. In March 2000, FDX began to roll out FedEx Home Delivery, a new business-to-residential delivery service aimed at capturing a share of the burgeoning e-commerce market. FedEx Home Delivery, which will initially serve only 50% of the U.S. population, is expected generate a $50 million loss in FY 01. In February 2001, FedEx Ground opened 85 Home Delivery facilities, thereby expanding coverage to 70% of the U.S.

The remaining 6.4% of FDX's revenues come from global logistics, time critical shipment services, customs brokerage, and LTL freight transportation in the western U.S.

Per Share Data ($) **(Year Ended May 31)**	**2001**	**2000**	**1999**	**1998**	**1997**	**1996**	**1995**	**1994**	**1993**	**1992**
Tangible Bk. Val.	NA	14.33	14.50	12.26	11.29	9.63	8.26	6.75	5.66	5.04
Cash Flow	NA	6.23	5.55	4.91	4.91	4.51	4.20	3.51	3.07	2.15
Earnings	1.99	2.32	2.10	1.69	1.56	1.35	1.32	0.91	0.50	-0.53
Dividends	Nil	Nil	Nil	Nil	Nil	Nil	Nil	Nil	Nil	Nil
Payout Ratio	Nil	Nil	Nil	Nil	Nil	Nil	Nil	Nil	Nil	Nil
Cal. Yrs.	2000	1999	1998	1997	1996	1995	1994	1993	1992	1991
Prices - High	49.85	61.87	46.56	42.25	22.50	21.50	20.18	18.12	14.02	11.12
- Low	30.56	34.87	21.81	21.00	16.71	14.62	13.37	11.09	8.60	7.84
P/E Ratio - High	25	27	22	25	14	16	15	20	28	NM
- Low	15	15	10	12	11	11	10	12	17	NM
Income Statement Analysis (Million $)										
Revs.	NA	18,257	16,773	15,873	11,520	10,274	9,392	8,479	7,808	7,550
Oper. Inc.	NA	2,376	2,198	2,047	1,477	1,344	1,244	1,113	926	834
Depr.	NA	1,155	1,034	964	778	720	652	583	562	577
Int. Exp.	NA	106	98.0	124	91.0	135	142	182	200	203
Pretax Inc.	NA	1,138	106	899	628	540	522	378	204	-147
Eff. Tax Rate	NA	40%	41%	45%	43%	43%	43%	46%	46%	NM
Net Inc.	NA	688	631	498	361	308	298	204	110	-114
Balance Sheet & Other Fin. Data (Million $)										
Cash	NA	68.0	325	230	122	93.0	358	393	155	78.0
Curr. Assets	NA	3,285	3,141	2,880	2,133	1,728	1,869	1,762	1,440	1,206
Total Assets	NA	11,527	10,648	9,686	7,625	6,699	6,433	5,992	5,793	5,463
Curr. Liab.	NA	2,891	2,785	2,804	1,963	1,618	1,779	1,536	1,449	1,385
LT Debt	NA	1,776	1,360	1,385	1,398	1,325	1,325	1,632	1,882	1,798
Common Eqty.	NA	4,785	4,663	3,961	2,962	2,576	2,246	1,925	1,671	1,580
Total Cap.	NA	6,906	6,316	5,620	4,520	3,965	3,627	3,560	3,626	3,501
Cap. Exp.	NA	1,627	1,550	1,880	1,471	1,412	1,061	1,089	867	771
Cash Flow	NA	1,843	1,665	1,462	1,139	1,028	950	787	672	443
Curr. Ratio	NA	1.1	1.1	1.0	1.1	1.1	1.1	1.1	1.0	0.9
% LT Debt of Cap.	NA	25.7	21.5	24.6	31.0	33.4	36.5	45.8	51.9	51.3
% Net Inc.of Revs.	NA	3.8	3.8	3.1	3.1	3.0	3.2	2.4	1.4	NM
% Ret. on Assets	NA	6.2	6.2	5.8	5.0	4.7	4.8	3.4	1.9	NM
% Ret. on Equity	NA	14.6	14.6	14.4	13.0	12.8	14.3	11.3	6.7	NM

Data as orig reptd.; bef. results of disc opers/spec. items. Per share data adj. for stk. divs. Bold denotes diluted EPS (FASB 128)-prior periods restated. E-Estimated. NA-Not Available. NM-Not Meaningful. NR-Not Ranked.

Office—942 South Shady Grove, Memphis, TN 38120. **Tel**—(901) 818-7200. **Website**—www.fedexcorp.com **Chrmn, Pres & CEO**—F. W. Smith. **EVP & CFO**—A. B. Graf Jr. **EVP & Secy**—K. R. Masterson. **Investor Contact**—Elizabeth Allen (901-818-7153). **Dirs**—R. H. Allen, J. L. Barksdale, R. L. Cox, R. D. DeNunzio, J. L. Estrin, P. Greer, J. R. Hyde III, S. A. Jackson, G. J. Mitchell, F. W. Smith, J. I. Smith, P. S. Walsh, P. S. Willmott. **Transfer Agent & Registrar**—First Chicago Trust Co. of New York, Jersey City, NJ. **Incorporated**—in Delaware in 1971. Reincorporated in Delaware in 1997. **Empl**— 197,000. **S&P Analyst:** Richard N. Stice

STANDARD & POOR'S
STOCK REPORTS

Harsco Corp.

NYSE Symbol **HSC**

In S&P MidCap 400

18-AUG-01

Industry: Manufacturing (Diversified)

Summary: This global industrial service provider and manufacturer has operations in steel mill services and railway services, as well as construction and gas equipment.

S&P Opinion: Accumulate (★★★★)

Recent Price • 33.38 | 52 Wk Range • 33.60-17.68 | Yield • 2.9% | 12-Mo. P/E • 16.0

Quantitative Evaluations

Outlook (1 Lowest—5 Highest)
• 3

Fair Value
• 33

Risk
• Low

Earn./Div. Rank
• A-

Technical Eval.
• **Bullish** since 7/01

Rel. Strength Rank (1 Lowest—99 Highest)
• 93

Insider Activity
• Neutral

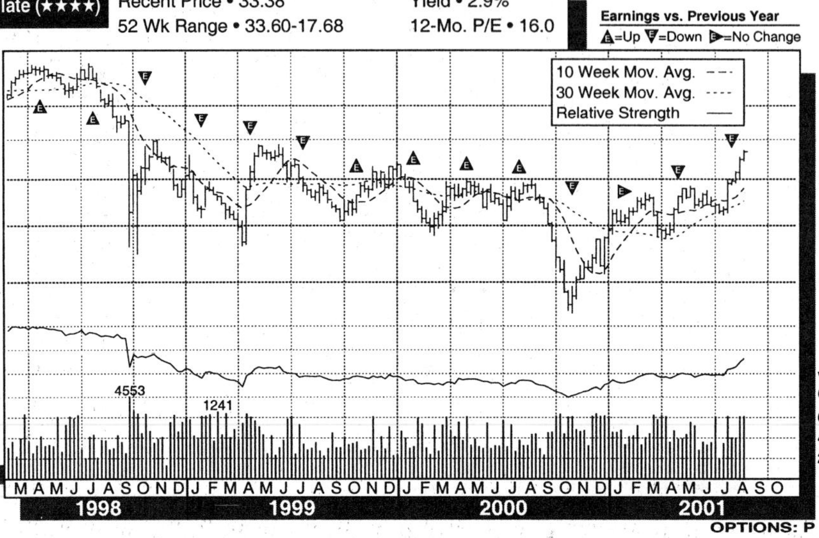

OPTIONS: P

Overview - 15-AUG-01

We look for 15% sales growth in 2001, as the inclusion of SGB Group for the full year will result in sharply higher sales in the infrastructure segment, outweighing declines in mill services and gas and fluid control. Operating margins will narrow, on sharply higher SG&A expenses for the integration of acquisitions, and severe margin contraction in gas and fluid control. Further penalized by higher interest expense, 2001 EPS will slightly trail 2000 levels. Assuming a stronger global economy in 2002, and a recovery in world steel production, sales should rise 8% to 10%. A rebound in the global steel industry should boost mill services, while a generally more vibrant economy will result in gains in infrastructure and gas and fluid control. Sales should also benefit from a likely decline in the U.S. dollar versus the euro. Aided by lower SG&A expenses, lower unit costs, and a decline in interest costs, EPS should post a solid gain in 2002.

Valuation - 15-AUG-01

Following release of second quarter EPS and a conference call, we upgraded the shares to accumulate, from hold, based on a more optimistic EPS outlook and valuation. Second quarter EPS exceeded average analyst estimates, as cost cutting and a stronger euro led to better than anticipated profit gains. We see EPS momentum picking up steam in the second half and continuing into 2002. Free cash flow per share improved substantially from first quarter levels, posting a positive $0.25 for the second quarter, versus a $0.94 deficit for the first quarter. The stock, recently trading at only 12X our 2002 EPS estimate, and with a yield of over 3.0%, represents solid value, and is worth accumulating. HSC should benefit from a change in investor preferences, as value investing becomes more fashionable, and investors begin to target mid-cap companies.

Key Stock Statistics

S&P EPS Est. 2001	2.40	Tang. Bk. Value/Share	16.94
P/E on S&P Est. 2001	13.9	Beta	0.70
S&P EPS Est. 2002	2.75	Shareholders	18,000
Dividend Rate/Share	0.96	Market cap. (B)	$ 1.3
Shs. outstg. (M)	39.8	Inst. holdings	53%
Avg. daily vol. (M)	0.110		

Value of $10,000 invested 5 years ago: $ 12,566

Fiscal Year Ending Dec. 31

	2001	2000	1999	1998	1997	1996
Revenues (Million $)						
1Q	526.6	449.5	405.1	401.3	390.7	366.7
2Q	532.3	457.3	431.4	456.3	426.3	387.7
3Q	—	533.2	426.0	446.1	407.4	395.8
4Q	—	539.4	458.3	431.1	403.1	407.4
Yr.	—	2,005	1,721	1,735	1,627	1,558
Earnings Per Share ($)						
1Q	0.25	0.50	0.35	0.52	0.37	0.31
2Q	0.62	0.70	0.58	0.71	0.50	0.45
3Q	E0.68	0.56	0.64	0.56	0.57	0.45
4Q	E0.85	0.65	0.65	0.55	0.62	0.47
Yr.	E2.40	2.42	2.21	2.34	2.06	1.67

Next earnings report expected: late October

Dividend Data (Dividends have been paid since 1939.)

Amount ($)	Date Decl.	Ex-Div. Date	Stock of Record	Payment Date
0.235	Sep. 26	Oct. 12	Oct. 16	Nov. 15 '00
0.240	Nov. 16	Jan. 11	Jan. 16	Feb. 15 '01
0.240	Mar. 15	Apr. 11	Apr. 16	May. 15 '01
0.240	Jun. 26	Jul. 12	Jul. 16	Aug. 15 '01

Harsco Corporation

Business Summary - 15-AUG-01

Harsco Corp. is a global provider of services and products to the steel, gas and energy, and infrastructure markets. HSC operates in three groups: Harsco Mill Services (38% of 2000 net sales), Harsco Gas and Fluid Control (27%), and Harsco Infrastructure (35%). HSC serves customers in the U.S. (58% of 2000 net sales), U.K. (14%) and other countries (28%).

In recent years, the company has shifted its core focus from being a manufacturing company to becoming an expanded provider of industrial services, in order to achieve higher and more consistent financial returns.

Mill Services Group provides specialized services to steel producers and non-ferrous metals industries through long-term contracts (average length of seven years, with a 90% to 95% renewal rate). This group includes the Heckett MultiServ division, which provides on-site services, equipment & technology to the steel producers; and through its Reed Materials unit processes materials for roofing shingles and industrial abrasives.

The Gas and Fluid Control Group provides a large variety of gas control and containment equipment, as well as process equipment and industrial pipe fittings. It includes Taylor-Wharton Gas Equipment, a producer of gas containment & control equipment; Sherwood, a producer of gas control products; Capital Manufacturing, a domestic leader in pipe fittings and conduit pipe products; American Welding and Tank, North America's largest producer of 120 to 2,000 gallon liquid petroleum gas tanks; Structural Composites Industries, a producer of composite gas cylinders; and Air-x-changers, a custom manufacturer of air-cooled heat exchangers.

The Infrastructure sector provides scaffolding, shoring and concrete forming equipment & services; railway maintenance of way equipment and services; and industrial grating and bridge decking products. This sector includes Harsco Track Technologies, the second largest supplier of railroad maintenance equipment & services in the world; Patent Construction Systems, a North American provider of scaffolding, shoring & concrete forming; IKG Industries, a provider of industrial grating and highway bridge decking; and Patterson-Kelley, a manufacturer of water heaters & boilers.

In June 2000, HSC acquired SGB Group PLC, for $334 million. SGB had annual sales of about $425 million, and was one of Europe's largest suppliers of scaffolding, forming and related access products and services. Following the transaction, HSC's debt rose to 56.5% of capital at the end of the second quarter. The company planned to implement a debt reduction program to strengthen its balance sheet and enable it to capitalize on future growth opportunities.

Backlog at year end 2000 stood at $258.9 million, versus $231.6 million a year earlier.

Per Share Data ($) (Year Ended Dec. 31)	2000	1999	1998	1997	1996	1995	1994	1993	1992	1991
Tangible Bk. Val.	16.94	9.77	9.74	12.65	9.80	8.38	7.28	6.03	9.41	8.78
Cash Flow	6.39	5.52	5.20	4.41	4.58	4.00	3.52	3.00	2.86	2.56
Earnings	2.42	2.21	2.34	2.06	2.39	1.93	1.73	1.61	1.76	1.46
Dividends	0.94	0.90	0.88	0.80	0.76	0.74	0.70	0.70	0.66	0.60
Payout Ratio	39%	41%	38%	39%	32%	38%	41%	43%	38%	41%
Prices - High	31.62	34.37	47.25	47.87	35.06	30.25	23.18	22.50	19.75	15.18
- Low	17.68	23.06	22.31	33.25	29.00	19.81	19.18	17.50	13.87	11.37
P/E Ratio - High	13	16	20	23	15	16	13	14	11	10
- Low	7	10	10	16	12	10	11	11	8	8
Income Statement Analysis (Million $)										
Revs.	2,003	1,721	1,735	1,627	1,558	1,496	1,358	1,422	1,625	1,943
Oper. Inc.	355	312	319	297	277	249	182	199	205	181
Depr.	159	136	131	117	109	105	90.2	69.6	57.1	57.7
Int. Exp.	50.1	27.0	20.5	16.7	21.5	28.9	34.4	20.0	19.2	18.9
Pretax Inc.	149	147	180	172	201	164	149	137	141	120
Eff. Tax Rate	31%	35%	37%	38%	38%	39%	40%	41%	35%	36%
Net Inc.	96.8	90.7	108	100	119	97.4	86.6	80.8	91.5	76.5
Balance Sheet & Other Fin. Data (Million $)										
Cash	56.4	51.3	41.6	222	45.9	76.7	44.0	59.0	50.0	120
Curr. Assets	726	613	587	714	509	534	537	600	598	662
Total Assets	2,181	1,660	1,624	1,477	1,324	1,311	1,315	1,428	991	1,060
Curr. Liab.	536	431	475	372	294	389	282	417	281	377
LT Debt	774	419	309	199	227	180	340	365	120	120
Common Eqty.	674	650	685	782	681	626	581	523	495	480
Total Cap.	1,537	1,122	1,050	1,018	943	842	951	921	632	624
Cap. Exp.	180	175	160	143	150	114	91.0	83.4	60.3	56.8
Cash Flow	256	227	239	217	228	202	177	150	149	134
Curr. Ratio	1.4	1.4	1.2	1.9	1.7	1.4	1.9	1.4	2.1	1.8
% LT Debt of Cap.	50.4	37.3	29.5	19.5	24.1	21.4	35.8	39.6	19.0	19.3
% Net Inc.of Revs.	4.8	5.3	6.2	6.2	7.7	6.5	6.4	5.7	5.6	3.9
% Ret. on Assets	5.0	5.5	6.9	7.2	9.1	7.4	6.3	6.7	9.1	7.5
% Ret. on Equity	14.6	13.6	14.7	13.7	18.2	16.1	15.6	16.0	19.1	16.7

Data as orig reptd.; bef. results of disc opers/spec. items. Per share data adj. for stk. divs. Bold denotes diluted EPS (FASB 128)-prior periods restated. E-Estimated. NA-Not Available. NM-Not Meaningful. NR-Not Ranked.

Office—350 Poplar Church Road, Post Office Box 8888, Camp Hill, PA 17001-8888. **Tel**—(717) 763-7064. **Website**—http://www.harsco.com **Chrmn, Pres & CEO**—D. C. Hathaway. **SVP & Secy**—P. C. Coppock. **SVP, CFO & Treas**—S. D. Fazzolari. **Investor Contact**—Eugene M. Truett (717-975-5677). **Dirs**—C. Hathaway, J J. Jasinowski, R. F. Nation, C. F. Scanlan, J. I. Scheiner, A. J. Sordoni III, J. P. Viviano, R. C. Wilburn. **Transfer Agent & Registrar**—Mellon Investor Services, L.L.C., South Hackensack, NJ. **Incorporated**—in Pennsylvania in 1899; reincorporated in Delaware in 1956. **Empl**— 19,700. **S&P Analyst:** Leo J. Larkin

STANDARD
&POOR'S
STOCK REPORTS

Insituform Technologies

Nasdaq Symbol **INSUA**

In S&P SmallCap 600

18-AUG-01

Industry: Manufacturing (Specialized)

Summary: This company provides patented methods of reconstructing deteriorated pipelines and manholes with little or no excavation.

S&P Opinion: Accumulate (★★★★)

Recent Price • 31.65
52 Wk Range • 43.20-26.48
Yield • Nil
12-Mo. P/E • 22.6

Quantitative Evaluations

Outlook
(1 Lowest—5 Highest)
• **4−**

Fair Value
• **42.40**

Risk
• **Average**

Earn./Div. Rank
• **B**

Technical Eval.
• **Neutral** since 8/01

Rel. Strength Rank
(1 Lowest—99 Highest)
• **27**

Insider Activity
• **Neutral**

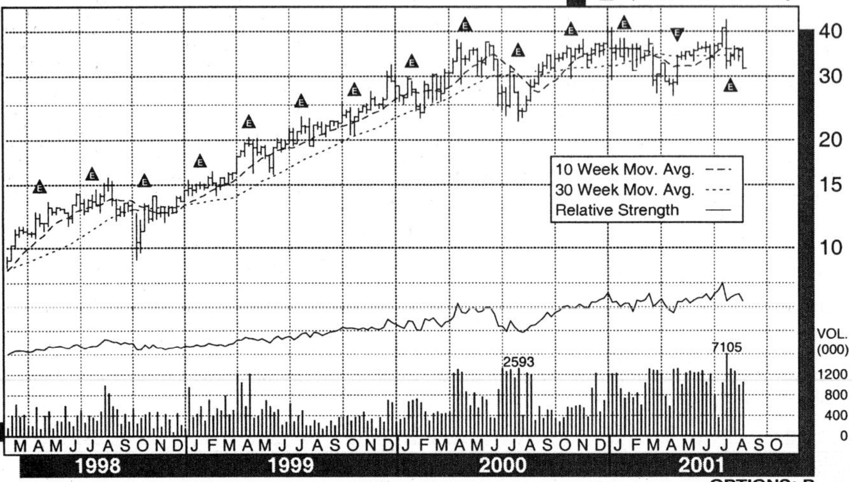

OPTIONS: P

Overview - 24-JUL-01

Internal revenues from the North American sewer rehabilitation business are expected to advance 14% in 2001, despite project startup delays in the first quarter and soft TiteLiner and tunneling revenues. We expect the recent acquisition of pipe bursting rehabilitation company Kinsel Industries to add over 10% to rehab segment revenues (80% of total revenues), and $0.03 to $0.05 to EPS, as INSUA broadens its client base. Gross margins may narrow somewhat as INSUA expands its product mix in the rehab segment, but operating margins should gradually benefit from $3 million per quarter in cost savings (direct labor, fixed costs and staff cuts). Based on a slower backlog conversion rate, and more modest revenue growth seen for the balance of the year, we recently cut our 2001 EPS projection by $0.10 to $1.55, and our 2002 estimate by $0.15 to $1.95.

Valuation - 24-JUL-01

Although second quarter earnings were in line with expectations, a more modest forecast for the second half triggered a 22% drop in the shares. However, we believe the prospects for the North American rehabilitation business remain strong, and are maintaining our accumulate opinion. The company plans to build its backlog -- a shift in strategy -- in an effort to avoid problems encountered in the first quarter when projects were delayed and backlog levels were too low. Technological and organizational changes should improve INSUA's competitive position for different sized piping sytems. As the company obtains greater leverage from operating costs and debt service, we expect cash to be used for share buybacks. Although the stock was recently trading on par with the P/E multiple of the S&P SmallCap 600, with 26% EPS growth seen for 2002, we see potential for capital gains.

Key Stock Statistics

S&P EPS Est. 2001	1.55	Tang. Bk. Value/Share	3.98
P/E on S&P Est. 2001	20.4	Beta	0.41
S&P EPS Est. 2002	1.95	Shareholders	1,100
Dividend Rate/Share	Nil	Market cap. (B)	$0.847
Shs. outstg. (M)	26.8	Inst. holdings	69%
Avg. daily vol. (M)	0.313		

Value of $10,000 invested 5 years ago: $ 42,200

Fiscal Year Ending Dec. 31

	2001	2000	1999	1998	1997	1996
Revenues (Million $)						
1Q	103.2	94.28	71.16	63.76	77.08	68.11
2Q	134.8	99.4	85.64	75.50	75.32	71.77
3Q	—	111.0	93.25	81.05	85.49	70.65
4Q	—	104.7	89.83	80.65	82.75	79.41
Yr.	—	409.4	339.9	301.0	320.6	289.9
Earnings Per Share ($)						
1Q	**0.18**	**0.24**	**0.16**	**0.11**	**0.05**	**0.08**
2Q	**0.42**	**0.33**	**0.25**	**0.16**	**0.01**	**0.14**
3Q	**E0.47**	**0.44**	**0.31**	**0.21**	**0.16**	**0.13**
4Q	**E0.48**	**0.36**	**0.29**	**0.18**	**0.14**	**0.19**
Yr.	**E1.55**	**1.37**	**1.00**	**0.66**	**0.36**	**0.17**

Next earnings report expected: mid October

Dividend Data

No cash has been paid.

A Division of The McGraw-Hill Companies

Insituform Technologies, Inc.

Business Summary - 24-JUL-01

Insituform Technologies (INSUA), continues to focus on accelerating its growth via acquisitions and being the low-cost provider of sewer rehabilitation services, specializing in the use of trenchless technologies to replace, maintain and install underground pipes. It now obtains over 74% of revenues from contracting, using its non-disruptive, Insituform Process technologies. INSUA has focused marketing of its rehabilitation technologies primarily on municipal wastewater markets worldwide; it expects this to remain the largest part of its business. Outside North America, it conducts direct installation operations through subsidiaries in the U.K., France, Spain, and the Netherlands.

Revenues and operating income by segment in 2000 were as follows: rehabilitation, 80% of revenues and 77% of operating income; tunneling 11% (9.3%); and TiteLiner 9% (13%). The geographic breakdown was: U.S., 81%; Canada, 5.4%; and other foreign, 13%.

In February 2001, the company acquired Kinsel Industries Inc. ($100 million revenues), a Houston-based provider of water and sewer pipe rehabilitation services including pipebursting, for $15.3 million in cash and notes, and $64.7 million in stock. INSUA plans to sell Kinsel's highway construction business.

The company provides a trenchless means of rehabilitating sewers, tunnels and pipelines through its Affholder unit. INSUA's TiteLiner Process lines new and existing steel pipelines with a corrosion and abrasion resistant polyethylene pipe. The company also offers the NuPipe Process in the U.S. and overseas, primarily to repair smaller or less damaged pipe. In February 2000, it acquired the New York and New Jersey licensees for the Insituform and Nupipe processes, for $5.2 million, boosting its U.S. population base 15%. During 2000, the company acquired the remaining 50% interest in its former joint venture in the Netherlands, and the remaining 33% interest in its French joint venture. INSUA also own 55% of a Mexican unit, United Pipeline de Mexico S.A., and nearly 80% of Video Injection S.A.

Pipeline technology involves licensing, selling and servicing trenchless reconstruction technology

The Insituform technology uses the INSUA manufactured Insitutube that serves as a carrier for liquid thermosetting plastic resins. At the job site, the tube is positioned in the pipe to be reconstructed through a manhole. Once the tube is in place and positioned tightly against the inner walls of the old pipe, heated water is used to cure the resin, forming a jointless, structural, corrosion-resistant new pipe (the Insitupipe) inside the old pipe.

The NuPipe subsidiary repairs pipe by first heating material which is then pulled into the pipe to be repaired. Once in place, the NuPipe is expanded tightly against the walls of the old pipe, forming a jointless, corrosion resistant pipe within a pipe.

Construction backlog at 2000 year end was $115 million, down 13% from a year earlier.

Per Share Data ($) (Year Ended Dec. 31)	2000	1999	1998	1997	1996	1995	1994	1993	1992	1991
Tangible Bk. Val.	3.98	2.98	2.70	2.37	1.99	1.69	5.15	4.45	3.91	5.74
Cash Flow	2.15	1.70	1.37	1.07	0.87	0.59	1.20	0.95	-0.15	1.97
Earnings	1.37	1.00	0.66	0.36	0.17	-0.04	0.68	0.51	-0.45	1.77
Dividends	Nil	Nil	Nil	Nil	Nil	Nil	Nil	Nil	Nil	Nil
Payout Ratio	Nil	Nil	Nil	Nil	Nil	Nil	Nil	Nil	Nil	Nil
Prices - High	41.50	32.43	15.75	10.18	13.37	16.62	15.37	25.75	26.50	20.62
- Low	22.50	14.00	7.75	5.37	6.12	11.12	10.50	11.25	14.00	3.25
P/E Ratio - High	30	32	24	28	79	NM	23	50	NM	12
- Low	16	14	12	15	36	NM	15	22	NM	2
Income Statement Analysis (Million $)										
Revs.	409	340	301	321	290	272	148	101	95.8	30.4
Oper. Inc.	81.7	NA	57.8	48.9	40.0	43.1	26.1	16.4	12.8	5.7
Depr.	18.7	18.2	19.1	19.2	19.2	16.8	7.5	6.3	4.2	1.6
Int. Exp.	9.3	9.0	9.1	8.8	6.2	6.4	3.1	1.4	0.2	NA
Pretax Inc.	58.2	45.7	31.8	17.2	9.9	4.3	16.5	11.0	-2.0	24.4
Eff. Tax Rate	39%	41%	41%	41%	51%	NM	37%	30%	NM	42%
Net Inc.	34.9	26.0	17.9	9.6	4.5	-1.0	9.8	7.3	-6.2	14.3
Balance Sheet & Other Fin. Data (Million $)										
Cash	64.1	68.2	76.9	45.7	13.5	11.4	17.7	16.1	14.3	25.9
Curr. Assets	201	174	170	161	131	121	71.7	56.3	43.7	37.8
Total Assets	355	312	305	298	268	260	162	129	87.4	58.1
Curr. Liab.	86.5	54.2	48.1	47.0	52.0	51.0	38.9	28.0	24.0	5.8
LT Debt	98.2	115	112	111	82.4	82.8	47.3	36.3	7.3	6.4
Common Eqty.	165	184	140	132	123	117	73.9	63.4	54.5	45.6
Total Cap.	266	301	255	250	209	208	124	101	63.4	52.2
Cap. Exp.	30.2	11.7	13.4	16.6	18.2	16.5	9.0	5.3	6.1	1.5
Cash Flow	53.6	44.2	37.0	28.9	23.7	15.8	17.3	13.6	-2.1	15.9
Curr. Ratio	2.3	3.2	3.5	3.4	2.5	2.4	1.8	2.0	1.8	6.5
% LT Debt of Cap.	36.9	38.1	43.9	44.4	39.4	39.8	38.3	35.9	11.6	12.3
% Net Inc.of Revs.	8.5	7.6	5.9	3.0	1.5	NM	6.6	7.2	NM	46.9
% Ret. on Assets	10.5	8.4	5.9	3.4	1.7	NM	6.7	6.6	NM	28.3
% Ret. on Equity	23.0	15.5	13.2	7.6	3.7	NM	14.2	12.2	NM	37.8

Data as orig reptd.; bef. results of disc opers/spec. items. Per share data adj. for stk. divs. Bold denotes diluted EPS (FASB 128)-prior periods restated. E-Estimated. NA-Not Available. NM-Not Meaningful. NR-Not Ranked.

Office—702 Spirit 40 Park Drive, Chesterfield, MO 63005. **Tel**—(314) 530-8000. **Website**—www.insituform.com **Chrmn, Pres & CEO**—A. W. Hooper. **VP & CFO**—J. A. White. **Secy**—H. Kailes.**Dirs**—R. W. Affholder, P. A. Biddelman, S. Cortinovis, J. Hinshaw, A. W. Hooper, T. N. Kalishman, S. Weinig, A. L. Woods. **Transfer Agent & Registrar**—American Stock Transfer & Trust Co., NYC. **Incorporated**—in Delaware in 1980. **Empl**— 1,771. **S&P Analyst:** Stewart Scharf

STANDARD
&POOR'S
STOCK REPORTS

ITT Industries

NYSE Symbol **ITT**

In S&P 500

18-AUG-01

Industry: Manufacturing (Diversified)

Summary: This diversified industrial manufacturer is the legal successor to the old ITT Corp.

S&P Opinion: Accumulate (★★★★)

Recent Price • 45.05 | 52 Wk Range • 49-29.75 | Yield • 1.3% | 12-Mo. P/E • 14.6

Quantitative Evaluations

Outlook (1 Lowest—5 Highest)
• 4

Fair Value
• 50

Risk
• Low

Earn./Div. Rank
• NR

Technical Eval.
• NA

Rel. Strength Rank (1 Lowest—99 Highest)
• 63

Insider Activity
• Neutral

Overview - 08-JUN-01

Modest revenue gains are expected in 2001. With demand for communications market equipment softening, sales gains from connectors should slow to a mid-single digit rate; pumps and specialty revenues should be flat to slightly higher, while defense sales should decline as some contracts wind down. Specialty products should also fall. Operating margins should benefit from new products, a more favorable sales mix and an improved cost structure; a lower tax rate should add approximately $0.11 to EPS. Foreign exchange rate fluctuations should hurt reported results. Free cash flow in 2001 could exceed 80% of net income. Longer term, revenues are expected to post 8% to 10% average annual growth, reflecting new products, expanded markets and acquisitions. The company's stated objectives include annual EPS growth of 14% to 16%, and segment operating margins of 12% by 2003.

Valuation - 08-JUN-01

The shares fluctuated widely in 2000, but have remained in a sustained uptrend since late 2000. Solid operating performance has helped ITT achieve its recent outperformance. We see EPS rising 11% in 2001, to $3.27, with a further 14% gain in 2002. Strong cash flow supports a modest cash dividend, debt reduction, and global expansion and other capital spending plans. We expect the company to add to organic growth via strategic acquisitions. Recent restructuring efforts are expected to create an improved cost structure. The company should see continued earnings growth via improved margins, new business, joint ventures, and acquisitions. The balance sheet is healthy, and despite a recent rebound, valuations remain at the low end of their historical range. With a positive operating outlook and favorable technical performance, we expect ITT to outperform.

Key Stock Statistics

S&P EPS Est. 2001	3.16	Tang. Bk. Value/Share	NM
P/E on S&P Est. 2001	14.3	Beta	0.77
S&P EPS Est. 2002	3.72	Shareholders	36,917
Dividend Rate/Share	0.60	Market cap. (B)	$ 4.0
Shs. outstg. (M)	87.9	Inst. holdings	70%
Avg. daily vol. (M)	0.329		

Value of $10,000 invested 5 years ago: $ 22,096

Fiscal Year Ending Dec. 31

	2001	2000	1999	1998	1997	1996
Revenues (Million $)						
1Q	1,186	1,205	1,092	1,099	2,167	2,201
2Q	1,184	1,224	1,192	1,125	2,251	2,241
3Q	—	1,173	1,106	1,048	2,060	2,045
4Q	—	1,215	1,242	1,220	2,299	2,231
Yr.	—	4,829	4,632	4,493	8,777	8,718
Earnings Per Share ($)						
1Q	**0.65**	**0.57**	**0.45**	**0.07**	**0.37**	**0.33**
2Q	**0.84**	**0.78**	**0.70**	**0.25**	**0.69**	**0.56**
3Q	**E0.76**	**0.72**	**0.60**	**0.23**	**-0.77**	**0.36**
4Q	**E0.91**	**0.87**	**0.80**	**-1.59**	**0.65**	**0.59**
Yr.	**E3.16**	**2.94**	**2.53**	**-0.86**	**0.94**	**1.85**

Next earnings report expected: mid October

Dividend Data (Dividends have been paid since 1996.)

Amount ($)	Date Decl.	Ex-Div. Date	Stock of Record	Payment Date
0.150	Oct. 17	Nov. 20	Nov. 22	Jan. 01 '01
0.150	Mar. 06	Mar. 14	Mar. 16	Apr. 01 '01
0.150	May. 15	May. 23	May. 25	Jul. 01 '01
0.150	Jul. 17	Aug. 29	Aug. 31	Oct. 01 '01

A Division of The McGraw-Hill Companies

Business Summary - 08-JUN-01

ITT Industries (formerly ITT Corp.) is the legal successor to the old ITT Corp. In a restructuring completed in December 1995, old ITT was divided into three separate, publicly owned entities. ITT Industries retained old ITT's industrial units, and two companies were spun off: ITT Hartford Group (insurance), and New ITT Corp. (hotels, gaming, entertainment and education). Old ITT shares were converted into ITT Industries shares on a one-for-one basis. One share each of New ITT and ITT Hartford were distributed to shareholders for each IIN share. After the discontinuation and spinoff of ITT Hartford Group (insurance) and New ITT Corp. (hotels, gaming and entertainment), ITT now produces mostly defense electronics and fluid technology products.

In 2000, the U.S. accounted for 59% of sales, Western Europe 25%, and Asia Pacific and other 16%.

Pumps & complementary products (36% of 2000 sales) include pumps, valves, heat exchangers, mixers and fluid measuring instruments and controls for residential, agricultural, commercial, municipal and industrial applications. Markets include water and wastewater treatment and industrial and process. Fluid Technology became the world's largest pump manufacturer (formerly third largest) following its May 1997 acquisition of Goulds Pumps, Inc.

Defense electronics (28%) includes tactical communications and electronic warfare systems, night vision devices, radar, satellite instruments and other. Commercial items include connectors, switches, cable assemblies and night vision devices. About 97% of segment sales are to government entities, including 84% to the U.S. government.

Specialty products (20%) include fluid handling materials, such as stainless steel and flexible tubing, specialty shock absorbers and brake friction materials for the transportation industry, engineered valves, controls and switches for industrial and aerospace applications, and products for the marine and leisure markets.

Connectors & switches (16%) include interconnects, cable assemblies, RF connectors, switches, rubber switchpads, input/output card kits, smart card connectors, LAN components, network systems, network services, and customer use tooling.

In 2000, the company completed two acquisitions that are expected to add an aggregate of approximately $150 million to annual revenues. The pace of acquisitions should accelerate in 2001.

Results in 2000 were led by 50% sales growth in the connectors and switches segment and strong organic growth in the water and wastewater pump business. The company warned, however, that demand for communication equipment had moderated in 2001.

In April 2001, ITT said it expected second quarter 2001 revenues of between $1.15 billion and $1.17 billion, segment operating margin of 12.4% to 12.6%, and earnings per share of $0.82 to $0.86.

Per Share Data ($) (Year Ended Dec. 31)	2000	1999	1998	1997	1996	1995	1994	1993	1992	1991
Tangible Bk. Val.	NM	NM	4.53	NM	3.81	2.26	50.41	64.08	59.93	69.47
Cash Flow	5.18	4.50	0.87	4.07	5.66	3.83	12.30	12.08	2.38	10.65
Earnings	2.94	2.50	-0.86	0.94	1.85	0.03	7.10	7.29	-2.47	6.42
Dividends	0.60	0.60	0.60	0.60	0.60	0.99	1.98	1.98	1.84	1.72
Payout Ratio	20%	24%	NM	64%	32%	NM	28%	27%	NM	26%
Prices - High	39.62	41.50	40.87	33.68	28.62	24.25	104.25	94.87	72.12	63.00
- Low	22.37	30.50	28.12	22.12	21.50	21.25	77.00	69.00	54.75	44.87
P/E Ratio - High	13	17	NM	36	15	NM	15	13	NM	10
- Low	8	12	NM	24	12	NM	11	9	NM	7
Income Statement Analysis (Million $)										
Revs.	4,829	4,632	4,493	8,777	8,718	8,884	23,620	22,762	21,651	20,421
Oper. Inc.	695	592	525	904	941	869	2,678	2,502	1,374	2,288
Depr.	202	181	196	378	433	423	592	576	553	535
Int. Exp.	93.1	84.8	126	133	169	175	413	920	1,050	1,073
Pretax Inc.	420	370	-160	187	371	71.0	1,259	1,282	-498	990
Eff. Tax Rate	37%	37%	NM	39%	40%	71%	31%	27%	NM	12%
Net Inc.	265	233	-98.0	114	223	21.0	852	910	-270	817
Balance Sheet & Other Fin. Data (Million $)										
Cash	88.7	182	880	192	122	94.0	4,816	4,321	5,659	2,853
Curr. Assets	1,506	1,628	2,382	2,377	2,289	2,502	NA	NA	NA	NA
Total Assets	4,611	4,530	5,049	6,221	5,491	5,879	100,854	70,560	58,764	53,867
Curr. Liab.	2,233	2,110	2,151	3,545	2,538	2,661	NA	NA	NA	NA
LT Debt	408	479	516	532	583	961	3,340	9,561	9,517	9,539
Common Eqty.	1,211	1,099	1,299	822	799	627	5,326	7,534	7,136	7,949
Total Cap.	1,620	1,578	1,815	1,386	1,492	1,709	8,979	17,407	17,013	18,712
Cap. Exp.	181	228	213	460	406	450	727	505	646	791
Cash Flow	466	414	98.0	492	656	429	1,414	1,450	279	1,299
Curr. Ratio	0.7	0.8	1.1	0.7	0.9	0.9	NA	NA	NA	NA
% LT Debt of Cap.	25.2	30.3	28.4	38.4	39.1	56.3	37.2	54.9	55.9	51.0
% Net Inc.of Revs.	5.5	5.0	NM	1.3	2.6	0.3	3.6	4.0	NM	4.0
% Ret. on Assets	5.8	4.9	NM	1.9	3.9	0.3	1.0	1.4	NM	1.6
% Ret. on Equity	22.9	19.4	NM	14.1	31.3	0.2	13.5	12.0	NM	10.0

Data as orig reptd.; bef. results of disc opers/spec. items. Per share data adj. for stk. divs. Bold denotes diluted EPS (FASB 128)-prior periods restated. E-Estimated. NA-Not Available. NM-Not Meaningful. NR-Not Ranked.

Office—4 W. Red Oak Lane, White Plains, NY 10604. **Tel**—(914) 641-2000. **Fax**—(914) 696-2950. **Website**—www.ittind.com **Chrmn, Pres & CEO**—L. J. Giuliano. **EVP & CFO**—D. J. Anderson.**VP & Treas**—D. E. Foley. **VP & Secy**—K. S. Stolar.**VP & Investor Contact**—Theodore Economou (914-641-2030). **Dirs**—R. V. Araskog, R. A. Burnett, C. J. Crawford, M. David-Weill, L. J. Giuliano, C. A. Gold, J. H. Hamre, R. W. LeBoeuf, L. S. Sanford. **Transfer Agent and Registrar**—Bank of New York, NYC. **Incorporated**—in Maryland in 1920; reincorporated in Delaware in 1968 and Indiana in 1995. **Empl**— 42,000. **S&P Analyst:** Efraim Levy

STANDARD &POOR'S STOCK REPORTS

Masco Corp.

NYSE Symbol **MAS**

In S&P 500

18-AUG-01

Industry: Building Materials

Summary: This company is one of the world's leading manufacturers of faucets, cabinets, coatings and other consumer brand-name home improvement and building products.

S&P Opinion: Accumulate (★★★★)

Recent Price • 25.76

52 Wk Range • 27-14.50

Yield • 2.0%

12-Mo. P/E • 24.3

Quantitative Evaluations

Outlook (1 Lowest—5 Highest) • **1−**

Fair Value • **23.60**

Risk • **Low**

Earn./Div. Rank • **B+**

Technical Eval. • **Bullish** since 6/01

Rel. Strength Rank (1 Lowest—99 Highest) • **70**

Insider Activity • **NA**

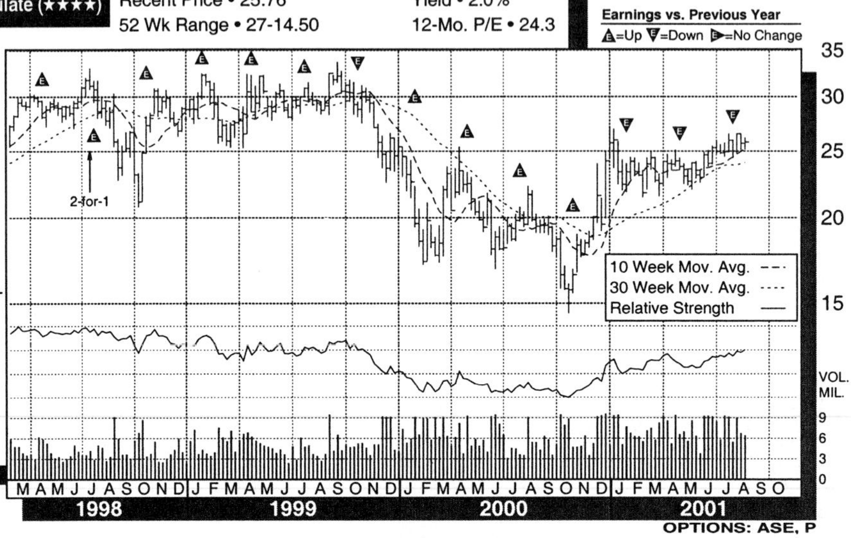

Overview - 13-AUG-01

Sales should rise in the high single digits in 2001, on the inclusion of recent acquisitions. However, we see little or no organic sales growth, and possibly a slight decline, with sales limited by slower economic conditions in the U.S. and Europe, the negative impact of weak foreign currencies, and the resultant softness in home improvement markets. Despite these near-term woes, we expect lower interest rates to start steadying the U.S. economy in the latter part of the year, and see MAS's customers concluding their inventory reduction programs around that time. These factors should allow the company's business to start turning around, and lead to sales growth of about 15% in 2002, including mid-single-digit internal growth. Margins should narrow in 2001, on difficult sales conditions and higher energy costs. However, a better sales setting and cost cutting initiatives should allow for improved margin comparisons in 2002.

Valuation - 13-AUG-01

The shares began to rebound in late 2000, as a downturn in interest rates started to give investors a more positive outlook on the economy, and on housing and home improvement markets. We agree with this view, and also expect Masco's strong brand names and greater home center presence to add to its market share. With MAS's strong management team also taking aggressive cost cutting actions, we see profits starting to firm in 2001's second half. Although sales and earnings will likely be uninspiring through year-end, we think investors will focus on a likely business recovery for MAS in 2002. With the shares recently trading at about 17 to 18 times our 2002 EPS forecast, which falls in the lower to middle part of the company's traditional forward P/E multiple, we would accumulate positions in anticipation of a rebound in Masco's business.

Key Stock Statistics

S&P EPS Est. 2001	1.25	Tang. Bk. Value/Share	2.14
P/E on S&P Est. 2001	20.6	Beta	0.80
S&P EPS Est. 2002	1.50	Shareholders	6,700
Dividend Rate/Share	0.52	Market cap. (B)	$ 11.9
Shs. outstg. (M)	460.2	Inst. holdings	69%
Avg. daily vol. (M)	1.365		

Value of $10,000 invested 5 years ago: $ 19,584

Fiscal Year Ending Dec. 31

	2001	2000	1999	1998	1997	1996
Revenues (Million $)						
1Q	1,911	1,746	1,391	1,039	854.0	764.0
2Q	2,085	1,871	1,567	1,085	913.0	787.0
3Q	—	1,893	1,704	1,122	1,003	843.0
4Q	—	1,733	1,645	1,099	990.0	843.0
Yr.	—	7,243	6,307	4,345	3,760	3,237
Earnings Per Share ($)						
1Q	**0.25**	**0.39**	**0.34**	**0.33**	**0.26**	**0.19**
2Q	**0.30**	**0.41**	**0.39**	**0.34**	**0.28**	**0.21**
3Q	**E0.35**	**0.41**	**0.15**	**0.37**	**0.30**	**0.26**
4Q	**E0.35**	**0.10**	**0.40**	**0.36**	**0.31**	**0.26**
Yr.	**E1.25**	**1.31**	**1.28**	**1.39**	**1.17**	**0.91**

Next earnings report expected: early November

Dividend Data (Dividends have been paid since 1944.)

Amount ($)	Date Decl.	Ex-Div. Date	Stock of Record	Payment Date
0.130	Sep. 14	Oct. 11	Oct. 13	Nov. 13 '00
0.130	Dec. 07	Jan. 10	Jan. 12	Feb. 12 '01
0.130	Mar. 16	Apr. 04	Apr. 06	May. 08 '01
0.130	Jun. 29	Jul. 11	Jul. 13	Aug. 13 '01

Masco Corporation

Business Summary - 13-AUG-01

Masco is one of the largest U.S. makers of brand name consumer products designed for the home improvement and homebuilding industries. The company derives the majority of its revenues from the sale of faucets, kitchen and bath cabinets, plumbing supplies and architectural coatings. Operations are concentrated in North America (82% of sales in 2000) and Europe (most of remaining 18%). Home Depot accounted for 26% of 2000 sales.

The plumbing products division (26% of 2000 sales) ranks as the world's leading faucet maker. MAS, which revolutionized faucets in 1954 with the Delta, also offers the Peerless, Damixa and Mariani brands, and private label faucets. The division also offers other bath products, including plumbing specialty products, gelcoat and acrylic bathtubs, tub and shower enclosures, and spa items; brand names include Alsons, Brass Craft, and Aqua Glass. It is also the largest U.S. maker of kitchen and bath cabinetry (35% of sales), featuring brands such as Kraftmaid, Merillat, Mill's Pride and StarMark.

MAS derives the rest of its sales from decorative architectural products (19% of sales), including stains, varnishes and paint, decorative bath and shower accessories and lock sets; the supply and installation of insulation products (12%); and other specialty products (8%), ranging from electric staple guns, radiators, and lock sets used primarily in the hospitality market.

In 2000 and early 2001, MAS acquired several businesses (combined annual sales of $1.3 billion), for a total of $1.4 billion in cash, stock and assumed debt. The most significant were Masterchem Industries, a maker and supplier of paint primer and related products; Tvilum-Scanbirk A/S, a Danish maker of ready-to-assemble cabinetry, shelving, storage units and workstations; and BSI Holdings, an installer of insulation and other products. In June 2001, Masco agreed to buy three additional companies (total annual sales of $500 million), including Milgard Manufacturing, a large maker of vinyl windows.

Historically, MAS's goal has been to boost sales 12% to 16% on an annual basis (on average, over any five-year cycle): 7% to 9% from internal growth, and 5% to 7% from acquisitions. However, with much weaker macroeconomic conditions slowing business, Masco has fallen well below its internal growth goals since 2000's third quarter; a 4% decline in the 2001 first quarter was the first organic sales decrease in about a decade, while organic sales were flat in the second quarter.

In late 2000, MAS adopted a plan to dispose of several unnamed businesses that no longer fit its long-term strategies. It said these units had annual sales of about $600 million, and an aggregate operating margin below the company average. MAS expected cash proceeds to exceed $400 million. Masco recorded fourth quarter charges of $0.20 a share to write down certain non-operating assets, and for the planned dispositions. In July 2001, MAS sold its INRECON unit ($200 million o f annual sales) to BELFOUR USA Group. INRECON repairs, remodels and restores facilities damaged by fire, wind, water and other disasters.

Per Share Data ($) (Year Ended Dec. 31)	2000	1999	1998	1997	1996	1995	1994	1993	1992	1991
Tangible Bk. Val.	42.78	3.14	4.99	4.53	4.29	4.09	4.43	4.56	4.13	5.96
Cash Flow	1.84	1.68	1.78	1.48	1.23	0.91	0.99	1.10	0.98	0.49
Earnings	1.31	1.28	1.39	1.18	0.92	0.63	0.61	0.72	0.60	0.15
Dividends	0.49	0.57	0.43	0.40	0.48	0.28	0.35	0.33	0.30	0.28
Payout Ratio	37%	45%	31%	34%	53%	44%	71%	45%	51%	192%
Prices - High	27.00	33.68	33.00	26.90	18.43	15.75	19.93	19.43	15.00	13.25
- Low	14.50	22.50	20.75	16.87	13.25	11.25	10.62	12.75	11.00	8.50
P/E Ratio - High	21	26	24	23	20	25	33	27	25	88
- Low	11	18	15	14	14	18	17	18	18	57
Income Statement Analysis (Million $)										
Revs.	7,243	6,307	4,345	3,760	3,237	2,927	4,468	3,886	3,525	3,141
Oper. Inc.	1,295	1,093	817	703	580	492	630	520	473	351
Depr.	238	182	136	116	100	90.0	121	116	114	103
Int. Exp.	191	120	85.3	79.8	74.7	73.8	105	106	101	127
Pretax Inc.	893	904	755	631	503	352	323	363	305	98.0
Eff. Tax Rate	34%	37%	37%	39%	41%	NM	40%	39%	40%	54%
Net Inc.	592	570	476	382	295	200	194	221	183	45.0
Balance Sheet & Other Fin. Data (Million $)										
Cash	169	231	542	441	474	60.5	71.0	125	54.0	70.0
Curr. Assets	2,308	2,110	1,863	1,627	1,431	965	1,891	1,644	1,466	1,376
Total Assets	7,744	6,635	5,167	4,334	3,702	3,779	4,390	4,021	3,987	3,786
Curr. Liab.	1,078	846	847	620	518	446	601	490	492	514
LT Debt	3,018	2,431	1,391	1,322	1,236	1,577	1,593	1,418	1,487	1,369
Common Eqty.	3,426	3,137	2,729	2,229	1,840	1,655	2,113	1,998	1,887	1,799
Total Cap.	6,444	5,788	4,321	3,714	3,183	3,332	3,705	3,417	3,374	3,168
Cap. Exp.	388	351	189	167	138	165	191	167	123	119
Cash Flow	830	751	612	498	395	290	314	337	298	148
Curr. Ratio	2.1	2.5	2.2	2.6	2.8	2.2	3.1	3.4	3.0	2.7
% LT Debt of Cap.	46.8	42.0	32.2	35.6	38.8	47.3	43.0	41.5	44.1	43.2
% Net Inc.of Revs.	8.2	9.0	11.0	10.2	9.1	6.8	4.3	5.7	5.2	1.4
% Ret. on Assets	8.2	9.3	10.0	9.5	7.9	5.0	4.5	5.5	4.7	1.2
% Ret. on Equity	18.0	19.3	19.2	18.8	16.9	10.6	9.3	11.4	9.9	2.5

Data as orig reptd.; bef. results of disc opers/spec. items. Per share data adj. for stk. divs. Bold denotes diluted EPS (FASB 128)-prior periods restated. E-Estimated. NA-Not Available. NM-Not Meaningful. NR-Not Ranked.

Office—21001 Van Born Rd., Taylor, MI 48180. **Tel**—(313) 274-7400. **Website**—http://www.masco.com **Chrmn & CEO**—R. A. Manoogian. **Pres & COO**—R. F. Kennedy. **Investor Contact**—Samuel Cypert (313-792-6646). **Dirs**—T. G. Denomme, P. A. Dow, A. F. Earley Jr., J. L. Hudson Jr., V. G. Istock, R. F. Kennedy, M. A. Kray Van Lokeren, W. B. Lyon, R. A. Manoogian, J. A. Morgan. **Transfer Agent & Registrar**—Bank of New York, NYC. **Incorporated**—in Michigan in 1929; reincorporated in Delaware in 1968. **Empl**— 48,600. **S&P Analyst:** Michael W. Jaffe

STANDARD &POOR'S
STOCK REPORTS

Quixote Corp.

Nasdaq Symbol **QUIX**

18-AUG-01

Industry: Manufacturing (Specialized)

Summary: This company manufactures highway safety products that both reduce the severity of accidents and help to prevent them.

S&P Opinion: Accumulate (★★★★)

Recent Price • 24.56
52 Wk Range • 31.25-13.78
Yield • 1.2%
12-Mo. P/E • 18.2

Quantitative Evaluations

Outlook (1 Lowest—5 Highest) • **3+**

Fair Value • **25.10**

Risk • **Average**

Earn./Div. Rank • **B**

Technical Eval. • **Bearish** since 7/01

Rel. Strength Rank (1 Lowest—99 Highest) • **39**

Insider Activity • **Neutral**

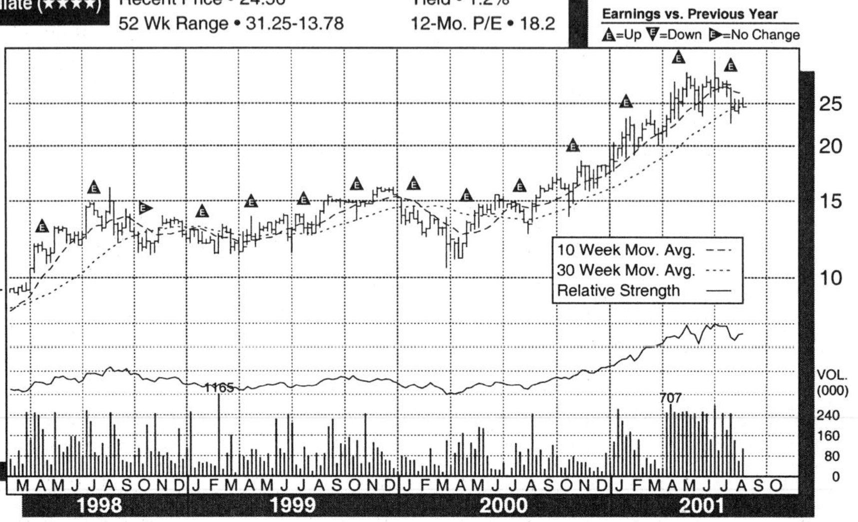

Overview - 06-AUG-01

After average revenue growth of 23% over the past three years, revenues should rise 16% in FY 01 (Jun.) and 15% in FY 02, driven by the development, acquisition and delivery of established and new highway safety products. Gross margin has narrowed in FY 01, as a result of an increased proportion of sales of lower-margin truck-mounted attenuators, and the absorption of the acquired National Signal business. We expect gross margin to narrow to 47.4% in FY 01, and to 46.1% in FY 02. However, as the company introduces a greater level of high-tech safety products, margins should widen. In FY 02, benefiting from leveraged gained on SG&A expenses, the operating margin, which had been trending higher, should approximate the level of FY 00. We expect EPS to rise 20% in FY 01, to $1.32, and increase 15% in FY 02, to $1.52.

Valuation - 06-AUG-01

The shares were recently up 29% in 2001, compared to a 6.2% decline for the S&P Capital Goods Index. We believe this contrast in performance is due to QUIX's recession-resistant characteristics. The Transportation Equity Act for the 21st Century, passed in May 1998, provides for $218 billion in federal funding over a six-year period, with 10% of the funds earmarked for highway safety. The company is the market share leader in the crash cushion market, with about an 85% share. QUIX's relationships with distributors across the U.S. have allowed it to bring various other highway safety products to market, and we expect these to increasingly be high tech, wider margin products. At a P/E multiple of 16X our FY 02 estimate, the shares were trading at a discount to the 18% growth rate that we forecast through the period. In valuing the company's discounted future free cash flows, we believe the shares are worth $34, and recommend accumulation.

Key Stock Statistics

S&P EPS Est. 2002	1.55	Tang. Bk. Value/Share	2.77
P/E on S&P Est. 2002	15.8	Beta	0.08
Dividend Rate/Share	0.30	Shareholders	1,367
Shs. outstg. (M)	7.4	Market cap. (B)	$0.182
Avg. daily vol. (M)	0.030	Inst. holdings	72%

Value of $10,000 invested 5 years ago: $ 41,324

Fiscal Year Ending Jun. 30

	2001	2000	1999	1998	1997	1996
Revenues (Million $)						
1Q	21.32	19.30	16.06	12.33	11.10	37.64
2Q	20.28	16.23	14.80	12.12	9.19	36.07
3Q	22.69	20.05	18.35	12.82	10.27	26.43
4Q	29.27	28.19	22.78	18.72	14.48	29.02
Yr.	93.55	83.77	71.99	55.99	45.04	129.2
Earnings Per Share ($)						
1Q	**0.29**	**0.23**	**0.20**	**0.20**	**0.08**	0.22
2Q	**0.17**	**0.13**	**0.11**	**0.08**	**-0.04**	0.06
3Q	**0.23**	**0.18**	**0.14**	**0.10**	**0.02**	-0.23
4Q	**0.66**	**0.58**	**0.47**	**0.38**	**0.29**	0.27
Yr.	**1.35**	**1.10**	**0.92**	**0.76**	**0.36**	**0.52**

Next earnings report expected: late October

Dividend Data (Dividends have been paid since 1993.)

Amount ($)	Date Decl.	Ex-Div. Date	Stock of Record	Payment Date
0.150	Nov. 14	Dec. 04	Dec. 06	Jan. 04 '01
0.150	May. 24	Jun. 04	Jun. 06	Jul. 06 '01

Quixote Corporation

Business Summary - 06-AUG-01

Quixote Corp. believes its products have prevented more than 30,000 traffic fatalities worldwide since 1969. The company is a leading developer, maker and marketer of highway safety products. It provides solutions to improve safety on the roads by minimizing the severity of crashes that occur, and by preventing crashes from occurring by directing or providing information. In FY 00 (Jun.), international sales climbed 56%, accounting for 12% of total sales.

In the area of severity minimization, the company offers various types of highway crash cushions that are currently installed in front of thousands of roadside hazards. QUIX's crash cushion systems and other barriers are designed to absorb or dissipate the force of impact in collisions between vehicles and fixed roadside objects, or slow moving vehicles. They employ the principles of momentum transfer and kinetic energy to safely decelerate errant vehicles.

QUIX also makes and sells products that prevent accidents and help control the flow of traffic by directing or guiding it. Products range from simple polyethylene guide posts that delineate a travel way to glare screens that are placed between travel medians, and to more intelligent products. Highway Information Systems, Inc., acquired in 1998, makes and markets highway advisory radio systems that help control traffic flow by informing motorists of accidents and traffic delays. Nu-Metrics, Inc., acquired in 1998, manufactures electronic wireless measuring and sensing devices used to gather and employ information to relieve traffic congestion.

Other safety products include the Groundhog line of permanent traffic monitors, which gather information on the volume, speed and class of vehicles as well as road surface conditions and transmit these data using the spread spectrum wireless method (RF) to a receiver unit. The company also offers remote traffic and weather information networks, which, using a tower and special detectors mounted in the road, can detect freezing conditions and provide valuable data to dispatch salt trucks or automatically activate anti-icing systems. QUIX is also a leading manufacturer of highway advisory radio systems.

The Federal Highway Administration (FHWA) endorses the installation of highway crash cushions as an effective safety program. Most company products are approved by the FHWA as acceptable highway hardware. The approval process makes the products eligible for federal funding, and creates a substantial barrier to entry in the industry.

Historically, federal funds have covered 75% to 90% of the cost of highway safety projects on roads constructed or maintained with federal assistance. The Transportation Equity Act for the 21st Century (TEA 21), passed in May 1998, provides for federal funding of about $218 billion over six years. States must set aside 10% of federal funds received yearly under TEA 21 for safety construction activities.

Per Share Data ($) (Year Ended Jun. 30)	2001	2000	1999	1998	1997	1996	1995	1994	1993	1992
Tangible Bk. Val.	NA	2.77	2.72	3.34	4.99	5.99	7.49	6.94	5.53	4.51
Cash Flow	NA	1.57	1.36	1.08	0.60	2.14	2.45	3.07	2.51	2.30
Earnings	1.35	1.10	0.92	0.76	0.36	0.32	0.76	1.37	1.17	1.05
Dividends	0.30	0.29	0.28	0.26	0.25	0.24	0.22	0.21	0.20	Nil
Payout Ratio	22%	26%	30%	34%	69%	75%	30%	15%	17%	Nil
Prices - High	31.25	20.06	16.12	16.12	9.87	10.87	13.25	22.75	18.00	15.75
- Low	17.50	10.50	11.25	8.00	6.75	5.50	7.25	10.75	11.75	11.00
P/E Ratio - High	23	18	18	21	27	34	18	16	15	15
- Low	13	10	12	10	19	17	10	7	10	10
Income Statement Analysis (Million $)										
Revs.	NA	83.8	72.0	56.0	45.0	129	185	177	145	129
Oper. Inc.	NA	19.1	9.1	10.9	7.7	22.7	29.0	31.9	29.4	27.9
Depr.	NA	3.8	3.4	2.3	1.9	14.5	15.6	11.5	9.6	8.9
Int. Exp.	NA	0.9	1.0	0.4	0.5	6.1	4.1	3.1	3.2	4.9
Pretax Inc.	NA	14.4	11.8	8.8	3.7	3.5	9.2	17.8	17.3	15.5
Eff. Tax Rate	NA	38%	36%	30%	21%	27%	35%	35%	45%	47%
Net Inc.	NA	8.9	7.6	6.1	2.9	2.6	6.0	11.6	9.4	8.3
Balance Sheet & Other Fin. Data (Million $)										
Cash	NA	1.5	2.2	3.9	18.5	2.3	2.2	1.0	4.1	10.6
Curr. Assets	NA	34.3	30.8	26.9	33.6	37.5	50.6	46.3	39.9	44.2
Total Assets	NA	73.3	71.8	59.1	55.2	130	170	123	110	101
Curr. Liab.	NA	12.2	12.2	11.7	13.0	17.9	40.1	26.6	25.4	20.0
LT Debt	NA	15.6	11.9	7.7	Nil	58.0	68.0	39.0	40.0	47.3
Common Eqty.	NA	43.1	46.0	38.9	41.7	47.6	59.0	54.1	41.9	33.6
Total Cap.	NA	60.5	59.3	47.4	42.2	108	130	96.2	84.5	81.0
Cap. Exp.	NA	1.4	2.3	1.4	1.3	24.4	38.4	11.0	16.7	5.2
Cash Flow	NA	12.8	11.0	8.5	4.8	17.1	21.5	23.2	19.0	17.2
Curr. Ratio	NA	2.8	2.5	2.3	2.6	2.1	1.3	1.7	1.6	2.2
% LT Debt of Cap.	NA	25.8	20.1	16.2	Nil	53.9	52.3	40.5	47.4	58.4
% Net Inc.of Revs.	NA	10.6	10.5	11.0	6.5	2.0	3.2	6.6	6.5	6.4
% Ret. on Assets	NA	12.3	11.6	10.8	3.1	1.7	4.1	9.9	8.9	8.0
% Ret. on Equity	NA	20.0	17.8	15.3	6.5	4.8	10.5	24.0	24.8	28.1

Data as orig reptd.; bef. results of disc opers/spec. items. Per share data adj. for stk. divs. Bold denotes diluted EPS (FASB 128)-prior periods restated. E-Estimated. NA-Not Available. NM-Not Meaningful. NR-Not Ranked.

Office—One East Wacker Dr., Chicago, IL 60601. **Tel**—(312) 467-6755. **Fax**—(312) 467-1356. **Website**—http://www.quixotecorp.com **Chrmn**—P. E. Rollhaus Jr. **Pres & CEO**—L. J. Jezuit. **VP, CFO & Treas**—D. P. Gorey. **VP, Secy & Investor Contact**—J. R. Riley. **Dirs**—J. H. DeVries, W. G. Fowler, L. J. Jezuit, L. C. McQuade, R. D. van Roijen Jr., P. E. Rollhaus Jr. **Transfer Agent**—Fleet National Bank, c/o EquiServe Ltd., Boston. **Empl**— 582. **S&P Analyst:** Markos N. Kaminis

STANDARD
&POOR'S
STOCK REPORTS

Raytheon Co.

NYSE Symbol **RTN**

In S&P 500

23-AUG-01 **Industry:** Electronics (Defense)

Summary: Raytheon, the second-largest U.S. military contractor, specializes in making high-tech missiles and electronics.

S&P Opinion: Accumulate (★★★★) Recent Price • 27 | 52 Wk Range • 36.68-24.67 | Yield • 3.0% | 12-Mo. P/E • NM

Quantitative Evaluations

Outlook (1 Lowest—5 Highest) • **2⁻**

Fair Value • **26.30**

Risk • **NA**

Earn./Div. Rank • **B+**

Technical Eval. • **NA**

Rel. Strength Rank (1 Lowest—99 Highest) • **40**

Insider Activity • **NA**

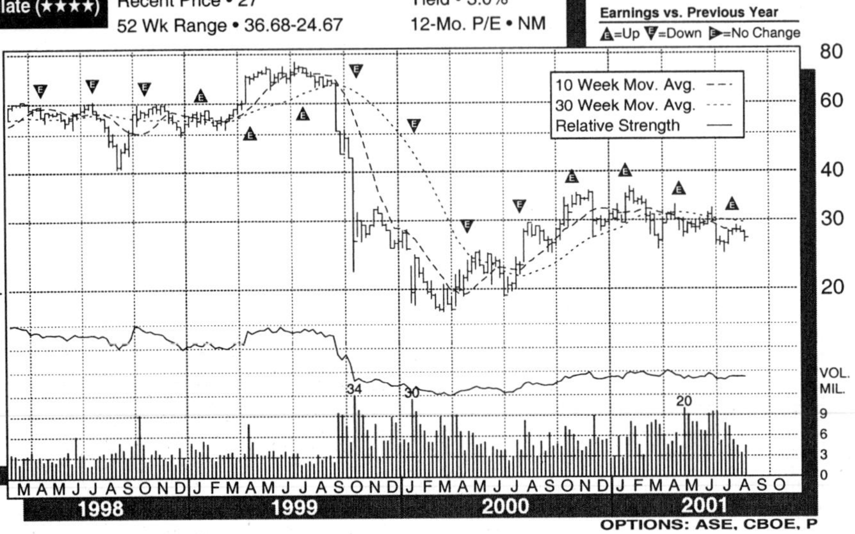

OPTIONS: ASE, CBOE, P

Overview - 23-AUG-01

Although RTN's missile and electronics offerings serve relatively faster growing segments of the otherwise mature domestic and international defense markets, the company is still not immune to the mediocre economics of the global weapons business. We believe U.S. military contractors, such as RTN, will continue to face tepid short- and long-term demand drivers, a highly political and intensely competitive weapons procurement process, and ongoing dependence on a single powerful customer (the Pentagon). We don't believe RTN will have much better luck in the international markets. The combination of relatively weak demand and intensifying competition from big European defense contractors should compress once-fat profit margins from international sales. Thus, we project RTN may generate short- and long-term average annual revenue growth in the middling 3%-6% range. Consequently, tepid sustainable volume growth and tough competitive landscapes should prevent RTN from posting average annual EPS growth and return on equity (ROE) higher than 7%-9% and 10%-13%, respectively.

Valuation - 23-AUG-01

We are maintaining our accumulate opinion on RTN, despite the company's mediocre management and underlying business fundamentals. Our relative valuation models, which compare RTN's P/E multiple of 16 (based on our 2001 operating EPS estimate of $1.70) to projections of 7%-9% sustainable EPS growth, would seem to indicate that RTN is trading at a premium. However, we put more stock in our intrinsic value models. These models (which incorporate several variables, including our projections of 10%-13% average ROE, a 7% long-term risk-free bond rate, and RTN's current net asset value of about $31 a share) indicate that RTN is worth $35-$45 a share.

Key Stock Statistics

S&P EPS Est. 2001	1.70	Tang. Bk. Value/Share	NM
P/E on S&P Est. 2001	15.9	Beta	0.58
S&P EPS Est. 2002	1.80	Shareholders	18,334
Dividend Rate/Share	0.80	Market cap. (B)	$ 9.4
Shs. outstg. (M)	342.9	Inst. holdings	66%
Avg. daily vol. (M)	0.811		

Value of $10,000 invested 5 years ago: $ 5,817

Fiscal Year Ending Dec. 31

	2001	2000	1999	1998	1997	1996
Revenues (Million $)						
1Q	3,968	4,231	5,025	4,575	2,899	2,788
2Q	4,307	4,124	5,210	5,078	3,325	3,127
3Q	—	4,160	4,776	4,436	3,445	3,032
4Q	—	4,380	4,830	5,441	4,004	3,384
Yr.	—	16,895	19,841	19,530	13,673	12,331
Earnings Per Share ($)						
1Q	**0.28**	**0.24**	**0.76**	**0.34**	0.78	0.78
2Q	**0.33**	**0.28**	**0.84**	**0.79**	0.89	0.88
3Q	**E0.44**	**0.39**	**-0.48**	**0.03**	0.89	0.80
4Q	**E0.65**	**0.55**	**0.21**	**1.08**	-0.31	0.75
Yr.	**E1.70**	**1.46**	**1.34**	**2.53**	**2.18**	**3.17**

Next earnings report expected: mid October

Dividend Data (Dividends have been paid since 1998.)

Amount ($)	Date Decl.	Ex-Div. Date	Stock of Record	Payment Date
0.200	Sep. 27	Oct. 04	Oct. 09	Nov. 06 '00
0.200	Dec. 20	Dec. 28	Jan. 02	Jan. 30 '01
0.200	Mar. 27	Apr. 04	Apr. 06	Apr. 30 '01
0.200	Jun. 27	Jul. 05	Jul. 09	Aug. 06 '01

A Division of The McGraw-Hill Companies

Raytheon Company

Business Summary - 23-AUG-01

RTN is now the world's largest maker of sophisticated military electronics and missiles, after gobbling up several large defense electronics businesses in the mid-1990s. However, the company's dominance in the military electronics and missile-making industries has come at a high price. RTN has had a difficult time integrating its far-flung defense operations. This has led to several asset writedowns, restructuring charges, and production problems. In addition, RTN's aggressive acquisition strategy has saddled the company with nearly $10 billion of debt, materially affecting its financial flexibility and R&D spending.

RTN's military electronics and missile segments (78% of 2000 revenues) primarily make sophisticated missiles and radar for the global military markets. Major competitors include Lockheed Martin, Northrop Grumman, Britain's BAE Systems and Europe's Matra BAE Dynamics. In 2000, 1999 and 1998, segment profit margins were 11%, 9.8% and 14%, respectively.

The Raytheon Aircraft segment (18%) makes small, piston-powered aircraft; turboprop-powered aircraft for commuter airlines; a line of corporate jets; and military training aircraft. Primary competitors include Bombardier's Lear division, General Dynamics' Gulfstream unit and Textron's Cessna division. Over the past several years, the unit has been missing out on the fractional ownership-fueled boom in business jet sales, in part due to new product delays, cost overruns and management turnover. Segment profitability has been eroding. In 2000, 1999 and 1998, segment profit margins were 5.1%, 6.0% and 9.7%, respectively.

Raytheon Aircraft also has its hands full with its aircraft financing and leasing arm, Raytheon Aircraft Credit Corp. One customer has stopped paying interest on about $160 million of loans. RACC is also negotiating with another customer, regarding another $160 million of loans. RTN would like to exit this business altogether. In recent periods, RTN has been selling off RACC's loan and lease portfolio. At June 30, 2001, total aircraft loans and leased aircraft (which are not included on RTN's consolidated balance sheet), stood at $1.7 billion, versus $3.2 billion at June 30, 2000.

RTN's small commercial electronics segment (4%), makes various components used in optical communications, satellite TV dishes, wireless communications products and auto radar devices. In 2000, 1999 and 1998, segment losses were $4 million, $30 million and $157 million, respectively.

In early 2001, Washington Group International sued RTN, regarding WGI's purchase of RTN's ailing engineering & construction division in 2000. WGI claims RTN fraudulently overstated the E&C unit's assets and understated liabilities, forcing WGI to file bankruptcy. We expect RTN to take after-tax charges of $530 million and $215 million in 2001 and 2002, respectively, representing costs RTN will expend to complete two power plant projects that it earlier indemnified.

Per Share Data ($) (Year Ended Dec. 31)	2000	1999	1998	1997	1996	1995	1994	1993	1992	1991
Tangible Bk. Val.	NM	NM	NM	NM	6.44	7.26	12.92	13.97	13.95	12.15
Cash Flow	3.50	3.46	4.75	4.07	4.77	4.77	3.29	3.62	3.48	3.40
Earnings	1.46	1.34	2.53	2.20	3.21	3.25	2.25	2.56	2.36	2.24
Dividends	0.80	0.80	0.80	0.80	0.79	0.75	0.72	0.53	0.66	0.61
Payout Ratio	55%	60%	32%	36%	25%	23%	32%	21%	28%	28%
Prices - High	35.81	76.56	60.75	60.50	56.12	47.25	34.43	34.25	26.75	22.06
- Low	17.50	22.18	40.68	41.75	43.37	31.43	30.25	25.25	20.31	16.43
P/E Ratio - High	25	57	24	28	17	15	15	13	11	10
- Low	12	17	16	19	14	10	13	10	9	7
Income Statement Analysis (Million $)										
Revs.	16,895	19,841	19,530	13,673	12,331	11,716	10,013	9,201	9,058	9,274
Oper. Inc.	2,319	2,251	2,797	2,036	1,602	1,584	1,353	1,207	1,196	1,128
Depr.	694	724	761	457	369	371	275	287	302	306
Int. Exp.	736	713	739	397	256	197	49.0	32.0	48.0	92.0
Pretax Inc.	877	828	1,467	790	1,083	1,192	900	1,047	956	873
Eff. Tax Rate	43%	45%	41%	33%	30%	34%	34%	34%	34%	32%
Net Inc.	498	457	864	527	761	792	597	693	635	592
Balance Sheet & Other Fin. Data (Million $)										
Cash	871	230	421	296	139	210	202	190	89.0	138
Curr. Assets	8,013	8,931	8,637	9,233	5,604	5,275	4,985	4,609	3,776	3,748
Total Assets	26,777	28,110	27,939	28,598	11,126	9,841	7,395	7,258	6,015	6,087
Curr. Liab.	4,865	7,886	6,680	11,886	4,692	3,690	3,283	2,910	2,137	2,716
LT Debt	9,054	7,298	8,163	4,406	1,500	1,488	24.5	24.4	25.3	39.3
Common Eqty.	10,823	10,959	10,856	10,425	4,598	4,292	3,928	4,298	3,843	3,323
Total Cap.	20,650	18,810	19,580	15,617	6,098	5,780	3,953	4,322	3,869	3,363
Cap. Exp.	431	532	509	459	406	329	267	310	308	349
Cash Flow	1,192	1,181	1,625	984	1,130	1,163	872	980	937	898
Curr. Ratio	1.6	1.1	1.3	0.8	1.2	1.4	1.5	1.6	1.8	1.4
% LT Debt of Cap.	43.8	38.8	41.7	28.2	24.6	25.8	0.6	0.6	0.7	1.2
% Net Inc.of Revs.	2.9	2.3	4.4	3.9	6.2	6.8	6.0	7.5	7.0	6.4
% Ret. on Assets	1.8	1.6	3.1	2.7	7.3	9.2	8.5	10.5	10.4	9.6
% Ret. on Equity	4.6	4.2	8.1	7.0	17.2	19.3	15.2	17.1	17.6	19.0

Data as orig. reptd.; bef. results of disc. opers. and/or spec. items. Per share data adj. for stk. divs. as of ex-div. date. Bold denotes diluted EPS (FASB 128). E-Estimated. NA-Not Available. NM-Not Meaningful. NR-Not Ranked. Historical/forecasted EPS based on ongoing operations.

Office—141 Spring St., Lexington, MA 02421. **Tel**—(781) 862 6600. **Website**—http://www.raytheon.com **Chrmn & CEO**—D. P. Burnham. **CFO**—F. A. Caine. **Treas**—R. A. Goglia. **Investor Contact**—Tim Oliver (781-860-2167). **Dirs**—B. B. Barrett, D. B. Burnham, F. Colloredo-Mansfeld, J. M. Deutch, T. E. Everhart, J. R. Galvin, L. D. Kozlowski, H. D. C. Meirelles, D. J. Picard, F. M. Poses, M. C. Ruettgers, W. B. Rudman, W. R. Spivey, A. M. Zeien. **Transfer Agent & Registrar**—EquiServe LLP, Boston. **Incorporated**—in Delaware in 1928. **Empl**— 93,700. **S&P Analyst:** Robert E. Friedman, CPA

STANDARD &POOR'S

STOCK REPORTS

Shaw Group

NYSE Symbol **SGR**

In S&P SmallCap 600

18-AUG-01

Industry: Engineering & Construction

Summary: This company supplies industrial piping systems, mainly for the electric power, refining and chemical industries.

S&P Opinion: Accumulate (★★★★)

Recent Price • 25.49

52 Wk Range • 63.48-22.25

Yield • Nil

12-Mo. P/E • 19.5

Quantitative Evaluations

Outlook (1 Lowest—5 Highest) • **3−**

Fair Value • **28.70**

Risk • **High**

Earn./Div. Rank • **B+**

Technical Eval. • **Bearish** since 6/01

Rel. Strength Rank (1 Lowest—99 Highest) • **7**

Insider Activity • **NA**

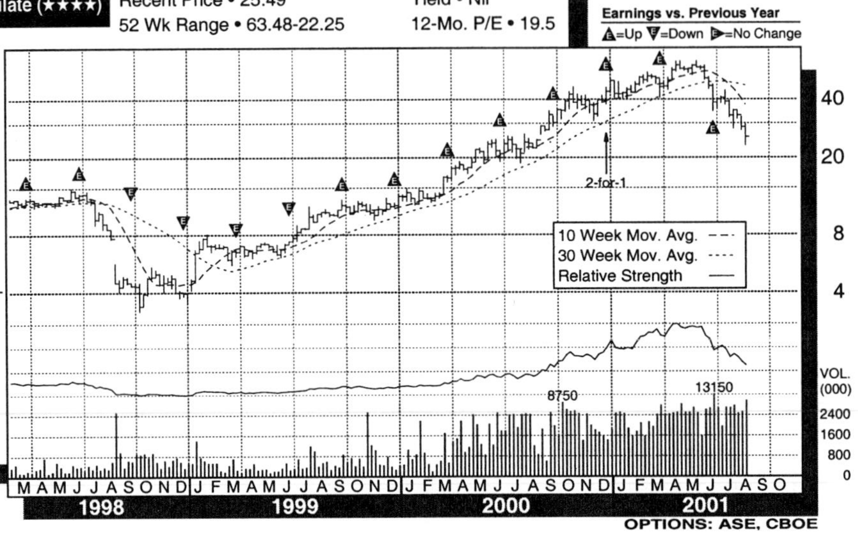

OPTIONS: ASE, CBOE

Overview - 15-AUG-01

Revenues from ongoing operations are expected to advance at least 20% in FY 01 (Aug.), with strength continuing in FY 02, primarily reflecting increased demand for power generation systems and higher pipe services volume from Stone & Webster. SGR derives 77% of its $3.6 billion backlog, which has risen 313% from a year ago, from power projects, with 81% U.S.-based. We expect international projects to increase as SGR expands capacity and hires more engineers and project managers. Gross margins are seen widening sequentially through FY 02 to over 17% of sales, while G&A expenses fall to near 9%, as strong engineering margins offset an increase in lower margin erection and maintenance services (versus fabricated work) driven by the S&W businesses. With third quarter earnings exceeding expectations, we raised our EPS estimates by $0.05, to $1.45 for FY 01 and $1.75 for FY 02.

Valuation - 15-AUG-01

Although the shares were recently trading 57% below their May 52-week high, due in part to some concern that federal caps on electricity prices would limit power-plant construction, we maintain our accumulate recommendation. With favorable prospects for natural gas projects, as well as for coal and nuclear plants, expected for several years, we do not see the FERC's (federal energy regulatory commission) ruling impacting orders. SGR plans to start six projects from its EntergyShaw joint venture, and recently received a contract to build a plant for the energy unit of FPL Group. We expect SGR to generate positive cash flow in FY 02, while cyclical downturns are mitigated by the diverse product mix of SGR's customers. With the shares trading at a PEG (P/E-to-EPS growth) ratio of less than 0.8X, and 8.5X our $3.25 EBITDA estimate, we suggest adding to positions.

Key Stock Statistics

S&P EPS Est. 2001	1.45	Tang. Bk. Value/Share	5.45
P/E on S&P Est. 2001	17.6	Beta	1.41
S&P EPS Est. 2002	1.75	Shareholders	152
Dividend Rate/Share	Nil	Market cap. (B)	$ 1.0
Shs. outstg. (M)	41.0	Inst. holdings	0%
Avg. daily vol. (M)	1.181		

Value of $10,000 invested 5 years ago: $ 20,684

Fiscal Year Ending Aug. 31

	2001	2000	1999	1998	1997	1996
Revenues (Million $)						
1Q	418.7	150.8	115.9	98.67	75.72	—
2Q	340.3	173.0	113.0	134.7	85.52	—
3Q	394.1	175.1	125.4	144.3	88.88	—
4Q	—	263.8	140.1	124.0	88.23	—
Yr.	—	762.7	494.0	501.6	338.4	222.0
Earnings Per Share ($)						
1Q	**0.32**	**0.22**	**0.12**	**0.18**	0.15	—
2Q	**0.28**	**0.22**	**0.18**	**0.21**	0.15	—
3Q	**0.42**	**0.23**	**0.21**	**0.23**	0.14	—
4Q	**E0.45**	**0.30**	**0.23**	**0.02**	0.15	—
Yr.	**E1.45**	**0.98**	**0.73**	**0.63**	**0.60**	0.47

Next earnings report expected: mid October

Dividend Data

Amount ($)	Date Decl.	Ex-Div. Date	Stock of Record	Payment Date
2-for-1	Nov. 13	Dec. 18	Dec. 01	Dec. 15 '00

The Shaw Group Inc.

Business Summary - 15-AUG-01

Shaw Group, a leading supplier of industrial piping systems, was founded in 1987 by current management. The company subsequently purchased the assets of Benjamin F. Shaw Co., a century-old pipe fabricator. Through internal expansion and a series of strategic acquisitions, SGR has expanded its fabrication and bending capacity, expanded its piping system products and services, and broadened its overall project scope to include engineering, pipe erection, construction and maintenance services. These actions have provided the company with the ability to achieve substantial economies of scale in purchasing raw materials, and in providing customers with a broad range of products and services.

SGR offers comprehensive design and engineering services, piping system fabrication, manufacturing and sale of specialty pipe fittings and design and fabrication of pipe support systems. It has also expanded its capabilities to include final on-site erection, turnkey construction and project maintenance. The company primarily serves the power generation (43% of FY 00 (Aug.) sales), process (42%), and environmental and infrastructure (3%) industries.

International revenues increased from $4.5 million in FY 99 to $170.9 million in FY 00 (22% of the total).

SGR operates facilities in California, Louisiana, New Hampshire, New Jersey, Oklahoma, South Carolina, Texas, Utah, Virginia, Australia, the U.K., Venezuela and Bahrain.

In July 2000, SGR acquired Stone & Webster (S&W), a Boston-based engineering and construction company, in exchange for $38 million in cash and 2.2 million common shares. SGR was the successful bidder for S&W in an auction that was part of a bankruptcy proceeding. It assumed liabilities of about $685 million, and incurred $6 million of acquisition costs. S&W, with more than 5,500 employees, provides full-service, value-added engineering, procurement, construction, consultation and environmental services to the power, governmental and industrial markets. SGR and S&W had combined FY 00 revenues of about $1.6 billion. In January 2001, the company sold S&W's cold storage business and office building in Houston, TX, for a total of $87 million.

In September 2000, SGR and Entergy Corp. formed EntergyShaw, a new, equally owned and jointly managed company. EntergyShaw's initial focus will be on construction of power plants in North America and Europe for Entergy's and Florida Power & Light's unregulated wholesale operations. EntergyShaw expects to generate approximately $100 million in revenues per turbine installed.

In October, the company sold publicly 2.4 million common shares at $63.50 each. Net proceeds of about $145 million were to be used for debt reduction.

SGR projects capital expenditures for FY 01 at $25 million.

Per Share Data ($) (Year Ended Aug. 31)	2000	1999	1998	1997	1996	1995	1994	1993	1992	1991
Tangible Bk. Val.	2.69	6.05	5.17	5.52	3.85	3.17	NA	NA	NA	NA
Cash Flow	1.53	1.27	1.03	0.92	0.69	0.38	0.29	NA	NA	NA
Earnings	0.98	0.73	0.63	0.60	0.47	0.25	0.20	0.32	0.17	NA
Dividends	Nil	Nil	Nil	Nil	Nil	Nil	Nil	Nil	NA	NA
Payout Ratio	Nil	Nil	Nil	Nil	Nil	Nil	Nil	Nil	NA	NA
Prices - High	50.50	12.75	13.96	13.37	18.50	5.37	13.25	9.75	NA	NA
- Low	11.37	4.09	3.18	6.25	4.37	1.93	1.37	7.25	NA	NA
P/E Ratio - High	51	17	22	22	39	22	68	31	NA	NA
- Low	12	6	5	10	9	8	7	23	NA	NA
Income Statement Analysis (Million $)										
Revs.	763	494	502	338	222	135	113	121	67.0	NA
Oper. Inc.	69.6	47.0	41.3	33.6	20.0	11.9	6.5	NA	NA	NA
Depr.	16.8	13.3	10.2	7.4	4.0	2.2	1.5	NA	NA	NA
Int. Exp.	8.0	8.6	8.5	6.8	4.0	2.8	1.7	NA	NA	NA
Pretax Inc.	46.7	26.8	23.3	20.0	13.0	6.5	4.4	NA	NA	NA
Eff. Tax Rate	35%	32%	30%	30%	32%	34%	31%	NA	NA	NA
Net Inc.	30.4	18.1	16.2	14.0	8.8	4.3	3.0	4.2	2.8	NA
Balance Sheet & Other Fin. Data (Million $)										
Cash	21.8	6.9	3.7	4.4	2.9	0.8	NA	NA	NA	NA
Curr. Assets	791	252	251	173	145	80.6	NA	NA	NA	NA
Total Assets	1,335	407	390	262	205	106	92.0	67.0	43.0	NA
Curr. Liab.	682	138	121	80.3	95.4	40.6	NA	NA	NA	NA
LT Debt	255	87.8	91.7	39.0	32.2	9.6	1.7	8.3	4.8	NA
Common Eqty.	377	174	171	138	73.3	54.1	NA	NA	NA	NA
Total Cap.	638	269	269	182	110	68.3	NA	NA	NA	NA
Cap. Exp.	20.6	18.0	14.6	15.8	18.1	4.6	4.7	NA	NA	NA
Cash Flow	47.2	31.4	26.4	21.4	12.8	6.5	4.5	NA	NA	NA
Curr. Ratio	1.2	1.8	2.1	2.2	1.5	2.0	NA	NA	NA	NA
% LT Debt of Cap.	39.9	32.7	34.0	21.5	29.2	14.1	NA	NA	NA	NA
% Net Inc.of Revs.	4.0	3.7	3.2	4.2	4.0	3.2	2.7	3.5	3.8	NA
% Ret. on Assets	3.5	4.5	5.0	6.0	5.6	4.3	3.8	4.7	NA	NA
% Ret. on Equity	11.0	10.5	10.5	13.3	13.8	NA	NA	NA	NA	NA

Data as orig reptd.; bef. results of disc opers/spec. items. Per share data adj. for stk. divs. Bold denotes diluted EPS (FASB 128)-prior periods restated. E-Estimated. NA-Not Available. NM-Not Meaningful. NR-Not Ranked.

Office—8545 United Plaza Blvd., Baton Rouge, LA 70809. **Tel**—(225) 932-2500. **Website**—http://www.shawgrp.com **Chrmn, Pres & CEO**—J. M. Bernhard Jr. **EVP & COO**—R. F. Gill. **EVP, CFO & Treas**—R. L. Belk. **Secy**—G. P. Graphia. **Dirs**—J. M. Bernhard Jr., W. H. Grigg, L. L. Grigsby, D. W. Hoyle, A. McAlister, J. W. Sinders Jr. **Transfer Agent & Registrar**—First Union National Bank, Charlotte, NC. **Incorporated**—in Louisiana in 1987. **Empl**— 13,000. **S&P Analyst:** Stewart Scharf

STANDARD & POOR'S
STOCK REPORTS

Stewart & Stevenson Services

Nasdaq Symbol **SSSS**

In S&P MidCap 400

18-AUG-01

Industry: Manufacturing (Diversified)

Summary: This diversified manufacturer of power generation equipment and specialized vehicles also distributes industrial machinery.

S&P Opinion: Accumulate (★★★★)

Recent Price • 31.61
52 Wk Range • 37.19-15.18
Yield • 1.1%
12-Mo. P/E • 18.7

Quantitative Evaluations

Outlook (1 Lowest—5 Highest)
• **3**

Fair Value
• **31.10**

Risk
• **Average**

Earn./Div. Rank
• **B**

Technical Eval.
• **Neutral** since 8/01

Rel. Strength Rank (1 Lowest—99 Highest)
• **68**

Insider Activity
• **Unfavorable**

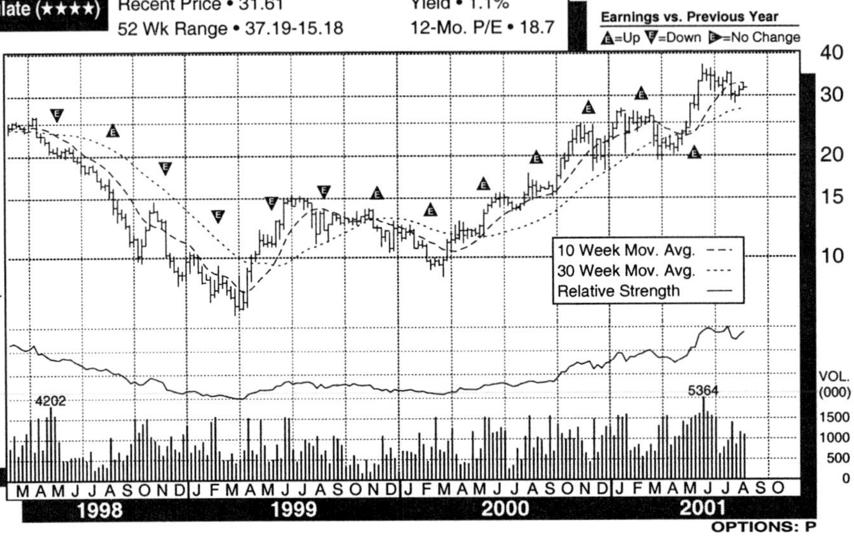

OPTIONS: P

Overview - 11-JUN-01

Despite a weak economic environment, we see SSSS achieving double digit sales growth in FY 02 (Jan.), on strength in the power products, tactical vehicles, and petroleum equipment segments. Power products sales should benefit from increasing demand for the company's diesel generators, on heightened concerns about energy availability and cost, particularly in California and Latin America. Tactical vehicle systems should post significant growth as a result of a planned ramp-up in production of tactical vehicles for the army. Results in the petroleum equipment segment should improve, on a continued increase in oil and gas exploration activities due to high oil and gas prices. Airline product sales should improve fractionally, as management works to return this business to profitability. Greater sales and cost reduction efforts should lead to widening margins in FY 02. Interest income should improve, as SSSS builds up its cash balances.

Valuation - 11-JUN-01

The shares have advanced significantly since the beginning of 2001, on expectations that the company would benefit from its exposure to the energy and defense sectors. We believe SSSS well positioned to continue to grow, even in a challenging economic environment. OPEC's desire to maintain oil prices bodes well for the power generation and petroleum products sectors. The company's tactical vehicles business has fixed rate production agreements with the U.S. Army, and it should therefore be unaffected by near-term economic fluctuations. With the stock trading at about 18X our FY 02 EPS estimate of $1.86 (excluding gains), and with projected EPS growth in excess of 45% for FY 02, we view the shares as attractive.

Key Stock Statistics

S&P EPS Est. 2002	2.17	Tang. Bk. Value/Share	13.50
P/E on S&P Est. 2002	14.6	Beta	0.76
Dividend Rate/Share	0.34	Shareholders	681
Shs. outstg. (M)	28.2	Market cap. (B)	$0.893
Avg. daily vol. (M)	0.224	Inst. holdings	81%

Value of $10,000 invested 5 years ago: $ 16,832

Fiscal Year Ending Jan. 31

	2002	2001	2000	1999	1998	1997
Revenues (Million $)						
1Q	341.5	259.2	188.9	305.0	329.4	219.5
2Q	—	265.1	200.6	323.5	345.9	240.8
3Q	—	284.2	234.7	321.1	299.0	336.8
4Q	—	338.9	287.4	257.1	334.3	390.1
Yr.	—	1,153	911.7	1,207	1,115	1,187
Earnings Per Share ($)						
1Q	**0.73**	**0.27**	**0.08**	**0.29**	0.30	0.20
2Q	**E0.40**	**0.27**	**0.11**	**0.30**	0.25	-0.23
3Q	**E0.44**	**0.30**	**0.26**	**-0.25**	0.11	0.22
4Q	**E0.60**	**0.38**	**0.17**	**-1.77**	**-0.89**	0.32
Yr.	**E2.17**	**1.23**	**0.62**	**-1.34**	**-0.44**	**0.14**

Next earnings report expected: late August

Dividend Data (Dividends have been paid since 1988.)

Amount ($)	Date Decl.	Ex-Div. Date	Stock of Record	Payment Date
0.085	Sep. 12	Oct. 27	Oct. 31	Nov. 10 '00
0.085	Dec. 11	Jan. 29	Jan. 31	Feb. 16 '01
0.085	Apr. 10	Apr. 26	Apr. 30	May. 11 '01
0.085	Jun. 13	Jul. 27	Jul. 31	Aug. 10 '01

Stewart & Stevenson Services, Inc.

18-AUG-01

Business Summary - 11-JUN-01

Stewart & Stevenson is a diversified industrial equipment producer and distributor that is primarily engaged in the custom fabrication of engine driven products. The company has four business segments.

The power products segment (53% of FY 01 (Jan.) sales) sells and rents various industrial equipment; sells components, replacement parts, accessories, and other materials supplied by independent manufacturers; and provides in-shop and on-site repair services for industrial equipment. In addition, it manufactures and packages power generation equipment .Some of the equipment sold or rented by the power products segment is acquired by the company from independent manufacturers, such as Detroit Diesel, John Deere, and GM, under distribution agreements.

The tactical vehicle systems segment (26%) assembles, and provides sustaining design engineering and service and support for, a family of medium tactical vehicles (FMTV) under contracts with the U.S. Army. In 1998, the company received a second multi-year contract from the U.S. Army that provides for continued production of the FMTV through FY 02, with a one-year option held by the U.S. Army that could extend the contracts through FY 03.

The petroleum equipment segment (9%) manufactures equipment for the oil and gas exploration, production and well stimulation industries. Its products include marine riser systems, blow-out preventers and controls, high pressure valves, coil tubing systems, acidizing and fracturing systems, and compression molded rubber products. Many of its products are manufactured according to proprietary designs and are covered by appropriate process and apparatus patents.

The airline products segment (10%) manufactures internal combustion and electric airline ground support equipment that includes aircraft tow tractors, gate pushback tractors, baggage tow tractors, beltloaders, air start units, and air conditioning units. This segment also manufactures mobile railcar movers. In addition, the company is engaged in other businesses such as the fabrication of gas compression equipment.

SSSS has an active acquisitions and dispositions program designed to enhance the company's long-term performance. In December 1999, SSSS acquired certain assets and liabilities of Thermo King of Northern California for about $6.2 million. This acquisition complemented the company's existing franchise agreements owned by the power products segment. In July 2000, the company sold its gas compressor leasing business for $57.5 million. During 1999, the company sold several non-core assets for about $6.8 million.

Capital spending in FY 01 declined to $35.4 million, from $38.6 million in FY 00.

Per Share Data ($) **(Year Ended Jan. 31)**	**2001**	**2000**	**1999**	**1998**	**1997**	**1996**	**1995**	**1994**	**1993**	**1992**
Tangible Bk. Val.	12.85	11.97	11.45	15.72	14.47	14.28	12.70	10.89	9.33	8.40
Cash Flow	2.02	1.42	-0.67	0.24	1.30	2.62	2.78	2.37	1.73	1.46
Earnings	1.23	0.62	-1.34	-0.44	0.51	1.87	2.05	1.73	1.35	1.18
Dividends	0.34	0.34	0.34	0.34	0.41	0.31	0.33	0.22	0.19	0.14
Payout Ratio	28%	55%	NM	NM	81%	17%	16%	13%	14%	12%
Cal. Yrs.	2000	1999	1998	1997	1996	1995	1994	1993	1992	1991
Prices - High	24.93	15.31	26.37	29.25	30.50	41.25	53.75	52.50	34.75	33.62
- Low	8.75	6.75	8.25	19.37	19.62	21.50	28.00	28.00	22.00	16.12
P/E Ratio - High	20	25	NM	NM	60	22	26	30	25	28
- Low	7	11	NM	NM	38	11	14	16	16	14
Income Statement Analysis (Million $)										
Revs.	1,153	912	1,207	1,115	1,187	1,234	1,138	982	813	686
Oper. Inc.	74.2	48.1	-42.5	29.8	92.2	126	131	109	77.8	64.3
Depr.	22.6	22.3	19.6	22.4	26.2	24.7	24.0	21.2	12.3	8.3
Int. Exp.	9.1	10.0	12.2	15.4	24.1	13.9	6.9	3.3	3.7	7.0
Pretax Inc.	55.1	26.1	-61.8	-22.6	25.6	91.9	102	84.8	64.6	52.5
Eff. Tax Rate	37%	33%	NM	NM	33%	33%	34%	33%	32%	32%
Net Inc.	34.8	17.5	-39.0	-14.5	16.8	61.8	67.6	56.8	44.0	35.7
Balance Sheet & Other Fin. Data (Million $)										
Cash	110	11.7	13.0	19.0	9.1	6.3	4.0	7.8	21.9	6.5
Curr. Assets	500	489	540	1,110	974	882	714	541	436	413
Total Assets	639	642	706	1,253	1,145	1,040	876	693	573	478
Curr. Liab.	188	212	285	562	321	330	311	241	199	166
LT Debt	66.6	78.3	83.5	147	320	211	117	68.0	44.5	27.9
Common Eqty.	361	335	320	527	479	472	419	359	306	272
Total Cap.	427	414	404	672	804	690	544	433	356	309
Cap. Exp.	5.8	38.6	39.6	31.7	25.0	24.8	33.4	30.6	75.1	26.2
Cash Flow	57.4	39.7	-19.4	7.9	43.1	86.5	91.5	78.0	56.3	44.0
Curr. Ratio	2.7	2.3	1.9	2.0	3.0	2.7	2.3	2.2	2.2	2.5
% LT Debt of Cap.	15.6	18.9	20.7	21.8	39.8	30.6	21.5	15.7	12.5	9.0
% Net Inc.of Revs.	3.0	1.9	NM	NM	1.4	5.0	5.9	5.8	5.4	5.2
% Ret. on Assets	5.4	2.6	NM	NM	1.5	6.5	8.6	8.9	8.3	7.9
% Ret. on Equity	10.0	5.3	NM	NM	3.5	10.0	17.4	17.1	15.1	15.2

Data as orig. reptd.; bef. results of disc. opers. and/or spec. items. Per share data adj. for stk. divs. as of ex-div. date. Bold denotes diluted EPS (FASB 128). E-Estimated. NA-Not Available. NM-Not Meaningful. NR-Not Ranked.

Office—2707 North Loop West, P.O. Box 1637, Houston, TX 77251-1637. **Tel**—(713) 868-7700. **Website**—http://www.ssss.com **Chrmn**—C. J. Stewart II. **Pres & CEO**—M. L. Grimes. **CFO**—J. H. Doster. **VP & Secy**—L. E. Wilson. **Treas & Investor Contact**—David R. Stewart (713-868-7657). **Dirs**--K. V. Attwell, M. L. Grimes, M. L. Lukens,, M. M. Luther, C. R. Ofner, D. E. Stevenson, C. J. Stewart II, C. J. Stewart III, R. S. Sullivan, D. M. Winick, H. Wolf. **Transfer Agent & Registrar**—Bank of New York, NYC. **Incorporated**—in Texas in 1947. **Empl**— 4,100. **S&P Analyst:** Robert McMillan

STANDARD
&POOR'S
STOCK REPORTS

Tetra Tech

Nasdaq Symbol **TTEK**

In S&P SmallCap 600

18-AUG-01

Industry: Services (Facilities & Environmental)

Summary: Tetra Tech provides specialized management consulting and technical services in three principal areas: resource management, infrastructure and communications.

S&P Opinion: Accumulate (★★★★) | Recent Price • 21.04 | 52 Wk Range • 37.56-17 | Yield • Nil | 12-Mo. P/E • 29.2

Quantitative Evaluations

Outlook (1 Lowest—5 Highest) • **5**

Fair Value • **34.50**

Risk • **Average**

Earn./Div. Rank • **B+**

Technical Eval. • **NA**

Rel. Strength Rank (1 Lowest—99 Highest) • **23**

Insider Activity • **Unfavorable**

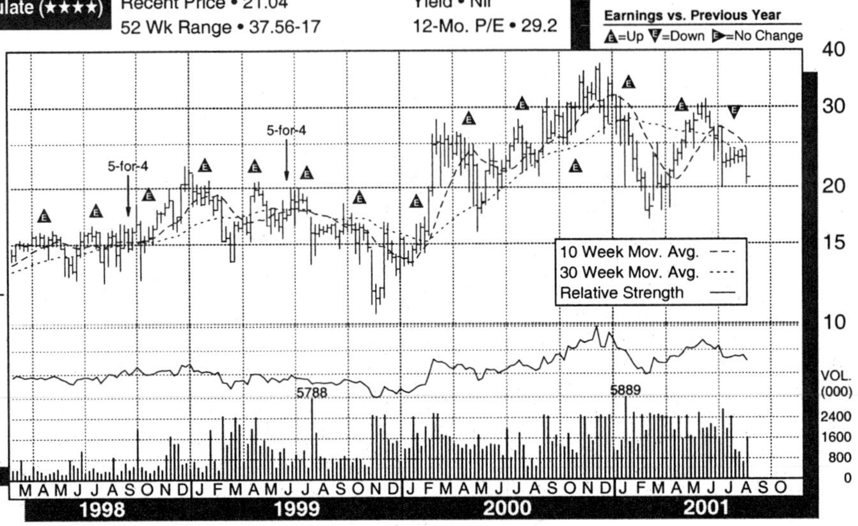

Overview - 24-JUL-01

Net revenues are projected to advance 25% in FY 01 (Sep.), with similar growth seen for FY 02, reflecting acquisitions in the infrastructure and communications groups, and a product mix shift toward infrastructure and resource management work. Internal revenues are likely to advance at least 10%. Growth in infrastructure will reflect more business from state and local governments, with a strong total funded backlog ($641 million at June 30). Gross margins should widen to nearly 24% of net revenues in FY 02, on a more favorable business mix, while SG&A expenses are well controlled, at 10% of revenues, despite development costs and higher process and systems costs. After taxes at a lower effective rate of 40%, we project FY 01 EPS of $1.10 (before a charge of $0.38 related to wireless customer Metricom's Chapter 11 filing), with a 23% gain, to $1.35, for FY 02.

Valuation - 24-JUL-01

The shares, which have traded erratically in 2001, were recently down 25% since May. Although terminated Metricom contracts accounted for 19% of total trade receivables, the next largest percentage customer (Sprint) accounts for only 3.7%. Thus, with third quarter earnings (before special charges) in line with expectations, and TTEK focusing on reducing A/R levels, we are maintaining our accumulate recommendation. We project cash flow generation of $80 million for FY 02, to be used in part to fund energy and water infrastructure acquisitions, which will represent a smaller portion of revenues than in FY 01 (nearly $50 million through the first nine months). We expect sequential improvement in the wireline and wireless segment to aid growth prospects. With a PEG ratio (P/E to EPS growth) of only 0.74X, and the book-to-bill ratio near historical levels of 1.0, we suggest adding to current positions.

Key Stock Statistics

S&P EPS Est. 2001	1.10	Tang. Bk. Value/Share	2.70
P/E on S&P Est. 2001	19.1	Beta	0.61
S&P EPS Est. 2002	1.35	Shareholders	1,911
Dividend Rate/Share	Nil	Market cap. (B)	$0.855
Shs. outstg. (M)	40.7	Inst. holdings	79%
Avg. daily vol. (M)	0.218		

Value of $10,000 invested 5 years ago: $ 23,951

Fiscal Year Ending Sep. 30

	2001	2000	1999	1998	1997	1996
Revenues (Million $)						
1Q	167.1	129.2	89.25	66.44	40.42	38.02
2Q	234.3	138.8	96.96	92.73	43.91	40.08
3Q	250.1	203.8	157.1	75.15	48.62	40.31
4Q	—	173.6	125.1	96.98	57.83	42.62
Yr.	—	598.1	432.1	297.6	190.8	161.0
Earnings Per Share ($)						
1Q	**0.22**	**0.19**	**0.14**	**0.12**	0.09	0.07
2Q	**0.25**	**0.20**	**0.17**	**0.13**	0.10	0.08
3Q	**-0.09**	**0.24**	**0.21**	**0.15**	0.12	0.09
4Q	**E0.34**	**0.35**	**0.22**	**0.18**	0.14	0.11
Yr.	**E1.10**	**0.97**	**0.74**	**0.57**	**0.46**	0.36

Next earnings report expected: mid November

Dividend Data

No cash dividends have been paid.

A Division of The McGraw-Hill Companies

Business Summary - 24-JUL-01

Tetra Tech aims to become the leading provider of specialized management consulting and technical services in its three principal business areas: resource management, infrastructure and communications. To achieve this objective, it plans to identify and expand into new business areas; expand service offerings and geographic presence through acquisitions; manage internal financial controls; and leverage its existing client base.

The company made nine acquisitions in FY 00 (Sep.), for $26.6 million. It is currently performing services under 1,000 active contracts, ranging from small site investigations to large, complex infrastructure projects.

Net revenues and operating income by segment in FY 00 were as follows: Resource Management, 42% of revenues and 40% of income from operations; infrastructure, 32% (26%); and communications, 26% (34%).

As a specialized management consultant, the company assists clients in defining problems and developing innovative and cost-effective solutions. Service offerings include: management consulting, research and development, applied science, engineering and architectural design, construction management, and operations and maintenance.

One of TTEK's major concentrations is water resource management, in which it has a leadership position in understanding the interrelationships of water quality and human activities. It supports high priority government programs for water quality improvement, environmental restoration, productive reuse of defense facilities and strategic environmental resource planning.

In the infrastructure area, the company focuses on development of water resource projects, institutional facilities, commercial, recreational and leisure facilities, and transportation projects.

In communications, TTEK focuses on delivery of technical solutions to build and manage communications infrastructure projects. Its capabilities support a wide range of technologies, including broadband and wireless communications.

The company has developed a diverse base of more than 700 clients, in both the public and private sectors. In FY 00, the Department of Defense, Environmental Protection Agency, and the Department of Energy accounted for 15%, 9.4% and 2.2% of net revenues, respectively. Private sector clients include companies in the chemical, mining, pharmaceutical, aerospace, automotive, petroleum, communications and utility industries. International business accounted for about 3% of net revenues in FY 00.

FY 00 EPS included $0.06 from the reversal of reserves related to government receivables, and a tax credit.

TTEK incurred apretax charge of $38.3 million ($0.38 a share, after tax) in the FY 01 third quarter, related to wireless network development contracts that the company has terminated as a result of the Chapter 11 filing of Metricom Inc.

Per Share Data ($) (Year Ended Sep. 30)	2000	1999	1998	1997	1996	1995	1994	1993	1992	1991
Tangible Bk. Val.	2.70	1.92	1.65	1.18	1.48	1.06	1.11	1.04	0.86	0.65
Cash Flow	1.30	1.06	0.74	0.61	0.49	0.45	0.43	0.41	0.40	0.58
Earnings	0.97	0.74	0.57	0.46	0.36	0.28	0.22	0.16	0.12	NA
Dividends	Nil	Nil	Nil	Nil	Nil	Nil	Nil	Nil	Nil	NA
Payout Ratio	Nil	Nil	Nil	Nil	Nil	Nil	Nil	Nil	Nil	NA
Prices - High	37.56	21.50	22.40	14.46	13.05	9.72	6.63	5.11	3.64	2.64
- Low	13.37	10.50	12.32	6.27	7.98	5.24	4.39	2.77	2.05	1.76
P/E Ratio - High	39	29	39	31	36	33	30	31	28	19
- Low	14	14	22	13	22	18	19	17	16	12
Income Statement Analysis (Million $)										
Revs.	598	432	298	191	161	87.9	67.8	51.2	43.5	38.0
Oper. Inc.	88.0	68.1	46.4	29.1	21.3	13.7	10.5	7.9	6.0	4.5
Depr.	13.7	12.7	6.6	4.5	3.6	1.9	1.4	1.1	0.8	0.9
Int. Exp.	7.4	3.6	2.3	0.3	1.1	Nil	Nil	Nil	0.3	1.1
Pretax Inc.	67.2	52.3	37.9	24.6	17.0	12.6	9.5	7.1	5.1	2.6
Eff. Tax Rate	40%	44%	42%	42%	40%	40%	40%	40%	40%	11%
Net Inc.	40.4	29.1	20.6	14.3	10.1	7.6	5.7	4.3	3.0	2.3
Balance Sheet & Other Fin. Data (Million $)										
Cash	7.6	8.2	4.9	12.3	6.1	13.1	15.9	13.4	9.0	1.0
Curr. Assets	297	195	142	80.9	57.9	72.3	42.9	35.8	27.4	17.6
Total Assets	526	380	267	160	88.5	92.9	51.6	38.6	30.1	20.1
Curr. Liab.	143	109	65.3	38.3	25.2	32.4	18.1	12.1	8.1	8.7
LT Debt	85.5	37.3	NA	Nil	Nil	19.0	Nil	Nil	NA	NA
Common Eqty.	284	221	152	108	63.3	41.5	33.5	26.4	22.0	2.8
Total Cap.	370	258	NA	121	63.3	60.5	33.5	26.5	NA	NA
Cap. Exp.	14.7	NA	NA	2.6	2.4	NA	NA	NA	NA	NA
Cash Flow	54.2	41.8	27.2	18.8	13.7	9.4	7.1	5.3	3.9	3.2
Curr. Ratio	2.1	1.8	2.2	2.1	2.3	2.2	2.4	3.0	3.4	2.0
% LT Debt of Cap.	23.1	14.4	NA	Nil	Nil	31.4	Nil	Nil	NA	NA
% Net Inc.of Revs.	6.8	6.7	6.9	7.5	6.3	8.6	8.4	8.4	7.0	6.2
% Ret. on Assets	8.9	9.0	9.7	11.5	11.1	10.5	12.7	12.5	12.1	NA
% Ret. on Equity	16.0	15.6	15.8	16.7	19.3	20.1	19.0	17.7	24.6	NA

Data as orig reptd.; bef. results of disc opers/spec. items. Per share data adj. for stk. divs. Bold denotes diluted EPS (FASB 128)-prior periods restated. E-Estimated. NA-Not Available. NM-Not Meaningful. NR-Not Ranked.

Office—670 N. Rosemead Blvd., Pasadena, CA 91107. **Tel**—(626) 351-4664. **Website**—http://www.tetratech.com **Chrmn, Pres & CEO**—Li-San Hwang. **VP, CFO & Treas**—J. M. Jaska. **VP & Secy**—R. A. Lemmon. **Dirs**—P. C. Haden, Li-San Hwang, J. C. Lewis, J. J. Shelton, D. A. Whalen. **Transfer Agent & Registrar**—U. S. Stock Transfer Corp., Glendale, CA. **Incorporated**—in Delaware in 1988. **Empl**— 6,601. **S&P Analyst:** Stewart Scharf

STANDARD &POOR'S
STOCK REPORTS

Union Pacific

NYSE Symbol **UNP**

In S&P 500

18-AUG-01 **Industry:** Railroads

Summary: UNP, which operates the largest U.S. railroad, has been thwarted in its attempts to sell its Overnite Transportation unit by poor market conditions and labor disruptions.

S&P Opinion: Accumulate (★★★★)

Recent Price • 53.95 | Yield • 1.5%
52 Wk Range • 60.70-37.50 | 12-Mo. P/E • 16.3

Quantitative Evaluations

Outlook (1 Lowest—5 Highest)
• 2

Fair Value
• 54.90

Risk
• Low

Earn./Div. Rank
• B

Technical Eval.
• Neutral since 7/01

Rel. Strength Rank (1 Lowest—99 Highest)
• 48

Insider Activity
• Neutral

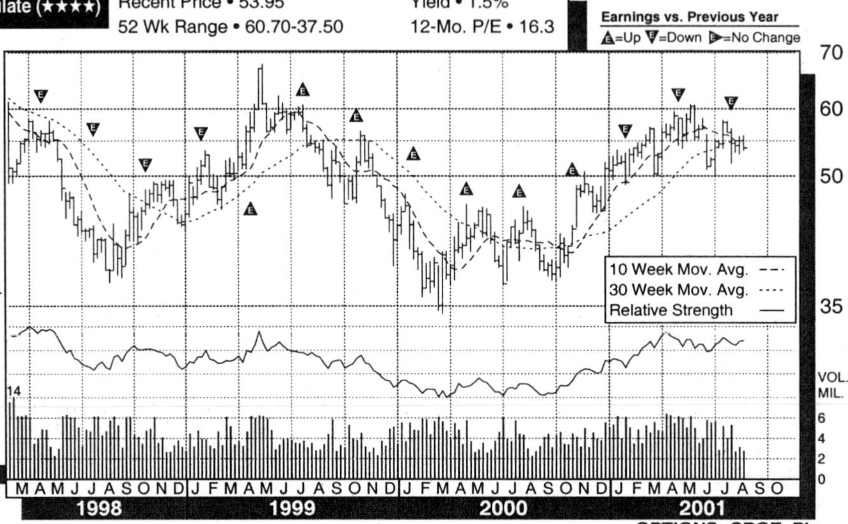

OPTIONS: CBOE, Ph

Overview - 30-JUL-01

Total revenues could rise 5.0% in 2002, after gaining an estimated 2.3% in 2000. Although all commodity groups should be lifted by an improving economy, revenue growth will see its largest contributions from the intermodal and energy segments. Gains are projected for intermodal, reflecting strength in Asian imports, and in energy, as a result of strong coal demand. Margin improvement is anticipated in rail operations, through employment reductions, higher productivity, better car utilization, and faster car cycle times. Fuel costs are expected to stabilize. Rail yields will improve. Overnite's traffic is expected to rebound. Overnite's margins will widen, as productivity increases and higher freight rates outweigh fuel expenses. Interest expense should decrease, as debt levels decline. We see 2002 EPS at $4.75, up from 2001's projected $4.00.

Valuation - 30-JUL-01

The shares have rallied since the fourth quarter of 2000, as investors shifted back into old economy stocks, and were encouraged by UNP's cost cutting efforts. In addition, demand for coal is allowing for revenue growth, despite the negative impact of a slowing economy on most other commodity groups. Although fuel costs remain high, they have begun to stabilize and are expected to remain relatively steady through the rest of the year. UNP has attempted to offset the weak economic conditions with operational improvements, which should provide future benefits. With UNP's price to sales and price to EBITDA ratios below its peer group average, and with increasing coal demand and more efficient operations, we believe the shares will outperform the broader market over the next six to 12 months. As a result, in April 2001, we upgraded the shares to accumulate, from avoid.

Key Stock Statistics

S&P EPS Est. 2001	4.00	Tang. Bk. Value/Share	35.07
P/E on S&P Est. 2001	13.5	Beta	0.36
S&P EPS Est. 2002	4.75	Shareholders	39,150
Dividend Rate/Share	0.80	Market cap. (B)	$ 13.4
Shs. outstg. (M)	247.9	Inst. holdings	75%
Avg. daily vol. (M)	0.688		

Value of $10,000 invested 5 years ago: NA

Fiscal Year Ending Dec. 31

	2001	2000	1999	1998	1997	1996
Revenues (Million $)						
1Q	2,943	2,913	2,740	2,586	2,810	1,968
2Q	2,998	2,979	2,773	2,362	2,883	2,012
3Q	—	3,070	2,893	2,404	2,825	1,996
4Q	—	2,952	2,867	2,684	2,561	2,810
Yr.	—	11,878	11,273	10,553	11,079	8,786
Earnings Per Share ($)						
1Q	**0.72**	**0.74**	**0.52**	**-0.25**	**0.52**	0.52
2Q	**0.95**	**0.96**	**0.77**	**-0.64**	**0.87**	0.90
3Q	**E1.15**	**1.00**	**0.86**	**0.13**	**0.96**	1.00
4Q	**E1.18**	**0.63**	**0.95**	**-1.83**	**-0.62**	0.93
Yr.	**E4.00**	**3.34**	**3.12**	**-2.57**	**1.74**	3.36

Next earnings report expected: mid October

Dividend Data (Dividends have been paid since 1900.)

Amount ($)	Date Decl.	Ex-Div. Date	Stock of Record	Payment Date
0.200	Nov. 16	Dec. 11	Dec. 13	Jan. 02 '01
0.200	Feb. 22	Mar. 12	Mar. 14	Apr. 02 '01
0.200	Jun. 01	Jun. 11	Jun. 13	Jul. 02 '01
0.200	Jul. 26	Sep. 10	Sep. 12	Oct. 01 '01

Union Pacific Corporation

Business Summary - 30-JUL-01

Union Pacific operates the largest U.S. railroad. The railroad expanded significantly in 1995 and 1996, when the company acquired the Chicago and North Western and Southern Pacific, respectively. Problems in integrating Southern Pacific, together with crew shortages, poor weather, and a series of derailments, led to a major service failure during 1997 and 1998. Service has returned to normal levels, but UNP continued to incur costs in 2000 to integrate the Southern Pacific, for which it paid $4.1 billion, into its system. The final integration should be completed in 2001. UNP has significantly restructured its operations since 1994, selling its waste management, oil and gas, and logistics units. The company has been thwarted in its efforts to sell its trucking unit, Overnite Transportation, because of poor market conditions, as well as Teamster picketing against certain Overnite facilities since October 1999.

Between mid-1997 and late 1998, UNP experienced serious operating problems on its rail system. Part of the problem stemmed from difficulties in integrating the information systems of the Southern Pacific and Union Pacific railroads. In 1999, service returned to normal levels, but UNP incurred $45 million of charges due to the merger. In 2000, the company incurred an additional $10 million in costs to integrate Southern Pacific. UNP has said it anticipates incurring additional merger integration costs in 2001. Such costs include severance for the elimination of 5,200 duplicate positions. UNP has also been incurring costs to relocate 4,700 positions, and to dispose of redundant rail lines and facilities.

The Union Pacific rail system (accounting for 90.6% of revenues in 2000) spans over 34,000 miles serving the western two-thirds of the US. It also maintains coordinated schedules with other carriers for the handling of freight to and from the Atlantic Coast, the Pacific Coast, the Southeast, the Southwest, Canada and Mexico. Energy (primarily coal) generated 21% of rail freight revenues in 2000, industrial products 19%, intermodal 19%, and chemicals 16%.

Overnite Transportation (9.4% of 2000 revenues) primarily offers less-than-truckload (LTL) service in the U.S., and in parts of Canada and Mexico. UNP, which intended to sell Overnite in the 1998 third quarter via an IPO, canceled plans for the offering. A charge of $547 million ($2.22 a share) was incurred in 1998, to write down goodwill related to Overnite. The Teamsters union, which has been attempting to organize Overnite since 1994, began picketing certain Overnite terminal facilities in October 1999. As of January 2001, 30 Overnite service centers had approximately 495 employees, less than 5% of Overnite's work force, who did not report to work.

UNP's other operations include the development and expansion of the company's technology and telecommunication assets, and self-insurance.

Per Share Data ($) (Year Ended Dec. 31)	2000	1999	1998	1997	1996	1995	1994	1993	1992	1991
Tangible Bk. Val.	35.07	32.29	29.93	30.79	30.51	26.62	20.36	17.38	16.43	14.02
Cash Flow	7.34	6.91	1.78	5.97	6.86	6.15	9.55	7.77	7.71	3.74
Earnings	3.34	3.22	-2.57	1.74	3.36	3.01	4.66	3.43	3.57	0.31
Dividends	0.80	0.80	1.03	1.72	1.72	1.72	1.66	1.54	1.42	1.30
Payout Ratio	24%	25%	NM	99%	51%	57%	36%	45%	40%	414%
Prices - High	52.81	67.87	63.75	72.98	74.50	70.12	67.12	67.00	60.50	51.75
- Low	34.25	39.00	37.31	56.25	48.25	45.62	43.75	56.87	44.37	32.62
P/E Ratio - High	16	21	NM	42	22	23	14	20	17	NM
- Low	10	12	NM	32	14	15	9	17	12	NM
Income Statement Analysis (Million $)										
Revs.	11,878	11,273	10,553	11,079	8,786	7,486	7,798	7,561	7,294	7,029
Oper. Inc.	2,043	2,887	1,446	2,296	2,295	1,983	2,501	2,282	2,119	1,939
Depr.	1,140	1,083	1,070	1,043	762	642	1,005	892	843	691
Int. Exp.	723	733	714	605	501	450	337	335	369	394
Pretax Inc.	1,310	1,202	-696	676	1,113	933	1,419	1,155	1,101	112
Eff. Tax Rate	36%	35%	NM	36%	34%	34%	33%	39%	34%	43%
Net Inc.	842	783	-633	432	733	619	958	705	728	64.0
Balance Sheet & Other Fin. Data (Million $)										
Cash	105	175	176	90.0	191	230	121	113	245	144
Curr. Assets	1,285	1,314	1,502	1,415	1,334	1,679	1,822	1,382	1,381	1,168
Total Assets	30,499	29,888	29,374	28,764	27,914	19,446	15,942	15,001	14,098	13,326
Curr. Liab.	2,962	2,885	2,932	3,247	3,056	1,899	2,505	2,089	2,084	1,868
LT Debt	9,644	9,926	10,011	8,285	7,900	6,232	4,090	4,069	3,989	3,913
Common Eqty.	8,662	8,001	7,393	8,225	8,225	6,364	5,131	4,885	4,639	4,163
Total Cap.	25,449	24,642	23,712	22,762	22,064	16,310	12,077	11,630	11,004	10,206
Cap. Exp.	1,783	1,834	2,111	2,101	1,360	1,058	1,597	1,520	1,525	1,191
Cash Flow	1,982	1,866	437	1,475	1,495	1,261	1,963	1,597	1,571	755
Curr. Ratio	0.4	0.5	0.5	0.4	0.4	0.9	0.7	0.7	0.7	0.6
% LT Debt of Cap.	37.9	40.3	42.2	36.3	35.8	38.2	33.9	35.0	36.3	38.3
% Net Inc.of Revs.	7.1	6.9	NM	3.9	8.3	8.3	12.8	9.3	10.0	0.9
% Ret. on Assets	2.8	2.6	NM	1.5	3.1	3.7	6.2	4.8	5.3	0.5
% Ret. on Equity	10.1	10.2	NM	5.3	10.0	10.8	19.1	14.8	16.5	1.5

Data as orig reptd.; bef. results of disc opers/spec. items. Per share data adj. for stk. divs. Bold denotes diluted EPS (FASB 128)-prior periods restated. E-Estimated. NA-Not Available. NM-Not Meaningful. NR-Not Ranked.

Office—1416 Dodge St., Omaha, NE 68179.**Tel**—(402) 271-5777. **Website**—http://www.up.com **Chrmn, CEO & Pres**—R. K. Davidson. **SVP & Secy**—C. W. von Bernuth. **EVP & CFO**—J. R. Young. **Investor Contact**—Mary S. Jones. **Dirs**—P. F. Anschutz, E. V. Conway, R. K. Davidson, T. J. Donohue, A. W. Dunham, S. F. Eccles, I. J. Evans, E. T. Gerry Jr., J. R. Hope, R. J. Mahoney, S. R. Rogel, R. D. Simmons, E. Zedillo Ponce de Leon. **Transfer Agent & Registrar**—Harris Trust and Savings Bank, Chicago. **Incorporated**—in Utah in 1969; R.R. incorporated in 1897. **Empl**—63,000. **S&P Analyst:** Richard N. Stice

STANDARD &POOR'S STOCK REPORTS

Waste Connections

Nasdaq Symbol **WCNX**

18-AUG-01

Industry: Waste Management

Summary: WCNX is a regional, integrated solid waste services company that provides solid waste collection, transfer, disposal and recycling services in secondary markets of the western U.S.

S&P Opinion: Accumulate (★★★★)

Recent Price • 32.62 | Yield • Nil
52 Wk Range • 37.31-21.37 | 12-Mo. P/E • 31.1

Quantitative Evaluations

Outlook (1 Lowest—5 Highest)
• 4−

Fair Value
• 40.20

Risk
• NA

Earn./Div. Rank
• NR

Technical Eval.
• Bullish since 5/01

Rel. Strength Rank (1 Lowest—99 Highest)
• 62

Insider Activity
• Neutral

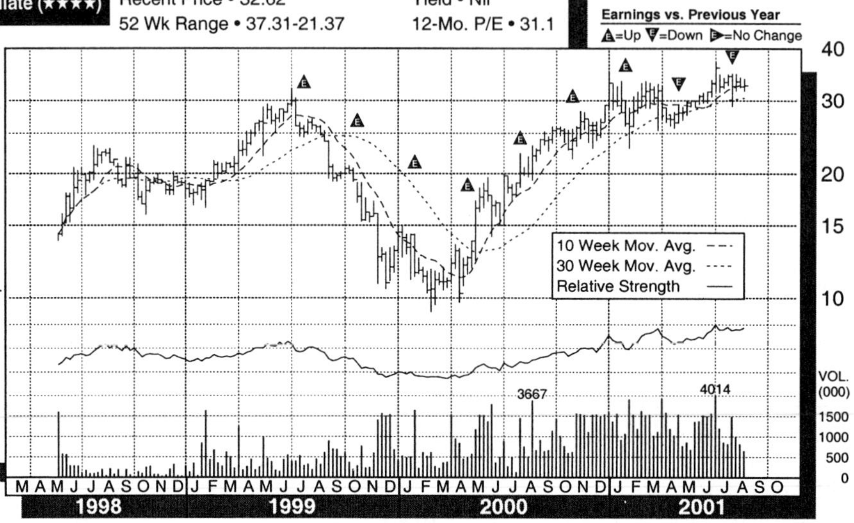

Overview - 07-AUG-01

We expect 25%-plus revenue growth to be derived primarily from acquisitions ($60 million in revenues) in the western U.S., where population growth is the strongest. Internal revenues should grow 5% to 6% (before 3%-4% negative effect from commodity recycling prices), with 3% to 4% from selective price hikes and 1% to 2% from volume. Gross margins should widen by 200 basis points to 45%, due mainly to synergies from tuck-in acquisitions and a greater landfill mix, as the internalization rate climbs to 63%, from 50% in 2000. EBITDA margins (before acquisition-related and stock compensation expenses) are likely to expand to near 37% from 34.3%, or $140 million, reflecting higher gross margins and well controlled SG&A expenses of 8%. Following higher depreciation and interest charges, and a 40% tax rate, we project EPS of $1.50 for 2001, rising 23% to $1.85 for 2002.

Valuation - 07-AUG-01

Despite soft market conditions, second quarter earnings were in line with expectations. With WCNX focusing on integrating operations and investing in information technology infrastructure, and the stock trading off its recent highs, we maintain our accumulate opinion. WCNX has a strong balance sheet (52% debt-to-capital), and will use solid free cash flow (seen at 9% to 10% of revenues, or $36 million) generated from a share offering and a recent $150 million convertible debt offering, for acquisitions and further debt paydowns. Although the major players in this sector have drastically reduced their acquisition budgets, and the company recently terminated a large transaction, WCNX's acquisition backlog remains strong as it targets deals in larger markets in the West. With debt-to-EBITDA averaging 3X and a P/E-to-EPS growth (PEG) ratio of only 0.75, we see potential for further capital gains.

Key Stock Statistics

S&P EPS Est. 2001	1.50	Tang. Bk. Value/Share	NM
P/E on S&P Est. 2001	21.7	Beta	NA
S&P EPS Est. 2002	1.85	Shareholders	123
Dividend Rate/Share	Nil	Market cap. (B)	$0.883
Shs. outstg. (M)	27.1	Inst. holdings	99%
Avg. daily vol. (M)	0.195		

Value of $10,000 invested 5 years ago: NA

Fiscal Year Ending Dec. 31

	2001	2000	1999	1998	1997	1996
Revenues (Million $)						
1Q	85.11	64.01	30.88	—	—	—
2Q	93.97	76.02	40.22	10.92	—	—
3Q	—	81.51	48.61	16.83	—	—
4Q	—	82.81	60.39	18.71	—	—
Yr.	—	304.4	182.6	54.04	35.01	—
Earnings Per Share ($)						
1Q	**0.18**	**0.26**	**-0.28**	—	—	—
2Q	**0.23**	**0.27**	**0.16**	**0.03**	—	—
3Q	**E0.42**	**0.32**	**0.24**	**0.10**	—	—
4Q	**E0.40**	**0.32**	**0.25**	**0.10**	—	—
Yr.	**E1.50**	**1.17**	**0.46**	**0.22**	**-0.45**	—

Next earnings report expected: late October

Dividend Data

The company has never paid cash dividends on its common stock and does not anticipate paying any in the foreseeable future.

Waste Connections, Inc.

Business Summary - 07-AUG-01

By focusing on secondary markets in western states, where it provides solid waste collection, transfer, disposal and recycling services to more than 700,000 commercial, industrial and residential customers, Waste Connections, Inc. (WCNX) believes it faces less competition from large waste firms, as these markets are generally more fragmented and less densely populated than markets in the eastern U.S. In addition, WCNX, which has an active acquisition program, is drawn to these markets because they contain a large number of independent solid waste services firms that it deems suitable for acquisition. WCNX also sees more opportunities to enter into exclusive arrangements -- a key element of its strategy -- in these markets.

WCNX has developed a two-pronged strategy tailored to the competitive and regulatory factors that affect its markets. In its exclusive markets, the company believes that controlling the waste stream by providing collection services under such arrangements is often more important than owning or operating landfills since regulations, in some cases, dictate the disposal facility to be used. The large size of many western states increases the cost of interstate and long haul disposal, heightening the effects of regulations that direct waste disposal, which may make it more difficult for a landfill to obtain the disposal volume necessary to operate profitably. In markets with these characteristics, the company believes that landfill ownership or vertical integration is not critical to its success.

More than 55% of the company's revenues are derived from services provided under exclusive franchise agreements, with the majority from long-term municipal contracts and governmental certificates, which provide the company with relatively consistent cash flow during the terms of the contracts. The balance is derived from competitive markets.

In markets where the company believes that competitive and regulatory factors make owning landfills advantageous, WCNX generally focuses on providing integrated services, from collection through disposal of solid waste in landfills it owns or operates.

As of April 2001, WCNX owned 65 collection operations, and operated or owned 32 transfer stations, 21 landfills and 16 recycling facilities. The company's customers are located in 15 states, 60% of which are in exclusive markets. Revenues by service in 2000 were: 72% collection, 13% disposal, 10% transfer, and 5% recycling and other. Revenues by customer were: 44% residential, 42% commercial, 9% industrial and construction, and 3% other.

From its inception in September 1997 through December 21, 2000, WCNX acquired 116 businesses, 26 of which occurred in 2000 for $172 million. In April 2001, it made six acquisitions with total annualized revenues of $24 million. WCNX is focusing its efforts on fragmented markets with several acquisition candidates and a potential revenue base of at least $15 million, usually in areas with a geog raphically dispersed population of 75,000 or less.

Per Share Data ($) **(Year Ended Dec. 31)**	**2000**	**1999**	**1998**	**1997**	**1996**	**1995**	**1994**	**1993**	**1992**	**1991**
Tangible Bk. Val.	NM	-0.89	-4.00	-5.69	NA	NA	NA	NA	NA	NA
Cash Flow	2.31	1.13	0.56	-2.24	NA	NA	NA	NA	NA	NA
Earnings	1.17	0.46	0.22	-3.61	NA	NA	NA	NA	NA	NA
Dividends	Nil	Nil	Nil	NA	NA	NA	NA	NA	NA	NA
Payout Ratio	Nil	Nil	Nil	NA	NA	NA	NA	NA	NA	NA
Prices - High	35.25	32.12	23.37	NA	NA	NA	NA	NA	NA	NA
- Low	9.25	10.50	13.75	NA	NA	NA	NA	NA	NA	NA
P/E Ratio - High	30	70	NM	NA	NA	NA	NA	NA	NA	NA
- Low	8	23	NM	NA	NA	NA	NA	NA	NA	NA
Income Statement Analysis (Million $)										
Revs.	304	183	54.0	6.2	22.2	NA	NA	NA	NA	NA
Oper. Inc.	104	55.4	12.2	0.9	0.6	NA	NA	NA	NA	NA
Depr.	27.2	14.7	4.1	0.4	1.1	NA	NA	NA	NA	NA
Int. Exp.	28.7	11.5	2.3	1.0	0.2	NA	NA	NA	NA	NA
Pretax Inc.	47.5	20.1	5.2	-5.4	1.8	NA	NA	NA	NA	NA
Eff. Tax Rate	41%	54%	46%	5.05%	28%	NA	NA	NA	NA	NA
Net Inc.	28.2	9.2	2.8	-5.1	1.3	NA	NA	NA	NA	NA
Balance Sheet & Other Fin. Data (Million $)										
Cash	2.5	2.4	2.7	0.8	0.1	NA	NA	NA	NA	NA
Curr. Assets	49.0	34.4	15.7	5.1	3.1	NA	NA	NA	NA	NA
Total Assets	810	617	149	18.9	15.3	NA	NA	NA	NA	NA
Curr. Liab.	59.4	44.1	24.4	4.3	2.4	NA	NA	NA	NA	NA
LT Debt	334	275	60.1	6.8	0.1	NA	NA	NA	NA	NA
Common Eqty.	334	219	61.1	-0.6	12.8	NA	NA	NA	NA	NA
Total Cap.	745	568	123	13.7	12.9	NA	NA	NA	NA	NA
Cap. Exp.	25.4	18.6	6.2	1.0	0.3	NA	NA	NA	NA	NA
Cash Flow	55.4	23.9	6.9	-4.7	2.4	NA	NA	NA	NA	NA
Curr. Ratio	0.8	0.8	0.6	1.2	1.3	NA	NA	NA	NA	NA
% LT Debt of Cap.	44.9	48.4	48.9	49.2	0.7	NA	NA	NA	NA	NA
% Net Inc.of Revs.	9.3	5.0	5.1	-25.6	5.8	NA	NA	NA	NA	NA
% Ret. on Assets	3.9	2.3	3.3	-35.9	8.4	NA	NA	NA	NA	NA
% Ret. on Equity	10.2	6.4	9.2	1228.7	10.0	NA	NA	NA	NA	NA

Data as orig reptd.; bef. results of disc opers/spec. items. Per share data adj. for stk. divs. Bold denotes diluted EPS (FASB 128)-prior periods restated. E-Estimated. NA-Not Available. NM-Not Meaningful. NR-Not Ranked.

Office—20 Coolidge Drive, Suite 350, Folsom, CA 95630. **Tel**—(916) 608-8200. **Website**—http://www.wasteconnections.com **Chrmn, Pres & CEO**—R. J. Mittelstaedt. **EVP & CFO**—S. F. Bouck. **EVP & Secy**—D. W. Chambliss. **VP & Treas**—E. J. Moser. **Dirs**—R. Davis, E. V. Dupreau, M. W. Harlan, R. J. Mittelstaedt, W. J. Razzouk. **Transfer Agent & Registrar**—Boston EquiServe, L.P. **Incorporated**—in Delaware in 1997. **Empl**—2,010. **S&P Analyst:** Stewart Scharf

Part Seven

Information Technology Stocks

STANDARD &POOR'S
STOCK REPORTS

Adobe Systems

Nasdaq Symbol **ADBE**

In S&P 500

18-AUG-01

Industry: Computer (Software & Services)

Summary: Adobe is a leading provider of graphic design, publishing and imaging software for Internet and print production.

S&P Opinion: Buy (★★★★★)

Recent Price • 32.76
52 Wk Range • 87.31-24.56
Yield • 0.2%
12-Mo. P/E • 28.7

Quantitative Evaluations

Outlook (1 Lowest—5 Highest)
• **2**

Fair Value
• **33.70**

Risk
• **Average**

Earn./Div. Rank
• **B+**

Technical Eval.
• **Bearish** since 7/01

Rel. Strength Rank (1 Lowest—99 Highest)
• **17**

Insider Activity
• **Unfavorable**

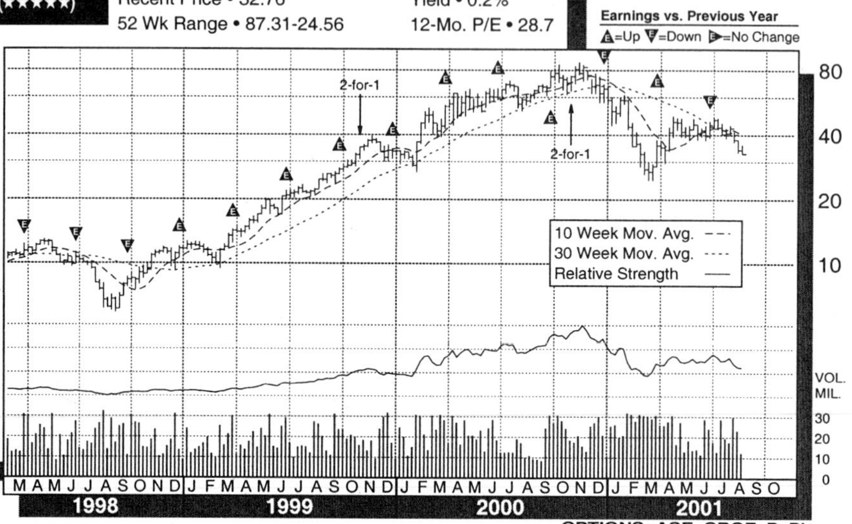

OPTIONS: ASE, CBOE, P, Ph

Overview - 19-JUN-01

We expect ADBE's revenues to increase about 21% in FY 01 (Nov.), fueled by the Web publishing solutions and ePaper (Acrobat) businesses. ADBE is capitalizing on three major technology industry trends: 1) digitization of content, 2) prevalence of rich media, and 3) prominence of paperless workflows. The company is the clear leader in the network publishing market, which is expected to grow to $11 billion by 2004. Despite a sluggish U.S. economy, ADBE should attain robust gross margins of 93% and operating margins of 31%, as a result of superb operating efficiencies and cost controls. Results should also benefit from well chosen venture investments. Share repurchases should continue to boost EPS comparisons. We believe EPS could rise some 40% in FY 01 (excluding extraordinary items), and over 25% annually over the long term.

Valuation - 19-JUN-01

We maintain our buy recommendation, in light of superb financial results, exciting new growth opportunities, and an appealing valuation. Despite a slowing U.S. economy and reined-in spending on information technology, ADBE continues to successfully leverage its core publishing and Internet technologies and brands to generate solid growth, while investing in research and development and masterfully controlling operating expenses. Investing in the shares is also a way to participate in the continuing expansion of the Internet, as ADBE is a financially solid profit generator with significant Web businesses (52% of second quarter FY 01 revenues). For example, the Adobe Acrobat PDF file format has become the standard for document transmission over the Internet. Recently trading at a forward P/E below our long-term EPS growth rate estimate, ADBE is an attractive blue-chip technology holding, as well as a value Internet infrastructure holding.

Key Stock Statistics

S&P EPS Est. 2001	1.34	Tang. Bk. Value/Share	3.10
P/E on S&P Est. 2001	24.4	Beta	1.09
S&P EPS Est. 2002	1.53	Shareholders	1,672
Dividend Rate/Share	0.05	Market cap. (B)	$ 7.8
Shs. outstg. (M)	238.9	Inst. holdings	74%
Avg. daily vol. (M)	4.092		

Value of $10,000 invested 5 years ago: NA

Fiscal Year Ending Nov. 30

	2001	2000	1999	1998	1997	1996
Revenues (Million $)						
1Q	329.0	282.2	226.9	197.8	226.5	193.6
2Q	344.1	300.1	245.9	227.3	228.3	204.3
3Q	—	328.9	260.9	222.9	230.0	180.9
4Q	—	355.2	281.8	246.7	227.1	207.7
Yr.	—	1,266	1,015	894.8	911.9	786.6
Earnings Per Share ($)						
1Q	**0.28**	**0.26**	**0.15**	**0.10**	0.16	0.11
2Q	**0.25**	**0.26**	**0.17**	**0.10**	0.14	0.07
3Q	**E0.31**	**0.30**	**0.22**	Nil	0.18	0.10
4Q	**E0.36**	**0.31**	**0.38**	**0.20**	0.16	0.23
Yr.	**E1.34**	**1.13**	**0.92**	**0.39**	**0.63**	0.51

Next earnings report expected: mid September

Dividend Data (Dividends have been paid since 1988.)

Amount ($)	Date Decl.	Ex-Div. Date	Stock of Record	Payment Date
2-for-1	Sep. 14	Oct. 25	Oct. 02	Oct. 24 '00
0.013	Dec. 14	Jan. 02	Jan. 04	Jan. 18 '01
0.013	Mar. 15	Mar. 22	Mar. 26	Apr. 09 '01
0.013	Jun. 14	Jun. 22	Jun. 26	Jul. 09 '01

Business Summary - 19-JUN-01

Adobe Systems Inc. develops computer software used to create, distribute and manage information across print and electronic media. Web designers use ADBE's page layout, digital video and digital imaging software to enable the virtual presentation of products and services on the Internet.

Web publishing products accounted for 42% and 39% of revenues in FY 00 (Nov.) and FY 99, respectively. Products include ActiveShare (online picture sharing), After Effects (sophisticated animation, motion composition and special effects), GoLive (website design and layout), LiveMotion (two-dimensional animation), PageMill (simple website authoring), PhotoShop (picture enhancement), and Premiere (digital video editing).

ADBE also offers cross-media publishing (previously called print publishing) products (31% and 35%): FrameMaker (authoring and publishing of documents, such as periodicals), Illustrator (illustration design), InDesign (page layout), InScope (collaboration), PageMaker (creation of business documents), and PressReady (professional printing).

ADBE is also the leader in providing solutions to integrate paper and digital document communications. In the FY 01 second quarter, ADBE released Acrobat 5.0, the cornerstone of its ePaper Solutions business (16% and 13%). Offerings provided are: Acrobat (publication and distribution of business documents using e-mail, the Internet, and intranets), Acrobat Capture (conversion of legacy documents into PDF files), Acrobat Messenger (transformation of paper documents into PDF files for workgroups), Create PDF Online (online conversion of documents into PDF files), PDF Merchant (encryption and distribution of Acrobat files), and Acrobat Reader with Web Buy (view, search and print of secure Acrobat files).

ADBE's primary printing system product is PostScript, a page description language that provides for rich printing output. The company sells software and licenses technologies to hardware manufacturers, software developers and service providers. The PostScript and original equipment manufacturer business accounted for 10% of FY 00 revenues and 14% of FY 99 revenues.

ADBE's investment program includes majority interests in four venture capital limited partnerships, as well as direct investments. The program invests in early stage companies with innovative technologies that may create new market opportunities for the company, or enhance its existing businesses. As of December 2000, these investments had a cost basis of $176.6 million, and a recorded fair market value of $162.7 million, and consisted of holdings in some 40 companies, including Digimarc (DMRC), FileNET (FILE), ImageX.com (IMGX), Shutterfly.com, and Tumbleweed Communications (TMWD).

Per Share Data ($) (Year Ended Nov. 30)	2000	1999	1998	1997	1996	1995	1994	1993	1992	1991
Tangible Bk. Val.	2.90	2.01	2.12	2.60	2.47	2.40	1.87	1.54	1.26	1.03
Cash Flow	1.29	1.12	0.59	0.83	0.69	0.52	0.24	0.38	0.28	0.32
Earnings	1.13	0.92	0.39	0.63	0.51	0.32	0.03	0.30	0.23	0.28
Dividends	0.06	0.05	0.05	0.05	0.05	0.05	0.05	0.05	0.04	0.04
Payout Ratio	6%	5%	13%	8%	10%	16%	NM	15%	17%	13%
Prices - High	87.31	39.50	12.96	13.28	16.06	18.56	9.62	9.25	8.56	8.46
- Low	26.71	9.42	5.90	8.12	7.12	6.81	5.12	3.90	3.15	3.34
P/E Ratio - High	77	43	33	21	31	59	NM	30	37	30
- Low	24	10	15	13	14	22	NM	13	14	12
Income Statement Analysis (Million $)										
Revs.	1,266	1,015	895	912	787	762	598	313	266	230
Oper. Inc.	457	337	220	296	229	242	182	94.5	83.5	84.6
Depr.	43.3	50.8	56.3	59.4	55.6	60.4	53.2	13.6	8.8	6.7
Int. Exp.	Nil	Nil	Nil	Nil	NM	Nil	Nil	Nil	Nil	NA
Pretax Inc.	444	374	168	296	245	164	40.0	91.1	69.5	83.6
Eff. Tax Rate	35%	37%	37%	37%	37%	43%	84%	37%	37%	38%
Net Inc.	288	238	105	187	153	93.5	6.3	57.0	43.6	51.6
Balance Sheet & Other Fin. Data (Million $)										
Cash	237	171	111	268	564	516	400	236	160	116
Curr. Assets	878	623	456	679	737	693	532	304	224	162
Total Assets	1,069	804	767	940	1,012	885	626	353	281	221
Curr. Liab.	315	268	251	225	231	186	169	73.7	56.8	36.9
LT Debt	Nil	Nil	Nil	Nil	Nil	Nil	Nil	Nil	Nil	Nil
Common Eqty.	753	512	516	715	707	698	457	279	225	183
Total Cap.	755	536	516	715	707	698	457	279	225	184
Cap. Exp.	29.8	42.2	59.7	33.9	45.9	34.1	28.5	14.4	11.9	12.2
Cash Flow	331	289	161	246	209	154	59.5	70.6	52.4	58.3
Curr. Ratio	2.8	2.3	1.8	3.0	3.2	3.7	3.2	4.1	4.0	4.4
% LT Debt of Cap.	Nil	Nil	Nil	Nil	Nil	Nil	Nil	Nil	Nil	Nil
% Net Inc.of Revs.	22.7	23.4	11.8	20.5	19.4	12.3	1.1	18.2	16.4	22.5
% Ret. on Assets	30.7	30.3	12.3	19.1	16.2	11.7	1.1	17.9	17.3	27.5
% Ret. on Equity	45.5	46.2	17.1	26.3	21.8	15.4	1.5	22.5	21.4	34.8

Data as orig reptd.; bef. results of disc opers/spec. items. Per share data adj. for stk. divs. Bold denotes diluted EPS (FASB 128)-prior periods restated. E-Estimated. NA-Not Available. NM-Not Meaningful. NR-Not Ranked.

Office—345 Park Avenue, San Jose, CA 95110-2704. **Tel**—(408) 536-6000. **Fax**—(408) 537-6000. **Website**—www.adobe.com **Chrmn**—C. M. Geschke. **CEO & Pres**—B. R. Chizen. **SVP & CFO**—M. J. Demo. **SVP & Secy**—C. M. Pouliot. **Investor Contact**—Mike Saviage (408-536-4416). **Dirs**—C. M. Baldwin, B. R. Chizen, C. M. Geschke, A. M. Perez, R. Sedgewick, J. E. Warnock, D. W. Yocam. **Transfer Agent & Registrar**—ComputerShare Investor Services LLC. **Incorporated**—in California in 1983; reincorporated in Delaware in 1997. **Empl**— 3,007. **S&P Analyst:** Scott H. Kessler

STANDARD
&POOR'S
STOCK REPORTS

Applied Materials

Nasdaq Symbol **AMAT**

In S&P 500

21-AUG-01

Industry: Equipment (Semiconductor)

Summary: This company is the world's largest manufacturer of wafer fabrication equipment for the semiconductor industry.

S&P Opinion: Buy (★★★★★)

Recent Price • 42.57 | Yield • Nil
52 Wk Range • 88.87-34.12 | 12-Mo. P/E • 24.6

Quantitative Evaluations

Outlook (1 Lowest—5 Highest)
• **2−**

Fair Value
• **44.30**

Risk
• **Average**

Earn./Div. Rank
• **B**

Technical Eval.
• **Neutral** since 8/01

Rel. Strength Rank (1 Lowest—99 Highest)
• **28**

Insider Activity
• **Neutral**

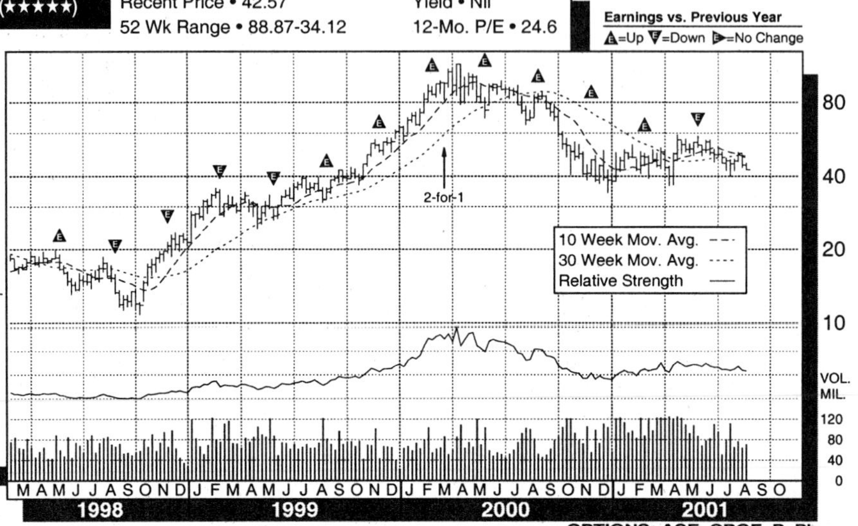

OPTIONS: ASE, CBOE, P, Ph

Overview - 21-AUG-01

We expect sales to fall 23% in FY 01 (Oct.), and rise 8% in FY 02. New orders have slowed decisively in 2001, and quarterly revenue runs have dropped below half the level seen at the cycle peak in the fourth fiscal quarter of FY 00. Chip makers are still investing in equipment to gain efficiencies from new technology, but are not spending to add capacity. AMAT has adopted cost-saving measures that should maintain profitability through the downturn. The company's most advanced products, which enable production of chips with linewidths (transistor size) of 0.13 micron and below using new copper interconnect materials, should help it gain substantial market share in next-generation wafer fabrication plants. We estimate FY 01 EPS at $1.07, and see $1.10 in FY 02, before a rebound to $2.75 in FY 03.

Valuation - 21-AUG-01

The shares of this leading chip equipment manufacturer have made a modest recovery since reaching lows in late 2000 and April 2001. The industry is at the bottom of cyclical downturn, in our view. A trade association forecasts that semiconductor equipment industry sales could decline as much as 35% in 2001. New order flow is currently very weak for AMAT and the industry, but we believe orders will begin to rise from low levels in 2002, indicating a new upturn. AMAT recently traded at 5.1X tangible book value, near cycle trough levels of 4X, which indicates modest downside risk. Although the next cycle peak might not come until 2004, AMAT traded above 10X tangible book at the prior cycle top. Overall, we believe AMAT's leading market position, sustainable competitive advantages of scale, and ample cash of $4.2 billion make it an attractive investment ahead of the next up cycle.

Key Stock Statistics

S&P EPS Est. 2001	1.07	Tang. Bk. Value/Share	8.39
P/E on S&P Est. 2001	39.8	Beta	2.26
S&P EPS Est. 2002	1.10	Shareholders	6,345
Dividend Rate/Share	Nil	Market cap. (B)	$ 35.2
Shs. outstg. (M)	813.1	Inst. holdings	64%
Avg. daily vol. (M)	13.710		

Value of $10,000 invested 5 years ago: $ 68,112

Fiscal Year Ending Oct. 31

	2001	2000	1999	1998	1997	1996
Revenues (Million $)						
1Q	2,731	1,667	742.5	1,308	835.8	1,041
2Q	1,909	2,190	1,118	1,176	900.9	1,128
3Q	1,334	2,732	1,434	884.5	1,057	1,115
4Q	—	2,920	1,566	673.2	1,280	861.0
Yr.	—	9,564	4,859	4,042	4,074	4,145
Earnings Per Share ($)						
1Q	**0.66**	**0.40**	**0.07**	**0.30**	0.04	0.23
2Q	**0.27**	**0.54**	**0.18**	**0.18**	0.14	0.25
3Q	**0.03**	**0.70**	**0.30**	**0.07**	0.24	0.23
4Q	—	**0.77**	**0.34**	**-0.17**	0.23	0.10
Yr.	—	**2.40**	**0.92**	**0.38**	**0.66**	**0.81**

Next earnings report expected: mid November

Dividend Data

No cash dividends have been paid.

A Division of The McGraw·Hill Companies

Applied Materials, Inc.

Business Summary - 21-AUG-01

As the largest supplier of wafer fabrication systems to the semiconductor industry, Applied Materials (AMAT) provides enabling technology that is critical for advanced semiconductor production. Rapid advances in semiconductor technology, which have allowed computers and other electronic goods to become smaller, faster and cheaper in recent years, would not have been possible without the efforts of companies like AMAT, in collaboration with chip makers such as Intel.

In FY 93 (Oct.), AMAT became the first chip equipment company to post revenues in excess of $1 billion. It is currently the world's largest semiconductor equipment company, with $9.6 billion in sales in FY 00. AMAT offers the most extensive range of products to the semiconductor market.

The company's products address most of the front-end equipment market for semiconductor wafer processing. However, the majority of sales come from deposition equipment, where AMAT commands a dominant market share. Deposition, a fundamental step in fabricating a semiconductor, is a process of layering either electrically insulating (dielectric) or electrically conductive material on the wafer. AMAT supplies equipment to perform the three main types of deposition: chemical vapor deposition (CVD), physical vapor deposition (PVD), and electroplating.

AMAT is also a leader in etch systems. Before etch processing begins, a wafer is patterned with photoresist during photolithography. Etching equipment is then used to selectively remove material from areas not covered by the photoresist.

The company also manufactures ion implantation equipment. During ion implantation, silicon wafers are bombarded by a high-velocity beam of electrically charged ions. These ions penetrate the wafer at selected sites and change the electrical properties of the implanted area.

In an effort to expand its served markets, AMAT has begun to aggressively compete in adjacent markets, such as rapid thermal processing (RTP) and chemical mechanical planarization (CMP). In October 1999, the company acquired Obsidian, Inc., a developer of slurry-free CMP technology that may reduce CMP costs and enhance precision in processing. Through earlier acquisitions, AMAT entered the rapidly growing metrology and wafer/reticle inspection markets. The acquisition of Etec Systems, the leader in mask pattern generation equipment, completed in March 2000, was expected to enable the company to penetrate new markets in the photomask area.

The company has increasingly sought to combine equipment systems into process modules to optimize the overall functionality of the tools and save customers time in setting up fabrication plants. The ability to bundle products can be a marketing advantage over competitors offering a smaller range of equipment.

Per Share Data ($) (Year Ended Oct. 31)	2000	1999	1998	1997	1996	1995	1994	1993	1992	1991
Tangible Bk. Val.	8.39	5.18	4.22	3.99	3.29	2.49	1.44	0.93	0.76	0.60
Cash Flow	2.82	1.26	0.76	0.95	1.02	0.77	0.40	0.21	0.12	0.09
Earnings	2.40	0.92	0.38	0.66	0.82	0.64	0.31	0.15	0.07	0.05
Dividends	Nil	Nil	Nil	Nil	Nil	Nil	Nil	Nil	Nil	Nil
Payout Ratio	Nil	Nil	Nil	Nil	Nil	Nil	Nil	Nil	Nil	Nil
Prices - High	115.00	64.50	23.50	27.09	11.18	14.96	6.81	5.00	2.42	1.18
- Low	34.12	21.43	10.78	8.67	5.43	4.62	4.53	2.01	1.00	0.60
P/E Ratio - High	48	70	77	41	14	23	22	33	36	25
- Low	14	23	35	13	7	7	14	13	15	13
Income Statement Analysis (Million $)										
Revs.	9,564	4,859	4,042	4,074	4,145	3,062	1,660	1,080	751	639
Oper. Inc.	3,149	1,257	910	1,429	1,078	777	396	199	96.1	76.5
Depr.	362	275	285	219	149	83.2	58.5	37.8	27.7	24.5
Int. Exp.	51.4	47.1	45.3	20.7	20.7	21.4	16.0	14.2	15.2	14.0
Pretax Inc.	2,948	1,056	438	799	922	699	331	150	58.9	40.4
Eff. Tax Rate	30%	31%	34%	38%	35%	35%	35%	34%	33%	35%
Net Inc.	2,064	726	289	498	600	454	214	100	39.5	26.2
Balance Sheet & Other Fin. Data (Million $)										
Cash	1,648	823	575	448	404	769	422	266	223	140
Curr. Assets	8,839	5,060	3,519	3,770	2,693	2,312	1,231	776	582	434
Total Assets	10,546	6,707	4,930	5,071	3,638	2,965	1,703	1,120	854	661
Curr. Liab.	2,760	1,669	1,118	1,402	935	862	496	381	248	200
LT Debt	573	584	617	623	275	280	209	121	118	124
Common Eqty.	7,104	4,337	3,121	2,942	2,370	1,784	966	599	474	325
Total Cap.	7,677	4,954	3,749	3,613	2,658	2,075	1,187	727	599	456
Cap. Exp.	383	204	449	339	453	266	186	99	67.0	67.0
Cash Flow	2,426	1,001	573	718	748	547	272	137	67.2	50.7
Curr. Ratio	3.2	3.0	3.1	2.7	2.9	2.7	2.5	2.0	2.3	2.2
% LT Debt of Cap.	7.5	11.8	16.4	17.3	10.3	13.5	17.6	16.7	19.8	27.2
% Net Inc.of Revs.	21.6	14.9	7.1	12.2	14.4	14.8	12.9	9.2	5.3	4.1
% Ret. on Assets	23.5	12.5	5.8	11.4	18.1	19.5	14.9	10.0	4.9	4.3
% Ret. on Equity	35.3	19.5	9.5	18.8	28.9	33.0	26.8	18.4	9.3	8.3

Data as orig reptd.; bef. results of disc opers/spec. items. Per share data adj. for stk. divs. Bold denotes diluted EPS (FASB 128)-prior periods restated. E-Estimated. NA-Not Available. NM-Not Meaningful. NR-Not Ranked.

Office—3050 Bowers Ave., Santa Clara, CA 95054-8039. **Tel**—(408) 727-5555. **Website**—http://www.AppliedMaterials.com **Chrmn & CEO**—J. C. Morgan. **Pres**—D. Maydan. **EVP & CFO**—J. R. Bronson. **Secy**—D. A. Slichter. **Investor Contact**—Carolyn Schwartz (408-748-5227). **Dirs**—M. Armacost, D. A. Coleman, H. M. Dwight Jr., P. V. Gerdine, P. R. Low, D. Maydan, M. Morio, J. C. Morgan, S.L. Miller, S. Shih. **Transfer Agent**—Harris Trust Co. of California, Chicago. **Incorporated**—in California in 1967; reincorporated in Delaware in 1987. **Empl**— 19,220. **S&P Analyst:** T. W. Smith, CFA

Atmel Corp.

Nasdaq Symbol **ATML**

In S&P MidCap 400

18-AUG-01

Industry: Electronics (Semiconductors)

Summary: This company makes and markets a broad range of logic, mixed-signal, non-volatile memory and RF semiconductors.

S&P Opinion: Buy (★★★★★)

Recent Price • 9.10 | 52 Wk Range • 21.93-7.62 | Yield • Nil | 12-Mo. P/E • 20.7

Quantitative Evaluations

Outlook (1 Lowest—5 Highest) **• 1−**

Fair Value **• 4.80**

Risk **• High**

Earn./Div. Rank **• B**

Technical Eval. **• Bearish** since 7/01

Rel. Strength Rank (1 Lowest—99 Highest) **• 19**

Insider Activity **• Neutral**

OPTIONS: ASE, CBOE, P, Ph

Overview - 31-JUL-01

We expect revenues to decline almost 25% in 2001, reflecting an industry-wide downturn in demand for semiconductors. Long-term growth prospects remain good, especially for high-end flash memory and specialty logic chips used in wireless communications end products, and we expect revenue to rise nearly 10% in 2002. Unit shipments of chips fell sharply in the first half of 2001, but ATML expects the third quarter to mark the bottom for shipment levels. Some chip segments may continue to suffer from a weak pricing environment. With ample capacity to handle higher unit volume runs when industry strength returns, ATML seems well positioned for growth. Margins are currently under pressure, but should widen in 2002 as the company boosts manufacturing efficiency. We estimate 2001 EPS at $0.12, and believe that 2002 EPS can reach $0.25.

Valuation - 31-JUL-01

The shares are stabilizing after hitting a 52-week low in early April. Despite a sharp industry downturn, the company is executing a steady strategy for long-term growth. ATML has taken substantial steps to reduce its cost structure and to decrease its dependence on low-margin commodity memory products. Chips for wireless communications now account for a majority of sales, and we view the stock as an attractive way to invest in the portable computing and communications boom. In 2000, the company started a new revenue stream from chips for smart cards, and for identification and security markets. The shares were recently trading at 2.4X tangible book value, a modest level compared to valuations for ATML's peer group. Despite near-term earnings pressure, we believe the stock can outperform the broader market over the next six to 12 months, as the industry regains vigor.

Key Stock Statistics

S&P EPS Est. 2001	0.12	Tang. Bk. Value/Share	4.10
P/E on S&P Est. 2001	75.8	Beta	2.75
S&P EPS Est. 2002	0.25	Shareholders	260,000
Dividend Rate/Share	Nil	Market cap. (B)	$ 4.2
Shs. outstg. (M)	464.0	Inst. holdings	41%
Avg. daily vol. (M)	4.513		

Value of $10,000 invested 5 years ago: $ 13,933

Fiscal Year Ending Dec. 31

	2001	2000	1999	1998	1997	1996
Revenues (Million $)						
1Q	525.9	429.2	290.0	260.4	252.9	240.1
2Q	367.0	478.8	311.1	288.2	224.9	268.8
3Q	—	530.4	340.2	273.8	240.1	280.3
4Q	—	574.3	388.7	288.7	240.3	281.1
Yr.	—	2,013	1,330	1,111	958.3	1,070
Earnings Per Share ($)						
1Q	0.12	0.09	0.04	0.07	0.10	0.11
2Q	Nil	0.13	0.04	-0.23	0.07	0.13
3Q	E-0.01	0.16	0.04	0.01	0.07	0.13
4Q	E0.01	0.18	0.08	0.03	-0.24	0.13
Yr.	E0.12	0.55	0.20	-0.13	0.01	0.50

Next earnings report expected: late October

Dividend Data

Amount ($)	Date Decl.	Ex-Div. Date	Stock of Record	Payment Date
2-for-1	Jul. 21	Aug. 28	Aug. 11	Aug. 25 '00

Atmel Corporation

Business Summary - 31-JUL-01

Founded in 1984, Atmel designs, makes and markets a broad range of high-performance non-volatile memory and logic integrated circuits. Its products are used in a wide range of applications, including telecommunications, computing, networking, consumer and automotive electronics, and the industrial markets. The company aims to leverage its expertise in non-volatile memories by combining them with microcontrollers, digital signal processors and other logic chips.

Production and sales are global in scope. Geographic distribution of revenue in 2000 was as follows: U.S. 36%, Asia 34%, Europe 28%, and rest of world 2%. The company sells to a diverse base of OEMs. Motorola accounted for 12% of sales in each of 2000 and 1999.

Atmel makes over 90% of its products at its own wafer fabrication plants. Headquartered in San Jose, CA, the company operates wafer fabs in Colorado Springs, CO; Irving, TX; Nantes, France; Rousset, France; Heilbronn, Germany; and North Tyneside, U.K. Wafer processing operations include BiCMOS, CMOS and Silicon Germanium (SiGe) technologies; the latter provides a cost-effective means of making RF (radio frequency) chips.

There are four reportable segments, each of which requires different design, development and marketing resources to produce and sell semiconductors: Non-volatile memories (52% of 2000 sales), Application specific integrated circuits (ASICs, 26%), Logic (7%), and Atmel Wireless and Microcontroller Group (WMG, formerly known as Temic, 15%).

The non-volatile memory segment focuses on flash memories, erasable programmable read-only memories (EPROMs), electrically erasable programmable read-only memories (EEPROMs). These types of products are generally standardized throughout the marketplace, and are thus subject to commodity pricing.

The ASICs segment includes semi-custom gate arrays and cell-based integrated circuits, as well as full custom application-specific integrated circuits and smartcards. The company's ASICs products are targeted toward customers whose high-end applications require high-speed, high-density, or low or mixed-signal voltages.

Logic products include microcontrollers, erasable programmable logic devices (EPLDs), and field programmable gate-arrays (FPGAs). Products are sold for a broad variety of consumer applications.

WMG manufactures analog, microcontroller and specialty products for the automotive, telecom, consumer and industrial markets. A prime focus is high-frequency products for cordless and cellular phones, and two-way pagers. Remote controls for keyless entry for automobiles is another end-product example.

In May 2000, ATML acquired Thomson-CSF Semiconducteurs Specifique, adding capabilities in making ASICs, especially for image sensors used in products such as digital cameras.

Per Share Data ($) (Year Ended Dec. 31)	2000	1999	1998	1997	1996	1995	1994	1993	1992	1991
Tangible Bk. Val.	4.10	1.99	1.84	1.97	2.00	1.51	0.99	0.66	0.47	0.43
Cash Flow	1.06	0.68	0.38	0.34	0.78	0.44	0.26	0.14	0.07	0.07
Earnings	0.55	0.20	-0.13	0.01	0.50	0.29	0.17	0.09	0.05	0.04
Dividends	Nil	Nil	Nil	Nil	Nil	Nil	Nil	Nil	Nil	Nil
Payout Ratio	Nil	Nil	Nil	Nil	Nil	Nil	Nil	Nil	Nil	Nil
Prices - High	30.68	15.75	5.31	12.21	10.59	9.18	4.70	2.41	1.06	1.17
- Low	9.37	3.40	1.50	4.37	4.53	3.84	2.06	0.96	0.47	0.42
P/E Ratio - High	56	79	NM	NM	21	32	28	26	22	31
- Low	17	17	NM	NM	9	13	12	10	10	11
Income Statement Analysis (Million $)										
Revs.	2,013	1,330	1,111	958	1,070	634	375	222	140	120
Oper. Inc.	671	344	270	206	416	226	122	59.4	26.8	23.6
Depr.	255	201	200	138	111	58.9	34.1	15.3	7.7	8.2
Int. Exp.	53.8	49.8	47.5	31.2	12.9	8.3	2.8	2.9	3.1	4.1
Pretax Inc.	416	129	-50.9	6.0	309	173	90.1	44.8	19.9	14.9
Eff. Tax Rate	36%	36%	NM	70%	35%	34%	34%	33%	30%	31%
Net Inc.	266	82.4	-50.0	1.8	202	114	59.5	30.0	13.9	10.3
Balance Sheet & Other Fin. Data (Million $)										
Cash	499	251	162	174	157	180	79.3	67.6	24.9	45.3
Curr. Assets	1,792	1,039	891	698	460	366	188	144	100	110
Total Assets	3,825	2,015	1,963	1,822	1,456	920	541	301	183	160
Curr. Liab.	1,189	552	399	384	336	233	124	54.8	27.9	23.6
LT Debt	669	654	771	571	279	88.5	46.5	24.0	23.0	21.2
Common Eqty.	1,895	801	732	786	790	589	358	218	132	115
Total Cap.	2,563	1,463	1,507	1,392	1,091	686	417	246	156	136
Cap. Exp.	961	172	188	312	511	229	183	73.9	14.2	7.3
Cash Flow	521	283	150	140	313	173	93.5	45.3	21.7	18.5
Curr. Ratio	1.5	1.9	2.2	1.8	1.4	1.6	1.5	2.6	3.6	4.7
% LT Debt of Cap.	26.1	44.7	51.2	41.0	25.6	12.9	11.2	9.7	14.8	15.6
% Net Inc.of Revs.	13.2	6.2	NM	0.2	18.9	18.0	15.8	13.5	10.0	8.6
% Ret. on Assets	9.1	4.1	NM	0.1	17.0	15.6	13.7	11.6	8.0	7.9
% Ret. on Equity	19.7	10.8	NM	0.2	29.3	24.1	19.9	16.1	11.1	13.6

Data as orig reptd.; bef. results of disc opers/spec. items. Per share data adj. for stk. divs. Bold denotes diluted EPS (FASB 128)-prior periods restated. E-Estimated. NA-Not Available. NM-Not Meaningful. NR-Not Ranked.

Office—2325 Orchard Pkwy., San Jose, CA 95131. **Tel**—(408) 441-0311. **Website**—http://www.atmel.com **Chrmn, Pres & CEO**—George Perlegos. **VP-Fin, CFO & Investor Contact**—Donald Colvin. **Secy**—M. A. Bertelsen. **Dirs**—P. Fougere, N. Hall, George Perlegos, Gust Perlegos, T. P. Thomas, T.-C. Wu. **Transfer Agent**—EquiServe, Providence, RI. **Incorporated**—in California in 1984; reincorporated in Delaware in 1999. **Empl**— 9,091. **S&P Analyst:** T. W. Smith, CFA

STANDARD
&POOR'S
STOCK REPORTS

BARRA

Nasdaq Symbol **BARZ**

In S&P SmallCap 600

20-AUG-01

Industry:
Computer (Software & Services)

Summary: This company develops, markets and supports application software and services used to analyze and manage portfolios of equity, fixed income and other financial instruments.

S&P Opinion: Buy (★★★★★)

Recent Price • 50.47
52 Wk Range • 61.50-29.91
Yield • Nil
12-Mo. P/E • 25.4

Quantitative Evaluations

Outlook
(1 Lowest—5 Highest)
• **4-**

Fair Value
• **58.80**

Risk
• **Average**

Earn./Div. Rank
• **B**

Technical Eval.
• **Bullish** since 7/01

Rel. Strength Rank
(1 Lowest—99 Highest)
• **78**

Insider Activity
• **Neutral**

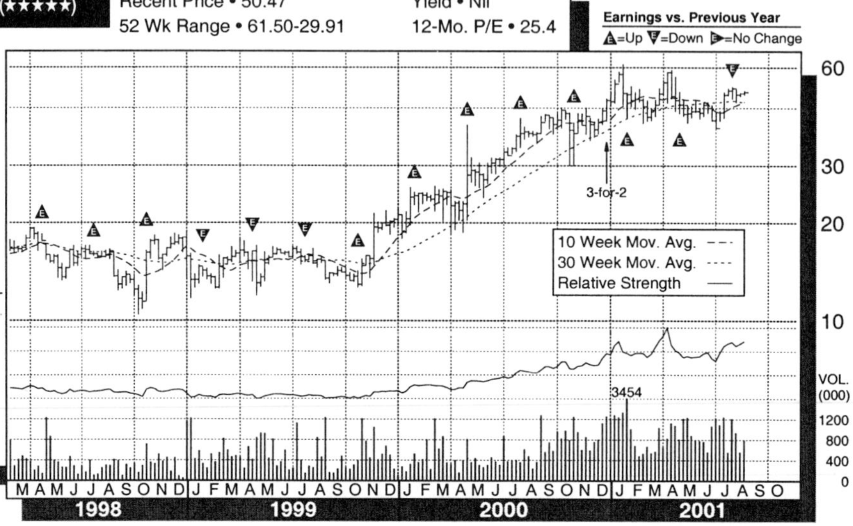

Overview - 20-AUG-01

Demand for Barra's risk management solutions remains strong. Its market leadership has been demonstrated in 2001 by several large licensing deals, notably with CalPERS, the largest U.S. public pension fund, and Merrill Lynch Investment Managers. On July 16, Barra completed the sale of its Symphony asset management unit. Although we expected that revenues from Symphony would have increased over the long term at a slightly faster pace than the equity market, the unit was a potential competitor with customers of BARZ's risk products, creating a conflict between the strategies of BARZ and the unit. Estimated initial proceeds from the sales were approximately $80 million, net of income taxes. The 50%-owned POSIT trading venture continues to benefit from increased institutional trading. Reflecting the short term effect of loss of earnings from Symphony, our projection is for essentially flat EPS of $2.02 for FY 02.

Valuation - 20-AUG-01

S&P is reiterating its buy opinion on BARZ. Recently trading at about 25X our 1EPS estimate for FY 02, the shares are valued at a moderate premium to the P/E of the S&P 500. EPS in fiscal 2002 are expected to increase 36% from pro forma earnings of $1.49 in fiscal 2001, adjusted to exclude results of Symphony. Moreover, we project earnings growth over the next three fiscal years of about 15% to 17%, reflecting the projected higher growth rate of the remaining businesses after the sale of the Symphony division. Cash flow should be equally strong, enabling the company to buy back its stock. This combination of superior earnings growth, strong free cash flow and attractive valuation leads us to expect superior capital appreciation for the shares over the next six to 12 months. Our price target range over that time frame is $59-$61.

Key Stock Statistics

S&P EPS Est. 2002	2.02	Tang. Bk. Value/Share	6.77
P/E on S&P Est. 2002	25.0	Beta	0.30
S&P EPS Est. 2003	2.35	Shareholders	3,600
Dividend Rate/Share	Nil	Market cap. (B)	$ 1.1
Shs. outstg. (M)	21.4	Inst. holdings	53%
Avg. daily vol. (M)	0.174		

Value of $10,000 invested 5 years ago: $ 51,617

Fiscal Year Ending Mar. 31

	2002	2001	2000	1999	1998	1997
Revenues (Million $)						
1Q	49.79	48.60	38.03	35.91	27.11	22.93
2Q	—	64.89	43.81	39.03	31.23	24.47
3Q	—	59.71	60.18	42.56	42.76	27.88
4Q	—	51.22	44.53	40.56	36.28	29.48
Yr.	—	224.4	186.6	158.1	137.4	104.8
Earnings Per Share ($)						
1Q	**0.45**	**0.47**	**0.02**	**0.21**	-0.33	0.13
2Q	—	**0.60**	**0.27**	**0.21**	0.17	0.09
3Q	—	**0.50**	**0.47**	**0.21**	**0.26**	0.20
4Q	—	**0.45**	**0.30**	**-0.03**	**0.22**	0.22
Yr.	—	**2.01**	**1.06**	**0.59**	**0.37**	**0.65**

Next earnings report expected: late October

Dividend Data

Amount ($)	Date Decl.	Ex-Div. Date	Stock of Record	Payment Date
3-for-2	Nov. 14	Dec. 19	Nov. 27	Dec. 18 '00

A Division of The McGraw-Hill Companies

BARRA, Inc.

Business Summary - 20-AUG-01

BARRA, Inc., with clients that include many of the world's largest portfolio managers, fund sponsors, pension and investment consultants, broker/dealers and master trustees, develops, markets and supports application software and information services used to analyze and manage portfolios of equity, fixed income and other financial instruments. In FY 00 (Mar.), BARZ reorganized its operations into two business units.

The company's Core Business unit (accounting for 50% of FY 00 revenues) provides portfolio risk management and enterprise risk management systems to investment professionals. These systems consist of three components: data, models and software applications. Portfolio risk products include the Aegis System, a suite of risk management software and applications for managing equity securities and derivatives, and the Cosmos System, which allows global fixed income portfolio managers to manage risk and optimize return in a multi-currency, global bond portfolio. The BARRA Total Risk System is a platform that addresses both the business and technology issues of delivering a consolidated view of financial risk across an enterprise.

The Ventures Business unit (50%) extends the Core Business segment's ideas into new markets and consists of several distinct, generally independent companies. POSIT (50% owned) is an electronic system for low-cost, confidential trade matching during the market day, through which clients enter buy and sell orders to trade single stocks and portfolios of securities among themselves.

On July 16, 2001, BARZ sold its 50%-owned Symphony asset management unit to John Nuveen. The company will initially receive net proceeds of $80 million in cash for its stake, after income taxes, with up to $12 million more in future contingency payments.

The Other Ventures segment of the Ventures business includes several properties. Bond Express is an aggregator of bond offerings and is the most widely used bond offering system of its type in the world. BARRA RogersCasey, Inc., offers investment consulting services, a variety of fund-of-funds and private equity products and plans, and the InvestWorks system. The Strategic Consulting Group provides consulting services to asset management firms. BARZ also owns a 16% stake in Data Downlink Corp., whose flagship product, .xls, aggregates, cross-indexes and distributes business databases. In addition, BARZ owns a 50% interest in Risk Reporting Ltd., which provides quarterly and annual reports that focus on identifying the risk of a pension fund.

Barra has repurchased shares of its stock in recent years. On June 18, 2001, directors expanded an earlier 500,000 share buyback to 750,000.

Per Share Data ($) (Year Ended Mar. 31)	2001	2000	1999	1998	1997	1996	1995	1994	1993	1992
Tangible Bk. Val.	6.77	3.51	2.99	2.24	2.20	1.60	1.56	1.36	1.18	0.95
Cash Flow	2.38	1.42	0.90	0.61	0.80	0.47	0.31	0.80	0.29	0.23
Earnings	2.01	1.07	0.59	0.37	0.64	0.40	0.23	0.20	0.22	0.19
Dividends	Nil	Nil	Nil	Nil	Nil	Nil	Nil	Nil	Nil	Nil
Payout Ratio	Nil	Nil	Nil	Nil	Nil	Nil	Nil	Nil	Nil	Nil
Cal. Yrs.	2000	1999	1998	1997	1996	1995	1994	1993	1992	1991
Prices - High	50.12	22.00	19.33	19.83	15.11	7.55	4.00	4.33	6.88	6.55
- Low	17.83	11.66	10.41	10.88	6.88	3.11	2.22	2.72	2.77	4.66
P/E Ratio - High	25	21	33	54	23	19	18	22	31	35
- Low	9	11	18	30	11	8	10	14	13	25
Income Statement Analysis (Million $)										
Revs.	224	187	158	137	105	61.0	51.8	45.6	39.2	32.6
Oper. Inc.	93.2	65.6	41.7	42.6	27.9	13.4	8.2	9.0	7.5	6.0
Depr.	8.2	7.7	6.7	5.1	3.2	1.3	1.5	1.0	1.3	0.7
Int. Exp.	Nil	Nil	Nil	NA	Nil	Nil	NA	NM	Nil	Nil
Pretax Inc.	88.5	52.7	32.0	29.1	25.0	12.6	7.3	5.9	6.7	5.3
Eff. Tax Rate	28%	26%	34%	44%	40%	41%	43%	39%	40%	42%
Net Inc.	45.3	23.4	13.0	7.9	13.5	7.5	4.0	3.6	4.0	3.1
Balance Sheet & Other Fin. Data (Million $)										
Cash	61.8	53.3	48.6	33.7	25.8	25.5	16.1	13.0	12.3	14.2
Curr. Assets	186	118	91.6	74.7	65.9	35.5	32.2	25.3	21.8	21.7
Total Assets	226	169	143	121	84.2	57.9	47.3	38.4	33.6	25.4
Curr. Liab.	68.0	67.7	51.6	47.2	32.6	22.3	17.7	12.3	11.3	8.1
LT Debt	Nil	Nil	Nil	Nil	0.5	0.4	0.5	0.3	Nil	Nil
Common Eqty.	155	96.8	88.2	70.8	48.4	34.1	27.1	24.1	21.4	17.3
Total Cap.	158	101	91.5	74.2	50.4	35.7	29.6	26.1	22.2	17.3
Cap. Exp.	4.4	5.8	8.7	8.8	3.7	1.4	2.4	1.1	3.3	1.2
Cash Flow	53.5	31.1	19.7	13.0	16.8	8.8	5.5	4.6	5.3	3.8
Curr. Ratio	2.7	1.7	1.8	1.6	2.0	1.6	1.8	2.1	1.9	2.7
% LT Debt of Cap.	Nil	Nil	Nil	Nil	0.9	1.1	1.6	1.3	Nil	Nil
% Net Inc.of Revs.	20.2	12.6	8.2	5.8	12.9	12.3	7.7	7.8	10.3	9.5
% Ret. on Assets	22.9	15.0	9.8	7.7	19.1	14.3	9.3	10.0	13.7	15.9
% Ret. on Equity	36.0	25.3	16.4	13.3	32.9	24.5	15.6	15.9	20.9	30.8

Data as orig reptd.; bef. results of disc opers/spec. items. Per share data adj. for stk. divs. Bold denotes diluted EPS (FASB 128)-prior periods restated. E-Estimated. NA-Not Available. NM-Not Meaningful. NR-Not Ranked.

Office—2100 Milvia St., Berkeley, CA 94704-1113. **Tel**—(510) 548-5442. **Fax**—(510) 548-4374. **Website**—http://www.barra.com **Chrmn**—A. Rudd. **Pres & CEO**—K. Duggirala. **CFO**—G. Stockett. **Secy**—M. L. Hekker. **Investor Contact**—Jennifer Hinchman (510-649-4548). **Dirs**—A. G. Battle, J. F. Casey, K. Duggirala, M. B. Hull, N. J. Laboe, C. W. Ostler, A. Rudd. **Transfer Agent & Registrar**—Mellon Investor Services, Ridgefield Park, NJ. **Incorporated**—in Delaware in 1998; originally incorporated in California in 1986. **Empl**— 667. **S&P Analyst:** Mark S. Basham

STANDARD &POOR'S
STOCK REPORTS

Check Point Software

Nasdaq Symbol **CHKP**

18-AUG-01

Industry: Computer (Software & Services)

Summary: This Israel-based company is a leading provider of network security products, including virtual private networks and firewalls.

S&P Opinion: Buy (★★★★★)

Recent Price • 36.17
52 Wk Range • 118.58-35.01
Yield • Nil
12-Mo. P/E • 35.1

Quantitative Evaluations

Outlook
(1 Lowest—5 Highest)
• **NA**

Fair Value
• **NA**

Risk
• **High**

Earn./Div. Rank
• **NR**

Technical Eval.
• **Neutral** since 8/01

Rel. Strength Rank
(1 Lowest—99 Highest)
• **13**

Insider Activity
• **NA**

OPTIONS: ASE, CBOE, P, Ph

Overview - 10-AUG-01

We expect revenues to increase approximately 40% in 2001. The company is benefiting from strong demand for its Internet security software products. CHKP continues to boost its leading market share for firewall software, while growing rapidly in the emerging virtual private network (VPN) market. Security has become a leading spending priority for many customers. We expect margins to widen slightly, as strong revenue growth outweighs the effects of increased spending on R&D and sales and marketing. CHKP's operating margin was an exceptionally strong 65% in the second quarter of 2001. Benefitting from a low Israeli tax rate, net margin was only slightly lower, at 61%. We project net margin of about 58% for 2001, with approximately a 57% advance in EPS.

Valuation - 10-AUG-01

We have a buy recommendation on the shares of CHKP, due to its attractive relative valuation to its growth rate and continued strong execution in a difficult economic environment. The company reported excellent results for the second quarter of 2001, as revenues rose 57%, versus our 50% growth estimate. Demand was strong in all segments and geographies. CHKP has emerged as a leader in the rapidly growing markets for firewalls and VPN software. As companies rely more and more on Internet-based networks, network security plays an increasingly vital role. We believe CHKP is well positioned for strong growth in an explosive market. We recently trimmed our 2001 EPS estimate to $1.33, from $1.35, primarily due to a challenging economic environment. In light of the company's leading position in a booming market, the stock is attractive despite its premium valuation, and we recommend purchasing the shares.

Key Stock Statistics

S&P EPS Est. 2001	1.33	Tang. Bk. Value/Share	2.33
P/E on S&P Est. 2001	27.2	Beta	1.77
S&P EPS Est. 2002	1.75	Shareholders	209
Dividend Rate/Share	Nil	Market cap. (B)	$ 8.5
Shs. outstg. (M)	235.5	Inst. holdings	51%
Avg. daily vol. (M)	7.971		

Value of $10,000 invested 5 years ago: $ 86,807

Fiscal Year Ending Dec. 31

	2001	2000	1999	1998	1997	1996
Revenues (Million $)						
1Q	145.0	78.17	43.77	31.96	13.68	—
2Q	—	90.67	50.05	34.27	17.26	—
3Q	—	116.0	57.80	35.22	22.41	8.03
4Q	—	140.4	67.95	40.49	29.59	11.62
Yr.	—	425.3	219.6	141.9	82.93	31.87
Earnings Per Share ($)						
1Q	**0.32**	**0.13**	**0.08**	**0.07**	0.03	—
2Q	—	**0.17**	**0.09**	**0.08**	0.04	—
3Q	—	**0.23**	**0.10**	**0.08**	0.05	—
4Q	—	**0.31**	**0.12**	**0.08**	**0.06**	0.03
Yr.	—	**0.84**	**0.39**	**0.30**	**0.18**	**0.07**

Next earnings report expected: NA

Dividend Data

Amount ($)	Date Decl.	Ex-Div. Date	Stock of Record	Payment Date
3-for-2	Jan. 18	Feb. 13	Feb. 01	Feb. 12 '01

Check Point Software Technologies Ltd.

Business Summary - 10-AUG-01

Check Point Software Technologies is a leading provider of network security software. Its main products include virtual private networks (VPNs), firewalls, intranet and extranet security, and managed service provider (MSP) management software.

The company offers solutions that enable secure, reliable and manageable business-to-business communications over virtually any Internet Protocol (IP) network. Check Point's products also include traffic control/quality of service and IP address management.

CHKP's Enterprise Security Management product line includes its FireWall-1 family, its VPN-1 family of virtual private networking solutions and some associated products. Firewall-1 integrates access control, authentication, network address translation, content security, auditing and enterprise policy management. VPN-1 helps protect the privacy and integrity of network communications by establishing a confidential communications channel for virtual private networking.

The company's Enterprise Traffic Control product line includes its FloodGate-1 bandwidth management solution, which alleviates traffic congestion on oversubscribed Internet and intranet links.

The Enterprise Infrastructure Management product line includes Meta IP, an automated solution for managing IP addressing and naming.

Firewall-1 and FloodGate-1 are based on CHKP's Stateful Inspection technology, which enables the screening of all communications attempting to pass through a gateway in a highly secure but efficient way. The company's Open Platform for Secure Enterprise Connectivity (OPSEC) integrates and centrally manages the entire enterprise security policy. More than 200 third party security applications, computer hardware, internetworking hardware, appliances and enterprise applications can be plugged into the OPSEC framework through published application programming interfaces (APIs).

The company promotes its products as strategic components of enterprise networks. CHKP has OEM/bundling relationships with server and workstation vendors such as Compaq and IBM, as well as internetworking device manufacturers such as Nortel Networks, 3Com, Nokia, and Alcatel.

While the company is based in Israel, 53% of its 1999 revenues in came from the U.S. As a result of its incorporation in Israel, CHKP receives certain tax benefit. Its tax rate was approximately 13% in 1999.

In January 2000, CHKP said it had exceeded 110,000 customer installations of its software, with VPNs accounting for 34,000.

Per Share Data ($) (Year Ended Dec. 31)	2000	1999	1998	1997	1996	1995	1994	1993	1992	1991
Tangible Bk. Val.	2.33	1.28	0.84	0.49	0.29	NA	NA	NA	NA	NA
Cash Flow	0.97	0.40	0.32	0.18	0.07	NA	NA	NA	NA	NA
Earnings	0.84	0.39	0.30	0.18	0.07	NA	NA	NA	NA	NA
Dividends	NA	Nil	Nil	Nil	Nil	NA	NA	NA	NA	NA
Payout Ratio	NM	Nil	Nil	Nil	NA	NA	NA	NA	NA	NA
Prices - High	118.58	37.25	7.95	8.41	Nil	NA	NA	NA	NA	NA
- Low	29.08	3.83	1.81	2.70	2.20	NA	NA	NA	NA	NA
P/E Ratio - High	NM	96	26	47	84	NA	NA	NA	NA	NA
- Low	NM	10	6	15	30	NA	NA	NA	NA	NA
Income Statement Analysis (Million $)										
Revs.	425	220	142	82.9	31.9	NA	NA	NA	NA	NA
Oper. Inc.	236	101	71.3	39.6	14.5	NA	NA	NA	NA	NA
Depr.	7.1	3.6	4.5	0.9	0.5	NA	NA	NA	NA	NA
Int. Exp.	0.8	0.3	4.9	0.6	0.4	NA	NA	NA	NA	NA
Pretax Inc.	258	110	73.8	41.8	15.6	NA	NA	NA	NA	NA
Eff. Tax Rate	14%	13%	5.30%	5.52%	2.25%	NA	NA	NA	NA	NA
Net Inc.	221	95.8	69.9	40.2	15.2	NA	NA	NA	NA	NA
Balance Sheet & Other Fin. Data (Million $)										
Cash	228	66.2	82.7	65.2	54.5	NA	NA	NA	NA	NA
Curr. Assets	540	299	116	84.4	64.0	NA	NA	NA	NA	NA
Total Assets	778	394	212	124	65.4	NA	NA	NA	NA	NA
Curr. Liab.	227	101	35.5	23.0	7.4	NA	NA	NA	NA	NA
LT Debt	Nil	Nil	Nil	Nil	Nil	NA	NA	NA	NA	NA
Common Eqty.	549	293	176	100	57.6	NA	NA	NA	NA	NA
Total Cap.	549	293	176	100	57.6	NA	NA	NA	NA	NA
Cap. Exp.	9.1	6.1	6.1	2.5	2.5	NA	NA	NA	NA	NA
Cash Flow	228	99	74.4	41.1	15.7	NA	NA	NA	NA	NA
Curr. Ratio	2.4	3.0	3.3	3.7	8.7	NA	NA	NA	NA	NA
% LT Debt of Cap.	Nil	Nil	Nil	Nil	Nil	NA	NA	NA	NA	NA
% Net Inc.of Revs.	52.0	43.6	49.2	48.5	47.8	NA	NA	NA	NA	NA
% Ret. on Assets	37.8	31.6	41.6	42.5	42.0	NA	NA	NA	NA	NA
% Ret. on Equity	52.6	40.9	50.7	51.0	48.6	NA	NA	NA	NA	NA

Data as orig reptd.; bef. results of disc opers/spec. items. Per share data adj. for stk. divs. Bold denotes diluted EPS (FASB 128)-prior periods restated. E-Estimated. NA-Not Available. NM-Not Meaningful. NR-Not Ranked.

Office—Three Lagoon Drive, Suite 400, Redwood City, CA 94065. **Tel**—(650) 628-2000. **Website**—www.checkpoint.com **Chrmn, CEO & Pres**—G. Shwed. **CFO**—E. Desheh. **Dirs**—I. Federman, S. Kramer, M. Nacht, R. Rothrock, D. Rubner, G. Shwed, A. Vieux. **Transfer Agent**—American Stock Transfer & Trust Co., NYC. **Incorporated**—in Israel in 1993. **Empl**— 951. **S&P Analyst:** Jonathan Rudy

STANDARD
&POOR'S
STOCK REPORTS

DoubleClick

Nasdaq Symbol **DCLK**

18-AUG-01

Industry:
Computer (Software & Services)

Summary: This company is a leading provider of global Internet advertising solutions for marketers and Web publishers.

S&P Opinion: Buy (★★★★★)

Recent Price • 9.87
52 Wk Range • 45.51-8

Yield • Nil
12-Mo. P/E • NM

Quantitative Evaluations

Outlook
(1 Lowest—5 Highest)
• **NA**

Fair Value
• **NA**

Risk
• **NA**

Earn./Div. Rank
• **NR**

Technical Eval.
• **Bearish** since 7/01

Rel. Strength Rank
(1 Lowest—99 Highest)
• **20**

Insider Activity
• **NA**

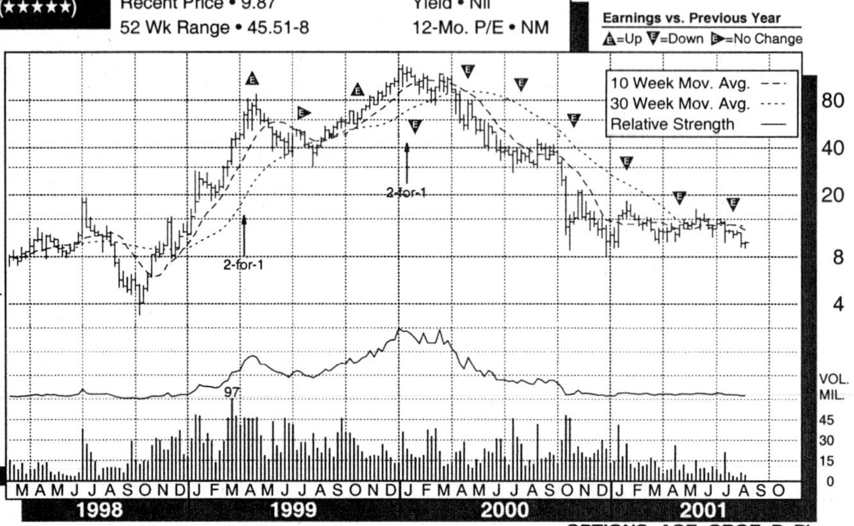

OPTIONS: ASE, CBOE, P, Ph

Overview - 16-JUL-01

Achieving revenue growth at DCLK, a leader in the online advertising segment, has proved extremely challenging since the first half of 2000, reflecting a difficult Internet advertising spending environment. We believe the worst may be over for Internet companies and the online advertising market, but we still expect DCLK's revenues to fall 16% in 2001. However, for the long term, we project annual sales gains of 50%. Even in a difficult marketing environment, the TechSolutions segment continues to post respectable results and margins. As a result of the April 2001 acquisition (for an undisclosed sum) of privately held FloNetwork Inc., whose customers include L.L. Bean, Procter & Gamble, Hallmark, and Continental Airlines, we expect DCLK to become the clear leader in e-mail marketing solutions.

Valuation - 16-JUL-01

In May 2001, we upgraded the shares to buy, from accumulate. Although the stock has performed relatively well in 2001, it fell dramatically in 2000 on negative publicity associated with online privacy, significant financial questions about many dot-coms, and a difficult online advertising spending climate. However, unlike many Internet companies, DCLK is financially sound, with a recent level of $814 million in cash and marketable securities ($6.21 a share). The company has used its strong balance sheet wisely. In addition to investing heavily in its high margin TechSolutions and Data businesses, the company has also greatly bolstered its research and e-mail marketing operations via acquisitions. Despite strong negative sentiment, we expect DCLK to emerge from the dot-com crash and economic slowdown as a stronger company, poised to benefit handsomely from an economic rebound.

Key Stock Statistics

S&P EPS Est. 2001	-0.24	Tang. Bk. Value/Share	6.19
P/E on S&P Est. 2001	NM	Beta	NA
S&P EPS Est. 2002	0.03	Shareholders	887
Dividend Rate/Share	Nil	Market cap. (B)	$ 1.3
Shs. outstg. (M)	130.9	Inst. holdings	54%
Avg. daily vol. (M)	0.829		

Value of $10,000 invested 5 years ago: NA

Fiscal Year Ending Dec. 31

	2001	2000	1999	1998	1997	1996
Revenues (Million $)						
1Q	114.9	110.1	22.09	13.00	—	—
2Q	101.9	128.1	30.99	17.29	—	—
3Q	—	135.2	44.95	20.78	—	—
4Q	—	132.3	93.69	29.11	—	—
Yr.	—	505.6	258.3	80.19	30.60	—
Earnings Per Share ($)						
1Q	**-0.48**	**-0.16**	**-0.09**	**-0.10**	—	—
2Q	**-0.29**	**-0.18**	**-0.07**	**-0.07**	—	—
3Q	**E-0.06**	**-0.09**	**-0.07**	**-0.07**	—	—
4Q	**E-0.02**	**-0.85**	**-0.38**	**-0.06**	—	—
Yr.	**E-0.24**	**-1.29**	**-0.51**	**-0.28**	**-0.14**	**-0.06**

Next earnings report expected: NA

Dividend Data

The company has never paid or declared a dividend on its common stock.

Business Summary - 16-JUL-01

The Internet has emerged as an attractive medium for advertisers, due to the rapid growth in the number of online users and usage, the increase in e-commerce, the interactive nature of the Web, and other factors. As a result, DoubleClick believes online advertising spending will grow significantly over the next several years, both domestically and internationally, and sees itself as well positioned to capitalize on this large market opportunity.

The company provides marketing and advertising solutions to thousands of advertisers, advertising agencies, Web publishers, and online merchants. DCLK's patented DART technology platform lets customers use preselected criteria to deliver ads in a targeted fashion. DART also measures ad performance and provides dynamic ad space inventory management. DCLK serves ads for more than 2,000 clients, up from 1,800 in 1999. In December 2000, the company delivered 63 billion targeted advertisements to Internet users, more than double the 30 million provided in 1999.

DoubleClick Media (50% and 49% of 2000 and 1999 revenues, respectively, accounting for revenue reductions for intersegment elimination) offers advertising and marketing solutions to publishers and advertisers. More than half of the companies that comprise the Fortune 100 used at least one of DCLK's networks in 2000. The company aggregates the advertising inventory of hundreds of websites into domestic and international networks, based on size, traffic and content. It enables advertisers to advertise on these networks, and to target users on a local, national and international basis.

DoubleClick Tech Solutions (40%, 28%) offers software and services that include the DART for Publishers, AdServer software for publishers and e-commerce merchants, DART for Advertisers, DARTmail. Professional services personnel provide education, consulting services and support. AdServer software allows firms to manage their advertising inventory, consumer data, advertising business processes, and relationships with advertisers and advertising agencies. This software was acquired via the October 1999 purchase of NetGravity, Inc., in exchange for 10.2 million shares.

DoubleClick Data Services (14%, 25%), through the Abacus division, provides information products and marketing research services to the direct marketing industry. Abacus has a database of consumer purchasing behavior gathered from more than 1,800 alliance members. This proprietary information and statistical modeling technology are used to provide direct marketers with information and analysis designed to increase response rates and profits from direct mail marketing campaigns. Abacus Direct Corp. was acquired in November 1999, in exchange for 21 million DCLK shares. DoubleClick Research provides research about the online advertising market and campaign management tools and planning systems. It was significantly bolstered by the February 2001 acquisition of @plan, for cash and stock valued at $90.7 million.

Per Share Data ($) (Year Ended Dec. 31)	2000	1999	1998	1997	1996	1995	1994	1993	1992	1991
Tangible Bk. Val.	6.19	2.38	3.79	0.39	NA	NA	NA	NA	NA	NA
Cash Flow	-1.01	-0.38	-0.50	-0.29	NA	NA	NA	NA	NA	NA
Earnings	-1.29	-0.51	-0.28	NA	-0.06	NA	NA	NA	NA	NA
Dividends	Nil	Nil	Nil	NA	Nil	NA	NA	NA	NA	NA
Payout Ratio	Nil	Nil	Nil	NA	Nil	NA	NA	NA	NA	NA
Prices - High	135.25	127.71	19.28	NA	NA	NA	NA	NA	NA	NA
- Low	8.00	11.00	3.37	NA	NA	NA	NA	NA	NA	NA
P/E Ratio - High	NM	NM	NM	NA	NM	NA	NA	NA	NA	NA
- Low	NM	NM	NM	NA	NM	NA	NA	NA	NA	NA
Income Statement Analysis (Million $)										
Revs.	506	258	80.2	30.6	NA	NA	NA	NA	NA	NA
Oper. Inc.	-85.4	-2.5	-18.7	-8.1	NA	NA	NA	NA	NA	NA
Depr.	33.4	14.6	2.2	0.4	NA	NA	NA	NA	NA	NA
Int. Exp.	12.1	9.4	0.1	0.3	NA	NA	NA	NA	NA	NA
Pretax Inc.	-155	-47.2	-18.2	-8.4	NA	NA	NA	NA	NA	NA
Eff. Tax Rate	NM	NM	NM	NA	NA	NA	NA	NA	NA	NA
Net Inc.	-156	-55.8	-18.2	-8.4	NA	NA	NA	NA	NA	NA
Balance Sheet & Other Fin. Data (Million $)										
Cash	194	119	127	2.7	NA	NA	NA	NA	NA	NA
Curr. Assets	773	422	169	19.4	NA	NA	NA	NA	NA	NA
Total Assets	1,299	729	184	21.7	NA	NA	NA	NA	NA	NA
Curr. Liab.	211	112	34.9	11.9	NA	NA	NA	NA	NA	NA
LT Debt	266	255	0.2	NA	NA	NA	NA	NA	NA	NA
Common Eqty.	817	362	148	9.4	NA	NA	NA	NA	NA	NA
Total Cap.	1,088	617	149	NA	NA	NA	NA	NA	NA	NA
Cap. Exp.	121	56.1	13.6	NA	NA	NA	NA	NA	NA	NA
Cash Flow	-123	-41.2	-15.9	-8.0	NA	NA	NA	NA	NA	NA
Curr. Ratio	3.7	3.8	4.8	1.6	NA	NA	NA	NA	NA	NA
% LT Debt of Cap.	24.4	41.4	0.2	NA	NA	NA	NA	NA	NA	NA
% Net Inc.of Revs.	NM	NM	NM	NA	NA	NA	NA	NA	NA	NA
% Ret. on Assets	NM	NM	NM	NA	NA	NA	NA	NA	NA	NA
% Ret. on Equity	NM	NM	NM	NA	NA	NA	NA	NA	NA	NA

Data as orig reptd.; bef. results of disc opers/spec. items. Per share data adj. for stk. divs. Bold denotes diluted EPS (FASB 128)-prior periods restated. E-Estimated. NA-Not Available. NM-Not Meaningful. NR-Not Ranked.

Office—450 W. 33rd St., New York, NY 10001. **Tel**—(212) 683-0001. **Website**—http://www.doubleclick.com **Chrmn**—K. J. O'Connor. **CEO, Pres & COO**—K. P. Ryan. **CFO, Treas & Secy**—S. R. Collins. **Dirs**—W. G. Gregory, D. A. Merriman, T. S. Murphy, M. E. Nunnelly, K. J. O'Connor, D. Peppers, K. P. Ryan, D. N. Strohm. **Transfer Agent & Registrar**—American Stock Transfer & Trust Co. (800-937-5449). **Incorporated**—in Delaware in 1996. **Empl**— 1,929. **S&P Analyst:** Scott H. Kessler

STANDARD
&POOR'S
STOCK REPORTS

Int'l Business Machines

NYSE Symbol **IBM**

In S&P 500

18-AUG-01

Industry: Computers (Hardware)

Summary: The world's largest technology company, IBM offers a diversified line of computer hardware equipment, application and system software, and related services.

S&P Opinion: Buy (★★★★★)

Recent Price • 104.59 | 52 Wk Range • 134.93-80.06 | Yield • 0.5% | 12-Mo. P/E • 22.3

Quantitative Evaluations

Outlook
(1 Lowest—5 Highest)
• **3+**

Fair Value
• **105**

Risk
• **Average**

Earn./Div. Rank
• **B**

Technical Eval.
• **Neutral** since 8/01

Rel. Strength Rank
(1 Lowest—99 Highest)
• **43**

Insider Activity
• **Unfavorable**

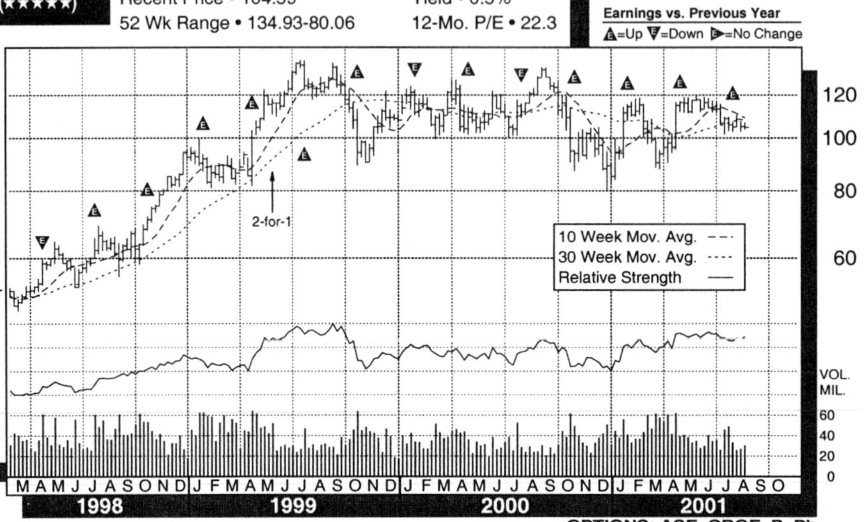

OPTIONS: ASE, CBOE, P, Ph

Overview - 20-JUL-01

We project flat revenues for 2001, but growth will exceed 5% when currency effects are excluded. The growth that we project on a constant currency basis reflects healthy gains for global services, partly offset by pressure on the company's hardware sales, due to slower information technology (IT) spending that we project for the year. In the first half of 2001, IBM's hardware sales benefited from its new mainframe release. Third quarter sales will likely be limited by weakness in the company's microelectronics unit, but the launch of the company's new Regatta server could bolster revenues in the fourth quarter. We expect gross margins to widen slightly in 2001, to 37.1%, from the 36.7% level of 2000, aided by stronger than expected gross margins in Services and Hardware. We project 2001 EPS at $4.80, up from $4.44 in 2000, and estimate EPS at $4.95 for 2002.

Valuation - 20-JUL-01

We continue to recommend buying the shares. We were impressed with the strength of IBM's 2001 first and second quarter earnings results, paced against the backdrop of a challenging U.S. economy. Favorable reviews of IBM's new server line show that the company continues to introduce compelling new technology, leveraging its healthy patent portfolio. In addition, we continue to like IBM for the long term, based on its leadership position in e-business consulting, and on the stock's attractive valuation. Although revenue growth may still not reach double-digits in 2001, the company's competitive position has been bolstered by important new server and storage offerings, as well as by its services capabilities. With the shares trading at an attractive P/E ratio (based on our EPS estimate for 2002) that represents a discount to peer levels, we believe the shares are undervalued.

Key Stock Statistics

S&P EPS Est. 2001	4.80	Tang. Bk. Value/Share	11.08
P/E on S&P Est. 2001	21.8	Beta	1.32
S&P EPS Est. 2002	4.95	Shareholders	673,270
Dividend Rate/Share	0.56	Market cap. (B)	$181.7
Shs. outstg. (M)	1737.4	Inst. holdings	50%
Avg. daily vol. (M)	5.700		

Value of $10,000 invested 5 years ago: $ 39,367

Fiscal Year Ending Dec. 31

	2001	2000	1999	1998	1997	1996
Revenues (Million $)						
1Q	21,044	19,348	20,317	17,618	17,308	16,559
2Q	21,568	21,651	21,905	18,823	18,872	18,183
3Q	—	21,781	21,144	20,095	18,605	18,062
4Q	—	25,616	24,182	25,131	23,723	23,143
Yr.	—	88,396	87,548	81,667	78,508	75,947
Earnings Per Share ($)						
1Q	**0.98**	**0.83**	**0.78**	**0.53**	0.59	0.35
2Q	**1.15**	**1.06**	**1.28**	**0.75**	0.73	0.63
3Q	—	**1.08**	**0.93**	**0.78**	0.69	0.61
4Q	—	**1.48**	**1.12**	**1.24**	**1.05**	0.98
Yr.	—	**4.44**	**4.12**	**3.28**	**3.00**	**2.50**

Next earnings report expected: mid October

Dividend Data (Dividends have been paid since 1916.)

Amount ($)	Date Decl.	Ex-Div. Date	Stock of Record	Payment Date
0.130	Oct. 31	Nov. 08	Nov. 10	Dec. 09 '00
0.130	Jan. 30	Feb. 07	Feb. 09	Mar. 10 '01
0.140	Apr. 24	May. 08	May. 10	Jun. 09 '01
0.140	Jul. 31	Aug. 08	Aug. 10	Sep. 10 '01

A Division of The McGraw-Hill Companies

International Business Machines Corporation

Business Summary - 20-JUL-01

International Business Machines (IBM), still the world's largest computer concern, is no longer just a computer vendor. Although hardware accounts for nearly 43% of sales, IBM has focused on key areas such as services (which provides 37% of sales, versus 15% in 1994), and software (about 14%). Software and services contributed 67% of 2000 pretax profits. Considered key growth engines, services and software have gained momentum as IBM has leveraged its unique capabilities in offering e-business (electronic business) solutions, in light of the fact that the Internet is emerging as a business tool in streamlining everything from supply chain management to customer service.

Hardware, once thought of as principally mainframes (System/390, now known as zSeries) and minicomputers (AS/400), has made a transition to more open systems. IBM, a leader in UNIX systems (with its RS6000, or pSeries), also offers entry level servers and workstations that use Intel microprocessors and run Microsoft operating systems. To broaden its server line to include highly scalable SMP (symmetric multiprocessing) systems, it acquired server maker Sequent Computer Systems, Inc., in 1999. In its PC business, IBM has introduced new manufacturing and distribution strategies aimed at maintaining low inventories.

The hardware division also includes the technology segment. The segment includes the company's hard disk drives, aimed at the market's high end; a new storage offering (Shark); and IBM's semiconductor unit, which includes custom logic and communications.

IBM Services has been growing at an average double-digit rate over the past several years. The unit's strong position in emerging e-business services, and 2000 year end services backlog of $85 billion, point to further healthy growth. In 1999, IBM sold its Global Network Services unit to AT&T for $5 billion in cash.

The software unit's sales growth has been in single-digits, but this masks the strength of its middleware offerings, and database and Web management software. To meet the slower growth of host-based software, IBM acquired software pioneer Lotus in 1995, and Tivoli Systems in 1996.

Global Financing (4% of sales) is primarily used to leverage IBM's financial structuring, portfolio management, etc., to expand the company's addressable base of customers and partners. Financing is increasingly becoming an important customer offering for computer hardware vendors.

Leading the world in U.S. patents in 1999, with 2,756 (latest available), IBM has been a leader in technological innovations, including semiconductor technology such as silicon germanium and silicon-on-insulator; and the use of copper (a better conductor than aluminum) to create the circuitry on silicon wafers.

Per Share Data ($) (Year Ended Dec. 31)	2000	1999	1998	1997	1996	1995	1994	1993	1992	1991
Tangible Bk. Val.	11.08	10.65	9.84	9.62	9.99	9.72	9.30	7.72	11.96	16.10
Cash Flow	6.95	7.40	5.63	4.99	4.30	3.57	3.05	-1.45	-0.91	2.00
Earnings	4.44	4.12	3.29	3.00	2.56	1.81	1.25	-3.50	-3.01	-0.25
Dividends	0.51	0.47	0.44	0.39	0.33	0.25	0.25	0.40	1.21	1.21
Payout Ratio	11%	11%	13%	13%	13%	14%	20%	NM	NM	NM
Prices - High	134.93	139.18	94.96	56.75	41.50	28.65	19.09	14.96	25.09	34.93
- Low	80.06	80.87	47.81	31.78	20.78	17.56	12.84	10.15	12.18	20.87
P/E Ratio - High	30	34	29	19	16	16	15	NM	NM	NM
- Low	18	20	15	11	8	10	10	NM	NM	NM
Income Statement Analysis (Million $)										
Revs.	88,396	87,548	81,667	78,508	75,947	71,940	64,052	62,716	64,523	64,792
Oper. Inc.	16,147	18,086	13,639	13,116	12,272	11,546	9,202	5,018	8,199	9,489
Depr.	4,513	6,159	4,475	4,018	3,676	3,955	4,197	4,710	4,793	5,149
Int. Exp.	717	727	713	760	747	748	1,247	1,319	1,461	1,566
Pretax Inc.	11,534	11,757	9,040	9,027	8,587	7,813	5,155	-8,797	-9,026	121
Eff. Tax Rate	30%	34%	30%	33%	37%	47%	41%	NM	NM	566%
Net Inc.	8,093	7,712	6,328	6,093	5,429	4,178	3,021	-7,987	-6,865	-564
Balance Sheet & Other Fin. Data (Million $)										
Cash	3,722	5,831	5,768	7,553	8,137	7,701	10,554	7,133	5,649	5,151
Curr. Assets	43,880	43,155	42,360	40,418	40,695	40,691	41,338	39,202	39,692	40,969
Total Assets	88,349	87,495	86,100	81,499	81,132	80,292	81,091	81,113	86,705	92,473
Curr. Liab.	36,406	39,578	36,827	33,507	34,000	31,648	29,226	33,150	36,737	33,624
LT Debt	18,371	14,124	15,508	13,696	9,872	10,060	12,548	15,245	12,853	13,231
Common Eqty.	20,377	20,264	19,186	19,564	21,375	22,170	22,288	18,613	27,624	37,006
Total Cap.	38,995	35,989	36,455	34,999	33,127	34,290	37,842	36,786	42,507	52,164
Cap. Exp.	5,616	5,959	6,520	6,793	5,883	4,744	3,078	3,154	4,751	6,502
Cash Flow	12,586	13,851	10,783	10,091	9,085	8,133	7,134	-3,324	-2,072	4,385
Curr. Ratio	1.2	1.1	1.1	1.2	1.2	1.3	1.4	1.2	1.1	1.2
% LT Debt of Cap.	47.1	39.2	42.5	39.1	29.8	29.3	53.2	41.4	30.2	25.4
% Net Inc.of Revs.	9.2	8.8	7.7	7.8	7.2	5.8	4.7	NM	NM	NM
% Ret. on Assets	9.2	8.9	7.6	7.5	6.8	5.2	3.7	NM	NM	NM
% Ret. on Equity	39.7	39.0	32.7	29.8	24.9	18.5	14.3	NM	NM	NM

Data as orig reptd.; bef. results of disc opers/spec. items. Per share data adj. for stk. divs. Bold denotes diluted EPS (FASB 128)-prior periods restated. E-Estimated. NA-Not Available. NM-Not Meaningful. NR-Not Ranked.

Office—New Orchard Rd., Armonk, NY 10504. **Tel**—(914) 499-1900. **Website**—http://www.ibm.com **Chrmn & CEO**—L. V. Gerstner Jr. **Vice Chrmn**—J. M. Thompson. **Pres. & COO**—S. J. Palmisano. **SVP & General Counsel**—L. R. Ricciardi. **SVP & CFO**—J. R. Joyce. **VP & Secy**—D. E. O'Donnell. **Investor Contact**—H. Parke III. **Shareholder Relations Dept** —914-499-7777. **Dirs**—C. Black, K. I. Chenault, J. Dormann, L. V. Gerstner Jr., N. O. Keohane, C. F. Knight, M. Makihara, L. A. Noto, S. J. Palmisano, J. B. Slaughter, S. Taurel, J. M. Thompson, A. Trotman, L. C. van Wachem, C. M. Vest. **Transfer Agent & Registrar**—First Chicago Trust Co. of New York, Jersey City, NJ. **Incorporated**—in New York in 1911. **Empl**— 316,303. **S&P Analyst:** M. Graham-Hackett

STANDARD & POOR'S STOCK REPORTS

KLA-Tencor Corp.

Nasdaq Symbol **KLAC**

In S&P 500

18-AUG-01

Industry: Equipment (Semiconductor)

Summary: KLA-Tencor is the world's leading manufacturer of yield monitoring and process control systems for the semiconductor industry.

S&P Opinion: Buy (★★★★★)

Recent Price • 47.98 | Yield • Nil
52 Wk Range • 67.37-25.50 | 12-Mo. P/E • 24.9

Quantitative Evaluations

Outlook (1 Lowest—5 Highest) • **2–**

Fair Value • **51.30**

Risk • **Average**

Earn./Div. Rank • **B**

Technical Eval. • **Neutral** since 8/01

Rel. Strength Rank (1 Lowest—99 Highest) • **31**

Insider Activity • **Unfavorable**

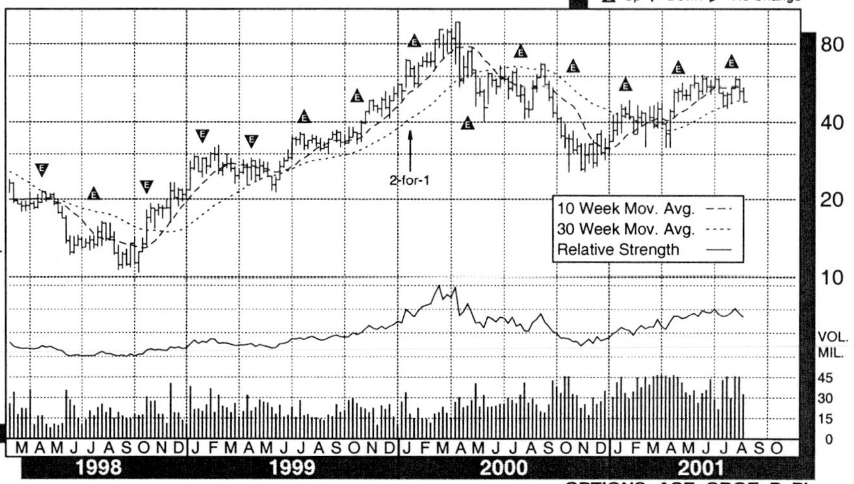

OPTIONS: ASE, CBOE, P, Ph

Overview - 01-AUG-01

We expect sales to decline about 6% in FY 02 (Jun.), based on newly adopted SAB 101 accounting rules that are more conservative in revenue recognition. The drop reflects a cyclical slowdown in the semiconductor equipment industry. In FY 03, we anticipate a rebound producing 17% sales growth. Chipmakers are presently spending little to add capacity, but continue to buy advanced tools to upgrade machinery for next-generation 300mm wafers, copper interconnect materials, and linewidths as small as 0.13 micron. KLAC introduced 19 new tool systems in FY 01. KLAC's reticle inspection and wafer inspection are considered by many customers to be a necessary part of the next-generation tool kit. Margins are expected to remain under pressure into 2002, despite the entry of new, higher margin products into the mix. We estimate FY 02 EPS (SAB 101 basis) at $1.60, with improvement to $2.00 in FY 03.

Valuation - 01-AUG-01

The shares of this leading semiconductor equipment company have risen from lows reached in late 2000, reflecting renewed investor interest in top-tier technology stocks. The company maintains a dominant position in yield monitoring and process control, and is benefiting as chipmakers convert their wafer fabrication plants to leading edge 0.13 micron technology. In the context of a cyclical industry downturn, KLAC's earnings and orders are faring well compared to those of many other equipment companies, based on the strength of its innovative yield management and process control systems. The shares were recently trading at 6X tangible book value, in line with valuations for peer companies. We believe the shares have room to rise further, in anticipation of the next industry upturn, and maintain our buy recommendation.

Key Stock Statistics

S&P EPS Est. 2002	1.60	Tang. Bk. Value/Share	9.20
P/E on S&P Est. 2002	30.0	Beta	2.42
S&P EPS Est. 2003	2.00	Shareholders	1,434
Dividend Rate/Share	Nil	Market cap. (B)	$ 8.9
Shs. outstg. (M)	185.4	Inst. holdings	79%
Avg. daily vol. (M)	8.056		

Value of $10,000 invested 5 years ago: $ 50,175

Fiscal Year Ending Jun. 30

	2001	2000	1999	1998	1997	1996
Revenues (Million $)						
1Q	534.6	273.0	205.2	312.4	261.1	149.1
2Q	573.1	330.8	193.4	326.4	242.2	165.8
3Q	528.8	413.0	210.9	274.2	252.3	187.5
4Q	602.6	482.1	233.6	253.4	276.2	192.6
Yr.	2,104	1,499	843.2	1,166	1,032	694.9
Earnings Per Share ($)						
1Q	**0.54**	**0.21**	**0.06**	**0.28**	**0.20**	0.26
2Q	**0.57**	**0.26**	**-0.10**	**0.29**	**0.20**	0.28
3Q	**0.48**	**0.38**	**0.11**	**0.17**	**0.21**	0.30
4Q	**0.67**	**0.47**	**0.14**	**0.02**	**0.01**	0.30
Yr.	**1.93**	**1.32**	**0.22**	**0.76**	**0.62**	**1.17**

Next earnings report expected: mid October

Dividend Data

No cash has been paid. A two-for-one stock split was effected in 1995.

KLA-Tencor Corporation

Business Summary - 01-AUG-01

KLA-Tencor (KLAC), formed via the April 1997 merger of two 20-year-old companies, KLA Instruments and Tencor Instruments, is the world's leading manufacturer of yield management and process monitoring systems for the semiconductor industry. Revenues rebounded to $1.50 billion in FY 00 (Jun.), from $0.84 billion in FY 99, reflecting an industrywide recovery from depressed conditions. KLAC maintained profitability during the down period, in contrast to losses posted by many other semiconductor equipment makers.

Maximizing yields, or the number of good die per wafer, is a key goal in manufacturing integrated circuits (ICs). Higher yields increase revenues obtained for each semiconductor wafer processed. As IC linewidths decrease, yields become more sensitive to the size and density of defects. KLAC's systems are used to improve yields by identifying defects, analyzing them to determine process problems, and, after corrective action has been taken, monitoring subsequent results to ensure that problems have been contained. Monitoring and analysis often take place at several points in the fabrication process, as wafers move through a production cycle consisting of hundreds of processing steps. With in-line systems, corrections can be made while the wafer is still in the production line, rather than waiting days for end-of-process testing and feedback.

The company's wafer inspection systems include unpatterned and patterned wafer inspection tools used to find, count and characterize particles and pattern defects on wafers both in engineering applications and in-line at various stages during the semiconductor manufacturing process. In July 2000, KLAC introduced the 2350, a new ultraviolet inspection system featuring ultra-broadband brightfield illumination that permits handling of defects at 0.13 micron design rules. It delivers a two-fold increase in throughput compared to previous generation 2100-series tools.

KLAC's 353UV Inspection System manages the quality of photomasks and reticles (used in copying circuit designs onto an IC during the photolithography process) throughout their useful lives. The TeraScan 570 tool, introduced in September 2000, provides a four-fold increase in throughput compared to the 300-series tools and can detect defects as small as 0.10 micron.

The film measurement division produces both film thickness and resistivity measurement tools. The company's metrology products measure the widths of circuit lines and the alignment of patterns from layer to layer in the process. The optical metrology product line is known as the 5000 series. KLAC introduced an electron-beam metrology system, the 8100 CD-SEM, in 1996. The 8300 CD-SEM (1999) extended the line to accommodate new generation 300 mm wafers.

KLAC sells systems to virtually all of the world's semiconductor manufacturers. In FY 00, international sales were 70% of the total, up from 60% in FY 99.

Per Share Data ($) (Year Ended Jun. 30)	2001	2000	1999	1998	1997	1996	1995	1994	1993	1992
Tangible Bk. Val.	NA	9.11	6.95	6.85	6.05	5.28	4.04	2.49	1.47	1.38
Cash Flow	NA	1.65	0.48	0.98	0.93	1.31	0.71	0.47	0.21	-0.08
Earnings	1.93	1.32	0.21	0.76	0.62	1.16	0.60	0.34	0.09	-0.23
Dividends	Nil	Nil	Nil	Nil	Nil	Nil	Nil	Nil	Nil	Nil
Payout Ratio	Nil	Nil	Nil	Nil	Nil	Nil	Nil	Nil	Nil	Nil
Prices - High	61.00	97.75	56.56	24.00	38.43	20.00	24.37	13.50	7.06	3.43
- Low	31.75	25.50	21.18	10.37	16.81	8.75	11.62	6.12	2.56	1.50
P/E Ratio - High	32	74	NM	32	62	17	41	40	81	NM
- Low	16	19	99	14	27	8	19	18	29	NM
Income Statement Analysis (Million $)										
Revs.	NA	1,499	843	1,166	1,032	695	442	244	167	156
Oper. Inc.	NA	370	80.6	226	259	194	118	50.8	20.4	5.3
Depr.	NA	63.3	48.2	38.9	52.3	16.3	10.6	10.7	9.6	10.7
Int. Exp.	NA	Nil	Nil	Nil	Nil	1.4	2.4	2.0	3.4	3.9
Pretax Inc.	NA	353	50.3	206	174	189	88.8	40.2	9.3	-16.3
Eff. Tax Rate	NA	28%	22%	35%	39%	36%	34%	25%	25%	NM
Net Inc.	NA	254	39.2	134	105	121	58.6	30.2	7.0	-16.6
Balance Sheet & Other Fin. Data (Million $)										
Cash	NA	844	696	216	349	124	119	139	52.4	23.7
Curr. Assets	NA	1,552	942	956	860	494	361	278	152	135
Total Assets	NA	2,204	1,585	1,548	1,343	713	546	322	199	188
Curr. Liab.	NA	495	352	351	325	169	133	66.0	58.0	50.8
LT Debt	NA	Nil	Nil	Nil	Nil	Nil	Nil	20.0	20.0	24.0
Common Eqty.	NA	1,709	1,233	1,198	1,015	537	404	227	114	103
Total Cap.	NA	1,709	1,233	1,198	1,019	544	413	256	141	138
Cap. Exp.	NA	78.7	56.8	64.4	56.8	39.1	19.0	5.8	3.2	5.1
Cash Flow	NA	317	87.4	173	158	137	69.3	40.9	16.6	-5.9
Curr. Ratio	NA	3.1	2.7	2.7	2.6	2.9	2.7	4.2	2.6	2.7
% LT Debt of Cap.	NA	Nil	Nil	Nil	Nil	NM	NM	7.8	14.2	17.4
% Net Inc.of Revs.	NA	16.9	4.7	11.5	10.2	17.5	13.2	12.3	4.2	NM
% Ret. on Assets	NA	13.4	2.5	9.3	11.5	19.2	13.5	11.5	3.5	NM
% Ret. on Equity	NA	17.3	3.2	12.1	15.3	25.7	18.5	17.6	6.3	NM

Data as orig reptd.; bef. results of disc opers/spec. items. Per share data adj. for stk. divs. Bold denotes diluted EPS (FASB 128)-prior periods restated. E-Estimated. NA-Not Available. NM-Not Meaningful. NR-Not Ranked.

Office—160 Rio Robles, San Jose, CA 95134. **Tel**—(408) 875-3000. **Website**—http://www.kla-tencor.com **Chrmn**—K. Levy. **Pres & CEO**—K. L. Schroeder. **CFO**—J. Kispert. **Secy**—L. W. Sonsini. **Dirs**—E. W. Barnholt, H. R. Bingham, R. T. Bond, R. J. Elkus Jr., K. Levy, D. O. Morton, K. L. Schroeder, J. D. Tompkins, L. Urbanek. **Transfer Agent & Registrar**—Boston Equiserve LLP. **Incorporated**—in Delaware in 1975. **Empl**— 6,578. **S&P Analyst:** T.W. Smith, CFA

STANDARD
&POOR'S
STOCK REPORTS

Linear Technology Corp.

Nasdaq Symbol **LLTC**

In S&P 500

18-AUG-01

Industry: Electronics (Semiconductors)

Summary: This rapidly growing company manufactures high-performance linear integrated circuits.

S&P Opinion: Buy (★★★★★)

Recent Price • 41.37
52 Wk Range • 74.12-32.68
Yield • 0.4%
12-Mo. P/E • 32.1

Quantitative Evaluations

Outlook (1 Lowest—5 Highest) • **1–**
Fair Value • **29.70**
Risk • **Average**
Earn./Div. Rank • **A**

Technical Eval. • **Neutral** since 8/01
Rel. Strength Rank (1 Lowest—99 Highest) • **31**
Insider Activity • **Neutral**

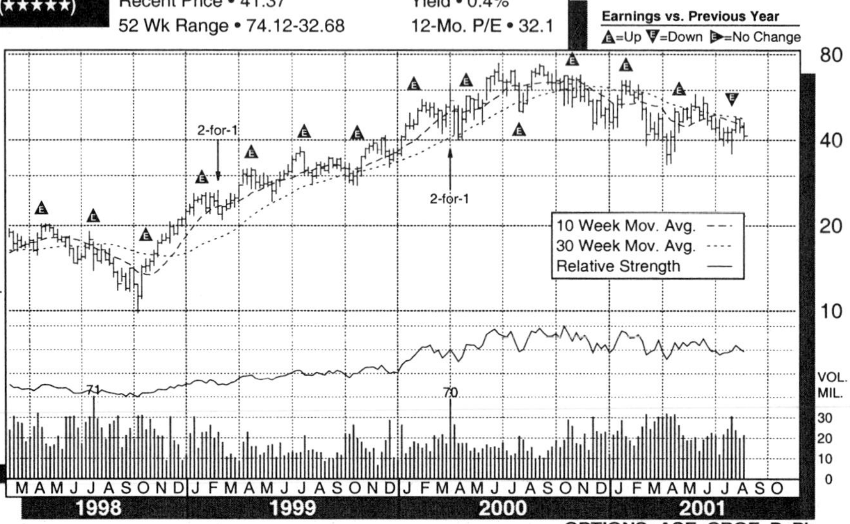

OPTIONS: ASE, CBOE, P, Ph

Overview - 31-JUL-01

Following two strong years, we expect sales to be down 36% in FY 02 (Jun.), reflecting a cyclical downturn in the semiconductor industry. We expect the industry to recover with the economy in FY 03, with LLTC's revenues rising about 50%. Bookings are very weak this summer for all products in all regions, but the heaviest period for order cancellations appears over. Communications markets account for about one third of total sales, with computer and industrial segments each accounting for one fourth. Cost saving measures are in place. Gross margin, which reached an industry leading 76.9% in the third quarter of FY 01, may narrow to 72% through the summer. Net margin may dip slightly below 40% at the nadir of the slowdown. The balance sheet is debt free, with ample cash assets. The quarterly dividend was recently boosted 33%. We estimate FY 02 EPS at $0.73, and see improvement to $1.20 in FY 03.

Valuation - 31-JUL-01

The shares of this leading analog chip maker are stabilizing after setting a 52-week low in April. The historical long-term rate of revenue growth for the cyclical semiconductor industry is near 17%. High-end analog makers like LLTC should exceed that pace. Although near-term order patterns have slowed, we expect orders to be rising by late 2001. We believe the company offers a good long-term outlook for revenue growth, combined with an exceptionally wide operating margin. LLTC has demonstrated smoother revenue and earnings growth than most other chipmakers. The shares trade at 45X our calendar 2002 EPS estimate of $1.00, and at 11X tangible book value, which represents a premium to the broader market, but in line with valuations for LLTC's peer group. The shares offer growth at a reasonable price for aggressive investors, and we maintain our buy recommendation.

Key Stock Statistics

S&P EPS Est. 2002	0.73	Tang. Bk. Value/Share	4.20
P/E on S&P Est. 2002	56.7	Beta	1.92
S&P EPS Est. 2003	1.20	Shareholders	1,448
Dividend Rate/Share	0.16	Market cap. (B)	$ 13.1
Shs. outstg. (M)	317.9	Inst. holdings	85%
Avg. daily vol. (M)	5.013		

Value of $10,000 invested 5 years ago: $ 52,967

Fiscal Year Ending Jun. 30

	2001	2000	1999	1998	1997	1996
Revenues (Million $)						
1Q	232.1	147.5	116.0	109.8	90.06	87.01
2Q	258.4	162.3	120.0	117.0	90.08	96.02
3Q	282.0	185.1	130.1	126.0	95.03	104.7
4Q	200.0	211.0	140.5	132.0	104.1	90.04
Yr.	972.6	705.9	506.7	484.8	379.3	377.8
Earnings Per Share ($)						
1Q	**0.31**	**0.18**	**0.14**	0.13	0.10	0.10
2Q	**0.34**	**0.20**	**0.15**	**0.14**	0.10	0.11
3Q	**0.38**	**0.23**	**0.15**	**0.15**	0.11	0.12
4Q	**0.26**	**0.27**	**0.17**	**0.15**	0.12	0.10
Yr.	**1.29**	**0.88**	**0.61**	**0.56**	**0.43**	0.43

Next earnings report expected: mid October

Dividend Data (Dividends have been paid since 1992.)

Amount ($)	Date Decl.	Ex-Div. Date	Stock of Record	Payment Date
0.030	Oct. 17	Oct. 25	Oct. 27	Nov. 15 '00
0.030	Jan. 16	Jan. 24	Jan. 26	Feb. 14 '01
0.040	Apr. 17	Apr. 25	Apr. 27	May. 16 '01
0.040	Jul. 24	Aug. 01	Aug. 03	Aug. 22 '01

Linear Technology Corporation

18-AUG-01

Business Summary - 31-JUL-01

Linear Technology Corp. (LLTC) has grown rapidly since incorporation in 1981. The company's annual revenues reached $100 million after 10 years of operations, and have since passed $700 million. LLTC designs, manufactures and markets a broad line of high-performance standard linear integrated circuits (ICs) that address a wide range of real-world signal processing applications. Real-world phenomena, such as temperature, pressure, sound, images, speed, acceleration, position and rotation, are specifically analog in nature, consisting of continuously varying information. Among the advantages offered by operating in the linear, as opposed to the digital, IC market, are smaller capital requirements, greater price stability and market diversity, and less Asian competition.

LLTC's products are used in a wide variety of applications, including telecommunications, notebook and desk-top PCs, computer peripherals, video/multimedia, cellular telephones and industrial. The company has expanded its customer base throughout its history. LLTC initially served primarily an industrial customer base, with a high percentage of revenues going to the military market. In the late 1980s and early 1990s, new products fueled substantial growth in the portable computer and hand-held device markets, and telecommunication and networking markets contributed to growth significantly in recent years.

The company's product line includes operational, instrumentation and audio amplifiers; voltage regulators, references, comparators and converters; switched-capacitor filters; communications interface circuits; one-chip data acquisition systems; pulse-width modulators and sample-and-hold devices.

LLTC is targeting the high-performance segments of the linear circuit market, which is characterized by higher precision, both high power or micropower, higher speed, more subsystem integration on a single chip and many other special features.

The company has wafer fabrication and manufacturing facilities in Milpitas, CA, and Camas, WA. In addition, it has built another wafer fabrication facility near Milpitas. LLTC also recently completed an addition to the Washington facility that doubled the production capacity there. The company operates test facilities in Singapore and Malaysia, and design facilities in Milpitas, CA, Boston, MA, Bedford, NH, Colorado Springs, CO, Raleigh, NC, and Singapore.

Sales by region broke down as follows in FY 00 (FY 99): North America 46% (46%), Europe 20% (24%), Asia Pacific and other 23% (18%), and Japan 11% (12%).

The company's backlog of released and firm orders was $298.4 million at July 2, 2000, well up from $89.4 million at June 27, 1999.

Per Share Data ($) (Year Ended Jun. 30)	2001	2000	1999	1998	1997	1996	1995	1994	1993	1992
Tangible Bk. Val.	NA	4.20	2.95	2.46	1.94	1.48	1.05	0.77	0.57	0.44
Cash Flow	NA	0.95	0.68	0.63	0.47	0.46	0.30	0.21	0.14	0.10
Earnings	1.29	0.88	0.61	0.56	0.43	0.43	0.28	0.19	0.12	0.09
Dividends	0.13	0.08	0.08	0.06	0.05	0.04	0.03	0.03	0.02	Nil
Payout Ratio	10%	9%	12%	11%	12%	9%	12%	15%	15%	Nil
Prices - High	65.12	74.75	41.59	22.62	18.75	12.56	11.40	6.43	4.93	3.18
- Low	32.68	35.06	20.87	9.78	10.12	5.43	5.75	4.56	2.59	1.96
P/E Ratio - High	50	85	68	40	44	29	41	34	40	37
- Low	25	40	34	17	24	13	21	24	21	21
Income Statement Analysis (Million $)										
Revs.	NA	706	507	485	379	378	265	201	151	119
Oper. Inc.	NA	399	280	268	201	201	129	88.2	58.6	40.1
Depr.	NA	25.0	22.0	20.1	12.4	10.2	8.6	6.3	5.8	4.5
Int. Exp.	NA	Nil	Nil	Nil	Nil	Nil	Nil	0.1	0.5	1.0
Pretax Inc.	NA	417	286	271	205	204	128	86.5	55.7	38.5
Eff. Tax Rate	NA	31%	32%	33%	34%	34%	34%	34%	35%	35%
Net Inc.	NA	288	194	181	134	134	84.6	56.8	36.4	25.0
Balance Sheet & Other Fin. Data (Million $)										
Cash	NA	230	787	638	443	322	250	177	128	95.3
Curr. Assets	NA	1,310	905	768	559	419	317	231	169	134
Total Assets	NA	1,507	1,047	893	680	530	368	268	196	160
Curr. Liab.	NA	169	125	123	89.0	86.3	56.0	42.9	32.4	33.5
LT Debt	NA	Nil	Nil	Nil	Nil	Nil	Nil	Nil	0.3	1.7
Common Eqty.	NA	1,322	907	756	589	440	309	223	163	124
Total Cap.	NA	1,339	922	770	591	443	312	225	164	126
Cap. Exp.	NA	80.3	39.1	24.4	21.9	70.0	22.0	16.2	7.6	9.8
Cash Flow	NA	313	216	201	147	144	93.2	63.2	42.2	29.6
Curr. Ratio	NA	7.8	7.2	6.2	6.3	4.9	5.7	5.4	5.2	4.0
% LT Debt of Cap.	NA	Nil	Nil	Nil	Nil	Nil	Nil	Nil	0.2	1.4
% Net Inc.of Revs.	NA	40.8	38.3	37.3	35.4	35.4	31.9	28.3	24.2	20.9
% Ret. on Assets	NA	22.5	20.0	23.0	22.2	29.8	26.6	24.3	20.3	17.5
% Ret. on Equity	NA	25.8	23.3	26.4	26.1	35.7	31.8	29.2	25.3	23.1

Data as orig reptd.; bef. results of disc opers/spec. items. Per share data adj. for stk. divs. Bold denotes diluted EPS (FASB 128)-prior periods restated. E-Estimated. NA-Not Available. NM-Not Meaningful. NR-Not Ranked.

Office—1630 McCarthy Blvd., Milpitas, CA 95035-7417. **Tel**—(408) 432-1900. **Fax**—(408) 434-6441. **Website**—http://www.linear.com **Chrmn & CEO**—R. H. Swanson Jr. **Pres**—C. B. Davies. **VP-Fin, CFO & Investor Contact**—Paul Coghlan. **Secy**—A. F. Schneiderman. **Dirs**—D. S. Lee, L. T. McCarthy, R. M. Moley, R. H. Swanson Jr., T. S. Volpe. **Transfer Agent & Registrar**—BankBoston, N.A. **Incorporated**—in California in 1981. **Empl**— 2,815. **S&P Analyst:** T. W. Smith, CFA

Mercury Interactive

Nasdaq Symbol **MERQ**

In S&P 500

18-AUG-01 **Industry:** Computer (Software & Services)

Summary: This company develops, markets and supports a family of automated testing and monitoring solutions for business-critical enterprise and web applications.

S&P Opinion: Buy (★★★★★)

Recent Price • 31.44 | 52 Wk Range • 162.50-30.60 | Yield • Nil | 12-Mo. P/E • 38.8

Quantitative Evaluations

Outlook (1 Lowest—5 Highest) • **4-**

Fair Value • **39.60**

Risk • **High**

Earn./Div. Rank • **NR**

Technical Eval. • **Bearish** since 7/01

Rel. Strength Rank (1 Lowest—99 Highest) • **8**

Insider Activity • **Unfavorable**

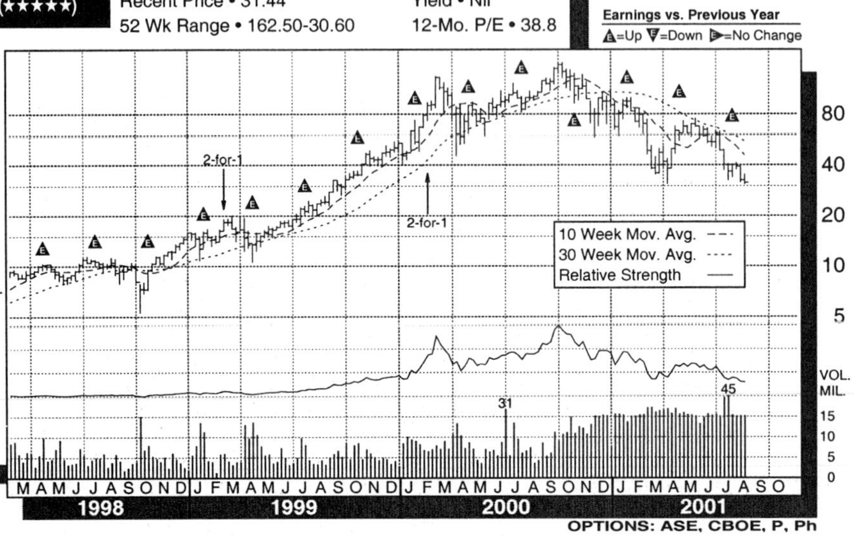

OPTIONS: ASE, CBOE, P, Ph

Overview - 24-JUL-01

Following discussions with management in mid-July that suggested that global IT spending would remain cautious through the end of the year, S&P expects 2001 revenues to rise to $398 to $402 million. This projection for 2001 revenues to increase about 30% is less than the 40% growth we forecast earlier this year, as well as the 36% we had been expecting just prior to these discussions. Operating margins will narrow slightly from the level of 2000, to about 20%. Interest income will likely be about $0.02 a share less each quarter than we had previously expected, due to lower available yields on fixed income investments. We estimate that EPS will advance 11% in 2001, to $0.78, from $0.70 in 2000. We project revenue growth of 37% to 39% for 2002, with a 32% increase in EPS to $1.03.

Valuation - 24-JUL-01

S&P is maintaining its buy opinion on MERQ. The stock has been volatile in 2001, trading in a range of $30 to $101. This volatility is attributable to the market's changing views of how to value high growth stocks such as MERQ amid general economic weakness and, particularly, a poor market for IT spending. MERQ has been able to meet growth expectations, so we like the company based on fundamentals. However, the shares tend to trade higher quickly and become overvalued when technology sector sentiment turns positive, but also to decline and become undervalued when pessimism is widespread. Since late June, the pessimistic view has been gaining, pressuring the shares toward the low end of 2001's wide trading range, and substantially below the $49 to $51 level that we view as appropriate, based on discounted cash flow analysis using our updated financial projections.

Key Stock Statistics

S&P EPS Est. 2001	0.77	Tang. Bk. Value/Share	3.57
P/E on S&P Est. 2001	40.8	Beta	1.29
S&P EPS Est. 2002	1.05	Shareholders	64,500
Dividend Rate/Share	Nil	Market cap. (B)	$ 2.6
Shs. outstg. (M)	82.6	Inst. holdings	89%
Avg. daily vol. (M)	3.310		

Value of $10,000 invested 5 years ago: $ 91,461

Fiscal Year Ending Dec. 31

	2001	2000	1999	1998	1997	1996
Revenues (Million $)						
1Q	90.70	60.40	37.60	22.20	15.40	11.00
2Q	96.00	69.60	42.50	27.20	17.50	12.10
3Q	—	79.50	47.50	30.60	19.60	14.20
4Q	—	97.50	60.10	41.00	24.20	17.25
Yr.	—	307.0	187.7	121.0	76.70	54.55
Earnings Per Share ($)						
1Q	**0.18**	**0.11**	**0.07**	**0.04**	**0.03**	**-0.01**
2Q	**0.18**	**0.14**	**0.09**	**0.05**	**0.03**	**0.01**
3Q	—	**0.18**	**0.15**	**0.07**	**-0.04**	**0.02**
4Q	—	**0.28**	**0.15**	**0.12**	**0.07**	**0.05**
Yr.	—	**0.70**	**0.39**	**0.28**	**0.10**	**0.07**

Next earnings report expected: mid October

Dividend Data

No cash dividends have been paid. The company intends to retain earnings for use in its business and does not expect to pay cash dividends in the foreseeable future. A stockholder rights plan was adopted in July 1996. The shares were split two for one in 1999 and in 2000.

Mercury Interactive Corporation

Business Summary - 24-JUL-01

Mercury Interactive Corp. is the leading provider of integrated performance management solutions that enable businesses to test and monitor their Web-based applications. MERQ's products allow corporate development organizations, system integrators and independent software developers to identify website performance problems with greater accuracy, speed and efficiency than traditional methods allow. The company is committed to its research and development efforts to help it carry out its strategy of offering advanced and innovative testing solutions for evolving business needs. Research and development expenses rose 36% in 2000, to $32.0 million, from $23.5 million in 1999.

Mercury's performance management solutions allow website developers to more quickly identify and correct problems before users experience them. Products can be categorized into four types: load testing, functional testing, test process management, and web performance monitoring.

Testing solutions include Astra LoadTest and LoadRunner. Astra LoadTest tests the scalability and performance of web applications by emulating the traffic of thousands of real users to identify and isolate bottlenecks. LoadRunner identifies and isolates performance problems across an enterprise's entire information infrastructure. This enables organizations to minimize testing cycles, optimize performance and accelerate application development.

Functional testing solutions include Astra QuickTest, WinRunner and XRunner. Astra QuickTest is an icon-based tool for recording and representing website user actions in a changing environment. WinRunner verifies that applications on the Windows platform work as expected. XRunner automates testing of X-Window-based applications.

Test Management and Monitoring solutions include Astra SiteManager for website testing management, TestDirector for enterprise testing management, and Topaz, a 24x7 performance monitoring solution.

In 1999, the company began offering organizations an alternative to product licensing with its LoadRunner ActiveTest hosting load testing service. In 2000, Mercury introduced ActiveWatch, a hosted performance monitoring service. As of early 2001, the company's hosted services were being provided to more than 400 customers.

Mercury markets its products through its direct sales and service organization, which focuses on major accounts, and indirectly through systems integrator and valued added resellers. The company has recently begun targeting indirect sales through private-labeling arrangements with application service providers. Representative customers include BMW, Citibank, Microsoft, Oracle, Siemens, Verizon and Wal Mart. International sales accounted for 32%, 34% and 35% of total revenues in 2000, 1999 and 1998, respectively.

Per Share Data ($) (Year Ended Dec. 31)	2000	1999	1998	1997	1996	1995	1994	1993	1992	1991
Tangible Bk. Val.	3.57	2.56	1.99	1.69	1.54	1.47	0.77	0.66	-1.09	NA
Cash Flow	0.81	0.46	0.33	0.15	0.12	-0.06	0.12	0.04	-0.33	NA
Earnings	0.70	0.39	0.28	0.10	0.07	-0.10	0.10	0.03	-0.38	NA
Dividends	Nil	Nil	Nil	Nil	Nil	Nil	Nil	Nil	Nil	NA
Payout Ratio	Nil	Nil	Nil	Nil	Nil	Nil	Nil	Nil	Nil	NA
Prices - High	162.50	55.12	15.81	7.03	6.00	7.25	5.43	5.75	NA	NA
- Low	40.12	10.50	5.28	2.37	2.37	2.93	1.75	3.25	NA	NA
P/E Ratio - High	NM	NM	56	NM	86	NM	57	NM	NA	NA
- Low	NM	NM	19	NM	34	NM	18	NA	NA	NA
Income Statement Analysis (Million $)										
Revs.	307	188	121	76.7	54.6	39.5	23.5	13.0	4.3	NA
Oper. Inc.	73.0	44.0	26.8	10.3	6.1	-4.3	5.8	1.8	-3.0	NA
Depr.	9.6	6.1	4.1	3.7	3.3	2.2	1.2	0.6	0.4	NA
Int. Exp.	12.8	Nil	Nil	Nil	Nil	Nil	0.0	0.1	0.0	NA
Pretax Inc.	80.9	42.0	27.3	9.6	5.8	-4.3	5.9	1.4	-3.3	NA
Eff. Tax Rate	20%	21%	20%	30%	20%	NM	15%	3.90%	Nil	NA
Net Inc.	64.7	33.1	21.8	6.7	4.6	-5.3	5.0	1.4	-3.3	NA
Balance Sheet & Other Fin. Data (Million $)										
Cash	226	113	96.1	57.2	71.0	77.8	33.3	33.7	6.3	NA
Curr. Assets	726	235	154	119	96.5	95.7	44.1	39.4	9.3	NA
Total Assets	976	297	204	143	117	113	49.6	41.7	11.1	NA
Curr. Liab.	173	97.7	58.0	30.4	18.5	20.2	10.4	8.2	4.8	NA
LT Debt	500	Nil	Nil	Nil	Nil	Nil	Nil	0.4	0.5	NA
Common Eqty.	303	200	146	113	99	92.6	39.2	33.0	-7.0	NA
Total Cap.	803	200	146	113	99	92.6	39.2	33.4	6.2	NA
Cap. Exp.	45.6	23.9	14.9	11.8	4.6	7.0	3.2	1.3	0.9	NA
Cash Flow	74.3	39.2	25.9	10.4	7.9	3.1	6.2	2.0	-2.9	NA
Curr. Ratio	4.2	2.4	2.6	3.9	5.2	4.7	4.2	4.8	1.9	NA
% LT Debt of Cap.	62.3	Nil	Nil	Nil	Nil	Nil	Nil	1.3	7.7	NA
% Net Inc.of Revs.	21.1	17.7	18.0	8.7	8.5	NM	21.5	10.5	NM	NA
% Ret. on Assets	10.2	13.2	12.6	5.1	4.0	NM	10.9	2.1	NM	NA
% Ret. on Equity	25.7	19.2	16.9	6.3	4.8	NM	13.8	NM	NM	NA

Data as orig reptd.; bef. results of disc opers/spec. items. Per share data adj. for stk. divs. Bold denotes diluted EPS (FASB 128)-prior periods restated. E-Estimated. NA-Not Available. NM-Not Meaningful. NR-Not Ranked.

Office—1325 Borregas Ave., Sunnyvale, CA 94089. **Tel**—(408) 822-5200. **Fax**—(408) 523-9911. **Website**—http://www.merc-int.com **Chrmn, Pres & CEO**—A. Landan. **COO**—K. Klein. **VP-Fin, & CFO**—S. Abrams. **Investor Contact**—Anne Marie McCauley (408-822-5359). **Dirs**—K. Klein, I. Kohavi, A. Landan, Y. Shamir, G. Yaron. **Transfer Agent & Registrar**—Mellon Investor Services, SF. **Incorporated**—in Delaware in 1989. **Empl**—1,418. **S&P Analyst:** Mark S. Basham

STANDARD &POOR'S
STOCK REPORTS

Roxio, Inc.

Nasdaq Symbol **ROXI**

In S&P SmallCap 600

23-AUG-01

Industry: Computer (Software & Services)

Summary: ROXI provides digital content management software solutions which enable individuals to personalize and store music, photos, video and data onto recordable compact discs (CDs).

S&P Opinion: Buy (★★★★★)

Recent Price • 12.50
52 Wk Range • 17-9.60
Yield • Nil
12-Mo. P/E • 59.5

Quantitative Evaluations

Outlook
(1 Lowest—5 Highest)
• **NA**

Fair Value
• **NA**

Risk
• **NA**

Earn./Div. Rank
• **NR**

Technical Eval.
• **NA**

Rel. Strength Rank
(1 Lowest—99 Highest)
• **62**

Insider Activity
• **NA**

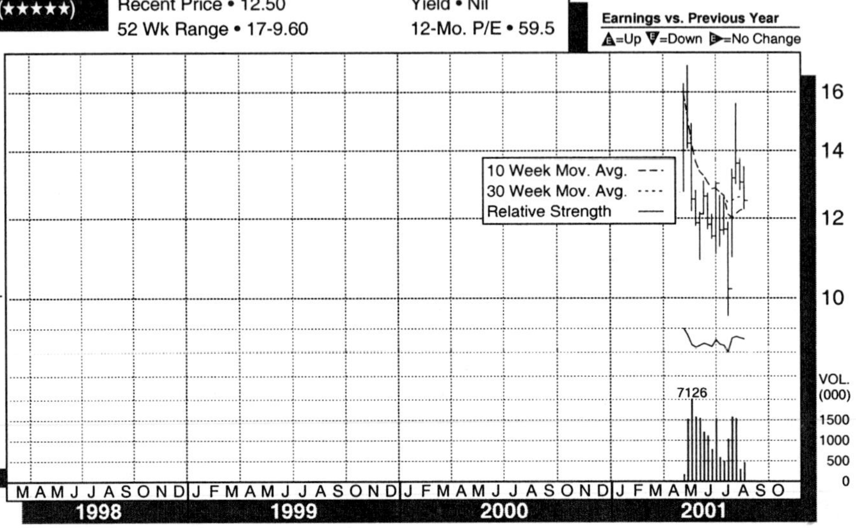

Overview - 23-AUG-01

We forecast revenue growth of 10% in FY 02 (Mar.) and 12% in FY 03. Revenue growth is currently being aided by ROXI's successful release of its Easy CD Creator software in the retail channel, as well as continued licensing of CD burning software by OEMs. Due to the increased level of retail sales in the company's revenue mix, we expect gross margin to narrow to 76.7% in FY 03 from our estimate of 79.5% in FY 02. We project operating margins approximating 4.6% in FY 02, expanding to 11.9% in FY 03, reflecting tight cost controls, balanced by continued R&D investments and lower stock-based compensation charges. Our FY 02 EPS estimate is $0.72, before an $0.08 one-time gain, and we project $1.03 for FY 03 (both before amortization of goodwill and stock-based compensation; including these items, we project FY 02 EPS of $0.42, and $0.83 for FY 03).

Valuation - 23-AUG-01

We initiated coverage of ROXI with a buy recommendation. The company is the leading maker of CD burning software, sales of which are currently benefiting from increased demand from consumers to manage new digital content being made available. Based on our discounted cash flow analysis, we estimate the intrinsic value of ROXI shares at $17-$18 per share, presenting opportunity for further appreciation. In addition, the shares are attractively priced on a price to sales basis (less than 2 -- a 60% discount to the average for software stocks). On a price to earnings basis, the shares are trading at a discount to the overall market, based on our calendar 2002 estimate of $0.62. However, we caution investors that we view investment in the shares as presenting higher than normal risk, with earnings highly dependent on successful new product introductions.

Key Stock Statistics

S&P EPS Est. 2002	0.72	Tang. Bk. Value/Share	0.85
P/E on S&P Est. 2002	17.4	Beta	NA
Dividend Rate/Share	Nil	Shareholders	NA
Shs. outstg. (M)	16.5	Market cap. (B)	$0.215
Avg. daily vol. (M)	0.183	Inst. holdings	52%

Value of $10,000 invested 5 years ago: NA

Fiscal Year Ending Mar. 31

	2002	2001	2000	1999	1998	1997
Revenues (Million $)						
1Q	36.95	—	—	—	—	—
2Q	—	—	—	—	—	—
3Q	—	—	—	—	—	—
4Q	—	—	—	—	—	—
Yr.	—	121.9	84.00	—	—	—
Earnings Per Share ($)						
1Q	**0.14**	—	—	—	—	—
2Q	—	—	—	—	—	—
3Q	—	—	—	—	—	—
4Q	—	—	—	—	—	—
Yr.	—	**0.22**	**-0.01**	—	—	—

Next earnings report expected: NA

Dividend Data

No cash dividends have been paid. The company currently intends to retain all available funds and any future earnings for use in the operation and expansion of its business and it does not anticipate paying any cash dividends for the foreseeable future.

Business Summary - 23-AUG-01

The leading provider of CD burning digital media software, Roxio was spun off from Adaptec, Inc., in May 2001. The company derives the majority of its sales from selling its CD recording software products to two customer bases: to original equipment manufacturers (OEMs, which include PC and CD recordable drive makers as well as integrators), and to distributors. Distributors resell the stand-alone deluxe versions of Roxio's products to retailers. While the mix of ROXI's sales in FY 01 (Mar.) was 59% from OEMs and 41% from distributors and direct sales, in the first quarter of FY 02, the mix reversed, with retail sales accounting for 59% of the company's revenues.

ROXI expects retail and direct sales to increase as a percentage of total revenues, as it expands its marketing efforts for its deluxe products. While this should dampen gross margins, ROXI's increased brand awareness through its successful retail penetration should drive software upgrade opportunities.

ROXI's software enables users to create, manage and move digital content, including music, photos, video and data, onto recordable CDs. ROXI offers two principal product families -- Easy CD Creator for Windows, and Toast for Macintosh. The company also plans to introduce a product for consumers for recording digital content on DVDs in 2001.

In 2000, ROXI's software was bundled with about 24 million CD recorders; the company believes this represented about 70% of the CD recorders shipped in 2000. In 2001, the forecast for the installed base of CD recorders is expected to reach 100 million.

In addition to its digital media software, the company also markets GoBack, a system recovery software product that allows PC users to quickly recover from system crashes, virus attacks, failed software installations and data loss. By working in the background to continuously keep an up-to-date record of a PC's hard drive, GoBack returns the hard drive to its former state, saving the user from having to periodically back up the drive.

The standard version of Easy CD Creator can be used to store any type of file on a CD, including presentations, photos, videos or data. Other features include the ability to create custom audio CDs from an existing CD collection and to convert an MP3 track to CD audio while playing the track.

ROXI's latest version of Easy CD Creator, Deluxe 5.0, provides an easier interface and better functionality for recording MP3s and digital photos.

The company also includes CD recording software with limited functionality in Microsoft Media Player 7 and RealNetworks RealJukebox, offering an upgrade to a full-featured version. ROXI also has an agreement with Microsoft to provide basic CD burning functionality for Windows XP (to be launched October 2001).

Per Share Data ($) **(Year Ended Mar. 31)**	**2001**	**2000**	**1999**	**1998**	**1997**	**1996**	**1995**	**1994**	**1993**	**1992**
Tangible Bk. Val.	0.85	NA	NA	NA	NA	NA	NA	NA	NA	NA
Cash Flow	1.22	0.52	NA	NA	NA	NA	NA	NA	NA	NA
Earnings	0.22	-0.01	NA	NA	NA	NA	NA	NA	NA	NA
Dividends	NA	Nil	NA	NA	NA	NA	NA	NA	NA	NA
Payout Ratio	NA	Nil	NA	NA	NA	NA	NA	NA	NA	NA
Cal. Yrs.	2000	1999	1998	1997	1996	1995	1994	1993	1992	1991
Prices - High	NA	NA	NA	NA	NA	NA	NA	NA	NA	NA
- Low	NA	NA	NA	NA	NA	NA	NA	NA	NA	NA
P/E Ratio - High	NA	NM	NA	NA	NA	NA	NA	NA	NA	NA
- Low	NA	NM	NA	NA	NA	NA	NA	NA	NA	NA
Income Statement Analysis (Million $)										
Revs.	122	84.0	NA	NA	NA	NA	NA	NA	NA	NA
Oper. Inc.	26.0	17.4	NA	NA	NA	NA	NA	NA	NA	NA
Depr.	16.6	16.7	NA	NA	NA	NA	NA	NA	NA	NA
Int. Exp.	Nil	Nil	NA	NA	NA	NA	NA	NA	NA	NA
Pretax Inc.	9.5	1.3	NA	NA	NA	NA	NA	NA	NA	NA
Eff. Tax Rate	62%	71%	NA	NA	NA	NA	NA	NA	NA	NA
Net Inc.	3.6	0.4	NA	NA	NA	NA	NA	NA	NA	NA
Balance Sheet & Other Fin. Data (Million $)										
Cash	Nil	37.5	NA	NA	NA	NA	NA	NA	NA	NA
Curr. Assets	38.2	NA	NA	NA	NA	NA	NA	NA	NA	NA
Total Assets	66.2	98.0	NA	NA	NA	NA	NA	NA	NA	NA
Curr. Liab.	23.3	NA	NA	NA	NA	NA	NA	NA	NA	NA
LT Debt	Nil	Nil	NA	NA	NA	NA	NA	NA	NA	NA
Common Eqty.	40.6	80.5	NA	NA	NA	NA	NA	NA	NA	NA
Total Cap.	42.9	80.5	NA	NA	NA	NA	NA	NA	NA	NA
Cap. Exp.	1.3	NA	NA	NA	NA	NA	NA	NA	NA	NA
Cash Flow	20.1	17.1	NA	NA	NA	NA	NA	NA	NA	NA
Curr. Ratio	1.6	NA	NA	NA	NA	NA	NA	NA	NA	NA
% LT Debt of Cap.	Nil	Nil	NA	NA	NA	NA	NA	NA	NA	NA
% Net Inc.of Revs.	2.9	0.4	NA	NA	NA	NA	NA	NA	NA	NA
% Ret. on Assets	5.8	NA	NA	NA	NA	NA	NA	NA	NA	NA
% Ret. on Equity	8.4	NA	NA	NA	NA	NA	NA	NA	NA	NA

Data as orig reptd.; bef. results of disc opers/spec. items. Pro forma data in 2000; bal. sh. as of Dec. 31, 2000. Per share data adj. for stk. divs. Bold denotes diluted EPS (FASB 128)-prior periods restated. E-Estimated. NA-Not Available. NM-Not Meaningful. NR-Not Ranked.

Office—461 South Milpitas Blvd., Milpitas, CA 95035. **Tel**—(408) 945-8600. **Website**—http://www.roxio.com **Pres & CEO**—W. C. Gorog. **SVP & COO**—T. J. Shea. **VP & CFO**—R. E. Carpenter. **Dirs**—R. J. Boyko, W. C. Gorog, J. C. Kaczorowski, R. Rodin. **Transfer Agent & Registrar**—Mellon Investor Services. **Incorporated**—in Delaware in 2000. **Empl**— 250. **S&P Analyst:** M. Graham-Hackett

STANDARD
&POOR'S
STOCK REPORTS

Symantec Corp.

Nasdaq Symbol **SYMC**

In S&P MidCap 400

18-AUG-01

Industry: Computer (Software & Services)

Summary: Symantec provides content security solutions, including antivirus software.

S&P Opinion: Buy (★★★★★)

Recent Price • 42.99
52 Wk Range • 73.50-27.37
Yield • Nil
12-Mo. P/E • NM

Quantitative Evaluations

Outlook
(1 Lowest—5 Highest)
• **5**

Fair Value
• **88.60**

Risk
• **High**

Earn./Div. Rank
• **B-**

Technical Eval.
• **Neutral** since 7/01

Rel. Strength Rank
(1 Lowest—99 Highest)
• **23**

Insider Activity
• **Unfavorable**

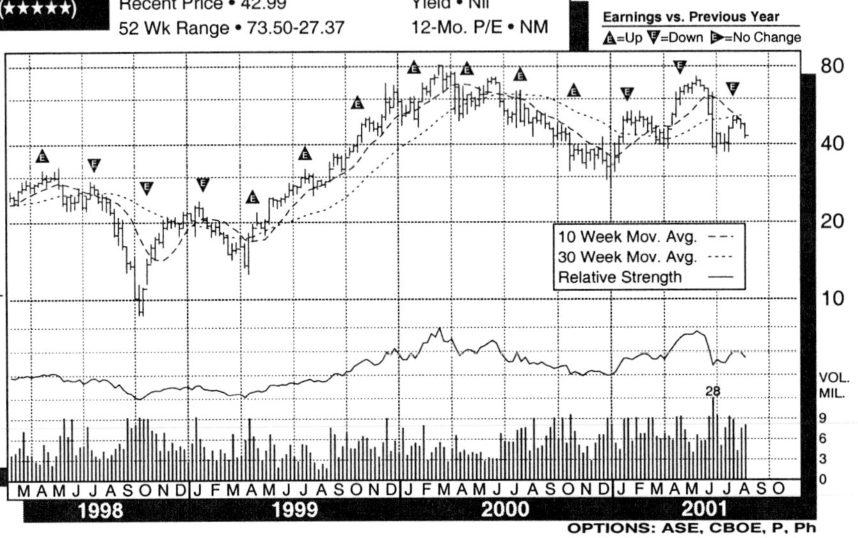

OPTIONS: ASE, CBOE, P, Ph

Overview - 15-AUG-01

Revenues should increase approximately 14% in FY 02 (Mar.). Comparisons will benefit from SYMC's recent acquisition of AXENT Technologies, as well as from the company's push into the enterprise market, adding to its traditional focus on the retail market. Enterprise business will continue to grow rapidly, helped by SYMC's agreements with IBM and Intel, as well as by other partnerships. On the retail side, despite intense competitive pressures, the company still managed to increase its revenues and add to its leading market share in recent quarters. SYMC has several new products in the pipeline, and this should further boost revenues. We expect operating margins to narrow slightly in FY 02 and, despite some near-term dilution from the AXENT acquisition, anticipate that EPS will climb in the low single digits in FY 02, from FY 01's $2.35 (excluding one-time items and goodwill amortization).

Valuation - 15-AUG-01

The shares have rebounded in 2001, following a disappointing 2000. SYMC has executed better than expected on its recent acquisition of AXENT Technologies. The company has also maintained its leadership in antivirus software, and dominates the market for mobile, remote, and telecommuting software. New products should contribute to solid revenue growth. SYMC's new products include Norton Internet Security software. In the retail market, we expect sales to benefit from high profile virus outbreaks, which create added awareness regarding antivirus software. Longer-term revenue growth should accelerate to the 25% range with AXENT included. Using a discount rate of approximately 15% in our discounted cash flow model, we arrive at an intrinsic value for SYMC of approximately $65-$70. Thus, with the stock at a significant discount to its intrinsic value, we recommend purchasing shares of SYMC.

Key Stock Statistics

S&P EPS Est. 2002	2.40	Tang. Bk. Value/Share	7.76
P/E on S&P Est. 2002	17.9	Beta	1.83
S&P EPS Est. 2003	2.88	Shareholders	663
Dividend Rate/Share	Nil	Market cap. (B)	$ 3.2
Shs. outstg. (M)	73.9	Inst. holdings	74%
Avg. daily vol. (M)	1.420		

Value of $10,000 invested 5 years ago: $ 41,942

Fiscal Year Ending Mar. 31

	2002	2001	2000	1999	1998	1997
Revenues (Million $)						
1Q	228.0	191.4	175.1	137.8	135.0	109.2
2Q	—	192.3	182.5	130.0	139.0	109.2
3Q	—	219.3	200.8	155.2	148.2	124.1
4Q	—	250.6	187.2	169.6	156.1	129.7
Yr.	—	853.5	745.7	592.6	578.4	472.2
Earnings Per Share ($)						
1Q	**-0.29**	**0.60**	**0.41**	**0.13**	**0.32**	**0.06**
2Q	—	**0.61**	**0.43**	**0.03**	**0.35**	**0.02**
3Q	—	**0.21**	**1.41**	**0.28**	**0.37**	**0.25**
4Q	—	**-0.37**	**0.49**	**0.43**	**0.40**	**0.15**
Yr.	—	**0.94**	**2.73**	**0.86**	**1.42**	**0.47**

Next earnings report expected: mid October

Dividend Data

No cash dividends have been paid.

STANDARD
&POOR'S
STOCK REPORTS

Symantec Corporation

18-AUG-01

Business Summary - 15-AUG-01

Symantec, a world leader in Internet security technology, provides a broad range of content and network security solutions to individuals and enterprises. SYMC is a leading provider of virus protection, firewall, virtual private network, vulnerability management, intrusion detection, remote management technologies and security services to consumers and enterprises around the world.

Symantec is organized in five operating segments: Consumer Products, Enterprise Security, Enterprise Administration, Services, and Other.

The Consumer Products segment accounted for 39% of total net revenues in FY 01 (Mar.). The segment's charter is to ensure that consumers and their information are secure and protected in a connected world. Primary product lines include Norton AntiVirus software for the protection, detection and elimination of computer viruses; and Norton Internet Security, a fully integrated suite that provides total Internet protection for the home computer. Others include Norton SystemWorks, Norton Utilities, and Norton CleanSweep.

The Enterprise Security and Administration segments represented approximately 60% of total net revenues in FY 01. The objective of the Enterprise Security segment is to provide a broad range of security solutions for SYMC's enterprise customers. This segment focuses on two areas: content and network security. The Enterprise Administration segment offers products that enable companies to be more effective and efficient within their IT (Information Technology) departments. Products include pcAnywhere and Ghost Corporate Edition.

The Services division provides fee-based technical support and consulting services to enterprise customers to assist them with the planning, design and implementation of enterprise security solutions in the anti-virus and Internet content filtering technologies.

The other business segment is comprised of sunset products, products nearing the end of their life cycle, and operations from the ACT! and Visual Cafe product lines, which were divested on December 31, 1999. SYMC received $75 million in cash for the Visual Cafe product line and approximately $20 million of unregistered common stock from Interact Commerce Corp. for the assets of ACT! and a four-year license of ACT! technology.

International revenues accounted for 45% of the total in FY 01, versus 41% in FY 00.

SYMC has acquired 23 companies since its initial public offering in 1989. In December 2000, SYMC acquired AXENT Technologies in a stock transaction valued at approximately $975 million. SYMC issued approximately 15 million shares to complete the transaction.

Per Share Data ($)										
(Year Ended Mar. 31)	**2001**	**2000**	**1999**	**1998**	**1997**	**1996**	**1995**	**1994**	**1993**	**1992**
Tangible Bk. Val.	7.76	8.87	4.75	5.56	3.93	3.35	2.77	2.23	2.91	3.35
Cash Flow	1.41	3.42	1.25	1.83	0.06	-0.38	1.12	Nil	-0.05	0.98
Earnings	0.68	2.73	0.86	1.42	0.47	-0.76	0.77	-0.37	-0.49	0.77
Dividends	Nil	Nil	Nil	Nil	Nil	Nil	Nil	Nil	Nil	Nil
Payout Ratio	Nil	Nil	Nil	Nil	Nil	Nil	Nil	Nil	Nil	Nil
Cal. Yrs.	2000	1999	1998	1997	1996	1995	1994	1993	1992	1991
Prices - High	81.62	69.31	32.62	27.75	23.12	33.25	19.62	20.50	51.00	44.75
- Low	27.37	12.50	8.68	12.00	8.75	16.12	9.87	9.25	5.87	13.00
P/E Ratio - High	NM	25	38	20	49	NM	25	NM	NM	46
- Low	NM	5	10	8	19	NM	13	NM	NM	13
Income Statement Analysis (Million $)										
Revs.	854	746	593	578	472	445	335	268	206	217
Oper. Inc.	291	191	90.0	126	57.6	-0.9	60.0	30.2	4.6	40.2
Depr.	32.0	42.9	24.0	25.2	22.7	19.7	13.3	11.1	10.4	5.2
Int. Exp.	Nil	0.0	1.8	1.2	1.4	1.5	2.4	2.3	NA	0.5
Pretax Inc.	141	257	83.2	112	30.3	-44.3	38.3	-16.0	-17.2	28.8
Eff. Tax Rate	55%	34%	40%	24%	14%	NM	26%	NM	NM	35%
Net Inc.	63.9	170	50.2	85.1	26.0	-39.7	28.5	-11.1	-11.5	18.7
Balance Sheet & Other Fin. Data (Million $)										
Cash	557	432	193	226	160	129	105	51.5	53.3	31.9
Curr. Assets	782	546	316	329	238	237	180	120	110	95.7
Total Assets	1,792	846	563	476	342	298	221	158	142	123
Curr. Liab.	413	227	217	153	109	102	84.5	52.7	45.9	45.5
LT Debt	2.4	1.6	1.5	6.0	15.0	15.5	25.4	25.6	26.2	1.6
Common Eqty.	1,377	619	345	318	218	180	111	80.1	69.6	75.6
Total Cap.	1,379	620	347	323	233	196	137	106	95.8	77.3
Cap. Exp.	61.2	28.5	25.1	26.3	27.1	35.8	17.7	7.3	15.4	12.7
Cash Flow	95.9	213	74.2	110	48.8	-20.0	41.8	-0.1	-1.1	23.9
Curr. Ratio	1.9	2.4	1.5	2.1	2.2	2.3	2.1	2.3	2.4	2.1
% LT Debt of Cap.	0.2	0.3	2.1	1.8	6.4	7.9	18.6	24.2	27.4	2.1
% Net Inc.of Revs.	7.5	22.8	8.5	14.7	5.5	NM	8.5	NM	NM	8.6
% Ret. on Assets	4.8	24.1	9.7	20.8	8.2	NM	13.9	NM	NM	18.8
% Ret. on Equity	6.4	35.3	15.2	31.8	13.0	NM	32.5	NM	NM	30.4

Data as orig reptd.; bef. results of disc opers/spec. items. Per share data adj. for stk. divs. Bold denotes diluted EPS (FASB 128)-prior periods restated. E-Estimated. NA-Not Available. NM-Not Meaningful. NR-Not Ranked.

Office—20330 Stevens Creek Blvd., Cupertino, CA 95014-2132. **Tel**—(408) 253-9600. **Website**—http://www.symantec.com **Chrmn, Pres & CEO**—J. W. Thompson. **SVP & CFO**—G. Myers. **Investor Contact**—Helyn Corcos (408-446-8891). **Dirs**—T. Amochaev, C. M. Boesenberg, P. K. Halvorsen, R. S. Miller, B. Owens, G. Reyes, D. H. Schulman, J. W. Thompson. **Transfer Agent**—Bank of Boston. **Incorporated**—in Delaware in 1988. **Empl**— 3,800. **S&P Analyst:** Jonathan Rudy

STANDARD
&POOR'S
STOCK REPORTS

Texas Instruments

NYSE Symbol **TXN**

In S&P 500

18-AUG-01 **Industry:** Electronics (Semiconductors)

Summary: One of the world's largest manufacturers of semiconductors, Texas Instruments also produces digital products.

S&P Opinion: Buy (★★★★★)

Recent Price • 33.14
52 Wk Range • 70.75-26.26
Yield • 0.3%
12-Mo. P/E • 43.0

Quantitative Evaluations

Outlook
(1 Lowest—5 Highest)
• 1-

Fair Value
• 18.40

Risk
• **Average**

Earn./Div. Rank
• **B+**

Technical Eval.
• **Bullish** since 8/01

Rel. Strength Rank
(1 Lowest—99 Highest)
• **45**

Insider Activity
• **Neutral**

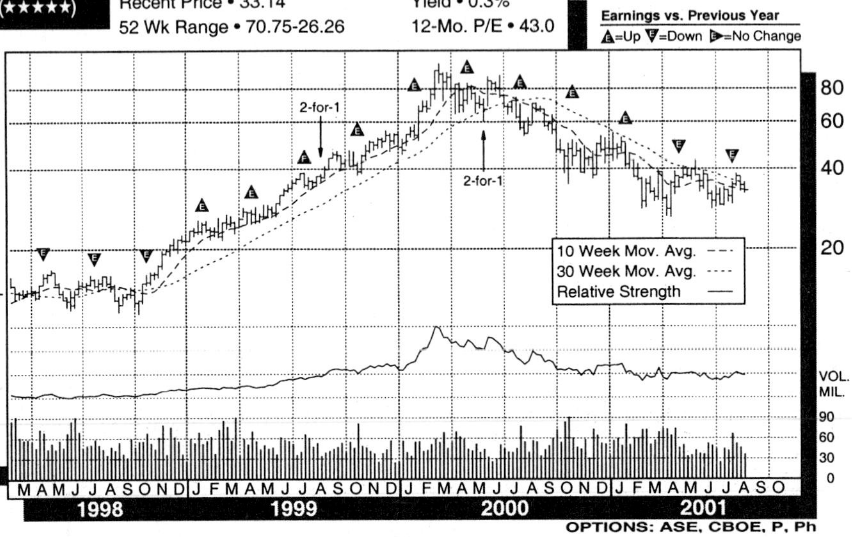

OPTIONS: ASE, CBOE, P, Ph

Overview - 02-AUG-01

We expect revenues to fall nearly 30% in 2001, and then to rise 17% in 2002, reflecting a slowdown in end markets for semiconductors and subsequent recovery. TXN's wireless segment, which had been the most negatively affected, saw orders start to increase in the second quarter. In addition, the rate of decline in semiconductor orders slowed, suggesting that a cycle bottom is being reached. Cost controls include layoffs of about 15% of the manufacturing work force. TXN has recently focused on the market for DSP solutions. The August 2000 acquisition of Burr-Brown Corp. added capacity and expertise in making high-end analog chips that are complementary to TXN's DSP chips. Operating margins will remain under pressure through 2001, reflecting lower revenues. We expect 2001 EPS (before charges) to drop to $0.13, from $1.22 in 2000. We forecast a rebound to $0.40 in 2002.

Valuation - 02-AUG-01

The shares are recovering from a low set in April 2001 and retested in July. Markets for wireless handsets and other electronics goods have softened with the economy in 2001. We expect revenue in the third quarter to be down 15% from the second quarter level, with growth resuming in late 2001, as the economy picks up. In the long run, TXN should prosper in the cyclical semiconductor industry. It has a commanding share (about 45%) of the digital signal processing (DSP) market; DSPs have a broad base of applications, primarily in communications. We believe the company's focus on DSP and analog will pay off as portable computing and communications markets grow. The shares were recently trading at 5.4X tangible book value, in line with peer companies. We believe a cyclical upturn for chipmakers is sufficiently near to raise our recommendation on TXN to buy, from hold.

Key Stock Statistics

S&P EPS Est. 2001	0.13	Tang. Bk. Value/Share	6.82
P/E on S&P Est. 2001	NM	Beta	1.77
S&P EPS Est. 2002	0.40	Shareholders	30,043
Dividend Rate/Share	0.09	Market cap. (B)	$ 57.5
Shs. outstg. (M)	1734.6	Inst. holdings	62%
Avg. daily vol. (M)	9.950		

Value of $10,000 invested 5 years ago: $ 60,596

Fiscal Year Ending Dec. 31

	2001	2000	1999	1998	1997	1996
Revenues (Million $)						
1Q	2,528	2,653	2,039	2,187	2,263	2,675
2Q	2,037	2,843	2,346	2,167	2,559	2,399
3Q	—	3,160	2,385	2,113	2,500	2,407
4Q	—	3,033	2,554	1,993	2,428	2,459
Yr.	—	11,875	9,468	8,460	9,750	9,940
Earnings Per Share ($)						
1Q	**0.13**	**0.25**	**0.14**	**0.01**	**0.07**	0.09
2Q	**-0.11**	**0.75**	**0.20**	**0.03**	**0.14**	0.03
3Q	—	**0.38**	**0.23**	**0.10**	**0.15**	-0.12
4Q	—	**0.37**	**0.26**	**0.12**	**-0.17**	-0.03
Yr.	—	**1.73**	**0.84**	**0.26**	**0.19**	**-0.03**

Next earnings report expected: mid October

Dividend Data (Dividends have been paid since 1962.)

Amount ($)	Date Decl.	Ex-Div. Date	Stock of Record	Payment Date
0.021	Oct. 19	Oct. 27	Oct. 31	Nov. 20 '00
0.021	Jan. 18	Jan. 29	Jan. 31	Feb. 12 '01
0.021	Apr. 18	Apr. 26	Apr. 30	May. 21 '01
0.021	Jul. 19	Jul. 27	Jul. 31	Aug. 20 '01

Texas Instruments Incorporated

Business Summary - 02-AUG-01

Texas Instruments is one of the world's top semiconductor and electronics companies, with design, sales or manufacturing operations in more than 28 countries. The company has increasingly concentrated on digital signal processors (DSPs) and analog integrated circuits. Semiconductors went from less than 60% of revenue in 1996 to 87% in 2000.

DSP and analog product lines are largely complementary. These chips work together to enable electronic devices to benefit from digitization of electronic signals. Analog technology converts "real-world" signals such as sound, light, and pressure into the "zeros and ones" of the digital world. DSP chips can then process the signal information in real time. Analog chips also convert the signal back to analog format.

The company believes the DSP market will grow dramatically in size in the next few years, driven by strong demand for devices such as wireless phones, modems, and computer networking gear. TXN also believes the increased use of digital components in embedded systems in automobiles, home appliances and manufacturing equipment will enhance market opportunities. Revenue from DSPs rose 29% in 2000; revenue from analog chips grew 28%. Together, these two categories represented 65% of TXN's 2000 semiconductor revenue; other chip products include standard logic, ASICs, RISC microprocessors, microcontrollers and digital imaging devices.

TXN's focused DSP strategy required multi-year restructuring. In 1997, the company sold its defense electronics business to Raytheon Co. In 1998, TXN sold its struggling dynamic random access memory (DRAM) operations to Micron Technology. In 2000, TXN acquired Toccata Technology, a developer of digital-audio amplifier technology; Dot Wireless, developer of CDMA third-generation wireless technology; Alantro Communications, a developer of wireless local area networking technology; and, most notably, Burr-Brown Corp., a high-end analog chip maker with expertise in data converters and amplifiers.

The company's semiconductor products are used in a wide variety of applications. Customers include original equipment manufacturers, contract manufacturers and distributors. In 2000, the top five customers represented 28% of semiconductor revenues. About 73% of sales were made outside the U.S. in 2000.

In addition to semiconductors, the company has two other principal segments. The Sensors & Controls (formerly Materials & Controls) segment (9% of 2000 sales) sells electrical and electronic controls, sensors, and radio frequency identification systems to the commercial and industrial market. The Educational & Productivity Solutions unit (4% of 2000 sales) is a leading supplier of educational and graphing calculators.

Per Share Data ($) (Year Ended Dec. 31)	2000	1999	1998	1997	1996	1995	1994	1993	1992	1991
Tangible Bk. Val.	6.71	5.38	4.18	3.79	2.69	2.70	2.05	1.59	1.11	1.02
Cash Flow	2.49	1.47	0.97	0.89	0.56	1.19	0.89	0.72	0.60	0.11
Earnings	1.73	0.84	0.26	0.19	-0.03	0.70	0.45	0.32	0.16	-0.34
Dividends	0.09	0.09	0.09	0.09	0.09	0.08	0.06	0.05	0.05	0.05
Payout Ratio	5%	10%	33%	45%	NM	11%	13%	14%	28%	NM
Prices - High	99.78	55.75	22.60	17.81	8.54	10.46	5.59	5.26	3.26	2.97
- Low	35.00	21.50	10.06	7.76	5.06	4.29	3.81	2.85	1.87	1.62
P/E Ratio - High	58	66	89	94	NM	15	12	17	21	NM
- Low	20	26	39	41	NM	6	8	9	12	NM
Income Statement Analysis (Million $)										
Revs.	11,875	9,468	8,460	9,750	9,940	13,128	10,315	8,523	7,440	6,784
Oper. Inc.	3,715	2,751	1,543	1,724	878	2,350	1,748	1,345	1,030	341
Depr.	1,376	1,055	1,144	1,109	904	756	665	617	610	590
Int. Exp.	75.0	75.0	75.0	94.0	108	69.0	58.0	55.0	57.0	59.0
Pretax Inc.	4,578	2,019	617	713	-23.0	1,619	1,042	696	369	-304
Eff. Tax Rate	33%	30%	34%	58%	NM	33%	34%	32%	33%	NM
Net Inc.	3,087	1,406	407	302	-46.0	1,088	691	476	247	-409
Balance Sheet & Other Fin. Data (Million $)										
Cash	745	662	540	1,015	978	1,553	1,290	888	859	601
Curr. Assets	8,115	6,055	4,846	6,103	4,454	5,518	4,017	3,314	2,626	2,381
Total Assets	17,720	15,028	11,250	10,849	9,360	9,215	6,989	5,993	5,185	5,009
Curr. Liab.	2,813	2,628	2,196	2,496	2,486	3,188	2,199	2,001	1,665	1,568
LT Debt	1,216	1,097	1,027	1,286	1,697	804	808	694	909	896
Common Eqty.	12,588	9,255	6,527	5,914	4,097	4,095	3,039	2,315	1,473	1,335
Total Cap.	14,273	11,346	7,935	7,200	5,794	4,899	3,847	3,009	2,856	2,851
Cap. Exp.	2,762	1,373	1,031	1,238	2,063	1,439	1,076	730	429	504
Cash Flow	4,463	2,461	1,551	1,411	858	1,844	1,356	1,073	820	147
Curr. Ratio	2.9	2.3	2.2	2.4	1.8	1.7	1.8	1.7	1.6	1.5
% LT Debt of Cap.	8.5	9.7	12.9	17.9	29.3	16.4	21.0	23.1	31.8	31.4
% Net Inc.of Revs.	26.0	14.8	4.8	3.1	NM	8.3	6.7	5.6	3.3	NM
% Ret. on Assets	18.6	10.6	3.7	3.0	NM	13.4	10.5	8.1	4.8	NM
% Ret. on Equity	27.9	17.6	6.5	6.0	NM	30.5	25.6	23.2	14.9	NM

Data as orig reptd.; bef. results of disc opers/spec. items. Per share data adj. for stk. divs. Bold denotes diluted EPS (FASB 128)-prior periods restated. E-Estimated. NA-Not Available. NM-Not Meaningful. NR-Not Ranked.

Office—12500 TI Boulevard, P.O. Box 660199, Dallas, TX 75266-0199. **Tel**—(972) 995-3773. **Website**—http://www.ti.com **Chrmn, Pres & CEO**—T. J. Engibous. **EVP & COO**—R. Templeton. **SVP, Treas & CFO**—W. A. Aylesworth. **SVP & Secy**—J. F. Hubach. **SVP & Investor Contact**—Terri West (214-480-5030). **Dirs**—J. R. Adams, D. L. Boren, J. B. Busey IV, D. A. Carp, T. J. Engibous, G. W. Fronterhouse, D. R. Goode, W. R. Sanders, R. J. Simmons. **Transfer Agent & Registrar**—ComputerShare Investor Services, L.L.C., Chicago. **Incorporated**—in Delaware in 1938. **Empl**— 42,481. **S&P Analyst:** T. W. Smith, CFA

STANDARD &POOR'S
STOCK REPORTS

Xilinx, Inc.

Nasdaq Symbol **XLNX**

In S&P 500

18-AUG-01

Industry: Electronics (Semiconductors)

Summary: Xilinx is the world's leading supplier of programmable logic chips and related development system software.

S&P Opinion: Buy (★★★★★)

Recent Price • 37.53 | 52 Wk Range • 92.50-29.79 | Yield • Nil | 12-Mo. P/E • NM

Quantitative Evaluations

Outlook (1 Lowest—5 Highest)
• **1-**

Fair Value
• **24.60**

Risk
• **Average**

Earn./Div. Rank
• **B**

Technical Eval.
• **Bearish** since 8/01

Rel. Strength Rank (1 Lowest—99 Highest)
• **31**

Insider Activity
• **Unfavorable**

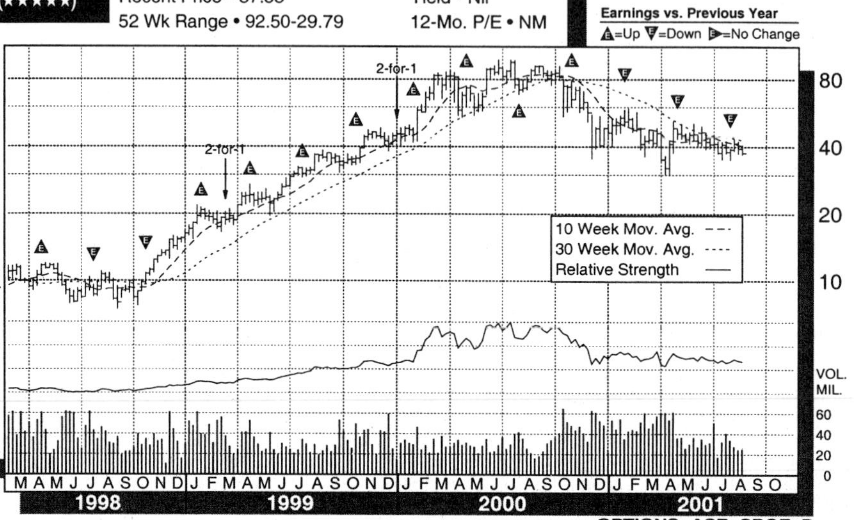

OPTIONS: ASE, CBOE, P

Overview - 14-AUG-01

Sales should decrease over 40% in FY 02 (Mar.), and then rise over 20% in FY 03, reflecting the current downturn in the semiconductor industry, followed by an expected cyclical recovery. Revenues might dip as much as 20% to 25% in the second quarter of FY 02 from the level of the first quarter, as large chip inventories continue to be used up. Demand for the company's chips for use in telecommunications and data processing equipment should pick up in 2002, as the economy strengthens. Gross margin is likely to average 54% in FY 02, below historical norms that are near 60%. Customer satisfaction with the advanced Virtex-II and Spartan product lines remains strong. We expect operating margins to narrow until mid-FY 02. Overall, we expect EPS (EBG basis, excluding goodwill, acquisition and other charges) to dip to $0.25 in FY 02, from FY 01's $1.08. We see $0.55 (EBG basis) for FY 03.

Valuation - 14-AUG-01

The shares of this chipmaker are stabilizing after setting a 52-week low in early April 2001. Surging end-market demand for telecommunications chips in 2000 has slowed sharply in 2001. Results will be muted until chip inventories at customers are used up; we expect this to occur by mid-2002. In the long-run, the high-end programmable logic device (PLD) market remains a high-growth segment, and we believe XLNX can deliver core EPS growth well in excess of the chip industry's historical 17% annual growth rate. The shares recently traded at 73X our FY 03 EPS estimate of $0.55 (EBG basis), a premium to XLNX's projected long-term growth rate of 27%, but in line with peer company valuations. Despite near-term earnings weakness, we expect this market-share leader in PLDs to outperform in the next industry upturn, and recommend purchase.

Key Stock Statistics

S&P EPS Est. 2002	0.25	Tang. Bk. Value/Share	5.82
P/E on S&P Est. 2002	NM	Beta	1.90
S&P EPS Est. 2003	0.55	Shareholders	940
Dividend Rate/Share	Nil	Market cap. (B)	$ 12.5
Shs. outstg. (M)	332.6	Inst. holdings	77%
Avg. daily vol. (M)	5.461		

Value of $10,000 invested 5 years ago: $ 40,688

Fiscal Year Ending Mar. 31

	2002	2001	2000	1999	1998	1997
Revenues (Million $)						
1Q	289.3	364.9	211.4	151.6	160.8	150.2
2Q	—	437.4	238.8	156.4	150.3	130.6
3Q	—	450.1	264.3	167.4	148.7	135.6
4Q	—	407.0	306.6	184.3	153.8	151.7
Yr.	—	1,659	1,021	662.0	613.6	568.1
Earnings Per Share ($)						
1Q	**0.05**	**0.27**	**0.15**	**0.09**	0.10	0.10
2Q	—	**0.32**	**0.17**	**0.09**	0.10	0.07
3Q	—	**-0.03**	**0.20**	**0.11**	**0.10**	0.08
4Q	—	**-0.49**	**1.36**	**0.12**	**0.10**	0.10
Yr.	—	**0.10**	**1.90**	**0.42**	**0.40**	**0.35**

Next earnings report expected: mid October

Dividend Data

No cash dividends have been paid, and Xilinx does not expect to pay any in the foreseeable future. A three-for-one stock split was effected in 1995.

A Division of The McGraw-Hill Companies

Xilinx, Inc.

Business Summary - 14-AUG-01

Founded in 1984, Xilinx is the leading supplier of programmable logic devices. These devices, commonly known as PLD chips, include field programmable gate arrays (FPGAs) and complex programmable logic devices (CPLDs). They are standard integrated circuits that are programmed by customers to perform desired logic operations. They provide high levels of integration, and create significant time and cost savings for electronic equipment manufacturers in the telecommunications, networking, computing and industrial markets.

While FPGAs account for the vast majority of XLNX's sales, the company also derives revenue from development and system software tools, and field engineering support. In FY 01 (Mar.), revenues were derived 62% from the U.S. (67% in FY 00), 20% (20%) from Europe, 10% (8%) from Japan, and 8% (5%) from Southeast Asia and other regions.

XLNX's FPGAs are proprietary integrated circuits designed by the company; they provide a unique combination of the high logic density usually associated with custom gate arrays, the time-to-market advantages of programmable logic and the availability of a standard product. XLNX has several product families, including the XC4000, Coolrunner, Spartan and Virtex lines. The Virtex-II product line, introduced in January 2001, offers very high-density chips of up to 10 million gates, used in applications that include optical networks, storage area networks, voice-over-Internet-protocol, video broadcasting, medical imaging, cellular base stations, and Internet infrastructure products.

Company products are classified as base, mainstream, advanced and support. Base products are manufactured using older 0.6-micron linewidth technology and accounted for only 6% of FY 01 sales (12% in FY 00). Mainstream products, produced using 0.50- and 0.35-micron processes, accounted for 35% of FY 01 revenues (53%). Advanced products are made with 0.25-micron and smaller technologies, and provided 51% of FY 01 sales (27%). Support products contributed nearly 8% of FY 01 sales (8%).

As a fabless semiconductor maker, XLNX does not directly manufacture wafers for its products. Instead, it contracts for wafer production from chip foundries, including United Microelectronics Corp. (UMC) in Taiwan and Seiko Epson Corp. in Japan. The company had invested $107 million in a manufacturing joint venture with UMC, known as United Silicon. In January 2000, XLNX converted its equity position in United Silicon into 222 million UMC shares (2%), creating a capital gain of $674 million ($398 million, after tax).

Revenue by end-market as of the fourth quarter of FY 01 was divided: 79% communications, 13% storage and servers, and 8% other.

Per Share Data ($) (Year Ended Mar. 31)	2001	2000	1999	1998	1997	1996	1995	1994	1993	1992
Tangible Bk. Val.	5.82	5.68	2.81	1.89	1.67	1.28	0.87	0.63	0.46	0.39
Cash Flow	0.36	2.03	0.52	0.50	0.43	0.39	0.24	0.18	0.13	0.09
Earnings	0.10	1.90	0.42	0.40	0.35	0.32	0.20	0.14	0.10	0.07
Dividends	Nil	Nil	Nil	Nil	Nil	Nil	Nil	Nil	Nil	Nil
Payout Ratio	Nil	Nil	Nil	Nil	Nil	Nil	Nil	Nil	Nil	Nil
Cal. Yrs.	2000	1999	1998	1997	1996	1995	1994	1993	1992	1991
Prices - High	98.31	48.56	16.75	14.62	11.62	13.87	5.16	4.54	2.58	2.70
- Low	35.25	15.31	7.43	7.12	6.12	4.52	2.41	1.95	1.20	1.04
P/E Ratio - High	NM	26	40	37	33	43	26	32	27	37
- Low	NM	8	18	18	18	14	12	14	13	14
Income Statement Analysis (Million $)										
Revs.	1,659	1,021	662	614	568	561	355	256	178	136
Oper. Inc.	586	371	214	207	192	208	107	76.0	50.2	39.2
Depr.	93.5	44.2	32.1	32.7	28.0	22.5	12.2	10.8	8.6	5.6
Int. Exp.	0.2	Nil	11.9	13.9	14.6	5.6	10.3	0.5	0.7	0.7
Pretax Inc.	61.1	1,030	184	183	166	171	94.8	67.4	43.6	33.8
Eff. Tax Rate	42%	37%	30%	31%	33%	41%	38%	39%	38%	37%
Net Inc.	35.3	652	129	127	110	102	59.3	41.3	27.2	21.3
Balance Sheet & Other Fin. Data (Million $)										
Cash	209	85.5	53.6	167	216	378	123	116	84.8	81.3
Curr. Assets	1,102	1,041	658	600	602	539	256	194	137	121
Total Assets	2,502	2,349	1,070	941	848	721	321	226	163	147
Curr. Liab.	350	245	167	126	97.3	103	76.1	51.1	35.7	33.0
LT Debt	Nil	Nil	Nil	250	250	250	0.9	2.2	3.9	5.0
Common Eqty.	1,918	1,777	879	550	491	368	244	173	123	109
Total Cap.	2,152	2,104	903	816	751	618	245	175	127	114
Cap. Exp.	223	144	40.9	29.7	26.8	60.5	26.2	12.3	9.8	7.2
Cash Flow	129	697	161	159	138	124	71.5	52.1	35.9	26.8
Curr. Ratio	3.1	4.3	3.9	4.8	6.2	5.2	3.4	3.8	3.8	3.7
% LT Debt of Cap.	Nil	Nil	Nil	30.6	33.3	40.4	0.4	1.3	3.1	4.4
% Net Inc.of Revs.	2.1	63.9	19.5	20.6	19.4	18.1	16.7	16.0	15.3	15.7
% Ret. on Assets	1.5	38.2	12.8	14.2	14.1	19.5	21.5	21.0	17.6	16.4
% Ret. on Equity	1.9	49.1	18.1	24.3	25.7	33.1	28.2	27.0	23.5	22.0

Data as orig reptd.; bef. results of disc opers/spec. items. Per share data adj. for stk. divs. Bold denotes diluted EPS (FASB 128)-prior periods restated. E-Estimated. NA-Not Available. NM-Not Meaningful. NR-Not Ranked.

Office—2100 Logic Dr., San Jose, CA 95124. **Tel**—(408) 559-7778. **Website**—http://www.xilinx.com **Chrmn**—B. V. Vonderschmitt. **Pres & CEO**—W. P. Roelandts. **SVP-Fin & CFO**—K. Chellam. **Secy**—T. R. Lavelle. **Investor Contact**—Maria Quillard (408-879-4988). **Dirs**—J. L. Doyle, J. G. Fishman, P. T. Gianos, W. G. Howard Jr., W. P. Roelandts, F. S. Sanda, D. L. Segers, R. W. Sevcik, E. Vanderslice, B. V. Vonderschmitt. **Transfer Agent & Registrar**—Equiserve, Boston. **Incorporated**—Organized in California in 1984; reincorporated in Delaware in 1990. **Empl**—2,678. **S&P Analyst:** T. W. Smith, CFA

STANDARD
&POOR'S
STOCK REPORTS

Amphenol Corp.

NYSE Symbol **APH**

18-AUG-01

Industry:
Electrical Equipment

Summary: Amphenol manufactures connectors, cable and interconnect systems for electronics, cable TV, telecommunications, aerospace, transportation and industrial applications.

S&P Opinion: Accumulate (★★★★)

Recent Price • 41.10 | Yield • Nil
52 Wk Range • 68.75-28.30 | 12-Mo. P/E • 15.7

Quantitative Evaluations

Outlook
(1 Lowest—5 Highest)
• **4**

Fair Value
• **55.30**

Risk
• **Average**

Earn./Div. Rank
• **B+**

Technical Eval.
• **Bullish** since 8/01

Rel. Strength Rank
(1 Lowest—99 Highest)
• **42**

Insider Activity
• **NA**

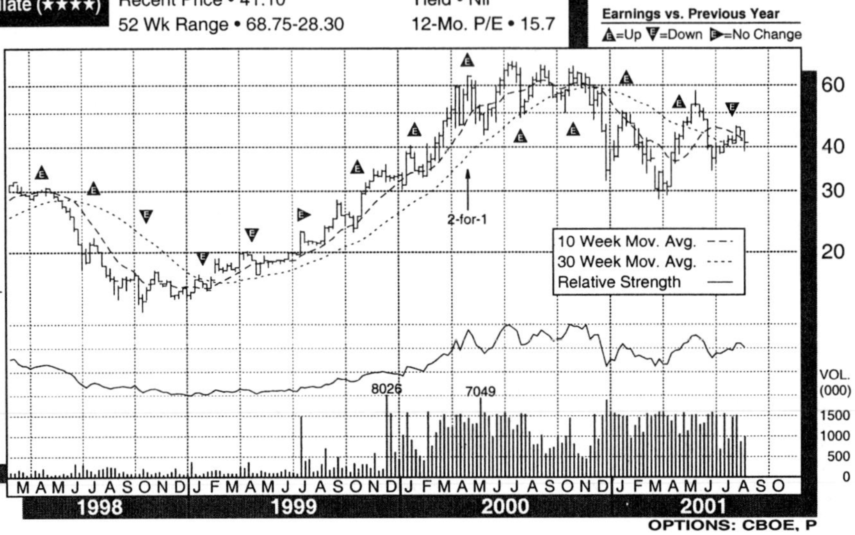

OPTIONS: CBOE, P

Overview - 02-AUG-01

Sales should fall some 15% in 2001, and seem likely to be little changed in 2002. Our 2001 forecast reflects a downturn in capital spending by communications customers, on drastic moderation in the U.S. economy and the reluctance of lenders to finance communications expenditures. We expect a steep decline in coaxial cable sales, and a high-single-digit drop in connector sales, as lower sales to communications customers outweigh increased sales to aerospace and industrial markets. Yet, with the domestic economy likely to firm and customer inventory reductions seeming near an end, we expect sequential sales gains in 2002. However, we do not see any major rebound during the year, with sales unlikely to match 2001's first quarter level. Margins should widen slightly in both years, on cost reduction measures and lower interest charges, as APH continues to reduce long term debt. Our 2002 forecast excludes benefits of about $0.33 under new accounting rules related to goodwill amortization.

Valuation - 02-AUG-01

The shares fell sharply from late 2000 through 2001's first quarter, as the exceptional growth seen in communications markets in recent years ended abruptly. They have since been trying to rebound, on a more positive economic outlook. It now appears that Amphenol's business will bottom over the last half of the year, but we do not expect a quick recovery. However, we think APH's long-term prospects remain solid, as greater build-out of the global communications infrastructure should take place. We thus expect Amphenol to record normalized long-term EPS growth of about 15%. With the shares recently trading at the lower end of their traditional P/E multiple range, we find APH undervalued. However, our forecast of a slow business recovery would limit the aggressiveness of our purchases.

Key Stock Statistics

S&P EPS Est. 2001	2.20	Tang. Bk. Value/Share	NM
P/E on S&P Est. 2001	18.7	Beta	1.44
S&P EPS Est. 2002	2.30	Shareholders	99
Dividend Rate/Share	Nil	Market cap. (B)	$ 1.7
Shs. outstg. (M)	41.7	Inst. holdings	43%
Avg. daily vol. (M)	0.240		

Value of $10,000 invested 5 years ago: $ 44,134

Fiscal Year Ending Dec. 31

	2001	2000	1999	1998	1997	1996
Revenues (Million $)						
1Q	316.7	300.1	237.2	228.5	211.8	194.8
2Q	274.1	335.5	247.4	227.9	227.0	198.9
3Q	—	354.7	256.9	229.0	223.5	184.9
4Q	—	369.4	269.1	233.4	222.1	197.6
Yr.	—	1,360	1,011	918.9	884.4	776.2
Earnings Per Share ($)						
1Q	**0.67**	**0.48**	**0.23**	**0.27**	**0.20**	**0.18**
2Q	**0.53**	**0.61**	**0.29**	**0.29**	**0.24**	**0.18**
3Q	**E0.46**	**0.67**	**0.32**	**0.23**	**0.24**	**0.18**
4Q	**E0.54**	**0.76**	**0.37**	**0.23**	**0.27**	**0.18**
Yr.	**E2.20**	**2.52**	**1.21**	**1.01**	**0.92**	**0.72**

Next earnings report expected: mid October

Dividend Data

No dividends have been paid.

Amphenol Corporation

Business Summary - 02-AUG-01

Amphenol makes fiber optic, electronic and electrical connectors, interconnect systems, and coaxial and flat ribbon cable. The company has adopted a strategy of focusing on optimizing its mix of higher-margin, higher-growth application specific products in its product offerings and maintaining continuing programs of productivity improvement. During 2000, Amphenol derived 65% of its revenues from communications markets, 20% from industrial and the remaining 15% from commercial and military aerospace.

APH makes a broad range of interconnect products and assemblies (74% of 2000 revenues) for voice, video and data communications systems, commercial and military aerospace systems, automotive and mass transportation applications, and industrial and factory automation equipment. Products include connectors, which facilitate electronic or fiber optic transmission.

In the communications area, the company supplies connector products for smart card acceptor devices used in mobile GSM telephones, cable modems and other applications to facilitate reading data from smart cards; fiber optic couplers used in fiber optic transmissions; input/output connectors used for linking PCs and peripheral equipment; and sculptured flexible circuits used for integrating circuit boards.

APH also makes a range of radio frequency connector products used in telecommunications, computer and office equipment, instrumentation equipment and local area networks. Radio frequency connectors are used in base stations, hand held sets and other components of cellular and personal communication networks.

APH's cable operations accounted for 26% of revenues in 2000. The Times Fiber subsidiary is the world's second largest producer of coaxial cable for the cable TV market. In the U.S., cable is sold in two forms: semi-flexible (primary trunk and feeder transmission cable for cable TV systems); and flexible (hook-ups from the feeder cable to the subscriber's residence). Coaxial cable for the international market is sold in 60 countries through a network of distributors and agents. International cable TV penetration is low; it is estimated that 31%, 29% and 16% of European, Asian and Latin American households, respectively, subscribe to cable TV service, versus 68% in the U.S.

The company also makes flat-ribbon cable, which is used to connect internal components in systems with space and component configuration limitations. The product is used in computer and office equipment components as well as in a variety of telecommunications applications.

International sales accounted for 49% of the 2000 total, with 50% of such sales in Europe.

Per Share Data ($) (Year Ended Dec. 31)	2000	1999	1998	1997	1996	1995	1994	1993	1992	1991
Tangible Bk. Val.	NM	NM	NM	NM	0.17	0.02	-0.79	-2.38	3.88	-1.42
Cash Flow	3.52	1.96	2.00	1.48	1.03	0.96	0.76	0.63	0.53	0.68
Earnings	2.52	1.21	1.01	0.92	0.72	0.67	0.46	0.29	0.13	-0.20
Dividends	Nil	Nil	Nil	Nil	Nil	Nil	Nil	Nil	Nil	Nil
Payout Ratio	Nil	Nil	Nil	Nil	Nil	Nil	Nil	Nil	Nil	Nil
Prices - High	70.37	35.75	32.00	28.31	13.81	15.18	12.56	8.25	5.31	4.62
- Low	30.31	14.71	13.50	10.75	9.37	9.37	7.06	3.25	2.56	3.50
P/E Ratio - High	28	30	32	31	19	23	28	28	41	NM
- Low	12	12	13	12	13	14	16	11	20	NA
Income Statement Analysis (Million $)										
Revs.	1,360	1,011	919	884	776	783	693	604	458	489
Oper. Inc.	287	201	185	187	167	162	132	110	69.2	84.0
Depr.	42.8	27.7	35.3	31.7	28.8	27.8	28.1	28.6	26.0	29.9
Int. Exp.	61.7	79.3	81.2	64.7	24.6	25.5	30.4	41.2	29.3	59.6
Pretax Inc.	173	76.2	64.8	88.2	110	105	69.5	38.1	11.4	-3.5
Eff. Tax Rate	38%	42%	42%	41%	38%	40%	39%	35%	24%	NM
Net Inc.	108	44.3	36.5	51.3	67.6	62.9	42.4	24.7	8.6	-6.5
Balance Sheet & Other Fin. Data (Million $)										
Cash	24.6	12.9	3.1	4.7	4.0	12.0	4.6	2.9	5.2	7.2
Curr. Assets	413	335	288	255	234	226	206	197	257	233
Total Assets	1,004	836	807	737	711	690	677	691	766	695
Curr. Liab.	243	146	124	117	97.0	104	110	100	106	91.0
LT Debt	700	746	952	937	219	195	234	365	458	334
Common Eqty.	29.2	-81.2	-292	-343	361	344	279	173	150	NA
Total Cap.	729	664	660	594	580	558	513	538	608	563
Cap. Exp.	53.1	23.5	26.3	24.1	20.4	20.4	10.9	6.0	6.7	10.0
Cash Flow	151	72.0	71.8	83.0	96.4	90.7	70.5	53.4	34.7	22.9
Curr. Ratio	1.7	2.3	2.3	2.2	2.4	2.2	1.9	2.0	2.4	2.6
% LT Debt of Cap.	96.0	112.2	144.3	158.0	38.0	35.0	45.7	67.8	75.4	NA
% Net Inc.of Revs.	7.9	4.4	4.0	5.8	9.0	8.0	6.1	4.1	1.9	NM
% Ret. on Assets	11.7	5.4	4.7	7.1	8.8	9.2	6.2	3.4	1.2	NM
% Ret. on Equity	NM	NM	NM	588.5	19.2	9.2	18.8	15.2	4.5	NM

Data as orig reptd.; bef. results of disc opers/spec. items. Per share data adj. for stk. divs. Bold denotes diluted EPS (FASB 128)-prior periods restated. E-Estimated. NA-Not Available. NM-Not Meaningful. NR-Not Ranked.

Office—358 Hall Ave., Wallingford, CT 06492-7530. **Tel**—(203) 265-8900. **Website**—www.amphenol.com **Chrmn, Pres & CEO**—M. H. Loeffler. **EVP, CFO & Investor Contact**—Edward G. Jepsen (203-265-8650). **Secy**—E. C. Wetmore. **Treas**—D. G. Reardon. **Dirs**—A. M. Clarkson, G. R. Durham, A. E. Lietz, H. R. Kravis, M. S. Lipschultz, M. H. Loeffler, M. W. Michelson, S. C. Nuttall, G. R. Roberts. **Transfer Agent & Registrar**—State Street Bank & Trust Co., Boston. **Incorporated**—in Delaware in 1932. **Empl**— 9,800. **S&P Analyst:** Michael W. Jaffe

STANDARD
&POOR'S
STOCK REPORTS

Autodesk, Inc.

Nasdaq Symbol **ADSK**

In S&P 500

18-AUG-01

Industry: Computer (Software & Services)

Summary: Autodesk develops, markets and supports computer-aided design and drafting (CAD) software, including its flagship AutoCAD program, for use on desktop computers and workstations.

S&P Opinion: Accumulate (★★★★)

Recent Price • 35.09 | Yield • 0.7%
52 Wk Range • 40.37-19.43 | 12-Mo. P/E • 20.9

Quantitative Evaluations

Outlook (1 Lowest—5 Highest)
• **5+**

Fair Value
• **48.30**

Risk
• **Average**

Earn./Div. Rank
• **B**

Technical Eval.
• **Bullish** since 7/01

Rel. Strength Rank (1 Lowest—99 Highest)
• **49**

Insider Activity
• **Unfavorable**

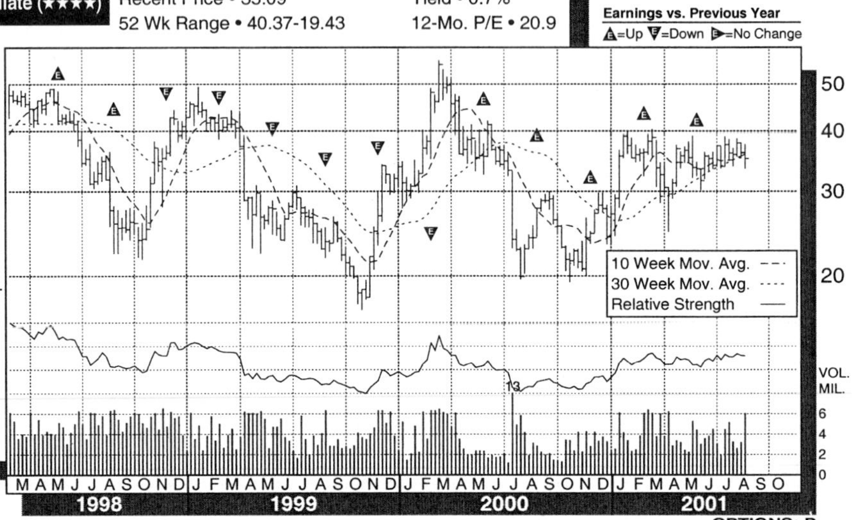

OPTIONS: P

Overview - 17-AUG-01

Revenues should increase approximately 7% in FY 02 (Jan.), after a 14% rise in FY 01. A revenue slowdown in FY 00 resulted largely from product transition issues in the U.S. related to the company's AutoCAD 2000 software. We expect the improvement in AutoCAD sales to continue in FY 02. However, ADSK will benefit mostly from the diversification of its product line, as many of the company's newer vertical market solutions are selling well. We also anticipate that, over time, revenues will be boosted as the company leverages the Internet with new product announcements. We expect operating margins to improve nicely, to low double digits, from high single digits. However, increased investment in Internet opportunities will adversely affect net income. Nevertheless, excluding amortization and one-time charges, EPS should increase approximately 12% in FY 02, to $2.10, from $1.87 in FY 01.

Valuation - 17-AUG-01

After weakness in FY 00, results have rebounded. Revenues advanced 3% in the first half of FY 02, despite a challenging economic environment, and earnings were better than expected. We believe the diversification of the company's product line over the past few years will continue to aid earnings growth. Although core AutoCAD sales have been weaker than expected, they have been improving lately. In addition, newer vertical market solutions have done well. We expect the company to benefit from Internet ventures, including buzzsaw.com, a building design and construction hub; and RedSpark, which is targeted toward manufacturing. With the shares trading at 16 times our FY 02 EPS estimate of $2.10, a significant stock repurchase program, and nearly $5.00 per share in cash and short term marketable securities, ADSK remains attractive.

Key Stock Statistics

S&P EPS Est. 2002	2.10	Tang. Bk. Value/Share	7.20
P/E on S&P Est. 2002	16.7	Beta	1.39
Dividend Rate/Share	0.24	Shareholders	1,023
Shs. outstg. (M)	53.9	Market cap. (B)	$ 1.9
Avg. daily vol. (M)	0.751	Inst. holdings	82%

Value of $10,000 invested 5 years ago: $ 17,077

Fiscal Year Ending Jan. 31

	2002	2001	2000	1999	1998	1997
Revenues (Million $)						
1Q	245.7	223.3	194.9	187.2	119.0	136.3
2Q	—	226.3	202.9	186.6	154.1	128.8
3Q	—	221.8	202.1	177.2	162.2	116.7
4Q	—	243.1	220.2	189.2	181.8	115.0
Yr.	—	936.3	820.2	740.2	617.1	496.7
Earnings Per Share ($)						
1Q	**0.50**	**0.41**	**-0.29**	**0.51**	**-1.15**	0.39
2Q	—	**0.35**	**0.01**	**0.43**	**0.34**	0.22
3Q	—	**0.32**	**0.02**	**0.39**	**0.41**	0.13
4Q	—	**0.51**	**0.41**	**0.50**	**0.60**	0.13
Yr.	—	**1.59**	**0.16**	**1.85**	**0.31**	**0.88**

Next earnings report expected: late August

Dividend Data (Dividends have been paid since 1989.)

Amount ($)	Date Decl.	Ex-Div. Date	Stock of Record	Payment Date
0.060	Sep. 19	Oct. 04	Oct. 06	Oct. 20 '00
0.060	Dec. 14	Jan. 03	Jan. 05	Jan. 19 '01
0.060	Mar. 22	Apr. 04	Apr. 06	Apr. 20 '01
0.060	Jun. 21	Jul. 03	Jul. 06	Jul. 20 '01

Business Summary - 17-AUG-01

Autodesk makes software products that are used across industries and in the home for architectural design and land development, manufacturing, utilities, telecommunications, and media and entertainment.

ADSK is organized into two reportable segments: the Design Solutions Segment and the Discreet Segment. The Design Solutions segment includes the following business divisions: Design Platforms Group, Manufacturing (formerly Mechanical Computer-Aided Design), Architecture, Engineering and Construction (AEC), and Geographic Information Solutions (GIS).

The Design Solutions segment sells design software for professionals, occasional users, and consumers who design, draft and diagram, in addition to mapping and geographic information systems technology to public and private users. End users of design software products include architects, engineers, construction firms, designers and drafters. The segment includes the company's flagship product, AutoCAD. With an installed base of more than 2.5 million units worldwide, AutoCAD is one of the world's leading computer aided design (CAD) tools. It is a general-purpose CAD tool for design, modeling, drafting, mapping, rendering and facility management tasks. The most current version, AutoCAD 2000i, was introduced in July 2000.

Design products also include Mechanical Desktop, a 3D mechanical design program; AutoCAD Architectural Desktop, an architectural design tool; AutoCAD Map, a CAD-based precision mapping and geographic information system analysis product; and AutoCAD LT, a low-cost CAD package offering 2-D and basic 3-D drafting capabilities.

The Discreet segment develops, assembles, markets, sells and supports nonlinear digital systems and software for creating, editing and compositing imagery. Its products are used in film and video postproduction, games and multimedia, broadcasters' graphics, programming and on-air event coverage, as well as by designers and architects for 3D visualization and conceptualization. Products include 3D Studio MAX, a 3D modeling and animation software package; flame*, a digital system used by creative professionals to create, edit and composite special visual effects in an on-line, real-time environment; and inferno*, which provides all the features of flame* with film tools, and increased image resolution and color control for digital film work.

In late 1999, the company spun off buzzsaw.com, a business-to-business (B2B) e-commerce hub for the building design and construction industry. In April 2000, ADSK spun off RedSpark Inc., a B2B e-commerce company targeting the manufacturing industry. Also in April, the company introduced Autodesk Point A, an online portal serving designers and engineers.

Per Share Data ($) (Year Ended Jan. 31)	2001	2000	1999	1998	1997	1996	1995	1994	1993	1992
Tangible Bk. Val.	7.41	8.89	8.24	6.29	5.40	7.39	6.85	6.25	5.58	5.43
Cash Flow	2.77	1.46	3.14	1.19	1.62	2.27	1.48	1.51	1.11	1.38
Earnings	1.59	0.16	1.85	0.31	0.88	1.76	1.14	1.25	0.88	1.16
Dividends	0.24	0.24	0.24	0.24	0.24	0.24	0.24	0.48	0.24	0.23
Payout Ratio	15%	150%	13%	77%	27%	14%	20%	38%	26%	20%
Cal. Yrs.	2000	1999	1998	1997	1996	1995	1994	1993	1992	1991
Prices - High	56.06	49.43	50.06	51.12	44.25	53.00	41.50	28.37	28.25	31.12
- Low	19.43	17.00	21.62	28.00	18.50	31.25	21.12	18.50	11.62	14.75
P/E Ratio - High	35	NM	27	NM	50	30	36	23	32	27
- Low	12	NM	12	NM	21	18	19	15	13	13
Income Statement Analysis (Million $)										
Revs.	936	820	740	632	510	547	465	419	368	285
Oper. Inc.	208	115	200	147	99	154	130	103	80.0	91.4
Depr.	68.8	79.7	63.2	43.9	34.8	25.2	17.4	13.1	11.3	11.2
Int. Exp.	Nil	Nil	Nil	Nil	Nil	Nil	Nil	NA	NA	NA
Pretax Inc.	41.7	23.9	147	55.0	66.5	138	89.1	96.8	69.8	92.3
Eff. Tax Rate	NM	59%	38%	72%	38%	37%	37%	36%	37%	37%
Net Inc.	93.2	9.8	90.6	15.4	41.6	87.8	56.6	62.2	43.9	57.8
Balance Sheet & Other Fin. Data (Million $)										
Cash	423	359	378	96.1	183	193	240	178	153	171
Curr. Assets	491	545	450	308	311	348	373	280	249	248
Total Assets	808	907	694	534	492	518	482	405	358	328
Curr. Liab.	334	299	232	199	150	144	155	102	84.1	57.0
LT Debt	Nil	Nil	Nil	Nil	Nil	Nil	Nil	Nil	Nil	Nil
Common Eqty.	460	602	460	303	244	342	323	297	268	267
Total Cap.	473	607	461	304	247	344	326	302	273	271
Cap. Exp.	32.4	14.9	30.4	15.0	17.4	16.3	20.0	21.5	11.0	9.9
Cash Flow	162	89.6	154	59.2	76.4	113	74.0	75.3	55.2	68.9
Curr. Ratio	1.5	1.8	1.9	1.5	2.1	2.4	2.4	2.7	3.0	4.3
% LT Debt of Cap.	Nil	Nil	Nil	Nil	Nil	Nil	Nil	Nil	Nil	Nil
% Net Inc.of Revs.	10.0	1.2	12.2	2.4	8.2	16.1	12.2	14.8	11.9	20.3
% Ret. on Assets	10.9	1.1	14.8	3.0	8.3	17.6	12.8	16.4	12.9	19.4
% Ret. on Equity	17.6	1.7	23.7	5.6	14.2	26.4	18.3	22.1	16.6	23.7

Data as orig. reptd.; bef. results of disc. opers. and/or spec. items. Per share data adj. for stk. divs. as of ex-div. date. Revs. in quarterly table for FY 98 and FY 97 are net of direct commissions. Bold denotes diluted EPS (FASB 128). E-Estimated. NA-Not Available. NM-Not Meaningful. NR-Not Ranked.

Office—111 McInnis Parkway, San Rafael, CA 94903. **Tel**—(415) 507-5000. **Website**—www.autodesk.com **Chrmn, CEO & Pres**—C. A. Bartz. **SVP & CFO**—S. Cakebread. **Dirs**—C. Bartz, M. A. Bertelsen, C. W. Beveridge, J. H. Dawson, P. K. Halvorsen, P. S. Otellini, M. A. Taylor, L. Wangberg. **Transfer Agent**—Harris Trust & Savings Bank, Chicago. **Incorporated**—in California in 1982; reincorporated in Delaware in 1994. **Empl**— 3,539. **S&P Analyst:** Jonathan Rudy

STANDARD &POOR'S STOCK REPORTS

Black Box

Nasdaq Symbol **BBOX**

In S&P SmallCap 600

18-AUG-01 **Industry:** Electrical Equipment

Summary: This company is a leading provider of a broad range of networking products, as well as on-site technical support.

S&P Opinion: Accumulate (★★★★) Recent Price • 48.01 52 Wk Range • 73.25-39.32 Yield • Nil 12-Mo. P/E • 14.9

Quantitative Evaluations

Outlook (1 Lowest—5 Highest) • **4−**

Fair Value • **60.30**

Risk • **High**

Earn./Div. Rank • **NR**

Technical Eval. • **Bearish** since 7/01

Rel. Strength Rank (1 Lowest—99 Highest) • **19**

Insider Activity • **Neutral**

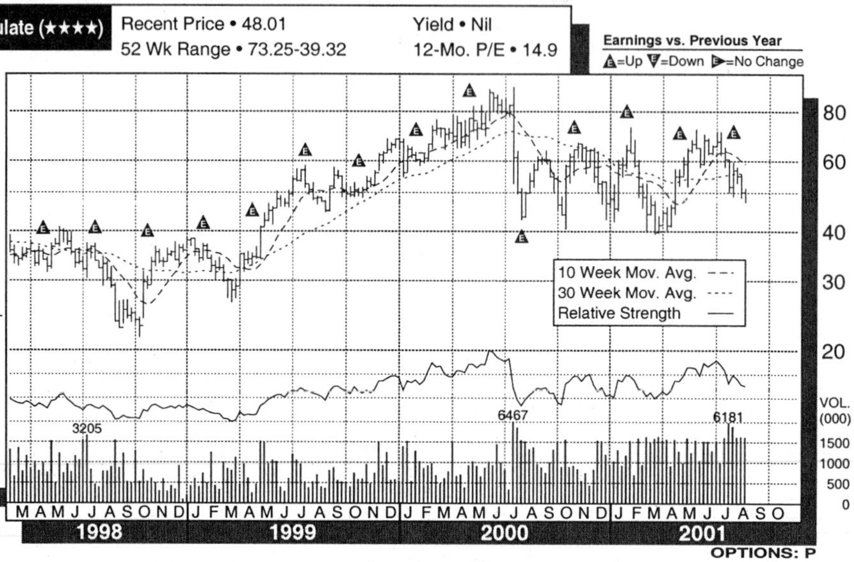

Overview - 06-AUG-01

After soaring 64% in FY 01 (Mar.), we expect revenue growth to slow to 7% in FY 02, as economic deceleration will likely impact orders for networking equipment and services. Growth is being driven by acquisitions of on-site service providers, international expansion and organically. BBOX is aggressively pursuing acquisitions in its on-site technical services unit, which was generating a majority of revenues at the end of the FY 02 first quarter. We expect gross margin to narrow, reflecting a rising proportion of on-site services business. However, gross margin pressures should be partly offset by acquisition synergies and cross-selling opportunities. A 2000 agreement with Home Depot is an example of BBOX's growing ability to manage large national customers. Additionally, BBOX has tailored its cost structure down, in order to match a less robust revenue outlook. We expect EPS to grow 19% in FY 02, to $3.82.

Valuation - 06-AUG-01

After an uptrend that began in April 1999, the shares fell significantly in July 2000, as the market reacted to a drop in same-store sales and lower free cash flow; the issue was resolved in the following quarter. Economic deceleration has since weighed on BBOX shares, but we expect that the stimulus introduced by the Federal Reserve's actions to lower interest rates should provide a boost. The long-term outlook for networking product sales and on-site services operations is being driven by the evolving telecommunications market. BBOX has been improving operating margins of acquired on-site service providers, moving toward a 15% goal it has targeted for the segment by the end of 2001. At a recent level of 14X our FY 02 EPS estimate, the shares are discounted to our 19% EPS growth projection through the period. In light of our view that BBOX can withstand a less appealing economic environment, we would add to holdings.

Key Stock Statistics

S&P EPS Est. 2002	3.82	Tang. Bk. Value/Share	2.68
P/E on S&P Est. 2002	12.6	Beta	1.58
S&P EPS Est. 2003	4.44	Shareholders	2,346
Dividend Rate/Share	Nil	Market cap. (B)	$0.941
Shs. outstg. (M)	19.6	Inst. holdings	96%
Avg. daily vol. (M)	0.691		

Value of $10,000 invested 5 years ago: $ 18,554

Fiscal Year Ending Mar. 31

	2002	2001	2000	1999	1998	1997
Revenues (Million $)						
1Q	207.1	171.1	97.52	73.10	64.20	52.86
2Q	—	210.2	117.9	79.13	68.93	56.17
3Q	—	220.5	127.1	84.79	74.64	57.66
4Q	—	225.2	157.3	92.96	76.14	62.87
Yr.	—	827.0	499.8	330.0	279.8	232.2
Earnings Per Share ($)						
1Q	**0.73**	**0.72**	**0.57**	**0.46**	0.39	0.31
2Q	—	**0.82**	**0.62**	**0.49**	0.42	0.34
3Q	—	**0.84**	**0.65**	**0.53**	**0.44**	0.35
4Q	—	**0.85**	**0.75**	**0.62**	**0.49**	0.41
Yr.	—	**3.22**	**2.60**	**2.09**	**1.75**	**1.40**

Next earnings report expected: mid October

Dividend Data

No dividends have been paid.

A Division of The McGraw-Hill Companies

Black Box Corporation

Business Summary - 06-AUG-01

Black Box is a leading worldwide direct marketer and technical service provider of computer communications and networking equipment and services. The company provides expert technical support 24 hours a day, seven days a week, and also provides fee-based on-site installation and technical services. Through its Black Box Catalog, available in nine languages, the company offers more than 40,000 products, approximately 90% of which are BBOX-labeled. While Black Box sells its products to businesses of all sizes, including many of the Fortune 1000 companies in the U.S., the majority of active customers are small and mid-size businesses, which lack in-house expertise.

During FY 00 (Mar.), the company significantly expanded its technical services offerings to include an increasing degree of on-site services. BBOX believes offering on-site services will allow it to further penetrate the telecommunications market. The company has expanded this business primarily through aggressive acquisition activity. From January 1998 through March of 2000, BBOX effected 33 acquisitions of on-site technical support providers. These providers averaged approximately 100 employees and $7 million in revenue. On-site revenues grew to 47% of total revenue in the FY 01 first quarter, from 6.8% in FY 98. As BBOX continues its strategy of building worldwide capabilities in selected markets, the percentage of on-site revenues should continue to grow.

The company services customers in 132 countries, and operates subsidiaries in five continents. In FY 00, 33% of revenues were generated outside North America, reflecting strong demand for computer systems and networks on a worldwide basis.

BBOX's primary marketing tool is its targeted mailing of a comprehensive, fully illustrated color catalog, as well as other direct promotional material mailed to systems design decision-makers. The company's catalogs present a wide choice of items, using a combination of product features and benefits, photographs, product descriptions, product specifications, compatibility charts, potential applications, and other helpful technical information.

The company differentiates itself from other direct marketers and distributors through its private label brand, and through its technical support. Black Box complements its products with 2000 technical support professionals, available by phone, free of charge, seven days a week, 24 hours a day, and via fee-based on-site cabling and installation services. In addition, BBOX's MIS and inventory management systems enable it to ship 95% of orders on the day of receipt.

Per Share Data ($) (Year Ended Mar. 31)	2001	2000	1999	1998	1997	1996	1995	1994	1993	1992
Tangible Bk. Val.	2.69	2.33	4.87	3.32	1.11	NM	NM	0.25	NA	NA
Cash Flow	4.27	3.21	2.50	2.11	1.75	1.46	1.31	1.42	NA	NA
Earnings	3.22	2.60	2.09	1.75	1.40	1.10	0.89	0.71	0.47	NA
Dividends	Nil	Nil	Nil	Nil	Nil	Nil	Nil	Nil	NA	NA
Payout Ratio	Nil	Nil	Nil	Nil	Nil	Nil	Nil	Nil	NA	NA
Cal. Yrs.	2000	1999	1998	1997	1996	1995	1994	1993	1992	1991
Prices - High	92.25	68.75	41.00	46.00	41.50	19.75	22.50	21.25	15.75	NA
- Low	40.50	26.37	21.50	20.75	13.25	12.65	8.62	11.25	13.25	NA
P/E Ratio - High	29	26	20	26	29	18	25	19	33	NA
- Low	13	10	10	12	9	11	9	10	28	NA
Income Statement Analysis (Million $)										
Revs.	827	500	330	280	232	193	165	142	NA	NA
Oper. Inc.	138	94.4	71.0	60.7	51.9	44.1	39.6	38.7	NA	NA
Depr.	20.9	11.4	7.6	6.3	6.2	6.1	6.8	11.3	NA	NA
Int. Exp.	11.3	3.2	0.6	2.7	3.6	5.8	NA	NA	NA	NA
Pretax Inc.	105	80.1	63.0	52.1	41.9	32.6	25.6	20.7	NA	NA
Eff. Tax Rate	39%	39%	40%	41%	42%	44%	43%	45%	NA	NA
Net Inc.	64.2	48.9	38.1	30.9	24.3	18.3	14.5	11.4	NA	NA
Balance Sheet & Other Fin. Data (Million $)										
Cash	6.2	8.6	5.9	10.6	1.4	1.9	2.5	2.2	NA	NA
Curr. Assets	267	195	117	100	83.9	62.8	54.2	52.9	NA	NA
Total Assets	653	452	246	185	173	156	152	186	NA	NA
Curr. Liab.	128	78.6	44.0	38.3	45.7	32.8	31.2	18.7	NA	NA
LT Debt	124	105	0.2	8.0	21.2	41.4	56.9	80.5	NA	NA
Common Eqty.	389	258	193	128	94.3	67.1	47.1	65.3	NA	NA
Total Cap.	524	373	202	147	128	123	121	168	NA	NA
Cap. Exp.	6.9	12.6	9.4	2.3	2.8	2.5	3.5	NA	NA	NA
Cash Flow	85.1	60.2	45.7	37.2	30.5	24.3	21.3	22.8	NA	NA
Curr. Ratio	2.1	2.5	2.7	2.6	1.8	1.9	1.7	2.8	NA	NA
% LT Debt of Cap.	23.7	28.2	0.1	5.4	16.6	33.7	47.1	47.9	NA	NA
% Net Inc.of Revs.	7.8	9.8	11.6	11.0	10.5	9.4	8.8	8.1	NA	NA
% Ret. on Assets	11.6	13.9	17.7	17.2	14.8	11.9	8.6	6.0	NA	NA
% Ret. on Equity	19.8	21.6	23.8	27.8	30.2	32.1	25.9	19.9	NA	NA

Data as orig reptd.; bef. results of disc opers/spec. items. Per share data adj. for stk. divs. Bold denotes diluted EPS (FASB 128)-prior periods restated. E-Estimated. NA-Not Available. NM-Not Meaningful. NR-Not Ranked.

Office—1000 Park Dr., Lawrence, PA 15055. **Tel**—(724) 746-5500. **Fax**—(724) 746-0746. **Website**—www.blackbox.com **Chrmn & CEO**—F. C. Young. **VP, CFO, Treas & Secy**—A. M. Baird. **Dirs**—W. F. Andrews, T. G. Greig, W. R. Newlin, B. D. Young, F. C. Young. **Transfer Agent & Registrar**—American Stock Transfer & Trust Co., NYC. **Incorporated**—in California in 1973; reincorporated in Delaware in 1989. **Empl**— 3,500. **S&P Analyst:** Markos N. Kaminis

STANDARD & POOR'S
STOCK REPORTS

Cadence Design Systems

NYSE Symbol **CDN**

In S&P MidCap 400

18-AUG-01

Industry: Computer (Software & Services)

Summary: This company is a leading producer of electronic design automation software.

S&P Opinion: Accumulate (★★★★)

Recent Price • 22.71 | Yield • Nil
52 Wk Range • 32.68-15.90 | 12-Mo. P/E • NM

Quantitative Evaluations

Outlook (1 Lowest—5 Highest)
• **3**

Fair Value
• **22.70**

Risk
• **Average**

Earn./Div. Rank
• **B-**

Technical Eval.
• **Bullish** since 7/01

Rel. Strength Rank (1 Lowest—99 Highest)
• **79**

Insider Activity
• **Unfavorable**

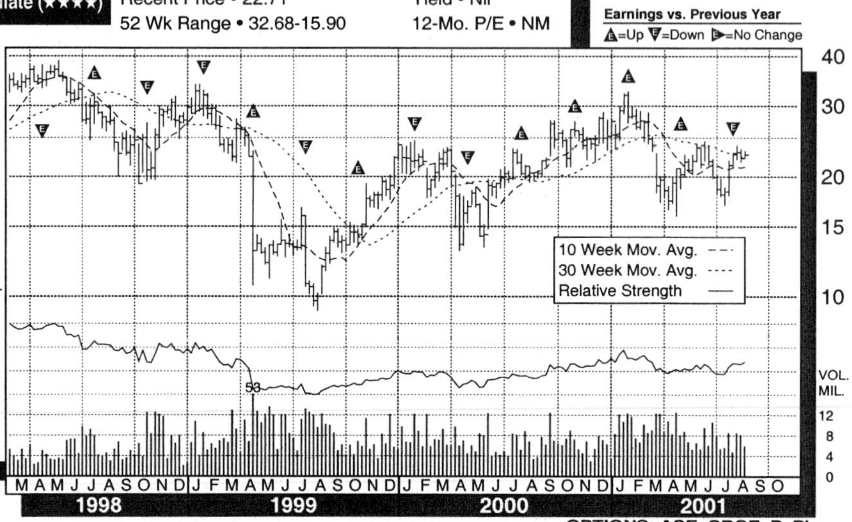

OPTIONS: ASE, CBOE, P, Ph

Overview - 18-JUL-01

We expect revenues to increase 15% in 2001, and 18% in 2002, as CDN completes a transition to a subscription licensing model. Although the changeover hurt revenues in recent quarters, earnings visibility is improving over time. About half of software bookings are now handled as subscription licenses. The design services segment recently encountered demand weakness and reduced staff by 150. However, customer interest in next generation EDA tools is up, and software sales are on track. Earnings improvement should continue, as the design cycles for semiconductors with linewidths of 0.18 and 0.13 microns heat up. CDN is improving the market strength of its product portfolio by focusing on complete front- to back-end solutions, and is accelerating from point tools to integrated process flows. Our 2001 EPS projection is $0.84, before goodwill amortization charges, with $1.10 seen for 2002.

Valuation - 18-JUL-01

The shares fell in February, as the economic outlook darkened for the entire electronics industry, and remain under pressure as the semiconductor sector cyclical downturn deepens. A shift in the sales model toward subscription (from time-based) licenses will restrict near-term operating results, but should aid predictability of future results as backlog grows. CDN is well positioned to capitalize on a continuing semiconductor technology shift toward deep sub-micron, system-on-a-chip product development. This should boost demand for CDN's software and services, which help chipmakers design high performance integrated circuits. The shares recently traded at 17X our 2001 EPS estimate of $1.10, below CDN's estimated long-term growth rate of 20%, creating an attractive PEG ratio below 1.0. We anticipate moderate outperformance, and are maintaining our accumulate recommendation.

Key Stock Statistics

S&P EPS Est. 2001	0.84	Tang. Bk. Value/Share	2.39
P/E on S&P Est. 2001	27.0	Beta	1.39
S&P EPS Est. 2002	1.10	Shareholders	42,007
Dividend Rate/Share	Nil	Market cap. (B)	$ 5.6
Shs. outstg. (M)	248.7	Inst. holdings	81%
Avg. daily vol. (M)	1.348		

Value of $10,000 invested 5 years ago: $ 14,029

Fiscal Year Ending Dec. 31

	2001	2000	1999	1998	1997	1996
Revenues (Million $)						
1Q	344.7	257.5	305.2	270.2	187.6	270.2
2Q	347.6	298.7	264.2	291.8	210.5	177.0
3Q	—	332.5	225.9	308.6	234.9	188.7
4Q	—	390.9	268.0	345.4	283.0	212.3
Yr.	—	1,280	1,093	1,216	915.9	741.5
Earnings Per Share ($)						
1Q	**0.01**	**-0.05**	**0.22**	Nil	0.18	0.14
2Q	**-0.12**	**0.02**	**-0.01**	**0.28**	0.14	0.15
3Q	—	**0.05**	**-0.17**	**-0.37**	0.24	0.18
4Q	—	**0.16**	**-0.09**	**0.20**	**0.26**	-0.36
Yr.	—	**0.19**	**-0.06**	**0.14**	**0.83**	**0.16**

Next earnings report expected: mid October

Dividend Data

No cash dividends have been paid. A two-for-one common stock split was effected in November 1997.

A Division of The McGraw-Hill Companies

Cadence Design Systems, Inc.

Business Summary - 18-JUL-01

As electronic devices become smaller, lighter, more powerful, and more mobile, the challenge of facilitating the design process for circuitry is creating opportunities for Cadence Design Systems. The company, formed via the 1988 merger of SDA Systems, Inc., into ECAD, Inc., is the largest supplier of electronic design automation (EDA) software and design and methodology services to the worldwide electronics industry. Its sophisticated EDA tools are used to develop circuits and systems that let customers manufacture increasingly complex electronic products with accelerated time to market schedules. These services greatly enhance customer competitiveness.

CDN works with customers to turn concepts into successful products. This requires partnering with customers to understand their design needs, explore options, and carefully evaluate tradeoffs before choosing the best path. Customers consist of large technology concerns, including ST Microelectronics, Texas Instruments, Agere Systems and Toshiba, as well as less well-known companies. Electronics products designed with company products and services include semiconductors, computer systems and peripherals, telecommunications and networking equipment, mobile and wireless devices, automotive electronics, and consumer products.

The company's product offerings include a variety of EDA tools that address the five major problems in circuit design: system level design, functional verification, automated digital integrated circuit (IC) design, custom IC (analog and mixed signal) design, and printed circuit board design and IC packaging. CDN also offers consulting and design services that help improve design environments, and that perform design projects for electronic system components. In addition, it offers standard support services, including product updates, telephone and Internet support, and metrics reporting. In 2000, products represented 49% of total sales, services 26%, and maintenance 25%.

Electronics design is a global business; international sales accounted for 44% of sales in 2000, down from 52% in 1999.

The company has added expertise and size through acquisitions. In February 2001, it acquired CadMOS Design Technology Inc., a privately held design tools firm in San Jose, CA, focusing on noise reduction in deep submicron design.

The company competes with small EDA software companies, as well as three larger competitors: Mentor Graphics, Synopsis, and Avant Corp. In May 2001, Avant pleaded no contested to charges related to theft of CDN's chip design code in a criminal case begun in 1995. Avant agreed to pay $27 million in fines. A hearing date related to possible restitution payments was set for June 4, 2001. With criminal matters settled, a related civil action by the company against Avant may now proceed.

Per Share Data ($) (Year Ended Dec. 31)	2000	1999	1998	1997	1996	1995	1994	1993	1992	1991
Tangible Bk. Val.	2.39	2.40	2.68	3.45	2.41	0.85	1.03	1.11	1.26	1.00
Cash Flow	0.98	0.62	0.58	1.09	0.44	0.77	0.34	0.13	0.38	0.01
Earnings	0.47	-0.06	0.14	0.83	0.16	0.52	0.19	0.00	0.27	-0.12
Dividends	Nil	Nil	Nil	Nil	Nil	Nil	Nil	Nil	Nil	Nil
Payout Ratio	Nil	Nil	Nil	Nil	Nil	Nil	Nil	Nil	Nil	Nil
Prices - High	28.93	34.12	23.50	29.12	22.18	14.12	4.83	5.41	6.63	7.69
- Low	13.00	9.18	15.93	13.06	10.68	4.27	2.27	1.83	2.91	3.22
P/E Ratio - High	62	NM	NM	35	NM	27	26	NM	25	NM
- Low	28	NM	21	16	NM	8	12	NM	11	NM
Income Statement Analysis (Million $)										
Revs.	1,280	1,093	1,216	916	741	548	429	369	435	392
Oper. Inc.	277	210	471	335	244	164	88.8	36.9	89.9	61.5
Depr.	207	164	102	56.6	51.7	46.0	30.1	25.7	24.2	25.6
Int. Exp.	Nil	Nil	3.6	2.5	1.9	2.2	1.1	0.7	0.9	2.7
Pretax Inc.	68.0	-11.4	113	260	90.5	135	49.3	-0.5	68.5	-11.8
Eff. Tax Rate	27%	NM	71%	30%	68%	28%	25%	NM	19%	NM
Net Inc.	50.0	-14.1	32.0	182	29.0	97.3	36.6	-0.6	55.4	-21.7
Balance Sheet & Other Fin. Data (Million $)										
Cash	85.2	111	183	207	286	97.0	97.0	93.0	92.0	111
Curr. Assets	557	480	580	609	491	207	192	218	249	246
Total Assets	1,477	1,460	1,406	1,024	717	374	361	339	370	350
Curr. Liab.	492	422	328	269	232	200	164	113	95.0	123
LT Debt	3.3	25.0	136	1.6	20.3	1.6	2.1	4.0	6.0	4.1
Common Eqty.	909	986	857	727	428	134	176	206	249	189
Total Cap.	924	1,011	1,053	729	463	155	180	213	263	212
Cap. Exp.	119	110	114	92.4	62.1	28.3	15.2	19.3	31.4	29.6
Cash Flow	257	150	134	238	80.9	143	66.7	25.1	79.0	2.6
Curr. Ratio	1.1	1.1	1.8	2.3	2.1	1.0	1.2	1.9	2.6	2.0
% LT Debt of Cap.	0.4	2.5	12.9	0.2	4.4	1.1	1.2	1.9	2.3	1.9
% Net Inc.of Revs.	3.9	NM	2.6	19.8	4.0	17.8	8.5	NM	12.7	NM
% Ret. on Assets	3.4	NM	1.4	20.9	5.4	26.5	10.9	NM	15.1	NM
% Ret. on Equity	5.3	NM	4.3	31.5	10.4	62.8	20.0	NM	24.6	NM

Data as orig reptd.; bef. results of disc opers/spec. items. Per share data adj. for stk. divs. Bold denotes diluted EPS (FASB 128)-prior periods restated. E-Estimated. NA-Not Available. NM-Not Meaningful. NR-Not Ranked.

Office—2655 Seely Ave., Bldg. 5, San Jose, CA 95134. **Tel**—(408) 943-1234. **Website**—http://www.cadence.com **Chrmn**—D. L. Lucas. **Pres & CEO**—H. R. Bingham. **SVP & CFO**—W. Porter. **SVP & Secy**—R. L. Smith McKeithen. **Dirs**—H. R. Bingham, S. L. Bostrom, L. Y. W. Liu, D. L. Lucas, A. Sangiovanni-Vincentelli, G. M. Scalise, J. B. Shoven, R. S. Siboni. **Transfer Agent**—Mellon Invesor Relations, Hackensack, NJ. **Incorporated**—in Delaware in 1988. **Empl**— 5,650. **S&P Analyst:** T. W. Smith, CFA

STANDARD &POOR'S STOCK REPORTS

Celestica

NYSE Symbol **CLS**

18-AUG-01

Industry: Computer (Software & Services)

Summary: This company is the world's third largest provider of manufacturing services to original equipment manufacturers in the electronics industry.

S&P Opinion: Accumulate (★★★★)

Recent Price • 39.47
52 Wk Range • 87-24
Yield • Nil
12-Mo. P/E • 40.7

Quantitative Evaluations

Outlook
(1 Lowest—5 Highest)
• **NA**

Fair Value
• **NA**

Risk
• **NA**

Earn./Div. Rank
• **NR**

Technical Eval.
• **Neutral** since 8/01

Rel. Strength Rank
(1 Lowest—99 Highest)
• **21**

Insider Activity
• **NA**

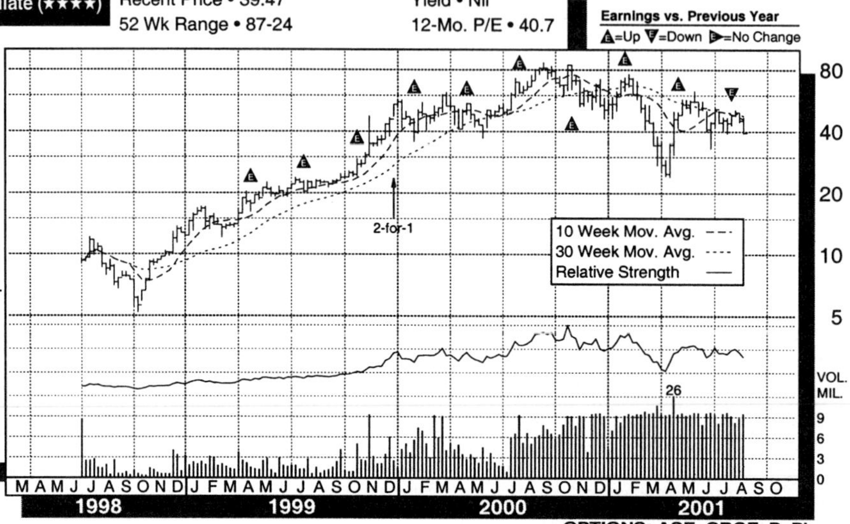

OPTIONS: ASE, CBOE, P, Ph

Overview - 10-AUG-01

Reflecting the difficult near-term economic environment, we now expect 2001 revenues to climb only about 8%-10%, down from a recent forecast of 35% growth. In the near term, the company should continue to see deferred orders and sluggish demand among electronics OEMs, particularly in the telecom and PC sectors. In the longer term, CLS should benefit from the overall trend among OEMs to increase the percentage of outsourcing that they do. We expect gross margins to widen to about 7.2%, from 7.1% in 2000, as the company increases its efforts to move to higher value added business and to increase efficiencies. These efforts will be made more challenging by large underutilized capacity due to the current downturn. Recent acquisitions will lead to higher operating expenses. We project 2001 cash EPS of $1.50, excluding amortization of goodwill and other intangibles and acquisition-related charges.

Valuation - 10-AUG-01

The shares have recovered somewhat in recent weeks from a large decline, but are still 48% off their 52-week highs. Despite weak near term conditions in the industry, we recently upgraded the shares of Celestica to accumulate, from hold. We feel the company's low cost manufacturing and diversified business mix provide competitive advantages during the current downturn. In addition, despite the current tech environment, CLS is still growing, unlike some if its competitors. Longer term, the potential for additional acquisitions and OEM divestiture deals provides the potential for upside to current earnings targets. Trading at 30 times our 2001 EPS estimate of $1.50, CLS is attractively priced at the low end of its historical P/E range and toward the lower end of its peer group.

Key Stock Statistics

S&P EPS Est. 2001	1.60	Tang. Bk. Value/Share	14.21
P/E on S&P Est. 2001	24.7	Beta	NA
S&P EPS Est. 2002	1.90	Shareholders	521
Dividend Rate/Share	Nil	Market cap. (B)	$ 6.5
Shs. outstg. (M)	203.4	Inst. holdings	54%
Avg. daily vol. (M)	2.039		

Value of $10,000 invested 5 years ago: NA

Fiscal Year Ending Dec. 31

	2001	2000	1999	1998	1997	1996
Revenues (Million $)						
1Q	2,693	1,612	1,082	738.7	—	—
2Q	2,661	2,092	1,250	773.6	—	—
3Q	—	2,600	1,357	811.6	—	—
4Q	—	3,448	1,609	925.3	—	—
Yr.	—	9,752	5,297	3,249	2,007	2,017
Earnings Per Share ($)						
1Q	**0.25**	**0.14**	**0.06**	**-0.43**	—	—
2Q	**0.06**	**0.20**	**0.08**	**-0.26**	—	—
3Q	—	**0.26**	**0.11**	**0.05**	—	—
4Q	—	**0.38**	**0.14**	**-0.03**	—	—
Yr.	—	**0.99**	**0.40**	**-0.47**	**-0.08**	—

Next earnings report expected: mid October

Dividend Data

No cash dividends have been paid. The shares were split two for one in 1999.

Celestica Inc.

Business Summary - 10-AUG-01

Capitalizing on a growing trend for original equipment manufacturers (OEMs) in the electronics industry to outsource production, Celestica is the world's third largest provider of electronics manufacturing services (EMS), with 2000 revenues of $9.8 billion. The company operates 34 facilities, in the U.S., Europe, South America, and Asia, with over 4,000,000 sq. ft. of manufacturing space.

The company got its start as a manufacturing unit of IBM, providing services only to IBM for more than 75 years. In 1993, CLS began providing EMS services to non-IBM customers. In October 1996, the company was purchased from IBM by an investor group led by Onex Corp. The company went public in 1998, selling 23.7 million subordinate voting shares for gross proceeds of U.S.$414 million. In March 2000, CLS sold publicly an additional 16.6 million subordinate voting shares, for gross proceeds of U.S.$757 million. Onex continues to own 100% of the multiple voting shares, which carry 25 votes per share, and controls about 87% of the company's voting rights.

CLS provides a wide variety of services to OEM customers, including the manufacture, assembly and test of complex printed circuit assemblies, and full system assembly of final products. In addition, the company provides a wide range of services including product design, worldwide distribution and after-sales support. CLS targets industry-leading OEMs primarily in the computer and communications sectors. It currently has about 50 OEM customers, including leading companies such as Cisco, Dell, EMC, Hewlett-Packard (HP), IBM, Lucent, Nortel, and Sun Microsystems. In 1999, the three largest customers, HP, Sun and Cisco, accounted for 55% of total revenue.

The company believes its competitive advantage lies in its advanced capabilities in technology, quality and supply chain management. Its manufacturing facilities are organized as customer-focused factories, with dedicated manufacturing lines and customer teams. CLS believes this enhances customer satisfaction and manufacturing flexibility. The company also regards its test facilities as among the best in the industry, allowing it to produce highly reliable products. CLS's large size, geographic reach, and expertise in supply chain management let it purchase materials effectively, and deliver products to customers faster, reducing overall product costs and reducing time to market.

CLS has completed 18 acquisitions since the beginning of 1997. Because of the advantages of size and geographic diversity in servicing global OEMs, the company believes the highly fragmented EMS industry will continue to see significant consolidation. In January 2000, CLS agreed to acquire three IBM plants, in Minnesota and Italy. Under the agreement, the company was to provide a variety of services to IBM, expected to lead to annualized revenues of about $1.5 billion.

Per Share Data ($) (Year Ended Dec. 31)	**2000**	**1999**	**1998**	**1997**	**1996**	**1995**	**1994**	**1993**	**1992**	**1991**
Tangible Bk. Val.	14.21	6.96	3.20	0.12	NA	NA	NA	NA	NA	NA
Cash Flow	1.92	1.17	0.37	0.65	NA	NA	NA	NA	NA	NA
Earnings	0.99	0.40	-0.47	-0.08	NA	NA	NA	NA	NA	NA
Dividends	Nil	Nil	Nil	NA	NA	NA	NA	NA	NA	NA
Payout Ratio	Nil	Nil	Nil	NA	NA	NA	NA	NA	NA	NA
Prices - High	87.00	57.00	13.75	NA	NA	NA	NA	NA	NA	NA
- Low	35.50	12.06	5.18	NA	NA	NA	NA	NA	NA	NA
P/E Ratio - High	88	NM	NM	NA	NA	NA	NA	NA	NA	NA
- Low	36	NM	NM	NA	NA	NA	NA	NA	NA	NA
Income Statement Analysis (Million $)										
Revs.	9,752	5,297	3,249	2,007	2,017	2,855	1,989	NA	NA	NA
Oper. Inc.	486	251	142	108	88.7	121	NA	NA	NA	NA
Depr.	213	127	NA	52.3	13.0	9.3	NA	NA	NA	NA
Int. Exp.	17.8	10.7	32.2	33.6	NA	NM	NA	NA	NA	NA
Pretax Inc.	276	104	-50.5	-4.7	53.8	103	68.3	NA	NA	NA
Eff. Tax Rate	25%	35%	NM	NM	46%	39%	39%	NA	NA	NA
Net Inc.	207	68.4	-48.5	-6.9	29.0	62.8	42.0	NA	NA	NA
Balance Sheet & Other Fin. Data (Million $)										
Cash	884	372	31.7	106	NA	NA	NA	NA	NA	NA
Curr. Assets	4,521	1,851	983	832	NA	NA	NA	NA	NA	NA
Total Assets	5,938	2,656	1,636	1,347	NA	NA	NA	NA	NA	NA
Curr. Liab.	2,258	851	627	468	NA	NA	NA	NA	NA	NA
LT Debt	131	132	133	219	NA	NA	NA	NA	NA	NA
Common Eqty.	3,469	1,658	850	363	NA	NA	NA	NA	NA	NA
Total Cap.	3,638	1,794	1,002	NA	NA	NA	NA	NA	NA	NA
Cap. Exp.	283	212	67.8	NA	NA	NA	NA	NA	NA	NA
Cash Flow	419	195	38.4	45.4	42.0	72.1	NA	NA	NA	NA
Curr. Ratio	2.0	2.2	1.6	1.8	NA	NA	NA	NA	NA	NA
% LT Debt of Cap.	3.6	7.3	13.3	NA	NA	NA	NA	NA	NA	NA
% Net Inc.of Revs.	2.1	1.3	NM	NM	1.4	2.2	2.1	NA	NA	NA
% Ret. on Assets	4.8	3.2	NM	NA	NA	NA	NA	NA	NA	NA
% Ret. on Equity	8.1	5.4	NM	NA	NA	NA	NA	NA	NA	NA

Data as orig reptd.; bef. results of disc opers/spec. items. Per share data adj. for stk. divs. Bold denotes diluted EPS (FASB 128)-prior periods restated. E-Estimated. NA-Not Available. NM-Not Meaningful. NR-Not Ranked.

Office—12 Concorde Place, 7th Floor, Toronto, ON, Canada M3C 3R8. **Tel**—(416) 448-2211. **Website**—http://www.celestica.com **Chrm**—R. L. Crandall. **Pres & CEO**—E. V. Polistuk. **EVP & CFO**—A. P. Puppi. **VP & Treas**—F. G. Thouret. **VP & Secy**—E. L. DelBianco. **VP & Contr**—P. J. Bar.**Dirs**—R. L. Crandall, W.A. Etherington, M. L. Hilson, R. S. Love, R. L. Martin, A. R. Melman, M. Naturo, E. V. Polistuk, A. P. Puppi, G. W. Schwartz, D. Tapscott. **Transfer Agent & Registrar**—Bank of Nova Scotia Trust Co. of New York, NYC. **Incorporated**—in Ontario in 1996. **Empl**—20,000. **S&P Analyst:** Jim Corridore

STANDARD
&POOR'S
STOCK REPORTS

EMC Corp.

NYSE Symbol **EMC**

In S&P 500

23-AUG-01 **Industry:** Computers (Peripherals)

Summary: This company is the leading supplier of enterprise data storage systems and software.

S&P Opinion: Hold (★★★)

Recent Price • 16.50 | Yield • Nil
52 Wk Range • 104.93-15.39 | 12-Mo. P/E • 24.3

Quantitative Evaluations

Outlook
(1 Lowest—5 Highest)
• **2−**

Fair Value
• **16.30**

Risk
• **Average**

Earn./Div. Rank
• **B+**

Technical Eval.
• **Bearish** since 5/01

Rel. Strength Rank
(1 Lowest—99 Highest)
• **6**

Insider Activity
• **Neutral**

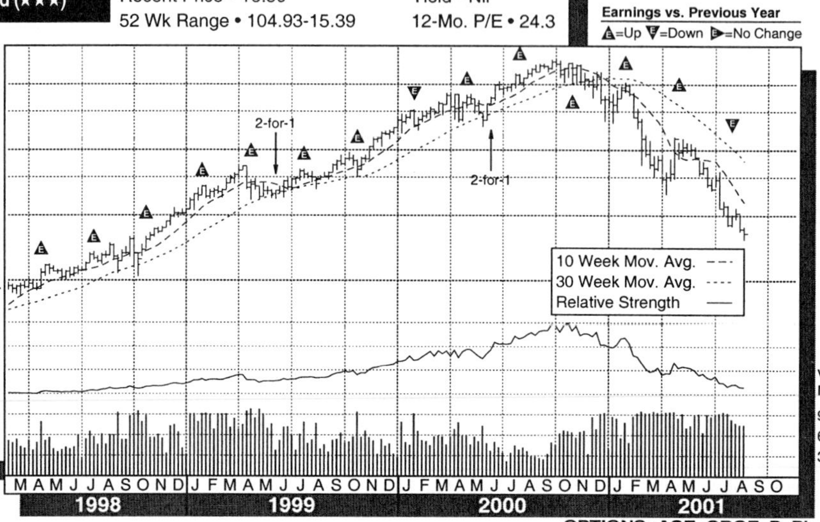

OPTIONS: ASE, CBOE, P, Ph

Overview - 27-JUL-01

We now see revenues increasing about 10% in 2001, in sharp contrast to recent expectations of up to 30% top line growth. The company is being affected by the economic slowdown and a resultant reduction in IT infrastructure spending. In addition, gross margins have been hampered by pricing pressures and unilateral pricing actions to keep products moving out the door, and by inefficient manufacturing utilization. We expect this issue to persist into the third quarter, and expect 2001 gross margins to drop into the high 40% area, from their historical 55% to 58% range. Despite tight control over operating costs, we now forecast that EPS will fall to $0.30 in 2001, a sharp decline from the $0.79 EMC reported in 2000. For the longer term, we see growth accelerating again once the economic picture clears, and we expect strong demand for the company's networked storage products, as well as for software and services.

Valuation - 27-JUL-01

The shares have been in a downtrend in 2001, punished by negative industry fundamentals and the long time it took EMC to admit that its business was slowing. Our accumulate recommendation takes into account quantitative and qualitative factors. Our discounted cash flow model indicates that EMC is currently trading at a modest discount to its intrinsic value. On a more relative basis, we see the current valuation of 40X our 2002 EPS estimate of $0.45 as an attractive entry point for the dominant company in what will inevitably be a fast growth category once economic activity accelerates again. Although EPS will decline in 2001, for the longer term, the company will continue to benefit from its leading market share in every segment in which it competes.

Key Stock Statistics

S&P EPS Est. 2001	0.30	Tang. Bk. Value/Share	3.88
P/E on S&P Est. 2001	55.0	Beta	1.97
S&P EPS Est. 2002	0.40	Shareholders	13,275
Dividend Rate/Share	Nil	Market cap. (B)	$ 34.2
Shs. outstg. (M)	2209.3	Inst. holdings	61%
Avg. daily vol. (M)	14.843		

Value of $10,000 invested 5 years ago: NA

Fiscal Year Ending Dec. 31

	2001	2000	1999	1998	1997	1996
Revenues (Million $)						
1Q	2,345	1,823	1,128	828.4	618.4	521.5
2Q	2,021	2,146	1,292	952.0	713.5	545.0
3Q	—	2,283	1,334	1,003	732.6	550.8
4Q	—	2,621	1,876	1,191	873.4	656.4
Yr.	—	8,873	6,716	3,974	2,938	2,274
Earnings Per Share ($)						
1Q	0.18	0.15	0.10	0.07	0.06	0.04
2Q	0.05	0.19	0.14	0.09	0.06	0.05
3Q	E0.02	0.20	0.14	0.10	0.06	0.05
4Q	E0.05	0.25	0.10	0.12	0.08	0.06
Yr.	E0.30	0.79	0.46	0.37	0.26	0.20

Next earnings report expected: mid September

Dividend Data

No cash dividends have been paid. The shares were split two for one in late 1997.

EMC Corporation

Business Summary - 27-JUL-01

EMC is the leader in the enterprise data storage industry. The company sells hardware, software and services for the storage, management, protection and sharing of electronic information. Faced with a severe economic and information technology spending slowdown in 2001, EMC recently said it would likely be unable to attain its goal of reaching $12 billion in revenues by the end of 2001. Revenue momentum has stalled from the 33% overall growth in 2000, when revenues hit $8.9 billion.

EMC's flagship product, Symmetrix, was introduced in 1991 to provide storage for mainframe computers. It was the first intelligent disk storage system that integrated software with large amounts of cache memory and arrays of industry standard disk drives. Since then, the company has become the leading supplier of enterprise storage systems and software for various computing platforms.

In October 1999, the company acquired Data General, for $1.1 billion in stock. EMC integrated Data General's CLARiiON product line into its primary storage line of business, and formed a new Data General division to sell AViiON servers and related services. CLARiiON Fibre Channel products are mid-range storage systems for Windows NT and UNIX platforms.

The Celerra file server is a high end network attached storage (NAS) device. A file server allows users to access and update files over a local area network (LAN) and store them in a central location. EMC's Connectrix storage area network (SAN) products, introduced in March 1999, facilitate the connection of a large number of servers to a single storage system through fibre channel links.

In 2000, revenues from information storage systems (including Symmetrix, CLARiiON, Celerra and Connectrix, accounted for 70% of the total, up from 68% in 1999.

EMC provides highly innovative software that provides customers with superior information management, sharing and protection capabilities. These capabilities include enhanced backup, disaster recovery, business continuance, data migration and data movement. Software provided 16% of revenues in 2000, up from 12% in 1999.

The company's global services organization offers consulting, installation, training, day-to-day support, parts delivery and system upgrades. The organization unites all of EMC's service functions, including customer service, professional services and technical training services. Revenue from storage services was 7% of the total in 2000, up from 5% in 1999. Revenue from other businesses, including Data General, accounted for 7% of revenues in 2000, down from 14% in 1999.

Per Share Data ($) (Year Ended Dec. 31)	2000	1999	1998	1997	1996	1995	1994	1993	1992	1991
Tangible Bk. Val.	3.72	2.38	1.60	1.19	0.83	0.62	0.45	0.28	0.12	0.10
Cash Flow	1.02	0.66	0.46	0.32	0.24	0.19	0.16	0.10	0.04	0.02
Earnings	0.79	0.46	0.37	0.26	0.20	0.17	0.15	0.08	0.02	0.01
Dividends	Nil	Nil	Nil	Nil	Nil	Nil	Nil	Nil	Nil	Nil
Payout Ratio	Nil	Nil	Nil	Nil	Nil	Nil	Nil	Nil	Nil	Nil
Prices - High	104.93	55.50	21.65	8.14	4.54	3.42	3.00	2.43	0.75	0.27
- Low	47.50	21.00	6.00	3.96	1.89	1.62	1.56	0.64	0.22	0.10
P/E Ratio - High	NM	NM	58	31	23	20	20	30	34	26
- Low	NM	NM	16	15	10	10	11	8	11	10
Income Statement Analysis (Million $)										
Revs.	8,873	6,716	3,974	2,938	2,274	1,878	1,377	783	349	232
Oper. Inc.	2,774	3,138	1,185	798	583	489	383	202	63.9	30.1
Depr.	517	447	203	136	86.9	53.6	32.7	21.7	17.4	9.3
Int. Exp.	14.6	33.5	20.2	15.5	12.0	12.9	15.3	6.0	4.8	1.9
Pretax Inc.	2,441	1,357	1,058	718	519	451	355	180	42.3	20.1
Eff. Tax Rate	27%	26%	25%	25%	26%	28%	30%	29%	32%	35%
Net Inc.	1,782	1,011	793	539	386	327	251	127	28.7	13.0
Balance Sheet & Other Fin. Data (Million $)										
Cash	1,983	1,109	1,530	955	727	380	241	345	55.1	16.8
Curr. Assets	6,100	4,320	3,105	2,627	1,754	1,319	902	650	217	112
Total Assets	10,628	7,173	4,569	3,490	2,294	1,746	1,318	830	321	190
Curr. Liab.	2,114	1,398	653	506	418	359	301	133	76.3	44.1
LT Debt	14.5	687	539	559	191	246	286	274	75.7	15.7
Common Eqty.	8,177	4,952	3,324	2,376	1,637	1,140	728	419	158	126
Total Cap.	8,494	5,764	3,914	2,980	1,874	1,386	1,014	693	239	146
Cap. Exp.	858	524	373	211	126	92.0	109	51.3	28.5	19.6
Cash Flow	2,299	1,458	997	675	473	380	283	149	46.1	22.3
Curr. Ratio	2.9	3.1	4.8	5.2	4.2	3.7	3.0	4.9	2.8	2.5
% LT Debt of Cap.	0.2	11.9	13.8	18.8	10.2	17.7	28.2	39.5	31.7	10.8
% Net Inc.of Revs.	20.1	15.0	20.0	18.3	17.0	17.4	18.2	16.2	8.2	5.6
% Ret. on Assets	20.0	15.8	19.7	18.6	19.1	21.3	22.8	20.9	11.2	7.4
% Ret. on Equity	27.1	34.4	27.8	26.8	27.8	35.0	42.7	41.6	20.0	11.0

Data as orig reptd.; bef. results of disc opers/spec. items. Per share data adj. for stk. divs. Bold denotes diluted EPS (FASB 128)-prior periods restated. E-Estimated. NA-Not Available. NM-Not Meaningful. NR-Not Ranked.

Office—35 Parkwood Drive, Hopkinton, MA 01748. **Tel**—(508) 435-1000. **Website**—http://www.emc.com **Chrmn**—M. C. Ruettgers. **Pres & CEO**—J. M. Tucci.**SVP & CFO**—W. J. Teuber Jr. **VP & Investor Contact**—Polly Pearson. **Dirs**—M. J. Cronin, J. R. Egan, R. J. Egan, W. P. Fitzgerald, J. F. Oliveri, M. C. Ruettgers, J. M. Tucci, A.M. Zeien. **Transfer Agent & Registrar**—EquiServe. **Incorporated**—in Massachusetts in 1979. **Empl**— 24,100. **S&P Analyst:** Jim Corridore

STANDARD
&POOR'S
STOCK REPORTS

Flextronics International

Nasdaq Symbol **FLEX**

18-AUG-01

Industry: Manufacturing (Specialized)

Summary: Flextronics is a leading provider of electronics contract manufacturing services to original equipment manufacturers in the PC, telecom, consumer and other industries.

S&P Opinion: Accumulate (★★★★)

Recent Price • 21.78 | Yield • Nil
52 Wk Range • 44.90-12.37 | 12-Mo. P/E • NM

Quantitative Evaluations

Outlook
(1 Lowest—5 Highest)
• **2-**

Fair Value
• **24.40**

Risk
• **NA**

Earn./Div. Rank
• **NR**

Technical Eval.
• **Neutral** since 8/01

Rel. Strength Rank
(1 Lowest—99 Highest)
• **22**

Insider Activity
• **Unfavorable**

Earnings vs. Previous Year
E=Up E=Down E=No Change

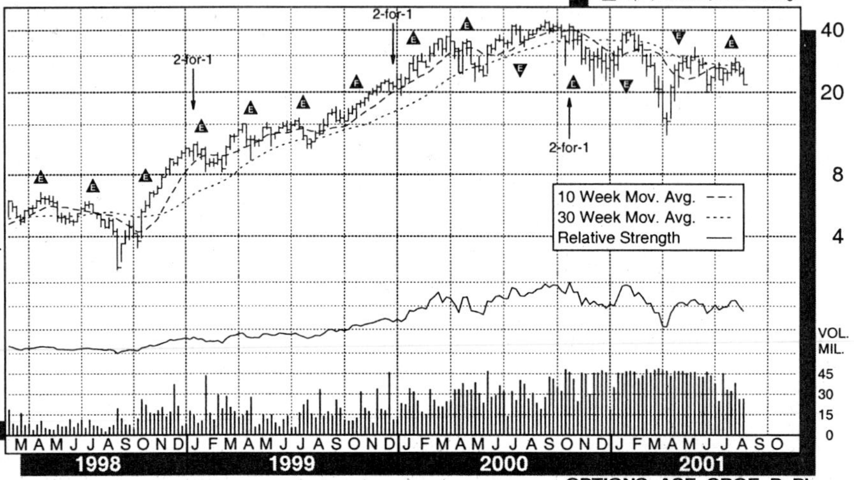

OPTIONS: ASE, CBOE, P, Ph

Overview - 14-AUG-01

We expect FY 02 (Mar.) revenues to climb only about 15%, reflecting the difficult economic environment that has impacted demand for the products FLEX makes, particularly in telecom and datacom. However, recent agreements with Ericsson, Alcatel, Microsoft and Motorola should allow the company to grow revenues at a time when most of its competitors are showing sharp revenue declines. In addition, the company is increasing penetration of its existing customer base, and in the long term, should benefit from rapid growth at these customers. Gross margins should narrow, on higher volume/lower mix issues, and acquisition costs should drive up SG&A expenses somewhat over the near term. We project FY 02 cash EPS (before amortization and one-time charges) of $0.75, down 14% from the $0.87 cash EPS the company reported for FY 01.

Valuation - 14-AUG-01

We still like the long term picture in the electronics manufacturing services industry, and particularly FLEX's position as the low cost producer in the industry. We now feel that much of the current economic difficulties being faced by the company and the sector are priced into the stock. The shares have recovered somewhat from a sharp correction earlier in the year and are now down about 14% for the year. At 33X our FY 02 EPS estimate, the shares are trading at the low end of their historical P/E range and at a slight premium to our expected five-year earnings growth rate of 30%. Given the company's conservative guidance, which expects hitting its earnings targets even with no improvement in the economic climate, we see opportunity for upside surprises if we do get some economic improvement by the end of the calendar year.

Key Stock Statistics

S&P EPS Est. 2002	0.75	Tang. Bk. Value/Share	6.32
P/E on S&P Est. 2002	29.0	Beta	NA
Dividend Rate/Share	Nil	Shareholders	2,094
Shs. outstg. (M)	482.0	Market cap. (B)	$ 10.5
Avg. daily vol. (M)	6.094	Inst. holdings	72%

Value of $10,000 invested 5 years ago: $ 96,800

Fiscal Year Ending Mar. 31

	2001	2000	1999	1998	1997	1996
Revenues (Million $)						
1Q	2,677	529.8	376.1	196.9	118.3	86.01
2Q	3,079	870.8	422.9	210.1	122.5	104.8
3Q	3,239	1,180	499.9	295.0	121.5	131.8
4Q	3,114	1,897	508.7	331.1	128.3	125.7
Yr.	12,110	5,740	1,808	1,113	490.6	448.4
Earnings Per Share ($)						
1Q	**-0.88**	**0.09**	**0.07**	0.05	0.04	0.03
2Q	**0.10**	**0.09**	**0.08**	0.05	0.05	0.04
3Q	**0.14**	**0.14**	**0.09**	**0.04**	**0.00**	0.05
4Q	**-0.41**	**0.14**	**0.06**	**0.01**	-0.03	-0.28
Yr.	**-1.01**	**0.52**	**0.28**	**0.13**	**0.08**	-0.17

Next earnings report expected: late August

Dividend Data

Amount ($)	Date Decl.	Ex-Div. Date	Stock of Record	Payment Date
2-for-1	Jul. 26	Oct. 17	Sep. 22	Oct. 16 '00

Flextronics International Ltd.

Business Summary - 14-AUG-01

Capitalizing on a growing trend for original equipment manufacturers (OEMs) to outsource production of their products, Flextronics International has been growing rapidly. Through a combination of internal growth and acquisitions, it has become one of the world's largest providers of electronic manufacturing services (EMS), with FY 01 (Mar.) pro forma revenues of $12.1 billion. FLEX provides services to OEMs in the telecom, networking, computer, consumer electronics and medical industries.

The company provides a wide range of integrated services, from initial product design to volume production and fulfillment. Manufacturing services range from printed circuit board (PCB) fabrication and assembly to full product assembly and testing. FLEX believes it has strengths in interconnect, miniaturization and packaging technologies. In addition, it provides engineering services, including design, PCB layout, quick-turn prototyping and test development, and also provides logistics services, including materials procurement, inventory management, packaging and distribution.

FLEX believes its size, global presence and expertise enable it to win large outsourced manufacturing programs from leading multinational OEMs. An OEM working with the company can achieve accelerated time-to-market and time-to-volume production, as well as reduced total production costs. By working closely with customers through the design, manufacturing and distribution process, FLEX believes it becomes an integral part of customer operations.

Customers include industry leaders such as Alcatel, Cisco, Compaq, Ericsson, Hewlett-Packard, Microsoft, Motorola, Nokia, Palm, Phillips and Siemens. In FY 01, the 10 largest customers accounted for 59% of net sales. No customer accounted for more than 10% of sales in FY 01.

The company operates manufacturing centers in 27 countries worldwide, with about 16 million sq. ft. of capacity. In recent years, FLEX has increased overall capacity substantially.

FLEX has been active on the acquisition front. In April 2000, it acquired The DII Group, Inc., an EMS company with 1999 revenues of $1.3 billion. In August 2000, Chatham Technologies was acquired, and in November 2000, FLEX acquired JIT Holdings ($562 million in revenues In FY 00). In May 2000, FLEX announced a complex agreement with Motorola under which Motorola would outsource $30 billion in revenues over the next five years, and purchased an equity instrument at a discount, for an initial payment of $100 million. However, in July 2001, the company announced that it would repurchase the equity instrument from Motorola and cancel the agreement, but would continue to work with Motorola and increase the amount of business the two companies do together.

Per Share Data ($) (Year Ended Mar. 31)	2001	2000	1999	1998	1997	1996	1995	1994	1993	1992
Tangible Bk. Val.	NA	6.04	2.22	2.28	0.95	0.58	0.56	0.64	NA	NA
Cash Flow	NA	0.86	0.55	0.67	0.35	-0.07	0.13	NA	NA	NA
Earnings	-1.01	0.52	0.28	0.13	0.06	-0.17	0.06	0.05	NA	NA
Dividends	Nil	Nil	Nil	Nil	Nil	Nil	Nil	NA	NA	NA
Payout Ratio	Nil	Nil	Nil	Nil	Nil	Nil	Nil	NA	NA	NA
Cal. Yrs.	2000	1999	1998	1997	1996	1995	1994	1993	1992	1991
Prices - High	44.90	24.68	10.92	6.18	4.90	3.78	2.06	NA	NA	NA
- Low	19.15	8.18	2.75	2.12	2.03	1.62	1.09	NA	NA	NA
P/E Ratio - High	NM	47	39	48	78	NM	32	NA	NA	NA
- Low	NM	16	10	16	32	NM	17	NA	NA	NA
Income Statement Analysis (Million $)										
Revs.	NA	4,307	1,808	1,113	491	448	237	NA	NA	NA
Oper. Inc.	NA	242	128	82.5	32.2	1.1	16.3	NA	NA	NA
Depr.	NA	83.0	50.4	30.9	13.6	10.4	6.1	NA	NA	NA
Int. Exp.	NA	31.0	21.9	17.7	3.9	2.7	0.7	NA	NA	NA
Pretax Inc.	NA	137	59.3	22.2	9.7	-13.6	7.6	NA	NA	NA
Eff. Tax Rate	NA	12%	13%	10%	23%	NM	19%	NA	NA	NA
Net Inc.	NA	121	51.5	19.9	7.5	-17.4	6.2	NA	NA	NA
Balance Sheet & Other Fin. Data (Million $)										
Cash	NA	619	173	89.4	23.6	4.8	NA	NA	NA	NA
Curr. Assets	NA	2,299	654	440	210	141	83.9	NA	NA	NA
Total Assets	NA	3,087	1,094	744	359	215	116	NA	NA	NA
Curr. Liab.	NA	1,256	413	315	235	114	50.5	NA	NA	NA
LT Debt	NA	214	197	190	Nil	13.4	Nil	NA	NA	NA
Common Eqty.	NA	1,593	466	215	83.6	70.8	57.7	NA	NA	NA
Total Cap.	NA	1,816	672	410	84.1	86.0	58.7	NA	NA	NA
Cap. Exp.	NA	250	148	99	38.0	NA	NA	NA	NA	NA
Cash Flow	NA	204	102	50.9	21.0	-7.0	12.3	NA	NA	NA
Curr. Ratio	NA	1.8	1.6	1.4	0.9	1.2	1.7	NA	NA	NA
% LT Debt of Cap.	NA	11.8	29.3	46.2	Nil	15.6	Nil	NA	NA	NA
% Net Inc.of Revs.	NA	2.8	2.8	1.8	1.5	NM	2.6	NA	NA	NA
% Ret. on Assets	NA	5.5	5.6	3.6	2.6	NM	5.7	NA	NA	NA
% Ret. on Equity	NA	11.6	15.1	13.3	9.7	NM	11.9	NA	NA	NA

Data as orig reptd.; bef. results of disc opers/spec. items. Per share data adj. for stk. divs. Bold denotes diluted EPS (FASB 128)-prior periods restated. E-Estimated. NA-Not Available. NM-Not Meaningful. NR-Not Ranked.

Office—11 UBI Road 1, #07-01/02, Meiban Industrial Building, Singapore 408723. **Tel**—(65) 844-3366. **Website**—www.flextronics.com **Chrmn & CEO**—M. E. Marks. **CFO**—R. R. B. Dykes. **Treas & Investor Contact**—Laurette Slawson (408-576-7233). **Dirs**—C. F. A. Ahkong, P. Foley, T. S. Lam, H. S. Leong, M. E. Marks, M. J. Moritz, R. L. Sharp. **Transfer Agent & Registrar**—Boston EquiServe L.P. **Incorporated**—in Singapore in 1990. **Empl**— 75,000. **S&P Analyst:** Jim Corridore

STANDARD
&POOR'S
STOCK REPORTS

International Rectifier

NYSE Symbol **IRF**

In S&P MidCap 400

18-AUG-01

Industry:
Electronics (Semiconductors)

Summary: This major worldwide supplier of power semiconductors is the leading producer in the power MOSFET (metal oxide semiconductor field effect transistor) market.

S&P Opinion: Accumulate (★★★★)

Recent Price • 33.15
52 Wk Range • 69.50-27.37
Yield • Nil
12-Mo. P/E • 24.6

Quantitative Evaluations

Outlook
(1 Lowest—5 Highest)
• **3-**

Fair Value
• **36.60**

Risk
• **Average**

Earn./Div. Rank
• **B**

Technical Eval.
• **Neutral** since 7/01

Rel. Strength Rank
(1 Lowest—99 Highest)
• **18**

Insider Activity
• **Neutral**

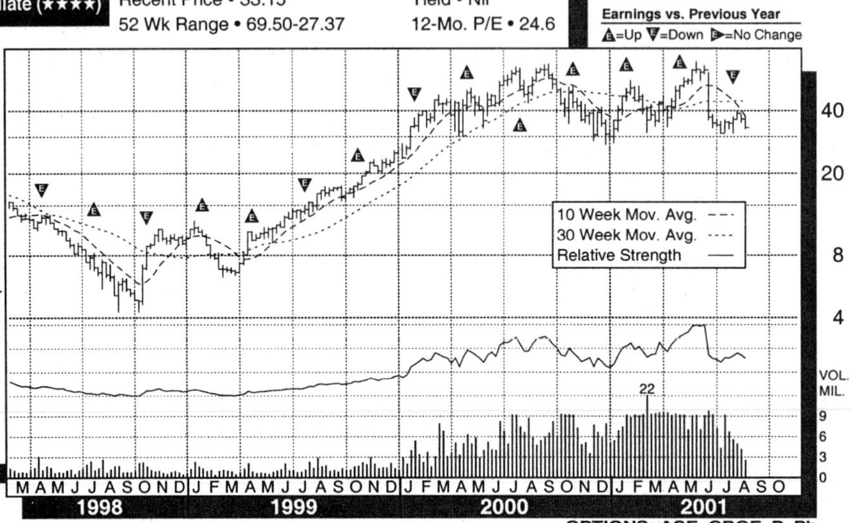

OPTIONS: ASE, CBOE, P, Ph

Overview - 30-JUL-01

We expect revenues to dip about 9% in FY 02 (Jun.), reflecting a sharp slowdown from the boom seen for most of FY 01. Demand in the datacom and telecom segments turned extremely weak in the spring, but should stabilize by autumn. Demand for IRF's power management chips in the automotive, home, aerospace, and industrial markets is holding up better. Lower demand for electronic goods will restrict results into early 2002. On May 15, 2001, IRF announced a strategic collaboration with Japanese power chip maker Sanken Electric Co., to join in design and development activities, and to cross-hold about $13 million of each other's shares. The company makes chips for Sony's Playstation 2 and Fujitsu's flat panel TVs. IRF took a restructuring charge of $86.4 million in the fourth quarter of FY 01. We expect the gross margin to dip to 37%, before improving in late 2001. We estimate FY 02 EPS at $1.50.

Valuation - 30-JUL-01

The shares have been consolidating since dropping 30% on the company's June 14, 2001, revenue warning. The semiconductor industry continues to suffer from high chip inventory levels and weak demand. Ultimately, demand for power management chips will rise again in response to the expansion of the Internet and mobile computing. The company reduced its debt burden in FY 01, and has ample cash of $850 million to pursue acquisitions. The shares recently traded at 22X our calendar 2002 EPS estimate of $2.45, which is at a discount to IRF's estimated long-term growth rate of 26%. The shares trade at 2.7X tangible book value, which is modest compared to most other chip companies. Given an attractive valuation, and some early evidence of a bottom in order patterns, we are upgrading our opinion to accumulate, from hold.

Key Stock Statistics

S&P EPS Est. 2002	1.50	Tang. Bk. Value/Share	13.70
P/E on S&P Est. 2002	22.1	Beta	2.29
S&P EPS Est. 2003	2.90	Shareholders	1,546
Dividend Rate/Share	Nil	Market cap. (B)	$ 2.1
Shs. outstg. (M)	62.6	Inst. holdings	81%
Avg. daily vol. (M)	0.851		

Value of $10,000 invested 5 years ago: $ 16,679

Fiscal Year Ending Jun. 30

	2001	2000	1999	1998	1997	1996
Revenues (Million $)						
1Q	249.4	152.2	127.5	133.1	115.2	126.1
2Q	268.1	171.1	132.8	144.6	118.0	141.0
3Q	276.0	198.0	137.6	140.4	122.8	154.1
4Q	185.1	232.0	147.5	133.8	130.2	155.7
Yr.	978.6	753.3	545.4	551.9	486.1	576.9
Earnings Per Share ($)						
1Q	**0.63**	**0.10**	Nil	0.12	0.06	0.25
2Q	**0.71**	**0.23**	**0.38**	**0.13**	0.07	0.30
3Q	**0.73**	**0.38**	**0.08**	**0.06**	0.08	0.35
4Q	**-0.78**	**0.52**	**-0.07**	**0.01**	-1.04	0.40
Yr.	**1.35**	**1.27**	**0.39**	**0.32**	**-0.84**	**1.29**

Next earnings report expected: mid October

Dividend Data

Annual dividends, paid since 1973, were omitted in 1982. The shares were split two for one in 1995.

International Rectifier Corporation

Business Summary - 30-JUL-01

International Rectifier, founded in 1947, is a leading designer and manufacturer of power semiconductors that refine electricity from wall outlets or batteries into a more usable form. The process, which the company calls power conversion, reduces costs and enhances the performance and efficiency of electrically powered products. IRF's products are used across a variety of markets, including information technology, automotive, industrial, consumer electronics and government/space.

Products offered by the company include MOSFETs (metal oxide semiconductor field effect transistors) and IGBTs (insulated gate bipolar transistors), which serve the switch function in power conversion to provide an even, usable flow of power for electronic equipment. The company's MOSFET and IGBT products accounted for about two-thirds of sales in recent years. IRF also supplies high-voltage ICs, high-performance diodes, high-power rectifiers and thyristors. It believes its full complement of power conversion technology represents a competitive advantage, enabling it to provide customers with integrated solutions to their power conversion needs. Based on industry sources, the company estimates that about 70% of the world's power MOSFETs are produced by IRF or under its patents.

IRF's products extend the battery life of portable electronic devices (laptop computers, cellular phones); increase automotive fuel efficiency and safety (electronic power steering, anti-lock braking systems); and reduce design and electricity costs of industrial automated equipment (motor controls) and major household appliances (refrigerators, washing machines). The company believes several factors will drive continued demand for efficient power semiconductor components and power conversion solutions, including the proliferation of portable electronics, rapid growth in electricity demand, and the high cost of installing electric power infrastructure in developing economies.

Based on statistics from the Semiconductor Industry Association (SIA), the company believes it is the leader in the field effect power transistor segment of the semiconductor industry with its MOSFETs and IGBTs. Industrywide revenues from sales of power MOSFETs and IGBTs were $2.69 billion in calendar 1998, a decrease of 4.6% from 1997 levels. However, industrywide revenues from sales of power MOSFETs and IGBTs increased to $3.13 billion in calendar 1999 and to about $4.0 billion in calendar 2000.

In FY 00 (Jun.), 36% of product sales came from North America, 24% from Europe, and 40% from Asia (including Japan and Asia Pacific). IRF has manufacturing facilities in North America, Europe and Asia, and also uses subcontract assembly in Asia.

In March 2000, the company acquired Zing Technologies, Inc., a supplier of power semiconductor modules and components, for about $28.5 million.

Per Share Data ($) (Year Ended Jun. 30)	2001	2000	1999	1998	1997	1996	1995	1994	1993	1992
Tangible Bk. Val.	NA	13.70	7.65	7.78	7.48	8.29	6.86	4.99	4.60	4.81
Cash Flow	NA	2.24	1.28	1.07	-0.12	1.88	1.33	0.78	0.28	0.61
Earnings	1.35	1.27	0.12	0.32	-0.84	1.29	0.84	0.39	-0.08	0.23
Dividends	Nil	Nil	Nil	Nil	Nil	Nil	Nil	Nil	Nil	Nil
Payout Ratio	Nil	Nil	Nil	Nil	Nil	Nil	Nil	Nil	Nil	Nil
Prices - High	69.50	67.43	26.00	14.75	23.75	27.00	26.00	12.18	7.50	8.06
- Low	27.81	23.50	6.25	4.25	10.87	11.25	11.06	6.50	4.81	3.68
P/E Ratio - High	51	53	NM	46	NM	21	31	31	NM	35
- Low	21	19	52	13	NM	9	13	17	NM	16
Income Statement Analysis (Million $)										
Revs.	NA	753	545	552	486	577	429	329	282	265
Oper. Inc.	NA	162	59.4	71.3	58.7	127	71.8	39.4	16.5	26.2
Depr.	NA	55.9	46.2	38.9	37.1	30.1	23.4	15.9	14.2	15.4
Int. Exp.	NA	6.0	11.1	7.3	4.0	0.4	0.4	3.6	3.6	1.4
Pretax Inc.	NA	102	31.2	24.6	-52.7	95.9	47.5	18.9	-2.6	10.5
Eff. Tax Rate	NA	28%	35%	33%	NM	31%	17%	17%	NM	12%
Net Inc.	NA	73.1	20.4	16.5	-43.2	66.5	39.4	15.7	-3.0	9.2
Balance Sheet & Other Fin. Data (Million $)										
Cash	NA	196	31.5	32.3	53.4	53.8	53.8	13.1	8.5	8.5
Curr. Assets	NA	592	306	317	316	277	234	157	128	136
Total Assets	NA	1,026	709	736	680	629	496	331	278	286
Curr. Liab.	NA	150	141	154	113	125	106	89.7	69.8	68.4
LT Debt	NA	4.6	158	154	143	48.0	23.9	27.0	12.0	12.0
Common Eqty.	NA	844	396	400	382	421	345	203	186	192
Total Cap.	NA	867	561	365	538	488	379	230	198	204
Cap. Exp.	NA	64.6	71.6	71.6	100	112	107	37.1	21.8	33.0
Cash Flow	NA	129	66.5	55.4	-6.1	96.6	62.8	31.6	11.1	24.6
Curr. Ratio	NA	3.9	2.2	2.1	2.8	2.2	2.2	1.7	1.8	2.0
% LT Debt of Cap.	NA	0.5	28.2	42.2	26.7	9.3	6.3	11.6	6.0	5.7
% Net Inc.of Revs.	NA	9.7	3.7	3.0	NM	11.5	9.2	4.8	NM	3.5
% Ret. on Assets	NA	8.4	2.8	2.3	NM	11.8	9.5	5.2	NM	3.4
% Ret. on Equity	NA	11.8	5.1	4.2	NM	17.3	14.4	8.1	NM	5.0

Data as orig reptd.; bef. results of disc opers/spec. items. Per share data adj. for stk. divs. Bold denotes diluted EPS (FASB 128)-prior periods restated. E-Estimated. NA-Not Available. NM-Not Meaningful. NR-Not Ranked.

Office—233 Kansas St., El Segundo, CA 90245. **Tel**—(310) 726-8000. **Fax**—(310) 322-3332. **Website**—http://www.irf.com **Chrmn**—E. Lidow. **CEO** —A. Lidow. **EVP & CFO**—M. P. McGee. **EVP & Secy**—L. M. Russell. **Investor Contact**—Shelley Wagers. **Dirs**—G. Krsek, A. Lidow, D. B. Lidow, E. Lidow, M. Matsuda, R. J. Mueller, J. D. Plummer, J. O. Vance, R. E. Vogt. **Transfer Agent & Registrar**—Mellon Investor Services, LA. **Incorporated**—in California in 1947; reincorporated in Delaware in 1979. **Empl**— 5,098. **S&P Analyst:** T.W. Smith, CFA

STANDARD
&POOR'S
STOCK REPORTS

Lexmark International

NYSE Symbol **LXK**

In S&P 500

18-AUG-01

Industry:
Computers (Peripherals)

Summary: This company develops, manufactures and supplies laser and inkjet printers and associated consumable supplies for the office and home markets.

S&P Opinion: Accumulate (★★★★)

Recent Price • 47.77 | Yield • Nil
52 Wk Range • 70.93-28.75 | 12-Mo. P/E • 22.0

Quantitative Evaluations

Outlook
(1 Lowest—5 Highest)
• **1+**

Fair Value
• **42.40**

Risk
• **Average**

Earn./Div. Rank
• **NR**

Technical Eval.
• **Bearish** since 7/01

Rel. Strength Rank
(1 Lowest—99 Highest)
• **25**

Insider Activity
• **Unfavorable**

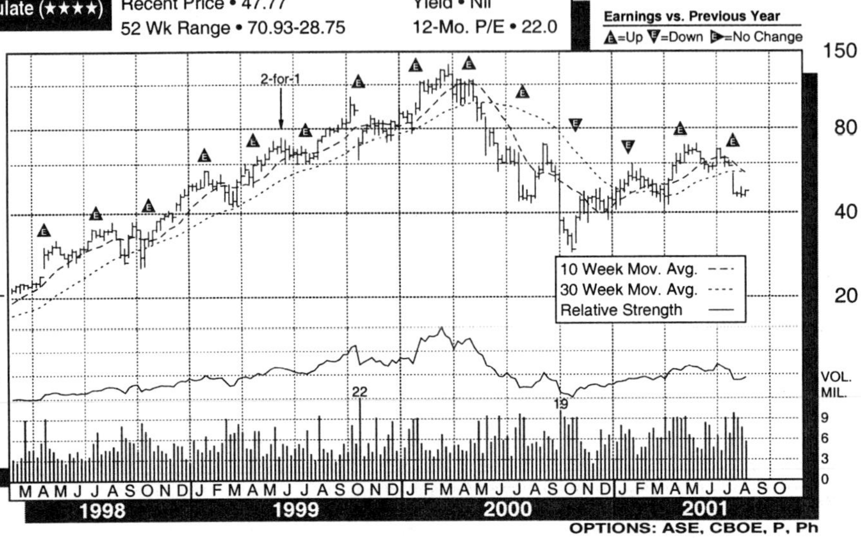

OPTIONS: ASE, CBOE, P, Ph

Overview - 25-JUL-01

We project a revenue increase of 10% for 2001, up from a gain of 10% in 2000, and we project an advance of 11% for 2002. Revenue gains should be aided in 2001 by better monochrome laser sales growth, and strong growth of inkjet printers in 2000 should translate into better supplies growth in 2001. We expect gross margins to widen moderately, from 33% in 2000 to 33.7% in 2001, as the impact of a more favorable product mix (growth in laser printers and supplies) is largely offset by aggressive pricing actions. Gross margins in 2002 should approximate 33.3%. Operating margins should remain at about 12%, as the company begins to benefit from new restructuring initiatives. We project 2001 EPS at $2.70, up from 2000's $2.35, excluding restructuring charges, and forecast $3.10 for 2002.

Valuation - 25-JUL-01

We continue to recommend accumulating the stock. The shares have outperformed the broader market since the beginning of 2001, and we believe they will continue to do so over the next six to 12 months, as investors are attracted to LXK's ability to generate EPS growth that exceeds that of its tech peers. In addition, the company has capitalized on growing printer demand, and has significantly expanded its market share; this bodes well for future high-margin aftermarket supplies sales. For 2002, LXK could benefit from the exit of Xerox from the office superstore, and should gain retail shelf space in this important market. However, a strong U.S. dollar, excess inventories, and stiff price competition will limit earnings growth in the second half of 2001. Still, we believe the shares, trading at a P/E multiple (based on our 2002 EPS estimate of $3.10) below that of LXK's peers, are attractive.

Key Stock Statistics

S&P EPS Est. 2001	2.62	Tang. Bk. Value/Share	6.11
P/E on S&P Est. 2001	18.2	Beta	1.20
S&P EPS Est. 2002	3.10	Shareholders	1,769
Dividend Rate/Share	Nil	Market cap. (B)	$ 6.1
Shs. outstg. (M)	128.2	Inst. holdings	89%
Avg. daily vol. (M)	2.021		

Value of $10,000 invested 5 years ago: $ 56,200

Fiscal Year Ending Dec. 31

	2001	2000	1999	1998	1997	1996
Revenues (Million $)						
1Q	999	891.7	787.0	672.1	583.4	587.8
2Q	988.0	893.0	817.3	697.3	556.3	555.3
3Q	—	926.6	845.0	743.8	618.3	547.6
4Q	—	1,096	1,003	907.4	735.0	686.9
Yr.	—	3,807	3,452	3,021	2,494	2,378
Earnings Per Share ($)						
1Q	**0.60**	**0.59**	**0.48**	**0.34**	0.20	0.14
2Q	**0.65**	**0.62**	**0.55**	**0.38**	0.23	0.20
3Q	**E0.59**	**0.50**	**0.56**	**0.41**	0.27	0.20
4Q	**E0.78**	**0.42**	**0.73**	**0.58**	**0.39**	0.29
Yr.	**E2.62**	**2.13**	**2.32**	**1.70**	**1.08**	**0.84**

Next earnings report expected: late October

Dividend Data

No dividends have been paid.

Lexmark International, Inc.

Business Summary - 25-JUL-01

Lexmark's primary focus is the monochrome and color workgroup laser printer market; it is a major supplier of these printers, second to Hewlett-Packard (H-P). The overall printer market, estimated by industry analysts to have exceeded $40 billion in 2000, is expected to post only modest growth through 2004, but LXK has concentrated on the faster growing markets for color inkjet printers and color laser printers, expected to grow at double-digit rates in volume terms. The company (formerly Lexmark International Group), spun off from IBM in 1991, has been publicly traded since November 1995.

Laser printers consist of two main markets: shared workgroup printers, which are typically directly attached to networks; and lower priced desktop printers. In the shared workgroup market, LXK believes it is second in worldwide market share, behind H-P. In the lower priced desktop laser printer market, LXK is one of three leading vendors. Overall, H-P dominates the laser printer market, with about a 60% share.

Although growth prospects are strong for inkjet printers, pricing is intensely competitive. LXK introduced the first desktop color printer priced at under $100 with its November 1997 launch of the $99 color inkjet printer, in a strategy aimed at building brand awareness and its installed base. In 1999, H-P introduced an inkjet printer (Apollo) priced under $100. The consumer market today consists largely of color inkjet printers. LXK's shipments of color inkjets rose at double digit rates from 1997 through 2000. In 2000, LXK's unit volumes grew at more than twice the industry average in color inkjets.

By expanding its installed base, growth in LXK's high margin consumable supplies helps to protect its operating performance in a price competitive marketplace. Consumable supplies are replaced one to three times a year, depending on type of printer and usage, and thus demand for laser and inkjet print cartridges grows faster than overall printer shipments.

In addition to its core printer business, the company makes supplies for IBM branded printers, after-market supplies for OEM products, and typewriters and typewriter supplies that are sold under the IBM trademark.

To meet accelerating demand, LXK completed a new facility in the Philippines in 1999, and built a new inkjet plant in Mexico; existing plants in Scotland and Mexico were expanded. Capital expenditures in 2000 were $297 million.

International sales, including exports from the U.S., represent about half of LXK's sales, with Europe accounting for two-thirds.

As of December 31, 2000, LXK had bought back $882 million worth of common shares under a $1 billion stock repurchase program.

Per Share Data ($) (Year Ended Dec. 31)	2000	1999	1998	1997	1996	1995	1994	1993	1992	1991
Tangible Bk. Val.	6.11	6.24	5.21	4.07	3.72	2.74	2.29	NA	NA	NA
Cash Flow	2.80	2.89	2.23	1.60	1.29	0.98	0.81	0.96	0.78	NA
Earnings	2.13	2.32	1.70	1.08	0.84	0.32	-0.23	-0.17	-0.56	-1.04
Dividends	Nil	Nil	Nil	Nil	Nil	Nil	NA	NA	NA	NA
Payout Ratio	Nil	Nil	Nil	Nil	Nil	Nil	NA	NA	NA	NA
Prices - High	135.87	104.00	51.00	19.00	13.87	11.18	NA	NA	NA	NA
- Low	28.75	42.09	17.50	9.56	6.68	7.75	NA	NA	NA	NA
P/E Ratio - High	64	45	30	18	16	35	NA	NA	NA	NA
- Low	13	18	10	9	8	24	NA	NA	NA	NA
Income Statement Analysis (Million $)										
Revs.	3,807	3,452	3,021	2,494	2,378	2,158	1,852	1,676	1,764	1,273
Oper. Inc.	548	557	458	352	300	268	242	210	205	NA
Depr.	91.2	80.1	75.6	77.5	69.2	99	127	139	165	NA
Int. Exp.	12.8	10.7	11.0	10.8	20.9	35.1	61.4	73.5	93.0	NA
Pretax Inc.	396	459	365	255	202	63.3	50.7	-9.4	-46.6	-110
Eff. Tax Rate	28%	31%	33%	36%	37%	24%	12%	NM	NM	NM
Net Inc.	285	319	243	163	128	48.1	44.6	-9.4	-57.3	-118
Balance Sheet & Other Fin. Data (Million $)										
Cash	68.5	93.9	149	43.0	119	151	37.3	NA	NA	NA
Curr. Assets	1,244	1,089	1,020	776	765	716	NA	NA	NA	NA
Total Assets	2,073	1,703	1,483	1,208	1,222	1,143	NA	NA	NA	NA
Curr. Liab.	979	736	606	548	421	488	NA	NA	NA	NA
LT Debt	149	149	149	57.0	163	175	215	NA	NA	NA
Common Eqty.	777	659	578	501	540	390	330	NA	NA	NA
Total Cap.	926	808	727	558	704	565	545	NA	NA	NA
Cap. Exp.	297	220	102	69.5	145	107	58.1	62.4	57.8	NA
Cash Flow	377	399	319	241	197	147	99	118	96.0	NA
Curr. Ratio	1.3	1.5	1.7	1.4	1.8	1.5	NA	NA	NA	NA
% LT Debt of Cap.	16.1	18.4	20.5	10.2	23.2	47.9	39.5	NA	NA	NA
% Net Inc.of Revs.	7.5	9.2	8.0	6.5	5.4	2.2	2.4	NM	NM	NA
% Ret. on Assets	15.1	20.0	18.1	13.4	10.8	4.6	NA	NA	NA	NA
% Ret. on Equity	39.7	51.5	45.1	31.3	27.5	7.0	NA	NA	NA	NA

Data as orig reptd.; bef. results of disc opers/spec. items. Per share data adj. for stk. divs. Bold denotes diluted EPS (FASB 128)-prior periods restated. E-Estimated. NA-Not Available. NM-Not Meaningful. NR-Not Ranked.

Office—One Lexmark Center Drive, Lexington, KY 40550. **Tel**—(859) 232-2000. **Website**—www.lexmark.com **Chrmn & CEO**—P. J. Curlander. **EVP & CFO**—G. E. Morin. **Investor Contact**—Mark D. Sisk (859-232-5934). **Dirs**—B. C. Ames, T. Beck, F. T. Cary, P. J. Curlander, W. R. Fields, R. E. Gomory, S. R. Hardis, J. F. Hardymon, R. Holland Jr., M. L. Mann, M. J. Maples, M. D. Walker. **Transfer Agent & Registrar**—Mellon Investor Services, Ridgefield Park, NJ. **Incorporated**—in Delaware in 1990. **Empl**— 13,000. **S&P Analyst:** Megan Graham-Hackett

STANDARD
&POOR'S
STOCK REPORTS

Maxim Integrated Products

Nasdaq Symbol **MXIM**

In S&P 500

22-AUG-01

Industry: Electronics (Semiconductors)

Summary: This company is a worldwide leader in design, development and manufacture of linear and mixed-signal integrated circuits.

S&P Opinion: Accumulate (★★★★)

Recent Price • 46.21
52 Wk Range • 90.12-33.55
Yield • Nil
12-Mo. P/E • 49.7

Quantitative Evaluations

Outlook
(1 Lowest—5 Highest)
• **1⁻**

Fair Value
• **43.70**

Risk
• **Average**

Earn./Div. Rank
• **B+**

Technical Eval.
• **Neutral** since 8/01

Rel. Strength Rank
(1 Lowest—99 Highest)
• **47**

Insider Activity
• **NA**

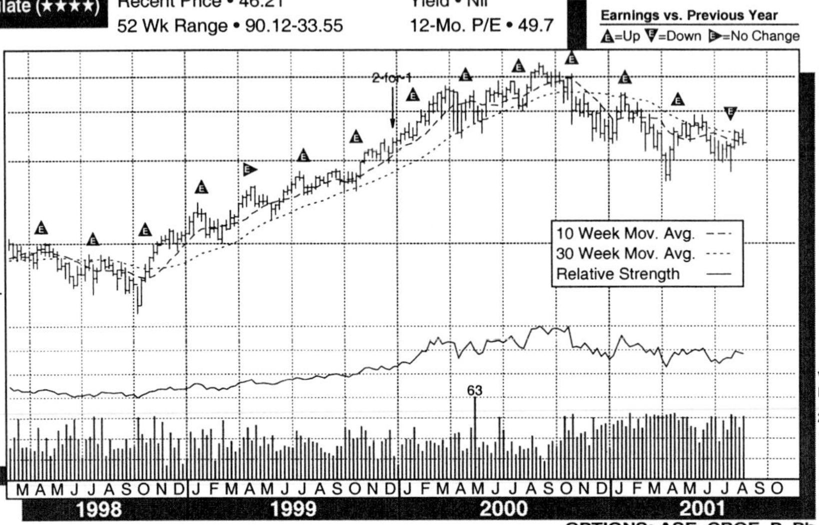

OPTIONS: ASE, CBOE, P, Ph

Overview - 22-AUG-01

We expect revenues to decline 13% in FY 02 (Jun.), reflecting a semiconductor industry downturn, tempered by the acquisition of Dallas Semiconductor in April 2001. Revenues for the first quarter of FY 02 are expected to be down 25% from the FY 01 fourth quarter. We expect revenue growth to pick up in 2002 as the economy strengthens and chip inventories clear. The company expects to maintain gross margin at an industry-leading level above 70% despite current low revenue levels. Linear and mixed-signal integrated circuits manufactured by MXIM are commonly known as analog circuits. Compared to the digital integrated market, the analog market is characterized by longer product life cycles, less foreign competition, and more stable growth rates that are less influenced by economic cycles. We estimate FY 02 EPS at $0.80, and foresee a rebound to $1.20 in FY 03.

Valuation - 22-AUG-01

The shares are rebounding from a 52-week low reached in April. We believe MXIM is currently in the most difficult part of the current industry downturn, with investors just beginning to look ahead to better results as the industry cycles up over the next two years. Maxim is exposed to a broad range of analog markets, and produces wide margins by industry norms. The operations acquired from Dallas Semiconductor added complementary product lines. Integration is proceeding smoothly, delivering scale advantages in research and marketing, and we view the acquisition favorably. The shares recently traded at 43X our calendar 2002 EPS estimate of $1.01, a premium to the broader market, but reasonable in light of MXIM's consistent performance in a cyclical growth industry and estimated long-term growth rate of 27%. We continue to recommend accumulating the shares.

Key Stock Statistics

S&P EPS Est. 2002	0.80	Tang. Bk. Value/Share	3.95
P/E on S&P Est. 2002	57.8	Beta	2.01
S&P EPS Est. 2003	1.20	Shareholders	2,869
Dividend Rate/Share	Nil	Market cap. (B)	$ 14.3
Shs. outstg. (M)	328.3	Inst. holdings	88%
Avg. daily vol. (M)	5.437		

Value of $10,000 invested 5 years ago: $ 61,871

Fiscal Year Ending Jun. 30

	2001	2000	1999	1998	1997	1996
Revenues (Million $)						
1Q	285.1	180.1	155.3	125.0	101.0	96.45
2Q	305.1	201.7	145.0	135.0	104.7	106.2
3Q	306.8	226.5	147.2	145.0	111.0	109.0
4Q	318.1	256.6	159.5	155.2	117.0	110.0
Yr.	1,577	864.9	607.0	560.2	433.7	421.6
Earnings Per Share ($)						
1Q	**0.29**	**0.18**	**0.17**	**0.13**	**0.11**	0.08
2Q	**0.31**	**0.20**	**0.15**	**0.14**	**0.12**	0.11
3Q	**0.33**	**0.23**	**0.15**	**0.15**	**0.12**	0.12
4Q	**-0.05**	**0.27**	**0.17**	**0.17**	**0.13**	0.12
Yr.	**0.93**	**0.88**	**0.65**	**0.59**	**0.47**	**0.43**

Next earnings report expected: late October

Dividend Data

No cash dividends have been paid.

Maxim Integrated Products, Inc.

Business Summary - 22-AUG-01

Maxim Integrated Products designs, develops, makes and markets a broad range of linear and mixed-signal integrated circuits known as analog circuits. Linear devices process signals representing real-world phenomena (such as temperature, pressure, sound or speed). Mixed-signal devices combine linear and digital functions.

The company initially generated most of its revenues from selling products that were second sources of a single competitor's integrated circuits, with distribution primarily to European customers. Although second-sourcing continues to be an important component of Maxim's product development program, current research emphasizes proprietary circuits. With more than 2,100 products introduced as of July 2000, the company has emerged as a leading developer of analog products.

Maxim operates wafer fabrication facilities in Beaverton, OR, and San Jose, CA. A Sunnyvale, CA, facility was closed in December 1998. A small portion of total wafer production is produced under contract by outside silicon foundries. The company spent $125 million on buildings and equipment in FY 00 (Jun.), and plans to spend about $170 million in FY 01.

The majority of processed wafers are shipped to Asian contractors that separate the chips and package them in various configurations. Assembled products are then tested for conformance with specific parameters at the company's test facility in the Philippines. In FY 00, Maxim began hiring staff and purchasing equipment for a second test facility, to be located in Thailand. Finished product is sold worldwide. International sales accounted for 57% of total revenue in FY 00, down from 59% in FY 99. Like many other analog chip makers, Maxim has a broad customer base of OEMs.

Maxim mainly serves four industry groups: communications, industrial control, instrumentation and data processing. Products include data converters, interface circuits, microprocessor supervisors, operational amplifiers, power supplies, multiplexers, switches, battery chargers, battery management circuits, RF circuits, fiber optic transceivers, sensors and voltage references. Applications for the company's products include broadband networks, cable systems, PBX, video and wireless communications, flow control, robotics, automatic test equipment, data recorders, measuring instruments, bar code readers, disk drives, hand-held computers/PDAs, mainframes, servers, personal computers and point of sale terminals. Products are also used in military and selected medical equipment.

In April 2001, the company acquired Dallas Semiconductor Corp. via an exchange of stock. The acquisition should add over $400 million to Maxim's annual revenue run. The Dallas operations are similar in nature to Maxim's, and will add complementary product lines in mixed-signal and digital chips. Savings from streamlining administrative overhead should be substantial.

Per Share Data ($) (Year Ended Jun. 30)	2001	2000	1999	1998	1997	1996	1995	1994	1993	1992
Tangible Bk. Val.	NA	3.95	3.23	2.42	3.65	1.32	0.76	0.57	0.44	0.34
Cash Flow	NA	0.94	0.70	0.64	1.06	0.48	0.19	0.12	0.09	0.08
Earnings	0.93	0.88	0.65	0.59	0.47	0.43	0.15	0.09	0.07	0.06
Dividends	Nil	Nil	Nil	Nil	Nil	Nil	Nil	Nil	Nil	Nil
Payout Ratio	Nil	Nil	Nil	Nil	Nil	Nil	Nil	Nil	Nil	Nil
Prices - High	70.12	90.12	48.31	22.75	19.09	10.93	10.46	3.64	3.06	1.85
- Low	33.55	45.62	19.93	11.15	10.53	5.15	3.53	2.71	1.53	1.20
P/E Ratio - High	75	NM	55	39	41	25	71	39	43	32
- Low	36	52	23	19	22	12	24	29	21	20
Income Statement Analysis (Million $)										
Revs.	NA	865	607	560	434	422	251	154	110	87.0
Oper. Inc.	NA	405	294	270	216	199	69.0	42.8	30.7	25.6
Depr.	NA	19.7	17.6	15.1	17.0	12.9	11.6	7.2	5.2	5.1
Int. Exp.	NA	Nil	Nil	Nil	0.1	0.0	0.0	0.1	0.1	0.4
Pretax Inc.	NA	425	297	270	208	190	60.0	37.6	26.6	21.0
Eff. Tax Rate	NA	34%	34%	34%	34%	35%	35%	36%	35%	35%
Net Inc.	NA	281	196	178	137	123	39.0	24.1	17.3	13.7
Balance Sheet & Other Fin. Data (Million $)										
Cash	NA	53.1	34.1	16.7	18.6	129	55.0	48.4	49.1	33.7
Curr. Assets	NA	931	729	508	377	265	162	100	91.3	67.9
Total Assets	NA	1,350	1,022	769	556	418	256	179	127	95.5
Curr. Liab.	NA	208	121	130	85.2	88.4	66.0	43.4	27.2	20.2
LT Debt	NA	Nil	Nil	Nil	Nil	Nil	Nil	0.0	0.2	0.7
Common Eqty.	NA	1,118	879	631	466	325	179	130	97.3	72.3
Total Cap.	NA	1,137	897	635	468	325	184	135	100	75.3
Cap. Exp.	NA	176	54.3	109	44.2	75.1	35.5	50.9	12.9	4.2
Cash Flow	NA	300	214	193	154	136	50.6	31.3	22.5	18.8
Curr. Ratio	NA	4.5	6.0	3.9	4.4	3.0	2.5	2.3	3.4	3.4
% LT Debt of Cap.	NA	Nil	Nil	Nil	Nil	Nil	NM	Nil	0.2	0.9
% Net Inc.of Revs.	NA	32.4	32.3	31.8	31.6	29.1	16.0	15.6	15.7	15.7
% Ret. on Assets	NA	23.7	21.9	26.9	28.1	36.6	17.9	15.6	15.2	16.0
% Ret. on Equity	NA	28.1	26.0	32.5	34.6	48.9	25.2	20.9	20.0	21.6

Data as orig reptd.; bef. results of disc opers/spec. items. Per share data adj. for stk. divs. Bold denotes diluted EPS (FASB 128)-prior periods restated. E-Estimated. NA-Not Available. NM-Not Meaningful. NR-Not Ranked.

Office—120 San Gabriel Dr., Sunnyvale, CA 94086. **Tel**—(408) 737-7600. **Website**—http://www.maxim-ic.com **Chrmn, Pres & CEO**—J. F. Gifford. **VP & CFO**—C. W. Jasper. **Dirs**—J. R. Bergman, J. F. Gifford, B. K. Hagopian, E. P. Karros, A. R. F. Wazzan. **Transfer Agent & Registrar**—Boston EquiServe. **Incorporated**—in Delaware in 1988. **Empl**— 4,185. **S&P Analyst:** T. W. Smith, CFA

STANDARD
&POOR'S
STOCK REPORTS

Mentor Graphics

Nasdaq Symbol **MENT**

In S&P MidCap 400

18-AUG-01

Industry:
Computer (Software & Services)

Summary: Mentor is a worldwide leader in electronic design automation systems for the integrated circuit and systems design markets.

S&P Opinion: Accumulate (★★★★)

Recent Price • 17
52 Wk Range • 33.62-15

Yield • Nil
12-Mo. P/E • 19.1

Quantitative Evaluations

Outlook
(1 Lowest—5 Highest)
• **4-**

Fair Value
• **21.20**

Risk
• **Average**

Earn./Div. Rank
• **B-**

Technical Eval.
• **Neutral** since 8/01

Rel. Strength Rank
(1 Lowest—99 Highest)
• **21**

Insider Activity
• **Unfavorable**

Earnings vs. Previous Year
▲=Up ▼=Down ▶=No Change

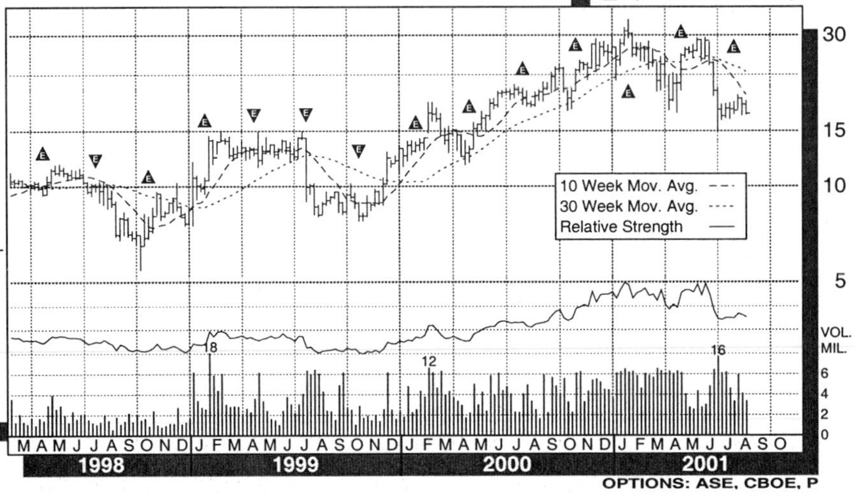

OPTIONS: ASE, CBOE, P

Overview - 30-JUL-01

We expect revenues to increase about 5% in 2001, driven by growth resulting from new product offerings, such as the Calibre and xCalibre verification tools for deep submicron design. The Calibre line won orders from Applied Micro Circuits and two major chip foundries in the second quarter of 2001. The company added 130 new customers in the quarter, broadening its customer base. Bookings for software have recently been sufficiently strong to outweigh weakness in the emulation and consulting segments; however, bookings turned weaker in June 2001. Operating margins are expected to trend slightly wider in 2001. The tax rate is running near 20% in 2001, down from 22% in 2000. Overall, we project EPS before goodwill amortization (EBG) of $1.13 for 2001, and estimate an advance to $1.40 (EBG) in 2002.

Valuation - 30-JUL-01

The shares rose from late 1999 to early 2001, reflecting an expansion in the electronics industry and improving prospects for circuit design software makers. However, a semiconductor industry slowdown worsened in 2001, restricting the ability of chipmakers to spend heavily on software tools. Thus far, MENT has compensated for weaker revenue growth with cost saving measures. The company has been aiming at entry into high growth areas, such as the programmable logic device (PLD) design market, that are relatively underserved by its competitors. The shares recently traded at about 13X our 2001 EPS estimate, a relatively modest P/E multiple in light of an estimated long-term growth rate near 20%. Despite some deferrals of orders this summer, we expect chip makers to step up their EDA software purchases as the next business cycle accelerates in late 2001, and recommend accumulating MENT shares.

Key Stock Statistics

S&P EPS Est. 2001	1.13	Tang. Bk. Value/Share	4.02
P/E on S&P Est. 2001	15.0	Beta	0.73
S&P EPS Est. 2002	1.40	Shareholders	807
Dividend Rate/Share	Nil	Market cap. (B)	$ 1.1
Shs. outstg. (M)	63.9	Inst. holdings	88%
Avg. daily vol. (M)	0.828		

Value of $10,000 invested 5 years ago: $ 12,142

Fiscal Year Ending Dec. 31

	2001	2000	1999	1998	1997	1996
Revenues (Million $)						
1Q	154.5	128.1	122.6	108.0	101.6	109.0
2Q	—	138.1	119.5	119.1	114.6	117.3
3Q	—	141.9	114.1	117.9	116.0	100.8
4Q	—	181.7	155.0	145.3	122.5	120.8
Yr.	—	589.8	511.1	490.4	454.7	447.9
Earnings Per Share ($)						
1Q	0.24	0.16	-0.13	-0.12	-0.43	0.06
2Q	—	0.09	Nil	0.01	0.06	0.04
3Q	—	0.22	0.09	0.12	0.03	Nil
4Q	—	0.35	0.08	-0.02	-0.14	-0.18
Yr.	—	0.81	0.03	-0.01	-0.48	-0.08

Next earnings report expected: NA

Dividend Data

Prior to omission in October 1993, cash dividends had been paid since 1988.

Mentor Graphics Corporation

Business Summary - 30-JUL-01

Founded in 1981, Mentor Graphics is a top-tier supplier of electronic design automation (EDA) software. EDA is technically advanced computer software that automates the design of complex semiconductors and electronic systems for supercomputers, automotive electronics, telephone switching, cellular base stations and handsets, network hubs and routers, signal processors, personal computers, personal digital assistants and smart cards.

The company is seeking to expand beyond its traditional EDA business to solve customer problems in design reuse, embedded systems design, and hardware/software co-design. MENT's goal is to enhance the competitiveness of its customers, which include leading companies in the communications, computer, semiconductor, aerospace, consumer electronics, networking, multimedia and transportation industries. In addition to software products, MENT's service division offers consulting, support and training to enhance customer success in the design and manufacture of hardware products. In 2000, system and software revenues constituted 58% of revenues, and service and support accounted for 42%. Software is the more profitable part of the business, with gross margins of 91% in 2000, compared to 64% for services. Total gross margin in 2000 was 80%, up from 77% in 1999.

The company's products are used to design, analyze, simulate, model, implement and verify the components of electronics systems. Four key areas of design work for which MENT markets and supports software products include field programmable gate array (FPGA) design and verification; physical verification of design and manufacturability; system-on-a-chip design; and printed circuit board (PCB) design. MENT's products allow for the integration of third party software tools developed by other commercial EDA vendors and by customers for their own internal use. The products help customers reduce development time in producing innovative hardware products of high quality.

The company's "design reuse" services, through the use of predefined building blocks of frequently used circuit functions, free designers to focus on optimizing system architecture.

MENT's software runs on UNIX, Windows NT and Linux platforms. Workstations are available in a broad range of price and performance levels from vendors including Sun Microsystems, Hewlett-Packard, IBM and Compaq. These computer manufacturers have a substantial installed base of workstations.

Marketing is conducted through direct channels in North America and through a sales force and distributors in the rest of the world. Sales outside of the Americas accounted for 52% of total revenues in 2000, versus 51% in 1999. The customer base is well diversified.

Marketing resources are focused on a limited number of emerging products, including the Calibre physical verification product. The Calibre solution is used by most of the world's largest semiconductor makers.

Per Share Data ($) (Year Ended Dec. 31)	2000	1999	1998	1997	1996	1995	1994	1993	1992	1991
Tangible Bk. Val.	4.02	4.49	4.49	4.31	4.69	5.45	4.60	4.11	4.86	6.14
Cash Flow	1.10	0.36	0.41	-0.06	0.26	1.47	1.00	-0.10	-0.56	-0.74
Earnings	0.81	0.03	-0.01	-0.48	-0.08	0.88	0.53	-0.69	-1.13	-1.43
Dividends	Nil	Nil	Nil	Nil	Nil	Nil	Nil	0.18	0.24	0.24
Payout Ratio	Nil	Nil	Nil	Nil	Nil	Nil	Nil	NM	NM	NM
Prices - High	29.31	15.06	11.81	13.12	18.50	22.87	17.25	15.50	22.25	19.00
- Low	11.56	7.50	5.43	6.50	7.37	12.37	9.37	7.87	5.25	11.50
P/E Ratio - High	36	NM	NM	NM	NM	26	33	NM	NM	NM
- Low	14	NM	NM	NM	NM	14	18	NM	NM	NM
Income Statement Analysis (Million $)										
Revs.	590	511	490	455	448	384	348	340	351	400
Oper. Inc.	21.2	76.2	61.4	10.0	55.0	84.6	56.4	23.0	-2.1	-3.7
Depr.	19.4	21.7	27.2	27.5	21.5	33.0	24.7	27.6	25.8	29.7
Int. Exp.	Nil	1.0	0.8	0.6	2.5	2.4	2.7	4.4	5.5	5.8
Pretax Inc.	70.5	2.9	0.0	-33.1	-1.4	57.3	30.9	-29.6	-48.3	-63.0
Eff. Tax Rate	22%	22%	NM	NM	NM	13%	11%	NM	NM	NM
Net Inc.	55.0	2.2	-0.5	-31.3	-5.0	49.9	27.5	-32.1	-50.9	-61.6
Balance Sheet & Other Fin. Data (Million $)										
Cash	109	95.6	119	84.4	197	201	138	110	109	144
Curr. Assets	337	291	305	272	338	303	238	198	208	294
Total Assets	531	449	464	402	513	462	394	354	379	446
Curr. Liab.	204	158	166	124	137	103	99	102	99	125
LT Debt	6.1	Nil	Nil	0.1	52.4	52.7	53.6	54.3	55.7	50.6
Common Eqty.	317	289	295	278	320	306	239	196	221	268
Total Cap.	325	290	296	278	372	358	293	250	277	318
Cap. Exp.	19.0	15.6	21.6	32.6	23.9	19.8	14.3	26.6	24.7	97.0
Cash Flow	74.4	24.0	26.7	-3.8	16.5	82.9	52.2	-4.5	-25.1	-31.9
Curr. Ratio	1.6	1.8	1.8	2.2	2.5	3.0	2.4	1.9	2.1	2.4
% LT Debt of Cap.	1.9	Nil	Nil	NM	14.1	14.7	18.3	21.7	20.1	15.9
% Net Inc.of Revs.	9.3	0.4	NM	NM	NM	13.0	7.9	NM	NM	NM
% Ret. on Assets	11.2	0.5	NM	NM	NM	11.6	7.1	NM	NM	NM
% Ret. on Equity	18.2	0.8	NM	NM	NM	18.3	12.2	NM	NM	NM

Data as orig. reptd.; bef. results of disc. opers. and/or spec. items. Per share data adj. for stk. divs. as of ex-div. date. Bold denotes diluted EPS (FASB 128). Bk. val. prior to 1994 incl. intangibles. E-Estimated. NA-Not Available. NM-Not Meaningful. NR-Not Ranked.

Office—8005 S.W. Boeckman Rd., Wilsonville, OR 97070-7777. **Tel**—(503) 685-7000. **Website**—www.mentor.com **Chrmn & CEO**—W. C. Rhines. **Pres**—G. K. Hinckley. **VP & Secy**—D. Freed. **Treas & Investor Contact**—Dennis Weldon (503-685-1462). **Dirs**—M. B. Congdon, J. R. Fiebiger, G. K. Hinckley, D. A. Hodges, K. McDonough, W. C. Rhines, F. K. Richardson. **Transfer Agent & Registrar**—American Stock Transfer & Trust Co., NYC. **Incorporated**—in Oregon in 1981. **Empl**— 2,750. **S&P Analyst:** T. W. Smith, CFA

STANDARD &POOR'S
STOCK REPORTS

Nokia Corp.

NYSE Symbol **NOK**

18-AUG-01

Industry: Communications Equipment

Summary: Nokia is a leading international provider of wireless telecommunications systems and equipment.

S&P Opinion: Accumulate (★★★★)

Recent Price • 17.08 | Yield • 1.2%
52 Wk Range • 53.75-16.90 | 12-Mo. P/E • 22.2

Quantitative Evaluations

Outlook (1 Lowest—5 Highest)
• **NA**

Fair Value
• **NA**

Risk
• **NA**

Earn./Div. Rank
• **NR**

Technical Eval.
• **Bearish** since 8/01

Rel. Strength Rank (1 Lowest—99 Highest)
• **12**

Insider Activity
• **Neutral**

OPTIONS: ASE, CBOE, P, Ph

Overview - 19-JUL-01

For 2001, we expect revenues to increase in mid-single digits, as increased sales of wireless phones (70% of total sales) offset weak spending on infrastructure products (30%). We project operating margins for Nokia networks in the mid-teens, with margins for Nokia mobile phones in the high teens. By continually introducing newer and higher-priced lines of phones, and by producing the largest volume of phones in the industry, Nokia should be able to counter fierce price competition for the foreseeable future. R&D spending will rise faster than sales, reflecting increased investment in development of third generation (3G) technologies. After factoring in a weak euro, we expect translated U.S. EPS of $0.64 in 2001.

Valuation - 19-JUL-01

The shares have fallen sharply, reflecting a weakening mobile market. NOK forecasts only modest mobile handset unit growth in 2001 from the 405 million units sold in 2000. Still, we expect the company to grow faster than the overall market rate and reach its long term goal of a dominant 40% mobile handset market share. More importantly, we expect handset operating margins to remain steady at around 17%, significantly higher than the margin of the company's peers. While competitors have resorted to aggressive discounting, NOK is emphasizing profitability. Although the mobile market is clearly decelerating from its earlier robust expansion, growth is still expected at a compound annual rate of about 15% for the next couple of years. We believe the company will emerge from this difficult environment in a stronger position. We would accumulate the stock, in light of NOK's leading worldwide market share in handsets, superior product portfolio, strong manufacturing capability, and an enormous 3G market opportunity that will eventually be available.

Key Stock Statistics

S&P EPS Est. 2001	0.64	Tang. Bk. Value/Share	1.77
P/E on S&P Est. 2001	26.7	Beta	2.00
S&P EPS Est. 2002	0.77	Shareholders	4,903
Dividend Rate/Share	0.21	Market cap. (B)	$ 80.1
Shs. outstg. (M)	4692.0	Inst. holdings	22%
Avg. daily vol. (M)	10.385		

Value of $10,000 invested 5 years ago: $ 80,359

Fiscal Year Ending Dec. 31

	2000	1999	1998	1997	1996	1995
Revenues (Million U.S. $)						
1Q	6,250	3,870	—	--	—	—
2Q	6,635	4,646	3,355	4,732	—	—
3Q	8,207	5,037	—	—	—	—
4Q	9,284	6,329	4,839	—	—	—
Yr.	30,376	21,034	15,054	10,154	7,723	8,489
Earnings Per ADS (U.S. $)						
1Q	**0.18**	**0.12**	—	--	—	—
2Q	**0.19**	**0.13**	**0.09**	0.10	—	—
3Q	**0.20**	**0.13**	—	0.07	—	—
4Q	**0.25**	**0.18**	**0.14**	**0.08**	—	—
Yr.	**0.77**	**0.58**	**0.41**	**0.26**	0.15	0.20

Next earnings report expected: NA

Dividend Data (Dividends have been paid since 1995.)

Amount (U.S. $)	Date Decl.	Ex-Div. Date	Stock of Record	Payment Date
0.211	—	Mar. 22	Mar. 26	Apr. 10 '01

Nokia Corporation

18-AUG-01

Business Summary - 19-JUL-01

Nokia has established itself as a key supplier of mobile handset communications devices. The company is a pioneer in the development of cellular systems, with strong positions in the global markets for Global System for Mobile Communications (GSM)-based cellular communications systems and mobile phones. It is the world's largest manufacturer of mobile phones, with an estimated market share of approximately 32% in 2000. In addition, Nokia is an important supplier of telecommunications equipment for fixed line telephony, and makes other electronics products.

Nokia is organized into two main business groups: Nokia Networks, and Nokia Mobile Phones. Nokia Networks (25% of 2000 revenues) supplies telecommunications infrastructure systems and equipment for use in fixed and mobile phone networks. Group sales climbed 36% in 2000. Sales were driven by continued GSM expansion; Nokia's total number of GSM customers rose to more than 100. Operators continue to invest in wireless data capabilities, such as GPRS, a forerunner of 3G. By year-end 2000, Nokia had delivered well over 50 GPRS networks, and had signed contracts to supply 3G networks to a total of 13 operators.

The Nokia Mobile Phones (72%) segment manufactures a complete range of cellular phones for all major analog and digital cellular systems. During 2000, the company launched 19 new products, including its first Bluetooth solution. Net sales in 2000 climbed 66%, driven by increasingly digitized European and North American markets. Over the past three years, NOK's mobile phone sales volume has consistently grown faster than the market. In 2000, the company outpaced the market in every quarter and in every region.

Nokia's total mobile phone unit volume in 2000 was 128.4 million units, up 64% from 1999's total of 78.5 million units. The company estimates that approximately 405 million units were sold in 2000, up from 280 million in 1999. Nokia forecasts that mobile phone users will rise from about 715 million in 2000 to more than 1 billion by the first half of 2002. It believes the replacement market for phones accounted for over 40% of total unit sales in 2000, and expected this share to rise to about 50% in 2001.

Other operations (3%), now known as Nokia Ventures Organization, focus on new business development and delivering Internet protocol technology-based products for the enterprise markets. This area increased 106% in 2000.

In 2000, the geographic breakdown of company sales was: Europe 52% of total sales; Americas 25%; and Asia-Pacific 23%.

Per ADS Data (U.S. $) (Year Ended Dec. 31)	2000	1999	1998	1997	1996	1995	1994	1993	1992	1991
Tangible Bk. Val.	1.77	1.50	NA	2.12	2.05	1.73	2.01	0.89	NA	NA
Cash Flow	1.03	2.90	0.53	0.37	0.26	0.30	NA	NA	NA	NA
Earnings	0.77	0.58	0.41	0.26	0.15	0.20	0.53	0.13	-0.10	-0.15
Dividends	0.16	0.11	0.07	0.04	0.03	0.03	0.01	NA	NA	NA
Payout Ratio	20%	19%	17%	14%	23%	15%	3%	NA	NA	NA
Prices - High	62.50	49.00	15.67	6.40	3.71	4.87	2.43	NA	NA	NA
- Low	27.62	15.57	4.15	3.44	1.96	1.95	1.25	NA	NA	NA
P/E Ratio - High	81	84	39	25	25	24	5	NA	NA	NA
- Low	36	27	10	14	13	10	2	NA	NA	NA
Income Statement Analysis (Million Euros)										
Euros Per ($)	1.06	0.94	0.19	0.19	0.22	0.23	0.19	0.17	0.22	0.25
Revs.	30,376	19,772	79,231	52,612	39,321	36,810	30,177	23,697	18,168	15,457
Oper. Inc.	6,785	4,573	17,827	11,216	6,502	6,837	4,605	2,461	1,238	842
Depr.	1,009	665	3,028	2,762	2,236	1,825	1,009	996	950	938
Int. Exp.	196	260	1,176	1,042	1,000	820	635	889	964	920
Pretax Inc.	5,862	3,845	14,603	8,371	3,898	4,933	4,002	1,146	-158	-324
Eff. Tax Rate	30%	31%	30%	27%	32%	16%	23%	26%	NM	NM
Net Inc.	3,938	2,577	9,992	5,998	3,044	4,087	2,995	767	-413	-604
Balance Sheet & Other Fin. Data (Million Euros)										
Euros Per ($)	1.06	0.99	0.20	0.19	0.22	0.23	0.21	0.17	0.19	0.00
Cash	1,409	1,023	4,314	12,247	7,045	4,214	5,268	3,297	3,118	NA
Curr. Assets	13,502	10,792	46,460	32,293	24,866	23,714	19,906	14,653	13,608	NA
Total Assets	19,890	14,279	59,660	41,738	33,275	32,761	27,849	22,647	21,238	NA
Curr. Liab.	8,594	6,372	26,476	18,376	14,907	15,955	11,319	11,520	10,111	NA
LT Debt	173	269	1,530	1,348	2,117	2,121	3,071	3,397	3,124	NA
Common Eqty.	10,808	7,378	30,379	21,524	15,148	12,855	11,641	5,955	6,291	NA
Total Cap.	11,227	7,849	32,285	23,067	18,071	16,349	16,044	10,444	10,546	NA
Cap. Exp.	1,580	1,302	4,527	2,402	2,028	3,299	1,967	1,186	838	868
Cash Flow	4,947	3,242	13,020	8,760	5,280	5,912	3,800	1,667	411	158
Curr. Ratio	1.6	1.7	1.8	1.8	1.7	1.5	1.8	1.3	1.3	NA
% LT Debt of Cap.	1.5	3.4	4.7	5.8	11.7	13.0	19.1	32.5	29.6	NA
% Net Inc.of Revs.	13.0	13.0	12.6	11.4	7.7	11.1	9.9	3.2	NM	NM
% Ret. on Assets	23.1	21.2	19.7	16.0	9.2	13.4	11.9	3.5	NM	NA
% Ret. on Equity	43.3	41.3	38.5	32.7	21.7	33.4	31.8	10.5	NM	NA

Data as orig reptd.; bef. results of disc opers/spec. items. Per share data adj. for stk. divs. Bold denotes diluted EPS (FASB 128)-prior periods restated. Prior to 1999, income statement and balance sheet data reported in Finnish Markka. E-Estimated. NA-Not Available. NM-Not Meaningful. NR-Not Ranked.

Office—Keilalahdentie 4, P.O. Box 226, Helsinki, Finland (U.S. office: 6000 Connection Drive, Irving, TX 75039). **Tel**—358 9 1807 289. **Website**—www.nokia.com **Chrmn & CEO**—J. Ollila. **Pres**—P. Ala-Pietila **EVP & CFO**—O-P. Kallasvuo. **U.S. Investor Contact**—Ulla James (972-894-4880). **Dirs**—P. Aitalo, E. Andersson, P. J. Collins, B. Holmstrom, J. K. Leskinen, J. Ollila, V. Vainio, R. F. W. van Oordt, I. Viinanen. **Depositary for ADRs**—Citibank N.A. **Empl**— 60,289. **S&P Analyst:** A. Bensinger

STANDARD &POOR'S STOCK REPORTS

Novellus Systems

Nasdaq Symbol **NVLS**

In S&P 500

18-AUG-01 **Industry:** Equipment (Semiconductor)

Summary: This company manufactures, markets and services automated wafer fabrication systems for the deposition of thin films.

S&P Opinion: Accumulate (★★★★) Recent Price • 45.93 52 Wk Range • 63.50-24.93 Yield • Nil 12-Mo. P/E • 21.6

Quantitative Evaluations

Outlook (1 Lowest—5 Highest) • **2⁻**

Fair Value • **46.30**

Risk • **High**

Earn./Div. Rank • **B**

Technical Eval. • **Neutral** since 8/01

Rel. Strength Rank (1 Lowest—99 Highest) • **31**

Insider Activity • **Unfavorable**

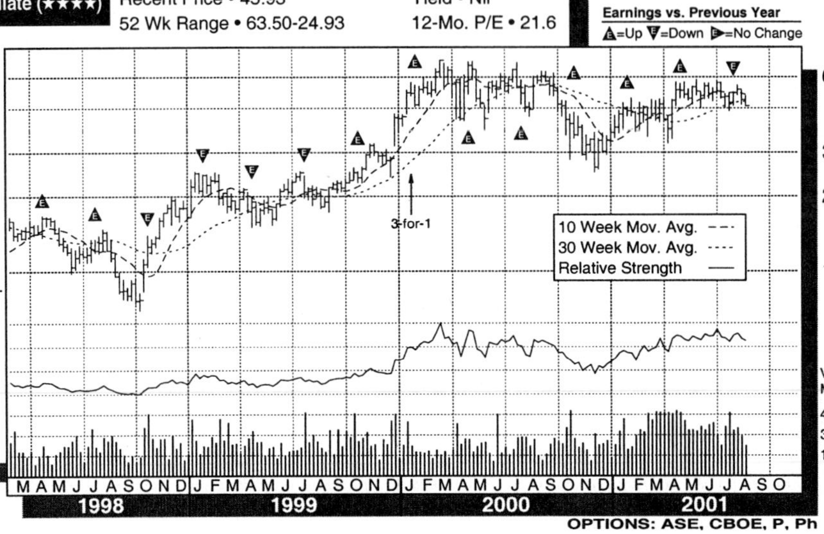

OPTIONS: ASE, CBOE, P, Ph

Overview - 03-AUG-01

Revenues are expected to rise about 3% in 2001, reflecting a slowdown in shipments after a strong industry expansion in 2000, offset by the benefits of an acquisition. NVLS acquired Gasonics International Corp., a leading supplier of dry resist removal and surface preparation equipment, on January 10, 2001, in exchange for about 9.24 million common shares. Although Intel and other large chipmakers made large capital expenditures in 2000, their budgets for spending on equipment in 2001 have come in much lower on average. Accordingly, bookings are running lower in all geographic regions. However, the company has a robust product portfolio of next-generation deposition tools, and will benefit from technology upgrades. We anticipate EPS of $1.45 in 2001, and $1.40 in 2002.

Valuation - 03-AUG-01

The shares of this semiconductor equipment manufacturer appear to have made a low for this industry downturn in late 2000 at about 2.2X tangible book value. We recommend accumulating the shares, recently trading closer to 4.7X tangible book value, because early signs of a cycle bottom for the industry are evident, and we believe a recovery is likely to become more apparent within our six-to-12-month investment horizon. Toward the top of the next multi-year cycle, we expect NVLS to trade near 6.0X a higher book value. Although capital equipment order trends for capacity expansion have stalled as part of an industry down cycle, technology buys of equipment for next generation wafer fabs are holding up better. NVLS has good technological strength, particularly in emerging copper interconnect solutions and tools to handle wafers with diameters of 300 mm and linewidths as small as 0.10 micron. Earnings should remain positive through the downturn.

Key Stock Statistics

S&P EPS Est. 2001	1.45	Tang. Bk. Value/Share	11.49
P/E on S&P Est. 2001	31.7	Beta	2.39
S&P EPS Est. 2002	1.40	Shareholders	734
Dividend Rate/Share	Nil	Market cap. (B)	$ 6.5
Shs. outstg. (M)	142.5	Inst. holdings	83%
Avg. daily vol. (M)	5.938		

Value of $10,000 invested 5 years ago: $ 76,327

Fiscal Year Ending Dec. 31

	2001	2000	1999	1998	1997	1996
Revenues (Million $)						
1Q	458.7	198.7	115.2	163.2	101.6	115.3
2Q	—	335.0	130.9	142.8	114.5	120.3
3Q	—	250.1	154.9	106.7	155.1	121.6
4Q	—	389.9	191.7	106.0	162.8	104.6
Yr.	—	1,174	592.7	518.8	534.0	461.7
Earnings Per Share ($)						
1Q	**0.55**	**0.19**	**0.08**	**0.20**	**0.15**	**0.26**
2Q	—	**0.57**	**0.10**	**0.15**	**-1.55**	**0.27**
3Q	—	**0.29**	**0.18**	**0.07**	**0.19**	**0.26**
4Q	—	**0.69**	**0.27**	**0.08**	**0.21**	**0.17**
Yr.	—	**1.75**	**0.64**	**0.50**	**-0.96**	**0.97**

Next earnings report expected: NA

Dividend Data

No cash has been paid.

Novellus Systems, Inc.

Business Summary - 03-AUG-01

As the Information Age calls steadily for smaller and more effective integrated circuits (ICs), demand grows for the advanced automated wafer fabrication equipment made by Novellus Systems. The company is a leading supplier of thin film deposition equipment to the semiconductor industry. Deposition, a fundamental process in semiconductor manufacture, must be repeated many times during a chip manufacturing cycle.

Novellus Systems is a leading manufacturer of chemical vapor deposition (CVD) systems, which are used to deposit both insulating and conductive material on the surface of a wafer by means of a chemical plasma. With its acquisition of the Thin Film Systems unit of Varian Associates in June 1997, the company expanded its presence in physical vapor deposition (PVD) as well. In the PVD process, conductive metals are sputtered on to a wafer surface. Novellus also offers electrofill systems that are used for depositing metal film layers using an electrically charged aqueous solution.

The acquisition of GaSonics International Corp. in January 2000 added photoresist and residue removal product lines. These products are used to prepare the device surface before the deposition process. The former GaSonics operations are now known as the Surface Integrity Group. The division also makes low pressure chemical vapor deposition (LPCVD) systems for the flat panel display industry.

The company aims to increase its market share in the worldwide thin film deposition market, and to strengthen its position as a leading supplier of semiconductor processing equipment. To attain this goal, NVLS's strategy is to provide customers with systems that achieve the highest levels of wafer throughput, yield (the percentage of functioning ICs to the total produced), and film quality. The company will continue to focus its marketing efforts on major semiconductor manufacturers. The company has sold at least one of its systems to each of the world's 20 largest semiconductor manufacturers. Sales to the 10 largest customers accounted for 56% of sales in 2000, down from 65% in 1999.

Although NVLS's original tool sets established the company as a leader in CVD, it has recently centered its product strategy around the emergence of the copper interconnect market. Copper has lower resistance and capacitance values than aluminum, the conductive metal generally used in integrated circuits. NVLS believes its SABRE tool had about 75% share of the copper electroplating systems market in 2000.

To maintain its technological leadership, the company spends heavily on research and development. In 1999, R&D expenditures totaled $120 million, equal to 20% of sales, versus $107 million (21%) in 1998.

The semiconductor industry that Novellus serves is global in scope. Export sales accounted for 66% of 2000 revenue, up from 64% in 1999.

Per Share Data ($) (Year Ended Dec. 31)	2000	1999	1998	1997	1996	1995	1994	1993	1992	1991
Tangible Bk. Val.	11.49	6.47	3.63	2.98	3.83	2.85	2.21	1.24	1.01	0.95
Cash Flow	2.04	0.89	0.73	-0.78	1.06	0.88	0.49	0.23	0.11	0.21
Earnings	2.39	0.64	0.50	-0.96	0.95	0.80	0.45	0.18	0.07	0.19
Dividends	Nil	Nil	Nil	Nil	Nil	Nil	Nil	Nil	Nil	Nil
Payout Ratio	Nil	Nil	Nil	Nil	Nil	Nil	Nil	Nil	Nil	Nil
Prices - High	70.25	42.79	19.77	22.12	10.75	14.54	9.41	6.16	4.41	4.54
- Low	24.93	14.95	6.95	7.95	5.25	7.12	4.29	2.33	1.29	1.75
P/E Ratio - High	29	67	39	NM	11	18	21	34	60	24
- Low	10	23	14	NM	6	9	9	13	18	9
Income Statement Analysis (Million $)										
Revs.	1,174	593	519	534	462	374	225	114	69.8	80.0
Oper. Inc.	328	130	103	112	148	123	67.7	27.1	10.9	24.7
Depr.	40.1	29.8	23.8	18.3	11.3	7.7	4.0	3.7	3.2	1.9
Int. Exp.	2.3	1.7	4.9	2.7	0.5	0.2	0.3	0.1	0.3	0.1
Pretax Inc.	342	114	80.0	-121	145	125	68.1	24.8	9.4	25.4
Eff. Tax Rate	31%	33%	34%	NM	35%	34%	34%	35%	34%	34%
Net Inc.	236	76.6	52.8	-95.7	94.0	82.5	44.9	16.1	6.2	16.8
Balance Sheet & Other Fin. Data (Million $)										
Cash	571	182	81.2	59.3	177	150	137	48.6	43.0	40.5
Curr. Assets	1,827	733	399	351	374	318	234	109	79.2	79.3
Total Assets	2,015	910	552	493	460	365	265	131	97.3	94.7
Curr. Liab.	505	140	111	127	86.1	92.0	50.8	25.7	13.9	12.8
LT Debt	Nil	Nil	65.0	65.0	Nil	Nil	Nil	Nil	0.8	1.0
Common Eqty.	1,511	770	375	301	374	273	214	105	82.7	80.9
Total Cap.	1,511	770	440	366	374	273	214	105	83.4	81.9
Cap. Exp.	68.5	28.8	36.1	36.2	35.2	19.3	6.9	6.6	5.1	10.2
Cash Flow	276	106	76.7	-77.4	105	90.2	48.9	19.8	9.5	18.7
Curr. Ratio	3.6	5.2	3.6	2.8	4.3	3.5	4.6	4.3	5.7	6.2
% LT Debt of Cap.	Nil	Nil	14.7	17.8	NM	NM	Nil	Nil	0.9	1.2
% Net Inc.of Revs.	20.1	12.9	10.2	NM	20.4	22.1	20.0	14.2	8.9	21.0
% Ret. on Assets	16.1	10.5	10.1	NM	22.8	26.0	21.7	13.9	6.6	20.1
% Ret. on Equity	20.7	13.4	15.6	NM	29.1	33.9	26.9	16.9	7.7	24.0

Data as orig reptd.; bef. results of disc opers/spec. items. Per share data adj. for stk. divs. Bold denotes diluted EPS (FASB 128)-prior periods restated. E-Estimated. NA-Not Available. NM-Not Meaningful. NR-Not Ranked.

Office—4000 North First Street, San Jose, CA 95134. **Tel**—(408) 943-9700. **Website**—www.novellus.com **Chrmn & Co-CEO**—R. S. Hill. **Pres & Co-CEO**—P. R. Hanley. **EVP, CFO & Secy**—R. H. Smith. **Treas & Investor Contact**—Robin Yim. **Dirs**—D. J. Guzy, R. S. Hill, J. D. Litster, T. Long, G. Possley, R. H. Smith, W. R. Spivey. **Transfer Agent & Registrar**—Mellon Investor Services, SF. **Incorporated**—in California in 1984. **Empl**—3,529. **S&P Analyst:** T. W. Smith, CFA

STANDARD & POOR'S STOCK REPORTS

NVIDIA Corp.

Nasdaq Symbol **NVDA**

In S&P MidCap 400

22-AUG-01

Industry: Electronics (Semiconductors)

Summary: This company develops and markets 3D graphics processors and related software to the mainstream PC market.

S&P Opinion: Accumulate (★★★★)

Recent Price • 83.77
52 Wk Range • 100-27.50
Yield • Nil
12-Mo. P/E • 58.2

Quantitative Evaluations

Outlook (1 Lowest—5 Highest)
• **NA**

Fair Value
• **NA**

Risk
• **NA**

Earn./Div. Rank
• **NR**

Technical Eval.
• **Neutral** since 8/01

Rel. Strength Rank (1 Lowest—99 Highest)
• **59**

Insider Activity
• **NA**

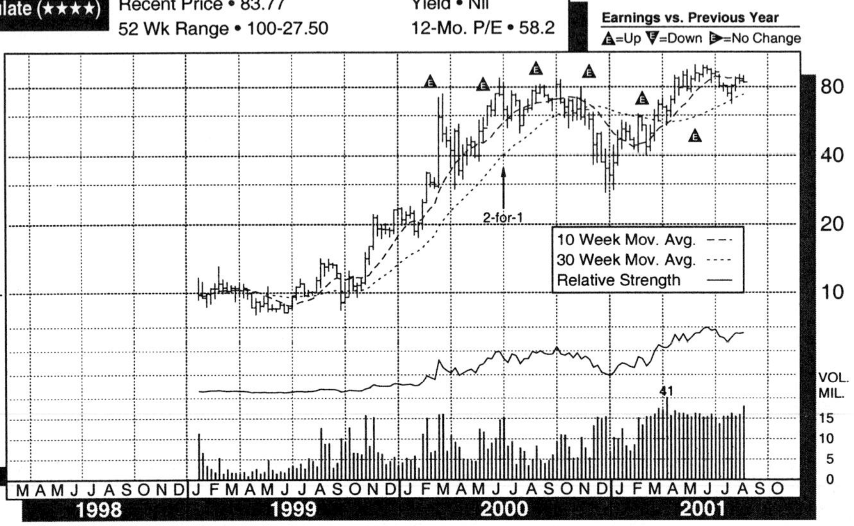

Overview - 22-AUG-01

We anticipate revenue growth above 55% in FY 02 (Jan.) and near 40% in FY 03, based on strong acceptance of the company's advanced graphics and multimedia processing chips by the consumer and professional computing markets. Besides offering a comprehensive product line for desktop PCs, the company is making inroads in the Apple Macintosh, mobile computing, and workstation markets. The company was chosen by Microsoft to develop graphics chips for use in the Xbox video game console, which is scheduled to debut November 8, 2001, and received a $200 million cash advance for the Xbox work. We expect operating margins to be steady at healthy levels into 2002. On August 14, 2001, NVIDIA announced a 2-for-1 stock split. We estimate pro forma EPS (excluding goodwill and acquisition charges) to rise to $1.80 in FY 02, from $1.25 in FY 01, and increase further to $2.40 in FY 03.

Valuation - 22-AUG-01

The shares have risen substantially in 2001 despite a cyclical downturn in the broader semiconductor market, based on the competitive strength of NVIDIA's graphics processors in their niche. The shares recently traded near 35X FY 03 earnings, which is attractive in light of an estimated long-term growth rate of 35%. Considering the advance funding from Microsoft for Xbox products, and NVIDIA's good record of steady releases of new products, the earnings visibility is better than at most other semiconductor makers. The company, on track to earn over $1 billion in revenue in FY 02, addresses markets estimated at $8 billion, and thus has room to grow. One cautionary note is that the ongoing weakness in the economy might deteriorate demand for end-products using NVIDIA's chips. We recommend accumulating the shares as a play on the increasing need for complex graphics displays in PCs and video games.

Key Stock Statistics

S&P EPS Est. 2002	1.80	Tang. Bk. Value/Share	5.93
P/E on S&P Est. 2002	46.5	Beta	NA
S&P EPS Est. 2003	2.40	Shareholders	357
Dividend Rate/Share	Nil	Market cap. (B)	$ 5.7
Shs. outstg. (M)	70.2	Inst. holdings	66%
Avg. daily vol. (M)	5.393		

Value of $10,000 invested 5 years ago: NA

Fiscal Year Ending Jan. 31

	2002	2001	2000	1999	1998	1997
Revenues (Million $)						
1Q	240.9	148.5	71.02	—	—	—
2Q	206.3	170.4	78.02	—	—	—
3Q	—	198.2	97.02	—	—	—
4Q	—	218.2	128.5	65.54	—	—
Yr.	—	735.3	374.5	158.2	29.10	—
Earnings Per Share ($)						
1Q	**0.31**	**0.23**	**0.09**	—	—	—
2Q	**0.39**	**0.28**	**0.10**	—	—	—
3Q	—	**0.35**	**0.14**	—	—	—
4Q	—	**0.38**	**0.20**	**0.14**	—	—
Yr.	—	**1.25**	**0.53**	**0.08**	**-0.14**	—

Next earnings report expected: early November

Dividend Data

Amount ($)	Date Decl.	Ex-Div. Date	Stock of Record	Payment Date
2-for-1	Aug. 14	Sep. 12	Aug. 28	Sep. 11 '01

NVIDIA Corp.

Business Summary - 22-AUG-01

NVIDIA designs, develops, and markets high-performance graphics processors and related software for personal computers and digital entertainment platforms. It has rapidly taken a prominent position in the graphics chip market.

Interactive 3D graphics displays are an integral part of many computing applications for workstations, consumer and commercial desktop PCs, Internet appliances and home gaming consoles. NVIDIA products are designed into products offered by virtually every top PC original equipment manufacturer. The company had 37 issued U.S. patents and 61 patent applications as of January 2001.

The company believes PC interactive 3D graphics capability represents one of the primary means by which users differentiate between systems. It thinks current PC users can easily differentiate the quality of graphics, and prefer PCs that provide a superior visual experience. NVIDIA believes these factors have dramatically increased demand for 3D graphics processors. It cites industry research that 3D graphics will be standard in every PC unit shipped by the end 2001, and estimates that 182 million 3D graphics processors were sold worldwide in 2000, with 356 million processors expected to be sold worldwide in 2005.

NVIDIA's current products provide high levels of visual quality, realistic imagery and motion, and complex object and scene interaction. The company offers a "top to bottom" family of graphics processors, serving various 3D and 2D sub-markets in a full spectrum of price points. At the high end is the NVIDIA GeForce3 GPU (graphics processing unit), which began shipment in January 2001, and is designed for the PC enthusiast and performance markets. It is fabricated on advanced 0.15 micron chip-making process technology. The prior generation NVIDIA GeForce2 Ultra shipped in August 2000, replacing the first-generation GeForce 256. A GeForce2 Mobile GPU was launched in January 2001.

Other products include the NVIDIA TNT2 graphics processor, which is designed for the mainstream PC market; and the NVIDIA TNT2 M64 and Vanta graphics processors, designed for the value and low-cost consumer and commercial desktop PC markets.

In March 2000, the company agreed to develop and supply graphics chips for Microsoft's Xbox video game console and in April 2000 received a $200 million advance against chip sales.

NVIDIA's sales are concentrated on a few big customers. Sales to Edom Technology, an Asian distributor, were 25% of sales in FY 01 (Jan.), and contract manufacturer Celestica represented another 11%.

The company has no fabrication plants of its own, relying instead on contract manufacturers including Taiwan Semiconductor for production.

Per Share Data ($)										
(Year Ended Jan. 31)	**2001**	**2000**	**1999**	**1998**	**1997**	**1996**	**1995**	**1994**	**1993**	**1992**
Tangible Bk. Val.	5.93	2.00	1.11	NM	NA	NA	NA	NA	NA	NA
Cash Flow	1.45	0.65	0.15	-0.09	NA	NA	NA	NA	NA	NA
Earnings	1.25	0.53	0.08	-0.14	NA	NA	NA	NA	NA	NA
Dividends	Nil	Nil	Nil	NA	NA	NA	NA	NA	NA	NA
Payout Ratio	Nil	Nil	Nil	NA	NA	NA	NA	NA	NA	NA
Cal. Yrs.	2000	1999	1998	1997	1996	1995	1994	1993	1992	1991
Prices - High	88.00	23.75	NA	NA	NA	NA	NA	NA	NA	NA
- Low	17.50	6.00	NA	NA	NA	NA	NA	NA	NA	NA
P/E Ratio - High	70	45	NA	NA	NA	NA	NA	NA	NA	NA
- Low	14	11	NA	NA	NA	NA	NA	NA	NA	NA
Income Statement Analysis (Million $)										
Revs.	735	375	158	29.1	3.9	NA	NA	NA	NA	NA
Oper. Inc.	146	63.4	8.5	-2.1	-2.2	NA	NA	NA	NA	NA
Depr.	15.7	9.0	4.0	1.4	0.8	NA	NA	NA	NA	NA
Int. Exp.	4.9	Nil	Nil	Nil	NA	NA	NA	NA	NA	NA
Pretax Inc.	147	56.2	4.5	-3.6	-3.1	NA	NA	NA	NA	NA
Eff. Tax Rate	32%	32%	7.96%	Nil	Nil	NA	NA	NA	NA	NA
Net Inc.	100	38.1	4.1	-3.6	-3.1	NA	NA	NA	NA	NA
Balance Sheet & Other Fin. Data (Million $)										
Cash	699	61.6	50.3	6.6	NA	NA	NA	NA	NA	NA
Curr. Assets	930	173	101	19.3	NA	NA	NA	NA	NA	NA
Total Assets	1,016	202	113	25.0	NA	NA	NA	NA	NA	NA
Curr. Liab.	110	76.2	47.1	3.2	NA	NA	NA	NA	NA	NA
LT Debt	300	1.5	2.0	1.9	NA	NA	NA	NA	NA	NA
Common Eqty.	406	125	64.2	6.9	NA	NA	NA	NA	NA	NA
Total Cap.	706	126	66.2	8.8	NA	NA	NA	NA	NA	NA
Cap. Exp.	36.3	11.6	7.9	0.2	NA	NA	NA	NA	NA	NA
Cash Flow	116	47.1	8.1	-2.2	NA	NA	NA	NA	NA	NA
Curr. Ratio	8.4	2.3	2.1	6.0	NA	NA	NA	NA	NA	NA
% LT Debt of Cap.	42.5	1.2	3.0	21.5	NA	NA	NA	NA	NA	NA
% Net Inc.of Revs.	13.6	10.2	2.6	NM	NA	NA	NA	NA	NA	NA
% Ret. on Assets	16.4	24.1	5.8	NM	NA	NA	NA	NA	NA	NA
% Ret. on Equity	37.7	40.4	11.3	NM	NA	NA	NA	NA	NA	NA

Data as orig reptd.; bef. results of disc opers/spec. items. Per share data adj. for stk. divs. Bold denotes diluted EPS (FASB 128)-prior periods restated. E-Estimated. NA-Not Available. NM-Not Meaningful. NR-Not Ranked.

Office—3535 Monroe Drive, Santa Clara, CA 95051. **Tel**—(408) 615-2500. **Fax**—(408) 615-2800. **Website**—http://www.nvidia.com **Pres & CEO**—J-H. Huang. **CFO & Secy**—C. B. Hoberg. **VP & Investor Contact**—Mary Ann Allencourt (408) 615-2750. **Dirs**—T. Coxe, J. C. Gaither, J-H. Huang, H. C. Jones Jr., W. J. Miller, A. B. Seawell, M. A. Stevens. **Transfer Agent & Registrar**—Mellon Investor Services, SF. **Incorporated**— in California in 1993 and reincorporated in Delaware in 1998. **Empl**— 796. **S&P Analyst:** T. W. Smith, CFA

STANDARD
&POOR'S
STOCK REPORTS

Oracle Corp.

Nasdaq Symbol **ORCL**

In S&P 500

18-AUG-01

Industry:
Computer (Software & Services)

Summary: This company is the world's largest supplier of information management software.

S&P Opinion: Accumulate (★★★★)

Recent Price • 14.72
52 Wk Range • 46.46-13
Yield • Nil
12-Mo. P/E • 33.5

Quantitative Evaluations

Outlook
(1 Lowest—5 Highest)
• **3+**

Fair Value
• **15.70**

Risk
• **Average**

Earn./Div. Rank
• **B+**

Technical Eval.
• **Bearish** since 8/01

Rel. Strength Rank
(1 Lowest—99 Highest)
• **19**

Insider Activity
• **Neutral**

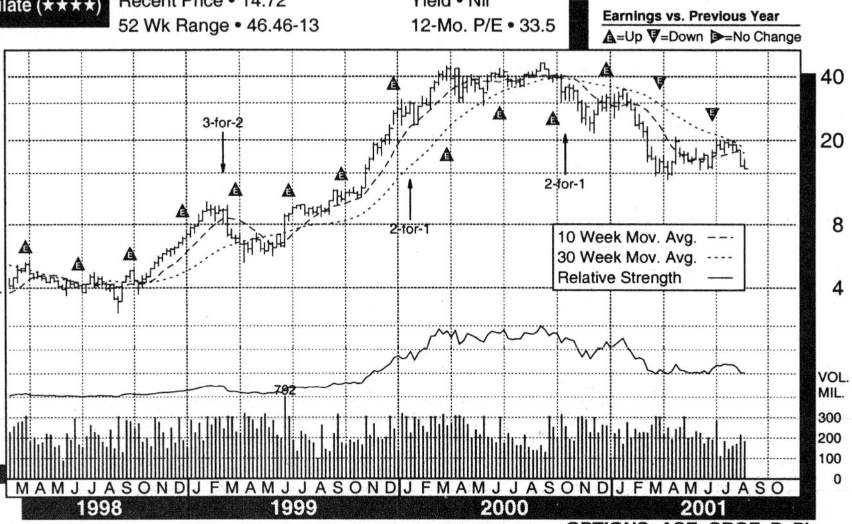

OPTIONS: ASE, CBOE, P, Ph

Overview - 20-JUN-01

We expect revenues to increase approximately 10% in FY 02 (May). Software license sales should grow faster than service revenues. The company's core database software business will likely benefit from the recent launch of its latest database platform, Oracle 9i. ORCL's flagship database product is geared toward the Internet, and the company continues to dominate the database market. We expect applications revenues to accelerate again, helping to drive revenue growth. ORCL is focusing on developing partnerships to provide services, rather than on expanding its internal consulting business. Operating margins should continue to widen, as management targets significant cost cutting and productivity enhancing measures. We expect EPS growth (excluding one-time gains) of approximately 18% in FY 02.

Valuation - 20-JUN-01

We continue to recommend accumulating the shares of this leading software company, despite the impact of the slowing global economy. The long-term positive benefits of the Internet are evident at Oracle. In addition to more rapid revenue growth for the long term, operating margins have improved dramatically, as the company has benefited from its own e-business technology. ORCL's operating margin widened to 34.8% in FY 01, from 30.4% in FY 00. Despite dramatic cost cutting, the company should continue its commitment to increasing investments in research and development. ORCL's strategy of selling an integrated suite of applications to compete with best-of-breed vendors will likely pay off over the long term. After selling off recently, the shares were trading at 33X our FY 02 EPS estimate of $0.52. With improved profitability, return on equity in excess of 40%, and 15% to 20% long-term earnings growth projected, we recommend accumulating the stock.

Key Stock Statistics

S&P EPS Est. 2002	0.50	Tang. Bk. Value/Share	1.15
P/E on S&P Est. 2002	29.4	Beta	1.84
Dividend Rate/Share	Nil	Shareholders	18,873
Shs. outstg. (M)	5613.6	Market cap. (B)	$ 82.6
Avg. daily vol. (M)	36.150	Inst. holdings	40%

Value of $10,000 invested 5 years ago: $ 32,976

Fiscal Year Ending May 31

	2001	2000	1999	1998	1997	1996
Revenues (Million $)						
1Q	2,262	1,985	1,749	1,369	1,052	771.8
2Q	2,660	2,322	2,056	1,614	1,311	967.2
3Q	2,674	2,449	2,079	1,749	1,373	1,020
4Q	3,264	3,374	2,943	2,413	2,079	1,464
Yr.	10,860	10,130	8,827	7,144	5,684	4,223
Earnings Per Share ($)						
1Q	**0.09**	**0.04**	**0.03**	Nil	0.02	0.01
2Q	**0.11**	**0.07**	**0.05**	0.03	0.03	0.02
3Q	**0.10**	**0.13**	**0.05**	**0.04**	0.03	0.02
4Q	**0.15**	**0.81**	**0.09**	**0.07**	0.06	0.04
Yr.	**0.44**	**1.05**	**0.22**	**0.14**	**0.14**	**0.10**

Next earnings report expected: mid September

Dividend Data

Amount ($)	Date Decl.	Ex-Div. Date	Stock of Record	Payment Date
2-for-1	Sep. 14	Oct. 13	Sep. 25	Oct. 12 '00

Oracle Corporation

Business Summary - 20-JUN-01

Oracle is the world's largest supplier of database software for information management. The company's software products fall into two broad categories: systems software and business applications software.

Systems software is a complete Internet platform to develop and deploy applications for computing on the Internet and corporate intranets. The Internet platform includes database management systems (DBMS) and development tools. The key component of Oracle's Internet platform is the Oracle8i relational DBMS, which enables storing, manipulating and retrieving relational, object-relational, multi-dimensional and other types of data. Oracle8i Lite is ORCL's mobile database for Internet computing. It is less complex than Oracle8i and requires no administration and can be used to temporarily store data and applications to be replicated back to Oracle8i.

The company also offers Oracle Application Server, an open-software platform for developing, deploying and managing distributed software application programs. It provides the infrastructure necessary to run Internet-computing applications. ORCL also provides application development tools supporting different approaches to software development for deployment running a web browser.

Business applications software automates the performance of specific business data processing functions for customer relationship management, supply chain management, financial management, procurement, project management, and human resources management. Oracle Applications Release 11.0 offers a fully Internet-enabled application. Oracle's Internet Business Solutions integrate the back office and front office of a company's business and capture information needed to provide a substantially completed view of a company's activities.

ORCL also offers consulting, education, support and systems integration services in support of its customers' use of its products. These services accounted for 56% of total revenues in FY 00 (May) and 58% in FY 99.

For customers that choose not to install their own applications, Oracle's Business On-Line delivers these applications across a network, through a hosting service. The applications can be accessed through a simple browser at significantly lower cost than traditional deployment.

In the first quarter of FY 00, the company opened a new Internet store. Within 18 months, ORCL expects as much as 80% of its revenues to go through the web store. The company had expected to save $1 billion a year from various cost cutting and productivity enhancing measures, but now has its sights set on $2 billion.

Per Share Data ($) (Year Ended May 31)	2001	2000	1999	1998	1997	1996	1995	1994	1993	1992
Tangible Bk. Val.	NA	1.15	1.29	0.51	0.40	0.32	0.21	0.13	0.09	0.08
Cash Flow	NA	1.10	0.43	0.19	0.18	0.14	0.10	0.06	0.03	0.02
Earnings	0.44	1.05	0.22	0.14	0.14	0.10	0.07	0.05	0.02	0.01
Dividends	Nil	Nil	Nil	Nil	Nil	Nil	Nil	Nil	Nil	Nil
Payout Ratio	Nil	Nil	Nil	Nil	Nil	Nil	Nil	Nil	Nil	Nil
Cal. Yrs.	2000	1999	1998	1997	1996	1995	1994	1993	1992	1991
Prices - High	46.46	28.34	7.47	7.02	5.66	3.61	2.29	1.86	0.70	0.41
- Low	21.50	5.25	2.95	3.48	2.92	1.97	1.29	0.66	0.29	0.13
P/E Ratio - High	NM	27	34	52	42	36	31	39	30	39
- Low	NM	5	14	26	22	20	17	14	12	13
Income Statement Analysis (Million $)										
Revs.	NA	10,130	8,827	7,144	5,684	4,223	2,967	2,001	1,503	1,178
Oper. Inc.	NA	6,475	2,619	1,740	1,565	1,124	797	485	297	165
Depr.	NA	314	320	329	265	220	148	65.2	56.2	50.9
Int. Exp.	NA	18.9	21.4	16.7	6.8	6.6	7.0	6.9	9.0	18.6
Pretax Inc.	NA	10,123	1,982	1,328	1,284	920	659	423	218	96.0
Eff. Tax Rate	NA	38%	35%	39%	36%	34%	33%	33%	35%	36%
Net Inc.	NA	6,297	1,290	814	821	603	442	284	142	62.0
Balance Sheet & Other Fin. Data (Million $)										
Cash	NA	7,872	1,786	1,920	890	841	586	465	358	177
Curr. Assets	NA	10,883	5,447	4,323	3,271	2,284	1,617	1,076	842	641
Total Assets	NA	13,077	7,260	5,819	4,624	3,357	2,425	1,595	1,184	956
Curr. Liab.	NA	5,862	3,046	2,484	1,922	1,455	1,055	682	551	406
LT Debt	NA	301	304	304	300	0.9	81.7	82.8	86.4	95.9
Common Eqty.	NA	6,461	7,391	2,958	2,370	1,870	1,211	741	528	435
Total Cap.	NA	7,028	7,831	3,278	2,676	1,880	1,321	862	623	541
Cap. Exp.	NA	263	347	328	391	308	262	251	41.3	46.6
Cash Flow	NA	6,611	1,290	1,142	1,086	823	589	349	198	112
Curr. Ratio	NA	1.9	1.8	1.7	1.7	1.6	1.5	1.6	1.5	1.6
% LT Debt of Cap.	NA	4.3	3.9	9.3	11.2	0.1	6.2	9.6	13.9	17.7
% Net Inc.of Revs.	NA	62.2	14.6	11.4	14.5	14.3	14.9	14.2	9.4	5.2
% Ret. on Assets	NA	61.9	19.7	15.6	20.6	20.9	22.0	20.4	13.2	6.7
% Ret. on Equity	NA	124.0	19.4	30.5	38.7	39.1	45.2	44.6	29.2	15.6

Data as orig reptd.; bef. results of disc opers/spec. items. Per share data adj. for stk. divs. Bold denotes diluted EPS (FASB 128)-prior periods restated. E-Estimated. NA-Not Available. NM-Not Meaningful. NR-Not Ranked.

Office—500 Oracle Parkway, Redwood Shores, CA 94065.**Reincorporated**—in Delaware in 1987.**Tel**—(415) 506-7000. **E-mail**—investor@oracle.com **Website**—http://www.oracle.com **Chrmn & CEO**—L. J. Ellison. **EVP & CFO**—J. O. Henley. **Dirs**—J. Berg, M. J. Boskin, L. J. Ellison, J. O. Henley, J. Kemp, K. Koplovitz, R. J. Lane, D. L. Lucas, R. A. McGinn. **Transfer Agent & Registrar**—Harris Trust & Savings Bank, Chicago. **Empl**— 41,320. **S&P Analyst:** Jonathan Rudy

STANDARD & POOR'S
STOCK REPORTS

Proxim, Inc.

Nasdaq Symbol **PROX**

In S&P SmallCap 600

18-AUG-01 **Industry:** Communications Equipment

Summary: PROX is the leading original equipment manufacturer supplier of spread spectrum wireless data networking products.

S&P Opinion: Accumulate (★★★★)

Recent Price • 9.92 | Yield • Nil
52 Wk Range • 68.75-5.62 | 12-Mo. P/E • NM

Quantitative Evaluations

Outlook (1 Lowest—5 Highest)
• **5**

Fair Value
• **14.50**

Risk
• **High**

Earn./Div. Rank
• **NR**

Technical Eval.
• **Bearish** since 6/01

Rel. Strength Rank (1 Lowest—99 Highest)
• **20**

Insider Activity
• **NA**

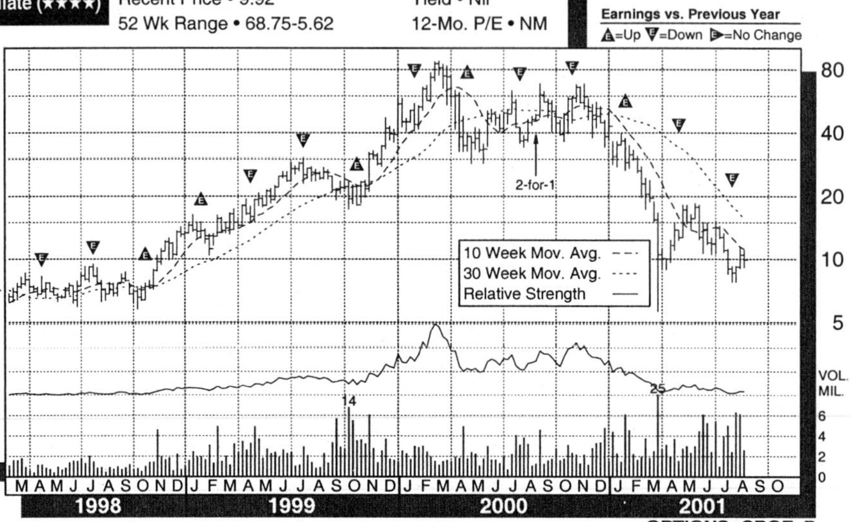

OPTIONS: CBOE, P

Overview - 14-AUG-01

For 2001, we expect sales to decline in the mid-single digits, hurt by weakness in the company's legacy vertical product line (about 30% of sales). Visibility remains extremely poor, as customers defer orders amid a weakening telecom spending market. Sales should receive a boost from the expected deployment of HomeRF 2.0 products, which will deliver data rates of 10 Mbps (up from the current rate of 1.6 Mbps) during the fourth quarter of 2001. As a result of the lower sales volume, gross margin will likely deteriorate to the low 40s, versus 47% in the prior year. SG&A expenses should decline in absolute dollars over the next several quarters, due to the implementation of aggressive cost control measures. Overall, we see EPS of $0.30 in 2001, down 41% from the $0.51 posted for 2000.

Valuation - 14-AUG-01

Despite a difficult near-term market, PROX's long term growth prospects remain robust, as the convergence of worldwide spectrum availability, emerging standards, and lower cost wireless and computing products will help drive strong wireless LAN growth for the next several years. The stock came under considerable scrutiny after Intel announced that it would support IEEE 802.11b technology, a wireless standard that competes with PROX's Home RF technology, for its next generation of consumer wireless networking devices. Still, we expect other major OEM partners such as Motorola and Siemens to begin to ramp HomeRF products, more than offsetting any weakness from Intel (about a 10% customer). From a technical standpoint, PROX's HomeRF products provide superior interference protection from cordless phones, microwave ovens and other wireless devices than 802.11b. The stock is attractive at 22X our 2002 estimate of $0.46, given PROX's leading position in the wireless LAN market.

Key Stock Statistics

S&P EPS Est. 2001	0.31	Tang. Bk. Value/Share	5.29
P/E on S&P Est. 2001	32.0	Beta	2.02
S&P EPS Est. 2002	0.46	Shareholders	117
Dividend Rate/Share	Nil	Market cap. (B)	$0.268
Shs. outstg. (M)	27.0	Inst. holdings	82%
Avg. daily vol. (M)	1.061		

Value of $10,000 invested 5 years ago: $ 5,736

Fiscal Year Ending Dec. 31

	2001	2000	1999	1998	1997	1996
Revenues (Million $)						
1Q	29.50	20.05	14.75	10.25	12.49	8.90
2Q	23.25	24.52	16.00	11.50	13.10	9.75
3Q	—	29.30	18.00	13.30	8.10	10.92
4Q	—	33.63	20.31	14.70	9.26	11.65
Yr.	—	107.5	69.07	49.71	42.95	41.22
Earnings Per Share ($)						
1Q	**-0.27**	**0.07**	**0.04**	**0.04**	0.08	0.06
2Q	**-2.38**	**0.01**	**0.05**	**0.06**	0.09	0.06
3Q	**E0.05**	**-0.10**	**0.09**	**0.08**	0.01	0.07
4Q	**E0.09**	**0.07**	**-0.05**	**0.05**	**-0.16**	0.15
Yr.	**E0.31**	**0.07**	**0.13**	**0.21**	**0.01**	**0.35**

Next earnings report expected: mid October

Dividend Data

Amount ($)	Date Decl.	Ex-Div. Date	Stock of Record	Payment Date
2-for-1	Jul. 18	Aug. 21	Aug. 01	Aug. 18 '00

Proxim, Inc.

Business Summary - 14-AUG-01

Proxim manufactures high performance wireless local area networking (LAN) and building-to-building network products based on radio frequency (RF) technology, producing wireless computer networking solutions for use in business and home environments. By eliminating the necessity for a physical network connection, these products let businesses input or retrieve time-sensitive data wherever needed. For example, hospitals can use the technology to input patient admission information anywhere in the hospital (not just at a fixed admitting station), and doctors can retrieve patient information and input their diagnoses at the point of care.

In 1994, PROX introduced the first 2.4 GHz wireless networking product line known as RangeLAN2. Since this product introduction, the 2.4 GHz frequency band has been approved for use by unlicensed wireless networks in virtually every developed country worldwide. The global acceptance of a common frequency standard for wireless networking has presented the company with new opportunities for international sales. In 2000, international sales accounted for 18% of total sales, down from 21% in 1999, as the company expanded its distribution channels.

The company's success is dependent on its ability to develop new products. In 1998, PRXM introduced the Symphony product family, delivering high-speed peer-to-peer cordless networking to the home and small office environment. In 2000, the company announced plans to develop a second generation of Symphony cordless networking products based on the SWAP (Shared Wireless Access Protocol) specification from the HomeRF Working Group that will support data rates up to 10Mbps. In 2000, PRXM introduced the RangeLAN-DS product family, which is based on 2.4 GHz direct sequence spread spectrum technology operating at up to 11 Mbps, and includes many of the innovative software and network management features provided by RangeLAN2 products. In 2000, the company also introduced the Harmony wireless LAN product family for the enterprise market, and the Stratum MP building-to-building wireless bridge.

A substantial portion of sales is derived from a limited number of customers, mostly original equipment manufacturers (OEMs). In 2000, Intermec accounted for 12% of total sales, versus 30% in 1999. PROX expects sales to a limited number of OEM customers to continue to account for a substantial portion of revenues for the foreseeable future. The company also distributes products indirectly to value added resellers, systems integrators, and end users.

In March 2001, PROX called off its merger with Netopia Inc., a developer of broadband Internet equipment solutions, due to weak market conditions. The original January purchase price had been $223 million.

Per Share Data ($) (Year Ended Dec. 31)	2000	1999	1998	1997	1996	1995	1994	1993	1992	1991
Tangible Bk. Val.	5.29	4.88	4.09	3.86	3.87	1.27	1.08	1.04	NA	NA
Cash Flow	0.37	0.21	0.28	0.08	0.41	0.21	0.07	0.01	-0.56	NA
Earnings	0.07	0.13	0.21	0.01	0.35	0.17	0.05	-0.01	NA	NA
Dividends	Nil	Nil	Nil	Nil	Nil	Nil	Nil	Nil	NA	NA
Payout Ratio	Nil	Nil	Nil	Nil	Nil	Nil	Nil	Nil	NA	NA
Prices - High	88.00	59.00	14.31	13.37	25.62	8.93	5.50	5.00	NA	NA
- Low	28.50	10.37	5.43	5.06	7.56	1.93	1.81	3.75	NA	NA
P/E Ratio - High	NM	NM	68	NM	72	51	110	NM	NA	NA
- Low	NM	NM	26	NM	21	11	36	NM	NA	NA
Income Statement Analysis (Million $)										
Revs.	107	69.1	49.7	43.0	41.2	22.1	11.3	8.1	4.1	2.7
Oper. Inc.	16.9	4.1	5.5	0.0	6.5	1.8	0.6	0.1	-1.7	NA
Depr.	8.7	2.2	1.7	1.6	1.0	0.5	0.3	0.2	0.2	NA
Int. Exp.	Nil	Nil	Nil	Nil	Nil	NA	NA	0.0	0.0	NA
Pretax Inc.	3.8	5.9	7.1	1.3	8.3	1.8	0.8	-0.1	-1.9	NA
Eff. Tax Rate	44%	47%	34%	93%	20%	NA	10%	NA	NM	NA
Net Inc.	2.1	3.1	4.7	0.1	6.7	2.8	0.7	-0.1	-1.9	-2.5
Balance Sheet & Other Fin. Data (Million $)										
Cash	69.7	87.4	66.7	62.3	54.2	6.2	11.3	13.3	1.2	NA
Curr. Assets	134	102	89.6	83.5	76.3	22.3	16.7	15.4	2.4	NA
Total Assets	198	147	94.2	89.1	81.4	24.1	17.4	15.8	2.8	NA
Curr. Liab.	12.4	12.0	8.8	10.4	5.7	5.7	2.2	1.5	1.0	NA
LT Debt	0.5	0.5	Nil	Nil	Nil	Nil	NA	NA	NA	NA
Common Eqty.	181	133	85.5	78.7	75.6	18.4	15.2	14.3	-3.6	NA
Total Cap.	186	135	85.5	78.9	75.6	18.4	15.2	14.3	-3.6	NA
Cap. Exp.	4.2	5.4	1.2	1.4	3.2	1.6	0.7	NA	NA	NA
Cash Flow	10.8	5.4	6.4	1.7	7.6	3.4	1.0	0.1	-1.7	NA
Curr. Ratio	10.8	8.5	10.2	8.0	13.3	3.9	7.6	10.6	2.4	NA
% LT Debt of Cap.	0.3	0.4	Nil	Nil	Nil	Nil	NA	NA	NA	NA
% Net Inc.of Revs.	2.0	4.5	9.5	0.2	16.1	12.9	6.6	NM	NM	NM
% Ret. on Assets	1.3	2.6	5.1	0.1	12.6	13.7	4.5	NM	NM	NM
% Ret. on Equity	1.4	2.9	5.7	0.1	14.1	16.9	5.0	NM	NM	NM

Data as orig reptd.; bef. results of disc opers/spec. items. Per share data adj. for stk. divs. Bold denotes diluted EPS (FASB 128)-prior periods restated. E-Estimated. NA-Not Available. NM-Not Meaningful. NR-Not Ranked.

Office—510 Deguigne Dr., Sunnyvale, CA 94086. **Tel**—(408) 731-2700. **Website**—www.proxim.com **Chrmn, Pres & CEO**—D. C. King. **VP-Fin & CFO**—K. E. Glover. **Secy**—J. D. Saper. **Dirs**—R. Chin, L. G. Denend, D. C. King, G. L. Reyes, J. D. Saper. **Transfer Agent & Registrar**—First National Bank of Boston. **Incorporated**—in Delaware in 1993. **Empl**— 233. **S&P Analyst:** A. Bensinger

STANDARD
&POOR'S
STOCK REPORTS

Rational Software

Nasdaq Symbol **RATL**

In S&P MidCap 400

18-AUG-01

Industry:
Computer (Software & Services)

Summary: This company develops software and services to help organizations develop and deploy software for e-business, e-infrastructure, and e-devices.

S&P Opinion: Accumulate (★★★★)

Recent Price • 14.25
52 Wk Range • 70.62-12.50
Yield • Nil
12-Mo. P/E • NM

Quantitative Evaluations

Outlook
(1 Lowest—5 Highest)
• 5

Fair Value
• 27.80

Risk
• High

Earn./Div. Rank
• B-

Technical Eval.
• Bearish since 7/01

Rel. Strength Rank
(1 Lowest—99 Highest)
• 8

Insider Activity
• NA

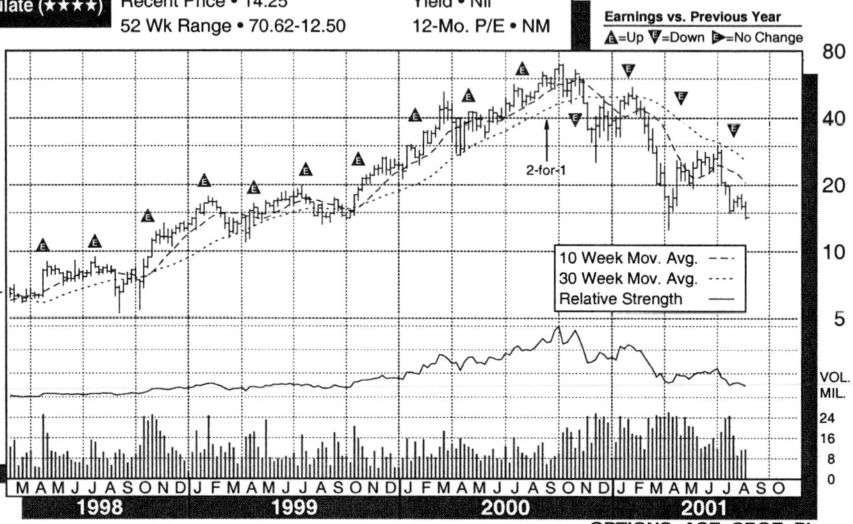

OPTIONS: ASE, CBOE, Ph

Overview - 13-JUL-01

We expect revenues to increase about 10% in FY 02 (Mar.), following a 42% gain in FY 01, as results have been restricted by the impact of the global economic slowdown. Both product and services revenues should contribute to gains, as the growth of the Internet fuels demand for RATL's products. The fastest growth should come from the company's wireless segment solutions, which currently account for only 10% of revenues. However, RATL's infrastructure solutions, which account for 45% of revenues, and e-business applications solutions, which provide 35% of revenues, should increase modestly in FY 02. We expect the company's profit margins to narrow considerably, due to lower than expected revenues, with a 15% operating margin and a 12% net margin projected. With more shares outstanding, operating EPS will likely drop about 28% in FY 02.

Valuation - 13-JUL-01

We are continuing our accumulate recommendation on the shares, despite concerns over the impact of the slowing global economy on RATL. The company provides software tools for the development of e-business, Internet infrastructure, and wireless device software, and will be hurt by the impact of lower spending on information technology in FY 02. However, we believe that for the long term, RATL is well positioned as a key provider of technology infrastructure for the Internet economy. Most companies that are developing software related to the Internet rely on RATL's development tools and services. Based on the company's strong market position and long-term annual growth prospects of 25% to 30%, we believe the shares are attractively valued at a recent level of 37X our recently reduced calendar 2001 EPS estimate of $0.55, and we would accumulate shares at these levels.

Key Stock Statistics

S&P EPS Est. 2002	0.52	Tang. Bk. Value/Share	2.17
P/E on S&P Est. 2002	27.4	Beta	2.28
S&P EPS Est. 2003	0.60	Shareholders	1,047
Dividend Rate/Share	Nil	Market cap. (B)	$ 2.9
Shs. outstg. (M)	201.7	Inst. holdings	79%
Avg. daily vol. (M)	2.428		

Value of $10,000 invested 5 years ago: $ 12,048

Fiscal Year Ending Mar. 31

	2002	2001	2000	1999	1998	1997
Revenues (Million $)						
1Q	175.8	170.3	117.4	82.97	38.36	32.00
2Q	—	187.5	128.2	94.66	46.26	34.00
3Q	—	215.5	146.2	109.1	82.31	39.10
4Q	—	241.7	180.4	125.1	87.25	40.30
Yr.	—	814.9	572.2	411.8	310.7	145.4
Earnings Per Share ($)						
1Q	**-0.13**	**0.10**	**0.08**	**0.05**	0.03	0.06
2Q	—	**0.10**	**0.10**	**0.07**	-0.37	0.07
3Q	—	**0.13**	**0.14**	**0.10**	**0.06**	-0.13
4Q	—	**0.03**	**0.13**	**0.12**	**0.06**	-0.45
Yr.	—	**0.35**	**0.45**	**0.33**	**-0.22**	**-0.31**

Next earnings report expected: mid October

Dividend Data

Amount ($)	Date Decl.	Ex-Div. Date	Stock of Record	Payment Date
2-for-1	Jul. 12	Sep. 05	Aug. 17	Sep. 01 '00

Rational Software Corporation

Business Summary - 13-JUL-01

Software is developed by teams of people who focus on different parts of the software development life cycle, such as analysis, design, coding and testing. When used in combination with one another, Rational Software's tools simplify customer software development environments, making it easier to develop software quickly, with the expected functionality and required levels of quality. Typical company customers build software in areas such as e-business, Web, intranet, n-tier, embedded, real-time, and software products.

The company's goal is to ensure the success of customers who depend on their ability to develop and deploy software. RATL creates and markets software an integrated family of tools, as well as services that unify cross-functional software teams, while also addressing the unique needs of team members. These tools span the critical phases of the software building process and are used with industry-standard hardware platforms and operating systems. In addition, the company provides a full range of technical consulting, training and support services.

The major components of RATL's product line include Rational ClearCase and Rational ClearQuest for configuration and change management; Rational RequisitePro for requirements management; Rational Rose for visual modeling; Rational Unified Process for software development process; Rational Robot, Rational TestFactory, Rational LoadTest, Rational Purify, Rational PureCoverage and Rational Visual Test, for various areas of automated testing; and Rational Apex for managing development teams and the components they generate. Each of the tools is available on a stand-alone basis, or integrated with the company's other tools, and each is supported by RATL's consulting services. Consulting arrangements focus on software architecture and development processes, and the successful adoption of object technology, regardless of programming language.

As of March 31, 2001, more than 917,000 licenses of the company's products had been sold to more than 52,000 customers worldwide. International sales accounted for 41% and 41% of revenues in FY 01 (Mar.) and FY 00, respectively.

RATL works with many strategic partners, including Microsoft, IBM, Intel, Sun Microsystems, Peoplesoft, Oracle, Hewlett-Packard and Silicon Graphics, for e-business as well as other application development platforms

In November 2000, the company announced that it would acquire the remaining 65% interest in Catapulse Inc. that it did not already own, for about $405 million in stock. The transaction was completed in February 2001. Catapulse was founded in October 1999 by two of RATL's co-founders.

Per Share Data ($) **(Year Ended Mar. 31)**	**2001**	**2000**	**1999**	**1998**	**1997**	**1996**	**1995**	**1994**	**1993**	**1992**
Tangible Bk. Val.	2.33	2.53	1.71	1.61	2.52	0.77	0.24	0.13	0.84	0.82
Cash Flow	NA	0.58	0.42	-0.10	-0.42	0.01	0.18	-0.19	0.18	0.11
Earnings	0.35	0.45	0.33	-0.22	-0.49	-0.07	0.09	-0.28	0.09	0.10
Dividends	Nil	Nil	Nil	Nil	Nil	Nil	Nil	Nil	Nil	Nil
Payout Ratio	Nil	Nil	Nil	Nil	Nil	Nil	Nil	Nil	Nil	Nil
Cal. Yrs.	2000	1999	1998	1997	1996	1995	1994	1993	1992	1991
Prices - High	70.62	26.84	13.68	20.43	22.12	6.00	2.53	3.75	3.84	2.25
- Low	21.15	10.93	5.25	3.53	3.96	1.78	1.03	1.73	2.06	0.75
P/E Ratio - High	NM	60	42	NM	NM	NM	28	NM	43	23
- Low	NM	25	16	NM	NM	NM	11	NM	23	8
Income Statement Analysis (Million $)										
Revs.	815	572	412	311	145	91.1	72.9	70.3	23.3	19.2
Oper. Inc.	150	138	89.5	39.1	23.3	8.7	8.1	1.0	5.5	3.6
Depr.	56.0	26.4	18.8	20.9	5.7	4.6	4.5	4.8	1.9	1.0
Int. Exp.	25.2	4.1	Nil	Nil	Nil	Nil	Nil	Nil	0.2	0.2
Pretax Inc.	113	123	84.6	-28.8	-38.5	-3.0	5.1	-13.4	3.2	2.3
Eff. Tax Rate	50%	30%	30%	NM	NM	NM	8.00%	NM	37%	28%
Net Inc.	72.1	85.3	59.2	-38.3	-43.0	-4.0	4.7	-13.8	2.0	1.7
Balance Sheet & Other Fin. Data (Million $)										
Cash	364	413	60.0	126	230	52.6	10.5	13.7	11.4	9.3
Curr. Assets	1,286	1,075	384	380	267	78.1	30.0	30.0	20.6	15.0
Total Assets	1,709	1,226	454	445	303	85.7	38.0	39.3	27.2	21.2
Curr. Liab.	360	243	156	152	59.7	32.6	22.2	28.1	6.8	5.5
LT Debt	500	500	Nil	0.2	1.7	Nil	0.7	3.0	0.6	0.7
Common Eqty.	959	637	294	287	240	50.9	12.1	6.5	17.4	14.5
Total Cap.	1,517	1,137	294	287	242	50.9	12.7	9.5	18.4	15.6
Cap. Exp.	76.2	24.5	21.7	9.1	3.6	2.8	3.2	5.3	0.5	1.5
Cash Flow	128	112	78.0	-17.4	-37.3	0.6	9.2	-9.0	3.9	2.7
Curr. Ratio	3.6	4.4	2.5	2.5	4.5	2.4	1.3	1.1	3.0	2.7
% LT Debt of Cap.	33.0	44.0	Nil	0.1	0.7	Nil	5.1	31.5	3.5	4.5
% Net Inc.of Revs.	8.8	14.9	14.4	NM	NM	NM	6.4	NM	8.7	8.7
% Ret. on Assets	4.9	10.2	13.2	NM	NM	NM	12.0	NM	7.8	8.9
% Ret. on Equity	8.4	16.2	20.4	NM	NM	NM	50.2	NM	11.8	12.8

Data as orig reptd.; bef. results of disc opers/spec. items. Per share data adj. for stk. divs. Bold denotes diluted EPS (FASB 128)-prior periods restated. E-Estimated. NA-Not Available. NM-Not Meaningful. NR-Not Ranked.

Office—18880 Homestead Rd., Cupertino, CA 95014-0721. **Tel**—(408) 863-9900; (800) 728-1212. **Website**—http://www.rational.com **Chrmn**—P. D. Levy. **CEO**—M. T. Devlin. **Pres & COO** —T. F. Bogan. **SVP, CFO & Secy**—T. A. Brennan. **Investor Contact**—David J. Henshall. **Dirs**—L. G. Denend, M. T. Devlin, P. D. Levy, J. E. Montague, A. R. Schleicher. **Transfer Agent & Registrar**—Mellon Investor Services, SF. **Incorporated**—in Delaware in 1982. **Empl**— 3,899. **S&P Analyst:** Jonathan Rudy

STANDARD
&POOR'S
STOCK REPORTS

RSA Security

Nasdaq Symbol **RSAS**

In S&P MidCap 400

18-AUG-01

Industry: Computer (Software & Services)

Summary: This company (formerly Security Dynamics Technologies) offers security products used to protect and manage access to computer-based information resources.

S&P Opinion: Accumulate (★★★★)

Recent Price • 17.93
52 Wk Range • 44.33-17.83
Yield • Nil
12-Mo. P/E • 6.8

Quantitative Evaluations

Outlook
(1 Lowest—5 Highest)
• **5+**

Fair Value
• **30.20**

Risk
• **High**

Earn./Div. Rank
• **NR**

Technical Eval.
• **Bearish** since 7/01

Rel. Strength Rank
(1 Lowest—99 Highest)
• **8**

Insider Activity
• **Unfavorable**

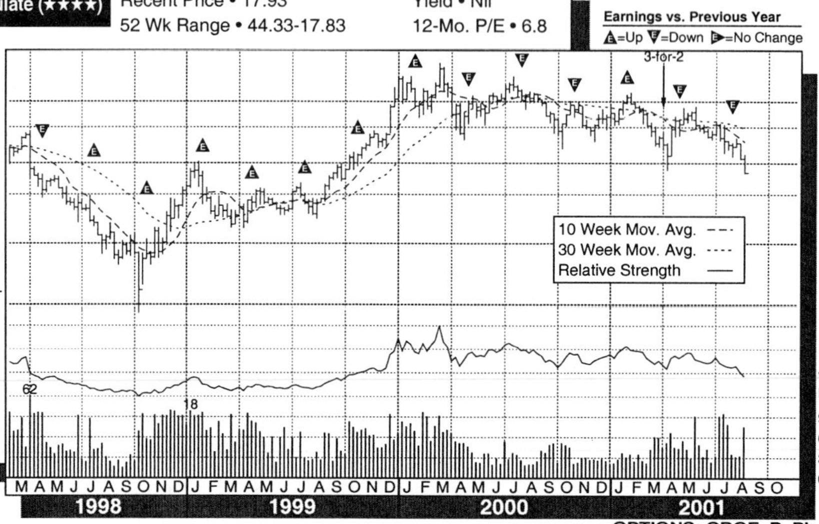

OPTIONS: CBOE, P, Ph

Overview - 16-JUL-01

We estimate revenue growth for 2001 at approximately 15%. Growth should be driven by the company's public key infrastructure (PKI) systems segment. Although the area provided only 5% of 1999 total revenues, we expect the percentage to more than double in 2001. PKI revenue will also benefit from the February 2001 acquisition of Xcert International. Revenues from the more mature authentication segment should grow solidly, in the mid- to high teens. However, encryption revenues will likely decline, year to year. We expect operating margins to narrow, as RSA will be negatively affected by a lower than previously expected revenue base. Excluding one-time gains and charges, operating EPS should decline slightly in 2001, from 2000's $0.61.

Valuation - 16-JUL-01

We currently have an accumulate recommendation on the shares, despite near-term concerns over the impact of the global economic slowdown on technology related spending. The company's SecurID authentication and BSAFE encryption products are industry standards, with dominant market shares. The company could face pricing pressures over the near term, due to the expiration of an encryption algorithm patent. However, a recent relaxation of government export restrictions on encryption will let RSAS compete internationally. PKI is an emerging industry, with potential to account for the majority of revenues in a few years. We believe the company is well positioned in this area with its Keon product, which combines RSAS's proven strengths in authentication and encryption. With an increasing need for e-security, and based on RSAS's strong industry position, we believe the shares remain attractive at 37X projected 2002 operating EPS of $0.68.

Key Stock Statistics

S&P EPS Est. 2001	0.56	Tang. Bk. Value/Share	8.56
P/E on S&P Est. 2001	32.0	Beta	2.35
S&P EPS Est. 2002	0.74	Shareholders	338
Dividend Rate/Share	Nil	Market cap. (B)	$ 1.0
Shs. outstg. (M)	57.2	Inst. holdings	78%
Avg. daily vol. (M)	0.864		

Value of $10,000 invested 5 years ago: $ 8,235

Fiscal Year Ending Dec. 31

	2001	2000	1999	1998	1997	1996
Revenues (Million $)						
1Q	76.34	63.30	48.67	40.25	26.44	12.17
2Q	80.78	66.70	51.81	43.37	29.66	14.07
3Q	—	72.03	55.66	40.80	34.83	20.36
4Q	—	78.12	61.99	46.92	39.73	23.50
Yr.	—	280.2	218.1	171.3	135.9	76.15
Earnings Per Share ($)						
1Q	**0.16**	**0.37**	**0.65**	**0.05**	0.09	0.06
2Q	**0.22**	**0.58**	**0.70**	**0.17**	0.10	0.07
3Q	—	**0.63**	**0.95**	**0.05**	0.04	0.01
4Q	—	**1.69**	**0.64**	**0.20**	**0.05**	0.13
Yr.	—	**3.21**	**2.92**	**0.46**	**0.27**	**0.24**

Next earnings report expected: mid October

Dividend Data

Amount ($)	Date Decl.	Ex-Div. Date	Stock of Record	Payment Date
3-for-2	Feb. 01	Mar. 26	Mar. 09	Mar. 23 '01

RSA Security Inc.

Business Summary - 16-JUL-01

Electronic security (e-security) has become a fundamental requirement for conducting all forms of electronic business, in order to create and ensure the same trust relationships that currently exist on paper. RSA Security (formerly Security Dynamics Technologies) helps organizations build secure, trusted foundations for e-business through its two-factor user authentication, encryption and public key management products and solutions.

Security requirements addressed by these products include user identification and authentication; access control and privilege management; data privacy, integrity and authentication; and security administration and audit.

The company's RSA SecurID solutions provide two-factor authentication services, designed to create a barrier against unauthorized access or intrusion. Two-factor means that the product combines two methods of user identification: something secret that the user knows (such as a personal identification number), and something that the user physically has (the RSA SecurID authenticator). As of December 31, 2000, the company had licensed more than 8 million authenticators to more than 7,000 customers worldwide.

RSA BSAFE tools are encryption components used by software developers to secure applications for electronic commerce. The company has the most widely deployed cryptographic software in the world, with more than 500 million licenses in use, as of December 2000.

The company's RSA Keon software provides a common foundation for securing Internet and e-business applications. Keon is a family of PKI (public key infrastructure) software modules used to manage digital certificates and provide an environment for authenticated, private and legally binding electronic communications and transactions.

RSAS has 23 U.S. patents and 31 foreign patents, expiring at various dates ranging from 2005 to 2018. On September 20, 2000, the patent describing the RSA public key encryption methodology expired. This has encouraged competitors to market competing products.

Until recently, the U.S. government only permitted exports of commercial encryption products (other than general purpose encryption toolkits) with key lengths of up to 56 bits. In January 2000, the U.S. Department of Commerce issued new regulations allowing encryption products of any key length to be exported to all end-users, other than governmental end-users. This has helped RSAS compete internationally in this arena.

In February 2001, RSAS acquired Xcert International, Inc., a privately held company that develops and delivers digital certificate-based products for securing e-business transactions. The purchase price was $67.5 million in cash.

Per Share Data ($) (Year Ended Dec. 31)	2000	1999	1998	1997	1996	1995	1994	1993	1992	1991
Tangible Bk. Val.	8.56	10.47	4.00	3.35	2.35	2.35	0.86	NA	NA	NA
Cash Flow	3.37	3.28	0.57	0.35	0.27	0.34	0.37	0.52	NA	NA
Earnings	3.21	2.92	0.46	0.27	0.24	0.15	0.08	0.06	NA	NA
Dividends	Nil	Nil	Nil	Nil	Nil	Nil	Nil	NA	NA	NA
Payout Ratio	Nil	Nil	Nil	Nil	Nil	Nil	Nil	NA	NA	NA
Prices - High	62.04	53.33	28.50	29.58	36.33	19.41	3.37	NA	NA	NA
- Low	23.50	9.50	3.62	14.00	14.16	2.93	2.33	NA	NA	NA
P/E Ratio - High	19	18	62	108	151	126	39	NA	NA	NA
- Low	7	3	8	51	59	19	27	NA	NA	NA
Income Statement Analysis (Million $)										
Revs.	280	218	171	136	76.1	33.8	17.6	12.1	8.9	6.1
Oper. Inc.	52.0	27.3	19.6	29.2	15.8	8.4	3.7	2.7	NA	NA
Depr.	10.0	9.2	6.8	4.4	1.8	0.7	0.3	0.1	NA	NA
Int. Exp.	Nil	Nil	Nil	Nil	Nil	Nil	Nil	Nil	Nil	Nil
Pretax Inc.	330	303	52.4	29.6	23.8	9.5	3.6	2.6	1.3	0.5
Eff. Tax Rate	38%	39%	45%	44%	45%	39%	35%	35%	39%	34%
Net Inc.	206	184	29.4	16.4	13.0	5.8	2.3	1.7	0.8	0.3
Balance Sheet & Other Fin. Data (Million $)										
Cash	335	1,383	158	95.7	9.5	44.6	17.5	2.8	NA	NA
Curr. Assets	414	1,454	216	206	125	98.4	31.4	6.6	NA	NA
Total Assets	590	1,512	281	232	140	102	32.6	7.3	5.5	3.7
Curr. Liab.	109	901	35.6	29.3	17.3	6.5	3.7	2.4	NA	NA
LT Debt	Nil	Nil	Nil	Nil	Nil	Nil	Nil	NA	NA	NA
Common Eqty.	481	611	243	199	121	95.0	28.9	-3.7	-5.4	-6.2
Total Cap.	481	611	245	202	123	95.0	28.9	NA	NA	NA
Cap. Exp.	39.5	13.7	18.9	10.9	9.2	1.5	0.8	0.2	NA	NA
Cash Flow	216	193	36.3	20.7	14.8	6.5	2.2	1.3	NA	NA
Curr. Ratio	3.8	1.6	6.1	7.0	7.2	15.1	8.5	2.8	NA	NA
% LT Debt of Cap.	Nil	Nil	Nil	Nil	Nil	Nil	Nil	NA	NA	NA
% Net Inc.of Revs.	73.4	84.2	17.2	12.0	17.1	17.2	13.2	13.8	9.0	5.3
% Ret. on Assets	19.6	20.5	11.5	8.8	10.8	8.7	11.6	26.3	17.5	NA
% Ret. on Equity	37.7	43.0	13.3	10.2	12.1	9.4	15.1	NM	NM	NA

Data as orig reptd.; bef. results of disc opers/spec. items. Per share data adj. for stk. divs. Bold denotes diluted EPS (FASB 128)-prior periods restated. E-Estimated. NA-Not Available. NM-Not Meaningful. NR-Not Ranked.

Office—36 Crosby Dr., Bedford, MA 01730. **Tel**—(617) 687-7000. **Website**—http://www.rsasecurity.com **Chrmn**—C. R. Stuckey Jr. **Pres & CEO**—A. W. Coviello Jr. **SVP & CFO**—J. F. Kennedy. **Investor Contact**—Steve Casey. **Dirs**—R. P. Badavas, D. J. Bidzos, A. W. Coviello, R. L. Earnest, T. Elgamal, J. B. Lassiter, III, J. K. Sims, C. R. Stuckey Jr. **Transfer Agent & Registrar**—Boston EquiServe. **Incorporated**— in Massachusetts in 1984; reincorporated in Delaware in 1986. **Empl**— 1,350. **S&P Analyst:** Jonathan Rudy

STANDARD
&POOR'S
STOCK REPORTS

Sanmina Corp.

Nasdaq Symbol **SANM**

In S&P 500

23-AUG-01

Industry: Electrical Equipment

Summary: This company is a leading provider of customized integrated manufacturing services to OEMs in the electronics industry.

S&P Opinion: Accumulate (★★★★)

Recent Price • 19 | Yield • Nil
52 Wk Range • 60.50-17.53 | 12-Mo. P/E • 22.4

Quantitative Evaluations

Outlook
(1 Lowest—5 Highest)
• **2−**

Fair Value
• **20.50**

Risk
• **Average**

Earn./Div. Rank
• **NR**

Technical Eval.
• **Neutral** since 7/01

Rel. Strength Rank
(1 Lowest—99 Highest)
• **17**

Insider Activity
• **NA**

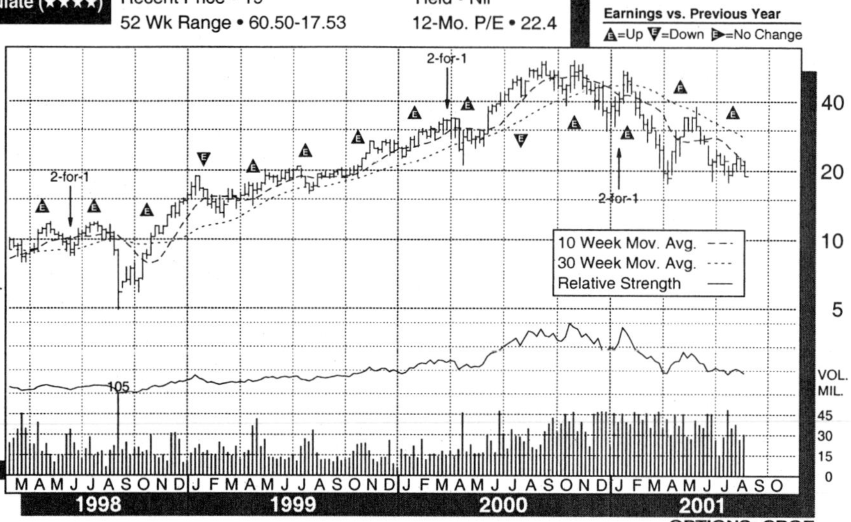

OPTIONS: CBOE

Overview - 23-AUG-01

We expect revenues in FY 02 (Sep.) to be down slightly from the estimated level of FY 01. The lack of growth reflects continued weakness in corporate information technology (IT) spending, and difficulties in the telecom sector, from which SANM derives most of its revenues. Despite the poor macroeconomic climate, the company should still benefit from its position with leading OEMs, expected new customer wins, and acquisition opportunities. Gross margins may narrow, on a less favorable business mix, but operating margins will be aided by cost controls and acquisition synergies. SANM's proposed acquisition of SCI Systems, subject to shareholder approval, is expected to be accretive to FY 02 earnings. Synergies gained from the transaction are expected to be $100 million to $150 million. We are forecasting FY 02 EPS of $0.70, a 22% decline from our FY 01 projection of $0.90.

Valuation - 23-AUG-01

The shares have corrected sharply, together with equities of the entire electronic manufacturing services (EMS) industry, and were recently down nearly 70% from their 52-week high. Trading at only 21X our FY 01 EPS target of $0.90, the shares were at a discount to the company's projected long-term EPS growth rate, the 25% annual industry growth rate, and SANM's peer group. The stock is attractive, as we still believe the long-term outlook for the company, and for the EMS industry as a whole, is exceptional, despite the harsh near-term telecom environment. In addition, SANM's proposed acquisition of SCI Systems will further enhance its capabilities and strengthen its position in the EMS space. For the longer term, the company's outlook is bolstered by its position at the high end of the telecom space, with industry leading margins, return on assets, and return on equity.

Key Stock Statistics

S&P EPS Est. 2001	0.90	Tang. Bk. Value/Share	4.54
P/E on S&P Est. 2001	21.1	Beta	2.34
Dividend Rate/Share	Nil	Shareholders	1,115
Shs. outstg. (M)	319.7	Market cap. (B)	$ 6.2
Avg. daily vol. (M)	6.089	Inst. holdings	89%

Value of $10,000 invested 5 years ago: $ 48,640

Fiscal Year Ending Sep. 30

	2001	2000	1999	1998	1997	1996
Revenues (Million $)						
1Q	1,390	459.7	275.5	159.1	88.87	52.17
2Q	1,191	555.3	281.1	172.2	96.70	63.22
3Q	776.6	1,001	309.5	197.1	105.4	71.18
4Q	—	1,272	348.6	194.2	114.2	78.51
Yr.	—	3,912	1,215	722.6	405.2	265.1
Earnings Per Share ($)						
1Q	**0.34**	**0.14**	Nil	**0.07**	**0.07**	0.04
2Q	**0.19**	**0.17**	**0.12**	**0.09**	0.07	0.05
3Q	**0.10**	**0.01**	**0.13**	**0.10**	0.07	0.05
4Q	—	**0.29**	**0.14**	**0.10**	0.07	0.06
Yr.	—	**0.64**	**0.38**	**0.36**	**0.17**	**0.21**

Next earnings report expected: late October

Dividend Data

Amount ($)	Date Decl.	Ex-Div. Date	Stock of Record	Payment Date
2-for-1	Dec. 13	Jan. 09	Dec. 18	Jan. 08 '01

A Division of The McGraw-Hill Companies

Sanmina Corporation

Business Summary - 23-AUG-01

Sanmina (SANM), which emphasizes a one-stop approach that includes everything from engineering design assistance to integration and testing of complete systems, has become a leading provider of electronic manufacturing services (EMS) to original equipment manufacturers (OEMs) in the electronics industry. It also provides sophisticated electronic assembly and turnkey manufacturing management services, and makes custom cable assemblies for electronics industry OEMs. The company has recently been actively participating in the consolidation of the contract manufacturing industry.

The company targets its services to customers in three rapidly growing electronics industry sectors: communications, which accounted for 72% of net sales in FY 00 (Sep.); industrial and medical instrumentation (12%); and computer systems (16%).

SANM's electronic assembly services involve the manufacture of complex printed circuit board assemblies using surface mount (SMT) and pin-through-hole (PTH) interconnection technologies; the manufacture of custom-designed backplane assemblies and complex multilayer printed circuit boards; and the testing and assembly of completed systems.

SMT and PTH printed circuit board assemblies are printed circuit boards on which electronic components, such as integrated circuits, capacitors, microprocessors and resistors have been mounted. Backplane assemblies are large printed circuit boards on which connectors are mounted to receive and interconnect printed circuit boards and other electronic components.

SANM locates its facilities close to customers, allowing it to meet their requirements on a quick-turn and cost-effective basis. The company's 46 manufacturing facilities comprise 5.6 million sq. ft., located in North America, Europe and Asia.

The company has been busy on the acquisition front over the past 18 months. In September 2000, SANM acquired the San Jose-based system integration and fulfillment operation of Lucent Technologies. In August 2000, the company acquired a design and engineering group from from Nortel Networks. In June 2000, SANM acquired Hadco Corp., a New Hampshire-based manufacturer of printed circuit boards and backplane assemblies, in exchange for about 19.3 million common shares. Also in June, the company acquired Essex AB, an EMS company with operations in Sweden and Finland.

Revenues are concentrated among a handful of customers. In FY 00 and FY 99, sales to the 10 largest customers accounted for 56% and 49% of total revenues, respectively. In FY 00, Nortel Networks accounted for 12% of sales, and was the only customer to provide over 10% of total sales.

Per Share Data ($) (Year Ended Sep. 30)	2000	1999	1998	1997	1996	1995	1994	1993	1992	1991
Tangible Bk. Val.	4.54	2.46	1.70	1.08	0.71	0.45	0.36	0.11	0.07	NA
Cash Flow	1.14	0.58	0.47	0.37	0.26	0.13	0.01	0.11	0.03	NA
Earnings	0.64	0.38	0.36	0.28	0.20	0.13	-0.03	0.06	0.00	NA
Dividends	Nil	Nil	Nil	Nil	Nil	Nil	Nil	Nil	Nil	NA
Payout Ratio	Nil	Nil	Nil	Nil	Nil	Nil	Nil	Nil	Nil	NA
Prices - High	60.50	27.31	15.62	11.34	7.09	3.57	1.96	1.84	NA	NA
- Low	21.06	12.37	4.90	4.75	2.53	1.60	0.95	0.62	NA	NA
P/E Ratio - High	95	72	44	41	35	28	NM	29	NA	NA
- Low	33	33	14	17	13	13	NM	10	NA	NA
Income Statement Analysis (Million $)										
Revs.	3,912	1,215	723	405	265	168	115	88.5	65.1	NA
Oper. Inc.	545	220	139	81.5	53.4	31.7	22.4	16.5	6.1	NA
Depr.	157	48.8	27.3	12.9	8.1	4.7	4.4	4.1	3.5	NA
Int. Exp.	Nil	Nil	0.7	5.1	5.2	0.7	0.1	2.6	1.6	NA
Pretax Inc.	330	148	107	67.1	45.3	28.0	3.6	9.9	NA	NA
Eff. Tax Rate	40%	37%	37%	39%	38%	39%	187%	40%	NA	NA
Net Inc.	197	93.7	68.2	40.9	28.1	17.0	-3.1	5.9	0.0	NA
Balance Sheet & Other Fin. Data (Million $)										
Cash	993	136	153	122	115	107	25.9	0.6	NA	NA
Curr. Assets	2,585	885	342	234	185	163	55.8	23.4	NA	NA
Total Assets	3,639	1,202	468	303	231	188	64.5	45.6	41.7	NA
Curr. Liab.	712	217	115	60.3	40.0	34.0	17.7	15.0	NA	NA
LT Debt	1,144	355	5.8	86.3	86.3	86.3	Nil	4.4	8.8	NA
Common Eqty.	1,701	626	344	156	104	67.1	46.7	26.1	20.9	NA
Total Cap.	2,907	982	350	242	190	154	46.7	30.6	29.6	NA
Cap. Exp.	199	65.3	29.0	30.2	21.8	9.9	4.1	3.1	NA	NA
Cash Flow	355	142	95.4	53.8	36.2	17.7	1.3	10.0	3.4	NA
Curr. Ratio	3.6	4.1	3.0	3.9	4.6	4.8	3.1	1.6	NA	NA
% LT Debt of Cap.	39.3	36.2	1.6	35.6	45.4	56.0	Nil	14.5	29.6	NA
% Net Inc.of Revs.	5.0	7.7	9.4	10.1	10.6	10.1	NM	6.7	NM	NA
% Ret. on Assets	7.0	10.1	17.7	15.3	13.4	13.5	NM	10.2	NA	NA
% Ret. on Equity	15.4	16.9	27.3	31.5	32.9	29.9	NM	45.1	NA	NA

Data as orig reptd.; bef. results of disc opers/spec. items. Per share data adj. for stk. divs. Bold denotes diluted EPS (FASB 128)-prior periods restated. E-Estimated. NA-Not Available. NM-Not Meaningful. NR-Not Ranked.

Office—2700 North First Street, San Jose, CA 95134. **Tel**—(408) 964-3500. **Website**—http://www.sanmina.com **Chrmn & CEO**—J. Sola. **Pres & COO**—R. W. Furr. **EVP & CFO**—R. A. Ackel. **Secy**—C. D. Mitchell.**Investor Relations**—(408-964-3500). **Dirs**—J. C. Bolger, N. R. Bonke, R. W. Furr, M. M. Rosati, J. M. Schell, J. Sola, B. V. Vonderschmitt. **Transfer Agent & Registrar**—Norwest Bank Minnesota, South St. Paul. **Incorporated**—in Delaware in 1989. **Empl**— 24,000. **S&P Analyst:** Richard N. Stice

STANDARD &POOR'S
STOCK REPORTS

Waters Corp.

NYSE Symbol **WAT**

In S&P MidCap 400

18-AUG-01

Industry: Electronics (Instrumentation)

Summary: WAT manufactures high performance liquid chromatography, thermal analysis and mass spectrometry products.

S&P Opinion: Accumulate (★★★★)

Recent Price • 28.48 | Yield • Nil
52 Wk Range • 90.93-22.33 | 12-Mo. P/E • 30.6

Quantitative Evaluations

Outlook
(1 Lowest—5 Highest)
• **4-**

Fair Value
• **30.90**

Risk
• **Average**

Earn./Div. Rank
• **NR**

Technical Eval.
• **Neutral** since 7/01

Rel. Strength Rank
(1 Lowest—99 Highest)
• **20**

Insider Activity
• **Neutral**

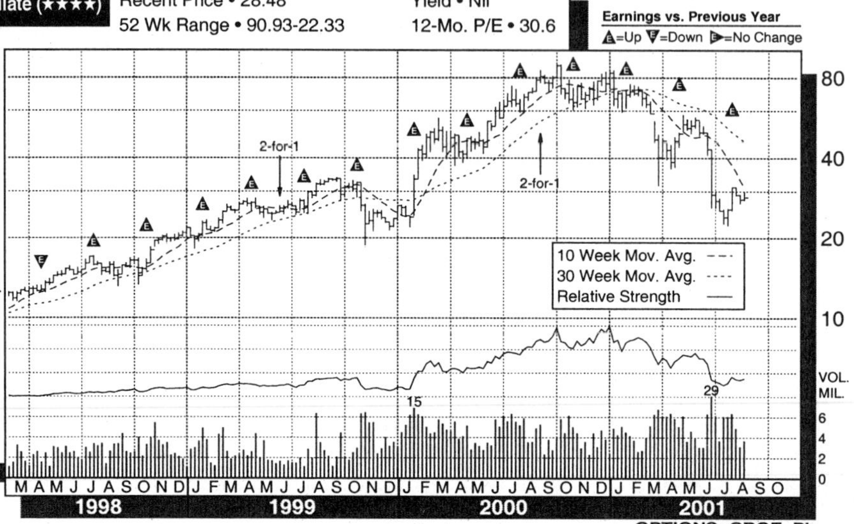

OPTIONS: CBOE, Ph

Overview - 24-JUL-01

Second quarter results were in line with our lowered estimates, reflecting weak demand for mass spectrometry instruments. The weak demand is attributed to purchase delays by some large pharmaceutical customers, which management believes is due in part to confusion surrounding the introduction of numerous new product offerings by itself and competitors. We now project net sales will increase 8.3% in 2001, to about $860 million, on solid demand for high performance liquid chromatography (HPLC) instruments. Mass spectrometry sales should grow about 9%-10%, on softening demand for drug discovery tools. HPLC instruments should increase 9%-11%. A lower effective tax rate should drive 10% EPS growth in 2001. For 2002, we see sales increasing 12%, and modest margin improvement driving 17% EPS growth. We project 2001 EPS of $1.27, and $1.49 for 2002.

Valuation - 24-JUL-01

We are upgrading WAT to accumulate, from hold, reflecting the improving outlook and valuation relative to its earnings growth rate. WAT holds a dominant share of the worldwide HPLC market, and leading market positions in both mass spectrometry and thermal analysis instruments. New collaborations with Variagenics and Caprion will extend WAT's penetration in key areas by leveraging its existing mass spectrometry and chemistry business to better compete in genomics and proteomics markets. WAT's strong product development pipeline should sustain future sales growth. WAT introduced several new products, extending its current lineup, at the Pittcon Conference in March. While weak biotech/pharmaceutical demand continues, demand should improve gradually through year-end. Trading at 19X our 2002 EPS estimate of $1.49, with 20% long-term EPS growth, we believe the stock will outperform.

Key Stock Statistics

S&P EPS Est. 2001	1.27	Tang. Bk. Value/Share	2.21
P/E on S&P Est. 2001	22.4	Beta	0.82
S&P EPS Est. 2002	1.49	Shareholders	259
Dividend Rate/Share	Nil	Market cap. (B)	$ 3.7
Shs. outstg. (M)	130.5	Inst. holdings	90%
Avg. daily vol. (M)	1.064		

Value of $10,000 invested 5 years ago: $ 36,318

Fiscal Year Ending Dec. 31

	2001	2000	1999	1998	1997	1996
Revenues (Million $)						
1Q	201.0	180.2	160.4	138.7	102.4	85.31
2Q	206.8	197.4	172.3	149.3	106.2	95.97
3Q	—	191.9	171.1	151.8	105.0	98.41
4Q	—	225.5	200.7	179.0	151.8	111.4
Yr.	—	795.1	704.4	618.8	465.5	391.1
Earnings Per Share ($)						
1Q	**0.28**	**0.23**	**0.17**	Nil	**0.10**	**0.07**
2Q	**0.29**	**0.28**	**0.21**	**0.15**	**0.12**	**-0.09**
3Q	—	**0.27**	**0.21**	**0.17**	**-0.35**	**0.05**
4Q	—	**0.37**	**0.32**	**0.24**	**0.04**	**0.12**
Yr.	—	**1.14**	**0.92**	**0.57**	**-0.08**	**0.15**

Next earnings report expected: mid October

Dividend Data

Amount ($)	Date Decl.	Ex-Div. Date	Stock of Record	Payment Date
2-for-1	Jul. 13	Aug. 28	Aug. 04	Aug. 25 '00

A Division of The McGraw-Hill Companies

Waters Corporation

Business Summary - 24-JUL-01

Waters Corp. helps scientists understand the complexities of natural products and synthetic chemical mixtures and the physical properties of materials. It operates in the analytical instrument industry, with manufacturing and distribution expertise in three complementary technologies: HPLC (high performance liquid chromatography) instruments, columns and other consumables, and related service; thermal analysis and rheology instruments; and mass spectrometry instruments that can be integrated and used together with other analytical instruments, particularly HPLC.

WAT is the world's largest maker of HPLC instruments, chromatography columns, and other consumables. It has the largest market share in the U.S., Europe, and non-Japan Asia, and a leading position in Japan. HPLC is the largest product segment of the analytical instrument market. Instruments are used in a broad range of industries to detect, identify, monitor and measure chemical, physical and biological composition of materials, and to purify a full range of compounds.

HPLC is the standard technique to identify and analyze the constituent components of various chemicals and materials. Its unique performance capabilities let it separate and identify 80% of all known chemicals and materials. As a result, HPLC is used to analyze substances in a wide variety of industries for R&D purposes, quality control, and process engineering applications. Pharmaceutical and life science industries use HPLC most often to identify new drugs.

The TA Instruments subsidiary makes and services thermal analysis and rheology instruments used for the physical characterization of polymers and related materials. Thermal analysis measures physical characteristics of materials as a function of temperature. Changes in temperature affect several characteristics of materials, such as their physical state, weight, dimension and mechanical and electrical properties, which may be measured by one or more thermal analysis techniques. As a result, thermal analysis techniques are widely used to develop, produce and characterize materials in industries such as plastics, chemicals, automobiles, pharmaceuticals and electronics.

The Micromass unit is a leader in the manufacture and support of organic, inorganic, stable isotope and ICP mass spectrometers typically coupled with HPLC, chemical electrophoresis, chemical electrophoresis chromatography, gas chromatography or elemental analysis systems. Mass spectrometry is an analytical technique to identify unknown compounds, quantify known materials, and elucidate the structural and chemical properties of molecules by measuring the masses of individual molecules that have been converted into ions. These products supply a diverse market with a strong emphasis on the life science, pharmaceutical, biomedical, clinical, environmental and geochemistry markets.

In 2000, international sales accounted for 57% of the total.

Per Share Data ($) (Year Ended Dec. 31)	2000	1999	1998	1997	1996	1995	1994	1993	1992	1991
Tangible Bk. Val.	2.21	0.97	NM	NM	NM	NA	-0.25	NA	NA	NA
Cash Flow	1.36	1.14	0.78	0.09	0.28	0.22	0.21	NA	NA	NA
Earnings	1.14	0.92	0.57	-0.08	0.15	0.14	0.12	NA	NA	NA
Dividends	Nil	Nil	Nil	Nil	Nil	Nil	NA	NA	NA	NA
Payout Ratio	Nil	Nil	Nil	Nil	Nil	Nil	NA	NA	NA	NA
Prices - High	90.93	33.84	21.87	12.10	8.40	4.56	NA	NA	NA	NA
- Low	21.96	18.12	9.12	5.78	4.18	3.31	NA	NA	NA	NA
P/E Ratio - High	80	37	39	NM	56	18	NA	NA	NA	NA
- Low	19	20	16	NM	28	13	NA	NA	NA	NA
Income Statement Analysis (Million $)										
Revs.	795	704	619	465	391	333	307	NA	NA	NA
Oper. Inc.	240	205	164	113	87.9	58.6	48.7	NA	NA	NA
Depr.	29.4	28.9	27.2	20.0	16.7	7.7	11.3	NA	NA	NA
Int. Exp.	Nil	8.9	18.3	13.7	14.7	30.3	19.9	NA	NA	NA
Pretax Inc.	211	168	102	7.5	31.1	17.2	18.4	NA	NA	NA
Eff. Tax Rate	26%	27%	27%	211%	36%	18%	18%	NA	NA	NA
Net Inc.	156	122	74.4	-8.3	19.9	14.1	15.1	NA	NA	NA
Balance Sheet & Other Fin. Data (Million $)										
Cash	75.5	3.8	5.5	3.1	0.6	3.2	22.8	NA	NA	NA
Curr. Assets	344	247	252	213	144	127	149	NA	NA	NA
Total Assets	692	584	578	552	366	300	321	NA	NA	NA
Curr. Liab.	221	198	186	171	83.0	70.9	69.8	NA	NA	NA
LT Debt	Nil	81.1	218	305	210	159	186	NA	NA	NA
Common Eqty.	452	292	150	62.3	57.8	58.1	53.6	NA	NA	NA
Total Cap.	452	373	377	376	275	223	246	NA	NA	NA
Cap. Exp.	35.4	19.4	15.0	18.2	10.1	6.3	NA	NA	NA	NA
Cash Flow	186	151	101	10.8	35.6	21.8	25.5	NA	NA	NA
Curr. Ratio	1.6	1.3	1.4	1.2	1.7	1.9	2.1	NA	NA	NA
% LT Debt of Cap.	Nil	21.7	57.8	81.1	76.4	71.1	75.7	NA	NA	NA
% Net Inc.of Revs.	19.6	17.4	12.0	NM	5.1	4.2	4.9	NA	NA	NA
% Ret. on Assets	24.4	21.1	13.2	NM	6.0	4.5	NA	NA	NA	NA
% Ret. on Equity	42.0	55.3	69.1	NM	32.7	79.6	NA	NA	NA	NA

Data as orig reptd.; bef. results of disc opers/spec. items. Per share data adj. for stk. divs. Bold denotes diluted EPS (FASB 128)-prior periods restated. E-Estimated. NA-Not Available. NM-Not Meaningful. NR-Not Ranked.

Office—34 Maple St., Milford, MA 01757. **Tel**—(508) 478-2000. **Website**—http://www.waters.com **Chrmn, Pres & CEO**—D. A. Berthiaume. **SVP-Fin & CFO**—P. S. Taymor. **VP & Investor Contact**—Brian Mazar. **Dirs**—J. Bekenstein, M. J. Berendt, D. A. Berthiaume, P. Caldwell, E. Conrad, L. H. Glimcher, W. J. Miller, T. P. Salice. **Transfer Agent & Registrar**—BankBoston, N.A.**Incorporated**—in Delaware in 1991. **Empl**—3,200. **S&P Analyst:** John Massey

Part Eight

Materials Stocks

STANDARD & POOR'S
STOCK REPORTS

Pactiv Corp.

NYSE Symbol **PTV**

In S&P 500

18-AUG-01

Industry: Containers and Packaging (Paper)

Summary: PTV, spun off by Tenneco in November 1999, is a leading provider of advanced packaging solutions for consumer, institutional and industrial markets.

S&P Opinion: Buy (★★★★★)

Recent Price • 16 | 52 Wk Range • 16.25-9.68 | Yield • Nil | 12-Mo. P/E • 17.0

Quantitative Evaluations

Outlook (1 Lowest—5 Highest) • **NA**

Fair Value • **NA**

Risk • **NA**

Earn./Div. Rank • **NR**

Technical Eval. • **NA**

Rel. Strength Rank (1 Lowest—99 Highest) • **85**

Insider Activity • **NA**

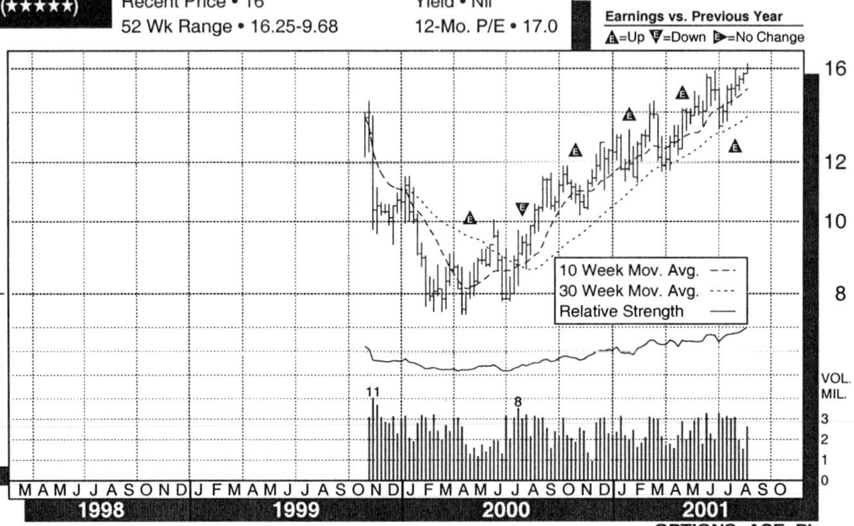

OPTIONS: ASE, Ph

Overview - 30-JUL-01

Revenues are expected to advance in the low single digits in 2001, as selective price hikes offset weak volume and a negative foreign currency effect. Strength in Hefty consumer products (tableware and OneZip food bags) should benefit the consumer packaging segment, while foodservice/food packaging sales are impacted by soft market conditions. Gross margins should widen to above 31% of sales, on an improved product mix and falling resin costs. EBITDA margins should widen by more than 100-basis point to over 19% of sales, as a restructuring of the protective/flexible packaging segment translates into group operating margins of 10% by the end of 2002, versus 5.9% recently and 4.4% in the first quarter of 2001. We expect free cash flow to exceed our earlier projections, rising significantly to $170 million, and forecast 2001 EPS growth of 15%, to $1.05, advancing to $1.20 in 2002.

Valuation - 30-JUL-01

With improved return on invested capital (recently up over 200 basis points to 8.6%; weighted average cost of capital at 8.3%), new products and cost-cutting initiatives, we maintain our strong buy recommendation. Although PTV was recently trading near its June 52-week high, and economic conditions remain weak, second quarter earnings were slightly above projections. Acquisitions are possible if PTV finds the right strategic fit, as multiples are sharply below the 7X EBITDA that packaging companies were paying for deals a few years ago. However, cash will be used primarily for debt paydowns, further reducing debt-to-capital from the recent 45% level. Debt-to-EBITDA is expected to stabilize near its current level of 2.3 times. The shares were recently trading at 14X our 2001 EPS estimate, a 42% discount to the projected P/E for the S&P 500, and a 19% discount to the multiple for PTV's peers.

Key Stock Statistics

S&P EPS Est. 2001	1.05	Tang. Bk. Value/Share	3.79
P/E on S&P Est. 2001	15.2	Beta	NA
S&P EPS Est. 2002	1.20	Shareholders	73,689
Dividend Rate/Share	Nil	Market cap. (B)	$ 2.5
Shs. outstg. (M)	158.7	Inst. holdings	77%
Avg. daily vol. (M)	0.488		

Value of $10,000 invested 5 years ago: NA

Fiscal Year Ending Dec. 31

	2001	2000	1999	1998	1997	1996
Revenues (Million $)						
1Q	695.0	738.0	666.0	633.0	—	—
2Q	745.0	820.0	738.0	738.0	—	—
3Q	—	778.0	754.0	696.0	—	—
4Q	—	798.0	763.0	724.0	—	—
Yr.	—	3,134	2,921	2,791	—	—
Earnings Per Share ($)						
1Q	**0.18**	**0.17**	**0.03**	—	—	—
2Q	**0.28**	**0.24**	**0.28**	—	—	—
3Q	**E0.27**	**0.24**	**0.01**	—	—	—
4Q	**E0.31**	**0.05**	**-1.00**	—	—	—
Yr.	**E1.05**	**0.70**	**-0.67**	**0.39**	—	—

Next earnings report expected: NA

Dividend Data

Directors plan to establish the company's dividend policy based on results of operations, its financial condition, and other business considerations.

Business Summary - 30-JUL-01

Pactiv Corp. is a global supplier of specialty packaging and consumer products. The company, formerly the Tenneco Packaging subsidiary of Tenneco Inc., was spun off by Tenneco in November 1999. PTV is seeking growth through highly focused internal programs, complemented by strategic acquisitions. Revenues increased from $900 million in 1995 to over $3.1 billion in 2000, in large part through acquisitions, including the 1995 purchase of Mobil Plastics with its Hefty brand product line. In January 2001, PTV sold its packaging polyethylene business to a unit of Tyco International Ltd. for $71 million. The business makes stretch film and institutional waste bags and can liners. The impact of the sale was expected to be slightly accretive to 2001 earnings.

The company operates two units: consumer products and food/foodservice packaging (73% of 2000 sales); and protective and flexible packaging (27%). PTV operates 79 manufacturing facilities in 17 countries. Foreign sales accounted for 18% of the total in 2000.

In April 2001, PTV sold its remaining 6% equity interest in Packaging Corp. of America (PCA) for $73 million. In February 2000, PTV sold publicly 37.5% of PCA for $398 million. Separately, the company sold part of its shared administrative services unit to Exult, Inc., as it continued to focus on core businesses and on cost reductions. In September 2000, PTV completed a $100 million repurchase program, buying back 11.7 million (7%) of its shares at an average price of $8.50 each.

The company manufactures consumer products such as foam and molded fiber disposable tableware, and disposable aluminum cookware. PTV sells many products under recognized brand names such as Hefty, Baggies, Hefty One-Zip, Kordite and E-Z Foil.

PTV manufactures food packaging products for the food processing industry, such as molded fiber egg cartons, foam meat trays, aluminum containers and modified atmosphere packaging.

The company also makes packaging for cushioning, bracing, surface protection and insulation in the automotive, computer, electronic, furniture, durable goods and building and construction products industries.

Flexible packaging products provide various efficient and attractive solutions for consumer, medical, pharmaceutical, chemical, hygiene and industrial applications. These products include liners for disposable diapers, wrap-around sleeves for glass and plastic bottles, and disposable surgical kits.

PTV recorded a pretax charge of $50 million ($0.21 a share, after tax) in the 2000 fourth quarter, to restructure its protective and flexible packaging business, and for a loss on the sale of the polyethylene business. A $20 million pretax gain reflected a reversal of a reserve for lower than expected transaction costs on PTV's spinoff. A gain of $134 million ($0.80 a share) on the sale of the stake in PCA was recorded in the 2000 first quarter.

A $0.01 decline in resin costs translates into a $0.05 per share EPS in crease.

Per Share Data ($) (Year Ended Dec. 31)	2000	1999	1998	1997	1996	1995	1994	1993	1992	1991
Tangible Bk. Val.	3.79	2.19	NA	NA	NA	NA	NA	NA	NA	NA
Cash Flow	1.84	0.43	1.43	NA	NA	NA	NA	NA	NA	NA
Earnings	0.70	-0.67	0.39	NA	NA	NA	NA	NA	NA	NA
Dividends	Nil	Nil	NA	NA	NA	NA	NA	NA	NA	NA
Payout Ratio	Nil	Nil	NA	NA	NA	NA	NA	NA	NA	NA
Prices - High	13.31	14.50	NA	NA	NA	NA	NA	NA	NA	NA
- Low	7.50	9.31	NA	NA	NA	NA	NA	NA	NA	NA
P/E Ratio - High	19	NM	NA	NA	NA	NA	NA	NA	NA	NA
- Low	11	NM	NA	NA	NA	NA	NA	NA	NA	NA
Income Statement Analysis (Million $)										
Revs.	3,134	2,921	2,791	NA	NA	NA	NA	NA	NA	NA
Oper. Inc.	570	498	466	NA	NA	NA	NA	NA	NA	NA
Depr.	185	184	175	NA	NA	NA	NA	NA	NA	NA
Int. Exp.	134	146	164	NA	NA	NA	NA	NA	NA	NA
Pretax Inc.	207	-159	124	NA	NA	NA	NA	NA	NA	NA
Eff. Tax Rate	44%	NM	46%	NA	NA	NA	NA	NA	NA	NA
Net Inc.	113	-112	66.0	NA	NA	NA	NA	NA	NA	NA
Balance Sheet & Other Fin. Data (Million $)										
Cash	26.0	12.0	18.0	NA	NA	NA	NA	NA	NA	NA
Curr. Assets	900	866	1,031	NA	NA	NA	NA	NA	NA	NA
Total Assets	4,341	4,588	4,749	NA	NA	NA	NA	NA	NA	NA
Curr. Liab.	512	920	1,703	NA	NA	NA	NA	NA	NA	NA
LT Debt	1,560	1,741	1,186	NA	NA	NA	NA	NA	NA	NA
Common Eqty.	1,539	1,350	1,286	NA	NA	NA	NA	NA	NA	NA
Total Cap.	3,595	3,432	2,848	NA	NA	NA	NA	NA	NA	NA
Cap. Exp.	135	1,129	NA	NA	NA	NA	NA	NA	NA	NA
Cash Flow	298	72.0	241	NA	NA	NA	NA	NA	NA	NA
Curr. Ratio	1.8	0.9	0.6	NA	NA	NA	NA	NA	NA	NA
% LT Debt of Cap.	43.4	50.7	41.6	NA	NA	NA	NA	NA	NA	NA
% Net Inc.of Revs.	3.6	NM	2.4	NA	NA	NA	NA	NA	NA	NA
% Ret. on Assets	2.5	NM	NA	NA	NA	NA	NA	NA	NA	NA
% Ret. on Equity	7.8	NM	NA	NA	NA	NA	NA	NA	NA	NA

Data as orig reptd.; bef. results of disc opers/spec. items. Data for 1998 is pro forma. Per share data adj. for stk. divs. Bold denotes diluted EPS (FASB 128)-prior periods restated. E-Estimated. NA-Not Available. NM-Not Meaningful. NR-Not Ranked.

Office—1900 West Field Court, Lake Forest, IL 60045. **Tel**—(847) 482-2000. **Website**—www.pactiv.com **Chrmn & CEO**—R. L. Wambold. **SVP & CFO**—A. A. Campbell. **Investor Contact**—Christine Hanneman (847-482-2429). **Secy**—K. A. Stewart. **Dirs**—L. D. Brady, R. J. Darnall, N. Henderson, R. B. Porter, P. T. Stecko, R. L. Wambold. **Incorporated**—in Delaware. **Empl**— 13,000. **S&P Analyst:** Stewart Scharf

Praxair

NYSE Symbol **PX**
In S&P 500

18-AUG-01 **Industry:** Chemicals

Summary: This company is the largest producer of industrial gases in North and South America, and one of the largest worldwide. It also provides ceramic and metallic coatings.

S&P Opinion: Buy (★★★★★)

Recent Price • 46.13 | Yield • 1.5%
52 Wk Range • 54-30.31 | 12-Mo. P/E • 19.9

Quantitative Evaluations

Outlook
(1 Lowest—5 Highest)
• **3⁻**

Fair Value
• **48.50**

Risk
• **Low**

Earn./Div. Rank
• **A**

Technical Eval.
• **Neutral** since 8/01

Rel. Strength Rank
(1 Lowest—99 Highest)
• **49**

Insider Activity
• **Unfavorable**

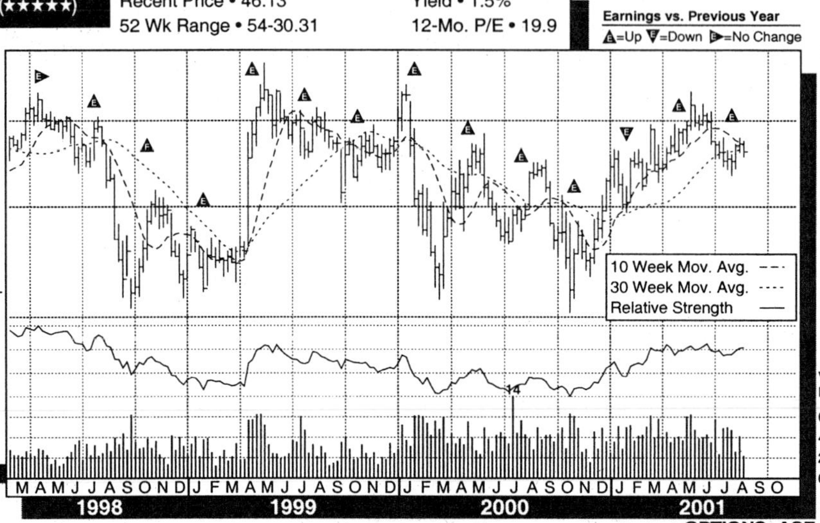

Overview - 05-JUN-01

We expect sales in 2001 to rise 5% to 7%, down from a 9% advance in 2000, as modest gains in volumes reflect the impact of slower global economic growth, and continued unfavorable currency rates. U.S. volumes comparisons will be negative at least through the first half, due to downturns in some markets. We expect a rise nearly in double digits for selling prices, partly as a result of efforts to recover higher energy costs, in addition to contractual pass-throughs of natural gas prices. Operating margins will benefit from new overhead cost savings, including a 3% work force reduction, although the impact of contractual pass-throughs of energy costs will remain a negative factor. At the end of 2000, PX closed a website that produced losses of about $12 million in 2000. Interest expense for 2001 will be similar to 2000 levels, and the tax rate is expected to remain at 23%. The 2000 fourth quarter included special restructuring charges of $0.73 a share.

Valuation - 05-JUN-01

After a retreat in 2000, the shares have turned up in 2001, with a 13% increase through the end of May. In mid-May, we upgraded PX for the second time in five months, this time to buy, from accumulate, as we see a further investor shift to basic material issues. We also view favorably actions announced by the company at the end of 2000. PX will concentrate on several less capital intensive, faster growing global markets, in addition to core industrial gases. The company is also taking restructuring and overhead cost reduction steps. We believe investors will view these actions positively, despite continued concerns about higher energy costs. Industrial gases fundamentals are positive, with growth in demand faster than that of the overall economy. The dividend was raised in early 2001, for the ninth consecutive year.

Key Stock Statistics

S&P EPS Est. 2001	3.04	Tang. Bk. Value/Share	7.93
P/E on S&P Est. 2001	15.2	Beta	1.11
S&P EPS Est. 2002	3.35	Shareholders	28,165
Dividend Rate/Share	0.68	Market cap. (B)	$ 7.4
Shs. outstg. (M)	160.6	Inst. holdings	81%
Avg. daily vol. (M)	0.670		

Value of $10,000 invested 5 years ago: $ 12,926

Fiscal Year Ending Dec. 31

	2001	2000	1999	1998	1997	1996
Revenues (Million $)						
1Q	1,335	1,230	1,118	1,201	1,158	1,090
2Q	1,314	1,265	1,149	1,234	1,178	1,093
3Q	—	1,275	1,169	1,201	1,190	1,115
4Q	—	1,273	1,203	1,197	1,209	1,151
Yr.	—	5,043	4,639	4,833	4,735	4,449
Earnings Per Share ($)						
1Q	**0.77**	**0.71**	**0.67**	**0.62**	**0.62**	**0.11**
2Q	**0.77**	**0.76**	**0.67**	**0.66**	**0.65**	**0.50**
3Q	**E0.74**	**0.76**	**0.69**	**0.66**	**0.65**	**0.54**
4Q	**E0.76**	**0.03**	**0.70**	**0.66**	**0.61**	**0.59**
Yr.	**E3.04**	**2.25**	**2.73**	**2.60**	**2.53**	**1.77**

Next earnings report expected: mid October

Dividend Data (Dividends have been paid since 1992.)

Amount ($)	Date Decl.	Ex-Div. Date	Stock of Record	Payment Date
0.155	Oct. 24	Dec. 05	Dec. 07	Dec. 15 '00
0.170	Jan. 30	Mar. 05	Mar. 07	Mar. 15 '01
0.170	Apr. 24	Jun. 05	Jun. 07	Jun. 15 '01
0.170	Jul. 24	Sep. 05	Sep. 07	Sep. 17 '01

Praxair, Inc.

Business Summary - 05-JUN-01

Since its 1992 spinoff from Union Carbide Corp., PX, the largest producer of industrial gases in North and South America, has expanded operations to 40 countries. Foreign sales accounted for 46% of total sales in 2000, with Brazil alone providing 11%. The purchase from CBI Industries of that company's Liquid Carbonic business in 1996 made PX the world's largest supplier of carbon dioxide. The acquisition added significantly to exposure to non-cyclical food and beverage markets. In December 2000, the company said it would concentrate on several less capital intensive, faster growing global markets, in addition to core industrial gases. PX also plans restructuring and overhead cost reduction steps. The company has reduced its capital spending in recent years, and has budgeted 2001 expenditures at $600 million to $700 million.

PX operates its industrial gases business through three operating segments: North America (60% of sales and 62% of profits in 2000), South America (14%, 19%), and Europe (10%, 14%). The industrial gases business involves the production, distribution and sale of atmospheric gases (oxygen, nitrogen, argon and rare gases), carbon dioxide, hydrogen, helium, acetylene, specialty gases and equipment for the production of industrial gases. Atmospheric gases are produced through air separation processes, primarily cryogenic, while other gases are produced by various methods. The company has also developed noncryogenic air separation processes that open new markets consisting of small users, and that help to optimize production capacity by lowering production costs. Major customers include aerospace, beverage, chemicals, electronics, food processing, health care, glass, metal fabrication, petroleum, primary metals and pulp/paper concerns. Consumption of industrial gases has historically increased 1.5X to 2X local industrial production growth in countries in which PX does business.

Industrial gases are supplied to customers through three basic methods: on-site/pipeline (23% of total 2000 sales), merchant (30%) and packaged (32%). The company has about 316 cryogenic air separation plants worldwide (195 in the U.S.), 90 carbon dioxide plants (23), and 37 hydrogen plants worldwide. In May 2000, PX raised its interest in S.A. White Martins (Brazil) to 98.6%, from 76%. White Martins is the largest producer of industrial gases in South America.

The Surface Technologies business (12%, 6%) applies metallic and ceramic coatings to parts and equipment provided by customers, provides aircraft engine and airframe component overhaul services, and sells specialty powders. It also manufactures thermal spray equipment. Other business segments (4%, -2%) include PX's industrial gases business in Asia, and the construction and sale of equipment to produce industrial gases.

Per Share Data ($) (Year Ended Dec. 31)	2000	1999	1998	1997	1996	1995	1994	1993	1992	1991
Tangible Bk. Val.	7.93	7.40	6.72	5.78	4.77	6.74	5.43	4.22	3.69	NA
Cash Flow	5.18	5.47	5.46	5.24	4.43	5.60	3.40	2.93	2.52	NA
Earnings	2.25	2.73	2.60	2.53	1.77	1.82	1.45	1.06	0.64	0.84
Dividends	0.62	0.56	0.50	0.44	0.38	0.32	0.28	0.25	0.13	NA
Payout Ratio	28%	21%	19%	17%	21%	18%	19%	24%	20%	NA
Prices - High	54.93	58.12	53.87	58.00	50.12	34.12	24.62	18.62	17.50	NA
- Low	30.31	32.00	30.68	39.25	31.50	19.75	16.25	14.12	13.62	NA
P/E Ratio - High	24	21	21	23	28	19	17	18	27	NA
- Low	13	12	12	16	18	11	11	13	21	NA
Income Statement Analysis (Million $)										
Revs.	5,043	4,639	4,833	4,735	4,449	3,146	2,711	2,438	2,604	2,469
Oper. Inc.	1,220	1,199	1,310	1,230	1,125	812	737	592	675	612
Depr.	471	445	467	444	420	279	273	253	247	236
Int. Exp.	224	204	260	216	220	125	112	108	230	177
Pretax Inc.	493	638	607	633	350	434	346	240	166	207
Eff. Tax Rate	21%	24%	21%	24%	31%	28%	24%	20%	22%	33%
Net Inc.	363	441	425	416	282	262	203	143	84.0	107
Balance Sheet & Other Fin. Data (Million $)										
Cash	31.0	76.0	34.0	43.0	63.0	15.0	63.0	34.0	24.0	82.0
Curr. Assets	1,361	1,335	1,394	1,497	1,666	930	840	691	691	824
Total Assets	7,762	7,722	8,096	7,810	7,538	4,134	3,520	3,255	3,344	3,451
Curr. Liab.	1,439	1,725	1,289	1,366	2,550	1,029	889	831	1,210	1,862
LT Debt	2,641	2,111	2,895	2,874	1,703	933	893	967	669	176
Common Eqty.	2,357	2,290	2,332	2,122	2,122	1,121	839	635	544	650
Total Cap.	5,156	4,835	5,789	5,592	4,195	2,462	2,286	2,099	1,774	1,208
Cap. Exp.	704	653	781	902	893	600	326	240	333	417
Cash Flow	834	886	892	860	696	758	476	396	331	343
Curr. Ratio	0.9	0.8	1.1	1.1	0.7	0.9	0.9	0.8	0.6	0.4
% LT Debt of Cap.	51.2	43.7	50.0	51.4	40.6	37.9	39.1	45.9	37.7	14.6
% Net Inc.of Revs.	7.2	9.5	8.8	8.8	6.3	8.4	7.5	5.9	3.2	4.3
% Ret. on Assets	4.7	5.6	5.3	5.4	4.9	6.9	5.9	4.3	NA	3.3
% Ret. on Equity	15.6	19.1	19.1	20.6	18.5	26.8	27.2	24.0	NA	16.5

Data as orig reptd.; bef. results of disc opers/spec. items. Per share data adj. for stk. divs. Bold denotes diluted EPS (FASB 128)-prior periods restated. E-Estimated. NA-Not Available. NM-Not Meaningful. NR-Not Ranked.

Office—39 Old Ridgebury Rd., Danbury, CT 06810-5113. **Tel**—(203) 837-2000; (800) 879-PRAXAIR. **Website**—http://www.praxair.com **Chrmn, Pres & CEO**—D. H. Reilley. **VP & CFO**—J. S. Sawyer. **VP & Secy**—D. H. Chaifetz. **Investor Contact**—Scott S. Cunningham. **Dirs**—A. Achaval, D. F. Frey, C. W. Gargalli, R. L. Kuehn Jr., R. W. LeBoeuf, B. F. Payton, G. J. Ratcliffe Jr., D. H. Reilley, H. M. Watson Jr. **Transfer Agent & Registrar**—Bank of New York, NYC. **Incorporated**—in Delaware in 1988. **Empl**— 23,430. **S&P Analyst:** Richard O'Reilly, CFA

STANDARD
&POOR'S
STOCK REPORTS

Smurfit-Stone Container Corp.

Nasdaq Symbol **SSCC**

18-AUG-01

Industry: Containers and Packaging (Paper)

Summary: Formed through the November 1998 merger of Jefferson Smurfit and Stone Container, SSCC is the world's largest paper-based packaging company.

S&P Opinion: Buy (★★★★★)

Recent Price • 16.89 | Yield • Nil
52 Wk Range • 17.80-9.12 | 12-Mo. P/E • 23.1

Quantitative Evaluations

Outlook (1 Lowest—5 Highest)
• **1−**

Fair Value
• **12.80**

Risk
• **NA**

Earn./Div. Rank
• **NR**

Technical Eval.
• **Bullish** since 8/01

Rel. Strength Rank (1 Lowest—99 Highest)
• **79**

Insider Activity
• **Neutral**

Earnings vs. Previous Year
▲=Up ▼=Down ▶=No Change

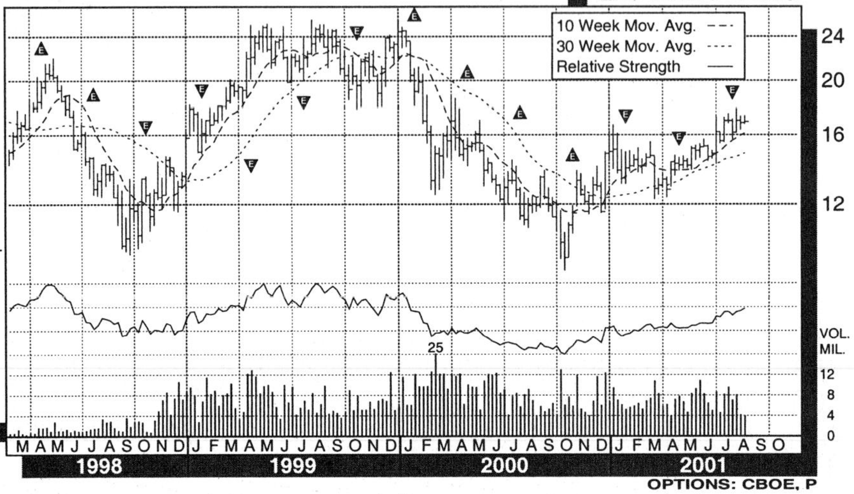

OPTIONS: CBOE, P

Overview - 26-JUL-01

We see sales little changed in 2001, followed by a mid-single-digits rise in 2002. In 2001, we expect a major volume reduction and a small decline in average corrugated pricing to be mostly offset by the full-year inclusion of St. Laurent Paperboard. Our volume outlook reflects our belief that the soft U.S. economy and strong U.S. dollar will stifle corrugated demand until early 2002. However, at that point, the current Federal Reserve easing program should firm up economic trends and boost corrugated demand. Much industry downtime has limited the corrugated pricing downturn during the current cycle, and we see a pick-up in demand bringing higher average prices in 2002. Margins should narrow sharply in 2001, hurt by the difficult sales conditions and high energy costs. However, we expect those trends to reverse in 2002. Interest charges should be lower in both years, on refinancings and lower debt levels.

Valuation - 26-JUL-01

The shares have started to rebound since late 2000, when lower interest rates made investors more optimistic about economic conditions and SSCC's business. We agree with this line of thinking, and believe that the Fed's easing program will start to firm up the economy by early 2002. SSCC's business had not shown any signs of recovery through the early summer of 2001, but we expect business prospects to look much better as we move into 2002, since corrugated box usage typically tracks the economic cycle. In light of our outlook, we recommend that investors take positions in the stock. The shares have been trading at a modest valuation of only about 14X our 2002 EPS forecast, and based on our forecast of the start of a strong business rebound for SSCC in 2002, we believe the stock will far outperform the broad market over the next 12 months.

Key Stock Statistics

S&P EPS Est. 2001	0.25	Tang. Bk. Value/Share	NM
P/E on S&P Est. 2001	67.6	Beta	1.16
S&P EPS Est. 2002	1.20	Shareholders	48,000
Dividend Rate/Share	Nil	Market cap. (B)	$ 4.1
Shs. outstg. (M)	243.6	Inst. holdings	56%
Avg. daily vol. (M)	1.146		

Value of $10,000 invested 5 years ago: $ 14,297

Fiscal Year Ending Dec. 31

	2001	2000	1999	1998	1997	1996
Revenues (Million $)						
1Q	2,183	2,035	1,705	764.0	778.0	916.0
2Q	2,115	2,191	1,730	764.0	785.0	844.0
3Q	—	2,328	1,792	758.0	832.0	834.0
4Q	—	2,242	1,924	1,183	843.0	816.0
Yr.	—	8,796	7,151	3,469	3,238	3,410
Earnings Per Share ($)						
1Q	**0.07**	**0.18**	**-0.43**	**0.03**	**-0.06**	**0.48**
2Q	**0.06**	**0.14**	**-0.11**	**0.02**	**-0.04**	**0.24**
3Q	**E0.06**	**0.32**	**-0.05**	**0.03**	**0.07**	**0.20**
4Q	**E0.06**	**0.28**	**1.29**	**-1.25**	**0.04**	**0.13**
Yr.	**E0.25**	**0.93**	**0.74**	**-1.56**	**0.01**	**1.04**

Next earnings report expected: early November

Dividend Data

The company does not intend to pay dividends on its common stock in the foreseeable future.

A Division of The McGraw-Hill Companies

Smurfit-Stone Container Corp.

Business Summary - 26-JUL-01

Smurfit-Stone Container, formed via the November 1998 merger of Jefferson Smurfit and Stone Container, is the world's leading paper-based packaging company. It further expanded its business through the May 2000 acquisition of Canada-based St. Laurent Paperboard, a producer of value-added packaging products. The transaction boosted SSCC's North American market share for corrugated to 19%, from 15%. SSCC is also the largest U.S. producer of multiwall industrial, consumer and grocery bags, folding cartons and boxboard. Jefferson Smurfit Group PLC holds a 33% stake in SSCC.

At 2000 year end, the company had annual production capacity of 8.2 million tons of containerboard, 594,000 tons of market pulp, 437,000 tons of kraft paper (used to make bags) and 848,000 tons of coated and uncoated boxboard. SSCC is also the world's largest collector and processor of recovered fiber. Corrugated containers are the largest business segment (68% of 2000 sales).

Shortly after its formation, SSCC announced a major restructuring. The plan included the shutdown of five less efficient containerboard mills that produced about 1.6 million tons annually (21% of SSCC's North American containerboard mill capacity prior to the St. Laurent acquisition; 4% of industry capacity). As of March 2001, the company had shut down six plants, with 1.8 million tons of annual capacity. SSCC also shut down 400,000 tons of market pulp capacity. By mid-2000, the merger and restructuring had exceeded SSCC's goal of $350 million of annual cost savings (before asset divestitures), six months ahead of the year-end target. SSCC achieved savings through optimization of production, elimination of redundant overhead costs, purchasing and logistical leverage, and lower interest charges related to working capital reductions.

In 1999, the company reduced debt by $1.8 billion through a non-core business and asset divestiture program instituted at the time of merger. Transactions included the $500 million sale of SSCC's 25% interest in Abitibi-Consolidated, the world's largest publications paper company; the sale of two newsprint facilities for $500 million; and the $710 million sale of 980,000 acres of owned or leased southern timberlands to Rayonier, Inc.

In May 2000, SSCC acquired St. Laurent Paperboard for $1.4 billion, including $631 million in cash, about 25 million common shares, and the assumption of $376 million of debt. St. Laurent (sales of U.S.$916 million in 1999) is a leading North American producer, supplier and converter of high quality, value-added specialty containerboard and high impact graphics packaging. The company expected to realize about $50 million of annual synergies from the combination.

In two separate transactions in January and May 2001, the company refinanced $1.3 billion of high coupon debt with lower coupon issues. The refinancings will reduce annual interest costs by about $25 million, and also extended debt maturities.

Per Share Data ($) (Year Ended Dec. 31)	2000	1999	1998	1997	1996	1995	1994	1993	1992	1991
Tangible Bk. Val.	NM	NM	NM	NM	NM	NM	-8.90	-9.01	NA	NA
Cash Flow	2.78	2.70	-0.21	1.23	2.42	3.60	1.43	0.01	NA	NA
Earnings	0.93	0.74	-1.56	0.01	1.05	2.23	0.12	-1.38	NA	NA
Dividends	Nil	Nil	Nil	Nil	Nil	Nil	Nil	Nil	NA	NA
Payout Ratio	Nil	Nil	Nil	Nil	Nil	Nil	Nil	Nil	NA	NA
Prices - High	25.00	25.75	22.00	21.62	16.12	20.37	23.12	NA	NA	NA
- Low	9.12	14.81	9.75	11.87	9.37	9.00	12.37	NA	NA	NA
P/E Ratio - High	27	NM	NM	NM	15	9	NM	NA	NA	NA
- Low	10	NM	NM	NM	9	4	NM	NA	NA	NA
Income Statement Analysis (Million $)										
Revs.	8,796	7,151	3,469	3,238	3,410	4,093	3,233	2,948	NA	NA
Oper. Inc.	1,418	863	193	342	543	783	423	266	NA	NA
Depr.	432	430	168	138	152	153	132	131	NA	NA
Int. Exp.	527	563	247	190	197	238	272	186	NA	NA
Pretax Inc.	434	339	-307	12.0	186	397	29.0	-193	NA	NA
Eff. Tax Rate	47%	50%	NM	92%	41%	39%	57%	NM	NA	NA
Net Inc.	219	163	-194	1.0	117	247	12.0	-130	NA	NA
Balance Sheet & Other Fin. Data (Million $)										
Cash	45.0	24.0	155	12.0	12.0	27.0	61.8	44.2	NA	NA
Curr. Assets	1,720	4,395	1,984	602	552	644	647	569	NA	NA
Total Assets	11,280	9,859	11,631	2,771	2,688	2,783	2,759	2,632	NA	NA
Curr. Liab.	1,250	1,569	1,349	531	525	597	636	527	NA	NA
LT Debt	5,298	4,619	6,428	2,025	1,934	2,111	2,392	2,368	NA	NA
Common Eqty.	2,455	1,847	1,634	-374	-375	-487	-730	-741	NA	NA
Total Cap.	9,079	7,396	9,256	2,013	1,922	1,952	1,886	1,848	NA	NA
Cap. Exp.	363	156	285	182	146	154	163	117	NA	NA
Cash Flow	651	593	-26.0	139	269	400	144	0.6	NA	NA
Curr. Ratio	1.4	2.8	1.5	1.1	1.1	1.1	1.0	1.1	NA	NA
% LT Debt of Cap.	58.4	62.5	69.4	101.0	100.6	108.0	126.8	128.0	NA	NA
% Net Inc.of Revs.	2.5	2.3	NM	NM	3.4	6.0	0.4	NM	NA	NA
% Ret. on Assets	2.1	1.5	NM	NM	4.3	8.9	Nil	NM	NA	NA
% Ret. on Equity	10.2	9.4	NM	NM	NM	NM	NM	NM	NA	NA

Data as orig reptd.; bef. results of disc opers/spec. items. Per share data adj. for stk. divs. Bold denotes diluted EPS (FASB 128)-prior periods restated. E-Estimated. NA-Not Available. NM-Not Meaningful. NR-Not Ranked.

Office—150 N. Michigan Ave., Chicago, IL 60601. **Tel**—(312) 346-6600. **Website**—www.smurfit-stone.com **Chrmn**—M. W. J. Smurfit. **Pres & CEO**—R. M. Curran. **Investor Contact**—Timothy McKenna (314-746-1254). **Dirs**—R. M. Curran, R. A. Giesen, A. E. Goldberg, H. E. Kilroy, J. J. O'Connor, J. K. Pearlman, T. A. Reynolds III, A. P. J. Smurfit, D. F. Smurfit, M. W. J. Smurfit. **Transfer Agent & Registrar**—Mellon Investor Services, Ridgefield Park, NJ. **Incorporated**—in Delaware in 1989. **Empl**— 39,700. **S&P Analyst:** Michael W. Jaffe

STANDARD &POOR'S
STOCK REPORTS

Westvaco Corp.

NYSE Symbol **W**

In S&P 500

23-AUG-01

Industry: Paper & Forest Products

Summary: This company produces paperboard for conversion into a variety of packaging products, premium packaging for consumer products and printing grade papers.

S&P Opinion: Buy (★★★★★)

Recent Price • 27 | Yield • 3.3%
52 Wk Range • 30.62-22.70 | 12-Mo. P/E • 14.7

Quantitative Evaluations

Outlook (1 Lowest—5 Highest) • **3**

Fair Value • **26.30**

Risk • **Low**

Earn./Div. Rank • **B**

Technical Eval. • **Bullish** since 7/01

Rel. Strength Rank (1 Lowest—99 Highest) • **76**

Insider Activity • **Neutral**

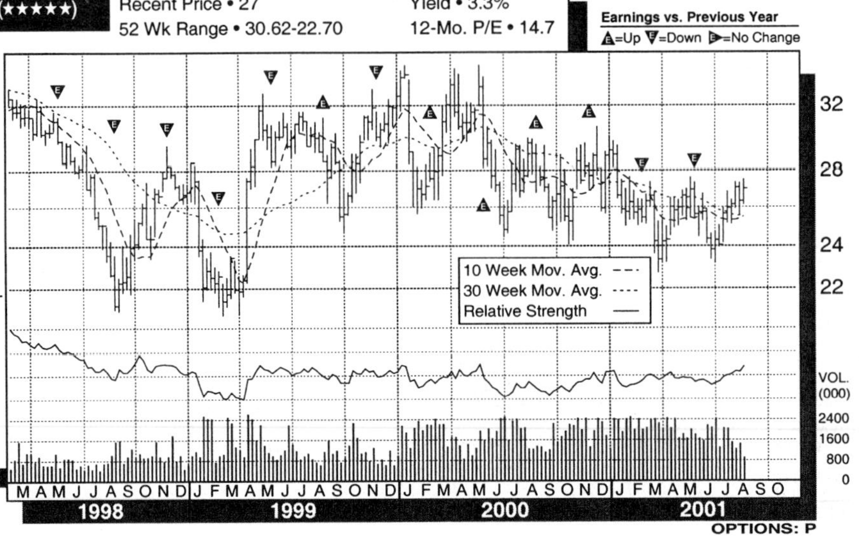

OPTIONS: P

Overview - 23-AUG-01

Sales should rise through FY 02 (Oct.), with FY 01 gains coming from the full-year inclusion of recent takeovers, and later gains stemming from a likely improvement in industry fundamentals. We see near-term coated papers volume remaining soft, as a muted U.S. economy has reduced orders and caused producers to take much downtime in a mostly unsuccessful attempt to hold up prices. We also see demand and pricing for consumer packaging remaining soft in the near-term, although entertainment packaging trends should stay strong. Yet, with the Fed's aggressive rate easing program likely to firm the economy in coming months, we expect paper and packaging demand and pricing to be revived in FY 02. Margins should narrow in FY 01, on difficult sales trends and higher energy prices, before getting a lift in FY 02 from a better sales picture and takeover synergies. Our FY 01 forecast includes $0.07 of land sales gains, but excludes more gains expected in the fourth quarter and $0.05 of tax credits.

Valuation - 23-AUG-01

The shares have been weak since early 2000, limited by economic worries and the softening of industry fundamentals during the past few quarters. Although W's current business trends have been poor, we have grown much more positive about its prospects. Our improved outlook centers around our belief that lower interest rates will start to firm the domestic economy in late 2001/early 2002. W's recent actions to center its business activities around packaging should pay off nicely at that time, as that will likely be one of the first forest industry sectors to benefit from an economic revival. With the shares recently trading at a reasonable early cycle valuation of about 16 times our FY 02 estimate, they should be a very attractive way to take part in the economic recuperation that we forecast.

Key Stock Statistics

S&P EPS Est. 2001	1.05	Tang. Bk. Value/Share	23.17
P/E on S&P Est. 2001	25.7	Beta	0.89
S&P EPS Est. 2002	1.70	Shareholders	6,600
Dividend Rate/Share	0.88	Market cap. (B)	$ 2.7
Shs. outstg. (M)	100.7	Inst. holdings	77%
Avg. daily vol. (M)	0.256		

Value of $10,000 invested 5 years ago: $ 11,133

Fiscal Year Ending Oct. 31

	2001	2000	1999	1998	1997	1996
Revenues (Million $)						
1Q	926.1	799.6	650.7	702.1	736.4	748.7
2Q	921.1	904.7	679.5	724.2	724.6	760.3
3Q	947.8	928.0	700.2	727.8	738.2	757.7
4Q	—	1,031	771.5	731.8	783.1	778.7
Yr.	—	3,663	2,802	2,886	2,982	3,045
Earnings Per Share ($)						
1Q	**0.33**	**0.50**	**0.25**	**0.32**	**0.35**	0.61
2Q	**0.18**	**0.70**	**0.27**	**0.34**	0.37	0.50
3Q	**0.28**	**0.53**	**0.35**	**0.31**	0.37	0.43
4Q	**E0.31**	**0.80**	**0.24**	**0.33**	0.51	0.55
Yr.	**E1.05**	**2.53**	**1.11**	**1.30**	**1.58**	2.09

Next earnings report expected: late November

Dividend Data (Dividends have been paid since 1892.)

Amount ($)	Date Decl.	Ex-Div. Date	Stock of Record	Payment Date
0.220	Aug. 22	Aug. 30	Sep. 01	Oct. 02 '00
0.220	Nov. 28	Dec. 06	Dec. 08	Jan. 02 '01
0.220	Feb. 27	Mar. 07	Mar. 09	Apr. 02 '01
0.220	May. 22	May. 30	Jun. 01	Jul. 02 '01

Westvaco Corporation

Business Summary - 23-AUG-01

Westvaco ranks as one of the largest U.S. producers of paper and paperboard. It also has a large international presence, (22% of sales in FY 00--Oct.), through a major paperboard and corrugated packaging position in Brazil, and from exports to more than 70 countries.

The paper and forest products industry tends to be extremely cyclical. However, W believes its emphasis on distinctive products and services enables it to record far more stable earnings than most of its competitors during industry downturns.

In FY 00, W produced 3,749,000 tons of paper and paperboard, up sharply from 2,992,000 tons in FY 99, on the inclusion of a number of acquisitions.

In FY 00, W combined its bleached board, consumer packaging, kraft and international packaging operations into a single packaging resources group. The division (59%) produces bleached paperboard, kraft paper and board, and premium packaging for consumer products markets. It makes these products in the U.S., Brazil and Europe.

The paper segment (32% of sales in FY 00) makes printing grade papers and envelopes; all operations are in the U.S.

In December 1999, the company acquired Temple-Inland's bleached paperboard mill in Evadale, TX, for $625 million. The mill's annual production capacity of 670,000 tons increased W's bleached paperboard capacity to 1.6 million tons. W projected $100 million of annual synergies and cost savings within three years.

W further expanded its packaging group through its January 2000 purchase of Mebane Packaging Group (annual sales of $130 million), a leading supplier of packaging for pharmaceutical products and personal care items; and its July 2000 acquisition of IMPAC Group (pro forma annual revenues of about $330 million), for total consideration of $500 million. IMPAC is a leading global supplier of high-value specialty packaging and printing solutions for a wide variety of consumer products markets. The company also acquired DuBOIS Holdings Ltd. (August 2000), a global licenser and European manufacturer of DVD packages; Sony Music Printing (Holland) BV (October 2000), a Netherlands-based maker of packaging for entertainment products; and a majority interest in Austria-based Alfred Wall AG (May 2001; sales of $127 million in 2000), one of Europe's leading suppliers of packaging for a wide range of consumer products. Finally, in August 2001, W bought Poly-Matrix, North America's largest producer of specialty plastic components for DVD, CD and other entertainment packaging.

At October 31, 2000, W owned 1,418,000 acres of timberland in the U.S. and Brazil. In FY 00, 32% of wood needed was harvested from its own forests. In May 2000, the company reported that it will try to sell about 200,000 acres of non-strategic parcels over the next two to three years.

W also makes a variety of specialty chemicals (9% of FY 00 sales).

Per Share Data ($) (Year Ended Oct. 31)	2000	1999	1998	1997	1996	1995	1994	1993	1992	1991
Tangible Bk. Val.	23.17	21.65	22.39	22.35	21.69	20.49	18.48	18.18	17.84	17.21
Cash Flow	5.63	3.90	4.06	4.25	4.45	5.08	3.21	2.51	3.21	3.22
Earnings	2.53	1.11	1.30	1.60	2.09	2.80	1.03	0.57	1.37	1.40
Dividends	0.88	0.88	0.88	0.88	0.88	0.77	0.73	0.73	0.73	0.71
Payout Ratio	35%	79%	68%	55%	42%	28%	71%	129%	53%	51%
Prices - High	34.75	33.50	34.12	37.50	33.12	31.87	26.50	25.33	27.50	26.50
- Low	24.06	20.81	21.00	25.00	25.37	24.08	19.75	20.00	21.33	17.08
P/E Ratio - High	14	30	26	23	16	11	26	45	20	19
- Low	10	19	16	16	12	9	19	35	16	12
Income Statement Analysis (Million $)										
Revs.	3,663	2,802	2,886	2,982	3,045	3,272	2,607	2,345	2,336	2,301
Oper. Inc.	869	601	577	580	637	771	485	429	471	481
Depr.	314	280	281	269	240	230	219	195	183	179
Int. Exp.	192	124	110	93.3	105	108	115	115	102	100
Pretax Inc.	404	148	204	247	336	470	162	92.9	206	226
Eff. Tax Rate	37%	25%	35%	34%	37%	40%	36%	39%	34%	39%
Net Inc.	255	111	132	163	212	283	104	56.5	136	137
Balance Sheet & Other Fin. Data (Million $)										
Cash	255	109	105	175	115	152	75.0	57.0	191	172
Curr. Assets	1,064	738	739	805	716	787	631	609	671	624
Total Assets	6,570	4,897	5,009	4,899	4,437	4,253	3,983	3,928	3,704	3,462
Curr. Liab.	567	425	467	406	419	429	362	365	353	314
LT Debt	2,687	1,502	1,526	1,513	1,153	1,147	1,234	1,258	1,055	970
Common Eqty.	2,333	2,171	2,246	2,279	2,210	2,081	1,862	1,824	1,777	1,699
Total Cap.	5,927	4,472	4,541	4,494	4,018	3,824	3,621	3,563	3,351	3,148
Cap. Exp.	214	229	423	621	522	290	215	433	318	303
Cash Flow	569	392	413	432	453	514	323	252	319	317
Curr. Ratio	1.9	1.7	1.6	2.0	1.7	1.8	1.7	1.7	1.9	2.0
% LT Debt of Cap.	45.3	33.6	33.6	33.7	28.7	30.0	34.1	35.3	31.5	30.8
% Net Inc.of Revs.	7.0	4.0	4.6	5.5	7.0	8.7	4.0	2.4	5.8	6.0
% Ret. on Assets	4.4	2.2	2.7	3.5	4.9	6.9	2.6	1.5	3.8	4.0
% Ret. on Equity	11.3	5.0	5.8	7.3	9.9	14.4	5.6	3.1	7.8	8.2

Data as orig. reptd.; bef. results of disc. opers. and/or spec. items. Per share data adj. for stk. divs. as of ex-div. date. Bold denotes diluted EPS (FASB 128). E-Estimated. NA-Not Available. NM-Not Meaningful. NR-Not Ranked.

Office—299 Park Ave., New York, NY 10171. **Tel**—(212) 688-5000. **Website**—http://www.westvaco.com **Chrmn, Pres & CEO**—J. A. Luke Jr. **SVP & CFO**—K. R. Osar. **Investor Contact**—Roger A. Holmes (203-461-7537). **Dirs**—S. W. Bodman III, W. L. L. Brown Jr., M. E. Campbell, T. W. Cole Jr., D. F. D'Alessandro, R. B. Kelson, D. S. Luke, J. A. Luke Jr., R. C. McCormack, W. R. Miller, J. L. Warner, R. A. Zimmerman. **Transfer Agent & Registrar**—Bank of New York, NYC. **Incorporated**—in Delaware in 1899. **Empl**— 17,100. **S&P Analyst:** Michael W. Jaffe

STANDARD & POOR'S STOCK REPORTS

Lubrizol Corp.

NYSE Symbol **LZ**

In S&P MidCap 400

18-AUG-01 **Industry:** Chemicals (Specialty)

Summary: Lubrizol is believed to be the largest supplier of chemical additives used in lubricants and fuels.

S&P Opinion: Accumulate (★★★★) Recent Price • 36.96 | 52 Wk Range • 37.69-18.25 | Yield • 2.8% | 12-Mo. P/E • 17.9

Quantitative Evaluations

Outlook (1 Lowest—5 Highest) • **3+**

Fair Value • **37.70**

Risk • **Low**

Earn./Div. Rank • **B+**

Technical Eval. • **Bullish** since 7/01

Rel. Strength Rank (1 Lowest—99 Highest) • **89**

Insider Activity • **Neutral**

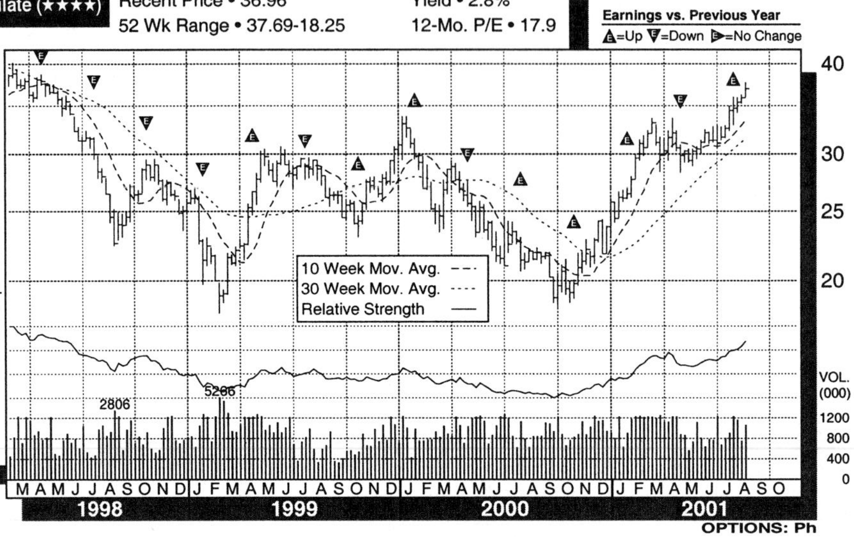

OPTIONS: Ph

Overview - 14-JUN-01

We see sales growing about 5% in 2001, reflecting recent successful industry price increases designed to recoup a climb in raw material costs during 2000. Prices increases have been most successful in North America and Europe. Volumes should rise modestly in 2001, after a 1% decline in 2000. Volumes will reflect growth of new product lines, acquisitions, and business obtained as a result of a recent litigation settlement. Gross margins will likely now begin to recover on the volume gains and as raw material and energy costs ease from first quarter's peaks. Operating expenses for 2001 will be up modestly as technology spending related to a new industry standard will be higher in the first half. At the end of 2000, LZ completed a second phase of a cost reduction plan, focusing on production and distribution activities; it will achieve additional savings of $13 million in 2001 for total annual savings of $20 million arising from a major plant downsizing. After a drop to about 30% in 2000, the tax rate for 2001 will rise to about 34.5%. A gain of $0.28 a share from litigation settlement was recorded in 2000.

Valuation - 14-JUN-01

The stock had been a poor performer over the past three years, reflecting disappointing EPS as a result of intense competitive pressures and slow industry conditions. In mid-June 2001, we raised our opinion to accumulate from hold on signs of improvement in poor industry fundamentals, successful cost reduction efforts, and a P/E multiple well below that of the overall market. LZ has gained some market share in several product lines, as a result of successful partnerships with customers. We feel LZ will be able to hold on to most of the recent price increases even in the face of declining raw material costs, boosting gross margins. Dividends will remain at current levels for the near term, and LZ should continue its stock buyback program.

Key Stock Statistics

S&P EPS Est. 2001	2.05	Tang. Bk. Value/Share	11.49
P/E on S&P Est. 2001	18.0	Beta	0.61
S&P EPS Est. 2002	2.20	Shareholders	4,992
Dividend Rate/Share	1.04	Market cap. (B)	$ 1.9
Shs. outstg. (M)	50.9	Inst. holdings	77%
Avg. daily vol. (M)	0.223		

Value of $10,000 invested 5 years ago: $ 15,446

Fiscal Year Ending Dec. 31

	2001	2000	1999	1998	1997	1996
Revenues (Million $)						
1Q	454.6	436.2	447.6	399.9	389.0	405.4
2Q	487.8	439.4	434.2	405.2	432.6	420.5
3Q	—	425.0	433.2	403.3	426.8	392.1
4Q	—	447.1	433.0	406.2	423.5	374.8
Yr.	—	1,776	1,748	1,615	1,674	1,593
Earnings Per Share ($)						
1Q	0.36	0.55	0.72	0.52	0.66	1.14
2Q	0.62	0.59	0.55	0.71	0.80	0.62
3Q	E0.55	0.44	0.37	0.30	0.66	0.53
4Q	E0.51	0.63	0.61	-0.27	0.53	0.48
Yr.	E2.05	2.22	2.25	1.27	2.66	2.79

Next earnings report expected: NA

Dividend Data (Dividends have been paid since 1935.)

Amount ($)	Date Decl.	Ex-Div. Date	Stock of Record	Payment Date
0.260	Sep. 25	Nov. 08	Nov. 10	Dec. 08 '00
0.260	Dec. 11	Feb. 07	Feb. 09	Mar. 09 '01
0.260	Apr. 23	May. 08	May. 10	Jun. 08 '01
0.260	Jul. 23	Aug. 08	Aug. 10	Sep. 10 '01

A Division of The McGraw-Hill Companies

The Lubrizol Corporation

Business Summary - 14-JUN-01

In response to modest annual growth in the worldwide lubricants additives industry and intense competition in its markets, this specialty chemicals company has taken steps since 1993 to improve its cost structure and expand into new market areas. It has consolidated production activities, shortened product development cycles, and reduced the number of product offerings. In the mid-90s, Lubrizol (LZ) reduced the number of its intermediate production units by about one-third, and it intends to reduce the number of units at least another 20% by 2001. Technical spending in the past few years remained well below that in 1995, although a small increase is projected for 2001, primarily for a new engine oil standard. LZ has successfully developed relationships with finished lubricant suppliers to reduce costs and jointly pursue business opportunities. In 1998, the company completed seven acquisitions, with total annual revenues of $162 million. In July 1998, LZ acquired the Adibis additives business (sales of $150 million in 1997) of British Petroleum. In March 2000, LZ acquired a leading supplier of additives for corrosion prevention in metalworking products, with annual revenues of $20 million.

LZ is the largest supplier of chemical additives for use in lubricants for transportation and industrial applications. It also makes fuel additives and other specialty chemicals. Chemical additives include detergents, dispersants, oxidation and wear inhibitors, viscosity improvers, and pour depressants. Lubricants are used in cars, trucks, buses, off-highway equipment, marine engines and industrial applications. Additives improve lubricants and fuels, allowing oil to withstand a broader range of temperatures, limit the buildup of sludge and deposits, reduce wear and inhibit the formation of foam and corrosion.

Chemicals for transportation (82% of sales and 85% of operating profits in 2000) consist of additives for engine oils (53% of sales); driveline oils (22%), such as automotive transmission fluids and gear oils; fuel products and refinery chemicals (5%); and additive components and viscosity improvers (2%). Chemicals for industry (18% and 15%) include industrial additives (10%) for hydraulic fluids, machine oils, metalworking compounds, and compressor lubricants; additives for coatings and inks and process chemicals (6%); and performance systems (2%), comprised of fluid metering devices and emission trap devices.

About 43% of sales in 2000 were made to customers in North America, with 33% of sales to Europe, 20% to Asia-Pacific region, and 7% to Latin America.

LZ had an active stock buyback program in the 1990s. In the five years through 1998, the company repurchased 19% of its common shares outstanding. In late 1999, LZ resumed the buyback program, which it had suspended at the end of 1998. It repurchased 3.23 million shares in 2000 for $76 million, with another 655,000 shares acquired for $20 million in the first quarter of 2001 .

Per Share Data ($) (Year Ended Dec. 31)	2000	1999	1998	1997	1996	1995	1994	1993	1992	1991
Tangible Bk. Val.	11.34	11.75	11.04	12.94	13.21	12.76	12.19	10.45	11.74	11.26
Cash Flow	4.11	4.07	2.84	4.16	4.13	3.54	3.60	2.14	2.65	2.58
Earnings	2.22	2.25	1.27	2.66	2.80	2.37	2.67	1.25	1.81	1.79
Dividends	1.04	1.04	1.04	1.01	0.97	0.93	0.89	0.85	0.81	0.77
Payout Ratio	47%	46%	82%	38%	35%	39%	33%	68%	44%	43%
Prices - High	33.87	31.37	40.18	46.93	32.37	37.37	38.62	36.37	35.31	30.00
- Low	18.25	18.00	22.37	30.37	26.50	25.50	28.50	26.62	23.37	21.25
P/E Ratio - High	15	14	32	18	12	16	14	29	20	17
- Low	8	8	18	11	9	11	11	21	13	12
Income Statement Analysis (Million $)										
Revs.	1,776	1,748	1,618	1,674	1,598	1,664	1,599	1,526	1,552	1,476
Oper. Inc.	280	326	242	319	276	269	263	223	220	222
Depr.	101	100	88.0	87.2	81.0	74.2	61.3	59.6	58.4	54.6
Int. Exp.	26.9	29.7	19.0	10.8	11.0	10.4	3.1	4.2	3.6	7.7
Pretax Inc.	170	195	119	231	251	226	251	120	177	178
Eff. Tax Rate	31%	37%	40%	33%	32%	33%	30%	29%	30%	31%
Net Inc.	118	123	71.2	155	170	152	176	85.0	125	124
Balance Sheet & Other Fin. Data (Million $)										
Cash	146	185	53.6	86.5	55.1	30.6	36.0	24.0	77.0	126
Curr. Assets	728	780	687	657	585	640	624	569	591	702
Total Assets	1,659	1,682	1,643	1,462	1,402	1,492	1,394	1,183	1,127	1,172
Curr. Liab.	282	311	270	262	227	266	254	224	206	262
LT Debt	379	365	390	182	158	194	114	55.3	23.3	35.0
Common Eqty.	752	790	769	815	819	849	832	732	819	794
Total Cap.	1,224	1,217	1,218	1,054	1,022	1,070	974	799	880	868
Cap. Exp.	85.8	64.9	93.4	101	94.0	189	161	128	95.8	82.0
Cash Flow	219	223	159	242	251	226	237	145	183	178
Curr. Ratio	2.6	2.5	2.5	2.5	2.6	2.4	2.5	2.5	2.9	2.7
% LT Debt of Cap.	30.9	30.0	32.1	17.3	15.4	18.2	11.7	6.9	2.6	4.0
% Net Inc.of Revs.	6.6	7.0	4.4	9.3	10.6	9.2	11.0	5.6	8.0	8.4
% Ret. on Assets	7.1	7.4	4.6	10.8	11.7	10.5	13.8	7.5	10.9	10.8
% Ret. on Equity	15.3	15.8	9.0	18.9	20.4	18.1	22.7	11.1	15.5	16.2

Data as orig reptd.; bef. results of disc opers/spec. items. Per share data adj. for stk. divs. Bold denotes diluted EPS (FASB 128)-prior periods restated. E-Estimated. NA-Not Available. NM-Not Meaningful. NR-Not Ranked.

Office—29400 Lakeland Blvd., Wickliffe, OH 44092-2298. **Tel**—(440) 943-4200. **Website**—http://www.lubrizol.com **Chrmn, Pres & CEO**—W. G. Bares. **VP, CFO & Treas**—C. P. Cooley. **Secy**—L. M. Reynolds. **Investor Contact**—Joanne Wanstreet. **Dirs**—W. G. Bares, J. A. Blumberg, P. G. Elliott, F. J. Farmer Sr., G. D. Harnett, V. F. Haynes, D. H. Hoag, W. P. Madar, R. A. Mitsch, M. T. Moore, D. E. Somers. **Transfer Agent & Registrar**—American Stock Transfer & Trust Co., NYC. **Incorporated**—in Ohio in 1928. **Empl**— 4,390. **S&P Analyst:** Richard O'Reilly, CFA

STANDARD
&POOR'S
STOCK REPORTS

Nucor Corp.

NYSE Symbol **NUE**

In S&P 500

22-AUG-01 **Industry:** Iron & Steel

Summary: Nucor, the largest U.S. minimill, is currently gaining market share in flat roll sheet and strip steel.

S&P Opinion: Accumulate (★★★★)

Recent Price • 48.27 | Yield • 1.4%
52 Wk Range • 56.50-29.50 | 12-Mo. P/E • 17.7

Quantitative Evaluations

Outlook
(1 Lowest—5 Highest)
• **5+**

Fair Value
• **62.70**

Risk
• **Low**

Earn./Div. Rank
• **A-**

Technical Eval.
• **Bearish** since 7/01

Rel. Strength Rank
(1 Lowest—99 Highest)
• **51**

Insider Activity
• **Unfavorable**

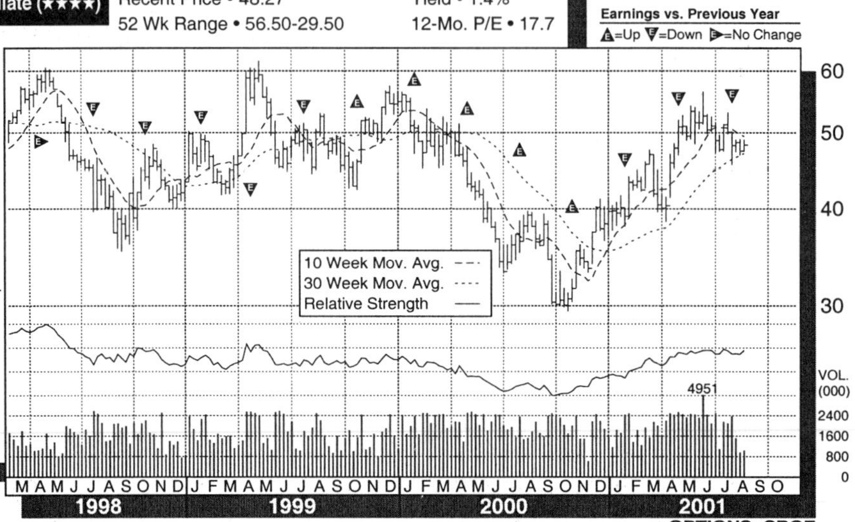

Overview - 22-AUG-01

As a result of weak demand for durable goods in 2001, continued pressure on prices from imports, and destocking of inventories, sales will decline by some 10% to 12%. Depressed prices will more than offset a 7% to 8% gain in the volume of tons shipped. Reduced revenue per ton will outweigh lower costs and result in sharply lower operating profit and EPS in 2001. Assuming a rebound in the economy, lower imports and restocking of inventories by distributors and original equipment manufacturers, sales should advance 5% to 7% in 2002. Benefiting from higher volume and more stable pricing, per ton profit and EPS will post a solid gain from 2001 depressed levels. Longer term EPS and cash flow per share will be aided by acquisitions, market share gains and implementation of new steelmaking technology.

Valuation - 22-AUG-01

Following second quarter EPS and a company conference call, we are maintaining our accumulate opinion on Nucor based on valuation. Recently selling at 14 times our estimate for free cash flow per share of $3.40 versus $1.60 estimated for 2001, Nucor is attractively priced given its strong growth prospects. Earlier, on May 22, 2001, we upgraded Nucor to accumulate from hold on news that Northwestern Steel & Wire, an Illinois-based manufacturer of steel beams, will cease operations. Northwestern's departure will remove some 1.7 million tons of steel beam capacity from the market, thereby leaving the field to Nucor and Texas Industries. Nucor also will benefit from what appears to be the permanent shutdown of Trico Steel, a 2.0 million ton per year flat roll minimill. Nucor's position in the flat roll market will also be enhanced by LTV's decision to discontinue some 2.0 million tons of production. Finally, we see Nucor gaining market share in plate products at the expense of its higher cost integrated rivals.

Key Stock Statistics

S&P EPS Est. 2001	1.85	Tang. Bk. Value/Share	27.46
P/E on S&P Est. 2001	26.1	Beta	1.02
S&P EPS Est. 2002	2.80	Shareholders	55,000
Dividend Rate/Share	0.68	Market cap. (B)	$ 3.8
Shs. outstg. (M)	77.6	Inst. holdings	67%
Avg. daily vol. (M)	0.245		

Value of $10,000 invested 5 years ago: $ 10,774

Fiscal Year Ending Dec. 31

	2001	2000	1999	1998	1997	1996
Revenues (Million $)						
1Q	1,028	1,200	893.8	1,139	1,010	876.1
2Q	1,079	1,214	997.2	1,128	1,035	911.1
3Q	—	1,163	1,027	1,011	1,102	937.5
4Q	—	1,009	1,092	873.1	1,037	922.4
Yr.	—	4,586	4,009	4,151	4,185	3,647
Earnings Per Share ($)						
1Q	0.42	0.94	0.32	0.74	0.74	0.60
2Q	0.43	0.98	0.58	0.82	0.83	0.63
3Q	E0.45	0.85	0.78	0.74	0.91	0.66
4Q	E0.55	1.03	1.12	0.70	0.87	0.94
Yr.	E1.85	3.80	2.80	3.00	3.35	2.83

Next earnings report expected: mid October

Dividend Data (Dividends have been paid since 1973.)

Amount ($)	Date Decl.	Ex-Div. Date	Stock of Record	Payment Date
0.150	Sep. 05	Sep. 27	Sep. 29	Nov. 10 '00
0.150	Dec. 05	Dec. 27	Dec. 29	Feb. 09 '01
0.170	Mar. 08	Mar. 28	Mar. 30	May. 11 '01
0.170	Jun. 05	Jun. 27	Jun. 29	Aug. 10 '01

Business Summary - 22-AUG-01

Nucor, the largest U.S. minimill and second largest steelmaker, continued its aggressive expansion with the October 1996 startup of its third thin slab flat roll minimill plant. The plant, in Berkeley County, SC, uses the same process that transforms steel scrap into a 2 inch thick slab, pioneered at NUE's Crawfordville, IN, and Hickman, AR, plants. This revolutionary process dramatically lowered the barriers to entry in the market for flat roll carbon sheet and strip, which account for about 50% of domestic steel industry shipments.

Aided by increased output at the new plant in Berkeley, Nucor produced 9.7 million tons of steel in 1997, becoming the second largest U.S. steelmaker, surpassing both LTV Corp. and Bethlehem Steel. It slid to third place in 1998, as Bethlehem's acquisition of Lukens let it surpass NUE's output for the year. However, through expansion at existing mills and construction of new mills, The company expects to increase its annual capacity to 13 million tons over the next several years. In 1999 and 2000, its production exceeded that of Bethlehem.

Although the company already has the broadest product line of any domestic steelmaker, commodity flat roll sheet is not the only market on which it has set its sights. In 1995, it began making stainless 409, a commodity stainless steel product used in auto exhaust systems. Although it has narrower margins than other grades of stainless steel, stainless 409 will help increase profitability, because stainless steel carries higher margins than carbon steel.

Raw materials comprise the major component of cost of sales. The average price of raw materials increased by less than 10% in 2000. In 1999, it decreased 20%, after being substantially unchanged in 1998, 1997 and 1996.

Shipments to outside customers totaled 9,779,000 tons in 2000, versus 8,734,000 tons in 1999. Steel production totaled 11,271,000 tons in 2000, versus 10,376,000 tons in 1999.

Nucor's principal competitors for traditional minimill construction market steel products include Bayou Steel, Birmingham Steel, Chaparral Steel, Florida Steel and Texas Industries.

Competition in flat roll carbon sheet includes the old line integrated companies and new minimill players such as BHP-North Star, Gallatin Steel and Steel Dynamics.

In May 2000, NUE signed a memorandum of understanding with the Rio Tinto Group and Lurgi Metalurgie for a joint venture to construct a hismelt plant at a Nucor facility in the U.S. Hismelt is a process that converts iron ore to liquid metal through the injection of non-coking coal and iron ore into a molten iron bath. Its environmental impact is more favorable than traditional technologies.

In November 2000, Nucor-Yamato and Voest-Alpine Schienen GmBh & Co. agreed to explore construction of a U.S. rail manufacturing mill.

Per Share Data ($) (Year Ended Dec. 31)	2000	1999	1998	1997	1996	1995	1994	1993	1992	1991
Tangible Bk. Val.	27.46	25.96	23.73	21.32	18.33	15.78	12.84	10.36	9.04	8.23
Cash Flow	6.97	5.74	5.88	5.83	4.91	5.15	4.41	2.83	2.04	1.83
Earnings	3.80	2.80	3.00	3.35	2.83	3.14	2.60	1.42	0.92	0.75
Dividends	0.60	0.51	0.46	0.40	0.32	0.28	0.18	0.16	0.14	0.13
Payout Ratio	16%	18%	15%	12%	11%	9%	7%	11%	15%	17%
Prices - High	56.43	61.81	60.62	62.93	63.00	63.25	72.00	57.25	39.93	22.37
- Low	29.50	41.62	35.25	44.75	45.12	42.00	48.75	38.00	20.93	14.25
P/E Ratio - High	15	22	20	19	22	20	28	40	44	30
- Low	8	15	12	13	16	13	19	27	23	19
Income Statement Analysis (Million $)										
Revs.	4,586	4,009	4,151	4,184	3,647	3,462	2,976	2,254	1,619	1,465
Oper. Inc.	737	631	665	678	570	605	528	323	223	189
Depr.	259	257	253	218	182	174	158	122	97.8	93.6
Int. Exp.	24.1	20.5	10.0	9.3	8.1	9.3	14.6	14.3	9.0	2.6
Pretax Inc.	478	379	415	460	388	432	357	187	117	96.0
Eff. Tax Rate	35%	35%	37%	36%	36%	37%	37%	34%	33%	33%
Net Inc.	311	245	264	294	248	276	227	124	79.2	64.7
Balance Sheet & Other Fin. Data (Million $)										
Cash	491	572	309	283	104	202	102	27.0	26.0	38.0
Curr. Assets	1,381	1,539	1,129	1,126	828	831	639	468	365	334
Total Assets	3,722	3,730	3,227	2,984	2,620	2,296	2,002	1,829	1,490	1,182
Curr. Liab.	558	531	487	524	466	477	382	350	272	229
LT Debt	460	390	215	168	153	107	173	352	247	73.0
Common Eqty.	2,131	2,262	2,073	1,876	1,609	1,382	1,123	902	784	712
Total Cap.	2,904	2,934	2,570	2,321	2,028	1,710	1,535	1,428	1,190	930
Cap. Exp.	415	375	503	307	537	263	185	364	379	218
Cash Flow	570	501	517	512	430	449	384	246	177	158
Curr. Ratio	2.5	2.9	2.3	2.1	1.8	1.7	1.7	1.3	1.3	1.5
% LT Debt of Cap.	15.9	13.3	8.4	7.2	7.5	6.3	11.3	24.7	20.7	7.8
% Net Inc.of Revs.	6.8	6.1	6.4	7.0	6.8	8.0	7.6	5.5	4.9	4.4
% Ret. on Assets	8.3	7.0	8.5	10.5	10.1	12.8	11.8	7.4	5.9	5.8
% Ret. on Equity	14.2	11.3	13.4	16.9	16.6	22.0	22.4	14.6	10.6	9.5

Data as orig reptd.; bef. results of disc opers/spec. items. Per share data adj. for stk. divs. Bold denotes diluted EPS (FASB 128)-prior periods restated. E-Estimated. NA-Not Available. NM-Not Meaningful. NR-Not Ranked.

Office—2100 Rexford Rd., Charlotte, NC 28211. **Tel**—(704) 366-7000. **Fax**—(704) 362-4208. **Website**—http://www.nucor.com **Chrmn**—P. C. Browning. **Pres & CEO**—D. R. Dimicco. **EVP & CFO**—T. S. Lisenby. **Dirs**—H. D. Aycock, P. C. Browning, D. R. Dimicco, B. Gantt, V. F. Haynes, J. D. Hlavacek, S. Siegel. **Transfer Agent & Registrar**—American Stock Transfer & Trust Co., NYC. **Incorporated**—in Delaware in 1958. **Empl**—7,900. **S&P Analyst:** Leo Larkin

STANDARD & POOR'S
STOCK REPORTS

Quanex Corp.

NYSE Symbol **NX**

In S&P SmallCap 600

18-AUG-01

Industry: Iron & Steel

Summary: Quanex produces hot rolled special bar quality carbon and alloy steel bars, air-bag components, and aluminum building products.

S&P Opinion: Accumulate (★★★★)

Recent Price • 27.29
52 Wk Range • 27.55-16.37
Yield • 2.3%
12-Mo. P/E • NM

Quantitative Evaluations

Outlook (1 Lowest—5 Highest)
• **4+**

Fair Value
• **31.60**

Risk
• **Low**

Earn./Div. Rank
• **B**

Technical Eval.
• **Bullish** since 4/01

Rel. Strength Rank (1 Lowest—99 Highest)
• **88**

Insider Activity
• **Neutral**

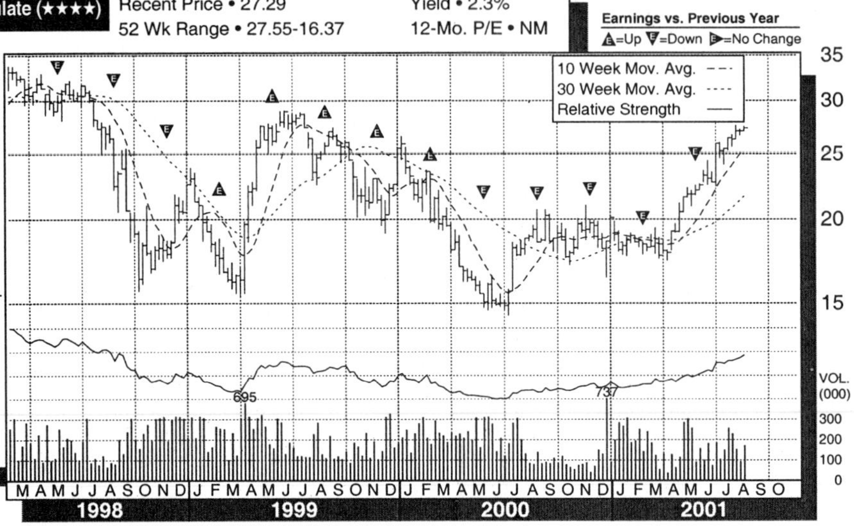

Overview - 14-JUN-01

In its FY 01 (Oct.) second quarter report, NX said operating results for the third quarter were expected to lag those of the FY 00 third quarter, but to show significant improvement from the level of the second quarter. Based on FY 01 first half results, and on its outlook for the second half, NX reaffirmed support for its earlier EPS guidance of $1.75 to $2.00 for FY 01. As a result of severe weakness in key durable goods markets in the first half of calendar 2001, we look for a 3% to 4% decline in sales in FY 01, mostly reflecting declines in volume and prices for steel, together with reduced sales from Piper Impact. Penalized by margin pressures in steel and aluminum, EPS, excluding unusual charges, will trail those of FY 00.

Valuation - 14-JUN-01

On June 5, 2001, we upgraded our investment opinion on NX and certain other steel stocks, on news that the Bush administration will initiate a section 201 trade investigation of the impact of imports on the U.S. steel industry. Although it is not clear that products made by NX will be covered by the investigation, we believe the action alone will act to deter imports. In addition to the favorable impact of a drop in imported steel, NX may ultimately gain market share in steel at the expense of several bankrupt competitors. The combination of less imported steel, market share gains, and an expected rebound in demand in calendar 2002 will help lift EPS. Finally, we were gratified at FY 01 second quarter results. Although EPS were in line with NX's pre-announcement, free cash flow per share showed dramatic improvement, both sequentially and year to year, thanks to much improved working capital management. We anticipate further improvement in EPS and free cash flow, and now recommend accumulating NX.

Key Stock Statistics

S&P EPS Est. 2001	1.75	Tang. Bk. Value/Share	15.39
P/E on S&P Est. 2001	15.6	Beta	0.57
S&P EPS Est. 2002	2.20	Shareholders	5,893
Dividend Rate/Share	0.64	Market cap. (B)	$0.365
Shs. outstg. (M)	13.4	Inst. holdings	73%
Avg. daily vol. (M)	0.032		

Value of $10,000 invested 5 years ago: $ 15,392

Fiscal Year Ending Oct. 31

	2001	2000	1999	1998	1997	1996
Revenues (Million $)						
1Q	193.8	199.3	183.1	181.0	194.9	188.8
2Q	213.8	243.3	202.9	203.4	217.1	218.3
3Q	—	254.1	206.6	204.8	225.1	225.5
4Q	—	237.5	217.5	208.2	195.6	263.1
Yr.	—	934.2	810.1	797.5	746.1	895.7
Earnings Per Share ($)						
1Q	**0.27**	**0.29**	**0.27**	**0.16**	0.23	0.30
2Q	**0.32**	**0.61**	**0.64**	**0.51**	0.61	0.60
3Q	**E0.51**	**0.05**	**0.79**	**0.66**	0.67	0.67
4Q	**E0.65**	**-1.78**	**0.85**	**-1.71**	0.59	0.84
Yr.	**E1.75**	**-0.73**	**2.56**	**-0.27**	**1.90**	**1.60**

Next earnings report expected: late August

Dividend Data (Dividends have been paid since 1988.)

Amount ($)	Date Decl.	Ex-Div. Date	Stock of Record	Payment Date
0.160	Aug. 30	Sep. 13	Sep. 15	Sep. 29 '00
0.160	Dec. 13	Dec. 20	Dec. 22	Dec. 29 '00
0.160	Feb. 22	Mar. 14	Mar. 16	Mar. 30 '01
0.160	May. 22	Jun. 13	Jun. 15	Jun. 29 '01

Quanex Corporation

Business Summary - 14-JUN-01

Quanex produces hot rolled special bar quality carbon and alloy steel bars, and aluminum building products. In August 1996, the company entered the market for impact extruded aluminum and steel products by acquiring Piper Impact.

In FY 00 (Oct.), NX incurred charges for the sale of Piper-Impact Europe in the second quarter and an asset impairment charge for Piper Impact in the fourth quarter. Excluding these charges, NX would have reported diluted EPS of $2.46 for FY 00.

Engineered steel products accounted for 36% of FY 00 sales. The segment includes steel bar operations, steel bar and tube heat treating services, and steel bar and tube wear and corrosion resistant finishing services. Steel bar operations, which account for the bulk of segment operations, are conducted by MacSteel at two plants. MacSteel makes hot rolled bars, including hot rolled steel bar quality carbon and steel bars used for camshafts, transmission gears, bearing cages, steering components, hydraulic mechanisms, seamless tube production, and track components for military vehicles. In recent years, NX has made incremental capacity additions to MacSteel's plants, improving product quality and adding volume. Operating profit was $57.7 million in FY 00, versus $60.4 million in FY 99.

The aluminum mill sheet products segment contributed 43% of sales in FY 00. It consists of Nichols-Homeshield (NH). NH uses state of the art aluminum minimill casting equipment to make coiled aluminum sheet from scrap and operates two finishing mills to supply a diverse mix of external customers in the construction, transportation and service centers markets. Operating profit in this segment increased to $21.5 million in FY 00, versus $15.3 million in FY 99.

The engineered products segment (10% of sales in FY 00) consists of Homeshield Fabricated Products and AMSCO. Homeshield Fabricated Products (HFP) makes a wide range of residential building products that are sold through distributors, as well as engineered products for OEMs. AMSCO manufactures aluminum window and patio door screens, window frames, and related accessories.

Piper Impact (11% of sales in FY 00) manufactures impact extruded aluminum and steel parts for the transportation, electronics and defense markets. The majority of Piper's sales are to Autoliv (formerly Morton International), in the form of air-bag components, including passenger and side impact air bags, smart bags with adjustable inflation speed, and bags with alternative inflation technologies. Piper incurred an $82.5 million loss in FY 00, versus an $853,000 loss in FY 99. NX is considering strategic alternatives for Piper, including its possible sale.

Per Share Data ($) (Year Ended Oct. 31)	2000	1999	1998	1997	1996	1995	1994	1993	1992	1991
Tangible Bk. Val.	16.17	17.66	15.50	12.62	7.66	10.27	8.12	7.76	8.54	9.94
Cash Flow	2.80	5.08	2.68	4.63	5.22	4.91	3.01	2.23	2.36	3.17
Earnings	-0.73	2.56	-0.27	1.98	2.41	2.20	0.96	0.18	0.28	1.02
Dividends	0.64	0.64	0.64	0.61	0.60	0.59	0.56	0.56	0.52	0.48
Payout Ratio	NM	25%	NM	31%	25%	27%	58%	NM	200%	47%
Prices - High	26.56	29.00	33.81	36.50	29.12	26.62	27.25	21.25	31.75	23.12
- Low	14.37	15.37	15.62	23.37	18.75	18.00	17.00	14.00	15.50	11.37
P/E Ratio - High	NM	11	NM	18	12	12	28	NM	NM	23
- Low	NM	6	NM	12	8	8	18	NM	NM	11
Income Statement Analysis (Million $)										
Revs.	934	810	797	746	896	891	699	616	572	589
Oper. Inc.	115	118	103	92.3	105	99	69.2	50.9	52.5	60.2
Depr.	48.4	45.9	41.8	37.3	38.4	32.4	27.8	27.7	26.4	25.1
Int. Exp.	13.3	12.8	10.5	14.0	11.4	10.7	13.9	15.1	15.5	17.7
Pretax Inc.	-15.4	60.3	-6.0	42.6	56.7	58.4	32.5	14.5	10.7	21.4
Eff. Tax Rate	NM	35%	NM	35%	42%	42%	42%	42%	42%	42%
Net Inc.	-10.0	39.3	-3.9	27.7	32.9	33.9	18.9	8.4	6.2	12.4
Balance Sheet & Other Fin. Data (Million $)										
Cash	22.4	25.9	26.3	26.9	36.0	45.2	88.1	89.9	96.9	31.1
Curr. Assets	236	212	210	187	263	242	259	243	250	164
Total Assets	646	690	674	686	718	547	564	529	535	446
Curr. Liab.	131	136	147	134	153	165	135	95.1	96.0	95.0
LT Debt	192	179	188	202	254	112	107	128	129	156
Common Eqty.	266	301	272	269	195	171	146	140	151	152
Total Cap.	486	524	494	519	473	312	363	372	383	341
Cap. Exp.	42.3	60.8	58.5	72.8	44.2	26.6	44.6	37.0	52.5	57.0
Cash Flow	38.4	85.2	38.0	65.0	71.3	66.3	40.7	30.2	30.0	37.0
Curr. Ratio	1.8	1.6	1.4	1.4	1.7	1.5	1.9	2.6	2.6	1.7
% LT Debt of Cap.	39.5	34.2	38.1	38.9	53.7	35.9	29.6	34.5	33.6	45.8
% Net Inc.of Revs.	NM	4.9	NM	3.7	3.7	3.8	2.7	1.4	1.1	2.1
% Ret. on Assets	NM	5.8	NM	3.9	5.2	6.1	3.4	1.6	1.2	2.8
% Ret. on Equity	NM	13.7	NM	12.0	18.0	16.8	9.0	1.7	2.2	8.0

Data as orig reptd.; bef. results of disc opers/spec. items. Per share data adj. for stk. divs. Bold denotes diluted EPS (FASB 128)-prior periods restated. E-Estimated. NA-Not Available. NM-Not Meaningful. NR-Not Ranked.

Office—1900 West Loop South, Suite 1500, Houston, TX 77027. **Tel**—(713) 961-4600. **Website**—www.quanex.com **Chrmn**—V. E. Oechsle. **Pres & CEO**—R. A. Jean. **VP & CFO**—T. M. Murphy. **Secy**—M. W. Conlon. **Investor Contact**—Valerie Calvert (713-977-5389). **Dirs**—D. J. Barger Jr., S. F. Davis, R. M. Flaum, R. A. Jean, V. E. Oechsle, C. E. Pfeiffer, V. R. Scorsone, M. J. Sebastian. **Transfer Agent & Registrar**—American Stock Transfer & Trust, NYC. **Incorporated**—in Michigan in 1927; reincorporated in Delaware in 1968. **Empl**— 3,361. **S&P Analyst:** Leo Larkin

Sigma-Aldrich Corp.

Nasdaq Symbol **SIAL**

In S&P 500

18-AUG-01

Industry:
Chemicals (Specialty)

Summary: SIAL makes and sells a wide range of biochemicals, organic chemicals, chromatography products and diagnostic reagents; it recently sold its metals component unit.

S&P Opinion: Accumulate (★★★★)

Recent Price • 41.81
52 Wk Range • 51.49-27.25
Yield • 0.8%
12-Mo. P/E • 10.8

Quantitative Evaluations

Outlook
(1 Lowest—5 Highest)
• **2+**

Fair Value
• **40.70**

Risk
• **Low**

Earn./Div. Rank
• **A+**

Technical Eval.
• **Bullish** since 8/01

Rel. Strength Rank
(1 Lowest—99 Highest)
• **45**

Insider Activity
• **NA**

OPTIONS: ASE, CBOE

Overview - 21-JUN-01

S&P sees chemical sales rising 10% to 12% in 2001, before the adverse impact of unfavorable exchange rates, on good growth in the scientific research, biotechnology and fine chemicals product units (over 90% of total chemical sales). The launch of new products and catalogs in 2000, together with price increases and geographical expansion, will continue to spur growth. Three acquisitions since mid-2000 will also contribute to gains, helped by the current launch of a new diagnostic test for heart attacks. Pretax margins will likely remain at 2000 levels, despite high investment and R&D spending, and greater interest expense. Two of the recent acquisitions expanding the diagnostic business will remain modestly dilutive through 2001. EPS comparisons will benefit from a reduction in shares outstanding. SIAL repurchased about 26% of its shares from November 1999 through early 2001, although the pace will now slow. EPS in the 2000 third quarter included acquisition charges of $0.07.

Valuation - 21-JUN-01

After a lackluster performance since early 1998, the stock surged from late 2000 to a record high in the second quarter of 2001. The increase reflected in part lessening investor concerns about Internet-based competitors. We are continuing our accumulate recommendation, as we are becoming more confident that the company can return to annual internal sales and earnings growth of 10% by 2002, and can boost return on equity to 20% by 2004. We expect SIAL to further leverage its balance sheet to finance additional buybacks and acquisitions. After a pullback, the shares are trading at a slight discount to the P/E multiple of the overall market, based on EPS forecast for 2001. Another positive factor is that the dividend has been raised each year since 1975, and this should continue in the future.

Key Stock Statistics

S&P EPS Est. 2001	1.95	Tang. Bk. Value/Share	7.34
P/E on S&P Est. 2001	21.4	Beta	0.16
S&P EPS Est. 2002	2.15	Shareholders	1,369
Dividend Rate/Share	0.33	Market cap. (B)	$ 3.2
Shs. outstg. (M)	75.7	Inst. holdings	76%
Avg. daily vol. (M)	0.292		

Value of $10,000 invested 5 years ago: $ 16,329

Fiscal Year Ending Dec. 31

	2001	2000	1999	1998	1997	1996
Revenues (Million $)						
1Q	305.6	290.1	333.0	306.2	279.1	262.4
2Q	—	273.8	318.4	294.6	278.6	258.8
3Q	—	269.8	323.9	300.4	286.1	255.8
4Q	—	262.6	252.1	293.1	283.4	257.5
Yr.	—	1,096	1,038	1,194	1,127	1,035
Earnings Per Share ($)						
1Q	0.48	0.45	0.44	0.43	0.40	0.36
2Q	E0.49	0.45	0.44	0.41	0.40	0.36
3Q	E0.49	0.35	0.44	0.41	0.41	0.36
4Q	E0.49	0.41	0.33	0.39	0.41	0.37
Yr.	E1.95	1.66	1.47	1.64	1.62	1.45

Next earnings report expected: NA

Dividend Data (Dividends have been paid since 1970.)

Amount ($)	Date Decl.	Ex-Div. Date	Stock of Record	Payment Date
0.083	Nov. 14	Dec. 13	Dec. 15	Jan. 02 '01
0.083	Feb. 20	Mar. 01	Mar. 05	Mar. 15 '01
0.083	May. 01	May. 30	Jun. 01	Jun. 15 '01
0.083	Aug. 14	Aug. 29	Aug. 31	Sep. 14 '01

Sigma-Aldrich Corporation

Business Summary - 21-JUN-01

Sigma-Aldrich, well known for its extensive catalog business, is one of the world's largest providers of research chemicals, diagnostic reagents, chromatography products, and related products. In May 2000, SIAL sold its B-Line Systems metals business (reported as discontinued operations in 1999) for $430 million, posting a gain of $172 million. The business manufactured metal components for strut, cable tray, pipe support and telecommunication systems and electrical enclosures. SIAL intends to boost annual sales growth for its continuing chemical business to 10% through continued global expansion by entering new countries, increasing the distribution of its catalogs, and acquisitions, joint ventures, and partnerships, especially in the life sciences product lines.

Foreign sales accounted for 50% of sales and 17% of pretax income in 2000.

SIAL distributes 85,000 chemical products under the Sigma, Aldrich, Fluka and Supelco brands names, for use primarily in research and development, in diagnosis of disease, and as specialty chemicals for manufacturing. About 75% of sales are to customers in the life sciences and the remaining 25% are used in high technology applications. The company itself produces about 40,000 products, accounting for over 50% of 2000 net sales of chemical products. Remaining products were purchased from outside sources.

The Scientific Research unit (56% of annual sales) supplies biochemicals, organic and inorganic compounds, reagents, and related equipment for university, governmental and agency research. The Biotechnology unit (20%) supplies products for molecular biology, cell biology, cell culture, protein analysis and chromatography. The December 1998 acquisition of Genosys added custom synthetic DNA products, synthetic peptides and genes to the life science product categories. The unit's first life science catalog was released in the 2000 second quarter.

The Fine Chemicals unit (17%) is a medium-sized supplier of bulk quantities of organic, inorganic and biochemicals to pharmaceutical, biotechnology, and industrial customers. Diagnostics (7%) includes reagents, controls and instrumentations marketed to hospitals and clinical laboratories, focuses on clinical chemistry, immunoassay and coagulation products. SIAL made two acquisitions in the 2000 third quarter, expanding its diagnostics businesses. In July, it acquired for $15 million First Medical. Inc., a developer of a rapid immunoassay system launched in May 2001 called Alpha Dx that diagnose Acute Myocardial Infarctions (AMI). In August, it purchased Amelung GmbH, a maker of coagulation instruments, for $28 million. SIAL expects to boost its coagulation sales from $15 million to over $30 million over the next two years.

SIAL also offers about 80,000 esoteric chemicals (under 1% of total sales) as a special service to customers that screen them for potential applications.

Per Share Data ($)										
(Year Ended Dec. 31)	**2000**	**1999**	**1998**	**1997**	**1996**	**1995**	**1994**	**1993**	**1992**	**1991**
Tangible Bk. Val.	7.34	11.58	10.96	10.56	9.42	8.27	7.02	5.93	5.14	4.43
Cash Flow	2.47	2.13	2.25	2.08	1.93	1.73	1.48	1.38	1.24	1.06
Earnings	1.66	1.47	1.64	1.62	1.48	1.32	1.10	1.07	0.96	0.80
Dividends	0.32	0.29	0.28	0.26	0.23	0.19	0.17	0.11	0.13	0.11
Payout Ratio	19%	20%	17%	16%	16%	14%	15%	11%	14%	14%
Prices - High	40.87	35.25	42.75	41.12	32.06	25.87	27.62	29.00	29.60	26.75
- Low	20.18	24.50	25.75	26.87	23.75	16.25	15.00	22.25	20.80	13.87
P/E Ratio - High	25	24	26	25	22	20	25	27	31	33
- Low	12	17	16	17	16	12	14	21	22	17
Income Statement Analysis (Million $)										
Revs.	1,096	1,038	1,194	1,127	1,035	960	851	739	654	589
Oper. Inc.	284	275	305	302	277	247	210	198	180	158
Depr.	67.6	66.9	61.8	48.1	45.2	40.9	36.7	29.7	27.4	25.8
Int. Exp.	10.2	Nil	0.9	0.7	1.8	1.6	2.9	2.4	5.4	8.0
Pretax Inc.	203	204	243	253	230	204	170	166	147	124
Eff. Tax Rate	31%	27%	31%	34%	36%	36%	35%	35%	35%	36%
Net Inc.	139	149	166	166	148	132	110	107	95.5	79.8
Balance Sheet & Other Fin. Data (Million $)										
Cash	31.1	43.8	24.3	46.2	104	84.0	9.7	10.3	44.9	28.1
Curr. Assets	714	775	773	707	667	610	502	451	416	391
Total Assets	1,348	1,432	1,433	1,244	1,100	985	852	753	616	597
Curr. Liab.	335	106	142	119	110	108	105	111	66.2	70.9
LT Debt	101	0.2	0.4	0.6	3.8	13.8	14.5	17.3	18.7	69.3
Common Eqty.	859	1,259	1,216	1,073	942	825	700	591	512	441
Total Cap.	960	1,260	1,217	1,061	946	839	714	608	543	520
Cap. Exp.	69.2	91.8	130	109	93.8	60.2	72.0	102	30.9	26.1
Cash Flow	207	216	228	214	193	173	147	137	123	106
Curr. Ratio	2.1	7.3	5.4	5.9	6.0	5.6	4.8	4.0	6.3	5.5
% LT Debt of Cap.	10.5	0.0	0.0	0.0	0.4	1.6	2.0	2.8	3.5	13.3
% Net Inc.of Revs.	12.7	14.3	13.9	14.7	14.3	13.7	13.0	14.5	14.6	13.5
% Ret. on Assets	10.0	10.4	12.4	14.2	14.2	14.3	13.7	15.6	15.7	14.0
% Ret. on Equity	13.1	12.0	14.5	16.4	16.7	17.3	17.1	19.4	20.0	19.7

Data as orig reptd.; bef. results of disc opers/spec. items. Per share data adj. for stk. divs. Bold denotes diluted EPS (FASB 128)-prior periods restated. E-Estimated. NA-Not Available. NM-Not Meaningful. NR-Not Ranked.

Office—3050 Spruce St., St. Louis, MO 63103. **Tel**—(314) 771-5765; (800) 521-8956. **E-mail**—sig-ald@sial.com **Website**—http://www.sial.com **Chrmn, Pres & CEO**—D. R. Harvey. **VP, CFO & Secy**—M. R. Hogan. **Treas & Investor Contact**—Kirk A. Richter. **Dirs**—A. E. Newman, N. V. Fedoroff, D. R. Harvey, D. M. Kipnis, W. C. O'Neil Jr., J. W. Sandweiss, D. D. Spatz, T. N. Urban. **Transfer Agent**—ComputerShare, Chicago. **Incorporated**—in Delaware in 1975. **Empl**— 6,218. **S&P Analyst:** Richard O'Reilly, CFA

Part Nine

Telecommunications Services Stocks

ALLTEL Corp.

NYSE Symbol **AT**
In S&P 500

18-AUG-01 **Industry:** Telephone

Summary: This company provides wireless and wireline communications and information services.

S&P Opinion: Buy (★★★★★)

Recent Price • 57.76 | Yield • 2.3%
52 Wk Range • 68.68-47.75 | 12-Mo. P/E • 13.6

Quantitative Evaluations

Outlook
(1 Lowest—5 Highest)
• **1**

Fair Value
• **54.30**

Risk
• **Low**

Earn./Div. Rank
• **A**

Technical Eval.
• **Bullish** since 6/01

Rel. Strength Rank
(1 Lowest—99 Highest)
• **43**

Insider Activity
• **Unfavorable**

OPTIONS: ASE, CBOE, P, Ph

Overview - 17-AUG-01

Revenue growth in 2001 should slow to 8% to 10%, as the wireless segment eliminates its wholesale roaming revenue stream, to make a transition to a retail focused, one-rate plan strategy. Reported earnings will appear weaker in the first half, due to declining roaming revenues and goodwill amortization related to wireless property acquisitions in 2000. Excluding goodwill and roaming revenue, margins should widen, as emerging businesses (long-distance, competitive local service, Internet, etc.) achieve profitability, and incumbent local operations benefit from cost reductions and economies. Interest expense should decline slightly. Reported results included net one-time gains of $3.48 a share in 2000 and $0.54 in the first half of 2001. EPS estimates for 2002 exclude $0.35/share in goodwill amortization.

Valuation - 17-AUG-01

In mid-August, we upgraded Alltel to buy, from accumulate. Over the prior month, the shares had fallen over 12%, largely due to AT's hostile $8.75 billion acquisition offer for CenturyTel, an independent ILEC and small wireless carrier. Given CTL management's rejection, we believe the merger is unlikely to take place, and AT's shares will rebound. Even if the acquisition is consummated, we see excellent synergies between the companies, which would contribute to long-term EPS growth and enhance the value of AT's wireless unit. Following a probable relaxation of regulatory spectrum caps by early 2002, we anticipate Alltel's regional wireless network (the 6th largest carrier in the U.S.) to be sold. Even without accretive M&A activity, we believe AT's shares would be fairly valued near 30X annualized first half free cash flow, implying over 20% appreciation in the coming 12 months.

Key Stock Statistics

S&P EPS Est. 2001	2.92	Tang. Bk. Value/Share	5.92
P/E on S&P Est. 2001	19.8	Beta	0.47
S&P EPS Est. 2002	3.63	Shareholders	255,000
Dividend Rate/Share	1.32	Market cap. (B)	$ 18.1
Shs. outstg. (M)	313.1	Inst. holdings	53%
Avg. daily vol. (M)	0.977		

Value of $10,000 invested 5 years ago: $ 24,375

Fiscal Year Ending Dec. 31

	2001	2000	1999	1998	1997	1996
Revenues (Million $)						
1Q	1,798	1,645	1,368	847.0	784.3	774.3
2Q	1,920	1,775	1,470	934.0	816.9	804.5
3Q	—	1,803	1,628	1,332	813.8	807.4
4Q	—	1,844	1,597	1,373	848.6	806.3
Yr.	—	7,067	6,302	5,194	3,264	3,192
Earnings Per Share ($)						
1Q	**1.19**	**0.68**	**0.59**	**0.66**	**0.54**	0.44
2Q	**0.70**	**3.15**	**0.67**	**0.84**	**0.92**	0.48
3Q	—	**1.53**	**0.47**	**-0.10**	**0.65**	0.10
4Q	—	**0.83**	**0.65**	**0.49**	**0.59**	0.51
Yr.	—	**6.20**	**2.59**	**1.89**	**2.70**	**1.52**

Next earnings report expected: late October

Dividend Data (Dividends have been paid since 1961.)

Amount ($)	Date Decl.	Ex-Div. Date	Stock of Record	Payment Date
0.330	Oct. 26	Dec. 06	Dec. 08	Jan. 03 '01
0.330	Jan. 25	Feb. 22	Feb. 26	Apr. 03 '01
0.330	Apr. 26	Jun. 06	Jun. 08	Jul. 03 '01
0.330	Jul. 26	Sep. 06	Sep. 10	Oct. 03 '01

ALLTEL Corporation

Business Summary - 17-AUG-01

Alltel's independent local exchange carrier (ILEC) operations, which accounted for 38.6% of 2000 segment operating profit, are the second largest in the U.S., and its wireless telephone services (50.8%) are the sixth largest. The company is leveraging strong cash flows from its ILEC operations to fund expanding Emerging Businesses (generating operating losses of $23.9 million in 2000), including competitive local exchange (CLEC) operations outside its incumbent service territory and long-distance services. During 2000, AT expanded its CLEC service into 17 additional markets in four new states, bringing its total CLEC presence to 43 markets covering 10 states. At the end of 2000, AT had approximately 1.1 million long-distance customers, up about 20% from the level in 1999.

The company's intent in rolling out Emerging Businesses is to expand margins through cross selling of additional services to existing customers. In AT's ILEC service territory (including 2.6 million customer lines), about 44% of all local phone customers also subscribed to the company's long-distance phone service at the end of 2000. Approximately 50% of AT's ILEC service territory is covered by its wireless phone services, with 13% of covered local customers also subscribing to wireless services. In its CLEC markets, the company seeks to provide bundled services (including local, long-distance and wireless) to higher volume medium and small business customers. These bundled services are provided at a discount to a la carte pricing, and are billed on a single, consolidated billing statement.

In addition to communications, AT has an Information Services division (10.7% of 2000 operating profit) that provides data processing and account management services to the financial institution and telecommunications industries. The unit's clients include 48 of the 50 leading U.S. banks. During 2000, Information Services processed 50% of all U.S. residential mortgages, and 34% of all U.S. consumer loans.

At the end of 2000, the Wireless division had more than 6.3 million customers in 21 states. The unit is undergoing two important transitions. The first is an effort to move analog customers to digital service (through new service contracts and subsidized phone upgrades), to provide greater service and reduce expenses. Variable costs for digital subscriber services are about 50% of those of older analog services. By the end of 2001, AT projects that more than 70% of its subscriber base will be digital, up from nearly 40% in 2000 and 10% in 1999. The second transition is to eliminate roaming fees, and move toward simple, one-rate pricing plans. As a result of reciprocal roaming agreements with Verizon Wireless, in May 2000, AT began to offer new rate plans that provide national wireless coverage with no toll or roaming charges.

Per Share Data ($) (Year Ended Dec. 31)	2000	1999	1998	1997	1996	1995	1994	1993	1992	1991
Tangible Bk. Val.	5.92	7.03	5.95	8.67	8.88	7.64	5.96	5.53	4.86	4.58
Cash Flow	9.39	5.19	4.44	5.10	3.77	4.02	3.34	2.84	2.54	2.50
Earnings	6.20	2.59	1.89	2.70	1.53	1.86	1.43	1.39	1.22	1.17
Dividends	1.29	1.22	1.16	1.11	1.05	0.98	0.90	0.82	0.76	0.71
Payout Ratio	21%	47%	61%	41%	69%	53%	63%	59%	62%	61%
Prices - High	82.93	91.81	61.37	41.62	35.62	31.12	31.37	31.25	25.00	21.62
- Low	47.75	56.31	38.25	29.75	26.62	23.25	24.00	22.87	17.62	15.87
P/E Ratio - High	13	35	32	15	23	17	22	22	20	18
- Low	8	22	20	11	17	12	17	16	14	14
Income Statement Analysis (Million $)										
Revs.	7,067	6,302	5,194	3,264	3,192	3,110	2,962	2,342	2,092	1,748
Depr.	988	862	707	451	424	410	362	272	245	217
Maint.	NA	NA	NA	NA	147	148	151	131	122	109
Constr. Credits	NA	NA	NA	NA	NA	Nil	NA	2.0	2.0	1.9
Eff. Tax Rate	40%	38%	42%	37%	37%	38%	38%	42%	36%	33%
Net Inc.	1,965	784	525	508	292	355	272	262	229	189
Balance Sheet & Other Fin. Data (Million $)										
Gross Prop.	12,113	10,291	8,233	5,531	5,114	4,842	4,697	4,235	3,297	2,913
Net Prop.	6,549	5,735	4,828	3,190	3,042	2,973	2,963	2,676	2,062	1,825
Cap. Exp.	1,165	1,006	869	546	464	523	596	426	367	308
Total Cap.	9,924	9,015	7,701	4,754	4,535	4,270	3,896	3,575	2,643	2,405
Fxd. Chgs. Cov.	12.1	5.8	4.5	5.4	5.2	4.5	4.1	5.4	4.8	4.0
Capitalization:										
LT Debt	4,612	3,750	3,492	1,874	1,756	1,762	1,846	1,596	1,018	992
Pfd.	0.5	2.1	14.0	14.8	15.7	16.3	17.1	18.0	19.1	21.3
Common	5,095	4,205	3,262	2,199	2,088	1,926	1,616	1,545	1,295	1,072
% Return On Revs.	27.8	12.4	10.1	15.6	9.1	11.4	9.2	11.2	10.9	10.8
% Return On Invest. Capital	25.3	14.3	23.7	16.6	16.2	16.6	10.9	11.6	12.7	11.4
% Return On Com. Equity	42.3	20.0	19.2	23.6	14.5	20.0	17.1	18.3	18.8	18.0
% Earn. on Net Prop.	43.7	45.1	47.5	24.5	23.4	23.0	16.6	14.0	15.8	14.3
% LT Debt of Cap.	47.5	47.1	51.6	45.8	45.4	47.6	53.1	50.5	43.7	47.6
Capital. % Pfd.	0.0	0.0	0.2	0.4	0.6	0.4	0.5	0.6	0.8	1.0
Capital. % Common	52.5	52.8	48.2	53.8	54.0	52.0	46.4	48.9	55.5	51.4

Data as orig reptd.; bef. results of disc opers/spec. items. Per share data adj. for stk. divs. Bold denotes diluted EPS (FASB 128)-prior periods restated. E-Estimated. NA-Not Available. NM-Not Meaningful. NR-Not Ranked.

Office—One Allied Drive, Little Rock, AR 72202. **Tel**—(501) 905-8000. **Website**—http://www.alltel.com **Chrmn & CEO**—J. T. Ford. **Pres & COO**—S. T. Ford. **SVP & CFO**—J. R. Gardner. **EVP & Secy**—F. X. Frantz. **VP & Investor Contact**—Kerry Brooks (501-905-8991). **Dirs**—J. R. Belk, J. T. Ford, S. T. Ford, D. E. Foster, L. L. Gellerstedt III, C. H. Goodman, E. A. Mahony, Jr., J. P. McConnell, J. Natori, G. W. Penske, F. E. Reed, F. W. Smith, R. Townsend. **Transfer Agent & Registrar**—First Union National Bank of North Carolina, Charlotte. **Incorporated**—in Delaware. **Empl**— 27,257. **S&P Analyst:** Craig K. Shere, CFA

STANDARD &POOR'S
STOCK REPORTS

Broadwing Inc.

NYSE Symbol **BRW**

In S&P MidCap 400

18-AUG-01 **Industry:** Telephone

Summary: Broadwing was formed through the merger of Cincinnati Bell and IXC Communications.

S&P Opinion: Buy (★★★★★)

Recent Price • 21.30
52 Wk Range • 30-15.40
Yield • Nil
12-Mo. P/E • NM

Quantitative Evaluations

Outlook (1 Lowest—5 Highest)
• **NA**

Fair Value
• **NA**

Risk
• **Average**

Earn./Div. Rank
• **B**

Technical Eval.
• **NA**

Rel. Strength Rank (1 Lowest—99 Highest)
• **28**

Insider Activity
• **Unfavorable**

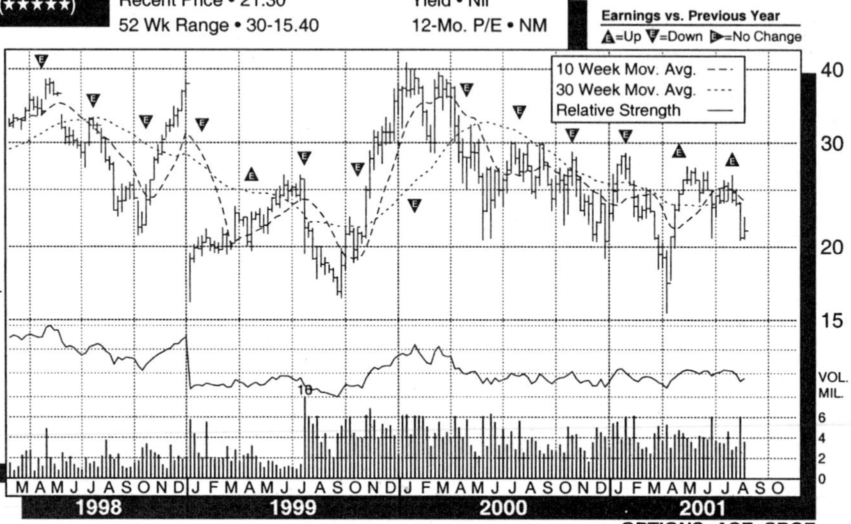

OPTIONS: ASE, CBOE

Overview - 13-JUL-01

We expect revenues to increase about 22% in 2001, with growth of about 45% in wireless and nearly 30% in broadband outweighing single digit increases in local communications. Gross margins will narrow, on an increased proportion of contributions from lower margin, growth businesses. SG&A expenses should decline as a percentage of revenue, with broadband services realizing significant economies of scale. Depreciation charges should rise about 17%, and amortization (mostly from goodwill related to the 1999 IXC Communications acquisition) should be flat. Equity in losses of unconsolidated affiliates should decline to $12.3 million, as BRW writes down its remaining carrying costs in Applied Theory. Interest expense should rise about 22%, BRW raises about $300 million in 2001 to help fund capital spending. We look for positive earnings (excluding amortization) in 2002, with positive free cash flow in the second half. Reported results for 2000 included one-time charges of $1.08 a share.

Valuation - 13-JUL-01

In the two months through mid-July, the stock declined about 2%, in sympathy with larger declines for pure play wholesale network providers. With significant contributions from stable ILEC operations (67% of first quarter EBITDA), and one of the most advanced, all optical U.S. networks, BRW is poised to maintain growth and expand market share as shakier competitors fall prey to the fiber glut. We are also optimistic about growth contributions from wireless operations and new long-distance services. We believe market interest in BRW will grow as it becomes earnings and cash flow positive. Based on a multiple of 25X projected 2004 free cash flow, discounted to the present, we estimate fair value at nearly twice current market value, and continue to recommend buying BRW.

Key Stock Statistics

S&P EPS Est. 2001	-0.52	Tang. Bk. Value/Share	NM
P/E on S&P Est. 2001	NM	Beta	1.66
S&P EPS Est. 2002	-0.06	Shareholders	105,000
Dividend Rate/Share	Nil	Market cap. (B)	$ 4.7
Shs. outstg. (M)	218.7	Inst. holdings	55%
Avg. daily vol. (M)	0.793		

Value of $10,000 invested 5 years ago: NA

Fiscal Year Ending Dec. 31

	2001	2000	1999	1998	1997	1996
Revenues (Million $)						
1Q	578.3	460.2	242.2	216.5	429.5	362.1
2Q	—	497.8	253.6	219.5	433.1	376.0
3Q	—	531.2	262.4	222.6	433.2	403.2
4Q	—	560.9	372.9	226.5	461.0	432.4
Yr.	—	2,050	1,131	885.1	1,757	1,574
Earnings Per Share ($)						
1Q	**-0.17**	**-0.28**	**0.18**	**0.16**	**0.42**	**0.31**
2Q	**E-0.14**	**-0.15**	**0.20**	**0.31**	**0.39**	**0.32**
3Q	**E-0.12**	**-0.12**	**0.19**	**0.35**	**0.38**	**0.34**
4Q	**E-0.09**	**-1.26**	**-0.25**	**0.16**	**0.22**	**0.37**
Yr.	**E-0.52**	**-1.82**	**0.24**	**0.59**	**1.41**	**1.35**

Next earnings report expected: NA

Dividend Data

No dividends have been paid since the 1999 merger of Cincinnati Bell and IXC Communications.

A Division of The McGraw·Hill Companies

Broadwing Inc.

Business Summary - 13-JUL-01

In November 1999, local phone carrier Cincinnati Bell completed the $3.2 billion acquisition of IXC Communications (Nasdaq: IIXC), and subsequently changed its name to Broadwing Inc. (NYSE: BRW). As of the end of 2000, BRW was organized into four business segments: Broadband, Local Communications, Wireless, and Other Communications.

The Broadband segment (47% of consolidated 2000 revenues, versus 45% pro forma for 1999) reflects the operations of Broadwing Communications (the IXC acquisition). This unit is a nationwide provider of data and voice communications services, with more than 18,000 route miles of fiber-optic transmission facilities. During 2000, Broadwing Communications sales were derived 41% from switched long distance services, 39% from broadband transport, and 20% from Internet services.

Local Communications (37% of 2000 revenue and 44% of pro forma 1999 revenue) operations are conducted by the Cincinnati Bell Telephone (CBT) subsidiary in a 2,400 square mile region of Cincinnati, OH. During 2000, CBT's sales stemmed 57% from local service revenues (the public switched telephone system and custom calling features), 25% from Network access provided to interexchange carriers, and 18% from Other services.

At the end of December 1998, BRW acquired an 80% ownership interest in AT&T Wireless' operations serving Greater Cincinnati and Dayton, Ohio. These operations represent the business activity of Broadwing Wireless (8.8% of 2000 revenue, versus 5.5% pro forma in 1999). The Wireless segment offers services over a digital wireless network using Time Division Multiple Access (TDMA) technology. The unit interconnects with AT&T PCS's national network for calls outside its regional service territory.

Broadwing's Other Communications segment (6.9% and 6.5%) combines the operations of Cincinnati Bell's Any Distance, Directory, ZoomTown.com and Public phone businesses. The "Any Distance" business resells long-distance services inside the Greater Cincinnati area. BRW's larger long-distance business was merged into Broadwing Communications in early 2000. Directory operations publishes Yellow Pages directories and sells advertising. ZoomTown provides managed web hosting nationally.

Per Share Data ($) (Year Ended Dec. 31)	2000	1999	1998	1997	1996	1995	1994	1993	1992	1991
Tangible Bk. Val.	NM	NM	0.28	2.83	3.17	2.29	2.69	2.48	2.79	2.74
Cash Flow	0.33	1.44	1.40	2.75	2.61	1.03	1.73	0.81	1.39	1.30
Earnings	-1.82	0.24	0.59	1.41	1.35	-0.19	0.57	-0.47	0.28	0.32
Dividends	Nil	0.30	0.40	0.40	0.40	0.40	0.40	0.40	0.40	0.40
Payout Ratio	Nil	125%	68%	28%	30%	NM	70%	NM	143%	127%
Prices - High	41.06	37.87	38.62	33.75	30.81	17.62	10.06	12.18	10.43	12.68
- Low	19.06	16.06	13.37	23.06	15.87	8.43	7.68	8.06	7.68	8.93
P/E Ratio - High	NM	NM	65	24	23	NM	18	NM	37	40
- Low	NM	NM	23	16	12	NM	13	NM	27	28
Income Statement Analysis (Million $)										
Revs.	2,050	1,131	885	1,757	1,574	1,336	1,228	1,090	1,136	1,088
Oper. Inc.	498	336	312	533	1,574	380	NA	NA	NA	NA
Depr.	460	181	111	185	173	162	154	159	137	121
Int. Exp.	164	61.7	24.2	35.5	33.9	52.8	NA	NA	NA	NA
Pretax Inc.	-498	71.3	126	297	285	19.6	NA	NA	NA	NA
Eff. Tax Rate	NM	47%	35%	35%	35%	29%	36%	3.10%	30%	36%
Net Inc.	-377	38.0	81.8	194	185	-25.3	72.6	-56.8	38.9	42.7
Balance Sheet & Other Fin. Data (Million $)										
Cash	37.9	80.0	10.1	9.9	2.0	2.9	NA	NA	NA	NA
Curr. Assets	463	413	197	450	391	341	NA	NA	NA	NA
Total Assets	6,478	6,509	1,041	1,499	1,671	1,592	NA	NA	NA	NA
Curr. Liab.	727	568	405	535	512	453	NA	NA	NA	NA
LT Debt	2,507	2,136	367	269	280	NA	NA	NA	NA	NA
Common Eqty.	1,892	2,003	142	580	634	478	NA	NA	NA	NA
Total Cap.	4,962	5,153	515	862	1,034	991	1,261	1,216	1,146	1,252
Cap. Exp.	844	381	143	233	156	115	NA	NA	NA	NA
Cash Flow	70.9	217	193	379	358	137	227	102	172	160
Curr. Ratio	0.6	0.7	0.5	0.8	NA	NA	NA	NA	NA	NA
% LT Debt of Cap.	50.5	41.5	713.0	NA	NA	NA	NA	NA	NA	NA
% Net Inc.of Revs.	NM	3.4	9.2	NA	NA	NA	NA	NA	NA	NA
% Ret. on Assets	NM	1.0	6.4	NA	NA	NM	NA	NA	NA	NA
% Ret. on Equity	NM	3.3	22.7	NA	NA	NA	NA	NA	NA	NA

Data as orig reptd.; bef. results of disc opers/spec. items. Per share data adj. for stk. divs. Bold denotes diluted EPS (FASB 128)-prior periods restated. E-Estimated. NA-Not Available. NM-Not Meaningful. NR-Not Ranked.

Office—201 E. Fourth St., Cincinnati, OH 45201. **Tel**—(513) 397-9900. **Website**—http://www.broadwing.com **Chrmn**—J. D. Kiggen. **Pres & CEO**—R. G. Ellenberger. **EVP & CFO**—K. W. Mooney. **Secy**—T. E. Taylor. **VP & Treas**—M. W. Peterson. **Investor Contact**—Hugh F. Anderson. **Dirs**—P. R. Cox, J. T. Crandall, R. G. Ellenberger, W. A. Friedlander, K. M. Hoguet, J. D. Kiggen, D. J. Meyer, M. D. Nelson, C. Redfield, D. B. Sharrock, J. M. Zrno. **Transfer Agent & Registrar**—Fifth Third Bank, Cincinnati. **Incorporated**—in Ohio in 1873; reincorporated in Ohio in 1983. **Empl**— 6,400. **S&P Analyst:** Craig K. Shere, CFA

STANDARD
&POOR'S
STOCK REPORTS

Sprint Corp. (PCS Group)

NYSE Symbol **PCS**

In S&P 500

18-AUG-01

Industry: Telecommunications (Cellular/Wireless)

Summary: Sprint PCS is one of the largest U.S. wireless communications carriers.

S&P Opinion: Buy (★★★★★)

Recent Price • 22.60
52 Wk Range • 54-15.72

Yield • Nil
12-Mo. P/E • NM

Quantitative Evaluations

Outlook
(1 Lowest—5 Highest)
• **NA**

Fair Value
• **NA**

Risk
• **NA**

Earn./Div. Rank
• **NR**

Technical Eval.
• **Neutral** since 8/01

Rel. Strength Rank
(1 Lowest—99 Highest)
• **36**

Insider Activity
• **Unfavorable**

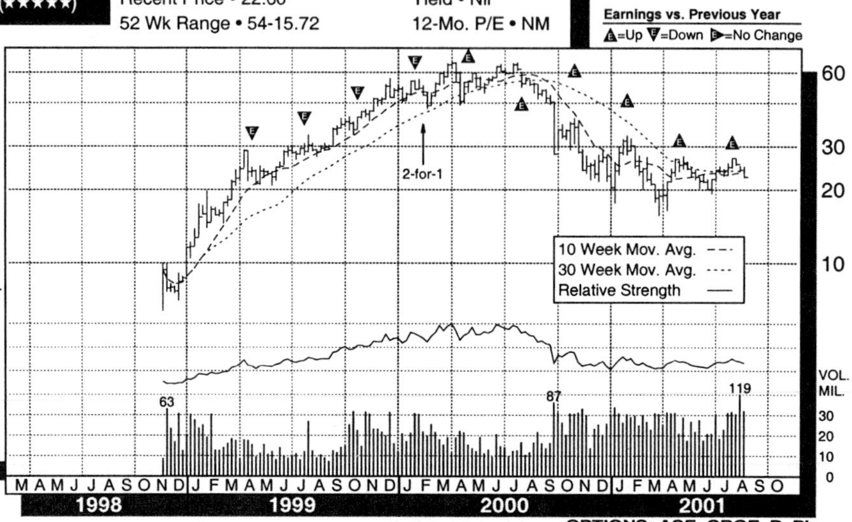

OPTIONS: ASE, CBOE, P, Ph

Overview - 18-JUL-01

We project PCS's 2001 revenue growth at over 45%, with the addition of more than 3.5 million direct customers, contributions from new wireless services, and increased usage per customer. Operating EBITDA should be approximately $2.1 billion, versus a negative $27 million, as a result of economies of scale, reduced levels of customer churn, and increased revenue per subscriber. Depreciation is expected to increase about 30%, and interest expense should rise appreciably, as a result of spending for capital investment and investment in affiliates (nearly $4 billion in 2001). Other losses should grow, reflecting full-year contributions from an equity interest in Pegaso PCS, a Mexican wireless carrier, and the absence of gains from the sale of assets to affiliates.

Valuation - 18-JUL-01

In mid-July, we upgraded the stock to buy, from accumulate. During the first quarter, PCS garnered over 20% of the net new subscriber additions for the eight leading wireless carriers (despite having under 11% of the total subscribers for the group). The company also enjoys one of the lowest customer attrition rates among the six national wireless carriers. In light of Sprint's monolithic CDMA network, we see the company rolling out 2.5G and 3G wireless services more quickly and cheaply than other carriers. If TDMA and GSM carriers are unable to acquire additional spectrum for their 3G migration toward WCDMA (a problem exacerbated by a recent court decision regarding NextWave licenses), PCS could ultimately enjoy a prolonged technological leadership status. Incorporating assumptions for declining new customer additions, our discounted cash flow analysis suggests that the stock would be fairly valued at more than 40% above current levels.

Key Stock Statistics

S&P EPS Est. 2001	-1.04	Tang. Bk. Value/Share	NM
P/E on S&P Est. 2001	NM	Beta	NA
S&P EPS Est. 2002	-0.17	Shareholders	64,000
Dividend Rate/Share	Nil	Market cap. (B)	$ 22.2
Shs. outstg. (M)	981.4	Inst. holdings	43%
Avg. daily vol. (M)	12.628		

Value of $10,000 invested 5 years ago: NA

Fiscal Year Ending Dec. 31

	2001	2000	1999	1998	1997	1996
Revenues (Million $)						
1Q	2,051	1,220	604.2	203.3	—	—
2Q	2,264	1,476	736.0	264.8	—	—
3Q	—	1,707	844.0	319.9	—	—
4Q	—	1,938	996.0	437.4	—	—
Yr.	—	6,341	3,180	1,225	258.0	—
Earnings Per Share ($)						
1Q	**-0.40**	**-0.54**	-0.70	**-0.48**	—	—
2Q	**-0.26**	**-0.48**	**-0.63**	**-0.49**	—	—
3Q	**E-0.18**	**-0.41**	**-0.66**	**-0.52**	—	—
4Q	**E-0.20**	**-0.53**	**-0.75**	-0.71	—	—
Yr.	**E-1.04**	**-1.95**	**-2.71**	-2.21	**-1.43**	—

Next earnings report expected: mid October

Dividend Data

No dividends have been paid.

A Division of The McGraw-Hill Companies

Sprint Corporation (PCS Group)

Business Summary - 18-JUL-01

Sprint PCS operates the only 100% digital wireless network in the U.S. using a single frequency and a single technology (K6). At the end of 2000, Sprint PCS had 9.85 million direct and resale customers, an increase of nearly 4.1 million from 1999. Sprint affiliates represented another 809,000 customers, an increase of 250,000 over 1999.

At the end of 2000, one million Sprint customers were accessing the Wireless Web. While only about half of these wireless web users subscribed to the company's personalized Internet services, the company is now the leading U.S. provider of wireless online services and expects to double its Wireless Web users in 2001. By 2005, Sprint anticipates that nearly all of its business customers and roughly 60% of consumer customers will be using its Wireless Web services. In early 2001, PCS forged an alliance with Palm Inc., the hand-held device maker, to provide wireless services to Palm users.

Sprint believes that its all digital, single spectrum system provides significant advantages. Competing systems that are burdened by a mix of analog and digital technologies and hampered by a mix of spectrum require duplicative operating systems, inefficient capital deployments and expensive additional spectrum capacity. The company believes its network efficiency permits transition to next-generation, high-speed data services at a cost that is a fraction of what competitors will have to spend. During the second half of 2001, Sprint plans to begin deployment of new 3G technology that will double its network's voice capacity and increase its online speeds 10-fold.

PCS markets its products through multiple distribution channels, including its own retail stores as well as other retail outlets. Equipment sales and subsequent service revenue generated by the company's largest third party retail chain accounted for 25% of total revenue in 2000, 28% in 1999 and 25% in 1998.

Given the high initial fixed investment needed to build a wireless system, Sprint's cost per subscriber has consistently declined as the firm has signed up additional subscribers. The company became EBITDA positive in the second quarter of 2000, and expects to achieve operating profitability in the second half of 2001.

Sprint PCS is a tracking share of Sprint Corp. After November 23, 2001, directors have the right to force an exchange of PCS shares for Sprint FON shares (thus consolidating the company). Until November 2002, redemption of PCS shares would require an approximate 10% premium to the market.

Per Share Data ($) (Year Ended Dec. 31)	2000	1999	1998	1997	1996	1995	1994	1993	1992	1991
Tangible Bk. Val.	13.95	NM	NM	NA	NA	NA	NA	NA	NA	NA
Cash Flow	-3.98	-1.04	-0.36	NA	NA	NA	NA	NA	NA	NA
Earnings	-1.95	-2.71	-2.21	-1.43	NA	NA	NA	NA	NA	NA
Dividends	Nil	Nil	Nil	Nil	NA	NA	NA	NA	NA	NA
Payout Ratio	Nil	Nil	Nil	Nil	NA	NA	NA	NA	NA	NA
Prices - High	66.93	56.81	11.68	NA	NA	NA	NA	NA	NA	NA
- Low	19.37	10.43	6.37	NA	NA	NA	NA	NA	NA	NA
P/E Ratio - High	NM	NM	NM	NA	NA	NA	NA	NA	NA	NA
- Low	NM	NM	NM	NA	NA	NA	NA	NA	NA	NA
Income Statement Analysis (Million $)										
Revs.	17,688	3,180	1,225	258	NA	NA	NA	NA	NA	NA
Oper. Inc.	-5,101	-1,714	-1,601	-1,082	NA	NA	NA	NA	NA	NA
Depr.	2,267	1,523	790	565	NA	NA	NA	NA	NA	NA
Int. Exp.	76.0	698	492	88.6	NA	NA	NA	NA	NA	NA
Pretax Inc.	-2,170	-3,889	-1,632	-1,865	NA	NA	NA	NA	NA	NA
Eff. Tax Rate	40%	NM	NM	NM	NA	NA	NA	NA	NA	NA
Net Inc.	-1,292	-2,481	-1,090	-1,171	NA	NA	NA	NA	NA	NA
Balance Sheet & Other Fin. Data (Million $)										
Cash	122	16.0	173	325	NA	NA	NA	NA	NA	NA
Curr. Assets	4,512	1,315	856	NA	NA	NA	NA	NA	NA	NA
Total Assets	23,649	17,924	15,138	NA	NA	NA	NA	NA	NA	NA
Curr. Liab.	5,004	2,578	2,674	NA	NA	NA	NA	NA	NA	NA
LT Debt	3,482	11,304	7,573	7,397	NA	NA	NA	NA	NA	NA
Common Eqty.	12,343	3,320	3,756	4,547	NA	NA	NA	NA	NA	NA
Total Cap.	17,101	15,206	12,342	11,944	NA	NA	NA	NA	NA	NA
Cap. Exp.	4,105	2,580	1,072	NA	NA	NA	NA	NA	NA	NA
Cash Flow	-3,552	-958	-300	NA	NA	NA	NA	NA	NA	NA
Curr. Ratio	0.9	0.5	0.3	NA	NA	NA	NA	NA	NA	NA
% LT Debt of Cap.	20.4	74.3	61.4	61.9	NA	NA	NA	NA	NA	NA
% Net Inc.of Revs.	7.3	NM	NM	NM	NA	NA	NA	NA	NA	NA
% Ret. on Assets	5.7	NM	NM	NA	NA	NA	NA	NA	NA	NA
% Ret. on Equity	11.2	NM	NM	NA	NA	NA	NA	NA	NA	NA

Data as orig. reptd.; bef. results of disc. opers. and/or spec. items. Per share data adj. for stk. divs. as of ex-div. date. Bold denotes diluted EPS (FASB 128). E-Estimated. NA-Not Available. NM-Not Meaningful. NR-Not Ranked.

Office—2330 Shawnee Mission Pkwy., Westwood, KS 66205 (P.O. Box 11315, Kansas City, MO 64112). **Tel**—(913) 624-3000. **Website**—www.sprintpcs.com **Chrmn & CEO**—W. T. Ersey. **Pres**—A. Sukawaty. **COO**—A. Kurtze. **CFO**—W. J. Gunter. **Investor Contact**—Kurt Fawkes (913-624-2268). **Dirs**—D. Ausley, W. L. Batts, W. T. Esrey, I. O. Hockaday Jr., R. T. LeMay, L. K. Lorimer, C. E. Rice, L. W. Smith, S. Turley. **Transfer Agents & Registrars**—UMB Bank, Kansas City, MO; Mellon Investor Services, NYC. **Incorporated**—in Kansas in 1938. **Empl**—84,100. **S&P Analyst:** Craig K. Shere, CFA

STANDARD &POOR'S
STOCK REPORTS

BCE Inc.

NYSE Symbol **BCE**

18-AUG-01

Industry: Telecommunications (Cellular/Wireless)

Summary: This diversified telecommunications holding company derives most of its revenues and earnings from Canadian telecommunications services.

S&P Opinion: Accumulate (★★★★)

Recent Price • 26.50 | 52 Wk Range • 29.56-21 | Yield • 2.9% | 12-Mo. P/E • NM

Quantitative Evaluations

Outlook (1 Lowest—5 Highest)
• **2−**

Fair Value
• **25.50**

Risk
• **Low**

Earn./Div. Rank
• **B+**

Technical Eval.
• **Bullish** since 6/01

Rel. Strength Rank (1 Lowest—99 Highest)
• **58**

Insider Activity
• **NA**

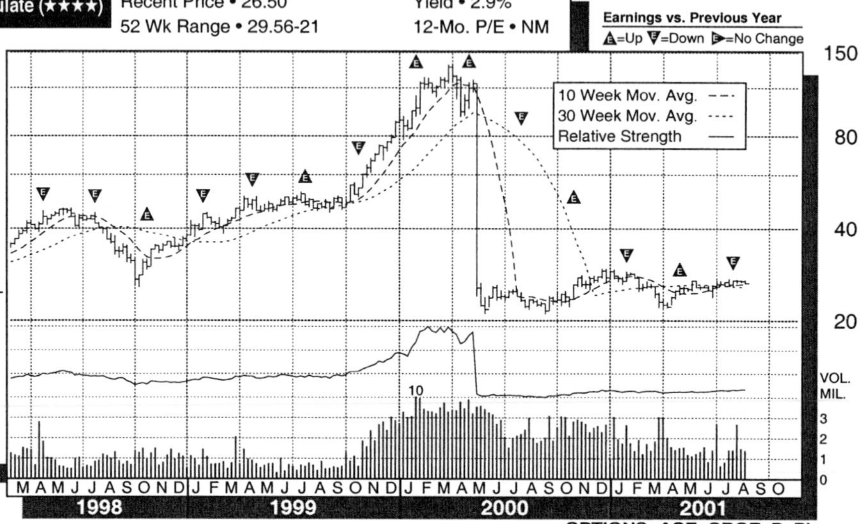

OPTIONS: ASE, CBOE, P, Ph

Overview - 04-MAY-01

Consolidated operating revenues are expected to climb 30% in 2001, benefiting from growth in connectivity segments and consolidation of various acquisitions. Operating margins will narrow from 36.9% to about 32.3%, due to costs of investments in growth businesses, and an increasing percentage of contributions from lower margin content, connectivity, and e-commerce units. Depreciation and amortization charges will rise nearly 29%. We anticipate an increase of nearly 13% in interest expense, but a significant reduction in taxes (due to a phased reduction of Canadian tax rates). In the first quarter of 2001, reported earnings included a one-time benefit of C$1.4 billion, stemming from gains on the sale of Nortel shares, less various restructuring and impairment charges. Excluding goodwill amortization and one-time items, cash earnings should decline over 7% in 2001.

Valuation - 04-MAY-01

In the month through early May, the shares rebounded nearly 15%, in line with the performance of the broader universe of telecommunications service providers. We are increasingly optimistic with regard to BCE's efforts to expand geographically (with wireless services in western Canada and broadband network services worldwide) and functionally (across connectivity, content and e-commerce). With growth investments beginning to mature, we look for strong double digit growth in cash earnings through 2004, well above other historical monopoly carriers. Taking a 20X multiple on projected 2004 core free cash flow less debt outstanding and discounting back, we arrive at a U.S.$ price target over 20% above current levels. We expect BCE to outperform the S&P 500 over the coming 12 months, and are maintaining our accumulate recommendation.

Key Stock Statistics

S&P EPS Est. 2001	1.63	Tang. Bk. Value/Share	NM
P/E on S&P Est. 2001	NA	Beta	1.31
S&P EPS Est. 2002	1.78	Shareholders	184,607
Dividend Rate/Share	1.20	Market cap. (B)	$ 21.5
Shs. outstg. (M)	810.0	Inst. holdings	17%
Avg. daily vol. (M)	0.346		

Value of $10,000 invested 5 years ago: NA

Fiscal Year Ending Dec. 31

	2001	2000	1999	1998	1997	1996
Revenues (Million Can. $)						
1Q	5,506	4,100	3,424	8,010	7,307	6,090
2Q	5,705	4,335	3,451	9,132	8,100	6,724
3Q	—	4,474	3,632	6,597	7,787	6,890
4Q	—	5,185	3,707	3,715	10,005	8,463
Yr.	—	18,094	14,214	27,454	33,191	28,167
Earnings Per Share (Can. $)						
1Q	0.83	0.16	-0.18	0.24	0.38	0.37
2Q	-0.04	0.16	7.23	0.39	0.43	0.33
3Q	—	1.10	0.19	5.70	0.67	0.36
4Q	—	-0.04	1.10	0.50	0.63	0.65
Yr.	—	1.26	8.35	7.07	2.11	1.70

Next earnings report expected: NA

Dividend Data (Dividends have been paid since 1881.)

Amount (Can. $)	Date Decl.	Ex-Div. Date	Stock of Record	Payment Date
0.300	Aug. 24	Sep. 13	Sep. 15	Oct. 15 '00
0.300	Nov. 24	Dec. 13	Dec. 15	Jan. 15 '01
0.300	Mar. 01	Mar. 13	Mar. 15	Apr. 15 '01
0.300	May. 24	Jun. 13	Jun. 15	Jul. 15 '01

Business Summary - 04-MAY-01

BCE is diversifying its revenue base from the more mature, slower growth telecommunications services offered by its majority-owned Bell Canada (BC) subsidiary (20% owned by SBC Communications). Through a series of investments and partnerships, the company has nurtured new growth initiatives in communications connectivity, content, and e-commerce.

BCE's connectivity initiatives are led by its BC and Teleglobe subsidiaries. In addition to local and long-distance services primarily provided in Quebec and Ontario, BC (which generated 78.5% of 2001 first quarter revenue) had nearly 800,000 ExpressVu satellite TV subscribers as of March 2001 (58% Canadian market share), 2.88 million Bell Mobility wireless phone subscribers, and 466,000 DSL subscribers. In February 2001, Bell Mobility won 20 spectrum licenses in eastern Canada (Ontario and Quebec) and western Canada (British Columbia and Alberta), for C$720 million ($1.40/pop/Mhz). The new spectrum expands the company's digital footprint to 95% in Ontario and Quebec, and will facilitate fourth quarter launches of 2.5G services in eastern Canada and initial wireless service in western Canada.

BCE also offers IP broadband network services in Canada and the U.S. through Nexxia (a Bell Canada subsidiary), and throughout the rest of the world through Teleglobe. Nexxia owns and operates a coast-to-coast network of 12 fibre strands. As of the 2001 first quarter, the unit had lit 16 light wavelengths on two strands to meet existing customer demand. Teleglobe is a BCE's global Nexxia equivalent, with operations in 29 countries. Teleglobe is in the process of completing a multi-billion dollar international Internet Backbone that will link virtually every major world market 200X as fast as its existing facilities. On November 1, 2000, BCE acquired the 77% stake in Teleglobe that it did not already own, for C$7.4 billion.

The company's content focus is spearheaded by 70%-owned Bell Globemedia. Formed in January 2001, Globemedia gathers under one umbrella Canada's leading print, broadcast and Internet brands.

BCE's commerce focus is spearheaded by BCE Emergis, a leading North American provider of business-to-business e-commerce solutions. At the end of 2000, 80% of all electronic payments in Canada went through Emergis solutions, and most Canadian insurance companies were using Emergis to handle health claims.

In May 2000, the company distributed a 35% interest in Nortel Networks to BCE shareholders. It retained an approximate 2% interest in Nortel at the end of 2000.

Per Share Data (U.S. $) (Year Ended Dec. 31)	2000	1999	1998	1997	1996	1995	1994	1993	1992	1991
Tangible Bk. Val.	NM	17.10	11.34	7.18	10.46	10.26	10.68	9.74	10.49	10.43
Cash Flow	3.13	8.85	8.16	5.76	3.87	4.39	4.37	3.12	4.63	4.86
Earnings	0.84	5.68	4.60	1.48	1.25	0.81	1.29	0.08	1.66	1.74
Dividends	0.58	0.92	0.88	0.95	0.99	0.99	0.98	0.99	1.07	1.12
Payout Ratio	69%	16%	19%	64%	80%	122%	76%	NM	65%	65%
Prices - High	137.50	98.31	46.62	34.00	25.37	17.50	19.37	19.00	21.62	21.31
- Low	21.00	37.31	25.62	22.00	17.18	14.50	15.81	16.00	16.06	16.68
P/E Ratio - High	NM	17	7	23	20	16	15	NM	13	12
- Low	NM	7	4	15	14	13	12	NM	10	10
Income Statement Analysis (Million U.S. $)										
Revs.	12,123	9,666	17,845	23,234	20,561	17,975	15,446	14,957	16,347	17,204
Oper. Inc.	4,557	3,871	4,096	5,616	5,197	4,399	3,928	3,925	5,126	5,747
Depr.	2,532	2,041	2,276	2,728	2,507	2,168	1,925	1,864	1,831	1,920
Int. Exp.	895	741	833	825	949	950	863	922	1,622	1,909
Pretax Inc.	1,803	4,366	3,903	2,441	2,027	1,455	1,633	100	2,055	2,167
Eff. Tax Rate	52%	15%	26%	52%	40%	41%	34%	NM	31%	32%
Net Inc.	594	3,712	2,989	990	841	571	840	120	1,093	1,150
Balance Sheet & Other Fin. Data (Million U.S. $)										
Cash	174	1,629	241	248	693	137	974	91.0	1,104	989
Curr. Assets	4,489	3,745	1,807	1,863	8,042	6,729	6,271	5,794	NA	NA
Total Assets	34,427	25,133	20,847	21,488	30,121	28,249	27,152	27,693	37,997	39,543
Curr. Liab.	7,714	3,769	3,771	3,887	6,743	6,214	5,920	6,768	12,448	12,127
LT Debt	9,409	5,970	6,019	6,204	8,623	8,672	8,150	7,883	10,191	11,365
Common Eqty.	10,828	11,011	7,765	8,003	7,681	7,328	7,216	7,313	8,713	9,281
Total Cap.	21,587	20,342	16,186	18,920	22,329	19,895	20,520	20,276	24,946	26,943
Cap. Exp.	3,237	2,453	NA	2,789	2,283	2,047	2,004	2,422	2,924	2,829
Cash Flow	3,126	5,690	5,205	3,668	3,293	2,739	2,699	1,913	2,849	2,988
Curr. Ratio	0.6	1.0	0.5	0.5	1.2	1.1	1.1	0.9	NA	NA
% LT Debt of Cap.	43.5	29.3	37.2	32.8	38.6	43.6	39.7	38.9	40.9	42.2
% Net Inc.of Revs.	4.8	4.3	16.7	NA	4.1	3.2	5.4	0.8	6.7	6.7
% Ret. on Assets	1.9	15.8	12.7	3.9	2.9	2.1	3.1	0.4	2.8	3.0
% Ret. on Equity	5.4	38.1	44.9	14.4	10.5	7.9	10.6	0.6	11.4	11.8

Data as orig reptd.; bef. results of disc opers/spec. items. Per share data adj. for stk. divs. Bold denotes diluted EPS (FASB 128)-prior periods restated. E-Estimated. NA-Not Available. NM-Not Meaningful. NR-Not Ranked.

Office—1000, rue de La Gauchetiere Ouest, Bureau 3700, Montreal, QC, Canada H3B 4Y7. **Tel**—(888) 932-6666. **Fax**—(514) 786-3964. **Website**—http://www.bce.ca **Chrmn & CEO**—J. C. Monty. **Pres**—M. J.Sabla. **CFO**—S. Vanaselja. **VP & Secy**—M. J. Ryan. **Investor Relations**—Sophie Argiriou (514-786-3845). **Dirs**—R. J. Currie, D. S. Kaufman, T. E. Kierans, B. M. Levitt, J. Maxwell, J. H. McArthur, J. C. Monty, J. E. Newall, G. Saint-Pierre, P. M. Tellier, V. L. Young. **Transfer Agents & Registrars**—Montreal Trust Co., Montreal; Bank of Montreal Trust Co., NYC; R-M Trust Co., London (U.K.). **Incorporated**—in Canada in 1880. **Empl**— 56,608. **S&P Analyst:** Craig K. Shere, CFA

STANDARD & POOR'S STOCK REPORTS

BellSouth Corp.

NYSE Symbol **BLS**

In S&P 500

18-AUG-01 **Industry:** Telephone

Summary: BLS, one of the largest U.S. telephone holding companies, provides local service in nine southeastern states, and also owns significant wireless and international assets.

S&P Opinion: Accumulate (★★★★) Recent Price • 38.92 Yield • 2.0%
52 Wk Range • 50.62-35.50 12-Mo. P/E • 18.7

Quantitative Evaluations

Outlook (1 Lowest—5 Highest) • **2**

Fair Value • **38.10**

Risk • **Low**

Earn./Div. Rank • **A-**

Technical Eval. • **Neutral** since 8/01

Rel. Strength Rank (1 Lowest—99 Highest) • **42**

Insider Activity • **Neutral**

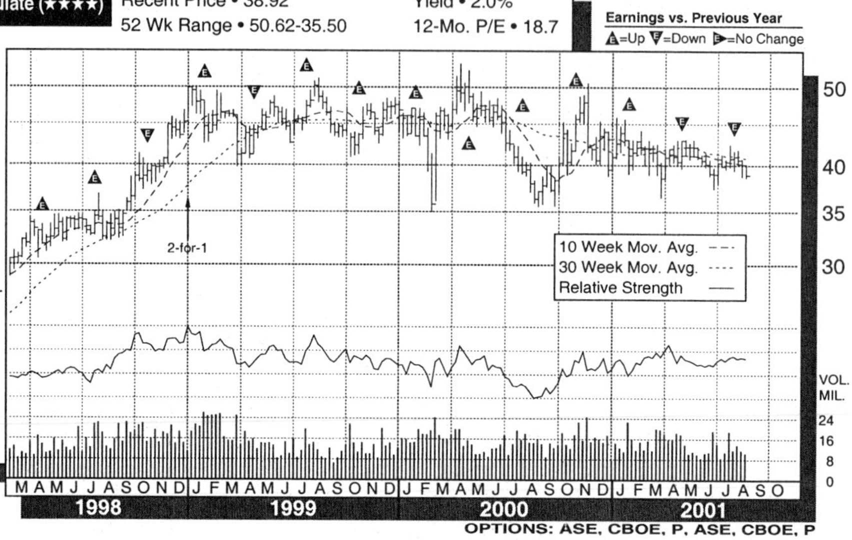

OPTIONS: ASE, CBOE, P, ASE, CBOE, P

Overview - 24-JUL-01

We look for 2001 revenues (including BLS's 40% interest in Cingular Wireless) to increase about 9%, with strong growth in wireless and international operations offsetting low single digit growth in domestic wireline communications. Margins should narrow, due to losses associated with investments in new DSL connections, Colombian wireless properties (acquired in July 2000), and a new branding campaign for Cingular. Profitability will also be hurt as foreign currency losses increase to about $0.08 a share, from $0.03 in 2000. Depreciation and amortization charges should rise over 10%, and interest expense should increase over 15%. Excluding foreign exchange losses and $0.03 a share in net positive one-time items in 2000, we look for operating EPS to rise over 5%.

Valuation - 24-JUL-01

In the six months through late July, the shares were flat, versus a nearly 10% decline in S&P's Local Telephone Index. The stock remains in a trading range that has existed since 1998; we believe it has failed to keep up with underlying developments. Near-term issues such as foreign currency losses, dilution from growth in new DSL lines, and a weak U.S. economy have kept the shares depressed. However, over the next year, several important catalysts (potential IPOs of Cingular Wireless and BLS's Latin American wireless investments, and approval to launch long-distance service throughout BLS's local service territory) could propel the stock to new highs. At recent levels, BLS was trading at under 16X our forward EPS estimates, near the low end of the three-year trading range. Moreover, assuming a long-term growth rate in excess of 9%, the PEG (P/E to growth rate) ratio was at about a 25% discount to the broader market. We recommend accumulating the shares.

Key Stock Statistics

S&P EPS Est. 2001	2.27	Tang. Bk. Value/Share	7.25
P/E on S&P Est. 2001	17.1	Beta	0.47
S&P EPS Est. 2002	2.57	Shareholders	891,893
Dividend Rate/Share	0.76	Market cap. (B)	$ 73.0
Shs. outstg. (M)	1875.3	Inst. holdings	46%
Avg. daily vol. (M)	2.330		

Value of $10,000 invested 5 years ago: $ 22,373

Fiscal Year Ending Dec. 31

	2001	2000	1999	1998	1997	1996
Revenues (Million $)						
1Q	5,919	6,487	5,973	5,426	4,845	4,541
2Q	5,985	6,752	6,148	5,664	4,923	4,620
3Q	—	6,903	6,422	5,865	5,193	4,928
4Q	—	6,160	6,681	6,168	5,600	5,050
Yr.	—	26,151	25,224	23,123	20,561	19,040
Earnings Per Share ($)						
1Q	0.47	0.53	0.32	0.45	0.35	0.48
2Q	0.47	0.56	0.51	0.41	0.33	0.32
3Q	E0.63	0.55	0.53	0.41	0.59	0.32
4Q	E0.65	0.59	0.55	0.51	0.37	0.32
Yr.	E2.27	2.23	1.80	1.78	1.64	1.44

Next earnings report expected: mid October

Dividend Data (Dividends have been paid since 1984.)

Amount ($)	Date Decl.	Ex-Div. Date	Stock of Record	Payment Date
0.190	Sep. 25	Oct. 10	Oct. 12	Nov. 01 '00
0.190	Nov. 27	Jan. 09	Jan. 11	Feb. 01 '01
0.190	Feb. 26	Apr. 10	Apr. 12	May. 01 '01
0.190	Jun. 25	Jul. 10	Jul. 12	Aug. 01 '01

BellSouth Corporation

Business Summary - 24-JUL-01

BellSouth is the third largest independent Regional Bell Operating Company (behind Verizon and SBC Communications) in terms of local phone lines and equity market capitalization. The company is the predominant telephone service provider in the Southeast, and owns 40% of the second largest U.S. wireless service provider, Cingular Wireless. BLS's business focuses on four general areas: Wireline Communications, Domestic Wireless, International, and Advertising and Publishing.

The wireline communications segment (62% of normalized 2000 revenue) includes local services, network access, long-distance, Internet access, and Digital Subscriber Lines (DSL). BLS ended 2000 with 215,000 DSL customers (expected to grow to 600,000 by the end of 2001). In February 2001, the company said it would exit the payphone business, with plans to divest 143,000 public payphones by the end of 2002. As of mid-2001, BLS had filed long-distance requests with state regulators in each of its local service territories except for Tennessee (a filing was expected in July). By September 2001, state regulators are expected to submit decisions in Louisiana, Alabama, Kentucky, Mississippi and South Carolina (to be followed by FCC filings).

Cingular Wireless (17% of 2000 normalized revenue) began operations in October 2000, through the merger of wireless operations of SBC and BLS. The joint venture launched a nationwide advertising campaign in January 2001, to reinforce brand awareness for the newly created brand. Cingular added 854,000 net subscribers in the first quarter of 2001, bringing its total customer base to 20,535,000. Also during the quarter, Cingular launched 2.5G GPRS-based services in its GSM markets, and the company's 85%-owned Salmon PCS division won a number of Spectrum rights in the FCC's 1,900 MHz auction. In May 2001, SBC said a much anticipated Cingular IPO was unlikely to come sooner than the end of the 2001, due to weak market conditions.

BLS's international operations (10%) consist primarily of wireless service providers operating in 15 countries in Latin America, Asia and Europe. The company has a stated goal of becoming the leading wireless communications provider in Latin America (where its investments represent a controlling interest in most businesses). In December 2000, shareholders approved a plan for BLS to issue separate tracking shares for its Latin American interests. However, weak markets have resulted in a postponement of the IPO.

The advertising and publishing unit (10%) publishes, prints and sells advertising in classified telephone directories in both paper and electronic formats. In 2000, the company printed more than 67 million white page, yellow page, and specialty directories.

Per Share Data ($) (Year Ended Dec. 31)	2000	1999	1998	1997	1996	1995	1994	1993	1992	1991
Tangible Bk. Val.	6.81	5.86	6.79	6.67	5.97	5.18	6.48	6.09	6.05	5.87
Cash Flow	4.84	4.24	3.97	3.64	3.31	2.52	2.70	2.08	2.39	2.31
Earnings	2.23	1.80	1.78	1.65	1.44	0.79	1.09	0.52	0.84	0.78
Dividends	0.76	0.76	0.72	0.72	0.72	0.70	0.69	0.69	0.69	0.69
Payout Ratio	34%	42%	40%	44%	50%	89%	63%	133%	82%	88%
Prices - High	53.50	51.31	50.00	29.06	22.93	21.93	15.87	15.96	13.87	13.75
- Low	34.93	39.75	27.06	19.06	17.62	13.40	12.62	12.59	10.84	11.34
P/E Ratio - High	24	29	28	18	16	28	15	31	16	18
- Low	16	22	15	12	12	17	12	24	13	15
Income Statement Analysis (Million $)										
Revs.	26,151	24,224	23,123	20,561	19,040	17,886	16,845	15,880	15,202	14,446
Depr.	4,935	4,671	4,357	3,964	3,719	3,455	3,206	3,104	3,100	3,016
Maint.	NA	NA	NA	NA	NA	NA	NA	NA	4,662	2,366
Constr. Credits	NA	NA	NA	NA	NA	NA	NA	NA	15.3	18.1
Eff. Tax Rate	36%	37%	39%	39%	38%	40%	37%	36%	36%	33%
Net Inc.	4,220	3,448	3,527	3,270	2,863	1,564	2,160	1,034	1,658	1,507
Balance Sheet & Other Fin. Data (Million $)										
Gross Prop.	24,157	61,009	57,974	53,828	50,059	46,869	44,199	41,975	39,801	38,403
Net Prop.	24,157	24,631	23,940	22,861	21,825	21,092	25,162	24,856	24,273	24,059
Cap. Exp.	6,995	6,200	5,212	4,858	4,455	4,203	3,600	3,486	3,189	3,102
Total Cap.	32,955	26,759	17,862	25,324	21,365	19,749	25,893	24,856	25,478	25,340
Fxd. Chgs. Cov.	5.9	6.5	7.4	7.1	6.8	6.2	6.1	3.3	4.4	3.8
Capitalization:										
LT Debt	12,463	9,113	8,715	7,348	8,116	7,924	7,435	7,381	7,360	7,745
Pfd.	Nil	Nil	Nil	Nil	Nil	Nil	Nil	Nil	Nil	Nil
Common	16,912	14,815	17,862	15,740	13,249	11,825	14,367	13,494	13,799	13,105
% Return On Revs.	16.1	14.2	15.3	15.9	15.0	8.7	12.8	6.5	10.9	10.4
% Return On Invest. Capital	20.7	17.7	26.0	14.0	12.2	19.1	11.1	6.8	9.5	9.1
% Return On Com. Equity	26.6	22.3	21.0	22.2	22.8	11.9	15.4	6.3	11.9	11.3
% Earn. on Net Prop.	50.9	47.1	43.8	41.8	39.6	33.9	11.3	7.0	9.2	8.6
% LT Debt of Cap.	42.4	38.1	29.8	31.8	37.9	40.1	34.1	35.4	34.8	37.1
Capital. % Pfd.	Nil	Nil	Nil	Nil	Nil	Nil	Nil	Nil	Nil	Nil
Capital. % Common	57.6	61.9	70.2	68.2	66.7	59.9	65.9	64.6	65.2	62.9

Data as orig reptd.; bef. results of disc opers/spec. items. Per share data adj. for stk. divs. Bold denotes diluted EPS (FASB 128)-prior periods restated. E-Estimated. NA-Not Available. NM-Not Meaningful. NR-Not Ranked.

Office—1155 Peachtree St., N.E., Atlanta, GA 30309-3610. **Tel**—(404) 249-2000. **Website**—http://www.bellsouth.com **Chrmn, Pres & CEO**—F. D. Ackerman. **EVP & CFO**—R. M. Dykes. **SVP & Secy**—C. E. Swearingen. **Investor Contact**—Nancy Humphries (800-241-3419). **Dirs**—F. D. Ackerman, R. V. Anderson, J. H. Blanchard, J. H. Brown, A. M. Codina, K. F. Feldstein, J. P. Kelly, J. M. Maglichotetti, J. G. Medlin Jr., L. F. Mullin, E. F. Murphy, R. B. Smith, W. S. Stavropoulos. **Transfer Agent & Registrar**—Mellon Investor Services, Ridgefield Park, NJ. **Incorporated**—in Georgia in 1983. **Empl**— 103,900. **S&P Analyst:** Craig K. Shere, CFA

STANDARD
&POOR'S
STOCK REPORTS

Vodafone Group

NYSE Symbol **VOD**

20-AUG-01

Industry:
Telecommunications (Cellular/Wireless)

Summary: This company is the leading provider of international wireless telecommunications services.

S&P Opinion: Accumulate (★★★★)

Recent Price • 18.25
52 Wk Range • 44.25-17.97
Yield • 1.1%
12-Mo. P/E • 65.2

Quantitative Evaluations

Outlook
(1 Lowest—5 Highest)
• 5

Fair Value
• 30.70

Risk
• Low

Earn./Div. Rank
• NR

Technical Eval.
• Bearish since 5/01

Rel. Strength Rank
(1 Lowest—99 Highest)
• 16

Insider Activity
• NA

OPTIONS: ASE, CBOE, P, Ph

Overview - 20-AUG-01

In FY 02 (Mar.), we look for VOD's proportionate interest in total group revenues to rise over 40%, fueled by customer growth, expanded service offerings, and acquisitions. Gross margins should widen, with operating synergies from the company's efforts to integrate acquisition efforts among a number of worldwide wireless telephone carriers in which it holds interests. Total interest expense should rise modestly, as debt financing of acquisitions and spectrum licenses and increased proportionate interests in debt of certain wireless divisions offset FY 01 debt reductions relating to the sale of non-strategic Mannesmann divisions. Estimates and comparisons exclude goodwill amortization (9.58 billion pounds in FY 01), as well as restructuring charges of 137 million pounds in FY 01. U.S. dollar estimates are based on a conversion rate of $1.445/British pound. Each ADR is equivalent to 10 ordinary shares.

Valuation - 20-AUG-01

Over the three months ended mid-August, VOD shares declined approximately 17%, on concerns of economic weakness and delays in availability of handsets compatible with new 3G services. Vodafone has one of the highest credit ratings among the world's pure play wireless carriers. We see VOD's co-branding, integrated roaming and centralized purchasing efforts exploiting synergies among its global wireless properties. As cash strapped competitors (such as BT and AT&T) continue to stumble with uncoordinated telecom investments, we see Vodafone in a position to make very attractive acquisitions. Excluding the cost of wireless licenses, our discounted free cash flow model suggests a current fair value of approximately $30 per share. Expecting shares to outperform the S&P 500 in the coming 12 months, we maintaining our accumulate recommendation.

Key Stock Statistics

S&P EPS Est. 2001	0.52	Tang. Bk. Value/Share	30.75
P/E on S&P Est. 2001	35.1	Beta	0.84
S&P EPS Est. 2002	0.51	Shareholders	43,875
Dividend Rate/Share	0.20	Market cap. (B)	$111.9
Shs. outstg. (M)	61334.0	Inst. holdings	1%
Avg. daily vol. (M)	5.861		

Value of $10,000 invested 5 years ago: $ 25,565

Fiscal Year Ending Mar. 31

	2000	1999	1998	1997	1996	1995
Revenues (Million U.S. $)						
1Q	—	—	—	—	—	—
2Q	—	—	—	1,211	1,046	880.3
3Q	—	—	—	—	—	—
4Q	—	—	—	—	—	—
Yr.	12,518	5,443	4,052	2,746	2,201	1,810
Earnings Per ADR (U.S. $)						
1Q	—	—	—	—	—	—
2Q	—	—	—	0.18	0.14	0.12
3Q	—	—	—	—	—	—
4Q	—	—	—	—	—	—
Yr.	**0.28**	**0.68**	**0.45**	**0.39**	0.32	0.24

Next earnings report expected: NA

Dividend Data (Dividends have been paid since 1989.)

Amount (U.S. $)	Date Decl.	Ex-Div. Date	Stock of Record	Payment Date
0.102	—	Jun. 07	Jun. 09	Aug. 21 '00
0.099	—	Nov. 21	Nov. 24	Feb. 19 '01
0.102	—	Jun. 06	Jun. 08	Aug. 20 '01

A Division of The McGraw-Hill Companies

Vodafone Group Plc

Business Summary - 20-AUG-01

Vodafone Group is a leading global wireless phone carrier, with interests in wireless networks boasting 188 million registered customers as of March 2001 (Vodafone's proportionate interests represented 83 million registered customers). In FY 02 (Mar.), the company is focusing on integrating acquired businesses, introducing new data and voice services and increasing cash flow.

Vodafone has maintained an unusually strong balance sheet for the wireless industry by using its stock (rather than cash) to fund acquisitions. In April 2000, VOD received final regulatory approval for its acquisition of German conglomerate Mannesmann for approximately 2.7 billion Vodafone shares. The acquisition gave VOD control of the largest German wireless operator (now called D2 Vodafone) and the second largest Italian carrier (Omnitel Vodafone). The company also used share and property exchanges to acquire a 100% interest in Ireland's Eircell in May 2001, a 25% interest in Switzerland's Swisscom in March 2001, an additional 52% interest in Spain's Airtel Movil in December 2000 and a 45% interest in America's Verizon Wireless in July 2000. Following the acquisition of Mannesman, VOD divested Mannesman's industrial and overlapping U.K. wireless operations (Orange) for cash consideration of over 26 billion pounds.

During FY 01, Vodafone also acquired wireless interests in Mexico, Kenya, China and Albania. Exploiting its stronger financial position, Vodafone acquired a controlling interest in J-Phone Communications of Japan in June 2001 through cash acquisitions of interests previously held by British Telecom, AT&T and two Japanese railway companies. The company also made cash investments in a number of global 3G spectrum licenses.

VOD is integrating its various wireless holdings through a co-branding campaign introducing the Vodafone brand to local markets, simplification of cross boarder roaming, streamlining global purchasing operations and concurrent launches of new wireless technologies. With many of its wireless markets near saturation penetration levels, VOD is now focused on reducing costs and increasing revenue per subscriber unit (ARPU). In order to drive ARPU higher, the company is rolling out new services in 2001 (including unified and instant messaging, mobile commerce, voice navigation, and other services). Vodafone is also expanding the applications offered through its Vizzavi wireless Internet portal (jointly owned with Vivendi Universal).

Per ADR Data (U.S. $) (Year Ended Mar. 31)	**2000**	**1999**	**1998**	**1997**	**1996**	**1995**	**1994**	**1993**	**1992**	**1991**
Tangible Bk. Val.	30.75	0.03	0.02	0.95	1.02	0.79	0.62	0.51	0.52	0.49
Cash Flow	1.11	0.06	0.42	0.53	0.44	0.34	0.32	0.33	0.28	NA
Earnings	0.28	0.68	0.45	0.37	0.32	0.24	0.24	0.25	0.21	0.21
Dividends	0.21	0.19	0.19	0.17	0.13	0.11	0.09	0.07	0.08	0.14
Payout Ratio	75%	42%	43%	44%	41%	44%	36%	30%	38%	66%
Cal. Yrs.	1999	1998	1997	1996	1995	1994	1993	1992	1991	1990
Prices - High	NA	33.40	15.05	8.70	9.00	7.05	6.07	4.81	4.90	4.47
- Low	NA	13.66	8.02	6.42	5.45	4.87	3.62	3.55	3.23	2.84
P/E Ratio - High	NA	73	34	23	29	29	25	19	23	21
- Low	NA	30	18	17	18	20	15	14	15	14
Income Statement Analysis (Million £)										
($) Per Pound	1.59	1.65	1.64	1.56	1.56	1.56	1.50	1.69	1.74	1.86
Revs.	7,873	3,360	2,471	1,749	1,402	1,153	851	664	585	537
Oper. Inc.	2,413	1,144	873	650	566	446	418	379	334	296
Depr.	1,432	297	238	154	117	92.3	79.9	68.9	60.8	50.7
Int. Exp.	456	109	65.8	36.6	16.6	2.9	0.7	1.3	1.4	1.0
Pretax Inc.	1,349	935	650	539	475	371	363	322	272	245
Eff. Tax Rate	51%	27%	31%	32%	35%	36%	33%	31%	32%	31%
Net Inc.	487	637	419	364	310	237	245	222	184	169
Balance Sheet & Other Fin. Data (Million £)										
($) Per Pound	1.59	1.62	1.66	1.53	1.53	1.60	1.49	1.46	1.74	1.75
Cash	159	6.1	15.3	41.8	13.0	16.0	127	157	80.0	38.6
Curr. Assets	2,517	792	591	495	341	308	334	306	219	179
Total Assets	153,368	3,644	2,502	2,422	1,763	1,410	1,054	869	657	616
Curr. Liab.	4,441	1,530	1,433	1,013	583	443	320	237	200	196
LT Debt	6,038	1,700	676	573	148	140	2.0	4.0	4.0	1.0
Common Eqty.	140,833	815	283	770	1,022	817	698	596	452	418
Total Cap.	148,398	2,635	1,061	1,402	1,172	961	701	601	456	419
Cap. Exp.	1,848	688	510	350	296	187	155	106	56.0	146
Cash Flow	1,919	934	657	518	427	330	325	291	245	NA
Curr. Ratio	0.6	0.5	0.4	0.5	0.6	0.7	1.0	1.3	1.1	0.9
% LT Debt of Cap.	4.1	64.5	63.7	40.9	12.6	14.6	0.3	0.6	0.9	0.1
% Net Inc.of Revs.	6.2	18.9	16.9	20.8	22.1	20.6	28.8	33.4	31.5	31.4
% Ret. on Assets	0.6	20.7	17.0	17.4	19.5	19.2	25.5	29.1	28.9	31.5
% Ret. on Equity	0.7	116.1	79.6	40.6	33.7	31.3	37.9	42.3	42.3	49.0

Data as orig. reptd.; bef. results of disc. opers. and/or spec. items. Per share data adj. for stk. divs. as of ex-div. date. Data for 2Q represents six mos. Bold denotes diluted EPS (FASB 128). E-Estimated. NA-Not Available. NM-Not Meaningful. NR-Not Ranked.

Office—The Courtyard, 2-4 London Rd, Newbury, Berkshire RG14 1JX, England. **Tel**—01635-33251. **Website**—http://www.vodafone-airtouch-plc.com **Chrmn**—Lord MacLaurin. **CEO**—C. Gent. **Secy**—S. R. Scott. **Financial Director & Investor Contact**—Ken J. Hydon. **Dirs**—J. Ackermann, P. R. Bamford, M. Boskin, A. Broers, T. Geitner, C. Gent, P. Hazen, J. M. Horn-Smith, P. Hughes, K. J. Hydon, Lord MacLaurin, A. Sarin, Sir D. Scholey, J. Schrempp, H. Schulte-Noelle. **Depositary for ADRs**—Bank of New York, NYC. **Incorporated**—in England in 1984. **Empl**— 56,800. **S&P Analyst:** Craig K. Shere, CFA

Part Ten

Utilities Stocks

STANDARD &POOR'S
STOCK REPORTS

Constellation Energy Group

NYSE Symbol **CEG**

In S&P 500

18-AUG-01

Industry: Electric Companies

Summary: This Maryand-based energy holding company intends to separate its operations into two publicly traded companies.

S&P Opinion: Buy (★★★★★)

Recent Price • 30.04
52 Wk Range • 52.06-29
Yield • 1.6%
12-Mo. P/E • 11.2

Quantitative Evaluations

Outlook
(1 Lowest—5 Highest)
• **3−**

Fair Value
• **31.30**

Risk
• **Low**

Earn./Div. Rank
• **A-**

Technical Eval.
• **Bearish** since 7/01

Rel. Strength Rank
(1 Lowest—99 Highest)
• **16**

Insider Activity
• **Unfavorable**

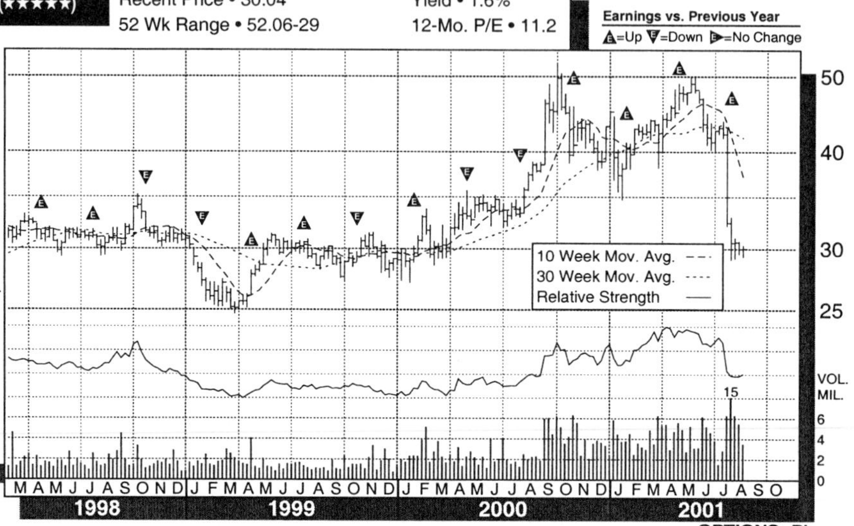

OPTIONS: Ph

Overview - 27-JUL-01

The planned separation of CEG into two publicly traded stand-alone companies is expected to take place by the end of 2001. The company will be renamed BGE Corp., and will then spin off the merchant energy business, which will be named Constellation Energy Group. BGE Corp. will then consist of the BGE utility and the units involved in retail energy services. Excluding the planned separation, EPS should grow around 9% in 2001 from 2000's operating EPS of $2.43. We had expected 25% growth, but our estimate was reduced by $0.20 due to the delay in closing the acquisition of the two Nine Mile Point nuclear units, and by another $0.15 due to the impact of the mild weather on its merchant energy business. Customer choice has been fully implemented in Maryland, with rate reductions retroactive to July 1, 2000. This was the result of the state's November 1999 regulatory order compelling Baltimore Gas & Electric to reduce residential rates by 6.5% and then freeze these rates through July 2006, and to freeze commercial and industrial rates through July 2004.

Valuation - 27-JUL-01

We are maintaining our buy recommendation for the stock. The shares have dropped more than 20% since CEG announced its reduced EPS expectations for 2001. We believe the stock has been oversold and that the shares, trading at about 9 times our proforma 2002 EPS estimate of $3.30, are significantly undervalued. With the pending formation of two publicly traded companies, shareholders will be provided with distinctly valued investments. CEG has reduced its annual dividend 71%, to $0.48, which is what BGE Corp. expects to pay after the separation. The new Constellation Energy Group will not pay a dividend, so as to maintain the financial resources needed for the continuing development and expansion of its merchant energy operations.

Key Stock Statistics

S&P EPS Est. 2001	2.65	Tang. Bk. Value/Share	20.88
P/E on S&P Est. 2001	11.3	Beta	0.11
S&P EPS Est. 2002	3.30	Shareholders	58,650
Dividend Rate/Share	0.48	Market cap. (B)	$ 4.9
Shs. outstg. (M)	163.7	Inst. holdings	55%
Avg. daily vol. (M)	1.664		

Value of $10,000 invested 5 years ago: $ 14,728

Fiscal Year Ending Dec. 31

	2001	2000	1999	1998	1997	1996
Revenues (Million $)						
1Q	1,165	992.2	932.3	866.1	887.7	861.3
2Q	822.8	868.0	820.0	767.6	746.4	731.7
3Q	—	981.6	970.5	934.0	860.8	826.0
4Q	—	1,036	1,064	790.4	812.6	734.3
Yr.	—	3,879	3,785	3,358	3,308	3,153
Earnings Per Share ($)						
1Q	**0.68**	**0.48**	**0.55**	**0.50**	0.43	0.62
2Q	**0.46**	**0.26**	**0.45**	**0.39**	0.05	0.36
3Q	**E1.03**	**0.98**	**0.91**	**1.08**	1.11	0.93
4Q	**E0.48**	**0.57**	**0.26**	**0.09**	**0.12**	-0.06
Yr.	**E2.65**	**2.30**	**2.18**	**2.06**	**1.72**	**1.85**

Next earnings report expected: mid October

Dividend Data (Dividends have been paid since 1910.)

Amount ($)	Date Decl.	Ex-Div. Date	Stock of Record	Payment Date
0.420	Oct. 02	Dec. 07	Dec. 11	Jan. 02 '01
0.120	Feb. 16	Mar. 08	Mar. 12	Apr. 02 '01
0.120	May. 18	Jun. 07	Jun. 11	Jul. 02 '01
0.120	Jul. 20	Sep. 06	Sep. 10	Oct. 01 '01

Constellation Energy Group, Inc.

Business Summary - 27-JUL-01

On October 23, 2000, Constellation Energy Group announced that it would separate its businesses into two stand-alone publicly traded companies. The merchant energy business, which includes wholesale generation and power marketing, will maintain the name Constellation Energy Group. The retail services business, which includes BGE (formerly Baltimore Gas & Electric), will be named BGE Corp. Shareholders will receive one share of each company's stock for each CEG share. The separation of the companies is expected to be completed during the second half of 2001.

BGE is a utility that serves more than 1.1 million electric customers and nearly 600,000 gas customers in central Maryland. The local economy includes service businesses, heavy industry, and the Port of Baltimore. In 2000, electricity accounted for 55.0% of revenues (59.6% in 1999); gas, 15.6% (12.6%); and nonregulated businesses, 29.4% (27.8%).

Electric revenues by customer class in 2000 were: commercial, 45.1% (44.3% in 1999); residential, 45.0% (46.0%); and industrial, 9.9% (9.6%).

In April 1999, Maryland enacted legislation providing all commercial and industrial customers with a choice of power supplier as of January 1, 2000. In November 1999, the Maryland Public Service Commission issued an order giving all customers the option to choose as of July 1, 2000. Under the order, BGE would reduce residential base rates by about 6.5% (about $54 million a year) from July 1, 2000, through July 1, 2006; transfer its generation assets to non-regulated subsidiaries; and be allowed to recover $528 million of stranded investments and restructuring costs.

On July 1, 2000 BGE transferred all of its non-nuclear generation assets to the Constellation Power Source Generation subsidiary of Constellation Power Source Holdings, whose other susidiaries include Constellation Power Source, which is involved in wholesale power marketing and trading; and Constellation Power, which develops, owns and operates domestic and international power projects. BGE also transferred its two Calvert Cliffs nuclear units to Constellation Nuclear, which, in December 2000, agreed to buy, for $815 million, the Nine Mile Point nuclear Unit 1 (a 100% interest) and Unit 2 (82%), which are located in upstate New York.

The nonregulated units of the retail services business include Constellation Energy Source, which provides businesses with customized energy products and services; BGE Home Products and Services, which sells appliances and home improvement services; Comfort Link, which provides cooling services for commercial customers; Constellation Investments, a financial business; and Constellation Real Estate Group, which manages CEG's real estate and its senior-living facilities.

Per Share Data ($) (Year Ended Dec. 31)	2000	1999	1998	1997	1996	1995	1994	1993	1992	1991
Tangible Bk. Val.	20.88	19.95	19.98	19.44	19.25	18.96	18.42	17.82	17.57	16.94
Earnings	2.30	2.18	2.06	1.72	1.85	2.02	1.93	1.85	1.63	1.52
Dividends	1.68	1.68	1.66	1.63	1.59	1.55	1.51	1.47	1.43	1.40
Payout Ratio	73%	77%	81%	95%	86%	77%	78%	79%	88%	92%
Prices - High	52.06	31.50	35.25	34.31	29.50	29.00	25.50	27.50	24.37	22.87
- Low	27.06	24.68	29.25	24.75	25.00	22.00	20.50	22.37	19.75	17.12
P/E Ratio - High	23	14	17	20	16	14	13	15	15	15
- Low	12	11	14	14	14	11	11	12	12	11
Income Statement Analysis (Million $)										
Revs.	3,879	3,787	3,358	3,308	3,153	2,935	2,783	2,669	2,491	2,459
Depr.	470	450	377	343	330	317	296	237	223	200
Maint.	NA	186	178	179	174	168	165	182	173	174
Fxd. Chgs. Cov.	3.1	3.0	2.8	2.9	2.6	2.6	2.6	2.8	2.4	2.1
Constr. Credits	NA	NA	9.7	5.3	10.0	21.8	33.5	22.5	22.1	37.5
Eff. Tax Rate	40%	36%	35%	36%	35%	33%	32%	31%	28%	27%
Net Inc.	345	326	328	283	311	338	324	310	264	234
Balance Sheet & Other Fin. Data (Million $)										
Gross Prop.	10,442	8,989	8,744	8,495	8,196	7,979	7,722	7,359	6,947	6,577
Cap. Exp.	1,079	436	339	373	361	458	483	478	389	456
Net Prop.	6,644	5,523	5,657	5,652	5,582	5,498	5,417	5,197	4,966	4,774
Capitalization:										
LT Debt	3,349	2,765	3,128	2,989	2,759	2,598	2,585	2,823	2,377	2,390
% LT Debt	52	48	51	49	46	44	45	47	43	47
Pfd.	Nil	Nil	-7.0	23.0	345	511	489	552	565	568
% Pfd.	Nil	Nil	NM	4.87	5.80	8.60	8.40	9.20	10	11
Common	3,153	2,993	2,982	2,870	2,857	2,813	2,718	2,621	2,535	2,153
% Common	48	52	49	47	48	48	47	44	46	42
Total Cap.	7,943	7,157	7,727	7,432	7,261	7,234	7,097	7,220	6,626	6,165
% Oper. Ratio	84.3	84.8	82.5	75.4	84.1	82.1	82.7	81.9	82.7	83.2
% Earn. on Net Prop.	13.3	13.6	13.1	11.9	12.1	12.7	9.1	9.5	8.8	8.9
% Return On Revs.	8.9	8.6	9.8	8.6	9.9	11.5	11.6	11.6	10.6	9.5
% Return On Invest. Capital	8.2	7.8	11.0	8.6	9.2	9.6	7.2	7.2	7.1	7.5
% Return On Com. Equity	11.2	10.9	10.5	8.9	9.6	10.8	10.6	10.4	9.5	9.0

Data as orig reptd (for Baltimore G&E pr. to 4/30/99); bef. results of disc opers/spec. items. Per share data adj. for stk. divs. Bold denotes diluted EPS (FASB 128)-prior periods restated. E-Estimated. NA-Not Available. NM-Not Meaningful. NR-Not Ranked.

Office—250 W. Pratt Street, Baltimore, MD 21201. **Tel**—(410) 234-5000. **Website**—http://www.contstellationenergy.com **Chrmn & CEO**—C. H. Poindexter. **Co-Pres**—E. Grubman, C. W. Shivery. **VP, CFO & Secy**—D. A. Brune. **Investor Contact**—Kevin J. Miller. **Dirs**—H. F. Baldwin, D. L. Becker, J. T. Brady, B. B. Byron, J. O. Cole, D. A. Colussy, E. A. Crooke, J. R. Curtiss, R. W. Gale, J. W. Geckle, F. A. Hrabowski III, R. J. Hurst, N. Lampton, C. R. Larson, C. H. Poindexter, G. L. Russell Jr., M. A. Shattuck III, M. D. Sullivan. **Transfer Agent & Registrar**—Co.'s office; Continental Stock Transfer and Trust Co., New York. **Incorporated**—in Maryland in 1906. **Empl**— 7,800. **S&P Analyst:** Justin McCann

STANDARD &POOR'S STOCK REPORTS

Dynegy Inc.

NYSE Symbol **DYN**

In S&P 500

18-AUG-01

Industry: Natural Gas

Summary: Dynegy trades electricity and related commodities, services and transports natural gas liquids, and operates a regulated Illinois utility.

S&P Opinion: Buy (★★★★★)

Recent Price • 41.01 | Yield • 0.7%
52 Wk Range • 59.87-38 | 12-Mo. P/E • 21.5

Quantitative Evaluations

Outlook (1 Lowest—5 Highest)
• **3**⁻

Fair Value
• **46**

Risk
• **NA**

Earn./Div. Rank
• **B**

Technical Eval.
• **Bearish** since 8/01

Rel. Strength Rank (1 Lowest—99 Highest)
• **25**

Insider Activity
• **Neutral**

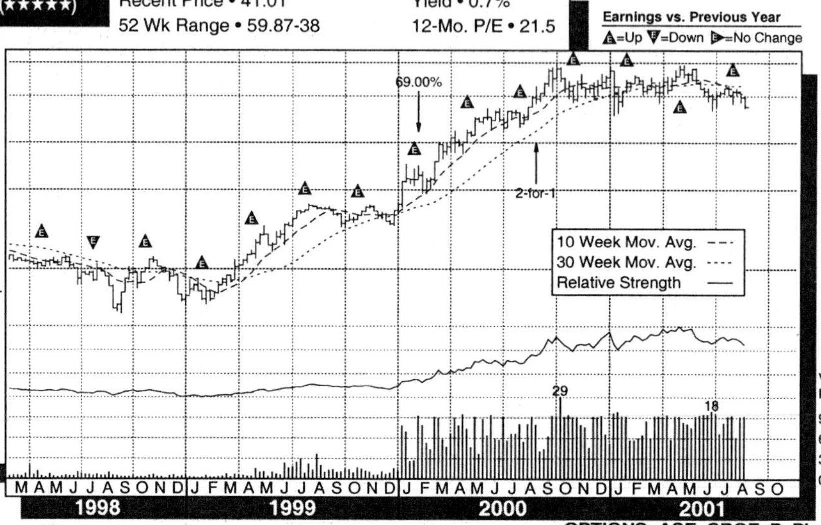

OPTIONS: ASE, CBOE, P, Ph

Overview - 14-AUG-01

Revenues should approximately double in 2001, spurred by contributions from DYN's online energy trading portal (Dynegydirect), growth in international origination and risk management activities, and contributions from newly constructed and acquired power plants. Margins should narrow, given dilution from communications investments and proportionately greater contributions from lower margin Dynegydirect transactions. We see equity earnings declining marginally, due to the absence of abnormally high returns in the summer of 2000 from jointly held California power plants. Ultimately, however, we look for a gain from the reversal of reserves for receivables due from California utilities. EPS for 2001 should advance more than 30%. Longer term EPS growth should exceed 25%, fueled by growing power generation, European energy marketing and broadband trading.

Valuation - 14-AUG-01

Over the three months ended mid-August, the shares fell more than 18%, as lower summer power prices and fears of a longer term power glut battered shares of independent power producers (IPPs). While there will no doubt be a decline in average "spark spreads" (margin of power prices over fuel costs), we believe fears of a capacity glut ignore demand growth, the need to retire older plants, and regional differences in supply/demand dynamics. Furthermore, DYN's energy marketing can actually benefit from lower prices. Less volatility makes risk management products more economical, and a more liquid wholesale market increases the total volume of DYN's marketing/trading activities. DYN's current P/E to growth rate (PEG) is less than 1X, versus about 2X for the S&P 500. Assuming a 1.5X PEG on a 25% growth rate, we estimate as much as 70% upside in DYN shares.

Key Stock Statistics

S&P EPS Est. 2001	2.07	Tang. Bk. Value/Share	6.49
P/E on S&P Est. 2001	19.8	Beta	0.68
S&P EPS Est. 2002	2.60	Shareholders	21,968
Dividend Rate/Share	0.30	Market cap. (B)	$ 9.8
Shs. outstg. (M)	326.0	Inst. holdings	57%
Avg. daily vol. (M)	1.900		

Value of $10,000 invested 5 years ago: $ 38,473

Fiscal Year Ending Dec. 31

	2001	2000	1999	1998	1997	1996
Revenues (Million $)						
1Q	14,168	5,349	3,045	3,316	3,272	1,647
2Q	10,812	5,720	3,161	3,278	2,684	1,163
3Q	—	8,366	4,585	4,587	3,657	1,495
4Q	—	10,010	4,639	3,078	3,765	2,954
Yr.	—	29,445	15,430	14,258	13,378	7,260
Earnings Per Share ($)						
1Q	**0.42**	**0.23**	**0.12**	**0.04**	0.02	0.19
2Q	**0.43**	**0.19**	**0.12**	**0.11**	0.15	0.09
3Q	**E0.82**	**0.73**	**0.22**	**0.19**	0.12	0.12
4Q	**E0.40**	**0.32**	**0.19**	**0.13**	**-0.65**	0.20
Yr.	**E2.07**	**1.48**	**0.65**	**0.48**	**-0.42**	**0.60**

Next earnings report expected: mid October

Dividend Data (Dividends have been paid since 1994.)

Amount ($)	Date Decl.	Ex-Div. Date	Stock of Record	Payment Date
0.075	Nov. 13	Nov. 29	Dec. 01	Dec. 15 '00
0.075	Jan. 19	Feb. 27	Mar. 01	Mar. 15 '01
0.075	May. 21	May. 29	May. 31	Jun. 15 '01
0.075	Jul. 23	Aug. 29	Aug. 31	Sep. 17 '01

A Division of The McGraw-Hill Companies

Dynegy Incorporated

Business Summary - 14-AUG-01

Dynegy fuels long-term growth through the synergistic combination of gas and power marketing capabilities with unregulated power generating plants. The company sees such a combination of skills and businesses providing an incremental return (which it calls the Merchant Leverage Effect), as a result of arbitrage opportunities across geographic lines and between fossil fuels and electricity. Dynegy ultimately hopes to replicate its domestic Merchant Leverage Effect in Canada, Europe and other markets as they open up to greater competition.

Dynegy added some 4,855 megawatts of generating capacity during 2000 through the $4 billion acquisition of Illinova, an Illinois electric utility, and construction of new power plants. The company ended 2000 with ownership in 39 facilities totaling 13,141 MW, and total megawatt hours produced during 2000 rose 74% from the prior year. During 2001, two first quarter acquisitions and three new plant constructions contributed another 2,860 MW to Dynegy's portfolio.

DYN's business is divided into four distinct segments: Dynegy Marketing and Trade (DMT), Transmission and Distribution, Midstream Services, and Dynegy Global Communications (DGC). DMT is the unit focused on the Merchant Leverage Effect. To augment its energy marketing, DYN in November 2000 launched Dynegydirect, an online trading portal that recorded nearly $25 billion in notional transactions through the second quarter of 2001 (approximately 40% representing new customer transactions for DYN). Transmission and Distribution represents the regulated power delivery business derived from the Illinova acquisition. Midstream Services consists primarily of North American midstream liquids operations and global liquefied petroleum gas transportation and natural gas liquids marketing operations.

DGC was formed in 2000 in an effort to transfer Dynegy's convergence prowess (combining physical assets with marketing and trading acumen) into the growing market for broadband communications. DGC began in September 2000, through the acquisition of an effective 80% interest in Extant, a wholesale communications provider, for $92 million in cash and 1.8 million DYN shares. Dynegy and Telstra Corp., an Australian telecommunications provider with a 20% interest in Extant, plan to invest $400 million through the end of 2001 to complete the buildout of Extant's nationwide connectivity network. In March 2001, DGC launched a European subsidiary through the acquisition of iaxis Limited, a London-based communications company with a European fiber optic network.

As of the first quarter of 2001, Chevron owned 26.6% of DYN's shares. The two companies have agreements giving DYN the power to market substantially all of Chevron's U.S. natural gas production outside of Alaska.

Per Share Data ($) (Year Ended Dec. 31)	2000	1999	1998	1997	1996	1995	1994	1993	1992	1991
Tangible Bk. Val.	6.49	4.03	3.15	4.52	2.67	3.81	3.36	5.96	5.99	NA
Cash Flow	2.71	1.22	0.93	1.41	0.55	0.58	0.93	1.30	1.29	NA
Earnings	1.48	0.65	0.48	-0.42	0.60	0.29	0.15	0.38	0.46	NA
Dividends	0.32	0.04	0.04	0.04	0.05	0.03	0.04	Nil	NA	NA
Payout Ratio	22%	5%	8%	NM	6%	13%	50%	Nil	NA	NA
Prices - High	59.87	17.93	12.68	17.48	17.93	8.51	8.87	9.51	NA	NA
- Low	17.11	7.33	6.79	10.66	6.25	6.06	5.79	7.33	NA	NA
P/E Ratio - High	40	27	27	NM	30	29	NM	25	NA	NA
- Low	12	11	14	NM	10	21	NM	19	NA	NA

Income Statement Analysis (Million $)	2000	1999	1998	1997	1996	1995	1994	1993	1992	1991
Revs.	29,445	15,430	14,258	13,378	7,280	3,666	584	591	602	NA
Oper. Inc.	1,130	343	225	490	Nil	127	73.3	90.0	99	NA
Depr.	389	129	103	379	0.5	44.9	33.8	33.4	31.9	NA
Int. Exp.	251	78.2	75.0	63.5	28.1	32.4	35.8	38.5	40.8	NA
Pretax Inc.	791	243	175	-140	170	65.2	5.5	23.0	28.4	NA
Eff. Tax Rate	33%	31%	29%	NM	33%	31%	50%	39%	36%	NA
Net Inc.	501	152	108	-87.7	113	44.8	2.8	13.9	18.2	NA

Balance Sheet & Other Fin. Data (Million $)	2000	1999	1998	1997	1996	1995	1994	1993	1992	1991
Cash	86.0	45.2	28.4	23.0	NM	16.3	1.6	2.2	NA	NA
Curr. Assets	10,150	2,805	2,117	2,019	456	763	118	98.0	NA	NA
Total Assets	21,406	6,525	5,264	4,517	1,278	1,875	757	745	795	NA
Curr. Liab.	9,405	2,539	2,026	1,753	393	706	102	85.0	NA	NA
LT Debt	3,174	1,499	1,247	1,202	333	523	372	387	456	NA
Common Eqty.	3,613	1,234	1,053	944	552	552	235	231	215	NA
Total Cap.	8,214	3,144	2,692	2,475	885	1,118	635	643	NA	NA
Cap. Exp.	769	365	299	220	Nil	129	26.6	57.0	65.1	NA
Cash Flow	855	281	211	291	114	89.7	36.6	47.3	50.1	NA
Curr. Ratio	1.1	1.1	1.0	1.2	1.2	1.1	1.2	1.2	NA	NA
% LT Debt of Cap.	38.6	47.7	46.3	40.5	37.6	46.8	58.6	60.2	NA	NA
% Net Inc.of Revs.	1.7	1.0	0.8	NM	1.6	1.2	0.5	2.4	3.0	NA
% Ret. on Assets	3.6	2.6	2.2	NM	7.3	3.4	0.4	Nil	NA	NA
% Ret. on Equity	19.2	13.2	10.8	NM	13.6	11.4	1.2	Nil	NA	NA

Data as orig reptd.; bef. results of disc opers/spec. items. Per share data adj. for stk. divs. Bold denotes diluted EPS (FASB 128)-prior periods restated. E-Estimated. NA-Not Available. NM-Not Meaningful. NR-Not Ranked.

Office—1000 Louisiana, Suite 5800, Houston, TX 77002. **Tel**—(713) 507-6400. **Website**—www.dynegy.com **Chrmn & CEO**—C. L. Watson. **Pres & COO**—S. W. Bergstrom. **SVP & CFO**—R. D. Doty. **VP & Secy**—K. E. Randolph. **Investor Contact**—Margaret Nollen (713-767-8707). **Dirs**—C. E. Bayless, S. W Bergstrom, D. W. Callahan, M. D. Capellas, D. L. Dienstbier, P. M. Eckert, J. Johnson, G. L. Kirkland, R. H. Matzke, H. J. Riley, Jr., S. Z. Rosenberg, J. J. Stewart, C. L. Watson, J. O. Winters. **Transfer Agent & Registrar**—Mellon Investor Services, Ridgefield Park, NJ. **Incorporated**—in Illinois in 1999. **Empl**— 5,778. **S&P Analyst:** Craig K. Shere, CFA

STANDARD & POOR'S
STOCK REPORTS

Kinder Morgan

NYSE Symbol **KMI**
In S&P 500

18-AUG-01 **Industry:** Natural Gas

Summary: KMI (formed through the 1999 merger of KN Energy and privately held Kinder Morgan) is one of the largest midstream energy companies in the U.S.

S&P Opinion: Buy (★★★★★)

Recent Price • 54.54 | Yield • 0.4%
52 Wk Range • 60-36.12 | 12-Mo. P/E • 34.5

Quantitative Evaluations
Outlook (1 Lowest—5 Highest) • **2-**
Fair Value • **50**
Risk • **Low**
Earn./Div. Rank • **B**
Technical Eval. • **NA**
Rel. Strength Rank (1 Lowest—99 Highest) • **63**
Insider Activity • **Unfavorable**

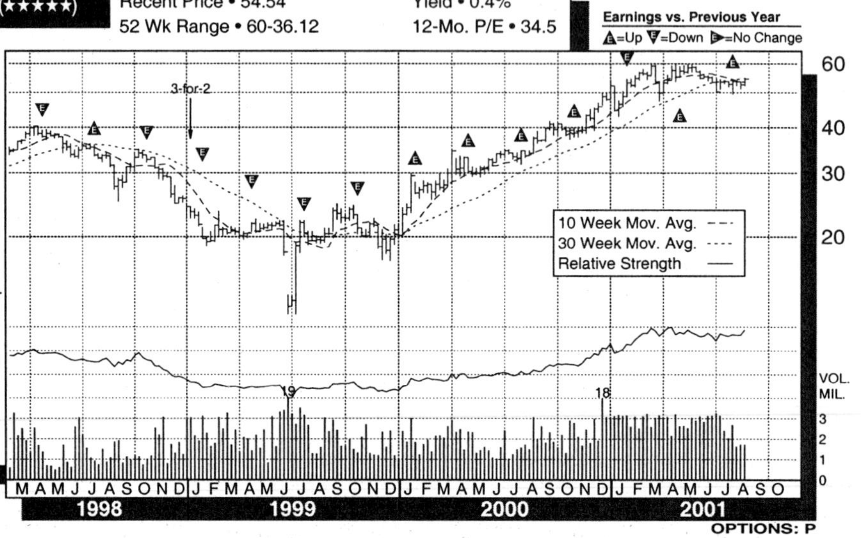

Overview - 20-APR-01

KMI's master limited partnership, Kinder Morgan Energy Partners (KMP), will provide the bulk of KMI's earnings growth this year. KMP, in turn, will grow earnings internally and through acquisitions. Internal growth sources include increased asset utilization of KMP's refined petroleum product pipelines amid well controlled costs and higher sales at the CO2 business. Externally, we expect KMP to continue making accretive, fee-based acquisitions, consolidating the still highly fragmented industries in which KMP operates. The $1.15 billion acquisition of GATX's pipeline and terminal assets was closed during the first quarter. At the KMI level, power earnings will double. The company recently signed a major long-term tolling deal with Williams. Interest expense should decline considerably on lower debt balances that are fixed at attractive rates. Overall, we expect KMI's EPS to increase 40%, in line with management's objectives.

Valuation - 20-APR-01

In our view, P/E to growth rate (PEG) ratios, which are used by analysts to justify high PEs, are often based on unrealistic growth rates. KMI is one of the few companies where management itself provides a bullish long-term growth estimate. Taking the midpoint of 25%, which we believe to be very reasonable, the stock trades at a PEG of just 1.0X, versus a 1.8 PEG average for KMI's group. As a result, we believe that, despite last year's strong price appreciation of 155%, the shares have significant upside potential. Intermediate-term growth should come from KMP, while long-term growth will be fueled by KMI's burgeoning power segment. That division inherited a very attractive contract for GE turbines, enabling cheap construction of power plants. Finally, KMI's telecom initiatives are in their infant stages and may provide for huge upside growth.

Key Stock Statistics

S&P EPS Est. 2001	1.87	Tang. Bk. Value/Share	16.72
P/E on S&P Est. 2001	29.2	Beta	0.10
S&P EPS Est. 2002	2.45	Shareholders	10,397
Dividend Rate/Share	0.20	Market cap. (B)	$ 6.3
Shs. outstg. (M)	115.4	Inst. holdings	58%
Avg. daily vol. (M)	0.384		

Value of $10,000 invested 5 years ago: $ 25,220

Fiscal Year Ending Dec. 31

	2001	2000	1999	1998	1997	1996
Revenues (Million $)						
1Q	347.5	480.5	406.7	1,167	489.5	385.9
2Q	218.8	549.8	408.2	1,040	357.9	277.1
3Q	—	749.1	471.1	1,045	515.1	304.3
4Q	—	931.7	459.5	1,139	782.7	475.9
Yr.	—	2,714	1,745	4,388	2,145	1,443
Earnings Per Share ($)						
1Q	**0.47**	**0.41**	**0.34**	**0.42**	**0.43**	**0.40**
2Q	**0.41**	**0.22**	**0.17**	**0.24**	**0.23**	**0.20**
3Q	—	**0.23**	**0.08**	**0.36**	**0.37**	**0.31**
4Q	—	**0.73**	**1.02**	**-0.05**	**0.59**	**0.52**
Yr.	—	**1.60**	**1.92**	**0.92**	**1.63**	**1.43**

Next earnings report expected: mid October

Dividend Data (Dividends have been paid since 1937.)

Amount ($)	Date Decl.	Ex-Div. Date	Stock of Record	Payment Date
0.050	Oct. 20	Oct. 27	Oct. 31	Nov. 14 '00
0.050	Jan. 17	Jan. 29	Jan. 31	Feb. 14 '01
0.050	Apr. 19	Apr. 26	Apr. 30	May. 15 '01
0.050	Jul. 20	Jul. 27	Jul. 31	Aug. 14 '01

Business Summary - 20-APR-01

In October 1999, KN Energy acquired Kinder Morgan, Inc., a private company that owned the the general partner of Kinder Morgan Energy Partners, L.P. (KMP)., the largest pipeline master limited partnership in the U.S. As part of the transaction, KN Energy changed its name to Kinder Morgan, Inc. (KMI).

KMI is one of the largest midstream energy companies in the U.S. With substantial natural gas assets, the company is poised to benefit from rising demand for natural gas that will be used to fuel electric generating facilities. In addition, the KMP master limited partnership is providing KMI, the general partner, with substantial earnings growth. Coupled with its ownership of 21% of limited partnership units, KMI receives nearly 60% of KMP's incremental distributions, as part of an incentive arrangement, and approximately 49% of KMP's total distributions.

The partnership owns and operates one of the largest refined petroleum product pipeline and terminal systems in the country. In addition, KMP is a major transporter of natural gas, operating more than 10,000 miles of pipeline; the leading provider of CO2 for use in enhanced oil recovery projects; and one of the largest operators of bulk terminals, with 29 facilities that transload more than 40 million tons of coal, petroleum coke and other products annually.

Through its Natural Gas Pipeline Company of America (NGPL) subsidiary, Kinder Morgan owns and operates 10,000 miles of interstate natural gas pipelines, field systems and related facilities, primarily consisting of two major interconnected transmission pipelines terminating near Chicago. In addition to serving Illinois, NGPL serves Indiana and Iowa and portions of Wisconsin, Nebraska, Kansas, Missouri and Arkansas. NGPL is also one the largest natural gas storage operators, with approximately 600 Bcf of total storage capacity, 210 Bcf of working capacity and 4.0 Bcf per day of peak deliverability.

Kinder Morgan Power constructs and operates power plants as an independent producer. Customers, which include power marketers and utilities, pay a fee to KMI for converting gas into electricity and assume all commodity price risks and rewards.

In February 2001, KMI announced an agreement under which Williams Energy Marketing and Trading will supply natural gas to and market 3,300 mw for 16 years for six 550 mw gas-fired plants. The first plant, currently under construction in Jackson, MI, is expected to begin commercial operation in July 2002. In constructing power plants, KMI utilizes its proprietary Orion technology.

At December 31, 2000, the retail natural gas business served approximately 218,000 customers, in Colorado, Nebraska and Wyoming, through 7,500 miles of distribution pipelines.

Per Share Data ($) (Year Ended Dec. 31)	2000	1999	1998	1997	1996	1995	1994	1993	1992	1991
Tangible Bk. Val.	15.70	14.79	17.65	12.63	11.42	10.11	9.52	8.94	8.39	8.09
Earnings	1.60	1.92	0.92	1.63	1.43	1.22	0.35	1.05	0.85	0.94
Dividends	0.20	0.65	0.76	0.73	0.70	0.67	0.65	0.61	0.57	0.52
Payout Ratio	13%	34%	83%	44%	49%	55%	187%	59%	67%	56%
Prices - High	54.25	24.68	40.33	36.00	27.50	20.16	17.91	20.00	13.33	12.50
- Low	19.87	12.18	22.33	24.08	18.00	13.50	13.83	12.44	9.22	9.27
P/E Ratio - High	34	13	44	22	19	17	52	19	16	13
- Low	12	6	24	15	13	11	40	12	11	10
Income Statement Analysis (Million $)										
Revs.	2,714	1,745	4,388	2,145	1,443	1,103	1,084	493	392	395
Depr.	108	144	196	56.0	51.2	49.9	50.3	26.2	24.2	21.4
Maint.	NA	NA	NA	NA	NA	NA	NA	14.4	7.3	7.4
Fxd. Chgs. Cov.	1.9	1.4	1.4	3.8	3.8	3.4	1.8	2.7	2.5	2.8
Constr. Credits	NA	Nil	Nil	Nil	NA	NA	NA	NA	NA	NA
Eff. Tax Rate	37%	34%	33%	32%	36%	36%	38%	37%	38%	39%
Net Inc.	184	155	60.0	77.5	63.8	52.5	15.3	24.3	19.6	21.6
Balance Sheet & Other Fin. Data (Million $)										
Gross Prop.	6,137	6,167	7,767	1,972	1,548	1,353	1,312	877	769	712
Cap. Exp.	137	94.3	257	311	120	79.4	70.6	63.1	60.1	59.4
Net Prop.	5,725	5,790	7,023	1,421	1,029	863	851	507	455	412
Capitalization:										
LT Debt	Nil	3,568	3,306	554	424	316	335	232	220	159
% LT Debt	Nil	68	73	47	45	42	45	53	53	46
Pfd.	Nil	Nil	7.0	7.0	7.0	7.6	8.7	9.9	11.5	13.6
% Pfd.	Nil	Nil	0.20	0.50	0.70	1.00	1.20	2.20	2.80	3.90
Common	1,797	1,666	1,217	606	520	427	394	202	185	175
% Common	100	32	27	52	55	57	53	46	44	50
Total Cap.	4,082	7,472	6,567	1,383	1,099	876	846	501	466	391
% Oper. Ratio	90.0	85.6	92.9	93.4	93.1	92.3	96.0	91.0	90.2	90.5
% Earn. on Net Prop.	9.2	4.8	8.3	6.3	14.3	13.3	6.4	9.2	8.9	9.5
% Return On Revs.	6.8	8.9	1.4	3.6	4.4	4.8	1.4	4.9	5.0	5.5
% Return On Invest. Capital	12.0	5.9	10.3	13.2	15.9	13.5	5.6	9.8	9.1	10.0
% Return On Com. Equity	10.6	10.7	6.5	13.8	13.4	12.7	3.7	12.1	10.3	11.3

Data as orig reptd.; bef. results of disc opers/spec. items. Per share data adj. for stk. divs. Bold denotes diluted EPS (FASB 128)-prior periods restated. E-Estimated. NA-Not Available. NM-Not Meaningful. NR-Not Ranked.

Office—500 Dallas, Suite #1000, Houston, TX 77002. **Tel**—(713) 369-9000. **Website**—www.kindermorgan.com **Chrmn & CEO**—R. D. Kinder. **Vice Chrmn & Pres**—W. V. Morgan. **VP & CFO**—C. P. Shaper. **VP & Secy**—M. B. Wyrsch. **VP & Treas**—E. W. Lundhagen. **Investor Contact**—Dax Sanders (713-369-9103). **Dirs**—E. H. Austin Jr., C. W. Battey, S. A. Bliss, T. A. Gardner, W. J. Hybl, R. D. Kinder, W. V. Morgan, E. Randall III, F. Sarofim, H. A. True III. **Transfer Agent & Registrar**—Bank of New York, NYC. **Incorporated**—in Kansas in 1927. **Empl**— 3,801. **S&P Analyst:** Ephraim Juskowicz

STANDARD
&POOR'S
STOCK REPORTS

Mirant Corp.

NYSE Symbol **MIR**

In S&P 500

23-AUG-01

Industry: Electric Companies

Summary: This international power company (formerly Southern Energy) has interests in electric generation, power distribution and energy marketing operations.

S&P Opinion: Buy (★★★★★)

Recent Price • 28 | Yield • Nil
52 Wk Range • 47.20-20.56 | 12-Mo. P/E • 17.8

Quantitative Evaluations

Outlook (1 Lowest—5 Highest)
• **NA**

Fair Value
• **NA**

Risk
• **NA**

Earn./Div. Rank
• **NR**

Technical Eval.
• **NA**

Rel. Strength Rank (1 Lowest—99 Highest)
• **19**

Insider Activity
• **NA**

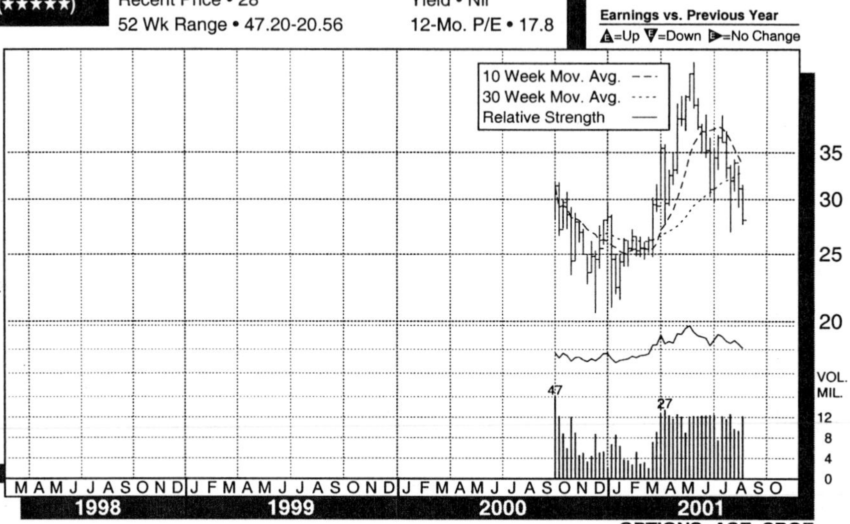

OPTIONS: ASE, CBOE

Overview - 23-AUG-01

Reported revenues should grow about 150% in 2001, reflecting the consolidation of the SCEM energy trading/ marketing business, contributions from the December 2000 acquisition of 5,154 MW of power from Potomac Electric Power Co. (PEPCO), and full-year contributions from other acquisitions and plant development. Gross margins should narrow substantially, reflecting the much narrower margins inherent in energy marketing operations. Depreciation and amortization charges should rise, as a result of significant growth in MIR's power plant portfolio, as well as special amortization charges for contractual supply obligations related to the PEPCO acquisition. EPS estimates for 2001 exclude $0.15 in net one time losses and for 2002 exclude goodwill amortization (about $0.20 a share in 2001).

Valuation - 23-AUG-01

Over the three months ended late August, Mirant shares declined over 35%, driven by fears of a "power glut" and severe weakness in the independent power producer (IPP) group. The company has beaten quarterly analyst estimates in each of the last two quarters, even after a $245 million provision for California receivables. Mirant has become far more than just an unregulated power company. Its energy marketing operations now rank among the 10 largest natural gas marketers in North America, with trading volumes some 10X the peak fuel needs for Mirant's own gas-fired electric plants. This success, combined with growth prospects from U.S. Mid-Atlantic and European operations, leads us to project a 20% to 25% EPS growth rate through 2004. MIR now trades around 11X our 2002 estimated EPS. The company's implied forward PEG (P/E to growth rate) is nearly 75% cheaper than the S&P 500. We look for the shares to handsomely outperform the broader market in the coming 12 months.

Key Stock Statistics

S&P EPS Est. 2001	1.98	Tang. Bk. Value/Share	1.54
P/E on S&P Est. 2001	14.1	Beta	NA
S&P EPS Est. 2002	2.65	Shareholders	NA
Dividend Rate/Share	Nil	Market cap. (B)	$ 9.9
Shs. outstg. (M)	340.4	Inst. holdings	47%
Avg. daily vol. (M)	2.116		

Value of $10,000 invested 5 years ago: NA

Fiscal Year Ending Dec. 31

	2001	2000	1999	1998	1997	1996
Revenues (Million $)						
1Q	8,182	—	—	—	—	—
2Q	7,928	—	—	—	—	—
3Q	—	42.81	—	—	—	—
4Q	—	7,934	—	—	—	—
Yr.	—	13,315	1,292	—	—	—
Earnings Per Share ($)						
1Q	**0.52**	—	—	—	—	—
2Q	**0.36**	—	—	—	—	—
3Q	—	**0.33**	—	—	—	—
4Q	—	**0.18**	—	—	—	—
Yr.	—	**1.15**	**1.22**	—	—	—

Next earnings report expected: late October

Dividend Data

No cash has been paid.

A Division of The McGraw-Hill Companies

Mirant Corporation

Business Summary - 23-AUG-01

Mirant Corp. (formerly Southern Energy) provides electricity and energy-related products and services worldwide. The company has built and acquired a broad portfolio of power plants, in which it holds net ownership interests totaling 17,807 megawatts (MW) of generating capacity. In addition, it has projects in construction and under advanced development that will add more than 7,000 MW. MIR also controls 1,858 MW of North American power through management contracts.

The company has a stated goal of increasing its owned and controlled North American generating capacity to 30,000 MW by 2004, from 14,400 MW, and its continental Europe capacity to a 10,000 MW to 12,000 MW in coming years, from 848 MW. Based on these growth goals, in October 2000, MIR projected that it could achieve EPS growth in excess of 20% in the coming four years.

Through its Southern Company Energy Marketing (SCEM), the company markets and trades electricity, gas, oil, coal and emission allowances. By the end of 2000, SCEM was the ninth largest U.S. natural gas marketer, marketing over 7 Bcf a day (about 10X the company's internal consumption). In December 2000, management stated its intention to double the size of gas marketing operations.

MIR was a wholly owned subsidiary of Southern Company (SO) until its October 2000 IPO. As a part of its full spin-off to SO shareholders in April 2001, Mirant assumed its current name (changed from Southern Energy).

As of December 2000, MIR's net ownership in North American power plants (excluding power controlled through contract) was 12,543 MW. The company has projects in construction and under advanced development totaling about 7,000 MW of net ownership. In December, the company closed on its acquisition of 5,154 MW of generation capacity from Potomac Electric Power Co. for $2.65 billion plus certain contractual power supply obligations.

In Europe, MIR owns a 26% interest in Bewag AG, an electric utility serving 2.1 million customers in Berlin, Germany. The company also has a 49% economic interest in, and operating control of, Western Power Distribution, which distributes electricity to about 1.4 million end users in southwest England. In addition, MIR has an interest in Hyder plc, which owns and operates the electricity network in South Wales, and the water distribution and waste water treatment business for all of Wales.

MIR also has net ownership of 3,160 MW of generation in the Philippines and China and 1,257 MW in South America and the Caribbean. As part of the company's interests in various power generating businesses, it also owns certain wholesale transmission lines in Germany, Chile and the Bahamas.

Per Share Data ($) (Year Ended Dec. 31)	2000	1999	1998	1997	1996	1995	1994	1993	1992	1991
Tangible Bk. Val.	0.31	1.03	NA	NA	NA	NA	NA	NA	NA	NA
Cash Flow	2.27	2.32	NA	NA	NA	NA	NA	NA	NA	NA
Earnings	0.98	1.22	NA	NA	NA	NA	NA	NA	NA	NA
Dividends	Nil	NA	NA	NA	NA	NA	NA	NA	NA	NA
Payout Ratio	Nil	NA	NA	NA	NA	NA	NA	NA	NA	NA
Prices - High	31.87	NA	NA	NA	NA	NA	NA	NA	NA	NA
- Low	20.56	NA	NA	NA	NA	NA	NA	NA	NA	NA
P/E Ratio - High	33	NA	NA	NA	NA	NA	NA	NA	NA	NA
- Low	21	NA	NA	NA	NA	NA	NA	NA	NA	NA
Income Statement Analysis (Million $)										
Revs.	13,315	2,268	NA	NA	NA	NA	NA	NA	NA	NA
Oper. Inc.	1,015	774	NA	NA	NA	NA	NA	NA	NA	NA
Depr.	333	270	NA	NA	NA	NA	NA	NA	NA	NA
Int. Exp.	615	502	430	NA	NA	NA	NA	NA	NA	NA
Pretax Inc.	502	674	NA	NA	NA	NA	NA	NA	NA	NA
Eff. Tax Rate	17%	19%	NA	NA	NA	NA	NA	NA	NA	NA
Net Inc.	332	362	NA	NA	NA	NA	NA	NA	NA	NA
Balance Sheet & Other Fin. Data (Million $)										
Cash	1,280	323	NA	NA	NA	NA	NA	NA	NA	NA
Curr. Assets	9,152	1,285	NA	NA	NA	NA	NA	NA	NA	NA
Total Assets	24,136	13,863	NA	NA	NA	NA	NA	NA	NA	NA
Curr. Liab.	9,775	3,215	NA	NA	NA	NA	NA	NA	NA	NA
LT Debt	7,133	5,985	NA	NA	NA	NA	NA	NA	NA	NA
Common Eqty.	4,136	3,102	NA	NA	NA	NA	NA	NA	NA	NA
Total Cap.	11,634	9,767	NA	NA	NA	NA	NA	NA	NA	NA
Cap. Exp.	616	747	NA	NA	NA	NA	NA	NA	NA	NA
Cash Flow	665	632	NA	NA	NA	NA	NA	NA	NA	NA
Curr. Ratio	0.9	0.4	NA	NA	NA	NA	NA	NA	NA	NA
% LT Debt of Cap.	61.3	61.3	NA	NA	NA	NA	NA	NA	NA	NA
% Net Inc.of Revs.	2.5	16.0	NA	NA	NA	NA	NA	NA	NA	NA
% Ret. on Assets	1.7	2.8	NA	NA	NA	NA	NA	NA	NA	NA
% Ret. on Equity	9.2	12.6	NA	NA	NA	NA	NA	NA	NA	NA

Data as orig reptd.; bef. results of disc opers/spec. items. Per share data adj. for stk. divs. Bold denotes diluted EPS (FASB 128)-prior periods restated. E-Estimated. NA-Not Available. NM-Not Meaningful. NR-Not Ranked.

Office—1155 Perimeter Center West, Atlanta, GA 30338. **Tel**—678-579-7000. **Website**—http://www.mirant.com **Chrmn**—A. W. Dahlberg. **Pres & CEO**—S. M. Fuller. **EVP & CFO**—R. D. Hill. **Investor Contact**—John Robinson (678-579-7782). **Dirs**—A. W. Dahlberg, H. A. Franklin, S. M. Fuller, E. B. Harris, W. L. Westbrook, A. D. Correll, W. M. Hjerpe, D. J. Lesar. **Transfer Agent**—Mellon Investor Services. **Incorporated**—in Delaware in April 1993. **Empl**— 7,000. **S&P Analyst:** Craig K. Shere, CFA

STANDARD
&POOR'S
STOCK REPORTS

TXU Corp.

NYSE Symbol **TXU**

In S&P 500

18-AUG-01

Industry: Electric Companies

Summary: This Dallas-based energy holding company (formerly Texas Utilities Co.) provides energy services to customers in Texas, the U.K., and Australia.

S&P Opinion: Buy (★★★★★)

Recent Price • 46.25 | Yield • 5.2%
52 Wk Range • 50-33.68 | 12-Mo. P/E • 13.6

Quantitative Evaluations

Outlook (1 Lowest—5 Highest) • **3+**

Fair Value • **47.80**

Risk • **Low**

Earn./Div. Rank • **B**

Technical Eval. • **Neutral** since 8/01

Rel. Strength Rank (1 Lowest—99 Highest) • **51**

Insider Activity • **Neutral**

OPTIONS: P

Overview - 01-JUN-01

EPS is expected to grow approximately 8% in 2001. This would follow a 7.5% rise in 2000 over 1999's operating EPS of $3.19. (Due to the different levels of shares outstanding, the reported EPS for the 1998 individual quarters do not add up to the full year EPS). TXU will continue to expand both its international business and its non-regulated domestic operations. It will seek growth in Europe through acquisitions, joint ventures and management service contracts. TXU intends to sell some of its generation plants in the U.K., since its energy trading operations do not require physical ownership of the plants. For the same reason, it is likely to sell or swap some of its generation plants in Texas. With the global merchant energy business expected to grow earnings at about 12% a year, we would expect TXU's consolidated EPS to grow at an average annual rate of around 10% for the next three years.

Valuation - 01-JUN-01

Despite the sharp rise in the shares, we would continue to buy TXU stock. With the shares trading at around 12 times our 2002 EPS estimate of $4.00 and a dividend yield of about 4.9%, the stock remains attractive for price appreciation and income. In 2000, after dropping nearly 27% in the early part of the year, the shares rebounded about 70% and finished the year up 24.6%. The stock had been hurt by the decline of power prices in the U.K and a PUCT order deferring consideration for 78% of the $1.65 billion regulatory asset securitization TXU requested. Texas legislation will allow TXU to completely recover its stranded costs and maintain existing rates until retail competition begins on January 1, 2002, at which time it will reduce its rates by 6% for a five year period. While this would reduce revenues by about $460 million, it would be more than offset by a $500 million increase from TXU's U.S. energy operations.

Key Stock Statistics

S&P EPS Est. 2001	3.70	Tang. Bk. Value/Share	NM
P/E on S&P Est. 2001	12.5	Beta	-0.23
S&P EPS Est. 2002	4.05	Shareholders	77,498
Dividend Rate/Share	2.40	Market cap. (B)	$ 11.9
Shs. outstg. (M)	256.9	Inst. holdings	51%
Avg. daily vol. (M)	0.916		

Value of $10,000 invested 5 years ago: $ 14,610

Fiscal Year Ending Dec. 31

	2001	2000	1999	1998	1997	1996
Revenues (Million $)						
1Q	8,375	4,776	4,468	2,499	1,494	1,464
2Q	6,127	4,592	3,729	3,236	1,588	1,691
3Q	—	5,834	4,435	4,380	2,265	1,930
4Q	—	6,807	4,486	4,621	2,598	1,466
Yr.	—	22,009	17,118	14,736	7,946	6,551
Earnings Per Share ($)						
1Q	**0.76**	**0.71**	**0.65**	**0.51**	0.51	0.56
2Q	**0.78**	**0.87**	**0.35**	**0.33**	0.72	0.90
3Q	**E1.34**	**1.25**	**1.31**	**1.04**	1.24	1.59
4Q	**E0.82**	**0.61**	**1.24**	**0.84**	**0.39**	0.30
Yr.	**E3.70**	**3.43**	**3.53**	**2.79**	**2.85**	**3.35**

Next earnings report expected: late October

Dividend Data (Dividends have been paid since 1917.)

Amount ($)	Date Decl.	Ex-Div. Date	Stock of Record	Payment Date
0.600	Aug. 18	Sep. 06	Sep. 08	Oct. 02 '00
0.600	Nov. 17	Dec. 06	Dec. 08	Jan. 02 '01
0.600	Feb. 16	Mar. 07	Mar. 09	Apr. 02 '01
0.600	May. 11	Jun. 06	Jun. 08	Jul. 02 '01

TXU Corp.

Business Summary - 01-JUN-01

This Dallas-based energy holding company serves about nine million customers in Texas, the U.K., and Australia. On May 15, 2000, the company changed its name from Texas Utilities Company to TXU Corp.

In May 1998, TXU acquired, for about $8 billion, the U.K.-based The Eastern Group (subsequently renamed TXU Europe Group), which has holdings that include Eastern, a British regional company with 2.7 million electricity customers and 700,000 gas customers. On August 3, 2000, TXU Europe acquired, for about $465 million, U.K.-based Norweb Energi, which has 1.8 million electricity customers and 400,000 gas customers. In January 2002, TXU Europe agreed to sell its 19.2% interest in Hidroelectrica Del Cantabrico, Spain's fourth largest integrated power company.

The company's main domestic subsidiary, TXU Electric Company, provides electricity and related services to around 2.3 million residential and about 310,000 commercial and industrial customers in the Dallas/Ft. Worth area. The area has seen significant growth in high technology enterprises, particularly in telecommunications and electronics. In recent years, the utility has averaged around 47,000 new customers a year.

TXU Electric's diverse fuel mix provides generating flexibility and reduces the risk of fluctuations in the cost or availability of any one fuel source. TXU Electric owns and operates two nuclear-fueled generating units at the Comanche Peak nuclear generating station, each with a net capacity of 1,150 megawatts.

Sources of power generation for TXU Electric in 2000 were: gas/oil, 33.4% (34.3% in 1999); lignite/coal, 36.6% (38.5%); nuclear, 16.5% (16.4%); and purchased power, 13.5% (10.8%).

In August 1997, the company acquired Lone Star Gas and Lone Star Pipeline, the local distribution and pipeline companies of ENSERCH Corp., for about $1.7 billion of stock and assumed debt.

TXU Lone Star Gas is one of the largest gas distribution companies in the U.S., and the largest in Texas, providing service to more than 1.37 million customers through over 24,000 miles of distribution mains. Lone Star Pipeline has one of the largest pipelines in the U.S., with approximately 7,200 miles of gathering and transmission pipelines in Texas.

In February 1999, the company acquired, for $1.0 billion, Kinetik Energy and Westar, the retail and natural gas distribution businesses privatized by the Government of Victoria, Australia. In 1995, it acquired Eastern Energy Ltd., an electricity distribution company serving around 500,000 customers in southeastern Australia.

In August 2000, TXU Communications contributed its telecommunications business to TXU Communications Ventures, a wholly owned subsidiary of Pinnacle One, in exchange for a 50% interest in Pinnacle One.

Per Share Data ($) (Year Ended Dec. 31)	2000	1999	1998	1997	1996	1995	1994	1993	1992	1991
Tangible Bk. Val.	NM	2.96	4.92	21.96	26.64	25.10	28.74	29.29	30.06	29.55
Earnings	3.43	3.53	2.79	2.85	3.35	-0.61	2.40	1.66	2.88	-1.98
Dividends	2.40	2.30	2.20	2.13	2.02	2.81	3.08	3.08	3.04	3.00
Payout Ratio	70%	65%	79%	75%	60%	NM	128%	186%	106%	NM
Prices - High	45.25	47.18	48.06	42.00	43.75	41.25	43.12	49.75	43.75	43.00
- Low	25.93	32.75	38.37	31.50	38.50	30.12	29.62	41.62	37.00	34.12
P/E Ratio - High	13	13	17	15	13	NM	18	30	15	NM
- Low	8	9	14	11	11	NM	12	25	13	NM
Income Statement Analysis (Million $)										
Revs.	22,009	17,118	14,736	7,946	6,551	5,639	5,664	5,435	4,908	4,893
Depr.	1,214	1,271	1,147	667	621	564	550	440	421	437
Maint.	NA	NA	NA	NA	344	290	305	350	301	309
Fxd. Chgs. Cov.	1.8	1.8	1.8	2.2	2.3	2.3	2.0	1.8	2.0	0.2
Constr. Credits	11.0	10.0	9.0	8.9	11.0	15.0	22.0	263	304	364
Eff. Tax Rate	27%	31%	42%	36%	31%	30%	33%	29%	22%	45%
Net Inc.	916	985	740	660	754	-139	543	369	619	-410
Balance Sheet & Other Fin. Data (Million $)										
Gross Prop.	32,051	33,090	31,110	25,287	25,562	24,616	24,001	23,722	22,994	21,902
Cap. Exp.	1,382	1,632	1,173	446	434	434	444	871	1,137	1,232
Net Prop.	23,301	23,640	22,867	18,571	17,599	17,746	17,669	17,818	17,484	16,768
Capitalization:										
LT Debt	16,986	17,875	16,566	8,759	8,668	9,175	7,888	8,380	7,932	7,951
% LT Debt	69	68	67	52	55	57	50	51	50	51
Pfd.	Nil	Nil	Nil	1,200	1,084	1,134	1,258	1,480	1,328	1,433
% Pfd.	Nil	Nil	Nil	7.20	6.90	7.10	8.00	9.00	8.40	9.20
Common	7,476	8,334	8,246	6,843	6,033	5,732	6,490	6,571	6,591	6,284
% Common	31	32	33	41	38	36	42	40	42	40
Total Cap.	29,084	30,671	29,078	20,362	19,226	19,393	19,168	19,823	17,613	17,228
% Oper. Ratio	90.3	87.5	86.9	80.7	69.4	68.3	76.5	78.2	76.3	76.8
% Earn. on Net Prop.	10.6	11.2	11.9	10.5	11.3	10.1	7.5	6.7	6.8	6.7
% Return On Revs.	4.2	5.8	5.0	8.3	11.5	NM	9.6	6.8	12.6	NM
% Return On Invest. Capital	8.4	8.5	8.9	9.6	10.4	NM	7.0	6.0	7.9	2.4
% Return On Com. Equity	11.4	11.9	9.8	10.3	12.8	NM	8.3	5.6	9.6	NM

Data as orig reptd.; bef. results of disc opers/spec. items. Per share data adj. for stk. divs. Bold denotes diluted EPS (FASB 128)-prior periods restated. E-Estimated. NA-Not Available. NM-Not Meaningful. NR-Not Ranked.

Office—Energy Plaza, 1601 Bryan Street, Dallas, TX 75201-3411. **Tel**—(214) 812-4600. **Website**—http://www.tu.com **Chrmn & CEO**—E. Nye. **Pres**—D. W. Biegler. **EVP & CFO**—M. J. McNally. **Secy**—P. B. Tinkham. **Treas**—K. Oliver. **Investor Contact**—David Anderson (812-4641); Tim Hogan (812-2756). **Dirs**—D. C. Bonham, J. S. Farrington, W. M. Griffin, K. Laday, J. E. Little, M. N. Maxey, E. Nye, J. E. Oesterreicher, C. R. Perry, H. H. Richardson. **Transfer Agent & Registrar**—Texas Utilities Shareholder Services, Dallas. **Incorporated**—in Texas in 1945. **Empl**— 16,540. **S&P Analyst:** Justin McCann

STANDARD
&POOR'S
STOCK REPORTS

AES Corp.

NYSE Symbol **AES**
In S&P 500

23-AUG-01

Industry:
Power Producers (Independent)

Summary: The world's largest independent power producer, AES produces and distributes electricity in both international and domestic markets.

S&P Opinion: Accumulate (★★★★)

Recent Price • 34.07
52 Wk Range • 72.81-33.60
Yield • Nil
12-Mo. P/E • 34.8

Quantitative Evaluations

Outlook
(1 Lowest—5 Highest)
• **4−**

Fair Value
• **43.90**

Risk
• **Average**

Earn./Div. Rank
• **B+**

Technical Eval.
• **Bearish** since 5/01

Rel. Strength Rank
(1 Lowest—99 Highest)
• **20**

Insider Activity
• **Unfavorable**

OPTIONS: ASE, CBOE, P, Ph

Overview - 23-AUG-01

We expect revenues to more than double in 2001, boosted by acquisitions, including that of IPALCO (parent of Indianapolis Power & Light), and growth in telecommunications and commercial energy marketing units. Margins should narrow, as increased contributions from lower-margin power distribution and losses from new business ventures offset the absence of fines and operating losses from California operations (over $0.05 in 2000). Excluding foreign exchange losses, we look for significant growth in equity earnings. EPS growth will be limited by a higher effective tax rate and more shares outstanding (diluted). Results for 2001 exclude $0.15 per share in one-time losses and $0.19 of foreign currency losses and for 2002 exclude goodwill amortization (equal to approximately $0.19 in 2001).

Valuation - 23-AUG-01

Over the three months ended late August, AES shares declined approximately 28%, on fears relating to Latin American economic and currency woes, power rationing in Brazil, and fears of a power glut in the U.S. While we are confident that existing businesses and announced projects can fuel 25% to 30% annual earnings growth for AES through 2005, we are increasingly concerned that AES's vast Brazilian (and other Latin American) investments may suffer from the currency and economic uncertainty in neighboring Argentina. Brazil's inflation rates have still not caught up with the effects of its 1998 devaluation, limiting AES's ability to raise prices while taking the full brunt of translation charges. Using very conservative multiples and discount rates based on our lowest 2005 EPS estimate, we arrive at a fair value estimate about 10% above current levels. From this fair value, we project 15% annual growth through 2005. We maintain our accumulate recommendation.

Key Stock Statistics

S&P EPS Est. 2001	1.81	Tang. Bk. Value/Share	5.21
P/E on S&P Est. 2001	18.8	Beta	1.43
S&P EPS Est. 2002	2.45	Shareholders	1,364
Dividend Rate/Share	Nil	Market cap. (B)	$ 18.2
Shs. outstg. (M)	532.3	Inst. holdings	63%
Avg. daily vol. (M)	2.207		

Value of $10,000 invested 5 years ago: $ 41,932

Fiscal Year Ending Dec. 31

	2001	2000	1999	1998	1997	1996
Revenues (Million $)						
1Q	2,545	1,476	638.0	575.0	261.0	172.0
2Q	2,215	1,538	640.0	565.0	261.0	174.0
3Q	—	1,761	847.0	612.0	358.0	205.0
4Q	—	1,916	1,128	646.0	531.0	284.0
Yr.	—	6,691	3,253	2,398	1,411	835.0
Earnings Per Share ($)						
1Q	**0.20**	**0.42**	**-0.04**	**0.18**	**0.13**	**0.10**
2Q	**0.21**	**0.25**	**0.18**	**0.20**	**0.13**	**0.09**
3Q	—	**0.29**	**0.14**	**0.21**	**0.14**	**0.06**
4Q	—	**0.46**	**0.28**	**0.24**	**0.16**	**0.12**
Yr.	—	**1.42**	**0.63**	**0.83**	**0.56**	**0.41**

Next earnings report expected: late October

Dividend Data

No cash dividends have been paid. The company does not contemplate paying cash dividends on its common stock in the foreseeable future.

AES Corporation

Business Summary - 23-AUG-01

As one of the world's largest power companies, AES appears to have the skills, capital and clout to take advantage of a worldwide trend toward deregulation and privatization of electric utility systems. Over the 16 months ended April 2001, the company and its affiliates made investments in and acquisitions of 12 different power businesses (primarily in Latin America) in transactions totalling over $7.5 billion and brought three newly constructed generating plants (1,264 MW) into operation. AES's decentralized corporate structure helps to facilitate rapid expansion, as regional subsidiaries can identify and evaluate potential acquisition opportunities without the limitations of a pre-planned, top-down corporate strategy.

AES's commitment to employee education and empowerment is integral to its cost competitiveness. By teaching employees to act like business owners, and by facilitating the sharing of knowledge across business units, the company is able to reduce the cost of power generation (down approximately 4.5% inflation adjusted during 2000). AES's efforts to move employees to a basis of salary plus bonus, rather than hourly pay, is a significant part of its strategy to transform employee thinking and incentives. During 2000, an additional 1,704 employees chose to switch from old-style hourly pay and overtime to straight salaries.

Although the company's historical power generating business has realized significant benefits from employee empowerment, the benefits related to more recently acquired businesses (electric distribution, telecommunications and retail energy sales) have yet to be determined. Thus far, worldwide electric distribution operations have been more effective in cutting staff than in reducing electricity losses from theft, inadequate metering, and inefficient collections. At the end of 2000, AES's interests in various energy distribution companies consisted of operations serving 6.2 million net customers, with annual sales in excess of 48,000 gigawatt hours.

At the end of 2000, the company held an average ownership interest of approximately 64% in 141 power plants (in existing operation or under construction) covering 25 nations. Also including pending acquisitions, AES's generating interests at the end of 2000 represented approximately 64,418 megawatts of power. Of total generating capacity in operation at the end of 2000, 38% was fueled by coal or petroleum coke, 18% by natural gas, 33% by hydroelectric power, 4% by oil, and the remaining 7% utilized multiple fossil fuels.

In addition to power generation and distribution, AES has begun developing telecom initiatives in Brazil. Due to the initial success with the company's deployment of a Brazilian fiber optic network, it is considering pursuing telecommunications efforts in several other locations, including Bolivia, El Salvador, Chile and the U.S.

Per Share Data ($) (Year Ended Dec. 31)	**2000**	**1999**	**1998**	**1997**	**1996**	**1995**	**1994**	**1993**	**1992**	**1991**
Tangible Bk. Val.	5.21	3.88	4.79	4.17	2.16	1.72	1.34	1.04	0.65	0.53
Earnings	1.42	0.63	0.83	0.56	0.41	0.35	0.33	0.24	0.20	0.17
Dividends	Nil	Nil	Nil	Nil	Nil	Nil	Nil	0.15	0.10	0.03
Payout Ratio	Nil	Nil	Nil	Nil	Nil	Nil	Nil	59%	48%	20%
Prices - High	72.81	38.18	29.00	24.81	12.53	6.00	5.94	5.66	6.10	5.54
- Low	34.25	16.40	11.50	11.18	5.25	4.00	3.93	4.20	2.67	3.07
P/E Ratio - High	51	61	35	45	31	17	18	23	30	34
- Low	24	26	14	20	13	11	12	17	13	19
Income Statement Analysis (Million $)										
Revs.	6,691	3,253	2,398	1,411	835	685	533	519	401	334
Depr.	582	278	196	114	65.0	55.0	43.4	41.7	33.7	29.2
Maint.	NA	NA	NA	NA	NA	NA	NA	NA	NA	NA
Fxd. Chgs. Cov.	1.8	NA	NA	NA	NA	NA	NA	NA	NA	NA
Constr. Credits	NA	NA	NA	NA	NA	NA	NA	NA	NA	NA
Eff. Tax Rate	25%	26%	27%	21%	31%	34%	30%	20%	14%	15%
Net Inc.	648	245	307	188	125	107	98.3	71.3	55.8	42.6
Balance Sheet & Other Fin. Data (Million $)										
Gross Prop.	19,150	NA	NA	NA	NA	NA	NA	NA	NA	NA
Cap. Exp.	2,150	NA	NA	NA	NA	NA	NA	NA	NA	NA
Net Prop.	17,846	NA	NA	NA	NA	NA	NA	NA	NA	NA
Capitalization:										
LT Debt	16,927	NA	NA	NA	NA	NA	NA	NA	NA	NA
% LT Debt	78	NA	NA	NA	NA	NA	NA	NA	NA	NA
Pfd.	NA	NA	NA	NA	NA	NA	NA	NA	NA	NA
% Pfd.	NA	NA	NA	NA	NA	NA	NA	NA	NA	NA
Common	4,811	NA	NA	NA	NA	NA	NA	NA	NA	NA
% Common	22	NA	NA	NA	NA	NA	NA	NA	NA	NA
Total Cap.	24,752	17,708	8,585	7,414	3,185	2,079	1,802	1,551	1,405	1,324
% Oper. Ratio	88.3	NA	NA	NA	NA	NA	NA	NA	NA	NA
% Earn. on Net Prop.	14.0	NA	NA	NA	NA	NA	NA	NA	NA	NA
% Return On Revs.	9.7	NA	NA	NA	NA	NA	NA	NA	NA	NA
% Return On Invest. Capital	9.8	NA	NA	NA	NA	NA	NA	NA	NA	NA
% Return On Com. Equity	17.4	NA	NA	NA	NA	NA	NA	NA	NA	NA

Data as orig. reptd.; bef. results of disc. opers. and/or spec. items. Per share data adj. for stk. divs. as of ex-div. date. Bold denotes diluted EPS (FASB 128). E-Estimated. NA-Not Available. NM-Not Meaningful. NR-Not Ranked.

Office—1001 North 19th St., Arlington, VA 22209. **Tel**—(703) 522-1315. **E-mail**—investing@aesc.com **Website**—www.aesc.com **Chrmn**—R. W. Sant. **Pres & CEO**—D. W. Bakke. **SVP & CFO**—B. J. Sharp. **SVP & Investor Contact**—Kenneth R. Woodcock. **Dirs**—D. W. Bakke, A. F. Emerson, R. F. Hemphill Jr., F. Jungers, P. Lader, J. H. McArthur, H. R. O'Leary, R. W. Sant, T. I. Unterberg, R. H. Waterman Jr. **Transfer Agent & Registrar**—First Chicago Trust Co., Jersey City, NJ. **Incorporated**—in Delaware in 1981. **Empl**— 26,606. **S&P Analyst:** Craig K. Shere, CFA

STANDARD & POOR'S
STOCK REPORTS

Allegheny Energy

NYSE Symbol **AYE**

In S&P 500

18-AUG-01

Industry: Electric Companies

Summary: This diversified energy company engages in electric generation and electric and natural gas delivery, and invests in and develops telecommunications and energy-related projects.

S&P Opinion: Accumulate (★★★★)

Recent Price • 43.63 | Yield • 3.9%
52 Wk Range • 55.09-35.12 | 12-Mo. P/E • 11.8

Quantitative Evaluations

Outlook
(1 Lowest—5 Highest)
• **3**

Fair Value
• **44.80**

Risk
• **NA**

Earn./Div. Rank
• **A-**

Technical Eval.
• **Bearish** since 6/01

Rel. Strength Rank
(1 Lowest—99 Highest)
• **36**

Insider Activity
• **NA**

OPTIONS: ASE, CBOE, P

Overview - 16-AUG-01

We expect revenues to climb about 150% in 2001, as a result of AYE's March acquisition of Merrill Lynch's Global Energy Marketing (GEM) unit, as well as the May acquisition of 1,710 MW of Midwest peaking plants from Enron. Gross margins will narrow appreciably, due to the high-volume, low-margin contributions from GEM. Excluding the impact of GEM, we see margins expanding, with increasing capacity utilization at AYE's coal powered, baseload generating plants and a full-year contribution from Mountaineer Gas (acquired in August 2000 for $323 million). Interest expense should rise over 15%, reflecting debt related to acquisitions and construction activity. EPS estimates for 2002 exclude goodwill amortization (equal to approximately $0.20 a share in 2001).

Valuation - 16-AUG-01

In the three months through mid-August, the shares fell nearly 20%, in sympathy with declines in both the utility and unregulated power sectors. Now trading at under 10X our 2002 EPS estimate, the stock's P/E ratio is near a 10-year low, and below the regulated utility average. Based on projected long-term annual EPS growth in excess of 10% (well above the average growth rate for the utility sector), the stock's P/E to growth ratio stands at about 50% that of the S&P 500. We anticipate that a planned fourth quarter IPO for Allegheny Energy Supply will garner valuations near the top of the independent power producer group, due to strong contributions from diversified energy marketing (spurred by the March acquisition of GEM from Merrill Lynch). As a result of strong earnings growth, cheap valuations, and a pending IPO for fast growing unregulated power operations, we anticipate that AYE will outperform the S&P 500 over the coming 12 months. We are maintaining our accumulate recommendation.

Key Stock Statistics

S&P EPS Est. 2001	4.05	Tang. Bk. Value/Share	14.98
P/E on S&P Est. 2001	10.8	Beta	0.27
S&P EPS Est. 2002	4.70	Shareholders	44,873
Dividend Rate/Share	1.72	Market cap. (B)	$ 5.4
Shs. outstg. (M)	124.7	Inst. holdings	42%
Avg. daily vol. (M)	0.732		

Value of $10,000 invested 5 years ago: $ 19,067

Fiscal Year Ending Dec. 31

	2001	2000	1999	1998	1997	1996
Revenues (Million $)						
1Q	1,814	866.8	690.0	645.5	615.0	648.0
2Q	3,456	865.3	643.4	627.6	542.8	551.0
3Q	—	1,058	741.4	726.6	595.1	554.0
4Q	—	1,221	733.7	576.7	616.6	574.7
Yr.	—	4,012	2,808	2,576	2,369	2,328
Earnings Per Share ($)						
1Q	**0.91**	**0.78**	**0.80**	**0.64**	0.64	0.43
2Q	**1.01**	**0.65**	**0.55**	**0.44**	0.42	0.44
3Q	**E1.26**	**0.69**	**0.63**	**0.68**	0.61	0.46
4Q	**E0.87**	**0.72**	**0.46**	**0.58**	**0.63**	0.40
Yr.	**E4.05**	**2.84**	**2.45**	**0.69**	**2.30**	**1.73**

Next earnings report expected: late October

Dividend Data (Dividends have been paid since 1935.)

Amount ($)	Date Decl.	Ex-Div. Date	Stock of Record	Payment Date
0.430	Sep. 07	Sep. 14	Sep. 18	Sep. 29 '00
0.430	Dec. 07	Dec. 14	Dec. 18	Dec. 29 '00
0.430	Mar. 01	Mar. 08	Mar. 12	Mar. 30 '01
0.430	Jun. 07	Jun. 14	Jun. 18	Jun. 29 '01

Allegheny Energy, Inc.

Business Summary - 16-AUG-01

Allegheny Energy is seeking to realize shareholder value through the transformation of its unregulated energy supply business into a national energy merchant, expansion of regulated energy delivery operations, and growth in diversified unregulated investments. In July 2001, the company filed with the SEC for an IPO for up to an 18% interest in its Allegheny Energy Supply (AES) subsidiary. AYE expects to conclude the AES IPO in the fourth quarter of 2001, spinning off the remaining interest in AES to AYE shareholders by the end of 2002.

AES (which contributed 24% of 2000 operating profit) has become a leading unregulated power producer and energy marketer as a result of deregulation, acquisitions and construction activities. During 1999 and 2000, AYE transferred approximately 6,150 MW of generating plants to AES at book value, as part of electric deregulation initiatives in Pennsylvania, Maryland, Virginia and Ohio. An additional 2,356 MW in West Virginia are expected to be transferred in 2002. AES also had nearly 4,300 MW of planned acquisitions and construction activity as of the beginning of 2001. By 2005, the subsidiary expects to own or control at least 18,000 MW of generation.

In March 2001, AES acquired Global Energy Markets (GEM), one of the 20 leading domestic energy marketing operations, from Merrill Lynch, for $490 million and a 2% interest in AES. As a part of the acquisition, Merrill Lynch will refer all client energy trading requests to AES for 30 months. GEM and AES's combined operations are expected to place the company among the 10 leading U.S. power marketers.

Allegheny Power (24% of 2000 operating profit) consists of the operations of three electric distribution companies; Monongahela Power, Patomac Edison, and West Penn Power. At the end of 2000, these subsidiaries served more than 1.4 million electric customers, with an aggregate 30.2 square mile service territory. In addition, Monongahela served approximately 230 natural gas customers, added through the acquisition of West Virginia Power in 1999 and Mountaineer Gas in 2000. The Mountaineer acquisitions, at a cost of $323 million, including the assumption of $100 million of debt, also contributed 375 natural gas wells, 11.7 Bcf of gas storage, and intrastate transmission pipelines.

AYE pursues additional unregulated investments through its Allegheny Ventures subsidiary. During 2000, the Ventures unit invested in a super-regional fiber optics company, launched retail high-speed Internet access service, and entered into partnerships with a number of distributed energy/power technology companies.

Per Share Data ($) (Year Ended Dec. 31)	2000	1999	1998	1997	1996	1995	1994	1993	1992	1991
Tangible Bk. Val.	13.80	14.97	16.49	18.31	17.68	17.52	17.11	16.49	15.59	15.32
Earnings	2.84	2.22	2.15	2.30	1.73	2.00	1.86	1.88	1.83	1.80
Dividends	1.72	1.72	1.72	1.72	1.69	1.65	1.64	1.63	1.60	1.58
Payout Ratio	61%	77%	74%	75%	98%	83%	88%	87%	88%	88%
Prices - High	48.75	35.18	34.93	32.59	31.12	29.25	26.50	28.43	24.37	23.25
- Low	23.62	26.18	26.62	25.50	28.00	21.50	19.75	23.43	20.75	17.43
P/E Ratio - High	17	16	15	14	18	15	14	15	13	13
- Low	8	12	11	11	16	11	11	12	11	10
Income Statement Analysis (Million $)										
Revs.	4,012	2,808	2,576	2,369	2,328	2,648	2,452	2,332	2,307	2,282
Depr.	248	257	270	266	263	256	224	210	198	190
Maint.	230	224	218	231	255	257	242	231	211	204
Fxd. Chgs. Cov.	3.1	3.3	3.3	3.2	3.3	3.0	3.0	2.8	2.8	3.0
Constr. Credits	7.3	6.9	5.0	NA	5.9	8.2	19.6	21.5	17.6	7.9
Eff. Tax Rate	37%	37%	39%	37%	38%	39%	35%	37%	34%	36%
Net Inc.	314	285	263	281	210	240	220	216	204	194
Balance Sheet & Other Fin. Data (Million $)										
Gross Prop.	9,507	8,840	8,630	8,451	8,207	7,813	7,587	7,177	6,680	6,256
Cap. Exp.	402	467	234	280	289	147	508	574	488	338
Net Prop.	5,539	5,207	5,234	5,296	5,296	5,113	5,057	4,788	4,440	4,162
Capitalization:										
LT Debt	2,634	2,328	2,349	2,193	2,397	2,273	2,178	2,008	1,952	1,748
% LT Debt	60	58	54	48	51	48	48	47	48	47
Pfd.	Nil	Nil	Nil	170	170	170	325	276	278	264
% Pfd.	Nil	Nil	Nil	3.70	3.60	3.70	7.10	6.50	6.90	7.10
Common	1,741	1,695	2,034	2,257	2,169	2,130	2,059	1,956	1,828	1,686
% Common	40	42	46	49	46	47	45	46	45	46
Total Cap.	5,372	5,062	5,351	5,784	5,878	5,709	5,693	5,280	4,645	4,271
% Oper. Ratio	86.6	83.1	82.9	80.9	83.2	84.1	84.2	83.9	84.6	84.7
% Earn. on Net Prop.	10.0	9.3	8.3	8.5	7.6	8.3	7.9	8.1	8.3	8.5
% Return On Revs.	7.8	10.2	10.2	11.9	9.1	9.1	9.0	9.3	8.8	8.5
% Return On Invest. Capital	10.5	9.2	11.9	8.1	10.9	10.5	7.2	7.8	8.2	8.5
% Return On Com. Equity	18.3	15.3	12.3	12.7	9.8	11.4	10.9	11.4	11.6	11.7

Data as orig reptd.; bef. results of disc opers/spec. items. Per share data adj. for stk. divs. Bold denotes diluted EPS (FASB 128)-prior periods restated. E-Estimated. NA-Not Available. NM-Not Meaningful. NR-Not Ranked.

Office—10435 Downsville Pike, Hagerstown, MD 21740-1766. **Tel**—(301) 790-3400. **Website**—www.alleghenypower.com **Chrmn, Pres & CEO**—A. J. Noia. **Secy**—M. L. Brooks. **SVP & CFO**—B. E. Walenczyk. **Investor Contact**—Gregory L. Fries (301-665-2713). **Dirs**—E. Baum, L. B. Campbell, W. F. Holland, F. A. Metz Jr., A. J. Noia, S. H. Rice, G. E. Sarsten. **Transfer Agent & Registrar**—Mellon Investor Services, Ridgefield Park, NJ. **Incorporated**—in Maryland in 1925. **Empl**— 5,600. **S&P Analyst:** Craig K. Shere, CFA

STANDARD
&POOR'S
STOCK REPORTS

Calpine Corp.

NYSE Symbol **CPN**

In S&P 500

18-AUG-01

Industry: Power Producers (Independent)

Summary: CPN acquires, develops, owns and operates power generation plants, and sells electricity and steam in the U.S. and Canada.

S&P Opinion: Accumulate (★★★★)

Recent Price • 29.28 | Yield • Nil
52 Wk Range • 58.04-29 | 12-Mo. P/E • 19.4

Quantitative Evaluations

Outlook
(1 Lowest—5 Highest)
• **4−**

Fair Value
• **41.20**

Risk
• **Average**

Earn./Div. Rank
• **NR**

Technical Eval.
• **Bearish** since 5/01

Rel. Strength Rank
(1 Lowest—99 Highest)
• **11**

Insider Activity
• **Neutral**

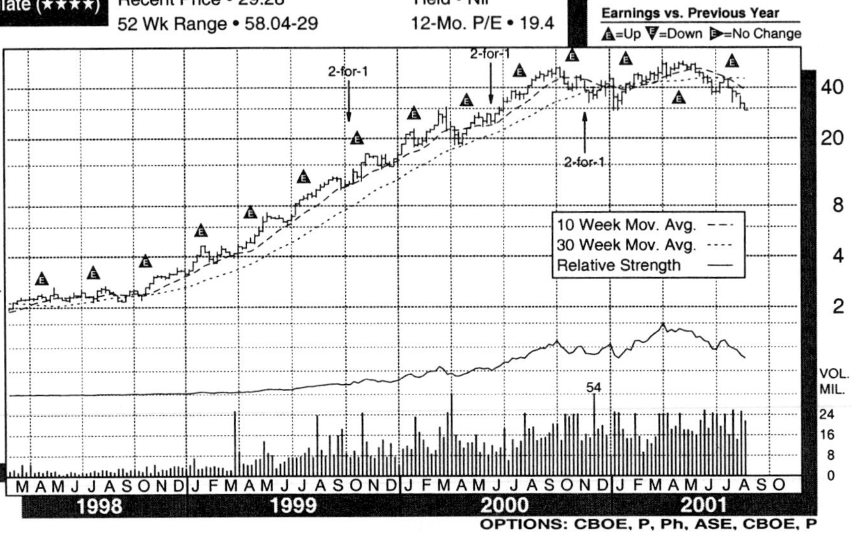

Overview - 21-JUN-01

Revenues should more than double in 2001, aided by construction of additional generating plants, acquisitions, and increased consolidation of power projects. Gross margins should narrow, with less attractive California electric prices, and reduced "spark spread" leverage, as second half gas prices fall, year to year. Income from unconsolidated investments will fall, due to declining interests in a Sumas, WA, power plant, and increased consolidation of investments. Depreciation charges as well as G&A expenses should continue to decline as a percentage of revenue. Interest expense will rise substantially, as interest costs for finished development projects are no longer capitalized, and additional debt is issued to bring CPN to its target of 65% debt to total capital. With more shares (fully diluted), we look for EPS to rise about 70%.

Valuation - 21-JUN-01

In late June, we downgraded Calpine to accumulate, from hold. The stock fell about 30% since late April, as the independent power producer (IPP) industry suffered from declining spot prices, enhanced regulatory price controls and California political threats. Despite strong value in the sector, poor technical performance warrants a less aggressive posture. Of our three buy-rated sector companies (CPN, DYN & MIR), Calpine is the only one without extensive power marketing operations and the only one focused solely on gas-fired power. Lacking the diversification of trading and multiple fuel exposure, Calpine offers a higher risk profile. Furthermore, apparent moves toward relaxed U.S. emission standards and news of new coal plant development could reduce competitive advantages for CPN's clean burning natural gas plants. Despite these concerns, Calpine is trading at a below market P/E multiple with nearly 3X the EPS growth potential.

Key Stock Statistics

S&P EPS Est. 2001	1.90	Tang. Bk. Value/Share	7.39
P/E on S&P Est. 2001	15.4	Beta	NA
S&P EPS Est. 2002	2.50	Shareholders	547
Dividend Rate/Share	Nil	Market cap. (B)	$ 8.7
Shs. outstg. (M)	298.7	Inst. holdings	88%
Avg. daily vol. (M)	5.822		

Value of $10,000 invested 5 years ago: NA

Fiscal Year Ending Dec. 31

	2001	2000	1999	1998	1997	1996
Revenues (Million $)						
1Q	1,230	235.4	145.9	55.15	39.23	31.67
2Q	1,613	363.7	190.7	141.6	67.74	50.32
3Q	—	678.9	263.6	186.2	92.91	70.90
4Q	—	1,005	247.5	173.0	76.44	61.66
Yr.	—	2,283	847.7	556.0	276.3	214.6
Earnings Per Share ($)						
1Q	**E0.30**	**0.07**	**0.02**	**-0.02**	-0.03	0.00
2Q	**0.32**	**0.19**	**0.08**	**0.07**	0.06	0.04
3Q	**E0.85**	**0.48**	**0.18**	**0.14**	0.11	0.10
4Q	**E0.45**	**0.34**	**0.12**	**0.08**	**0.06**	0.02
Yr.	**E1.90**	**1.11**	**0.43**	**0.27**	**0.21**	**0.16**

Next earnings report expected: late October

Dividend Data

Amount ($)	Date Decl.	Ex-Div. Date	Stock of Record	Payment Date
2-for-1	Oct. 26	Nov. 15	Nov. 06	Nov. 14 '00

Calpine Corporation

Business Summary - 21-JUN-01

Calpine is embarking on the largest power plant construction program in the history of the United States. From nearly 5,900 megawatts of generating capacity at the end of 2000, CPN's goal is to have 70,000 MW of capacity up and running by the end of 2005. This represents a 64% compound annual growth rate in generating power. At the end of 2000, the company had 14,028 MW of new plants under construction and was in the process of developing another 15,142 MW of specifically identified generating facilities.

Apart from 850 MW of geothermal plants in California (The "Geysers"), all of Calpine's existing and planned generating plants are gas-fired facilities. CPN believes this focus provides it with a number of competitive advantages including reduced plant development costs, the ability to invest in improved turbine technology, the capacity to become the primary customer for key suppliers (turbine manufacturers and construction companies) and the critical mass to acquire direct control of natural gas properties.

Calpine estimates that by the end of 2005, its plants will consume over 10% of all the natural gas produced in North America. The company's goal is to supply at least 25% of its fuel requirements from company owned drilling properties. Between July 2000 and April 2001, CPN closed five natural gas property acquisitions for approximately $1.38 billion in cash, stock and assumed debt. These acquisitions bring the company's daily gas production to 390 MMcf, enough to fuel 2,300 MW of generation. Longer term, Calpine is evaluating opportunities in the importation of liquefied natural gas, deployment of gas pipelines from Northern Canada and Alaska and development of economical coal gasification technologies.

As of early 2001, Calpine had the largest fleet of gas turbines in the world (46 in operation, 19 in plants under construction, and 180 on order). The company believes this dominance has allowed it to attract top engineering personnel, interface more with suppliers, and develop proprietary turbine technology. In December 2000, CPN acquired Power Systems Mfg., a combustion turbine component engineering and manufacturing firm, for approximately $43 million in stock and estimated future cash payments.

Longer term, Calpine has stated its intention to fuel growth through possible entry into high reliability power systems and expansion internationally. In May 2000, the company established c*Power, a division focused on highly reliable, high quality electricity back-up systems for data centers and telecommunications developers. In May 2001, Calpine acquired WRMS Engineering, an engineering firm focused on facilities with uninterrupted power generation.

Per Share Data ($) (Year Ended Dec. 31)	2000	1999	1998	1997	1996	1995	1994	1993	1992	1991
Tangible Bk. Val.	7.39	3.61	1.64	1.37	1.28	1.05	NA	NA	NA	NA
Earnings	1.11	0.43	0.27	0.21	0.16	0.11	NA	NA	NA	NA
Dividends	Nil	Nil	Nil	Nil	Nil	Nil	NA	NA	NA	NA
Payout Ratio	Nil	Nil	Nil	Nil	Nil	Nil	NA	NA	NA	NA
Prices - High	52.96	16.37	3.45	2.86	2.50	NA	NA	NA	NA	NA
- Low	16.09	3.15	1.59	1.54	2.00	NA	NA	NA	NA	NA
P/E Ratio - High	48	38	13	14	16	NA	NA	NA	NA	NA
- Low	14	7	6	7	13	NA	NA	NA	NA	NA
Income Statement Analysis (Million $)										
Revs.	2,283	847	556	276	214	224	NA	NA	NA	NA
Depr.	154	87.2	74.3	46.8	36.6	42.1	NA	NA	NA	NA
Maint.	NA	NA	NA	NA	NA	NA	NA	NA	NA	NA
Fxd. Chgs. Cov.	2.8	1.8	1.7	1.9	NA	1.4	NA	NA	NA	NA
Constr. Credits	NA	NA	NA	NA	NA	Nil	NA	NA	NA	NA
Eff. Tax Rate	40%	39%	37%	35%	33%	41%	NA	NA	NA	NA
Net Inc.	325	96.2	46.3	34.7	18.6	12.8	NA	NA	NA	NA
Balance Sheet & Other Fin. Data (Million $)										
Gross Prop.	7,788	3,094	1,298	868	732	NA	NA	NA	NA	NA
Cap. Exp.	2,967	930	98.2	107	24.0	NA	NA	NA	NA	NA
Net Prop.	7,459	2,866	1,094	720	631	658	NA	NA	NA	NA
Capitalization:										
LT Debt	5,553	2,277	1,066	743	564	589	NA	NA	NA	NA
% LT Debt	71	70	79	76	74	78	NA	NA	NA	NA
Pfd.	Nil	Nil	Nil	Nil	Nil	Nil	NA	NA	NA	NA
% Pfd.	Nil	Nil	Nil	Nil	Nil	Nil	NA	NA	NA	NA
Common	2,237	965	287	240	203	162	NA	NA	NA	NA
% Common	29	30	21	24	27	22	NA	NA	NA	NA
Total Cap.	8,394	3,595	1,513	1,125	867	851	NA	NA	NA	NA
% Oper. Ratio	83.2	91.0	78.5	71.5	68.8	72.6	NA	NA	NA	NA
% Earn. on Net Prop.	11.6	15.8	24.4	21.0	10.5	NA	NA	NA	NA	NA
% Return On Revs.	14.2	11.4	8.3	12.6	8.7	5.7	NA	NA	NA	NA
% Return On Invest. Capital	7.1	7.4	7.1	7.9	NA	NA	NA	NA	NA	NA
% Return On Com. Equity	20.3	15.4	17.6	15.7	NA	NA	NA	NA	NA	NA

Data as orig. reptd. (pro forma in 1995); bef. results of disc. opers. and/or spec. items. Per share data adj. for stk. divs. as of ex-div. date. Bold denotes diluted EPS (FASB 128). E-Estimated. NA-Not Available. NM-Not Meaningful. NR-Not Ranked.

Office—50 W. San Fernando St., San Jose, CA 95113. **Tel**—(408) 995-5115. **Website**—www.calpine.com **Chrmn, Pres & CEO**—P. Cartwright. **EVP, CFO & Secy**—A. B. Curtis. **SVP-Fin**—R. D. Kelly. **SVP & Investor Contact**—Rick Barraza. **Dirs**—P. Cartwright, A. B. Curtis, K. T. Derr, J. E. Garten, M. P. Polsky, S. C. Schwab, G. J. Stathakis, J. O. Wilson. **Transfer Agent & Registrar**—First Chicago Trust Co. of New York, Jersey City, NJ. **Incorporated**—in Delaware on 1996; previously incorporated in California in 1984. **Empl**— 1,883. **S&P Analyst:** Craig K. Shere, CFA

STANDARD & POOR'S STOCK REPORTS

CMS Energy

NYSE Symbol **CMS**

In S&P 500

18-AUG-01

Industry: Electric Companies

Summary: This energy holding company's principal subsidiary is Consumers Energy, the largest utility in Michigan and the fifth largest gas and 12th largest electric utility in the U.S.

S&P Opinion: Accumulate (★★★★)

Recent Price • 24.19
52 Wk Range • 32.25-23.65
Yield • 6.0%
12-Mo. P/E • 96.8

Quantitative Evaluations

Outlook (1 Lowest—5 Highest)
• **4−**

Fair Value
• **30.40**

Risk
• **Low**

Earn./Div. Rank
• **B**

Technical Eval.
• **Bearish** since 7/01

Rel. Strength Rank (1 Lowest—99 Highest)
• **28**

Insider Activity
• **Neutral**

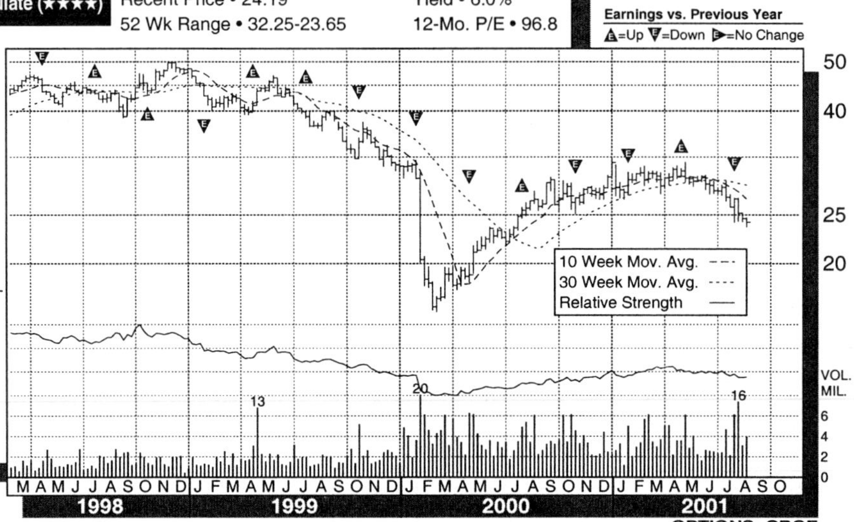

OPTIONS: CBOE

Overview - 24-MAY-01

EPS in 2001 is expected to grow more than 8% from 2000's operating EPS of $2.53 (which excludes numerous one-time items, including a $2.37 write-off of the Loy Yang plant in Australia). The decline in 2000 (from 1999's operating EPS of $2.89) reflected, in part, a regulatory securitization order that prevented Consumers Energy from retroactively offsetting the impact of a 5% residential rate reduction. However, securitization recovery will be allowed on a prospective basis. As of the end of 2000, CMS had completed about $1.2 billion of its $1.4 billion asset sale and debt reduction program. In February 2001, CMS netted proceeds of nearly $296 million from the issuance of 10 million new CMS shares. However, due to unfavorable market conditions, the planned IPO of up to a 50% stake in its oil and gas unit was indefinitely deferred. Through the development and expansion of its non-utility operations, the company believes it will be able to realize average annual EPS growth of approximately 10%.

Valuation - 24-MAY-01

We recommend accumulating CMS shares. While down nearly 8% year to date, with the dividend yielding about 5.0% and the stock trading at less than 11X our 2002 EPS estimate of $3.05, the shares are an attractive investment. After a nearly 36% drop in 1999 and an additional 48% in the first two months of 2000, the stock nearly doubled from its early 2000 low and finished the year up 1.5%. The rebound reflected the enactment of Michigan's electric restructuring legislation, which provided CMS with the full recovery of its stranded costs, and authorized securitization financing (on a prospective basis) to fund a 5% rate reduction. Given CMS's potential (beginning in 2002) for annual EPS growth of about 10%, we believe the stock is still undervalued.

Key Stock Statistics

S&P EPS Est. 2001	2.65	Tang. Bk. Value/Share	12.15
P/E on S&P Est. 2001	9.1	Beta	0.28
S&P EPS Est. 2002	2.85	Shareholders	66,783
Dividend Rate/Share	1.46	Market cap. (B)	$ 3.2
Shs. outstg. (M)	132.0	Inst. holdings	64%
Avg. daily vol. (M)	1.517		

Value of $10,000 invested 5 years ago: $ 9,539

Fiscal Year Ending Dec. 31

	2001	2000	1999	1998	1997	1996
Revenues (Million $)						
1Q	4.13	1,825	1,538	1,374	1,295	1,283
2Q	4,421	1,595	1,353	1,132	1,024	938.0
3Q	—	2,391	1,488	1,286	1,032	929.0
4Q	—	3,187	1,768	1,349	1,436	1,183
Yr.	—	8,998	6,103	5,141	4,787	4,333
Earnings Per Share ($)						
1Q	**0.85**	**0.65**	**0.80**	**0.32**	**0.78**	**0.83**
2Q	**0.40**	**0.71**	**0.67**	**0.62**	**0.55**	**0.53**
3Q	**E0.17**	**0.49**	**0.78**	**0.80**	**0.69**	**0.65**
4Q	**E1.23**	**-1.44**	**0.17**	**0.44**	**0.59**	**0.43**
Yr.	**E2.65**	**0.36**	**2.17**	**2.22**	**2.61**	**2.44**

Next earnings report expected: late October

Dividend Data (Dividends have been paid since 1989.)

Amount ($)	Date Decl.	Ex-Div. Date	Stock of Record	Payment Date
0.365	Oct. 23	Oct. 31	Nov. 02	Nov. 22 '00
0.365	Jan. 29	Feb. 05	Feb. 07	Feb. 22 '01
0.365	Apr. 27	May. 03	May. 07	May. 22 '01
0.365	Jul. 27	Aug. 03	Aug. 07	Aug. 22 '01

CMS Energy Corporation

Business Summary - 24-MAY-01

CMS Energy is the holding company for Consumers Energy (formerly Consumers Power Co.), an electric and gas utility serving Michigan's lower peninsula, and for CMS Enterprises, which is engaged in domestic and international energy-related businesses.

Contributions by segment in 2000 were: electric utility, 29.7% of revenues, $481 million in operating income; natural gas transmission, 10.1% and $227 million; gas utility, 13.3% and $98 million; oil and gas exploration and production, 1.5% and $31 million; international energy distribution, 2.9% and $22 million; marketing, services and trading, 36.6% and $14 million; independent power production, 5.6% and a loss of $140 million; and other, 0.3% and a loss of $6 million.

In February 2001, CMS deferred indefinitely its plans (announced in October 2000) for an IPO of up to 50% of its oil and gas subsidiary. Earlier, in May 2000, the company said it would not proceed with a plan to create, through an IPO, a tracking stock representing a 20% interest in Consumers Energy. It also withdrew a plan to cut its annual dividend from $1.46 to $0.40.

Consumers Energy provides electricity to 1.69 million customers in 61 of the 68 counties in the lower peninsula of Michigan and gas to 1.61 million customers in 54 of these counties. It has four generating plants that use coal as a fuel source, and that produced 73% of its power generation in 2000. The utility owns and operates the Palisades nuclear facility, which produced 23% of its power generation in 2000. In 2000, 37% of Consumers' gas supply was purchased under long-term contracts, and nearly 43% on the spot market.

In October 1999, the company exchanged 6,132,600 new CMS shares for all 8,709,823 Class G shares, issued in 1995 to reflect the performance of the Consumers Gas Group.

In March 1999, CMS acquired Panhandle Eastern Pipeline Co., Trunkline Gas Co. and the Trunkline LNG Co. terminal from Duke Energy, for $2.2 billion, including $300 million in Panhandle debt. The companies now operate as subsidiaries of CMS Gas Transmission, CMS's international gas pipeline unit, which is involved in projects in the U.S., Latin America, Africa and Australia.

The company's other businesses include CMS Oil and Gas Co., which conducts oil and gas exploration and development operations in the U.S. and six other countries; CMS MST, which offers energy marketing, risk management and energy management services; CMS Electric and Gas, which manages and operates international natural gas and electric distribution systems; and CMS Generation, an independent power production company with ownership interests in operating projects throughout the U.S., and in Australia, Argentina, Chile, Ghana, India, Jamaica, Morocco, the Philippines, Thailand, the United Arab Emirates and Venezuela.

Per Share Data ($) (Year Ended Dec. 31)	2000	1999	1998	1997	1996	1995	1994	1993	1992	1991
Tangible Bk. Val.	12.15	13.23	20.30	19.49	17.86	15.94	12.40	10.39	7.73	13.23
Earnings	0.32	2.42	2.22	2.61	2.45	2.27	2.09	1.90	-3.72	-3.26
Dividends	1.46	1.39	1.26	1.14	1.02	0.90	0.78	0.60	0.48	0.48
Payout Ratio	NM	57%	57%	44%	42%	40%	37%	32%	NM	NM
Prices - High	32.25	48.43	50.12	44.06	33.75	30.00	25.00	27.50	22.75	33.00
- Low	16.06	30.31	38.75	31.12	27.81	22.62	19.62	18.12	14.87	16.62
P/E Ratio - High	NM	20	23	17	14	13	12	14	NM	NM
- Low	NM	13	17	12	11	10	9	10	NM	NM
Income Statement Analysis (Million $)										
Revs.	8,998	6,103	5,141	4,787	4,333	3,890	3,619	3,482	3,073	2,941
Depr.	637	595	484	477	441	416	379	365	348	283
Maint.	298	216	176	174	178	186	192	206	203	172
Fxd. Chgs. Cov.	1.6	1.7	1.8	2.3	2.3	2.1	2.1	1.9	NM	NM
Constr. Credits	NA	Nil	Nil	16.0	8.0	8.0	6.0	5.0	3.0	5.0
Eff. Tax Rate	58%	19%	29%	30%	37%	37%	31%	31%	NM	NM
Net Inc.	41.0	277	242	268	240	204	179	155	-297	-262
Balance Sheet & Other Fin. Data (Million $)										
Gross Prop.	14,087	14,278	11,253	10,705	10,147	9,701	9,125	8,605	8,101	7,618
Cap. Exp.	1,032	1,124	1,295	711	659	535	575	548	484	348
Net Prop.	7,835	8,121	6,040	5,435	5,280	5,074	4,826	4,583	4,326	4,121
Capitalization:										
LT Debt	7,913	7,075	5,486	3,347	2,945	3,012	2,817	2,520	2,823	2,009
% LT Debt	77	74	71	60	59	62	66	69	76	62
Pfd.	Nil	Nil	Nil	238	356	356	356	163	163	163
% Pfd.	Nil	Nil	Nil	4.28	7.10	7.30	8.30	4.40	4.40	5.00
Common	2,361	2,456	2,216	1,977	1,702	1,469	1,107	966	727	1,060
% Common	23	26	29	36	34	30	26	27	20	33
Total Cap.	11,221	10,359	8,486	6,456	5,962	5,648	5,043	4,349	4,263	3,902
% Oper. Ratio	88.9	84.7	86.9	86.9	87.6	87.8	88.9	90.0	93.0	91.8
% Earn. on Net Prop.	9.1	12.9	13.5	13.9	13.1	9.6	8.5	7.8	5.1	5.9
% Return On Revs.	0.5	4.5	4.7	5.6	5.5	5.2	4.9	4.5	NM	NM
% Return On Invest. Capital	9.5	10.0	12.0	9.9	11.5	8.9	8.7	8.7	NM	1.7
% Return On Com. Equity	1.7	11.9	11.5	14.6	15.1	15.8	17.3	18.3	NM	NM

Data as orig reptd.; bef. results of disc opers/spec. items. Per share data adj. for stk. divs. Bold denotes diluted EPS (FASB 128)-prior periods restated. E-Estimated. NA-Not Available. NM-Not Meaningful. NR-Not Ranked.

Office—Fairlane Plaza South, Suite 1100, 330 Town Center Dr., Dearborn, MI 48126. **Tel**—(313) 436-9200. **Website**—http://www.cmsenergy.com **Chrmn & CEO**—W. T. McCormick Jr. **EVP & COO, Gas**—W. J. Haener. **EVP & COO, Electric**—D. W. Joos. **EVP & CFO**—A. M. Wright. **VP & Secy**—T. A. McNish. **VP, Treas & Investor Contact**—Laura L. Mountcastle (517-788-2590). **Dirs**—J. M. Deutch, J. M. Duderstadt, K. R. Flaherty, E. D. Holton, W. T. McCormick Jr., W. U. Parfet, P. A. Pierre, K. L. Way, K. Whipple, J. B. Yasinsky. **Transfer Agent & Registrar**—Co.'s office, Jackson, MI. **Incorporated**—in Maine in 1910; reincorporated in Michigan in 1968. **Empl**— 11,652. **S&P Analyst:** Justin McCann

STANDARD &POOR'S
STOCK REPORTS

Dominion Resources

NYSE Symbol **D**

In S&P 500

18-AUG-01 **Industry:** Electric Companies

Summary: This energy holding company's principal subsidiaries are Virginia Electric & Power Co. and Consolidated Natural Gas.

S&P Opinion: Accumulate (★★★★) Recent Price • 62 | 52 Wk Range • 69.99-50.06 | Yield • 4.2% | 12-Mo. P/E • 22.0

Quantitative Evaluations

Outlook (1 Lowest—5 Highest) • 3⁻

Fair Value • 63.40

Risk • Low

Earn./Div. Rank • B

Technical Eval. • **Bearish** since 6/01

Rel. Strength Rank (1 Lowest—99 Highest) • 56

Insider Activity • Neutral

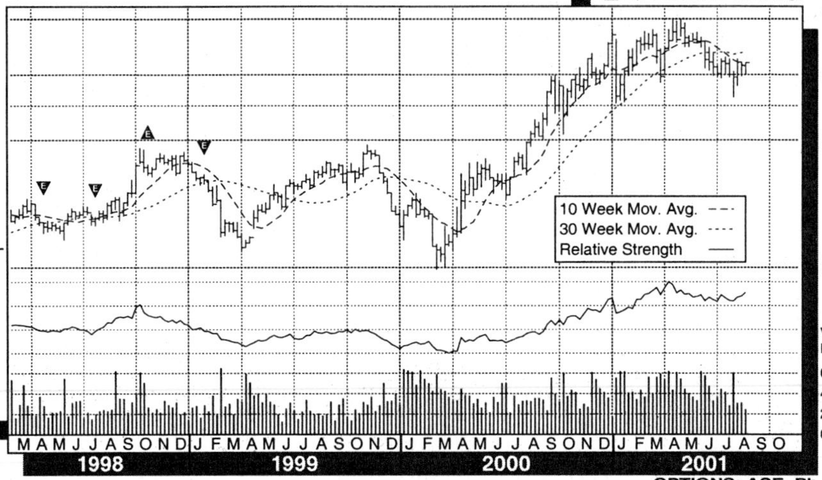

OPTIONS: ASE, Ph

Overview - 08-JUN-01

We expect EPS in 2001 to grow nearly 25% from 2000's operating EPS of $3.33 (excluding one-time net charges of about $1.49 a share), which were up over 10% from 1999 operating EPS of $3.01 (excluding an extraordinary non-cash charge of $1.33, and other one-time charges and costs of $0.13). The Consolidated Natural Gas acquisition has made D the fourth largest U.S. electric and natural gas utility, with over $9 billion in annual revenues. The merger could realize combined revenue and cost savings gains of $150 million to $200 million by 2002. Having exited markets in the U.K. and South America, the company will focus on expansion (through acquisitions and/or alliances) of its operations in the Midwest to Northeast. The April 2001 acquisition of the Millstone nuclear units is expected to add about $0.05 to EPS in both 2001 and 2002. Over the 2002 through 2004 period, we expect D to realize average annual EPS growth of about 10%.

Valuation - 08-JUN-01

Given the recent decline in the shares, we have upgraded our opinion on D Stock to accumulate from hold. The shares are down about 8% year to date (compared to approximate declines of 4% and 18% for the respective S&P Indexes of Electric and Natural Gas Companies). In 2000, the stock rebounded more than 90% from its yearly low (which was down nearly 30% from the then five-year high reached in the fall of 1999), and finished the year up 70.7% (versus gains of 42.3% and 74.7% for the respective Electric and Natural Gas Indexes). In November 2000, the company sold publicly 6 million common shares, with proceeds of about $354 million to be used for new acquisitions and/or the reduction of debt. With the dividend yielding around 4%, the stock is an attractive investment at around 13 times our 2002 EPS estimate of $4.60.

Key Stock Statistics

S&P EPS Est. 2001	4.20	Tang. Bk. Value/Share	14.22
P/E on S&P Est. 2001	14.8	Beta	0.10
S&P EPS Est. 2002	4.90	Shareholders	188,737
Dividend Rate/Share	2.58	Market cap. (B)	$ 15.4
Shs. outstg. (M)	248.1	Inst. holdings	46%
Avg. daily vol. (M)	0.724		

Value of $10,000 invested 5 years ago: $ 21,691

Fiscal Year Ending Dec. 31

	2001	2000	1999	1998	1997	1996
Revenues (Million $)						
1Q	3,198	2,005	1,293	1,774	1,855	1,239
2Q	2,309	2,056	1,315	1,585	1,635	1,121
3Q	—	2,351	1,663	1,549	2,060	1,287
4Q	—	2,781	1,250	1,178	1,887	1,195
Yr.	—	9,260	5,520	6,086	7,678	4,842
Earnings Per Share ($)						
1Q	**1.20**	**0.63**	—	**0.72**	0.93	0.85
2Q	**0.62**	**-0.44**	—	**-0.42**	0.43	0.53
3Q	**E1.36**	**1.07**	—	**2.17**	1.12	0.91
4Q	**E0.92**	**0.49**	**0.33**	**0.28**	**0.53**	0.36
Yr.	**E4.20**	**1.76**	**2.81**	**2.75**	**2.15**	**2.65**

Next earnings report expected: mid October

Dividend Data (Dividends have been paid since 1925.)

Amount ($)	Date Decl.	Ex-Div. Date	Stock of Record	Payment Date
0.645	Oct. 20	Nov. 21	Nov. 24	Dec. 20 '00
0.645	Feb. 16	Feb. 28	Mar. 02	Mar. 20 '01
0.645	Apr. 27	May. 30	Jun. 01	Jun. 20 '01
0.645	Jul. 20	Aug. 29	Aug. 31	Sep. 20 '01

Dominion Resources, Inc.

Business Summary - 08-JUN-01

On January 28, 2000, Dominion Resources, the holding company for Virginia Electric & Power Co., completed the acquisition of Consolidated Natural Gas (CNG). D also owns two other subsidiaries: Dominion Energy, an independent power and natural gas company, and Dominion Capital, a financial services and real estate firm.

The CNG operations acquired are engaged in the exploration and production, purchasing, gathering, transmission, storage and distribution of natural gas. The utilities supply gas to approximately 1.7 million retail customers in Ohio, Pennsylvania and West Virginia. CNG Transmission operates an interstate pipeline system serving its distribution units and nonaffiliated utilities in the Midwest, the mid-Atlantic states and the Northeast.

The newly formed Dominion Exploration and Production, Inc. (which includes CNG Producing) is involved in the development, exploration, and operation of oil and natural gas reserves in the Gulf of Mexico, the Southwest, the Appalachian region and Canada.

Virginia Electric & Power Co. provides electric service in Virginia and to a lesser extent in North Carolina. The service territory is characterized by government installations, high-technology centers and financial services businesses. Fuel sources in 2000 were: coal, 42% (38% in 1999); nuclear, 33% (35%); net purchased power, 20% (19%); oil, 3% (4%); and other, 2% (4%).

In August 1998, the Virginia State Corporation Commission approved Virginia Power's rate case settlement, which called for: a $100 million annual reduction retroactive to March 1, 1998, and an additional $50 million annual reduction beginning March 1, 1999; the write-off of $220 million in regulatory assets; and an incentive mechanism that allowed the company to grow its earnings and benefit from future efficiency gains.

In April 2001, Dominion completed the acquisition (agreed to in August 2000) of the Connecticut-based Millstone nuclear station for $1.28 billion in cash. The assets include a 100% interest in Millstone Unit 2 (870 megawatts), a 93.47% interest in Unit 3 (1,150 megawatts), and a 100% interest in Unit 1, which was retired in 1998 for future decommissioning.

Dominion Energy provides non-utility electric power generation outside of Virginia Power's service territory and is active in the development, exploration and operation of oil and natural gas reserves. In October 2000, the company completed its exit from Latin America with the sale (announced in July 2000) of its natural gas and electricity assets in Argentina for $145 million. Earlier, in April 2000, it completed the sale of its Latin American generation business for $405 million.

In October 2000, D completed the sale (announced in May 2000) of CNG's Virginia Natural Gas subsidiary for $533 million. The company is also in the process of divesting its Dominion Capital subsidiary.

Per Share Data ($) (Year Ended Dec. 31)	2000	1999	1998	1997	1996	1995	1994	1993	1992	1991
Tangible Bk. Val.	14.20	24.80	26.56	16.55	27.21	26.73	26.51	26.38	25.21	24.41
Earnings	1.85	2.81	2.75	2.15	2.65	2.45	2.81	3.12	2.66	2.94
Dividends	2.58	2.58	2.58	2.58	2.58	2.58	2.55	2.48	2.40	2.31
Payout Ratio	139%	92%	94%	120%	97%	105%	91%	79%	92%	79%
Prices - High	67.93	49.37	48.93	42.87	44.37	41.62	45.37	49.50	41.00	38.12
- Low	34.81	36.56	37.81	33.25	36.87	34.87	34.87	38.25	34.12	29.87
P/E Ratio - High	37	18	18	20	17	17	16	16	15	13
- Low	19	13	14	15	14	14	12	12	13	10
Income Statement Analysis (Million $)										
Revs.	9,260	5,520	6,086	7,678	4,842	4,652	4,491	4,434	3,791	3,786
Depr.	1,176	716	734	819	615	551	533	510	450	450
Maint.	NA	NA	NA	NA	251	261	263	280	281	305
Fxd. Chgs. Cov.	2.0	2.4	1.8	2.4	3.1	2.4	2.6	2.8	2.5	2.4
Constr. Credits	NA	Nil	Nil	Nil	Nil	6.7	6.4	5.1	9.5	11.8
Eff. Tax Rate	31%	31%	35%	34%	31%	30%	26%	29%	32%	31%
Net Inc.	415	551	536	399	472	425	478	559	475	511
Balance Sheet & Other Fin. Data (Million $)										
Gross Prop.	31,011	18,646	18,106	19,520	16,816	15,977	15,415	15,009	14,147	13,388
Cap. Exp.	1,385	737	755	649	484	578	721	1,127	941	815
Net Prop.	14,849	10,764	10,637	12,533	10,509	10,322	10,245	10,207	9,687	9,278
Capitalization:										
LT Debt	10,486	7,321	5,071	7,196	4,728	4,612	4,711	4,751	4,404	4,393
% LT Debt	58	58	44	49	45	45	47	48	47	49
Pfd.	509	509	1,074	1,074	824	824	816	829	829	735
% Pfd.	2.83	4.05	9.40	7.30	7.90	8.10	8.10	8.20	8.90	8.20
Common	6,992	4,752	5,315	5,040	4,924	4,742	4,586	4,436	4,131	3,878
% Common	39	38	46	34	47	47	45	44	44	43
Total Cap.	20,955	14,427	13,475	14,658	12,474	12,111	12,016	11,897	11,173	10,237
% Oper. Ratio	80.5	80.9	64.4	83.6	81.6	80.0	76.9	79.3	78.2	76.6
% Earn. on Net Prop.	11.9	9.7	9.4	13.0	11.5	11.2	10.2	9.2	8.8	9.7
% Return On Revs.	4.5	10.0	8.8	5.2	9.8	9.1	10.6	12.6	12.5	13.5
% Return On Invest. Capital	10.7	7.9	8.4	7.6	9.8	8.6	8.8	9.9	9.8	11.2
% Return On Com. Equity	7.1	10.9	10.4	8.0	9.8	9.1	10.6	11.9	10.5	12.1

Data as orig reptd.; bef. results of disc opers/spec. items. Per share data adj. for stk. divs. Bold denotes diluted EPS (FASB 128)-prior periods restated. E-Estimated. NA-Not Available. NM-Not Meaningful. NR-Not Ranked.

Office—120 Tredegar Street, Richmond, VA 23219. **Tel**—(804) 819-2000. **Website**—http://www.dom.com **Chrmn, Pres & CEO**—T. E. Capps. **EVP & CFO**—T. N. Chewning. **SVP & Treas**—G. S. Hetzer. **VP & Secy**—P. A. Wilkerson. **Investor Contacts**—Tom Wohlfarth (2150) / Suzette Mata (2154). **Dirs**—W. S. Barrack Jr., T. E. Capps, G. A. Davidson Jr., J. W. Harris, B. J. Lambert III, R. L. Leatherwood, M. A. McKenna, S. A. Minter, K. A. Randall, F. S. Royal, S. D. Simmons, R. H. Spilman, D. A. Wollard. **Transfer Agent & Registrar**—Co.'s office. **Incorporated**—in Virginia in 1909. **Empl**— 15,600. **S&P Analyst:** Justin McCann

STANDARD
&POOR'S
STOCK REPORTS

Duke Energy

NYSE Symbol **DUK**

In S&P 500

18-AUG-01

Industry: Electric Companies

Summary: DUK provides electric service to around two million customers in North and South Carolina, and is one of the largest U.S. transporters and marketers of natural gas.

S&P Opinion: Accumulate (★★★★)

Recent Price • 38.15 | Yield • 2.9%

52 Wk Range • 47.74-32.40 | 12-Mo. P/E • 14.3

Quantitative Evaluations

Outlook
(1 Lowest—5 Highest)
• **3−**

Fair Value
• **38.20**

Risk
• **Low**

Earn./Div. Rank
• **A-**

Technical Eval.
• **Bearish** since 7/01

Rel. Strength Rank
(1 Lowest—99 Highest)
• **38**

Insider Activity
• **Neutral**

OPTIONS: ASE, CBOE, P, Ph

Overview - 09-AUG-01

After an anticipated 19% increase in 2001 (over 2000's operating EPS of $2.10), we expect EPS to grow about 12% in 2002. We then expect EPS to grow at an annual rate of between 10% to 15% over the next several years, led by the expansion of DUK's non-regulated and international operations. In 2000, these operations accounted for 90% of DUK's consolidated revenues and 53% of its EBIT. DUK will continue to benefit from the strength and volatility of electricity and natural gas prices in the wholesale markets. In the fourth quarter of 2000, DUK took a charge of $0.18 as a provision against receivable balances related to its California energy sales. California, however, accounts for a relatively minor portion of its wholesale energy operations. DUK will continue to develop energy assets in the key regional centers of the Northeast, the West and the Gulf Coast. In addition to the natural gas operations, DUK is one of the largest and lowest-cost U.S. electric utilities.

Valuation - 09-AUG-01

We recommend accumulating the stock. Following its strong 70% gain in 2000 (versus respective increases of 42% and 75% for the S&P Indexes of Electric and Natural Gas Companies), the shares are down nearly 14% year to date (compared to respective declines of around 9% and 28% for the Electric and Gas indexes), reflecting a shift away from energy stocks and concerns about California. Given the decline, the stock is attractive at around 13 times our 2002 EPS estimate of $2.80. Duke is developing domestic energy assets in the most attractive regional centers. Internationally, DUK's Latin American acquisitions will enable it to engage in cross-border trading and marketing as markets in South and Central America become deregulated. The dividend will not be increased until the payout ratio has been reduced to approximately 50% of earnings.

Key Stock Statistics

S&P EPS Est. 2001	2.50	Tang. Bk. Value/Share	11.21
P/E on S&P Est. 2001	15.3	Beta	-0.08
S&P EPS Est. 2002	2.80	Shareholders	152,392
Dividend Rate/Share	1.10	Market cap. (B)	$ 29.4
Shs. outstg. (M)	771.9	Inst. holdings	59%
Avg. daily vol. (M)	2.962		

Value of $10,000 invested 5 years ago: $ 19,200

Fiscal Year Ending Dec. 31

	2001	2000	1999	1998	1997	1996
Revenues (Million $)						
1Q	16,491	7,236	4,160	4,115	3,786	—
2Q	15,580	10,926	4,691	4,014	3,113	—
3Q	—	15,691	6,694	5,298	4,821	—
4Q	—	15,411	6,197	4,183	4,590	—
Yr.	—	49,318	21,742	17,610	16,309	4,758
Earnings Per Share ($)						
1Q	**0.73**	**0.53**	**0.41**	**0.45**	**0.42**	—
2Q	**0.53**	**0.44**	**0.39**	**0.38**	**0.21**	—
3Q	**E0.78**	**1.03**	**0.59**	**0.58**	**0.41**	—
4Q	**E0.46**	**0.38**	**-0.27**	**0.30**	**0.20**	—
Yr.	**E2.50**	**2.38**	**1.12**	**1.71**	**1.25**	**1.44**

Next earnings report expected: NA

Dividend Data (Dividends have been paid since 1926.)

Amount ($)	Date Decl.	Ex-Div. Date	Stock of Record	Payment Date
2-for-1	Dec. 20	Jan. 29	Jan. 03	Jan. 26 '01
0.275	Jan. 04	Feb. 14	Feb. 16	Mar. 16 '01
0.275	Apr. 26	May. 09	May. 11	Jun. 18 '01
0.275	Jun. 26	Aug. 15	Aug. 17	Sep. 17 '01

Duke Energy Corporation

Business Summary - 09-AUG-01

Duke Energy was formed in June 1997 through the merger of Duke Power and PanEnergy.

Contributions by business segment in 2000 were: the electric operations (10% of revenues, 45% of operating income); Natural Gas Transmission (2%, 14%); Duke Ventures (1%, 15%); North American Wholesale Energy (68%, 11%); International Energy (2%, 9%); Field Services (15%, 8%); and other (2%, -2%).

On March 31, 2000, Duke completed the combination of its gas gathering and processing business with the gas processing and marketing (GPM) unit of Phillips Petroleum to form a new company called Duke Energy Field Services (DEFS). Upon the closing of the transaction, Duke owned 69.7% of DEFS, the largest midstream natural gas liquids business in the U.S. One year earlier, on March 31, 1999, DUK completed the acquisition of the natural gas and natural gas liquids business of Union Pacific Resources for $1.35 billion.

The Electric Operations segment provides for the generation, transmission, distribution and sale of electricity in central and western North Carolina and the western portion of South Carolina. Within this territory, DUK serves (through its Duke Power and Nantahala Power and Light Co. units) about two million customers.

Fuel sources in 2000 were: coal, 51%; nuclear, 48%; hydroelectric, 0.5%; and oil and gas, 0.5%.

The company's North American Wholesale Energy segment (NAWE) is involved in asset development, operation and management, mainly through Duke Energy North America (DENA), and commodity sales and services related to natural gas and power, primarily through Duke Energy Trading and Marketing (DETM). NAWE also develops new energy commodity business lines through Duke Energy Merchants (DEM).

The Natural Gas Transmission unit is involved in the interstate transportation and storage of natural gas. DUK's 10,300 mile Northeast Pipeline system includes Texas Eastern Transmission Corp. and the Algonquin Gas Transmission Co. In March 1999, it sold the Panhandle Eastern Pipe Line Co. and the Trunkline Gas and LNG companies to CMS Energy for $2.2 billion.

The International Energy operations are conducted through Duke Energy International (DEI). In August 1999, DEI acquired a 40% interest in the Paranpanema utility in the Brazilian state of Sao Paulo. In January 2000, it increased its ownership to 95%. From August 1999 through April 2000, DEI acquired the generation businesses of Dominion Resources in Argentina, Belize, Bolivia and Peru for $405 million. During 2000, it acquired Mobil Europe Gas, a gas marketing company located in the Netherlands.

Duke Ventures is comprised of businesses involved in real estate projects in the southeastern U.S., financial services, and the provision of fiber optic networks.

Per Share Data ($) (Year Ended Dec. 31)	**2000**	**1999**	**1998**	**1997**	**1996**	**1995**	**1994**	**1993**	**1992**	**1991**
Tangible Bk. Val.	11.21	10.69	10.09	9.36	11.56	11.09	10.46	9.96	9.76	9.65
Earnings	2.38	1.13	1.71	1.25	1.69	1.63	1.44	1.40	1.10	1.30
Dividends	1.10	1.10	1.10	1.08	1.04	1.00	0.96	0.92	0.88	0.84
Payout Ratio	46%	98%	64%	86%	62%	62%	67%	66%	80%	65%
Prices - High	45.21	32.65	35.50	28.28	26.50	23.93	21.50	22.43	18.75	17.50
- Low	22.87	23.37	26.56	20.93	21.68	18.68	16.43	17.68	15.68	13.37
P/E Ratio - High	19	29	21	23	16	15	15	16	17	13
- Low	10	21	16	17	13	11	11	12	14	10
Income Statement Analysis (Million $)										
Revs.	49,318	21,742	17,610	16,309	4,758	4,677	4,489	4,282	3,961	3,817
Depr.	1,167	968	909	841	492	458	460	488	491	432
Maint.	NA	NA	NA	NA	NA	416	430	376	404	356
Fxd. Chgs. Cov.	4.3	3.2	4.8	3.7	4.2	4.3	4.1	4.2	3.1	3.5
Constr. Credits	63.0	82.0	88.0	109	112	23.1	27.4	27.1	21.2	70.0
Eff. Tax Rate	33%	31%	36%	39%	40%	40%	38%	40%	37%	34%
Net Inc.	1,776	847	1,260	974	730	715	639	626	508	584
Balance Sheet & Other Fin. Data (Million $)										
Gross Prop.	34,615	30,436	27,128	25,448	14,946	14,937	14,489	13,760	14,953	14,337
Cap. Exp.	5,634	NA	2,159	1,323	646	713	772	655	588	807
Net Prop.	24,469	20,995	16,875	15,736	9,386	9,361	9,264	8,924	8,882	8,699
Capitalization:										
LT Debt	12,425	10,087	7,191	6,530	3,538	3,711	3,567	3,285	3,202	3,160
% LT Debt	55	52	46	45	39	40	40	39	39	40
Pfd.	247	313	313	489	684	684	780	781	780	731
% Pfd.	1.09	1.61	2.00	3.40	7.50	7.50	8.80	9.30	9.60	9.20
Common	10,056	8,998	8,150	7,540	4,889	4,785	4,533	4,338	4,151	4,066
% Common	44	46	52	52	54	52	51	52	51	51
Total Cap.	29,225	24,225	19,882	18,673	11,737	11,824	11,501	10,895	9,798	9,558
% Oper. Ratio	94.3	93.8	90.6	91.8	81.4	91.1	82.6	81.0	81.7	81.5
% Earn. on Net Prop.	16.8	9.5	14.9	15.4	14.5	14.5	8.6	9.2	8.2	8.2
% Return On Revs.	3.6	3.9	7.2	6.0	15.3	15.3	14.2	14.6	12.8	15.3
% Return On Invest. Capital	11.2	7.6	13.2	11.2	16.9	12.6	7.9	8.5	8.4	9.1
% Return On Com. Equity	18.4	9.6	15.5	14.1	14.2	14.3	13.3	12.5	11.1	13.5

Data as orig. reptd.; bef. results of disc. opers. and/or spec. items. Per share data adj. for stk. divs. as of ex-div. date. Bold denotes diluted EPS (FASB 128). E-Estimated. NA-Not Available. NM-Not Meaningful. NR-Not Ranked.

Office—526 S. Church St., Charlotte, NC 28202-1904. **Tel**—(704) 594-6200. **Website**—http://www.duke-energy.com **Chrmn, Pres & CEO**—R. B. Priory. **EVP & CFO**—R. P. Brace. **Secy**—R. W. Blackburn. **SVP & Treas**—D. L. Hauser. **VP & Investor Contact**—Sue A. Becht. **Dirs**—A. Bernhardt, Sr., R. J. Brown, W. A. Coley, W. T. Esrey, A. M. Gray, D. R. Hendrix, H. S. Hook, G. D. Johnson Jr., M. Lennon, L. E. Linbeck Jr., J. G. Martin, R. B. Priory, R. M. Robinson II. **Transfer Agent & Registrar**—Company's office. **Incorporated**—in New Jersey in 1917; reincorporated in North Carolina in 1964. **Empl**— 23,000. **S&P Analyst:** Justin McCann

STANDARD
&POOR'S
STOCK REPORTS

Edison International

NYSE Symbol **EIX**

In S&P 500

18-AUG-01

Industry:
Electric Companies

Summary: Edison International is the holding company for Southern California Edison. Other businesses include electric power generation, financial investments and real estate development.

S&P Opinion: Accumulate (★★★★)

Recent Price • 14
52 Wk Range • 26.62-6.25
Yield • Nil
12-Mo. P/E • NM

Quantitative Evaluations

Outlook
(1 Lowest—5 Highest)
• **1**

Fair Value
• **10.70**

Risk
• **Low**

Earn./Div. Rank
• **B**

Technical Eval.
• **Bullish** since 7/01

Rel. Strength Rank
(1 Lowest—99 Highest)
• **83**

Insider Activity
• **NA**

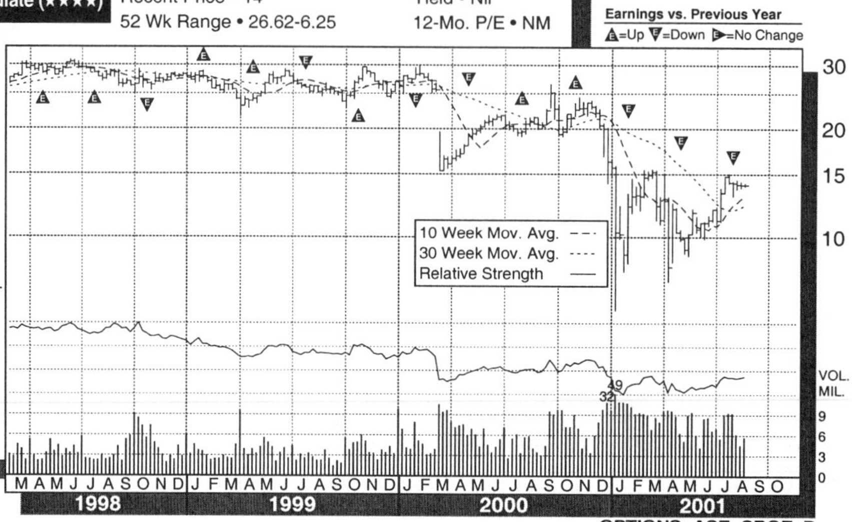

OPTIONS: ASE, CBOE, P

Overview - 10-AUG-01

EIX's Southern California Edison (SCE) subsidiary is working for legislation that will enable it to avoid the prospect of bankruptcy. However, a plan approved by the California state senate on July 20 would leave it about $1 billion short of that needed to regain creditworthiness. While the state assembly may approve a plan more closely resembling the April 9 memorandum of understanding (MOU) with the Governor, the outlook for a bill that can pass both state branches remains uncertain. Under the MOU, SCE would be able to recover an estimated $3.5 billion in net undercollected revenues (as a result of a rate freeze preventing the pass through of its purchased power costs), repay its debt, and restore its investment grade credit rating. In addition to the $2.76 billion that would be received from the sale of SCE's transmission system, the plan would enable the utility to sell about $2 billion in securitized bonds (that would be covered by a surcharge over a 15-year period).

Valuation - 10-AUG-01

We have lowered our opinion on EIX stock to accumulate from buy. Given the recent rise in the shares, we believe the upside potential over the near term has been reduced. While the stock gained 27% on the first day of trading following the announcement of the April 9 agreement with the Governor, it subsequently retreated some 25% before rebounding more than 50% to its recent level. The shares are still about 30% below their price level in the fall of 2000, which was just prior to the collapse that resulted from the realization that SCE's liquidity crisis could result in a potential bankruptcy. While the stock should benefit from favorable developments, the volatile shares will remain speculative until the legislative and financial uncertainties are resolved.

Key Stock Statistics

S&P EPS Est. 2001	-0.85	Tang. Bk. Value/Share	14.04
P/E on S&P Est. 2001	NM	Beta	-0.22
S&P EPS Est. 2002	1.80	Shareholders	89,910
Dividend Rate/Share	Nil	Market cap. (B)	$ 4.6
Shs. outstg. (M)	325.8	Inst. holdings	60%
Avg. daily vol. (M)	1.344		

Value of $10,000 invested 5 years ago: $ 10,418

Fiscal Year Ending Dec. 31

	2001	2000	1999	1998	1997	1996
Revenues (Million $)						
1Q	2,462	2,723	2,088	1,909	2,001	1,968
2Q	—	2,749	2,116	2,243	2,167	1,814
3Q	—	3,653	2,957	3,441	2,738	2,568
4Q	—	2,590	2,509	2,615	2,329	2,195
Yr.	—	11,717	9,670	10,208	9,235	8,544
Earnings Per Share ($)						
1Q	**-1.89**	**0.32**	**0.40**	**0.38**	0.35	0.38
2Q	**-0.31**	**0.40**	**0.37**	**0.40**	0.34	0.35
3Q	**E0.95**	**1.10**	**0.73**	**0.60**	0.70	0.63
4Q	**E0.40**	**-7.83**	**0.28**	**0.46**	**0.36**	0.27
Yr.	**E-0.85**	**-5.84**	**1.79**	**1.84**	**1.73**	**1.63**

Next earnings report expected: late October

Dividend Data

Amount ($)	Date Decl.	Ex-Div. Date	Stock of Record	Payment Date
0.280	Sep. 21	Oct. 03	Oct. 05	Oct. 31 '00
Div Omitted	Dec. 22			Jan. 31 '01

A Division of The McGraw-Hill Companies

Edison International

Business Summary - 10-AUG-01

Edison International is the holding company for the regulated Southern California Edison utility (SCE), as well as several non-regulated subsidiaries.

SCE provides electric service to 4.3 million customers in a 50,000 square mile area of central and Southern California (excluding Los Angeles and certain other cities). In 1999 (latest available), it accounted for 67% of revenues (versus 1999's 78%); diversified operations accounted for 33% (22%).

On April 9, 2001, EIX and the Governor of California announced an agreement under which the state would pay SCE about $2.76 billion for its transmission system and a 10-year contract under which SCE (and the Edison Mission Energy "Sunrise" power plant) would sell power to the state at cost-based pricing. The plan, which would require the approval of the state legislature and the California Public Utility Commission, also included a securitized $2 billion bond issuance, that would further enable the utility to repay its creditors.

SCE owns 37 hydro electric plants and one diesel-fueled generating plant. It also has a 75% interest in the San Onofre 2 and 3 nuclear generating units. SCE's power sources in 2000 were: purchased 58.6%; nuclear 22.3%; coal 13.7%; and hydro 5.4%.

EIX's diversified operations include Edison Mission Energy (EME), which develops, owns and operates independent power facilities; Edison Capital, a provider of capital and financial services to support the growth of energy and infrastructure projects; and Edison Source, a retail provider of energy services and energy marketing. In June 2001, EIX agreed to sell Edison Select, a provider of consumer products and services. Earlier, in January 2001, it sold Edison Utility Services, which offers services to electric utilities in the U.S. and Canada.

In December 1999, Midwest Generation, an EME subsidiary, acquired all of the coal and gas-fired generation assets (with a total capacity of 9,772 megawatts) of Commonwealth Edison for $4.8 billion. In July 1999, EME acquired 2 electric generating facilities (each with capacity of about 2,000 mw) in the U.K. for approximately $2.0 billion. Earlier, in March 1999, it acquired the 1,884 megawatt (mw) coal-fired Homer City Generating Station in western Pennsylvania for $1.8 billion.

On March 31, 1998, the right to choose an electric supplier was provided to all California customers as a result of legislation passed in September 1996. The legislation also included a nonbypassable competitive transition charge for recovery of stranded costs; a 10% rate reduction (implemented in 1998) for residential and small commercial customers, to be financed by rate reduction bonds; a rate freeze for industrial, agricultural and large commercial customers through March 31, 2002; and formation of a generation power exchange and an independent system operator to manage and control the transmission system and ensure reliability.

Per Share Data ($) (Year Ended Dec. 31)	2000	1999	1998	1997	1996	1995	1994	1993	1992	1991
Tangible Bk. Val.	7.43	14.04	13.55	13.65	14.12	13.40	12.76	12.45	12.49	12.12
Earnings	-5.84	1.79	1.84	1.73	1.64	1.66	1.52	1.43	1.66	1.60
Dividends	1.11	1.07	1.04	1.00	1.25	1.00	1.10	1.42	1.39	1.35
Payout Ratio	NM	60%	56%	58%	76%	60%	73%	99%	84%	84%
Prices - High	30.00	29.62	31.00	27.81	20.37	18.00	20.50	25.75	23.81	23.68
- Low	14.12	21.62	25.12	19.37	15.00	14.37	12.37	19.87	20.12	18.00
P/E Ratio - High	NM	17	17	16	12	11	13	18	14	15
- Low	NM	12	14	11	9	9	8	14	12	11
Income Statement Analysis (Million $)										
Revs.	11,717	9,670	10,208	9,235	8,545	8,405	8,345	7,821	7,984	7,502
Depr.	1,933	1,794	1,662	1,362	1,173	1,014	945	922	807	764
Maint.	NA	NA	411	406	331	359	332	363	361	382
Fxd. Chgs. Cov.	-1.0	2.0	1.7	2.3	3.2	3.3	2.9	2.6	3.1	2.9
Constr. Credits	NA	Nil	12.0	17.0	26.0	33.0	28.0	36.0	37.0	28.0
Eff. Tax Rate	NM	32%	40%	40%	44%	42%	40%	36%	39%	38%
Net Inc.	-1,943	623	668	700	717	739	681	639	739	703
Balance Sheet & Other Fin. Data (Million $)										
Gross Prop.	25,737	27,203	17,223	24,661	21,134	20,717	20,127	19,441	18,652	17,523
Cap. Exp.	1,488	1,231	963	783	744	NA	1,137	1,259	844	986
Net Prop.	17,903	19,683	10,326	14,117	11,703	12,148	12,417	12,303	11,937	11,184
Capitalization:										
LT Debt	13,660	15,050	8,543	8,871	7,475	7,195	6,347	6,459	6,320	5,745
% LT Debt	85	74	63	59	51	50	48	50	49	48
Pfd.	Nil	Nil	Nil	609	709	709	721	634	637	558
% Pfd.	Nil	Nil	Nil	4.05	4.80	5.00	5.50	4.90	4.90	4.70
Common	2,420	5,211	5,099	5,527	6,397	6,360	6,144	5,948	5,954	5,681
% Common	15	26	37	37	44	45	47	46	46	47
Total Cap.	21,609	26,252	18,520	19,452	19,943	19,638	18,305	17,476	15,618	13,260
% Oper. Ratio	86.4	92.9	96.9	87.8	82.7	83.6	84.4	84.4	83.2	83.6
% Earn. on Net Prop.	NM	11.6	6.4	10.2	12.4	11.2	10.5	10.0	11.0	11.0
% Return On Revs.	NM	6.4	6.5	7.6	8.4	8.8	8.2	8.2	9.3	9.4
% Return On Invest. Capital	7.8	3.6	7.9	10.5	7.1	7.9	7.0	7.1	8.6	10.1
% Return On Com. Equity	NM	12.1	12.6	11.7	11.2	11.8	11.3	10.7	12.5	12.5

Data as orig reptd.; bef. results of disc opers/spec. items. Per share data adj. for stk. divs. Bold denotes diluted EPS (FASB 128)-prior periods restated. E-Estimated. NA-Not Available. NM-Not Meaningful. NR-Not Ranked.

Office—2244 Walnut Grove Ave., Rosemead, CA 91770. **Tel**—(626) 302-2222. **Website**—http://www.edisoninvestor.com **Chrmn, Pres & CEO**—J. E. Bryson. **SVP & CFO**—T. F. Craver. **Secy**—B. P. Ryder. **Investor Contact**—Jo Ann Goddard (626-302-2515). **Dirs**—J. E. Bryson, W. Christopher, S. E. Frank, J. C. Hanley, C. F. Huntsinger, C. D. Miller, L. G. Nogales, R. L. Olson, J. M. Rosser, R. H. Smith, T. C. Sutton, D. M. Tellep, E. Zapanta. **Transfer Agent & Registrar**—Wells Fargo Bank Minnesota N.A., St. Paul. **Incorporated**—in California in 1909. **Empl**— 18,555. **S&P Analyst:** Justin McCann

STANDARD
&POOR'S
STOCK REPORTS

El Paso Corp.

NYSE Symbol **EPG**

In S&P 500

18-AUG-01 **Industry:** Natural Gas

Summary: EPG (formerly El Paso Energy), which recently acquired Coastal Corp., operates in all areas of the energy business.

S&P Opinion: Accumulate (★★★★)

Recent Price • 47.39 Yield • 1.8%
52 Wk Range • 75.30-44.50 12-Mo. P/E • NM

Quantitative Evaluations

Outlook (1 Lowest—5 Highest) • **3−**

Fair Value • **46.90**

Risk • **Low**

Earn./Div. Rank • **B+**

Technical Eval. • **Bearish** since 5/01

Rel. Strength Rank (1 Lowest—99 Highest) • **26**

Insider Activity • **Neutral**

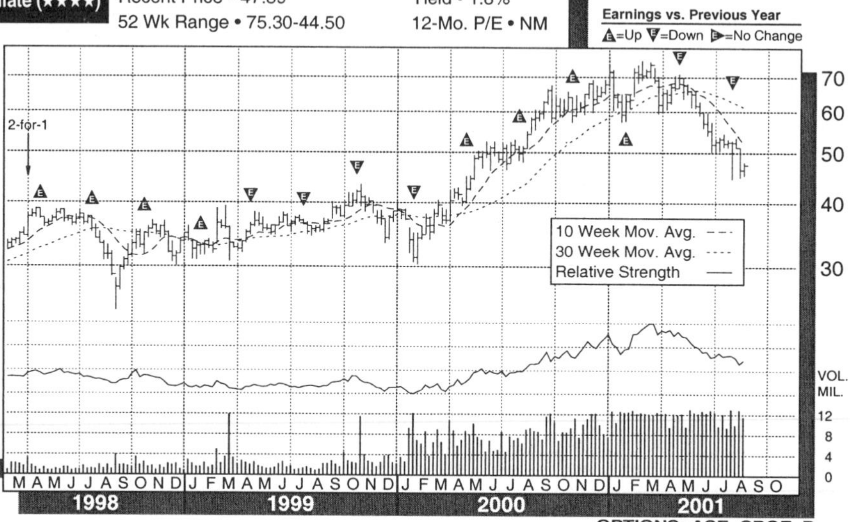

OPTIONS: ASE, CBOE, P

Overview - 02-JUL-01

EPG's recent acquisition of Coastal Corp. (CGP) accelerates contributions of nonregulated businesses to earnings. We are especially impressed with CGP's exploration and production activities, as its five-year average annual domestic reserve replacement rate is 400%, at a cost of only $0.89 per Mcfe. With prior results restated to conform with pooling of interests accounting, we expect EBIT at the Production segment to more than double in 2001, fueled in part by a 7% production increase. A majority of production volumes have been hedged, decreasing EBIT volatility. A large portion of EPG's 2001 capital budget has been allocated to Production, demonstrating the company's bullishness on this segment. Merchant Energy Group (MEG) should contribute about $1.3 billion of EBIT, reflecting a doubling of North American trading volumes, $125 million a quarter of fee-based income, and the addition of CGP's petroleum assets.

Valuation - 02-JUL-01

For the longer term, we expect EPG to benefit from recent deregulation of energy markets in Europe and Asia, and from new financial services and liquefied natural gas (LNG) initiatives. El Paso Field Services will provide substantial future earnings growth, as it develops its burgeoning master limited partnership. However, the recent investigation of possible violation by EPG of the affiliate standards in awarding shipping contracts for its California pipeline system should continue to put pressure on the stock price. Adding the recent weakening in natural gas prices due to seasonal inventory build and a lack of weather-related demand, we recently trimmed our 2001 EPS estimate to $3.30 from $3.34. With the shares trading at only 13x our 2002 EPS estimate, we believe EPG will outperform the market over the long term.

Key Stock Statistics

S&P EPS Est. 2001	3.30	Tang. Bk. Value/Share	15.25
P/E on S&P Est. 2001	14.4	Beta	0.59
S&P EPS Est. 2002	3.85	Shareholders	75,700
Dividend Rate/Share	0.85	Market cap. (B)	$ 24.1
Shs. outstg. (M)	509.2	Inst. holdings	69%
Avg. daily vol. (M)	3.286		

Value of $10,000 invested 5 years ago: $ 25,605

Fiscal Year Ending Dec. 31

	2001	2000	1999	1998	1997	1996
Revenues (Million $)						
1Q	17,754	3,106	2,275	1,619	1,831	606.0
2Q	13,363	4,227	2,600	1,296	979.0	587.0
3Q	—	6,987	3,263	1,615	1,251	745.0
4Q	—	7,543	2,443	1,252	1,577	1,072
Yr.	—	21,950	10,581	5,782	5,638	3,010
Earnings Per Share ($)						
1Q	**-0.78**	**0.70**	**-0.62**	**0.48**	**0.42**	**-0.50**
2Q	**-0.26**	**0.56**	**0.17**	**0.45**	**0.37**	**0.34**
3Q	—	**0.57**	**0.17**	**0.43**	**0.37**	**0.34**
4Q	—	**0.61**	**-0.78**	**0.49**	**0.43**	**0.30**
Yr.	—	**2.44**	**-1.06**	**1.85**	**1.59**	**0.52**

Next earnings report expected: late October

Dividend Data (Dividends have been paid since 1992.)

Amount ($)	Date Decl.	Ex-Div. Date	Stock of Record	Payment Date
0.206	Oct. 26	Nov. 28	Nov. 30	Jan. 02 '01
0.212	Jan. 26	Feb. 28	Mar. 02	Apr. 02 '01
0.212	Apr. 17	May. 30	Jun. 01	Jul. 02 '01
0.212	Jul. 17	Sep. 05	Sep. 07	Oct. 01 '01

El Paso Corporation

Business Summary - 02-JUL-01

To better reflect its increasing reliance on the entire energy process, this energy giant changed its name from El Paso Natural Gas Co. to El Paso Energy in August 1998. Following the February 2001 introduction of a telecom strategy, the company changed its name to El Paso Corp. In January 2001, EPG acquired Coastal Corp. (CGP), in exchange for about 264 million common shares and the assumption of $6 billion of debt. EPG was attracted to CGP by potential synergies between the two companies. The acquisition substantially expanded EPG's pipeline network, and increased its exposure to the lucrative exploration and production (E&P) business. Sonat, another integrated energy company, was acquired in October 1999, for $6 billion. Both transactions were accounted for as poolings of interests.

EPG provides energy services through four business segments. Pipeline Group (PG) manages 60,000 miles of interstate pipelines, moving more natural gas than any other energy company in the world. PG's pipeline system consists of ANR, Colorado Interstate Gas, El Paso Natural Gas, Southern Natural Gas and Tennessee Gas Pipeline. In addition, EPG owns 1,900 miles of pipelines in Australia. Several pipelines were divested to comply with FTC orders related to the Sonat and CGP acquisitions.

The Merchant Energy Group (MEG) buys, sells and trades natural gas, power, natural gas transmission capacity, gas storage, and other energy commodities. It also acquires, develops, constructs, owns, operates and manages domestic power generation facilities. In addition, MEG has significant petroleum shipping, terminal and refining capacity. Through EPG's physical assets and knowledge of the energy marketplace, MEG provides customers with solutions to meet energy supply and financial risk management requirements. MEG's activities are organized into four units: North America, Petroleum Markets, International and Europe.

With more than 6 trillion cubic feet of natural gas equivalent reserves and more than 10 million net acres, the Production segment is one of the largest U.S. E&P companies. El Paso Field Services (EPFS) provides customers with wellhead-to-wire services, including gas gathering and transportation, products extraction, dehydration, purification, compression and intrastate gas transmission services. Together with its general partnership interest in El Paso Energy Partners (NYSE: EPN), EPFS has interests in 24,000 miles of intrastate pipeline and gathering systems, 35 processing and treating plants, and eight offshore platforms. The company purchased certain natural gas assets from PG&E in December 2000, for $840 million in cash and assumption of debt.

El Paso Global Networks (which is not yet a reporting segment) is focusing on developing a bandwidth merchanting platform to provide end-to-end liquidity in the commercially undeveloped broadband industry.

Per Share Data ($) (Year Ended Dec. 31)	2000	1999	1998	1997	1996	1995	1994	1993	1992	1991
Tangible Bk. Val.	15.25	10.47	13.06	15.39	13.77	9.71	9.98	9.60	9.01	8.69
Cash Flow	4.82	1.61	3.92	3.60	1.93	2.28	2.11	1.96	2.08	1.83
Earnings	2.44	-1.06	1.85	1.59	0.53	1.24	1.23	1.23	1.06	0.98
Dividends	0.82	0.79	0.76	0.73	0.69	0.66	0.60	0.55	0.38	NA
Payout Ratio	34%	NM	41%	46%	131%	53%	49%	44%	35%	NA
Prices - High	74.25	43.43	38.93	33.75	26.62	16.25	20.93	20.18	15.75	NA
- Low	30.31	30.68	24.68	24.43	14.31	12.37	14.81	15.12	9.50	NA
P/E Ratio - High	30	NM	21	21	50	13	17	16	15	NA
- Low	12	NM	13	15	27	10	12	12	9	NA
Income Statement Analysis (Million $)										
Revs.	21,950	10,581	5,782	5,638	3,010	1,038	870	909	803	730
Oper. Inc.	2,155	1,482	775	757	370	284	302	283	258	241
Depr.	589	609	269	236	101	72.1	65.0	54.0	73.0	61.3
Int. Exp.	538	453	267	238	110	86.3	78.8	75.4	68.1	97.9
Pretax Inc.	1,012	-287	377	340	65.0	133	148	151	123	114
Eff. Tax Rate	28%	NM	34%	38%	39%	36%	40%	39%	38%	37%
Net Inc.	582	-242	225	186	38.0	85.4	90.0	92.0	76.0	71.9
Balance Sheet & Other Fin. Data (Million $)										
Cash	688	545	90.0	116	200	39.0	28.0	Nil	49.0	170
Curr. Assets	10,076	2,911	1,209	1,629	1,965	369	299	304	364	606
Total Assets	27,445	16,657	10,069	9,532	9,532	2,535	2,332	2,270	2,051	2,094
Curr. Liab.	10,467	3,702	2,162	2,464	2,712	643	452	356	373	469
LT Debt	6,574	5,548	3,177	2,119	2,215	772	779	796	637	639
Common Eqty.	3,569	2,947	2,108	1,959	1,638	712	710	708	669	633
Total Cap.	14,623	11,601	6,914	5,993	5,280	1,798	1,794	1,801	1,508	1,493
Cap. Exp.	1,336	1,086	406	293	119	166	173	164	246	NA
Cash Flow	1,171	367	494	422	139	157	155	146	150	133
Curr. Ratio	1.0	0.8	0.6	0.7	0.7	0.6	0.7	0.9	1.0	1.3
% LT Debt of Cap.	45.0	47.8	46.0	35.4	42.0	42.9	43.4	44.2	42.2	42.8
% Net Inc.of Revs.	2.7	NM	3.9	3.3	1.3	8.2	10.3	10.1	9.5	9.9
% Ret. on Assets	2.6	NM	2.3	2.0	0.7	3.5	4.0	4.3	3.2	NA
% Ret. on Equity	17.9	NM	11.1	10.3	3.2	12.0	12.9	13.4	9.4	NA

Data as orig reptd.; bef. results of disc. opers./spec. items. Per share data adj. for stk. divs. Bold denotes diluted EPS (FASB 128)-prior periods may be restated. E-Estimated. NA-Not Available. NM-Not Meaningful. NR-Not Ranked.

Office—1001 Louisiana Street, Houston, TX 77002. **Tel**—(713) 420-2131. **Website**—http://www.epenergy.com **Chrmn, Pres & CEO**—W. A. Wise. **Vice Chrmn**—D. A. Arledge. **EVP & CFO**—H. B. Austin. **Secy**—D. L. Siddall. **Investor Contact**—Bruce Connery (713-420-5855). **Dirs**—W. A. Wise, B. Allumbaugh, D. A. Arledge, J. M. Bissell, J. C. Braniff, J. F. Gibbons, A. W. Hall Jr., R. L. Kuehn Jr., J. C. MacNeil Jr., T. R. McDade, M. Wallop, W. A. Wise, J. B. Wyatt. **Transfer Agent & Registrar**—BankBoston, N.A. **Incorporated**—in Delaware in 1928. **Empl**— 15,000. **S&P Analyst:** John Kartsonas

STANDARD
&POOR'S
STOCK REPORTS

Energy East

NYSE Symbol **EAS**

In S&P MidCap 400

18-AUG-01 **Industry:** Electric Companies

Summary: EAS serves more than 1.3 million electricity customers and 600,000 natural gas customers in New York and New England.

S&P Opinion: Accumulate (★★★★) Recent Price • 20.24 52 Wk Range • 23.50-16.96 Yield • 4.5% 12-Mo. P/E • 10.3

Quantitative Evaluations

Outlook
(1 Lowest—5 Highest)
• **4−**

Fair Value
• **24.50**

Risk
• **NA**

Earn./Div. Rank
• **B+**

Technical Eval.
• **NA**

Rel. Strength Rank
(1 Lowest—99 Highest)
• **49**

Insider Activity
• **NA**

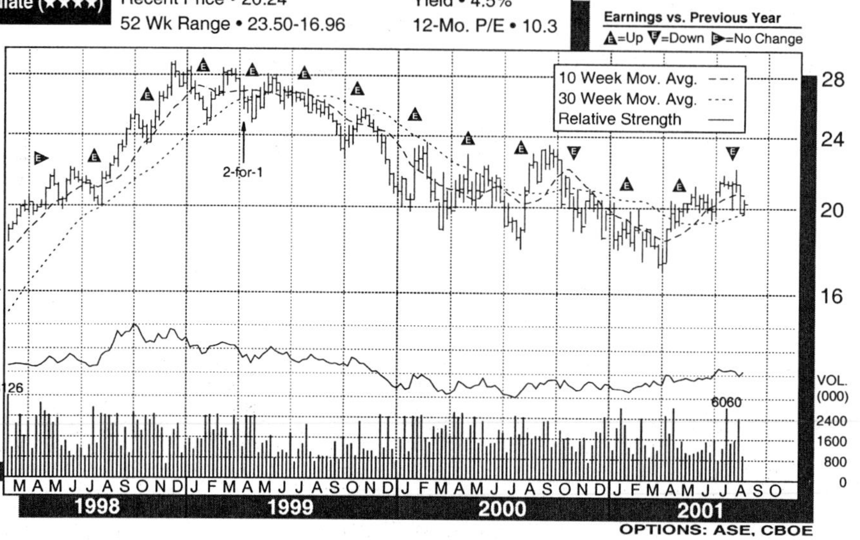

OPTIONS: ASE, CBOE

Overview - 14-AUG-01

Total revenues should climb over 40% in 2001, with full-year contributions from the February 2000 acquisition of Connecticut Energy (CNE) and the September 2000 acquisitions of CMP Group (CTP), CTG Resources (CTG), and Berkshire Energy (BERK). Operating margins will narrow, as contributions from lower margin acquired businesses outweigh merger-related synergies. Annual goodwill amortization related to acquisitions in 2000 will be about $21 million. Investment income will drop, with the remaining cash proceeds of EAS's 1999 generation divestitures absorbed by the four 2000 acquisitions. EPS comparisons will benefit from $150 million to $200 million in annual share repurchases. Aided by merger synergies and ongoing share repurchases, we see 8% to 10% EPS growth in each of 2001 and 2002. However, EPS will likely be hurt by a pending New York electric rate case.

Valuation - 14-AUG-01

In the two months through mid-August, the shares declined less than 2%, versus a decline of nearly 6% in the broader utility sector. We believe EAS's low P/E ratio, below both its historical average and the broader utility sector, offers significant downside protection. Although it may hurt earnings, we see final resolution of the NYSEG electric rate case, expected in September, leading to P/E expansion as uncertainty is alleviated. The pending RGS acquisition, announced in February, should provide significant synergies. With more than 200 contiguous miles of service territory, and offsetting winter/summer peaking requirements, the companies are a natural fit. With a payout ratio near the low end of its desired range, EAS is also likely to continue annual dividend increases. Based on attractive valuations and a solid dividend, we see the shares outperforming the S&P 500 in the coming 12 months.

Key Stock Statistics

S&P EPS Est. 2001	2.18	Tang. Bk. Value/Share	6.59
P/E on S&P Est. 2001	9.3	Beta	0.24
S&P EPS Est. 2002	2.30	Shareholders	31,484
Dividend Rate/Share	0.92	Market cap. (B)	$ 2.4
Shs. outstg. (M)	116.3	Inst. holdings	44%
Avg. daily vol. (M)	0.326		

Value of $10,000 invested 5 years ago: $ 22,078

Fiscal Year Ending Dec. 31

	2001	2000	1999	1998	1997	1996
Revenues (Million $)						
1Q	1,271	684.4	654.4	637.6	588.1	618.8
2Q	849.0	571.9	507.9	548.3	470.4	452.9
3Q	—	651.1	571.0	698.7	492.8	456.6
4Q	—	1,052	545.0	614.8	578.6	531.1
Yr.	—	2,960	2,279	2,499	2,130	2,059
Earnings Per Share ($)						
1Q	**0.98**	**0.83**	**0.71**	**0.57**	0.57	0.68
2Q	**0.23**	**0.50**	**0.48**	**0.23**	0.17	0.13
3Q	**E0.32**	**0.30**	**0.41**	**0.35**	0.19	0.06
4Q	**E0.65**	**0.45**	**0.42**	**0.34**	**0.34**	0.33
Yr.	**E2.18**	**2.07**	**2.03**	**1.51**	**1.28**	**1.19**

Next earnings report expected: NA

Dividend Data (Dividends have been paid since 1910.)

Amount ($)	Date Decl.	Ex-Div. Date	Stock of Record	Payment Date
0.220	Oct. 13	Oct. 19	Oct. 23	Nov. 15 '00
0.230	Jan. 12	Jan. 18	Jan. 22	Feb. 15 '01
0.230	Apr. 12	Apr. 19	Apr. 23	May. 15 '01
0.230	Jul. 13	Jul. 19	Jul. 23	Aug. 15 '01

Energy East Corporation

Business Summary - 14-AUG-01

In February 2001, Energy East announced an agreement to acquire RGS Energy Group, the parent of Rochester Gas & Electric, for approximately $2.4 billion in cash, stock, and assumption of debt. The merger, approved by EAS shareholders in June, is expected to close in early 2002, subject to certain regulatory requirements. With more than 200 miles of contiguous service territory, management believes the merger will generate approximately $50 million in annual cost savings. The combined company would serve nearly 3 million Northeast electric and gas customers.

EAS has transformed itself from a vertically integrated upstate New York utility into a super-regional energy distribution company. As part of this process, the company has divested power plants, and acquired a number of Northeast electric and gas distributions companies. As of the end of 2000, the company and its acquired businesses served approximately 1.4 million electric and 600,000 natural gas customers in an aggregate 33,000 square mile service territory covering New York, Maine, Connecticut, and Massachusetts.

The company's divestiture of generating assets began in 1999, with the sale of seven coal fired stations for $1.3 billion (after tax). In December 2000, the company agreed to sell its 18% interest in the Nine Mile Point 2 nuclear power plant, for $65 million at closing, plus five annual principal and interest payments totaling $85 million. The transaction is expected to close in the second half of 2001. As a part of the NMP2 sale agreement, the buyer will provide the sellers with electricity at pre-negotiated prices for 10 years, after which the sellers will receive revenue sharing payments through 2021.

During 2000, EAS completed four acquisitions. In February 2000, the company acquired Connecticut Energy (serving 160,000 Connecticut gas customers), for $617 million in cash, stock, and the assumption of debt. In September, EAS closed on its acquisitions of CMP Group (53,000 Maine electric customers), CTG Resources (142,000 Connecticut gas customers) and Berkshire Energy (34,000 Massachusetts gas customers), for an aggregate $1.9 billion in cash, stock, and assumption of debt. Revenues during 2000 were derived 68.3% from electric delivery, 26.1% from natural gas delivery, and 0.6% from other sources.

The company repurchased about 8 million common shares in 2000, at an average price of $20.51 a share, and 1.3 million shares, at an average price of $18.43 a share, during the first half of 2001.

Per Share Data ($) (Year Ended Dec. 31)	2000	1999	1998	1997	1996	1995	1994	1993	1992	1991
Tangible Bk. Val.	6.59	13.12	13.04	13.09	12.06	11.54	10.77	10.57	10.64	10.29
Earnings	2.07	2.03	1.51	1.28	1.19	1.25	1.19	1.04	1.20	1.18
Dividends	0.88	0.84	0.78	0.70	0.70	0.70	1.00	1.09	1.07	1.05
Payout Ratio	43%	41%	51%	54%	59%	56%	84%	105%	89%	89%
Prices - High	23.62	28.62	29.00	17.87	13.18	13.37	15.25	18.25	16.37	14.81
- Low	17.93	20.56	16.53	10.31	10.18	9.50	8.87	14.37	13.06	12.00
P/E Ratio - High	11	14	19	14	11	11	13	18	14	13
- Low	9	10	11	8	9	8	7	14	11	10
Income Statement Analysis (Million $)										
Revs.	2,960	2,279	2,013	2,130	2,059	2,010	1,899	1,800	1,692	1,556
Depr.	166	639	145	199	189	185	178	165	159	152
Maint.	108	85.8	112	110	108	117	107	112	103	110
Fxd. Chgs. Cov.	3.6	0.0	3.9	3.5	3.1	3.0	2.8	2.4	2.5	2.4
Constr. Credits	NA	Nil	Nil	Nil	NA	1.4	4.0	4.0	4.0	8.0
Eff. Tax Rate	40%	48%	39%	39%	38%	37%	35%	34%	33%	33%
Net Inc.	237	236	214	185	178	197	188	166	184	169
Balance Sheet & Other Fin. Data (Million $)										
Gross Prop.	6,989	4,295	6,047	5,962	5,916	5,755	5,630	5,462	5,261	5,063
Cap. Exp.	156	70.0	126	124	214	163	247	265	265	244
Net Prop.	3,893	2,261	2,836	4,066	3,982	3,964	3,987	3,920	3,833	3,753
Capitalization:										
LT Debt	2,390	1,245	1,412	1,450	1,481	1,581	1,651	1,631	1,777	1,789
% LT Debt	58	47	59	42	46	45	46	46	49	52
Pfd.	Nil	Nil	54.4	159	159	166	266	266	267	269
% Pfd.	Nil	Nil	2.20	4.60	4.90	4.70	7.40	7.60	7.40	7.80
Common	1,717	1,404	1,713	1,803	1,611	1,744	1,665	1,616	1,586	1,405
% Common	42	53	72	53	50	50	47	46	44	41
Total Cap.	4,564	2,862	3,612	4,188	4,205	4,471	4,586	4,483	4,568	4,455
% Oper. Ratio	87.9	111.4	82.8	84.7	83.0	83.2	83.0	83.3	80.9	80.0
% Earn. on Net Prop.	16.8	17.5	13.9	8.0	8.8	8.5	8.2	7.8	8.5	8.5
% Return On Revs.	8.0	10.4	10.6	8.7	8.7	9.8	9.9	9.2	10.9	10.8
% Return On Invest. Capital	10.5	13.3	12.1	10.2	7.1	7.2	7.1	6.8	7.4	7.5
% Return On Com. Equity	15.2	15.1	11.6	9.8	9.6	10.4	10.3	9.1	10.6	10.7

Data as orig. reptd.; bef. results of disc opers. and/or spec. items. Per share data adj. for stk. divs. as of ex-div. date. Bold denotes diluted EPS (FASB 128). E-Estimated. NA-Not Available. NM-Not Meaningful. NR-Not Ranked.

Office—Ithaca-Dryden Rd., P.O. Box 3287, Ithaca, NY 14851-3287. **Tel**—(607) 347-4131. **Website**—www.engyeast.com **Chrmn, Pres & CEO**—W. W. von Schack. **EVP & Secy**—K. M. Jasinski. **Investor Contact**—Thorn Dickinson (607-347-2561). **Dirs**—R. Aurelio, J. A. Carrigg, A. P. Casarett, J. J. Castiglia, L. B. DeFleur, P. L. Gioia, J. M. Keeler, B. E. Lynch, W. G. Rich, W. W. von Schack. **Transfer Agent**—Mellon Investor Services, Ridgefield Park, NJ. **Incorporated**—in New York in 1852. **Empl**— 5,721. **S&P Analyst:** Craig K. Shere, CFA

STANDARD &POOR'S STOCK REPORTS

Entergy Corp.

NYSE Symbol **ETR**

In S&P 500

18-AUG-01

Industry: Electric Companies

Summary: This electric utility holding company, which serves customers in Arkansas, Louisiana, Mississippi and Texas, has terminated its merger agreement with FPL Group.

S&P Opinion: Accumulate (★★★★)

Recent Price • 38.95

52 Wk Range • 44.67-30.43

Yield • 3.2%

12-Mo. P/E • 11.9

Quantitative Evaluations

Outlook (1 Lowest—5 Highest) • **3+**

Fair Value • **37.90**

Risk • **Low**

Earn./Div. Rank • **B**

Technical Eval. • **Bearish** since 6/01

Rel. Strength Rank (1 Lowest—99 Highest) • **56**

Insider Activity • **NA**

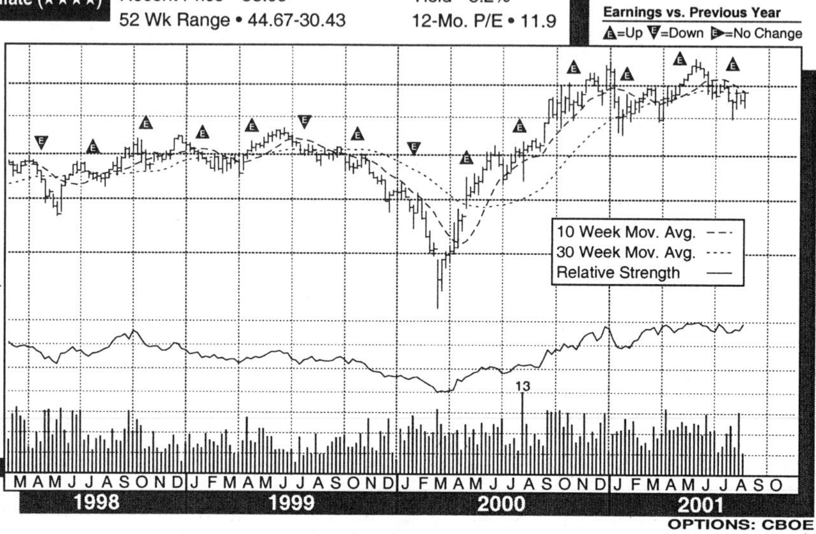

Overview - 02-AUG-01

Following an anticipated 2% to 3% increase in 2001 (over 2000's operating EPS of $3.12), we expect EPS to grow nearly 8% in 2002. In 2000, operating EPS grew 44% (aided by favorable weather and 7% fewer shares) over the prior year's $2.17. On April 2, 2001, ETR and FPL Group announced they agreed to terminate their planned merger into a new holding company. The termination reflected serious differences over management structure and the development of the non-regulated operations. The combined company would have been the largest U.S. power producer, the second largest generator of nuclear power, and one of the largest marketers of electricity and natural gas. Since the initiation in July 1999 of what is now a $1.06 billion share repurchase program, ETR had bought back (through year-end 2000) 28.9 million shares for $779 million. In December 1999, ETR announced a five-year, $9.8 billion capital investment program, with $4.2 billion for the utilities, $3.9 billion for expansion of wholesale operations, and $1.7 billion for purchase and operation of additional nuclear plants.

Valuation - 02-AUG-01

We have raised our opinion on the stock to accumulate from hold. With the shares down around 10% year to date (equal to the approximate 10% decline for the S&P Index of Electric Companies) and about 15% from 2001 high, we believe the stock is undervalued at around 11 times our 2002 EPS estimate of $3.45. In 2000, the shares gained 64% (versus a 42% rise for the Index), benefiting from higher EPS expectations and the anticipated merger with FPL Group. The decline in 2001 has reflected the sector shift away from electric utility stocks. With the termination of the merger, we expect ETR to grow EPS at an average annual rate of around 8% to 10% for the next several years.

Key Stock Statistics

S&P EPS Est. 2001	3.20	Tang. Bk. Value/Share	31.83
P/E on S&P Est. 2001	12.2	Beta	-0.04
S&P EPS Est. 2002	3.45	Shareholders	73,619
Dividend Rate/Share	1.26	Market cap. (B)	$ 8.6
Shs. outstg. (M)	220.7	Inst. holdings	74%
Avg. daily vol. (M)	0.835		

Value of $10,000 invested 5 years ago: $ 19,208

Fiscal Year Ending Dec. 31

	2001	2000	1999	1998	1997	1996
Revenues (Million $)						
1Q	2,653	1,811	1,640	2,313	2,046	1,604
2Q	2,495	2,138	2,316	2,509	2,178	1,853
3Q	—	3,432	3,065	4,587	2,798	2,138
4Q	—	2,635	1,752	2,085	2,540	1,569
Yr.	—	10,016	8,773	11,495	9,562	7,164
Earnings Per Share ($)						
1Q	**0.69**	**0.42**	**0.25**	**0.20**	**0.47**	**-0.38**
2Q	**1.06**	**1.04**	**0.81**	**0.83**	**0.61**	**0.83**
3Q	**E1.21**	**1.34**	**1.16**	**1.02**	**0.33**	**1.22**
4Q	**E0.24**	**0.19**	**-0.02**	**0.96**	**-0.36**	**0.16**
Yr.	**E3.20**	**2.97**	**2.25**	**3.00**	**1.03**	**1.83**

Next earnings report expected: mid October

Dividend Data (Dividends have been paid since 1988.)

Amount ($)	Date Decl.	Ex-Div. Date	Stock of Record	Payment Date
0.315	Oct. 27	Nov. 08	Nov. 10	Dec. 01 '00
0.315	Jan. 26	Feb. 09	Feb. 13	Mar. 01 '01
0.315	Apr. 04	May. 11	May. 15	Jun. 01 '01
0.315	Jul. 27	Aug. 10	Aug. 14	Sep. 01 '01

Entergy Corporation

Business Summary - 02-AUG-01

As the holding company for Entergy Arkansas, Entergy Gulf States, Entergy Louisiana, Entergy Mississippi and Entergy New Orleans, ETR provides electricity to 2.5 million U.S. retail customers. It also owns System Energy Resources, which has a 90% interest in the Grand Gulf 1 nuclear plant.

On April 2, 2001, Entergy agreed to terminate its merger agreement (announced on July 31, 2000) with the Florida-based FPL Group (FPL). The companies agreed not to seek a break-up fee, unless one of the parties agreed to a substantially comparable transaction with 9 months of the merger termination.

Revenues by segment in 2000 were: domestic electric, 72.1% (71.5% in 1999); competitive businesses, 26.3% (27.1%); and natural gas and steam, 1.6% (1.4%).

Fuel sources for domestic utilities and System Energy in 2000 were: natural gas 42% (45% in 1999); nuclear 39% (35%); coal 15% (16%); and fuel oil 4% (4%).

In August 1998, ETR cut its dividend 33% and announced the planned sale of its international distribution operations and some non-core domestic units.

In November 1998, ETR sold London Electricity (acquired in February 1997 for $2.1 billion) for $3.185 billion. Also in November, it sold Melbourne-based CitiPower (acquired in January 1996 for A$1.575 billion) for A$1.7 billion. In June 1999, ETR sold its 5.1% interest in Buenos Aires-based Edesur, S.A. for $87.5 million.

ETR's domestic nuclear business provides services to nuclear facilities owned by other utilities. In November 2000, it acquired, for $967 million, the Indian Point 3 and James A. FitzPatrick nuclear facilities in New York. Also in November, it agreed to acquire, in a transaction valued at $602 million, the Indian Point 1 and 2 units; closing was expected in September of 2001. (Unit 1 was shut down and placed in storage in the 1970s.) Earlier, in July 1999, ETR acquired the Pilgrim nuclear station in Massachusetts, for $81 million.

Power marketing and trading units are operated by Entergy Power, EMPC and ET&M. In January 2001, ETR formed an energy commodity trading joint venture, Entergy-Koch L.P., with $1 billion in total assets. ETR's global power development business acquires or develops power generation projects worldwide.

In December 1993, ETR acquired Entergy Gulf States (formerly Gulf States Utilities), which owns 70% of the River Bend nuclear plant, for $2.3 billion. In 1988, the Public Utility Commission in Texas (PUCT) placed in abeyance $1.4 billion of River Bend plant investment and $157 million of deferred costs. In March 1998, a PUCT order disallowed recovery of the $1.4 billion of abeyant plant costs and the $157 million of deferred costs. In June 1999, a PUCT approved settlement agreement limited potential recovery of the reduced value of the plant to $115 million, and prohibited action on ETR's appeal until January 1, 2002.

Per Share Data ($) (Year Ended Dec. 31)	2000	1999	1998	1997	1996	1995	1994	1993	1992	1991
Tangible Bk. Val.	31.83	29.71	28.82	19.72	25.77	28.25	27.74	27.16	24.23	23.31
Earnings	2.97	2.25	3.00	1.03	1.83	2.13	1.49	2.62	2.48	2.64
Dividends	1.22	1.20	1.50	1.80	1.80	1.80	1.80	1.65	1.45	1.25
Payout Ratio	41%	53%	50%	175%	98%	85%	121%	63%	58%	47%
Prices - High	43.87	33.50	32.43	30.25	30.37	29.25	37.37	39.87	33.62	29.87
- Low	15.93	23.68	23.25	22.37	24.87	20.00	21.25	32.50	26.12	21.87
P/E Ratio - High	15	15	11	29	17	14	25	15	14	11
- Low	5	11	8	22	14	9	14	12	11	8
Income Statement Analysis (Million $)										
Revs.	10,016	8,773	11,495	9,562	7,164	6,274	5,963	4,485	4,116	4,051
Depr.	785	745	985	980	791	691	657	444	425	399
Maint.	NA	NA	NA	NA	NA	NA	410	307	302	283
Fxd. Chgs. Cov.	2.8	2.3	1.9	1.9	2.5	2.3	1.6	2.4	2.1	2.1
Constr. Credits	56.0	52.0	23.0	18.0	18.3	18.0	21.8	14.0	12.0	15.0
Eff. Tax Rate	40%	38%	24%	59%	50%	41%	24%	36%	34%	34%
Net Inc.	711	595	786	301	420	485	342	458	438	482
Balance Sheet & Other Fin. Data (Million $)										
Gross Prop.	29,865	28,178	26,892	29,102	25,109	24,080	23,557	23,180	15,051	14,813
Cap. Exp.	1,494	1,196	1,144	847	572	618	676	512	427	397
Net Prop.	18,501	17,279	16,816	19,517	16,223	15,821	15,917	16,022	10,736	10,812
Capitalization:										
LT Debt	8,014	7,253	7,349	9,304	7,838	7,081	7,367	7,679	5,326	5,493
% LT Debt	52	49	50	55	51	49	49	50	52	53
Pfd.	335	338	338	1,003	928	954	1,001	900	705	690
% Pfd.	2.18	2.30	2.28	5.80	6.00	6.60	6.90	5.90	6.80	6.60
Common	7,003	7,118	7,107	6,693	6,641	6,472	6,351	6,536	4,279	4,208
% Common	46	48	48	39	43	45	44	43	42	41
Total Cap.	19,095	18,539	18,942	22,156	19,876	18,897	19,959	19,917	12,088	12,348
% Oper. Ratio	89.0	88.3	86.8	81.3	82.4	80.6	82.1	77.9	76.7	73.7
% Earn. on Net Prop.	8.6	7.3	8.3	10.1	7.9	7.7	6.7	7.4	8.9	9.8
% Return On Revs.	7.1	6.8	6.8	3.1	5.9	7.7	5.7	10.2	10.6	11.9
% Return On Invest. Capital	7.1	7.0	14.8	7.7	6.2	6.3	5.5	6.3	8.7	9.3
% Return On Com. Equity	9.6	7.8	10.7	3.7	6.3	7.6	5.3	12.6	10.3	11.6

Data as orig reptd.; bef. results of disc opers/spec. items. Per share data adj. for stk. divs. Bold denotes diluted EPS (FASB 128)-prior periods restated. E-Estimated. NA-Not Available. NM-Not Meaningful. NR-Not Ranked.

Office—639 Loyola Ave., New Orleans, LA 70113. **Tel**—(504) 576-4000. **Website**—http://www.entergy.com **Chrmn**—R. v.d. Luft. **CEO**—J. W. Leonard. **Pres**—D. C. Hintz. **EVP & CFO**—C. J. Wilder. **SVP & Secy**—M. G. Thompson. **VP-Investor Relations**—Nancy Morovich (504-576-4947). **Dirs**—M. S. Bateman, W. F. Blount, G. W. Davis, S. DeBree, N. C. Francis, J. W. Leonard, R. v.d. Luft, T. F. McLarty, III. P. W. Murrill, J. R. Nichols, W. A. Percy, D. H. Reilley, W. C. Smith, B. A. Steinhagen. **Transfer Agent & Registrar**—Mellon Investor Services, Ridgefield Park, NJ. **Incorporated**— in Delaware in 1994; in Florida in 1949. **Empl**— 14,100. **S&P Analyst:** Justin McCann

STANDARD &POOR'S
STOCK REPORTS

MDU Resources Group

NYSE Symbol **MDU**

In S&P MidCap 400

18-AUG-01

Industry: Natural Gas

Summary: MDU is involved in electric and natural gas distribution, natural gas storage, gathering and transmission, construction materials and mining, and oil and natural gas production.

S&P Opinion: Accumulate (★★★★)

Recent Price • 30.40 | Yield • 3.0%
52 Wk Range • 40.37-23.81 | 12-Mo. P/E • 12.9

Quantitative Evaluations

Outlook (1 Lowest—5 Highest)
• 2−

Fair Value
• 29.60

Risk
• Low

Earn./Div. Rank
• A-

Technical Eval.
• **Bearish** since 6/01

Rel. Strength Rank (1 Lowest—99 Highest)
• 38

Insider Activity
• Neutral

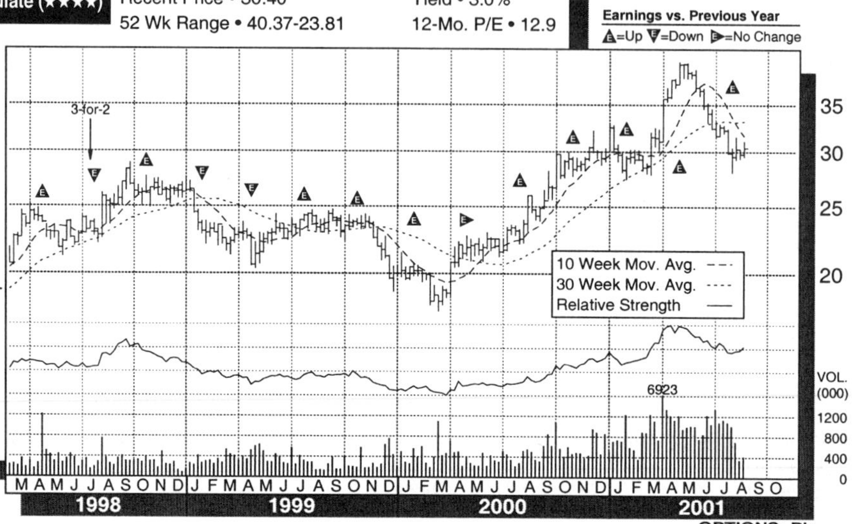

OPTIONS: Ph

Overview - 01-AUG-01

Earnings in the first half of 2001 were aided by 54% higher natural gas and oil production, with most of the increase coming from eastern Montana and the coalbeds in the Powder River Basin. Natural gas accounts for 77% of MDU's reserve base. The construction materials and mining (CM&M) segment is gaining from increased federal funding for highway construction. CM&M should see double-digit volume growth this year. Utility services will be aided by an expected 78% increase in revenues, as gross margin percentage should be unchanged. Pipeline and energy services will benefit from an anticipated 9% increase in throughput. Overall, EPS should grow 38% in 2001, reflecting the strong commodity environment, with approximately $300 million of operating cash flow. MDU expects to invest approximately $500 million in capital expenditures, including acquisitions.

Valuation - 01-AUG-01

The shares were recently down 1.0% year to date, compared to a 26% decline for the Natural Gas index, mainly reflecting the recent deterioration in natural gas prices. Stocks, such as MDU, that have stable utility businesses to support growth areas should continue benefiting amid general market volatility. In addition, the shares offer an attractive dividend yield of nearly 3.0%. Despite its acquisition binge, the company has maintained a ratio of long-term debt to total capitalization of just 25%. MDU's diverse businesses reduce the risk typically associated with acquisitions. Given our 2001 earnings estimates for each segment and applying the average peer group multiple, we get a weighted average multiple of 14.5X our EPS estimate, which represents upside potential of approximately 22%.

Key Stock Statistics

S&P EPS Est. 2001	2.50	Tang. Bk. Value/Share	13.55
P/E on S&P Est. 2001	12.2	Beta	-0.18
S&P EPS Est. 2002	2.68	Shareholders	13,600
Dividend Rate/Share	0.92	Market cap. (B)	$ 2.1
Shs. outstg. (M)	67.9	Inst. holdings	33%
Avg. daily vol. (M)	0.121		

Value of $10,000 invested 5 years ago: $ 25,756

Fiscal Year Ending Dec. 31

	2001	2000	1999	1998	1997	1996
Revenues (Million $)						
1Q	641.2	372.0	259.1	170.1	139.8	126.5
2Q	546.0	363.0	290.2	179.7	125.4	110.2
3Q	—	530.8	375.6	270.0	163.7	133.8
4Q	—	607.9	354.9	276.8	178.8	144.2
Yr.	—	1,874	1,280	896.6	607.7	514.7
Earnings Per Share ($)						
1Q	0.49	0.23	0.23	0.39	0.33	0.30
2Q	0.63	0.35	0.33	-0.12	0.20	0.20
3Q	—	0.63	0.52	0.42	0.32	0.19
4Q	—	0.56	0.42	-0.01	0.39	0.35
Yr.	—	1.80	1.52	0.66	1.24	1.05

Next earnings report expected: late October

Dividend Data (Dividends have been paid since 1937.)

Amount ($)	Date Decl.	Ex-Div. Date	Stock of Record	Payment Date
0.220	Nov. 16	Dec. 12	Dec. 14	Jan. 01 '01
0.220	Feb. 15	Mar. 06	Mar. 08	Apr. 01 '01
0.220	May. 17	Jun. 12	Jun. 14	Jul. 01 '01
0.230	Aug. 16	Sep. 11	Sep. 13	Oct. 01 '01

MDU Resources Group, Inc.

Business Summary - 01-AUG-01

MDU Resources Group (MDU) is a natural resources company that conducts its business through the following segments: electric (18% of 2000 operating income), natural gas distribution (4%), utility services (8%), pipeline and energy services (13%), natural gas and oil production (31%), and construction materials and mining (26%).

MDU's construction materials and mining unit conducts business through Knife River Corp. This operation mines, processes, and sells construction aggregates (crushed rock, sand, and gravel) and supplies ready-mixed concrete. The unit also produces and sells asphalt for commercial and roadway applications. Knife River operates in Alaska, California, Hawaii, Montana, Oregon and Wyoming. In September 2000, Knife River agreed to sell its coal operations for $28.8 million cash.

Wholly-owned WBI Holdings is comprised of the Fidelity Exploration & Production Co., and Williston Basin subsidiaries. Fidelity is involved in the acquisition, exploration, development and production of natural gas and oil resources in the Rocky Mountains and Gulf of Mexico. In 2000, natural gas production rose 19% from 1999 levels, while oil production rose 7.1%.

Williston Basin, the pipeline and energy services segment, operates over 3,800 miles of transmission, gathering and storage lines and 24 compressor stations. Through three underground storage fields located in Montana and Wyoming, storage services are provided to local distribution companies, producers and natural gas marketers. Williston Basin's system is strategically located near five natural gas producing basins.

MDU's electric and natural gas distribution segments conduct business through Montana-Dakota Utilities, which generates, transmits, and distributes electricity, and distributes natural gas in North and South Dakota, Montana, and Wyoming. MDU also operates through Great Plains Natural Gas, which distributes natural gas to the southeastern North Dakota and western Minnesota markets, and transports substantially all of Montana-Dakota's natural gas.

The utility services segment is a diversified infrastructure construction company that specializes in electric, natural gas, and telecommunications utility construction and interior industrial electrical, exterior lighting, and traffic signalization.

In 2000, MDU acquired a number of businesses, including construction materials and mining businesses, a coal bed natural gas development operation, utility services businesses, a natural gas distribution business, and an energy services company. These acquisitions were funded with common stock, cash, and the conversion of a note receivable, totaling $286 million.

Per Share Data ($) (Year Ended Dec. 31)	2000	1999	1998	1997	1996	1995	1994	1993	1992	1991
Tangible Bk. Val.	13.55	11.74	10.39	8.84	8.21	7.90	7.66	7.45	7.10	6.94
Earnings	1.80	1.52	0.66	1.24	1.05	0.95	0.92	0.89	0.81	0.87
Dividends	0.86	0.81	0.78	0.75	0.73	0.72	0.70	0.68	0.65	0.64
Payout Ratio	48%	53%	117%	61%	70%	75%	77%	76%	80%	73%
Prices - High	33.00	27.18	28.87	22.33	15.66	15.38	14.33	14.72	11.94	11.05
- Low	17.62	18.81	18.83	14.00	13.25	11.44	11.27	11.50	9.72	8.77
P/E Ratio - High	18	18	44	18	15	16	16	17	15	13
- Low	10	12	29	11	13	12	12	13	12	10
Income Statement Analysis (Million $)										
Revs.	1,874	1,280	897	608	515	464	450	440	353	367
Depr.	111	81.8	77.8	65.8	62.7	54.8	48.1	45.2	39.7	36.6
Maint.	NA	NA	NA	NA	NA	NA	NA	21.5	17.8	18.3
Fxd. Chgs. Cov.	4.7	4.6	4.8	3.7	3.0	3.5	3.4	3.2	2.8	2.9
Constr. Credits	NA	NA	Nil	Nil	Nil	Nil	NA	NA	NA	NA
Eff. Tax Rate	39%	37%	34%	36%	26%	36%	32%	34%	24%	31%
Net Inc.	111	84.1	34.1	54.6	45.5	41.6	39.8	38.8	35.4	38.0
Balance Sheet & Other Fin. Data (Million $)										
Gross Prop.	2,496	2,042	1,811	1,510	1,370	1,287	1,234	1,165	1,094	1,031
Cap. Exp.	409	171	191	112	112	115	82.0	103	73.0	46.0
Net Prop.	1,601	1,248	1,085	840	753	716	692	664	625	595
Capitalization:										
LT Debt	728	564	413	299	281	237	218	232	250	221
% LT Debt	45	45	42	43	43	40	39	41	44	41
Pfd.	16.4	16.5	16.6	16.7	16.8	17.0	17.0	17.1	17.2	17.3
% Pfd.	1.01	1.32	1.70	2.40	2.60	2.90	3.00	3.00	3.00	3.20
Common	881	670	551	386	351	337	327	318	303	297
% Common	54	54	56	55	54	57	58	56	53	56
Total Cap.	1,907	1,463	1,153	821	764	798	775	692	725	691
% Oper. Ratio	92.1	91.4	86.7	86.7	81.5	85.5	86.8	85.5	81.2	81.4
% Earn. on Net Prop.	15.2	13.7	7.4	14.0	15.2	12.9	8.8	9.9	108.0	11.6
% Return On Revs.	5.9	6.6	3.8	9.0	8.8	9.0	8.9	8.8	10.8	10.4
% Return On Invest. Capital	9.4	9.2	12.4	14.6	12.3	11.4	9.1	9.0	8.6	9.5
% Return On Com. Equity	14.2	13.7	7.1	14.6	13.0	12.3	12.1	12.3	11.5	12.7

Data as orig reptd.; bef. results of disc opers/spec. items. Per share data adj. for stk. divs. Bold denotes diluted EPS (FASB 128)-prior periods restated. E-Estimated. NA-Not Available. NM-Not Meaningful. NR-Not Ranked.

Office—Schuchart Building, 918 E. Divide Ave., P.O. Box 5650, Bismarck, ND 58506. **Tel**—(701) 222-7900. **Website**—http://www.mdu.com **Chrmn, Pres & CEO**—M. A. White. **EVP, Treas & CFO**—W. L. Robinson. **VP & Secy**—L. H. Loble II. **Chrmn**—J. A. Schuchart. **Investor Contact**—Phyllis Rittenbach (800-437-8000). **Dirs**—B. R. Albertson, T. Everist, D. W. Johnson, D. C. Kane, R. L. Nance, J. L. Olson, H. J. Pearce, H. A. Scott Jr., J. T. Simmons, Sister T. Welder, M. A. White. **Transfer Agent & Registrar**—Wells Fargo Bank Minnesota, N.A., St. Paul, MN.**Incorporated**—in Delaware in 1924. **Empl**— 4,087. **S&P Analyst:** John Kartsonas

STANDARD & POOR'S
STOCK REPORTS

PPL Corp.

NYSE Symbol **PPL**
In S&P 500

18-AUG-01 **Industry:** Electric Companies

Summary: This Pennsylvania-based holding company for PPL Utilities also has holdings in the U.K., Europe and Latin America.

S&P Opinion: Accumulate (★★★★)
Recent Price • 42.43
52 Wk Range • 62.36-29.50
Yield • 2.5%
12-Mo. P/E • 10.5

Quantitative Evaluations
Outlook (1 Lowest—5 Highest)
• **3−**
Fair Value
• **44.80**
Risk
• **Low**
Earn./Div. Rank
• **B+**

Technical Eval.
• **Bearish** since 7/01
Rel. Strength Rank (1 Lowest—99 Highest)
• **22**
Insider Activity
• **NA**

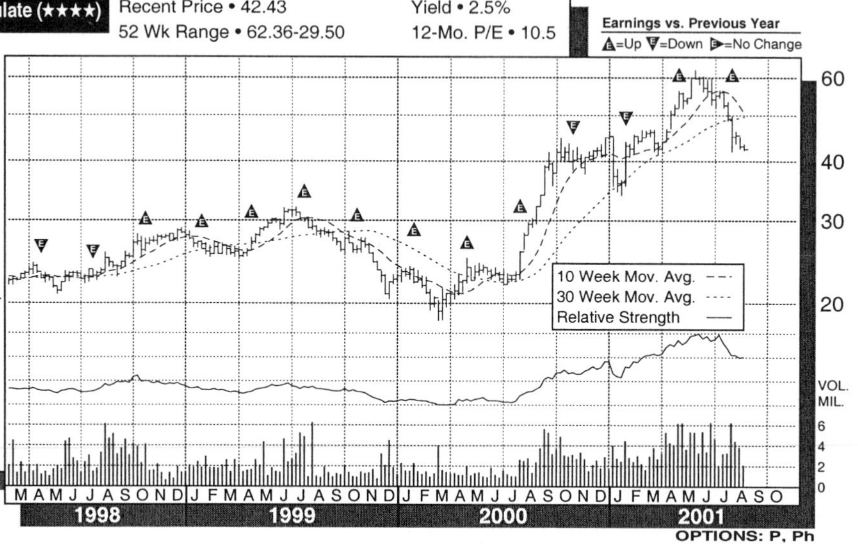

OPTIONS: P, Ph

Overview - 15-MAY-01

Operating EPS in 2001 is expected to grow more than 20% from the $3.28 earned in 2000, which was up nearly 40% from the $2.35 earned in 1999. EPS in 2000 was aided by the reversal of the one-year 4% retail rate reduction implemented on January 1, 1999. (Operating EPS for 1999 excludes several gains from asset sales.) Results in 2001 and 2002 should benefit from the increased margins of the wholesale energy marketing and trading operations, as well as from higher earnings from the international operations. Through the planned securitization of its regulated operations, PPL expects to obtain low-cost funds for the expansion of its generation projects. With the acquisition and development of generation facilities in the Northeast and Far West, PPL will become one of the top 12 owners of generating capacity in the U.S. We expect EPS to grow an additional 15% in 2002.

Valuation - 15-MAY-01

We would continue to accumulate PPL stock. After a dramatic 97.5% advance in 2000 (more than double the 42.3% gain for the S&P Index of Electric Companies), the shares have gained an additional 24% year to date (versus an approximate 1% decline for the S&P Index). Despite this exceptional outperformance, the stock remains attractive at about 12 times our 2002 EPS estimate of $4.60. Thereafter, aided by the expansion of its generation projects, PPL could realize annual EPS growth of 12% to 15% through 2005. In 1999, the company sold $2.42 billion in "transition" bonds (that securitized a portion of the $2.97 billion of stranded costs it was authorized to recover) and used the proceeds to repurchase about $1.7 billion of high coupon debt and approximately 7 million shares of its common stock. The financing savings from PPL's pending securitization of its regulated operations should add around $0.10 to EPS from 2002 through 2004.

Key Stock Statistics

S&P EPS Est. 2001	4.10	Tang. Bk. Value/Share	13.30
P/E on S&P Est. 2001	10.3	Beta	0.15
S&P EPS Est. 2002	4.60	Shareholders	117,293
Dividend Rate/Share	1.06	Market cap. (B)	$ 6.2
Shs. outstg. (M)	146.0	Inst. holdings	40%
Avg. daily vol. (M)	0.910		

Value of $10,000 invested 5 years ago: $ 23,895

Fiscal Year Ending Dec. 31

	2001	2000	1999	1998	1997	1996
Revenues (Million $)						
1Q	1,566	1,413	1,067	880.2	785.8	789.2
2Q	1,409	1,297	1,004	838.0	686.0	669.1
3Q	—	1,458	1,386	1,166	777.8	714.6
4Q	—	1,505	1,133	902.0	799.2	737.4
Yr.	—	5,683	4,590	3,786	3,049	2,910
Earnings Per Share ($)						
1Q	1.52	0.99	0.76	0.60	0.72	0.73
2Q	0.80	0.64	0.40	0.32	0.39	0.38
3Q	E0.98	0.94	1.07	0.81	0.25	0.49
4Q	E0.80	0.79	0.93	0.56	0.44	0.45
Yr.	E4.10	3.36	3.14	2.29	1.80	2.05

Next earnings report expected: late October

Dividend Data (Dividends have been paid since 1946.)

Amount ($)	Date Decl.	Ex-Div. Date	Stock of Record	Payment Date
0.265	Aug. 25	Sep. 06	Sep. 08	Oct. 01 '00
0.265	Nov. 17	Dec. 06	Dec. 08	Jan. 01 '01
0.265	Feb. 23	Mar. 07	Mar. 09	Apr. 01 '01
0.265	May. 25	Jun. 06	Jun. 08	Jul. 01 '01

A Division of The McGraw-Hill Companies

PPL Corporation

Business Summary - 15-MAY-01

PPL Corporation (formerly PP&L Resources) is the holding company formed in April 1995 by Pennsylvania Power & Light (now operating as PPL Electric Utilities), its main subsidiary, which supplies electricity to some 1.3 million customers in a 10,000-square-mile area in 29 counties of central-eastern Pennsylvania. Important cities served are Allentown, Bethlehem, Harrisburg, Lancaster, Scranton, Wilkes-Barre and Williamsport.

The company's revenues by business segment in 2000 were: electric, 55.7% (62.6% in 1999); wholesale energy marketing and trading, 36.6% (31.4%); and energy-related businesses, 7.7% (6.0%).

In August 1998, PPL acquired Penn Fuel Gas (now operating as PPL Gas Utilities), a natural gas distributor with 105,000 customers in Pennsylvania and a few hundred in Maryland, for about $135 million in new stock.

The PPL Global subsidiary invests in international electric projects. In 1999, it increased its interest in the Chilean electric distribution company, Empressa Emel S. A., to 95.4%. In June 2000, it acquired an 84.7% interest in the Brazilian electric utility, Cia Energetica do Maranhao (CEMAR), for $289 million. It also owns a 51% equity interest (49% voting interest) in Western Power Distribution in the U.K., and has holdings in Argentina, Bolivia, El Salvador, Peru, Spain and Portugal.

PPL's other unregulated businesses include: PPL EnergyPlus, which markets wholesale and retail electricity in the U.S. and Canada; and PPL Generation, which operates an expanding fleet of domestic power plants. In 1999, PPL acquired generating assets in Maine for $89 million and 11 hydroelectric plants in Montana for $757 million. In 2000, PPL Generation produced about 40.6 billion kilowatt hours (kWh) in its Pennsylvania plants, with coal accounting for 56% of the fuel source used for power generation; nuclear, 39%; gas and oil, 3%; and hydroelectric, 2%.

In December 1996, Pennsylvania enacted legislation to restructure its electric utility industry. The legislation called for a three-year phase-in (that began in 1999) of retail customer choice, and allowed utilities to recover PUC-approved transition or stranded costs through a non-bypassable transition charge. In August 1998, the PUC issued an order that allowed Pennsylvania Power & Light to recover (over 11 years beginning January 1, 1999) $2.97 billion in stranded costs, with the authorization to issue transition bonds that would securitize up to $2.85 billion of its stranded costs.

In April 2001, PPL announced its plan to obtain low-cost funds for its generation expansion projects through the securitization of its regulated electricity transmission and distribution business. The process would involve the separation of the regulated units from PPL Corporation and its non-regulated businesses and the solicitation of power supply contracts for all of its electricity needs from 2002 through the end of 2009.

Per Share Data ($) (Year Ended Dec. 31)	2000	1999	1998	1997	1996	1995	1994	1993	1992	1991
Tangible Bk. Val.	13.30	11.20	11.87	16.77	16.73	16.13	15.06	15.28	15.03	14.56
Earnings	3.36	3.14	2.29	1.80	2.05	2.05	1.41	2.07	2.02	2.01
Dividends	1.06	1.00	1.34	1.67	1.67	1.67	1.67	1.65	1.60	1.55
Payout Ratio	32%	32%	59%	93%	81%	81%	118%	80%	79%	77%
Prices - High	46.12	32.00	28.93	24.25	26.00	26.50	27.25	31.00	28.25	26.37
- Low	18.37	20.37	20.87	19.00	21.62	17.87	18.62	26.12	23.87	20.87
P/E Ratio - High	14	10	13	13	13	13	19	15	14	13
- Low	5	6	9	11	11	9	13	13	12	10
Income Statement Analysis (Million $)										
Revs.	5,683	4,590	3,786	3,049	2,910	2,752	2,725	2,727	2,744	2,560
Depr.	261	257	338	374	363	302	289	271	261	239
Maint.	261	215	182	184	191	186	180	231	201	207
Fxd. Chgs. Cov.	3.0	3.2	3.5	3.3	3.8	3.2	3.0	3.4	2.9	2.8
Constr. Credits	NA	NA	Nil	NA	NA	12.1	13.1	15.6	14.9	12.0
Eff. Tax Rate	36%	26%	39%	43%	45%	43%	42%	40%	40%	38%
Net Inc.	513	478	379	296	329	350	244	348	347	348
Balance Sheet & Other Fin. Data (Million $)										
Gross Prop.	11,418	10,717	10,489	10,336	10,242	10,235	9,998	9,684	9,054	8,758
Cap. Exp.	460	318	304	310	360	403	505	488	422	374
Net Prop.	5,948	5,644	4,363	6,766	6,905	7,122	7,127	6,997	6,855	6,754
Capitalization:										
LT Debt	4,717	4,103	3,092	2,698	2,968	2,967	3,092	2,788	2,785	2,767
% LT Debt	69	72	60	47	48	50	54	49	49	49
Pfd.	97.0	Nil	347	347	466	466	466	506	227	596
% Pfd.	1.42	Nil	6.70	6.10	7.50	7.90	7.80	8.80	9.60	11
Common	2,012	1,613	1,790	2,809	2,745	2,497	2,454	2,426	2,367	2,298
% Common	29	28	35	49	44	42	41	42	42	41
Total Cap.	6,880	7,328	5,317	8,075	8,075	8,356	8,290	8,232	7,037	6,972
% Oper. Ratio	84.0	84.8	79.8	82.1	80.9	79.1	81.6	79.4	79.1	77.2
% Earn. on Net Prop.	28.6	22.3	10.3	8.0	8.0	8.1	7.1	8.1	8.4	8.7
% Return On Revs.	9.0	10.4	10.0	9.7	11.3	12.7	9.0	12.8	12.6	13.6
% Return On Invest. Capital	14.3	11.3	13.1	9.4	6.5	6.8	6.6	7.6	8.5	8.7
% Return On Com. Equity	28.3	28.1	16.5	10.7	12.3	12.8	8.7	13.1	13.1	13.4

Data as orig reptd.; bef. results of disc opers/spec. items. Per share data adj. for stk. divs. Bold denotes diluted EPS (FASB 128)-prior periods restated. E-Estimated. NA-Not Available. NM-Not Meaningful. NR-Not Ranked.

Office—Two North Ninth St., Allentown, PA 18101. **Tel**—(610) 774-5151. **Website**—http://www.pplweb.com **Chrmn, Pres & CEO**—W. F. Hecht. **EVP & CFO** —J. R. Biggar. **SVP & Secy**—R. J. Grey. **Investor Contact**—T. J. Paukovits (610-774-4124). **Dirs**—F. M. Bernthal, J. W. Conway, E. A. Deaver, W. J. Flood, E. D. Gates, W. F. Hecht, S. Heydt, F. A. Long, W. K. Smith. **Transfer Agents & Registrars**—Co.'s office; Wells Fargo Bank Minnesota, South St. Paul, MN. **Incorporated**—in Pennsylvania in 1920; reincorporated in Pennsylvania in 1994. **Empl**— 11,893. **S&P Analyst:** Justin McCann

STANDARD &POOR'S STOCK REPORTS

UtiliCorp United

NYSE Symbol **UCU**

In S&P MidCap 400

24-AUG-01 **Industry:** Electric Companies

Summary: This international electric and gas utility has operations in North America, Europe, New Zealand, Australia and Jamaica.

S&P Opinion: Accumulate (★★★★) Recent Price • 31.28 | 52 Wk Range • 37.85-23.25 | Yield • 3.8% | 12-Mo. P/E • 13.5

Quantitative Evaluations

Outlook (1 Lowest—5 Highest)
• **4-**

Fair Value
• **35.70**

Risk
• **Low**

Earn./Div. Rank
• **A-**

Technical Eval.
• **Neutral** since 8/01

Rel. Strength Rank (1 Lowest—99 Highest)
• **48**

Insider Activity
• **Unfavorable**

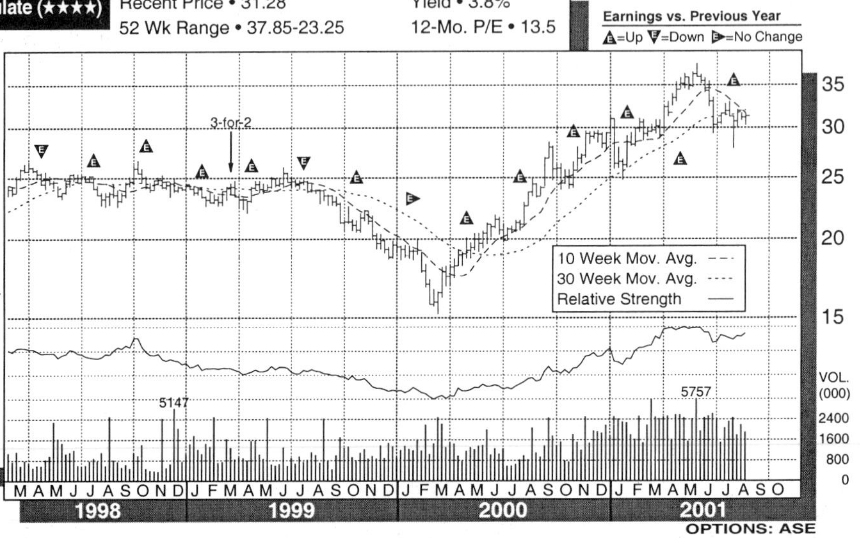

OPTIONS: ASE

Overview - 24-AUG-01

We see revenues climbing over 50% in 2001, fueled by strong growth in wholesale and capacity services operations at Aquila (ILA), UCU's unregulated energy marketing subsidiary, and contributions from St. Joseph Light & Power, acquired in December 2000. Margins will narrow, with a greater proportion of contributions from lower margin energy marketing activity, losses from UCU's Kansas City fiber optic buildout, foreign exchange losses, and the expiration of management fees from Quanta Services (PWR). Based on a proven track record for UCU's value chain strategy, we believe a recurring portion of annual earnings will be derived from the profitable disposition of investments, subsidiaries, and unbundled utility operations. Earnings in 2002 will benefit from a recovery in UCU's PWR investment, reduced dilution from fiber optic deployment, and profitability in Australian communications interests. EPS estimates for 2001 exclude a gain of $0.50 from the April IPO of a 20% interest in Aquila.

Valuation - 24-AUG-01

In the three months through late August, the shares declined about 13%, in sympathy with weakness in the utility sector and in shares of ILA. UCU intends to spin off its remaining ILA interest to shareholders in the coming year. We estimate that UCU shares trade at only 12X EPS, excluding contributions from and the market value of ILA. Although this is in line with the broader utility sector, we believe UCU deserves a premium, in light of above average growth prospects for the company's Services and International Networks operations. Furthermore, we believe UCU's successful value chain strategy warrants premium valuations. Based on growth opportunities for UCU's Aquila holdings and modest multiples for UCU's core businesses, we continue to see the shares outperforming the S&P 500.

Key Stock Statistics

S&P EPS Est. 2001	2.55	Tang. Bk. Value/Share	17.94
P/E on S&P Est. 2001	12.3	Beta	0.18
S&P EPS Est. 2002	2.80	Shareholders	44,017
Dividend Rate/Share	1.20	Market cap. (B)	$ 3.7
Shs. outstg. (M)	115.3	Inst. holdings	44%
Avg. daily vol. (M)	0.602		

Value of $10,000 invested 5 years ago: $ 20,997

Fiscal Year Ending Dec. 31

	2001	2000	1999	1998	1997	1996
Revenues (Million $)						
1Q	11,980	4,750	3,801	2,896	2,060	1,084
2Q	10,441	5,771	3,970	2,565	1,550	765.0
3Q	—	8,086	6,464	3,809	2,257	892.6
4Q	—	10,369	4,386	3,294	3,060	1,590
Yr.	—	28,975	18,622	12,563	8,926	4,332
Earnings Per Share ($)						
1Q	**0.69**	**0.59**	**0.57**	**0.53**	**0.72**	**0.53**
2Q	**1.21**	**0.31**	**0.27**	**0.29**	**0.25**	**0.37**
3Q	**E0.90**	**0.80**	**0.46**	**0.36**	**0.31**	**0.19**
4Q	**E0.58**	**0.50**	**0.45**	**0.45**	**0.39**	**0.37**
Yr.	**E2.55**	**2.21**	**1.75**	**1.63**	**1.65**	**1.46**

Next earnings report expected: early November

Dividend Data (Dividends have been paid since 1939.)

Amount ($)	Date Decl.	Ex-Div. Date	Stock of Record	Payment Date
0.300	Nov. 08	Nov. 20	Nov. 22	Dec. 12 '00
0.300	Feb. 07	Feb. 20	Feb. 22	Mar. 12 '01
0.300	May. 02	May. 18	May. 22	Jun. 12 '01
0.300	Aug. 08	Aug. 20	Aug. 22	Sep. 12 '01

UtiliCorp United Inc.

24-AUG-01

Business Summary - 24-AUG-01

UtiliCorp has developed a value chain strategy, involving the acquisition of deregulating or privatized utility operations, enhancement of operations (through business combinations, separation of business functions and development of complementary services), and the ultimate divestiture of segregated business units. The company has identified a number of traditional utility operations that it believes can be segregated into profitable, stand-alone businesses, including billing and customer service, plant construction and maintenance, electricity generation, electric and gas distribution, and telecommunications connections (using regulated rights of way).

The company is organized into three distinct parts: Networks, Energy Merchant, and Services. Domestic Network operations (63% of 2000 earnings before interest and taxes) provide gas and/or electric utility service to approximately 1.3 million customers in seven midwestern states. International Networks (28% of 2000 EBIT) includes ownership interests in electric, natural gas and broadband networks in Australia and New Zealand that serve approximately 2.2 million customers and provide electric distribution services to 500,000 customers in Canada. As a part of its value chain strategy, the Networks unit announced an agreement in April 2001 to sell its generation assets in British Columbia for net proceeds of $77 million; in December 2000, it sold the retail business of its Canadian utility operations (originally acquired in August 2000) for about $75 million. Also in December, the company closed on its $280 million acquisition (including stock and assumed debt) of St. Joseph Light and Power.

Energy Merchant operations (34% of 2000 EBIT) are conducted through wholly owned Aquila, Inc. During 2000, Aquila was North America's fourth largest wholesale marketer of natural gas and power on a combined basis. Aquila also has a growing presence in Western Europe. During 2000, Aquila marketed approximately 12 Bcf/day of natural gas, 189.9 MMWhs of power, and 18.3 million tons of coal. As a part of UCU's value chain strategy, the company sold 20% of Aquila in an IPO in April 2001; the remainder is to be spun off to shareholders within 12 months.

Services operations (6% of 2000 EBIT) include UCU's 36% interest in Quanta Services (a specialty contractor serving the utility, telecommunications and cable TV industries) and a domestic broadband communications business. In April 2000, the Services unit entered into a partnership to construct broadband fiber-optic networks to support cable TV, telephone, and high speed Internet. As of March 2001, broadband construction had primarily been limited to the Kansas City area.

Per Share Data ($) (Year Ended Dec. 31)	2000	1999	1998	1997	1996	1995	1994	1993	1992	1991
Tangible Bk. Val.	17.94	16.35	15.82	14.49	14.55	13.73	13.55	13.51	12.44	12.97
Earnings	2.21	1.75	1.63	1.65	1.47	1.15	1.39	1.30	0.88	1.49
Dividends	1.20	1.20	1.20	1.17	1.17	1.15	1.13	1.08	1.07	1.03
Payout Ratio	54%	69%	74%	71%	80%	100%	82%	83%	121%	69%
Prices - High	31.31	26.00	26.62	26.04	20.16	19.75	21.25	22.66	19.33	19.58
- Low	15.18	18.56	22.50	16.75	17.16	17.58	16.75	18.08	14.75	13.41
P/E Ratio - High	14	15	16	16	14	17	15	17	22	13
- Low	7	11	14	10	12	15	12	14	17	9
Income Statement Analysis (Million $)										
Revs.	28,975	18,622	12,563	8,926	4,332	2,799	1,515	1,572	1,299	1,075
Depr.	225	194	150	130	128	145	140	135	123	53.9
Maint.	NA	NA	NA	NA	NA	NA	49.3	NA	NA	NA
Fxd. Chgs. Cov.	2.2	2.0	2.0	2.0	1.7	2.3	2.4	2.1	1.7	2.2
Constr. Credits	NA	Nil	Nil	NA	NA	NA	NA	NA	NA	NA
Eff. Tax Rate	33%	28%	39%	39%	43%	40%	34%	26%	37%	36%
Net Inc.	207	161	132	134	106	79.8	94.4	86.4	52.9	73.5
Balance Sheet & Other Fin. Data (Million $)										
Gross Prop.	5,930	5,210	4,762	3,801	3,658	3,411	2,557	2,445	2,221	2,088
Cap. Exp.	139	129	122	133	134	109	132	141	150	134
Net Prop.	3,655	3,665	3,314	2,480	2,407	2,280	1,634	1,580	1,454	1,366
Capitalization:										
LT Debt	2,796	2,552	1,476	1,359	1,471	1,355	977	1,010	891	928
% LT Debt	61	63	51	54	55	58	50	52	54	55
Pfd.	Nil	Nil	Nil	Nil	25.0	25.4	53.8	83.9	95.1	97.1
% Pfd.	Nil	Nil	Nil	Nil	1.00	1.10	2.80	4.30	5.80	5.70
Common	1,800	1,525	1,446	1,164	1,158	946	907	852	661	670
% Common	39	37	49	46	44	41	47	44	40	40
Total Cap.	4,614	4,155	3,503	3,044	3,125	2,706	2,238	2,227	1,830	1,873
% Oper. Ratio	99.2	98.6	98.6	98.0	94.5	86.0	88.0	92.2	89.4	86.3
% Earn. on Net Prop.	16.0	14.9	14.4	16.3	15.6	3.4	11.3	8.1	9.7	12.0
% Return On Revs.	0.7	0.9	1.1	1.5	2.4	2.9	6.2	5.5	4.1	6.8
% Return On Invest. Capital	10.2	9.4	9.2	8.8	10.4	10.6	9.0	6.1	8.2	9.4
% Return On Com. Equity	12.4	10.8	10.1	11.5	9.9	8.4	10.4	10.0	7.0	11.3

Data as orig reptd.; bef. results of disc opers/spec. items. Per share data adj. for stk. divs. Bold denotes diluted EPS (FASB 128)-prior periods restated. E-Estimated. NA-Not Available. NM-Not Meaningful. NR-Not Ranked.

Office—20 West Ninth, Kansas City, MO 64105. **Tel**—(816) 421-6600. **Website**—http://www.utilicorp.com **Chrmn & CEO**—R. C. Green Jr. **Pres & COO**—R. K. Green. **SVP & CFO**—P. Lowe. **VP, Treas & Secy**—D. J. Wolf. **Investor Contact**—Kay McMillan (816-467-3087). **Dirs**—J. R. Baker, H. Cain, R. C. Green Jr., R. K. Green, I. O. Hockaday Jr., S. O. Ikenberry, R. F. Jackson Jr., L. P. Kline. **Transfer Agent & Registrar**—First Chicago Trust Co. of New York. **Incorporated**—in Missouri in 1950; reincorporated in Delaware in 1986. **Empl**— 4,060. **S&P Analyst:** Craig K. Shere, CFA

STANDARD
&POOR'S
STOCK REPORTS

Williams Companies

NYSE Symbol **WMB**

In S&P 500

18-AUG-01 **Industry:** Natural Gas

Summary: WMB, which provides a full range of energy services, spun off its communications subsidiary to existing shareholders via a tax-free dividend.

S&P Opinion: Accumulate (★★★★) Recent Price • 31.91 Yield • 2.3%
52 Wk Range • 48-30 12-Mo. P/E • 25.3

Quantitative Evaluations

Outlook
(1 Lowest—5 Highest)
• **3–**

Fair Value
• **33.70**

Risk
• **Low**

Earn./Div. Rank
• **B**

Technical Eval.
• **Neutral** since 8/01

Rel. Strength Rank
(1 Lowest—99 Highest)
• **32**

Insider Activity
• **Neutral**

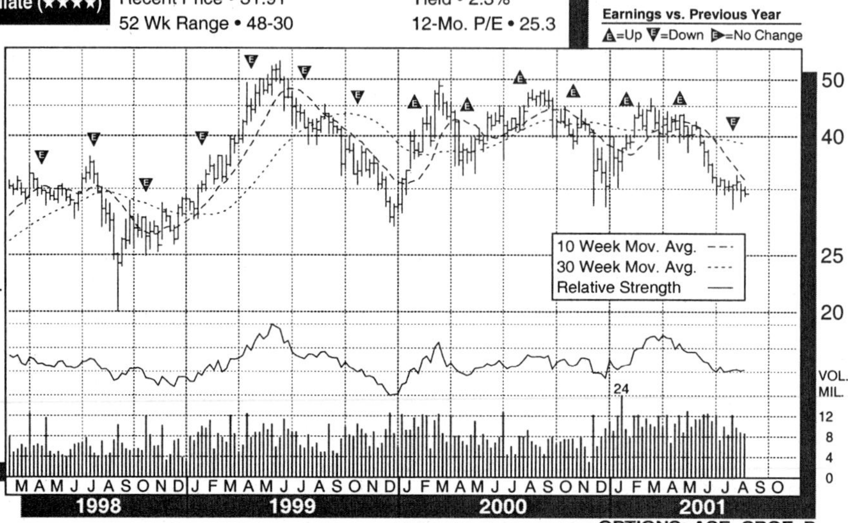

OPTIONS: ASE, CBOE, P

Overview - 03-AUG-01

Results in the first half of 2001 reflected a strong commodity price environment in the U.S., as well as improved refining volumes and margins. Profits in the Energy Marketing and Trading group more than doubled, aided by high volatility in the natural gas market. The Exploration and Production unit posted strong results, on higher realized prices and slightly greater production. However, going into the second half, we expect lower profits in these two segments, on relatively weaker commodity prices. WMB's merchant services operations will benefit from the merger with Barrett Resources, which will provide a natural hedge to the unit's activities. Williams Energy Partners, the company's master limited partnership, should contribute approximately $23 million in profit in 2001.

Valuation - 03-AUG-01

The stock was recently down 8% in 2001, versus losses of 25.5% and 8.3% for the S&P natural gas index and the broader market, respectively. Lower natural gas prices, due to weaker than expected demand as well as the California refund situation, have put pressure on the stock in the last two months. After two orders by the Federal Energy Regulatory Commission that required WMB to relinquish "excessive" profits made in California last winter, we downgraded the shares to accumulate, from buy. A decision is expected in the fall. Meanwhile, our energy-only estimate for 2001 EPS of $1.75 is unchanged. With the energy-only component trading at a P/E to growth rate of 1.1X, versus a peer average of 1.6X, we still advise investors to accumulate the shares. Our 2001 consolidated EPS estimate excludes the solutions business, which has been classified as discontinued.

Key Stock Statistics

S&P EPS Est. 2001	2.36	Tang. Bk. Value/Share	13.26
P/E on S&P Est. 2001	13.5	Beta	0.51
S&P EPS Est. 2002	2.70	Shareholders	14,815
Dividend Rate/Share	0.72	Market cap. (B)	$ 16.4
Shs. outstg. (M)	514.2	Inst. holdings	59%
Avg. daily vol. (M)	2.032		

Value of $10,000 invested 5 years ago: NA

Fiscal Year Ending Dec. 31

	2001	2000	1999	1998	1997	1996
Revenues (Million $)						
1Q	3,088	2,428	1,944	1,960	1,001	893.7
2Q	2,821	2,859	1,993	1,781	1,021	837.5
3Q	—	2,882	2,207	1,901	1,121	842.2
4Q	—	3,229	2,449	2,017	1,267	957.8
Yr.	—	10,398	8,593	7,658	4,410	3,531
Earnings Per Share ($)						
1Q	**0.78**	**0.27**	**0.13**	**0.16**	**0.31**	**0.31**
2Q	**0.69**	**0.78**	**0.04**	**0.14**	**0.32**	**0.24**
3Q	—	**0.27**	**0.06**	**0.07**	**0.19**	**0.21**
4Q	—	**0.57**	**0.13**	**-0.05**	**0.19**	**0.31**
Yr.	—	**1.95**	**0.12**	**0.32**	**1.04**	**1.07**

Next earnings report expected: late October

Dividend Data (Dividends have been paid since 1974.)

Amount ($)	Date Decl.	Ex-Div. Date	Stock of Record	Payment Date
0.150	Jan. 22	Mar. 07	Mar. 09	Mar. 26 '01
Stk.	Mar. 30	Apr. 24	Apr. 09	Apr. 23 '01
0.150	May. 18	Jun. 06	Jun. 08	Jun. 25 '01
0.180	Jul. 23	Aug. 22	Aug. 24	Sep. 10 '01

The Williams Companies, Inc.

Business Summary - 03-AUG-01

The Williams Companies operates in two broad categories: gas pipelines and energy services. The gas pipeline group, comprised of Williams Gas Pipeline Co. and its subsidiaries, owns and operates a combined total of approximately 27,300 miles of pipelines, with total annual throughput of approximately 3,800 trillion Btu of natural gas with peak-day delivery capacity of approximately 17 Bcf of natural gas. Pipeline subsidiaries include Transcontinental Gas Pipe Line, Northwest Pipeline, Kern River Gas Transmission, Texas Gas Transmission and Williams Gas Pipelines Central. The company also has interests in other pipelines and pipeline projects, including Alliance (14.8%) and the Gulfstream (50%).

The Williams Energy Services subsidiary is comprised of four business units. At year-end 2000, Exploration and Production had total proved reserves of 1.2 Tcf of natural gas equivalent, primarily located in New Mexico, Wyoming and Colorado. Midstream Gas & Liquids owns and operates gas gathering, processing and treating, natural gas liquids (NGLs) transportation, fractionation and storage facilities. In October 2000, WMB acquired midstream assets in western Canada from TransCanada Pipelines, for $540 million. The Petroleum Services unit owns and operates a petroleum products pipeline system, 78 petroleum products terminals, two ethanol production plants, two refineries, and 277 convenience stores/travel centers. In February 2001, WMB sold a 40% stake in Williams Energy Partners L.P. (NYSE: WEG) in an IPO. WEG is engaged in the storage, transportation and distribution of refined petroleum products and ammonia. Energy Marketing and Trading buys, sells and transports a full suite of energy-related commodities, including power, natural gas, refined products, NGLs, crude oil, propane, liquefied natural gas, liquefied petroleum gas and emission credits.

Following an October 1999 private placement and IPO, WMB held an 86% stake in Williams Communications Group (NYSE: WCG). WCG's activities are organized into three business units. Network owns or leases and operates a nationwide inter-city fiber optic network, which is extending locally and globally to provide Internet, data, voice and video services exclusively to communications service providers. Broadband Media, created in the 2000 first quarter, primarily consists of Vyvx Services, a provider of live and non-live video transmission services worldwide for news, sports, advertising and entertainment events. Strategic Investments includes certain domestic and international investments. In March 2001, WMB spun off its WCG stake to shareholders via a tax-free dividend.

In January 2001, the company agreed to sell its Solutions unit to a private equity firm. In August, WMB acquired Barrettt Resources, an exploration and production company, for cash and stock valued at about $2.8 billion.

Per Share Data ($) (Year Ended Dec. 31)	2000	1999	1998	1997	1996	1995	1994	1993	1992	1991
Tangible Bk. Val.	13.26	11.69	8.34	9.35	10.35	9.68	5.15	5.25	4.58	4.27
Cash Flow	3.79	2.04	1.82	2.49	2.35	2.19	1.00	1.44	1.09	1.08
Earnings	1.95	0.36	0.32	1.04	1.08	0.93	0.82	0.75	0.42	0.39
Dividends	0.60	0.60	0.60	0.54	0.47	0.36	0.28	0.26	0.25	0.23
Payout Ratio	31%	167%	171%	52%	43%	39%	34%	35%	62%	59%
Prices - High	49.75	53.75	36.93	28.62	19.50	14.83	11.12	10.62	6.81	6.54
- Low	29.50	28.00	20.00	18.12	14.16	8.16	7.37	5.95	4.64	4.22
P/E Ratio - High	26	NM	NM	28	18	16	14	14	16	17
- Low	15	NM	NM	17	13	9	9	8	11	11
Income Statement Analysis (Million $)										
Revs.	10,398	8,593	7,658	4,410	3,531	2,856	1,751	2,438	2,448	2,092
Oper. Inc.	2,602	1,591	1,372	1,414	1,271	998	465	584	452	436
Depr.	832	742	646	500	411	369	150	211	184	172
Int. Exp.	1,010	668	515	405	360	278	146	166	162	163
Pretax Inc.	1,415	316	247	543	545	401	247	377	172	151
Eff. Tax Rate	39%	51%	45%	33%	34%	25%	33%	38%	26%	27%
Net Inc.	873	162	147	351	362	299	165	185	128	110
Balance Sheet & Other Fin. Data (Million $)										
Cash	1,211	1,092	503	81.3	115	90.0	36.0	64.0	212	48.0
Curr. Assets	15,477	6,517	3,532	2,256	1,890	1,344	1,457	627	743	448
Total Assets	40,197	25,289	18,647	13,879	12,419	10,495	5,226	5,020	4,982	4,247
Curr. Liab.	16,804	5,772	4,439	3,027	2,199	2,050	1,474	733	978	687
LT Debt	10,532	9,746	6,366	4,565	4,377	2,874	1,308	1,605	1,683	1,540
Common Eqty.	5,892	5,585	4,155	3,430	3,260	3,014	1,406	1,624	1,268	1,070
Total Cap.	20,693	18,475	13,193	9,973	9,425	7,456	3,476	3,954	3,772	3,325
Cap. Exp.	4,904	3,513	1,708	1,162	819	828	326	529	586	317
Cash Flow	1,705	901	786	840	763	669	306	431	298	271
Curr. Ratio	0.9	1.1	0.8	0.7	0.9	0.7	1.0	0.9	0.8	0.7
% LT Debt of Cap.	50.9	52.8	48.3	45.8	46.4	38.5	37.6	40.6	44.6	46.3
% Net Inc.of Revs.	8.4	1.9	1.9	7.9	10.3	46.1	9.4	9.5	5.2	5.3
% Ret. on Assets	2.7	0.7	0.9	2.7	3.2	16.8	3.4	4.4	2.7	2.6
% Ret. on Equity	15.2	3.3	3.7	10.2	11.2	13.5	11.0	14.5	9.3	9.4

Data as orig reptd.; bef. results of disc opers/spec. items. Per share data adj. for stk. divs. Bold denotes diluted EPS (FASB 128)-prior periods restated. E-Estimated. NA-Not Available. NM-Not Meaningful. NR-Not Ranked.

Office—One Williams Center, Tulsa, OK 74172. **Tel**—(918) 573-2000. **Website**—http://www.williams.com **Chrmn, Pres & CEO**—K. E. Bailey. **SVP-Fin & CFO**—J. D. McCarthy. **Secy**—D. M. Higbee. **Investor Contact**—Richard George (918-573-3679). **Dirs**—K. E. Bailey, H. M. Chapman, G. A. Cox, T. H. Cruikshank, W. E. Green, W. R. Howell, J. C. Lewis, C. M. Lillis, G. A. Lorch, F. T. Macinnis, P. C. Meinig, G. R. Parker, J. D. Stoney, J. H. Williams. **Transfer Agent & Registrar**—First Chicago Trust Co. of New York, Jersey City, NJ. **Incorporated**—in Nevada in 1949; reincorporated in Delaware in 1987. **Empl**— 22,625. **S&P Analyst:** John Kartsonas